FINANCIAL
ACCOUNTING

SIXTH CANADIAN EDITION

Robert Libby

Cornell University

Patricia A. Libby

Ithaca University

Daniel Short

Texas Christian University

George Kanaan

Concordia University

Maureen Sterling

University of Windsor

Mc
Graw
Hill
Education

Financial Accounting
Sixth Canadian Edition

The Internet addresses listed in the text were accurate at the time of publication. The
inclusion of a Web site does not indicate an endorsement by the authors or McGraw-Hill Ryerson, and McGraw-Hill Ryerson does not guarantee the accuracy of the information presented at these sites.

ISBN-13: 978-1-25-910569-2
ISBN-10: 1-25-910569-5

2 3 4 5 6 7 8 9 10 TCP 1 2 3 4 5 6 0 9 8

Printed and bound in Canada.

Care has been taken to trace ownership of copyright material contained in this text;
however, the publisher will welcome any information that enables them to rectify any
reference or credit for subsequent editions.

Portfolio and Program Manager: *Karen Fozard*
Product Manager: *Keara Emmett*
Executive Marketing Manager: *Joy Armitage Taylor*
Product Developer: *Amy Rydzanicz*
Senior Product Team Associate: *Stephanie Giles*
Supervising Editor: *Jeanette McCurdy*
Photo/Permissions Researcher: *Karen Hunter*
Copy Editor: *Julie van Tol*
Print Proofreader: *Rodney Rawlings*
Production Coordinator: *Sarah Strynatka*
Manufacturing Production Coordinator: *Sheryl MacAdam*
Cover Image: © *Baramee Thaweesombat | Dreamstime.com*
Cover and eBook Interior Design: *Dave Murphy*
Print Interior Design: *Michelle Losier*
Page Layout: *Tom Dart*
Printer: *Transcontinental Printing Group*

About the Authors

Robert Libby

Robert Libby is the David A. Thomas Professor of Management at the Johnson Graduate School of Management at Cornell University, where he teaches the introductory financial accounting course. He has previously taught at the University of Illinois, Pennsylvania State University, University of Texas at Austin, University of Chicago, and University of Michigan. He received his B.S. from Pennsylvania State University and his M.A.S. and Ph.D. from the University of Illinois; he is also a CPA. Bob is a widely published author specializing in behavioural accounting.

Patricia A. Libby

Patricia Libby is Associate Professor of Accounting at Ithaca College, where she teaches the undergraduate financial accounting course. She has previously taught graduate and undergraduate financial accounting at Eastern Michigan University and the University of Texas. Before entering academe, she was an auditor with Price Waterhouse (now PricewaterhouseCoopers) and a financial administrator at the University of Chicago. She received her B.S. from Pennsylvania State University, her M.B.A. from DePaul University, and her Ph.D. from the University of Michigan; she is also a CPA. Pat conducts research on using cases in the introductory course and other parts of the accounting curriculum.

Daniel G. Short

Now retired, Daniel Short was Professor of Accounting and Dean of the M. J. Neeley School of Business at Texas Christian University. Over the course of his career, he held various positions: Dean, Richard T. Farmer School of Business at Miami University (Ohio); Dean, College of Business at Kansas State University; and Associate Dean, McCombs School of Business at the University of Texas at Austin, where he taught the undergraduate and graduate financial accounting courses. He has also taught at the University of Michigan and the University of Chicago. Dan received his undergraduate degree from Boston University and his M.B.A. and Ph.D. from the University of Michigan. He has won numerous awards for his outstanding teaching abilities, and has published articles in accounting and business journals.

George Kanaan

George Kanaan is Professor of Accountancy and Associate Dean at the John Molson School of Business at Concordia University, where he teaches the introductory financial accounting course. George previously taught undergraduate and graduate courses at universities in Canada, China, and Lebanon. He received his B.A. from the Lebanese University, his M.A. from Southern Illinois University at Carbondale, and his Ph.D. from the University of Wisconsin–Madison. He has conducted research on disclosures related to pension accounting, deferred income taxes, and the effects of changing prices. George's research has been published in *The Journal of Accounting, Auditing and Finance*, and *Managerial Finance*.

Maureen Sterling

Maureen Sterling (formerly Gowing) is Associate Professor of Accounting at the Odette School of Business at the University of Windsor. She has developed and taught Ph.D. research seminars as well as M.B.A. and undergraduate courses in both managerial and financial accounting. She acquired extensive experience in valuation while working as a financial analyst in the oil and securities industries, and did forensic work at the Vancouver Stock Exchange. Maureen obtained her B.A. from Carleton University, her M.B.A. from the University of Toronto, and her Ph.D. from Queen's University. She is also a CPA-CMA. Maureen is a member of the Academic Advisory Committee of the Chartered Professional Accountants of Canada (CPA Canada) and a member of the editorial board of Contemporary Accounting Research. She has conducted research on the effects of personal values on ethical reasoning, and has published in academic journals, such as the *Journal of Business Ethics* and *Business Ethics: A European Review*.

Contents in Brief

Contents

Operating Decisions and the Statement of Earnings   110

Adjustments, Financial Statements, and the Quality of Earnings   173

CHAPTER **FIVE**

Reporting and Interpreting Cash Flows   239

FOCUS COMPANY: NATIONAL BEVERAGE CORP.—PRODUCING VALUE FOR CUSTOMERS AND CASH FLOWS TO SHAREHOLDERS

CHAPTER **SIX**

Reporting and Interpreting Sales Revenue, Receivables, and Cash   301

FOCUS COMPANY: GILDAN ACTIVEWEAR INC.—BUILDING BRANDS TO BUILD GROSS PROFIT: MANAGING PRODUCT DEVELOPMENT, PRODUCTION, AND WORKING CAPITAL

Reporting and Interpreting Cost of Sales and Inventory   364

FOCUS COMPANY: REITMANS (CANADA) LIMITED—
MARKETING FASHIONABLE APPAREL TO YOUNG AND
CONTEMPORARY CUSTOMERS

Reporting and Interpreting Property, Plant, and Equipment; Natural Resources; and Intangibles   424

FOCUS COMPANY: WESTJET AIRLINES—MANAGING EARNINGS THROUGH CONTROL OF PRODUCTIVE CAPACITY

Reporting and Interpreting Current Liabilities   492

FOCUS COMPANY: SEARS CANADA INC.—MANAGING CAPITAL STRUCTURE

CHAPTER **TEN**

Reporting and Interpreting Non-current Liabilities   547

FOCUS COMPANY: BELL CANADA ENTERPRISES (BCE)—
FINANCING GROWTH WITH LONG-TERM DEBT

CHAPTER **ELEVEN**

Reporting and Interpreting Shareholders' Equity   606

FOCUS COMPANY: BELL CANADA ENTERPRISES,
INC.—FINANCING CORPORATE GROWTH WITH CAPITAL
SUPPLIED BY OWNERS

CHAPTER **TWELVE**

Communicating Accounting Information and Analyzing Financial Statements   658

FOCUS COMPANY: CANADIAN TIRE CORPORATION, LIMITED—FINANCIAL ANALYSIS: BRINGING IT ALL TOGETHER

CHAPTER THIRTEEN

Reporting and Interpreting Investments in Other Corporations   730

Since it was first published, *Financial Accounting* has grown to be a market-leading financial accounting textbook on which both students and instructors rely. The authors of the Sixth Canadian Edition continue to make financial accounting more relevant and interesting to students. How? By helping the instructor and student become partners in learning, using a remarkable learning approach that keeps students engaged and involved in the material from the first day of class.

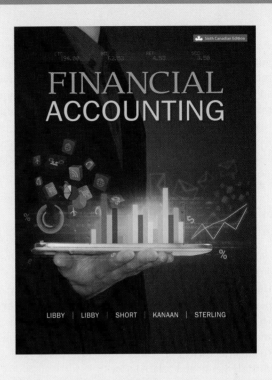

Financial Accounting's distinctive focus-company approach motivates students by involving them in the business decisions of a real company and demonstrating how financial accounting makes a difference in the success of a firm. That, combined with pedagogical features and technology tools that serve a variety of learning styles, makes *Financial Accounting* the textbook that both students and instructors agree is the best of its kind on the market today.

Financial Accounting provides leadership by focusing on

CURRENCY. *Financial Accounting* keeps your students' learning up to date, preparing them for the courses and jobs they will have in the future. International Financial Reporting Standards (IFRS) are completely integrated within each chapter, and an Accounting Standards for Private Enterprises box concludes each chapter. In addition, the financial statements, financial data, and articles used in both the instruction and the problem material continue to be updated.

RELEVANCE—THE PIONEERING FOCUS-COMPANY APPROACH. The authors first introduced their focus-company approach as the best method for helping students understand financial statements and real-world implications of financial

accounting for future managers. **This approach shows how relevant accounting is and motivates students by explaining accounting in a real-world context.** Throughout each chapter, the material focuses on a familiar company, its decisions, and its financial statements. This provides the perfect setting for discussing the importance of accounting and how businesses use accounting information. Furthering the real-world applicability, the end-of-chapter cases tie directly to the financial statements of the Consolidated Financial Statements of the Canadian Tire Corporation, Limited, conveniently located in Appendix A, and to the Consolidated Financial Statements of Sears Canada Inc., available on *Connect* online. These financial statements give students valuable practice reading and interpreting real financial data. In addition, real-world excerpts expand on topics, with insight into how real firms use financial accounting to their competitive advantage.

CLARITY. Do students complain that their textbook is hard to read? They don't if they're reading *Financial Accounting*. It is the proven choice for presenting financial accounting with a clear, relevant approach that keeps students engaged throughout the course. To continue to meet the changing needs of financial accounting instructors and students, the organization of the material has been refined to ensure maximum readability for students and flexibility for instructors.

Inside the Textbook: A Complete Learning System

Financial Accounting offers a host of pedagogical tools that complement the way you like to teach and the ways your students like to learn. Some of these offer information and tips that help you present a complex subject, while others highlight issues relevant to what your students read online and in the papers, or view on mobile devices or TV. Either way, *Financial Accounting*'s pedagogical support will make a real difference in your course and in your students' learning.

ACCOUNTING STANDARDS FOR PRIVATE ENTERPRISES

Not all companies are public, and not all students will end up working in one that is. Because of this, and because private enterprises are not required to use IFRS, this box was developed. **Accounting Standards for Private Enterprises** boxed features address the differences between ASPE and IFRS; for example, why a statement of changes in equity isn't necessary or what details aren't reported in financial statements and related notes.

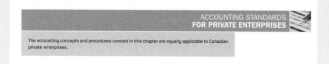

INTERNATIONAL PERSPECTIVE

The **International Perspective** sections make students aware of differences in accounting methods used in various countries. Financial statements and real-world excerpts related to international companies are included in the end-of-chapter material as well.

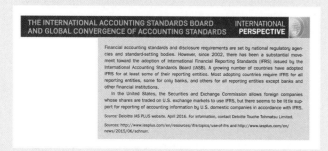

FINANCIAL ANALYSIS

These features tie important chapter concepts to real-world decision-making examples. They also highlight alternative viewpoints, and add to the critical thinking and decision-making focus of the text.

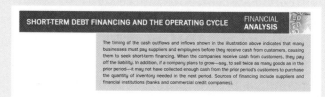

PAUSE FOR FEEDBACK AND SELF-STUDY QUIZ

Research shows that students learn best when they are actively engaged in the learning process. This active-learning feature engages the student, provides interactivity, and promotes efficient learning. These quizzes ask students to pause at strategic intervals throughout each chapter to ensure they understand key points before moving ahead.

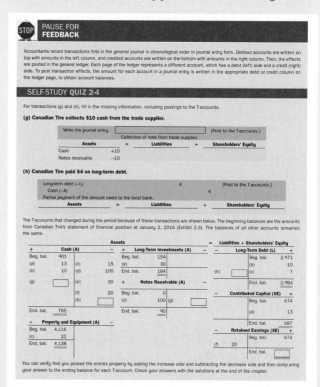

FOCUS ON CASH FLOWS

The early and consistent coverage of cash flows encourages students to think more critically about the decisions they will face as managers, and the impact those decisions will have on the company's cash flow. Each of Chapters 2 through 12 includes a discussion and analysis of changes in the cash flow of the focus company, and an exploration of the decisions that caused those changes.

KEY RATIO ANALYSIS

Students will be better prepared to use financial information if they understand how to evaluate elements of financial performance while learning how to measure and report them. For this reason, we include relevant key ratios in the **Key Ratio Analysis** sections. Each box presents a ratio analysis for the chapter's focus company as well as for comparative companies. Cautions are also provided to help students understand the limitations of certain ratios.

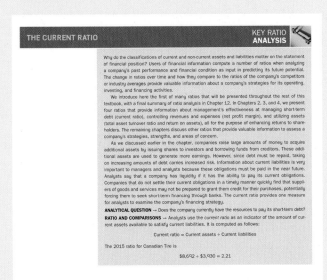

A QUESTION OF ACCOUNTABILITY

The more students are exposed to ethical situations, the more likely they will be to consider the effects their choices will have on others. These boxes appear throughout the text, conveying to students the importance and consequences of acting responsibly in business practice.

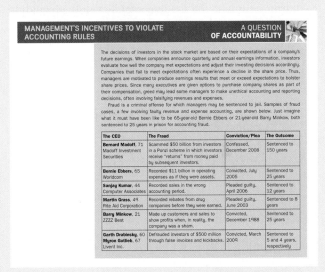

ORGANIZATION OF THE CHAPTER

This framework, at the beginning of each chapter, provides a powerful visual schematic of the content, and of what questions will be answered.

ALL JOURNAL ENTRIES TIED TO THE ACCOUNTING EQUATION

In early chapters, all journal entries marked with (A), (L), (SE), (R), and (E), or with (X) if a contra account, and with + and – signs assist students in transaction analysis. All journal entries end with a summary of the effects of each transaction on the fundamental accounting equation as well as on cash and net earnings, when appropriate.

REAL-WORLD EXCERPT

These excerpts appear throughout the text and include financial statement information from focus companies and others, news articles, analysts' reports, and press releases.

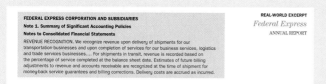

ICONS

Easily identifiable margin icons indicate what types of skills are being addressed in the end-of-chapter material.

 International coverage

 An ethical dilemma

 Cash flow analysis

 Ratio analysis

 Written work, for developing communication skills

 Exercises to be solved using the Excel template provided

 Problems and cases requiring analysis, for developing the ability to use financial information to guide business decisions

Flexible End-of-Chapter Content and Organization

Each chapter is followed by an extensive selection of end-of-chapter material that examines and integrates multiple concepts presented in the chapter. To maintain the real-world emphasis, these are often based on real Canadian, U.S., and international companies, and require analysis, conceptual thought, calculation, and written communication. Assignments suitable for individual or group written projects and oral presentations are also included.

Chapter Take-Aways Bulleted end-of-chapter summary complementing the learning objectives outlined at the beginning of the chapter.

Key Ratios Summary of the key ratios presented in the chapter.

Finding Financial Information Easy-to-review graphic highlighting where to find the financial data discussed in the chapter.

Questions Chapter concepts are covered, allowing students and faculty to ensure that these have been grasped.

Mini-Exercises (NEW) Short assignments covering specific learning objectives from the chapter.

Exercises Assignments that cover multiple learning objectives from the chapter.

Problems Detailed assignments integrating various topics discussed in the chapter. Cross-references to the Alternate Problems appear in blue.

Alternate Problems Additional problems that are similar in level and content to the end-of-chapter problems and include cross-references to the Problems in blue.

Comprehensive Problems Problems in selected chapters that cover topics from earlier chapters to refresh, reinforce, and build an integrative understanding of the course material.

Cases and Projects This section includes Finding and Interpreting Financial Information, Financial Reporting and Analysis Cases, Critical Thinking Cases, and Financial Reporting and Analysis Team Project.

Continuing Case (NEW) The continuing case revolves around Penny's Pool Service & Supply Inc. and its largest supplier, Pool Corporation Inc. In the first five chapters, the continuing case follows the establishment, operations, and financial reporting for Penny's. In Chapter 5, Pool Corporation, a real publicly traded corporation, is also introduced in more detail. The Pool Corporation example is then extended to encompass each new topic in the remaining chapters.

Financial Statements The consolidated financial statements of two dynamic companies—the Canadian Tire Corporation, Limited, and Sears Canada Inc.—are referenced in the text's problem material. Excerpts from the financial statements for the Canadian Tire Corporation, Limited, appear in Appendix A in the text, and Sears Canada Inc.'s financial statements are available online.

What's New in the Sixth Canadian Edition

Based on market feedback, the primary goals of the Sixth Edition are to

- Simplify explanations of complex topics.
- Provide a better match of end-of-chapter material to instructor and student needs.
- Accurately reflect the exciting changes taking place in the accounting environment.
- Provide real-world excerpts from financial statements of Canadian and international companies, prepared in conformity with International Financial Reporting Standards.
- Provide instructors with more flexibility in key topical coverage.

As a result, the authors have made the detailed revisions noted in the following sections:

Chapter One

- Changed the focus company to Canadian Tire Corporation, Limited.
- Revised the main learning objectives and added two learning objectives for the supplementary material.
- Shortened the statement of cash flows to cover the essential elements of the statement in this introductory chapter.
- Added a section on ethical conduct.
- Added a *New* **CONTINUING CASE** to the end-of-chapter problems, based on the activities of Penny's Pool Service & Supply Inc. and its supplier, Pool Corporation. These cases summarize key points emphasized in each chapter in a consistent context throughout the text. In Chapter 1, students prepare a basic statement of earnings, a statement of shareholders' equity, and a statement of financial position based on Penny's estimates for the first year.
- New and updated real companies, as well as modified accounts, names, and amounts for fictional companies in end-of-chapter exercises, problems, and cases. Addition of mini-exercises.

Chapter Two

- Changed the focus company to Canadian Tire Corporation, Limited.
- Expanded on the qualitative characteristics of accounting information.
- Introduced the trial balance (moved from Chapter 4 in 5e) and updated it as needed to reflect the continuing illustration of Canadian Tire's hypothetical transactions.
- Reduced the coverage of cash flows to identifying transactions as operating, investing, or financing.

- Added a *New* **CONTINUING CASE** to the end-of-chapter problems. In this case, students prepare journal entries, post to T-accounts, prepare a trial balance and classified statement of financial position identify investing and financing activities affecting cash flows, and compute and interpret the current ratio based on the statement of financial position for Penny's Pool Service.
- New and updated real companies, as well as modified accounts, names, and amounts for fictional companies in end-of-chapter exercises, problems, and cases. Addition of mini-exercises.

Chapter Three

- Changed the focus company to Canadian Tire Corporation, Limited.
- Expanded the coverage related to the statement of earnings (covered in Chapter 6 in 5e).
- Added an illustration to highlight the difference between cash basis and accrual basis accounting.
- Revised the transaction analysis process.
- Updated the trial balance to reflect the continuing illustration of Canadian Tire's hypothetical transactions.
- Reduced the coverage of cash flows with a focus on transactions affecting the cash T-account.
- Added an appendix on earnings measurement and comprehensive income (covered in Chapter 6 in 5e).
- Added a *New* **CONTINUING CASE** to the end-of-chapter problems. In this case, students prepare journal entries for operating activities and prepare a multiple-step statement of earnings for Penny's Pool Service.
- New and updated real companies, as well as modified accounts, names, and amounts for fictional companies in end-of-chapter exercises, problems, and cases. Addition of mini-exercises.

Chapter Four

- Changed the focus company to Canadian Tire Corporation, Limited.
- Revised the steps in the adjustment process for improved clarity.
- Deleted Appendix 4A that covered a practical aspect of recording certain transactions.
- Revised the continuing Demonstration Case and shortened its solution.
- Added two *New* **CONTINUING CASES** to the end-of-chapter problems. The first asks students to prepare adjusting entries for Penny's Pool Service. The second introduces Penny's supplier, Pool Corporation, a public company, and asks students to prepare a detailed classified statement of earnings and statement of financial position, and to compute specific ratios.
- New and updated real companies, as well as modified accounts, names, and amounts for fictional companies in end-of-chapter exercises, problems, and cases. Addition of mini-exercises.

Chapter Five

- Changed the focus company to National Beverage Corporation.
- Added learning objectives for the three end-of-chapter appendices.
- Added Appendix 5C to illustrate the preparation of the statement of cash flows using the T-account approach.
- Added a *New* **CONTINUING CASE** to the end-of-chapter problems. Students are asked to prepare a complete statement of cash flows for Pool Corporation, a public company.
- New and updated real companies, as well as modified accounts, names, and amounts for fictional companies in end-of-chapter exercises, problems, and cases. Addition of mini-exercises.

Chapter Six

- Updated focus and comparison companies.
- Revised the learning objectives.
- Deleted Appendix 6B and integrated the recording of sales discounts and returns into the chapter.
- Added a *New* **CONTINUING CASE** to the end-of-chapter problems. Students are asked to make summary entries for bad debts and compute the amount to be reported as net sales for Pool Corporation, a public company.

- New and updated real companies, as well as modified accounts, names, and amounts for fictional companies in end-of-chapter exercises, problems, and cases. Addition of mini-exercises.

Chapter Seven

- Changed the focus company to Reitmans (Canada) Limited.
- Reorganized the learning objectives to reflect the reorganization of the chapter.
- Added two learning objectives for the supplementary material.
- Moved the discussion of the periodic inventory system to two appendices.
- Incorporated the recording of purchase discounts and returns into the chapter.
- Added a *New* **CONTINUING CASE** to the end-of-chapter problems. Students are asked to compute the cost of sales using two different inventory costing methods, FIFO and weighted average cost; record specific purchase and sale transactions; and compare the effects of both methods on earnings and cash flows for Pool Corporation, a public company.
- New and updated real companies, as well as modified accounts, names, and amounts for fictional companies in end-of-chapter exercises, problems, and cases. Addition of mini-exercises.

Chapter Eight

- Updated the focus and comparison companies.
- Split the Demonstration Case into two cases: accounting for and reporting of property, plant, equipment, and intangible assets; and accounting for natural resources.
- Added a *New* **CONTINUING CASE** to the end-of-chapter problems. Students are asked to record the acquisition, depreciation, and disposal of equipment for Pool Corporation, a public company.
- New and updated real companies, as well as modified accounts, names, and amounts for fictional companies in end-of-chapter exercises, problems, and cases. Addition of mini-exercises.

Chapter Nine

- Changed the focus company to Sears Canada Inc.
- Added two learning objectives related to the appendices.
- Added one Self-Study Quiz.
- Shortened Appendix 9A by eliminating the real-world excerpts.

- Added a *New* **CONTINUING CASE** to the end-of-chapter problems. Students are asked to record and report the effects of specific transactions related to current liabilities for Pool Corporation, a public company.

- New and updated real companies, as well as modified accounts, names, and amounts for fictional companies in end-of-chapter exercises, problems, and cases. Addition of mini-exercises.

Chapter Ten

- Updated the focus and comparison companies.

- Added three learning objectives related to the appendices.

- Added journal entries to record the issuance of notes, payment of interest, and principal under various scenarios.

- Added two appendices.

- Added a *New* **CONTINUING CASE** to the end-of-chapter problems. Students are asked to compute the issue price of bonds, interest expense, and the carrying amount of the bonds for Pool Corporation, a public company.

- New and updated real companies, as well as modified accounts, names, and amounts for fictional companies in end-of-chapter exercises, problems, and cases. Addition of mini-exercises.

Chapter Eleven

- Updated the focus and comparison companies.

- Added a learning objective related to Appendix 11A.

- Added a *New* **CONTINUING CASE** to the end-of-chapter problems. Students are asked to record transactions related to the repurchase of shares for Pool Corporation, a public company, as well as declaration and distribution of dividends.

- New and updated real companies, as well as modified accounts, names, and amounts for fictional companies in end-of-chapter exercises, problems, and cases. Addition of mini-exercises.

Chapter Twelve

- Updated the focus company to Canadian Tire Corporation, Limited, and changed the comparison companies.

- Added two learning objectives.

- Expanded the coverage by including the Players in the Accounting Communication Process and the Disclosure Process (covered in Chapter 6 in 5e).

- Added a *New* **CONTINUING CASE** to the end-of-chapter problems. Students are asked to compute specific ratios for Pool Corporation, a public company.

- New and updated real companies, as well as modified accounts, names, and amounts for fictional companies in end-of-chapter exercises, problems, and cases. Addition of mini-exercises.

Chapter Thirteen

- Changed the focus company to BCE Inc.

- Deleted the appendix.

- Added a *New* **CONTINUING CASE** to the end-of-chapter problems. Students are asked to record specific transactions related to passive investments in securities for Pool Corporation, a public company.

- New and updated real companies, as well as modified accounts, names, and amounts for fictional companies in end-of-chapter exercises, problems, and cases. Addition of mini-exercises.

Market Leading Technology

LEARN WITHOUT LIMITS ▇connect

McGraw-Hill *Connect®* is an award-winning digital teaching and learning platform that gives students the means to better connect with their coursework, with their instructors, and with the important concepts that they will need to know for success now and in the future. With *Connect*, instructors can take advantage of McGraw-Hill's trusted content to seamlessly deliver assignments, quizzes, and tests online. McGraw-Hill *Connect* is a learning platform that continually adapts to each student, delivering precisely what they need, when they need it, so class time is more engaging and effective. *Connect* makes teaching and learning personal, easy, and proven.

CONNECT KEY FEATURES

SmartBook®

As the first and only adaptive reading experience, SmartBook is changing the way students read and learn. SmartBook creates a personalized reading experience by highlighting the most important concepts a student needs to learn at that moment in time. As a student engages with SmartBook, the reading experience continuously adapts by highlighting content based on what each student knows and doesn't know. This ensures that he or she is focused on the content needed to close specific knowledge gaps, while it simultaneously promotes long-term learning.

Connect Insight®

Connect Insight is *Connect*'s new one-of-a-kind visual analytics dashboard, now available for instructors, that provides at-a-glance information regarding student performance, and which is immediately actionable. By presenting assignment, assessment, and topical performance results together with a time metric that is easily visible for aggregate or individual results, Connect Insight gives instructors the ability to take a just-in-time approach to teaching and learning, which was never before available. Connect Insight presents data that helps instructors improve class performance in a way that is efficient and effective.

SIMPLE ASSIGNMENT MANAGEMENT

With *Connect*, creating assignments is easier than ever, so instructors can spend more time teaching and less time managing.

- Assign SmartBook learning modules.
- Draw from a variety of text specific questions, resources, and test bank material to assign online.
- Instructors can edit existing questions and create their own questions.
- Streamline lesson planning, student progress reporting, and assignment grading to make classroom management more efficient than ever.

When it comes to studying, time is precious. *Connect* helps students learn more efficiently by providing feedback and practice material when they need it, where they need it.

- Automatically score assignments, giving students immediate feedback on their work and comparisons with correct answers.
- Access and review each response; manually change grades or leave comments for students to review.
- Track individual student performance—by question or assignment, or in relation to the class overall—with detailed grade reports.
- Reinforce classroom concepts with practice tests and instant quizzes.
- Integrate grade reports easily with Learning Management Systems, including Blackboard, D2L, and Moodle.

The *Connect* Instructor Library is a repository for additional resources to improve student engagement in and out of the class. It provides all the critical resources instructors need to build their course.

- Access instructor resources.
- View assignments and resources created for past sections.
- Post your own resources for students to use.

INSTRUCTOR SUPPORT

The following resources are available online to support instructors:

- **Instructor's Manual.** Includes a chapter outline, detailed lecture notes, suggested activities, and a reading list for each chapter.
- **Solutions Manual.** Provides solutions for end-of-chapter questions, mini-exercises, exercises, problems, and cases.
- **PowerPoint® Presentations.** These slides for use in your classroom are completely customized for the Sixth Canadian Edition of *Financial Accounting*.
- **Computerized Test Bank.** Includes more than 1,800 true/false, multiple choice, and essay questions.
- **Instructor's Excel® Template Solutions.** These Excel template solutions accompany the templates available to students online.

The McGraw-Hill Education team is ready to help you assess and integrate any of our products, technology, and services into your course for optimal teaching and learning performance. Whether it's helping your students improve their grades or putting your entire course online, the McGraw-Hill Education team is here to help you do it. Contact your Learning Solutions Consultant today to learn how to maximize all of McGraw-Hill Education's resources!

For more information, please visit us online: http://www.mheducation.ca/he/solutions

Writing and adapting a successful textbook requires a team effort and we have enjoyed working with excellent teammates. Throughout the process of writing this textbook, many people stepped forward with tremendous efforts that enabled us to accomplish our goals. First and foremost, we are deeply indebted to Robert Libby, Patricia Libby, and Daniel Short, authors of the U.S. edition, for developing the pedagogical approach used in this text. Their approach helped us tremendously in shaping this Sixth Canadian Edition.

We would like to recognize the sincere and devoted efforts of the many people who added their input to the process of developing this book. We received invaluable advice and suggestions during the manuscript development and revision process. For this assistance, we thank the following colleagues:

SIXTH EDITION REVIEWERS

Darrin Ambrose	*University of Calgary*
Robert Ducharme	*University of Waterloo*
Ian Dunn	*Western University*
Sonya von Heyking	*University of Lethbridge*
Aadil Murali Juma	*McMaster University*
Michael Khan	*University of Toronto*
Sohyung Kim	*Brock University*
Douglas Kong	*University of Toronto*
Randy Linton	*University of Regina*
Robert Madden	*St. Francis Xavier University*
John Shepherd	*Kwantlen Polytechnic University*
Mumsy Ullattikulam	*Langara College*

We also received invaluable input and support through the years from present and former colleagues and students. We are indebted to the following individuals who helped adapt, critique, and shape the ancillary package for the Canadian market: Ambrose Chan, CPA; Shannon Butler, Carleton University; Lynn De Grace, McGill University; Robert Ducharme, University of Waterloo; Ian Feltmate, Acadia University; Ross Meacher, CPA.

We applaud the extraordinary efforts of a talented group of individuals at McGraw-Hill Education who made all of this come together. We especially thank Keara Emmett for her involvement in the planning stage of this project, Amy Rydzanicz for tirelessly following the development process through various stages of the final product, Jeanette McCurdy who managed the final production of this book, and all the marketing and sales people who helped bring this book to both instructors and students. We also thank all those who worked behind the scenes to ensure the successful completion of this book. Special thanks to Julie van Tol who edited and proofread our work.

We thank the Canadian Tire Corporation, Limited, and Sears Canada Inc. for permitting us to use their financial statements to provide students with real-world examples of financial statements and accompanying notes. We are also grateful to all the focus companies that allowed us to use excerpts from their financial statements and notes to illustrate the main ideas in each chapter.

Special thanks go to our families for their support, patience, and understanding while we worked on completing this Sixth Canadian Edition of the book. We dedicate the book to them.

George Kanaan
Maureen Sterling

To Our Student Readers

This book is aimed at two groups of readers:

1. *Future managers*, who will need to interpret and use financial statement information in business decisions.

2. *Future accountants*, who will prepare financial statements for those managers.

Future managers need a firm basis for using financial statement information in their careers in marketing, finance, banking, manufacturing, human resources, sales, information systems, or other areas of management. Future accountants need a solid foundation for further professional study.

Both managers and accountants must understand how to *use financial statements in making real business decisions* to perform their duties successfully. The best way to learn this is to study accounting in real business contexts. This is the key idea behind our focus-company approach, which we introduce in the first chapter. Each chapter's material is integrated with a focus company, its decisions, and its financial statements. The focus companies are drawn from different industries, providing you with a broad range of experience in realistic business and financial accounting practices. In each chapter, you *will actually work with these real companies' statements* and with those of additional contrast companies.

When you complete this course, you will be able to read and understand financial statements of real companies. We help you achieve this goal by

1. Selecting learning objectives and content based on the way that seasoned managers use financial statements in modern businesses. We emphasize the topics that count.

2. Recognizing that students using this book have no previous exposure to accounting and financial statements, and often little exposure to the business world. We take you through the financial statements three times, at increasing levels of detail (in Chapter 1, Chapters 2 through 5, and Chapters 6 through 13). This is the secret to our "building-block approach."

3. Helping you "learn how to learn" by teaching efficient and effective approaches for learning the material. Keep these learning hints in mind throughout.

4. Providing regular feedback in Self-Study Quizzes, which occur throughout each chapter. Complete the quizzes before you move on. Check your answers against the solutions at the end of the chapter. If you are still unclear about any of the answers, refer back to the chapter material before moving on.

5. Repeating the key terms and their definitions. A handy index is provided on *Connect*.

6. Introducing the Key Financial Ratios used to assess different elements of financial performance at the same time you are learning how to measure and report those elements. These will show you what kinds of accounting information managers use and how they interpret it.

7. At the end of each chapter, test what you have learned by working through the Demonstration Cases. *Working problems is one of the keys to learning accounting.*

Good luck in your financial accounting course.

George Kanaan
Maureen Sterling

Financial Statements and Business Decisions

After studying this chapter, you should be able to do the following:

LO1-1 Recognize the information conveyed in each of the four basic financial statements and how the information is used by different decision makers (investors, creditors, and managers).

LO1-2 Identify the role of International Financial Reporting Standards (IFRS) in determining the content of financial statements and how companies ensure the accuracy of their financial statements.

SUPPLEMENTARY MATERIAL

LO1-S1 Describe the different types of business entities.

LO1-S2 Identify typical career opportunities for professional accountants.

Source: Courtesy of Canadian Tire Corporation

Focus Company: **Canadian Tire Corporation**

VALUING AN INVESTMENT USING FINANCIAL STATEMENT INFORMATION

Canadian Tire Corporation (CTC) (www.canadiantire.ca) has been in business for over 90 years. It offers a range of products and services to Canadians through a portfolio of the leading retail banners in Canada, including Canadian Tire; various FGL Sports banners, with the largest being Sport Chek, Sports Experts, and Atmosphere; Mark's; PartSource; and Gas+. CTC's retail business is supported and strengthened through Canadian Tire Financial Services, which markets financial and other products and services, including credit cards, in-store financing, product warranties, and retail and broker deposits. CT Real Estate Investment Trust's primary business is owning, developing, and leasing income-producing commercial properties. CT REIT's geographically diversified portfolio of properties is made up, largely, of stand-alone Canadian Tire stores, retail developments anchored by a Canadian Tire store and/or stores operating under other CTC retail banners, two distribution centres, a mixed-use commercial property, and development lands.

Canadian Tire became a corporation on December 1, 1927. Its shares trade on the Toronto Stock Exchange under the symbol CTC. The company has grown by expanding the number of Canadian Tire stores over time and by acquiring existing companies, such as the Forzani Group (currently FGL Sports) and Mark's Work Warehouse (currently Mark's).

UNDERSTANDING THE BUSINESS

THE PLAYERS

The success story of Canadian Tire began in 1923 when brothers John W. and Alfred J. Billes sold Hamilton Tire and Garage Ltd. to create Canadian Tire Corporation. As is common in new businesses, the founders, or investors, also functioned as managers of the business.

When the investors started the company, Canadian Tire needed additional money to expand its operations. It borrowed money from local banks and other lenders, or *creditors*, and used these funds to expand the business. Canadian Tire's leadership in offering a wide selection of quality products and services in many locations helped the company become the leading retailer in Canada.

Investors who buy small percentages of large corporations are called *shareholders*. They hope to gain from their investment in two ways—they expect to receive a portion of what the company earns in the form of cash payments called *dividends*, and they hope to eventually sell their share of the company at a higher price than they paid.

Creditors lend money to a company for a specific length of time. They gain by charging interest on the money they lend. The exchanges of money between Canadian Tire and its lenders and owners are called *financing activities*. Canadian Tire's purchases or sales of stores, are called *investing activities*.

THE BUSINESS OPERATIONS

To understand any company's financial statements, you must first understand its operations. Selling household items, garden products, sportswear, auto parts, and financial services requires that Canadian Tire gain access to and transport their products and services to individuals who need them. Acquiring products and access to services requires that Canadian Tire negotiate with its *suppliers*.

Canadian Tire sells many products and services to its *customers* through its own network of stores and provides them with options to pay for the items they purchase.

THE ACCOUNTING SYSTEM

Managers (often called **internal decision makers**) need information about the company's business activities to control and improve the operating, investing, and financing activities of the firm. Shareholders and creditors (often called **external decision makers**) need information about these same business activities to assess whether the company will be able to pay back its debts with interest and pay dividends. All businesses must have an **accounting** system that collects and processes financial information about an organization's business activities and reports that information to decision makers. Canadian Tire's **business activities** include the following:

- **Financing Activities:** borrowing or paying back money to lenders and receiving additional funds from shareholders, or paying them dividends.

- **Investing Activities:** buying or selling items, such as retail stores, buildings, and equipment used to store and then distribute goods and services to customers.

- **Operating Activities:** the day-to-day process of obtaining products and services from suppliers, storing and then delivering them to customers, collecting cash from customers, and paying suppliers.

Exhibit 1.1 outlines the two parts of the accounting system. Internal managers typically require continuous detailed information because they must plan and manage the day-to-day operations of the organization. Developing accounting information for internal decision makers is called *managerial*, or *management, accounting* and is the subject of a separate accounting course. The focus of this text is accounting for external decision makers, called *financial accounting*, and the four basic financial statements and related disclosures that are periodically produced by that system.

Purchase products and access to services demanded by customers

Collect cash from customers and pay suppliers

THE BUSINESS OPERATIONS

Market the products and series available for sale

Sell products and services to customers

LO1-1

Recognize the information conveyed in each of the four basic financial statements and how the information is used by different decision makers (investors, creditors, and managers).

ACCOUNTING is a system that collects and processes (analyzes, measures, and records) useful financial information about an organization and reports that information to decision makers.

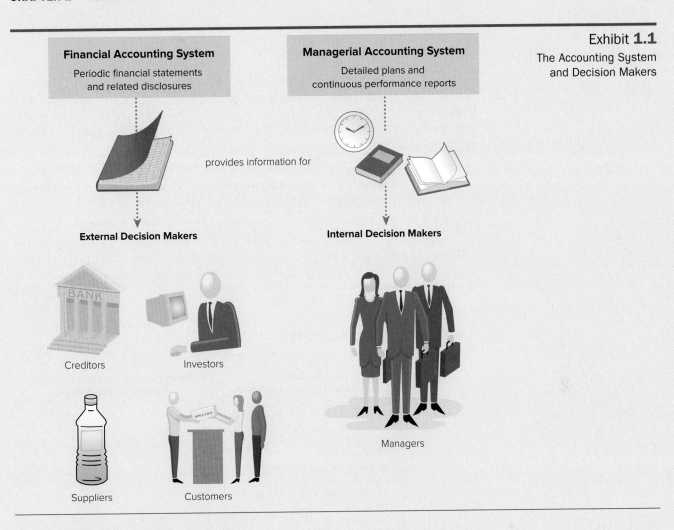

Exhibit **1.1**
The Accounting System
and Decision Makers

WHY STUDY FINANCIAL ACCOUNTING?

No matter what your business career goals are, you will use financial accounting information to make decisions. You may want to work for an investment firm, a bank, or an accounting firm that would be involved in the financing of companies like Canadian Tire. We will focus much of our discussion on the perspectives of *investors*, *creditors*, and *preparers* of financial statements. However, you might not be aware that managers within the firm also make direct use of financial statements. For example, *marketing managers* and *credit managers* use customers' financial statements to decide whether to extend credit to their customers. *Supply chain managers* analyze suppliers' financial statements to see whether the suppliers have the resources to meet demand and invest in future development. Both the employees' unions and company *human resource managers* use financial statements as a basis for contract negotiations over pay rates. Financial statement figures even serve as a basis for calculating employee bonuses. Regardless of the functional area of management in which you are employed, you will use financial statement information.

We begin this process with a brief but comprehensive overview of the four basic financial statements and the people and organizations involved in their preparation and use. This overview provides you with a context in which you can learn the more detailed material that is presented in the chapters that follow. In particular, we focus on how two primary users of the statements, investors (owners) and creditors (lenders), relied on each of Canadian Tire's four basic financial statements in their decisions to invest in or lend money to Canadian Tire. Later in the chapter, we discuss a broader range of uses of financial statement data in marketing, management, human resources, and other business contexts.

YOUR GOALS FOR CHAPTER 1

To understand the way shareholders and creditors use Canadian Tire's financial statements in their decisions, we must first understand what specific information is reported in the four basic financial statements for a company. *Focus your attention on learning the general content, structure, and use of the statements, and do memorize the definitions of every term used in this chapter.* Specifically, you should focus on these questions:

1. What type of information does a statement convey, and where can you find it?

2. How are the elements within a statement related? These *relationships* are usually described by an equation that tells you how the elements fit together.

3. How is the information useful to shareholders' and creditors' decisions?

The Pause for Feedback and Self-Study Quiz features that occur throughout the chapter will test your ability to answer these questions. Remember that, since this chapter is an overview, each concept discussed in this chapter will be discussed again, in Chapters 2 through 5.

ORGANIZATION OF THE CHAPTER

The Four Basic Financial Statements: An Overview	Responsibilities for the Accounting Communication Process
• The Statement of Financial Position • The Statement of Comprehensive Income • The Statement of Changes in Equity • The Statement of Cash Flows • Relationships among the Four Financial Statements • Notes to Financial Statements • Summary of the Four Basic Financial Statements	• International Financial Reporting Standards (IFRS) • Ensuring the Accuracy of Financial Statements

Supplemental material:
Appendix 1A: Types of Business Entities
Appendix 1B: Employment in the Accounting Profession Today

THE FOUR BASIC FINANCIAL STATEMENTS: AN OVERVIEW

Four financial statements are normally prepared by profit-making organizations for use by shareholders, creditors, and other external decision makers.

1. On its **statement of financial position**, Canadian Tire reports the economic resources it owns and the sources of financing for those resources.

2. On its **statement of earnings** (the main component of the statement of comprehensive income), Canadian Tire reports its ability to sell goods for more than their cost to acquire and sell.

3. On its **statement of changes in equity**, Canadian Tire reports additional contributions from or payments to shareholders, and the amount of earnings the company reinvested for future growth.

4. On its **statement of cash flows**, Canadian Tire reports its ability to generate cash and how it was used.

The four basic financial statements can be prepared at any point in time and can apply to any time span (such as one year, one quarter, or one month). Like most companies, Canadian Tire prepares financial statements for external users at the end of each quarter (known as *quarterly reports*) and at the end of the year (known as *annual reports*).

The Statement of Financial Position[1]

The purpose of the **statement of financial position (balance sheet)** is to report the financial position (amount of assets, liabilities, and shareholders' equity) of an accounting entity at a particular point in time. We can learn a lot about what the statement of financial position reports just by reading the statement from the top. The statement of financial position of Canadian Tire is shown in Exhibit 1.2.

A **STATEMENT OF FINANCIAL POSITION (BALANCE SHEET)** reports the financial position (assets, liabilities, and shareholders' equity) of an accounting entity at a point in time.

Exhibit **1.2**
Statement of Financial Position

REAL-WORLD EXCERPT

*Canadian Tire
Corporation*

CANADIAN TIRE CORPORATION			
Statement of Financial Position			
At January 2, 2016			
(in millions of Canadian dollars)			
Assets			
Cash	$	901	Amount of cash in the company's bank accounts
Short-term investments		96	Investments in highly liquid assets
Accounts receivable		6,521	Amounts owed by customers from prior sales
Inventories		1,765	Products stored but not sold
Prepaid expenses		96	Rent and insurance paid in advance
Property and equipment		4,116	Land, stores and sales equipment
Goodwill		437	Economic resource that lacks physical substance
Other assets		1,056	A variety of assets that are covered in future chapters
Total assets		$14,988	
Liabilities			
Accounts payable[2]	$	920	Amounts owed to suppliers for purchases of goods
Accrued liabilities		1,037	Amounts owed to suppliers of services
Provisions		262	Estimated liabilities whose amount and timing of payment are not known with certainty
Short-term borrowings		89	Amounts owed to lenders within one year
Income tax payable		61	Tax owed to the government
Long-term debt		2,996	Amounts owed on written debt contracts payable after one year
Other liabilities		3,833	A variety of liabilities that are covered in future chapters
Total liabilities		$ 9,198	
Shareholders' Equity			
Contributed capital		674	Amounts invested in the business by shareholders
Retained earnings		4,172	Past earnings not distributed to shareholders
Other components		944	A variety of equity items that are explained in future chapters
Total shareholders' equity		5,790	
Total liabilities and shareholders' equity		$14,988	

Name of the entity
Title of the statement
Date of the statement
Unit of measure

The accompanying notes are an integral part of these financial statements.

This statement is an adaptation of Canadian Tire's actual statement of financial position. A more detailed statement of financial position is presented in Chapter 2.

Source: Canadian Tire Corporation, Annual Report 2015.

Structure   The *heading* of the statement of financial position identifies four significant items related to the statement:

1. *name of the accounting entity*—Canadian Tire Corporation
2. *title of the statement*—Statement of Financial Position
3. *specific date of the statement*—At January 2, 2016
4. *unit of measure*—(in millions of Canadian dollars)

An **ACCOUNTING ENTITY** is the organization for which financial data are to be collected.

The organization for which financial data are to be collected and reported is called an **accounting entity**. The accounting entity must be precisely defined. On the statement of financial position, the accounting entity itself, not the business owners, is viewed as owning its debts and the resources it uses.

The heading of the statement indicates the time dimension of the report. The statement of financial position is like a financial snapshot, clearly stating the entity's financial position *at a specific point in time*—in this case, January 2, 2016—which is stated clearly on the statement. Financial information is normally reported in the currency of the country in which the entity must legally report its financial results. In this case, Canadian Tire reports in Canadian dollars. Similarly, U.S. companies report in U.S. dollars and Mexican companies in Mexican pesos. Medium-sized companies, such as Canadian Tire, often report their financial figures in millions; that is, they round the last six digits to the nearest million. The listing of merchandise inventories at $1,765 on Canadian Tire's statement of financial position actually means $1,765,000,000. The amounts shown in the rest of this chapter are in millions of Canadian dollars, except where otherwise noted.

Canadian Tire's statement of financial position has three major captions: assets, liabilities, and shareholders' equity. The **basic accounting equation** explains their relationship:

The **BASIC ACCOUNTING EQUATION** is, Assets = Liabilities + Shareholders' Equity

Assets	**=**	**Liabilities**	**+**	**Shareholders' Equity**
Economic resources (e.g., cash, inventory, buildings)		Financing from creditors (e.g., amounts owed to suppliers, employees, banks)		Financing from shareholders (e.g., contributed capital, retained earnings)

The basic accounting equation shows what we mean when we refer to a company's *financial position*: the economic resources that the company owns and the sources of financing for those resources.

Elements   *Assets* are economic resources controlled by the entity as a result of past business events. Assets have the potential to contribute cash to the entity in the future. Canadian Tire lists seven items under the assets category, and those named are common to many companies. The specific items listed as assets on a company's statement of financial position depend on the nature of its operations. Canadian Tire has listed all economic resources that provide and sell essential retail services and products. The company expects each of these economic resources to provide future benefits to the company.

To start its operations, Canadian Tire needed *cash* to purchase land on which to build stores *(property)*, and fixtures and equipment *(equipment)* to store the variety of products and services it offers to its customers. Canadian Tire needed to have insurance to protect its resources against potential losses; advance payment *(prepaid expenses)* of any insurance premiums provide future economic benefits (i.e., insurance protection). Canadian Tire then purchased the variety of products to sell to its customers, leading to the value assigned to *inventories*. When Canadian Tire sells its products and services to customers, it sells them either for cash or on credit and receives promises to pay, called *accounts receivable*, which are collected in cash later. When Canadian Tire has excess cash that is not needed for operations, it invests this cash in highly liquid assets, such as certificates of deposit with banks *(short-term investments)* that are convertible back into cash with a three-month period. As Canadian Tire grew more profitable, it expanded its business activities by acquiring other businesses, including assets that are not easily identifiable or measured. These assets are known as *goodwill* and include such items as customer loyalty and a reputation for good service. Because of the complexity of its operations, Canadian Tire also controls resources reported as *other assets*, which are explained in future chapters.

Every asset on the statement of financial position is initially measured at the total cost incurred to acquire it. Statements of financial position do not, generally, report the amounts for which the assets could currently be sold.

Liabilities are the entity's obligations that result from past business events. They arise primarily from purchasing goods or services on credit and borrowing cash to finance the business.

There are seven types of liabilities listed on Canadian Tire's statement of financial position. When Canadian Tire purchases products and services from suppliers on credit without a formal contract, it must pay the equivalent amount in cash within a short period of time. The obligation to pay is reported as *accounts payable*. Canadian Tire also receives services from other providers, such as employees and telecommunications companies, and it must pay for these services. Unpaid amounts are reported as *accrued liabilities*. *Provisions* are estimated amounts payable in the future, but the exact amount and timing of the payment depend on future events. As a profitable company, Canadian Tire must pay income taxes, which are reported as *income tax payable*. The company has borrowed from banks and other creditors according to formal, written lending agreements. The amounts payable within 12 months from the date of the statement are reported as *short-term borrowings*; the amounts payable after 12 months are reported as *long-term debt*. The company also reports a variety of other obligations under *other liabilities*, which are identified and described in future chapters.

Shareholders' equity indicates the amount of financing provided by owners of the business, and reinvested earnings.[2] Shareholders' equity arises from three sources: (1) *contributed capital*, or the investment of cash and other assets in the business by the owners; (2) *retained earnings*, or the amount of earnings reinvested in the business (and, thus, not distributed to shareholders in the form of dividends); and (3) *other components*, which includes specific elements of equity that are covered in future chapters.

INTERPRETING ASSETS, LIABILITIES, AND SHAREHOLDERS' EQUITY ON THE STATEMENT OF FINANCIAL POSITION

FINANCIAL ANALYSIS

The value of Canadian Tire's assets is important to its creditors and its owners. Assets, by definition, must have the potential to produce cash and, therefore, provide a basis for judging whether the company has sufficient resources available to continue to operate the business. Assets are also important because they could be sold for cash if Canadian Tire goes out of business.

Creditors are interested in Canadian Tire's liabilities because they must know if the company will have sufficient sources of cash to pay its debts. Canadian Tire's debts are also relevant to its bankers' decisions to lend more money to the company, because existing creditors share the bankers' claims against Canadian Tire's assets. Legal ownership of assets remains with the creditors, to secure the company's repayment of debt. If a business does not pay its creditors, the creditors may force the sale of assets sufficient to meet their claims.

In some situations, the sale of assets may not cover all of the company's debts; thus, creditors often take a loss. This is because the assets were acquired with the intent of producing future cash for the company in the normal course of its operations. These assets may not be valued by external parties as having the same potential to produce cash for them as the assets had for Canadian Tire. Thus, creditors may not be able to sell the assets for the amount of the debt.

Canadian Tire's shareholders' equity, or net worth, is important to creditors because, legally, their claims for repayment of obligations must be settled before those of the owners. If Canadian Tire goes out of business and its assets are sold, the proceeds of that sale must be used to pay back creditors before the shareholders receive any money. Shareholders provide resources for the company to use in the future, with no promise of any future repayment. They are entitled to what is left only after creditors' claims have been settled. Thus, creditors consider shareholders' equity a protective cushion.

A Note on Format   A few additional formatting conventions are worth noting here. Assets may be listed on the statement of financial position in either increasing or decreasing order of their convertibility to cash. Most Canadian companies, including Canadian Tire, list their assets beginning with the most-liquid asset, cash, and ending with the least-liquid assets, which are not readily convertible to cash, such as goodwill. In contrast, many international companies, such as the Benetton Group, list their least-liquid assets first and most-liquid assets last. Similarly, liabilities may be listed by either increasing or decreasing order of maturity (due date). International Accounting Standard (IAS) 1 allows companies to use either format to report their assets and liabilities.

Most financial statements include the monetary unit sign (in Canada, $) beside the first amount in a group of items (e.g., the cash amount in the assets). Also, it is common to place a single underline below the last item in a group before a total or subtotal (e.g., Other assets). A double underline is placed below group totals (e.g., Total assets). The same conventions are followed in all four basic financial statements.

PAUSE FOR FEEDBACK

We just learned that the statement of financial position reports dollar amounts for a company's assets, liabilities, and shareholders' equity at a specific point in time. These elements are related in the basic accounting equation: Assets = Liabilities + Shareholders' Equity. Before you move on, complete the following questions to test your understanding of these concepts.

SELF-STUDY QUIZ 1-1

1. Canadian Tire's *assets* are listed in one section and *liabilities* and *shareholders' equity* in another. Notice that the two sections balance, in conformity with the basic accounting equation. In the following chapters, you will learn that the accounting equation is the basic building block for the entire accounting process. Your task here is to verify that total assets ($14,988) is correct, using the numbers for liabilities and shareholders' equity presented in Exhibit 1.2.

2. Restate the accounting equation with shareholders' equity on the left-hand side. Use this format of the accounting equation to explain, in plain language, what the value of total shareholders' equity means.

3. Learning which items belong in each of the categories on the statement of financial position is an important first step in understanding their meaning. Mark each item in the following list as an asset (A), a liability (L), or shareholders' equity (SE), without referring to Exhibit 1.2.

_____ Accounts payable

_____ Accounts receivable

_____ Cash

_____ Contributed capital

_____ Property and equipment

_____ Inventories

_____ Long-term debt

_____ Goodwill

_____ Retained earnings

After you complete your answers, check them with the solutions at the end of the chapter.

The **STATEMENT OF COMPREHENSIVE INCOME** reports the change in shareholders' equity during an accounting period from business activities, excluding exchanges with shareholders.

The Statement of Comprehensive Income

Structure   The **statement of comprehensive income** reports the *change* in shareholders' equity, during an accounting period, arising from business activities other than investments by shareholders (such as the issuance of shares) or distributions to shareholders (such as dividends). The statement of comprehensive income has two parts. The first part reports the accountant's primary measure of a company's performance: revenues generated less expenses incurred during the accounting period. Accountants label this measure of performance "net earnings."[3] The second part reports other comprehensive income, which includes changes in values of assets and liabilities that are not recognized in the statement of earnings.

Companies can present all items of income and expenses either in one statement of comprehensive income or in two related statements—a **statement of earnings** (or income statement[4]) reporting the revenues and expenses of the accounting period that have already affected net earnings, and a statement of comprehensive income reporting additional income and expense items that will affect net earnings in the future. Canadian Tire uses the two-statement approach. We will focus our attention in this chapter on the statement of earnings. The statement of comprehensive income will be covered in Chapter 11.

A quick reading of Canadian Tire's statement of earnings (Exhibit 1.3) indicates its purpose and content. The heading of the statement, again, identifies the name of the entity, title of the statement, and unit of measure used in the statement. Unlike the statement of financial position, which reports financial information as of a certain date, the statement of earnings reports information for a *specified period of time* (e.g., for the year ended January 2, 2016). The time period covered by the financial statements (one year in this case) is called an **accounting period**.

Notice that Canadian Tire's statement of earnings has three major captions: revenues, expenses, and net earnings. The equation that describes their relationship is:

Revenues	–	Expenses	=	Net Earnings
Cash and promises received from delivery of goods and services		Resources used to earn the period's revenues		Revenues earned minus expenses incurred

Revenues — **Expenses** = **Net earnings**

Elements   Companies earn *revenues* from the sale of goods or services to customers (in Canadian Tire's case, from the sale of various household and garden items, sportswear and equipment, auto products, and petroleum products). Revenues normally are amounts expected to be received for goods or services that have been delivered to a customer, *whether or not the customer has paid for the goods or services*. Retail stores, such as Tim Hortons, Dollarama, and Canadian Tire, often receive cash at the time of sale. Canadian Tire also allows commercial customers to purchase goods on credit and receives a promise of future payment called an account receivable, which is collected in cash at a later date. In either case, the business recognizes the total of cash and credit sales made during a specific accounting period as revenue for that period. Various terms are used in financial statements to describe different sources of revenue (e.g., provision of services, sale of goods, rental of property). Canadian Tire's revenues consist mainly of sale of goods to customers, rendering of services, and interest on unpaid balances on customers' purchases from Canadian Tire.

Statement
of
Earnings

Revenues
– Expenses

Net earnings

Exhibit **1.3**
Statement of Earnings

REAL-WORLD EXCERPT

Canadian Tire Corporation

CANADIAN TIRE CORPORATION		
Statement of Earnings		
For the Year Ended January 2, 2016		
(in millions of Canadian dollars, except per share amounts)		
Revenues		
Sale of goods	$10,650	
Other revenues	1,630	
		$12,280
Expenses		
Cost of producing revenue	$ 8,144	
Selling, general, and administrative expenses	3,042	
Interest expense	93	
Total pretax expenses		11,279
Earnings before income taxes		1,001
Income tax expense		(265)
Net earnings		$ 736
Earnings per share		$ 8.66

Name of the entity
Title of the statement
Accounting period
Unit of measure

Revenue earned from sale of products

Revenue earned from services rendered, interest on receivables from customers, and other revenues sources

Cost of products and services sold to customers

Other operating expenses (marketing, utilities, delivery costs, etc.)

Interest and other costs incurred in connection with the borrowing of funds

Income taxes related to the period's pretax earnings

The accompanying notes are an integral part of these financial statements.

This statement is an adaptation of Canadian Tire's actual statement of earnings for 2015.

Source: Canadian Tire Corporation, Annual Report, 2015.

Expenses represent the monetary value of resources the entity used up, or consumed, to earn revenues during the period. Canadian Tire lists four items as expenses on the statement of earnings. The cost of producing revenue is Canadian Tire's total cost of products and services sold to customers during the year. These include the costs of products purchased from suppliers and services rendered by others. The cost of products sold is the most significant expense for merchandising companies, and most of these companies use the term *cost of sales* (or *cost of goods sold*) on their statement of earnings. *Selling, general, and administrative expenses* include items such as the salaries of personnel, marketing and promotion of the company's products through print and electronic media, and the cost of buildings, equipment, and tools used (called *depreciation*) to store the goods that were sold. *Interest expense* is a finance cost that Canadian Tire incurred in connection with the funds it borrowed from creditors. Finally, as a corporation, Canadian Tire must pay income tax to the government based on its pretax earnings. Canadian Tire's *income tax expense* for 2015 is approximately 26.5 percent of its pretax earnings.

Expenses may require immediate payment of cash, payment of cash at a future date, or use of some other resource, such as an inventory item, that may have been paid for in a previous period. For accounting purposes, the expense reported in one accounting period may actually be paid for in cash in another accounting period. Nevertheless, the company recognizes all expenses (cash and credit) incurred during a specific accounting period, regardless of the timing of the cash payment. For example, if Canadian Tire used $1 million for telecommunication services throughout its stores in December 2015, but it did not pay the $1 million until mid-January 2016, this amount would be recognized as an expense for the accounting period ending on January 2, 2016. This is because the services provided by the telecommunications company were used during the accounting period in the process of generating revenue for Canadian Tire during that period.

Net earnings (also called *net income* or *profit*) is the excess of total revenues over total expenses incurred to generate revenue during a specific period. Canadian Tire's net earnings for the year measures its success in selling products and services for more than it cost to generate those sales. If total expenses exceed total revenues, a loss is reported. (Losses are normally noted by parentheses around the reported figure.) When revenues and expenses are equal for the period, the business has operated at breakeven.

We noted earlier that revenues are not necessarily the same as cash collections from customers, and expenses are not necessarily the same as cash payments to suppliers. As a result, the amount of net earnings normally *does not equal* the net cash generated by operations. This latter amount is reported on the statement of cash flows discussed later in the chapter.

ANALYZING THE STATEMENT OF EARNINGS: BEYOND THE BOTTOM LINE

FINANCIAL ANALYSIS

Investors and creditors closely monitor a firm's net earnings because they reflect the firm's ability to sell goods and services for more than the cost to produce and deliver them. Investors buy the company's shares when they believe that net earnings will improve and lead to a higher share price. Lenders also rely on future earnings to provide the resources to repay loans. The details of the statement are also important. For example, Canadian Tire had to sell $12,280 (all dollar amounts in millions) worth of products and services in 2015 to earn $736. If a competitor were to lower its prices by just 5 percent, forcing Canadian Tire to do the same in order to retain its market share, or if Canadian Tire had to triple marketing expenses to catch up to a competitor, its net earnings could easily turn into a net loss. These and other factors help investors and creditors estimate the company's future net earnings based on past information.

PAUSE FOR FEEDBACK

As noted above, the statement of earnings reports revenues, expenses, and net earnings for a stated period of time. To practice your understanding of these concepts, complete the following questions.

SELF-STUDY **QUIZ 1-2**

1. Learning which items belong in each of the statement of earnings categories is an important first step in understanding their meaning. Mark each statement of earnings item in the following list as either a revenue (R) or an expense (E), without referring to Exhibit 1.3.

   _____ Cost of sales   _____ Sales   _____ General and administrative

2. During 2015, Canadian Tire delivered products and services to customers for which the customers paid, or promised to pay in the future, amounts totalling $12,280. During the same period, it collected $12,275 in cash from its customers. Without referring to Exhibit 1.3, indicate which of the two amounts will be shown on Canadian Tire's statement of earnings as sales revenue for 2015. Explain.

3. During the year 2015, Canadian Tire delivered products and services to customers that cost $8,144. During the same period, it paid its suppliers an amount of $8,094 for purchases of products and services. Without referring to Exhibit 1.3, indicate which of the two amounts will be shown on Canadian Tire's statement of earnings as cost of sales for 2015. Explain.

After you complete your answers, check them with the solutions at the end of the chapter.

The Statement of Changes in Equity

The **STATEMENT OF CHANGES IN EQUITY** reports all changes to shareholders' equity during the accounting period.

Structure The **statement of changes in equity** reports all changes to shareholders' equity during the accounting period. Canadian Tire prepares a separate statement of changes in equity, shown in Exhibit 1.4 in a condensed format. The heading identifies the name of the entity, title of the statement, and unit of measure used. Like the statement of earnings, the statement of changes in equity covers a specific period of time, which in this case is one year. This statement reports the way that net earnings, distribution of net earnings (dividends), and other changes to shareholders' equity affected the company's financial position during the accounting period. We focus on retained earnings in this chapter and discuss the other components of equity in Chapter 11.

RETAINED EARNINGS refers to the accumulated earnings of a company that are not distributed to the shareholders as dividends.

Retained earnings refers to the accumulated earnings of a company that are not distributed to the shareholders as dividends and are reinvested in the business. Net earnings achieved during the year increases the balance of retained earnings. The declaration of dividends to the shareholders decreases retained earnings.[5] The retained earnings equation that describes these relationships is

$$\text{Beginning retained earnings} + \text{Net earnings} - \text{Dividends}$$
$$= \text{Ending retained earnings}$$

Exhibit **1.4**

Statement of Changes in Equity

REAL-WORLD EXCERPT

Canadian Tire Corporation

	Name of the entity Title of the statement Accounting period Unit of measure
Last-period ending balances	
Net earnings reported on the statement of earnings	
Issuance of new shares to investors	
Repurchase of the company's shares	
Dividends declared during the period	
A variety of changes affecting other components of equity	
Ending balances reported on the statement of financial position	

CANADIAN TIRE CORPORATION
Statement of Changes in Equity
For the Year Ended January 2, 2016
(in millions of Canadian dollars)

	Contributed Capital	Retained Earnings	Other Components
Balance as at January 3, 2015	$699	$4,075	$858
Net earnings for the year		736	
Issuance of shares	8		
Repurchase of shares	(33)		
Distribution of dividends		(639)	
Other changes			86
Balance as at January 2, 2016	$674	$4,172	$944

The accompanying notes are an integral part of these financial statements.

This statement is an adaptation of Canadian Tire's actual statement of changes in equity.

Source: Canadian Tire Corporation, Annual Report, 2015.

Statement of Changes in Equity

Equity, beginning of the period
+ Net earnings for the year
+ Other comprehensive income
− Dividends
+/− Other changes, net

Equity, end of the period

Elements The statement begins with Canadian Tire's balances to contributed capital, retained earnings, and other equity components at January 3, 2015 (the beginning of the accounting period). The net earnings reported on the statement of earnings for the current period is added to the beginning balance of retained earnings, and dividends declared during the year are subtracted from this amount. During 2015, Canadian Tire reported net earnings of $736, as shown in Exhibit 1.3, and declared a total of $639 in dividends to its shareholders. The net result is that retained earnings at January 2, 2016 (the end of the accounting period), increased by $97 ($4,172 − $4,075).

The ending retained earnings amount of $4,172 is the same as that reported in Exhibit 1.2 on Canadian Tire's statement of financial position. The ending balances of contributed capital and other components are also reported on the statement of financial position.

INTERPRETING RETAINED EARNINGS

FINANCIAL ANALYSIS

Reinvestment of net earnings, or retained earnings, is an important source of financing for Canadian Tire, representing about 28 percent of its financing. Creditors closely monitor a firm's retained earnings, because the firm's policy on dividend payments to its shareholders affects its ability to repay its debts. Every dollar Canadian Tire pays to shareholders as a dividend is not available for use in paying back its debt to creditors. The reverse is also true; every dollar used to repay creditors is unavailable either for distribution to investors as dividends or for retention and reinvestment in the company's future growth. Investors examine retained earnings to determine whether the company is reinvesting a sufficient portion of net earnings to support future growth.

PAUSE FOR FEEDBACK

The statement of retained earnings explains changes to the retained earnings balance caused by net earnings and dividends during the reporting period. Check your understanding of these relationships by completing the following question.

SELF-STUDY QUIZ 1-3

Canadian Tire's retained earnings reflect the way that the net earnings and distribution of dividends affected the financial position of the company during the accounting period. Assume that, in a prior period, Canadian Tire's financial statements reported the following amounts: beginning retained earnings, $4,405; total assets, $13,642; dividends, $512; cost of sales, $12,162; and net earnings, $640. Without referring to Exhibit 1.4, compute ending retained earnings.

After you complete your answer, check it with the solutions at the end of the chapter.

The Statement of Cash Flows

Structure The **statement of cash flows** divides Canadian Tire's cash inflows (receipts) and outflows (payments) into three primary categories of cash flows in a typical business: cash flows from operating, investing, and financing activities. Canadian Tire's statement of cash flows is presented in Exhibit 1.5 in a summarized form. The specifics of a complete statement of cash flows are discussed in Chapter 5. The heading identifies the name of the entity, the title of the statement, and the unit of measure used. Like the statement of earnings, the statement of cash flows covers a specified period of time, which in this case is one year.

As discussed earlier in this chapter, reported revenues do not always equal cash collected from customers because some sales may be on credit. Also, expenses reported on the statement of earnings may not be equal to cash paid out during the period because expenses may be incurred in one period and paid for in another. As a result, net earnings (revenues minus expenses) does *not* usually equal the amount of cash received minus the amount paid during the period. Because the statement of earnings does not provide any information concerning cash flows, accountants prepare the statement of cash flows to report inflows and outflows of cash.

The **STATEMENT OF CASH FLOWS** reports cash inflows and outflows that are related to operating, investing, and financing activities during the accounting period.

Exhibit **1.5**
Statement of Cash Flows

REAL-WORLD EXCERPT

Canadian Tire Corporation

Name of the entity	
Title of the statement	
Accounting period	
Unit of measure	
Cash flows directly related to earnings from operations	
Cash flows from purchase/sale of property, equipment, and investments	
Cash flows from and to investors and creditors	
Change in cash during the period	
Last period's ending cash balance	
Ending cash on the statement of financial position	

CANADIAN TIRE CORPORATION Statement of Cash Flows For the Year Ended January 2, 2016 (in millions of Canadian dollars)	
Cash flows from operating activities	$979
Cash flows from investing activities	(299)
Cash flows from financing activities	(427)
Net increase in cash during the year	253
Cash, beginning of year	648
Cash, end of year	$901

The accompanying notes are an integral part of these financial statements.

This statement is an adaptation of Canadian Tire's actual statement of cash flows.

Source: Canadian Tire Corporation, Annual Report, 2015.

Statement of Cash Flows

+/− CFO
+/− CFI
+/− CFF

Change in cash

The statement of cash flows equation describes the causes of the change in cash reported on the statement of financial position from the end of the last period to the end of the current period:

+/− **Cash flows from operating activities**
+/− **Cash flows from investing activities**
+/− **Cash flows from financing activities**

Change in cash

Note that each of the three cash flow sources can be either positive or negative.

Elements   *Cash flows from operating activities (CFO)* are cash flows that are directly related to generating earnings. For example, when customers pay Canadian Tire for the products and services it delivered to them, the company lists the amounts collected as cash collected from customers. When Canadian Tire pays salaries or bills received for its suppliers of merchandise inventory, it includes the amounts in cash paid to employees and suppliers.[6]

Cash flows from investing activities (CFI) include cash flows related to the acquisition or sale of the company's property, equipment, and investments. This year, Canadian Tire had two cash outflows for investing activities: purchase of additional property and equipment, and intangible assets. The company also sold some of its property, equipment, and investments.

Cash flows from financing activities (CFA) are directly related to the financing of the company itself. They involve both receipts and payments of cash to investors and creditors (except for suppliers). During 2015, Canadian Tire's main financing activities included borrowing from creditors, paying cash dividends to its shareholders, repurchases of the company's shares, and repayment of debt that became due.

INTERPRETING THE STATEMENT OF CASH FLOWS

FINANCIAL
ANALYSIS

Many analysts believe that the statement of cash flows is particularly useful for predicting future cash flows that may be available for payment of debt to creditors and dividends to investors. Bankers often consider the operating activities section to be the most important, because it indicates the company's ability to generate cash from sales to meet its current cash needs. Any amount left can be used to repay debt or expand the company.

Shareholders will invest in a company if they believe that it will eventually generate more cash from operations than it uses, so that cash will become available to pay dividends and to expand. The statement of cash flows shows that Canadian Tire has invested in new retail and distribution capacity during 2015, a good sign if demand continues to increase. It also indicates that Canadian Tire used more funds for financing activities than it generated during the year. The cash generated from operations was sufficient to cover the company's cash needs for both investing and financing activities.

PAUSE FOR
FEEDBACK STOP

The statement of cash flows reports inflows and outflows of cash for a stated period of time, classified into three categories: operating, investing, and financing activities. Answer the following questions to test your understanding of the concepts involved.

SELF-STUDY QUIZ 1-4

1. During the period 2015, Canadian Tire delivered products and services to customers that paid, or promised to pay in the future, amounts totalling $12,280. During the same period, it collected $12,275 in cash from its customers. Without referring to Exhibit 1.5, indicate which of the two numbers will be shown on Canadian Tire's statement of cash flows for 2015.

2. Learning which items belong in each category on the statement of cash flows is an important first step in understanding their meaning. Mark each item in the following list as a cash flow from operating activities (O), investing activities (I), or financing activities (F), without referring to Exhibit 1.5. Also, place parentheses around the letter only if it is a cash *outflow*.

   _____ Cash paid for dividends

   _____ Cash paid for interest

   _____ Cash received from bank borrowings

   _____ Cash paid for taxes

   _____ Cash paid to purchase property and equipment

   _____ Cash collected from customers

After you complete your answers, check them with the solutions at the end of the chapter.

Relationships among the Four Financial Statements

Our discussion of the four basic financial statements focused on the different elements reported on each of the statements, how the elements are related through the equation for each statement, and how the elements are important to the decisions of investors, creditors, and other external users. We have also discovered how the statements, all of which are outputs from the same system, are related to one another. In particular, we learned these points:

1. Net earnings from the statement of earnings results in an increase in ending retained earnings on the statement of changes in equity.

2. Ending retained earnings from the statement of changes in equity is one of the three components of shareholders' equity on the statement of financial position.

3. The change in cash on the statement of cash flows added to the cash balance at the beginning of the year equals the balance of cash at the end of the year, which appears on the statement of financial position.

Thus, as external users, we can think of the statement of earnings (and the statement of comprehensive income) as explaining, through the statement of changes in equity, how the operations of the company changed its financial position during the year. The statement of cash flows explains how the operating, investing, and financing activities of the company affected the cash balance on the statement of financial position during the year. These relationships are illustrated in Exhibit 1.6 for Canadian Tire's financial statements.

Exhibit **1.6**

Relationships among Canadian Tire's Statements

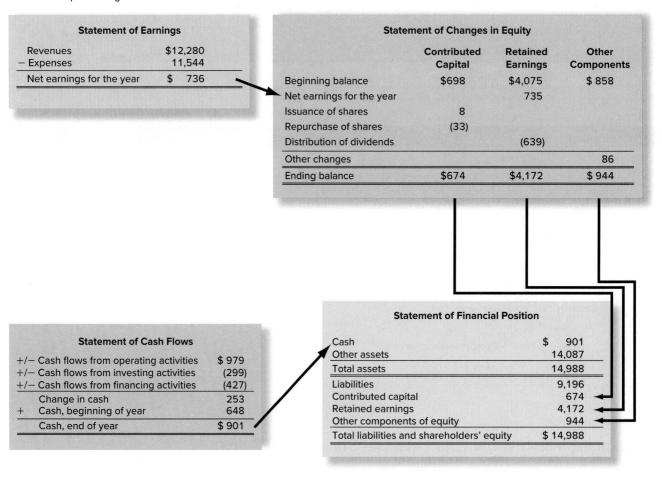

MANAGERIAL USES OF FINANCIAL STATEMENTS

FINANCIAL
ANALYSIS

In our discussion of financial analysis thus far, we have focused on the perspectives of investors and creditors. In addition, managers within the firm often make direct use of financial statements. For example, Canadian Tire's marketing managers and credit managers use customers' financial statements to decide whether to extend credit to them for their purchases of Canadian Tire's products. Canadian Tire's purchasing managers analyze financial statements of suppliers to judge whether the suppliers have the resources to meet Canadian Tire's demand for the many products that it sells to its customers. Both Canadian Tire's human resource managers and the employees' union use the company's financial statements as a basis for contract negotiations over pay rates. The net earnings figure even serves as a basis for computing employee bonuses.

When Canadian Tire's managers examine the financial statements of the company's customers and suppliers, they rely on these statements as the best source of financial information available to external users, because they do not have access to internal financial information produced by their customers and their suppliers. However, when they make internal decisions regarding Canadian Tire's operations, they rely on more detailed financial information obtained through the company's managerial accounting system.

Notes to Financial Statements

At the bottom of each of the four basic financial statements you will typically find the following statement: "The accompanying notes are an integral part of these financial statements." This is the accounting equivalent of the nutritional content on pre-packaged food. It warns users that failure to read the notes to these financial statements will result in incomplete knowledge of the company's financial health. **Notes** provide supplemental information about the financial condition of a company, without which the financial statements cannot be fully understood.

There are three basic types of notes. The first type provides descriptions of the accounting rules applied in the company's statements. The second presents additional detail about a line on the financial statements. For example, Canadian Tire's note referring to property and equipment lists the types of assets that are grouped together under this item. The third type of note presents additional financial disclosures about items not listed on the statements themselves. For example, Canadian Tire is exposed to significant risks; the risks related to credit and fluctuations in exchange rates are disclosed in a note. We will discuss many note disclosures throughout the book, because understanding their content is critical to understanding the company.[7]

NOTES provide supplemental information about the financial condition of a company, without which the financial statements cannot be fully understood.

Summary of the Four Basic Financial Statements

We learned a lot about the content of the four basic statements. Exhibit 1.7 summarizes this information. Take a few minutes to review the information in the exhibit before you move on to the next section of the chapter.

Exhibit **1.7**

Summary of Four Basic Financial Statements

Financial Statement	Purpose	Structure	Examples of Content
Statement of Financial Position	Reports the financial position (economic resources and sources of financing) of an accounting entity *at a point in time*.	**Statement of Financial Position** Assets = Liabilities + Shareholders' Equity	cash, trade receivables, plant and equipment, notes payable, contributed capital
Statement of Earnings	Reports the net earnings achieved *during the accounting period*.	**Statement of Earnings** Revenues − Expenses Net earnings	sales revenue, cost of sales, selling expense, interest expense
Statement of Changes in Equity	Reports the way that elements of comprehensive income, dividends, and changes to contributed capital affected the financial position of the company *during the accounting period*.	**Statement of Changes in Equity** Equity, beginning of the period + Net earnings for the year + Other comprehensive income − Dividends +/− Other changes, net Equity, end of the period	retained earnings, elements of comprehensive income, distributions of dividends, increase in contributed capital
Statement of Cash Flows	Reports inflows (receipts) and outflows (payments) of cash *during the accounting period* in the operating, investing, and financing categories.	**Statement of Cash Flows** +/− CFO +/− CFI +/− CFF Change in cash	cash collected from customers, cash paid to suppliers, cash paid to purchase equipment, cash borrowed from banks

RESPONSIBILITIES FOR THE ACCOUNTING COMMUNICATION PROCESS

Effective communication means that the recipient understands what the sender intends to convey. For decision makers to use the information in Canadian Tire's financial statements effectively, they have to understand what information each statement conveys. Understandability is the foundation of effective communication.

Decision makers also need to understand the *measurement rules* applied in computing the numbers on the statements. A swim coach would never try to evaluate a swimmer's time in the "100 freestyle" without first asking whether the time was for a race in metres or in yards. Likewise, a decision maker should never attempt to use accounting information without first understanding the measurement rules that were used to develop the information. The measurement rules used to develop the information in financial statements are based on **International Financial Reporting Standards (IFRS)**. These encompass broad principles, specific rules, practices, and conventions of general application that are used by organizations to record transactions and report financial statement information to interested users.

International Financial Reporting Standards (IFRS)

How Are Accounting Standards Determined? The accounting system that we use today has a long history. Its foundations are normally traced back to the works of an Italian monk and mathematician, Fr. Luca Pacioli. In 1494, he described an approach developed by Italian merchants to account for their activities as owner-managers of business ventures. Many others wrote works on accounting after Pacioli, but prior to 1933, each company's management largely determined its own financial reporting practices. Thus, little uniformity in practice existed among companies.

In contrast, today there are organizations that determine the accounting standards which must be followed in identifying, measuring, classifying, and reporting accounting information. In Canada, the **Accounting Standards Board (AcSB)** is the private-sector body given primary responsibility to set the detailed rules that become accepted accounting standards. The AcSB is responsible for establishing standards of accounting and reporting by publicly accountable enterprises, private enterprises, government organizations, and not-for-profit organizations. These standards or recommendations, which are published in *CPA Canada Handbooks*, have expanded over time because of the increasing diversity and complexity of business practices.

For Canadian publicly accountable enterprises,[8] the AcSB has determined that they must prepare their financial statements in accordance with International Financial Reporting Standards. IFRS are a single set of globally accepted high-quality standards, produced by the **International Accounting Standards Board (IASB)**, which is an independent standard-setting board responsible for the development and publication of IFRS. An older set of International Accounting Standards (IAS) were issued by the Board of the International Accounting Standards Committee, and they complement the accounting standards issued by the IASB.

This book focuses on the accounting and financial reporting by publicly accountable enterprises. The accounting and financial reporting standards used by other types of organizations are covered in advanced accounting courses. Differences between the accounting standards applicable to Canadian publicly accountable enterprises and Canadian private enterprises are highlighted at the end of each chapter.

Most managers do not need to learn all of the details included in all accounting standards. Our approach is to focus on those standards, appropriate to an introductory course, that have the greatest effect on the numbers presented in financial statements.

Why Are Accounting Standards Important to Managers and External Users? Accounting standards are of great interest to the companies that must prepare the statements and to the readers of these statements. IFRS and IAS provide

INTERNATIONAL FINANCIAL REPORTING STANDARDS (IFRS) are guidelines for the measurement rules used to develop the information in financial statements.

The **ACCOUNTING STANDARDS BOARD** (AcSB) is the private-sector body given the primary responsibility to set the detailed rules that become accepted accounting standards.

The **INTERNATIONAL ACCOUNTING STANDARDS BOARD (IASB)** is an independent standard-setting board that is responsible for the development and publication of International Financial Reporting Standards.

guidance to companies in selecting the accounting methods that best reflect the results of their operations and financial situation, and on reporting them in an understandable manner. These globally accepted accounting standards also prevent managers from deliberately manipulating and reporting values that serve their personal interests by using accounting practices not in conformity with IFRS. Widely divergent accounting practices reduce the *comparability* of financial information from different companies operating in the same line of business. IFRS enhance the comparability by limiting the number of acceptable alternative accounting methods across companies and over time. Furthermore, understanding IFRS and IAS enables external users to assess the quality of the information presented in the financial statements and related notes.

Companies, their managers, and their owners are most directly affected by the information presented in the financial statements. Companies incur the cost of preparing the statements and bear the major economic consequences of their publication. These economic consequences include, among others, the following:

1. Changes to the selling price of a company's shares.

2. Changes to the amount of bonuses received by management and employees.

3. The loss of competitive advantage over other companies.

THE INTERNATIONAL ACCOUNTING STANDARDS BOARD AND GLOBAL CONVERGENCE OF ACCOUNTING STANDARDS   INTERNATIONAL **PERSPECTIVE**

Financial accounting standards and disclosure requirements are set by national regulatory agencies and standard-setting bodies. However, since 2002, there has been a substantial movement toward the adoption of International Financial Reporting Standards (IFRS) issued by the International Accounting Standards Board (IASB). A growing number of countries have adopted IFRS for at least some of their reporting entities. Most adopting countries require IFRS for all reporting entities, some for only banks, and others for all reporting entities except banks and other financial institutions.

In the United States, the Securities and Exchange Commission allows foreign companies whose shares are traded on U.S. exchange markets to use IFRS, but there seems to be little support for reporting of accounting information by U.S. domestic companies in accordance with IFRS.

Source: Deloitte IAS PLUS website. April 2016. For information, contact Deloitte Touche Tohmatsu Limited.

Sources: http://www.iasplus.com/en/resources/ifrs-topics/use-of-ifrs and http://www.iasplus.com/en/news/2015/06/schnurr.

Canadian Tire's share price can be determined in part based on the net earnings computed in compliance with IFRS. This presents the possibility that changes in accounting standards can affect the price buyers are willing to pay for companies. Employees who receive part of their pay based on reaching stated net earnings targets are directly concerned with any changes in how the net earnings figure is determined. Managers and owners are often concerned that publishing more information in financial statements will give away trade secrets to other companies that compete with them. As a consequence of these and other concerns, changes in accounting standards are actively debated and political lobbying often takes place. The accounting standards that are eventually issued are often a compromise among the conflicting wishes of interested parties.

Ensuring the Accuracy of Financial Statements

Ethical Conduct Ethics are standards of conduct for judging right from wrong, honest from dishonest behaviour, and fair from unfair practices. Intentional misreporting of financial statements is both unethical and illegal. However, many situations are less clear cut and require that individuals weigh one moral principle (e.g., honesty) against another (e.g., loyalty to a friend). When money is involved, people can easily fool themselves into believing that bad acts are justified. To avoid falling prey to this tendency, when faced with an ethical dilemma, people should follow a three-step process:

1. Identify the effects of the decision on both parties, those who will benefit from the situation (often the manager or employee involved) and those who will be harmed (other employees, owners, creditors, the environment).

2. Identify alternative courses of action.

3. Choose the alternative that you would like to see reported on the news. That is usually the ethical choice.

Management Responsibility and the Demand for Auditing

Who is responsible for the accuracy of the amounts reported in Canadian Tire's financial statements? Primary responsibility for setting up systems to prevent and detect unethical behaviour lies with management, as represented by the highest officer of the company and its highest financial officer.[9] Companies take three important steps to assure investors that the company's records are accurate: (1) they develop and maintain a system of internal controls over both the records and the assets of the company, (2) they hire outside independent auditors to attest to the fairness of the statement presentations, and (3) they form a committee of the board of directors to oversee the integrity of these two safeguards. These responsibilities are often reiterated in a formal report on **management responsibility for financial statements (management certification)**, which indicates management's primary responsibility for financial statement information and the steps to ensure the accuracy of the company's records (see Exhibit 1.8). The three safeguards outlined above and management certification are required for all Canadian companies with publicly traded shares. Managers of companies that prepare fraudulent financial statements are subject to criminal and civil penalties.

The report on **MANAGEMENT RESPONSIBILITY FOR FINANCIAL STATEMENTS (MANAGEMENT CERTIFICATION)** indicates management's primary responsibility for financial statement information and the steps to ensure the accuracy of the company's records.

ANNUAL REPORT

Exhibit 1.8
Management Responsibility
for Financial Statements
and Independent Auditor's Report

REAL-WORLD EXCERPT
*Canadian
Tire Corporation*

Management's Responsibility for Financial Statements

The Management of Canadian Tire Corporation, Limited is responsible for the accompanying consolidated financial statements. The financial statements have been prepared by Management in accordance with International Financial Reporting Standards, which recognize the necessity of relying on some best estimates and informed judgments. All financial information in our Management's Discussion and Analysis is consistent with the consolidated financial statements.

To discharge its responsibilities for financial reporting and safeguarding of assets, Management depends on the company's systems of internal control. These systems are designed to provide reasonable assurance that the financial records are reliable and form a proper basis for the timely and accurate preparation of financial statements. Management meets the objectives of internal control on a cost-effective basis through the prudent selection and training of personnel, adoption and communication of appropriate policies, and employment of an internal audit program.

The Board of Directors oversees Management's responsibilities for the consolidated financial statements primarily through the activities of its Audit Committee, which is composed solely of directors who are neither officers nor employees of the Company. This Committee meets with Management and the Company's independent auditors, Deloitte LLP, to review the consolidated financial statements and recommend approval by the Board of Directors. The Audit Committee is also responsible for making recommendations with respect to the appointment of, and for approving remuneration and the terms of engagement of, the Company's auditors. The Audit Committee also meets with the auditors, without the presence of Management, to discuss the results of their audit.

The consolidated financial statements have been audited by Deloitte LLP, who were appointed by shareholder vote at the annual shareholders' meeting. Their report is presented below.

Michael B. Medline
President and Chief Executive Officer
February 17, 2016

Dean McCann
Executive Vice-President and Financial Officer

Independent Auditor's Report

To the Shareholders of Canadian Tire Corporation, Limited

We have audited the accompanying consolidated financial statements of Canadian Tire Corporation, Limited, which comprise the consolidated balance sheets as at January 2, 2016, and January 3, 2015, and the consolidated statements of income, consolidated statements of comprehensive income, consolidated statements of cash flows, and consolidated statements of changes in equity for the years ended January 2, 2016, and January 3, 2015, and a summary of significant accounting policies and other explanatory information.

Management's Responsibility for the Consolidated Financial Statements

Management is responsible for the preparation and fair presentation of these consolidated financial statements in accordance with International Financial Reporting Standards, and for such internal control as management determines is necessary to enable the preparation of consolidated financial statements that are free from material misstatement, whether due to fraud or error.

Auditor's Responsibility

Our responsibility is to express an opinion on these consolidated financial statements based on our audits. We conducted our audits in accordance with Canadian generally accepted auditing standards. Those standards require that we comply with ethical requirements and plan and perform the audit to obtain reasonable assurance about whether the consolidated financial statements are free from material misstatement.

An audit involves performing procedures to obtain audit evidence about the amounts and disclosures in the consolidated financial statements. The procedures selected depend on the auditor's judgment, including the assessment of the risks of material misstatement of the consolidated financial statements, whether due to fraud or error. In making those risk assessments, the auditor considers internal control relevant to the entity's preparation and fair presentation of the consolidated financial statements in order to design audit procedures that are appropriate in the circumstances, but not for the purpose of expressing an opinion on the effectiveness of the entity's internal control. An audit also includes evaluating the appropriateness of accounting policies used and the reasonableness of accounting estimates made by management, as well as evaluating the overall presentation of the consolidated financial statements.

We believe that the audit evidence we have obtained in our audits is sufficient and appropriate to provide a basis for our audit opinion.

Opinion

In our opinion, the consolidated financial statements present fairly, in all material respects, the financial position of Canadian Tire Corporation, Limited, as at January 2, 2016, and January 3, 2015, and its financial performance and its cash flows for the years then ended in accordance with International Financial Reporting Standards.

Deloitte LLP
Chartered Professional Accountants
Licensed Public Accountants
February 17, 2016
Toronto, Ontario

Source: Canadian Tire Corporation, Annual Report, 2015.

Three steps to ensure the accuracy of records:

System of Controls	External Auditors	Board of Directors

The role of the independent auditor is described in more detail in the **independent audit report**, which describes the auditor's opinion of the fairness of the financial statements and the evidence gathered to support that opinion (see Exhibit 1.8). It is important to note that the main difference between the report of management and the report of the independent auditor concerns the responsibility for the financial information included in the company's annual report. As the report of the independent auditor indicates, the auditor's responsibility is to express an opinion on Canadian Tire's financial statements that have been prepared by its accounting personnel and reviewed by the *audit committee* of the *board of directors*, which assumes responsibility for the quality of the content of these financial statements.[10]

In Canada, professional accountants were previously designated as *Chartered Accountant (CA), Certified General Accountant (CGA),* or *Certified Management Accountant (CMA).* Efforts to unify the profession began in 2011 and have resulted in the unification of the accounting profession in Quebec in 2012 and the establishment of Chartered Professional Accountants of Canada (CPA Canada) effective January 1,

2013. The previous three accounting designations became one designation: *Chartered Professional Accountant (CPA)*. The CPA designation is granted on completion of the CPA professional educational program and practical experience requirements.[11] Professional accountants can offer various accounting services to the public, as indicated in Appendix 1B.

An **audit** is an examination of the financial reports to ensure that they represent what they claim and conform to IFRS. In performing an audit, the independent auditor examines the underlying transactions and the accounting methods used to account for these transactions. Because of the enormous number of transactions that total billions of dollars each year for a major enterprise, such as Canadian Tire, the auditor does not examine each transaction. Rather, professional approaches are used to ascertain beyond reasonable doubt that transactions were measured and reported properly.[12]

Many opportunities exist for managers to intentionally prepare misleading financial reports. An audit performed by an independent auditor is the best protection available to the public. When that protection fails, however, the independent auditor is sometimes found liable for losses incurred by those who rely on the statements. In this regard, the Canadian Public Accountability Board was created in 2003 to provide public oversight for auditors of public companies.

Legal Liability, Professional Conduct, and Independence

The vast majority of accountants, auditors, managers, and owners do act in an honest and responsible manner. However, when the top officers in an organization collude to deceive other parties, they may temporarily succeed. In many cases, even the most diligent audit may not immediately uncover the results of fraud involving collusion of the top officers of a corporation. Examples include well-publicized cases such as Livent Inc. and SNC-Lavalin Group Inc. in Canada, American Investment Group Inc. (AIG) in the United States, Siemens AG in Germany, and Parmalat S.p.A. in Italy. However, those who were involved in fraudulent behaviour were eventually identified and sanctioned by the appropriate legal authorities.

Misrepresentations by managers highlight the importance of ensuring the integrity of the financial reporting system by the public accounting profession. Disclosure of financial information that does not faithfully represent actual business events imposes significant costs on the shareholders, creditors, and employees of companies who make important investment, lending, and career decisions. Recent reforms of the accounting profession and the imposition of new government regulations both in Canada and in the United States make it more difficult and costly for company managers to engage in fraudulent activities.

If financial statements are to be of any value to decision makers, users must have confidence in the fairness of the information. These users will have greater confidence in the information if they know that the people who were associated with auditing the financial statements were required to not only obey the law but also conform to professional standards of ethics and competence.

The Canadian accounting profession requires its members to adhere to a code of professional conduct and standards of independence. These standards are enforced through a disciplinary process. The provincial CPA institutes all stress how important it is for each member to behave in ways that enhance the reputation of the profession through voluntary compliance. In addition, CPA Canada places professional and ethical behaviour as the most important of the enabling competencies possessed by its members.[13]

Failure to comply with professional rules of conduct can result in serious penalties for professional accountants, including rescinding the professional designation of an offending member. The potential economic effects of damage to reputation and malpractice liability provide strong incentives to abide by professional standards. Thus, the profession recognizes that its members' reputations for ethical conduct and competence are their most important assets. Finally, recent changes in laws and securities regulation permit the assessment of personal financial penalties on professional

An **AUDIT** is an examination of the financial reports to ensure that they represent what they claim and conform to **IFRS**.

accountants who are found guilty of non-compliance, and they must compensate for the financial harm done to others.

Financial statement fraud is a fairly rare event, due in part to the diligent efforts of practising professional accountants. In fact, many such frauds are first identified by the firm's accounting staff or its external auditors, who advise regulatory authorities of possible wrongdoing. In doing so, these "whistle blowers" place the interest of the public at large ahead of their own interests and act accordingly. However, in case of malpractice, independent auditors may be held liable for losses suffered by those who relied on the audited financial statements.

ACCOUNTING STANDARDS FOR PRIVATE ENTERPRISES (ASPE)

The use of IFRS is required of all Canadian publicly accountable enterprises. However, corporations that do not have their shares traded on organized exchange markets and other private for-profit enterprises (proprietorships and partnerships) are not required to use IFRS. Instead, Canadian private enterprises may prepare their financial statements in accordance with a set of Canadian accounting standards that exclude inappropriate financial reporting complexities.[14]

The AcSB's decision to allow Canadian private enterprises to use accounting standards that deviate from IFRS recognizes that the information needs of external users of the financial statements of private enterprises differ from the information needs of users of the financial statements of publicly accountable enterprises. The major difference between the two types of enterprises is that external users of the private enterprise's financial statements do not include the many individual investors that typically purchase shares of publicly accountable enterprises. Hence, lenders are often the major external stakeholders in private enterprises and may obtain additional information from these companies upon request.

The financial statements prepared by both types of companies are based on the same conceptual foundations, but they may differ with respect to the details that are reported in the financial statements and related notes. Differences related to the basic financial statements are highlighted below. Other differences between IFRS and accounting standards for private enterprises (ASPE) will be highlighted in future chapters.

Financial Reporting Issue	IFRS	ASPE
Basic financial statements	The four basic financial statements are	The four basic financial statements are
	1. *Statement of comprehensive income.* This statement includes all revenues, expenses, gains, and losses reported in the statement of earnings as well as income and loss items that are not included in the computation of net earnings, such as gains and losses resulting from the measurement of specific financial assets and liabilities at fair value.	1. *Income statement.* This statement includes all revenues, expenses, gains, and losses for the period. Private enterprises are not required to report comprehensive income or loss.
	2. *Statement of changes in equity.* This statement reports the changes to various components of equity, including contributed capital, retained earnings, and accumulated other comprehensive income or loss.	2. *Statement of retained earnings.* This statement reports the changes to retained earnings during the period, which result primarily from net earnings and dividends.
	3. *Statement of financial position.* Some publicly accountable enterprises have continued to use the title "balance sheet" after adopting IFRS.	3. *Balance sheet*
	4. *Statement of cash flows* Publicly accountable enterprises must use IFRS for external reporting.	4. *Statement of cash flows* Private enterprises may use IFRS for external reporting. They may also choose to follow neither IFRS nor ASPE, particularly if they are not dependent on significant external sources of financing for their operations.

DEMONSTRATION **CASE**

At the end of most chapters, one or more demonstration cases are presented. These cases provide an overview of the primary issues discussed in the chapter. Each demonstration case is followed by a recommended solution. You should read the case carefully and then prepare your own solution before you study the recommended solution. *This self-evaluation is highly recommended*. The introductory case presented here reviews the elements reported on the statement of earnings and statement of financial position and how the elements within each are related.

Ivanko Inc. has been in operation for many years. It sells clothing, cosmetics, furniture, and home appliances. Following is a list of the financial statement items and amounts adapted from recent statements of earnings and financial position. The numbers are presented in *thousands* of dollars for the year ended December 31, 2016.

Cash	$ 507	Other liabilities	$ 4,351
Contributed capital	1,506	Property and equipment	5,154
Cost of sales	6,638	Retained earnings	1,029
Depreciation and amortization	460	Sales revenue	11,162
Intangible assets and goodwill	1,774	Selling, general, and administrative expenses	4,066
Income tax expense	132	Total assets	12,649
Finance costs, net	188	Total liabilities	9,550
Inventories	3,415	Total liabilities and shareholders' equity	12,649
Loans and borrowings	3,705	Total pretax expenses	10,643
Net earnings	387	Total shareholders' equity	3,099
Other assets	1,297	Trade and other receivables	512
Other components of equity	639	Trade payables	1,494

Required:

1. Prepare a statement of financial position and a statement of earnings for the year, following the formats in Exhibits 1.2 and 1.3.

2. Specify what information these two statements provide.

3. Indicate the other two statements that would be included in Ivanko's annual report.

4. Securities regulations require that the financial statements of Ivanko be subject to an independent audit. Suggest why Ivanko might voluntarily subject its financial statements to an independent audit if there were no such requirement.

SUGGESTED **SOLUTION**

1.

IVANKO INC.
Statement of Earnings
For the Year Ended December 31, 2016
(in thousands of Canadian dollars)

Sales revenue	$11,162
Expenses	
Cost of sales	6,638
Selling, general, and administrative expenses	4,066
Depreciation and amortization	460
Finance costs, net	188
Total pretax expenses	10,643
Earnings before income tax	219
Income tax expense	132
Net earnings	$ 387

IVANKO INC.
Statement of Financial Position
At December 31, 2016
(in thousands of Canadian dollars)

Assets		
Cash	$	507
Trade and other receivables		512
Inventories		3,415
Property and equipment		5,154
Intangible assets and goodwill		1,774
Other assets		1,287
Total assets		$12,649
Liabilities		
Trade payables		1,494
Loans and borrowings		3,705
Other liabilities		5,351
Total liabilities		9,550
Shareholders' equity		
Contributed capital		1,506
Retained earnings		1,029
Other components		564
Total shareholders' equity		3,099
Total liabilities and shareholders' equity		$12,649

2. The statement of financial position reports the amount of assets, liabilities, and shareholders' equity of an accounting entity at a point in time. The statement of earnings reports the accountant's primary measure of performance of a business, revenues less expenses, during the accounting period.
3. Ivanko Inc. would also present a statement of changes in equity and a statement of cash flows.
4. Users will have greater confidence in the accuracy of financial statement information if they know that the people who audited the statements were required to meet professional standards of ethics and competence.

LO1-S1

Describe the different types of business entities.

APPENDIX 1A: TYPES OF BUSINESS ENTITIES

This textbook emphasizes *accounting for profit-making business entities.* The three main types of business entities are sole proprietorship, partnership, and corporation. Specific aspects of the three types of business entities are compared in Exhibit 1.9. A *sole proprietorship* is an unincorporated business owned by one person; it is usually small in size and is common in the service, retailing, and farming industries. Often the owner is the manager. Legally, the business and the owner are not separate entities. The owner is responsible for the debts of the business and has *unlimited liability.*[15] However, accounting views the business as a separate entity that must be accounted for separately from its owner.

Exhibit **1.9**

Comparison of Three Types of Business Entities

	Proprietorship	Partnership	Corporation
Number of owners	One owner	Two or more owners	Many owners
Legal status of entity	Not separate from that of its owner	Not separate from that of its owners	Separate legal entity
Responsibility of owners for debts of business entity	Unlimited legal liability	Unlimited legal liability	Owners' liability limited to their investment
Accounting status	Each entity is separate from its owners for accounting purposes		

A *partnership* is an unincorporated business owned by two or more persons known as *partners.* The agreements among the owners are specified in a partnership contract that deals with matters such as division of profit among partners and distribution of resources of the business on termination of its operations. A partnership is not legally separate from its owners. Legally, each partner in a general partnership is responsible for the debts of the business (each general partner has *unlimited liability*). The partnership, however, is a separate business entity to be accounted for separately from its several owners.

A *corporation* is a business incorporated federally under the *Canada Business Corporations Act* or provincially under similar provincial acts. The owners are called shareholders, or stockholders. Ownership is represented by shares of capital that usually can be bought and sold freely. After the business organizers file an application for incorporation and receive approval, a charter is issued by either the federal or the provincial government. This charter gives the corporation the right to operate as a legal entity, separate from its owners. The shareholders enjoy *limited liability.* Shareholders cannot lose more than they paid for their shares. The corporate charter specifies the types and amounts of share capital that can be issued. Most provinces require a minimum of two shareholders and a minimum amount of resources to be contributed at the time of organization. The shareholders elect a governing board of directors, which, in turn, employs managers and exercises general supervision of the corporation. Accounting also views the corporation as a separate business entity that must be accounted for separately from its owners. Limited liability companies (LLCs) and limited liability partnerships (LLPs) have many characteristics similar to corporations. Accounting firms are typically organized as LLPs.

In terms of economic importance, the corporation is the dominant form of business organization in Canada. This dominance is caused by the many advantages of the corporate form: (1) limited liability for the shareholders, (2) continuity of life, (3) ease in transferring ownership (shares), and (4) opportunities to raise large amounts of money by selling shares to a large number of people. The primary disadvantages of a corporation are (1) loss of control by shareholders, (2) complex reporting procedures for a variety of government agencies, and (3) potential for double taxation of earnings (profits are taxed when they are earned and again when they are distributed to shareholders as dividends). In this textbook, we emphasize the corporate form of business. Nevertheless, the accounting concepts and procedures that we discuss also apply to other types of businesses. The main differences among these three types of entities appear in the equity section of the statement of financial position.

APPENDIX 1B: EMPLOYMENT IN THE ACCOUNTING PROFESSION TODAY

LO1-S2

Identify typical career opportunities for professional accountants.

Based on an Act of Parliament in 1902, accounting has legally attained the stature of professions such as law, medicine, engineering, and architecture. The act was amended in 2010 and now applies to all individuals with the title of Chartered Professional Accountant (CPA). As with all recognized professions, accounting is subject to professional competence requirements, is dedicated to service to the public, requires a high level of academic study, and rests on a common body of knowledge. The CPA designation is granted only on completion of requirements specified by CPA Canada. Specific requirements include a university degree with a specified number of accounting courses, good character, a minimum of two years of relevant professional experience, and successful completion of a professional examination. Currently, all accountants must be licensed by the government to engage in professional practice, and they must meet ongoing tests of competence to retain their licence. Similar accounting designations exist in other countries, most notably the Certified Public Accountant (CPA) in the United States.

Accountants are usually engaged in professional practice or employed by businesses, government entities, and not-for-profit organizations. The accounting profession is continuously changing. While many accountants still provide traditional accounting and tax services to businesses, individual clients, and government organizations, other areas of practice have become increasingly common in the accounting profession today. Demand for value-added accounting services (e.g., financial analysis, evaluation and implementation of new information technology and business processes, management advisory and consulting services, forensic accounting, and environmental accounting) is reshaping the nature of educational programs that prepare students to become professional accountants.

Practice of Public Accounting

Although an individual may practice public accounting, usually two or more individuals organize an accounting firm in the form of a partnership (in many cases, a limited liability partnership, or LLP). Accounting firms vary in size from a one-person office to regional firms to the "Big Four" firms (Deloitte & Touche, Ernst & Young, KPMG, and PricewaterhouseCoopers), which have hundreds of offices worldwide. Accounting firms usually render at least three types of services: audit or assurance services, management consulting services, and tax services.

Audit or Assurance Services   Audit or assurance services are independent professional services that improve the quality of information or its context for decision makers. The most important assurance service performed by CPAs in public practice is financial statement auditing. The purpose of an audit is to lend credibility to the financial reports; that is, to ensure that they fairly represent what they claim. An audit involves an examination of the financial reports (prepared by the management of the business) to ensure that they conform to the applicable accounting standards. Other areas of assurance services include integrity and security of electronic commerce and reliability of information systems.

Management Consulting Services   Many independent accounting firms offer management consulting services. These services are usually accounting based and encompass such activities as the design and installation of accounting, data processing, and profit-planning and control (budget) systems; financial advice; forecasting; internal controls; cost-effectiveness studies; and operational analysis. To maintain their independence, professional accountants are prohibited from performing specific consulting services for the public companies that they audit.

Tax Services   Accountants in public practice usually provide income tax services to their clients. These services include both tax planning as a part of the decision-making process and the determination of the income tax liability (reported on the annual income tax return). Because of the increasing complexity of provincial and federal tax laws, a high level of competence is required, which accountants specializing in taxation can provide. The accountant's involvement in tax planning is often quite significant. Most major business decisions have significant tax impacts; in fact, tax-planning considerations often govern certain business decisions.

Employment by Organizations

Many accountants, including CPAs, are employed by profit-making, not-for-profit, and government organizations. An organization, depending on its size and complexity, may employ from a few to hundreds of accountants. In a business enterprise, the chief financial officer (usually a vice-president or controller) is a member of the management team. This responsibility usually entails a wide range of management, financial, and accounting duties.

In a business entity, accountants are typically engaged in a wide variety of activities, such as general management, general accounting, cost accounting, profit planning and control (budgeting), internal auditing, and computerized data processing. A primary function of the accountants in organizations is to provide data that are useful for internal managerial decision making and for controlling operations. The functions of external reporting, tax planning, control of assets, and a host of related responsibilities are normally also performed by accountants in industry.

Employment in the Public and Not-for-Profit Sectors

The vast and complex operations of governmental units, from the local to the international level, create a need for accountants. The same holds true for other not-for-profit organizations, such as charitable organizations, hospitals, and universities. Accountants employed in the public and not-for-profit sectors perform functions similar to those performed by their counterparts in private organizations.

A survey of positions occupied by accounting professionals and related salaries is available at https://www.roberthalf.ca/en/finance/the-salary-guide-for-accounting-and-finance.

CHAPTER **TAKE-AWAYS**

1-1. Recognize both the information conveyed in each of the four basic financial statements and how the information is used by different decision makers (investors, creditors, and managers).

The *statement of financial position* reports financial values for assets, liabilities, and shareholders' equity at a specific point in time.

The *statement of comprehensive income* reports the net earnings (revenues minus expenses) for a period, as well as changes in equity during that period, except those resulting from exchanges with owners.

The *statement of changes in equity* reports the way that net earnings, the distribution of net earnings (dividends), and other changes to shareholders' equity affected the company's financial position during a specific period.

The *statement of cash flows* reports inflows and outflows of cash for a specific period.

The statements are used by investors and creditors to evaluate different aspects of the firm's financial position and performance.

1-2. Identify the role of International Financial Reporting Standards (IFRS) and International Accounting Standards (IAS) in determining the content of financial statements and how companies ensure the accuracy of their financial statements. IFRS are the broad principles, specific rules, and practices used to develop and report the information in financial statements. Knowledge of IFRS is necessary to accurately interpret the numbers in financial statements.

Management has primary responsibility for the accuracy of a company's financial information. Auditors are responsible for expressing an opinion on the fairness of the financial statement presentations based on their examination of the reports and records of the company.

Users will have confidence in the accuracy of financial statement numbers only if the people associated with their preparation and audit have reputations for ethical behaviour and competence. Management and auditors can also be held legally liable for fraudulent financial statements and malpractice.

In this chapter, we studied the basic financial statements that communicate financial information to external users. Chapters 2, 3, 4, and 5 will provide a more detailed look at financial statements and examine how to translate data about business transactions into these statements. Learning the relationship between business transactions and financial statements is the key to using financial statements in planning and decision making. Chapter 2 begins our discussion of how the accounting function collects data about business transactions and processes the data to provide periodic financial statements, with emphasis on the statement of financial position. To accomplish this purpose, Chapter 2 discusses key accounting concepts, the accounting model, transaction analysis, and analytical tools. We examine typical business activities of Canadian Tire to demonstrate the concepts in Chapters 2, 3, and 4.

FINDING **FINANCIAL INFORMATION**

STATEMENT OF FINANCIAL POSITION
Assets = Liabilities + Shareholders' Equity

STATEMENT OF CHANGES IN EQUITY

	Equity, beginning of the period
+	Net earnings
+/−	Other comprehensive income/loss
−	Dividends
+/−	Other changes, net
	Equity, end of the period

STATEMENT OF EARNINGS

	Revenues
−	Expenses
	Net earnings

STATEMENT OF CASH FLOWS

+/−	Cash flows from operating activities
+/−	Cash flows from investing activities
+/−	Cash flows from financing activities
	Change in cash

QUESTIONS

1. Define *accounting*.
2. Briefly distinguish financial accounting from managerial accounting.
3. The accounting process generates financial reports for both internal and external users. Identify some of the groups of users.
4. Briefly distinguish investors from creditors.
5. What is an accounting entity? Why is a business treated as a separate entity for accounting purposes?
6. What information should be included in the heading of each of the four primary financial statements?
7. What are the purposes of (a) the statement of earnings, (b) the statement of financial position, (c) the statement of cash flows, and (d) the statement of changes in equity?
8. Explain why the statement of earnings and statement of cash flows are dated, for example, "For the Year Ended December 31, 2017," whereas the statement of financial position is dated, for example, "At December 31, 2017."
9. Briefly explain the importance of assets and liabilities to the decisions of investors and creditors.
10. Briefly define *net earnings* and *net loss*.
11. Explain the accounting equation for the statement of earnings. Define the three major items reported on the statement of earnings.
12. Explain the accounting equation for the statement of financial position. Define the three major components reported on the statement of financial position.
13. Explain the accounting equation for the statement of cash flows. Explain the three major components reported on the statement.
14. Explain the accounting equation for retained earnings. Explain the major items that affect the ending balance of retained earnings.
15. Financial statements discussed in this chapter are aimed at *external* users. Briefly explain how a company's *internal* managers in different functional areas (e.g., marketing, purchasing, human resources) might use financial statement information from their own or other companies.
16. Briefly describe how accounting standards are determined in Canada, including the role of the AcSB.
17. Briefly explain the responsibility of company management, the board of directors, and the independent auditors in the internal control and financial reporting process.
18. (Appendix 1A) Briefly differentiate among a sole proprietorship, a partnership, and a corporation.
19. (Appendix 1B) List and briefly explain the three primary services that accountants in public practice provide.

connect MINI-EXERCISES

LO1-1

M1-1   **Matching Elements with Financial Statements**

Match each element with its financial statement by entering the appropriate letter in the space provided.

Element	Financial Statement
_____ (1) Expenses	A. Statement of financial position
_____ (2) Cash flow from investing activities	B. Statement of earnings
_____ (3) Assets	C. Statement of shareholders' equity
_____ (4) Dividends	D. Statement of cash flows
_____ (5) Revenues	
_____ (6) Cash flow from operating activities	
_____ (7) Liabilities	
_____ (8) Cash flow from financing activities	

LO1-1

M1-2 **Matching Financial Statement Items to Financial Statement Categories**

Mark each item in the following list as an asset (A), liability (L), or shareholders' equity (SE) item that would appear on the statement of financial position or a revenue (R) or expense (E) that would appear on the statement of earnings.

_____ (1) Retained earnings   _____ (6) Inventories

_____ (2) Accounts receivable   _____ (7) Interest expense

_____ (3) Sales revenue   _____ (8) Accounts payable

_____ (4) Property and equipment   _____ (9) Land

_____ (5) Cost of sales

LO1-1

M1-3 **Identifying Important Accounting Abbreviations**

The following is a list of important abbreviations used in the chapter. These abbreviations also are used widely in business. For each abbreviation, give the full designation. The first one is an example.

Abbreviation	Full Designation
(1) AcSB	Accounting Standards Board
(2) IFRS	_____
(3) CPA	_____
(4) IASB	_____

connect EXERCISES

LO1-1

Leon's Furniture Ltd.

E1-1 **Preparing a Statement of Financial Position**

Leon's Furniture Ltd. is one of Canada's largest retailers, selling a wide range of merchandise, including furniture, major appliances, and home electronics. A recent statement of financial position contained the following items (in millions).

Cash and cash equivalents	$ 18
Contributed capital	31
Dividends payable	7
Income tax payable	35
Intangible assets and goodwill	739
Inventories	267
Loans and borrowings	315
Other assets	93
Other components of equity	8
Other liabilities	460
Property, plant, and equipment	334
Retained earnings	510
Total assets	1,563
Total liabilities and shareholders' equity	?
Trade receivables	112
Trade and other payables	197

Required:

1. Prepare a statement of financial position as at December 31, 2015, solving for the missing amount.

2. Explain how an investor should interpret the following items: dividends payable, retained earnings, and total assets.

LO1-1

E1-2 **Completing a Statement of Financial Position and Inferring Net Earnings**

Terry Lloyd and Joan Lopez organized Read More Store as a corporation; each contributed $50,000 cash to start the business and received 4,000 shares of capital. The store completed its first year of operations on December 31, 2017. On that date, the following financial items were determined: cash on hand and in the bank, $48,900; amounts due from customers from sales of books, $25,000; unused portion of store and office equipment, $49,000; amounts owed to publishers for books purchased,

$7,000; one-year note for $3,000, signed on January 15, 2017, and payable to a local bank. No dividends were declared or paid to the shareholders during the year.

Required:

1. Complete the following statement of financial position as at December 31, 2017.

2. What was the amount of net earnings for the year?

Assets		Liabilities	
Cash	$	Trade payables	$
Trade receivables		Note payable	
Store and office equipment		Interest payable	120
		Total liabilities	$
		Shareholders' Equity	
		Contributed capital	$
		Retained earnings	12,780
		Total shareholders' equity	
Total assets	$	Total liabilities and shareholders' equity	$

LO1-1

E1-3 Analyzing Revenues and Expenses and Preparing a Statement of Earnings

Assume that you are the owner of The University Shop, which specializes in items that interest students. At the end of September 2018, you find (for September only) the following:

a. Sales, per the cash register tapes, of $119,000, plus one sale on credit (a special situation) of $1,000.

b. With the help of a friend (who majored in accounting), you determined that all of the goods sold during September had cost $40,000 to purchase.

c. During the month, according to the cheque book, you paid $38,000 for salaries, rent, supplies, advertising, and other expenses; however, you have not yet paid the $600 monthly utilities for September.

Required:

1. On the basis of the data given, what was the amount of net earnings for September (disregard income taxes)? Show computations. (*Hint:* A convenient form to use has the following major side captions: revenue from sales, expenses, and the difference—net earnings for the period.)

2. As a manager of what use is this information if you are deciding whether or not to purchase a new cash register at a cash cost of $2,500?

LO1-1

Corus
Entertainment Inc.

E1-4 Preparing a Statement of Earnings and Inferring Missing Values

Corus Entertainment Inc. is a Canadian integrated media and entertainment company that delivers engaging, interactive, and informative content to millions of people every day. Its television services include YTV, Teletoon, and the Oprah Winfrey Network (Canada). It also owns many radio stations in the major Canadian markets. A recent annual statement of earnings contained the following items (in thousands of Canadian dollars). Solve for the missing amounts and prepare a condensed statement of earnings for the year ended August 31, 2015. (*Hint:* First order the items as they would appear on the statement of earnings and then solve for the missing values.)

Cost of sales	$533,529
Interest expense	46,332
Net earnings	165,749
Revenues	?
Depreciation expense	26,903
Income tax expense	39,759
Total expenses excluding income taxes	?
Earnings before income tax	?

LO1-1

E1-5 Analyzing Revenues and Expenses and Completing a Statement of Earnings

Home Realty Inc. has been operating for three years and is owned by three investors. J. Doe owns 60 percent of the 9,000 shares that are outstanding and is the managing executive in charge. On

December 31, 2017, the following financial items for the entire year were determined: commissions earned and collected in cash, $150,000; rental service fees earned and collected, $15,000; expenses paid including salaries, $62,000; commissions, $35,000; payroll taxes, $2,500; rent, $2,200; utilities, $1,600; promotion and advertising, $8,000; income taxes, $18,500; and miscellaneous expenses, $500. At December 31, $16,000 of commissions were earned but not collected, and the rent for December ($200) was not paid. Complete the following statement of earnings:

Revenues		
Commissions	$_____	
Rental service fees		
Total revenues		$_____
Expenses		
Salaries	$_____	
Commission		
Payroll tax		
Rent		
Utilities		
Promotion and advertising		
Miscellaneous		
Total expenses (excluding income taxes)		
Earnings before income taxes		$_____
Income tax expense		
Net earnings		$_____

LO1-1

E1-6 **Inferring Values by Using the Statement of Earnings and Statement of Financial Position Equations**

Review the chapter explanations of the statement of earnings and the statement of financial position equations. Apply these equations in each independent case to compute the two missing amounts for each case. Assume that it is the end of 2016, the first full year of operations for the company.

(*Hint:* Organize the listed items as they are presented in the statement of financial position and statement of earnings equations and then compute the missing amounts.)

Independent Cases	Total Revenues	Total Expenses	Net Earnings (Loss)	Total Assets	Total Liabilities	Shareholders' Equity
A	$91,700	$76,940		$140,200	$69,000	
B		74,240	$14,740	107,880		$79,010
C	69,260	76,430		97,850	69,850	
D	58,680		21,770		17,890	78,680
E	84,840	78,720			25,520	79,580

As a creditor how would you use this information to decide whether or not to lend $50,000, repayable over five years, to either Company B or Company C?

LO1-1

E1-7 **Preparing a Statement of Earnings and a Statement of Financial Position**

Ducharme Corporation was organized by five individuals on January 1, 2017. At the end of January 2017, the following monthly financial data are available:

Total revenues	$299,000
Total expenses (excluding income taxes)	189,000
Income tax expense (all unpaid as at January 31)	34,500
Cash balance, January 31, 2017	65,150
Receivables from customers (all considered collectible)	34,500
Merchandise inventory (by inventory count at cost)	96,600
Payables to suppliers for merchandise purchased from them (will be paid during February 2017)	26,450
Contributed capital (2,600 shares)	59,800
No dividends declared in January 2017	

Required:

1. Prepare a summarized statement of earnings for the month of January 2017.

2. Prepare a statement of financial position at January 31, 2017.

LO1-1

E1-8   **Computing Ending Balance of Retained Earnings**

Sultan Inc. was organized on January 1, 2017. It reported the following for its first two years of operations:

Net earnings for 2017	$ 31,000
Dividends for 2017	14,200
Total shareholders' equity at end of 2017	130,000
Net earnings for 2018	42,000
Dividends for 2018	18,700
Total shareholders' equity at end of 2018	250,000

Required:

Compute the ending balance of retained earnings for Sultan Inc. as at December 31, 2018. Show computations.

LO1-1

E1-9   **Analyzing and Interpreting a Statement of Earnings**

Pest Away Corporation was organized by three individuals on January 1, 2017, to provide insect extermination services. At the end of 2017, the following statement of earnings was prepared.

PEST AWAY CORPORATION
Statement of Earnings
For the Year Ended December 31, 2017

Revenues		
Service revenue (cash)	$192,000	
Service revenue (credit)	24,000	
Total revenues		$216,000
Expenses		
Salaries	$ 76,000	
Rent	21,000	
Utilities	12,000	
Advertising	14,000	
Supplies	25,000	
Interest	8,000	
Total expenses		156,000
Earnings before income tax		60,000
Income tax expense		21,000
Net earnings for the year		$ 39,000

Required:

1. What was the average amount of monthly revenue?
2. What was the amount of monthly rent?
3. Explain why supplies are reported as an expense.
4. Explain why interest is reported as an expense.
5. What was the average income tax rate for Pest Away Corporation?
6. What does the amount of total revenues mean to an external decision maker?
7. Can you determine how much cash the company had on December 31, 2017? Explain.

LO1-1

Saputo Inc.

E1-10   **Focusing on Cash Flows: Matching Cash Flow Items to Categories**

Saputo Inc. is a Canadian company that produces, markets, and distributes a wide variety of products to customers in over 50 countries. Its products include cheese, fluid milk, yogurt, dairy ingredients, and snack cakes. The following items were taken from its recent statement of cash flows. Note that different companies use slightly different titles for the same item. Without referring to Exhibit 1.5, mark each item in the list as a cash flow from operating activities (O), investing activities (I), or financing activities (F). Place parentheses around the letter only if it is a cash outflow.

_____ (1)   Cash paid to suppliers
_____ (2)   Cash received from customers
_____ (3)   Dividends paid

_____ (4)   Issuance of share capital
_____ (5)   Interest paid
_____ (6)   Proceeds from disposal of investment
_____ (7)   Purchases of property, plant, and equipment
_____ (8)   Repurchase of share capital

LO1-1   **E1-11**   **Preparing a Statement of Cash Flows**
NITSU Manufacturing Corporation is preparing the annual financial statements for its shareholders. A statement of cash flows must be prepared. The following data on cash flows were developed for the entire year ended December 31, 2017: cash inflow from operating revenues, $270,000; cash expended for operating expenses, $180,000; sale of unissued NITSU shares for cash, $30,000; cash dividends declared and paid to shareholders during the year, $22,000; and payments on long-term borrowings, $80,000. During the year, a tract of land was sold for $15,000 cash (which was the same price that NITSU had paid for the land in 2016), and $38,000 cash was expended for two new machines. The machines were used in the factory. The beginning-of-the-year cash balance was $63,000.

Required:
Prepare a statement of cash flows for 2017. Follow the format illustrated in the chapter.

connect PROBLEMS

LO1-1   **P1-1**   **Preparing a Statement of Earnings and a Statement of Financial Position** (AP1-1)
Assume that you are the president of Nuclear Company. At December 31, 2017, the end of the first year of operations, the following financial data for the company are available:

Cash	$ 25,000
Receivables from customers (all considered collectible)	12,000
Inventory of merchandise (based on physical count and priced at cost)	90,000
Equipment owned, at cost less used portion	45,000
Payables to suppliers of merchandise	47,370
Salary payable for 2017 (on December 31, 2017, this was owed to an employee, but the amount was not paid until January 10, 2018)	2,000
Total sales revenue	140,000
Expenses, including the cost of the merchandise sold (excluding income taxes)	89,100
Income taxes expense (at 30% of pretax earnings); all paid during 2017	?
Contributed capital, 7,000 shares outstanding	87,000
No dividends were declared or paid during 2017.	

Required (show computations):
1. Prepare a summarized statement of earnings for the year ended December 31, 2017.
2. Prepare a statement of financial position at December 31, 2017.
3. How would a creditor make use of the information on receivables from customers and the payables to suppliers of merchandise?

LO1-1   **P1-2**   **Analyzing a Student's Business, and Preparing a Statement of Earnings and a Statement of Financial Position** (AP1-2)

Upon graduation from high school, William Nitter accepted a job as a plumber's assistant for a large local plumbing company. After three years of hard work, William received a plumbing licence and decided to start his own business. He had saved $24,000, which he invested in the business. His lawyer had advised him to start as a corporation. First, he transferred the $24,000 from his savings account to a business bank account for William's Plumbing Services Inc. and was issued shares. He then purchased a used panel truck for $18,000 cash and second-hand tools for $3,000, rented space in a small building, inserted an advertisement in the local paper, and opened his business on July 1, 2017. Immediately, William was very busy; after one month, he employed an assistant.

Although William knew practically nothing about the financial side of the business, he realized that a number of reports were required and that expenses and collections from clients had to be controlled carefully. At December 31, 2017, prompted in part by concern about his income tax situation, William recognized the need for financial statements. His wife, Jennifer, developed some financial statements for the business. On December 31, 2017, with the help of a friend, she gathered the following data for the six months just ended. Bank account deposits of collections for plumbing services totalled $64,000. The following cheques had been written: plumber's assistant, $17,000; payroll taxes, $750; oil, gas, and maintenance for the truck, $2,400; rent, $2,500; supplies purchased and used on jobs, $17,100; utilities and telephone, $1,850; insurance, $700 for the past six months; and miscellaneous expenses (including advertising), $900. Also, uncollected invoices to customers for plumbing services amounted to $6,000. The $500 rent for December had not been paid. William estimated the cost of using the truck and tools (depreciation) during the three months to be $2,400. The average income tax rate for income from his business is 30 percent.

Required:

1. Prepare a statement of earnings for William's Plumbing Services Inc. for the six months of July through December 2017. Use the following main captions: revenue from services, expenses, earnings before income taxes, and net earnings.

2. Prepare a statement of financial position for William's Plumbing Services Inc. as at December 31, 2017.

3. Do you think that William may have a need for one or more additional financial reports for 2017 and thereafter? Explain.

4. As an owner, how can William use the information conveyed by both the statement of earnings and the statement of financial position to decide whether or not to apply for a bank loan, payable in one year?

■ LO1-1

P1-3   **Comparing Net Earnings with Cash Flow (A Challenging Problem)** (AP1-3)

Choice Chicken Company was organized on January 1, 2017. At the end of the first quarter (three months) of operations, the owner prepared a summary of its activities as shown in the first row of the following tabulation:

Summary of Transactions	Computation of	
	Net earnings	Cash
a. Services performed for customers, $85,000, of which $15,000 remained uncollected at the end of the quarter.	+$85,000	+$70,000
b. Cash borrowed from the local bank, $25,000 (one-year note).		
c. Small service truck purchased at the end of the quarter to be used in the business for two years starting the next quarter: cost, $8,000 cash.		
d. Wages earned by employees, $36,000, of which one-sixth remained unpaid at the end of the quarter.		
e. Service supplies purchased for use in the business, $4,000 cash, of which $1,000 were unused (still on hand) at the end of the quarter.		
f. Other operating expenses, $31,000, of which one-half remained unpaid at the end of the quarter.		
Based only on these transactions, compute the following for the quarter: Net earnings (or loss) Cash inflow (or outflow)		

Required:

1. For each of the six transactions given in this tabulation, enter what you consider the correct amounts. Enter a zero when appropriate. The first transaction is illustrated.

2. For each transaction, explain the basis for your responses.

■ LO1-1

P1-4   **Evaluating Data to Support a Loan Application (A Challenging Problem)**

On January 1, 2019, three individuals organized West Company as a corporation. Each individual invested $10,000 cash in the business. On December 31, 2019, they prepared a list of resources owned (assets) and a list of debts (liabilities) to support the company's request for a loan of $70,000 submitted to a local bank. None of the three investors had studied accounting. The two lists prepared were as follows:

Company resources	
Cash	$ 12,000
Service supplies inventory (on hand)	7,000
Service trucks (four practically new)	68,000
Personal residences of organizers (three houses)	190,000
Service equipment used in the business (practically new)	30,000
Amounts due from customers (for services already completed)	15,000
Total	$322,000
Company obligations	
Unpaid wages to employees	$ 19,000
Unpaid taxes	8,000
Owed to suppliers	10,000
Owed on service trucks and equipment (to a finance company)	50,000
Loan from organizer	15,000
Total	$102,000

Required:

Prepare a short memo indicating the following:

1. Which of these items do not belong on the statement of financial position (bear in mind that the company is considered to be separate from the owners)?

2. What additional questions would you raise about measurement of items on the lists? Explain the basis for each question.

3. If you were advising the local bank on its loan decision, which amounts on the lists would create special concerns? Explain the basis for each concern and include any recommendations that you have.

4. In view of your responses to (1) and (2), calculate the amount of shareholders' equity as at December 31, 2019. Show your computations.

LO1-1

P1-5 **Using Financial Reports: Applying the Accounting Equation to Liquidate a Company**
On June 1, 2018, Bland Corporation prepared a statement of financial position just prior to going out of business. The totals for the three main components showed the following:

Assets (no cash)	$90,000
Liabilities	50,000
Shareholders' equity	40,000

Shortly thereafter, all of the assets were sold for cash.

Required:

1. How would the statement of financial position appear immediately after the sale of the assets for cash for each of the following cases? Use the format given here.

	Cash Received for the Assets	Balances Immediately after Sale Assets	– Liabilities	= Shareholders' Equity
Case A	$ 90,000	$ _____	$ _____	$ _____
Case B	80,000	$ _____	$ _____	$ _____
Case C	100,000	$ _____	$ _____	$ _____
Case D	35,000	$ _____	$ _____	$ _____

2. How should the cash be distributed in each separate case? (*Hint:* creditors must be paid in full before owners receive any payment.) Use the format given here:

	To Creditors	To Shareholders	Total
Case A	$ _____	$ _____	$ _____
Case B	$ _____	$ _____	$ _____
Case C	$ _____	$ _____	$ _____
Case D	$ _____	$ _____	$ _____

ALTERNATE PROBLEMS

■ LO1-1   **AP1-1**   **Preparing a Statement of Earnings and a Statement of Financial Position** (P1-1)

Assume that you are the president of McClaren Corporation. At June 30, 2018, the end of the first year of operations, the following financial data for the company are available:

Cash	$13,150
Receivables from customers (all considered collectible)	9,500
Inventory of merchandise (based on physical count and priced at cost)	57,000
Equipment used in the business	36,000
Payables to suppliers of merchandise	31,500
Salary payable for 2018 (on June 30, 2018, this was owed to an employee, but the amount was not paid until July 7, 2018)	1,500
Total sales revenue	90,000
Expenses, including the cost of the merchandise sold (excluding income taxes)	60,500
Income taxes expense (at 30% of pretax earnings); all paid during 2018	?
Contributed capital, 5,000 shares outstanding	?
No dividends were declared or paid during 2018.	

Required (show computations):

1. Prepare a summarized statement of earnings for the year ended June 30, 2018.

2. Prepare a statement of financial position as at June 30, 2018.

3. How would a creditor make use of the information on receivables from customers and the payables to suppliers of merchandise?

■ LO1-1   **AP1-2**   **Analyzing a Student's Business, and Preparing a Statement of Earnings and a Statement of**

Financial Position (P1-2)

While pursuing his undergraduate studies, Bruno Clarke needed to earn sufficient money for the coming academic year. Unable to obtain a job with a reasonable salary, he decided to try the lawn care business for three months during the summer. After a survey of the market potential, Bruno bought a used pick-up truck on June 1 for $3,000. On each door he painted "Bruno's Lawn Service, Tel: 555-9623." He also spent $1,800 for mowers, trimmers, and tools. To acquire these items, he borrowed $5,000 cash by signing a note payable, promising to pay the $5,000 plus interest of $150 at the end of the three months (ending August 31).

At the end of the summer, Bruno realized that he had done a lot of work, and his bank account looked good. This fact prompted him to become concerned about how much profit the business had earned.

A review of the cheque stubs showed the following: bank deposits of collections from customers totalled $25,200. The following cheques had been written: gas, oil, and lubrication, $1,840; mower repair, $150; helpers, $9,500; payroll taxes, $400; truck repairs, $410; payment for assistance in preparing payroll tax forms, $50; insurance, $240; telephone, $210; miscellaneous supplies used, $160; and $5,150 to pay off the note, including interest (on August 31). A notebook kept in the truck, plus some unpaid bills, reflected that customers still owed him $1,250 for lawn services rendered and that he owed $200 for gas and oil (credit card charges). He estimated that the cost for use of the truck and the other equipment (depreciation) for three months amounted to $1,000.

Required:

1. Prepare a quarterly statement of earnings for Bruno's Lawn Service for the months of June, July, and August 2017. Use the following main captions: revenues from services, expenses, and net earnings. Because this is a sole proprietorship, the company will not be subject to income tax.

2. Prepare a statement of financial position for Bruno's Lawn Service as at August 31, 2017. Bruno's business is a proprietorship with one equity item: Bruno Clarke, capital.

3. Do you see a need for one or more additional financial reports for this business for 2017 and thereafter? Explain.

4. As an owner, how can Bruno use the information conveyed by both the statement of earnings and the statement of financial position to decide whether or not to apply for a bank loan, payable in one year?

LO1-1

AP1-3 **Comparing Net Earnings with Cash Flow (A Challenging Problem)** (P1-3)

New Delivery Company was organized on January 1, 2018. At the end of the first quarter (three months) of operations, the owner prepared a summary of its operations as shown in the first row of the following tabulation:

Summary of Transactions	Computation of	
	Net Earnings	Cash
a. Services performed for customers, $66,000, of which one-sixth remained uncollected at the end of the quarter.	$66,000	$55,000
b. Cash borrowed from the local bank, $45,000 (one-year note).		
c. Small service truck purchased at the end of the quarter to be used in the business for two years starting the next quarter: cost, $9,500; paid 20% down, balance on credit.		
d. Wages earned by employees, $21,000, of which one-half remained unpaid at the end of the quarter.		
e. Service supplies purchased for use in the business, $3,800 cash, of which one-fifth were unused (still on hand) at the end of the quarter.		
f. Other operating expenses, $36,000, of which one-sixth remained unpaid at the end of the quarter.		
Based only on these transactions, compute the following for the quarter: Net earnings (or loss) Cash inflow (or outflow)		

Required:

1. For each of the six transactions given in this tabulation, enter what you consider to be the correct amounts. Enter a zero when appropriate. The first transaction is illustrated.

2. For each transaction, explain the basis for your responses.

CASES AND PROJECTS

FINDING AND INTERPRETING FINANCIAL INFORMATION

LO1-1

CP1-1 **Finding Financial Information**

Refer to the financial statements of Canadian Tire Corporation in Appendix A at the end of this book.

Canadian Tire
Corporation

Required:

Look at the statement of earnings, statement of financial position, and statement of cash flows closely and attempt to infer the types of information they report. Then answer the following questions based on the report.

1. On what day of the year does Canadian Tire's fiscal year end?

2. For how many years does it present complete

    a. statements of financial position (balance sheets)?

    b. statements of earnings (or income)?

    c. statements of cash flows?

3. Are its financial statements audited by independent accountants? How do you know?

4. Did its total assets increase or decrease over the last year?

5. What was the balance of merchandise inventories at the end of the most current year?

6. Write out its basic accounting equation in Canadian dollars at year-end.

LO1-1

CP1-2 **Finding Financial Information**

Go to *Connect* for the financial statements of Sears Canada Inc. and related notes.

Sears Canada Inc.

Required:

1. What is the amount of net earnings (net income) for the current fiscal year?

2. What amount of revenue was earned in the current fiscal year?

3. How much inventory does the company have at the end of the current fiscal year?

4. By what amount did cash and cash equivalents* change during the year?

5. Who is the auditor for the company?

*Cash equivalents are short-term investments that are readily convertible into cash and whose value is unlikely to change.

■ LO**1-1**

Canadian Tire
Corporation vs.
Sears Canada Inc.

CP1-3   **Comparing Companies**

Refer to the financial statements and the accompanying notes of Canadian Tire Corporation given in Appendix A and of Sears Canada Inc. on *Connect*.

Required:

1. Total assets is a common measure of the size of a company. Which company had the higher total assets at the end of the most recent year?

2. Net sales is also a common measure of the size of a company. Which company had the higher net sales for the most recent year?

3. Growth during a period is calculated as

    Growth rate = [(Ending amount − Beginning amount)/Beginning amount] × 100

    Which company had the higher growth rate in total assets during the most recent year? Which company had the higher growth rate in net sales during the most recent year?

FINANCIAL REPORTING AND ANALYSIS CASE

■ LO**1-1**

Sears Canada Inc.

CP1-4   **Using Financial Reports: Identifying and Correcting Deficiencies in a Statement of Earnings and a Statement of Financial Position**

Performance Corporation was organized on January 1, 2017. At the end of 2017, the company had not yet employed an accountant; however, an employee who was "good with numbers" prepared the following statements at that date:

Performance Corporation December 31, 2017	
Income from sales of merchandise	$175,000
Total amount paid for goods sold during 2017	(90,000)
Selling costs	(25,000)
Depreciation (on service vehicles used)	(10,000)
Income from services rendered	52,000
Salaries and wages paid	(62,000)

Performance Corporation December 31, 2017		
Resources		
Cash		$ 32,000
Merchandise inventory (held for resale)		42,000
Service vehicles		50,000
Retained earnings (net earnings of 2017)		30,000
Grand total		$154,000
Debts		
Payable to suppliers		$ 22,000
Note owed to bank		25,000
Due from customers		13,000
Total		$ 60,000
Supplies on hand (to be used in rendering services)	$ 15,000	
Accumulated depreciation* (on service vehicles)	10,000	
Contributed capital, 6,500 shares	65,000	
Total		90,000
Grand total		$150,000

*Accumulated depreciation represents the cost related to the used portion of the asset and should be subtracted from the asset balance.

Required:

1. List all of the deficiencies that you can identify in these statements. Give a brief explanation of each one.

2. Prepare a proper statement of earnings for Performance Corporation for 2017 (correct net earnings is $30,000) and a proper statement of financial position at December 31, 2017 (correct total assets are $142,000).

CRITICAL THINKING CASES

■ LO**1-1,1-2**

CP1-5   **Making Decisions as a Manager: Reporting the Assets and Liabilities of a Business**

Emmanuel Lucas owns and operates Emmanuel's Shop (a sole proprietorship). An employee prepares a financial report for the business at each year-end. This report lists all of the resources (assets) owned by Emmanuel, including such personal items as the home he owns and occupies. It also lists all of the debts of the business, but not his personal debts.

Required:

1. From an accounting point of view, do you disagree with what is being included in and excluded from the report of business assets and liabilities? Explain.

2. Upon questioning, Emmanuel responded, "Don't worry about it; we use it only to support a loan from the bank." How would you respond to this comment?

LO1-2

CP1-6   **Making Decisions as an Owner: Deciding about a Proposed Audit**

You are one of three partners who own and operate Sam's Cleaning Service. The company has been operating for 10 years. One of the other partners has always prepared the company's annual financial statements. Recently you proposed that the statements be audited each year because it would benefit the partners and preclude possible disagreements about the division of net earnings. The partner who prepares the statements proposed that his nephew Roger, who has a lot of financial experience, can do the job and at little cost. Your other partner remained silent.

Required:

1. What position would you take on the proposal? Justify your response.

2. What would you strongly recommend? Give the basis for your recommendation.

LO1-2

CP1-7   **Evaluating Compliance with the Code of Professional Conduct and Auditor Responsibilities**

A key factor that an auditor provides is independence. CPA Canada's *Independence Standards – Harmonized Rule of professional conduct 204* state that "a member or firm shall not perform an audit or review engagement for an entity if the member, firm or a network firm, has a direct financial interest or a material indirect financial interest in the entity." (Source: https://www.cpacanada.ca/en/the-cpa-profession/cpas-and-what-we-do/what-cpas-do/professional-conduct-auditor-independence-rule-204/rule-204-harmonized-standards, June 2016 version, 204.4 (2) (b).)

Required:

Do you consider the following circumstances to suggest a lack of independence? Explain your position. (Use your imagination. Specific answers are not provided in the chapter.)

1. James Slater is a partner with a large audit firm and is assigned to the CGI audit. James owns 10 shares of CGI.

2. Maria Tsoukas has invested in a mutual fund company that owns 100,000 shares of Sears Canada Inc. She is the auditor of Sears.

3. Bob Fisher is a clerk/typist who works on the audit of the Bank of Montreal. He has just inherited 70,000 shares of the Bank of Montreal. (Bob enjoys his work and plans to continue despite his new wealth.)

4. Nancy Chen worked on weekends as the controller for a small business that a friend started. Nancy quit the job in mid-year and now has no association with the company. She works full-time for a large accounting firm and has been assigned to do the audit of her friend's business.

5. Sylvia Bertone borrowed $100,000 for a home mortgage from First City National Bank. The mortgage was granted on normal credit terms. Sylvia is the partner in charge of the First City audit.

FINANCIAL REPORTING AND ANALYSIS TEAM PROJECT

LO1-1,1-2

CP1-8   **Team Project: Examining an Annual Report**

As a team, select an industry to analyze. A list of companies classified by industry can be obtained by accessing www.fpinfomart.ca and then choosing Companies by Industry. You can also find a list of industries and companies within each industry via http://ca.finance.yahoo.com/investing. A list of industries can be obtained by clicking on Order Annual Reports under Tools.

Each group member should acquire the annual report for one publicly traded company in the industry, with each member selecting a different company. (Library files, the SEDAR service at www.sedar.com, and the company's website are good sources.)

Required:

On an individual basis, each group member should write a short report answering the following questions about the selected company. Discuss any patterns that you observe as a team. Then, as a team, write a short report comparing and contrasting your companies, using the six attributes listed below.

1. What types of products or services does it sell?

2. On what day of the year does its fiscal year end?

3. For how many years does it present complete
   a. statements of financial position (or balance sheets)?
   b. statements of earnings and statements of comprehensive income?
   c. statements of cash flows?
4. Are its financial statements audited by independent auditors? If so, by whom?
5. Did its total assets increase or decrease over the last year?
6. Did its net earnings increase or decrease over the last year?

connect   CONTINUING CASE

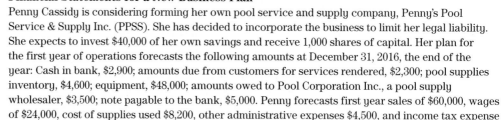

■ LO1-1   **CC1-1**   **Financial Statements for a New Business Plan**

Penny Cassidy is considering forming her own pool service and supply company, Penny's Pool Service & Supply Inc. (PPSS). She has decided to incorporate the business to limit her legal liability. She expects to invest $40,000 of her own savings and receive 1,000 shares of capital. Her plan for the first year of operations forecasts the following amounts at December 31, 2016, the end of the year: Cash in bank, $2,900; amounts due from customers for services rendered, $2,300; pool supplies inventory, $4,600; equipment, $48,000; amounts owed to Pool Corporation Inc., a pool supply wholesaler, $3,500; note payable to the bank, $5,000. Penny forecasts first year sales of $60,000, wages of $24,000, cost of supplies used $8,200, other administrative expenses $4,500, and income tax expense of $4,000. She expects to pay herself a $10,000 dividend as the sole shareholder of the company.

Required:

If Penny's estimates are correct, what would the following first year financial statements look like for Penny's Pool Service & Supply (use Exhibits 1.2, 1.3, and 1.4 as models).

1. Statement of earnings for the year ended December 31, 2016
2. Statement of shareholders' equity as at December 31, 2016
3. Statement of financial position as at December 31, 2016

SOLUTIONS TO SELF-STUDY QUIZZES

Self-Study Quiz 1-1 (all amounts are in thousands of dollars)

1. Assets ($14,988) − Liabilities ($9,198) = Shareholders' Equity ($5,790).
2. Shareholders' Equity = Assets − Liabilities

   This equation means that shareholders' equity is a residual value that results from subtracting the value of the total liabilities from the value of total assets. This is the accounting value of the shareholders' investment in Canadian Tire. It also means that the value of shareholders' equity depends on the values assigned to total assets and total liabilities.
3. L, A, A, SE, A, A, L, A, SE (reading down the columns).

Self-Study Quiz 1-2

1. E, R, E (reading down the columns).
2. Sales revenue in the amount of $12,280 is recognized because sales revenue is normally reported on the statement of earnings when the goods or services have been delivered to customers who have either paid or promised to pay for them in the future.
3. Cost of sales is $8,144 because expenses are the dollar amount of resources used up to earn revenues during the period, regardless of the amount that Canadian Tire paid to its suppliers during the same period.

Self-Study Quiz 1-3

Ending retained earnings = Beginning retained earnings + Net earnings − Dividends
$$= \$4,405 + 640 - 512$$
$$= \$4,533$$

Self-Study Quiz 1-4

1. An amount of $12,275 is recognized on the statement of cash flows because this number represents the actual cash collected from customers related to current and prior years' sales.
2. (F), (O), F, (O), (I), O.

ENDNOTES

1. Some companies, including Canadian Tire, refer to this statement as a "balance sheet," a title that was commonly used prior to the adoption of IFRS in Canada. In this book, we use the title *statement of financial position*, which is more common than *balance sheet*.

2. Canadian Tire reported a total amount of $1,957 for both accounts payable and accrued liabilities. The total amount is divided in two separate amounts for illustrative purposes.

3. Many companies, including Canadian Tire, refer to this measure as "net income," while others prefer to use the term "profit." The three terms—net earnings, net income, and profit—are synonymous. We use *net earnings* because it is consistent with other terms used in financial statements, such as *earnings per share* and *retained earnings*.

4. The title "statement of earnings" is more commonly used than "income statement" by Canadian publicly accountable enterprises. Other titles, such as "statement of operations" or "statement of income," used by Canadian Tire, are also used by some companies. All these titles are synonymous.

5. Retained earnings decrease when expenses exceed revenues, resulting in a loss. The complete process of declaring and paying dividends is discussed in Chapter 11.

6. Alternative ways to present cash flows from operating activities are discussed in Chapter 5.

7. The basic financial statements and related notes are part of more elaborate documents called annual reports that are produced by public companies. Annual reports are normally split into two sections. The first is non-financial and usually includes a letter to shareholders from the chairperson of the company's board of directors and the chief executive officer; descriptions of the company's management philosophy, products, and successes (and occasionally failures); exciting prospects and challenges for the future; and beautiful photographs of products, facilities, and personnel.

   The second section includes the core of the report. The principal components of this financial section include summarized financial data for five or ten years, management's discussion and analysis of the company's financial condition and results of operations, four financial statements and related notes, auditor's report, recent stock price information, a summary of quarterly financial data, and a list of directors and officers of the company.

8. The *CPA Canada Handbook* defines a publicly accountable enterprise as "an entity, other than a not-for-profit organization, that: (i) has issued, or is in the process of issuing, debt or equity instruments that are, or will be, outstanding and traded in a public market (a domestic or foreign stock exchange or an over-the-counter market, including local and regional markets); or (ii) holds assets in a fiduciary capacity for a broad group of outsiders as one of its primary businesses. Banks, credit unions, insurance companies, securities brokers/dealers, mutual funds and investment banks typically meet the second criterion above." Preface to *CPA Canada Handbook: Accounting*.

9. Legally, this is enforced by the Ontario Securities Commission (OSC) through National Instrument 52-109—Certification of Disclosure in Issuers' Annual and Interim Filings. Chief executive and chief financial officers must sign a legal document with every financial report filed with the OSC. That document certifies that the CEO and CFO have designed or supervised the design of a financial data collection and reporting system that will result in financial statements free of material misstatement and fraud. This is an assurance of the quality of financial information disclosed by companies listed on Canadian stock exchanges.

10. A typical audit report for Canadian public companies consists of the auditor's responsibility and opinion.

11. Refer to CPA Canada (www.cpacanada.ca) for details of the educational and experience requirements.

12. The Auditing and Assurance Standards Board (AASB) of the Canadian Institute of Chartered Accountants sets standards for auditing of public companies. The AASB has produced new Canadian Auditing Standards that are essentially the International Standards on Auditing issued by the International Auditing and Assurance Standards Board.

13. Chartered Professional Accountants of Canada (2012). The Chartered Professional Accountant Competency Map, p. 10. Accessible through CPA Canada's website, www.cpacanada.ca.

14. Not-for-profit organizations and pension plans are subject to different sets of accounting standards. The accounting standards applicable to the various types of organizations are compiled in different parts of the *CICA Handbook*. Part I of the *Handbook* includes IFRS. Part II includes accounting standards for private enterprises.

15. Liability means being responsible to pay for any debt owed or damage done to others. Unlimited liability means that an owner's personal assets may be seized and sold to obtain the funds necessary to pay the debt. In contrast, limited liability means only the assets of the business are at risk not the personal assets of the shareholders. Members of the board of directors, executives, and officers of companies, as well as employees, however, do *not* enjoy limited liability for any damage caused by their wilful wrongdoing. Because a corporation is considered a legally separate entity, directors and executives may find themselves being sued for damages by their employer.

Investing and Financing Decisions and the Statement of Financial Position

After studying this chapter, you should be able to do the following:

LEARNING OBJECTIVES

LO2-1 Define the objective of financial reporting, the qualitative characteristics of accounting information, and the related key accounting assumptions and principles.

LO2-2 Define the elements of a classified statement of financial position.

LO2-3 Identify what constitutes a business transaction, and recognize common account titles used in business.

LO2-4 Apply transaction analysis to simple business transactions in terms of the accounting model: Assets = Liabilities + Shareholders' Equity.

LO2-5 Determine the impact of business transactions on the statement of financial position by using two basic tools: journal entries and T-accounts.

LO2-6 Prepare a trial balance and a classified statement of financial position, and analyze the company using the current ratio.

LO2-7 Identify investing and financing transactions and demonstrate how they impact cash flows.

Source: Courtesy of Canadian Tire Corporation

Focus Company: **Canadian Tire Corporation**

EXPANSION STRATEGY IN THE RETAIL INDUSTRY

Almost all Canadians recognize the Canadian Tire brand name (www.canadiantire.ca). With about 20.9 million retail square feet in its 498 stores across Canada, from coast to coast to coast, the company competes successfully in the Canadian retail marketplace against nationwide companies, such as Hudson's Bay Company and Sears Canada. Dealers contract with Canadian Tire to manage and operate the stores, while the company provides training and operations support and financing for its 481 dealers. The company employs almost 12,000 full-time and 16,000 part-time employees. In addition to retail sales, Canadian Tire, through its subsidiaries, operates a wholesale business to develop, source, and import private label and exclusive licensed apparel brands. Digital technology has transformed retailing, and the company provides a variety of digital services to its customers, suppliers, employees, and partners to complement the face to face customer experience.

Canadian Tire achieved its growth through acquisition of related wholesale and retail organizations, and geographic expansion of sales. Expanding the company's sales required the acquisition of productive capacity, which was financed by both shareholders and creditors. The company's growth over time is highlighted through the increase in its assets, liabilities, and shareholders' equity between the years 2006 and 2015, as reported on its statements of financial position at January

2, 2016, and compared to December 30, 2006. The amounts below and throughout this chapter are in thousands of Canadian dollars, except where noted.

	Assets	=	Liabilities	+	Shareholders' Equity
January 2, 2016	$14,988		$9,198		$5,790
December 30, 2006	5,805		3,020		2,785
Change	$ 9,183		$6,178		$3,005

Year	Sales	Total Assets
2006	8,253	5,805
2007	8,606	6,765
2008	9,121	7,784
2009	8,687	8,874
2010	9,213	11,049
2011	10,387	12,339
2012	11,427	13,229
2013	11,786	13,630
2014	12,463	14,553
2015	12,280	14,988

Sales ━━■━━

Total Assets ━━■━━

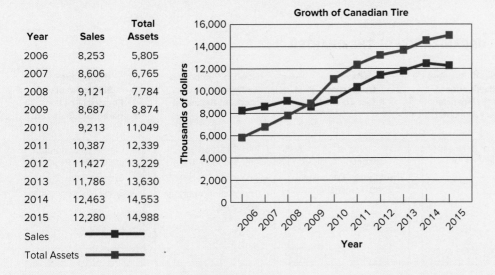

Source: Annual reports of Canadian Tire Corporation.

The company's annual growth in sales and total assets since 2006 are plotted on the graph.

UNDERSTANDING THE BUSINESS

Canadian Tire sells its products across Canada. For repeat customers and growth, the company's strategy includes customizing products and services to the needs of each community. In addition, Canadian Tire has invested in a nationwide Jumpstart program that financially supports the provision of sports equipment to young Canadians who wish to participate in organized sports.

The company's financial performance, reported in its audited financial statements, helps users understand how well Canadian Tire has implemented its strategy in the past, and to evaluate future growth potential.

Financial statements are intended to communicate the economic facts, measured in monetary units, in a standardized, formal way. Therefore, by applying accounting principles consistently, accountants formally communicate comparable estimates that faithfully represent important economic facts about companies like Canadian Tire and its competitors. Recall from Chapter 1 that financial statements include four components: the statement of financial position, the statement of comprehensive income (and its main component, the statement of earnings), the statement of changes in equity, and the statement of cash flows. In this chapter, we focus on the statement of financial position, and we examine how this financial statement communicates the results, or consequences, of Canadian Tire's strategy by answering the following questions:

- What type of business activities cause changes in amounts reported on the statement of financial position from one period to the next?
- How do specific activities affect each of these amounts?
- How do companies keep track of these amounts?

In this chapter, we focus on typical asset acquisition activities (often called *investing activities*) in which Canadian Tire engages, along with the related *financing activities*, such as borrowing funds from creditors and selling shares to investors, to provide the cash necessary to acquire the assets. We examine only those activities that affect amounts reported on the statement of financial position. Operating activities that affect amounts reported on both the statement of earnings and the statement of financial position are covered in Chapters 3 and 4. To begin, let us return to the basic concepts introduced in Chapter 1.

ORGANIZATION OF THE CHAPTER

Overview of Accounting Concepts	What Types of Business Activities Cause Changes in Financial Statement Amounts?	How Do Transactions Affect Accounts?	How Do Companies Keep Track of Account Balances?	How Is the Statement of Financial Position Prepared and Analyzed?
• Concepts Emphasized in Chapter 2 • Elements of the Classified Statement of Financial Position	• Nature of Business Transactions • Accounts	• Principles of Transaction Analysis • Analyzing Canadian Tire's Transactions	• The Direction of Transaction Effects • Analytical Tools • Transaction Analysis Illustrated	• Classified Statement of Financial Position • Current Ratio • Some Misconceptions

Supplemental material:
Appendix C: The Formal Recordkeeping System (on *Connect*)

LO2-1

Define the objective of financial reporting, the qualitative characteristics of accounting information, and the related key accounting assumptions and principles.

OVERVIEW OF ACCOUNTING CONCEPTS

The key accounting terms and concepts we defined in Chapter 1 are part of a theoretical framework developed over many years. The framework prescribes the nature, function, and limitations of both financial accounting and financial statements. The essential elements of this framework are embodied in the IASB *Framework for the Preparation and Presentation of Financial Statements,*[1] which identifies concepts that form the foundation for financial reporting. This framework is the subject of a major project undertaken jointly by the IASB and the Financial Accounting Standards Board (FASB) of the United States. The first phase of this project was completed in 2010, and work continues on the remaining phases.[2] This conceptual framework establishes the concepts that underlie the estimates and judgments embodied in financial statements. It also provides guidance to accounting standard setters in developing new accounting standards and in revising existing standards. Exhibit 2.1 presents an overview of the key concepts discussed in the next five chapters. An understanding of the accounting concepts will be helpful as you study, because learning and remembering *how* the accounting process works is much easier if you know *why* it works a certain way. A clear understanding of these concepts will also help you in future chapters as we examine more complex business activities.

Concepts Emphasized in Chapter 2

Objective of Financial Reporting   The **primary objective of external financial reporting** is to provide financial information about the reporting entity that is useful to existing and potential investors, lenders, and other creditors in making decisions about providing resources to the entity. To achieve this objective, financial reports must enable *decision makers* not only to assess the amounts, timing, and

The **PRIMARY OBJECTIVE OF EXTERNAL FINANCIAL REPORTING** is to provide financial information about the reporting entity that is useful to existing and potential investors, lenders, and other creditors in making decisions about providing resources to the entity.

uncertainty of future cash inflows and outflows but also to understand the financial value of both the assets owned and claims against those assets (liabilities and equity). These decision makers include average investors, creditors, and experts who provide financial advice. All decision makers are expected to have a reasonable understanding of accounting concepts and procedures (this may be one of the reasons you are studying accounting). Of course, as we discussed in Chapter 1, many other groups, such as suppliers and customers, also use financial statements.

To provide financial information about the reporting entity that is useful to existing and potential investors, lenders, and other creditors in making decisions about providing resources to the entity.

Qualitative Characteristics of Useful Accounting Information:

- Fundamental characteristics: **relevance, faithful representation**
- Enhancing characteristics: **comparability, verifiability, timeliness, understandability**

Elements to Be Measured and Reported:

- **Assets, liabilities, shareholders' equity, investments by owners, distribution to owners**
- Revenues, expenses, gains and losses
- Comprehensive income

Concepts for Measuring and Reporting Information:

- **Assumptions: separate entity, stable monetary unit, continuity (going concern),** periodicity
- **Principles: mixed-attribute measurement,** revenue recognition, full disclosure
- **Constraints: cost**

Concepts in red are discussed in Chapters 1 and 2. Those not in black type will be discussed in future chapters.

Exhibit 2.1

Financial Accounting and Reporting Conceptual Framework

Most users are interested in information to assist them in projecting the future cash inflows and outflows of a business. For example, creditors and potential creditors need to assess an entity's ability to pay interest on a loan over time and repay the initial amount borrowed, called the *principal*. Investors and potential investors want to assess the entity's ability to pay dividends in the future. They also want to evaluate how successful the company might be in the future, so that as the share price rises, investors can then sell their shares for more than they paid.

Qualitative Characteristics of Useful Accounting Information To fulfill the primary objective of providing useful information, the conceptual framework provides guidance on the essential characteristics that determine the usefulness of accounting information. There are two fundamental qualitative characteristics—relevance and faithful representation—supported by four enhancing qualitative characteristics: comparability, verifiability, timeliness, and understandability.[3] Accounting information that embodies the best balance of these characteristics will be of high quality to external decision makers. These six characteristics are presented in Exhibit 2.2 and discussed below, along with important constraints on accounting measurement.

Relevance Information disclosed in financial statements is **relevant information** if it can influence users' decisions by helping them assess the economic effect of past activities and/or predict future events. For example, the various elements of a statement of earnings have predictive value if they help users predict future levels of net earnings or its subcomponents, such as earnings from operations. The *predictive value* of the statement of earnings is enhanced if non-recurring items are presented separately on a multiple-step statement of earnings, because these items are transient in nature. Similarly, information presented on the statement of earnings has *confirmatory value* if it confirms or changes prior expectations based on previous evaluations. Comparison of predicted results with actual results is helpful in improving the quality of the prediction process.

RELEVANT INFORMATION can influence a decision; it has predictive and/or confirmatory value.

Exhibit **2.2**

Qualitative Characteristics of Accounting Information

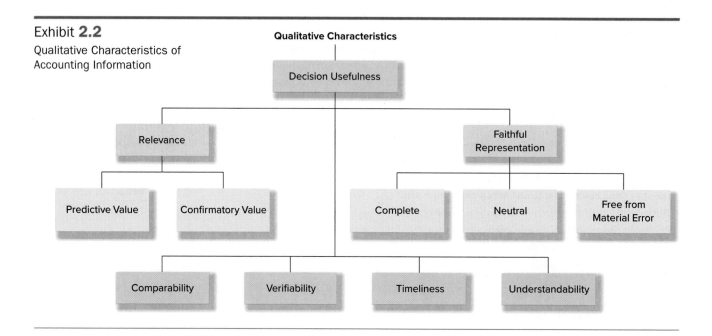

Faithful Representation   To be useful for decision making, information provided in financial statements must be a **faithful representation** of the economic phenomena it is supposed to represent, thus reflecting the substance of the underlying transactions. The information must be complete, neutral, and free from material error. For example, deferred revenue that is recognized prematurely as revenue for the period overstates the amount of revenue reported on the statement of earnings, causing a lack of faithful representation of current-period revenues.

The usefulness of accounting information is enhanced when it is neutral; that is, free from bias in its measurement and presentation. Bias in measurement occurs when the item being measured is consistently understated or overstated. For example, a consistent understatement of administrative expenses leads to a biased higher amount of net earnings. In this context, the development of accounting standards for measurement and reporting of transaction effects should not result in favouring one group of users over others. The measurement and reporting of liabilities, for example, should not result in consistent under reporting of liabilities on the statement of financial position, because this would favour owners over creditors and may influence investment and credit decisions of financial statement users.

Information that faithfully represents the underlying transactions must reflect the economic substance of the transactions and how they affect the economic condition of the company rather than their legal form. For example, when a company leases equipment, the monthly or annual payment represents an expense that is reported on the statement of earnings. However, the specific provisions of the lease contract may indicate that it is essentially a purchase of an asset, which is financed by the seller. Regardless of the legal form of the lease contract, if the underlying substance of the transaction reflects a purchase transaction, then accountants must classify the transaction as a purchase and account for the equipment as an asset and the future lease payments as a liability.

Comparability   **Comparability** of accounting information across businesses is enhanced when similar accounting methods have been applied. It enables users to identify similarities and discrepancies between two sets of financial reports produced by two different companies. This quality is also important when comparing information provided by the same company over time. The comparability of financial reports is enhanced if consistent information is made available by using the same accounting

FAITHFUL REPRESENTATION suggests that information provided in financial statements must reflect the substance of the underlying transactions.

COMPARABILITY of accounting information across businesses is enhanced when similar accounting methods have been applied.

methods over time as well. Changes in accounting methods reduce the comparability of information and necessitate disclosure of the effects of the change in order to maintain comparability.

Verifiability   Information presented in financial statements is **verifiable** if independent accountants can agree on the nature and amount of the transaction. For example, the historical cost of a piece of land that is reported on a company's statement of financial position at year-end is usually highly verifiable. The cost of acquisition is based on the purchase price and related costs that result from actual exchanges with external parties. However, the appraised market value of the land at that date is a subjective estimate that reflects the appraiser's past experience. It is not verifiable because it is not based on an actual exchange transaction. However, if a company is considering the sale of land, its market value would be relevant for that decision even though it is less verifiable than the land's historical cost.[4]

Information is **VERIFIABLE** if independent accountants can agree on the nature and amount of the transaction.

Timeliness   Information that is not available to users in a timely manner loses its relevance because it cannot be considered in making decisions. **Timely** information enhances both its predictive and confirmatory values. The relevance of accounting information for decision making declines as time passes. For this reason, companies produce quarterly reports and issue press releases to convey timely information to investors, creditors, and other user groups.

TIMELY information enhances both its predictive and confirmatory values.

Understandability   Information cannot be useful if it is not properly understood. **Understandability** is the quality of information that enables users to comprehend its meaning. It is assumed that users of accounting information have a reasonable knowledge of business and economic activities as these are reflected in financial reports. It is also assumed that users are willing to study the information with reasonable diligence.[5] In this context, the classification and presentation of information within the financial statements and related notes enhance its understandability.

UNDERSTANDABILITY is the quality of information that enables users to comprehend its meaning.

Constraints of Accounting Measurement   Accurate interpretation of financial statements requires that the statements' reader be aware of important constraints of accounting measurement.

Cost   Companies produce and disseminate accounting information to users with the expectation that the benefits to users of such information exceed the cost of producing it. The **cost constraint** suggests that information should be produced only if the perceived benefits of increased decision usefulness exceed the expected costs of providing that information. Such benefits may be difficult to measure, but the costs of producing additional information can be estimated with reasonable accuracy. When standard setters, such as the Accounting Standards Board, require companies to disclose specific information, known as *mandatory* disclosure, they have determined implicitly that the benefits to users exceed the costs the company will incur to produce the information. For example, the regulation introduced by the CSA concerning internal control over financial reporting imposed additional costs on companies to evaluate the effectiveness of internal control procedures put in place to discourage corporate fraud by managers and other employees.[6] The perceived benefits of this new regulation include increased verifiability and decision usefulness of the accounting information disclosed in financial statements. While the cost of improving internal control procedures can be estimated, the related benefits to users of financial statements may be difficult to measure.

The **COST CONSTRAINT** suggests that information should be produced only if the perceived benefits of increased decision usefulness exceed the expected costs of providing that information.

In other cases, the company's managers may decide that *voluntary* disclosure of information about specific aspects of the company's operations would be beneficial to users. In such cases, the costs of disclosure should not exceed the expected benefits. In this context, the cost constraint plays an important role in determining whether new information should be produced and communicated to users.

PRUDENCE suggests that care should be taken not to overstate assets and revenues or understate liabilities and expenses.

Prudence   **Prudence** requires that special care be taken to avoid (1) overstating assets and revenues and (2) understating liabilities and expenses. Users of financial statements often want to know about possible sources of trouble for the company. For example, creditors need to know how secure their investments will be if the company's fortunes deteriorate, but they may not be interested in whether the company might do exceptionally well. They care more about the downside risk than the upside potential. For this reason, financial statements that show assets at historical cost but reduce these amounts when current values are significantly lower help satisfy the needs of creditors. This lower-of-cost-or-market guideline attempts to offset managers' natural optimism about their business operations, which sometimes creeps into the financial reports that they prepare. More companies have perished through excessive optimism than through excessive caution. Prudence is viewed as a constraint rather than a desirable quality of accounting information, because the prudent reporting of accounting information contradicts the concept of neutrality and is likely to result in bias in the values reported on financial statements.

In summary, the usefulness of accounting information depends on many players, each contributing his or her share in the process of preparing and disseminating information that is credible. Credibility of the information conveyed in financial reports depends on those who establish accounting standards, those who are responsible for the preparation of financial reports, and those responsible for ensuring compliance with the accounting standards. The standard-setting process alone, no matter how meticulous, cannot establish and sustain trust. Compliance in practice; appropriate audit procedures; and professional codes of conduct, oversight, and public disciplinary procedures all work together to enhance the credibility of those who are legally responsible for the periodic production and communication of accounting information to a variety of users.

Recognition and Measurement Concepts   Before we discuss accountants' definitions for elements of the statement of financial position, we should consider three assumptions and a measurement concept that underlie much of our application of these definitions. The **separate-entity assumption** states that the activities of each business must be accounted for separately from the activities of its owners, all other persons, and other entities. Separation of the owners' resources (and obligations) from those of the business entity is necessary for a proper evaluation of the entity's results of operations and its financial position. For example, a building purchased by the owner of a real estate development and management company for personal use should not be mixed with buildings owned by the company. Under the **stable monetary unit assumption**, accounting information should be measured and reported in the national monetary unit (Canadian dollars in Canada, euros in countries that use it, pesos in Mexico, etc.), without any adjustment for changes in purchasing power (e.g., inflation) even if the entity has business operations in many countries.

The SEPARATE-ENTITY ASSUMPTION states that the activities of each business must be accounted for separately from the activities of its owners.

The STABLE MONETARY UNIT ASSUMPTION states that accounting information should be measured and reported in the national monetary unit without any adjustment for changes in purchasing power.

The use of a specific unit of measure allows for meaningful aggregation of financial amounts. Furthermore, accountants assume that the unit of measure has a stable value over time, even though the price we pay to purchase a specific item, such as a chocolate bar, tends to increase over time. Canadian Tire's statement of financial position includes many assets purchased in different years and measured in Canadian dollars. The stable monetary unit assumption allows accountants to combine dollar amounts from various years, even though the purchasing power of the monetary unit has changed over time.

For accounting purposes, a business is normally assumed to continue operating long enough to carry out its objectives and to meet contractual commitments. The **continuity (going-concern) assumption** states that businesses are assumed to continue to operate into the foreseeable future. Violation of this assumption means that assets and liabilities should be valued and reported on the statement of financial position as if the company were to be liquidated (i.e., discontinued, with all assets sold and all debts paid). In all future chapters, unless indicated otherwise, we assume that businesses meet the continuity assumption.

The CONTINUITY (GOING-CONCERN) ASSUMPTION states that businesses are assumed to continue to operate into the foreseeable future.

Finally, accountants measure the elements of the statement of financial position using what is called a **mixed-attribute measurement model**. Most elements of the statement of financial position are recorded at their cash-equivalent value on the date of the transaction. This is called the **historical cost principle or cost principle**. For example, assets are initially recorded at the cash paid plus the monetary value of all non-cash considerations (any assets, privileges, or rights) given on the exchange date. We will discuss the conditions under which these values are adjusted to other amounts, such as their market value, starting in Chapter 6 of this text. With these assumptions in mind, we are now ready to discuss accountants' precise definitions of the elements of the statement of financial position.

One advantage of this approach is that many assets are acquired according to legal contracts that clearly state the acquisition cost. For example, Canadian Tire owns property that it acquired several years ago and reports it on the statement of financial position at historical cost. Although the market price or economic value of the land has risen over time, its recorded value remains unchanged at its original cost because this amount is a verifiable measure based on an actual exchange that occurred in the past. It would be desirable to show on the statement of financial position the land's fair value; that is, the price at which it could be sold instead of its outdated historical cost. However, Canadian Tire did not acquire the land in order to resell it but rather to use it as sites for retail outlets that would generate revenue. Moreover, the land's fair value may not be reliable if different real estate appraisers produce different values for the same piece of land. Accountants continue, therefore, to rely on historical cost measures for reporting purposes because they are factual, although they may not be useful for specific decision-making purposes. Furthermore, as long as Canadian Tire remains a going concern it is unlikely to sell the land at its fair value. The land retains usefulness, often referred to as the asset's value-in-use, to Canadian Tire. If Canadian Tire has no intent to sell the land, then its fair value is not specifically relevant to understanding the financial health of the company. We will discuss the use of alternative measurement bases for asset valuation and the conditions under which historical cost measures are adjusted to other amounts, such as their fair value, starting in Chapter 6 of this text.

Assets, liabilities, and equity are the key elements of a corporation's statement of financial position, as we learned in Chapter 1. Let us examine the definitions in more detail.

Elements of the Classified Statement of Financial Position

Assets are economic resources controlled by an entity as a result of past transactions or events and from which future economic benefits may be obtained. These are the resources that the entity has and can use in its future operations. When Canadian Tire purchases an asset, it acquires the right for future benefits to be derived from that asset, as well as any future risks and obligations arising from control of the asset. External users of Canadian Tire's financial statements care about its assets because they embody future financial benefits. For lenders, Canadian Tire's assets and their productivity are the basis upon which they can generate forecasts about how readily the company can repay its financial obligations. For Canadian Tire's shareholders, the increase in the value of their investment will depend in large part on the realized future benefits arising from assets under the company's control.

To make financial statements more useful to investors, creditors, and analysts, specific *classifications* of information are included on the statements. Various classifications are used in practice, and you should not be confused when you notice slightly different formats used by different companies.

Let us explore Canadian Tire's simplified statement of financial position, presented in Exhibit 2.3. First, notice the title of the statement: Consolidated Statement of Financial Position. *Consolidated* means that the classified elements of Canadian Tire's statement of financial position are combined with those of other companies under its

The **MIXED-ATTRIBUTE MEASUREMENT MODEL** is applied to measuring different assets and liabilities.

The **HISTORICAL COST PRINCIPLE** or **COST PRINCIPLE** requires that assets be recorded at their cash-equivalent value on the date of the transaction, and that such value be reported on the statement of financial position at subsequent dates.

LO2-2

Define the elements of a classified statement of financial position.

ASSETS are economic resources controlled by an entity as a result of past transactions or events and from which future economic benefits may be obtained.

control (e.g., FGL Sports).[7] For convenience, the amounts for the various elements of the statement of financial position are shown in thousands of Canadian dollars. Two amounts are shown for each element: one at January 2, 2016, and the other at January 3, 2015, one year earlier. This system allows investors to compare, at a glance, the value of each classified element from year to year, and then analyze these changes to understand whether the company's financial position has improved or deteriorated over time.

Canadian Tire's statement of financial position is shown in *column*, or *report*, format, with assets listed first, followed by liabilities, and then shareholders' equity. Other companies may choose an account format with the assets listed on the left-hand side and liabilities and shareholders' equity listed on the right. Both formats are standard ways of communicating the same information. We now explain the various elements that appear on Canadian Tire's statement of financial position.

Exhibit 2.3 presents Canadian Tire's statement of financial position, with amounts rounded to the nearest thousand dollars. Notice that Canadian Tire's fiscal year ends on January 2. The choice of year-ends will be discussed in Chapter 4.

Typically, the assets of a company include the following:

1. Current assets (short term)

    a. Cash

    b. Short-term investments

    c. Accounts receivable

    d. Inventories

    e. Prepaid expenses (i.e., expenses paid in advance of use)

    f. Other current assets

2. Non-current assets (long term)

    a. Property and equipment (at cost less accumulated depreciation)

    b. Financial assets

    c. Goodwill

    d. Intangible assets

    e. Other (miscellaneous) assets

CURRENT ASSETS are assets that will be used or turned into cash, normally within one year. Inventory is always considered to be a current asset, regardless of the time needed to produce and sell it.

Canadian Tire lists its assets *in order of liquidity*; meaning, how soon an asset is expected by management to be transformed into cash. Notice that several of Canadian Tire's assets are categorized as current assets. **Current assets** are those economic resources that Canadian Tire will typically transform into cash or use within the next year or the operating business cycle of the company, whichever is longer. Under current assets, *cash* appears first because it is the most liquid asset. *Short-term investments* represent the reported values for shares of other companies, certificates of deposit with banks and other financial assets purchased as investments of excess cash.

Any *receivable* represents an amount of money owed to Canadian Tire. *Accounts receivable* consist primarily of *trade receivables*, which are amounts owed by customers who purchased products and services on credit. These amounts are normally collected within one year of the statement's date.

Inventories refers to goods that (1) are held for sale to customers in the normal course of business or (2) are used to produce goods or services for sale. Inventory is always considered to be a current asset, no matter how long it takes to produce and sell. Canadian Tire's inventory would include a variety of housewares, appliances, auto parts, sportswear and equipment, and outdoor products not yet sold to customers. *Prepaid expenses* (e.g., insurance premiums and rent paid in advance for use of equipment) reflect available benefits (e.g., monthly insurance protection, office space) that the company will use within one year. *Other current assets*, when reported, will include a number of assets with smaller balances that are combined.

Exhibit **2.3**

Canadian Tire's Statement of Financial Position

REAL-WORLD EXCERPT

Canadian Tire Corporation

CANADIAN TIRE CORPORATION Consolidated Statement of Financial Position (in thousands of Canadian dollars)		
Assets	**January 2, 2016**	**January 3, 2015**
Current assets		
Cash	$ 901	$ 648
Short-term investments	96	289
Accounts receivable	5,790	5,786
Inventories	1,765	1,624
Prepaid expenses	96	104
Other current assets	44	45
Total current assets	8,692	8,496
Non-current assets		
Long-term receivables	731	684
Long-term investments	154	176
Property and equipment	4,116	3,892
Goodwill	437	437
Intangible assets	810	815
Other non-current assets	48	39
Total non-current assets	6,296	6,043
Total assets	$14,988	$14,539
Liabilities and shareholders' equity		
Current liabilities		
Accounts payable[8]	$ 920	$ 870
Accrued Liabilities	1,037	1,091
Provisions	262	250
Short-term borrowings	89	200
Income taxes payable	62	55
Current portion of long-term debt	24	588
Other current liabilities	1,536	1,555
Total current liabilities	3,930	4,609
Non-current liabilities		
Long-term debt	2,971	2,132
Other non-current liabilities	2,297	2,167
Total non-current liabilities	5,268	4,299
Total liabilities	9,198	8,908
Shareholders' equity		
Contributed capital	674	698
Retained earnings	4,172	4,075
Other components	944	858
Total shareholders' equity	5,790	5,631
Total liabilities and shareholders' equity	$14,988	$14,539

Annotations (left margin):

- *Amount of cash in the company's bank accounts* — Cash
- *Investment in highly liquid assets* — Short-term investments
- *Amounts owed by customers from prior sales* — Accounts receivable
- *Products stored but not sold* — Inventories
- *Rent, advertising, and insurance paid in advance* — Prepaid expenses
- *A variety of current assets* — Other current assets
- *Amounts owed on loans receivable after one year* — Long-term receivables
- *Investment in financial assets that are convertible to cash after one year* — Long-term investments
- *Land, stores, and sales equipment* — Property and equipment
- *An intangible asset that results from the acquisition of another business* — Goodwill
- *Assets that do not have physical substance but have a long life* — Intangible assets
- *A variety of assets that are covered in future chapters* — Other non-current assets
- *Amounts owed to suppliers for prior purchases* — Accounts payable
- *Amounts owed to suppliers of services* — Accrued Liabilities
- *Estimated liabilities whose amounts and timing of payment are not known with certainty* — Provisions
- *Amounts owed to lenders within one year* — Short-term borrowings
- *Amount of taxes owed to the government* — Income taxes payable
- *Amounts owed on written debt contracts within one year* — Current portion of long-term debt
- *A variety of current liabilities* — Other current liabilities
- *Amounts owed on written debt contracts after one year* — Long-term debt
- *A variety of non-current liabilities* — Other non-current liabilities
- *Amounts invested in the business by shareholders* — Contributed capital
- *Past earnings not distributed to shareholders* — Retained earnings
- *Adjustments to assets and liabilities that are explained in future chapters* — Other components

Note: This statement is an adaptation of Canadian Tire's actual statement of financial position. Some of the elements of the actual statement were combined for illustrative purposes.

Source: Canadian Tire Corporation, Annual Report 2015.

ANALYSIS OF CHANGES IN INVENTORY AND ACCOUNTS RECEIVABLE

FINANCIAL ANALYSIS

Investors analyze the financial statements of a company to decide whether or not to purchase its shares or to lend it money. One important decision factor is how easily a company can access cash to pay both debts to its creditors and dividends to its shareholders. In a normal business cycle, Canadian Tire would purchase products for sale in its retails stores. These products, called *inventories*, are stored in warehouses until they are sold. The faster these products are sold to customers, the faster these assets are transformed into cash. Let us examine the company's ability to access cash, assuming for simplicity that Canadian Tire's inventories consist of products held for sale.

Notice that the balance of accounts receivable increased slightly from $5,786* at January 3, 2015, to $5,790 at January 2, 2016, indicating that the amount of sales on credit exceeded the cash collected from customers. An investor would also observe that cash increased from $648 at January 3, 2015, to $901 at January 2, 2016. Investors would examine the statement of cash flows to gain clearer insight as to how events in the past year resulted in the change in cash (see Chapter 5). For the moment, this brief analysis would reassure an investor that the first two elements reported on the statement of financial position are relevant in answering an important question about how easily Canadian Tire can access cash to pay its debts to creditors and dividends to shareholders.

*We assume, for simplicity, that this amount is the result of trade transactions.

NON-CURRENT ASSETS are considered to be long term because they will be used or turned into cash over a period longer than the next year.

Following the current assets section, Canadian Tire reports a number of non-current assets. **Non-current assets** are considered to be long term because they will be used or turned into cash over a period longer than the next year. *Property, plant, and equipment* includes all land, buildings, machinery, and equipment, such as tools, furniture, and other fixtures that will be used for the storage of the many products that Canadian Tire sells. Non-current assets are also called *fixed assets* or *capital assets*—they have a physical form you can touch, and, therefore, each asset is *tangible*.

Canadian Tire's receivables from others and investments in shares of other corporations can be classified as either short-term or long-term assets depending on management's intention from holding these financial assets and how soon they will be converted into cash. *Goodwill* is an intangible asset that arises when a company purchases another business to control its operating, investing, and financing decisions. Often, the purchase price of a business exceeds the fair value of all of the identifiable assets owned by the business minus all of the identifiable liabilities owed to others. Goodwill reflects assets that are not easily identifiable or measured, such as customer confidence, quality of products, reputation for good service, and financial standing of the acquired business. The amount of $437 that Canadian Tire reported at January 2, 2016, resulted from the acquisition of FGL Sports, Mark's, and other companies, over time. *Intangible assets* have no physical substance but have a long life. They are usually not acquired for resale but are directly related to the operations of the business. Intangible assets include such items as franchises, patents, trademarks, and copyrights. Their values arise from the *legal rights* and *privileges* of ownership, which are recognized if they are purchased from external parties or as a result of internal development. Canadian Tire's intangibles include software, banners, and trademarks, among others and are reported at a net value of $810 at January 2, 2016. Intangible assets, including goodwill, are discussed in more detail in Chapter 8.

Other non-current assets, when reported, will include a number of assets that are combined because of their relatively small values.

UNRECORDED BUT VALUABLE ASSETS

FINANCIAL
ANALYSIS

Many very valuable intangible assets, such as trademarks, patents, and copyrights, that are developed inside a company (not purchased), are not reported on the statement of financial position. For example, Tim Hortons's statement of financial position or related notes do not report any value for its trademark because it was developed internally over time through research, development, and advertising (it was not purchased). Likewise, the Coca-Cola Company does not report any asset for its patented Coke formulas, although it does report more than US$6.5 billion in various trademarks that it has purchased.

Liabilities are present debts or obligations arising from an entity's past transactions that will be paid with assets or services. They represent future outflows of assets (mainly cash) or services to the *creditors* that provided the corporation with the resources needed to conduct its business. When the corporation borrows money, creditors receive not only full payment of the amount owed to them but also interest on the borrowed amount.

Typically, the liabilities of a company include the following:

1. Current liabilities (short term)
    a. Accounts payable
    b. Short-term debt (or borrowings)
    c. Income taxes payable
    d. Accrued liabilities
    e. Provisions
    f. Other current liabilities
2. Non-current liabilities (long term)
    a. Long-term debt (or borrowings)
    b. Provisions
    c. Other liabilities

Just as assets are reported in order of liquidity, liabilities are usually listed by order of time to maturity (how soon an obligation must be paid). **Current liabilities** are short-term obligations that will be settled within the coming year by providing cash, goods, other current assets or services. Normally, the cash from converting current assets is used to pay current liabilities.

LIABILITIES are present debts or obligations arising from an entity's past transactions that will be paid with assets or services.

CURRENT LIABILITIES are short-term obligations that will be settled within the coming year by providing cash, goods, other current assets or services.

ANALYSIS OF CHANGE IN CURRENT LIABILITIES

FINANCIAL
ANALYSIS

Using both current assets and current liabilities for Canadian Tire, we can improve our analysis of the availability of cash to repay debts to creditors and dividends to shareholders.

Canadian Tire's statement of financial position shows that the company owes $679 less in current liabilities at January 2, 2016, than it did at January 31, 2015. As investors, we would tentatively conclude that the company has reduced its reliance on suppliers and other creditors to finance its current assets. However, investors must learn far more about the business cycle for the products and services marketed by the company, Canadian Tire's main competitors, and the outlook for the industry sectors in which Canadian Tire operates before coming to a firm conclusion.

At the beginning of this chapter, we stated that investors are most interested in relevant information that helps them predict future cash inflows and outflows. From this very preliminary analysis, investors can predict that, because Canadian Tire has decreased its current liabilities by $679, a smaller amount of cash is needed in the year 2016 to repay the outstanding debt to creditors compared to the amount of $4,609 that was settled during the year 2015.

NON-CURRENT LIABILITIES are all of the entity's obligations not classified as current liabilities.

Non-current liabilities are all of the entity's obligations not classified as current liabilities. They include *long-term debt (or borrowings)* from banks and other lenders; *provisions*, which are estimated liabilities characterized by uncertainty about the exact amount to be paid and the timing of the payment; and *other liabilities*, which include a number of other liabilities. These various types of non-current liabilities will be covered in future chapters.

ENVIRONMENTAL LIABILITIES—THE GREENING OF ACCOUNTING STANDARDS

A QUESTION OF ACCOUNTABILITY

For many years, companies faced growing pressure to estimate and disclose environmental liabilities, such as the cleanup of hazardous waste. IFRS require Canadian publicly accountable enterprises to report their best estimate of probable liabilities, including environmental liabilities, in the notes to the financial statements. For example, Suncor Energy Inc., which mines oil from the tar sands of northern Alberta, reported environmental liabilities exceeding $5,505 million in its 2015 financial statements, representing approximately 14.3 percent of its total liabilities at December 31, 2015. It is estimated, however, that a significant percentage of companies under report or fail to report such liabilities, often because of the way disclosure rules are applied.

A key economic concern for many Canadian companies is how to manage their resources in an economically sustainable way. Canadian Tire, like many Canadian companies, is subject to environmental regulation, and has disclosed the following information in its annual information form for 2015:*

REAL-WORLD EXCERPT

Canadian Tire Corporation

MANAGEMENT'S DISCUSSION AND ANALYSIS
Environmental risk

Environmental risk within Canadian Tire is primarily associated with the storage, handling, and recycling of certain materials, such as oil, lubricants, and other substances used in the servicing of automobiles, tires, paint, lawn chemicals, and electronics sold in Canadian Tire and PartSource stores. The Company has established and follows comprehensive environmental policies and practices to avoid a negative impact on the environment, to comply with environmental laws and to protect its reputation.

Environmental risk within Petroleum is primarily associated with the storage and handling of gasoline, oil, and propane. Environmental contamination, if not prevented or remediated, could result in fines and sanctions and damage the Company's reputation. The Company mitigates its environmental risks through a comprehensive regulatory compliance program, which includes environmental investigations and the remediation of contaminated sites as required. Petroleum also has environmental insurance coverage.

Other companies, such as Suncor Energy Inc. and Bombardier Inc., publish detailed reports on environmental sustainability or corporate social responsibility, which include both financial and non-financial performance indicators that measure their progress toward meeting sustainable development targets.

Source: Canadian Tire Corporation, Annual Report, 2015.

SHAREHOLDERS' EQUITY (OWNERS' EQUITY or STOCKHOLDERS' EQUITY) is the financing provided by the owners and the operations of the business.

Shareholders' equity (owners' equity or stockholders' equity) is the financing provided to the corporation by both its owners and the operations of the business. One key difference between shareholders and creditors is that creditors are entitled to settlement of their legal claims on the corporation's assets before the shareholders receive a penny, even if this consumes all of the corporation's assets. Consequently, shareholders have a residual claim on the corporation's assets.

Shareholders *invest* in a company because they expect to receive two types of cash flow: dividends, which are a distribution of the corporation's earnings (a return on shareholders' investment), and gains from selling their investment in the corporation for more than they paid (known as *capital gains*).

Typically, the shareholders' equity of a corporation includes the following:

1. Contributed capital

2. Retained earnings (accumulated earnings that have not been declared as dividends)

3. Other components

Financing provided by shareholders is referred to as **contributed capital**. Shareholders invest in the business by providing cash and sometimes other assets, and receive shares as evidence of ownership. Investors in the company's shares typically include financial institutions (mutual funds, pension funds, etc.), the company's directors and executive officers, other corporate employees, and the general public. Canadian Tire's contributed capital of $674 at January 2, 2016, has resulted from contributions by shareholders at different points in the company's history.

Financing provided by operations is referred to as *earned capital* or **retained earnings**. Most companies that operate profitably retain part of their earnings for reinvestment in their business. The other part is distributed as dividends to shareholders. Earnings that are not distributed to shareholders but instead are reinvested in the business by management are called retained earnings. Canadian Tire's retained earnings equalled $4,172 at January 2, 2016, and represent the amount of earnings that have not been distributed to shareholders since the company was incorporated. Canadian Tire's growth over time has been financed by a substantial reinvestment of retained earnings. In addition to contributed capital and retained earnings, shareholders' equity includes other components that are explained in Chapter 11.

CONTRIBUTED CAPITAL results from shareholders providing cash (and sometimes other assets) to the business.

RETAINED EARNINGS refers to the accumulated earnings of a company that are not distributed to the shareholders as dividends.

PAUSE FOR FEEDBACK STOP

We just learned the elements of the statement of financial position (assets, liabilities, and shareholders' equity) and how assets and liabilities are usually classified (current or non-current). Current assets (including inventory) are expected to be used or transformed into cash within the next 12 months, and current liabilities are expected to be paid or settled within the next 12 months with cash, services, or other current assets.

SELF-STUDY QUIZ 2-1

The following is a list of items from a recent statement of financial position for Tim Hortons Inc. Indicate on the line provided whether each of the following is categorized on the statement of financial position as a current asset (CA), a non-current asset (NCA), a current liability (CL), a non-current liability (NCL), or shareholders' equity (SE).

_____ Accrued liabilities	_____ Long-term debt	_____ Property and equipment
_____ Inventories	_____ Retained earnings	_____ Notes receivable (due in five years)
_____ Accounts receivable	_____ Accounts payable	_____ Cash

After you have completed your answers, check them with the solutions at the end of the chapter.

Now that we have reviewed several of the basic accounting concepts and terms, we need to understand the economic activities of a business that result in changes in amounts reported in financial statements and the process used in generating the financial statements.

LO2-3

Identify what constitutes a business transaction, and recognize common account titles used in business.

WHAT TYPES OF BUSINESS ACTIVITIES CAUSE CHANGES IN FINANCIAL STATEMENT AMOUNTS?

Nature of Business Transactions

Accounting focuses on specific events that have an economic impact on the entity. Any event that is recorded as a part of the accounting process is called a **transaction**. The first step in translating the results of business events to financial statement

A **TRANSACTION** is (1) an exchange between a business and one or more external parties to a business or (2) a measurable internal event, such as adjustments for the use of assets in operations.

amounts is determining which events to include. As the definitions of assets and liabilities indicate, only economic resources and debts *resulting from past transactions* are recorded on the statement of financial position. Transactions include two types of events:

1. *External events:* These are *exchanges* of assets, goods, or services by one party for assets, services, or promises to pay (liabilities) by one or more other parties. Examples include the purchase of a machine from a supplier, the sale of merchandise to customers, borrowing of cash from a bank, and investment of cash in the business by the owners. Transactions that affect elements of the statement of financial position are discussed in this chapter, and those that affect elements of the statement of earnings will be covered in Chapter 3.

2. *Internal events:* These include certain events that are not exchanges between the business and other parties but, nevertheless, have a direct and measurable effect on the accounting entity. Examples include using up insurance paid in advance and using buildings and equipment over several years. Accounting for internal events will be discussed in Chapter 4.

Throughout this textbook, the word "transaction" will be used in the broad sense to include both types of events.

Some important events that have an economic impact on the company, however, are *not* reflected in the financial statements. In most cases, signing a contract is not considered to be a transaction because it involves *the exchange only of promises* not of assets, such as cash, goods, services, or property. For example, assume that Canadian Tire signs an employment contract with a new regional manager. From an accounting perspective, no transaction has occurred because no exchange of assets, goods, or services has been made. Each party to the contract has exchanged promises; the manager agrees to work and Canadian Tire agrees to pay the manager for work rendered. For each day the new manager works, however, the exchange of services for pay results in a transaction that Canadian Tire must record. Because of their importance, long-term employment contracts, leases, and other commitments may need to be disclosed in notes to the financial statements.

How does the accounting staff at Canadian Tire record external and internal events that cause changes in the amounts reported on the company's statement of financial position? The recording of transactions has evolved over time. Advances in computer hardware and software technology have paved the way for efficient recording of transactions and instantaneous preparation of financial statements. However, the basic system of recording transactions has withstood the test of time and has been in use for more than 500 years. The basic tenets of manual and computerized recording systems are discussed in this chapter and elaborated on further in Chapters 3 and 4.

Accounts

An **ACCOUNT** is a standardized format that organizations use to accumulate the monetary effects of transactions on each financial statement item.

An **account** is a standardized record that organizations use to accumulate the monetary effects of transactions on each financial statement item. The cumulative result of all transactions that affect a specific account, or its ending balance, is then reported on the appropriate financial statement. To facilitate the recording of transactions, each company establishes a *chart of accounts*; that is, a list of accounts and their unique numeric codes. The chart of accounts is organized by financial statement element, with asset accounts listed first (by order of liquidity), followed by liabilities (by order of time to maturity), shareholders' equity, revenue, and expense accounts, in that order. In formal recordkeeping systems, including computerized accounting systems, use of appropriate account numbers is essential if the monetary effects of similar transactions are to be grouped correctly. Exhibit 2.4 lists account titles that are quite common and used by most companies. This list is helpful when you are completing assignments and are unsure of an account title.

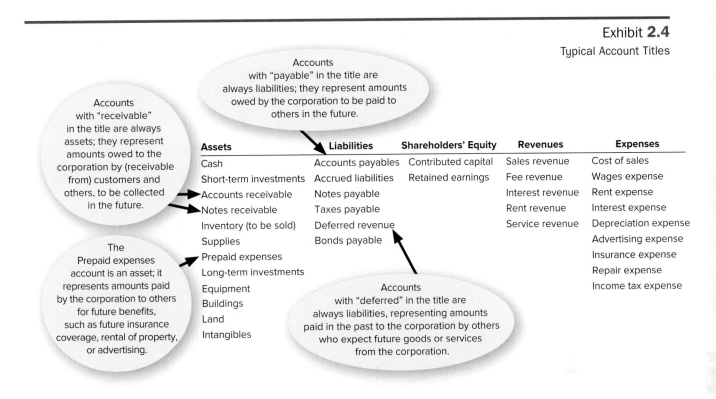

Exhibit **2.4**
Typical Account Titles

Every company creates its own chart of accounts to fit the nature of its business activities. For example, a small lawn care service may have an asset account called lawn-mowing equipment, but a large corporation, such as the Royal Bank of Canada, is unlikely to report such an account. These differences will become more apparent as we examine the statements of financial position of various companies. Because each company has a different chart of accounts, you should *not* try to memorize a typical chart of accounts, but you should understand the nature of each typical account. Then when you see a company that uses a slightly different title, you will understand what it means. For example, some companies use the term "trade accounts receivable" or "merchandise inventory" (same as inventory). *When you prepare homework problems, you will either be given the company's account names or be expected to select appropriate descriptive names, similar to the ones in Exhibit 2.4.* Once a name is selected for an account, you must use that exact name in all transactions affecting that account.

The accounts you see in the financial statements are actually summations (or aggregations) of a number of specific accounts in a company's recordkeeping system. For example, Canadian Tire keeps separate accounts for the products it sells but combines them as *inventories* on the statement of financial position. Equipment, buildings, and land are also combined into an account called *property and equipment*. Since our aim is to understand financial statements of actual companies, we focus on aggregated accounts.

HOW DO TRANSACTIONS AFFECT ACCOUNTS?

Managers make business decisions that often result in transactions affecting financial statements. For example, the decisions to expand the number of stores, advertise a new product, change an employee benefit package, and invest excess cash would all affect the financial statements. Sometimes, these decisions have unintended consequences as well. For example, the decision to purchase additional inventory for cash in anticipation of a major sales initiative will increase inventory and decrease cash.

LO2-4

Apply transaction analysis to simple business transactions in terms of the accounting model: Assets = Liabilities + Shareholders' Equity.

But, if there is no demand for the additional inventory, the lower cash balance will also reduce the company's ability to pay its other obligations.

Because business decisions often involve an element of risk, business managers should understand how transactions impact the accounts on the financial statements. The process for determining the effects of transactions is called *transaction analysis*.

Principles of Transaction Analysis

Transaction analysis is the process of studying each transaction to determine its economic effect on the entity in terms of the accounting equation (A = L + SE, also known as the *fundamental accounting model*). We outline the process in this section of the chapter, and create a visual tool representing the process (the transaction analysis model). The basic accounting equation and two fundamental concepts are the foundation for this model. Recall from Chapter 1 that the accounting equation for a business that is organized as a corporation is as follows:

Assets (A) = Liabilities (L) + Shareholders' Equity (SE)

The two concepts underlying the transaction analysis process follow:

1. Every transaction affects at least two accounts; it is critical to correctly identify the accounts affected and the direction of the effect (increase or decrease).

2. The accounting equation must remain in balance after each transaction.

Success in performing transaction analysis depends on a clear understanding of how the transaction analysis model is constructed, based on these concepts. *Study this material well. You should not move on to a new concept until you understand and can apply all prior concepts.*

Dual Effects　　The idea that every transaction has *at least two effects* on the basic accounting equation is known as the *dual effects* concept.[9] Most transactions with external parties involve an *exchange* by which the business entity both receives something and gives up something in return. For example, suppose that Canadian Tire purchased some office supplies for cash. In this exchange, Canadian Tire would receive supplies (an increase in an asset) and, in return, would give up cash (a decrease in an asset):

Transaction	Canadian Tire Received	Canadian Tire Gave
Purchased paper for cash	Supplies (increased)	Cash (decreased)

In analyzing this transaction, we determined that the accounts affected were office supplies and cash. As we discussed in Chapter 1, however, most supplies are purchased on credit (i.e., money is owed to suppliers). In that case, Canadian Tire would engage in *two* transactions:

1. **The purchase of an asset on credit** In the first transaction, Canadian Tire would receive office supplies (an increase in an asset) and would give in return a promise to pay later, called accounts payable (an increase in a liability).

2. **The eventual payment** In the second transaction, Canadian Tire would eliminate, or receive back, its promise to pay (a decrease in the accounts payable liability) and would give up cash (a decrease in an asset).

Transaction	Canadian Tire Received	Canadian Tire Gave
1. Purchased paper for credit	Office supplies (increased)	Accounts payable (increased) [a promise to pay]
2. Paid on its accounts payable	Accounts payable (decreased) [a promise was eliminated]	Cash (decreased)

As noted earlier, not all important business events result in a transaction that affects the financial statements. Most important, signing a contract involving *the exchange of promises to perform a future business transaction does not result in a transaction* that is recorded. For example, if Canadian Tire sent an order to its paper supplier for more paper without making any payment, and the supplier accepted the order but did not fill it immediately, then no transaction has taken place for accounting purposes, because Canadian Tire and the paper supplier have exchanged only promises.[10] From the supplier's perspective, the same holds true. No transaction has taken place, so the supplier's financial statements are not affected. As soon as the paper is shipped to Canadian Tire, however, the supplier gives up inventory in exchange for a promise from Canadian Tire to pay for the paper it receives, and Canadian Tire exchanges its promise to pay for the paper it receives. Because a *promise* has been exchanged for *goods*, a transaction has taken place, and the financial statements of both Canadian Tire and the supplier will be affected.

Balancing the Accounting Equation   The accounting equation must remain in balance after each transaction. Total assets (resources) must equal total liabilities plus shareholders' equity (claims to resources). If the correct accounts have been identified and the appropriate direction of the effect on each account has been determined, then the equation should remain in balance.

Systematic transaction analysis for investing and financing activities includes the following steps:

> Step 1:   **Ask → What was received and what was given?**
>
> - **Identify the accounts affected by their titles** (e.g., cash and accounts payable). Make sure that at least two accounts change.
> - **Classify each by type of account.** Was each account an asset (A), a liability (L), or shareholders' equity (SE)?
> - **Determine the direction of the effect.** Did the account increase (+) or decrease (−)?
>
> Step 2:   **Verify → Is the accounting equation in balance? (A = L + SE)**

Analyzing Canadian Tire's Transactions

To illustrate the use of the transaction analysis process, let us consider typical Canadian Tire transactions that are also common to most businesses. This chapter presents transactions affecting accounts reported on the statement of financial position. Assume that Canadian Tire engaged in the following transactions during January 2016, the month following the statement of financial position in Exhibit 2.3. The month will end on January 31. For simplicity, account titles are based on that statement of financial position. Note that monetary amounts are usually preceded by the symbol of the currency used in the exchange transactions (e.g., $ for Canadian dollars, € for euros). In the following illustration, all amounts are in thousands of Canadian dollars.

(a) Canadian Tire issues shares to new investors in exchange for $13 in cash.

(b) The company borrows $10 from its local bank, signing a note to be paid in two years.

Transactions (a) and (b) are *financing* transactions. Companies that need cash for *investing* purposes (to buy or build additional facilities as part of their plans for growth) often seek funds by selling shares to investors, as in transaction (a), or borrowing from creditors, usually banks, as in transaction (b).

(c) For expansion, Canadian Tire opened a new store. The company purchased new shelving racks, counters, and other equipment for $22; paid $15 in cash; and signed a note for $7, payable to the supplier in two years.

Assets		=	Liabilities	+	Shareholders' Equity
Cash	Property and equipment		Long-term debt		Contributed capital
(a) +13		=			+13
(b) +10		=	+10		
(c) −15	+22	=	+7		

Step 2: **Is the accounting equation in balance?**

Assets $7 = Liabilities $7 + Shareholders' Equity $0

Notice that more than two accounts were affected by transaction (c).

The analysis of transactions (d) through (f) follows. The effects are listed in the chart at the end of Self-Study Quiz 2-2. Space is left in the chart for your answers to the quiz, transactions (g) and (h), which follow transaction (f).

(d) Canadian Tire lends $100 to a trade supplier in financial difficulty. The trade supplier signs notes agreeing to repay the amount borrowed in six months.

Step 1: **What was received and what was given?** (account name, type of account, amount, and direction of effect)

Received: Written promise from the trade supplier, Notes receivable (+A) $100   **Given:** Cash (−A) $100

Step 2: **Is the accounting equation in balance?**

Assets $0 = Liabilities $0 + Shareholders' Equity $0

(e) Canadian Tire purchases shares issued by another company as a long-term investment, paying $30 in cash. The number of shares purchased allows Canadian Tire to exert significant influence over decisions made by that company.

Step 1: **What was received and what was given?** (account name, type of account, amount, and direction of effect)

Received: Share certificates from the other company, Long-term investments (+A) $30   **Given:** Cash (−A) $30

Step 2: **Is the accounting equation in balance?**

Assets $0 = Liabilities $0 + Shareholders' Equity $0

Purchasing and selling property and equipment, and investments in the shares of other corporations are *investing* transactions.

(f) Canadian Tire's board of directors declares cash dividends of $20 for shareholders. The dividends are paid immediately.

Step 1: **What was received and what was given?** (account name, type of account, amount, and direction of effect)

Received: Earnings retained in the business distributed to investors, Retained earnings (−SE) $20   **Given:** Cash (−A) $20

Step 2: **Is the accounting equation in balance?**

Assets −$20 = Liabilities $0 + Shareholders' Equity −$20

PAUSE FOR FEEDBACK

Transaction analysis involves identifying (by title) accounts affected in a transaction, recognizing that at least two accounts are affected, classifying the accounts (asset, liability, or shareholders' equity), and determining the direction of the effect on the account (increase or decrease). If all accounts and effects are correct, then the fundamental accounting equation (A = L + SE) will remain in balance. *The most effective way to develop your transaction analysis skills is to practice with many transactions.*

SELF-STUDY QUIZ 2-2

Review the analysis in transactions (a) through (f) and complete the transaction analysis steps in the chart following the transactions (g) and (h). *Repeat the steps until they become a natural part of your thought process.*

(g) Canadian Tire collects $10 cash on notes receivable from the trade supplier. (*Hint:* Think about what is received and what is given.)

> Step 1: **Identify and classify accounts and effects.**
>
> Step 2: **Is the accounting equation in balance?**

(h) Canadian Tire paid $4 on long-term debt.

> Step 1: **Identify and classify accounts and effects.**
>
> Step 2: **Is the accounting equation in balance?**

Include these effects on the following chart.

	Cash	Notes receivable	Long-term Investments	Property and equipment	=	Long-term debt	+	Contributed capital	Retained earnings
			Assets		=	**Liabilities**	+	**Shareholders' Equity**	
(a)	13				=			+13	
(b)	+10				=	+10			
(c)	−15			+22	=	+7			
(d)	−100	+100			=				
(e)	−30		+30		=				
(f)	−20				=				−20
(g)					=				
(h)					=				

After you complete your answers, check them with the solutions at the end of the chapter.

(*i*) Canadian Tire's board of directors approved the construction of a new store at a meeting in January 2016 and the borrowing of $20 from the local bank to finance the construction of the new store in March 2016.

Unlike transactions (*a*) through (*h*), which reflect exchanges between Canadian Tire and external parties, these two decisions of the board of directors are not transactions because no exchanges have taken place yet. The company's board of directors made commitments that will likely translate into actions in March 2016. Specific statement of financial position accounts will be affected only when the actual exchanges occur in March 2016. However, to improve on the representational faithfulness of financial statements, such commitments will normally be disclosed in a financial statement note.

HOW DO COMPANIES KEEP TRACK OF ACCOUNT BALANCES?

For most organizations, recording transaction effects and keeping track of account balances in the manner just presented is impractical. To handle the multitude of daily transactions that businesses generate, companies establish accounting systems, usually computerized, that follow a cycle. The accounting cycle, illustrated in Exhibit 2.5, highlights the primary activities performed during the accounting period to analyze, record, and post transactions. In this chapter and in Chapter 3, we will illustrate these activities *during the period*. In Chapter 4, we will complete the accounting cycle by discussing and illustrating activities *at the end of the period* to adjust the records, prepare financial statements, and close the accounting records.

LO2-5

Determine the impact of business transactions on the statement of financial position by using two basic tools: journal entries and T-accounts.

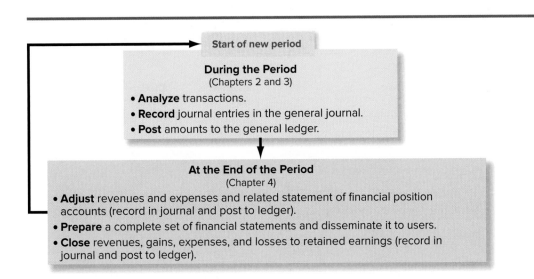

Exhibit **2.5**
The Accounting Cycle

During the accounting period, transactions that result in exchanges between the company and other external parties are analyzed and recorded in the *general journal* in chronological order, and the related accounts are updated in the *general ledger*. These formal records are based on two very important tools used by accountants: journal entries and T-accounts. From the standpoint of accounting systems design, these analytical tools are more-efficient mechanisms for reflecting the effects of transactions and for determining account balances for financial statement preparation. *As future business managers, you should develop your understanding and use of these tools in financial analysis. For those studying accounting, this knowledge is the foundation for understanding the accounting system and future accounting coursework.* After we explain how to perform transaction analysis by using these tools, we illustrate their use in financial analysis.

The Direction of Transaction Effects

As we saw earlier, transactions change the balances of assets, liabilities, and shareholders' equity accounts. To reflect these effects efficiently, we need to structure the transaction analysis model in a manner that shows the *direction* of the effects. One very useful tool for summarizing the transaction effects and determining the balances for individual accounts is a **T-account**, as shown in Exhibit 2.6. Notice the following:

- Each T-account has two sides: a left side, known as the debit side, and a right side, known as the credit side.

The **T-ACCOUNT** is a tool for summarizing transaction effects for each account, determining balances, and drawing inferences about a company's activities.

DEBIT (dr) is on the left side of an account.

CREDIT (cr) is on the right side of an account.

- The increase symbol, +, is located on the left side of the T for accounts that appear on the left side of the accounting equation (assets), and on the right side of the T for accounts that are on the right side of the equation (liabilities and shareholders' equity).

- The term **debit** (dr for short) is always written on the left side of each account, and the term **credit** (cr for short) is always written on the right side.

Exhibit **2.6**

Transaction Analysis Model

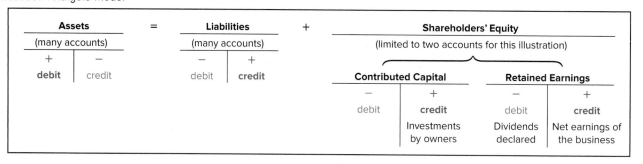

From this transaction analysis model, we can observe the following:

- Asset accounts increase on the left (debit) side. They have debit balances. It would be highly unusual for an asset account, such as inventories, to have a negative (credit) balance.

- Liabilities and shareholders' equity accounts increase on the right (credit) side, creating credit balances.

To remember which accounts are increased by debit and which accounts are increased by credit, recall that a debit (left) increases asset accounts, because assets are on the left side of the accounting equation (A= L + SE). Similarly, a credit (right) increases liability and shareholders' equity accounts because they are on the right side of the accounting equation.

In summary,

Assets	=	Liabilities	+	Shareholders' Equity
↑ with debits		↑ with credits		↑ with credits
Accounts have debit balances		Accounts have credit balances		Accounts have credit balances

In Chapter 3, we will add revenue and expense account effects. Until then, as you are learning to perform transaction analysis, you should refer to this model often until you can construct it on your own without assistance.

Many students have trouble with accounting because they forget that the term "debit" is simply the left side of an account and the term "credit" is simply the right side of an account. Perhaps someone once told you that you were a credit to your school or your family. As a result, you may think that credits are good and debits are bad. Such is not the case. Just remember that *debit is on the left* and *credit is on the right*.

If you have identified the correct accounts and effects through transaction analysis, the accounting equation will remain in balance. Moreover, *the total monetary value of all debits equals the total monetary value of all credits* in a transaction. For an extra measure of assurance, add this equality check (debits = credits) to the transaction analysis process.

From Exhibit 2.6, we learned that each account can increase and decrease. In the transaction analysis model, the effect of a transaction on each element can be represented with a T, with one side increasing and the other side decreasing. The balances of asset accounts that appear on the left side of the accounting equation are increased on the left side of the T. The balances of liability and shareholders' equity accounts that are on the right side of the accounting equation are increased on the right side of the T. In accounting, the left side of the T is called the debit side and the right side is called the credit side. Most accounts have a balance on the positive side.

SELF-STUDY **QUIZ 2-3**

The following is a list of items from a recent statement of financial position for Tim Hortons Inc. Indicate on the line provided whether each of the following accounts usually has a debit (dr) or a credit (cr) balance.

_____ Accrued liabilities   _____ Long-term debt   _____ Property and equipment

_____ Inventories   _____ Retained earnings   _____ Notes receivable (due in five years)

_____ Accounts receivable   _____ Accounts payable   _____ Cash

After you have completed your answers, check them with the solutions at the end of the chapter.

Analytical Tools

The Journal Entry In a bookkeeping system, transactions are initially recorded in chronological order in a *general journal* (see Appendix C, available on *Connect*, for a detailed illustration of formal recordkeeping procedures). After analyzing the business documents (such as purchase invoices, receipts, and cash register tapes) that describe a transaction, the bookkeeper prepares the formal journal entry and enters the effects on the accounts by using debits and credits. The **journal entry**, then, is an accounting method for expressing the effects of a transaction on various accounts, using the double-entry bookkeeping system explained previously. The journal entry for transaction (*c*) in the Canadian Tire illustration is written as follows:

A **JOURNAL ENTRY** is an accounting method for expressing the effects of a transaction on various accounts, using the double-entry bookkeeping system.

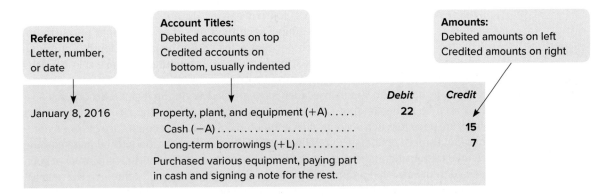

Reference: Letter, number, or date	Account Titles: Debited accounts on top Credited accounts on bottom, usually indented	Amounts: Debited amounts on left Credited amounts on right		
			Debit	*Credit*
January 8, 2016	Property, plant, and equipment (+A)		22	
	Cash (−A)			15
	Long-term borrowings (+L)			7
	Purchased various equipment, paying part in cash and signing a note for the rest.			

Notice the following:

- It is useful to include a date or some form of reference for each transaction. The debited accounts are written first (on top) with the amounts recorded in the left column. The credited accounts are written below the debits and are indented to the right in manual records; the credited amounts are written in the right column. The order of the debited accounts or credited accounts does not matter, as long as the debits are on top and the credits are on the bottom and indented to the right.

- Total debits ($22) equal total credits ($15 + $7).

- Three accounts are affected by this transaction. Any journal entry that affects more than two accounts is called a *compound entry*. Although this is the only transaction in the preceding illustration that affects more than two accounts, many transactions in subsequent chapters will require compound journal entries.

- As you can see in the illustration of a formal bookkeeping system in Exhibit 2.7, an additional line is written below the journal entry as an explanation of the transaction.

Recording external transactions in the journal is based on legal documents that highlight the contractual commitments between Canadian Tire and other parties. For example, Canadian Tire signed a contract with a supplier to purchase equipment for $22. It issued a cheque for $15 to transfer cash to the manufacturer and promised to pay $7 in two years. Consequently, the effects of this transaction are recorded in the journal and reflected in Canadian Tire's financial statements. The equipment supplier retains legal control of the equipment until it is fully paid after two years. For accounting purposes, however, Canadian Tire has control of and will use this resource to generate revenue over the next two years. This highlights the focus on the economic substance of a transaction rather than its legal form in reporting information to financial statement users. While recording external transactions in the journal requires legal documents, some legal contracts, such as signing a contract to hire a new employee, are not reflected in the financial statements.

While you are learning to perform transaction analysis, use the symbol A, L, or SE next to each account title, as in the preceding journal entry, for all homework problems. Specifically identifying accounts as assets (A), liabilities (L), or shareholders' equity (SE) clarifies the transaction analysis and makes journal entries easier to write. For example, if cash is to be increased, we will write "Cash (+A)." Throughout subsequent chapters, we include the direction of the effect along with the symbol to help you understand the effects of each transaction on the financial statements.

A note of caution: Many students try to memorize journal entries without understanding or using the transaction analysis model. The task becomes increasingly difficult as more detailed transactions are presented in subsequent chapters. In the long run, *memorizing, understanding, and using the transaction analysis model* presented here will save you time and prevent confusion.

The T-Account By themselves, journal entries do not provide the balances in accounts. After the journal entries have been recorded, the bookkeeper posts (transfers) the monetary values to each account affected by the transaction to determine the new account balances. In most computerized accounting systems, this happens automatically upon recording the journal entry.

As a group, the accounts are called a *general ledger*. In the manual accounting system used by some small organizations, the ledger is often a three-ring binder with a separate page for each account. In a computerized system, accounts are part of a database and stored on a disk. See Exhibit 2.7 for an illustration of a journal page and the related cash ledger page. Note that the cash effects from the journal entries have been posted to the cash ledger page. The three digits under the "Ref." column in the general journal are examples of account codes used in the chart of accounts.

Exhibit 2.8 shows the T-accounts for the cash and long-term borrowings accounts for Canadian Tire, based on transactions (*a*) through (*h*). Notice that for cash, which is an asset, increases are shown on the left and decreases are on the right side of the T-account. For long-term borrowings, however, increases are shown on the right and decreases on the left, since notes payable is a liability. Some small businesses still use handwritten, or manually maintained, accounts in this T-account format. Computerized systems retain the concept but not the format of the T-account.

Exhibit **2.7**

Posting Transaction Effects
from the Journal to the Ledger

General Journal   Page G1

Date	Account Titles and Explanations (in millions)	Ref.	Debit	Credit
Jan. 3	Cash	101	13	
	Contributed capital			13
	Investment by shareholders.			
Jan. 6	Cash	101	10	
	Long-term debt	201		10
	Borrowed from bank.			
Jan. 8	Property and equipment	140	**22**	
	Cash	101		15
	Long-term debt	201		7
	Purchased equipment paying part cash			
	and the rest due on a note payable.			

General Ledger   **Cash**   101

Date	Explanation	Ref.	Debit	Credit	Balance
	Balance				901
Jan. 3	Investment by shareholders.	G1	13		914
Jan. 6	Borrowed from bank.	G1	10		924
	Purchased equipment				
	paying part cash and the				
Jan. 8	rest due on a note payable.	G1		15	917

General Ledger   **Property and Equipment**   140

Date	Explanation	Ref.	Debit	Credit	Balance
	Balance				4,116
	Purchased equipment				
	paying part cash and				
	the rest due on a				
Jan. 8	note payable.	G1	22		4,138

General Ledger   **Cash**   201

Date	Explanation	Ref.	Debit	Credit	Balance
	Balance				2,971
Jan. 6	Investment by shareholders.	G1		10	2,981
Jan. 8	Borrowed from bank.	G1		7	2,984

In Exhibit 2.8, notice that the ending balance is indicated on the positive side with a double underline. To find the account balances, we can express the T-accounts as equations:

	Cash	Long-Term Debt
Beginning balance	$901	$2,971
+ "+" side	+ 26	+ 17
− "−" side	− 79	− 4
Ending balance	$765	$2,984

Exhibit **2.8**

T-Accounts Illustrated

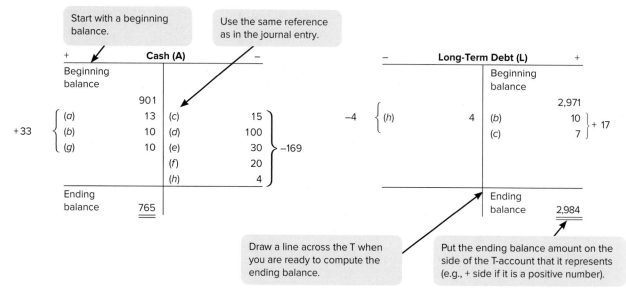

A word on terminology: the words "debit" and "credit" are used as verbs, nouns, and adjectives. For example, we can say that Canadian Tire's cash account was debited (verb) when shares were issued to investors, meaning that the amount was entered on the left side of the T-account. Or we can say that a credit (noun) was entered on the right side of an account. Cash may be described as a debit account (adjective). These terms will be used instead of "left" and "right" throughout the rest of the textbook.

The next section illustrates the steps to follow in analyzing the effects of transactions, recording the effects in journal entries, and determining account balances by using T-accounts.

Transaction Analysis Illustrated

In this section, we will use the monthly transactions of Canadian Tire that were presented earlier to demonstrate transaction analysis and the use of journal entries and T-accounts. We analyze each transaction, checking to make sure that the accounting equation remains in balance and that debits equal credits. The amounts from Canadian Tire's statement of financial position at January 2, 2016, have been inserted as the beginning balances in the T-accounts, located together at the end of the illustration. After reviewing or preparing each journal entry, trace the effects to the appropriate T-accounts by using the transaction letters (*a*) to (*h*) as a reference. The first transaction has been highlighted for you.

Study this illustration carefully, including the explanations of transaction analysis. Careful study is *essential* to the understanding of (1) the accounting model, (2) transaction analysis, (3) the dual effects of each transaction, and (4) the dual-balancing system. *The most effective way to learn these critical concepts that affect material throughout the rest of the textbook is to practise, practise, practise.*

(a) Canadian Tire issues shares to new investors in exchange for $13 in cash.

Cash (+A)		13	
Contributed capital (+SE)			13
Issued shares for cash.			

Assets	=	**Liabilities**	+	**Shareholders' Equity**	
Cash +13				Contributed capital	+13

These effects have been posted to the appropriate T-accounts at the end of the illustration. To post the amounts, transfer or copy the debit or credit amount on each line to the appropriate T-account indicated in order to accumulate balances for each account. For example, the $13 debit is listed in the debit (increase) column of the cash T-account.

(b) The company borrows $10 from its local bank, signing a note to be paid in two years.

Cash (+A)   10
   Long-term debt (+L)   10
Borrowed money from the local bank, payable
in two years.

Assets		=	Liabilities		+	Shareholders' Equity
Cash	+10		Long-term debt	+10		

(c) For expansion, Canadian Tire opened a new store. The company purchased new shelving racks, counters, and other equipment for $22; paid $15 in cash; and signed a note for $7, payable to the supplier in two years.

Property and equipment (+A)   22
   Cash (−A)   15
   Long-term debt (+L)   7
Purchased various equipment, paying part in cash
and signing a note for the rest, payable in two
years.

Assets		=	Liabilities		+	Shareholders' Equity
Property and equipment	+22		Long-term debt	+7		
Cash	−15					

(d) Canadian Tire lends $100 to a trade supplier in financial difficulty. The trade supplier signs notes agreeing to repay the amount borrowed within six months.

Notes receivable (+A)   100
   Cash (−A)   100
Lent money to a trade supplier; to be repaid within
six months.

Assets		=	Liabilities	+	Shareholders' Equity
Cash	−100				
Notes receivable	+100				

(e) Canadian Tire purchases shares issued by another corporation as a long-term investment, paying $30 in cash.

Long-term Investments (+A)   30
   Cash (−A)   30
Purchased shares in another corporation as a long-
term investment.

Assets		=	Liabilities	+	Shareholders' Equity
Cash	−30				
Investments	+30				

(f) Canadian Tire's board of directors declares cash dividends of $20 for shareholders. The dividends are paid immediately.

Retained earnings (−SE)   20
   Cash (−A)   20
Declared and paid dividends to shareholders.

Assets		=	Liabilities	+	Shareholders' Equity	
Cash	−20				Retained earnings	−20

PAUSE FOR FEEDBACK

Accountants record transactions first in the general journal in chronological order in journal entry form. Debited accounts are written on top with amounts in the left column, and credited accounts are written on the bottom with amounts in the right column. Then, the effects are posted in the general ledger. Each page of the ledger represents a different account, which has a debit (left) side and a credit (right) side. To post transaction effects, the amount for each account in a journal entry is written in the appropriate debit or credit column on the ledger page, to obtain account balances.

SELF-STUDY QUIZ 2-4

For transactions (g) and (h), fill in the missing information, including postings to the T-accounts.

(g) Canadian Tire collects $10 cash from the trade supplier.

Write the journal entry. [ ] [Post to the T-accounts.]

Collection of note from trade supplier.

Assets		=	Liabilities	+	Shareholders' Equity
Cash	+10				
Notes receivable	−10				

(h) Canadian Tire paid $4 on long-term debt.

Long-term debt (−L)	4	[Post to the T-accounts.]
Cash (−A)		4
Partial payment of the amount owed to the local bank.		

Assets	=	Liabilities	+	Shareholders' Equity

The T-accounts that changed during the period because of these transactions are shown below. The beginning balances are the amounts from Canadian Tire's statement of financial position at January 2, 2016 (Exhibit 2.3). The balances of all other accounts remained the same.

Assets   **= Liabilities + Shareholders' Equity**

+	Cash (A)		−
Beg. bal.	901		
(a)	13	(c)	15
(b)	10	(d)	100
(g)	[ ]	(e)	30
		(f)	20
		(h)	[ ]
End. bal.	765		

+	Property and Equipment (A)	−
Beg. bal.	4,116	
(c)	22	
End. bal.	4,138	

+	Long-Term Investments (A)		−
Beg. bal.	154		
(e)	30		
End. bal.	184		

+	Notes Receivable (A)		−
Beg. bal.	0		
(d)	100	(g)	[ ]
End. bal.	90		

−	Long-Term Debt (L)		+
		Beg. bal.	2,971
		(b)	10
(h)	[ ]	(c)	7
		End. bal.	2,984

−	Contributed Capital (SE)		+
		Beg. bal.	674
		(a)	13
		End. bal.	687

−	Retained Earnings (SE)		+
		Beg. bal.	674
(f)	20		
		End. bal.	[ ]

You can verify that you posted the entries properly by adding the increase side and subtracting the decrease side and then comparing your answer to the ending balance for each T-account. Check your answers with the solutions at the end of the chapter.

INFERRING BUSINESS ACTIVITIES FROM T-ACCOUNTS

FINANCIAL
ANALYSIS

T-accounts are useful primarily for instructional and analytical purposes. In many cases, we will use T-accounts to determine what transactions a company engaged in during a period. For example, the primary transactions affecting trade payables for a period are purchases of assets on account and cash payments to suppliers. If we know the beginning and ending balances of trade payables and all of the amounts that were purchased on credit during a period, we can determine the amount of cash paid, p. A T-account will include the following:

−		Trade Payables (L)	+
		Beg. bal.	600
Cash payments to suppliers	?	Purchases on account	1,500
		End. bal.	300

Solution:

Beginning balance	+	Purchases on account	−	Cash payments to suppliers	=	Ending balance
$600	+	$1,500	−	p	=	$ 300
		$2,100	−	p	=	$ 300
				p	=	$1,800

HOW IS THE STATEMENT OF FINANCIAL POSITION PREPARED AND ANALYZED?

As discussed in Chapter 1, a statement of financial position is one of the financial statements that will be communicated to users, especially those external to the business. Although no operating activities occurred yet (they will be illustrated in Chapter 3), it is possible to prepare a statement of financial position based solely on the investing and financing activities recorded above. Usually, businesses will create a **trial balance** spreadsheet first for internal purposes before preparing financial statements for external users. A trial balance lists the titles of the T-accounts in one column, usually in financial statement order (assets, liabilities, shareholders' equity, revenues, and expenses), with their ending debit or credit balances in the next two columns. Debit balances are indicated in the left column and credit balances are indicated in the right column. Then the two columns are totaled to provide a check on the equality of the debits and credits. Errors in a computer-generated trial balance may exist if wrong accounts and/or amounts are used in the journal entries.[11]

Canadian Tire's trial balance follows. The account balances that did not change are taken from Canadian Tire's statement of financial position at January 2, 2016, in Exhibit 2.3. The accounts that did change due to the investing and financing transactions illustrated in this chapter are shaded; their balances are taken from the T-accounts summarized earlier.

LO2-6

Prepare a trial balance and a classified statement of financial position and analyze the company using the current ratio.

A **TRIAL BALANCE** is a list of all accounts with their balances to provide a check on the equality of the debits and credits.

CANADIAN TIRE CORPORATION
TRIAL BALANCE
As at January 31, 2016

($ in thousands)	Debit	Credit
Cash	$ 765	
Short-term investments	96	
Accounts receivable	5,790	
Notes receivable	90	
Inventories	1,765	
Prepaid expenses	96	
Other current assets	44	
Long-term receivables	731	
Long-term investments	184	
Property and equipment	4,138	
Goodwill	437	
Intangible assets	810	
Other non-current assets	48	
Accounts payable		$ 920
Accrued liabilities		1,037
Provisions		262
Short-term borrowings		89
Income taxes payable		62
Current portion of long-term debt		24
Other current liabilities		1,536
Long-term debt		2,984
Other non-current liabilities		2,297
Contributed capital		687
Retained earnings		4,152
Other components		944
Total	**$14,994**	**$14,994**

Classified Statement of Financial Position

The statement of financial position in Exhibit 2.9 was prepared from the trial balance above. Notice several additional features in Exhibit 2.9:

- The assets and liabilities are classified into two categories: *current* and *non-current*. Current assets are those to be used or transformed into cash within the upcoming year, whereas non-current assets are those that will last longer than one year. Current liabilities are those obligations to be paid or settled within the next 12 months with current assets.

- Dollar signs are indicated at the top and bottom of both the asset section and the liabilities and shareholders' equity section.

- The statement includes comparative data. That is, it compares the account balances at January 31, 2016, with those at January 2, 2016. When multiple periods are presented, the most recent statement of financial position amounts are usually listed on the left.

At the beginning of the chapter, we presented the changes in Canadian Tire's total assets from 2003 to 2015. We questioned what made the accounts change and what the process was for reflecting the changes. Now we can see that the assets have changed again in one month, along with liabilities and shareholders' equity, because of the transactions illustrated in this chapter.

	Assets	=	Liabilities	+	Shareholders' Equity
January 31, 2016	14,994		9,211		5,783
January 2, 2016	14,988		9,198		5,790
Change	+ 6		+ 13		− 7

Exhibit **2.9**
Canadian Tire's Statement
of Financial Position

CANADIAN TIRE CORPORATION
Consolidated Statement of Financial Position
(in thousands of Canadian dollars)

Assets	January 31, 2016	January 2, 2016
Current assets		
Cash	$ 765	$ 901
Short-term investments	96	96
Accounts receivable	5,790	5,790
Notes receivable	90	–
Inventories	1,765	1,765
Prepaid expenses	96	96
Other current assets	44	44
Total current assets	**8,646**	**8,692**
Non-current assets		
Long-term receivables	731	731
Long-term investments	184	154
Property and equipment	4,138	4,116
Goodwill	437	437
Intangible assets	810	810
Other non-current assets	48	48
Total non-current assets	**6,348**	**5,564**
Total assets	**$14,994**	**$14,988**
Liabilities and Equity		
Current liabilities		
Accounts payable	$ 920	$ 920
Accrued liabilities	1,037	1,037
Provisions	262	262
Short-term borrowings	89	89
Income taxes payable	62	62
Current portion of long-term debt	24	24
Other current liabilities	1,536	1,536
Total current liabilities	**3,930**	**3,930**
Non-current liabilities		
Long-term debt	2,984	2,971
Other non-current liabilities	2,297	2,297
Total non-current liabilities	**5,281**	**5,268**
Total liabilities	**9,211**	**9,198**
Equity		
Contributed capital	687	674
Retained earnings	4,152	4,172
Other components	944	944
Total equity	**5,783**	**5,790**
Total liabilities and equity	**$14,994**	**$ 14,988**

UNDERSTANDING FINANCIAL STATEMENTS OF FOREIGN COMPANIES

INTERNATIONAL PERSPECTIVE

The adoption of IFRS by many countries has made it easier to read foreign companies' financial statements. However, there are still some differences in the structure of the statements and account titles that may cause confusion. A single, consistent format has not been mandated. Consequently, various formats have evolved over time, with those by Canadian and U.S. companies differing from those typically used internationally, particularly by European companies. The formatting differences are shown below:

Order of Listing Assets, Liabilities, and Shareholders' Equity	Format Typically Used by Canadian Companies	Alternative Format Typically Used by European Companies
Similar accounts are shown, but the order of liquidity (for assets) and the order of maturity (for liabilities) differ	**Assets:** Current Non-current **Liabilities:** Current Non-current **Shareholders' Equity**	**Assets:** Non-current Current **Shareholders' Equity** **Liabilities:** Non-current Current

Canadian companies typically list assets in **decreasing order of liquidity, but European companies have typically listed their assets in increasing order of liquidity.** Similarly, companies may emphasize longer-term financing sources by listing equity before liabilities and, within liabilities, by listing non-current liabilities before current liabilities (**decreasing time to maturity**). The key to avoiding confusion is to be sure to **pay attention to the subheadings** in the statement. Any account under the heading "liabilities" must be a liability.

THE CURRENT RATIO

KEY RATIO ANALYSIS

Why do the classifications of current and non-current assets and liabilities matter on the statement of financial position? Users of financial information compute a number of ratios when analyzing a company's past performance and financial condition as input in predicting its future potential. The change in ratios over time and how they compare to the ratios of the company's competitors or industry averages provide valuable information about a company's strategies for its operating, investing, and financing activities.

We introduce here the first of many ratios that will be presented throughout the rest of this textbook, with a final summary of ratio analysis in Chapter 12. In Chapters 2, 3, and 4, we present four ratios that provide information about management's effectiveness at managing short-term debt (current ratio), controlling revenues and expenses (net profit margin), and utilizing assets (total asset turnover ratio and return on assets), all for the purpose of enhancing returns to shareholders. The remaining chapters discuss other ratios that provide valuable information to assess a company's strategies, strengths, and areas of concern.

As we discussed earlier in the chapter, companies raise large amounts of money to acquire additional assets by issuing shares to investors and borrowing funds from creditors. These additional assets are used to generate more earnings. However, since debt must be repaid, taking on increasing amounts of debt carries increased risk. Information about current liabilities is very important to managers and analysts because these obligations must be paid in the near future. Analysts say that a company has liquidity if it has the ability to pay its current obligations. Companies that do not settle their current obligations in a timely manner quickly find that suppliers of goods and services may not be prepared to grant them credit for their purchases, potentially forcing them to seek short-term financing through banks. The current ratio provides one measure for analysts to examine the company's financing strategy.

ANALYTICAL QUESTION → Does the company currently have the resources to pay its short-term debt?

RATIO AND COMPARISONS → Analysts use the *current ratio* as an indicator of the amount of current assets available to satisfy current liabilities. It is computed as follows:

$$\text{Current ratio} = \text{Current assets} \div \text{Current liabilities}$$

The 2015 ratio for Canadian Tire is

$$\$8,692 \div \$3,930 = 2.21$$

Comparisons over Time			Comparisons with Competitors	
Canadian Tire Corporation			Hudson's Bay Company*	Sears Canada Inc.*
2013	2014	2015	2015	2015
1.85	1.84	2.21	1.36	1.92

*The fiscal years of both Hudson's Bay and Sears Canada ended on January 30, 2016.

INTERPRETATIONS

In General→ The current ratio is a very common ratio. Creditors and security analysts use the current ratio to measure the ability of the company to pay its short-term obligations with short-term assets. Generally, the higher the ratio, the more cushion a company has to pay its current obligations if future economic conditions take a downturn. While a high ratio above 1.0 normally suggests good liquidity, today, many strong companies use sophisticated management techniques to minimize funds invested in current assets, and, as a result, have current ratios below 1.0. Likewise, when compared to ratios of other companies in the same industry, too high a ratio suggests inefficient use of resources.

Focus Company Analysis→ Canadian Tire's current ratio at January 2, 2016, indicates that the company has $2.21 for each $1.00 in current liabilities. The increase in this ratio is the result of an increase in current assets coupled with a decrease in current liabilities. Canadian Tire's ratio is higher than those of its competitors, Hudson's Bay Company and Sears Canada Inc. Since all three companies have ratios exceeding 1.0, this suggests that they have sufficient liquidity to meet their short-term obligations.

A Few Cautions→ The current ratio may be a misleading measure of liquidity if significant funds are tied up in assets that are not easily converted into cash. A company with a high current ratio might still have liquidity problems if the majority of its current assets are slow-moving inventory. Analysts recognize that managers can manipulate the current ratio by engaging in particular types of transactions just before the close of the fiscal year. For example, the current ratio can be improved by paying creditors immediately prior to the preparation of financial statements.

> **SELECTED FOCUS COMPANY CURRENT RATIOS—2015**
>
> Gildan Activewear 5.38
>
>
>
> Reitmans (Canada) Limited. 2.64
>
>
>
> WestJet Airlines Ltd. 0.97

As you can see, using the relevant financial information from financial statements to calculate a single ratio is only the first step toward understanding whether a company is healthy enough to merit your investment money. The real challenges are discovering why the ratios have changed over time, comparing the ratios with competitors' ratios, developing a keen understanding of the industry and businesses, and using all this knowledge to predict the future for a company.

PAUSE FOR FEEDBACK

We just learned that the current ratio measures a company's ability to pay short-term obligations with short-term assets; a liquidity measure. It is computed by dividing current assets by current liabilities. A ratio between 1.0 and 2.0 is normally considered good, although some companies may need a higher ratio, while other companies with good cash management systems can have a ratio below 1.0 (i.e., more current liabilities than current assets).

SELF-STUDY QUIZ 2-5

Dollarama Inc. is the leading dollar store operator in Canada, with more than 900 locations across the country. The company offers a broad assortment of everyday consumer products, general merchandise, and seasonal items. It reported the following balances on its recent statements of financial position (in millions). Compute Dollarama's current ratio for the three years.

	Current Assets	Current Liabilities	Current Ratio
January 31, 2016	$617	$227	
February 1, 2015	548	215	
February 2, 2014	459	164	

What does this ratio suggest about Dollarama's liquidity in the current year and over time?

After you complete your answers, check them with the solutions at the end of the chapter.

INVESTING AND FINANCING ACTIVITIES

LO2-7

Identify investing and financing transactions and demonstrate how they are reported on the statement of cash flows.

Recall from Chapter 1 that companies report cash inflows and outflows over a period in their statement of cash flows. This statement divides all transactions that affect cash into three categories:

- Operating activities are covered in Chapter 3.
- Investing activities include buying and selling non-current assets and investments.
- Financing activities include borrowing and repaying debt, including short-term bank loans, issuing and repurchasing shares, and paying dividends.

Only transactions affecting cash are reported on the statement. An important step in constructing and analyzing the statement of cash flows is identifying the various transactions as operating (**O**), investing (**I**), or financing (**F**). Let us analyze the cash T-account for Canadian Tire's transactions in this chapter. Refer to transactions *(a)–(h)* illustrated on previous pages, and remember that **you must see cash in the transaction for it to affect the statement of cash flows.**

		+	Cash (A)		−	
	Bal.	901				
From investors + F	*(a)*	13	15	*(c)*	− I	For non-current assets
From bank + F	*(b)*	10	100	*(d)*	− I	To trade supplier
From trade supplier + I	*(g)*	10	30	*(e)*	− I	For investment in other companies
			20	*(f)*	− F	To shareholders
			4	*(h)*	− F	To bank
	Bal.	765				

The eight transactions we have analyzed for Canadian Tire are issuing shares, borrowing from a bank, purchasing equipment, lending to a trade supplier, purchasing shares in other companies, declaring and paying dividends, collecting cash on a note receivable, and paying down a bank loan. All of these transactions affected cash. Four of the eight transactions relate to investment activities, and the other four relate to financing activities.

PAUSE FOR FEEDBACK

As we discussed, every transaction affecting cash can be classified as an operating (discussed in Chapter 3), investing, or financing activity. Investing activities relate to purchasing/selling investments or property and equipment, or lending funds to/receiving repayment from others. Financing activities relate to borrowing from or repaying banks, issuing shares to or repurchasing shares from investors, or paying dividends to investors.

SELF-STUDY QUIZ 2-6

Lance Inc. manufactures and sells snack products. Indicate whether the following transactions from a recent statement of cash flows were investing (I) or financing (F) activities, and show the direction of the effect on cash (+ means increases cash; − means decreases cash):

Transaction	Type of Activity (I or F)	Effect on Cash Flows (+ or −)
1. Paid dividends	_____	_____
2. Sold property	_____	_____
3. Repaid debt	_____	_____
4. Purchased vending machines	_____	_____
5. Issued new shares	_____	_____

After you complete your answers, check them with the solutions at the end of the chapter.

Some Misconceptions

Some people confuse bookkeeping with accounting. In effect, they confuse a part of accounting with the whole. Bookkeeping involves routine data entry, a clerical task that requires only minimal knowledge of accounting. A bookkeeper may record the repetitive and uncomplicated transactions in most businesses and may maintain the simple records of a small business. In contrast, the accountant is a highly trained professional, competent in the design of information systems, analysis of complex transactions, financial reporting, interpretation of financial data, auditing, taxation, and management consulting.

Another prevalent misconception is that all transactions are subject to precise and objective measurement, and that the accounting results reported in the financial statements are exactly what happened during that period. In reality, accounting numbers are influenced by estimates, as subsequent chapters will illustrate. Some people believe that financial statements report the entity's market value (including its assets), but they do not. To understand and interpret financial statements, you must be aware of their limitations as well as their usefulness. You should understand what the financial statements do and do not try to accomplish.

Finally, financial statements are often thought to be inflexible because of their quantitative nature. As you study accounting, you will learn that it requires considerable *professional judgment* on the part of the accountant to capture the economic essence of complex transactions. Accountants develop professional judgment after years of experience in analyzing business transactions and in applying accounting principles and financial reporting standards in preparing and auditing financial reports. Accounting is stimulating intellectually; it is not a cut-and-dried subject. It calls on your intelligence, analytical ability, creativity, and judgment. Accounting is a communication process involving an audience (users) with a wide diversity of knowledge, interest, and capabilities; therefore, it will call on your ability as a communicator. The language of accounting uses concisely written phrases and symbols to convey information about the resource flows measured for specific organizations.

To understand financial statements, you must have a certain level of knowledge of the concepts and the measurement procedures used in the accounting process. You should learn what accounting is really like and appreciate the reasons for using certain procedures. This level of knowledge cannot be gained by reading a list of the concepts and a list of the misconceptions. Neither can a generalized discussion of the subject matter suffice. A certain amount of involvement, primarily problem solving (similar to the requirement in mathematics courses), is essential in the study of accounting focused on the needs of the user. Therefore, we provide problems aimed at the desirable knowledge level for the user as well as the preparer of financial statements.

ACCOUNTING STANDARDS
FOR PRIVATE ENTERPRISES

As noted in Chapter 1, the accounting standards applicable for the reporting of financial information by private enterprises may differ from IFRS, especially the accounting for complex transactions and the extent of detail reported in the notes to the financial statements. Differences in the application of accounting standards may lead to different values for assets, liabilities, and equity, which are reported on the statement of financial position. A few differences are highlighted below.

Financial Reporting Issue	IFRS	ASPE
Presentation of assets, liabilities, and shareholders' equity	Publicly accountable enterprises have a choice between two ways of presenting their assets and liabilities. The choice depends upon which method provides the most relevant information. Companies may list their assets in increasing order of liquidity, with the least-liquid assets listed at the top of the assets. Hence, non-current assets are presented before current assets. IFRS similarly emphasize longer-term financing sources by listing equity before liabilities and, within liabilities, by listing non-current liabilities before current liabilities (decreasing time to maturity). However, assets should be reported by decreasing order of liquidity and liabilities by increasing time to maturity if such classification provides more relevant information to users of financial statements.	Private enterprises report their assets in a decreasing order of liquidity, with the most-liquid asset (cash) presented first. Similarly, liabilities are reported in order of time to maturity. Current assets are presented before non-current assets, and current liabilities appear before non-current liabilities.
Asset valuation	Publicly accountable enterprises may choose to report their assets using either the cost model or the revaluation model. For example, property, plant, and equipment can be reported at fair value (e.g., net sales price) provided that the company uses this method consistently over time. This allows the company to record increases and decreases in the values of these assets.	Private enterprises are required to report assets at historical cost and are not permitted to record increases in these assets over time.

DEMONSTRATION CASE

On April 1, 2014, three ambitious college students started Terrific Lawn Maintenance Corporation. Completed transactions (summarized) through April 7, 2017, for Terrific Lawn Maintenance Corporation follow:

a. Issued 1,500 shares in exchange for $9,000 cash. Each investor received 500 shares.

b. Acquired rakes and other hand tools (equipment) for $600 but with a list price of $690; paid the hardware store $200 cash and signed a three-month note for the balance.

c. Ordered three lawn mowers and two edgers from Lawn Supply Inc. for $4,000.

d. Purchased four acres of land as a future site of a storage garage; paid cash, $5,000.

e. Received the mowers and edgers that had been ordered, signing a note to pay Lawn Supply in full, in 18 months.

f. Sold one acre of land to the city for a park. Accepted a note for $1,250 as payment to be received at April 10, 2017.

g. One of the owners borrowed $3,000 from a local bank for personal use.

Required:

1. Set up T-accounts for cash, notes receivable (from the city), equipment (for hand tools and mowing equipment), land, short-term notes payable (to the hardware store), long-term notes payable (to the equipment supply company), and contributed capital. Indicate beginning balances of $0 in the T-accounts. Analyze each transaction by using the process outlined in the chapter. Prepare journal entries in chronological order. Enter the effects of the transactions in the appropriate T-accounts. Identify each amount with its letter in the preceding list. Use the following transaction analysis model:

Assets		=	Liabilities		+	Shareholders' Equity			
+	–		–	+					
debit	credit		debit	credit		**Contributed Capital**		**Retained Earnings**	
						–	+	–	+
						debit	credit	debit	credit
							Investment by owners	Dividends declared	Net earnings

2. Use the balances in the T-accounts developed in (1) to prepare a classified statement of financial position for Terrific Lawn Mainte-nance Corporation at April 7, 2017. Show the account balances for all assets, liabilities, and shareholders' equity.

3. Identify transactions (a)–(g) as investing or financing activities affecting cash flows and the direction of each effect. Use +I for invest-ing inflow, −I for investing outflow, +F for financing inflow, and −F for financing outflow.

We strongly recommend that you prepare your own answers to these requirements and then check your answers with the following solution.

SUGGESTED **SOLUTION**

1. Transaction Analysis:

Received:	Given:
a. Cash (+A) $9,000	Contributed capital (+SE) 9,000
b. Equipment (+A) $600	Cash (−A) $200
	Short-term notes payable (+L) $400
c. Not a transaction—a promise to pay for a promise to deliver from the supplier	
d. Land (+A) $5,000	Cash (−A) $5,000
e. Equipment (+A) $4,000	Long-term notes payable (+L) $4,000
f. Notes receivable (+A) $1,250	Land (2A) $1,250 (one-fourth of cost of the land)
g. Not a transaction of the business—separate-entity assumption	

Journal Entries:

(a) Cash (+A)   9,000
     Contributed capital (+L))   9,000

Assets	=	Liabilities	+	Shareholders' Equity
Cash +9,000				Contributed capital +9,000

(b) Equipment (+A)   600
     Cash (−A)   200
     Short-term notes payable (+L)   400

Assets	=	Liabilities	+	Shareholders' Equity
Equipment +600		Short-term notes payable +400		
Cash −200				

The historical cost principle states that assets should be recorded at the amount paid on the date of the transaction. This is $600, not the list price of $690.

(c) This is not a transaction; no exchange has taken place. No accounts are affected.

(d) Land (+A)   5,000
     Cash (−A)   5,000

Assets	=	Liabilities	+	Shareholders' Equity
Land +5,000				
Cash −5,000				

(e) Equipment (+A)   4,000
     Long-term notes payable (+L)   4,000

Assets	=	Liabilities	+	Shareholders' Equity
Equipment +4,000		Long-term notes payable +4,000		

(f) Notes receivable (+A)   1,250
     Land (−A)   1,250

Assets	=	Liabilities	+	Shareholders' Equity
Notes receivable +1,250				
Cash −1,250				

(g) This is not a transaction that involves the company. The separate-entity assumption states that transactions of the owners are separate from transactions of the business.

T-Accounts:

Assets	=	Liabilities + Shareholders' Equity

Cash (A)

+		−
Beg. bal.	0	
(a)	9,000	(b) 200
		(d) 5,000
End. bal.	3,800	

Notes Receivable (A)

+		−
Beg. bal.	0	
(f)	1,250	
End. bal.	1,250	

Short-Term Notes Payable (L)

−	+	
	Beg. bal.	0
	(b)	400
	End. bal.	400

Equipment (A)

+		−
Beg. bal.	0	
(b)	600	
(e)	4,000	
End. bal.	4,600	

Land (A)

+		−
Beg. bal.	0	
(d)	5,000	(f) 1,250
End. bal.	3,750	

Long-Term Notes Payable (L)

−	+	
	Beg. bal.	0
	(e)	4,000
	End. bal.	4,000

Contributed Capital (SE)

−	+	
	Beg. bal.	0
	(a)	9,000
	End. bal.	9,000

2. Statement of financial position:

TERRIFIC LAWN MAINTENANCE CORPORATION
Statement of Financial Position
At April 7, 2017

Assets		Liabilities	
Current Assets		Current Liabilities	
Cash	$ 3,800	Short-term notes payable	$ 400
Notes receivable	1,250	Total current liabilities	400
Total current assets	5,050	Long-term notes payable	4,000
		Total liabilities	4,400
Equipment	4,600	Shareholders' Equity	
Land	3,750	Contributed capital	9,000
Total assets	**$13,400**	**Total liabilities and**	
		shareholders' equity	**$13,400**

Notice that the statement of financial position presented earlier in the text listed assets on the top and liabilities and shareholders' equity on the bottom. It is also acceptable practice to prepare a statement of financial position with assets on the left side and liabilities and shareholders' equity on the right side, as in the preceding example.

3. Cash Flows:

Cash (A)

+		−
Beg. bal.	0	
(a)	9,000	(b) 200
		(d) 5,000
End. bal.	3,800	

Only transactions (a), (b), and (d) affect cash flows (as shown in the cash T-account).

CHAPTER **TAKE-AWAYS**

2-1. Define the objective of financial reporting, qualitative characteristics of accounting information, and the related key accounting assumptions and principles.

Objective:

- The primary objective of external financial reporting is to provide financial information about a business to help external parties, primarily investors, and creditors make sound financial decisions.

Qualitative characteristics of useful financial information:

- Relevance that allows users to assess past activities and/or predict future activities.
- Faithful representation requires information to be complete, neutral, and free from material error.
- To enhance the two fundamental qualitative characteristics, information should be comparable (to other companies and over time), verifiable, timely, and understandable.

Key recognition, measurement, and disclosure concepts:

Assumptions:

- Separate-entity assumption—transactions of the business are accounted for separately from transactions of the owner.
- Continuity (going-concern) assumption—a business is expected to continue to operate into the foreseeable future.
- Stable monetary unit assumption—financial information is reported in the national monetary unit without adjustment for changes in purchasing power.

Principles:

- Mixed-attribute measurement model—most elements of the statement of financial position are recorded according to the historical cost principle—financial statement elements should be recorded at their cash-equivalent cost on the date of the transaction; however, these values may be adjusted to other amounts, such as market value depending on certain conditions.

2-2. Define the elements of a classified statement of financial position.

Elements of the statement of financial position are as follows:

- Assets—these are probable future economic benefits owned by the entity as a result of past transactions.
- Liabilities—these are present debts or obligations of the entity as a result of past transactions, which will be paid with assets or services.
- Shareholders' equity—residual interest of owners in the assets of the entity after settling liabilities. This is the financing provided by the owners (contributed capital) and the operations of the business (earned capital).

2-3. Identify what constitutes a business transaction, and recognize common account titles used in business.

A transaction includes the following:

- An exchange of cash, goods, services, or promises between a business and one or more external parties to a business (not the exchange of a promise for a promise).

or

- A measurable internal event, such as adjustments for the use of assets in operations.

An account is a standardized format that organizations use to accumulate the dollar effects of transactions of each financial statement item. Typical account titles include the following:

- *Assets*—cash, accounts receivable, inventory, prepaid expenses, investments, property (buildings and land) and equipment, and intangibles (rights without physical substance).
- *Liabilities*—accounts payable, notes payable, accrued liabilities, deferred revenue, and taxes payable.
- *Shareholders' equity*—contributed capital and retained earnings.

2-4. Apply transaction analysis to simple business transactions in terms of the accounting model: Assets = Liabilities + Shareholders' Equity.

To determine the economic effect of a transaction on the entity in terms of its accounting equation, each transaction is analyzed as to the accounts (at least two) that are affected. In an exchange, the company receives something and gives something. If the accounts, direction of the effects, and amounts are correctly analyzed, the accounting equation must stay in balance. The transaction analysis model is as follows:

Assets	=	Liabilities	+	Shareholders' Equity			
(many accounts)		(many accounts)		(limited to two accounts for this illustration)			

+	−		−	+		Contributed Capital		Retained Earnings	
debit	credit		debit	**credit**		−	+	−	+
						debit	**credit**	debit	**credit**
							Investments by owners	Dividends declared	Net earnings of the business

Systematic transaction analysis includes (1) determining the accounts that were received and were given in the exchange, including the type of each account (A, L, or SE), amounts, and direction of the effect, and (2) determining that the accounting equation remains in balance.

2-5. Determine the impact of business transactions on the statement of financial position by using two basic tools: journal entries and T-accounts.

- Journal entries express the effects of a transaction on accounts by using the debit-credit framework. The accounts and amounts to be debited are listed first. Then the accounts and amounts to be credited are listed below the debits and indented, resulting in debits on the left and credits on the right. A brief description of the transaction is then included for future reference:

(date or reference)	Property and equipment	22	
	Cash (−A)		15
	Long-term debt (+L)		7

- T-accounts summarize transaction effects for each account. These tools can be used to determine balances and draw inferences about a company's activities.

+	Assets	−		−	Liabilities and Shareholders' Equity	+
Beginning balance					Beginning balance	
Increases		Decreases		Decreases		Increases
Ending balance						Ending balance

2-6. Prepare a trial balance and a classified statement of financial position and analyze the company using the current ratio.

Classified statements of financial position are structured as follows:

- Assets are categorized as current assets (those to be used or turned into cash within the year, with inventory always considered to be a current asset) and non-current assets, such as long-term investments, property and equipment, and intangible assets.
- Liabilities are categorized as current liabilities (those that will be paid within the next year or the operating cycle, whichever is longer) and non-current liabilities.
- Shareholders' equity accounts are listed as contributed capital first, followed by retained earnings (earnings reinvested in the business) and other components.

The current ratio (current assets ÷ current liabilities) measures a company's liquidity; that is, the ability of the company to pay its short-term obligations with current assets.

2-7. Identify investing and financing transactions, and how they impact the statement of cash flows.

A statement of cash flows reports the sources and uses of cash for the period by the type of activity that generated the cash flow: operating, investing, or financing. Investing activities are purchasing and selling long-term assets, making loans, and receiving payment from loans to others. Financing activities are borrowing and repaying loans to banks, issuing and repurchasing shares, and paying dividends.

In this chapter, we discussed the fundamental accounting model and transaction analysis. Journal entries and T-accounts were used to record the results of transaction analysis for investing and financing decisions that affect specific accounts. In Chapter 3, we continue our detailed look at financial statements, in particular the statement of earnings. The purpose of Chapter 3 is to build on your knowledge by discussing concepts for the measurement of revenues and expenses and by illustrating transaction analysis for operating decisions.

KEY **RATIOS**

The current ratio measures the ability of the company to pay its short-term obligations with current assets. Although a ratio between 1.0 and 2.0 indicates that sufficient current assets are available to meet obligations when they become due, many companies with sophisticated cash management systems have ratios below 1.0. The ratio is computed as follows:

$$\text{Current ratio} = \frac{\text{Current assets}}{\text{Current liabilities}}$$

FINDING **FINANCIAL INFORMATION**

STATEMENT OF FINANCIAL POSITION
Current Assets
  Cash
  Accounts receivable
  Notes receivable
  Inventory
  Prepaid expenses
Non-current Assets
  Investments
  Property and equipment
  Goodwill
Current Liabilities
  Bank borrowings
  Accounts payable
  Notes payable
  Accrued liabilities
Non-current Liabilities
  Long-term debt
Shareholders' Equity
  Contributed capital
  Retained earnings

STATEMENT OF CASH FLOWS
Under Investing Activities
  + Sales of non-current assets for cash
  − Purchases of non-current assets for cash
  − Loans to others
  + Receipt of cash on loans to others
Under Financing Activities
  + Borrowing from banks
  − Repayment of loans from banks
  + Issuance of shares
  − Repurchase of shares
  − Payment of dividends

STATEMENT OF EARNINGS
To be presented in **Chapter 3**

NOTES
To be discussed in future chapters

QUESTIONS

1. What is the primary objective of financial reporting for external users?
2. Define the following:
    a. Asset
    b. Current asset
    c. Liability
    d. Current liability
    e. Contributed capital
    f. Retained earnings
3. Explain why information must be relevant and representationally faithful to be useful.
4. Explain what the following assumptions and principle mean in accounting:
    a. Separate-entity assumption
    b. Unit-of-measure assumption
    c. Continuity assumption
    d. Cost principle
5. Why is it important to have accounting assumptions?
6. How is the current ratio computed and how is it interpreted?
7. For accounting purposes, what is an account? Explain why accounts are used in an accounting system.

8. What are the limitations of using the historical cost principle as a basis for valuation of assets subsequent to acquisition?

9. What is the fundamental accounting model?

10. Define a business transaction in the broad sense and give examples of the two different kinds of transactions.

11. Explain what debit and credit mean.

12. Briefly explain what is meant by transaction analysis. What are the two steps in transaction analysis?

13. What two equalities in accounting must be maintained in transaction analysis?

14. What is a journal entry?

15. What is a T-account? What is its purpose?

16. What transactions are classified as investing activities in a statement of cash flows? What transactions are classified as financing activities?

17. What is the difference between a bookkeeper and an accountant?

connect   MINI-EXERCISES

LO2-1,2-5   **M2-1**   **Matching Definitions with Terms**

Match each definition with its related term by entering the appropriate letter in the space provided. There should be only one definition per term (that is, there are more definitions than terms).

Term	Definition
_____ (1) Continuity assumption	A. = Liabilities + Shareholders' Equity
_____ (2) Historical cost principle	B. Reports assets, liabilities, and shareholders' equity
_____ (3) Credits	C. Accounts for a business separately from its owners
_____ (4) Assets	D. Increase assets; decrease liabilities and shareholders' equity
_____ (5) Account	E. An exchange between an entity and other parties
	F. The concept that businesses will operate into the foreseeable future
	G. Decrease assets; increase liabilities and shareholders' equity
	H. The concept that assets should be recorded at the amount paid on the date of the transaction
	I. A standardized format used to accumulate data about each item reported on financial statements

LO2-3   **M2-2**   **Identifying Events as Accounting Transactions**

For each of the following events, which ones result in an exchange transaction for Dittman Company (Y for yes and N for no)?

_____ (1) Six investors in Dittman Company sold their shares to another investor.

_____ (2) The founding owner, Megan Dittman, purchased additional shares in another company.

_____ (3) The company borrowed $2,500,000 from a local bank.

_____ (4) Dittman Company purchased a machine and signed a note, payable in one year.

_____ (5) The company lent $300,000 to a supplier.

_____ (6) Dittman Company ordered supplies from Staples to be delivered next week.

LO2-3   **M2-3**   **Classifying Accounts on a Statement of Financial Position**

The following are accounts of Rosa-Perez Company:

_____ (1) Accounts payable		_____ (9) Long-term investments	
_____ (2) Accounts receivable		_____ (10) Notes payable (due in three years)	
_____ (3) Buildings		_____ (11) Notes receivable (due in six months)	
_____ (4) Cash		_____ (12) Prepaid rent	
_____ (5) Contributed capital		_____ (13) Retained earnings	
_____ (6) Land		_____ (14) Supplies	
_____ (7) Merchandise inventory		_____ (15) Utilities payable	
_____ (8) Income taxes payable		_____ (16) Wages payable	

In the space provided, classify each as it would be reported on a statement of financial position. Use the following symbols:

CA for current asset   CL for current liability   SE for shareholders' equity

NCA for non-current asset   NCL for non-current liability

LO2-3   **M2-4**   **Determining Financial Statement Effects of Several Transactions**

For each of the following transactions of Dennen Inc. for the month of January 2018, indicate the accounts, amounts, and direction of the effects on the accounting equation. A sample is provided.

a. *(Sample)* Borrowed $30,000 from a local bank.

b. Lent $10,000 to an affiliate; accepted a note due in one year.

c. Sold 100 additional shares to investors for $500 cash.

d. Purchased $15,000 of equipment, paying $5,000 cash and signing a note for the rest due in one year.

e. Declared and paid $2,000 in dividends to shareholders.

Assets	=	Liabilities	+	Shareholders' Equity
a. *Sample:* Cash 130,000		Notes payable 130,000		

LO2-4   **M2-5**   **Identifying Effects on Elements of the Statement of Financial Position**

Complete the following table by entering either "increases" or "decreases" in columns (1) and (2), and either "debit" or "credit" in columns (3) and (4).

	(1) Debit	(2) Credit	(3) Increases	(4) Decreases
Assets	_____	_____	_____	_____
Liabilities	_____	_____	_____	_____
Shareholders' equity	_____	_____	_____	_____

LO2-5   **M2-6**   **Recording Simple Transactions**

For each transaction in M2-4 (including the sample), write the journal entry in the proper form.

LO2-5   **M2-7**   **Completing T-Accounts**

For each transaction in M2-4 (including the sample), post the effects to the appropriate T-accounts and determine ending account balances. Beginning balances are provided.

Cash		Accounts Receivable		Equipment	
Beg. bal. 900		Beg. bal. 1,000		Beg. bal. 15,100	

Notes Payable		Contributed Capital		Retained Earnings	
	Beg. bal. 3,000		Beg. bal. 4,000		Beg. bal. 10,000

LO2-6   **M2-8**   **M2-8 Preparing a Trial Balance**

Complete M2-7, and then prepare a trial balance for Dennen Inc. as of January 31, 2018.

LO2-6   **M2-9**   **Preparing a Simple Classified Statement of Financial Position**

Starting with the beginning balances in M2-7 and given the transactions in M2-4 (including the sample), prepare a statement of financial position for Dennen Inc. as of January 31, 2018, with a classification of the assets and liabilities into current and non-current categories.

LO2-7   **M2-10**   **Identifying Transactions as Investing or Financing Activities on the Statement of Cash Flows**

For the transactions in M2-4 (including the sample), identify each as an investing (I) activity or financing (F) activity on the statement of cash flows.

■ LO2-1,2-2,2-3,2-4

E2-1

Matching Definitions with Terms

Match each definition with its related term by entering the appropriate letter in the space provided. There should be only one definition per term (that is, there are more definitions than terms).

Term	Definition
_____ (1) Transaction	A. Economic resources to be used or turned into cash within one year.
_____ (2) Continuity assumption	B. Reports assets, liabilities, and shareholders' equity.
_____ (3) Statement of financial position	C. Business transactions are separate from the transactions of the owners.
_____ (4) Liabilities	D. Increase assets; decrease liabilities and shareholders' equity.
_____ (5) Assets = Liabilities + Shareholders' Equity	E. An exchange between an entity and other parties.
_____ (6) Note payable	F. The concept that businesses will operate into the foreseeable future.
_____ (7) Historical cost principle	G. Decrease assets; increase liabilities and shareholders' equity.
_____ (8) Account	H. The concept that assets should be recorded at the amount paid on the exchange date.
_____ (9) Dual effects	I. A standardized format used to accumulate data about each item reported on financial statements.
_____ (10) Retained earnings	J. Amounts owed from customers.
_____ (11) Current assets	K. The fundamental accounting model.
_____ (12) Separate-entity assumption	L. The account that is credited when money is borrowed from a bank.
_____ (13) Debits	M. The concept that states that accounting information should be measured and reported in the national monetary unit.
_____ (14) Accounts receivable	N. Cumulative earnings of a company that are not distributed to the owners.
_____ (15) Stable monetary unit assumption	O. Probable debts or obligations to be paid with assets or services.
_____ (16) Shareholders' equity	P. Every transaction has at least two effects.
	Q. Financing provided by owners and by business operations.
	R. Probable economic resources expected to be used or turned into cash beyond the next 12 months.

■ LO2-1

E2-2

Qualitative Characteristics of Accounting Information

Match each qualitative characteristic of useful accounting information with the related definition by entering the appropriate letter in the space provided. There should be only one definition per term (that is, there are more definitions than terms).

Qualitative Characteristics	Definition
_____ (1) Relevance	A. Application of the same accounting methods over time.
_____ (2) Timeliness	B. Agreement between what really happened and the disclosed information.
_____ (3) Predictive value	C. The information is available prior to the decision.
_____ (4) Confirmatory value	D. The accounting information does not favour a particular group.
_____ (5) Verifiability	E. The information helps reduce uncertainty in the future.
_____ (6) Faithful representation	F. The information provides input to evaluate previous expectations.
_____ (7) Neutrality	G. The information allows the evaluation of one alternative against another alternative.
_____ (8) Comparability	H. The information has a bearing on a specific decision.
_____ (9) Consistency	I. The information can be depended upon.
	J. Implies that qualified persons working independently arrive at similar conclusions.

LO2-1

E2-3 **Assessing the Relevance and Faithful Representation of Information**

Paula Romanov is the credit manager of Pinnacle Inc. She is considering whether to extend credit to Mak Inc., a new customer. Pinnacle sells most of its goods on credit but is very careful in extending credit to new customers. Tim Mak, the owner of Mak Inc., provided the following documents to Paula to assist her in her evaluation:

1. A detailed analysis of the sales revenue and earnings that Mak Inc. expects to achieve within the next 12 months.
2. Projections of the company's sales during the next five years.
3. The company's monthly bank statements for the past three years.
4. A report of the company's credit history prepared by Mak's employees.
5. A letter signed by all four company officers indicating that they are prepared to personally guarantee the amount of credit that Pinnacle approves.
6. Brief resumés of the four company officers along with descriptions of the functions they perform in the company.
7. Eight letters of reference from close friends and relatives of the four company officers.

Required:

Analyze each of the items above with respect to the characteristics of relevance (predictive value and confirmatory value) and faithful representation (complete, neutral, and free from material error). Explain whether or not each item possesses these characteristics.

LO2-3

E2-4 **Identifying Events as Accounting Transactions**

Which of the following events results in an exchange transaction for O'Brien Company (Y for yes and N for no)?

_____ (1) O'Brien purchased a machine and signed a note payable, payable in six months.
_____ (2) Six investors in O'Brien Company sold their shares to another investor.
_____ (3) The company lent $150,000 to a member of the board of directors.
_____ (4) O'Brien Company ordered supplies from Office Max to be delivered next week.
_____ (5) The founding owner, Meaghan O'Brien, purchased additional shares in another company.
_____ (6) The company borrowed $1,000,000 from a local bank.

LO2-1,2-3

E2-5 **Identifying Account Titles**

The following are independent situations.

a. A company purchases a piece of land for $100,000 cash. An appraiser for the buyer valued the land at $105,000.
b. A telecommunications company purchases the patent (an intangible asset) on a software application for its wireless communication system. The company paid $250,000 cash and signed a note for $550,000, payable in one year at an annual interest rate of 5 percent.
c. A company orders and receives five laptops for office use for which it signs a note promising to pay $12,000 within three months.
d. A company makes a cash payment of $5,400 for prepaid services.
e. A manufacturing company signs a contract for the construction of a new warehouse for $500,000. At the signing, the company writes a cheque for $50,000 as a deposit on the future construction.
f. A publishing firm purchases the copyright (an intangible asset) to a manuscript for an introductory accounting text from the author for $40,000.
g. A company purchases a new delivery truck that has a list, or sticker, price of $35,000 for $32,000 cash.
h. A company purchases on account women's clothing for sale to customers. The supplier's invoice of $2,430 is payable within 30 days.
i. A new company is formed and sells 2,000 shares for $22 per share to investors.
j. A company purchases 400 shares of Canadian Tire Corporation for $2,432 cash.
k. A local company is a sole proprietorship (one owner); its owner buys a car for $10,000 for personal use. Answer from the company's point of view.
l. A manufacturing firm pays dividends of $100,000 to shareholders in cash.
m. A company pays $1,500 principal on its note payable.

Required:

1. Indicate the appropriate elements on the classified statement of financial position (use account titles), if any, that are affected in each of the preceding events. Consider what is given and what is received.

2. At what amount would you record the land in (*a*)? The truck in (*g*)? What measurement principle are you applying?

3. What accounting concept did you apply for situation (*k*)?

■ LO2-3,2-5   **E2-6**   **Classifying Accounts and Their Usual Balances**

WestJet Airlines   As described in a recent annual report, WestJet Airlines provides quality travel services to many destinations in North America.

Required:

For each of the following accounts from WestJet's recent statement of financial position, complete the following chart by indicating whether the account is classified as a current asset (CA), a non-current asset (NCA), a current liability (CL), a non-current liability (NCL), or shareholders' equity (SE), and whether the account usually has a debit or a credit balance.

Account	Statement of Financial Position Classification	Debit or Credit Balance
1. Advance ticket sales (deferred revenue)		
2. Cash and cash equivalents		
3. Contributed capital		
4. Intangible assets		
5. Inventory		
6. Long-term borrowings		
7. Prepaid expenses		
8. Property and equipment		
9. Retained earnings		
10. Accounts payable		
11. Accounts receivable		

■ LO2-4   **E2-7**   **Determining Financial Statement Effects of Several Transactions**

The following events occurred for Mitka Ltd.:

a. Received investment of $32,000 cash by organizers.

b. Purchased land for $18,000 in land; paid $6,000 in cash and signed a mortgage note with a local bank for the balance (due in five years).

c. Borrowed cash from a bank and signed a note for $11,000.

d. Lent $300 to an employee who signed a note due in three months.

e. Paid the bank the amount borrowed in (*c*).

f. Purchased $8,000 of equipment, paying $4,000 in cash and signing a note due to the manufacturer.

Required:

For each of the events (*a*) through (*f*), perform transaction analysis and indicate the account, amount, and direction of the effects (+ for increase and – for decrease) on the accounting equation. Check that the accounting equation remains in balance after each transaction. Use the following headings:

Event	Assets	=	Liabilities	+	Shareholders' Equity

■ LO2-4   **E2-8**   **Determining Financial Statement Effects of Several Transactions**

Tim Hortons Inc.   Tim Hortons Inc. is one of the largest quick-service restaurants in North America. The company operates a chain of coffee and doughnut shops across Canada and the United States specializing in fresh coffee, baked goods, and homestyle lunches. The following activities occurred during a recent year. The amounts are rounded to millions of dollars.

a. Purchased additional property and equipment for $186.7 in cash.

b. Repurchased its own shares for $225.2 cash. The shares were originally sold for the same amount.

c. Declared $110.2 in dividends and paid $130.5 during the year.

d. Several investors in Tim Hortons shares sold their shares to other investors on the stock exchange for $3.5.

e. Repaid $7.7 in principal on long-term debt obligations.

f. Paid $175.9 in income taxes.

Required:

For each of these events, perform transaction analysis and indicate the account, amount, and direction of the effects on the accounting equation. Check that the accounting equation remains in balance after each transaction. Use the following headings:

Event	Assets	=	Liabilities	+	Shareholders' Equity

LO2-5   **E2-9**   **Recording Investing and Financing Activities**

Refer to E2-7.

Required:

For each of the events in E2-7, prepare journal entries, checking that debits equal credits.

LO2-5   **E2-10**   **Analyzing the Effects of Transactions in T-Accounts**

Grady Service Company Inc. was organized by Chris Grady and five other investors. The following events occurred during the year:

a. Received $63,000 cash from the investors; each was issued 1,400 shares.

b. Purchased equipment for use in the business at a cost of $16,000; one-fourth was paid in cash, and the company signed a note for the balance, payable in six months.

c. Signed an agreement with a cleaning service to pay it $200 per week for cleaning the corporate offices.

d. Lent $2,500 to one of the investors, who signed a note due in six months.

e. Issued shares to additional investors, who contributed $6,000 in cash and a lot of land valued at $15,000.

f. Paid the amount of the note payable in (b).

g. Conor Mulkeen borrowed $10,000 for personal use from a local bank and signed a note payable in one year.

Required:

1. Prepare journal entries for each transaction. If an event does not require a journal entry, explain the reason. Use the account titles listed in (2).

2. Create T-accounts for the following accounts: cash, note receivable, equipment, land, note payable, and contributed capital. Beginning balances are zero. For each of the preceding transactions, record the effects of the transaction in the appropriate T-accounts. Include good referencing and totals for each T-account.

3. Using the balances in the T-accounts, fill in the following amounts for the accounting equation:

Assets $_____ = Liabilities $_____ + Shareholders' Equity $_____

LO2-4,2-6   **E2-11**   **Inferring Investing and Financing Transactions, and Preparing a Statement of Financial Position**

During its first week of operations ending January 7, 2017, FastTrack Sports Inc. completed six transactions with the dollar effects indicated in the following schedule:

Accounts	Dollar Effect of Each of the Six Transactions						Ending Balance
	1	**2**	**3**	**4**	**5**	**6**	
Cash	$15,000	$75,000	$(5,000)	$(4,000)	$(9,500)		
Note receivable (short term)				4,000			
Store fixtures					9,500		
Land			16,000			$4,000	
Note payable (due in three months)		75,000	11,000			4,000	
Contributed capital	15,000						

Required:

1. Write a brief explanation of each transaction. Explain any assumptions that you made.

2. Compute the ending balance in each account and prepare a classified statement of financial position for FastTrack Sports Inc. on January 7, 2017.

LO2-6

E2-12   **Inferring Investing and Financing Transactions, and Preparing a Statement of Financial Position**

During its first month of operations, March 2018, Faye's Fashions Inc. completed seven transactions with the dollar effects indicated in the following T-accounts:

Cash				Short-Term Investments				Short-Term Note Receivable	
(a)	50,000	4,000	(b)	(d)	6,000	2,000	(f)	(c)	4,000
(f)	2,000	4,000	(c)						
		6,000	(d)						
		3,000	(e)						

Computer Equipment			Delivery Truck			Long-Term Note Payable		
(g)	4,000		(b)	25,000		(e)	3,000	21,000	(b)

Contributed Capital	
	50,000 (a)
	4,000 (g)

Required:

1. Write a brief explanation of transactions (a) through (g). Explain any assumptions that you made.

2. Compute the ending balance in each account and prepare a classified statement of financial position for Faye's Fashions Inc. at the end of March 2018.

LO2-5

BMW Group

E2-13   **Recording Journal Entries**

BMW Group, headquartered in Munich, Germany, manufactures several automotive brands, including BMW, MINI, and Rolls-Royce. Financial information is reported in euros (€), using IFRS as applicable to the European Union. The following transactions were adapted from the annual report of the BMW Group; amounts are in millions of euros:

a. Declared €937 in dividends to be paid next month.

b. Issued additional shares for €19 cash.

c. Paid €1,516 in dividends declared in prior months.

d. Borrowed €7,977 and signed long-term notes, payable in the distant future.

e. Lent €27 to trade suppliers, who signed notes to repay the loans in three months.

f. Purchased equipment for €6,890, paying €5,236 in cash and signing a note for the balance.

g. Purchased investments for €2,073 cash.

Required:

Prepare journal entries for each transaction. Be sure to use good referencing, and categorize each account as an asset (A), a liability (L), or shareholders' equity (SE). If a transaction does not require a journal entry, explain the reason.

LO2-5,2-6

E2-14   **Analyzing the Effects of Transactions by Using T-Accounts, Preparing a Statement of Financial Position, and Interpreting the Current Ratio as a Manager of the Company**

Massimo Company has been operating for one year (2016). You are a member of the management team investigating expansion ideas, all of which will require borrowing funds from banks. At the start of 2017, Massimo's T-account balances were as follows:

Assets:

Cash		Short-Term Investments		Property and Equipment	
1,000		2,000			2,500

Liabilities:

Short-Term Notes Payable		Long-Term Notes Payable	
	2,200		300

Shareholders' Equity:

Contributed Capital		Retained Earnings	
	1,000		2,000

Required:

1. Using the data from these T-accounts, complete the accounting equation on January 1, 2017:

   Assets $_____ = Liabilities $_____ + Shareholders' Equity $_____

2. Enter in the T-accounts the following transactions that occurred in 2017:

   a. Paid one-half of the principal on the long-term note payable.

   b. Sold $1,000 of the investments for $1,000 cash.

   c. Sold one-half of the property and equipment for $1,250 cash.

   d. Borrowed $2,000 from the bank and signed a note promising to pay the principal and interest at an annual rate of 5 percent in three years.

   e. Paid $500 in dividends to shareholders.

3. Compute ending balances in the T-accounts to complete the statement of financial position on December 31, 2017:

   Assets $_____ = Liabilities $_____ + Shareholders' Equity $_____

4. Using the ending balances in the T-accounts, prepare a classified statement of financial position at December 31, 2017, in good form.

5. Calculate the current ratio at December 31, 2017. If the industry average for the current ratio is 1.50, what does your computation suggest to you about Massimo Company? Would you support expansion by borrowing? Why or why not?

LO2-5

E2-15 **Explaining the Effects of Transactions on Specific Accounts by Using T-Accounts**

Heavey and Lovas Furniture Repair Service, a company with two shareholders, began operations on June 1, 2017. The following T-accounts indicate the activities for the month of June.

Cash (A)			Notes Receivable (A)			Tools and Equipment (A)		
(a)	17,000	(b) 10,000	(c)	1,500	(d) 500	(a)	3,000	(f) 800
(d)	500	(c) 1,500						
(f)	800	(e) 1,000						

Building (A)		Notes Payable (L)			Contributed Capital (SE)		
(b)	50,000	(e) 1,000	(b)	40,000		(a)	20,000

Required:

Explain transactions (a) through (f), which resulted in the entries in the T-accounts; that is, what activity made the account increase or decrease?

LO2-5

E2-16 **Inferring Typical Investing and Financing Activities in Accounts**

The following T-accounts indicate the effects of normal business transactions:

Equipment			Note Receivable			Notes Payable		
1/1	500		1/1	150			100	1/1
	250	?		?	225	?	170	
31/12	100		31/12	170			180	31/12

Required:

1. Describe the typical investing and financing transactions that affect each T-account; that is, what economic events made these accounts increase or decrease?

2. For each T-account, compute the missing amounts.

LO2-7

Performance Sports
Group Ltd.

E2-17 **Identifying Investing and Financing Activities Affecting Cash Flows**

Performance Sports Group Ltd. is a leading developer and manufacturer of ice hockey, roller hockey, and lacrosse equipment as well as related apparel. The company holds the top market share position in both ice and roller hockey. Its products are marketed under the Bauer Hockey, Mission Roller Hockey, Maverik Lacrosse, and Cascade Sports brand names. The following are several of Bauer's investing and financing activities that were reflected in a recent annual statement of cash flows:

   a. Issuance of shares

   b. Purchase of property, plant, and equipment

   c. Issuance of long-term debt

   d. Principal repayment of long-term debt

   e. Purchase of investments

   f. Repurchase of shares

   g. Proceeds from disposition of property, plant, and equipment

Required:

For each of these, indicate whether the activity is investing (I) or financing (F), and indicate the direction of the effect on cash flows (+ = increases cash; − = decreases cash).

■ **LO2-7**   **E2-18**   **Preparing the Investing and Financing Section of the Statement of Cash Flows**

Hilton Hotels Corporation constructs, operates, and franchises domestic and international hotel
Hilton Hotels   and hotel-casino properties. Information from the company's recent annual statement of cash
Corporation   flows indicates the following investing and financing activities during that year (simplified):

Payment of debt principal	$ 24
Purchase of investments	139
Sale of property (assume sold at cost)	230
Issuance of shares	60
Purchase and renovation of properties	370
Additional borrowing from banks	992
Receipt of principal payment on a note receivable	125

Required:

Prepare the investing and financing sections of the statement of cash flows for Hilton hotels. Assume that the company's year-end is December 31, 2017.

 PROBLEMS

■ **LO2-2,2-5**   **P2-1**   **Identifying Accounts on a Classified Statement of Financial Position and Their Normal**
Saputo Inc.   **Debit or Credit Balances** (AP2-1)

Saputo Inc. is Canada's leading processor of dairy products. The company produces, markets, and distributes a wide array of products of the utmost quality, including cheese, fluid milk, yogurt, dairy ingredients, and snack cakes. Saputo's products are distributed in many countries, primarily in Canada, the United States, and Argentina. The following are several of the accounts that appeared on the company's recent statement of financial position:

Account	Statement of Financial Position Classification	Debit or Credit Balance
1. Cash and cash equivalents		
2. Deferred income tax liabilities		
3. Retained earnings		
4. Income taxes payable		
5. Prepaid expenses		
6. Contributed capital		
7. Trademarks and other intangibles		
8. Accounts payable		
9. Accrued liabilities		
10. Bank loans (short term)		
11. Property, plant, and equipment		
12. Long-term investments		
13. Accounts receivable		
14. Long-term debt		

Required:

For each account, indicate how it normally should be categorized on a classified statement of financial position. Use CA for current asset, NCA for non-current asset, CL for current liability, NCL for non-current liability, and SE for shareholders' equity. Also indicate whether the account normally has a debit or a credit balance.

■ **LO2-3,2-4,2-6**   **P2-2**   **Determining Financial Statement Effects of Various Transactions, and Interpreting the**
 eXcel   **Current Ratio** (AP2-2)

East Hill Home Healthcare Services was organized on January 1, 2016, by four friends. Each organizer invested $10,000 in the company and, in turn, was issued 8,000 shares. To date, they are the only shareholders. At the end of 2017, the accounting records reflected total assets of $700,000 ($50,000 cash, $500,000 land, $50,000 equipment, and $100,000 buildings), total liabilities of $200,000 (short-term notes payable of $100,000 and long-term notes payable of $100,000), and shareholders' equity of $500,000 ($100,000 contributed capital and $400,000 retained earnings). The following summarized events occurred during January 2018:

a. Sold 9,000 additional shares to the original organizers for a total of $90,000 cash.

b. Purchased a building for $60,000, equipment for $15,000, and four acres of land for $14,000; paid $9,000 in cash and signed a note for the balance (due in 15 years). (*Hint*: Five different accounts are affected.)

c. Sold one acre of land acquired in (*b*) for $3,500 cash to another company.

d. Purchased short-term investments for $18,000 cash.

e. One shareholder reported to the company that he sold 300 East Hill shares to another shareholder for $3,000 cash.

f. Lent $5,000 to one of the shareholders for moving costs, receiving a signed six-month note from the shareholder.

Required:

1. Was East Hill Home Healthcare Services organized as a sole proprietorship, a partnership, or a corporation? Explain the basis for your answer.

2. During January 2018, the records of the company were inadequate. You were asked to prepare the summary of the preceding transactions. To develop a quick assessment of their economic effects on East Hill Home Healthcare Services, you have decided to complete the tabulation that follows and to use plus (+) for increases and minus (−) for decreases for each account. The first event is used as an example.

	Assets						=	**Liabilities**	+	**Shareholders' Equity**	
	Cash	Short-term investments	Notes receivable	Land	Building	Equipment		Short-term notes payable	Long-term notes payable	Contributed capital	Retained earnings
Beg.	50,000			500,000	100,000	50,000 =	100,000	100,000 +	100,000	400,000
(a)	190,000									190,000	

3. Did you include the transaction between the two shareholders, event (*e*), in the tabulation? Why or why not?

4. Based only on the completed tabulation, provide the following amounts at January 31, 2018 (show computations):

    a. Total assets

    b. Total liabilities

    c. Total shareholders' equity

    d. Cash balance

    e. Total current assets

5. Compute the current ratio at January 31, 2018. What does this suggest about the company?

LO2-6

P2-3 **Recording Transactions in T-Accounts, Preparing a Statement of Financial Position from a Trial Balance, and Evaluating the Current Ratio** (AP2-3)

Injection Plastics Company has been operating for three years. At December 31, 2017, the accounting records reflected the following:

Cash	$21,000	Intangibles	$ 3,000
Investments (short term)	2,000	Accounts payable	15,000
Accounts receivable	3,000	Accrued liabilities	2,000
Inventories	24,000	Short-term borrowings	7,000
Notes receivable (long term)	1,000	Notes payable (long-term)	48,000
Equipment	48,000	Contributed capital	90,000
Factory building	90,000	Retained earnings	30,000

During the year 2018, the following summarized transactions were completed:

a. Purchased equipment that cost $18,000; paid $6,000 cash and signed a one-year note for the balance.

b. Issued 2,000 additional shares for $12,000 cash.

c. Lent $7,000 to a manager, who signed a two-year note.

d. Purchased short-term investments for $9,000 in cash.

e. Paid $5,000 on the note in transaction (*a*).

f. Borrowed $12,000 cash on December 31, 2018, from the bank and signed a note, payable June 30, 2019.

g. Purchased a patent (an intangible asset) for $3,000 cash.

h. Built an addition to the factory for $25,000; paid $9,000 in cash and signed a three-year note for the balance.

i. Hired a new president at the end of the year. The contract was for $85,000 per year plus options to purchase company shares at a set price based on company performance.

j. Returned defective equipment to the manufacturer, receiving a cash refund of $1,000.

Required:

1. Create a T-account for each of the accounts on the statement of financial position and enter the balances at the end of 2017 as beginning balances for 2018.

2. Record each of the transactions for 2018 in a T-account (including referencing) and determine the ending balances.

3. Explain your response to transaction (*i*).

4. Prepare a trial balance at December 31, 2018.

5. Prepare a classified statement of financial position at December 31, 2018.

6. Compute the current ratio at December 31, 2018. What does this ratio suggest about Injection Plastics Company?

 LO2-7

P2-4   **Identifying Effects of Transactions on the Statement of Cash Flows** (AP2-4)
Refer to P2-3.

Required:
Using the transactions (*a*) through (*j*) in P2-3, indicate whether each transaction is an investing (I) or financing (F) activity for the year and the direction of the effect on cash flows (+ for increase and − for decrease). If there is no effect on cash flows, write NE.

 LO2-5,2-6

Bayer AG

P2-5   **Recording Transactions, Preparing Journal Entries, Posting to T-Accounts, Preparing a Statement of Financial Position, and Evaluating the Current Ratio** (AP2-5)
Bayer AG, with headquarters in Leverkusen, Germany, is an international research-based group of companies active in health care, nutrition, and high-tech materials. Popular products include ASPIRIN, Alka-Seltzer, and One-A-Day vitamins. The following is Bayer's (simplified) statement of financial position as at December 30, 2015:

BAYER AG	
Statement of Financial Position	
At December 31, 2015 (in millions of euros)	
ASSETS	
Current assets	
Cash and cash equivalents	€ 1,853
Receivables	10,585
Inventories	8,478
Other assets	1,311
	22,227
Non-current assets	
Investments	223
Property, plant, and equipment	11,428
Goodwill	16,168
Intangible assets	15,653
Other assets	4,535
	48,007
Total assets	**70,234**
LIABILITIES AND SHAREHOLDERS' EQUITY	
Current liabilities	
Trade accounts payable	€ 5,363
Financial liabilities	3,376
Provisions	4,912
Other current liabilities	1,852
	15,503

Non-current liabilities	
Provisions	14,252
Deferred income taxes	689
Financial liabilities	18,484
Other liabilities	1,088
	34,513
Shareholders' equity	
Contributed capital	8,284
Retained earnings	11,934
	20,218
Total liabilities and shareholders' equity	**70,234**

Source: Bayer AG Corp. International, Annual Report 2015.

Assume that the following transactions occurred in the first quarter of 2016:

a. Issued additional shares for €60 in cash.

b. Borrowed €615 from banks due in two years.

c. Declared and paid €560 in dividends to shareholders.

d. Purchased additional intangibles for €64 cash.

e. Purchased property, plant, and equipment; paid €1,514 in cash and €5,410 with additional long-term bank loans.

f. Acquired additional investments; paid €623 in cash.

g. Lent €125 to an associated company that signed a six-month note.

h. Sold investments costing €461 for the same amount in cash.

Required:

1. Prepare a journal entry for each transaction.

2. Create a T-account for each financial statement account and include the December 31, 2015, balances. Post each journal entry to the appropriate T-accounts.

3. Prepare a statement of financial position for Bayer based on the T-account ending balances at March 31, 2016.

4. Compute Bayer's current ratio at March 31, 2016. What does this suggest about the company?

LO2-7

Bayer AG

P2-6 **Preparing the Investing and Financing Sections of a Statement of Cash Flows** (AP2-6)
Refer to P2-5.

Required:
Based on the transactions that occurred in 2016, prepare the investing and financing sections of the statement of cash flows of Bayer for the first quarter of 2016.

LO2-6

Le Château Inc.

P2-7 **Using Financial Reports: Preparing a Classified Statement of Financial Position, and Analyzing the Current Ratio** (AP2-7)
The accounts below, in alphabetical order, are adapted from Le Château Inc.'s recent statement of financial position (amounts in thousands of dollars):

	Current Year	Prior Year		Current Year	Prior Year
Accounts payable and accrued liabilities	$17,865	$16,133	Inventories	$113,590	$115,357
Accounts receivable	1,180	2,025	Long-term debt	61,132	39,510
Cash	—	1,195	Other non-current liabilities	10,966	12,827
Contributed capital	56,522	52,406	Prepaid expenses and other current assets	1,954	1,698
Deferred revenue	3,216	3,452	Property and equipment, net	48,332	58,091
Intangible assets	3,434	2,961	Retained earnings	3,832	39,577
			Short-term debt	14,957	17,422

Required:

1. Prepare, in good form, a classified statement of financial position (with two years reported) for Le Château Inc. Assume a fiscal year-end of January 31.

2. Compute the company's current ratio for the current year. How would you interpret this ratio for Le Château?

LO2-5,2-6

P2-8   Analyzing the Effects of Transactions Using T-Accounts, Preparing a Statement of Financial Position, and Interpreting the Current Ratio over Time as a Bank Loan Officer (AP2-8)

Lee Delivery Company Inc. was organized at the beginning of 2017. The following transactions occurred during 2017 (the company's first year of operations):

a. Received $40,000 cash from the organizers in exchange for shares in the new company.

b. Purchased land for $16,000 and signed a one-year note (at a 6 percent annual interest rate).

c. Bought two used delivery trucks for operating purposes at the start of the year at a cost of $10,000 each; paid $5,000 cash and signed a promissory note for the balance, payable over the next three years (at an annual interest rate of 7 percent).

d. Sold one-fourth of the land for $4,000 to Birkins Moving, which promised to pay in six months.

e. Paid $2,000 cash to a truck repair shop for a new motor for one of the trucks. (*Hint:* Increase the account you used to record the purchase of the trucks since the usefulness of the truck has been improved.)

f. Traded the other truck and $6,000 cash for a new one. The old truck's fair value is $10,000.

g. Shareholder Jonah Lee paid $27,500 cash for a vacant lot (land) for his personal use.

h. Collected the amount of the note due from Birkins Moving in (*d*).

i. Paid one-third of the principal of the note due for the delivery trucks in (*c*).

Required:

1. Set up appropriate T-accounts with beginning balances of $0 for cash, short-term notes receivable, land, equipment, short-term notes payable, long-term notes payable, and contributed capital. Using the T-accounts, record the effects of these transactions on Lee Delivery Company.

2. Prepare a classified statement of financial position for Lee Delivery Company at the end of 2017. Compute the current ratio at that date.

3. At the end of the next two years, Lee Delivery Company reported the following amounts on its statements of financial position:

	December 31, 2018	December 31, 2019
Current assets	$52,000	$ 47,000
Non-current assets	38,000	73,000
Total assets	90,000	120,000
Short-term notes payable	23,000	40,000
Long-term notes payable	17,000	20,000
Total liabilities	40,000	60,000
Shareholders' equity	50,000	60,000

4. Compute the company's current ratio for 2017, 2018, and 2019. What is the trend and what does this suggest about the company?

5. At the beginning of 2020, Lee Delivery Company applied to your bank for a $50,000 short-term loan to expand the business. The vice-president of the bank asked you to review the information and make a recommendation on lending the funds based solely on the results of the current ratio. What recommendation would you make to the bank's vice-president about lending the money to Lee Delivery Company?

ALTERNATE PROBLEMS

LO2-2,2-5

Celestica Inc.

AP2-1   Identifying Accounts on a Classified Statement of Financial Position and Their Normal Debit or Credit Balances (P2-1)

According to a recent annual report of Celestica Inc., the company is a "key player in the new technology-driven global economy." The company provides a broad range of services, including "design, prototyping, assembly, testing, product assurance, supply chain management, worldwide distribution, and after-sales service." The following are several of the accounts from a recent statement of financial position:

(1) Trade accounts receivable	(8) Retained earnings
(2) Short-term borrowings	(9) Trade accounts payable
(3) Contributed capital	(10) Cash and short-term investments
(4) Long-term debt	(11) Accrued liabilities
(5) Prepaid expenses and other assets	(12) Other long-term liabilities
(6) Intangible assets	(13) Inventories
(7) Property, plant, and equipment	(14) Income taxes payable

Required:

Indicate how each account normally should be categorized on a classified statement of financial position. Use CA for current asset, NCA for non-current asset, CL for current liability, NCL for non-current liability, and SE for shareholders' equity. Also indicate whether the account normally has a debit or a credit balance.

■ LO2-3,2-4   **AP2-2**   **Determining Financial Statement Effects of Various Transactions, and Interpreting the Current Ratio** (P2-2)

Adamson Inc. is a small manufacturing company that makes model trains to sell to toy stores. It has a small service department that repairs customers' trains for a fee. The company has been in business for five years. At December 31, 2016 (the company's fiscal year-end), the accounting records reflected total assets of $500,000 (cash, $120,000; equipment, $70,000; buildings, $310,000), total liabilities of $200,000 (short-term notes payable, $140,000; long-term notes payable, $60,000), and total shareholders' equity of $300,000 (contributed capital, $220,000; retained earnings, $80,000). During the current year, 2017, the following summarized events occurred:

a. Borrowed $110,000 cash from the bank and signed a 10-year note.

b. Purchased equipment for $30,000, paying $3,000 in cash and signing a note due in six months for the balance.

c. Issued 10,000 shares for $100,000 cash.

d. Purchased a delivery truck (equipment) for $10,000; paid $5,000 cash and signed a short-term note payable for the remainder.

e. Lent $2,000 cash to the company president, Clark Adamson, who signed a note promising to pay the amount and annual interest at the rate of 10 percent in one year.

f. Built an addition on the factory for $200,000 and paid cash to the contractor.

g. Purchased $85,000 in long-term investments.

h. Returned a $3,000 piece of equipment purchased in (*b*) because it proved to be defective; received a reduction of the note payable equal to the value of the defective equipment.

i. A shareholder sold $5,000 of his shares in Adamson Incorporated to her neighbour for $6,400.

Required:

Prepare a summary of the preceding transactions. To develop a quick assessment of the transaction effects on Adamson Incorporated, you have decided to complete the tabulation that follows and to use plus (+) for increases and minus (−) for decreases for each account. The first transaction is used as an example.

		Assets				=	Liabilities		+	Shareholders' Equity	
	Cash	Notes receivable	Long-term investments	Equipment	Building		Short-term notes payable	Long-term notes payable		Contributed capital	Retained earnings
Beg.	120,000			70,000	310,000 =		140,000	60,000 +		220,000	80,000
(a)	+110,000								+110,000		

1. Did you include all transactions in the tabulation? If not, which one did you exclude and why?

2. Based on beginning balances plus the completed tabulation, calculate the following amounts at the end of 2017 (show computations):

    a. Total assets

    b. Total liabilities

    c. Total shareholders' equity

    d. Cash balance

    e. Total current assets

3. Compute the company's current ratio at the end of the year. What does this ratio suggest to you about Adamson Incorporated?

LO2-5,2-6   **AP2-3**   **Recording Transactions in T-Accounts, Preparing a Statement of Financial Position, and Evaluating the Current Ratio** (P2-3)

Gildan Activewear Inc.

Gildan Activewear Inc. specializes in manufacturing and selling T-shirts, sport shirts, and fleece. The following is adapted from a recent statement of financial position dated January 3, 2016, the end of the company's fiscal year. Amounts are in thousands of dollars:

Cash and cash equivalents	$ 50,675	Accounts payable and accrued liabilities	$ 232,268
Accounts receivable	306,132	Long-term debt	375,000
Inventories	851,033	Other long-term liabilities	38,569
Prepaid expenses	42,934	Contributed capital	164,504
Other current assets	2,840	Retained earnings	2,022,846
Property, plant, and equipment, net	1,044,389	Other components of equity	1,093
Intangible assets	336,753		
Goodwill	190,626		
Other non-current assets	8,898		

Assume that the following transactions occurred in the first quarter of fiscal year 2016, ended on March 31, 2016:

a. Received $630 on sale of intangibles at cost.

b. Paid $14,000 in principal on long-term debt.

c. Purchased $3,400 in non-current investments for cash.

d. Sold equipment at its cost for $600 cash.

e. Purchased additional intangibles for $5,400 cash.

f. Issued additional shares for $1,500 in cash.

g. Purchased property, plant, and equipment; paid $12,450 in cash and $9,400 with additional long-term bank loans.

h. Sold other non-current assets at cost for $310 cash.

i. Declared and paid $9,000 in dividends to shareholders.

Required:

1. Create a T-account for each of the accounts on the statement of financial position; enter the balances at January 3, 2016.

2. Record each of the transactions for the first quarter ended March 31, 2016, in a T-account (including referencing) and determine the ending balances.

3. Prepare a trial balance at March 31, 2016.

4. Prepare a classified statement of financial position at March 31, 2016.

5. Compute the current ratio at March 31, 2016. What does this suggest about Gildan Activewear?

LO2-7   **AP2-4**   **Identifying Effects of Transactions on the Statement of Cash Flows** (P2-4)

Refer to AP2-3.

Gildan Activewear Inc.

Required:

Using transactions (*a*) through (*i*) in AP2-3, indicate whether each transaction is an investing (I) or financing (F) activity for the year and the direction of the effect on cash flows (+ for increase and − for decrease). Indicate no effect on cash flows related to investing or financing with NE.

LO2-5,2-6   **AP2-5**   **Recording Transactions, Preparing Journal Entries, Posting to T-Accounts, Preparing a Statement of Financial Position, and Evaluating the Current Ratio** (P2-5)

BCE Inc.

BCE Inc., Canada's largest communications company, provides a comprehensive and innovative suite of broadband communications and content services to consumer, residential, business, and government customers in Canada. The following is BCE's (simplified) statement of financial position from a recent year:

BCE INC.
Statement of Financial Position
At December 31, 2015
(in millions of Canadian dollars)

ASSETS

Current assets

Cash and cash equivalents	$ 613
Receivables	3,009
Inventories	416
Prepaid expenses	393
Other assets	377
Total current assets	**4,808**

Non-current assets

Property, plant, and equipment, net	21,630
Long-term investments	1,119
Intangible assets	11,176
Goodwill	8,377
Other non-current assets	883
Total assets	**$47,993**

LIABILITIES AND SHAREHOLDERS' EQUITY

Current liabilities

Trade payables and accrued liabilities	$ 4,287
Income taxes payable	148
Dividends payable	576
Debt due within one year	4,895
Other current liabilities	86
Total current liabilities	**9,992**

Non-current liabilities

Long-term debt	15,390
Other liabilities	5,282
Total liabilities	**30,664**
Shareholders' equity	**17,329**
Total liabilities and shareholders' equity	**$47,993**

Source: BCE Inc., Annual Report 2015.

Assume that the following transactions (in millions of dollars) occurred in fiscal year 2016 (ending on December 31, 2016):

a. Issued additional shares for $200 in cash.

b. Borrowed 6,300 from creditors; due in 10 years.

c. Purchased additional investments for $1,500 cash; one-fifth were long term and the rest were short term.

d. Purchased property, plant, and equipment; paid $4,650 in cash and $850 with additional long-term bank loans.

e. Lent $250 to associated companies that signed a six-month note.

f. Sold short-term investments costing $200 for $200 cash.

Required:

1. Prepare a journal entry for each transaction.
2. Create a T-account for each item on the statement of financial position and include the December 31, 2016, balances. Post each journal entry to the appropriate T-account.
3. Prepare a trial balance as at December 31, 2016.
4. Prepare a statement of financial position for BCE based on the T-account ending balances at December 31, 2016.
5. Compute BCE's current ratio for fiscal year 2016. What does this suggest about the company?

LO2-7

BCE Inc.

AP2-6 **Preparing the Investing and Financing Sections of a Statement of Cash Flows** (P2-6)
Refer to AP2-5.

Required:
Based on the transactions that occurred in fiscal year 2016, prepare the investing and financing sections of BCE's statement of cash flows for that year.

LO2-6

AP2-7 **Using Financial Reports: Preparing a Classified Statement of Financial Position, and Analyzing the Current Ratio** (P2-7)
The accounts below, in alphabetical order, are adapted from a recent statement of financial position for Big Burgers Inc. (amounts are in thousands of dollars):

	Current Year	Prior Year		Current Year	Prior Year
Accounts and notes receivable	$ 795.9	$ 745.5	Long-term debt	$ 8,937.4	$ 8,357.3
Accrued liabilities	2,344.2	2,144.0	Notes payable (short term)	544.0	–
Cash and cash equivalents	4,260.4	1,379.8	Other long-term liabilities	1,869.0	1,758.2
Contributed capital	2,814.2	2,202.6	Other non-current assets	1,245.0	1,338.4
Current maturities of long-term debt	658.7	862.2	Prepaid expenses and other current assets	646.4	585.0
Intangible assets, net	1,950.7	1,828.3	Property and equipment, net	20,108.0	20,903.1
Inventories	147.0	147.5	Retained earnings	12,331.9	11,998.9
Long-term investments	1,035.4	1,109.9	Accounts payable	689.4	714.3

Required:

1. Construct, in good form, a classified statement of financial position (with two years reported) for Big Burgers Inc.

2. Compute the company's current ratio at the end of the current year. How do you interpret this ratio for Big Burgers?

LO2-5,2-6

Le Château Inc.

AP2-8 **Analyzing the Effects of Transactions by Using T-Accounts, Preparing a Statement of Financial Position, and Interpreting the Current Ratio as a Bank Loan Officer** (P2-8)
Chu Delivery Company Inc. was organized in 2018. The following transactions occurred during 2018:

a. Received $40,000 cash from organizers in exchange for shares in the new company.

b. Purchased land for $12,000, signing a one-year note.

c. Bought two used delivery trucks for operating purposes at the start of the year at a cost of $10,000 each; paid $4,000 cash and signed a note due in three years for the rest (ignore interest).

d. Sold one-fourth of the land for $3,000 to Pablo Moving, which signed a six-month note.

e. Paid $1,000 cash to a truck repair shop for a new motor for one of the trucks. (*Hint:* Increase the account you used to record the purchase of the trucks since the productive life of the truck has been improved.)

f. Shareholder Jingbi Chu paid $27,600 from her personal savings to purchase a vacant lot (land) for her personal use.

Required:

1. Set up appropriate T-accounts with beginning balances of zero for cash, short-term notes receivable, land, equipment, short-term notes payable, long-term notes payable, and contributed capital. Using the T-accounts, record the effects of these transactions by Chu Delivery Company.

2. Prepare a classified statement of financial position for Chu Delivery Company at December 31, 2018.

3. At the end of the next two years, Chu Delivery Company reported the following amounts on its statements of financial position:

	December 31, 2019	December 31, 2020
Current assets	$42,000	$ 47,000
Non-current assets	38,000	53,000
Total assets	**80,000**	**100,000**
Short-term notes payable	23,000	40,000
Long-term notes payable	17,000	10,000
Total liabilities	**40,000**	**50,000**
Shareholders' equity	**40,000**	**50,000**

Compute the company's current ratio for 2018, 2019, and 2020. What is the trend and what does this suggest about the company?

4. At the beginning of 2021, Chu Delivery Company applied to your bank for a $100,000 loan to expand the business. The vice-president of the bank asked you to review the information and make a recommendation on lending the funds based solely on the results of the current ratio. What recommendation would you make to the bank's vice-president about lending the money to Chu Delivery Company?

≡ connect CASES AND PROJECTS

FINDING AND INTERPRETING FINANCIAL INFORMATION

LO2-1,2-2,2-3,2-4,2-7

CP2-1

Canadian Tire
Corporation

Finding Financial Information

Refer to the financial statements and the accompanying notes of Canadian Tire Corporation in Appendix A at the end of this book.

Required:

1. Is the company a corporation, a partnership, or a proprietorship? How do you know?
2. Use the company's statement of financial position to determine the amounts in the accounting equation (A = L + SE).
3. The company shows on the statement of financial position that merchandise inventories are reported at $1,764.5 million. Does this amount represent the expected selling price? Why or why not?
4. What is the company's fiscal year-end? Where did you find the exact date?
5. What are the company's non-current liabilities?
6. Compute the company's current ratio, and explain its meaning.
7. How much cash did the company spend on purchasing property and equipment each year (capital expenditures)? Where did you find the information?

LO2-1,2-2,2-3,2-4,2-7

CP2-2

Sears Canada Inc.

Finding Financial Information

Go to *Connect* for the financial statements of Sears Canada Inc. and related notes.

Required:

1. Use the company's statement of financial position to determine the amounts in the accounting equation (A = L + SE) as at January 30, 2016.
2. If the company were liquidated at the end of the current year (January 30, 2016), are the shareholders guaranteed to receive $554.2 million?
3. What are the company's non-current liabilities?
4. What is the company's current ratio?
5. Did the company have a cash inflow or outflow from investing activities? How much?

LO2-3,2-7   **CP2-3**

Canadian Tire
Corporation vs.
Sears Canada Inc.

Comparing Companies within an Industry

Refer to the financial statements and the accompanying notes of Canadian Tire Corporation (Appendix A) and Sears Canada Inc. (*Connect*) and the Industry Ratio Report (Appendix B) on *Connect*.

Required:

1. Which company is larger in terms of total assets?
2. Compute the current ratio for both companies. Compared to the industry average (from the Industry Ratio Report), are these two companies more or less able to satisfy short-term obligations with current assets? Explain.
3. In the most recent year, how much cash, if any, was spent buying back (repurchasing) each company's own common shares?
4. How much did each company pay in dividends for the most recent year?
5. What account title does each company use to report any land, buildings, and equipment it may have?

FINANCIAL REPORTING AND ANALYSIS CASES

LO2-6,2-7   **CP2-4**   **Broadening Financial Research Skills: Locating Financial Information on the SEDAR Database**

The Securities Commissions regulate companies that issue shares on the stock market. They receive financial reports from public companies electronically under a system called SEDAR (System for Electronic Document Analysis and Retrieval). Using the Internet, anyone may search the database for the reports that have been filed.

Using your Web browser, access the SEDAR database at www.sedar.com. To search the database, select English, then Company Profiles; click on the letter T under Public Companies to get a list of all company names that start with T. Select Thomson Reuters Corporation (TRC), then click on "View this company's public documents" at the lower left corner of the next screen.

Required:

1. Look at SEDAR filings by clicking on the most recent Interim financial statements/report—English. Then locate the statement of financial position.
    a. What was the amount of TRC's total assets at the end of the most recent quarter reported?
    b. Did long-term debt increase or decrease for the quarter?
    c. Compute the current ratio. What does this suggest about the company?

2. Look at the statement of cash flow in the interim report.
    a. What amount did TRC spend on capital expenditures for the most recent quarter reported?
    b. What was the total amount of cash flows from (used in) financing activities for the most recent quarter reported?

LO2-1,2-2,2-6   **CP2-5**   **Using Financial Reports: Evaluating the Reliability of a Statement of Financial Position**

Betsey Jordan asked a local bank for a $50,000 loan to expand her small company. The bank asked Betsey to submit a financial statement of the business to supplement the loan application. Betsey prepared the following statement of financial position:

Statement of Financial Position At June 30, 2017	
Assets	
Cash and investments	$ 9,000
Inventory	30,000
Equipment	46,000
Personal residence (monthly payments, $2,800)	300,000
Other assets	20,000
Total assets	**$405,000**
Liabilities	
Short-term debt to suppliers	$ 62,000
Long-term debt on equipment	38,000
Total debt	100,000
Shareholders' equity	**305,000**
Total liabilities and shareholders' equity	**$405,000**

Required:

1. The statement of financial position has several flaws. However, there is at least one major deficiency. Identify it and explain its significance.

2. As a bank manager, would you lend the company money? Explain.

LO2-6   **CP2-6**   **Using Financial Reports: Analyzing the Statement of Financial Position**

Smiley Corp. and Tsang Inc. were organized in 2005. Both companies operate in the same line of business. The statements of financial position of the two companies at December 31, 2017, are as follows:

Smiley Corp. Statement of Financial Position December 31, 2017	
Assets	
Cash	$ 17,000
Accounts receivable	30,000
Inventory	16,000
Property, plant, and equipment	117,600
Total	$180,600
Liabilities and Shareholders' Equity	
Liabilities:	
Notes payable (short-term)	$ 18,600
Accounts payable	14,400
Total liabilities	33,000
Shareholders' equity:	
Contributed capital	90,000
Retained earnings	57,600
Total shareholders' equity	147,600
Total	$180,600

Tsang Inc. Statement of Financial Position December 31, 2017	
Assets	
Cash	$ 7,200
Accounts receivable	14,400
Inventory	7,600
Property, plant, and equipment	244,400
Total	$273,600
Liabilities and Shareholders' Equity	
Liabilities:	
Notes payable (short-term)	$ 33,600
Accounts payable	64,800
Total liabilities	98,400
Shareholders' equity:	
Contributed capital	108,000
Retained earnings	67,200
Total shareholders' equity	175,200
Total	$273,600

Required:

1. Eric Frechette wants to invest in one of these two companies by purchasing all of its shares. As a financial adviser to Mr. Frechette, which company would you select as an investment? Provide justification for your selection.

2. Each company applied to Development Bank for a loan of $20,000, payable in four months. As a bank loan officer, would you lend each company the requested amount? Explain.

CRITICAL THINKING CASES

LO2-1,2-2,2-6 CP2-7   **Making a Decision as a Financial Analyst: Preparing and Analyzing a Statement of Financial Position**

Your best friend from home writes you a letter about an investment opportunity that has come her way. A company is raising money by issuing shares and wants her to invest $20,000 (her recent inheritance from her great-aunt's estate). Your friend has never invested in a company before and, knowing that you are a financial analyst, asks that you look over the statement of financial position and send her some advice. An *unaudited* statement of financial position, in only moderately good form, is enclosed with the letter:

DEWEY, CHEETUM, AND HOWE INC. Statement of Financial Position For the Year Ending December 31, 2018	
Accounts receivable	$ 8,000
Cash	1,000
Inventory	8,000
Furniture and fixtures	52,000
Delivery truck	12,000
Buildings (estimated market value)	98,000
Total assets	$179,000
Accounts payable	$ 16,000
Payroll taxes payable	13,000
Long-term notes payable	15,000
Mortgage payable	50,000
Total liabilities	94,000
Contributed capital	80,000
Retained earnings	5,000
Total shareholders' equity	85,000
Total liabilities and shareholders' equity	$179,000

There is only one footnote, and it states that the building was purchased for $65,000, has been depreciated by $5,000 on the books, and still carries a mortgage (shown in the liability section). The footnote further states that, in the opinion of the company president, the building is "easily worth $98,000."

Required:

1. Draft a new statement of financial position for your friend, correcting any errors you note. (If any of the account balances need to be corrected, you may need to adjust the balance of retained earnings accordingly.) If no errors or omissions exist, say so.

2. Write a letter to your friend explaining the changes you made to the statement of financial position, if any, and offer your comments on the company's apparent financial condition based only on this information. Suggest other information your friend might want to review before coming to a final decision on whether to invest.

LO2-3,2-4,2-6   CP2-8

Manipulating Financial Statements: Ethical Considerations

Technology N Motion is a publicly traded company that is facing financial difficulties. To survive, the company needs large new bank loans. As the chief financial officer of the company, you approached several banks, but each has asked for your audited financial statements for 2017, the most recent fiscal year. You called for a meeting with other corporate officers to discuss how the financial statements could be improved. The suggestions made by your colleagues include the following:

a. We owe $20 million to our suppliers. We could show half this amount as a liability on our statement of financial position and report the other half as contributed capital. This will improve our financial position.

b. We own land that is worth at least $8 million in today's market, but it cost us only $3 million when we bought it. Why not show the land at $8 million on the company's statement of financial position, which increases both the total assets and shareholders' equity by $5 million?

c. We owe FirstRate Software $2 million, due in 30 days. I can ask their chief financial officer to let us delay the payment of this debt for a year, and our company could sign him a note that pays 8 percent interest.

Required:

Evaluate each of these three proposals to improve Technology N Motion's financial statements by considering both accounting and ethical issues.

LO2-3   CP2-9

Nortel Networks
Corporation

Evaluating an Ethical Dilemma: Analyzing Management Incentives

Nortel Networks Corporation (Nortel), based in Brampton, Ontario, is a global supplier of networking solutions and services. In 2005, the company released the findings of an independent review as a result of continuing problems with its accounting. The review revealed that three former company executives, the chief executive officer, the chief financial officer, and the controller, used accounting practices that increased reported earnings from late 2002 to mid-2003. Through Nortel's internal investigation, several problems had become known, not the least of which was $900 million of inappropriately reported liabilities and approximately $250 million of overstated net earnings. This mattered to the executives who received a bonus if earnings before tax exceeded specific levels.

In April 2004, Nortel issued a news release announcing the appointment of its new chief executive officer (CEO), Mr. William Owens, and the termination of its previous CEO, for cause. The previous CEO left his position on April 28 and left the company's board of directors on May 21, 2004. Neither the chairman of the board of directors nor the new CEO would comment on the termination. A month earlier the chief financial officer and the controller had been placed on paid leave of absence and they too were fired. A day later, the U.S. Securities and Exchange Commission announced that it was investigating Nortel, and then the Ontario Securities Commission launched its own investigation. But the worst was yet to come.

In May 2004, a U.S. federal grand jury subpoenaed Nortel for accounting records and other documents prepared for the previous four years during which the previous CEO, an accountant, had served as chief financial officer. A few days later, the Ontario Public Service Employees Union Pension Trust filed a class action lawsuit to recover losses arising from its investment in Nortel shares between April 2003 and 2005, based on fraudulent financial information. By August 2004, the Royal Canadian Mounted Police began a Canadian criminal investigation into the former CEO's activities. The cost to Nortel has been over $2.4 billion in cash awarded to the Ontario pension fund in April 2005, and the company sued the former CEO to recover this money from him personally. Pursuant to the independent review, 12 senior executives agreed to repay a total of $8.6 million in bonuses they received from the company in the past.

Required:

1. Describe the parties that were harmed or helped by this fraud.

2. Explain how greed may have contributed to this fraud.

3. Why do you think the independent auditors failed to catch the fraud?

FINANCIAL REPORTING AND ANALYSIS TEAM PROJECT

LO2-3,2-7   **CP2-10**   **Team Project: Analyzing the Statement of Financial Position and Ratios**
As a team, select an industry to analyze. A list of companies classified by industry can be obtained by accessing www.fpinfomart.ca and then choosing Companies by Industry on the left-hand side. You can also find a list of industries and companies within each industry via http://ca.finance. yahoo.com/investing. A list of industries can be obtained by clicking on Order Annual Reports under Tools.

Each group member should acquire the annual report for a different publicly traded company in the industry. (Library files, the SEDAR service at www.sedar.com, and the company's website are good sources.)

Required:

Each team member should write a short report answering the following questions about the selected company. Discuss any patterns that you as a team observe. Then, as a team, write a short report comparing and contrasting your companies.

1. For the most recent year, what are the top three asset accounts by size? What percentage is each account of the total assets (Calculated as Asset A ÷ Total Assets)?

2. What are the major investing and financing activities (by dollar size) for the most recent year? (Look at the statement of cash flows.)

3. Perform a ratio analysis.

   a. What does the current ratio measure in general?

   b. Compute the current ratio for the last three years. (You may find prior years' information in the section in the annual report called "Selected Financial Information," or search for prior years' annual reports.)

   c. What do your results suggest about the company?

   d. If available, find the industry ratio for the most recent year, compare it to your results, and discuss why you believe your company differs from or is similar to the industry ratio.

connect   CONTINUING CASE

LO2-5,2-6,2-7   **CC2-1**   **Accounting for the Establishment of a New Business (the Accounting Cycle)**
Penny Cassidy has decided to start her business, Penny's Pool Service & Supply Inc. (PPSS). There is much to do when starting a new business. Here are some transactions that have occurred in the business in March 2016.

   a. Received $25,000 cash and a large delivery van with a value of $36,000 from Penny, who was given 4,000 shares in exchange.

   b. Purchased land with a small office and warehouse by paying $10,000 cash and signing a 10-year mortgage note payable to the local bank for $80,000. The land has a value of $18,000 and the building's value is $72,000. Use separate accounts for land and buildings.

   c. Purchased a new computer from Dell for $2,500 cash and office furniture for $4,000, signing a short-term note payable in six months.

   d. Hired a receptionist for the office at a salary of $2,500 per month, starting in April 2016.

   e. Paid $1,000 on the note payable to the bank at the end of March 2016 (ignore interest).

   f. Purchased short-term investments in shares of other companies for $5,000 cash.

   g. Ordered $10,000 in inventory from Pool Corporation Inc., a pool supply wholesaler, to be received in April 2016.

Required:

1. For each of the events, prepare journal entries if a transaction of the business exists, checking that debits equal credits. If a transaction does not exist, explain why there is no transaction for the business.

2. Create T-accounts, and post each of the transactions to determine balances at March 31, 2016. Because this is a new business, beginning balances are $0.

3. Prepare a trial balance on March 31, 2016, to check that debits equal credits after the transactions are posted to the T-accounts.

4. From the trial balance, prepare a classified statement of financial position (with current assets and current liabilities sections) at March 31, 2016 (before the beginning of operations in April).

5. For each of the events, indicate if it is an investing activity (I) or financing activity (F), and the direction (+ for increases; − for decreases) and amount of the effect on cash flows using the following structure. Write NE if there is no effect on cash flows.

	Type of Activity **(I, F, or NE)**	**Effect on Cash Flows** **(+ or − and amount)**
(a)		
(b) etc.		

6. Calculate the current ratio at March 31, 2016. What does this ratio indicate about the ability of PPSS to pay its current liabilities?

SOLUTIONS TO SELF-STUDY QUIZZES

Self-Study Quiz 2-1
Column 1: CL, CA, CA. Column 2: NCL, SE, CL. Column 3: NCA, NCA, CA.

Self-Study Quiz 2-2
(*g*) Cash (A) is received +3. The trade supplier's written promise to pay is "given back" (paid off); Notes receivable (A) −3. The equation remains the same because assets increase and decrease by the same amount.

(*h*) Cash (A) is given −4. Canadian Tire's written promise to the bank is "given back" (paid off); Long-term notes payable −4. There is a $4 decrease on the left side of the equation and a $4 decrease on the right side.

If your answers did not agree with these, go back and make sure that you have completed each of the steps for each transaction.

Self-Study Quiz 2-3
Column 1: cr, dr, dr. Column 2: cr, cr, cr. Column 3: dr, dr, dr.

Self-Study Quiz 2-4
(*g*) Journal entry:

Cash (+A)	3	
Notes receivable (−A)		3

(*h*) Effects on the accounting equation:

Assets		=	**Liabilities**		+	**Shareholders' Equity**
Cash	−4		Long-term debt	−4		

Posting to ledger accounts:
Cash: (*g*) 300; (*h*) 4   Notes receivable: (*g*) 300   Long-term borrowings: (*h*) 4
Ending balance of Retained earnings = $28,481

Self-Study Quiz 2-5
Current Ratio:
January 31, 2016 $617 ÷ $227 = 2.72
February 1, 2015 $548 ÷ $215 = 2.55
February 2, 2014 $459 ÷ $164 = 2.80

Dollarama has a high level of liquidity, which has decreased over the three years. It is a cash-oriented business with a strong cash management system. The nature of its business requires a build-up in its inventories, which represents a significant percentage of the company's assets. This may be a cause for concern in case of economic downturn and a slow-moving inventory.

Self-Study Quiz 2-6
F −, 2. I +, 3. F −, 4. I −, 5. F +

ENDNOTES

1. International Accounting Standards Committee (1989). Framework for the Preparation and Presentation of Financial Statements. Adopted by the International Accounting Standards Board, 2001.

2. International Accounting Standards Board (2010). Conceptual Framework for Financial Reporting 2010.

3. *Ibid.*

4. In the original conceptual frameworks produced by the FASB and the IASB, verifiability was considered a component of reliability, which also encompassed accuracy and freedom from bias. In the revised conceptual framework, reliability has been replaced with faithful representation as the second fundamental qualitative characteristic. A critical review of the primary qualitative characteristics and their relative significance for performance evaluation and investment and credit decisions is provided in Patricia C. O'Brien, "Changing the Concepts to Justify the Standards," *Accounting Perspectives* 8, No. 4 (2009): 263–275, and in Patricia C. O'Brien and William R. Scott, "Contracting Theory," *CA Magazine* 145, No. 3 (2012): 44–46.

5. To help users better understand the contents of its financial reports, IBM includes on its website (www.ibm.com/investor/help) a glossary of terms and provides basic explanations of the information contained in financial statements.

6. Canadian Securities Administrators, "National Instrument 52-109 Certification of Disclosure in Issuers' Annual and Interim Filings (NI 52-109)" (October 2008). Accessed May 7, 2016, from the OSC website, www.osc.gov.on.ca/en/home.htm.

7. The basic rules for consolidation of financial statements are covered in Chapter 14 (on *Connect*).

8. Canadian Tire reported total amounts of $1,957 and $1,961 at January 2, 2016, and January 3, 2015, respectively, for both accounts payable and accrued liabilities. Each amount is divided in two separate amounts for illustrative purposes.

9. From this concept, accountants have developed what is known as the double-entry system of recordkeeping.

10. Contracts of this nature that are likely to result in significant future liabilities must be noted in the financial statements as commitments.

11. In homework assignments, if you have an error in your trial balance (the two column totals are not equal), errors can be traced and should be corrected. To find errors, reverse your steps. Check that:

    - You copied the ending balances in all of the T-accounts (both the amount and whether it is a debit or a credit)correctly to the trial balance.
    - You computed the ending balances in the T-accounts correctly.
    - You posted the transaction effects correctly from the journal entries to the T-accounts (amount, account, and whether a debit or credit).
    - You prepared the journal entries correctly (amount, account, and whether a debit or credit).

Operating Decisions and the Statement of Earnings

After studying this chapter, you should be able to do the following:

LO3-1 Describe a typical business operating cycle and explain the necessity for the periodicity assumption.

LO3-2 Explain how business activities affect the elements of the statement of earnings.

LO3-3 Explain the accrual basis of accounting and apply the revenue recognition principle and the matching process to measure net earnings.

LO3-4 Apply transaction analysis to examine and record the effects of operating activities on the financial statements.

LO3-5 Prepare a classified statement of earnings and explain the difference between net earnings and cash flow from operations.

LO3-6 Compute and interpret the total asset turnover ratio and the return on assets.

SUPPLEMENTARY MATERIAL

LO3-S1 Explain earnings measurement and comprehensive income.

ValeStock/Shutterstock.com

Focus Company: **Canadian Tire Corporation**

OFFERING PRODUCTS TAILORED TO CLIENTS' NEEDS

Canadian Tire (www.canadiantire.ca) has grown over time through careful attention to customer demand and by innovative provision of products and services. In the past three years, the company has continued to implement renewal of the design and format if its retail stores; improve key operations, such as the returns process; broaden its product offerings; and improve on product quality. In addition, Canadian Tire has carefully culled unprofitable stores. It offers a broad range of retail goods and services, including general merchandise, apparel, sporting goods, petroleum, and financial services throughout Canada, coupled with a robust Web presence and in-store online technology to keep closely connected to the customers' needs. The company has attributed its success in large part to its very strong relationship with its dealers, who are closest to regional customers; its focus on strengthening brand recognition; and its enthusiastic and nimble response to shifts in the application of technology in retailing.

Canadian Tire has grown both organically, by enlarging its network of existing stores, and inorganically, by acquiring new companies, such as the Forzani Group (renamed FGL Sports) and Mark's Work Wearhouse. The company owns a significant real estate portfolio of 273 properties that were purchased as it expanded. The activities relating to managing these assets, such as development, purchase, leasing, and sale, are conducted by the company's Real Estate Investment Trust.

UNDERSTANDING THE BUSINESS

To become a leading merchandising company, Canadian Tire has developed its brand recognition. It has implemented a strategy of acquiring and developing high-quality private brand labels, such as Mastercraft® tools, Denver Hayes® and Windriver® clothing, and Woods® outdoor equipment. In addition, the company has a "Tested for Life" product development process, whereby 15,000 Canadians have tested and endorsed the quality of Canadian Tire's products before they were displayed for sale in the retail stores. With this array of products, the company has a superior warehouse management system and uses third parties to implement the logistics of obtaining and delivering products to the dealer network. To maintain and improve its profitability in these day-to-day operations, the company purchases, distributes, and sells inventory according to a company-wide plan.

Financial analysts develop their own set of expectations about Canadian Tire's future performance. The published statement of earnings provides the primary basis for comparing analysts' projections to the actual results of operations. We discuss these comparisons and the stock market's reactions to Canadian Tire's results through-out this chapter as we learn about revenue recognition and measurement. To understand how business plans and the results of operations are reflected on the statement of earnings, we need to answer the following questions:

1. How do business activities affect the statement of earnings?
2. How are these activities recognized and measured?
3. How are these activities reported on the statement of earnings?

In this chapter, we focus on Canadian Tire's operating activities, which include sales of its many products to consumers through its various stores, including FGL Sports, Mark's, and Canadian Tire Bank, among others. The results of these activities are reported on the statement of earnings.

ORGANIZATION OF THE CHAPTER

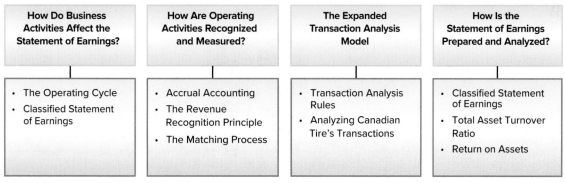

How Do Business Activities Affect the Statement of Earnings?	How Are Operating Activities Recognized and Measured?	The Expanded Transaction Analysis Model	How Is the Statement of Earnings Prepared and Analyzed?
• The Operating Cycle • Classified Statement of Earnings	• Accrual Accounting • The Revenue Recognition Principle • The Matching Process	• Transaction Analysis Rules • Analyzing Canadian Tire's Transactions	• Classified Statement of Earnings • Total Asset Turnover Ratio • Return on Assets

Supplemental material:
Appendix 3A: Earnings Measurement and Comprehensive Income
Appendix C: The Formal Recordkeeping System (on *Connect*)

HOW DO BUSINESS ACTIVITIES AFFECT THE STATEMENT OF EARNINGS?

The Operating Cycle

The long-term objective for any business is *to turn cash into more cash*. For companies to stay in business, this excess cash must be generated from operations (i.e., from the activities for which the business was established), not from borrowing money or selling non-current assets.

LO3-1

Describe a typical business operating cycle and explain the necessity for the periodicity assumption.

The **OPERATING (CASH-TO-CASH) CYCLE** is the time it takes for a company to pay cash to suppliers, sell goods and services to customers, and collect cash from customers.

Companies acquire inventory and the services of employees and then sell inventory or services to customers. The **operating (cash-to-cash) cycle** begins when a company receives goods to sell (or, in the case of a service company, has employees work), pays for them, and sells to customers; it ends when customers pay cash to the company. The length of time for completion of the operating cycle depends on the nature of the business.

The operating cycle for Canadian Tire is relatively short. It spends cash to purchase finished products ready for transport and sale to customers. In some companies, inventory is paid for well before it is sold. Toys "R" Us, for example, builds its inventory for months prior to the year-end holiday season. It borrows funds from banks to pay for the inventory and repays the loans with interest when cash is received from customers. In other companies, cash is received from customers well after a sale takes place. For example, car dealerships often sell cars over time, with monthly payments from customers due over several years. Companies attempt to shorten the operating cycle by creating incentives to encourage customers to buy sooner or pay faster, in order to improve the company's cash flows.

Purchase goods and services

BEGIN OPERATING CYCLE

Typical Operating Cycle

Receive cash from customers

Pay cash to suppliers

Sell goods and services to customers

SHORT-TERM DEBT FINANCING AND THE OPERATING CYCLE

FINANCIAL ANALYSIS

The timing of the cash outflows and inflows shown in the illustration above indicates that many businesses must pay suppliers and employees before they receive cash from customers, causing them to seek short-term financing. When the companies receive cash from customers, they pay off the liability. In addition, if a company plans to grow—say, to sell twice as many goods as in the prior period—it may not have collected enough cash from the prior period's customers to purchase the quantity of inventory needed in the next period. Sources of financing include suppliers and financial institutions (banks and commercial credit companies).

Managers know that reducing the time needed to turn cash into more cash (i.e., shortening the operating cycle) means higher net earnings and faster growth. Managers may purchase additional inventory or other assets for growth or repay debt with the excess cash, or they may distribute it to owners.

Until a company ceases activities, the operating cycle is repeated continuously. However, decision makers require periodic information about the financial condition and performance of a business. To measure net earnings for a specific period of time, accountants follow the **periodicity assumption**, which assumes that the long life of a company can be reported in shorter time periods, such as months, quarters, and years.[1] Two types of issues arise in reporting periodic net earnings to users:

1. Recognition issues. *When* should the effects of operating activities be recognized (recorded)?

2. Measurement issues. *What amounts* should be recognized?

Before we examine the rules accountants follow as they resolve these issues, let us review the elements of financial statements that are affected by operating activities.

> The **PERIODICITY ASSUMPTION** means that the long life of a company can be reported in shorter periods.

Classified Statement of Earnings

The statement of earnings includes a number of sections and subtotals to aid the user in identifying the company's earnings from operations for the year, and to highlight the effect of other items on net earnings.

Most manufacturing and merchandising companies use the following basic structure:

> **LO3-2**
>
> Explain how business activities affect the elements of the statement of earnings.

$$
\begin{array}{rl}
& \text{Net sales} \\
- & \text{Cost of sales} \\
= & \text{Gross profit} \\
- & \text{Operating expenses} \\
= & \text{Earnings from operations} \\
+/- & \text{Non-operating revenues/expenses and gains/losses} \\
= & \text{Earnings before income taxes} \\
- & \text{Income tax expense} \\
= & \text{Earnings from continuing operations} \\
+/- & \text{Earnings/loss from discontinued operations} \\
= & \text{Net earnings}
\end{array}
$$

The operating expenses consist mainly of distribution costs, administrative expenses, and other operating expenses.

Exhibit 3.1 shows a recent statement of earnings for Canadian Tire. As we indicated in Chapter 1, the statement of earnings is the main part of a statement of comprehensive income. We continue to focus our attention on the statement of earnings in this chapter, but we briefly discuss comprehensive income later in the chapter.

Canadian Tire reports its statement of earnings in a *multiple-step* format, which is very common.[2] Classification of the various elements of the statement of earnings helps financial statement users assess the company's operating performance and predict its future profitability.

The statement of earnings includes three major sections:

1. Results of continuing operations

2. Results of discontinued operations

Net earnings (the sum of 1 and 2)

3. Earnings per share

All companies report information for sections 1 and 3, while some companies report information in section 2, depending upon their particular circumstances. The bottom line, net earnings, is the sum of sections 1 and 2. First, we will focus on the most common and most relevant section, continuing operations.

Exhibit **3.1**

Statement of Earnings

REAL-WORLD EXCERPT

Canadian Tire Corporation

CONSOLIDATED STATEMENT OF EARNINGS For the Year Ended (in millions of Canadian dollars, except for earnings per share)		
	January 2, 2016	January 3, 2015
Sales	$12,280	$12,463
Cost of sales[3]	(8,144)	(8,417)
Gross profit	4,136	4,046
Operating expenses		
Salaries and wages	(1,128)	(1,141)
Other operating expenses	(1,968)	(1,929)
Total operating expenses	(3,096)	(3,070)
Earnings from operations	1,040	976
Other income (expenses and losses)		
Finance costs	(107)	(128)
Finance income	14	19
Other income	54	11
Earnings before income taxes	1,001	878
Income tax expense	(265)	(239)
Net earnings for the year	$ 736	$ 639
Earnings per share	$ 8.66	$ 7.65

← Operating activities (central focus of business)

← Includes rent, insurance, repairs, utilities, and advertising

⟵ Subtotal of operating revenues minus operating expenses

⟵ Peripheral activities (not the main focus of the business)

⟵ Subtotal of all income minus all expenses except income taxes

⟵ Net earnings divided by weighted average number of shares outstanding

Note: This statement of earnings is an adaptation of Canadian Tire's actual consolidated statement of earnings for 2015.

Continuing Operations This section of the statement of earnings presents the results of continuing operations. As we discuss the elements of the statement of earnings, it is useful to refer to the conceptual framework outlined in Exhibit 2.1 in Chapter 2.

REVENUES are increases in assets or settlements of liabilities from ongoing operations.

EXPENSES are decreases in assets or increases in liabilities to generate revenues during the period.

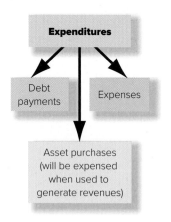

Operating Revenues **Revenues** are defined as increases in assets or settlements of liabilities from *ongoing operations* of the business. Operating revenues result from the sale of goods or services. Canadian Tire earns revenue when it sells goods and renders services to customers. It recognizes revenue in the statement of earnings when the significant risks and rewards of ownership have been transferred to the buyer, which is mainly upon delivery of goods or services. When revenues are earned, assets, usually cash or accounts receivable, often increase. Sometimes, a company receives cash in exchange for a promise to provide goods or services in the future. At that point, revenue is not earned, but a liability account, deferred revenue, is created. When the company provides the promised goods or services to the customer, revenue is recognized and the liability is settled.

Operating Expenses **Expenses** are decreases in assets or increases in liabilities from ongoing operations, and are incurred to generate revenues during the period. Some students confuse the terms "expenditures" and "expenses." An expenditure is any outflow of cash for any purpose, whether to buy equipment, pay off a bank loan, or pay employees their wages. An expense is more narrowly defined; it will only result when an asset, such as equipment or supplies, is *used to generate revenue during a period*, or when an amount is *incurred to generate revenues during a period*, such as using electricity, even if the amount will be paid in the future. Therefore, *not all expenditures are expenses*, and *expenses are necessary to generate revenues.*

Canadian Tire purchases a variety of products from suppliers for resale to consumers, pays employees to receive merchandise from suppliers, prepares them for display in the company's stores, sells products and services to customers, and performs administrative tasks. The company uses electricity to operate equipment and lights in its facilities, and advertises the products and services it sells. Without incurring these expenses, Canadian Tire would have nothing in its stores to sell and could not generate revenues. Although some of the expenses may result from expenditures of cash at the time they are incurred, some expenses may be incurred after cash was paid, in the past, while other expenses may be incurred before cash is paid, in the future. When an expense occurs, assets such as supplies inventory decrease (are used up), *or* liabilities such as salaries payable or utilities payable increase.

The following are primary operating expenses for most merchandising companies:

1. *Cost of sales* is the cost of products sold to customers. For example, when Canadian Tire purchases tires from suppliers, it may pay for transport and handling, in addition to the purchase price. All of these costs are included in the cost of the asset "inventories." As inventories are sold, they become an expense, called cost of sales. In companies with a manufacturing or merchandising focus, the cost of sales (also called cost of goods sold) is usually the most significant expense. The cost of sales for Canadian Tire is $8,144 and represents about 66.3 percent of the sales for 2015.[4] The difference between sales—net of sales discounts, returns and allowances—and cost of sales is known as **gross profit (or gross margin)**.[5]

2. *Operating expenses* are the usual expenses, other than cost of sales, that are incurred in operating a business during a specific accounting period. The expenses reported will depend on the nature of the company's operations. International Accounting Standard 1 requires companies to classify their expenses either by function—such as marketing and promotion, distribution, and administrative—or by nature of the expense. Classification by nature includes the three main costs of production: materials, labour, and property and equipment use.

Canadian Tire, like most companies, classifies its expenses by function.[6] Salaries and wages expenses include the salaries of all personnel who support the sales effort, such as sales personnel, legal counsel, accountants, and computer technicians. Other operating expenses include a variety of expenses related to marketing and promotion of the company's products through various print and electronic media, distribution of the company's products to its customers, rental of warehouse space, insurance, utilities, and telecommunications services. Canadian Tire did not provide details of its operating expenses in its statement of earnings, but it reported the major expenses in a note to its financial statements.

Another subtotal, **earnings from operations**, also called operating income, equals net sales less cost of sales and operating expenses.

Non-operating Items Not all activities affecting a statement of earnings are central to continuing operations. Any revenues, expenses, gains, or losses that result from these other activities are not included as part of earnings from operations but instead categorized as other income or expenses. Typically, these include the following:

- *Investment income* (or *investment, interest,* or *dividend revenue*). Using excess cash to purchase certificates of deposit or shares in other corporations are investing activities for Canadian Tire, not a central operation (purchasing and selling products and services). Therefore, any interest or dividends earned on the investment are not included as operating revenue.

- *Financing costs.* Likewise, since borrowing money is a financing activity, any cost of using that money (called interest) is not an operating expense. In addition to interest expense, Canadian Tire incurs other financing costs when other currencies,

GROSS PROFIT (or **GROSS MARGIN**) is net sales less cost of sales.

EARNINGS FROM OPERATIONS (operating income) equals net sales less cost of sales and operating expenses.

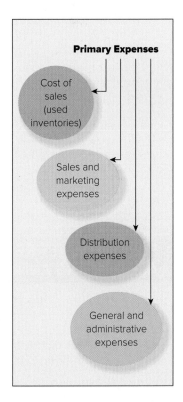

Primary Expenses

Cost of sales (used inventories)

Sales and marketing expenses

Distribution expenses

General and administrative expenses

such as the U.S. dollar, are the basis for purchase or sale transactions. Except for financial institutions, incurring interest expense or earning investment income are *not* part of the central operations of most businesses, including Canadian Tire. We say these are peripheral (normal but not central) transactions.

- *Gains (or losses) on disposal of assets.* Companies dispose of (either sell or abandon) property and equipment from time to time to maintain modern facilities. Selling land for more than the original cost does not result in earning revenue because the transaction is not the central operating focus for the business. **Gains** (with an account called *gain on disposal of assets*) are increases in assets or decreases in liabilities from *peripheral* transactions. **Losses** are decreases in assets or increases in liabilities from *peripheral* transactions. Abandoning or getting rid of property and equipment results in losses to the company. In 2015, Canadian Tire reported other income of $57, which resulted primarily from selling short-term investments and realizing a gain on the transaction.

GAINS are increases in assets or decreases in liabilities from peripheral transactions.

LOSSES are decreases in assets or increases in liabilities from peripheral transactions.

EARNINGS BEFORE INCOME TAXES (pretax earnings) equals revenues minus all expenses except income tax expense.

The non-operating items that are subject to income taxes are added to or subtracted from earnings from operations to obtain the **earnings before income taxes** (or pretax earnings).

Income Tax Expense   Income tax expense is the last expense listed on the statement of earnings. All for-profit corporations are required to compute income taxes owed to federal, provincial, and foreign governments. Income tax expense is calculated as a percentage of earnings before income taxes, reflecting the difference between income, which includes revenues and gains, and expenses and losses. It is determined by using applicable tax rates. Canadian Tire's effective tax rate in 2015 was 26.5 percent (income tax expense ÷ earnings before income taxes). This indicates that for every dollar of earnings before income taxes that Canadian Tire incurred in 2015, the company incurred $0.265 in income taxes.

Discontinued Operations   Companies may dispose of a major line of business or a geographical area of operations during the accounting period, or decide to discontinue a specific operation in the near future. When the decision is made to discontinue a major component of a business, the net earnings or loss from that component, as well as any gain or loss on subsequent disposal, are disclosed separately on the statement of earnings as *discontinued operations*. Because of their non-recurring nature, the financial results of discontinued operations are not useful in predicting future recurring net earnings; hence, they are presented separately from the results of continuing operations.

Earnings per Share   Corporations are required to disclose earnings per share on the statement of earnings or in the notes to the financial statements. This ratio is widely used in evaluating the operating performance and profitability of a company. At this introductory level, we can compute earnings per share simply as net earnings divided by the average number of shares outstanding during the period. Please note, however, that the calculation of the ratio is actually more complex and beyond the scope of this course. Instead, we used the actual number computed by Canadian Tire. For 2015, Canadian Tire reported $8.66 for each share owned by shareholders,

STOCK MARKET REACTIONS TO ACCOUNTING ANNOUNCEMENTS

FINANCIAL ANALYSIS

Stock market analysts and investors use accounting information to make investment decisions. The stock market, which is based on investors' expectations about future company performance, often reacts negatively when a company does not meet previously specified operating results. A company can experience difficulty even if it does not report a loss. Any unexpected deviation of actual performance from the operating plan, such as lower than expected quarterly earnings, needs to be explained.

On May 12, 2016, Canadian Tire announced the results of its first quarter ending April 2, 2016. On the day of the announcement, the price per share closed at $145.37, an increase of $6.31 over the closing price on the previous day.* Canadian Tire reported net earnings of $0.90 per share for the first quarter of 2016 compared to net earnings of $0.88 for the first quarter of 2015, which reflects an improvement in its operating performance. Prior to the earnings announcement, investors had built expectations of the company's performance based on available information. They expected the company to earn $0.84 for the first quarter of 2016. The increase in share price on the day of the earnings announcement suggests that investors were pleased with the company's actual results and reacted positively when the reported earnings per share figure exceeded their expectations.

This is a clear example of how external users react to information. Accounting information has a pervasive effect on all forms of corporate decision making, as well as on the economic decisions that investors and creditors make.

*Sources: Canadian Tire's website, and http://web.tmxmoney.com/pricehistory.php?m_symbol=CTC.A, accessed June 4, 2016.

HOW ARE OPERATING ACTIVITIES RECOGNIZED AND MEASURED?

You probably determine your personal financial position by the balance in your bank account. Your financial performance is measured as the difference between your account balance at the end of the period and the balance at the beginning of the period (i.e., whether you end up with more or less cash). If you have a higher account balance, cash receipts exceeded cash disbursements for the period. Many local retailers and other small businesses use **cash basis accounting**, which records revenues when cash is received and expenses when cash is paid, regardless of when the revenues are earned or the expenses incurred. This basis is often quite adequate for these organizations, which usually do not have to report to external users. The following table illustrates the application of cash basis accounting for the first three years of a new business, Jade Company:

CASH BASIS ACCOUNTING records revenues when cash is received and expenses when cash is paid.

Statements of Earnings	Year 1	Year 2	Year 3	Total
Sales on credit	$ 60,000	$60,000	$60,000	$180,000
Cash receipts from customers	20,000	70,000	90,000	180,000
Cash payments for:				
Salaries to employees	(30,000)	(30,000)	(30,000)	(90,000)
Insurance for three years	(12,000)	(0)	(0)	(12,000)
Supplies	(3,000)	(7,000)	(5,000)	(15,000)
Net operating cash flows	**$(25,000)**	**$33,000**	**$55,000**	**$ 63,000**

In this illustration, $60,000 in sales was earned each year by Jade Company. However, because the sales were on account, customers spread out their payments over three years. Salaries to employees were paid in full each year. Insurance was prepaid at the beginning of the first year for equal coverage over the three years. Supplies were purchased on credit and used evenly over the three years. However, the company paid part of the first year purchases in the second year.

Using cash basis accounting may lead to an incorrect interpretation of future company performance. Simply looking at the first year, investors and creditors might interpret the negative cash flows as a problem with the company's ability to generate cash flows in the future. However, the other two years show positive cash flows. Likewise, performance over time appears uneven, when in actuality it is not. Sales were earned evenly each year, although collections from customers were not. The years in which insurance and supplies were paid for are not the same as the years in which these resources were used.

LO3-3

Explain the accrual basis of accounting and apply the revenue recognition principle and matching process to measure net earnings.

ACCRUAL BASIS ACCOUNTING records revenues when earned and expenses when incurred, regardless of the timing of cash receipts or payments.

ACCRUAL BASIS Income Measurement
Revenues (when earned)
− Expenses (when incurred)
Net earnings

Accrual Accounting

Financial statements created under cash basis accounting normally postpone or accelerate recognition of revenues and expenses long after or before goods and services are produced and delivered. They also do not necessarily reflect all assets and liabilities of a company on a particular date. For these reasons, cash basis financial statements are not very useful to external decision makers. Therefore, IFRS require accrual basis accounting for financial reporting purposes.

In **accrual basis accounting**, revenues and expenses are recognized when the transaction that causes them occurs, not necessarily when cash is received or paid. *Revenues are recognized when they are earned and expenses when they are incurred.* The *revenue recognition principle* and the *matching process* determine when revenues and expenses are to be recorded under accrual basis accounting.

Using the same information for Jade Company, we can apply the accrual basis of accounting.

Statements of Earnings	Year 1	Year 2	Year 3	Total
Sales revenue (earned)	$60,000	$60,000	$60,000	$180,000
Expenses (resources used or incurred):				
Salaries expense	(30,000)	(30,000)	(30,000)	(90,000)
Insurance expense	(4,000)	(4,000)	(4,000)	(12,000)
Supplies expenses	(5,000)	(5,000)	(5,000)	(15,000)
Net earnings	**$21,000**	**$21,000**	**$21,000**	**$ 63,000**

Regardless of when cash is received, Jade Company reported revenues when earned. Likewise, the company used insurance coverage and supplies evenly over the three years, despite prepaying the entire amount of insurance at the beginning of the first year and paying part of the first year's purchases in the second year. The net earnings of $21,000 in the first year is a better predictor of future cash flows and performance than net operating cash flows reported under cash basis accounting. To determine when revenues and expenses are recognized and recorded under accrual basis accounting, accountants are guided by the *revenue recognition principle* and the *matching process.*

The Revenue Recognition Principle

Companies engage in a series of events that lead to the recognition of revenue. For example, after purchasing inventory items, such as kitchen utensils or garden accessories, Canadian Tire stores these finished products in the company's warehouses and markets them to consumers through various media before they are sold to customers either for cash or on credit. Each activity (purchase of inventory items, storage, promotion, sale, and collection from customers) contributes to the recognition of revenue. It is difficult, however, to estimate and recognize the value each activity adds to the amount eventually recognized as revenue. Instead, accountants attempt to identify the most critical event that leads to a flow of future benefits to Canadian Tire from all of these activities.

To guard against identification of critical events that may favour earlier recognition of revenue and increase net earnings, the following five conditions must be met for revenue to be recognized, according to the **revenue recognition principle**. If any of the following conditions are not met, revenue is normally not recognized and cannot be recorded:[7]

The **REVENUE RECOGNITION PRINCIPLE** states that revenues are recognized when the significant risks and rewards of ownership are transferred to the buyer, it is probable that future economic benefits will flow to the entity, and the benefits and the costs associated with the transaction can be measured reliably.

a. *The entity has transferred to the buyer the significant risks and rewards of ownership of the goods.* In most cases, the transfer of the risks and rewards of ownership coincides with the transfer of the legal title or the passing of possession to the buyer.

b. *The entity retains neither continuing managerial involvement to the degree usually associated with ownership nor effective control over the goods sold.* If the entity retains significant risks of ownership, the transaction is not a sale and revenue is not recognized. An entity may retain a significant risk of ownership in a number of ways. For example, if the buyer has the right to rescind the purchase for a reason specified in the sales contract and the entity is uncertain about the probability of return, then revenue cannot be recognized at the point of sale.

c. *The amount of revenue can be measured reliably.* There are no uncertainties as to the amount to be collected.

d. *It is probable that the economic benefits associated with the transaction will flow to the entity.* The consideration received for the sale of goods is either cash or the customer's promise to pay cash in the future. For cash sales, collection is not an issue since it is received on the date of the exchange. For sales on credit, the company reviews the customer's ability to pay. If the customer is considered creditworthy, collecting cash from the customer is reasonably likely.

e. *The costs incurred or to be incurred with respect to the transaction can be measured reliably.* Companies that provide service after sale may incur additional costs related to the sale transaction. In general, the costs to be incurred after the shipment of the goods can normally be measured reliably when the other conditions for the recognition of revenue have been satisfied. However, revenue cannot be recognized when the expenses cannot be measured reliably.

If *any* of the previous conditions are *not* met, revenue is normally *not* recognized and should not be recorded. For most businesses, these conditions are met at the point of delivery of goods or services.[8]

Companies usually disclose their revenue recognition practices in a note to the financial statements. The following excerpt from Canadian Tire's note describes how it recognizes its revenue from selling goods and rendering services.

REAL-WORLD EXCERPT

Canadian Tire Corporation
2015 FINANCIAL STATEMENTS

Canadian Tire Corporation
Notes to Consolidated Financial Statements

3. Significant Accounting Policies

Revenue
The Company recognizes revenue when the amount can be reliably measured, when it is probable that future economic benefits will flow to the entity, and when specific criteria have been met for each of the Company's activities as described below.

Sale of goods
Revenue from the sale of goods includes merchandise sold to Dealers and Mark's Work Wearhouse Ltd. ("Mark's") and FGL Sports Ltd. ("FGL Sports") franchisees, the sale of gasoline through agents, and the sale of goods by Mark's, PartSource, and FGL Sports corporately owned stores to the general public. This revenue is recognized when the goods are delivered, less an estimate for the sales and warranty returns. Revenue from the sale of goods is measured at the fair value of the consideration received less an appropriate deduction for actual and expected returns, discounts, rebates, and warranty and loyalty program costs, net of sales taxes. If there is any uncertainty regarding the right of a customer to return goods, no revenue is recognized until the uncertainty is resolved. However, in the case of warranties, if warranty claims can be reasonably estimated, revenue is then recorded for the net amount.
...

Services rendered
Service revenue includes Roadside Assistance Club membership revenue; insurance premiums and reinsurance revenue; extended warranty contract fees; merchant, interchange, and processing fees; cash advance fees; foreign exchange fees; and service charges on the loans receivable of the Financial Services operating segment, as well as Mark's clothing alteration revenue. Service revenue is recognized according to the contractual provisions of the arrangement, which is generally when the service is provided or over the contractual period.

Merchant, interchange, and processing fees, cash advance fees, and foreign exchange fees on credit card transactions are recognized as revenue at the time transactions are completed. Revenue from separately priced extended warranty contracts is recorded on a straight-line basis over the term of the contracts.

Reinsurance premiums are recorded on an accrual basis and are included in net income on a pro rata basis over the life of the insurance contract, with the unearned portion deferred in the Consolidated Balance Sheets. Premiums that are subject to adjustment are estimated based on available information. Any variances from the estimates are recorded in the periods in which they become known.
....

Exhibit 3.2 shows excerpts from the revenue recognition policies used by other companies that offer different types of products and services. Note that the point in time when revenue should be recognized depends on the nature of the products sold and services provided by the company.

Although businesses expect to receive cash in exchange for their goods and services at the time of delivery, the timing of cash receipts from customers does not dictate when businesses report revenues. Instead, the key to determining when to report revenues is whether or not the business has done what it promised to do. Thus, cash can be received (1) *before* the goods or services are delivered, (2) at the *same* time as the goods or services are delivered, or (3) *after* the goods or services are delivered, as shown in Exhibit 3.3.

Exhibit **3.2**

Timing of Revenue Recognition

Company Name	Typical Timing of Revenue Recognition
Bell Canada Enterprises Inc. (*Telecommunications*)	We recognize revenues from the sale of products or the rendering of services when they are earned; specifically, when all the following conditions are met: • the significant risks and rewards of ownership are transferred to customers and we retain neither continuing managerial involvement nor effective control • there is clear evidence that an arrangement exists • the amount of revenue and related costs can be measured reliably • it is probable that the economic benefits associated with the transaction will flow to the company In particular, we recognize the following: • fees for local, long distance, and wireless services when we provide the services • other fees, such as network access fees, licence fees, hosting fees, maintenance fees, and standby fees over the term of the contract • subscriber revenues when customers receive the service • advertising revenue, net of agency commissions, when advertisements are aired or delivered on the Internet • revenues from the sale of equipment when the equipment is delivered and accepted by customers • revenues on long-term contracts as services are provided, equipment is delivered and accepted, and contract milestones are met • advertising revenue, net of agency commissions, when advertisements are aired on radio or TV, posted on our website, or appear on the company's advertising panels and street furniture
Sears Canada Inc. (*Department store*)	2.15 Revenue recognition Revenue is measured at the fair value of the consideration received or receivable, excluding sales taxes. Revenue is reduced for estimated customer returns, discounts, and other similar allowances. 2.15.1 Sale of goods Revenue from the sale of goods is recognized upon delivery of goods to the customer. In the case of goods sold in-store, delivery is generally complete at the point of sale. For goods subject to delivery, such as furniture or major appliances, and goods sold online or through the catalogue, delivery is complete when the goods are delivered to the customers' selected final destination or picked up from a catalogue/online agent. In the case of goods subject to installation, such as home improvement products, revenue is recognized when the goods have been delivered and the installation is complete. 2.15.2 Rendering of services Revenue from a contract to provide services is recognized by reference to the stage of completion of the contract. *Extended warranty service contracts* The Company sells extended warranty service contracts with terms of coverage generally between 12 and 60 months. Revenue from the sale of each contract is deferred and amortized on a straight-line basis over the term of the related contract. *Product repair, handling, and installation services* Product repair, handling, and installation services revenue is recognized once the services are complete. These services are performed within a short timeframe. ... 2.15.5 Customer loyalty program The Sears Club Points Program (the "Program") allows members to earn points from eligible purchases made on any tender accepted by the Company. Members can then redeem points in accordance with the Program rewards schedule for merchandise. When points are earned, the Company defers revenue equal to the fair value of the awards adjusted for expected redemptions. When awards are redeemed, the redemption value of the awards is charged against deferred revenue and recognized as revenue. The expected future redemption rates are reviewed on an ongoing basis and are adjusted based upon expected future activity.

2.15.6 Gift cards

The Company sells gift cards through its retail stores, websites, and third parties with no administrative fee charges or expiration dates. No revenue is recognized at the time gift cards are sold. Revenue is recognized as a merchandise sale when the gift card is redeemed by the customer. The Company also recognizes income when the likelihood of the gift card being redeemed by the customer is remote, which is generally at the end of 18 months subsequent to issuance, estimated based on historical redemption patterns.

Sources: BCE, Annual Report 2015; Sears Canada Inc., Annual Report. 2015.

Exhibit **3.3**

Recording Revenues versus Cash Receipts

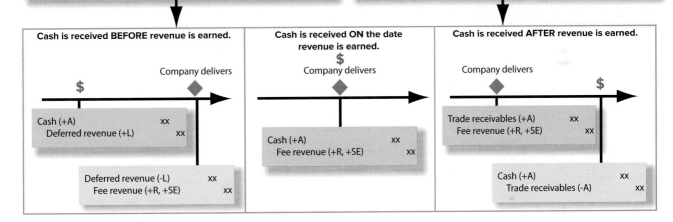

- If cash is received before the company delivers goods or services, the liability account Deferred Revenue is recorded because the company still owes goods or services. Examples include companies that sell magazine subscriptions and companies that sell insurance. Although not corporations, colleges and universities also receive tuition revenue and sell season tickets to sporting events and plays before any revenue is earned.

- If cash is received after goods or services are delivered, the receivable account created when the revenue was recorded is reduced because the customers have paid the company what they owed.

Cash is received BEFORE revenue is earned.

Company delivers

Cash (+A)   xx
   Deferred revenue (+L)   xx

Deferred revenue (-L)   xx
   Fee revenue (+R, +SE)   xx

Cash is received ON the date revenue is earned.

Company delivers

Cash (+A)   xx
   Fee revenue (+R, +SE)   xx

Cash is received AFTER revenue is earned.

Company delivers

Trade receivables (+A)   xx
   Fee revenue (+R, +SE)   xx

Cash (+A)   xx
   Trade receivables (-A)   xx

The revenue recognition principle's five recognition criteria are as follows: (1) the significant risks and rewards of ownership are transferred to customers, (2) the company retains neither continuing managerial involvement nor effective control over the goods sold, (3) the amount of revenue can be measured reliably, (4) it is probable that the economic benefits associated with the transaction will flow to the company, and (5) the costs related to the transaction can be measured reliably. Regardless of when cash is received, revenue is earned and recorded when these criteria are met.

SELF-STUDY **QUIZ 3-1**

This self-study quiz allows you to practice applying the revenue recognition principle under accrual accounting. Complete this quiz now to make sure you can apply this principle. The following transactions are samples of typical monthly operating activities of Canadian Tire.

1. Indicate the account titles that are affected and the type of account for each (A for asset, L for liability, and R for revenue).

2. Identify the amount of revenue that is recognized in January, the revenue that has been earned in December, and the revenue that will be earned in future periods (deferred revenue).

3. Compute the revenue recognized in January and compare it to the amount of cash received in January.

4. Which amount—revenue recognized in January or cash received in January—is a better measure of Canadian Tire's operating performance? Explain.

Refer to Canadian Tire's statement of earnings presented in Exhibit 3.1 for account titles. All amounts are in thousands of dollars.

Activity	Accounts Affected and Type of Account	Cash Received in January	Amount of Revenue Earned in		Deferred Revenue
			December	January	
(a) In January, Canadian Tire sold merchandise to customers for $480 cash.					
(b) In January, Canadian Tire sold different products to retail outlets for $520, of which $120 was in cash and the rest was on account.					
(c) In January, Canadian Tire received $2,400 in cash from customers for prior sales, of which $2,200 related to December sales.					
(d) In January, Canadian Tire signed contracts with new customers and received $50 in cash. The company provided $40 in services to these customers during January; the remainder of the services will be provided over the next three months.					
Totals					

After you complete your answers, check them with the solutions at the end of the chapter.

The Matching Process

The **MATCHING PROCESS** requires that expenses be recorded when incurred in earning revenue.

The **matching process** requires that expenses be recorded when incurred in earning revenue. In other words, all of the resources consumed in earning revenues during a specific period must be recognized in that same period, *a matching of costs with benefits.* The costs of generating revenue include expenses incurred, such as the following:

- Salaries to employees who *worked during the period* (wages expense)
- Utilities for the electricity *used during the period* (utilities expense)
- Inventory items (e.g., home renovation products, footwear, clothing, furniture) that are *sold during the period* (cost of sales)
- Facilities *rented during the period* (rent expense)
- *Use* of buildings and equipment for production purposes *during the period* (depreciation expense)

Some of these expenses are matched directly to sales revenue, such as the cost of sales and sales commissions. Other expenses, such as utilities, rent of facilities, insurance, and interest, may not be identifiable with specific sources of revenue but need to be incurred in order to generate revenue during the period.

As with revenues and cash receipts, expenses are recorded as incurred, *regardless of when cash is paid.* Cash may be paid before, during, or after an expense is incurred, as shown in Exhibit 3.4. An entry will be made on the date the expense is incurred and another one on the date of the cash payment, if at different times.

Exhibit **3.4**
Recording Expenses versus Cash Payments

- For example, fresh fruits and packaging supplies are acquired prior to their use. These items are recorded as inventory, an asset, when they are purchased, but are not expensed until they are used. Similarly, companies usually pay for rent in advance of using rental property and record the cash outlay in the Prepayments asset account, representing future benefits to the company. This asset is allocated over time to Rent expense as the property is used. In addition, part of the cost of long-term assets, such as equipment used in operations, needs to be matched with the revenues generated in the period. The portion of the assets that was used up is recognized as depreciation expense.

- In some cases, resources are used to generate revenues prior to a cash outlay. Canadian Tire's payroll expense represents the amount earned by managers and employees who prepare the products for sale to customers. It is an expense for that period. While employees are usually paid after they provide their services, wages expense and wages payable should be recorded when the service is provided by the employees.

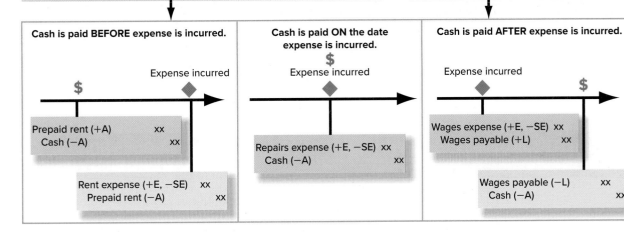

Cash is paid BEFORE expense is incurred.	**Cash is paid ON the date expense is incurred.**	**Cash is paid AFTER expense is incurred.**

Prepaid rent (+A)   xx
  Cash (−A)   xx

Rent expense (+E, −SE)   xx
  Prepaid rent (−A)   xx

Repairs expense (+E, −SE) xx
  Cash (−A)   xx

Wages expense (+E, −SE) xx
  Wages payable (+L)   xx

Wages payable (−L)   xx
  Cash (−A)   xx

PAUSE FOR FEEDBACK

The *matching process* requires that costs incurred to generate revenues be recognized in the same period—that costs be matched with revenues. Regardless of when cash is paid, expense is recorded when incurred.

SELF-STUDY QUIZ 3-2

This self-study quiz allows you to practice applying the *matching process* under accrual accounting. It is important to complete this quiz now to make sure you can apply this process.

The following transactions are samples of typical monthly operating activities of Canadian Tire.

1. Indicate the account titles that are affected and the type of account for each (A for asset, L for liability, and E for expense).

2. If an expense is to be recognized in January, indicate the amount. If an expense is not to be recognized in January, indicate why.

3. Compute the amount of expenses recognized in January and compare this amount to the cash paid in January.

Refer to Canadian Tire's statement of earnings presented in Exhibit 3.1 for account titles. All amounts are in thousands of dollars.

Activity	Accounts Affected and Type of Account	Cash Paid in January	Amount of Expense Incurred in January OR Why an Expense Is Not Recognized
(a) In January, Canadian Tire paid $900 to suppliers on account for merchandise inventory received in December. These purchases were not sold to customers yet.			
(b) In January, the cost of merchandise sold to customers was $320. These items were purchased in previous months.			
(c) In January, Canadian Tire paid $150 for rent of warehousing facilities for January, February, and March.			
(d) In January, the cost of products sold to retail outlets was $340. These items were produced in previous months.			
(e) In late January, Canadian Tire received a utility bill for $5 payable in February for electricity used in January.			
Totals			

After you complete your answers, check them with the solutions at the end of the chapter.

MANAGEMENT'S INCENTIVES TO VIOLATE ACCOUNTING RULES

A QUESTION OF ACCOUNTABILITY

The decisions of investors in the stock market are based on their expectations of a company's future earnings. When companies announce quarterly and annual earnings information, investors evaluate how well the company met expectations and adjust their investing decisions accordingly. Companies that fail to meet expectations often experience a decline in the share price. Thus, managers are motivated to produce earnings results that meet or exceed expectations to bolster share prices. Since many executives are given options to purchase company shares as part of their compensation, greed may lead some managers to make unethical accounting and reporting decisions, often involving falsifying revenues and expenses.

Fraud is a criminal offense for which managers may be sentenced to jail. Samples of fraud cases, a few involving faulty revenue and expense accounting, are shown below. Just imagine what it must have been like to be 65-year-old Bernie Ebbers or 21-year-old Barry Minkow, both sentenced to 25 years in prison for accounting fraud.

The CEO	The Fraud	Conviction/Plea	The Outcome
Bernard Madoff, 71 Madoff Investment Securities	Scammed $50 billion from investors in a Ponzi scheme in which investors receive "returns" from money paid by subsequent investors.	Confessed, December 2008	Sentenced to 150 years
Bernie Ebbers, 65 Worldcom	Recorded $11 billion in operating expenses as if they were assets.	Convicted, July 2005	Sentenced to 25 years
Sanjay Kumar, 44 Computer Associates	Recorded sales in the wrong accounting period.	Pleaded guilty, April 2006	Sentenced to 12 years
Martin Grass, 49 Rite Aid Corporation	Recorded rebates from drug companies before they were earned.	Pleaded guilty, June 2003	Sentenced to 8 years
Barry Minkow, 21 ZZZZ Best	Made up customers and sales to show profits when, in reality, the company was a sham.	Convicted, December 1988	Sentenced to 25 years
Garth Drabinsky, 60 **Myron Gotlieb**, 67 Livent Inc.	Defrauded investors of $500 million through false invoices and kickbacks.	Convicted, March 2009	Sentenced to 5 and 4 years, respectively

Many others are affected by fraud. Shareholders lose the value of their investment, employees may lose their jobs (and pension funds, as in the case of Enron), and customers and suppliers may become wary of dealing with a company operating under the cloud of fraud. As a manager, you may face an ethical dilemma in the workplace. The ethical choice is the decision you will be proud of 20 years later.

THE EXPANDED TRANSACTION ANALYSIS MODEL

LO3-4

Apply transaction analysis to examine and record the effects of operating activities on the financial statements.

We have seen the variety of business activities affecting the statement of earnings, and how they are measured. Now we need to determine how these business activities are recorded in the accounting system and reflected in the financial statements. Chapter 2 covered investing and financing activities affecting assets, liabilities, and contributed capital. We now expand the transaction analysis model presented in that chapter to include operating activities.

Transaction Analysis Rules

The complete transaction model presented in Exhibit 3.5 includes all five elements: assets, liabilities, shareholders' equity, revenues, and expenses. Recall that the retained earnings account is the accumulation of all past revenues and expenses, minus any earnings distributed as dividends to shareholders (i.e., earnings not retained in the business). Retained earnings increase when net earnings are realized and decrease when a loss occurs.

Some students attempt to memorize journal entries at the outset of the introductory accounting course. However, they often become overwhelmed by the number and complexity of transactions as the course progresses. To avoid this pitfall, you should instead be able to construct the transaction analysis model in Exhibit 3.5 on your own and use it to analyze transactions. It will be very beneficial in completing assignments and analyzing more-complex transactions in future chapters. Now let us study Exhibit 3.5 carefully to remember how the model is constructed and to understand the impact of operating activities on both the statement of financial position and the statement of earnings:

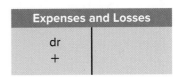

- All accounts can increase or decrease, although revenues and expenses tend to increase throughout a period. For accounts on the left side of the accounting equation, the increase symbol, +, is written on the left side of the T-account. For accounts on the right side of the accounting equation, the increase symbol, +, is written on the right side of the T-account, *except for expenses, which increase on the left side of the T-account.*

- Debits (dr) are written on the left side of each T-account and credits (cr) are written on the right.

- Every transaction affects at least two accounts.

- Revenues increase net earnings, retained earnings, and shareholders' equity. Therefore, revenues have *credit* balances; that is, to increase a revenue account, you credit it, which increases net earnings and retained earnings. Recording revenue results in either increasing an asset (such as cash or accounts receivable) or decreasing a liability (such as deferred subscriptions revenue).

- Expenses decrease net earnings, thus decreasing retained earnings and shareholders' equity. Therefore, expenses have *debit* balances (opposite of the balance in retained earnings); that is, to increase an expense, you debit it, which decreases net earnings and retained earnings. Recording an expense results in either decreasing an asset (such as supplies when used) or increasing a liability (such as wages payable when money is owed to employees).

- When revenues exceed expenses, the company reports net earnings, increasing retained earnings and shareholders' equity. However, when expenses exceed revenues, a loss results that decreases retained earnings and, thus, shareholders' equity.

In summary:

REVENUES	EXPENSES
• Increase net earnings and shareholders' equity	• Decrease net earnings and shareholders' equity
• ↑ with credits	• ↑ with debits
• Accounts have credit balances	• Accounts have debit balances

---

Exhibit **3.5**

Expanded Transaction Analysis Model

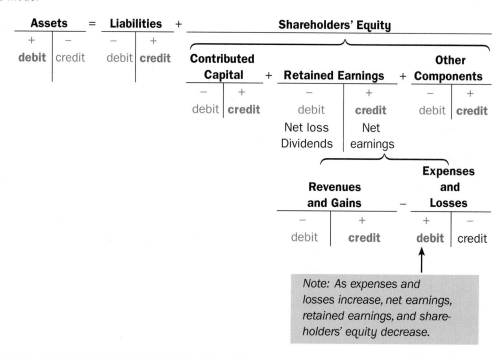

The steps to follow in analyzing transactions presented in Chapter 2 are now modified to determine the effects of earning revenues and incurring expenses. When a transaction occurs, the questions to ask are as follows:

Transaction Analysis Steps:

Step 1: **Ask → Was a revenue earned by delivering goods or services?**

If so, credit the revenue account and debit the account for what was received.

or Ask → Was an expense incurred to generate a revenue in the current period?

If so, debit the expense account and credit the account for what was received.

or Ask → If no revenue was earned or expense incurred, what was received and given?

- **Identify the accounts affected by title (e.g., cash, deferred revenue).** *Make sure that at least two accounts change.*
- **Classify the accounts by type.** Was each account an asset (A), a liability (L), shareholders' equity (SE), a revenue/gain (R), or an expense/loss (E)?
- **Determine the direction of the effect. Did the account increase [+] or decrease [−]?**

Step 2: **Verify → Is the accounting equation in balance? (A = L + SE)**

You should refer to the expanded transaction analysis model until you can construct it on your own without assistance. Study the following illustration carefully to make sure that you understand the impact of operating activities on both the statement of financial position and the statement of earnings.

Analyzing Canadian Tire's Transactions

Now we continue activities for Canadian Tire, building on the company's trial balance presented at the end of Chapter 2. It included only the effects of the investing and financing transactions that occurred during the month of February 2016.

CANADIAN TIRE CORPORATION Trial Balance As at January 31, 2016		
(in thousands)	**Debit**	**Credit**
Cash	$ 765	
Short-term investments	96	
Accounts receivable	5,790	
Notes receivable	90	
Inventories	1,765	
Prepaid expenses	96	
Other current assets	44	
Long-term receivables	731	
Long-term investments	184	
Property and equipment	4,138	
Goodwill	437	
Intangible assets	810	
Other non-current assets	48	
Accounts payable		$ 920
Accrued liabilities		1,037
Provisions		262
Short-term borrowings		89
Income taxes payable		62
Current portion of long-term debt		24
Long-term debt		2,984
Other non-current liabilities		2,297
Contributed capital		687
Retained earnings		4,152
Other components		944
Total	**$14,994**	**$14,994**

Using the transaction analysis steps, we analyze, record, and post to the T-accounts the effects of this chapter's operating activities that also occurred during the same accounting period. Because we illustrated eight investing and financing transactions in Chapter 2 using referencing of (*a*) to (*h*), we start with transaction (*i*) in this chapter. You will notice that in each journal entry in which a revenue or expense is recorded, we insert (+R → +SE) for revenues or (+E → −SE) for expenses to emphasize the effect of the transaction on the accounting equation and to help you verify that the equation remains in balance. In Chapter 4, we will complete the accounting cycle with the activities at the end of the period (January 31). All amounts are in millions of Canadian dollars, and the effects are posted to the appropriate T-accounts at the end of the illustration.

(*i*) Canadian Tire sold merchandise to customers for $480 in cash. The cost of these sales was $320.

(*Note:* This requires two entries, one for the revenue earned and one for the expense incurred in generating the revenue.)

Cash (+A)		480	
Sales revenue (+R → +SE)			480
To record cash sales.			
Cost of sales (+E → −SE)		320	
Inventories (−A)			320
To record cost of sales.			

Assets		=	Liabilities	+	Shareholders' Equity	
Cash	+480				Sales revenue	+480
Inventories	−320				Cost of sales	−320

These effects are posted to the appropriate T-accounts in Exhibit 3.6 (see the shaded amounts).

Recall that revenues are recognized when Canadian Tire sells goods and renders services regardless of the timing of cash receipts, and expenses are recognized when incurred regardless of the timing of cash payments. To highlight the difference between accrual basis accounting and cash basis accounting, we show after each transaction its net effect on net earnings and on cash.

Effect of adjustment on

Net earnings: ↑ 160
Cash: ↑ 480

(j) Canadian Tire sold different products to retail outlets for $520; $120 was received in cash and the rest was due from the outlets. The cost of products sold was $360.

Cash (+A)		120	
Accounts receivable (+A)		400	
Sales revenue (+R → +SE)			520
To record sales, partly for cash and the rest on account.			
Cost of sales (+E → −SE)		360	
Inventories (−A)			360
To record cost of sales.			

Assets		=	Liabilities	+	Shareholders' Equity	
Cash	+120				Sales revenue	+520
Accounts receivable	−400				Cost of sales	−360
Inventories	−360					

Effect of transaction on

Net earnings: ↑ 160
Cash: ↑ 120

(k) Canadian Tire received $1,400 from customers for prior sales made on account.

Cash (+A)		1,400	
Accounts receivable (−A)			1,400
To record collection from customers.			

Assets		=	Liabilities	+	Shareholders' Equity
Cash	+1,400				
Accounts receivable	−1,400				

Effect of transaction on

Net earnings: No effect
Cash: ↑ 1,400

(l) Canadian Tire signed contracts with new dealers and received $50 cash. The company earned $40 immediately by performing services for this client; the rest will be earned in February.

Cash (+A)		50	
Service revenue (+R → +SE)			40
Deferred service revenue (+L)			10
To record the receipt of cash for current and future services.			

Assets		=	Liabilities		+	Shareholders' Equity	
Cash	+50		Deferred service revenue	+10		Service revenue	+40

Effect of transaction on

Net earnings: ↑ 40
Cash: ↑ 50

(m) At the beginning of January, Canadian Tire paid $223 in advance for the following: $60 for insurance covering the next four months beginning January 1, $150 for rent of warehousing facilities for the next three months beginning January 1, and $13 for advertising to be run in February.

Prepaid expenses (+A)			223	
Cash (−A)				223

To record payment of cash for insurance, rent, and advertising.

Assets		=	Liabilities	+	Shareholders' Equity
Cash	−223				
Prepaid expenses	+223				

Effect of transaction on

Net earnings: No effect

    Cash: ↓ 223

(n) Canadian Tire paid $25 for telecommunication services, repairs, and fuel for delivery vehicles, all considered other operating expenses.

Other operating expenses (+E → −SE)		25	
Cash (−A)			25

To record payment for various expenses.

Assets		=	Liabilities	+	Shareholders' Equity	
Cash	−25				Other operating expenses	−25

Effect of transaction on

Net earnings: ↓ 25

    Cash: ↓ 25

(o) Canadian Tire ordered and received $695 in merchandise inventories; $80 was paid in cash and the rest was on account with suppliers.

Inventories (+A)		695	
Cash (−A)			80
Accounts payable (+L)			615

To record purchase of supplies with partial payment.

Assets		=	Liabilities		+	Shareholders' Equity
Cash	−80		Accounts payable	+615		
Inventories	+695					

Effect of transaction on

Net earnings: No effect

    Cash: ↓ 80

(p) Canadian Tire paid $80 in cash to employees for work in January.

Salaries and wages expense (+E → −SE)		80	
Cash (−A)			80

To record payment to employees.

Assets		=	Liabilities	+	Shareholders' Equity	
Cash	−80				Salaries and wages expense	−80

Effect of transaction on

Net earnings: ↓ 80

    Cash: ↓ 80

PAUSE FOR **FEEDBACK**

We just illustrated the steps in analyzing and recording transactions, including those involving earning revenue and incurring expenses. Now it is your turn.

SELF-STUDY **QUIZ 3-3**

For transactions (q) through (s), fill in the missing information. Be sure to post journal entries to the T-accounts in Exhibit 3.6.

(q) Canadian Tire received $71 in cash: $1 in interest earned on notes receivable and $71 in payments made on notes receivable from the trade supplier.

Effect of transaction on	Assets		=	Liabilities	+	Shareholders' Equity	
Net earnings: _____	Cash	+71				Interest revenue	+1
Cash: _____	Notes receivable	+70					

Write the journal entry, post the effects to the T-accounts, and show the effects on net earnings and cash.

(r) Canadian Tire paid $490 on accounts owed to suppliers.

Effect of transaction on	Assets	=	Liabilities	+	Shareholders' Equity
Net earnings: _____					
Cash: _____	Write the journal entry; post the effects to the T-accounts.				
	Show the effects on the accounting equation and on net earnings and cash.				

(s) Canadian Tire sold land for $35. The cost of the land is $5.

Effect of transaction on			
Net earnings: _____	Cash (+A)		35
Cash: _____	Property and equipment (−A)		5
	Gain on sale of land (Gain → +SE)		30
	To record sale of land at a gain.		

	Assets	=	Liabilities	+	Shareholders' Equity

Show the effects on the accounting equation, on net earnings, and on cash.

After you complete your answers, check them with the solutions at the end of the chapter.

Exhibit 3.6 shows the T-accounts that changed during the period because of transactions (*i*) through (*s*). The balances of all other accounts remained the same. The amounts from Canadian Tire's trial balance at the end of Chapter 2 have been included as the beginning balances in Exhibit 3.6 for the assets, liabilities, and shareholders' equity accounts. However, the accounts that are reported on the statement of earnings have zero beginning balances so that the effects of transactions on revenue and expense accounts can be accumulated over the period.

You can verify that you posted the entries for transactions (*q*) through (*s*) properly by adding the increase side and subtracting the decrease side, and then comparing your answer to the ending balance given in each of the T-accounts.

Exhibit **3.6**

T-Accounts

The beginning balances of financial statement accounts are taken from Exhibit 2.9.

ASSETS

+	Cash (A)		−
Beg. bal.	765		
(i)	480	(m)	223
(j)	120	(n)	25
(k)	1,400	(o)	80
(l)	50	(p)	80
(q)			
(s)	35	(r)	
End. bal.	2,023		

+	Accounts Receivable (A)		−
Beg. bal.	5,790		
(j)	400	(k)	1,400
End. bal.	4,790		

+	Inventories (A)		−
Beg. bal.	1,765	(i)	320
		(j)	360
(o)	695		
End. bal.	1,780		

+	Prepaid Expenses (A)		−
Beg. bal.	96		
(m)	223		
End. bal.	319		

+	Notes Receivable (A)		−
Beg. bal.	90		
		(q)	
End. bal.	20		

+	Property and Equipment, net (A)		−
Beg. bal.	4,138	(s)	5
End. bal.	4,133		

LIABILITIES

− Deferred Service Revenue (L) +	
	(l) 10
End. bal. 10	

− Accounts Payable (L) +		
	Beg.bal 920	
(r)	(o) 615	
	End.bal 1,045	

REVENUES AND GAINS

− Sales Revenue (R) +	
	(i) 480
	(j) 520
End. bal. 1,000	

− Service Revenue (R) +	
	(l) 40
End.bal 40	

− Interest Revenue (R) +	
(q)	
End. bal. 1	

− Gain on Sale of Land (G) +	
	(s) 30
End. bal. 30	

EXPENSES

+ Cost of Sales (E) −	
(i) 320	
(j) 360	
End. bal. 680	

+ Salaries and Wages Expenses (E) −	
(p) 80	
End.bal 80	

+ Other Operating Expenses (E) −	
(n) 25	
End. bal. 25	

HOW IS THE STATEMENT OF EARNINGS PREPARED AND ANALYZED?

LO3-5

Prepare a statement of earnings and explain the difference between net earnings and cash flow from operations.

As we discussed in Chapter 2, companies can prepare financial statements at any point in time. Before we consider creating any statements for Canadian Tire, however, we must first determine that the debits equal credits after all of the transactions illustrated above by generating a trial balance. Accounts are listed in financial statement order: assets, liabilities, shareholders' equity, revenues/gains, and expenses/losses. The account balances that did not change are taken from Canadian Tire's trial balance at January 31, 2016. The accounts that did change due to the operating transactions illustrated in this chapter are shaded; their balances are taken from the T-accounts summarized on the previous page. Notice that new revenue, gain, and expense accounts are added to the previous list of accounts.

CANADIAN TIRE CORPORATION Unadjusted Trial Balance As at January 31, 2016		
($ in thousands)	Debit	Credit
Cash	$ 2,023	
Short-term investments	96	
Accounts receivable	4,790	
Notes receivable	20	
Inventories	1,780	
Prepaid expenses	319	
Other current assets	44	
Long-term receivables	731	
Long-term investments	184	
Property and equipment	4,133	
Goodwill	437	
Intangible assets	810	
Other non-current assets	48	

Accounts payable		$ 1,045
Accrued liabilities		1,037
Deferred service revenue		10
Provisions		262
Short-term borrowings		89
Income taxes payable		62
Current portion of long-term debt		24
Other current liabilities		1,536
Long-term debt		2,984
Other non-current liabilities		2,297
Contributed capital		687
Retained earnings		4,152
Other components		944
Sales revenue		1,000
Service revenue		40
Interest revenue		1
Gain on sale of land		30
Cost of sales	680	
Salaries and wages	80	
Other operating expenses	25	
Total	$16,200	$16,200

Although debits do equal credits, why is the trial balance labelled "unadjusted"? Does it make sense that cash was prepaid for insurance and rent but no expense was recorded to show the amount of insurance and rent used during February? And didn't Canadian Tire use property and equipment during February to generate revenues? The answer to these questions is that no end-of-period adjustments have been made yet to reflect all revenues earned and expenses incurred during the month. Therefore, the trial balance is **unadjusted** until adjustments are made, as we discuss in Chapter 4.

Classified Statement of Earnings

The following classified or multiple-step statement of earnings is presented to highlight its structure *but note that, because it is based on unadjusted balances, it would not be presented to external users.*

CANADIAN TIRE CORPORATION	
Consolidated Statement of Earnings	
Unadjusted	
For the Month Ended January 31, 2016	
(in millions of Canadian dollars)	
Revenues	
Sales revenue	$1,000
Service revenue	40
Total revenues	1,040
Cost of sales	(680)
Gross profit	360
Operating expenses	
Salaries and wages	80
Other operating expenses	25
Total operating expenses	105
Earnings from operations	255
Other revenues and gains (expenses and losses)	
Interest revenue	1
Gain on sale of land	30
Earnings before income taxes	$ 286

This statement of earnings does not at this point reflect all revenues earned or expenses incurred in January. For example,

- The prepaid expenses account includes rent and insurance covering January and future months, but the expenses are not yet recorded for the amounts used in January. This is true of the equipment used during the month as well. Until adjusted, assets are overstated and expenses are understated.

- We have not calculated income taxes expense for the amount incurred in January and owed within the next quarter. Thus, both expenses and liabilities are understated.

- Deferred service revenue (a liability account) has not been updated for any amount of service revenue earned in January. In this case, liabilities are overstated and revenues are understated.

Chapter 4 will describe the adjustment process to update the accounting records. After the adjustments are made, the amount of income tax expense and net earnings will be determined and reported in the statement of earnings.

OPERATING ACTIVITIES

FOCUS ON
CASH FLOWS

In this chapter, we focus on cash flows from operating activities: *cash from* operating sources, primarily customers, and *cash to* suppliers and others involved in operations. The accounts most often associated with operating activities are current assets—such as accounts receivable, inventories, and prepaid expenses—and current liabilities, such as accounts payable, wages payable, and deferred revenue.

As discussed in Chapter 2, companies report cash inflows and outflows over a period of time in their **statement of cash flows** that is divided into three categories:

- **O** - Operating activities primarily with customers and suppliers, payments for interest, and income from investments. Although interest relates to borrowing, a financing activity, interest paid may be classified as an operating activity because it enters into the determination of net earnings or loss (IAS 7—Statement of Cash Flows, para. 33).

- **I** - Investing activities include buying and selling non-current assets and investments.

- **F** - Financing activities include borrowing and repaying debt, including short-term bank loans, issuing and repurchasing shares, and paying dividends.

Only transactions affecting cash are reported on the statement. An important step in constructing and analyzing the cash flow statement is identifying the various transactions as operating, investing, or financing. Let us analyze the cash T-account for Canadian Tire's transactions in this chapter, adding to transactions *(a)–(h)* from Chapter 2. Refer to transactions *(i)–(s)* illustrated earlier in the chapter, and remember, **if you see cash in a transaction, it will be reflected on the statement of cash flows.**

		+	Cash (A)	−		
		Bal.	901			
From investors	+ F	(a)	13	15	(c)	−I	For non-current assets
From bank	+ F	(b)	10	100	(d)	−I	To trade supplier
From trade supplier	+ I	(g)	10	30	(e)	−I	For investment in other companies
From customers	+ O	(i)	480	20	(f)	−F	To shareholders
From customers	+ O	(j)	120	4	(h)	−F	To bank
From customers	+ O	(k)	1,400	223	(m)	−O	For prepaid expenses
From customers	+ O	(l)	50	25	(n)	−O	For utilities, repairs and fuel
From trade supplier	+ I	(q)	71	80	(o)	−O	To trade suppliers
From investing activity	+ I	(s)	35	80	(p)	−O	To employees
				490	(r)	−O	To trade suppliers
		Bal.	2,023			

Operating activities contributed $2,050 in cash receipts during January and resulted in cash payments of $898, for a net cash inflow of $1,152.⁹ The cash flow from operating activities is different from earnings from operations of $286 that is based on accrual accounting. The difference between $286 and a net cash inflow of $1,152 is because revenue is recognized when earned, regardless of when cash is received, and expenses are recognized when incurred, regardless of when cash is paid.

To remain in business in the long run, companies must generate positive cash flows from operations. Cash is needed to pay suppliers and employees. When cash from operations is negative over a period of time, the only other ways to obtain the necessary funds are to (1) sell non-current assets, which reduces future productivity; (2) borrow from creditors at increasing interest rates to compensate for the increased risk of default on the debt; and (3) issue additional shares, where investor expectations about poor future performance drive the stock price down. There are clearly negative implications associated with generating funds through sources not directly related to operating activities.

Canadian Tire experienced net inflow of cash from operating activities over the five-year period 2011–2015, as shown below. Furthermore, the cash flow from operations differs from the reported net earnings. These differences are the result of using accrual basis accounting, where the reported revenues differ from cash receipts and the reported expenses differ from cash payments for operating purposes.

	2011	2012	2013	2014	2015
Cash flow from operations	$1,406	$743	$893	$575	$979
Net earnings	467	499	564	639	736

PAUSE FOR FEEDBACK

Every transaction affecting cash can be classified as an operating, investing, or financing effect.

Operating effects relate to receipts of cash from customers and payments to suppliers (employees, utilities, and other suppliers of goods and services for operating the business).

Investing effects relate to purchasing/selling investments or property and equipment or lending funds to/receiving repayment from others.

Financing effects relate to borrowing or repaying banks, issuing shares to investors, repurchasing shares from investors, or paying dividends to investors.

SELF-STUDY QUIZ 3-4

Canadian Tire Corporation

The transactions below relate to typical activities of the corporation. Indicate whether the transaction affected cash flow as an operating (O), investing (I), or financing (F) activity, and indicate the direction of the effect on cash (+ for increases; − for decreases):

Transactions		Type of Activity (O, I, or F)	Effect on Cash Flows (+ or −)
1.	Payment of dividends to shareholders	____	____
2.	Receipt of cash from customers	____	____
3.	Purchase of property and equipment for cash	____	____
4.	Payment of income taxes	____	____
5.	Payment of cash to suppliers	____	____
6.	Repayment of long-term debt	____	____
7.	Receipt of interest on investments	____	____
8.	Cash proceeds of long-term debt	____	____
9.	Issuance of shares	____	____
10.	Payment of interest on borrowings	____	____
11.	Payment of cash to employees	____	____
12.	Sale of property for cash	____	____

After you complete your answers, check them with the solutions at the end of the chapter.

TOTAL ASSET TURNOVER RATIO AND RETURN ON ASSETS

KEY RATIO
ANALYSIS

In Chapter 2, we discussed the current ratio, a tool to evaluate the company's ability to pay its short-term obligations with current assets—a liquidity measure. We now introduce two ratios to assess managers' use of assets in total to improve net earnings. These two ratios focus on the use of assets to generate revenue and net earnings, respectively. As we will see in other chapters, similar analysis of the use of specific types of assets provides additional information for decision makers.

LO3-6

Compute and interpret the total asset turnover ratio and the return on assets.

TOTAL ASSET TURNOVER RATIO

ANALYTICAL QUESTION → How effective is management at generating sales from assets (resources)?

RATIO AND COMPARISONS → The total asset turnover ratio is useful in answering this question. It is computed as follows:

$$\text{Total asset turnover ratio} = \frac{\text{Sales (or operating) revenues}}{\text{Average total assets}^*}$$

*Average total assets = (Beginning total assets + Ending total assets) ÷ 2

The 2015 ratio for Canadian Tire is

$$\$12,280/[(\$14,553 + \$14,988)/2] = 0.81$$

Comparisons over Time			Comparisons with Competitors	
Canadian Tire			Hudson's Bay Company*	Sears Canada Inc.*
2013	**2014**	**2015**	**2015**	**2015**
0.88	0.88	0.81	1.03	1.85

*The fiscal years of both Hudson's Bay and Sears Canada ended on January 30, 2016.

INTERPRETATIONS

In General → The total asset turnover ratio measures the sales generated per dollar of assets. A high total asset turnover ratio signifies efficient management of assets; a low total asset turnover ratio signifies less-efficient management. A company's products and business strategy contribute significantly to its total asset turnover ratio. However, when competitors are similar, management's ability to control the firm's assets is vital in determining its success. Stronger financial performance improves the total asset turnover ratio.

Creditors and security analysts use this ratio to assess a company's effectiveness at controlling current and non-current assets. In a well-run business, creditors expect the ratio to fluctuate because of seasonal upswings and downturns. For example, as inventory is built up prior to a high-sales season, companies need to borrow funds. The total asset turnover ratio declines with this increase in assets. Eventually, the season's high sales provide the cash needed to repay the loans. The total asset turnover ratio then rises with the increased sales.

Focus Company Analysis → Canadian Tire's total asset turnover ratio was relatively stable for the two years 2013 and 2014, but decreased for 2015, suggesting a decrease in management's effectiveness in using assets to generate revenue. Its assets increased during 2015, but its revenue did not keep pace with the increased assets.

Compared to its competitors, Canadian Tire's 2015 total asset turnover ratio is lower than the ratios of both Hudson's Bay and Sears Canada. The difference in ratios is due in part to differences in operating strategy and the mix of products and services offered by these companies. Sears's relatively higher ratio is due to lower reported amounts for receivables and intangible assets, which reduce its total assets.

SELECTED FOCUS COMPANY TOTAL ASSET TURNOVER RATIOS—2015	
BCE	0.47
WestJet Airlines	0.82
Gildan Activewear	1.09

A Few Cautions → The total asset turnover ratio may decrease because of seasonal fluctuation, but a declining ratio may also be caused by changes in corporate policies leading to a rising level of assets. Examples include relaxing credit policies for new customers and reducing collection efforts in accounts receivable. A detailed analysis of the changes in the key components of assets is needed to determine the causes of a change in the total asset turnover ratio, and thus in management's decisions. Remember that any one ratio is not sufficient as a basis for investment decisions.

RETURN ON ASSETS (ROA)

ANALYTICAL QUESTION → How well has management used the total invested capital provided by debt holders and shareholders during the period?

RATIO AND COMPARISONS → Analysts refer to the rate of return on assets (ROA) as a useful measure in addressing this issue. It is computed as follows:

$$\text{Return on assets} = \frac{\text{Net earnings} + \text{Interest expense (net of tax)}}{\text{Average total assets}}$$

Both the total asset turnover ratio and the return on assets measure management's effectiveness at utilizing the company's resources: the first in generating revenue during the period, the second in generating after-tax return on the use of assets.

The return on assets takes into consideration the resources contributed by both shareholders and creditors. For this reason, the return to shareholders or net earnings is augmented by the return to creditors, which is interest expense. Interest expense is measured net of income tax because it represents the net cost of the funds provided by the creditors to the corporation. The returns to both shareholders and creditors are measured net of tax in the numerator of this ratio.

The 2015 ratio for Canadian Tire is

$$\frac{\$736 + \$107^* \times (1 - 0.265)^{**}}{[(\$14{,}553 + 14{,}988)/2]} = 0.055 \text{ (or 5.5\%)}$$

*As disclosed in Note 33 to Canadian Tire's financial statements.
**Income tax rate = income tax expense ÷ earnings before income taxes.

Comparisons over Time			Comparisons with Competitors	
Canadian Tire			Hudson's Bay Company*	Sears Canada Inc.*
2013	**2014**	**2015**	**2015**	**2015**
5.4%	5.2%	5.5%	4.0%	−3.7%

*The fiscal years of both Hudson's Bay and Sears Canada ended on January 30, 2016.

SELECTED FOCUS COMPANY COMPARISONS: RETURN ON ASSETS—2015	
BCE	7.2
WestJet Airlines	8.3
Gildan Activewear	11.7

INTERPRETATIONS

In General → ROA measures how much the firm earned from the use of its assets. It is the broadest measure of profitability and management effectiveness, independent of financing strategy. ROA allows investors to compare management's investment performance against alternative investment options. Firms with higher ROA are doing a better job of selecting new investments, all other things being equal. Company managers often compute the measure on a division-by-division basis and use it to evaluate division managers' relative performance.

Focus Company Analysis → The ratio decreased slightly in 2014 but recovered in 2015. Both Hudson's Bay and Sears Canada were less effective than Canadian Tire in using invested capital to generate return to both investors and creditors. Sears's ratio is negative because it reported a net loss for 2015.

A Few Cautions →Effective analysis of ROA requires an understanding of why ROA differs from prior levels and from the ROA of the company's competitors. Analysis of the differences in ROA over time and across companies can be facilitated by a decomposition of this ratio into two other ratios, as shown later in Chapter 12.

PAUSE FOR
FEEDBACK

The total asset turnover ratio measures management's effectiveness in utilizing the company's resources to generate revenue during the period, while the return on assets measures management's effectiveness at utilizing total assets in generating after-tax return for both creditors and shareholders. We just illustrated the computation of both ratios for Canadian Tire and explained how these ratios should be interpreted. Now it is your turn to compute and interpret these ratios for another company.

SELF-STUDY **QUIZ 3-5**

Sears Canada Inc.

Sears Canada is one of the biggest Canadian retailers. It operates a large number of department stores, which sell home fashions, appliances, apparel, home electronics, and garden products. It also sells merchandise online. Selected information about the company's resources and operations are presented below (amounts in millions of Canadian dollars):

	2015	2014	2013	2012	2011	2010
Total assets	$1,633	$1,774	$2,392	$2,479	$2,834	$3,072
Total revenue	3,146	3,425	3,992	4,301	4,619	4,939
Net earnings	(68)	(338)	446	101	(60)	115
Interest expense	6	7	11	13	9	17
Tax rate	8%	6%	9%	11%	14%	34%

Required:

1. Complete the following table by computing the total asset turnover ratio and the return on assets for 2015 and 2014.

	2015	2014	2013	2012	2011
Total asset turnover ratio			1.64	1.62	1.56
Return on assets (ROA)			18.7%	4.0%	−2.0%

2. What conclusion can you draw from these ratios about the company's effectiveness in managing the economic resources under its control?

After you complete your answers, check them with the solutions at the end of the chapter

ACCOUNTING STANDARDS
FOR PRIVATE ENTERPRISES

The accounting concepts and procedures covered in this chapter are equally applicable to Canadian private enterprises.

DEMONSTRATION **CASE**

This case is a continuation of the Terrific Lawn Maintenance Corporation case introduced in Chapter 2. The company was established with supplies, property, and equipment purchased ready for business. The statement of financial position at April 7, 2017, based on investing and financing activities, is as follows:

TERRIFIC LAWN MAINTENANCE CORPORATION
Statement of Financial Position
At April 7, 2017

Assets		**Liabilities**	
Current Assets		*Current Liabilities*	
Cash	$ 3,800	Short-term notes payable	$ 400
Notes receivable	1,250	Total current liabilities	400
Total current assets	5,050	Long-term notes payable	4,000
		Total liabilities	4,400
Equipment	4,600	*Shareholders' Equity*	
Land	3,750	Contributed capital	9,000
Total assets	**$13,400**	**Total liabilities and**	**$13,400**
		shareholders' equity	

The following completed activities occurred during the rest of April 2017:

a. Purchased and used gasoline for mowers and edgers, paying $90 in cash at a local gas station.

b. In early April, received from the city $1,600 cash in advance for lawn maintenance service for April through July ($400 each month). The entire amount was recorded as deferred revenue.

c. In early April, purchased insurance costing $300 covering six months, April through September. The entire payment was recorded as prepaid expenses.

d. Mowed lawns for residential customers who are billed every two weeks. A total of $5,200 of service was billed in April.

e. Residential customers paid $3,500 on their accounts.

f. Paid wages every two weeks. Total cash paid in April was $3,900.

g. Received a bill for $320 from the local gas station for additional gasoline purchased on account and used in April. The bill will be paid in May.

h. Paid $700 on the long-term note owed to XYZ Lawn Supply and $40 in interest.

i. Paid $100 on accounts payable.

j. Collected $1,250 on the note owed by the city to the company as well as $12 in interest.

Required:

1. a. On a separate sheet of paper, set up T-accounts for cash, accounts receivable, notes receivable, prepaid expenses, equipment, land, accounts payable, deferred revenue, short-term notes payable, long-term notes payable, contributed capital, mowing revenue, interest revenue, fuel expense, wages expense, and interest expense. Beginning balances for asset, liability, and equity accounts should be taken from the preceding statement of financial position. Beginning balances for operating accounts are $0. Indicate these balances on the T-accounts.

   b. Analyze each transaction using the steps outlined in Chapter 2. Please refer to the expanded transaction analysis model presented in this chapter.

   c. On a separate sheet of paper, prepare journal entries to record the transactions above in chronological order and indicate their effects on the accounting model (Assets = Liabilities + Shareholders' Equity) as well as their effects on net earnings and cash. Verify that the accounting equation is in balance.

   d. Enter the effects of each transaction in the appropriate T-accounts. Identify each amount with its letter in the list of activities.

   e. Compute balances in each of the T-accounts.

2. On the cash T-account, identify each transaction as O for operating activity, I for investing activity, and F for financing activity.

3. Use the amounts in the T-accounts to prepare an unadjusted classified statement of earnings for Terrific Lawn Maintenance Corporation for the month ended April 30, 2017. (Adjustments to accounts will be presented in Chapter 4.)

We strongly recommend that you prepare your own answers to these requirements and then check your answers with the following solution.

SUGGESTED **SOLUTION**

1. b. and c. Transaction analysis, journal entries, effects on accounting equation, and effects on net earnings and cash:

(a)

| Fuel expense (+E → −SE) | | | 90 | |
| Cash (−A) | | | | 90 |

Assets	=	**Liabilities**	+	**Shareholders' Equity**
Cash	−90			Fuel expense	−90

Effect of transaction on
Net earnings: ↓ 90
Cash: ↓ 90

(b)

| Cash (+A) | | | 1,600 | |
| Deferred revenue (+L) | | | | 1,600 |

Assets	=	**Liabilities**	+	**Shareholders' Equity**
Cash	+1,600	Deferred revenue	+1,600	

Effect of transaction on
Net earnings: No effect
Cash: ↑ 1,600

(c)

| Prepaid expenses (+A) | | | 300 | |
| Cash (−A) | | | | 300 |

Assets	=	**Liabilities**	+	**Shareholders' Equity**
Cash	−300			
Prepaid expense	+300			

Effect of transaction on
Net earnings: No effect
Cash: ↓ 300

(d)

| Accounts receivable (+A) | | | 5,200 | |
| Mowing revenue (+R → +SE) | | | | 5,200 |

Assets	=	**Liabilities**	+	**Shareholders' Equity**
Accounts receivable	+5,200			Mowing revenue	+5,200

Effect of transaction on
Net earnings: ↑ 5,200
Cash: No effect

(e)

| Cash (+A) | | | 3,500 | |
| Accounts receivable (−A) | | | | 3,500 |

Assets	=	**Liabilities**	+	**Shareholders' Equity**
Cash	+3,500			
Accounts receivable	−3,500			

Effect of transaction on
Net earnings: No effect
Cash: ↑ 3,500

(f)

| Wage expense (+E → −SE) | | | 3,900 | |
| Cash (−A) | | | | 3,900 |

Assets	=	**Liabilities**	+	**Shareholders' Equity**
Cash	−3,900			Wages expense	−3,900

Effect of transaction on
Net earnings: ↓ 3,900
Cash: ↓ 3,900

(g)

| Fuel expense (+E → −SE) | | | 320 | |
| Accounts payable (+L) | | | | 320 |

Assets	=	**Liabilities**	+	**Shareholders' Equity**
		Accounts payable	+320	Fuel expense	−320

Effect of transaction on
Net earnings: ↓ 320
Cash: No effect

(h)

Long-term notes payable (−L)			700	
Interest expense (+E → −SE)			40	
Cash (−A)				740

Assets	=	**Liabilities**	+	**Shareholders' Equity**
Cash	−740	Long-term notes payable	−700	Interest expense	−40

Effect of transaction on
Net earnings: ↓ 40
Cash: ↓ 740

(i)

| Accounts payable (−L) | | | 100 | |
| Cash (−A) | | | | 100 |

Assets	=	**Liabilities**	+	**Shareholders' Equity**
Cash	−100	Accounts payable	−100	

Effect of transaction on
Net earnings: No effect
Cash: ↓ 100

(j)

Cash (+A)	1,262	
Notes receivable (−A)		1,250
Interest revenue (+R → +SE)		12

Effect of transaction on

Net earnings: ↓ 12

Cash: ↓ 1,262

Assets		=	Liabilities	+	Shareholders' Equity	
Cash	+1,262				Interest revenue	+12
Notes receivable	−1,250					

1. a., d, and e. T-Accounts:

The beginning balances of the statement of financial position accounts are taken from the solutions to the demonstration case in Chapter 2.

ASSETS

+	Cash (A)		−		+	Accounts Receivable (A)		−		+	Notes Receivable (A)		−
Beg. bal.	3,800				*(d)*	5,200	*(e)*	3,500		Beg. bal.	1,250		
(b)	1,600	*(a)*	90		End. bal.	1,700						*(j)*	1,250
(e)	3,500	*(c)*	300							End. bal.	0		
(j)	1,262	*(f)*	3,900										
		(h)	740										
		(i)	100										
End. bal.	5,032												

+	Prepaid Expenses (A)	−		+	Equipment (A)	−		+	Land (A)	−
(c)	300			Beg. bal.	4,600			Beg. bal.	3,750	
End. bal.	300			End. bal.	4,600			End. bal.	3,750	

LIABILITIES

−	Accounts Payable (L)		+		−	Deferred Revenue (L)		+		−	Short-Term Notes Payable (L)		+
(h)	100	*(g)*	320				*(b)*	1,600				Beg.bal	700
		End. bal.	220				End. bal.	1,600				End. bal.	700

−	Long-Term Notes Payable (L)		+
		Beg. bal.	4,000
(h)	700		
		End. bal.	3,300

SHAREHOLDERS' EQUITY

−	Contributed Capital (SE)	+
		Beg. bal.	9,000
		End. bal.	9,000

REVENUES

−	Mowing Revenue (R)	+		−	Interest Revenue (R)	+
		(d)	5,200			*(j)*	12
		End. bal.	5,200			End. bal.	12

EXPENSES

+	Wages Expense (E)	−		+	Fuel Expense (E)	−		+	Interest Expense (E)	−
(f)	3,900			*(a)*	90			*(h)*	40	
End. bal.	3,900			*(g)*	320			End. bal.	40	
				End. bal.	410					

2.

			Cash (A)				
		+			**−**		
	Beg.		3,800				
From customers +O	(b)		1,600	90	(a)	−O	For fuel
From customers +O	(e)		3,500	300	(c)	−O	For insurance
$12 for interest +O;				3,900	(f)	−O	To employees
$1,250 for principal + I;	(j)		1,262				
				740	(h)	−O	$40 for interest; −F; $700 for principal
				100	(i)	−O	To suppliers
			5,032				

3.

TERRIFIC LAWN MAINTENANCE CORPORATION
Unadjusted Statement of Earnings
For the Month Ended April 30, 2017

Revenues	
Mowing revenue	$5,200
Operating Expenses	
Fuel expense	410
Wages expense	3,900
Total operating expenses	4,310
Earnings from operations	890
Other items	
Interest revenue	12
Interest expense	(40)
Earnings before income tax	862
Income tax expense	0
Net earnings	$ 862
Earnings per share for the month	$ 0.57*

← To be computed and recorded after adjustments are made to revenue and expense accounts (Chapter 4)

*862/1,500 shares

APPENDIX 3A: EARNINGS MEASUREMENT AND COMPREHENSIVE INCOME

LO3-S1

Explain earnings measurement and comprehensive income.

Earnings Measurement

The measurement of earnings continues to be a subject of debate. Accountants have attempted over the years to estimate the true earnings that an entity achieves during a specific period. Until recently, the dominant approach to earnings measurement has focused on measurement of revenues and expenses. The revenue recognition principle, matching process, and mixed-attribute measurement model were predominant in measuring revenues, expenses, gains, and losses that are reported on the statement of earnings. Consequently, the values of assets and liabilities reported on the statement of financial position did not necessarily reflect their current values but the values that resulted from the application of these accounting concepts and measurement rules. For example, depreciation of property and equipment reflects an allocation of historical acquisition costs instead of a decline in the current value of these assets over time.

More recently, the desire to provide more relevant information for decision-making purposes has focused the attention of accounting standard setters toward measuring the current values of assets and liabilities. While the measurement of assets and liabilities at their current values is consistent with economic theory and leads to an estimation of economic earnings, the actual determination of current value is not a simple task. Different measures of current value have been proposed over time and are currently used in determining the values reported on the statement of financial position. Ideally, companies should measure their assets and liabilities at fair value, or exit value, which is defined as "the price that would be received to sell an asset or paid to transfer a liability in an orderly transaction between market participants at the measurement date."[10] Because of practical difficulties in determining a price for an asset or liability in the absence of an active market, accounting standard setters have provided guidance to accountants for the measurement of fair value under different circumstances.

The lack of active markets for many assets and liabilities has resulted in the use of different valuation approaches, ranging from historical cost to exit value. Hence, mixed attributes of assets and liabilities are measured and reported in financial statements. The following table summarizes the valuation bases that are currently permitted by IFRS for the reporting of asset and liability values on the statement of financial position:

Asset or Liability Group	Valuation Basis
Financial assets (e.g., investment in shares of other corporations, trade receivables, notes receivable)	Amortized cost or fair value
Inventories	Lower of cost and net realizable value
Property, plant, and equipment	Depreciated cost or recoverable amount
Investment properties (e.g., commercial real estate properties)	Depreciated cost or fair value
Intangible assets	Amortized cost or fair value
Financial liabilities	Amortized cost or fair value
The concepts of amortized cost, net realizable value and recoverable amount are discussed in later chapters.	

Because end-of-period valuations are not based on actual exchange transactions between the company and outside parties, the gains and losses that result from such valuations are usually reported separately in a statement of comprehensive income, and distinguished from gains and losses that have been realized through actual transactions. This also leads to the preparation of a statement of changes in equity that reconciles the values reported on the statement of financial position to those reported on the statement of comprehensive income. The effects of the various asset and liability valuation methods on the values reported on financial statements are discussed in later chapters.[11]

Statement of Comprehensive Income

The statement of earnings includes the results of operations for a specific accounting period as well as the effects of discontinued operations. Over the years, accounting academics and standard setters have debated whether the statement of earnings should include additional elements reflecting unrealized changes in the values of specific assets and liabilities. Hence, publicly accountable enterprises are now required to disclose additional information in a statement of comprehensive income. The additional components of income reflect the financial effect of events that cause changes in shareholders' equity, other than investments by shareholders or distributions to shareholders. The additional components of income, or *other comprehensive income*, include unrealized gains and losses on certain financial instruments, as well as other items discussed in advanced accounting courses. The net earnings and other comprehensive income totals are then combined to create a final total called comprehensive income (the bottom line for this statement).

The statement of comprehensive income for Canadian Tire for the year ended January 2, 2016 (see Exhibit 3.7), includes specific adjustments to net earnings. Measurement of the various components of other comprehensive income (loss) is rather complex and is covered in advanced accounting courses.

CANADIAN TIRE COMPANY Consolidated Statements of Comprehensive Income For the Year Ended January 2, 2016 (in millions of Canadian dollars)	Year Ended January 2, 2016	Year Ended January 3, 2015
Net income	$ 736.9	$ 639.3
Other comprehensive income		
Items that may be reclassified subsequently to net earnings:		
Cash flow hedges:		
Gains	275.6	114.0
Reclassification of gains to non-financial assets	(207.4)	(77.5)
Reclassification of gains to income	(3.0)	(1.5)
Available-for-sale financial assets:		
(Losses)	(0.5)	(0.1)
Reclassification of gains to income	–	(0.1)
Item that will not be reclassified subsequently to net income:		
Actuarial gains (losses)	0.8	(13.2)
Other comprehensive income	$ 65.5	$ 21.6

Source: Canadian Tire Corporation, Annual Report 2015.

Exhibit 3.7

Statement of Comprehensive Income

REAL-WORLD EXCERPT

Canadian Tire Corporation

CHAPTER **TAKE-AWAYS**

3-1. Describe a typical business operating cycle and explain the necessity for the periodicity assumption.

- The operating cycle, or the cash-to-cash cycle, is the time it takes to purchase goods or services from suppliers, sell the goods or services to customers, and collect cash from customers.
- The periodicity assumption means that we can measure and report financial information periodically by assuming that the long life of the company can be cut into shorter periods.

3-2. Explain how business activities affect the elements of the statement of earnings.

Elements on the classified statement of earnings are as follows:

a. Revenues are increases in assets or settlements of liabilities from ongoing operations.

b. Expenses are decreases in assets or increases in liabilities from ongoing operations.

c. Gains are increases in assets or settlements of liabilities from peripheral activities.

d. Losses are decreases in assets or increases in liabilities from peripheral activities.

3-3. Explain the accrual basis of accounting and apply the revenue recognition principle and matching process to measure net earnings.

When applying accrual accounting concepts, revenues are recognized (recorded) when earned and expenses are recognized when incurred.

- Based on the revenue recognition principle, we recognize revenues when the earnings process is complete or nearly complete, an exchange has taken place, and collection is probable.
- Based on the matching process, we recognize expenses when incurred in generating revenue.

3-4. Apply transaction analysis to examine and record the effects of operating activities on the financial statements.

The expanded transaction analysis model includes revenues and expenses:

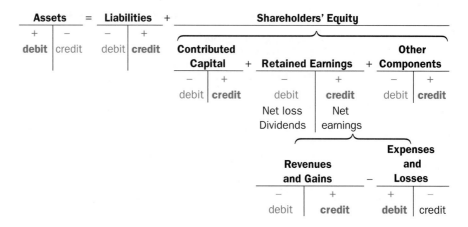

3-5. Prepare a classified statement of earnings and explain the difference between net earnings and cash flow from operations.

A classified statement of earnings includes a number of sections and subtotals to aid the user in identifying the company's earnings from operations for the year, and to highlight the effect of other items on net earnings. Net earnings is the difference between revenues/gains and expenses/losses, whereas cash flow from operations equals the difference between cash receipts and cash payments related to operations. Net earnings differs from cash flow from operations because the revenue recognition principle and matching process result in the recognition of revenues and related expenses that are independent of the timing of cash receipts and payments.

3-6. Compute and interpret the total asset turnover ratio and the return on assets.

The total asset turnover ratio (sales ÷ average total assets) measures the sales generated from the use of assets. The higher the ratio, the more efficient the company is at managing assets. The return on assets (ROA) measures how much the company earned from the use of assets. It provides information on profitability and management's effectiveness in utilizing assets. An increasing ROA over time suggests increased efficiency. ROA is computed as the sum of net earnings and interest expense (net of tax) divided by average total assets.

In this chapter, we discussed the operating cycle and accounting concepts relevant to income determination: the periodicity assumption, definitions for the statement of earnings elements (revenues, expenses, gains, and losses), the revenue recognition principle, and the matching process. These accounting principles are defined in accordance with the accrual basis of accounting, which requires revenues to be recorded when earned and expenses to be recorded when incurred in generating revenues during the period. We expanded the transaction analysis model introduced in Chapter 2 by adding revenues and expenses. In Chapter 4, we discuss the activities at the end of the accounting period: the adjustment process, the preparation of adjusted financial statements, and the closing process.

KEY **RATIOS**

The total asset turnover ratio measures the sales generated from the use of assets. A high ratio suggests that the company is managing its assets (resources used to generate revenues) efficiently. It is computed as follows:

$$\text{Total asset turnover ratio} = \frac{\text{Sales (or operating) revenues}}{\text{Average total assets}^*}$$

The return on assets measures how much the company earned from the use of assets during the period. A high ratio suggests that the company is managing its assets efficiently. It is computed as follows:

$$\text{Return on assets (ROA)} = \frac{\text{Net earnings + Interest expense (net of tax)}}{\text{Average total assets}^*}$$

*(Beginning total assets + Ending total assets) ÷ 2

FINDING **FINANCIAL INFORMATION**

STATEMENT OF FINANCIAL POSITION
Current Assets
    Cash
    Accounts and notes receivable
    Inventories
    Prepaid expenses
Non-current Assets
    Long-term investments
    Property, and equipment
    Intangibles
Current Liabilities
    Accounts payable
    Notes payable
    Accrued liabilities
    Deferred revenue
Non-current Liabilities
    Long-term debt
Shareholders' Equity
    Contributed capital
    Retained earnings

STATEMENT OF EARNINGS
Revenues
    Sales (from various operating activities),
    investment income
Expenses
    Cost of sales, rent, wages, interest,
    depreciation, insurance, etc.
Pretax Earnings
    Income tax expense
Net Earnings

STATEMENT OF CASH FLOWS
Under Operating Activities
    + Cash from customers
    + Cash from interest
    − Cash to suppliers
    − Cash to employees
    − Cash for interest
    − Cash for income taxes

NOTES
**Under Summary of Significant Accounting
Policies**
    Description of company's revenue
    recognition policy

QUESTIONS

1. Assume that you have just opened a small gift store that specializes in gift items imported from Asia. Explain the typical business operating cycle for your store.

2. Explain what the periodicity assumption means in accounting.

3. Write the statement of earnings equation and define each element.

4. Explain the difference between
   a. revenues and gains
   b. expenses and losses

5. Define *accrual accounting* and contrast it with *cash basis accounting*.

6. What conditions must normally be met for revenue to be recognized under the accrual basis of accounting?

7. Explain the matching process.

8. Explain why shareholders' equity is increased by revenues and decreased by expenses.

9. Explain why revenues are recorded as credits and expenses as debits.

10. Complete the following matrix by entering either "debit" or "credit" in each cell:

Item	Increase	Decrease
Revenues		
Expenses		
Gains		
Losses		

11. Complete the following matrix by entering either "increase" or "decrease" in each cell:

Item	Debit	Credit
Revenues		
Expenses		
Gains		
Losses		

12. Identify whether each of the following transactions results in a cash flow effect from operating, investing, or financing activities, and indicate the effect on cash (+ for increase and − for decrease). If there is no cash flow effect, write "none":

Transaction	Operating, Investing, or Financing Effect	Direction of the Effect
Cash paid to suppliers		
Sale of goods on account		
Cash received from customers		
Purchase of investments for cash		
Cash paid for interest		
Issuance of shares for cash		

13. State the equation for the total asset turnover ratio, and explain how it is interpreted.
14. State the equation for the return on assets and explain how it is interpreted.
15. (Appendix 3A) Briefly explain how net earnings are measured and why publicly accountable enterprises are required to prepare a statement of comprehensive income.

connect   MINI-EXERCISES

LO3-1,3-2,3-3   M3-1   Matching Definitions with Terms

Match each definition with its related term by entering the appropriate letter in the space provided. There should be only one definition per term (that is, there are more definitions than terms).

Term	Definition
____ (1) Losses	A. Record revenues when earned and measurable (the significant risks and rewards of ownership are transferred to the buyer, it is probable that future economic benefits will flow to the entity, and the benefits and the costs associated with the transaction can be measured reliably).
____ (2) Matching process	
____ (3) Revenues	B. The time it takes to purchase goods or services from suppliers, sell goods or services to customers, and collect cash from customers.
____ (4) Periodicity assumption	C. Record expenses when incurred in earning revenue.
____ (5) Operating cycle	D. Decreases in assets or increases in liabilities from ongoing operations.
	E. Report the long life of a company in shorter time periods.
	F. Increases in assets or decreases in liabilities from ongoing operations.
	G. Decreases in assets or increases in liabilities from peripheral transactions.

LO3-3   M3-2   Reporting Cash Basis versus Accrual Basis Earnings

Mostert Music Company had the following transactions in March:

a. Sold instruments to customers for $15,000; received $10,000 in cash and the rest on account.
b. Determined that the cost of the instruments sold was $9,000.
c. Purchased $3,000 of new instruments inventory; paid $1,000 in cash and the rest on account.
d. Paid $750 in wages for the month.
e. Received a $200 bill for utilities that will be paid in April.
f. Received $3,000 from customers as deposits on orders of new instruments to be sold to customers in April.

Complete the following statements:

Cash Basis Statement of Earnings		Accrual Basis Statement of Earnings	
Revenues	$_____	Revenues	$_____
Cash sales	_____	Sales to customers	_____
Customer deposits	_____		
Expenses		Expenses	
Inventory purchases	_____	Cost of sales	_____
Wages paid	_____	Wages expense	_____
	_____	Utilities expense	_____
Net earnings	_____	Net earnings	_____

Does the cash basis or the accrual basis of accounting provide a better indication of the operating performance of Mostert Music Company in March? Explain.

LO3-2,3-3 **M3-3** **Identifying Revenues**

Craig's Bowling Inc. operates several bowling centres (for games and equipment sales). The following transactions occurred in November 2017. If revenue is to be recognized in **November**, indicate the account title and amount of revenue. If revenue is not to be recognized in November, explain why.

Activity	Account Title and Amount of Revenue
a. Craig's collected $15,000 from customers for games played in November.	
b. Craig's sold bowling equipment inventory for $8,000; received $3,000 in cash and the rest on account.	
c. Craig's received $4,000 from customers on account who purchased merchandise in October.	
d. The men's and ladies' bowling leagues gave Craig's a deposit of $2,500 for the upcoming fall season.	

LO3-2,3-3 **M3-4** **Identifying Expenses**

Craig's Bowling Inc. operates several bowling centres (for games and equipment sales). The following transactions occurred in November 2017. If expense is to be recognized in **November**, indicate the account title and amount of expense. If expense is not to be recognized in November, explain why.

Activity	Account Title and Amount of Revenue
a. Craig's sold bowling merchandise costing $6,800.	
b. Craig's paid $800 on the electricity bill for October (recorded as expense in October).	
c. Craig's paid $3,500 to employees for work in November.	
d. Craig's purchased $1,500 in insurance for coverage from October 1 to December 31.	
e. Craig's paid $700 to plumbers for repairing a broken pipe in the restrooms.	
f. Craig's received the November electricity bill for $900 to be paid in December.	

LO3-4 **M3-5** **Recording Revenues**

For each of the transactions in M3-3, write the journal entry in good form.

LO3-4 **M3-6** **Recording Expenses**

For each of the transactions in M3-4, write the journal entry in good form.

LO3-4 **M3-7** **Determining the Financial Statement Effects of Operating Activities Involving Revenues**

Craig's Bowling Inc. operates several bowling centres (for games and equipment sales). The following transactions occurred in November 2017. For each of the following transactions, complete the tabulation, indicating the amount and effect (+ for increase and – for decrease) of each transaction. (Remember that A = L + SE, R – E = NE, and NE affects SE through retained earnings.) Write "N" if there is no effect. The first transaction is provided as an example.

	Statement of Financial Position			Statement of Earnings		
Transaction	**Assets**	**Liabilities**	**Shareholders' Equity**	**Revenues**	**Expenses**	**Net Earnings**
a. Craig's collected $15,000 from customers for games played in November.	+15,000	N	+15,000	+15,000	N	+15,000
b. Craig's sold bowling equipment inventory for $8,000; received $3,000 in cash and the rest on account.						

c. Craig's received $4,000 from customers on account who purchased merchandise in October.					
d. The men's and ladies' bowling leagues gave Craig's a deposit of $2,500 for the upcoming fall season.					

LO3-4

M3-8　**Determining the Financial Statement Effects of Operating Activities Involving Expenses**

Craig's Bowling Inc. operates several bowling centres (for games and equipment sales). The following transactions occurred in November 2017. For each of the following transactions, complete the tabulation, indicating the amount and effect (+ for increase and − for decrease) of each transaction. (Remember that A = L + SE, R − E = NE, and NE affects SE through retained earnings.) Write "N" if there is no effect. The first transaction is provided as an example.

	Statement of Financial Position			Statement of Earnings		
Transaction	**Assets**	**Liabilities**	**Shareholders' Equity**	**Revenues**	**Expenses**	**Net Earnings**
a. Craig's sold bowling merchandise costing $6,800.	−6,800	N	−6,800	N	+6,800	−6,800
b. Craig's paid $800 on the electricity bill for October (recorded as expense in October).						
c. Craig's paid $3,500 to employees for work in November.						
d. Craig's purchased $1,500 in insurance for coverage from October 1 to December 31.						
e. Craig's paid $700 to plumbers for repairing a broken pipe in the restrooms.						
f. Craig's received the November electricity bill for $900 to be paid in December.						

LO3-5

M3-9　**Preparing a Simple Statement of Earnings**

Given the transactions in M3-7 and M3-8 (including the examples), prepare a statement of earnings for Craig's Bowling Inc. for the month of November 2017.

LO3-5

M3-10　**Identifying the Operating Activities in a Statement of Cash Flows**

Given the transactions in M3-7 and M3-8 (including the examples), indicate how the transactions will affect the statement of cash flows for Craig's Bowling Inc. for the month of November 2017. Create a table similar to the partial table below for transactions a. through j. Use O for operating, I for investing, and F for financing activities and indicate the direction of their effects on cash (+ for increases in cash; − for decreases in cash). Also include the amount of cash to be reported on the statement. If there is no effect on the statement of cash flows, write "N."

Transaction	Type of Activity (O, I, or F)	Effect on Cash Flows (+ or − and amount)
a		
b		
etc.		

■ LO3-6   **M3-11**   **Computing and Interpreting the Total Asset Turnover Ratio and the Return on Assets Ratio**

The following data are from annual reports of Jen's Jewellery Company:

	2018	2017	2016
Total assets	$ 60,000	$ 53,000	$ 41,000
Sales revenue	163,000	151,000	132,000
Net earnings	45,000	40,000	25,000
Interest expense (after tax)	1,500	1,200	1,000

Compute Jen's total asset turnover and the return on assets ratio for 2017 and 2018. What do these results suggest to you about Jen's Jewellery Company?

connect EXERCISES

■ LO3-2   **E3-1**   **Inferring Statement of Earnings Values**

Supply the missing dollar amounts for the 2017 statement of earnings of Ultimate Style Company for each of the following independent cases:

	Case A	Case B	Case C	Case D	Case E
Sales revenue	$900	$700	$410	$?	$?
Selling expense	?	150	80	400	250
Cost of sales	?	380	?	500	310
Income tax expense	?	30	20	40	30
Gross profit	400	?	?	?	440
Earnings before income tax	200	90	?	190	?
Administrative expense	150	?	60	100	80
Net earnings	170	?	50	?	80

■ LO3-2   **E3-2**   **Preparing a Statement of Earnings**

The following data were taken from the records of Village Corporation at December 31, 2017:

Sales revenue	$70,000
Gross profit	24,500
Selling (distribution) expense	8,000
Administrative expense	?
Earnings before income tax	10,000
Income tax rate	30%
Number of shares outstanding	4,000

Required:

Prepare a complete statement of earnings for the company (showing both gross profit and earnings from operations). Show all computations. (*Hint:* Set up the side captions starting with sales revenue and ending with earnings per share; use the amounts and percentages given to infer missing values.)

■ LO3-2,3-3   **E3-3**   **Identifying Revenues**

Revenues are normally recognized when the entity has transferred to the buyer the significant risks and rewards of ownership of the goods, it retains neither continuing managerial involvement to the degree usually associated with ownership nor effective control over the goods, it is probable that future economic benefits will flow to the company, and the benefits from and costs associated with the transaction can be measured reliably. The amount recorded is the cash-equivalent sales price. Assume that the following events and transactions occurred in **September** 2017:

   a. A customer purchases a ticket from WestJet for $435 cash to travel the following January. Answer from WestJet's standpoint.

   b. General Motors issues $26 million in new shares.

   c. Hall Construction Company signs a contract with a customer for the construction of a new $500,000 warehouse. At the signing, Hall receives a cheque for $50,000 as a deposit on the future construction. Answer from Hall's standpoint.

   d. On September 1, 2017, a bank lends $10,000 to a company. The loan carries a 6 percent annual interest rate, and the principal and interest are due in a lump sum on August 31, 2018. Answer from the bank's standpoint.

e. A popular ski magazine company receives a total of $1,800 from subscribers on September 30, the last day of its fiscal year. The subscriptions begin in the next fiscal year. Answer from the magazine company's standpoint.

f. Sears Canada sells a $100 lamp to a customer who charges the sale on his store credit card. Answer from the standpoint of Sears.

g. A customer orders and receives 10 personal computers from Dell Inc.; the customer promises to pay $20,000 within three months. Answer from Dell's standpoint.

h. Sam Shell Dodge sells a truck with a list, or sticker, price of $24,000 for $21,000 cash.

i. The Hudson's Bay Company orders 1,000 men's shirts from Gildan Activewear Inc. at $18 each for future delivery. The terms require payment in full within 30 days of delivery. Answer from Gildan's standpoint.

j. Gildan Activewear completes production of the shirts described in (i) and delivers the order. Answer from Gildan's standpoint.

k. Gildan receives payment from the Hudson's Bay Company for the order described in (i). Answer from Gildan's standpoint.

Required:

For each of the September transactions, indicate the account title and amount of revenue. If revenue is not to be recognized in September, explain why. Use the following headings in structuring your solution:

Event or Transaction	Account Title and Amount of Revenue
a.	
b.	
etc.	

LO3-2,3-3   **E3-4**   **Identifying Expenses**

Revenues are normally recognized when goods or services have been provided and payment or promise of payment has been received. Expense recognition is guided by an attempt to match the costs associated with the generation of those revenues to the same time period. Assume that the following events and transactions occurred in January 2017:

a. A new grill is installed at a McDonald's restaurant. On the same day, payment of $14,000 is made in cash.

b. On January 1, 2017, Carousel Mall has janitorial supplies costing $1,000 in storage. An additional $600 worth of supplies is purchased during January. At the end of January, $900 worth of janitorial supplies remains in storage.

c. A Concordia University employee works eight hours, at $15 per hour, on January 31; however, payday is not until February 3. Answer from the university's point of view.

d. Wang Company pays $3,600 for a fire insurance policy on January 2. The policy covers the current month and the next 11 months. Answer from Wang's point of view.

e. Amber Incorporated has its delivery van repaired in January for $280 and charges the amount on account.

f. Ziegler Company, a farm equipment company, receives its phone bill at the end of January for $230 for January calls. The bill has not been paid to date.

g. Spina Company receives and pays in January a $2,100 invoice from a consulting firm for services received in January.

h. Felicetti's Taxi Company pays a $600 invoice from a consulting firm for services received and recorded in accounts payable in December.

i. Dell Inc. pays its computer service technicians $85,000 in salary for the two weeks ended January 7. Answer from Dell's standpoint.

j. Turner Construction Company pays $4,500 in workers' compensation insurance for the first three months of the year.

k. McGraw-Hill Ryerson Limited uses $1,200 worth of electricity and natural gas in its headquarters building for which it has not yet been billed.

l. Gildan Activewear Inc. completes production of 500 men's shirts ordered by Bon Ton Department Store at a cost of $9 each and delivers the order. Answer from Gildan's standpoint.

m. The campus bookstore receives 500 accounting textbooks at a cost of $70 each. The terms indicate that payment is due within 30 days of delivery.

n. During the last week of January, the campus bookstore sells 450 accounting textbooks received in (m) at a sales price of $100 each.

o. Sam Shell Dodge pays its salespeople $3,500 in commissions related to December automobile sales. Answer from Sam Shell Dodge's standpoint.

p. On January 31, Sam Shell Dodge determines that it will pay its salespeople $4,200 in commissions related to January sales. The payment will be made in early February. Answer from Sam Shell Dodge's standpoint.

Required:

For each of the January transactions, indicate the account title and amount of the expense. If an expense is not to be recognized in September, explain why.

Use the following headings in structuring your solution:

Event or Transaction	Account Title and Amount of Expense
a.	
b.	
etc.	

LO3-2,3-3,3-5 **E3-5** **Identifying Revenues and Expenses**

Peter's Curling Inc. operates several curling centres for games and equipment sales. The following transactions occurred in October 2017.

Required:

1. For each transaction, indicate in the appropriate column the account titles that are affected and the type of account (A for asset, L for liability, R for revenue, and E for expense), and the amount of cash received or paid.

2. If a revenue or expense is to be recognized in October, indicate the amount. If a revenue or expense is not to be recognized in October, indicate why.

3. Explain why the difference between revenues and expenses is not equal to the net cash flow during October 2017.

Activity	Account Affected and Type of Account	Cash Received (Paid) in October	Amount of Revenue Earned or Expense Incurred in October OR Why a Revenue or an Expense Is Not Recognized
(a) The curling league gave Peter's a deposit of $2,600 for the upcoming fall season.			
(b) Peter's received $2,500 from customers on account who purchased merchandise in September.			
(c) Peter's paid $1,900 for the September electricity bill and received the October bill for $2,200, which will be paid in November.			
(d) Peter's sold curling equipment inventory for $7,000; received $3,000 in cash and the rest on account; cost of sales is $4,200.			
(e) Peter's collected $13,000 from customers for games played in October.			
(f) Peter's paid $1,400 to plumbers for repairing a broken pipe in the washrooms.			
(g) Peter's paid $4,700 to employees for work in October.			
(h) Peter's purchased and paid for $1,800 in insurance for coverage from October 1 to December 31.			
Totals			

LO3-3

E3-6   **Timing of Revenue Recognition**

Modern Equipment Corp. manufactures special-purpose machines for use in the mining industry. In late April, the company received an order from Kross Mining Company (KMC) for a special-purpose machine to be delivered in two months. The specific events related to the production of this machine are shown below.

April 29   KMC placed an order for a special-purpose machine to be manufactured and delivered in two months.

May 3   Raw materials and components are ordered so that the machine can be manufactured.

May 4   Modern Equipment receives written confirmation of the order from KMC.

May 12   Manufacture of the machine is completed.

May 13   The machine is shipped to KMC.

May 14   KMC receives the machine.

May 15   Modern Equipment receives written confirmation that the machine was delivered to KMC.

May 16   An invoice is sent to KMC.

June 16   KMC receives free after-sales service for the machine.

June 19   A cheque is received from KMC in full payment.

June 25   The cheque is cleared by the bank.

Required:

When should Modern Equipment Corp. recognize revenue from the sale of the machine? Explain.

LO3-4

E3-7   **Determining the Financial Statement Effects of Operating Activities**

Peter's Curling Inc. operates several curling centres (for games and equipment sales). The following transactions occurred in the month of October. For each of the transactions below, complete the tabulation, indicating the amount and effect (+ for increase and − for decrease) of each transaction. (Remember that A = L + SE, R − E = NE, and NE affects SE through retained earnings.) Write "N" if there is no effect. The first transaction is provided as an example.

	Statement of Financial Position			Statement of Earnings		
Transaction	**Assets**	**Liabilities**	**Shareholders' Equity**	**Revenues**	**Expenses**	**Net Earnings**
(a) Peter's collected $13,000 from customers for games played in October.	+13,000	N	+13,000	+13,000	N	+13,000
(b) Peter's sold $7,000 in curling equipment inventory; received $3,000 in cash and the rest on account; cost of sales is $4,200.						
(c) Peter's received $2,500 from customers on account who purchased merchandise in September.						
(d) The curling league gave Peter's a deposit of $2,600 for the upcoming fall season.						
(e) Peter's paid $1,900 for the September electricity bill and received the October bill for $2,200 to be paid in November.						
(f) Peter's paid $4,700 to employees for work in October.						
(g) Peter's purchased $1,800 in insurance for coverage from October 1 to December 31.						
(h) Peter's paid $1,400 to plumbers for repairing a broken pipe in the washrooms.						

LO3-4,3-5

E3-8 **Preparing a Statement of Earnings**

Refer to the transactions in E3-7 (including the example), and prepare a statement of earnings for Peter's Curling Inc. for the month of October 2017. Use an income tax rate of 40 percent.

LO3-4

E3-9 **Determining Financial Statement Effects of Various Transactions**

The following transactions occurred during a recent year:

  a. Issued shares to organizers for cash (example).

  b. Borrowed cash from the local bank.

  c. Purchased equipment on credit.

  d. Earned revenue; collected cash.

  e. Incurred expenses on credit.

  f. Earned revenue; billed the customer.

  g. Paid cash on account.

  h. Incurred expenses; paid cash.

  i. Earned revenue; collected three-fourths in cash and the rest on credit.

  j. Experienced theft of $100 cash.

  k. Declared and paid cash dividends.

  l. Collected cash from customers on account.

  m. Incurred expenses; paid four-fifths in cash and the rest on credit.

  n. Paid income tax expense for the period.

Required:

Complete the tabulation below for each of the transactions, indicating the effect (+ for increase and − for decrease) of each transaction. (Remember that A = L + SE, R − E = NE, and NE affects SE through retained earnings.) Write "N" if there is no effect. The first transaction is provided as an example.

	Statement of Financial Position			Statement of Earnings		
Transaction	Assets	Liabilities	Shareholders' Equity	Revenues	Expenses	Net Earnings
(a) (example)	+	N	+	N	N	N

LO3-4

Saputo Inc.

E3-10 **Determining Financial Statement Effects of Various Transactions**

Saputo Inc. produces, markets, and distributes a wide variety of products, including cheese, fluid milk, yogurt, dairy ingredients, and snack cakes. It is the largest dairy processor in Canada and serves customers in over 50 countries.

The following transactions occurred during a recent year. Amounts are in millions of dollars.

  a. Issued $30 in shares to investors (example).

  b. Purchased $149 of additional property, plant, and equipment for cash.

  c. Incurred $309 in selling expenses with two-thirds paid in cash and the rest on account.

  d. Purchased on account $6,128 of raw materials used in processing various dairy products.

  e. Earned $7 interest on investments; received 50 percent in cash.

  f. Paid $21 on bank loans.

  g. Sold $8,422 of products to customers on account; the cost of the products sold was $6,263.

  h. Incurred $9 in interest expense (not yet paid).

  i. Declared and paid cash dividends of $184.

Required:

Complete the tabulation below for each of the transactions, indicating the effect (+ for increase and − for decrease) of each transaction. (Remember that A = L + SE, R − E = NE, and NE affects SE through retained earnings.) Write "N" if there is no effect. The first transaction is provided as an example.

	Statement of Financial Position			Statement of Earnings		
Transaction	Assets	Liabilities	Shareholders' Equity	Revenues	Expenses	Net Earnings
(a) (example)	+30	N	+30	N	N	N

■ **LO3-4**

Sysco

E3-11 **Recording Journal Entries**

Sysco, formed in 1969, is the largest U.S. marketer and distributor of food service products, serving nearly 400,000 restaurants, hotels, schools, hospitals, and other institutions. The following summarized transactions are typical of those that occurred in a recent year (dollars in millions).

a. Borrowed $181 from financial institutions, signing short-term notes.

b. Provided $39,323 in service to customers during the year, with $28,558 on account and the rest received in cash.

c. Purchased equipment for $96 in cash.

d. Purchased inventory for $32,305 on account.

e. Paid $3,500 in salaries during the year.

f. Received $39,043 on account paid by customers.

g. Purchased and used fuel of $750 in delivery vehicles during the year (paid for in cash).

h. Declared and paid $597 in dividends for the year.

i. Paid $32,074 cash on accounts payable.

j. Incurred $68 in utility usage during the year; paid $55 in cash and the rest on account.

Required:

Prepare a journal entry to record each of the transactions. Determine whether the accounting equation remains in balance and debits equal credits after each entry.

■ **LO3-4,3-5**

E3-12 **Analyzing the Effects of Transactions in T-Accounts**

Lisa Fruello and Emilie Dumont had been operating a catering business for several years. In March 2017, the partners were planning to expand by opening a retail sales shop and decided to form the business as a corporation called Travelling Gourmet Inc. The following transactions occurred in March 2017:

a. Received $80,000 cash from each of the two shareholders to form the corporation, in addition to $2,000 in accounts receivable, $5,300 in equipment, a van (equipment) appraised at a fair market value of $13,000, and $1,200 in supplies.

b. Purchased a vacant store for sale in a good location for $360,000, making a $72,000 cash down payment and signing a 10-year mortgage from a local bank for the rest.

c. Borrowed $50,000 from the local bank and signed a 5 percent, one-year note.

d. Purchased for $10,830 cash, food and paper supplies that were used in March.

e. Catered four parties in March for $4,200; $1,600 was billed and the rest was received in cash.

f. Made and sold food at the retail store for $11,900 cash.

g. Received a $420 telephone bill for March to be paid in April.

h. Paid $363 in gas for the van in March.

i. Paid $6,280 in wages to employees who worked in March.

j. Paid a $300 dividend from the corporation to each owner.

k. Paid $50,000 in exchange for equipment (refrigerated display cases, cabinets, tables, and chairs) and renovated and decorated the new store for $20,000 cash (added to the cost of the building).

Required:

1. Set up appropriate T-accounts for cash, accounts receivable, supplies, equipment, building, accounts payable, note payable, mortgage payable, contributed capital, retained earnings, food sales revenue, catering sales revenue, supplies expense, utilities expense, wages expense, and fuel expense.

2. Record in the T-accounts the effects of each transaction for Travelling Gourmet Inc. in March. Identify the amounts, with the letters starting with (*a*). Compute ending balances.

3. Show the effects (direction and amount) of each transaction on net earnings and cash.

■ **LO3-4,3-5**

E3-13 **Recording Journal Entries**

Rowland & Sons Air Transport Service Inc. has been in operation for three years. The following transactions occurred in February:

February 1 Paid $1,900 for rent of hangar space in February.

2 Purchased fuel costing $450 on account for the next flight to Winnipeg.

4 Received customer payment of $950 to ship several items to Montreal next month.

7 Flew cargo from Ottawa to Edmonton; the customer paid $1,240 for the air transport.

10 Paid pilot $4,000 in wages for flying in January.

14 Paid $600 for an advertisement in the local paper, to run on February 19.

18 Flew cargo for two customers from Regina to Calgary for $1,800; one customer paid $500 cash and the other asked to be billed.

25 Purchased spare parts for the planes costing $1,350 on account.

27 Declared a $1,300 cash dividend to be paid in March.

Required:

1. Prepare a journal entry to record each transaction. Be sure to categorize each account as an asset (A), a liability (L), shareholders' equity (SE), revenue (R), or an expense (E).

2. Show the effects (direction and amount) of each transaction on net earnings and cash.

LO3-3,3-4,3-5,3-6

E3-14

Analyzing the Effects of Transactions in T-Accounts, and Computing Cash Basis versus Accrual Basis Earnings

Stacey's Piano Rebuilding Company has been operating for one year (2016). At the start of 2017, its statement of earnings accounts had zero balances and the account balances on its statement of financial position were as follows:

Cash	$10,000	Accounts payable	$16,000
Accounts receivable	50,000	Deferred revenue (deposits)	6,400
Supplies	2,400	Note payable (due in three years)	80,000
Equipment	16,000	Contributed capital	16,000
Land	12,000	Retained earnings	36,000
Building	64,000		

Required:

1. Create T-accounts for the accounts reported on the statement of financial position and for these additional accounts: rebuilding fees revenue, rent revenue, wages expense, and utilities expense. Enter the beginning balances.

2. Enter the following January 2017 transactions in the T-accounts, using the letter of each transaction as the reference:

   a. Received a $600 deposit from a customer who wanted her piano rebuilt.

   b. Rented a part of the building to a bicycle repair shop; received $820 for rent in January.

   c. Rebuilt and delivered five pianos to customers who paid $18,400 in cash.

   d. Received $7,200 from customers as payment on their accounts.

   e. Received an electric and gas utility bill for $520 to be paid in February.

   f. Ordered $960 in supplies.

   g. Paid $2,140 on account to suppliers.

   h. Received from Sam Mensa, the major shareholder, a $920 tool (equipment) to use in the business in exchange for the company's shares.

   i. Paid $15,000 in wages to employees for work in January.

   j. Declared and paid a cash dividend of $2,600.

   k. Received and paid for the supplies ordered in (*f*).

3. Using the data from the T-accounts, calculate the amounts for the following on January 31, 2017:
   Revenues, $_____ − Expenses, $_____ = Net earnings, $_____ Assets, $_____ = Liabilities, $_____ + Shareholders' Equity, $_____

4. Calculate the company's net earnings for January by using the cash basis of accounting. Why does this differ from the net earnings in (3) above?

5. Calculate the return on assets for January 2017. If the company had a return on assets of 6 percent in December 2016 and 5 percent in November 2016, what does your computation suggest to you about Stacey's Piano Rebuilding Company? What would you state in your report?

LO3-4

E3-15

Analyzing the Effects of Transactions on the Statement of Cash Flows

Refer to E3-14.

Required:

Use the following chart to identify whether each of the transactions in E3-14 results in a cash flow effect from operating (O), investing (I), or financing (F) activities, and indicate the direction and the effect on cash (+ for increase and − for decrease). If there is no cash flow effect, write "none." The first transaction is provided as an example.

Transaction	Type of Activity (O, I, or F)	Effect on Cash Flows (+ or − and amount)
(a)	O	+600

LO3-4   **E3-16**   **Preparing a Statement of Earnings, Identifying Cash Flow Effects, and Analyzing Results**
Refer to E3-14.

Required:
Use the ending balances in the T-accounts in E3-14 to respond to the following:

1. Prepare a statement of earnings in good form for the month of January 2017.

2. Identify the operating activities (O), investing (I), and financing (F) activities affecting cash flows for January 2017. Include the direction and amount of the effect. If there is no effect on cash flows, use N.

3. Evaluate the success of this company based on the results of the first month of operations.
   Hint: Compare net earnings to cash flows from operations.

LO3-6   **E3-17**   **Computing and Explaining the Total Asset Turnover Ratio**
The following data are from annual reports of Justin's Jewellery Company:

	2017	2016	2015
Total assets	$ 60,000	$ 50,000	$ 40,000
Total liabilities	12,000	10,000	5,000
Total shareholders' equity	48,000	40,000	35,000
Sales	154,000	144,000	130,000
Net earnings	5,000	3,800	25,000

Required:
Compute Justin's total asset turnover ratio and its return on assets for 2016 and 2017. What do these results suggest to you about Justin's Jewellery Company?

LO3-4,3-6   **E3-18**   **Analyzing the Effects of Transactions by Using T-Accounts and Interpreting the Total Asset Turnover Ratio as a Financial Analyst**
Internet Marketing Inc. (IMI), which has been operating for three years, provides marketing consulting services worldwide for online companies. You are a financial analyst assigned to report on the effectiveness of IMI's management team at managing its assets. At the start of 2017 (its fourth year), IMI's T-account balances were as follows. Amounts are in thousands of dollars.

ASSETS

Cash	Accounts Receivable	Long-Term Investments
3,200	8,000	6,400

LIABILITIES

Accounts Payable	Deferred Revenue	Long-Term Debt
2,400	5,600	1,600

SHAREHOLDERS' EQUITY

Contributed Capital	Retained Earnings
4,800	3,200

REVENUES

Consulting Fee Revenue	Investment Income

EXPENSES

Wages Expense	Travel Expense	Utilities Expense

Rent Expense

Required:

1. Using the data from these T-accounts, complete the accounting equation on January 1, 2017.
   Assets, $_____ = Liabilities, $_____ + Shareholders' Equity, $_____

2. Enter the following 2017 transactions in the T-accounts:

   a. Provided $58,000 in services to clients; received $48,000 in cash and the rest on account.

   b. Received $5,600 cash from clients on account.

   c. Received $400 in cash as income on investments.

   d. Paid $36,000 for wages, $12,000 for travel, $7,600 in rent, and $1,600 on accounts payable.

   e. Received $1,600 in cash from clients in advance of services that IMI will provide next year.

   f. Received a utility bill for $800 for services used in 2017.

   g. Paid $480 in dividends to shareholders.

  3. Compute ending balances in the T-accounts to determine the missing amounts on December 31, 2017:
   Revenues, $_____ – Expenses, $_____ = Net earnings, $_____
   Assets, $_____ = Liabilities, $_____ + Shareholders' Equity, $_____

  4. Calculate the total asset turnover ratio for 2017. If the company had a total asset turnover ratio of 2.00 in 2016 and of 1.80 in 2015, what does your computation suggest to you about IMI? What would you state in your report?

LO3-6

E3-19 **Computing and Interpreting the Total Asset Turnover Ratio and the Return on Assets**
Bianca Corp. and Uzma Inc. operate in the same industry. The companies' total assets, revenue, and net earnings for the years 2016–2019 are provided below. All amounts are in thousands of dollars.

	2019	2018	2017	2016
Bianca Corp.				
Total assets	$ 40,000	$ 50,000	$ 60,000	$ 65,000
Revenue	130,000	144,000	154,000	150,000
Net earnings	25,000	3,800	5,000	4,800
Interest expense, net of tax	1,000	800	700	800
Uzma Inc.				
Total assets	$ 65,000	$ 60,000	$ 50,000	$ 40,000
Revenue	150,000	154,000	144,000	130,000
Net earnings	4,800	5,000	3,800	25,000
Interest expense, net of tax	400	500	400	300

Required:

 1. Compute the total asset turnover ratio and the return on assets for each company for each of the years 2017, 2018, and 2019.

 2. Based on the two sets of ratios that you computed, which company was more efficient in managing its assets during the 2016–2019 period? Explain.

connect PROBLEMS

LO3-4,3-5,3-6 **P3-1** **Preparing a Statement of Earnings and a Partial Statement of Financial Position, and Evaluating the Return on Assets** (AP3-1)
Fashion World Inc. reported the following accounts and balances in its unadjusted trial balance as at December 31, 2017 (in thousands of Canadian dollars). Note that the accounts are listed in alphabetical order:

Accumulated depreciation	$ 28,600	Note payable, 5%, due March 1, 2019	$ 35,000
Cash	14,000	Prepaid expenses	1,050
Contributed capital (1,000 shares)	50,000	Rent expense	13,850
Cost of sales	158,500	Retained earnings, January 1, 2017	19,550
Depreciation expense	9,600	Salaries expense	30,500
Furniture and equipment, at cost	68,800	Sales revenue	232,250
Insurance expense	750	Supplies expense	1,100
Investments (long term)	37,000	Supplies inventory	950
Merchandise inventory	26,000	Trade accounts payable	34,400
Other operating expenses	7,700	Trade accounts receivable	30,000

Additional information is as follows:

 a. All of these accounts have "normal" debit and credit balances.

 b. The note payable was signed on March 1, 2016.

 c. The company is subject to an income tax rate of 30 percent.

Required:

1. Identify the accounts that would be listed in a statement of earnings.

2. Prepare the statement of earnings for Fashion World Inc. for the year ended December 31, 2017.

3. Prepare the assets section only of a classified statement of financial position as at December 31, 2017.

4. Compute the return on assets (ROA) based on your answers to the previous requirements. Assume that the company reported total assets of $186,200 at December 31, 2016. How would you interpret the ROA?

LO3-4　　**P3-2**　**Recording Journal Entries** (AP3-2)

Chad Polovick organized a new company, CapUniverse Inc. The company operates a small store in an area mall and specializes in baseball-type caps with logos printed on them. Chad, who is never without a cap, believes that his target market is college students. You have been hired to record the transactions occurring in the first two weeks of operations:

May 1　Issued 2000 shares for $20 per share.

May 1　Borrowed $60,000 from the bank to provide additional funding to begin operations. The note is due in two years with interest at 10 percent annually.

May 1　Paid $1,500 for the current month's rent and another $1,500 for next month's rent.

May 1　Paid $2,400 for a one-year fire insurance policy (recorded as a prepaid expense).

May 3　Purchased furniture and fixtures for the store for $15,000 on account. The amount is due within 30 days.

May 4　Purchased for $2,800 cash a supply of University of Waterloo, York University, and Saint Mary's University baseball caps to be sold online.

May 5　Placed advertisements on Google for a total of $350 cash.

May 9　Sold caps for a total of $1,700, half of which was charged on account. The cost of the caps sold was $900.

May 10　Made full payment for the furniture and fixtures purchased on account on May 3.

May 14　Received $210 from a customer on account.

Required:

Prepare a journal entry to record each of the transactions. Be sure to categorize each account as an asset (A), liability (L), shareholders' equity (SE), revenue (R), or expense (E). Note that the transaction on May 9 requires two entries, one to recognize revenue and one for the related expense.

LO3-4,3-5,3-6　　**P3-3**　**Analyzing the Effects of Transactions by Using T-Accounts, Preparing a Statement of Earnings, and Evaluating the Total Asset Turnover Ratio and the Return on Assets as a Manager** (AP3-3)

Joanne Beauport, a connoisseur of fine chocolate, opened Joanne's Chocolates Inc. in Newtown on March 1, 2017. The shop specializes in a selection of gourmet chocolates and a line of gourmet ice cream. You have been hired as manager. Your duties include maintaining the store's financial records. The following transactions occurred in March 2017, the first month of operations:

a. Received contributions of $60,000 in total from four shareholders to form the corporation.

b. Paid store rent for three months at $1,600 per month (recorded as prepayment).

c. Purchased supplies for $800 cash.

d. Purchased chocolates on account for $6,000, due in 30 days.

e. Issued additional shares to new investors for $10,000 cash.

f. Used the money from (e) to purchase a computer for $4,000 (for recordkeeping and inventory tracking). The rest was used to buy furniture and fixtures for the store.

g. Placed a grand-opening advertisement in the local paper for $850 cash.

h. Sold chocolates for $4,200; $3,750 was in cash and the rest on account. The cost of the chocolates sold was $2,100.

i. Made a $1,000 payment on accounts payable.

j. Incurred and paid employee wages of $2,520.

k. Collected accounts receivable of $200 from customers.

l. Made a repair on one of the display cases for $268 cash.

m. Made cash sales of $5,500 during the rest of the month. The cost of the chocolates and ice cream sold was $2,900.

Required:

1. Set up appropriate T-accounts for cash, accounts receivable, supplies, merchandise inventory, prepaid rent, equipment, furniture and fixtures, accounts payable, notes payable, interest payable,

contributed capital, sales revenue, cost of sales, advertising expense, wages expense, repair expense, and interest expense. All accounts begin with zero balances.

2. Record in the T-accounts the effects of each transaction for Joanne's Chocolates Inc. in March, referencing each transaction in the accounts with the transaction letter. Show the ending balances in the T-accounts.

3. Prepare a statement of earnings for March 2017.

4. Write a short memo to Joanne offering your opinion on the results of operations during the first month of business.

5. After three years in business, you are being evaluated for a salary increase. One measure is how efficiently you managed the assets of the business. The following data are available:

	2019*	2018	2017
Total assets	$112,000	$63,000	$49,000
Total liabilities	63,000	28,000	21,000
Total shareholders' equity	49,000	35,000	28,000
Total sales	119,000	105,000	70,000
Net earnings	28,000	14,000	5,600

*At the end of 2019, Joanne decided to open a second store, requiring loans and inventory purchases prior to the opening in early 2017.

Compute the total asset turnover ratio and the return on assets for 2018 and 2019, and evaluate the results. Do you think your salary should be increased? Why? The company is subject to an income tax rate of 30 percent.

LO3-4

P3-4 **Analyzing the Effects of Transactions on the Statement of Cash Flows** (AP3-4)
Refer to P3-3.

Required:
For each transaction in P3-3, identify whether the cash flow relates to operating (O), investing (I), or financing (F) activities. Indicate the direction and the effect on cash (+ for increase and − for decrease). If there is no cash flow effect, write "none."

LO3-4,3-5,3-6 **P3-5**

Analyzing the Effects of Transactions by Using T-Accounts, Preparing Financial Statements, and Evaluating the Total Asset Turnover Ratio and the Return on Assets (AP3-5)
The following are the summary account balances from a recent statement of financial position of Modern Sportswear Inc. The accounts are followed by a list of transactions for the month of January 2018. All amounts are shown in millions of dollars:

Cash	$ 635	Accounts payable	$1,822
Long-term borrowings	2,229	Income tax payable	300
Accounts receivable	1,503	Prepaid expenses	16
Inventories	551	Retained earnings	4,266
Deferred income taxes (credit)	2,518	Other non-current assets	1,126
Property and equipment, net	10,759	Contributed capital	3,455

The accounts have normal debit or credit balances, but they are not necessarily listed in good order. The following additional information is also available:

a. Purchased new equipment costing $150 by issuing long-term debt.

b. Received $900 on accounts receivable.

c. Received and paid the telephone bills for $1.

d. Earned $500 in sales to customers on account; the cost of sales was $300.

e. Paid employees $100 for wages earned in January.

f. Paid half of the income taxes payable.

g. Purchased inventory for $223 on account.

h. Prepaid rent for February for a warehouse for $12.

i. Paid $10 of long-term borrowings and $1 in interest on the debt.

j. Purchased a patent (an intangible asset) for $8 cash.

Required:

1. Set up T-accounts for the preceding list and enter the respective balances. (You will need additional T-accounts for statement of earnings accounts.)

2. For each transaction, record the effects in the T-accounts. Label each by using the letter of the transaction. Compute ending balances.

3. Show the effects (direction and amount) of each transaction on net earnings and cash.

4. Prepare in good form a multiple-step statement of earnings for the month of January 2018 and a classified statement of financial position as at January 31, 2018.

5. Compute the company's total asset turnover ratio. What does this ratio suggest to you about Modern Sportswear Inc.?

LO3-4,3-6   **P3-6**   **Determining and Interpreting the Effects of Transactions on Statement of Earnings Categories and Return on Assets** (AP3-6)

Apple Inc.

Apple Inc. popularized both the personal computer and the easy-to-use graphic interface. Today it competes against many companies that rely on the Windows and Android operating systems. The company's statement of earnings for a recent year is presented below (in millions of U.S. dollars):

Net sales	$182,795
Cost of sales	112,258
Gross profit	70,537
Operating expenses:	
Research and development	6,041
Selling, general, and administrative	11,993
Total operating expenses	18,034
Earnings from operations	52,503
Other income/(expense), net	980
Earnings before provision for income taxes	53,483
Provision for income taxes	13,973
Net earnings	$ 39,510

Required:

1. Compute the return on assets based on the information presented in the statement of earnings. Apple's total assets averaged $220,420 million for that year and its interest expense equaled $516.

2. Assume that the following hypothetical *additional* transactions occurred during the fiscal year. Complete the following tabulation, indicating the sign and amount of the effect of each additional transaction (+ for increase, − for decrease, and "N" for no effect). Consider each item independently and ignore income taxes.

   a. Recorded sales on account of $700 and related cost of sales of $475.

   b. Incurred additional research and development expense of $100, which was paid in cash.

   c. Issued additional shares for $350 cash.

   d. Declared and paid dividends of $90.

Transaction	Gross Profit	Earnings from Operations	Return on Assets
a.			
b.			
c.			
d.			

LO3-4,3-6   **P3-7**   **Recording Journal Entries and Identifying Transaction Effects on the Total Assets Turnover Ratio and Cash Flows**

Cedar Fair

Cedar Fair L.P. (Limited Partnership) is one of the largest amusement park operators in the world, owning 11 amusement parks, four outdoor water parks, one indoor water park, and five hotels. Parks in the United States include Cedar Point in Ohio; Valleyfair near Minneapolis/St. Paul; Dorney Park and Wildwater Kingdom near Allentown, Pennsylvania; Worlds of Fun/Oceans of Fun in Kansas City; and Great America in Santa Clara, California. It also operates Canada's Wonderland, near Toronto. The following are summarized transactions similar to those that occurred in a recent year (amounts in thousands of dollars):

a. Guests at the parks paid $596,042 cash in admissions.

b. The primary operating expenses (such as employee wages, utilities, and repairs and maintenance) for the year were $433,416, with $401,630 paid in cash and the rest on account.

c. Interest incurred and paid on long-term debt was $153,326.

d. The parks sell food and merchandise and operate games. The cash received during the year for these combined activities was $365,693. The cost of merchandise sold during the year was $92,057.

e. Cedar Fair purchased and built additional buildings, rides, and equipment during the year, paying $90,190 in cash.

f. Guests may stay in some of the parks at accommodations owned by the company. During the year, accommodations revenue was $82,994; $81,855 was paid by the guests in cash and the rest was on account.

g. Cedar Fair paid $47,100 on notes payable.

h. The company purchased $147,531 in food and merchandise inventory for the year, paying $119,431 in cash and the rest on account.

i. The selling, general, and administrative expenses (such as the president's salary and advertising for the parks; those not classified as operating expenses) for the year were $140,426; $34,044 was paid in cash and the rest was on account.

j. Cedar Fair paid $11,600 on accounts payable during the year.

Required:

1. Prepare a journal entry to record each of these transactions. Use the letter of each transaction as its reference.

2. Show the effects (direction and amount) of each transaction on net earnings and cash.

3. Indicate the direction of the effect (increase, decrease, or no effect) of each of the transactions (*a*) through (*j*) on the total asset turnover ratio, and provide an explanation for your answer. Cedar Fair's total asset turnover ratio was 0.56 in the previous year. For example, transaction (*a*) increases the ratio. Both sales and total assets would increase. Since the ratio is less than 1.0, the increase in sales (the numerator) is proportionally higher than the increase in total assets (the denominator).

4. Use the following chart to identify whether each transaction results in a cash flow effect from operating (O), investing (I), or financing (F) activities, and indicate the direction and amount of the effect on cash (+ for increase and − for decrease). If there is no cash flow effect, write "none." The first transaction is provided as an example.

Transaction	Operating, Investing, or Financing Effect	Direction and Amount of the Effect
(a)	O	+596,042

P3-8

Computing and Analyzing the Total Asset Turnover Ratio and the Return on Assets

A summary of selected historical results is presented below for three Canadian companies: Gildan Activewear, WestJet Airlines, and Le Groupe Jean Coutu. Each of these companies has grown in size over time by acquiring assets and investing in other companies. (Amounts are in millions of dollars.)

	2015	2014	2013	2012	2011	2010
Gildan Activewear						
Total assets	2,834	$2,593	$2,044	$1,896	$1,890	$1,328
Total revenue	2,959	2,360	2,184	1,948	1,726	1,311
Net earnings	305	360	320	148	240	198
Interest expense, net of tax	13	5.3	7.3	7.3	3.3	0.5
Operating cash flow	354	264	427	220	1 64	302
WestJet Airlines						
Total assets	5,129	4,646	4,143	3,747	3,474	3,384
Total revenue	4,029	3,599	3,338	3,427	3,072	2,607
Net earnings	368	284	269	242	149	90
Interest expense, net of tax	38	37	25	36	40	44
Operating cash flow	876	572	608	722	506	419
Le Groupe Jean Coutu						
Total assets	1,380	1,344	1,165	1,393	1,073	1,060
Total revenue	2,855	2,814	2,733	2,740	2,733	2,613
Net earnings	214	219	437	558	230	183
Interest expense, net of tax	0.0	0.0	0.0	0.6	2	2
Operating cash flow	226	278	284	224	245	214

Required:

1. Complete the following table by computing the total asset turnover ratio and the return on assets for each company for each of the years 2014 and 2015.

	2015	2014	2013	2012	2011
Gildan Activewear					
Total asset turnover ratio			1.11	1.03	1.07
Return on assets (ROA)			16.60%	8.20%	15.10%
WestJet Airlines					
Total asset turnover ratio			0.85	0.95	0.90
Return on assets (ROA)			4.70%	7.70%	5.51%
Le Groupe Jean Coutu					
Total asset turnover ratio			2.14	2.22	2.56
Return on assets (ROA)			34.10%	45.30%	21.75%

2. Based on the computed ratios, rank these companies from most successful to least successful in implementing their growth strategies and effectively utilizing their assets.

3. Which of these three companies appears to be in the best position at the end of 2015 to pay off its short-term liabilities? What additional information would help you provide a more definite answer to this requirement? Explain.

ALTERNATE PROBLEMS

■ **LO3-4,3-5**   **AP3-1**   **Preparing a Statement of Earnings and a Partial Statement of Financial Position, and Evaluating the Total Asset Turnover Ratio and the Return on Assets** (P3-1)

You were recently offered a position as an intern in the accounting firm Faitou and Dowal LLP. On your first day at work, your supervisor wanted to test your knowledge of accounting. She gave you the following list of accounts and related balances of New Look Corp. as at December 31, 2018, and asked you to complete the requirements below

(Amounts in thousands of dollars)	Debit	Credit
Accumulated depreciation—furniture and fixtures		$ 90
Cash	$ 410	
Contributed capital (10,000 shares)		500
Cost of sales	2,600	
Depreciation expense	10	
Deferred revenue		30
Furniture and fixtures	370	
Interest receivable	10	
Interest revenue		10
Merchandise inventory	860	
Note receivable, due on September 30, 2020	240	
Other operating expenses	400	
Prepaid expenses	15	
Retained earnings, January 1, 2018		1,400
Salaries expense	295	
Salaries payable		15
Sales revenue		3,500
Trade accounts payable		190
Trade accounts receivable	525	
Total	$5,735	$5,735

Required:

1. Prepare the statement of earnings for New Look Corp. for the year ended December 31, 2018. The company is subject to an income tax rate of 40 percent and pays its income taxes within three months.

2. By how much would net earnings change if depreciation expense was omitted in the preparation of the statement of earnings?

3. Prepare the liabilities and shareholders' equity sections of a classified statement of financial position for New Look Corp. as at December 31, 2018.

4. Compute the total asset turnover ratio and the return on assets based on your answers to the previous requirements, and explain the meaning of each ratio. Assume that the company reported total assets of $2,150 at December 31, 2017.

LO3-4   **AP3-2**   **Recording Journal Entries** (P3-2)

Sandro Spina is the president of TemPro Inc., a company that provides temporary employees for not-for-profit companies. TemPro has been operating for five years; its revenues are increasing with each passing year. You have been hired to help Sandro in analyzing the following transactions for the first two weeks of April:

April 1 Purchased office supplies for $2,600 on account.
  3 Received the April telephone bill for $1,950 to be paid in May.
  5 Billed the local United Way $23,500 for temporary services provided.
  8 Paid $3,005 for supplies purchased and recorded on account last period.
  8 Placed an advertisement in the local paper for $1,400 cash.
  9 Purchased a new computer for the office costing $2,300 cash.
  10 Paid employee wages of $11,900. Of this amount, $3,800 had been earned and recorded in the wages payable account in the prior period.
  11 Received $12,500 on account from the local United Way office for services provided on April 5.
  12 Purchased land as the site of a future office for $50,000. Paid $10,000 down and signed a note payable for the balance. The note is due in five years and has an annual interest rate of 10 percent.
  13 Issued 3,000 additional shares for cash at $45 per share in anticipation of building a new office.
  14 Billed Family & Children's Service $14,500 for services rendered.

Required:

Prepare a journal entry to record each of the transactions. Be sure to categorize each account as an asset (A), a liability (L), shareholders' equity (SE), a revenue (R), or an expense (E).

LO3-4,3-5,3-6 AP3-3   **Analyzing the Effects of Transactions by Using T-Accounts, Preparing a Statement of Earnings, and Evaluating the Total Asset Turnover Ratio and the Return on Assets as a Manager** (P3-3)

Alpine Stables Inc. was established on April 1, 2017. The company provides stables, care for animals, and grounds for riding and showing horses. You have been hired as the new assistant controller. The following transactions for April 2017 are provided for your review:

a. Received contributions from five investors of $60,000 in cash ($12,000 each), a barn valued at $100,000, and land valued at $90,000. Each investor received 3,000 shares.

b. Built a small barn for $62,000. The company paid half the amount in cash on April 1, 2017, and signed a three-year note payable for the balance.

c. Provided animal care services to customers, all on credit, for $35,260.

d. Rented stables to customers who cared for their own animals, and received cash payment of $13,200.

e. Received from a customer $2,400 to board her horse in April, May, and June (record as deferred revenue).

f. Purchased hay and feed supplies on account for $3,180 to be used in the summer.

g. Paid $1,240 in cash for water utilities expense incurred in the month.

h. Paid $2,700 on accounts payable for previous purchases.

i. Received $10,000 from customers on accounts receivable.

j. Paid $6,000 in wages to employees who worked during the month.

k. Purchased a one-year insurance policy for $3,600 at the end of the month.

l. Received an electric utility bill for $1,800 for usage in April; the bill will be paid in May.

m. Paid $500 cash dividend to each of the investors at the end of the month.

Required:

1. Set up appropriate T-accounts. All accounts begin with zero balances.

2. Record in the T-accounts the effects of each transaction for Alpine Stables in April, referencing each transaction in the accounts with the transaction letter. Show the ending balances in the T-accounts.

3. Prepare a statement of earnings at April 30, 2017, as well as a classified statement of financial position as at date.

4. Write a short memo to the five owners, offering your opinion on the results of operations during the first month of business.

5. After three years in business, you are being evaluated for a promotion to chief financial officer. One measure is how efficiently you managed the assets of the business. The following data are available:

	2019*	2018	2017
Total assets	$480,000	$320,000	$300,000
Total liabilities	125,000	28,000	30,000
Total shareholders' equity	49,000	292,000	270,000
Total sales	450,000	400,000	360,000
Net earnings	50,000	30,000	(10,000)

*At the end of 2019, Alpine Stables decided to build an indoor riding arena for giving lessons year-round. The company borrowed construction funds from a local bank and the arena was opened in early 2017.

Compute the total asset turnover ratio and the return on assets for 2018 and 2019 and evaluate the results. Do you think you should be promoted? Why? Ignore interest on the long-term note related to (b).

 LO3-4

AP3-4   **Analyzing the Effects of Transactions on the Statement of Cash Flows** (P3-4)
Refer to AP3-3.

Required:
For each transaction in AP3-3 identify whether the cash flow relates to from operating (O), investing (I), or financing (F) activities, and indicate the direction and the effect on cash (+ for increase and − for decrease). If there is no cash flow effect, write "none."

 LO3-4,3-5,3-6   **AP3-5**   **Analyzing the Effects of Transactions by Using T-Accounts, Preparing Financial**

Canada Post

Statements, and Evaluating the Total Asset Turnover Ratio and the Return on Assets (P3-5)
The following are several December 31, 2014, account balances (in millions of dollars) from a recent annual report of Canada Post Corporation, followed by several typical transactions. The corporation's vision is described in the annual report as follows:

Canada Post will be a world leader in providing innovative physical and electronic delivery solutions, creating value for our customers, employees, and all Canadians.

Account	Balance	Account	Balance
Property, plant, and equipment, net	$2,676	Equity (debit)	$2,011
Accounts payable	583	Receivables	894
Short-term investments	689	Other non-current assets	2,097
Accrued liabilities	487	Cash	677
Long-term borrowings	1,134	Investments (long-term)	551
Deferred revenues	133	Other non-current liabilities	7,258

These accounts have normal debit or credit balances, but are not necessarily in good order. The following hypothetical transactions (in millions of dollars) occurred the next month (from January 1, 2015, to January 31, 2015):

a. Provided delivery service to customers, receiving $564 in accounts receivable and $60 in cash.

b. Purchased new equipment costing $540; signed a long-term note.

c. Paid $74 in cash to rent equipment, with $64 for rental this month and the rest for rent for the first few days in February.

d. Spent $396 in cash to maintain and repair facilities and equipment during the month.

e. Collected $675 from customers on account.

f. Borrowed $90 by signing a long-term note (ignore interest).

g. Paid employees $279 earned during the month.

h. Purchased for cash and used $49 in supplies.

i. Paid $184 on accounts payable.

j. Ordered $72 in spare parts and supplies.

Required:

1. Prepare T-accounts for the preceding list and enter the respective balances. (You will need additional T-accounts for statement of earnings accounts.)

2. For each transaction, record the effects in the T-accounts. Label each by using the letter of the transaction. Compute ending balances.

3. Show the effects (direction and amount) of each transaction on net earnings and cash.

4. Prepare in good form a multiple-step statement of earnings for January 2015.

5. Prepare in good form a classified statement of financial position as at January 31, 2015.

6. Compute the company's total asset turnover ratio and its return on assets. What do these ratios suggest to you about Canada Post? Assume that the long-term note of $90 was signed on January 31, and that interest has not accrued yet.

AP3-6

Barnes & Noble Inc.

Determining and Interpreting the Effects of Transactions on Statement of Earnings Categories and Return on Assets (P3-6)

Barnes & Noble Inc. revolutionized bookselling by making its stores public spaces and community institutions where customers may browse, find a book, relax over a cup of coffee, talk with authors, and join discussion groups. Today it is fighting increasing competition not only from traditional sources but also from online booksellers. Presented here is a recent statement of earnings (in millions of dollars):

Net sales	$5,121
Cost of sales	3,540
Gross margin	1,581
Operating expenses:	
Selling and administrative	1,251
Depreciation and amortization	174
Pre-opening expenses	13
Total operating expenses	1,438
Earnings from operations	143
Other income and expenses:	
Interest expense	2
Earnings before provision for income taxes	141
Provision for income taxes	56
Net earnings	$ 85

Required:

Assume that the following hypothetical *additional* transactions occurred during the fiscal year: (*a*) recorded and received interest income of $14, (*b*) purchased $95 of additional inventory on open account, (*c*) recorded and paid additional advertising expense of $19, and (*d*) issued additional common shares for $90 cash.

Complete the following tabulation, indicating the sign of the effect of each *additional* transaction (+ for increase, − for decrease, and NE for no effect). Assume that the company's return on assets is less than one prior to these transactions. Consider each item independently and ignore income taxes.

Transaction	Earnings (Loss) from Operations	Net Earnings	Return on Assets
(*a*)			
(*b*)			
(*c*)			
(*d*)			

---

connect **CASES AND PROJECTS**

FINDING AND INTERPRETING FINANCIAL INFORMATION

CP3-1

Canadian Tire Corporation

Finding Financial Information

Refer to the financial statements and the accompanying notes of Canadian Tire Corporation in Appendix A.

Required:

1. State the amount of the largest expense on the statement of earnings for 2015 and describe the transaction represented by the expense.

2. Assuming that all net sales are on credit, how much cash did Canadian Tire Corporation collect from customers? (*Hint:* Use a T-account for trade and other receivables and for loans receivable to infer collections.)

3. A shareholder has complained that "more dividends should be paid because the company had net earnings of $735.9 million in 2015. Since this amount is all cash, more of it should go to the shareholders." Explain why the shareholder's assumption that net earnings equal net cash inflow is not valid. If you believe that the assumption is valid, state so and support your position concisely.

4. Describe and contrast the purpose of a statement of earnings versus a statement of financial position.

5. Compute the company's total asset turnover ratio and its return on assets for 2015. Explain their meaning.

LO3-2,3-4,3-6 CP3-2   **Finding Financial Information**

Sears Canada Inc.

Go to *Connect* for the financial statements of Sears Canada Inc.

Required:

1. What is the company's revenue recognition policy? (*Hint:* Look in the notes to the financial statements.)

2. How much inventory did the company buy during the year? (*Hint:* Refer to Note 7 to the financial statements, and use a T-account for inventories to infer how much was purchased.)

3. Refer to the consolidated statement of net loss and comprehensive loss and compute the ratio of selling, administrative, and other expenses to revenue for the years ended January 30, 2016, and January 31, 2015. By what percentage did these expenses increase or decrease from fiscal year 2014 to 2015? (*Hint:* Percentage change = [Current-year amount − Prior-year amount]/Prior-year amount.)

4. Compute the company's total asset turnover ratio for the year ended January 30, 2016, and explain its meaning.

LO3-2,3-3,3-5 CP3-3   **Comparing Companies within an Industry**

Canadian Tire
Corporation vs.
Sears Canada Inc.

Refer to the financial statements of Canadian Tire Corporation (Appendix A) and Sears Canada Inc. (on *Connect*), and the Industry Ratio Report (Appendix B on *Connect*).

Required:

1. What title does each company give its statement of earnings? Explain what the term "consolidated" means.

2. Which company had higher net earnings at the end of its fiscal year?

3. Compute the total asset turnover ratio and the return on assets for each company for the most recent year. Which company is utilizing assets more effectively to generate sales and net earnings? Explain.

4. Compare the total asset turnover ratio and the return on assets for both companies to the industry average. On average, are these two companies utilizing assets to generate sales and net earnings better or worse than their competitors?

5. How much cash was provided by operating activities by each company during the most recent year? What was the percentage change in operating cash flows for each company during the most recent year? (*Hint:* Percentage change = [Current-year amount − Prior-year amount] ÷ Prior-year amount.)

6. How much did each company pay in income taxes during the last fiscal year reported in the financial statements? Where did you find this information?

7. What segments does Canadian Tire report in the notes to its financial statements? What does Sears Canada report about segments?

FINANCIAL REPORTING AND ANALYSIS CASE

LO3-4,3-5   CP3-4   **Using Financial Reports: Analyzing Changes in Accounts and Preparing Financial Statements**

Pete's Painting Service was organized as a corporation on January 20, 2017, by three individuals, each receiving 5,000 shares of capital from the new company. The following is a schedule of the *cumulative* account balances immediately after each of the first 10 transactions ending on January 31, 2017.

	CUMULATIVE BALANCES									
Accounts	(a)	(b)	(c)	(d)	(e)	(f)	(g)	(h)	(i)	(j)
Cash	$75,000	$70,000	$85,000	$71,000	$61,000	$64,000	$60,000	$49,000	$44,000	$60,000
Accounts receivable			12,000	12,000	12,000	26,000	26,000	26,000	26,000	10,000
Office fixtures		22,000	22,000	22,000	22,000	22,000	22,000	22,000	22,000	22,000
Land				18,000	18,000	18,000	18,000	18,000	18,000	18,000
Accounts payable					3,000	3,000	3,000	10,000	5,000	5,000
Note payable (long term)		17,000	17,000	21,000	21,000	21,000	21,000	21,000	21,000	21,000
Contributed capital	75,000	75,000	75,000	75,000	75,000	75,000	75,000	75,000	75,000	75,000
Retained earnings							(4,000)	(4,000)	(4,000)	(4,000)
Paint revenue			27,000	27,000	27,000	44,000	44,000	44,000	44,000	44,000
Supplies expense					5,000	5,000	5,000	8,000	8,000	8,000
Wages expense					8,000	8,000	8,000	23,000	23,000	23,000

Required:

1. Analyze the changes in this schedule for each transaction, and then explain the transaction. Transaction (*a*) is an example:

   a. Cash increased $75,000, and contributed capital (shareholders' equity) increased $75,000. Therefore, transaction (*a*) was an issuance of shares of the corporation for $75,000 cash.

2. Based only on the preceding schedule after transaction (*j*), prepare a statement of earnings, a statement of shareholders' equity, and a statement of financial position.

3. For each of the transactions, indicate the type of effect on cash flows (O for operating, I for investing, or F for financing) and the direction (+ for increase and − for decrease) and amount of the effect. If there is no effect, write "none." The first transaction is provided as an example.

Transaction	Operating, Investing, or Financing Effect	Direction and Amount of the Effect
(a)	F	+75,000

CRITICAL THINKING CASES

CP3-5 | **LO3-3,3-6** | **Making a Decision as a Bank Loan Officer: Analyzing and Restating Financial Statements That Have Major Deficiencies (A Challenging Case)**

Tom Martinez started and operated a small boat repair service company during 2018. He is interested in obtaining a $100,000 loan from your bank to build a dry dock to store boats for customers in the winter months. At the end of the year, he prepared the following statements based on information stored in a large filing cabinet:

MARTINEZ COMPANY Profit for 2018		
Service fees collected during 2018		$ 55,000
Cash dividends received		10,000
Total		65,000
Expense for operations paid during 2018	$22,000	
Cash stolen	500	
New tools purchased during 2018 (cash paid)	1,000	
Supplies purchased for use on service jobs (cash paid)	3,200	
Total		26,700
Net earnings		$ 38,300
Assets Owned at the End of 2018		
Cash in chequing account		$ 29,300
Service garage (at current market value)		32,000
Tools and equipment		18,000
Land (at current market value)		30,000
Shares in ABC Industrial		130,000
Total		$239,300

The following is a summary of completed transactions:

a. Received the following contributions to the business from the owner when it was started in exchange for 1,000 shares in the new company:

Building	$21,000	Land	$20,000
Tools and equipment	17,000	Cash	1,000

b. Earned service fees during 2018 of $87,000; of the cash collected, $20,000 was for deposits from customers on work to be done by Martinez during 2019.

c. Received the cash dividends on shares of ABC Industrial purchased by Tom as a personal investment six years earlier.

d. Incurred expenses during 2018, $61,000.

e. Determined amount of supplies on hand (unused) at the end of 2018, $700.

Required:

1. Did Tom prepare the statement of earnings on a cash basis or on an accrual basis? Explain how you can tell. Which basis should be used? Explain why.

2. Reconstruct the correct entries under accrual accounting principles and post the effects to T-accounts.

3. Prepare an accrual-based statement of earnings for 2018 and a statement of financial position at the end of 2018. Explain (using footnotes) the reason for each change that you make to the statement of earnings.

4. What additional information would assist you in formulating your decision regarding the loan to Tom?

5. Based on the revised statements and additional information needed, write a letter to Tom explaining your decision at this time regarding the loan.

LO3-3   **CP3-6**   **Proper Measurement of Net Earnings**

Paula Manolakos purchased La Forêt Inc., a bakery, from Gianni Fiori. The purchase agreement included a provision that required Paula to pay Gianni 25 percent of the bakery's net earnings in each of the next five years. The agreement stated that the bakery's net earnings would be measured in a "fair and reasonable manner," but did not state that it would be measured in accordance with the applicable financial reporting standards. Neither Paula nor Gianni was familiar with accounting concepts.

In measuring net earnings, Paula used the following accounting policies:

a. Revenue was recognized when cash was received from customers. Because of the nature of the business, most customers paid in cash, but a few customers purchased merchandise on account and were allowed to pay in 30 days.

b. Paula set her annual salary at $60,000, which Gianni has agreed was reasonable. She also paid $30,000 per year to her spouse and to each of her two teenage children. These family members did not work in the business on a regular basis, but they did help during busy periods.

c. Weekly expenditures for eggs, milk, flour, and other supplies were charged directly to supplies expense, as were the weekly groceries for Paula's family.

d. The bakery had modern baking equipment valued at $50,000 at the time Paula purchased the company. The statement of earnings for the first year included a $50,000 equipment expense related to these assets.

e. Income taxes expense included the amount paid by the corporation (which was computed correctly), as well as the personal income taxes paid by various members of Paula's family on the salaries they earned for working in the business.

Gianni was disappointed, however, when Paula reported net earnings for the first year that was far below his expectations.

Required:

1. Discuss the fairness and reasonableness of Paula's accounting policies. Identify the accounting principle or assumption that may have been violated.

2. Do you think that the net cash flow from operations (cash receipts minus cash payments) is higher or lower than the net earnings reported by Paula? Explain.

3. What advice would you give Gianni to ensure that the bakery's net earnings would be measured properly in future years?

■ LO3-3   **CP3-7**   **Evaluating an Ethical Dilemma**

Mike Kruk is the manager of a Vancouver regional office for an insurance company. As the regional manager, his compensation package comprises a base salary, commissions, and a bonus when the region sells new policies in excess of its quota. Mike has been under enormous pressure lately, stemming largely from two factors. First, he is experiencing mounting personal debt because of a family member's illness. Second, compounding his worries, the region's sales of new policies have dipped below the normal quota for the first time in years.

You have been working for Mike for two years, and like everyone else in the office, you consider yourself lucky to work for such a supportive boss. You also feel great sympathy for his personal problems over the last few months. In your position as accountant for the regional office, you are only too aware of the drop in new policy sales and the impact this will have on the manager's bonus. While you are working late at year-end, Mike stops by your office.

Mike asks you to change the manner in which you have accounted for a new property insurance policy for a large local business. A cheque for the premium, substantial in amount, came in the mail on December 31, the last day of the reporting year. The premium covers a period beginning on January 5. You deposited the cheque and correctly debited cash and credited a *deferred revenue* account. Mike says, "Hey, we have the money this year, so why not count the revenue this year? I never did understand why you accountants are so picky about these things anyway. I'd like you to change the way you have recorded the transaction. I want you to credit a *revenue* account. And anyway, I've done favours for you in the past, and I am asking for such a small thing in return." With that, he leaves for the day.

Required:

1. How should you handle this situation?

2. What are the ethical implications of Mike's request?

3. Who are the parties who would be helped or harmed if you complied with the request?

4. If you fail to comply with his request, how will you explain your position to him in the morning?

FINANCIAL REPORTING AND ANALYSIS TEAM PROJECT

■ LO2-2,2-3,2-5,2-6   **Team Project: Analyzing Statement of Earnings and Ratios**

    CP3-8   As a team, select an industry to analyze. A list of companies classified by industry can be obtained

by accessing www.fpinfomart.ca and then choosing Companies by Industry on the left-hand side. You can also find a list of industries and companies within each industry via http://ca.finance. yahoo.com/investing (click on Order Annual Reports under Tools).

Each team member should acquire the annual report for a different publicly traded company in the industry. (Library files, the SEDAR service at www.sedar.com, and the company's website are good sources.)

Required:

On an individual basis, each team member should write a short report that answers the following questions about the selected company. Discuss any patterns across the companies that you as a team observe. Then, as a team, write a short report comparing and contrasting your companies.

1. For the most recent year, what is/are the major revenue account(s)? What percentage is each of total operating revenues (computed as Revenue A ÷ Total revenues)?

2. For the most recent year, what is/are the major expense account(s)? What percentage is each of total operating expenses (computed as Expense A ÷ Total expenses)?

3. Perform a ratio analysis:

    a. What do the total asset turnover ratio and the return on assets measure in general?

    b. Compute these ratios for the last three years.

    c. What do your results suggest about the company?

    d. If available, find the industry ratios for the most recent year, compare them with your results, and discuss why you believe your company's ratios differ from or are similar to the industry ratios.

4. Describe the company's revenue recognition policy, if reported. (Usually found in note 2 to the financial statements, titled Significant Accounting Policies.)

5. Cash from operating activities as a percentage of net earnings measures how liberal (i.e., speeding up revenue recognition or delaying expense recognition) or conservative (i.e., taking care not to record revenues too early or expenses too late) a company's management is in choosing among various revenue and expense recognition policies. A ratio above 1.0 suggests more conservative policies, and a ratio below 1.0 suggests more liberal policies. Compute the percentage for the last three years. What do your results suggest about the company's choice of accounting policies?

LO2-4,2-5,2-6 CC3-1 **Accounting for Operating Activities in a New Business (the Accounting Cycle)**
Penny's Pool Service & Supply Inc. (PPSS) had the following transactions related to operating the business in its first year's busiest quarter ended September 30, 2016:

a. Placed and paid for $2,600 in advertisements with several area newspapers (including the online versions), all of which ran in the newspapers during the quarter.

b. Cleaned pools for customers for $19,200, receiving $16,000 in cash with the rest owed by customers who will pay when billed in October.

c. Paid Pool Corporation Inc. a pool supply wholesaler, $10,600 for inventory received by PPSS in May.

d. As an incentive to maintain customer loyalty, PPSS offered customers a discount for prepaying next year's pool cleaning service. PPSS received $10,000 from customers who took advantage of the discount.

e. Paid the office receptionist $4,500, with $1,500 owed for work in the prior quarter and the rest for work in the current quarter. The amount due for work completed last quarter was recorded as an expense and a liability, wages payable.

f. Paid $310 to a mechanic to repair the company van.

g. Paid $220 for phone, water, and electric utilities used during the quarter.

h. Received $75 cash in interest earned during the current quarter on short-term investments.

i. Received a property tax bill for $600 for use of the land and building in the quarter; the bill will be paid next quarter.

j. Paid $2,400 for the next quarter's insurance coverage.

Required:

1. Prepare journal entries to record the above transactions, checking that debits equal credits.

2. Prepare a multiple-step statement of earnings for the quarter ended September 30, 2016, based only on these quarterly transactions.

3. Calculate the net profit margin ratio at September 30, 2016 (using earnings before taxes in place of net earnings). What does this ratio indicate about the ability of PPSS to control operations?

SOLUTIONS TO SELF-STUDY QUIZZES

Self-Study Quiz 3-1

Accounts Affected and Type of Account	Cash Received in January	Amount of Revenue Earned in December	January	Deferred Revenue
(a) Cash (A)	$ 480			
Sales (R)			$ 480	
(b) Cash (A)	120			
Accounts receivable (A)				
Sales (R)			520	
(c) Cash (A)	2,400			
Sales (R)			200	
Accounts receivable (A)		$2,200		
(d) Cash (A)	50			
Sales (R)			40	
Deferred revenue (L)				$10
Totals	**$3,050**	**$2,200**	**$1,240**	**$10**

The total cash received in January, $3,450, is not equal to the amount of revenue recognized for January, $1,240. The cash received in January includes $2,200 for revenue recorded for December and $10 for revenue to be recognized in the future. On the other hand, the revenues for January include $400 to be collected at a later date. Revenues reflect the efforts made in January, not earlier or later, and are, therefore, a better measure of operating performance than cash receipts.

Self-Study Quiz 3-2

Accounts Affected and Type of Account	Cash Paid in January	Amount of Expense Recognized in January OR Why an Expense Is Not Recognized
(a) Cash (A) 　　Accounts payable (L)	$900	December purchase, paid in January; supplies expensed when used or sold
(b) Inventories (A) 　　Cost of sales (E)		$320 (of used inventory)
(c) Cash (A) 　　Other operating expenses (E) 　　Prepaid expenses (A)	150	$50 incurred in January; $100 not incurred until future months
(d) Inventories (A) 　　Cost of sales (E)		$340 (of used inventory)
(e) Accounts payable (L) 　　Other operating expense (E)		$5 incurred in January to be paid in the future
Totals	**$1,050**	**$715—Expenses for January**

If your answers did not agree with ours, we recommend that you go back to each transaction to make sure that you have completed each of the steps for each transaction.

Self-Study Quiz 3-3

(q)

Effect of transaction on
Net earnings: ↑ 1
Cash: ↑ 71

Cash (+A)	71	
Interest revenue (+R →+SE)		1
Notes receivable (−A)		70

(r)

Effect of transaction on
Net earnings: No effect
Cash: ↓ 490

Accounts payable (−L)	490	
Cash (−A)		490

Assets	=	Liabilities	+	Shareholders' Equity
Cash　−490		Accounts payable　−490		

(s)

Effect of transaction on
Net earnings: ↑ 30
Cash: ↑ 35

Assets	=	Liabilities	+	Shareholders' Equity
Cash　　　　　　　+35				Gain on sale of land　+30
Property and equipment　−5				

Self-Study Quiz 3-4
1. F−; 2. O+; 3. I−; 4. O−; 5. O−; 6. F−; 7. I+ or O+; 8. F+; 9. F+; 10. F− or O−; 11. O−; 12. I+

Self-Study Quiz 3-5

1.

	2015	2014	2013	2012	2011
Total asset turnover ratio	1.84	1.64	1.64	1.62	1.56
Return on assets (ROA)	−3.7%	−16.0%	18.7%	4.0%	−2.0%

2. The total asset turnover ratio increased slightly in 2012 and 2013, remained stable in 2014, and increased again in 2015. This indicates that Sears has been able in the last year to improve on using its total assets to generate revenues. The company's sales decreased steadily from $4,939 in 2010 to $3,146 in 2015. Its total assets also decreased over the 2010 to 2015 period. The decline in sales, which is due to the economic downturn that started in 2008, has resulted in net losses from operations in 2014 and 2015. The significant increase in net earnings for 2013 was due to a gain on termination of leases. The net losses in the last two years are the result of the increased competition that Sears has faced from its competitors. Consequently, the return on assets is negative for both 2014 and 2015.

ENDNOTES

1. In addition to the audited annual statements, most businesses prepare quarterly financial statements (also known as *interim reports* covering a three-month period) for external users. The securities commissions require publicly accountable enterprises to do so.

2. Another common format, *single step*, reorganizes all accounts on the multiple-step format. All revenues are listed together and all expenses except income taxes are listed together. The expenses subtotal is then subtracted from the revenue subtotal to arrive at earnings before income taxes, the same subtotal as on the multiple-step statement. For example, Canadian Tire's statement of earnings is presented in Exhibit 1.3 in Chapter 1 using the single-step format. Many companies use some variation of the single-step and multiple-step formats.

3. Canadian Tire uses the term *cost of producing revenue,* which includes cost of sales. We use the latter term for simplicity and consistency throughout this book.

4. All amounts in this chapter are in millions of Canadian dollars, except where noted otherwise.

5. Sales discounts, returns, and allowances are covered in Chapter 7.

6. The expenses that are deducted from revenue to obtain earnings from operations can alternatively be classified by nature to reflect the main elements of the costs of production and sale—namely, the cost of raw materials and consumables used, changes in inventories of finished products and work in progress, employee benefit costs, and depreciation and amortization expenses. For example, the Danish company ECCO Sko A/S, which produces and markets footwear products worldwide, classifies its operating expenses by nature (see, for example, page 58 of its 2015 annual report at http://media.ecco.com/GroupCommunication/Annualreport2015/).

7. International Accounting Standards Board, 2009.
International Accounting Standard 18, Revenue, paragraph 14. The IASB issued in May 2014 International Financial Reporting Standard (IFRS) 15, Revenue from Contracts with Customers, that will supersede IAS 18. Companies that prepare IFRS-based financial reports are expected to implement the new standard for reporting periods beginning on or after January 1, 2018. The core revenue recognition principle that we discuss in this chapter will not change. **Companies will recognize revenue when goods and services are transferred to customers in an amount they expect to receive.** The major changes relate to complex contracts that require transfer of multiple goods or services, such as when Apple sells electronic devices and a warranty together in a single sale. For these types of sales contracts, companies will determine the separate obligations and split the sales price among them. They will then recognize each part of the revenue when they have provided each promised good or service. Accounting for complex sales transactions will be covered in your intermediate accounting course.

8. Further discussion of the application of the revenue recognition principle to special circumstances is provided in Chapter 6.

9. We classified the interest of $5 received from the trade supplier as an investing activity for this illustration because it is a return on an investment. Alternatively, it may be classified as operating cash flow because it enters into the determination of net earnings or net loss.

10. International Accounting Standards Board, International Financial Reporting Standard 13—Fair Value Measurement, (May 2011): para. 9.

11. An excellent review of fair value accounting of financial assets and liabilities, and its role in the 2007–2009 financial crisis, is provided in M. Magnan, "Fair Value Accounting and the Financial Crisis: Messenger or Contributor?" *Accounting Perspectives* 8, No. 3 (2009), pp. 189–213. In another article in the same journal, A. R. Abdel-Khalik argues that historical cost information is essential in evaluating management's stewardship of the economic resources entrusted to them, stating that fair value accounting does not provide information for this purpose. See A. R. Abdel-Khalik, "Fair Value Accounting and Stewardship," *Accounting Perspectives* 9, No. 4 (2010), pp. 253–269.

Adjustments, Financial Statements, and the Quality of Earnings

After studying this chapter, you should be able to do the following:

LEARNING OBJECTIVES

LO4-1 Explain the purpose of adjustments and analyze the adjustments necessary at the end of the period to update statement of financial position and statement of earnings accounts.

LO4-2 Prepare a statement of earnings with earnings per share, a statement of changes in equity, and a statement of financial position.

LO4-3 Compute and interpret the net profit margin ratio and the return on equity.

LO4-4 Explain the closing process at the end of the period.

Monkeybusinessimages/iStockphoto.com

Focus Company: **Canadian Tire Corporation**

ESTIMATING REVENUES AND EXPENSES AT YEAR-END

The end of the accounting period is a very busy time for Canadian Tire Corporation (www. canadiantire.ca). The last day of the fiscal year for Canadian Tire falls on the Saturday closest to December 31 of each year.[1]

The financial statements, however, are not distributed to users on that day. They are released only after management and the external auditors make many critical evaluations.

• Management must ensure that the correct amounts are reported on the statement of financial position and the statement of earnings. This often requires estimations, assumptions, and judgments about the timing of revenue and expense recognition, and the values for assets and liabilities.

• The auditors have to (1) assess the strength of the controls established by management to safeguard the company's assets and ensure the accuracy of the financial records, and (2) evaluate the appropriateness of estimates and accounting principles used by management in determining revenues and expenses.

Managers of most companies understand the need to present financial information fairly so as not to mislead users. This is one reason why external auditors examine the company's records on a test, or sample, basis. To maximize the chance of detecting any errors significant enough to affect users' decisions, auditors allocate more of their testing to transactions most likely to be in error. End-of-period adjustments are the most complex portion of the annual recordkeeping process; they are prone to unintentional error. Typical end-of-period adjustment errors include failure to provide adequate provision for product warranty, failure to include items that should be expensed, and end-of-period transactions recorded in the wrong period (called *cut-off errors*). These adjustments receive much attention from the auditors.

For fiscal year 2015, Canadian Tire's year-end estimation and auditing process took until February 17, 2016, the date on which the auditor, Deloitte LLP, completed the audit work and signed its audit opinion. At that point, the financial statements were made available to the public.

UNDERSTANDING THE BUSINESS

Managers are responsible for preparing financial statements that are useful to investors, creditors, and others. Financial information is most useful for analyzing the past and predicting the future when it is considered by users to be of *high quality*. High-quality information is relevant (that is, material and able to influence users' decisions) and faithfully represents the substance of the underlying transactions (that is, complete, free from error, and unbiased in portraying economic reality).

Users expect revenues and expenses to be reported in the proper period, based on the revenue recognition principle and matching process discussed in Chapter 3. Revenues must be recorded when earned and expenses must be recorded when incurred, regardless of when cash is received or paid. Operating activities take place over one accounting period or over several periods; for example, using insurance that has been prepaid or owing salaries to employees for past work. Because recording these and similar activities daily is often very costly, most companies wait until the end of the period to record *adjustments* to revenue and expense accounts to reflect the proper amounts in the correct period. These entries update the records and are the focus of this chapter.

In this chapter, we emphasize the use of the analytical tools introduced in Chapters 2 and 3 (journal entries and T-accounts) to help you understand how the necessary adjustments are analyzed and recorded at the end of the accounting period. These tools provide the foundation for additional adjustments that require estimation and judgments by management, which we discuss in future chapters. Then we prepare financial statements by using adjusted account balances. Finally, we illustrate how we prepare the accounting records for the next accounting period by performing a process called "closing the books."

ORGANIZATION OF THE CHAPTER

Adjusting Revenues and Expenses	Preparing Financial Statements	Closing the Books
• Accounting Cycle	• Statement of Earnings	• End of the Accounting Cycle
• Purpose of Adjustments	• Statement of Changes in Equity	• Post-closing Trial Balance
• Types of Adjustments	• Statement of Financial Position	
• Adjustment Process	• Net Profit Margin Ratio	
• Materiality and Adjusting Entries	• Return on Equity	

Supplemental material:

Appendix C: The Formal Recordkeeping System (on *Connect*)

ADJUSTING REVENUES AND EXPENSES

Accounting Cycle

The ACCOUNTING CYCLE is the process used by entities to analyze and record transactions, adjust the records at the end of the period, prepare financial statements, and prepare the records for the next cycle.

The **accounting cycle** is the process used by entities to analyze and record transactions, adjust the records at the end of the period, prepare financial statements, and prepare the records for the next cycle. *During* the accounting period, transactions that result in exchanges between the company and other external parties are analyzed and recorded in the general journal in chronological order (journal entries), and the related accounts are updated in the general ledger (T-accounts), in a manner similar to our Canadian Tire illustrations in Chapters 2 and 3. In this chapter, we examine the *end-of-period* steps that focus primarily on adjustments to record revenues and expenses in the proper period and to update the statement of financial position accounts for reporting purposes. Exhibit 4.1 presents the fundamental steps in the accounting cycle.

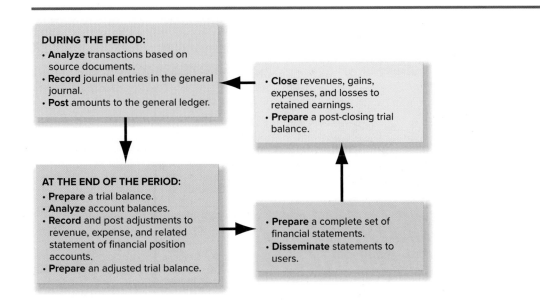

Exhibit **4.1**
The Accounting Cycle

Purpose of Adjustments

Accounting systems are designed to record most recurring, daily transactions, particularly those involving cash. As cash is received or paid, it is recorded in the accounting system. In general, this focus on cash works well, especially when cash receipts and payments occur in the same period as the activities that produce revenues and expenses. However, cash is not always received in the period in which the company earns revenue; likewise, cash is not always paid in the period in which the company incurs an expense.

How does the accounting system record revenues and expenses when one transaction is needed to record a cash receipt or payment and another transaction is needed to record a revenue when it is earned or an expense when it is incurred? The solution to the problem created by such differences in timing is to record **adjusting entries** at the end of every accounting period, so that

- Revenues are recorded when earned (the *revenue recognition principle).*

- Expenses are recorded when incurred to generate revenue during the same period (the *matching process*).

- *Assets* are reported at amounts that represent the probable future benefits remaining at the end of the period.

- *Liabilities* are reported at amounts that represent the probable future sacrifices of assets or services owed at the end of the period.

Companies wait until *the end of the accounting period* to adjust their accounts, because adjusting the records daily would be very costly and time-consuming. Adjusting entries are required every time a company wants to prepare financial statements for external users.

Types of Adjustments

Exhibit 4.2 describes the four types of adjustments (two in which cash was already received or paid and two in which cash will be received or paid). Each of these types of adjustments involves two entries:

LO4-1

Explain the purpose of adjustments and analyze the adjustments necessary at the end of the period to update statement of financial position and statement of earnings accounts.

ADJUSTING ENTRIES are entries necessary at the end of the accounting period to identify and record all revenues and expenses of that period.

1. One entry to record the cash receipt or payment during the period, and
2. One entry to record the revenue or expense in the proper period through an adjusting entry prepared at the end of the period.

Exhibit **4.2**

Four Types of Adjustments

In practice, almost every account, *except cash*, could require an adjustment. Rather than trying to memorize an endless list of specific examples, you should focus instead on learning the general types of adjustments that are needed and the process that is used to determine how to adjust the accounts. We will illustrate the process involved in analyzing and adjusting the accounts by reviewing all the adjustments needed for Canadian Tire before preparing January's financial statements based on adjusted balances.

When a customer pays for goods or services before the company delivers them, the company records the amount of cash received in a deferred revenue account. **Deferred revenue** is a liability representing the company's promise to perform or deliver the goods or services in the future. Recognition of (recording) the revenue is deferred (postponed) until the company meets its obligation.

Sometimes, companies perform services or provide goods (i.e., earn revenue) before customers pay. Because the cash that is owed for these goods has not yet been

DEFERRED REVENUES are previously recorded liabilities that need to be adjusted at the end of the accounting period to reflect the amount of revenues earned.

EXAMPLES:
• Deferred ticket revenue
• Deferred subscription revenue

ADJUSTING ENTRY:
↓ Liability and ↑ Revenue

received, the revenue that was earned has not been recorded. Revenues that have been earned but have not yet been recorded at the end of the accounting period are called **accrued revenues**.

Exhibit 4.3 summarizes the process involved in adjusting deferred revenues and accrued revenues, using deferred fees and interest revenue as examples. The first column indicates the classification of the revenue, either deferred or accrued. The remaining columns indicate the timing and type of journal entry required. AJE in the exhibit refers to "adjusting journal entry." Note that in both cases the goal is the same—to record revenues in the proper period. Also note that adjusting entries affect one account on the statement of financial position and one account on the statement of earnings, but *cash is never adjusted.* Cash was recorded when received prior to the end of the period, or will be recorded when collected in a future period.

ACCRUED REVENUES are previously unrecorded revenues that need to be recorded at the end of the accounting period to reflect the amount earned and its related receivable account.

EXAMPLES:
• Interest receivable
• Rent receivable

ADJUSTING ENTRY:
↑ Asset and ↑ Revenue

Exhibit 4.3
Illustration of Adjusting Deferred and Accrued Revenues

	During the period	End of period	Next period
	Entry when **cash is received before** the company performs (earns revenue)	**AJE** needed because the company has performed (earned a revenue) during the period	Entry when **cash is received after** the company performs (earns revenue)
Deferred Revenues	Cash (+A) Deferred fee revenue (+L)	Deferred fee revenue (−L) Fee revenue (+R, +SE)	
Accrued Revenues		Interest receivable (+A) Interest revenue (+R, +SE)	Cash (+A) Interest receivable (−A)

Revenues recorded in the proper period

Assets represent resources with probable future benefits to the company. Many assets are used over time to generate revenues, including supplies, prepaid rent, prepaid insurance, buildings, equipment, and intangible assets, such as patents and copyrights. These assets are **deferred expenses**. At the end of every period, an adjustment must be made to record the amount of the asset that was used during the period.

Numerous expenses are incurred in the current period without being paid for until the next period. Common examples include interest expense incurred on debt, wages expense for the wages owed to employees, and utilities expense for water, gas, and electricity used during the period for which the company has not yet received a bill. These **accrued expenses** accumulate (accrue) over time but are not recognized until the end of the period in an adjusting entry.

Exhibit 4.4 summarizes the process involved in adjusting deferred expenses and accrued expenses, using prepaid insurance and wages expense as examples. AJE refers, again, to adjusting journal entry. Note that in both cases the goal is to record expenses in the proper period. In addition, note that the adjusting journal entry involves one account on the statement of financial position and one account on the statement of earnings, and cash is never affected. Cash was recorded when paid prior to the end of the period or will be recorded in a future period.

DEFERRED EXPENSES are previously acquired assets that need to be adjusted at the end of the accounting period to reflect the amount of expense incurred in using the assets to generate revenue.

EXAMPLES:
• Supplies
• Prepaid expenses (e.g., rent, insurance)
• Buildings and equipment

ADJUSTING ENTRY:
↑ Expense and ↓ Asset

ACCRUED EXPENSES are previously unrecorded expenses that need to be recorded at the end of the accounting period to reflect the amount incurred and its related payable account.

EXAMPLES:
• Interest payable
• Wages payable
• Property taxes payable

ADJUSTING ENTRY:
↑ Expense and ↑ Liability

Adjustment Process

Throughout the rest of the text, you will discover that nearly every account, except cash, on a company's statement of financial position will need to be adjusted, often requiring management to make judgments and estimates. In this chapter, we will illustrate common adjusting entries. In analyzing adjustments at the end of the period, there are three steps:

Exhibit **4.4**

Illustration of Adjusting
Deferred and Accrued Expenses

	During the period	End of period	Next period
	Entry when **cash is paid before** the company incurs an expense	**AJE** needed because the company has incurred an expense during the period	Entry when **cash is paid after** the company incurs an expense

Deferred Expenses	Prepaid insurance (+A)
	  Cash (−A)
		Insurance expense (+E, −SE)
		  Prepaid insurance (−A)	

Accrued Expenses		Wages expense (+E, −SE)
		  Wages payable (+L)
			Wages payable (−L)
			  Cash (−A)

Expenses recorded
in the proper period

Step 1: **Ask: Was revenue earned or an expense incurred that has not yet been recorded?**
If the answer is YES, the revenue or expense account must be increased—credit the revenue account or debit the expense account in the adjusting entry.

Step 2: **Ask: Was the related cash received or paid in the past or will it be received or paid in the future?**

If cash *was received* in the past, a deferred revenue (liability) account was recorded in the past) ⟶ now, reduce the liability account (usually deferred revenue) that was recorded when cash was received, because the entire liability or part of it has been settled since then.

If cash *will be received* in the future ⟶ increase the receivable account (such as interest receivable or rent receivable) to record what is owed by others to the company (creates accrued revenue).

If cash *was paid* in the past, a deferred expense account (asset) was recorded in the past) ⟶ now, reduce the asset account (such as supplies or prepaid expenses) that was recorded in the past because the entire asset or part of it has been used since then.

If cash *will be paid* in the future ⟶ increase the payable account (such as interest payable or wages payable) to record what is owed by the company to others (creates an accrued expense).

NOTE: Cash is never included in the adjusting entry, because it was recorded already in the past or will be recorded in the future.

Step 3: **Compute the amount of revenue earned or expense incurred and record the adjusting entry.**

Sometimes the amount is given or known. At other times it must be computed, or sometimes estimated.

What are the adjustments needed for Canadian Tire at the end of January 2016? We start by reviewing the unadjusted trial balance from Chapter 3.

A trial balance is a schedule prepared for internal purposes and is not considered to be a financial statement for external users. Exhibit 4.5 presents an unadjusted trial balance for Canadian Tire at January 31, 2016, based on the balances of the T-accounts illustrated in Chapters 2 and 3, plus other accounts that may be needed but currently have zero balances. Several common adjustments are indicated in the margin of Exhibit 4.5 and will be illustrated in this chapter.

Exhibit **4.5**

Trial Balance for
Canadian Tire
Corporation

CANADIAN TIRE CORPORATION
Unadjusted Trial Balance
As at January 31, 2016

($ in millions)	Debit	Credit
Cash	$ 2,023	
Short-term investments	96	
Accounts receivable	4,790	
Notes receivable	20	
Inventories	1,780	
Prepaid expenses	319	
Other current assets	44	
Long-term receivables	731	
Long-term investments	184	
Property and equipment	6,959	
Accumulated depreciation		$2,826
Goodwill	437	
Intangible assets	810	
Other non-current assets	48	
Accounts payable		1,045
Accrued liabilities		1,037
Deferred service revenue		10
Provisions		262
Short-term borrowings		89
Income taxes payable		62
Current portion of long-term debt		24
Other current liabilities		1,536
Long-term debt		2,984
Other non-current liabilities		2,297
Contributed capital		687
Retained earnings		4,172
Other components		944
Dividends declared	20	
Sales revenue		1,000
Service revenue		40
Interest revenue		1
Gain on sale of land		30
Cost of sales	680	
Salaries and wages expense	80	
Other operating expenses	25	
Totals	**$19,046**	**$19,046**

May need an accrual for any amount earned from customers but not yet recorded

May need an adjustment if merchandise sold has not been recorded

May need an adjustment for the amount of insurance, rent, and advertising used during the period

Represents the historical cost of property and equipment

Represents the portion of the cost of property and equipment used in the past

May need an accrual for any wages, utilities, and interest incurred

May need an adjustment for the amount earned during the period

Needs an accrual for the amount of income tax expense incurred during the period

Represents the beginning balance of retained earnings

Revenue from selling food products and beverages

Revenue from services provided to customers

Revenue earned during the period on note receivable

May need an adjustment if merchandise sold has not been recorded

Summary expense for salaries and wages of all employees

Summary expense for many operating expenses, including insurance, rent, and utilities

Debits = Credits

Canadian Tire's trial balance in Exhibit 4.5 lists several accounts that suggest adjusting entries are necessary. Note that you can identify them as deferrals or accruals by whether cash is received or paid in the past or the future.

Account	Cash Received or Paid in the Past		Revenue Earned or Expense Incurred (during the month)		Cash to Be Received or Paid in the Future
Deferred service revenue	Deferred revenue	⟶	All or a portion may have been earned by month-end.		
Accounts receivable			Customers may owe Canadian Tire for merchandise delivered but not recorded.	⟶	Accrued revenue
Prepaid expenses	Deferred expense	⟶	All or a portion of the prepaid rent, insurance, and advertising may have been used by month-end.		
Property and equipment	Deferred expense	⟶	These non-current assets have been used during the month to generate revenues. A portion of their historical cost is recorded as an expense.		
Accrued liabilities			Canadian Tire owes (1) amounts due for utilities used during the month but not yet billed and (2) wages to employees for work during the last week of January. Neither has yet been recorded as an expense.	⟶	Accrued expense
Debt			Canadian Tire owes interest on borrowed funds.	⟶	Accrued expense
Income taxes payable			Income tax expense needs to be recorded for the period.	⟶	Accrued expense

We will now use the adjustment process to record adjusting entries for Canadian Tire at the end of January.[2] Study the following illustration carefully to understand the steps in the adjustment process, paying close attention to the computation of the amounts in the adjustment and the effects on the account balances. First, we adjust the deferred revenues and accrued revenues and then the deferred expenses and accrued expenses, using the three-step adjustment process.

For each of the following adjustments, we shorten the term "adjusting journal entry" to AJE for ease of labelling. Also, as you learned in Chapters 2 and 3, it is important to continue to check that debits equal credits in each entry and that the accounting equation remains in balance. In the following adjustments, all entries and the accounting equation are in balance.

Deferred Revenues

(AJE 1) Deferred Service Revenue Canadian Tire provided additional services in January for $10 to new clients that had previously paid initial fees to Canadian Tire.

Step 1: **Was revenue earned that is not yet recorded? Yes**. Because Canadian Tire provided services to clients, the company has earned service revenue that is not yet recorded. Record an increase in the revenue account.

Step 2: **Was the related cash received in the past or will it be received in the future?** Canadian Tire received cash **in the past** from clients for future services and recorded the amount received in the deferred service revenue liability account. At January 31, the liability account must be reduced by $10 because Canadian Tire performed the services during the current period.

Step 3: **Compute the amount of revenue earned.** The amount of the revenue that was earned is given as $10. The adjusting journal entry reflects the changes to the accounts.

31/1—AJE 1		
Deferred service revenue (−L)	10	
Service revenue (+R, +SE)		10

Assets	=	Liabilities	+	Shareholders' Equity
		Deferred service revenue −10		Service revenue +10

− Deferred Service Revenue (L) +		− Service Revenue (R) +	
	Ch. 3 bal. 10		Ch. 3 bal. 40
AJE 1 10			AJE 1 10
	End. bal. 0		End. bal. 50

Effect of adjustment on
Net earnings: ↑ 10
  Cash: No effect

For other companies, additional examples of deferred revenues include magazine subscriptions; season tickets to sporting events, plays, and concerts; airline tickets sold in advance; and rent paid in advance by renters. Each of these requires an adjusting entry at the end of the accounting period to report the amount of revenue earned during the period.

Accrued Revenues

(AJE 2) Accounts Receivable Canadian Tire sold merchandise on account for $30 on January 31, but the sales invoices had not been recorded yet. The cost of merchandise sold in $20.

Step 1: **Was revenue earned that is not yet recorded? Yes.** Revenue has been earned during January, but cash will be received in the future, requiring an *accrual of revenue*. Record an increase in the revenue account.

Step 2: **Was the related cash received in the past or will it be received in the future?** Canadian Tire will receive payment from clients for past sales. Because cash will be received **in the future**, a receivable needs to be increased. Increase accounts receivable.

Step 3: **Compute the amount of revenue earned.** The amount of the revenue that was earned is given as $30. The adjusting journal entry reflects the changes to the accounts.

31/1—AJE 2		
Accounts receivable (+A)	30	
Sales revenue (+R, +SE)		30
Cost of sales (+E, −SE)	20	
Inventories (−A)		20

Assets	=	Liabilities	+	Shareholders' Equity
Accounts receivable +30				Sales revenue +30
Inventories −20				Cost of sales −20

+ Accounts Receivable (A) −		− Sales Revenue (R) +	
Ch. 3 bal. 4,790			Ch. 3 bal. 1,000
AJE 2 30			AJE 2 30
End. bal. 4,820			End. bal. 1,030

+ Cost of Sales (E) −		+ Inventories (A) −	
Ch. 3 bal. 680		Ch. 3 bal. 1,780	
AJE 2 20			AJE 2 20
End. bal. 700		End. bal. 1,760	

Effect of adjustment on
Net earnings: ↑ 30
  Cash: No effect

Effect of adjustment on
Net earnings: ↓ 20
  Cash: No effect

Deferred Expenses

(AJE 3) Prepaid expenses At the beginning of January 2016, Canadian Tire paid a total of $223 for future expenses, including insurance ($60), rent ($150), and advertising ($13). The payment for insurance covers four months; one month has passed (January), and three months of future insurance benefits remain. The payment for rent covers three months; one month has passed, and two months of future rent benefits remain. The payment for advertising relates to March 2016 and has not been used yet. In addition to the payment of $223 in January, Canadian Tire has paid an amount of $96 prior to January 2016 to cover future expenses as reflected on its statement of financial position at January 2, 2016. For illustrative purposes, we assume that this amount relates to prepaid insurance, rent, and advertising expenses that the $96 was used to generate revenue in January.

Step 1: **Was expense incurred that is not yet recorded? Yes**. The company used insurance coverage for one month, rental space for one month, and advertising during January, but no entry has been made to record expenses in the appropriate accounts. Record an increase in insurance expense, rent expense, and advertising expense.

Step 2: **Was the related cash paid in the past or will it be paid in the future? In the past**. At the beginning of January, Canadian Tire acquired insurance coverage for the next four months and prepaid rent for the next three months. It had also paid for advertising in future periods. The payments were recorded in the prepaid expenses account, which must now be reduced at month-end because insurance, rent, and advertising have been used during the month. Record a decrease in the prepaid expenses account.

Step 3: **Compute the amount of expense incurred.** One month has expired for the prepaid amounts for insurance and rent, and the amount of prepaid expenses at January 2, 2016, has been used in January:

(1) Insurance: $60 ÷ 4 months = $15 used in January

(2) Rent: $150 ÷ 3 months = $50 used in January

(3) Other prepaid expenses: $96 (given)

Three expense accounts are affected by the adjustment—insurance expense, rent expense, and advertising expense. All three expense accounts are categorized as other operating expenses. For this reason, the beginning balance of prepaid expenses ($96) was not allocated to insurance, rent, and advertising expenses to simplify this illustration. The adjusting journal entry reflects the changes to the accounts.

Effect of adjustment on

Net earnings: ↓ 161

Cash: No effect

31/1—AJE 3		
Other operating expenses (+E, −SE)	161	
Prepaid expenses (−A)		161
Cost of sales (+E, −SE)	20	
Inventories (−A)		20

Assets	=	**Liabilities**	+	**Shareholders' Equity**
Prepaid expenses −161				Other operating expenses −161

+	**Prepaid Expenses (A)**	−	+	**Other Operating Expenses (E)**	−
Ch. 3 bal.	96		Ch. 3 bal.	25	
Purchased	223	AJE 3 161	AJE 3	161	
End. bal.	158		End. bal.	186	

(AJE 4) Property and Equipment Before illustrating the adjustment process, notice that the property and equipment account is stated at the original cost of $6,959 in the trial balance but was stated at $4,133 (original cost minus the portion allocated to past operations) in previous chapters. Unlike supplies that are purchased and then used over a relatively short period, property and equipment represents deferred expenses

that will be used over many years. Property and equipment increases when assets are *acquired* and decreases when they are *sold*. However, these assets are also *used* over time to generate revenue. Thus, a part of their cost should be expensed in the same period (the matching process). Accountants say that these assets depreciate over time as they are used. In accounting, *depreciation is an allocation of an asset's cost over its estimated useful life to the organization.*

To keep track of the asset's historical cost, the amount that has been used is not subtracted directly from the asset account. Instead, it is accumulated in a new kind of account called a contra account. A **contra account** is an account that is an offset to, or reduction of, the primary account. It is *directly related to another account, but has a balance on the opposite side of the T-account.* As a contra account increases, the net amount (the account balance less the contra-account balance) decreases. For property and equipment, the contra account is called *accumulated depreciation.*[3] This is the first of several contra accounts you will learn about throughout the text. We will designate contra accounts with an X in front of the type of account to which it is related (e.g., accumulated depreciation [XA] for contra asset).

Since assets have debit balances, accumulated depreciation has a credit balance. On the statement of financial position, the amount that is reported for property and equipment is its **carrying amount (book value or net book value)**, which equals the ending balance in the property and equipment account minus the ending balance in the accumulated depreciation account. For Canadian Tire, accumulated depreciation has a credit balance of $2,826:

A **CONTRA ACCOUNT** is an account that is an offset to, or reduction of, the primary account.

The **CARRYING AMOUNT** (**BOOK VALUE**, or **NET BOOK VALUE**) of an asset is the difference between its acquisition cost and accumulated depreciation, its related contra account.

+ Property and Equipment (A) −		− Accumulated Depreciation (XA) +	
Beginning bal.	Sell		Beginning bal.
Buy			Used
Ending balance			Ending balance = **Carrying amount**

↑
Amount reported
on the statement of
financial position

Depreciation is discussed in much greater detail in Chapter 8. Until then, we will give you the amount of depreciation estimated by the company for the period. Canadian Tire estimates depreciation to be $312 per year.

Step 1: **Was expense incurred that is not yet recorded? Yes.** The company used buildings and equipment during January. Record an increase in the depreciation expense account.

Step 2: **Was the related cash paid in the past or will it be paid in the future?** Canadian Tire purchased property and equipment **in the past** to be used over several years to generate revenue. The acquisitions were recorded in the property, plant, and equipment asset account. The carrying amount must now be reduced to record the depreciation for January. Reduce the carrying value by increasing the accumulated depreciation contra account.

Step 3: **Compute the amount of expense incurred.** The property, plant, and equipment has been used to generate revenues for one month. Thus, we need to calculate depreciation expense for one month: Monthly depreciation = $312 ÷ 12 months = $26 per month

31/1—AJE 4		
Depreciation expense (+E, −SE)	26	
Accumulated depreciation—Property and equipment (+XA → −A)		26

Assets	=	Liabilities	+	Shareholders' Equity
Accumulated depreciation—Property and equipment −26				Depreciation expense −26

Effect of adjustment on

Net earnings: ↓ 26

Cash: No effect

Note that increasing the contra asset account decreases total assets.

+	Depreciation Expense (E)	−	−	Accumulated Depreciation—Property + and Equipment (XA) +
Ch. 3 bal.	0		Ch. 3 bal.	2,826
AJE 4	26		AJE 4	26
End. bal.	26		End. bal.	2,852

Accrued Expenses

(AJE 5) Accrued Expenses (Salaries, Utilities, and Interest) By January 31, Canadian Tire owed the following amounts: (1) $5 for use of natural gas and electricity (utilities) during January, (2) $13 to its employees for the last four days in January, and (3) interest on both short-term and long-term debt.

Step 1:   **Was expense incurred that is not yet recorded? Yes.** During January, the company used gas and electricity, employees' labour, and money borrowed from creditors, but by the end of January, not all of these expenses had been recorded. Record an increase in each of the following expense accounts: other operating expenses (for the utilities), salaries and wages expenses (for the salaries of employees), and interest expense.

Step 2:   **Was the related cash paid in the past or will it be paid in the future? In the future.** Each of the expenses will need to be paid in the next period, but no liability has yet been recorded. Thus, liabilities on the statement of financial position need to be increased. Although individual liability accounts—such as utilities payable, salaries and wages payable, and interest payable—could be increased, Canadian Tire records all of these accrued expenses in one account, accrued liabilities. Increase the liability.

Step 3:   **Compute the amount of expense incurred.** Each of the amounts is computed or estimated by Canadian Tire at the end of February. These amounts are as follows:
(1) Utilities: Amount given as $5, which is estimated by Canadian Tire based on reviewing prior utility bills.
(2) Salaries: The amount of salaries and wages owed to employees is given at $13.
(3) Interest on debt: $11 computed by Canadian Tire based on the total amount borrowed and the interest rate that Canadian Tire is required to pay to creditors for the debt.

Effect of adjustment on

Net earnings: ↓ 29
Cash: No effect

31/1—AJE 5		
Other operating expenses (+E, −SE)	5	
Salaries and wages expenses (+E, −SE)	13	
Interest expense (+E, −SE)	11	
Accrued liabilities (+L)		29

Assets	=	Liabilities	+	Shareholders' Equity	
		Accrued liabilities +29		Other operating expenses	−5
				Salaries and wages expenses	−13
				Interest expense	−11

+	Other Operating Expenses (E)	−	+	Salaries and Wages Expenses (E)	−
Ch. 3 bal.	25		Ch. 3 bal.	80	
AJE 3	161		AJE 5	13	
AJE 5	5		End. bal.	93	
End. bal.	191				

+	Interest Expense (E)	−	−	Accrued Liabilities (L)	+
Ch. 3 bal.	0			Ch. 2 bal.	1,037
AJE 5	11			AJE 5	29
End. bal.	11			End. bal.	1,066

(AJE 6) Income Taxes Payable The final adjusting journal entry is to record the accrual of income taxes that will be paid in the next quarter (an unrecorded expense). This adjusting entry is recorded last because all other adjustments should be incorporated in computing earnings before income taxes (i.e., balances from the unadjusted trial balance plus the effects of all the previous adjustments):

	Revenues and Gains	Expenses and Losses	
Unadjusted totals	$1,071	$ 785	From Exhibit 4.5
AJE 1	10		
AJE 2	30	20	
AJE 3		161	
AJE 4		26	
AJE 5		29	
	$1,111	− $1,021	= $90 Pretax earnings

Assume that Canadian Tire's average income tax rate is 30 percent.

Step 1: **Was expense incurred that is not yet recorded? Yes**. Companies incur taxes on earnings. Hence, income tax expense must be recorded at the end of the period based on all adjusted revenues, gains, expenses, and losses. Record an increase in the income tax expense account.

Step 2: **Was the related cash paid in the past or will it be paid in the future? In the future**. Income taxes are due at the end of each quarter. So the tax liabilities on the statement of financial position must be increased. Increase the income tax payable liability account.

Step 3: **Compute the amount of expense incurred. Income taxes are computed on the pretax earnings after all other adjustments have been made: $90** pretax earnings × 0.30 = $27 income tax expense for January

31/1—AJE 6		
Income tax expense (+E, −SE)	27	
Income taxes payable (+L)		27

Assets	=	Liabilities		+	Shareholders' Equity	
		Income taxes payable	+27		Income tax expense	−27

+	Income Tax Expense (E)	−		−	Income Tax Payable (L)	+
Ch. 3 bal.	0				Ch. 3 bal.	62
AJE 6	27				AJE 6	27
End. bal.	27				End. bal.	89

Effect of adjustment on

Net earnings: ↓ 27

Cash: No effect

In all the adjustments we completed, you may have noticed that *the cash account was never adjusted.* The cash has already been received or paid by the end of the period, or will be received or paid after the end of the period. Adjustments are required to record revenues and expenses in the proper period because the cash part of the transaction occurs at a different point in time. In addition, *each adjusting entry always included one account on the statement of earnings and one account on the statement of financial position.* Now it is your turn to practise the adjustment process.

PAUSE FOR **FEEDBACK** STOP

Adjustments are necessary at the end of the accounting cycle to record all revenues and expenses in the proper period and to reflect the proper valuation for assets and liabilities.

- *Deferred revenues* (liabilities) have balances at the end of the period because cash was received before it was earned. If all or part of the liability has been satisfied by the end of the period, revenue needs to be recorded and the liability reduced.

- *Accrued revenue* adjustments are necessary when the company has earned revenue, but the cash will be received in the next period. Since nothing has yet been recorded, revenue needs to be recognized and an asset (a receivable) increased.

- *Deferred expenses* (assets) have balances at the end of the period because cash was paid in the past by the company for the assets. If all or part of the asset has been used to generate revenues in the period, an expense needs to be recorded and the asset reduced.

- *Accrued expense* adjustments are necessary when the company has incurred an expense but the cash will be paid in the next period. Since nothing has yet been recorded, an expense needs to be recognized and a liability (a payable) increased.

SELF-STUDY QUIZ 4-1

For practice, complete the following adjustments using the three-step process outlined in the chapter: (1) determine if revenue was earned or an expense incurred, (2) determine if cash was received or paid in the past or will be received or paid in the future, and (3) compute the amount.

B.C. Flippers, a scuba diving and instruction business, completed its first year of operations on December 31, 2017. For each of the following adjustments, identify the type of adjustment, determine the amount of the adjustment, and record the adjusting journal entry.

AJE 1: B.C. Flippers received $6,000 from customers on November 15, 2017, for diving trips in December and January. The $6,000 was recorded in deferred revenue on that date. By the end of December, one-third of the diving trips had been completed.

AJE 2: On December 1, 2017, B.C. Flippers provided advanced diving instruction to 10 customers who will pay the business $800 in January. No entry was made when the instruction was provided.

AJE 3: On September 1, 2017, B.C. Flippers paid $24,000 for insurance for the 12 months beginning on September 1. The amount was recorded as prepaid insurance on September 1.

AJE 4: On March 1, 2017, B.C. Flippers borrowed $300,000 at a 6 percent annual interest rate. Interest totalling $15,000 has accrued until December 31, 2017, but is payable on March 1, 2018.[4]

(1) Revenue earned or expense incurred?	(2) Cash received/ paid in the past or cash to be received/ paid in the future?	(3) Amount	Adjustment Journal Entry Accounts	Debit	Credit
AJE 1					
AJE 2					
AJE 3					
AJE 4					

After you complete your answers, check them with the solutions at the end of the chapter.

Materiality and Adjusting Entries

The term "materiality" describes the relative significance of financial statement information in influencing economic decisions made by financial statement users. **Materiality** suggests that minor items that would not influence the decisions of financial statement users are to be treated in the easiest and most convenient manner. An item of information, or an aggregate of items, is material if it is probable that its omission or misstatement would influence or change a decision. It is a practical concept that provides scope for accountants to be cost effective when they record the effects of transactions and prepare financial disclosure. The concept of materiality allows accountants to estimate amounts and even to ignore specific accounting principles if the results of their actions do not have a material effect on the financial statements. This concept is also of particular importance to the audit process. Auditors use professional judgment to decide whether both individual transactions and aggregated small transactions will result in a *material* misstatement of the financial position of the company.

The process of making adjusting entries can be simplified if we account for immaterial items in the easiest and most convenient manner. For example, businesses purchase many assets that provide benefits for a long period of time. Some of these assets have a very low cost, such as pencil sharpeners and wastebaskets. The proper accounting treatment for such assets is to depreciate their acquisition cost to expense over their useful lives. However, the cost of such assets can be directly charged to expense accounts rather than to asset accounts, in accordance with the materiality concept, thus eliminating the need for an adjusting entry to record periodic depreciation expense. Furthermore, adjusting entries to record accrued expenses or revenues may be ignored if the monetary amounts are immaterial.

The accountant's decision to treat a specific item as immaterial depends on a number of considerations and is a matter of professional judgment. Traditional guidelines in the auditing profession imply that an item is material if it exceeds 1 to 1.5 percent of total assets or sales, or 5 to 10 percent of net earnings. Materiality depends on the nature of the item and its monetary value. If an employee has been stealing small amounts of money systematically, these amounts should not be judged as immaterial because they indicate a weakness in the company's internal control system that should be corrected.[5] Accountants must also consider the combined effect of numerous immaterial events. While each item may be immaterial when considered by itself, the combined effect of many items may be material.

ADJUSTMENTS AND INCENTIVES

A QUESTION OF ACCOUNTABILITY

Owners and managers of companies are most directly affected by the information presented in financial statements. If the financial performance and condition of the company appear strong, the company's share price rises. Shareholders usually receive dividends, and the value of their investment increases. Managers often receive bonuses based on the strength of a company's financial performance, and many in top management are compensated with options to buy their company's shares at prices below market.* The higher the market value, the more compensation they earn. When actual performance lags behind expectations, managers, and owners may be tempted to manipulate accruals and deferrals to make up part of the difference. For example, managers may record cash received in advance of being earned as revenue in the current period or may fail to accrue certain expenses at year-end.

Evidence from studies of large samples of companies indicates that some do engage in such behaviour. This research is borne out by enforcement actions of the securities commissions against companies and sometimes against their auditors. These enforcement actions most often relate to accrual of revenue and receivables that should be deferred to future periods. In many of these cases, the firms involved, their managers, and their auditors are penalized for such actions. Furthermore, owners suffer because the company's share price is affected negatively by news of an investigation by a securities commission.

For example, in June 2004, the Ontario Securities Commission (OSC) charged four top management personnel of Atlas Cold Storage Income Trust with misleading investors after the warehouse operator restated two years of earnings. The OSC indicated that, in preparing Atlas Cold's financial statements, the four executives understated some costs and expenses and recorded some expenses in the wrong periods. These errors resulted in overstatements of net earnings for 2001, 2002, and the second quarter of 2003. The restatement (correction) of the company's financial results erased a total of $42.6 million of net earnings for 2001 and 2002, widened the loss for the third quarter of 2003, and caused suspension of payments to investors.

In September 2006, the OSC reached a settlement agreement with Ronald Perryman, the company's vice-president of finance, who "demonstrated a lack of due diligence that contributed, in part, to the presentation of an improved picture of the financial performance of Atlas for the period including the financial years 2001, 2002, and the first two reporting periods of 2003." Perryman agreed (a) to resign all positions as an officer or director of any issuer, (b) not to become or act as a director or officer of any issuer for 10 years, (c) to be reprimanded, and (d) to pay the sum of $20,000 in respect of the costs of the investigation and hearing in this matter.**

*M. Nelson, J. Elliott, and R. Tarpley. "How Are Earnings Managed? Examples from Auditors," *Accounting Horizons*, Supplement 2003, pp. 17–35.

**In the Matter of the Securities Act, R.S.O. 1990, c. S.5, as Amended and in the Matter of Patrick Gouveia, Andrew Peters, Ronald Perryman, and Paul Vickery, Ontario Securities Commission website. Accessed October 17, 2016.

PREPARING FINANCIAL STATEMENTS

Based on the transactions that have been recorded during January and the adjustments that were recorded at January 31, 2016, we can now prepare financial statements reflecting the operating activities for January. Recall from prior chapters what the four statements are and how they relate to each other:

Because net earnings is a component of retained earnings on the statement of financial position, it is necessary to compute net earnings first by preparing the statement of earnings (#1). The statement of changes in equity (#2) is then prepared because it reports the changes and ending balances in contributed capital and retained earnings, providing the connection to the statement of financial position (#3). Finally, the sources and uses of cash are reported on the statement of cash flows (#4), and the ending balance for cash on the statement equals the cash balance on the statement of financial position:

Statement	Formula
#1 Statement of Earnings	Revenues − Expenses = Net Earnings
#2 Statement of Changes in Equity	Beginning Retained Earnings + Net Earnings − Dividends Declared = Ending Retained Earnings Beginning Contributed Capital + Share Issuances − Share Repurchases = Ending Contributed Capital Ending Shareholders' Equity
#3 Statement of Financial Position	Assets = Liabilities + Shareholders' Equity (includes Cash)
#4 Statement of Cash Flows	Cash provided by (or used in) operating activities +/− Cash provided by (or used in) investing activities +/− Cash provided by (or used in) financing activities Change in Cash + Beginning Cash Ending Cash

As you learned in Chapter 1, these four financial statements are interrelated; that is, the numbers from one statement flow into the next statement as indicated in the coloured financial statement elements above. Thus, if a number on the statement of earnings changes or is in error, it will affect other statements. Although shareholders' equity includes three main elements, we report changes to both contributed capital and retained earnings in this chapter and discuss changes to other components of equity in future chapters. Refer to Exhibit 1.6 of Chapter 1 for an alternative way of presenting the relationships among the four financial statements.

Before we prepare a complete set of financial statements, let us update the trial balance to reflect the adjustments and to provide us with adjusted balances for the statements.[6] In Exhibit 4.6, any account that changed due to adjustments is highlighted. The balances are taken from the T-accounts following each adjustment. For example, in the case of the income taxes payable account, the balance is based on the last adjustment (AJE 6) made to the accounts. Again, we note that the total debits equal the total credits in each of the columns. It is from these adjusted balances that we will prepare a statement of earnings, a statement of changes in equity (which includes a column for retained earnings), and a statement of financial position.

Statement of Earnings

The statement of earnings is prepared first, because net earnings is a component of retained earnings. The January statement of earnings for Canadian Tire is based on transactions in Chapters 2 and 3 and adjustments in this chapter. Note that a few of the expense accounts have been combined into specific categories on the statement of earnings.

Exhibit 4.6

Adjusted Trial Balance for Canadian Tire Corporation

CANADIAN TIRE CORPORATION Adjusted Trial Balance As at January 31, 2016		
($ in millions)	**Debit**	**Credit**
Cash	2,023	
Short-term investments	96	
Accounts receivable	4,820	
Notes receivable	20	
Inventories	1,760	
Prepaid expenses	158	
Other current assets	44	
Long-term receivables	731	
Long-term investments	184	
Property and equipment	6,959	
Accumulated depreciation		2,852
Goodwill	437	
Intangible assets	810	
Other non-current assets	48	
Accounts payable		1,045
Accrued liabilities		1,066
Provisions		262
Short-term borrowings		89
Income taxes payable		89
Current portion of long-term debt		24
Other current liabilities		1,536
Long-term debt		2,984
Other non-current liabilities		2,297
Contributed capital		687
Retained earnings		4,172
Other Components		944
Dividends declared	20	
Sales revenue		1,030
Service revenue		50
Interest revenue		1
Gain on sale of land		30
Cost of sales	700	
Salaries and wages expense	93	
Other operating expenses	191	
Depreciation expense	26	
Interest expense	11	
Income taxes expense	27	
Totals	19,158	19,158

You will note that the earnings per share (EPS) ratio is reported on the statement of earnings (Exhibit 4.7). It is widely used in evaluating the operating performance and profitability of a company and is the only ratio required to be disclosed on the statement or in the notes to the financial statements. The actual computation of the ratio is quite complex and appropriate for advanced accounting courses. We simplify the earnings per share computation:[7]

$$\text{Earnings per share} = \frac{\text{Net earnings available to common shareholders}}{\text{Weighted-average number of common shares outstanding during the period}}$$

The denominator is the average number of shares outstanding (the number at the beginning of the period, plus the number at the end of the period, divided by two). For Canadian Tire, we use 48,509,000, the average number of shares outstanding as disclosed in its 2015 annual report.

$$\text{Earnings per share} = \$63,000,000 \text{ net earnings} \div 76,151,321 \text{ shares}$$
$$= \$0.83 \text{ for January 2016}$$

Exhibit **4.7**

Consolidated Statement of Earnings

CANADIAN TIRE CORPORATION Consolidated Statement of Earnings For the Month Ended January 31, 2016 (in millions of Canadian dollars)	
Revenues	
Sales revenue	$ 1,030
Service revenue	50
Total revenues	1,080
Cost of sales	700
Gross profit	380
Operating expenses	
Salaries and wages	93
Other operating expenses	191
Depreciation expense	26
Total operating expenses	310
Earnings from operations	70
Other non-operating items	
Interest revenue	1
Interest expense	(11)
Gain on sale of land	30
Earnings before income taxes	90
Income taxes expense	27
Net earnings	$ 63
Earnings per share	$ 0.83

As was indicated in Chapter 1, Canadian Tire and all Canadian publicly accountable enterprises are required to prepare a statement of comprehensive income that can be combined with the statement of earnings. The preparation of such a statement is beyond the scope of this textbook.

DIFFERENT EARNINGS FOR DIFFERENT PURPOSES

FINANCIAL
ANALYSIS

In recent years, many companies reported different measures of earnings in addition to net earnings, as determined by IFRS, because they believe that use of these non-IFRS financial measures provides more insight into and understanding of their performance.

Most companies, including the focus companies used in this book, report one or more supplemental measures of operating performance. The most common measure is EBITDA (earnings before interest, taxes, depreciation, and amortization), which excludes interest expense, income tax expense, and depreciation and amortization expense from the computation of net earnings. The management discussion and analysis section of Canadian Tire's annual report for fiscal year 2015 and the 10-year financial review include the following details:

Additionally, the Company considers earnings before interest, tax, depreciation and amortization, and the change in fair value of the redeemable financial instrument ("adjusted EBITDA") to be an effective measure of CTC's profitability on an operational basis. Adjusted EBITDA is a non-GAAP financial metric and is commonly regarded as an indirect measure of operating cash flow, a significant indicator of success for many businesses.

	2015	2014	2013	2012	2011
Net earnings	$ 736	$ 639	$ 564	$ 499	$ 467
Adjusted EBITDA	1,519	1,359	1,236	1,138	1,058

Canadian Tire indicates that adjusted EBITDA is also commonly regarded as an indirect measure of operating cash flow, a significant indicator of success for many businesses. Investors are usually cautioned about relying on such measures of operating performance, which are not prepared in accordance with IFRS and may not be comparable across companies because of differences in the methods of computing such measures.

Statement of Changes in Equity

The final amount from the statement of earnings, net earnings, is carried forward to the retained earnings column of the statement of changes in equity. Dividends declared during January 2016 are deducted to arrive at the ending balance at January 31, 2016. The issuance of additional shares (from Chapter 2) is added to the beginning balance of contributed capital. Other components of equity are unchanged for this illustration.

CANADIAN TIRE CORPORATION **Statement of Changes in Equity** **For the Month Ended January 31, 2016** **(in thousands of Canadian dollars)**				
	Contributed Capital	**Retained Earnings**	**Other Components**	**Shareholders' Equity**
Beginning balance	$674	$4,172	$944	$5,790
Issuance of shares	13			13
Net earnings		63		63
Distribution of dividends		(20)		(20)
Ending balance	$687	$4,215	$944	$5,846

From event (a) in Chapter 2
From the statement of earnings
From event (f) in Chapter 2
Included in the statement of financial position

Statement of Financial Position

The ending balances under the contributed capital, retained earnings, and other components headings of the statement of changes in equity are included on the statement of financial position. You will notice that the contra-asset account accumulated depreciation has been subtracted from the property, plant, and equipment account to reflect its carrying amount (or net book value) at month-end for financial reporting purposes. Also, recall that assets are listed in order of liquidity, while liabilities are listed in order of time to maturity. Current assets are those used or turned into cash within one year. Current liabilities are obligations to be settled within one year. The balances at January 2, 2016, are presented for comparative purposes.

In addition to preparing the basic financial statements, companies provide further information about specific elements of these statements in notes that follow the statements. The additional details supporting the reported numbers facilitate analysis of the company's operating performance and financial condition. A closer look at note disclosures related to financial statements is provided in future chapters.

CANADIAN TIRE CORPORATION Consolidated Statement of Financial Position (in millions of Canadian dollars)		
Assets	**January 31, 2016**	**January 2, 2016**
Current assets		
Cash	$ 2,023	$ 901
Short-term investments	96	96
Accounts receivable	4,820	5,790
Notes receivable	20	–
Inventories	1,760	1,765
Prepaid expenses	158	96
Other current assets	44	44
Total current assets	8,921	9,330
Property and equipment, net	4,107	4,116
Long-term receivables	731	731
Long-term investments	184	154
Goodwill	437	437
Intangible assets	810	810
Other non-current assets	48	48
Total assets	**$15,238**	**$14,988**
Liabilities and shareholders' equity		
Current liabilities		
Accounts payable	$ 1,045	$ 920
Accrued liabilities	1,066	1,037
Provisions	262	262
Short-term borrowings	89	89
Income taxes payable	89	62
Current portion of long-term debt	24	24
Other current liabilities	1,536	1,536
Total current liabilities	4,111	3,930
Long-term debt	2,984	2,971
Other non-current liabilities	2,297	2,297
Total liabilities	9,392	9,198
Shareholders' equity		
Contributed capital	687	674
Retained earnings	4,215	4,172
Other components	944	944
Total shareholders' equity	5,846	5,790
Total liabilities and shareholders' equity	**$15,238**	**$14,988**

CASH FLOW FROM OPERATIONS, NET EARNINGS, AND THE QUALITY OF EARNINGS

FOCUS ON
CASH FLOWS

As presented in the previous chapters, the statement of cash flows explains the difference between the ending and beginning balances in the cash account during the accounting period. Put simply, the statement of cash flows is a categorized list of all transactions of the period that affected the cash account. The three categories are operating, investing, and financing activities. *Since the adjustments made in this chapter did not affect cash, the cash flow categories identified in the cash T-account at the end of Chapter 3 remain the same.*

Many standard financial analysis texts warn analysts to look for unusual deferrals and accruals when they attempt to predict future periods' earnings. They often suggest that wide disparities between net earnings and cash flow from operations are a useful warning sign. For example, Subramanyan suggests the following:

> Accounting accruals determining net income rely on estimates, deferrals, allocations, and valuations. These considerations sometimes allow more subjectivity than do the factors determining cash flows. For this reason, we often relate cash flows from operations to net income in assessing its quality. *Some users consider earnings of higher quality when the ratio of cash flows from operations divided by net income is greater* [emphasis added]. This derives from a concern with revenue recognition or expense accrual criteria yielding high net income but low cash flows.*

The cash flows from operations to net earnings ratio is illustrated and discussed in more depth in Chapter 13.

*K. Subramanyan, *Financial Statement Analysis* (New York, McGraw-Hill/Irwin, 2009), p. 412.

NET PROFIT MARGIN RATIO AND RETURN ON EQUITY

KEY RATIO ANALYSIS

Evaluating company performance is the primary goal of financial statement analysis. Company managers, as well as competitors, use financial statements to better understand and evaluate a company's business strategy. Analysts, investors, and creditors use these same statements to evaluate performance as part of their share valuation and credit evaluation judgments. In Chapter 3, we introduced the return on assets to examine managers' effectiveness at using assets to generate earnings. We now discuss two other measures of profitability. The net profit margin ratio compares net earnings to the revenues generated during the period, and the return on equity relates net earnings to shareholders' investment in the business.

LO4-3

Compute and interpret the net profit margin ratio and the return on equity.

NET PROFIT MARGIN RATIO

ANALYTICAL QUESTION → How effective is management at controlling revenues and expenses to generate more earnings?

RATIO AND COMPARISONS → The net profit margin ratio is useful in answering this question. It is computed as follows:

$$\text{Net profit margin ratio} = \frac{\text{Net earnings}}{\text{Net sales (or Operating revenues)}^*}$$

*Net sales is sales revenue less any returns from customers, and other reductions. For companies in the service industry, total operating revenues equals net sales.

The 2015 ratio for Canadian Tire is,

$$\frac{\$736}{\$12,280} = 0.060 (6.0\%)$$

Comparisons over Time			Comparisons with Competitors	
Canadian Tire			Hudson's Bay Company	Sears Canada Inc.
2013	2014	2015	2015	2015
4.8%	5.1%	6.0%	3.5%	−2.2%

*The fiscal years of both companies, Hudson's Bay Company and Sears Canada Inc., ended on January 30, 2016.

INTERPRETATIONS

In General → The net profit ratio margin measures how much profit is earned as a percentage of revenues generated during the period. A rising net profit margin ratio signals more efficient management of sales and expenses. Differences among industries result from the nature of the products or services provided and the intensity of competition. Differences among competitors in the same industry reflect how each company responds to changes in competition (and demand for the product or the service) and changes in managing sales volume, sales price, and costs. Financial analysts expect well-run businesses to maintain or improve their net profit margin ratio over time.

SELECTED FOCUS COMPANY NET PROFIT MARGIN RATIOS—2015

BCE Inc., 12.7

Canadian Tire 6.0

Gildan Activewear 10.3

Focus Company Analysis → Canadian Tire's net profit margin ratio increased over the period 2013–2015. The increase in the ratio in 2015 reflects strong retail sales growth at Canadian Tire and FGL Sports, strong gross profit contribution from Canadian Tire Gas+'s higher per litre gas margins, and increased credit card charges on increased accounts receivables in the Financial Services segment. These increases were partially offset by a reduction in retail sales and gross profit rates at Mark's and an increase in selling, general, and administrative expenses compared to fiscal year 2014. Canadian Tire's ratio surpassed the ratios of both of its competitors.

A Few Cautions → The decisions that management makes to maintain the company's net profit margin ratio in the current period may have negative long-run implications. Analysts should perform additional analysis of the ratio to identify trends in each component of revenues and expenses. This involves dividing each line on the statement of earnings by net sales. Statements presented with these percentages are called *common-sized statements of earnings*, as discussed in Chapter 12. Changes in the percentages of the individual components of net earnings provide information on shifts in management's strategies.

RETURN ON EQUITY

ANALYTICAL QUESTION → How well has management used shareholder investment to generate net earnings during the period?

RATIO AND COMPARISONS → The return on equity (ROE) helps in answering this question. It is computed as follows:

$$\text{Return on equity} = \frac{\text{Net earnings}}{\text{Average shareholders' equity*}}$$

*Average shareholders' equity = (Beginning shareholders' equity + Ending shareholders' equity) ÷ 2

The 2015 ratio for Canadian Tire is,

$$\frac{\$736}{[(\$5,631 + \$5,790) \div 2]} = 0.129(12.9\%)$$

Comparisons over Time			Comparisons with Competitors	
Canadian Tire			Hudson's Bay Company	Sears Canada Inc.
2013	2014	2015	2015	2015
11.1%	11.5%	12.9%	13.9%	−12.1%

INTERPRETATIONS

In General → ROE measures how much the firm earned as a percentage of shareholders' investment. In the long run, firms with higher ROE are expected to have higher share prices than firms with lower ROE, all other things being equal. Managers, analysts, and creditors use this ratio to assess the effectiveness of the company's overall business strategy (its operating, investing, and financing strategies).

SELECTED FOCUS COMPANY RETURNS ON EQUITY—2015

BCE Inc., 16.8

Canadian Tire 12.9

Gildan Activewear 14.5

Focus Company Analysis → Canadian Tire's ROE increased over the three-year period, 2013–2015. This indicates that Canadian Tire's utilization of resources has generated a higher level of return on shareholders' investment, particularly in 2015, because of increased net earnings relative to the increase in shareholders' equity. Compared to Canadian Tire, Hudson's Bay achieved a higher return on equity in 2015, but Sears Canada's decreased sales resulted in a net loss for the year and a negative ratio.

A Few Cautions → An increasing ROE can also indicate that a manufacturing company is failing to invest in research and development or in modernization of plant and equipment. While such a strategy will decrease expenses and, thus, increase ROE in the short run, it normally results in future declines in ROE as the company's products, plant, and equipment reach the end of their life cycles. As a consequence, experienced decision makers evaluate ROE in the context of a company's business strategy.

More detailed analysis of ROE and its relationship to other financial ratios is covered in Chapter 12.

PAUSE FOR **FEEDBACK**

Adjustments are necessary at the end of the accounting cycle to ensure that all revenues and expenses are recorded in the proper period and to reflect the proper valuation for assets and liabilities. If adjustments are omitted, the reported amounts for assets, liabilities, equity, revenues, expenses, and net earnings will be incorrect and the related ratios are likely to be misleading.

SELF-STUDY QUIZ 4-2

Refer to Exhibits 4.5 and 4.6. Compute the net profit margin for Canadian Tire based on information disclosed in (1) the unadjusted trial balance and (2) the adjusted trial balance. Why are the two ratios different? Is the difference between the two ratios significant? Explain.

After you complete your answers, check them with the solutions at the end of the chapter.

CLOSING THE BOOKS

End of the Accounting Cycle

The statement of financial position accounts are updated continuously throughout the accounting period, and the ending balance for the current period becomes the beginning account balance for the next period. The balances in these accounts, called **permanent (real) accounts**, are not reduced to zero at the end of the accounting period. For example, the ending cash balance of one accounting period must be the beginning cash balance of the next accounting period. The only time a permanent account has a zero balance is when the item represented is no longer owned or owed.

In contrast, revenue, expense, gain, loss, and dividend accounts are used to accumulate transaction effects for the *current accounting period only*; they are called **temporary (nominal) accounts**. The final step in the accounting cycle, closing the books, is done to prepare statement of earnings accounts for the next accounting cycle. Therefore, at the end of each period, the balances in the temporary accounts are transferred, or closed, to the retained earnings account by recording **closing entries**.

The closing entries have two purposes:

1. To transfer the balances in the temporary accounts to retained earnings.
2. To establish a zero balance in each of the temporary accounts to start the accumulation in the next accounting period.

The closing process requires three journal entries: one entry to close the revenue and expense accounts, another entry to close the expense and loss accounts, and a final entry to close the dividends declared account. Revenue and gain accounts, which have credit balances, are closed by debiting the total amount to **income summary**, a temporary account used only during the closing process to facilitate closing temporary accounts. Expense and loss accounts, which have debit balances, are closed by crediting the total amount to income summary. The balance of the income summary account reflects the net earnings (or loss) and is then closed to the retained earnings account. In this way, the statement of earnings accounts are again ready for their temporary accumulation function for the next period.

Closing entries are dated the last day of the accounting period, entered in the usual format in the journal, and immediately posted to the ledger (or T-accounts). We illustrate the closing process by preparing the closing entries for Canadian Tire at January 31, 2016, although, in practice, companies close their records only at the end of the fiscal year:

LO4-4

Explain the closing process at the end of the period.

PERMANENT (REAL) ACCOUNTS are the statement of financial position accounts whose ending balances are carried into the next accounting period.

TEMPORARY (NOMINAL) ACCOUNTS are statement of earnings (and sometimes dividends declared) accounts that are closed to retained earnings at the end of the accounting period.

CLOSING ENTRIES transfer balances in temporary accounts to retained earnings and establish zero balances in temporary accounts.

INCOME SUMMARY is a temporary account used only during the closing process to facilitate closing temporary accounts.

Sales Revenue (R)				Cost of Sales (E)			
Closing	1,030	Sales in January	1,030	Cost of sales in January	700	Closing	700
		End. bal.	0			End. bal.	0

Income Summary (T)			
Cost of sales in January	700	Sales in January	1,030
...		...	
...		...	
Closing	63		
		End. bal.	0

Dividends Declared (SE)			
Dividends declared in January	20	Closing	20
		End. bal.	0

Retained Earnings (SE)			
		Ch. 3 bal.	4,172
Dividends declared	20	Net earnings	63
		End. bal.	4,215

Sales revenue (−R)	1,030	
Service revenue (−R)	50	
Interest revenue (−R)	1	
Gain on sale of land (−R)	30	
Income summary (+T)		1,111
To close the revenue accounts to income summary.		
Income summary (−T)	1,048	
Cost of sales (−E)		700
Salaries and wages expenses (−E)		93
Other operating expenses (−E)		191
Depreciation expense (−E)		26
Interest expense (−E)		11
Income tax expense (−E)		27
To close the expense accounts to income summary.		
Income summary (−T)	63	
Retained earnings (+SE)		63
To close the income summary account to retained earnings.		
Retained earnings (−SE)	20	
Dividends declared (+SE)		20
To close the dividends declared account to retained earnings.		

Post-closing Trial Balance

The **POST-CLOSING TRIAL BALANCE** should be prepared as the last step of the accounting cycle to check that debits equal credits and that all temporary accounts have been closed.

After the closing process is complete, all of the statement of earnings accounts have a zero balance. These accounts are then ready for recording revenues and expenses in the new accounting period. The ending balance in retained earnings is now up to date (matches the amount on the statement of financial position) and is carried forward as the beginning balance for the next period. A **post-closing trial balance** should be prepared as the last step of the accounting cycle to check that debits equal credits and that all temporary accounts have been closed.

ACCRUALS AND DEFERRALS: JUDGING EARNINGS QUALITY

FINANCIAL ANALYSIS

Most of the adjustments discussed in this chapter, such as the allocation of prepaid insurance or the determination of accrued interest revenue, involve direct calculations and require little judgment on the part of the company's management. In later chapters, we will discuss many other adjustments that involve difficult and complex estimates about the future. These include, for example, estimates of customers' ability to make payments to the company for purchases on account, the useful lives of new machines, and future amounts that a company may owe on warranties of products sold in the past. Each of these estimates and many others can have significant effects on the stream of net earnings that companies report over time.

When attempting to value firms based on their statement of financial position and statement of earnings information, analysts also evaluate the estimates that form the basis for the adjustments. Managers who make relatively pessimistic estimates that reduce current net earnings are judged to be *prudent* in deciding on financial reporting strategies, and the financial reports they produce are given more credence. The resulting net earnings numbers are often said to be of *higher quality* because they are less influenced by management's natural optimism. Firms that consistently make optimistic estimates resulting in reporting higher net earnings, however, are judged to be *aggressive*. Analysts judge these companies' operating performance to be of lower quality.

ACCOUNTING STANDARDS FOR PRIVATE ENTERPRISES

The accounting concepts and procedures related to adjusting and closing the appropriate accounts are equally applicable to private enterprises.

DEMONSTRATION CASE

We take our final look at the accounting activities of Terrific Lawn Maintenance Corporation by illustrating the activities at the end of the accounting cycle: adjustment process, financial statement preparation, and closing process. Chapter 2 presented investing and financing activities, and Chapter 3 presented operating activities. No adjustments had been made to the accounts to reflect all revenues earned and expenses incurred in April, however. The trial balance for Terrific Lawn on April 30, 2017, based on the unadjusted balances in Chapter 3, is as follows:

TERRIFIC LAWN MAINTENANCE CORPORATION
Unadjusted Trial Balance
At April 30, 2017

	Debit	Credit
Cash	5,032	
Accounts receivable	1,700	
Prepaid expenses	300	
Equipment *(cost)*	4,600	
Accumulated depreciation *(used cost)*		0
Land	3,750	
Accounts payable		220
Wages payable		0
Utilities payable		0
Deferred revenue		1,600
Notes payable (short term)		400
Interest payable		0
Income tax payable		0
Notes payable (long term)		3,300
Contributed capital		9,000
Retained earnings		0
Mowing revenue		5,200
Interest revenue		12
Fuel expense	410	
Wages expense	3,900	
Interest expense	40	
Insurance expense	0	
Utilities expense	0	
Depreciation expense	0	
Income tax expense	0	
Totals	19,732	19,732

Additional information is as follows:

a. The $1,600 in deferred revenue represents four months of service (April through July).

b. Prepaid expenses include insurance costing $300, providing coverage for six months (April through September).

c. Mowers, edgers, rakes, and hand tools (equipment) have been used in April to generate revenue. The company estimates $300 in depreciation each year.

d. Wages have been paid through April 28. Wages earned in April by the employees during the last two days will be paid in May. They accrue at $200 per day.

e. An extra telephone line was installed in April at an estimated cost of $52, including hook-up and usage charges. The bill will be received and paid in May. No entry has yet been recorded.

f. Interest accrues on the outstanding short-term and long-term notes payable at an annual rate of 6 percent. The $3,700 in principal has been outstanding all month.

g. The estimated income tax rate for Terrific Lawn is 35 percent for both federal and provincial income taxes.

Required:

1. Prepare the adjusting entries for April, using the account titles shown in the trial balance. In your analysis, be sure to use the three-step process outlined in this chapter: (1) determine if revenue was earned or an expense incurred that needs to be recorded for the period, (2) determine if cash was or will be received or paid, and (3) compute the amount. In addition, show the effect of the adjustment on net earnings and cash.

2. Prepare an adjusted trial balance.

3. Prepare a statement of earnings, a statement of changes in equity, and a statement of financial position based on the amounts in the adjusted trial balance. Include earnings per share on the statement of earnings. The company issued 1,500 shares.

4. Prepare the closing entry for April 30, 2017.

5. Compute the company's net profit margin, return on equity, and total asset turnover ratios for the month.

6. For each of the items (a), (b), and (c) above, indicate the effect of omitting the required adjustment on the elements of the statement of financial position and statement of earnings. Use O for overstatement, U for understatement, and N for no effect. Ignore the effects of income taxes on overstatements or understatements of revenues and expenses.

Transaction	Statement of Financial Position			Statement of Earnings		
	Assets	**Liabilities**	**Shareholders' Equity**	**Revenues**	**Expenses**	**Net Earnings**
(a)						
(b)						
(c)						

We strongly recommend that you prepare your own answers to these requirements and then check your answers with the following solution.

SUGGESTED **SOLUTION**

1. Adjusting entries:

AJE		Debit	Credit	Effect of Adjustment on	
a.	Deferred revenue (−L)	400		Net earnings:	↑400
	Mowing revenue (+R, + SE)		400	Cash:	No effect
	Revenue earned in April = $1,600 × 1/4 = $400.				
b.	Insurance expense (+E, −SE)	50		Net earnings:	↓5
	Prepaid expenses (−A)		50	Cash:	No effect
	Insurance used in April = $300 × 1/6 = $50.				
c.	Depreciation expense (+E, −SE)	25		Net earnings:	↓25
	Accumulated depreciation—Equipment (+XA → −A)		25	Cash:	No effect
	Depreciation expense for April = $300 × 1/12 = $25.				
d.	Wages expense (+E, −SE)	400		Net earnings:	↓400
	Wages payable (+L)		400	Cash:	No effect
	Wages incurred in April = $200 per day × 2 days = $400				

e.   Utilities expense (+E, −SE)   52   Net earnings: ↓52
       Utilities payable (+L)   52   Cash: No effect
       Estimated amount incurred in April

f.   Interest expense (+E, −SE)   37   Net earnings: ↓37
        Interest payable (+L)   37   Cash: No effect
       Interest incurred in April = $3,700 × 0.12 × 1/12 = $37

g.   Income tax expense (+E, −SE)   244   Net earnings: ↓244
       Income taxes payable (+L)   244   Cash: No effect

	Revenues	*Expenses*	
Unadjusted balances	$5,212	$4,350	From trial balance
AJE a	400		
AJE b		50	
AJE c		25	
AJE d		400	
AJE e		52	
AJE f		37	
	$5,612	− $4,914	= $698 pretax earnings × 0.35 tax rate
			$244 (rounded)

Note that all the adjustments affected net earnings because the revenue and expense accounts had to be increased to record all the revenues earned and the expenses incurred during the period. These adjustments affected specific asset and liability accounts, but none of the adjustments affected the cash account, because adjustments are internal transactions that do not involve an exchange with an outside party.

2. Adjusted trial balance:

TERRIFIC LAWN MAINTENANCE CORPORATION Adjusted Trial Balance At April 30, 2017		
(in thousands of dollars)	**Debit**	**Credit**
Cash	5,032	
Accounts receivable	1,700	
Prepaid expenses	250	
Equipment *(cost)*	4,600	
Accumulated depreciation		25
Land	3,750	
Accounts payable		220
Wages payable		400
Utilities payable		52
Deferred revenue		1,200
Notes payable (short term)		400
Interest payable		37
Income taxes payable		244
Notes payable (long term)		3,300
Contributed capital		9,000
Retained earnings		0
Mowing revenue		5,600
Interest revenue		12
Fuel expense	410	
Wages expense	4,300	
Interest expense	77	
Insurance expense	50	
Utilities expense	52	
Depreciation expense	25	
Income tax expense	244	
Totals	20,490	20,490

3. Financial statements:

TERRIFIC LAWN MAINTENANCE CORPORATION Statement of Earnings For the Month Ended April 30, 2017	
Operating Revenues:	
Mowing revenue	$5,600
Operating Expenses:	
Fuel expense	410
Wages expense	4,300
Insurance expense	49
Utilities expense	52
Depreciation expense	25
	4,837
Earnings from Operations	763
Other items:	
Interest revenue	12
Interest expense	(77)
Earnings before income taxes	698
Income tax expense	244
Net earnings	$ 454
Earnings per share (for the month) ($454 ÷ 1,500 shares)	$ 0.30

TERRIFIC LAWN MAINTENANCE CORPORATION Statement of Changes in Equity For the Month Ended April 30, 2017			
	Contributed Capital	**Retained Earnings**	**Total**
Balance, April 1, 2017	$ 0	$ 0	$ 0
Issuance of shares	9,000		9,000
Net earnings	454	454	
Dividends			0
Balance, April 30, 2017	$9,000	$454	$9,454

TERRIFIC LAWN MAINTENANCE CORPORATION Statement of Financial Position At April 30, 2017			
Assets		**Liabilities**	
Current Assets:		**Current Liabilities:**	
Cash	$ 5,032	Accounts payable	$ 220
Accounts receivable	1,700	Wages payable	400
Prepaid expenses	250	Utilities payable	52
Total current assets	6.982	Deferred revenue	1,200
		Notes payable (short term)	400
		Interest payable	37
		Income taxes payable	244
		Total current liabilities	2,553
		Notes payable (long term)	3,300
Equipment (net of $25 accumulated depreciation	4,575	Total liabilities	5,853
Land	3,750	**Shareholders' Equity**	
		Contributed capital	9,000
		Retained earnings	454
		Total shareholders' equity	9,454
Total assets	$15,307	Total liabilities and shareholders' equity	$15,307

4. Closing entries:

Mowing revenue (−R)	5,600	
Interest revenue (−R)	12	
Income summary (+T)		5,612
Income summary (−T)	5,158	
Fuel expense (−E)		410
Wages expense (−E)		4,300
Utilities expense (−E)		52
Insurance expense (−E)		50
Depreciation expense (−E)		25
Interest expense (−E)		77
Income tax expense (−E)		244
Income summary (−T)	454	
Retained earnings (+SE)		454

5. Ratios

a. Net profit margin ratio for April:

$$\frac{\text{Net earnings}}{\text{Net sales}} = \$454 \div \$5,600 = 0.081 \text{ or } 8.1\%$$

Return on equity for April:

$$\frac{\text{Net earnings}}{\text{Average shareholders' equity}} = \frac{\$454}{(\$9,000 + \$9,454) \div 2} = 0.492 \text{ or } 4.92\%$$

6.

	Statement of Financial Position			Statement of Earnings		
Transaction	Assets	Liabilities	Shareholders' Equity	Revenues	Expenses	Net Earnings
(a)	N	O, $400	U, $400	U, $400	N	U, $400
(b)	O, $50	N	O, $50	N	U, $50	O, $50
(c)	O, $25	N	O, $25	N	U, $25	O, $25

CHAPTER TAKE-AWAYS

4-1. Explain the purpose of adjustments and analyze the adjustments necessary at the end of the period to update statement of financial position and statement of earnings accounts.

- Adjusting entries are necessary at the end of the accounting period to measure earnings properly, correct errors, and provide for adequate valuation of financial statement accounts. There are four types of adjustments:
- Deferred revenues—previously recorded liabilities created when cash was received in advance that must be adjusted for the amount of revenue earned during the period.
- Accrued revenues—revenues that were earned during the period but have not yet been recorded (cash will be received in the future).
- Deferred expenses—previously recorded assets (prepaid rent, supplies, and equipment) that must be adjusted for the amount of expense incurred during the period.
- Accrued expenses—expenses that were incurred during the period but have not yet been recorded (cash will be paid in the future).

The analysis involves the following steps:

Step 1: Determine if revenue was earned or an expense was incurred. Record an increase in the revenue or expense account.

Step 2: Determine whether cash was received or paid in the past or will be received or paid in the future. If in the past, the existing asset or liability is overstated and needs to be reduced. If in the future, the related receivable or payable account needs to be increased.

Step 3: Compute the amount of revenue earned or expense incurred in the period.

- Recording adjusting entries has no effect on the cash account.

4-2. Prepare a statement of earnings with earnings per share, a statement of changes in equity, and a statement of financial position.

Adjusted account balances are used in preparing the following financial statements:

- Statement of Earnings: Revenues − Expenses = Net earnings (including earnings per share computed as net earnings divided by the weighted-average number of common shares outstanding during the period).
- Statement of Changes in Equity: (Beginning contributed capital + Issuance of shares − Repurchase of shares) + (Beginning retained earnings + Net earnings − Dividends declared) = Ending shareholders' equity.
- Statement of Financial Position: Assets = Liabilities + Shareholders' Equity.
- Statement of Cash Flows: Since adjustments never affect cash, the statement of cash flows is not changed.

4-3. Compute and interpret the net profit margin ratio and the return on equity.

The net profit margin ratio (net earnings ÷ net sales) measures how much profit is earned as a percentage of revenues generated during the period. A rising net profit margin ratio signals more efficient management of revenues and expenses. The return on equity measures how well management used shareholders' investment to generate revenue during the period. Managers, analysts, and creditors use this ratio to assess the effectiveness of the company's overall business strategy (its operating, investing, and financing strategies).

4-4. Explain the closing process at the end of the period.

Temporary accounts (revenues, expenses, gains, and losses) are closed to a zero balance at the end of the accounting period to allow for the accumulation of these items in the following period and to update retained earnings for the period's net earnings. To close these accounts, debit each revenue and gain account with a credit to income summary, credit each expense and loss account with a debit to income summary, and then record the difference to retained earnings. The dividends declared account should also be closed and the balance transferred to retained earnings.

Each year, many companies report healthy net earnings but file for bankruptcy. Some investors consider this situation to be a paradox, but sophisticated analysts understand how this situation can occur. The statement of earnings is prepared under the accrual concept (revenue is reported when earned and the related expense is reported when incurred). The statement of earnings does not report cash collections and cash payments. Troubled companies usually file for bankruptcy because they cannot meet their cash obligations (e.g., they cannot pay their suppliers or meet their required interest payments). The statement of earnings does not help analysts assess the cash flows of a company. The statement of cash flows discussed in Chapter 5 is designed to help statement users evaluate a company's cash inflows and outflows.

KEY **RATIOS**

The net profit margin ratio measures how much each sales dollar generated in net earnings during the period. A high or rising ratio suggests that the company is managing its sales and expenses efficiently. It is computed as follows:

$$\text{Net profit margin ratio} = \frac{\text{Net earnings}}{\text{Net sales (or Operating revenues)}}$$

Return on equity measures how much the firm earned for each dollar of shareholders' investment. It is computed as follows:

$$\text{Return on equity} = \frac{\text{Net earnings}}{\text{Average shareholders' equity}}$$

FINDING **FINANCIAL INFORMATION**

STATEMENT OF FINANCIAL POSITION
Current Assets
Accruals include
   Interest receivable
   Rent receivable
   Deferrals include
   Inventory
   Prepaid expenses
Non-current Assets
Deferrals include
   Property and equipment
   Intangibles
Current Liabilities
Accruals include
   Interest payable
   Wages payable
   Utilities payable
   Income tax payable
Deferrals include
   Deferred revenue

STATEMENT OF EARNINGS
Revenues
   Include end-of-period adjustments
Expenses
   Include end-of-period adjustments
Earnings before Income Taxes
   Income tax expense
Net earnings

STATEMENT OF CASH FLOWS
Adjusting Entries Do Not Affect Cash

NOTES
In Various Notes, if Not on the Financial Statements
Details of accrued liabilities

Interest paid, interest and dividends received, income taxes paid, significant non-cash transactions (if not reported on the statement of cash flows)

QUESTIONS

1. Explain the accounting information processing cycle.
2. Identify, in sequence, the phases of the accounting information processing cycle.
3. What is the purpose of recording adjusting entries.
4. List the four types of adjusting entries, and give an example of each type.
5. What is a contra asset? Give an example of one.
6. Explain why adjusting entries are entered in the journal on the last day of the accounting period and then posted to the ledger.
7. Explain how the financial statements relate to each other.
8. What is the equation for each of the following: (a) statement of earnings, (b) retained earnings component of the statement of changes in equity, (c) statement of financial position, and (d) statement of cash flows.
9. Explain the effect of adjusting entries on cash.
10. How is earnings per share computed and interpreted?
11. Contrast an unadjusted trial balance with an adjusted trial balance. What is the purpose of each?
12. Why does net earnings differ from cash flow from operations? Explain.
13. What is the practical importance of the concept of materiality to preparers, auditors, and users of financial statements?
14. What is meant by the "quality of earnings"?
15. What is the purpose of closing entries? Why are they recorded in the journal and posted to the ledger?
16. Differentiate among permanent, temporary, real, and nominal accounts.
17. Why are the statement of earnings accounts closed, but the statement of financial position accounts are not?
18. What is a post-closing trial balance? Is it a useful part of the accounting information processing cycle? Explain.
19. How is the net profit margin ratio computed and interpreted?
20. How is the return on equity computed and interpreted?

LO4-1   M4-1   Preparing a Trial Balance

Hagadorn Company has the following adjusted accounts and balances at year-end (June 30, 2017):

Accounts payable	$ 250	Income taxes payable	$ 50
Accounts receivable	420	Interest expense	70
Accrued expenses payable	160	Interest revenue	60
Accumulated depreciation	250	Inventories	710
Buildings and equipment	1,400	Land	300
Cash	175	Long-term debt	1,460
Contributed capital	400	Prepaid expenses	30
Cost of sales	780	Salaries expense	640
Depreciation expense	150	Sales revenue	2,400
Deferred fees	90	Rent expense	460
Income taxes expense	135	Retained earnings	150

Prepare an adjusted trial balance in good form for the Hagadorn Company at June 30, 2017.

LO4-1   M4-2   Matching Definitions with Terms

Match each definition with its related term by entering the appropriate letter in the space provided.

Definition	Term
_____ (1) Revenue not yet earned; collected in advance.	A. Accrued expense
_____ (2) Rent not yet collected; already earned.	B. Deferred expense
_____ (3) Property taxes incurred; not yet paid.	C. Accrued revenue
_____ (4) Rent revenue collected; not yet earned.	D. Deferred revenue
_____ (5) An expense incurred; not yet paid or recorded.	
_____ (6) Office supplies on hand to be used next accounting period.	
_____ (7) An expense not yet incurred; paid in advance.	
_____ (8) Revenue earned; not yet collected.	

LO4-1   M4-3   Matching Definitions with Terms

Match each definition with its related term by entering the appropriate letter in the space provided.

Definition	Term
_____ (1) At year-end service revenue of $1,000 was collected in cash but was not yet earned.	A. Accrued expense
	B. Deferred expense
_____ (2) Interest of $550 on a note receivable was earned at year-end, although collection of the interest is not due until the following year.	C. Accrued revenue
	D. Deferred revenue
_____ (3) At year-end, wages payable of $5,600 had not been recorded or paid.	
_____ (4) Office supplies were purchased during the year for $700, and $100 of them remained on hand (unused) at year-end.	

LO4-1   M4-4   Recording Adjusting Entries (Deferred Accounts)

In each of the following transactions (*a*) through (*c*) for Romney's Marketing Company, use the three-step process illustrated in the chapter to record the adjusting entry at year-end December 31, 2018. The process includes (1) determining if revenue was earned or an expense incurred, (2) determining whether cash was received or paid in the past or will be received or paid in the future, and (3) computing the amount of the adjustment.

a. Collected $1,200 rent for the period December 1, 2018, to April 1, 2019, which was credited to deferred rent revenue on December 1, 2018.

b. Purchased a machine for $32,000 cash on January 1, 2014. The company estimates annual depreciation for the year 2018 at $3,200.

c. Paid $5,000 for a two-year insurance premium on July 1, 2018; debited prepaid insurance for that amount.

LO4-1   M4-5   Determining Financial Statement Effects of Adjusting Entries (Deferred Accounts)

For each of the transactions in M4-4, indicate the amounts and direction of effects of the adjusting entry on the elements of the statement of financial position and the statement of earnings. Using the following format, indicate + for increase, − for decrease, and N for no effect.

	Statement of Financial Position			Statement of Earnings		
Transaction	Assets	Liabilities	Shareholders' Equity	Revenues	Expenses	Net Earnings
a.						
b.						
c.						

LO4-1

M4-6   Recording Adjusting Entries (Accrued Accounts)

In each of the following transactions (*a*) through (*c*) for Romney's Marketing Company, use the three-step process illustrated in the chapter to record the adjusting entry at year-end December 31, 2018. The process includes (1) determining if revenue was earned or an expense incurred, (2) determining whether cash was received or paid in the past or will be received or paid in the future, and (3) computing the amount of the adjustment.

a. Estimated electricity usage at $450 for December; to be paid in January 2019.

b. On September 1, 2018, loaned $6,000 to an officer who will repay the loan principal and interest in one year at an annual interest rate of 5 percent.

c. Owed wages to 10 employees who worked four days at $200 each per day at the end of December 2018. The company will pay employees at the end of the first week of January 2019.

LO4-2

M4-7   Determining Financial Statement Effects of Adjusting Entries (Accrued Accounts)

For each of the transactions in M4-6, indicate the amounts and direction of effects of the adjusting entry on the elements of the balance sheet and income statement. Using the following format, indicate + for increase, – for decrease, and N for no effect.

	Statement of Financial Position			Statement of Earnings		
Transaction	Assets	Liabilities	Shareholders' Equity	Revenues	Expenses	Net Earnings
a.						
b.						
c.						

M4-8   Reporting an Income Statement with Earnings per Share

Romney's Marketing Company has the following adjusted trial balance at December 31, 2018. No dividends were declared. However, 500 shares ($0.10 par value per share) issued at the end of the year for $3,000 are included below:

	Debit	Credit
Cash	1,500	
Accounts receivable	2,200	
Interest receivable	100	
Prepaid insurance	1,600	
Notes receivable (long-term)	2,800	
Equipment	15,290	
Accumulated depreciation		3,000
Accounts payable		2,400
Accrued expenses payable		3,920
Income taxes payable		2,700
Deferred rent revenue		500
Contributed capital (800 shares)		3,700
Retained earnings		2,000
Sales revenue		38,500
Interest revenue		100
Rent revenue		800
Wages expense	19,500	
Depreciation expense	1,800	
Utilities expense	380	
Insurance expense	750	
Rent expense	9,000	
Income tax expense	2,700	
Total	57,620	57,620

Prepare a multi-step statement of earnings in good form for 2018. Include earnings per share.

LO4-2   **M4-9   Reporting a Statement of Shareholders' Equity**
Refer to M4-8. Prepare a statement of shareholders' equity in good form for 2018.

LO4-2   **M4-10   Reporting a Statement of Financial Position and Explaining the Effects of Adjustments on the Statement of Cash Flows**

1. Refer to M4-8. Prepare a classified statement of financial position in good form at December 31, 2018.

2. Explain how the adjustments in M4-4 and M4-6 affected the operating, investing, and financing activities on the statement of cash flows.

LO4-3   **M4-11   Computing Net Profit Margin Ratio and Return on Equity**
Compute the net profit margin ratio and the return on equity for 2018 based on the statement of earnings and the statement of changes in equity in M4-8 and M4-9.

LO4-4   **M4-12   Recording Closing Entries**
Refer to the adjusted trial balance in M4-8. Prepare the closing entries on December 31, 2018.

connect EXERCISES

LO4-1,4-4   **E4-1   Identifying Adjusting Entries from an Unadjusted Trial Balance**
As stated in its annual report, Unik Computer Corporation is an information technology company, developing and marketing hardware, software, solutions, and services. The following trial balance lists accounts that Unik uses. Assume that the balances are unadjusted at the end of the fiscal year ended December 31, 2018:

UNIK COMPUTER CORPORATION
Unadjusted Trial Balance
At December 31, 2018
(millions of dollars)

	Debit	Credit
Cash	$ 10,200	
Short-term investments	100	
Accounts receivable	19,300	
Inventories	7,900	
Prepaid expenses	14,400	
Property, plant, and equipment	18,900	
Accumulated depreciation		$ 8,100
Intangible assets	50,700	
Accounts payable		24,200
Accrued liabilities		17,300
Income taxes payable		6,200
Deferred revenue		900
Long-term debt		24,700
Contributed capital		14,000
Retained earnings		17,800
Product revenue		91,700
Services revenue		26,300
Interest revenue		400
Cost of products sold	69,300	
Cost of services sold	20,300	
Interest expense	300	
Research and development costs	3,600	
Other operating expenses	14,500	
Income tax expense	2,100	
	$231,600	$231,600

Required:

1. Based on the information in the unadjusted trial balance, list the deferred accounts that may need to be adjusted at December 31 and the related statement of earnings account in each case (no computations are necessary).

2. Based on the information in the unadjusted trial balance, list the accrual accounts that may need to be recorded at December 31 and the related statement of earnings account in each case (no computations are necessary).

3. Which accounts should be closed at the end of the year? Why?

LO4-1 **E4-2** **Recording Adjusting Entries**

Evans Company completed its first year of operations on December 31, 2017. All of the 2017 entries have been recorded, except for the following:

a. At year-end, employees earned wages of $6,000, which will be paid on the next payroll date, January 6, 2018.

b. At year-end, the company had earned interest revenue of $3,000. The cash will be collected March 1, 2018.

Required:

1. What is the annual reporting period for this company?

2. Identify whether each transaction above is a deferral or an accrual. Using the process illustrated in the chapter, prepare the required adjusting entry for transactions (a) and (b). Include appropriate dates and write a brief explanation of each entry.

3. Why are these adjustments made?

LO4-1,4-2 **E4-3** **Recording Adjusting Entries and Reporting Balances in Financial Statements**

Dion Ltée is making adjusting entries for the year ended December 31, 2018. In developing information for the adjusting entries, the accountant learned the following:

a. Paid a one-year insurance premium of $1,800 on October 1, 2018, for coverage beginning on that date.

b. At December 31, 2018, obtained the following data relating to shipping supplies. The company uses a large amount of shipping supplies that are purchased in volume, stored, and used as needed:

Shipping supplies on hand, January 1, 2018	$24,000
Purchases of shipping supplies during 2018	72,000
Shipping supplies on hand, per inventory December 31, 2018	22,000

Required:

1. Using the process illustrated in the chapter, record the adjusting entry for insurance at December 31, 2018, assuming that the bookkeeper debited the full amount paid on October 1, 2018, to prepaid insurance.

2. Using the process illustrated in the chapter, record the adjusting entry for shipping supplies at December 31, 2018, assuming that the purchases of shipping supplies were debited in full to shipping supplies inventory.

3. What amount should be reported on the 2018 statement of earnings for insurance expense? For shipping supplies expense?

4. What amount should be reported on the December 31, 2018, statement of financial position for prepaid insurance? For shipping supplies inventory?

LO4-1 **E4-4** **Recording Seven Typical Adjusting Entries**

Divtek's Variety Store is completing the accounting process for the year just ended on December 31, 2017. The transactions during 2017 have been journalized and posted. The following data with respect to adjusting entries are available:

a. Wages earned by employees during December 2017, unpaid and unrecorded at December 31, 2017, amounted to $2,700. The last payroll was December 28; the next payroll will be January 11, 2018.

b. Office supplies inventory at January 1, 2017, was $450. Office supplies purchased and debited to office supplies inventory during the year amounted to $500. The year-end count showed $275 of supplies on hand.

c. One-fourth of the basement space is rented to Heald's Specialty Shop for $560 per month, payable monthly. On December 31, 2017, the rent for November and December 2017 had not been collected or recorded. Collection is expected January 10, 2018.

d. The store used delivery equipment that cost $60,500; the estimated depreciation for 2017 was $12,100.

e. On July 1, 2017, a two-year insurance premium amounting to $2,400 was paid in cash and debited in full to prepaid insurance. Coverage began on July 1, 2017.

f. The remaining basement space of the store is rented for $1,600 per month to another merchant, M. Carlos Inc. Carlos sells compatible, but not competitive, merchandise. On November 1, 2017, the store collected six months' rent in the amount of $9,600 in advance from Carlos; it was credited in full to deferred rent revenue when collected.

g. Divtek's Variety Store operates a repair shop to meet its own needs. The shop also does repairs for M. Carlos. At the end of December 31, 2017, Carlos had not paid $800 for completed repairs. This amount has not yet been recorded as repair shop revenue. Collection is expected during January 2018.

Required:

1. Identify each of these transactions as a deferred revenue, deferred expense, accrued revenue, or accrued expense.

2. Using the process illustrated in the chapter, prepare for each situation the adjusting entry that should be recorded for Divtek's Variety Store at December 31, 2017.

LO4-1

E4-5 **Determining Financial Statement Effects of Seven Typical Adjusting Entries**
Refer to E4-4.

Required:

For each of the transactions in E4-4, indicate the amount and direction of the effects of the adjusting entry on the elements of the statement of financial position and statement of earnings. Use the following format: + for increase, − for decrease, and "N" for no effect.

	Statement of Financial Position			Statement of Earnings		
Transaction	Assets	Liabilities	Shareholders' Equity	Revenues	Expenses	Net Earnings
a.						
b.						
c.						
etc.						

LO4-1

E4-6 **Recording Seven Typical Adjusting Entries**
Cardon's Boat Yard Inc. repairs, stores, and cleans boats for customers. It is completing the accounting process for the year just ended on November 30, 2018. The transactions during 2018 have been journalized and posted. The following data with respect to adjusting entries are available:

a. Cardon's winterized (cleaned and covered) three boats for customers at the end of November, but did not prepare the bill of $2,700 for the service it provided until December.

b. On October 1, 2018, Cardon's paid $1,200 to the local newspaper for an advertisement to run every Thursday for 12 weeks. All ads have been run except for three Thursdays in December to complete the 12-week contract.

c. On April 1, 2018, Cardon's borrowed $300,000 at an annual interest rate of 4 percent to expand its boat storage facility. The loan requires Cardon's to pay the interest quarterly until the note is repaid in three years. Cardon's paid quarterly interest on July 1 and October 1, 2018.

d. The Kwan family paid Cardon's $4,500 on November 1, 2018, to store its sailboat for the winter until May 1, 2019. Cardon's credited the full amount to deferred storage revenue on November 1.

e. Cardon's used boat-lifting equipment that cost $220,000; the estimated depreciation for fiscal year 2018 is $22,000.

f. Boat repair supplies on hand at December 1, 2017, totalled $16,500. Repair supplies purchased and debited to supplies inventory during the year amounted to $46,000. The year-end inventory count showed $12,400 of the supplies remaining on hand.

g. Wages earned by employees during November 2018, unpaid and unrecorded at November 30, 2018, amounted to $3,800. The next payroll date will be December 5, 2018.

Required:

1. Identify each of these transactions as a deferred revenue, a deferred expense, an accrued revenue, or an accrued expense.

2. Using the process illustrated in the chapter, prepare for each situation the adjusting entry that should be recorded for Cardon's at November 30, 2018.

E4-7 **Determining Financial Statement Effects of Seven Typical Adjusting Entries**
Refer to E4-6.

Required:

For each of the transactions in E4-6, indicate the amount and direction of the effects of the adjusting entry on the elements of the statement of financial position and statement of earnings. Use the following format: + for increase, − for decrease, and "N" for no effect.

Transaction	Statement of Financial Position			Statement of Earnings		
	Assets	Liabilities	Shareholders' Equity	Revenues	Expenses	Net Earnings
a.						
b.						
c.						
etc.						

E4-8 **Recording Transactions Including Adjusting and Closing Entries (Nonquantitative)**
The following accounts are used by Britt's Knits Inc.

Code	Account	Code	Account
A	Cash	J	Contributed capital
B	Office supplies	K	Retained earnings
C	Accounts receivable	L	Service revenue
D	Office equipment	M	Interest revenue
E	Accumulated depreciation	N	Wage expense
F	Note payable	O	Depreciation expense
G	Wages payable	P	Interest expense
H	Interest payable	Q	Supplies expense
I	Deferred service revenue	R	None of the above

Required:

For each of the following nine independent situations, prepare the journal entry by entering the appropriate code(s) and amount(s). The first transaction is used as an example.

	Debit		Credit	
Independent Situations	**Code**	**Amount**	**Code**	**Amount**
a. Accrued wages, unrecorded and unpaid at year-end, $400 (example).	N	400	G	400
b. Service revenue earned but not yet collected at year-end, $600.				
c. Dividends declared and paid during the year, $900.				
d. Office supplies on hand during the year, $400; supplies on hand at year-end, $160.				
e. Service revenue collected in advance and not yet earned, $800.				
f. Depreciation expense for the year, $1,000.				
g. At year-end, interest on note payable not yet recorded or paid, $220.				
h. Balance at year-end in service revenue account, $56,000. Prepare the closing entry at year-end.				
i. Balance at year-end in Interest expense account, $460. Prepare the closing entry at year-end.				

■ LO4-1,4-2   **E4-9**   **Determining Financial Statement Effects of Three Adjusting Entries**

Terbish Company started operations on January 1, 2017. It is now December 31, 2017, the end of the fiscal year. The part-time bookkeeper needs your help to analyze the following three transactions:

a. During 2017, the company purchased office supplies that cost $1,600. At the end of 2017, office supplies of $400 remained on hand.

b. On January 1, 2017, the company purchased a special machine for cash at a cost of $12,000. The machine's cost is estimated to depreciate at $1,200 per year.

c. On July 1, 2017, the company paid cash of $600 for a one-year premium on an insurance policy on the machine; coverage begins on July 1, 2017.

Required:

Complete the following schedule of the amounts that should be reported for 2017:

Selected Statement of Financial Position Amounts at December 31, 2017	Amount to Be Reported
Assets	
Equipment	$_____
Accumulated depreciation	_____
Carrying amount of equipment	_____
Office supplies inventory	_____
Prepaid insurance	_____
Selected Statement of Earnings Amounts for the Year Ended December 31, 2017	
Expenses	
Depreciation expense	$_____
Office supplies expense	_____
Insurance expense	_____

■ LO4-1   **E4-10**   **Determining Financial Statement Effects of Interest on Two Notes**

Note 1: On April 1, 2017, Warren Corporation received a $30,000, 5 percent note from a customer in settlement of a $30,000 open account receivable. According to the terms, the principal of the note and interest are payable at the end of 12 months. Warren's fiscal year ends on December 31, 2017.

Note 2: On August 1, 2017, to meet a cash shortage, Warren Corporation obtained a $30,000, 6 percent loan from a local bank. The principal of the note and interest expense are payable at the end of six months.

Required:

For the relevant transaction dates of each note, indicate the amounts and direction of effects on the elements of the statement of financial position and the statement of earnings. Using the following format, indicate + for increase, – for decrease, and N for no effect. (**Reminder:** Assets = Liabilities + Shareholders' equity; Revenues – Expenses = Net earnings; and net earnings accounts are closed to retained earnings, a component of shareholders' equity.)

	Statement of Financial Position			Statement of Earnings		
Date	Assets	Liabilities	Shareholders' Equity	Revenues	Expenses	Net Earnings
Note 1 April 1, 2017						
December 31, 2017						
March 31, 2018						
Note 2 August 1, 2017						
December 31, 2017						
January 31, 2018						

■ LO4-1   **E4-11**   **Inferring Transactions**

Deere & Company

Deere & Company is the world's leading producer of agricultural equipment; a leading supplier of a broad range of industrial equipment for construction, forestry, and public works; a producer and marketer of a broad line of lawn and grounds care equipment; and a provider of credit, managed health care plans, and insurance products for businesses and the general public. The following information is taken from an annual report (in millions of dollars):

Income Taxes Payable			Dividends Payable			Interest Payable		
	Beg. bal.	321		Beg. bal.	192		Beg. bal.	130
(a) ?	(b)	1,907	(c) ?	(d)	775	(e) 317	(f)	?
	End. bal.	279		End. bal.	210		End. bal.	103

Required:

1. Identify the nature of each of the transactions (a) through (f). Specifically, what activities cause the accounts to increase and decrease?
2. Compute the amounts of transactions (a), (c), and (f).

LO4-1

E4-12 Analyzing the Effects of Errors on Financial Statement Items

Cohen & Boyd Inc., publishers of movie and song trivia books, made the following errors in adjusting the accounts at year-end (December 31):

a. Did not accrue $1,400 owed to the company by another company renting part of the building as a storage facility.
b. Did not record $15,000 depreciation on equipment costing $115,000.
c. Failed to adjust the deferred fee revenue account to reflect that $1,500 was earned by the end of the year.
d. Recorded a full year of accrued interest expense on a $17,000, 9 percent note payable that has been outstanding only since November 1 of the current year.
e. Failed to adjust prepaid insurance to reflect that $650 of insurance coverage has been used.

Required:

1. For each error, prepare (a) the adjusting journal entry that was made, if any; (b) the entry that should have been made at year-end; and (c) the entry to correct the error.
2. Using the following headings, indicate the effect of each error and the amount of the effect (i.e., the difference between the entry that was or was not made and the entry that should have been made). Use O if the effect overstates the item, U if the effect understates the item, and NE if there is no effect.

Transaction	Statement of Financial Position			Statement of Earnings		
	Assets	Liabilities	Shareholders' Equity	Revenues	Expenses	Net Earnings
a.						
b.						
c.						
etc.						

3. Explain the concept of materiality and how it might affect the adjusting entries you prepared in (1).

LO4-1,4-2

E4-13 Analyzing the Effects of Adjusting Entries on the Statement of Earnings and Statement of Financial Position

On December 31, 2017, Mica Company prepared a statement of earnings and a statement of financial position but failed to take into account four adjusting entries. The statement of earnings, prepared on this incorrect basis, reflected pretax earnings of $30,000. The statement of financial position (before the effect of income taxes) reflected total assets, $90,000; total liabilities, $40,000; and shareholders' equity, $50,000. The data for the four adjusting entries follow:

a. Depreciation of $9,000 for the year on equipment that cost $75,000 was not recorded.
b. Wages amounting to $17,000 for the last three days of December 2017 were not paid and not recorded (the next pay date is January 10, 2018).
c. An amount of $9,600 was collected on December 1, 2017, for rental of office space for the period December 1, 2017, to February 28, 2018. The $9,600 was credited in full to deferred rent revenue when collected.
d. Income taxes were not recorded. The income tax rate for the company is 30 percent.

Required:

Complete the following tabulation to correct the financial statements for the effects of the four errors (indicate deductions with parentheses):

Items	Net Earnings	Total Assets	Total Liabilities	Shareholders' Equity
Balances reported	$30,000	$90,000	$40,000	$50,000
Effect of depreciation	———	———	———	———
Effect of wages	———	———	———	———
Effect of rent revenue	———	———	———	———
Adjusted balances	———	———	———	———
Effect of income taxes	———	———	———	———
Correct balances	═══	═══	═══	═══

 LO4-1,4-2,4-3　E4-14 **Reporting a Correct Statement of Earnings with Earnings per Share to Include the Effects of Adjusting Entries and Evaluating the Net Profit Margin Ratio as an Auditor**

Barton Inc. completed its first year of operations on December 31, 2017. Because this is the end of the fiscal year, the company bookkeeper prepared the following tentative statement of earnings:

Statement of Earnings, 2017		
Rental revenue		$114,000
Expenses:		
Salaries and wages expense	$28,500	
Maintenance expense	12,000	
Rent expense (on location)	9,000	
Utilities expense	4,000	
Gas and oil expense	3,000	
Miscellaneous expenses (items not listed elsewhere)	1,000	
Total expenses		57,500
Net earnings		$ 56,500

You are an independent accountant hired by the company to audit its accounting systems and review its financial statements. In your audit, you developed additional data as follows:

a. Unpaid wages for the last three days of December amounting to $310 were not recorded.

b. The unpaid $400 telephone bill for December 2017 has not been recorded.

c. Depreciation on rental cars, amounting to $23,000 for 2017, was not recorded.

d. Interest on a $20,000, one-year, 10 percent note payable dated October 1, 2017, was not recorded. The full amount of interest is payable on the maturity date of the note.

e. The deferred rental revenue account has a balance of $4,000 as at December 31, 2017, which represents rental revenue for the month of January 2018.

f. Maintenance expense includes $1,000, which is the cost of maintenance supplies still on hand at December 31, 2017. These supplies will be used in 2018.

g. The income tax expense is $7,000. Payment of income tax will be made in 2018.

Required:

1. For each item, (*a*) through (*g*), what adjusting entry, if any, do you recommend that Barton should record at December 31, 2017? If none is required, explain why.

2. Prepare a correct statement of earnings for 2017 in good form, including earnings per share, assuming that 7,000 shares are outstanding. Show computations.

3. Compute the net profit margin ratio based on the corrected information. What does this ratio suggest? If the industry average for net profit margin ratio is 18 percent, what might you infer about Barton?

 LO4-3　　**E4-15** **Evaluating the Effect of Adjusting Deferred Subscriptions on Cash Flows and Performance as a Manager**

You are the regional sales manager for Weld News Company. Weld is making adjusting entries for the year ended March 31, 2018. On September 1, 2017, $12,000 cash was received from customers in your region for two-year magazine subscriptions beginning on that date. The magazines are published and mailed to customers monthly. These were the only subscription sales in your region during the year.

Required:

1. What amount should be reported as cash from operations on the 2018 statement of cash flows?
2. What amount should be reported on the 2018 statement of earnings for subscriptions revenue?
3. What amount should be reported on the March 31, 2018, statement of financial position for deferred subscriptions revenue?
4. Prepare the adjusting entry at March 31, 2018, assuming that the subscriptions received on September 1, 2017, were recorded for the full amount in deferred subscriptions revenue.
5. The company expects your region's annual revenue target to be $4,000.
   a. Evaluate your region's performance, assuming that the revenue target is based on cash sales.
   b. Evaluate your region's performance, assuming that the revenue target is based on accrual accounting.

■ LO4-1,4-2,4-4 **E4-16**   **Recording Four Adjusting Entries, Completing a Trial Balance, Preparing Financial Statements, and Recording Closing Entries**

Cayuga Ltd. prepared the following trial balance at the end of its first year of operations ending December 31, 2018. To simplify the case, the amounts given are in thousands of dollars. Other data not yet recorded at December 31, 2018, are as follows:

a. Insurance expired during 2018, $4
b. Depreciation expense for 2018, $4
c. Wages payable, $8
d. Income tax expense, $9

	Unadjusted		Adjustments		Adjusted	
Account Title	**Debit**	**Credit**	**Debit**	**Credit**	**Debit**	**Credit**
Cash	38					
Accounts receivable	9					
Prepaid insurance	6					
Machinery (20-year life, no residual value)	80					
Accumulated depreciation		8				
Accounts payable		9				
Wages payable						
Income taxes payable						
Contributed capital (4,000 shares)		68				
Retained earnings (deficit)	4					
Revenues (not detailed)		84				
Expenses (not detailed)	32					
Totals	169	169				

Required:

1. Prepare the adjusting entries for 2018.
2. Show the effects (direction and amount) of the adjusting entries on net earnings and cash.
3. Complete the trial balance adjustments and adjusted columns.
4. Using the adjusted balances, prepare a statement of earnings, a statement of changes in equity, and a statement of financial position.
5. What is the purpose of "closing the books" at the end of the accounting period?
6. Using the adjusted balances, prepare the closing entries for 2018.

■ LO4-2,4-3,4-4 **E4-17**   **Preparing Financial Statements, Closing Entries, and Analyzing the Net Profit Margin Ratio and Return on Equity**

Liner Company has the following adjusted trial balance at December 31, 2017. No dividends were declared; however, 400 additional shares were issued during the year for $2,000:

	Debit	Credit
Cash	$ 2,700	
Accounts receivable	3,000	
Interest receivable	120	
Prepaid expenses	600	
Notes receivable	3,000	
Equipment	12,000	
Accumulated depreciation		$ 2,000
Accounts payable		1,600
Accrued liabilities		3,820
Income taxes payable		2,900
Deferred rent revenue		600
Contributed capital (500 shares)		2,400
Retained earnings		1,000
Sales revenue		45,000
Interest revenue		120
Rent revenue		300
Wages expense	20,600	
Depreciation expense	2,000	
Utilities expense	1,220	
Insurance expense	600	
Rent expense	10,000	
Income tax expense	3,900	
Total	$59,740	$59,740

Required:

1. Prepare a statement of earnings in good form for 2017. Include earnings per share.
2. Prepare closing entries and post the effects to the appropriate ledger accounts.
3. Prepare a statement of financial position in good form at December 31, 2017.
4. Compute Liner Company's net profit margin ratio and return on equity for the year. What do these ratios mean?

■ LO4-3

Chipotle Mexican
Grill Inc.

E4-18   Analyzing and Evaluating Return on Equity from a Security Analyst's Perspective
Chipotle Mexican Grill Inc. is one of the fast-growing restaurant chains. Selected statement of earnings and statement of financial position amounts (in thousands) for two recent years are presented below:

	Current Year	Prior Year
Net earnings	$ 445,374	$ 327,438
Average shareholders' equity	1,775,325	1,392,107

Required:

1. Compute the return on equity for the current and prior years and explain the meaning of the change.
2. Would security analysts more likely increase or decrease their estimates of share value on the basis of this change? Explain.

■ LO4-3

Telus Corp.

E4-19   Evaluating Profitability by Using the Net Profit Margin Ratio and Return on Equity
Telus Corp. is a leading Canadian telecommunications company. It provides a wide range of communications products and services including data, Internet protocol (IP), voice, wireless, entertainment, and video. Selected information about the company's resources and operations for fiscal years 2011 through 2015 are presented below (amounts in millions of Canadian dollars):

	2015	2014	2013	2012	2011
Total shareholders' equity	$ 7,672	$ 7,454	$ 8,015	$ 7,686	$ 7,513
Total revenue	12,502	12,002	11,404	10,921	10,397
Net earnings	1,382	1,425	1,294	1,204	1,130

Required:

1. Compute the net profit margin ratio and the return on equity for the years 2012 to 2015.

2. As a potential investor, how do you interpret these ratios?

3. What additional information would you require before deciding whether or not to invest in Telus's shares?

≡connect PROBLEMS

LO4-1
Mattel Inc.

P4-1 Preparing a Trial Balance (AP4-1)

Mattel Inc. is a worldwide leader in the design, manufacture, and marketing of toys and family products. Mattel markets its products in many countries under well-known brands, such as Barbie®, Monster High®, American Girl®, Thomas & Friends®, and Fisher-Price®. The following is a list of accounts and amounts reported in the company's financial statements for 2015. The accounts have normal debit or credit balances and their balances are rounded to the nearest thousand dollars. The company's fiscal year ends on December 31.

Accounts payable	$ 651,681	Interest income	$ 8,263
Accounts receivable	1,145,099	Inventories	587,521
Accrued liabilities	658,225	Long-term debt	2,100,000
Accumulated other comprehensive loss	848,899	Other non-current assets	1,230,159
Advertising and promotion expenses	717,852	Other non-current liabilities	473,863
Cash and equivalents	892,814	Other selling and administrative expenses	1,547,584
Contributed capital	2,231,239	Prepaid expenses	571,429
Cost of sales	2,896,255	Property, plant, and equipment, net	741,147
Goodwill	1,384,520	Retained earnings (deficit), January 1, 2015	?
Income tax expense	94,499	Sales revenue	5,702,613
Income taxes payable	18,752	Short-term borrowings	16,914
Interest expense	85,270		

Required:

1. Prepare an adjusted trial balance at December 31, 2015. List the accounts in the following order: assets, liabilities, shareholders' equity, revenues, and expenses.

2. How did you determine the amount for retained earnings (deficit)?

LO4-1,4-2

P4-2 Recording Adjusting Entries and Determining Their Financial Statement Effects (AP4-2)

Chandra Company's fiscal year ends on June 30. It is June 30, 2018, and all of the 2018 entries have been made, except the following adjusting entries:

a. On March 30, 2018, Chandra paid $3,200 for a six-month premium for property insurance starting on that date. Cash was credited and prepaid insurance was debited for this amount.

b. At June 30, 2018, wages of $900 were earned by employees but not yet paid. The employees will be paid on the next pay date, July 15, 2018.

c. On June 1, 2018, Chandra collected maintenance fees of $450 for two months. At that date, Chandra debited cash and credited deferred maintenance revenue for $450.

d. Depreciation must be recognized on a service truck that cost $19,000 on July 1, 2017. Depreciation of the truck was estimated at $4,000 per year.

e. Cash of $4,200 was collected on May 1, 2018, for services to be rendered evenly over the next year, beginning on May 1 (deferred service revenue was credited).

f. On February 1, 2018, the company borrowed $16,000 from a local bank and signed a 9 percent note for that amount. The principal and interest are payable on January 32, 2019.

g. On June 15, 2018, the company received from the city a tax bill for $500, covering property taxes on land for the first half of 2018. The amount is payable during July 2018.

h. The company earned service revenue of $2,000 on a special job that was completed on June 29, 2018. Collection will be made during July 2018; no entry has been recorded.

Required:

1. Indicate whether each transaction relates to a deferred revenue, a deferred expense, an accrued revenue, or an accrued expense.

2. Prepare the adjusting entry required for each transaction at June 30, 2018.

3. Show the effects (direction and amount) of the adjusting entries on net earnings and cash.

LO4-1,4-2   **P4-3**   **Recording Adjusting Entries and Determining Their Financial Statement Effects** (AP4-3)

Lamorte Towing Company is at the end of its fiscal year, December 31, 2017. The following data that must be considered were developed from the company's records and related documents:

a. On January 1, 2017, the company purchased a new hauling van at a cash cost of $24,600. Depreciation estimated at $4,000 for the year has not been recorded for 2017.

b. During 2017, office supplies amounting to $1,000 were purchased for cash and debited to supplies inventory. At the end of 2013, the inventory of supplies remaining on hand (unused) was $400. The inventory of supplies on hand at December 31, 2017, was $250.

c. On December 31, 2017, the company completed repairs on one of its trucks at a cost of $1,200; the amount is not yet recorded and, by agreement, will be paid during January 2018.

d. On December 31, 2017, property taxes on land owned during 2017 were estimated at $1,500. The taxes have not been recorded, and will be paid in 2018 when billed.

e. On December 31, 2017, the company completed a contract for another company for $6,000 payable by the customer within 30 days. No cash has been collected, and no journal entry has been made for this transaction.

f. On July 1, 2017, a one-year insurance premium on equipment in the amount of $1,200 was paid and debited in full to prepaid insurance on that date. Coverage began on July 1.

g. On October 1, 2017, the company borrowed $11,000 from the local bank on a one-year, 6 percent note payable. The principal plus interest is payable on September 30, 2018.

h. Earnings before any of the adjustments or income taxes equalled $30,000. The company's income tax rate is 40 percent. (*Hint:* compute adjusted pretax earnings based on transactions (*a*) through (*g*) to determine the income tax expense for 2017.)

Required:

1. Indicate whether each transaction relates to a deferred revenue, a deferred expense, an accrued revenue, or an accrued expense.

2. Prepare the adjusting entry required for each transaction at December 31, 2017.

3. Using the following headings, indicate the effect of each adjusting entry and the amount of each. Use + for increase, – for decrease, and "N" for no effect.

Transaction	Statement of Financial Position			Statement of Earnings		
	Assets	Liabilities	Shareholders' Equity	Revenues	Expenses	Net Earnings
a.						
b.						
c.						
etc.						

LO4-1,4-3,4-4   **P4-4**   **Inferring Year-End Adjustments, Computing Earnings per Share and Net Profit Margin Ratio, and Recording Closing Entries** (AP4-4)

Savory Ltd. is completing the information-processing cycle at its fiscal year end, December 31, 2018. Following are the correct account balances at December 31, 2018, both before and after the adjusting entries for 2018:

	Trial Balance, December 31, 2018					
	Before Adjusting Entries		Adjustments		After Adjusting Entries	
Items	Debit	Credit	Debit	Credit	Debit	Credit
a. Cash	$ 12,600				$ 12,600	
b. Service revenue receivable					560	
c. Prepaid insurance	840				560	
d. Equipment	168,280				168,280	
e. Accumulated depreciation, equipment		$ 42,100				$ 54,000
f. Accrued advertising payable						6,580
g. Contributed capital		112,000				112,000
h. Retained earnings, January 1, 2018		19,600				19,600
i. Service revenue		64,400				64,960
j. Salary expense	56,380				56,380	
k. Depreciation expense					11,900	
l. Insurance expense					280	
m. Advertising expense					6,580	
	$238,100	$238,100			$257,140	$257,140

Required:

1. Compare the amounts in the columns before and after the adjusting entries to reconstruct the adjusting entries made in 2018. Explain each adjustment.

2. Compute the amount of net earnings, assuming that it is based on the amounts (a), before adjusting entries, and (b), after adjusting entries. Which net earnings amount is correct? Explain.

3. Compute the earnings per share, assuming that 4,000 shares are outstanding all year.

4. Compute the net profit margin ratio and the return on equity, assuming that contributed capital did not change during the year. What do the computed ratios suggest to you about the company?

5. Prepare the closing entries at December 31, 2018.

■ LO4-1,4-2,4-4   **P4-5**   **Recording Adjusting and Closing Entries and Preparing a Statement of Earnings, Including Earnings per Share, and a Statement of Financial Position** (AP4-5)

Sutton Inc., a small service company, keeps its records without the help of an accountant. After much effort, an outside accountant prepared the following unadjusted trial balance as at the end of the company's fiscal year, December 31, 2017:

Account Titles	Debit	Credit
Cash	$ 60,000	
Accounts receivable	13,000	
Service supplies inventory	800	
Prepaid insurance	1,000	
Service trucks	20,000	
Accumulated depreciation, service trucks		$ 12,000
Other assets	11,200	
Accounts payable		3,000
Note payable (three years; 5% due each December 31)		20,000
Contributed capital (5,000 shares outstanding)		28,200
Retained earnings		7,500
Service revenue		77,000
Other expenses, excluding income tax	41,700	
Totals	$147,700	$147,700

Data not yet recorded at December 31, 2017, were as follows:

a. Supplies inventory on December 31, 2017, reflecting $200 remaining on hand.

b. Insurance expired during 2017, $400.

c. Depreciation expense for 2017, $4,000.

d. Wages earned by employees not yet paid on December 31, 2017, $1,100.

e. Income tax expense, $7,350.

Required:

1. Prepare the adjusting entries at December 31, 2017.

2. Show the effects (direction and amount) of the adjusting entries on net earnings and cash.

3. Prepare a statement of earnings for 2017 and a statement of financial position at December 31, 2017, including the effects of transactions (*a*) through (*e*).

4. Assume that you forgot to adjust the balance of the service supplies inventory account. How would this error affect the amount of net earnings for the year? Does this error lead to a material effect on net earnings? Explain.

5. Prepare the closing entries at December 31, 2017.

■ LO4-2,4-3,4-4   **P4-6**   **Preparing Both a Statement of Earnings and a Statement of Financial Position from a Trial Balance and Closing Entries** (AP4-6)

Juan Real Estate Company (organized as a corporation on April 1, 2013) has completed the accounting cycle for the year, ended March 31, 2018. Juan has also completed a correct trial balance as follows:

JUAN REAL ESTATE COMPANY Adjusted Trial Balance At March 31, 2018		
Account Titles	**Debit**	**Credit**
Cash	$ 53,000	
Accounts receivable	44,800	
Office supplies inventory	300	
Automobiles (company cars)	30,000	
Accumulated depreciation, automobiles		$ 10,000
Office equipment	3,000	
Accumulated depreciation, office equipment		1,000
Accounts payable		20,250
Salaries and commissions payable		1,500
Note payable, long term		30,000
Contributed capital (30,000 shares)		35,000
Retained earnings (on April 1, 2017)		7,350
Dividends declared	8,000	
Sales commissions earned		77,000
Management fees earned		13,000
Operating expenses (detail omitted to conserve your time)	48,000	
Depreciation expense (including $500 on office equipment)	5,500	
Interest expense	2,500	
Totals	$195,100	$195,100

Required:

1. Prepare a statement of earnings for the reporting year ended March 31, 2018. Include income tax expense, assuming a 30 percent tax rate. Use the following major captions: revenues, expenses, earnings before income taxes, income tax, net earnings, and earnings per share (list each item under these captions as appropriate).

2. Prepare the journal entry to record income taxes for the year (not yet paid).

3. Prepare a statement of financial position at the end of the reporting year, March 31, 2018. Use the following captions (list each item under these captions as appropriate):

   Assets
   Current assets
   Non-current assets

   Liabilities
   Current liabilities
   Non-current liabilities

   Shareholders' Equity
   Contributed capital
   Retained earnings

4. Compute the net profit margin ratio and the return on equity. What do these ratios suggest?

5. Prepare the closing entries at March 31, 2018.

LO4-1,4-2,4-3,4-4
P4-7
Recording Adjusting and Closing Entries, Preparing a Statement of Earnings Including Earnings per Share, and Preparing a Statement of Financial Position (AP4-7)
It is your first day on the job as a trainee for an entry position in the accounting department of Alimex Inc., a merchandising company. The company controller provides you with the following *unadjusted* trial balance as at December 31, 2017, with accounts listed in alphabetical order:

	Debit	Credit
Accounts payable		$ 33,000
Accounts receivable	$100,000	
Accumulated depreciation, equipment		9,000
Cash	11,000	
Contributed capital (15,000 shares)		60,000
Cost of sales	129,000	
Deferred revenue		11,240
Equipment, at cost	60,000	
Merchandise inventory	18,200	
Other operating expenses	1,400	
Note receivable, due December 31, 2018	24,000	
Prepaid income taxes	1,040	
Prepaid rent	16,800	
Rent expense	11,000	
Retained earnings, January 1, 2017		70,000
Sales revenue		301,000
Wages expense	111,800	
	$484,240	**$484,240**

Additional information is as follows:

a. Wages owed to employees totalled $8,000 as at December 31, 2017.

b. The note receivable was obtained by Alimex on September 1, 2017. The note carries an annual interest rate of 5 percent, payable to Alimex at maturity only.

c. The balance in prepaid rent represents a payment August 1, 2017, for 12 months of rent, beginning on that date.

d. The equipment has a useful life of 20 years. Depreciation expense for 2017 was estimated at $3,000.

e. Cash dividends of $1 per share were declared on December 31, 2017, payable on January 25, 2018.

f. The company is subject to an income tax rate of 20 percent. Income taxes are due March 15, 2018.

Journal entries related to these transactions have not been recorded yet.

Required:

1. Prepare in proper form the adjusting journal entries as at December 31, 2017, for items (*a*) through (*f*) above. Create new accounts, if necessary. (*Hint:* complete requirement 2 before making the adjusting entry related to item (*f*).)

2. Show the effects (direction and amount) of the adjusting entries on net earnings and cash.

3. Prepare a multiple-step statement of earnings for the year ended December 31, 2017. Alimex did not issue or repurchase any shares during 2017.

4. Prepare a classified statement of financial position as at December 31, 2017.

5. Prepare the closing entries at December 31, 2017.

6. Compute the net profit margin ratio and total asset turnover for 2017, and explain the meaning of each ratio. Total assets equalled $200,000 at January 1, 2017.

■ LO4-3

George Weston
Limited
Metro Inc.
Maple Leaf Foods
Inc.

P4-8 **Using Financial Reports: Evaluating Profitability by Using the Net Profit Margin Ratio and Return on Equity**

A summary of selected historical results is presented below for three Canadian companies: George Weston Limited, Metro Inc., and Maple Leaf Foods Inc. Each of these companies has grown in size over time by acquiring assets and investing in other companies. (Amounts are in millions of dollars.)

	2015	2014	2013	2012
George Weston Limited				
Total shareholders' equity	$14,930	$14,249	$ 8,901	$8,072
Total revenue	46,894	43,918	33,582	
Net earnings	864	134	904	
Operating cash flow	3,367	2,851	1,738	
Metro Inc.				
Total shareholders' equity	2,657	2,684	2,800	2,533
Total revenue	12,224	11,590	11,400	
Net earnings	519	456	704	
Operating cash flow	678	432	566	
Maple Leaf Foods, Inc.				
Total shareholders' equity	2,053	2,245	1,642	958
Total revenue	3,293	3,157	4,406	
Net earnings	42	712	512	
Operating cash flow	159	(362)	260	

Required:

1. Compute the net profit margin ratio and the return on equity for each company for each of the years 2013 through 2015 using the table below:

	2015	2014	2013
George Weston Limited			
Net profit margin			
Return on equity (ROE)			
Quality of earnings			
Metro Inc.			
Net profit margin			
Return on equity (ROE)			
Quality of earnings			
Maple Leaf Foods Inc.			
Net profit margin			
Return on equity (ROE)			
Quality of earnings			

2. Based on the computed ratios, rank these companies from most successful to least successful in generating net earnings for shareholders.

3. Assume that you are interested in investing in one of these three companies. Which company would you choose? Write a brief report to justify your choice.

4. Analysts examine both net earnings and cash flow from operating activities in evaluating a company. One measure that relates these two numbers is the quality of earnings ratio, which equals cash flow from operations divided by net earnings. The higher the ratio, the higher the quality of earnings. Compute this ratio for 2013–2015, and rank the three companies from highest to lowest, based on the quality of their earnings.

■ LO4-1   **P4-9**   **Recording Journal Entries and Inferring Adjustments**

Stay 'N Shape was started by Jennifer Long several years ago to provide physical fitness services to its customers. The following balances were extracted from the company's general ledger as at the following dates:

	May 31, 2017	April 30, 2017
Deferred revenue	$ 4,500	$ 3,000
Accounts receivable	44,000	59,000
Prepaid rent	?	4,900
Prepaid insurance	?	1,200
Notes payable	20,000	20,000
Supplies inventory	?	7,200
Supplies expense	17,200	

Additional information about several transactions that occurred in May is provided below:

a. Some customers pay for services in advance. The remaining customers are sent invoices for services used and are allowed one month to pay their invoices. During May, the company received from customers a total of $62,000 in cash, including an amount of $7,000 that was paid by customers in advance.

b. At the end of April, the company paid rent for the next five months and recorded the amount as prepaid rent.

c. The balance of prepaid insurance at April 30 represents the cost of insuring the company's premises and equipment for one month. In May, the company received an invoice from the insurance company for a renewal of the company's insurance policy for one year. The insurance premium was increased by 10 percent over the amount of the premium of the previous year because the company filed a few insurance claims. The company paid the one-year insurance premium.

d. The note payable carries annual interest of 6 percent and is due on June 30, 2017, along with accrued interest. The company recognizes interest expense on a monthly basis.

e. An invoice for $780 pertaining to advertising work done during May was received on May 2.

f. Supplies amounting to $17,200 were purchased on account during May and debited to the supplies expense account. A physical count of supplies on hand on May 31 valued the inventory at $11,500.

Required:

Prepare journal entries to record the following transactions and events:

1. The receipt of cash from customers and the recognition of all revenues earned in May.
2. Rent expense for May.
3. Payment of the premium for the new insurance policy.
4. Interest expense that accrued in May.
5. The invoice for advertising work, received on May 2.
6. The adjustment to the supplies inventory account.

ALTERNATE PROBLEMS

LO4-1
Starbucks
Corporation

AP4-1 **Preparing a Trial Balance** (P4-1)

Starbucks Corporation purchases and roasts high-quality, whole-bean coffees and sells them along with fresh-brewed coffees, Italian-style espresso beverages, a variety of pastries and confections, coffee-related accessories and equipment, and a line of premium teas. In addition to sales through its company-operated retail stores, Starbucks also sells coffee and tea products through other distribution channels. The following is a simplified list of accounts and amounts reported in financial statements. The accounts have normal debit or credit balances and the dollars are rounded to the nearest million. The fiscal year ended on September 27, 2015.

Accounts payable	$ 684
Accounts receivable	719
Accrued liabilities	1,985
Cash and cash equivalents	1,530
Contributed capital	43
Cost of sales	7,788
Deferred income tax assets	1,210
Depreciation and amortization expenses	894
Deferred revenue	984
General and administrative expenses	1,197
Goodwill	1,575
Income tax expense	1,144
Interest expense	71
Interest income	43
Inventories	1,306
Long-term investments	664
Long-term debt	2,348
Net sales revenues	19,163
Other assets	416
Other intangible assets	520
Other long-term liabilities	625
Other operating expenses	522
Prepaid expenses	334
Property, plant, and equipment, net	4,088
Retained earnings, beginning of year	?
Short-term investments	81
Store operating expenses	5,411

Required:

Prepare an adjusted trial balance at September 27, 2015. How did you determine the amount for retained earnings?

■ LO4-1,4-2   **AP4-2**   **Recording Adjusting Entries and Determining Their Financial Statement Effects** (P4-2)
e**X**cel

Zumra Company's fiscal year ends on December 31. It is December 31, 2018, and all of the 2018 entries have been made, except the following adjusting entries:

a. On September 1, 2018, Zumra collected six months' rent of $8,400 on storage space. At that date, Zumra debited cash and credited deferred rent revenue for $8,400.

b. On October 1, 2018, the company borrowed $18,000 from a local bank and signed a 5 percent note for that amount. The principal and interest are payable on the maturity date, September 30, 2019.

c. Depreciation of $2,500 must be recognized on a service truck purchased on July 1, 2018, at a cost of $15,000.

d. Cash of $3,000 was collected on November 1, 2018, for services to be rendered evenly over the next year beginning on November 1. Deferred service revenue was credited when the cash was received.

e. On November 1, 2018, Zumra paid a one-year premium for property insurance, $9,000, for coverage starting on that date. Cash was credited and prepaid insurance was debited for this amount.

f. The company earned service revenue of $4,000 on a special job that was completed December 29, 2018. Collection will be made during January 2019. No entry has been recorded.

g. At December 31, 2018, wages earned by employees totalled $14,000. The employees will be paid on the next payroll date, January 15, 2019.

h. On December 31, 2018, the company estimated it owed $500 for 2018 property taxes on land. The tax will be paid when the bill is received in January 2019.

Required:

1. Indicate whether each transaction relates to a deferred revenue, a deferred expense, an accrued revenue, or an accrued expense.

2. Prepare the adjusting entry required for each transaction at December 31, 2018.

3. Show the effects (direction and amount) of the adjusting entries on net earnings and cash.

LO4-1,4-2   AP4-3   Recording Adjusting Entries and Determining Their Financial Statement Effects (P4-3)

Bill's Catering Company is at its accounting year-end, December 31, 2018. The following data that must be considered were developed from the company's records and related documents:

a. During 2018, office supplies amounting to $1,200 were purchased for cash and debited in full to supplies inventory. At the beginning of 2018, the supplies on hand amounted to $450. The inventory of supplies at December 31, 2018 was $400.

b. On December 31, 2018, the company catered an evening gala for a local celebrity. The $7,500 bill was payable by the end of January 2019. No cash has been collected, and no journal entry has been made for this transaction. (Ignore cost of sales.)

c. On October 1, 2018, a one-year insurance premium on equipment in the amount of $1,200 was paid and debited in full to prepaid insurance on that date. Coverage began on November 1.

d. On December 31, 2018, repairs on one of the company's delivery vans were completed at a cost estimate of $600; the amount has not yet been paid or recorded. The repair shop will bill Bill's Catering at the beginning of January 2019.

e. In November 2018, Bill's Catering signed a lease for a new retail location, providing a down payment of $2,100 in rent for the first three months. The amount was debited to prepaid rent. The lease began on December 1, 2018.

f. On July 1, 2018, the company purchased new refrigerated display counters at a cash cost of $18,000. Depreciation of $2,600 has not been recorded for 2018.

g. On November 1, 2018, the company lent $4,000 to one of its employees on a one-year, 3 percent note. The principal plus interest is payable by the employee on October 31, 2019.

h. Earnings before any of the adjustments or income taxes totalled $22,400. The company's income tax rate is 30 percent. Compute the adjusted net earnings, taking into consideration transactions (a) through (g) to determine the income tax expense for 2018.

Required:

1. Indicate whether each transaction relates to a deferred revenue, a deferred expense, an accrued revenue, or an accrued expense.

2. Prepare the adjusting entries required at December 31, 2018, for transactions (a) through (g).

3. Using the following headings, indicate the effect of each adjusting entry and the amount of each. Use + for increase, – for decrease, and "N" for no effect:

Transaction	Statement of Financial Position			Statement of Earnings		
	Assets	Liabilities	Shareholders' Equity	Revenues	Expenses	Net Earnings
a.						
b.						
c.						
etc.						

LO4-1,4-3,4-4   AP4-4   Inferring Year-End Adjustments, Computing Earnings per Share and the Net Profit Margin Ratio, and Recording Closing Entries (P4-4)

Gilca Ltd. is completing the information-processing cycle at the end of its fiscal year, December 31, 2017. The correct account balances at December 31, 2017, both before and after the adjusting entries for 2017, are shown below:

	Trial Balance, December 31, 2017						
	Before Adjusting Entries		**Adjustments**		**After Adjusting Entries**	
Items	**Debit**	**Credit**	**Debit**	**Credit**	**Debit**	**Credit**
a. Cash	$ 18,000				$ 18,000	
b. Service revenue receivable					1,500	
c. Prepaid expenses	1,200				800	
d. Property, plant, and equipment	210,000				210,000	
e. Accumulated depreciation, PP&E		$ 52,500				$ 70,000
f. Income taxes payable						6,500
g. Deferred revenue		16,000				8,000
h. Contributed capital		110,000				110,000
i. Retained earnings, January 1, 2017		21,700				21,700
j. Service revenue		83,000				92,500
k. Salary expense	54,000				54,000	
l. Depreciation expense					17,500	
m. Rent expense					400	
n. Income tax expense					6,500	
	$283,200	$283,200			$308,700	$308,700

Required:

1. Compare the amounts in the columns before and after the adjusting entries to reconstruct the adjusting entries made in 2017. Explain each adjustment.

2. Compute the net earnings for 2017, assuming that it is based on the amounts (a) before adjusting entries and (b) after adjusting entries. Which net earnings amount is correct? Explain.

3. Compute the earnings per share, assuming that 5,000 shares are outstanding.

4. Compute the net profit margin ratio and the return on equity, assuming that contributed capital did not change during the year. What do the computed ratios suggest to you about the company?

5. Prepare the closing entries at December 31, 2017.

■ LO4-1,4-2,4-4 **AP4-5**   **Recording Adjusting and Closing Entries, Preparing a Statement of Earnings Including Earnings per Share, and Preparing a Statement of Financial Position** (P4-5)

Mitakis Inc., a small service repair company, keeps its records without the help of an accountant. After much effort, an outside accountant prepared the following unadjusted trial balance as at the end of the company's fiscal year, December 31, 2018:

Account Titles	Debit	Credit
Cash	$19,600	
Accounts receivable	7,000	
Supplies inventory	1,300	
Prepaid insurance	900	
Equipment	27,000	
Accumulated depreciation, equipment		$12,000
Other assets	5,100	
Accounts payable		2,500
Note payable (two years; 7% due each December 31)		5,000
Contributed capital (4,000 shares)		16,000
Retained earnings		10,300
Service revenue		48,000
Other expenses, excluding income tax	32,900	
Totals	$93,800	$93,800

Data not yet recorded at December 31, 2018, include the following:

a. Depreciation expense for 2018, $3,000.

b. Insurance expired during 2018, $450.

c. Wages earned by employees not yet paid on December 31, 2018, $1,100.

d. Supplies inventory on December 31, 2018, reflecting $600 remaining on hand.

e. Income tax expense, $2,950.

Required:

1. Prepare the adjusting entries at December 31, 2018.

2. Show the effects (direction and amount) of the adjusting entries on net earnings and cash.

3. Prepare a statement of earnings for 2018 and a statement of financial position at December 31, 2018. Include the effects of transactions (*a*) through (*e*).

4. Compute the net earnings for the year, assuming that you did not make an adjustment to the balance of the supplies inventory account. Does this error cause a material change to net earnings? Explain.

5. Prepare the closing entries at December 31, 2018.

■ LO4-3,4-4   **AP4-6**   **Preparing Both a Statement of Earnings and a Statement of Financial Position from a Trial Balance** (P4-6)

ACME Pest Control Services (organized as a corporation on September 1, 2012) has completed the accounting cycle for the second year, ended August 31, 2017. ACME Pest Control has also completed a correct trial balance as follows:

ACME PEST CONTROL SERVICES Trial Balance At August 31, 2017		
Account Titles	**Debit**	**Credit**
Cash	$ 26,000	
Accounts receivable	30,800	
Supplies inventory	1,300	
Service vehicles (company vans)	60,000	
Accumulated depreciation, automobiles		$ 20,000
Equipment	14,000	
Accumulated depreciation, equipment		4,000
Accounts payable		16,700
Salaries payable		1,100
Note payable, long term		34,000
Contributed capital (10,000 shares)		40,000
Retained earnings (on September 1, 2013)		4,300
Dividends declared	2,000	
Sales revenue		38,000
Maintenance contract revenue		17,000
Operating expenses (detail omitted to conserve your time)	27,000	
Depreciation expense (including $2,000 on equipment)	12,000	
Interest expense	2,000	
Totals	$175,100	$175,100

Required:

1. Prepare a statement of earnings for the reporting year ended August 31, 2017. Include income tax expense, assuming a 30 percent tax rate. Use the following major captions: revenues, expenses, net earnings before income tax, income tax, net earnings, and earnings per share (list each item under these captions as appropriate).

2. Prepare the journal entry to record income taxes for the year (not yet paid).

3. Prepare a statement of financial position at the end of the reporting year, August 31, 2017. Use the following captions (list each item under these captions as appropriate):

   Assets
   Current assets
   Non-current assets

   Liabilities
   Current liabilities
   Non-current liabilities

   Shareholders' Equity
   Contributed capital
   Retained earnings

4. Compute the net profit margin ratio and the return on equity. What do these ratios suggest?

5. Prepare the closing entries at August 31, 2017.

■ LO4-1,4-2,4-3,4-4

AP4-7

Recording Adjusting and Closing Entries, Preparing a Statement of Earnings Including Earnings per Share, and Preparing a Statement of Financial Position (P4-7)

Claudia Pederzolli is enrolled in a co-op program in accounting that provides an opportunity for alternating study and work terms. For the second work term, Claudia was offered a position at the local branch of a CPA firm. After three weeks on the job, she was asked to assist her supervisor in preparing the financial statements of Sakura Ltd., a long-time client of the CPA firm. Claudia was provided with the following *unadjusted* trial balance for Sakura Ltd. as at December 31, 2017, as well as additional information to prepare the required financial statements:

	Debit	Credit
Cash	$ 247,000	
Accounts receivable	485,000	
Note receivable	60,000	
Property, plant, and equipment	500,000	
Accumulated depreciation		$ 140,625
Accounts payable		70,400
Note payable		30,000
Deferred rent revenue		6,000
Contributed capital (100,000 shares)		620,000
Retained earnings—January 1, 2017		165,000
Sales revenue		999,000
Cost of sales	502,000	
Salaries expense	222,000	
Other operating expenses	15,025	
	$2,031,025	$2,031,025

Additional information is as follows:

a. The company lent $60,000 to an employee on October 1, 2017, and recorded the note receivable. According to the terms of the note, interest at an annual rate of 5 percent will be paid when the note matures on March 15, 2019.

b. The company borrowed $30,000 on December 1, 2017, and signed a note, payable at December 31, 2018. Interest on the note is 4 percent per year and is payable at the beginning of each month, starting January 1, 2018.

c. A portion of the building was rented to Senecal Inc. on November 1, 2017, for three months for a total amount of $6,000. Sakura received the amount in cash from Senecal on that date and recorded it as deferred rent revenue.

d. Depreciation on the property, plant, and equipment was estimated at $15,625 for 2017.

e. Dividends of $0.60 per share were declared in December 2017, payable January 15, 2018.

f. Sakura Ltd. is subject to an income tax rate of 30 percent. The company will pay income taxes on March 15, 2018.

Journal entries related to these events have not been recorded yet.

Required:
Assume the role of Claudia Pederzolli and answer the following requirements:

1. Prepare the adjusting journal entries as at December 31, 2017, for items (*a*) through (*f*) above. Create new accounts, if necessary. (*Hint:* complete (2) before making the adjusting entry related to item (*f*).)

2. Show the effects (direction and amount) of the adjusting entries on net earnings and cash.

3. Prepare a multiple-step statement of earnings for the year ended December 31, 2017. Sakura Ltd. did not issue or repurchase any shares during 2017.

4. Prepare a classified statement of financial position as at December 31, 2017.

5. Prepare the closing entries at December 31, 2017.

6. Compute the net profit margin ratio and the return on equity for 2017, and explain the meaning of each ratio.

COMPREHENSIVE PROBLEMS (CHAPTERS 1–4)

■ LO4-1,4-2,4-3,4-4

COMP4-1

Recording Transactions (Including Adjusting and Closing Entries), Preparing a Complete Set of Financial Statements, and Performing Ratio Analysis

Brothers Anthony and Christopher Gaber began operations of their tool and die shop (A & C Tools Inc.) on January 1, 2016. The company's fiscal year ends on December 31. The trial balance on January 1, 2017, was as follows:

Account No.	Account Titles	Debit	Credit
01	Cash	$ 3,000	
02	Accounts receivable	5,000	
03	Service supplies inventory	12,000	
04	Land		
05	Equipment	60,000	
06	Accumulated depreciation (equipment)		$ 6,000
07	Other assets (not detailed, to simplify)	4,000	
11	Accounts payable		5,000
12	Notes payable		
13	Wages payable		
14	Interest payable		
15	Income taxes payable		
21	Contributed capital (65,000 shares)		65,000
31	Retained earnings		8,000
35	Service revenue		
40	Depreciation expense		
41	Income tax expense		
42	Interest expense		
43	Other expenses		
	Totals	$84,000	$84,000

Transactions and events during 2017 are as follows:

a. Borrowed $10,000 cash on a 6 percent note payable, dated March 1, 2017.

b. Purchased land for future building site; paid cash, $9,000.

c. Earned revenues for 2017 of $160,000, including $50,000 on credit.

d. Sold 3,000 additional shares for $1 cash per share.

e. Recognized other expenses for 2017, $85,000, including $20,000 on credit.

f. Collected accounts receivable, $24,000.

g. Purchased additional assets, $10,000 cash (debit other assets account).

h. Paid accounts payable, $13,000.

i. Purchased service supplies on account, $18,000 (debit to Account No. 03).

j. Signed a $25,000 service contract to start February 1, 2018.

k. Declared and paid cash dividend, $15,000.

   Data for adjusting entries are as follows:

l. Service supplies inventory on hand at December 31, 2017, $12,000 (debit other expenses account).

m. Depreciation on the equipment estimated at $6,000 per year.

n. Accrued interest on notes payable (to be computed).

o. Wages earned since the December 24 pay date but not yet paid, $15,000.

p. Income tax expense for 2017 payable in 2018, $8,000.

Required:

1. Set up T-accounts for the accounts on the trial balance and enter their beginning balances.

2. Record transactions (*a*) through (*k*) and post them to the T-accounts.

3. Record and post the adjusting entries (*l*) through (*p*).

4. Prepare a statement of earnings (including earnings per share), a statement of changes in equity for 2017, and a statement of financial position at December 31, 2017.

5. Record and post the closing entries.

6. Prepare a post-closing trial balance.

7. Compute the following ratios for 2017 and explain what they mean:

    a. Current ratio

    b. Total asset turnover ratio

    c. Net profit margin ratio

    d. Return on equity

LO4-1,4-2,4-3,4-4

COMP4-2

Recording Transactions (Including Adjusting and Closing Entries), Preparing a Complete Set of Financial Statements, and Performing Ratio Analysis

Serena and Bill Davis began operations of their furniture repair shop, Rumours Furniture Inc., on January 1, 2013. The company's fiscal year ends December 31. The trial balance on January 1, 2017, was as follows (in thousands of dollars):

Account No.	Account Titles	Debit	Credit
01	Cash	$ 5	
02	Accounts receivable	4	
03	Supplies inventory	2	
04	Small-tools inventory	6	
05	Equipment		
06	Accumulated depreciation (equipment)		
07	Other assets (not detailed to simplify)	9	
11	Accounts payable		$ 7
12	Notes payable		
13	Wages payable		
14	Interest payable		
15	Income taxes payable		
16	Deferred revenue		
21	Contributed capital (15,000 shares)		15
31	Retained earnings		4
35	Service revenue		
40	Depreciation expense		
41	Income tax expense		
42	Interest expense		
43	Other expenses		
	Totals	$26	$26

Transactions during 2017 (summarized in thousands of dollars) follow:

a. Borrowed $25 cash on July 1, 2017, on an 8 percent note, payable on June 30, 2018.

b. Purchased equipment for $18 cash on July 1, 2017.

c. Sold 5,000 additional shares for $1 cash per share.

d. Earned revenues for 2017: $74, including $15 on credit.

e. Recognized other expenses for 2017: $35, including $9 on credit.

f. Purchased additional small-tools inventory, $3 cash.

g. Collected accounts receivable, $8.

h. Paid accounts payable, $11.

i. Purchased supplies on account, $10 (debit to Account No. 03).

j. Received a $3 deposit on work to start January 15, 2018.

k. Declared and paid cash dividend, $12.

    Data for adjusting entries are as follows:

l. Service supplies inventory of $4 and small-tools inventory of $9 on hand at December 31, 2017 (debit other expenses account).

m. Depreciation on the equipment estimated at $4 per year.

m. Accrued interest on notes payable (to be computed).

o. Wages earned since the December 24 pay date but not yet paid, $4.

p. Income tax expense payable in 2018, $4.

Required:

1. Set up T-accounts for the accounts on the trial balance and enter their beginning balances.
2. Record transactions (*a*) through (*k*) and post them to the T-accounts.
3. Record and post the adjusting entries (*l*) through (*p*).
4. Prepare a statement of earnings (including earnings per share) for 2017, a statement of changes in equity for 2017, and a statement of financial position at December 31, 2017.
5. Record and post the closing entries.
6. Prepare a post-closing trial balance.
7. Compute the following ratios for 2017 and explain what they mean:
   a. Current ratio
   b. Total asset turnover ratio
   c. Net profit margin ratio
   d. Return on equity

connect CASES AND PROJECTS

FINDING AND INTERPRETING FINANCIAL INFORMATION

LO4-1,4-3,4-4 CP4-1 | **Finding Financial Information**

Canadian Tire Corporation

Refer to the financial statements of Canadian Tire Corporation in Appendix A at the end of this book.

Required:

1. How much did the company pay in interest for the 2015 fiscal year? Where did you find this information?
2. To what account is accumulated depreciation related?
3. What company accounts would not appear on a post-closing trial balance?
4. Prepare the closing entry for inventories.
5. What is the company's basic earnings per share for the two years reported?
6. Compute the company's net profit margin ratio for 2014 and 2015 based on information reported on the statement of earnings. How would you interpret the results?

LO4-3,4-4 CP4-2 | **Finding Financial Information**

Sears Canada Inc.

Go to *Connect* for the financial statements of Sears Canada Inc.

Required:

1. What is the balance of the prepaid expenses account at the end of the most recent year? Where did you find this information?
2. What is the difference between prepaid rent and deferred rent revenue?
3. Describe in general terms what accrued liabilities are.
4. What would generate the interest income that is reported in Note 5 to the financial statements?
5. Which company accounts would not have balances on a post-closing trial balance?
6. Give the closing entry, if any, for prepaid expenses.
7. What is the company's earnings per share (basic only) for the two years reported?
8. Compute the company's net profit margin ratio for the two years reported. What do the results suggest to you about Sears Canada Inc.?

LO4-3 CP4-3 | **Comparing Companies over Time**

Canadian Tire Corporation vs. Sears Canada Inc.

Refer to the financial statements of Canadian Tire Corporation (Appendix A) and Sears Canada Inc. (on *Connect*), and the Industry Ratio Report (Appendix B on *Connect*).

Required:

1. What was the cost of sales for each company's most recent fiscal year? Where did you find the information?
2. Compute the percentage of cost of sales to sales for each company if possible. Compute the same ratio for the previous two fiscal years and comment on the results.
3. Compute each company's net profit margin ratio for the years shown in its annual report. What do your results suggest about each company over the two-year period?

4. Compute each company's return on equity for the most recent year. Which company is more profitable? Explain.

5. Compare each company's net profit margin ratio and return on equity for the most recent year to the industry averages for both ratios in the Industry Ratio Report. Were these two companies performing better or worse than the average company in the industry?

FINANCIAL REPORTING AND ANALYSIS CASES

LO4-1

CP4-4   Analyzing the Effects of Adjustments

Seneca Land Company, a closely held corporation, invests in commercial rental properties. Seneca's fiscal year ends on December 31. At the end of each year, numerous adjusting entries must be made because many transactions completed during the current and prior years have economic effects on the financial statements of the current and future years. Assume that the current year is 2017.

Required:

This case concerns four transactions that have been selected for your analysis. Answer the questions for each.

Transaction (*a*): On July 1, 2016, the company purchased office equipment costing $14,000 for use in the business. The company estimates that the equipment will have a useful life of 10 years and no residual value.

1. Over how many accounting periods will this transaction directly affect Seneca's financial statements? Explain.

2. Assuming that depreciation expense is $1,400 per year, how much depreciation expense was reported on the 2016 and 2017 statements of earnings?

3. How should the office equipment be reported on the statement of financial position at December 31, 2018?

4. Would Seneca make an adjusting entry at the end of each year during the life of the equipment? Explain your answer.

Transaction (*b*): On September 1, 2017, Seneca collected $24,000 for rent of office space. This amount represented rent for a six-month period, September 1, 2017, through February 28, 2018. Deferred rent revenue was increased (credited), and cash was increased (debited) for $24,000.

1. Over how many accounting periods will this transaction affect Seneca's financial statements? Explain.

2. How much rent revenue on this office space should Seneca report on the 2017 statement of earnings? Explain.

3. Did this transaction create a liability for Seneca as of the end of 2017? Explain. If yes, how much?

4. Should Seneca make an adjusting entry on December 31, 2017? Explain. If your answer is yes, prepare the adjusting entry.

Transaction (*c*): On December 31, 2017, Seneca owed wages of $7,500 to employees because they worked the last three days in December 2017. The next payroll date is January 5, 2018.

1. Over how many accounting periods does this transaction affect Seneca's financial statements? Explain.

2. How would this $7,500 amount affect Seneca's statement of earnings for 2017 and the statement of financial position at December 31, 2017?

3. Should Seneca make an adjusting entry on December 31, 2017? Explain. If your answer is yes, prepare the adjusting entry.

Transaction (*d*): On January 1, 2017, Seneca agreed to supervise the planning and subdivision of a large tract of land for a customer, J. Ray. This service job involves four separate phases. By December 31, 2017, three phases had been completed to Ray's satisfaction. The remaining phase will be done during 2018. The total price for the four phases (agreed on in advance by both parties) was $60,000. Each phase involves about the same amount of services. On December 31, 2017, Seneca had not collected any cash for the services already performed.

1. Should Seneca record any service revenue on this job for 2017? Explain. If yes, prepare the adjusting entry to record the revenue.

2. What entry will Seneca make when it completes the last phase, assuming that the full contract price is collected on the completion date, February 15, 2018?

LO4-1,4-3,4-4 CP4-5 Using Financial Reports: Inferring Adjusting and Closing Entries and Answering Analytical Questions

Rowland Company was organized on January 1, 2016. At the end of the first year of operations, December 31, 2016, the bookkeeper prepared the following trial balances (amounts in thousands of dollars):

Account No.	Account Titles	Unadjusted Trial Balance		Adjustments		Adjusted Trial Balance	
		Debit	Credit	Debit	Credit	Debit	Credit
11	Cash	40				40	
12	Accounts receivable	17				17	
13	Prepaid insurance	2				1	
14	Rent receivable					2	
15	Property, plant, and equipment	46				46	
16	Accumulated depreciation						11
17	Other assets	6				6	
18	Accounts payable		27				27
19	Wages payable						3
20	Income taxes payable						5
21	Deferred rent revenue						4
22	Note payable (10%; dated January 1, 2013)		20				20
23	Contributed capital (1,000 shares)		30				30
24	Retained earnings	3				3	
25	Revenues (total)		105				103
26	Expenses (total including interest)	68				83	
27	Income tax expense					5	
	Totals	**182**	**182**			**203**	**203**

Required:

1. Based on inspection of the two trial balances, prepare the 2016 adjusting entries recorded by the bookkeeper (provide brief explanations).

2. Based on these data, prepare the 2016 closing entries with brief explanations.

3. Answer the following questions (show computations):

   a. How many shares were outstanding at year-end?

   b. What was the amount of interest expense included in the total expenses?

   c. What was the balance of retained earnings on December 31, 2016?

   d. What was the average income tax rate?

   e. How would the rent receivable and deferred rent revenue accounts be reported on the statement of financial position?

   f. Explain why cash increased by $40,000 during the year even though net earnings was comparatively very low.

   g. What was the amount of earnings per share for 2016?

   h. What was the average selling price of the shares?

   i. When was the insurance premium paid and over what period of time did the coverage extend?

   j. What was the net profit margin ratio for the year?

   k. What was the return on equity for the year?

LO4-1,4-2 CP4-6 Using Financial Reports: Analyzing Financial Information in a Sale of a Business (A Challenging Case)

Robert Brissette, a local massage therapist, decided to sell his practice and retire. He has had discussions with a therapist from another province who wants to relocate. The discussions are at the complex stage of agreeing on a price. The financial statements of Robert's practice, Brissette Stress Reduction, played an important role in this process. Robert's secretary, Kelsey Doucette, maintained the records, under his direction. Each year, Kelsey developed a statement of net earnings on a cash basis from the records she maintained, but she did not prepare a statement of financial position. Upon request, Robert provided the other therapist with the following statements for 2018 prepared by Kelsey:

BRISSETTE STRESS REDUCTION Statement of Earnings 2018		
Therapy fees collected		$130,000
Expenses paid:		
Rent for office space	$19,500	
Utilities expense	360	
Telephone expense	2,200	
Office salaries expense	23,500	
Office supplies expense	900	
Miscellaneous expenses	1,400	
Total expenses		47,860
Net earnings		$ 82,140

Upon agreement of the parties, you have been asked to examine the financial figures for 2018. The other therapist said, "I question the figures because, among other things, they appear to be on a 100 percent cash basis." Your investigations revealed the following additional data at December 31, 2018:

a. Of the $130,000 in therapy fees collected in 2018, $30,000 was for services performed prior to 2018.

b. At the end of 2018, therapy fees of $6,000 for services performed during the year were uncollected.

c. Office equipment owned and used by Brissette Stress Reduction cost $8,000. It is depreciated at a rate of $800 per year.

d. An inventory of office supplies at December 31, 2018, reflected $400 worth of items purchased during the year that were still on hand. Also, the records for 2017 indicate that the supplies on hand at the end of that year were about $250.

e. At the end of 2018, Kelsey, whose salary is $24,000 per year, had not been paid for the last week of December because the next payday is January 8, 2019.

f. The $140 phone bill for December 2018 was not paid until January 11, 2019.

g. The payment for office rent was for 13 months, including January 2019.

Required:

1. Prepare a correct statement of earnings for 2018 based on the information above. Show your computations for any amounts changed from those in the statement prepared by Kelsey. (*Hint:* use four column headings: Item, Cash Basis per Brissette's Statement, $; Explanation of Changes; and Corrected Basis, $.)

2. Write a memo to support your schedule prepared in (1). The purpose should be to explain the reasons for your changes and to suggest other important items that should be considered in the pricing decision.

LO4-1,4-3   CP4-7   Using Financial Reports: Preparing Statements of Earnings for Different Periods

Wong's Insurance Agency adjusts its accounts at the end of each month. The adjusted balances of the revenue and expense accounts at two different dates of the year appear below. The company's fiscal year starts on January 1:

	September 30, 2018	June 30, 2018
Commissions earned	$72,000	$45,000
Salaries expense	18,000	12,000
Rent expense	11,250	7,500
Depreciation expense	1,350	900
Advertising expense	14,000	7,500

The company is subject to an income tax rate of 40 percent.

Required:

Prepare statements of earnings for two separate time periods: the quarter ending September 30, 2018, and the nine-month period ending September 30, 2018. Explain how you determined the amounts for each time period and show supporting computations.

LO4-1,4-2   CP4-8   Using Financial Reports: Analyzing Financial Information from Real Financial Statements

WestJet Airlines

The current liabilities of WestJet Airlines include the advance ticket sales account. The company's recent annual reports show the following trend in the balance of this account over a three-year period:

	2015	2014	2013
Advance ticket sales (in thousands)	$620,216	$575,781	$551,022

The first note to the company's financial statements, titled *Significant accounting policies*, includes the following disclosure about revenue recognition:

Guest revenues, including the air component of vacation packages, are recognized when air transportation is provided. Tickets sold but not yet used are included in the consolidated statement of financial position as advance ticket sales.

Required:

1. What does the balance in the advance ticket sales account represent?

2. Why does WestJet recognize guest revenue when transportation is provided, rather than when cash is received?

3. How does WestJet Airlines normally settle this liability?

4. Should WestJet recognize flight expenses, such as jet fuel, salaries of flight crew, and cost of food and beverage, in the period when the flights occur or during the period when tickets are sold? Explain.

5. Explain the most probable reason for the increase in the amount of this liability from 2013 to 2015.

6. Based on the trend in the amount of this liability, would you expect the annual amounts of guest revenue to increase, decrease, or remain stable over the three-year period? Explain.

 CP4-9   **Using Financial Reports: Analyzing Financial Information from Real Financial Statements**

Leon's Furniture Limited

Leon's Furniture Limited, one of Canada's largest retailers, sells a wide range of merchandise including furniture, major appliances and home electronics. Selected information from the company's financial statements for the year ended December 31, 2015, is provided below (in thousands of dollars):

	December 31, 2015	December 31, 2014
Statement of Financial Position		
Trade receivables	$ 117,832	$112,721
Customers' deposits	112,446	97,705
Dividends payable	7,141	7,105
Income taxes payable	7,266	34,773
Deferred warranty plan revenue	145,155	143,365
Loans and borrowings	287,357	315,363
Other information		
Sales for fiscal year 2015	$2,031,718	
Income taxes paid during the year	52,297	23,514

Required:

1. Compute the amount of cash collected from customers during the year. Assume that all sales for fiscal year 2015 were on credit.

2. Explain the nature of the deferred warranty plan revenue account. What would have caused the account balance to change during the year?

3. The company's board of directors declared dividends of $28,501 during the year. Prepare a summary journal entry to record the amount of dividends paid during the year.

4. The company is required to pay income taxes in advance on a quarterly basis even though the exact amount of income taxes expense is not calculated until the end of the fiscal year. Compute the amount of income taxes expense for 2015 and prepare the related adjusting journal entry at December 31, 2015.

5. The company's loans and borrowings include a short-term bank loan for $50,000. Assume that the company signed for this loan on October 31, 2015, to be repaid on October 31, 2017. Interest on the loan, at an annual rate of 4.5 percent, is payable each year on October 31. Prepare the adjusting journal entry that should be made on December 31, 2015, to recognize interest expense for fiscal year 2015.

6. Assume that the company's accountant did not record the journal entry you prepared for (5) above. What would be the effect of this error (overstatement, understatement, no effect) on the following:

   a. Total assets at December 31, 2015.

   b. Net earnings for the year 2015, assuming that the company is subject to an income tax rate of 30 percent.

   c. Current liabilities at December 31, 2015.

CRITICAL THINKING CASES

LO4-1,4-2,4-3 CP4-10   **Using Financial Reports: Evaluating Financial Information as a Bank Loan Officer**
Magliochetti Moving Corp. has been in operation since January 1, 2017. It is now December 31, 2017, the end of the company's fiscal year. The company has not done well financially during the first year, although revenue has been fairly good. The three shareholders manage the company, but they have not given much attention to recordkeeping. In view of a serious cash shortage, they have applied to your bank for a $20,000 loan. You requested a complete set of financial statements. The following annual financial statements for 2017 were prepared by a clerk and then were given to the bank:

MAGLIOCCHETTI MOVING CORP.				
Statement of Earnings **For the Period Ended** **December 31, 2017**			**Statement of Financial Position** **At December 31, 2017**	
Transportation revenue	$85,000	**Assets**		
Expenses:		Cash		$12,000
Salaries expense	17,000	Receivables		3,000
Maintenance expense	12,000	Inventory of maintenance supplies		6,000
Other expenses	18,000	Equipment		40,000
Total expenses	47,000	Prepaid expenses		4,000
Net earnings	$38,000	Other assets		27,000
		Total assets		$82,000
		Liabilities		
		Accounts payable		$ 9,000
		Shareholders' Equity		
		Contributed capital (10,000 shares outstanding)		35,000
		Retained earnings		38,000
		Total liabilities and shareholders' equity		$82,000

After briefly reviewing the statements and looking into the situation, you requested that the statements be redone (with some expert help) to "incorporate depreciation, accruals, inventory counts, income taxes, and so on." As a result of a review of the records and supporting documents, the following additional information was developed:

a. The inventory of maintenance supplies of $6,000 shown on the statement of financial position has not been adjusted for supplies used during 2017. An inventory count of the maintenance supplies on hand (unused) on December 31, 2017, showed $1,800. Supplies used should be debited to maintenance expense.

b. The insurance premium paid in 2017 was for 2017 and 2018; therefore, the prepaid insurance at December 31, 2017, amounted to $2,000. The total insurance premium was debited to prepaid insurance when paid in 2017.

c. The equipment cost $40,000 when purchased January 1, 2017. Depreciation expense of $5,000 has not been recorded for 2017.

d. Unpaid (and unrecorded) salaries at December 31, 2017, amounted to $2,200.

e. At December 31, 2017, transportation revenue collected in advance amounted to $7,000. This amount was credited to transportation revenue when the cash was collected.

f. The company is subject to an income tax rate of 30 percent.

Required:

1. Record the six adjusting entries required on December 31, 2017, based on the preceding additional information.

2. Recast the preceding statements after taking into account the adjusting entries. Use the following format for the solution:

	Changes			
Items	**Amounts Reported**	**Plus**	**Minus**	**Correct Amounts**
(List here each item from the two statements)				

3. Omission of the adjusting entries caused the following:

a. Net earnings to be overstated or understated (select one) by $_____.

b. Total assets to be overstated or understated (select one) by $_____.

      c. Total liabilities to be overstated or understated (select one) by $_____.

   4. Use both the unadjusted and adjusted balances to calculate the following ratios for the company: (a) earnings per share, (b) net profit margin ratio, and (c) return on equity. Explain the causes of the differences and the impact of the changes on the financial analysis.

   5. Write a letter to the company explaining the results of the adjustments, your analysis, and your decision regarding the loan.

LO4-1,4-3   **CP4-11**   **Making a Decision as an Auditor: Effects of Errors on Net Earnings, Assets, and Liabilities**

Megan Company was careless about its financial records during its first year of operations, 2013. It is December 31, 2016, the end of the company's fiscal year. An external auditor examined the records and discovered numerous errors, all of which are described below. Assume that each error is independent of the others.

	Effect on					
	Net Earnings		**Assets**		**Liabilities**	
Independent Errors	**2016**	**2017**	**2016**	**2017**	**2016**	**2017**
(a) Depreciation expense for 2016, not recorded in 2016, $950.	O $950	N	O $950	O $950	N	N
(b) Wages earned by employees during 2016, not recorded in 2016, but will be paid in 2017, $500.						
(c) Revenue earned during 2016 but not collected or recorded until 2017, $600; will be collected in 2017.						
(d) Amount paid in 2016 and recorded as expense in 2016, but it is not an expense until 2017, $200.						
(e) Revenue collected in 2016 and recorded as revenue in 2016, but it is not earned until 2017, $900.						
(f) Sale of services for cash in 2016. Recorded as a debit to cash and as a credit to accounts receivable, $300.						
(g) On December 31, 2016, bought land on credit for $8,000, but did not record the transaction until payment was made on February 1, 2017.						

Required:

Analyze each error and indicate its effect on 2016 and 2017 net earnings, assets, and liabilities if not corrected. Do not assume any other errors. Use these codes to indicate the effect of each dollar amount: O = overstated, U = understated, and N = no effect. Write an explanation of your analysis of each transaction to support your response.

   A sample explanation of analysis of errors that are not corrected is provided below, using the first error as an example:

   a. Failure to record depreciation in 2016 caused depreciation expense to be too low; therefore, net earnings was overstated by $950. Accumulated depreciation is also too low by $950, which causes assets to be overstated by $950 until the error is corrected.

LO4-3   **CP4-12**   **Making Decisions as a Manager: Evaluating the Effects of Business Strategy on Return on Equity**

Sony

Sony is a world leader in the manufacture of consumer and commercial electronics as well as the entertainment and insurance industries.

Required:

Using the table below, indicate the most likely effect of each of the following changes in business strategy on Sony's return on equity for the current period and future periods (+ for increase, − for decrease, and NE for no effect), assuming all other things are unchanged. Explain your answer for each. Treat each item independently.

   a. Sony decreases its investment in research and development aimed at products to be brought to market in more than one year.

   b. Sony begins a new advertising campaign for a movie to be released during the next year.

c. Sony issues additional shares for cash, the proceeds to be used to acquire other high-technology companies in future periods.

Strategy Change	Current-Period ROE	Future Periods' ROE
(a)		
(b)		
(c)		

FINANCIAL REPORTING AND ANALYSIS TEAM PROJECT

LO4-1,4-2,4-3 CP4-13

Team Project: Analyzing Accruals, Earnings per Share, Net Profit Margin Ratio, and Return on Equity

As a team, select an industry to analyze. A list of companies classified by industry can be obtained by accessing www.fpinfomart.ca and then choosing Companies by Industry. You can also find a list of industries and companies within each industry via http://ca.finance.yahoo.com/investing (click on Order Annual Reports under Tools).

Each group member should acquire the annual report for a different publicly traded company in the industry. (Library files, the SEDAR service at www.sedar.com, and the company's website are good sources.)

Required:

On an individual basis, each team member should write a short report answering the following questions about the selected company. Discuss any patterns across the companies that you as a team observe. Then, as a team, write a short report comparing and contrasting your companies.

1. From the statement of earnings, what are the company's earnings per share for the last three years?
2. Perform a ratio analysis:
   a. What does the net profit margin measure in general?
   b. What does the return on equity measure in general?
   c. Compute these ratios for the last three years.
   d. What do your results suggest about the company? (You may refer to the management discussion and analysis section of the annual report to learn about the company's stated reasons for any change over time.)
   e. If available, find the industry ratio for the most recent year, compare it to your results, and discuss why you believe the ratio for your company differs from or is similar to the industry ratio.
3. List the accounts and amounts of accrued liabilities on the most recent statement of financial position. (You may find the detail in the notes to the statements.) What is the ratio of the total accrued liabilities to the total liabilities?

connect CONTINUING CASE

LO4-1

CC4-1

Adjusting Accounts at Year-End (the Accounting Cycle)

Penny's Pool Service & Supply Inc. (PPSS) is completing the accounting process for the year just ended, December 31, 2017. The transactions during 2017 have been journalized and posted. The following data with respect to adjusting entries are available:

a. PPSS owed $800 wages to the office receptionist and three assistants for working the last two days in December. The employees will be paid in January 2018.
b. On October 1, 2017, PPSS received $24,000 from customers who prepaid pool cleaning service for one year beginning on November 1, 2017.
c. The company received a $520 utility bill for December utility usage. It will be paid in January 2018.
d. PPSS borrowed $30,000 from a local bank on May 1, 2017, signing a note with a 6 percent interest rate. The note and interest are due on May 1, 2018.
e. On December 31, 2017, PPSS cleaned and winterized a customer's pool for $800, but the service was not yet recorded on December 31.
f. On August 1, 2017, PPSS purchased a two-year insurance policy for $4,200, with coverage beginning on that date. The amount was recorded as prepaid insurance when paid.
g. On December 31, 2017, PPSS had $3,100 of pool cleaning supplies on hand. During 2017, PPSS purchased supplies costing $23,000 from Pool Corporation Inc. and had $2,400 of supplies on hand on December 31, 2016.

   h. PPSS estimated that depreciation on its buildings and equipment was $8,300 for the year.

   i. At December 31, 2017, $110 of interest on investments was earned that will be received in 2018.

   Required:
   Prepare adjusting entries for Penny's Pool Service & Supply Inc. on December 31, 2017.

■ LO4-2,4-3　　**CC4-2**　**Preparing a Statement of Earnings and Statement of Financial Position and Computing Selected Ratios for a Public Company)**

Pool Corporation, Inc., is the world's largest wholesale distributor of swimming pool supplies and equipment. It is a publicly traded corporation that trades on the NASDAQ exchange under the symbol POOL.

   It sells these products to swimming pool repair and service businesses like Penny's Pool Service & Supply, Inc., swimming pool builders, and retail swimming pool stores. The majority of these customers are small, family-owned businesses like Penny's. Its trial balance and additional information adapted from a recent year ended December 31 are presented below. All numbers are in thousands.

Account Title	Debit	Credit
Cash and cash equivalents	$　17,487	
Receivables, net	110,555	
Product inventories, net	386,924	
Prepaid expenses and other current assets	23,035	
Property and equipment, net	41,394	
Intangible assets	188,841	
Other non-current assets, net	30,386	
Accounts payable		$　177,437
Accrued expenses and other current liabilities		53,398
Current portion of long-term debt		22
Long-term debt		247,300
Other long-term liabilities		40,719
Contributed capital		173,227
Retained earnings, January 1		34,526
Net sales		1,793,318
Cost of sales	1,261,728	
Selling and administrative expenses	406,523	
Interest expense	7,755	
Provision for income taxes	45,319	
	$2,519,947	$2,519,947

   Required:

   1. Prepare a classified statement of earnings (with earnings per share) and a statement of financial position for the current year. The number of shares outstanding used in computing earnings per share was 48,158.

   2. Compute the following ratios: debt-to-equity, total assets turnover, return on assets, net profit margin, and return on equity. As a shareholder of this company, how would you interpret these ratios? Total assets and total shareholders' equity equaled $728,545 and $285,182, respectively at the beginning of the year.

SOLUTIONS TO SELF-STUDY QUIZZES

Self-Study Quiz 4-1

	(1) Revenue earned or expense incurred?	(2) Cash received/paid in the past or cash to be received/ paid in the future?	(3) Amount	Adjusting journal entry accounts	Debit	Credit
AJE 1	Trip revenue earned	Received in past: *Deferred revenue*	$6,000 × 1/3 = $2,000 earned	Deferred revenue (−L) Trip revenue (+R, +SE)	2,000	2,000

AJE 2	Instruction revenue earned	To be received: *Accrued revenue*	$800 earned (given)	Accounts receivable (+A) Instruction revenue (+R, +SE)	800	800
AJE 3	Insurance expense incurred	Paid in past: *Prepaid expense*	$24,000 ÷ 12 = $2,000 per month $2,000 × 4 months = $8,000 used	Insurance expense (+E, −SE) Prepaid insurance (−A)	8,000	8,000
AJE 4	Interest expense incurred	To be paid: *Accrued expense*	$300,000 × 0.06 × 10/12 = $15,000 incurred and owed	Interest expense (+E, −SE) Interest payable (+L)	15,000	15,000

Self-Study Quiz 4-2

Net profit margin ratio based on the unadjusted trial balance:

> Earnings before income taxes = $255
>
> Income tax expense = $255 × 40% = $102; Net earnings = $255 − $102 = $153
>
> Net profit margin = $153 ÷ $1,040 = 0.147 or 14.7%
>
> Net profit margin based on the adjusted trial balance:
>
> Net profit margin = $63 ÷ $1,080 = 0.058 or 5.8%

The difference between the two ratios is due to the end-of-period adjustments, which increased revenues by $40 and increased expenses by $232, thus, lowering net earnings significantly from $255 to $63. The difference between the two ratios, 8.9%, represents 153.4% of the correct ratio. It is certainly a material difference. Clearly, if adjustments to the revenue and expense accounts are not made, net earnings will be overstated as well as the net profit margin ratio. Inaccurate information is not useful for decision making. Thus, what appears to be a set of very intricate procedures, when properly executed, actually contributes to the decision usefulness of financial statements.

ENDNOTES

1. A firm's fiscal year does not have to conform to the calendar year (January 1 to December 31). Some companies choose a fiscal year that ends on a date that is more convenient than December 31 to prepare its financial statements. For example, a retail company may choose a fiscal year that ends on January 31, after the busy shopping period during the holiday season. In some cases, companies choose a fiscal year-end that is defined as "the last Saturday of the month" or "the Sunday closest to the end of the month," which results in financial information covering 52 weeks in some years and 53 weeks in other years.

2. Companies can choose fiscal periods other than actual month-ends, and financial statements can cover different accounting periods (month, quarter, or year). Adjusting entries may be prepared monthly, quarterly, and/or annually to ensure that proper amounts are included on the financial reports presented to external users.

3. Valuation of property, plant, and equipment is discussed in Chapter 8.

4. The computation of interest is relatively simple: Interest × Amount borrowed × Annual interest rate = Time. For this example, interest has accrued for 10 months, from March 1 to December 31, 2017. The amount accrued is computed as follows: $300,000 × 0.06 × (10 months/12) = $15,000. Interest computations are covered in more detail in Chapter 9.

5. In fact, a bank employee was able to accumulate a large sum of money by altering a computer program to round off amounts of exchange transactions to the nearest cent and by transferring the fractional amounts to a specific account under his control. Even though the amounts involved per transaction were very small, the volume of banking transactions resulted in the accumulation of a relatively large amount. Fortunately, the employee's fraud was detected a few years later and an appropriate penalty was imposed on him.

6. For a discussion and illustration of the use of a worksheet for end-of-period adjustments, refer to Appendix C on *Connect*.

7. If there are preferred dividends (discussed in Chapter 11), the amount is subtracted from net earnings in the numerator. Outstanding shares are those that are currently held by the shareholders.

Reporting and Interpreting Cash Flows

After studying this chapter, you should be able to do the following:

Courtesy of National Beverage Corp.

Focus Company: **National Beverage Corp.**

PRODUCING VALUE FOR CUSTOMERS AND CASH FLOWS TO SHAREHOLDERS

In the highly competitive beverage market dominated by giants Coca-Cola and PepsiCo, National Beverage (http://www.nationalbeverage.com) aims at value-conscious consumers seeking flavour variety. With over 50 different flavours available in its well-known Shasta and Faygo carbonated soft drinks, combined with Everfresh juices, LaCroix waters, and Rip It energy products, National Beverage can meet all of the beverage needs of a wide variety of consumers and retailers. For its value strategy of earning profits for shareholders, National Beverage must also be a cost-effective producer. It maintains product quality and cost discipline through centralized purchasing, and by owning and operating all of its production and bottling facilities. Its 12 plants are strategically located near customer distribution centres in different markets, thereby reducing distribution costs and allowing National Beverage to tailor its products and media promotions to regional tastes. Through difficult economic times, sales and earnings at National Beverage continue to grow. As Nick Caporella, chairman and CEO of the company since its founding, said in a recent annual report, there are a number of keys to the company's strong performance:

- Brands that sparkle in tough times
- Fortress statement of financial position
- Investor focus that yields appreciation
- Investor cash—returned appropriately

Although it may be puzzling, profitable operations do not always ensure positive cash flow. As we have seen in earlier chapters, this occurs because the timing of revenues and expenses does not always match those of cash inflows and outflows. As a consequence, National Beverage must carefully manage cash flows as well as profits. For the same reasons, financial analysts must consider the information provided in National Beverage's statement of cash flows in addition to information reported on its statement of financial position and statement of earnings.

UNDERSTANDING THE BUSINESS

Net earnings is an important indicator of performance, but cash flow is also critical to a company's success. Cash flow permits a company to expand its operations, replace worn assets, take advantage of new investment opportunities, pay its creditors, and pay dividends to its owners. Some financial analysts go as far as saying that "cash flow is king." Both managers and analysts need to understand the various sources and uses of cash that are associated with business activity.

The statement of cash flows focuses attention on a firm's ability to generate cash internally, its management of operating assets and liabilities, and the details of its investments and external financing. It is designed to help both managers and analysts answer important cash-related questions such as these:

- Will the company have enough cash to pay its short-term debts to suppliers, employees, taxation authorities, and other creditors without additional borrowing?

- Is the company adequately managing its accounts receivable, inventory, and other current assets?

- Has the company made necessary investments in new productive capacity?

- Did the company generate enough cash flow internally to finance necessary investments, or did it rely on external financing?

- Is the company changing the proportion of debt and equity in its capital structure?

We begin our discussion with an overview of the statement of cash flows. Then, we examine the information reported in each section of the statement in depth. The chapter ends with a discussion of additional cash flow disclosures.

ORGANIZATION OF THE CHAPTER

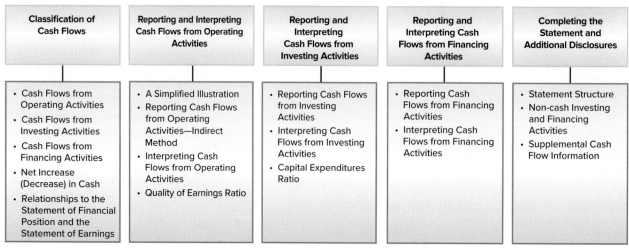

Classification of Cash Flows	Reporting and Interpreting Cash Flows from Operating Activities	Reporting and Interpreting Cash Flows from Investing Activities	Reporting and Interpreting Cash Flows from Financing Activities	Completing the Statement and Additional Disclosures
• Cash Flows from Operating Activities • Cash Flows from Investing Activities • Cash Flows from Financing Activities • Net Increase (Decrease) in Cash • Relationships to the Statement of Financial Position and the Statement of Earnings	• A Simplified Illustration • Reporting Cash Flows from Operating Activities—Indirect Method • Interpreting Cash Flows from Operating Activities • Quality of Earnings Ratio	• Reporting Cash Flows from Investing Activities • Interpreting Cash Flows from Investing Activities • Capital Expenditures Ratio	• Reporting Cash Flows from Financing Activities • Interpreting Cash Flows from Financing Activities	• Statement Structure • Non-cash Investing and Financing Activities • Supplemental Cash Flow Information

Supplemental material:

Appendix 5A: Adjustment for Gains and Losses on the Sale of Long-Lived Assets—Indirect Method
Appendix 5B: Reporting Cash Flows from Operating Activities—Direct Method
Appendix 5C: T-account Approach—Indirect Method
Appendix 5D: Spreadsheet Approach—Statement of Cash Flows, Indirect Method

CLASSIFICATION OF CASH FLOWS

Basically, the statement of cash flows explains how the cash balance at the beginning of the period changed to another cash balance at the end of the period. For the purpose of this statement, the definition of cash includes cash and cash equivalents. **Cash equivalents** are short-term, highly liquid investments that are both

1. readily convertible to known amounts of cash, and
2. less than three months to their maturity and subject to an insignificant risk of changes in value.

Generally, an investment qualifies as a cash equivalent only when it has an original maturity of three months or less from the date of acquisition.[1] Examples of cash equivalents are Treasury bills (a form of short-term government debt), money market funds, and commercial paper (short-term notes payable issued by large corporations).

As you can see in Exhibit 5.1, the statement of cash flows reports cash inflows and outflows based on three broad categories: (1) operating activities, (2) investing activities, and (3) financing activities. Together, these three cash flow categories explain the change in cash from the beginning balance to the ending balance on the statement of financial position. To improve comparability, International Accounting Standard 7— Statement of Cash Flows defines each category included in the required statement. These definitions (with explanations) are presented in the following sections.[2]

LO5-1

Classify cash flow items into cash flows from operating, investing, and financing activities.

A **CASH EQUIVALENT** is a short-term, highly liquid investment with an original maturity of less than three months, and subject to an insignificant risk of changes in value.

Exhibit **5.1**
Consolidated Statement of Cash Flows

REAL-WORLD EXCERPT
National Beverage Corp.
ANNUAL REPORT

NATIONAL BEVERAGE CORP.
Consolidated Statements of Cash Flows
For the Year Ended May 2, 2015*
(amounts in thousands)

Operating activities	
Net earnings (loss)	$(49,311)
Adjustments for items not affecting cash:	
Depreciation and amortization	9,404
Change in non-cash working capital items related to operations:	
Accounts receivable (increase)	(1,746)
Inventories (decrease)	990
Prepaid expenses (decrease)	355
Accounts payable (decrease)	(710)
Accrued liabilities (increase)	2,384
Income tax payable (increase)	54
Cash flows from operating activities	60,042
Investing activities	
Purchases of property, plant, and equipment	(11,630)
Proceeds from sale of property, plant, and equipment	1,905
Purchase of short-term investments	(6,532)
Proceeds from sale of short-term investments	4,869
Cash flows used in investing activities	(11,388)
Financing activities	
Repayment of principal on long-term debt	(18,400)
Repurchase of shares	(7,455)
Payment of dividends	(275)
Cash flows used in financing activities	(26,130)
Increase in cash and cash equivalents	22,524
Cash and cash equivalents, beginning of period	29,932
Cash and cash equivalents, end of period	$52,456

The balances of certain accounts have been adjusted to simplify the presentation.

*National Beverage's fiscal year ends on the last Saturday closest to April 30 each year.
Source: National Beverage Corp., Annual Report 2015.

Cash Flows from Operating Activities

Cash flows from operating activities (cash flows from operations) are the cash inflows and cash outflows that directly relate to revenues and expenses from normal operations. There are two alternative approaches for presenting the operating activities section of the statement:

1. The **direct method** reports the components of cash flows from operating activities listed as gross receipts and gross payments:

Inflows	Outflows
Cash received from	*Cash paid for*
Customers	Purchase of goods for resale and services (electricity, etc.)
Dividends and interest on investments	Salaries and wages
	Income taxes
	Interest on borrowings

The difference between the inflows and outflows is called the *net cash inflow (outflow) from operating activities*. National Beverage experienced a net cash inflow of $60,042 from its operations for fiscal year 2015. Although IAS 7 encourages companies to use the direct method, it is rarely seen in Canada. Many financial executives have reported that they do not use it because it is more expensive to implement than the indirect method. Attempts by standard setters to require use of the direct method are usually met with intense opposition from the preparer community.

2. The **indirect method** of presenting the operating activities section of the statement of cash flows starts with net earnings for the period and then eliminates non-cash items to arrive at net cash inflow (outflow) from operating activities:

Net earnings
+/− Adjustments for non-cash items
Net cash inflow (outflow) from operating activities

Notice in Exhibit 5.1 that National Beverage reported net earnings of $49,311 but generated positive cash flows from operating activities of $60,042. Why do net earnings and cash flows from operating activities differ? Recall that the statement of earnings is prepared under the accrual concept, whereby revenues are recorded when earned without regard to when the related cash is collected. Similarly, expenses are recorded in the same period as the revenues without regard to when the related cash payments are made.

For now, the most important thing to remember about the two methods is that they are simply alternative ways to compute the same amount. The total amount of *cash flows from operating activities is always the same* (an inflow of $60,042 in National Beverage's case), *whether it is computed by using the direct or the indirect method*, as illustrated below:

Direct		Indirect	
Cash collected from customers	$644,079	Net earnings	$49,311
Cash payments to suppliers	(426,405)	Depreciation and amortization	9,404
Cash payments for other expenses	(131,356)		
Cash payments for interest	(928)		
Cash payments for income taxes	(25,348)	Changes in non-cash operating working capital items	1,327
Net cash provided by operating activities	$ 60,042	Net cash provided by operating activities	$60,042

Cash Flows from Investing Activities

Cash flows from investing activities are cash inflows and outflows related to the acquisition or sale of long-lived productive assets and investments in the securities of other companies. Typical cash flows from investing activities include the following:

Inflows	Outflows
Cash received from	*Cash paid for*
Sale or disposal of property, plant, and equipment	Purchase of property, plant, and equipment
Sale or maturity of investments in securities	Purchase of investments in securities

The difference between these cash inflows and outflows is called *net cash inflow (outflow) from investing activities.*

For National Beverage, this amount was an outflow of $11,388 for fiscal year 2015. Most of the activity was related to purchases and sales of short-term investments and the purchase and sale of property, plant, and equipment. Since total purchases exceeded cash collected from sales, there was a net cash outflow.

Cash Flows from Financing Activities

Cash flows from financing activities are cash inflows and outflows related to external sources (owners and creditors) to finance the enterprise and its operations. Usual cash flows from financing activities include the following:

Inflows	Outflows
Cash received from	*Cash paid for*
Borrowing on notes, mortgages, bonds, etc. from creditors	Repayment of principal to creditors
Issuing shares to shareholders	Interest on borrowings if it is classified as a financing activity
	Repurchasing shares from shareholders
	Dividends to shareholders

The difference between these cash inflows and outflows is called *net cash inflow (outflow) from financing activities.*

For National Beverage, this amount was an outflow of $26,130 for fiscal year 2015. The financing activities section of the statement shows that National Beverage paid $18,400 of principal on long-term debt, repurchased shares (that it issued previously) for $7,455, and paid cash dividends of $275 to shareholders.

Net Increase (Decrease) in Cash

The combination of the net cash flows from operating activities, investing activities, and financing activities must equal the net increase (decrease) in cash for the reporting period. For fiscal year 2015, National Beverage reported a net increase of $22,524, which explains the change in cash and cash equivalents on the statement of financial position from the beginning balance of $29,932 to the ending balance of $52,456:

(in thousands)	
Net cash provided by operating activities	$(60,042)
Net cash used in investing activities	(11,388)
Net cash used in financing activities	(26,130)
Net increase in cash and cash equivalents	22,524
Cash and cash equivalents at beginning of period	29,932
Cash and cash equivalents at end of period	$ 52,456

Beginning and ending balances from the statement of financial position

The three main sections of the statement of cash flows are a) cash flows from operating activities, which are related to generating earnings from normal operations; b) cash flows from investing activities, which are related to the acquisition and sale of productive assets; and c) cash flows from financing activities, which are related to external financing of the enterprise. The net cash inflow or outflow for the year is the same amount as the increase or decrease in cash and cash equivalents for the year on the statement of financial position. To make sure you understand the appropriate classifications of the different cash flows, answer the following questions before you move on.

SELF-STUDY QUIZ 5-1

Canadian Tire Corporation
Canadian Tire Corporation is a network of businesses engaged in retail, financial services, and petroleum. A listing of some items that are reported on its statement of cash flows follows. Without referring to Exhibit 5.1, indicate whether each item is disclosed in the operating activities (O), investing activities (I), or financing activities (F) section of the statement.

_____ *a.* Purchase of short-term investments
_____ *b.* Net earnings
_____ *c.* Change in accounts receivable
_____ *d.* Additions to property, plant, and equipment
_____ *e.* Change in prepayments and other current assets
_____ *f.* Change in inventories
_____ *g.* Change in accrued liabilities
_____ *h.* Depreciation and amortization
_____ *i.* Issuance of shares
_____ *j.* Change in accounts payable

After you complete your answers, check them with the solutions at the end of the chapter.

To give you a better understanding of the statement of cash flows, we now discuss in more detail National Beverage's statement and the way that it relates to the statement of financial position and the statement of earnings. Then, we examine the way that each section of the statement describes a set of important decisions that National Beverage management made. We also discuss the way financial analysts use each section to evaluate the company's performance.

Relationships to the Statement of Financial Position and the Statement of Earnings

Preparing and interpreting the statement of cash flows require analyzing the accounts that are reported on both the statement of financial position and the statement of earnings. As we discussed in previous chapters, accountants record transactions as journal entries that are posted to specific ledger accounts. The accounts' balances are then used to prepare the statement of earnings and the statement of financial position. Companies cannot prepare the statement of cash flows by using amounts recorded in the specific accounts because these amounts are based on accrual accounting. Instead, accountants must analyze the amounts recorded under the accrual basis and adjust them to a cash basis. To prepare the statement of cash flows, they need the following data:

1. *Comparative statements of financial position*, which are used to compute the cash flows from all activities (operating, investing, and financing).

2. A *complete statement of earnings*, which is used primarily to identify cash flows from operating activities.

3. *Additional details* concerning selected accounts because often the net change in an account balance during the year does not reveal the underlying nature of the cash flows.

Our approach to preparing and understanding the statement of cash flows focuses on the changes in the accounts that are reported on the statement of financial position. It relies on a simple algebraic manipulation of the accounting equation:

$$\text{Assets} = \text{Liabilities} + \text{Shareholders' equity}$$

First, assets can be split into cash and non-cash assets:

$$\text{Cash} + \text{Non-cash assets} = \text{Liabilities} + \text{Shareholders' equity}$$

If we move the non-cash assets to the right side of the equation, then

$$\text{Cash} = \text{Liabilities} + \text{Shareholders' equity} - \text{Non-cash assets}$$

Given this relationship, the change in cash (Δ) between the beginning and end of the period must equal the changes (Δ) in the amounts on the right side of the equation during the same period:

$$\Delta\text{Cash} = \Delta\text{Liabilities} + \Delta\text{Shareholders' equity} - \Delta\text{Non-cash assets}$$

Thus, *any transaction that changes cash must be accompanied by a change in liabilities, shareholders' equity, or non-cash assets.*

In general, increases in cash are associated with decreases in non-cash asset accounts and increases in liability and shareholders' equity accounts. In contrast, cash decreases when non-cash assets increase, and when liabilities or shareholders' equity decrease:

Decrease in non-cash assets
Increase in liabilities and shareholders' equity $\longrightarrow$ Cash inflow

Increase in non-cash assets
Decrease in liabilities and shareholders' equity $\longrightarrow$ Cash inflow

Exhibit 5.2 illustrates this concept along with a sample of cash transactions that affect different asset, liability, and equity accounts.

Next, we use the following preliminary steps to prepare the statement of cash flows:

1. Determine the change in each account on the statement of financial position by subtracting this year's ending balance from last year's ending balance (which is this year's beginning balance).

2. Classify each change as relating to operating (O), investing (I), or financing (F) activities, based on National Beverage's financial statements.

Exhibit 5.3 shows National Beverage's comparative statements of financial position at the end of fiscal years 2014 and 2015, and its statement of earnings for fiscal year 2015. *The financial position accounts related to generating earnings (operating items) should be marked with an O.* These accounts include the following:

- most current assets (other than short-term investments that relate to investing activities);[3]

- most current liabilities (other than amounts owed to investors and financial institutions,[4] all of which relate to financing activities);

- retained earnings, because it increases by the amount of net earnings or decreases by the amount of net loss, which is the starting point of the operating section. (Retained earnings also decreases by the amount of dividends declared, which is a financing outflow noted by an F.)

Exhibit 5.2

Selected Cash Transactions and Their Effects on Other Statement of Financial Position Accounts

Category	Transaction	Effect on Cash	Other Account Affected
Operating	Collect accounts receivable	+Cash	−Accounts receivable (A)
	Pay accounts payable	−Cash	−Accounts payable (L)
	Prepay rent	−Cash	+Prepaid rent (A)
	Pay interest	−Cash	−Retained earnings (SE)
	Sell for cash	+Cash	+Retained earnings (SE)
Investing	Purchase equipment for cash	−Cash	+Equipment (A)
	Sell investment securities for cash	+Cash	−Investments
Financing	Pay back debt to bank	−Cash	−Notes payable—Bank (L)
	Issue shares for cash	+Cash	+Contributed capital (SE)

In Exhibit 5.3, all of the relevant current assets and liabilities have been marked with an O. These items include accounts receivable, inventories, prepaid expenses, accounts payables, and accrued liabilities. As we have noted, retained earnings is also relevant to operations.

Exhibit 5.3

National Beverage Inc.: Comparative Statements of Financial Position and Current Statement of Earnings

Related Cash Flow Section Change in Cash		**NATIONAL BEVERAGE CORP.** **Consolidated Statements of Financial Position** **(amounts in thousands)**		
		May 2, 2015	**May 3, 2014**	**Change**
	Assets			
	Current assets			
I	Cash and cash equivalents	$52,456	$ 29,932	+$22,524
O	Short-term investments	4,348	2,685	+1,663
O	Accounts receivable	59,951	58,205	+1,746
O	Inventories	42,924	43,914	−990
	Prepaid expenses	8,050	8,405	−355
	Total current assets	167,729	143,141	
I*	Property, plant, and equipment (net)	80,021	79,700	+321
	Total assets	$247,750	$222,841	
	Liabilities			
	Current liabilities			
O	Accounts payable	44,896	45,606	−710
O	Accrued liabilities	21,257	18,873	+2,384
O	Income taxes payable	98	44	+54
	Total current liabilities	66,251	64,523	
F	Long-term debt	33,717	52,117	−18,400
	Total liabilities	99,968	116,640	
	Shareholders' Equity			
F	Contributed capital	18,009	25,464	−7,455
O and F	Retained earnings	129,773	80,737	+49,036
	Total shareholders' equity	147,782	106,201	
	Total liabilities and shareholders' equity	$247,750	$222,841	

The balances of certain accounts have been adjusted to simplify the presentation.

*The accumulated depreciation/amortization accounts are also related to operations because depreciation and amortization expenses are added back to net earnings.

NATIONAL BEVERAGE CORP. Consolidated Statement of Earnings For the Fiscal Year Ended May 2, 2015 (amounts in thousands)	
Net sales	$645,825
Cost of sales	426,685
Gross profit	219,140
Operating expenses:	
Selling, general, and administrative expenses	134,095
Depreciation and amortization	9,404
Total operating expenses	143,499
Earnings from operations	75,641
Interest expense	928
Earnings before income taxes	74,713
Provision for income taxes	25,402
Net earnings	$ 49,311

The balances of certain accounts have been adjusted to simplify the presentation.
Source: National Beverage Corp., Annual Report 2015.

The financial position accounts related to investing activities should be marked with an I. These include all of the remaining assets on the statement of financial position. In Exhibit 5.3, these are property and equipment and computer software.

The financial position accounts related to financing activities should be marked with an F. These include all of the remaining liability and shareholders' equity accounts on the statement of financial position. In Exhibit 5.3, these accounts include contributed capital and retained earnings (for decreases resulting from dividends declared).

In the next sections of this chapter, we use this information to prepare each section of the statement of cash flows.

REPORTING AND INTERPRETING CASH FLOWS FROM OPERATING ACTIVITIES

The operating activities section can be prepared in one of two formats: the direct method and the indirect method. The next section presents a comparison of the direct and indirect methods by using a simplified illustration. Then we reconstruct the operating activities section of National Beverage's statement of cash flows by using the indirect method.

A Simplified Illustration

The simplified example below illustrates the difference between the computation of cash flows from operating activities using the *direct* versus the *indirect* method. We first show the effects of a series of summary transactions on the accounting equation and the statement of cash flows. Then we show how the transaction effects on operating activities can be grouped to prepare the operating activities section of the statement of cash flows.

LO5-2

Report and interpret cash flows from operating activities by using the indirect method.

Sample Corporation reported the following account balances at December 31, 2016:

SAMPLE CORPORATION Statement of Financial Position At December 31, 2016		
Assets		
Cash		$19,200
Accounts receivable		22,000
Merchandise inventory		75,000
Prepaid expenses		15,000
Property, plant, and equipment	$1,13,500	
Less: Accumulated depreciation	20,000	93,500
Total assets		$224,700
Liabilities and Shareholders' Equity		
Liabilities		
Accounts payable		$14,000
Salaries payable		1,500
Income tax payable		4,500
Long-term borrowings		54,000
Total liabilities		74,000
Shareholders' equity		
Contributed capital	$1,26,000	
Retained earnings	24,700	150,700
Total liabilities and shareholders' equity		$224,700

The following summary transactions occurred during 2017:

1. Purchased merchandise for $62,000 on account, and paid $59,000 to various suppliers.

2. Sold merchandise on account for $140,000 and collected $145,000 in cash from customers. The cost of merchandise sold was $69,000.

3. Salaries expense totalled $28,000 but only $27,000 was paid to employees during the year.

4. Interest expense of $5,000 was paid in full.

5. Other operating expenses totalled $15,800, including expenses of $5,000 that were prepaid and $10,800 that were paid during the year.

6. Purchased a new building for $20,000 and issued shares in full payment.

7. Declared and paid cash dividend of $6,000.

8. Depreciation expense was $7,000 for the year.

9. Income tax expense for 2017 totalled $9,000; the company paid $10,500 to the tax authorities.

The effects of these transactions on the accounting equation and cash flows are shown in Exhibit 5.4. Note that some of the accounts we use, such as prepaid expenses; property, plant, and equipment; accrued liabilities; and retained earnings, are groupings of many accounts. The main ideas that we present in this illustration do not change with the addition of more detailed accounts.

Study Exhibit 5.4 carefully, particularly the amounts entered in the revenues and expenses columns, comparing them to the amounts in the column showing cash flows from operating activities.

Exhibit 5.4

Effects of Summary Transactions on the Accounting Equation

Transaction	Assets					=	Liabilities				+	Shareholders' Equity					Effect on Cash Flows		
	Cash	Accounts Receivable	Merchandise Inventory	Prepaid Expenses	Property, Plant, and Equipment (net)		Accounts Payable	Salaries Payable	Income Tax Payable	Long-Term Borrowings		Common Shares	Retained Earnings	Revenues	Expenses	Description of Item	Operating Activities	Investing Activities	Financing Activities
Balance, January 1, 2017	19,200	22,000	75,000	15,000	93,500		14,000	1,500	4,500	54,000		126,000	24,700						
1a. Purchase of merchandise			62,000				62,000												
1b. Payment to suppliers	(59,000)						(59,000)										(59,000)		
2a. Credit sales		140,000												140,000		Sales			
2b. Cost of merchandise sold			(69,000)												(69,000)	Cost of sales			
2c. Collection from customers	145,000	(145,000)															145,000		
3a. Salaries expense								28,000							(28,000)	Salaries			
3b. Payments to employees	(27,000)							(27,000)									(27,000)		
4. Payment of interest	(5,000)														(5,000)	Interest	(5,000)		
5. Other operating expenses	(10,800)			(5,000)											(15,800)	Other expenses	(10,800)		
6. Purchase of building					20,000							20,000							
7. Payment of dividends	(6,000)												(6,000)						(6,000)
8. Depreciation/amortization expense					(7,000)										(7,000)	Depreciation			
9a. Income tax expense for the year									9,000						(9,000)	Income tax			
9b. Payment of income taxes	(10,500)								(10,500)								(10,500)		
Balance, December 31, 2017	45,900	17,000	68,000	10,000	106,500		17,000	2,500	3,000	54,000		146,000	18,700	140,000	(133,800)		32,700	-	(6,000)

The detailed transaction effects in Exhibit 5.4 can be used to prepare the operating activities section of the statement of cash flows by listing the cash receipts and cash payments related to operations:

SAMPLE CORPORATION
Statement of Cash Flows (Partial)
For the Year Ended December 31, 2017
(Direct Method)

Operating Activities		
Collections from customers		$145,000
Payments:		
to suppliers	$59,000	
to employees	27,000	
for interest	5,000	
for other operating expenses	10,800	
for income taxes	10,500	
Total payments		112,300
Net cash flows from operating activities		$ 32,700

These amounts appear in the operating activities column in Exhibit 5.4.

Let us now turn our attention to the reporting of cash flow from operations under the indirect method. The starting point of the computation is net earnings, which is the difference between revenues (including gains) and expenses (including losses). We know that the revenues earned by the company in 2017 do not necessarily result in an equal amount of cash collections from customers during the year. In fact, the amount of cash received from customers during the year could be equal to, lower than, or higher than the amount of revenues. Similarly, the amount of expenses incurred during the year may not equal the amount of cash payments for these expenses. Given that revenues and expenses include both cash and non-cash components, we need to remove the non-cash revenues and non-cash expenses from net earnings in order to obtain the cash components. Exhibit 5.5 shows how we can decompose the revenues and expenses into cash and non-cash components.

Exhibit 5.5

Decomposition of Revenues and Expenses into Cash and Non-cash Components

Transaction	A Operating Revenue or Expense (Accrual Amount)	B Cash − Component	C Difference (Non-cash = Component)
Sales	$140,000	$145,000	$ (5,000)
Cost of sales	(69,000)	(59,000)	(10,000)
Salaries expense	(28,000)	(27,000)	(1,000)
Interest expense	(5,000)	(5,000)	-0-
Other operating expenses	(15,800)	(10,800)	(5,000)
Depreciation expense	(7,000)	-0-	(7,000)
Income tax expense	(9,000)	(10,500)	1,500
Cash/accrual earnings from operations	$ 6,200	$ 32,700	$(26,500)

The amounts in column A are taken from the revenues and expenses columns in Exhibit 5.4, and the amounts in column B are the corresponding cash receipts or payments that appear in the operating activities column of the same exhibit. The earnings from operations, $6,200, is made up of a $32,700 cash component and a $26,500 non-cash component.

The non-cash components of revenue and expense accounts are reflected in related accounts on the statement of financial position. For example, salary expense totalled $28,000 for 2017, but the company paid only $27,000. The unpaid amount of $1,000 is a liability, salary payable, which must be paid in the future. Hence, it increases the balance of salaries payable from $1,500 to $2,500.

As indicated previously, the direct method focuses on the cash elements of net earnings by computing cash receipts and cash payments for operating purposes and reporting the details found in column B of Exhibit 5.5 to arrive at net cash flows from operating activities. In contrast, the indirect method starts with net earnings and eliminates the non-cash elements reported in column C of Exhibit 5.5 to arrive at the same result. In general,

Net earnings = Cash elements +/− Non-cash elements
Cash elements = Net earnings +/− Non-cash elements

Hence, the net cash flows from operating activities can be computed indirectly as

Net cash flows from operating activities = $6,200 + $26,500 = $32,700

The decomposition of net earnings into cash and non-cash components, as presented in Exhibit 5.5, requires a reconstruction of all the transactions that occurred during the year. Such details are not publicly available. But because transactions that affect revenue or expense accounts also affect, primarily, the current asset or current liability accounts, we can use the changes in the statement of financial position accounts to compute the non-cash components of net earnings, which are identified in column C of Exhibit 5.5. This process, which is explained in detail in the next section, leads to an alternative way of computing and reporting the net cash flows from operating activities.

SAMPLE CORPORATION
Statement of Cash Flows (Partial)
For the Year Ended December 31, 2017
(Indirect Method)

Operating Activities		
Net earnings from operations		$6,200
Add (deduct) items not affecting cash:		
Depreciation expense	$7,000	
Decrease in accounts receivable	5,000	
Decrease in merchandise inventory	7,000	
Decrease in prepaid expenses	5,000	
Increase in accounts payable	3,000	
Increase in salaries payable	1,000	
Decrease in income tax payable	(1,500)	
Net adjustments		26,500
Net cash flows from operating activities		$32,700

Notice that the adjustments listed above are the same amounts that appear in column C in Exhibit 5.5, except they show the non-cash component of the cost of sales ($10,000) as the result of a decrease in merchandise inventory by $7,000 and an increase in accounts payable by $3,000.

Before proceeding further, remember the following:

1. Cash flow from operating activities is always the same regardless of whether it is computed by using the direct method or the indirect method.

2. The investing and financing sections are always presented in the same manner, regardless of the format of the operating section.

Reporting Cash Flows from Operating Activities—Indirect Method

The indirect method of reporting cash flows from operating activities starts with net earnings and eliminates the non-cash components of revenues and expenses. The general structure of the operating activities section is as follows:

Operating Activities
Net earnings
Add/subtract items not affecting cash:
+ Depreciation expense
+ Decreases in non-cash current assets
− Increases in non-cash current assets
+ Increases in current liabilities
− Decreases in current liabilities
Net Cash Flows from Operating Activities

To keep track of all the additions and subtractions made to convert net earnings to cash flows from operating activities, it is helpful to set up a schedule to record the computations. We construct such a schedule for National Beverage in Exhibit 5.6.

Exhibit **5.6**

National Beverage Inc.: Schedule for Net Cash Flows from Operating Activities, Indirect Method (in thousands of dollars)

Conversion of net earnings to net cash flows from operating activities:

Item	Amount	Explanation
Net earnings, accrual basis	$49,311	From statement of earnings.
Add (subtract) to convert to cash basis:		
Depreciation and amortization expense	+9,404	Add because depreciation expense is a non-cash expense.
Increase in accounts receivable	−1,746	Subtract because cash collected from customers is less than accrual basis revenues.
Decrease in inventories	+990	Add because cost of sales is more than purchases.
Decrease in prepaid expenses	+355	Add because accrual basis expenses are more than cash prepayments for expenses.
Decrease in accounts payable	−710	Subtract because purchases on account (due to suppliers) are less than cash payments to suppliers.
Increase in accrued liabilities	+2,384	Add because cash payments for expenses are less than accrual basis expenses.
Increase in income taxes payable	+54	Add because cash payments for expenses are less than accrual basis expenses.
Net cash inflow from operating activities	$60,042	Reported on the statement of cash flows.

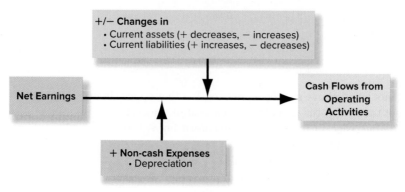

We begin our schedule presented in Exhibit 5.6 with net earnings of $49,311 taken from National Beverage's statement of earnings (Exhibit 5.3). Completing the operating section by using the indirect method involves two steps:

Step 1: **Adjust net earnings for the effect of depreciation and amortization expenses.** Recording depreciation and amortization expenses does not affect the cash account (or any other current asset or liability). It affects a non-current asset (such as property, plant, and equipment; net or intangible assets). *Since depreciation and amortization expenses are subtracted in computing net earnings, but do not affect cash, we always add them back* to convert net earnings to cash flows from operating activities.[5] In the case of National Beverage, we need to remove the effect of depreciation and amortization expenses by adding back $9,404 to net earnings (see Exhibit 5.6).[6]

Step 2: **Adjust net earnings for changes in current assets and current liabilities marked as operating (O).** Each *change* in operating current assets (other than cash and short-term investments) and liabilities (other than amounts owed to owners and financial institutions) causes a difference between net earnings and cash flows from operating activities.[7] When converting net earnings to cash flows from operating activities, apply the following general rules:

- Add the change when a current asset decreases or a current liability increases.
- Subtract the change when a current asset increases or a current liability decreases.

Understanding what makes these current assets and current liabilities increase and decrease is the key to understanding the logic of these additions and subtractions.

Change in Accounts Receivable We illustrate this logic with the first operating item (O) listed on National Beverage's statement of financial position (Exhibit 5.3), accounts receivable. Remember that the statement of earnings (loss) reflects sales revenue, but the statement of cash flows must reflect cash collections from customers. As the following accounts receivable T-account illustrates, when sales revenues are recorded, accounts receivable increase, and when cash is collected from customers, accounts receivable decrease:

Accounts Receivable (A)

Change	Beginning balance	58,205		
+1,746	Sales revenue (on account)	645,825	Collections from customers	644,079
	Ending balance	59,951		

In the National Beverage example, the amount of accounts receivable at the beginning of the fiscal year 2015 ($58,205) is normally collected from customers during that fiscal year. In addition, most of the sales made during that fiscal year are collected in cash from customers. However, customers who purchase the company's products on account toward the end of the fiscal year will likely pay the amounts due during the next fiscal year. This is reflected in the ending balance of accounts receivable ($59,951). Hence, the amount of cash collections from customers is $644,079 (= $58,205 + $645,825 − $59,951). The cash received is lower than sales revenue. As a result, sales revenue must be decreased to determine the amount of cash collected from customers during the year. This can also be determined by adjusting sales revenue for the change in accounts receivable during the year. The increase in accounts receivable ($59,951 − $58,205 = $1,746) is subtracted from sales revenue.[8] In contrast, a decrease in accounts receivable signals that the cash collected from customers exceeds the sales revenue. Hence, the decrease in accounts receivable is added to sale revenue.

This same underlying logic is used to determine adjustments for the other current assets and liabilities.

To summarize, the statement of earnings reflects revenues of the period, but cash flows from operating activities must reflect cash collections from customers. Sales on account increase the balance in accounts receivable, and collections from customers decrease the balance:

Accounts Receivable (A)	
Beg. bal.	58,205
Increase	1,746
End. bal.	59,951

The statement of financial position for National Beverage indicates an *increase* in accounts receivable of $1,746 for the period, which means cash collected from customers is less than revenue. To convert net earnings to cash flows from operating activities, the amount of the increase in accounts receivable must be *subtracted* from net earnings in Exhibit 5.6. (A decrease would be added.)

Change in Inventory

The statement of earnings reflects merchandise sold for the period, whereas cash flows from operating activities must reflect cash purchases.

Both the change in inventory and the change in accounts payable (borrowing from suppliers) determine the magnitude of this difference. It is easiest to think about the change in inventory in terms of the simple case in which the company pays cash to trade suppliers. We address the added complexity involved when purchases are made on account when we discuss the adjustment for the change in accounts payable.

As shown in the inventories T-account, purchases of goods increase the balance in inventory, and recording the cost of sales decreases the balance in inventory. Therefore, the change in inventory is the difference between purchases and cost of sales:

Inventories (A)			Inventories (A)		
Beg. bal.			Beg. bal.	43,914	
Purchases	Cost of sales				Decrease 990
End. bal.			End. bal.	42,924	

National Beverage's statement of financial position indicates that inventory *decreased* by $990, which means that the cost of purchases is less than the cost of merchandise sold. The decrease must be *added* to net earnings to convert to cash flows from operating activities in Exhibit 5.6. (An increase would be subtracted.)

Change in Prepaid Expenses

The statement of earnings reflects expenses of the period, but cash flows from operating activities must reflect the cash payments. Cash paid in advance increases the balance in prepaid expenses, and expenses recognized during the period decrease the balance:

Prepaid Expenses (A)			Prepaid Expenses (A)		
Beg. bal.			Beg. bal.	8,405	
Purchases	Services used (expense)				Decrease 355
End. bal.			End. bal.	8,050	

National Beverage's statement of financial position shows that prepaid expenses *decreased* by $355 during the year, indicating that new cash prepayments are less than the amount of expenses. The decrease must be *added* to net earnings in Exhibit 5.6. (An increase would be subtracted.)

Change in Accounts Payable

Cash flow from operations must reflect cash purchases, but not all purchases are for cash. Purchases on account increase accounts payable, and cash paid to suppliers decreases accounts payable:

Accounts Payable (L)

		Beg. bal.	45,606
Decrease	710		
		End. bal.	44,896

National Beverage's accounts payable *decreased* by $710, indicating that cash payments were more than purchases on account, and this decrease (the extra payments) must be *subtracted* from net earnings in Exhibit 5.6. (An increase would be added.)

Change in Accrued Liabilities The statement of earnings reflects all accrued expenses, but the statement of cash flows must reflect actual payments for those expenses. Recording accrued expenses increases the accrued liabilities balance, and cash payments for the expenses decrease it:

Accrued Liabilities (L)		**Accrued Liabilities (L)**	
	Beg. bal.	Beg. bal.	18,873
Payment of accruals	Accrued expenses	Increase	2,384
	End. bal.	End. bal.	21,257

National Beverage's accrued liabilities *increased* by $2,384, which indicates that cash paid for the expenses is less than accrual basis expenses. The increase must be *added* to net earnings in Exhibit 5.6. (A decrease would be subtracted.)

Change in Income Tax Payable Cash flow from operations must reflect cash payments to the tax authorities, but the statement of earnings must reflect income tax expense based on accrual basis accounting. Recognition of income tax expense increases income tax payable, and cash paid to the tax authorities decreases it:

Income Taxes Payable (L)		**Income Taxes Payable (L)**	
	Beg. bal.	Beg. bal.	44
Cash payments	Income taxes expense	Increase	54
	End. bal.	End. bal.	98

National Beverage's income taxes payable *increased* by $54, indicating that cash payments were less than income tax expense, and this increase must be *added* to net earnings in Exhibit 5.6. (A decrease would be subtracted.)

Summary We can summarize the additions and subtractions that are required to reconcile net earnings with cash flows from operating activities as follows:

	Additions and Subtractions to Reconcile Net Earnings to Cash Flows from Operating Activities	
Item	**When item increases**	**When item decreases**
Depreciation and amortization	+	NA
Accounts receivable	−	+
Inventories	−	+
Prepaid expenses	−	+
Accounts payable	+	−
Accrued liabilities	+	−
Income tax payable	+	−

Notice in this table that an increase in a current asset or a decrease in a current liability is always subtracted to reconcile net earnings to cash flows from operating activities. A decrease in a current asset or an increase in a current liability is always added to reconcile net earnings to cash flows from operating activities. The statement of cash flows for National Beverage (Exhibit 5.1) shows the same additions and subtractions to reconcile net earnings to cash flows from operating activities described in Exhibit 5.6.

It is important to note again that the net cash inflow or outflow from operating activities is the same regardless of whether the direct or indirect method of presentation is used (in this case, an inflow of $60,042). The two methods differ only in terms of the details reported on the statement. We show in Appendix 5B how cash flows from operations can be computed by using the direct method.

REAL-WORLD EXCERPT

Domino's Pizza Enterprises Ltd.

ANNUAL REPORT

Domino's Pizza Enterprises Ltd. is the largest pizza chain in Australia. It is also the largest franchisee for the Domino's Pizza brand in the world. Australian companies prepare their financial statements in accordance with Australian Accounting Standards, which are based on IFRS. As we noted before, IAS 7 encourages companies to report their cash flows from operations using the direct method. But Australian Accounting Standards require Australian companies to use the direct method. Hence, Domino's cash flow from operations is presented as follows:

STATEMENT OF CASH FLOWS
For the Year Ended 1 July, 2015
(in millions of Australian dollars)

Cash Flows from Operating Activities	
Receipts from customers	780.2
Payments to suppliers and employees	(653.5)
Interest received	0.8
Interest and other costs of finance paid	(2.5)
Income taxes paid	(20.0)
Net cash generated by operating activities	106.0

Note that Domino's combines payments to suppliers and employees, but other companies report these items separately. Like Canadian companies that choose the direct method, Domino's reports the indirect presentation in a note to the financial statements.

PAUSE FOR FEEDBACK

The indirect method for reporting cash flows from operating activities reports a conversion of net earnings to net cash flow from operating activities. The conversion involves additions and subtractions for 1) expenses (such as depreciation expense) and revenues that do not affect current assets or current liabilities, and for 2) changes in each of the individual current assets (other than cash and short-term investments) and current liabilities (other than short-term debt to financial institutions and current maturities of long-term debt, which relate to financing). This is done to reflect differences in the timing of accrual basis net earnings and cash flows. To test whether you understand these concepts, answer the following questions before you move on.

SELF-STUDY QUIZ 5-2

National Supermarkets Inc.
Indicate which of the following items taken from the statement of cash flows of National Supermarkets Inc. would be added (+), subtracted (−), or not included (0) in the reconciliation of net earnings to cash flow from operations.

_____ *a.* Increase in inventories
_____ *b.* Repayment of loans and borrowings
_____ *c.* Depreciation expense
_____ *d.* Decrease in accounts receivable
_____ *e.* Increase in accounts and other payable
_____ *f.* Increase in prepaid expenses

After you complete your answers, check them with the solutions at the end of the chapter

Interpreting Cash Flows from Operating Activities

LO5-3

Analyze and interpret the quality of earnings ratio.

The operating activities section of the statement of cash flows focuses attention on the firm's ability to generate cash internally through operations, and its management of working capital (current assets minus current liabilities). Many analysts regard this as the most important section of the statement because, in the long run, operations are the only sustainable source of cash. Investors should not invest in a company if they believe that it will not be able to pay them dividends or make reinvestments with cash generated from operations. Similarly, creditors should not lend money if they believe that cash generated from operations will not be available to pay back the loan. For example, many Internet-based companies crashed when investors lost faith in their ability to turn business ideas into cash from operations.

A common rule followed by financial and credit analysts is to avoid firms with rising net earnings but falling cash flow from operations. Rapidly rising inventories require the use of cash until goods are sold. Similarly, rapidly rising accounts receivable reflect a delay in the collection of cash. Rising inventories and accounts receivable often predict a slump in net earnings as revenues fall. This increases the need for external financing as overall cash inflows from operations decline. A true understanding of the meaning of the difference between net earnings and cash flow from operations requires a detailed understanding of its causes.

In fiscal year 2015, National Beverage reported that cash flow from operations was higher than net earnings What caused this relationship? To answer this question, we must carefully analyze how National Beverage's operating activities are reported in its statement of cash flows. To properly interpret this information, we must also learn more about the beverage industry. National Beverage normally reports higher cash flow from operations than net earnings because of the effect of depreciation and amortization expenses, which reduce net earnings but do not require cash outflows. At the same time, it carefully manages the assets and liabilities that relate to operating activities, keeping the total changes in these assets and liabilities to a minimum. Many analysts compute the quality of earnings ratio as a general sign of the ability to generate cash through operations.

QUALITY OF EARNINGS RATIO

KEY RATIO ANALYSIS

ANALYTICAL QUESTION → How much cash does each dollar of net earnings generate?

RATIO AND COMPARISONS → The quality of earnings ratio is useful in answering this question. It is computed as follows:

$$\text{Quality of earnings ratio} = \frac{\text{Cash flows from operating activities}}{\text{Net earnings}}$$

National Beverage's ratio for the year 2014 is

$$\$60,042 / \$49,311 = 1.22$$

Comparisons over Time				Comparisons with Competitors	
National Beverage*				Coca-Cola	PepsiCo
2012	2013	2014		2014	2014
0.86	1.20	1.22		1.49	1.60

*The fiscal year of National Beverage ends in early May. Hence, we noted the year includes eight months of the company's activities. Both the Coca-Cola Company and PepsiCo Inc. have fiscal years that end in December.

ANALYTICAL QUESTION → How much cash does each dollar of net earnings generate?

RATIO AND COMPARISONS → The quality of earnings ratio is useful in answering this question. It is computed as follows:

$$\text{Quality of earnings ratio} = \frac{\text{Cash flows from operating activities}}{\text{Net earnings}}$$

National Beverage's ratio for the year 2014 is

$$\$60,042/\$49,311 = 1.22$$

Comparisons over Time				Comparisons with Competitors	
National Beverage*				Coca-Cola	PepsiCo
2012	2013	2014		2014	2014
0.86	1.20	1.22		1.49	1.60

*The fiscal year of National Beverage ends in early May. Hence, we noted the year includes eight months of the company's activities. Both the Coca-Cola Company and PepsiCo Inc. have fiscal years that end in December.

INTERPRETATIONS

In General → The quality of earnings ratio measures the portion of earnings that was generated in cash. All other things being equal, a higher quality of earnings ratio indicates a greater ability to finance operating and other cash needs from operating cash inflows.[9] A higher ratio also indicates that it is less likely that the company is using aggressive revenue recognition policies to increase net earnings. A ratio that is greater than 1.0 indicates that each dollar of earnings is supported by more than one dollar of operating cash flows. When the ratio does not equal 1.0, analysts must establish the source of the difference to determine the significance of the findings. There are four potential causes of any difference:

1. **The corporate life cycle (growth or decline in sales).** When sales are increasing, receivables and inventory normally increase faster than accounts payable. This often reduces operating cash flows below the reported net earnings, which, in turn, reduces the ratio. When sales are declining, the opposite occurs and the ratio increases.

2. **Seasonality.** Seasonal (from quarter to quarter) variations in sales and purchases of inventory can cause the ratio to deviate from 1.0 during particular quarters.

3. **Changes in revenue and expense recognition.** Aggressive revenue recognition or failure to accrue appropriate expenses will inflate net earnings and reduce the ratio.

4. **Changes in management of operating assets and liabilities.** Inefficient management will increase operating assets and decrease liabilities, which will reduce operating cash flows and reduce the ratio. More efficient management will have the opposite effect.

Focus Company Analysis → National Beverage's quality of earnings ratio increased from 0.86 in 2012 to 1.22 in 2014. In comparison with its competitors, National Beverage has a lower quality of earnings ratio than both Coca-Cola and PepsiCo. National Beverage's lower ratio would prompt financial analysts to read the management's discussion and analysis sections of the annual reports of the three companies to determine the causes of such differences.

A Few Cautions → The quality of earnings ratio can be interpreted only based on an understanding of the company's business operations and strategy. For example, a low ratio can be due simply to normal seasonal changes. However, it can also indicate obsolete inventory, slowing sales, or failed expansion plans. To test for these possibilities, analysts often analyze this ratio in tandem with the accounts receivable turnover and inventory turnover ratios.

SELECTED FOCUS COMPANY COMPARISONS—2015

WestJet Airlines 2.01%

Gildan Activewear 0.73%

Canadian Tire 0.90%

FRAUD AND CASH FLOWS FROM OPERATIONS

A QUESTION OF ACCOUNTABILITY

The statement of cash flows often gives outsiders the first hint that financial statements may contain errors and irregularities. The importance of this indicator as a predictor is receiving more attention following corporate scandals. For example, *Investors Chronicle* reported on an accounting fraud at a commercial credit company, suggesting that

> ... a look at Versailles's cash flow statement—an invaluable tool in spotting creative accounting—should have triggered misgivings. In the company's last filed accounts ... Versailles reported operating profits of ... $25 million but a cash outflow from operating activities of $24 million ... such figures should ... have served as a warning. After all, what use is a company to anyone if it reports only accounting profits which are never translated into cash?*

As noted in earlier chapters, unethical managers sometimes attempt to reach earnings targets by manipulating accruals and deferrals of revenues and expenses to inflate net earnings. Since these adjustments do not affect the cash account, they have no effect on the statement of cash flows. As a consequence, a growing difference between net earnings and cash flow from operations can be a sign of such manipulations. This could be an early warning sign of operating and financial difficulties that may lead to bankruptcy.

*James Chapman, "Creative Accounting: Exposed!" *Investor's Chronicle.*

REPORTING AND INTERPRETING CASH FLOWS FROM INVESTING ACTIVITIES

LO5-4

Report and interpret cash flows from investing activities.

Reporting Cash Flows from Investing Activities

Preparing this section of the statement of cash flows requires analyzing the accounts related to property, plant, and equipment; intangible assets; and investments in the securities of other companies. Normally, the relevant statement of financial position accounts include short-term investments and non-current asset accounts, such as long-term investments and property, plant, and equipment. The following relationships are the ones that you will encounter most frequently:

Related Statement of Financial Position Account(s)	Investing Activity	Cash Flow Effect
Property, plant, and equipment and intangible assets (e.g., patents)	Purchase of property, plant, and equipment or intangible assets for cash	Outflow
	Sale of property, plant, and equipment or intangible assets for cash	Inflow
Short- or long-term investments in shares and bonds issued by other companies	Purchase of investment securities for cash	Outflow
	Sale (maturity) of investment securities for cash	Inflow

Typical investing activities include the following:

1. Cash expenditures that include the acquisition of tangible productive assets, such as buildings and equipment, or intangible assets, such as trademarks and patents. *Only purchases paid for with cash or cash equivalents are included.*

2. Cash proceeds from the sale of productive assets or intangible assets. This is the amount of cash that was received from the sale of assets, regardless of whether the assets were sold at a gain or a loss.

3 Purchase of short- or long-term investments for cash. These investments can include shares or bonds issued by other companies, guaranteed investment certificates, or government securities with maturities of more than three months. (Remember that securities with maturities of three months or less are cash equivalents.)

4. Cash proceeds from the sale or maturity of short- or long-term investments. Again, this is the amount of cash that was received from the sale, regardless of whether the assets were sold at a gain or a loss.

In the case of National Beverage, the analysis of changes in the statement of financial position (shown in Exhibit 5.3) indicates that two non-current assets (noted with an I) have changed during the period: property and equipment (net), and intangible assets. To determine the causes of changes in these assets, accountants need to search the related company records.

Property, Plant, and Equipment—Net The company's property, plant, and equipment (PPE) account increased by an amount of $321, net of accumulated depreciation. Typically, the net change in PPE is the result of three main changes: (1) purchase of new assets, (2) disposal of old assets, and (3) periodic depreciation of these assets. The purchase of assets increases the balance of PPE, the disposal of assets decreases the balance by the carrying amount (original cost − accumulated depreciation) of the assets disposed of, and the periodic depreciation increases the accumulated depreciation, which, in turn, reduces the balance of PPE.

During fiscal year 2015, National Beverage purchased new property, plant, and equipment for cash in the amount of $11,630, which is a cash outflow. The company also sold old equipment for a cash inflow of $1,905, which is equal to its carrying amount. These transactions are listed in the schedule of investing activities in Exhibit 5.7. These amounts, less the depreciation expense of $9,404, which is added to the net earnings in the operations section of the statement of cash flows, explain the net increase in PPE of $321:

Property, Plant, and Equipment—Net			
Beg. bal.	79,700	Sale	1,905
Purchase	11,630	Depreciation	9,404
End. bal.	80,021		

Cash purchases and sales of property, plant, and equipment are listed separately on the statement of cash flows.

Short-Term Investments   National Beverage's records indicate that it purchased short-term investments during the year for $6,532 in cash, which is a cash outflow. The company also sold short-term investments for a cash inflow of $4,869, which is equal to their carrying amount. These two amounts explain the net increase of $1,663 in short-term investments:

Short-Term Investments (A)			
Beg. bal.	2,685		
Purchase	6,532	Sale	4,869
End. bal.	4,348		

These investing items are listed in the schedule of investing activities in Exhibit 5.7 and result in a cash outflow of $11,388.

Exhibit 5.7

National Beverage: Schedule for Net Cash Flow from Investing Activities (amounts in thousands)

Items from Statement of Financial Position and Account Analysis	Cash Inflow (Outflows)	Explanation
Purchase of property, plant, and equipment	$(11,630)	Payment in cash for property and equipment.
Proceeds from disposal of property, plant, and equipment	1,905	Receipt of cash from sale of equipment.
Purchase of short-term investments	(6,532)	Payment in cash for new investments.
Proceeds from sale of short-term investments	4,869	Receipt of cash from sale of investments.
Net cash inflow (outflow) from investing activities	$(11,388)	Reported on the statement of cash flows

---

LO5-5

Analyze and interpret the capital expenditures ratio.

Interpreting Cash Flows from Investing Activities

Two common ways of assessing a company's ability to finance its expansion needs from internal sources are the capital expenditures ratio and free cash flow.

CAPITAL EXPENDITURES RATIO

ANALYTICAL QUESTION → To what degree was the company able to finance purchases of property and equipment, intangibles, and other businesses with cash provided by operating activities?

RATIO AND COMPARISONS→ This ratio is computed as follows:

$$\text{Capital expenditures ratio} = \frac{\text{Cash flow from operating activities}}{\text{Cash paid for capital expenditures}}$$

National Beverage's ratio for 2014 is,

$$\$60{,}042/\$11{,}630 = 5.16$$

Comparisons over Time			Comparisons with Competitors	
National Beverage*			Coca-Cola	PepsiCo
2012	2013	2014	2014	2014
4.15	4.32	5.16	4.41	3.67

*The fiscal year of National Beverage ends in early May. Hence, we noted the year that includes eight months of the company's activities. Both the Coca-Cola Company and PepsiCo Inc. have fiscal years that end in December.

INTERPRETATIONS

In General → The capital expenditures ratio reflects the portion of purchases of property and equipment, intangible assets, and acquisition of other businesses financed from operating activities without the need for outside debt or equity financing or the sale of property, plant, and equipment; intangibles; or other investments. A high ratio indicates less need for outside financing for current and future expansion. This provides the company with opportunities for strategic acquisitions, avoids the cost of additional debt, and reduces the risks of bankruptcy that come with additional leverage (see Chapter 10).

Focus Company Analysis→ National Beverage's ratio increased from 4.15 in 2012 to 5.16 in 2014. It generated more than sufficient cash to meet its investing needs and used the excess cash from operations to reduce its debt. This is consistent with the company's strategy discussed at the beginning of the chapter: to maintain a "fortress statement of financial position." National Beverage has maintained a ratio that is higher than those of its larger competitors, Coca-Cola and PepsiCo.

A Few Cautions→ Since the needs for investment in both tangible and intangible assets differ dramatically across industries (e.g., airlines versus takeout pizzerias), a particular firm's ratio should be compared only with its prior years' figures or with other firms in the same industry. Also, a high ratio may indicate a failure to upgrade a company's productive capacity, which can limit its ability to compete in the future.

SELECTED FOCUS COMPANY COMPARISONS—2015

WestJet Airlines 0.77%

Gildan Activewear 0.67%

Canadian Tire 0.83%

FREE CASH FLOW

Managers and analysts also often calculate **free cash flow**[10] as a measure of the firm's ability to pursue long-term investment opportunities. It is normally calculated as follows:

   Free cash flow = Cash flows from operating activities − Dividends − Capital expenditures

Any positive free cash flow is available for additional capital expenditures, investments in other companies, and mergers and acquisitions, without the need for external financing. While free cash flow is considered a positive sign of financial flexibility, it can also represent a hidden cost to shareholders. Sometimes, managers use free cash flow to pursue unprofitable investments just for the sake of growth or for perquisites for management use (such as fancy offices and corporate jets). In these cases, the shareholders would be better off if free cash flow were paid as additional dividends or used to repurchase the company's shares in the open market.

REPORTING AND INTERPRETING CASH FLOWS FROM FINANCING ACTIVITIES

Reporting Cash Flows from Financing Activities

Financing activities are associated with generating capital from creditors and owners. This section reflects changes in two current liabilities, *notes payable to financial institutions* (often called *short-term debt*) and *current portion of long-term debt*, as well as changes in *non-current liabilities and shareholders' equity accounts*. These financial position accounts relate to the issuance and retirement of debt, repurchase of shares, and payment of dividends. The following relationships are the ones that you will encounter most frequently:

Related Statement of Financial Position Account(s)	Financing Activity	Cash Flow Effect
Short-term debt	Borrowing cash from bank or other financial institution	Inflow
	Repayment of loan principal	Outflow
Long-term debt	Long-term borrowings for cash	Inflow
	Repayment of principal on long-term borrowings	Outflow
Contributed capital	Issuance of shares for cash	Inflow
	Repurchase (retirement) of shares for cash	Outflow
Retained earnings	Payment of cash dividends	Outflow

Financing activities are associated with generating capital from creditors and owners. Typical financing activities include the following:

1. **Proceeds from issuance of short- and long-term debt.** This represents cash received from borrowing from banks and other financial institutions, and from issuance of long-term debt (e.g., notes) to the public. *If the debt is issued for other than cash* (e.g., issued directly to a supplier of equipment to pay for a purchase), *it is not included in the statement.*

2. **Principal payments on short- and long-term debt.** Cash outflows associated with debt include the periodic repayment of principal as well as interest payments. Cash repayments of principal are listed as cash flows from financing activities.

3. **Proceeds from the issuance of shares.** This represents cash received from the sale of shares to investors. *If the shares are issued for other than cash* (e.g., issued directly to an employee as part of salary), *the amount is not included in the statement.*

4. **Purchase of shares for retirement.** This cash outflow includes cash payments for repurchase of the company's own shares from shareholders.

5. **Interest and dividends.** Cash flows from interest and dividends received and paid should be classified in a consistent manner from period to period as operating, investing, or financing activities. Cash dividends are usually reported as a financing activity because they are payments to shareholders. Alternatively, dividends paid may be classified as a component of cash flows from operating activities in order to assist users to determine the ability of an entity to pay dividends out of operating cash flows.

   Dividends received may be classified as investing cash flows because they represent returns on investments. Alternatively, they may be classified as operating cash flows because they enter into the determination of net earnings or net loss.

   Interest paid may be classified as financing cash flow because it is a cost of obtaining financial resources, and interest received may be classified as investing cash flow because it is a return on investments. Alternatively, they may be classified as operating cash flows because they enter into the determination of net earnings or net loss.

To compute cash flows from financing activities, you should review changes in debt and shareholders' equity accounts. In the case of National Beverage, analysis of changes in the account balances on the statement of financial position indicates that long-term debt, contributed capital, and retained earnings changed during the period (noted with an F in Exhibit 5.3).

Short- and Long-Term Debt Additional borrowing or principal repayments on borrowings from banks are financing cash flows. The appropriate amounts are determined by analyzing the long-term debt account. National Beverage's repaid $18,400 in principal on long-term debt during 2015.

Long-Term Debt (L)			
		Beg. bal.	52,117
Repayment of amount borrowed	18,400		
		End. bal.	33,717

Contributed Capital National Beverage's change in contributed capital results from two types of decisions: issuance of shares to current or new shareholders for cash and repurchase of outstanding shares for cash. National Beverage did not issue any shares in fiscal year 2015, but it repurchased shares for $7,455, the same amount it received when the shares were issued. This amount is listed in the schedule of financing activities in Exhibit 5.8.

Exhibit **5.8**

National Beverage: Schedule for Net Cash Flow from Financing Activities (amounts in thousands)

Item from Statement of Financial Position and Account Analysis	Cash Inflow (Outflow)	Explanation
Repayment of principal on long-term debt	(18,400)	Cash payments of principal on long-term debt.
Repurchase of shares	(7,455)	Cash payments to repurchase shares.
Payment of dividends	(275)	Payment of cash dividends to shareholders.
Net cash inflow from financing activities	$ 26,130	Reported on the statement of cash flows.

Contributed Capital (SE)			
		Beg. bal.	25,464
Repurchase of shares	7,455		
		End. bal.	18,009

Retained Earnings Retained earnings increase when National Beverage reports net earnings. They decrease when dividends are declared. National Beverage reported net earnings of $49,311 during fiscal year 2015; it declared and paid $275 in dividends to shareholders. The dividend payment is listed on the schedule of financing activities in Exhibit 5.8.

Retained Earnings (SE)			
		Beg. bal.	80,737
		Net earnings	49,311
Dividends declared	275		
		End. bal.	129,773

Dividends Payable Companies usually pay dividends on a quarterly basis, and cash payments to shareholders are typically made within three or four weeks from the date of dividend declaration. The dividends declared during fiscal year 2015 were all paid in that year.

Dividends Payable (L)			
		Beg. bal.	0
Payment to shareholders	275	Dividends declared	275
		End. bal.	0

Interpreting Cash Flows from Financing Activities

The long-term growth of a company is normally financed from three sources: internally generated funds (cash from operating activities), the issuance of shares, and money borrowed on a long-term basis. As we discuss in Chapter 10, companies can adopt a number of different capital structures (the balance of debt and equity). The financing sources that management uses to fund growth will have an important impact on the firm's risk and return characteristics. The statement of cash flows shows how management has elected to fund its growth. This information is used by analysts who wish to evaluate the capital structure and growth potential of a business.

INTERPRETATION OF CASH FLOW PATTERNS

FINANCIAL ANALYSIS

The statement of cash flows depicts the relationships among the operating, investing, and financing activities. Throughout this chapter, we have illustrated the reporting and interpretation of National Beverage's cash flows for fiscal year 2015. These cash flows are specific to one company for a specified time period. To generalize, the table below shows the eight possible patterns of cash flows generated from (used for) operating, investing, and financing activities. A general explanation for each observed pattern is also provided:

Analysis of Cash Flow Patterns

	1	2	3	4	5	6	7	8
Cash Flow from Operating	+	+	+	+	−	−	−	−
Cash Flow from Investing	+	−	+	−	+	−	+	−
Cash Flow from Financing	+	−	−	+	+	+	−	−

A general explanation of each pattern follows:

1. The company is using cash generated from operations, from the sale of non-current assets, and from financing to build its cash reserves. This is a very liquid company, possibly looking for acquisitions. This pattern is very unusual.

2. The company is using cash generated from operations to buy non-current assets and to reduce its debt or distribute cash dividends to shareholders. This pattern reflects a mature, successful firm.

3. The company is using cash from operations and from the sale of non-current assets to reduce its debt or distribute cash dividends to shareholders. It is actually downsizing its operations.

4. The company is using cash from operations and from borrowing (or from equity investment) to expand. This pattern is typical of many growing companies.

5. The company's operating cash flow problems are covered by the sale of non-current assets and by borrowing or shareholder contributions. The company is selling its non-current assets to stay in business, and the fact that investors are willing to supply the financing indicates that they apparently expect a turnaround in operating cash flows.

6. The company is experiencing a shortfall in cash flow from operations and from investing activities. The deficiency in cash is financed by long-term borrowings or investments by shareholders. This pattern is most typical of a young, fast-growing company.

7. The company is financing operating cash flow shortages, paying its debtholders and/or its shareholders via the sale of non-current assets. The company is actually shrinking.

8. The company is using cash reserves to finance operations, pay long-term creditors and/or investors, and acquire new non-current assets. This unusual scenario is possible only if cash previously accumulated is being used to meet these cash outflows.

Source: Adapted from M. T. Dugan, B. E. Gup, and W. D. Samson, "Teaching the Statement of Cash Flows," *Journal of Accounting Education,* Vol. 9, 1991, pp. 33–52.

National Beverage's statement of cash flows for fiscal years 2011–2015 showed the following pattern of cash flows (in thousands of dollars):

	2015	2014	2013	2012	2011
Net cash provided by (used in) operating activities	$60,042	$52,382	$40,264	$37,696	$55,302
Net cash provided by (used in) investing activities	(11,630)	(12,062)	(9,616)	(9,852)	(11,312)
Net cash provided by (used in) financing activities	(26,130)	(28,655)	(48,007)	410	(105,184)

This pattern of cash flows reflects a mature, successful company that used cash from operations to invest in non-current assets and to reduce its debt or distribute cash dividends to shareholders.

PAUSE FOR **FEEDBACK**

Cash flows can be generated from or used in operating, investing, and financing activities. The sources and uses of cash flows provide an indication of the phase that the company is experiencing in its life cycle. For example, successful companies generate cash flows from operations for use in investing and financing activities, but companies that sell their long-lived assets to finance their operations and pay their creditors may not survive for long. Check your understanding of the different patterns of cash flows by answering the following questions before you move on.

SELF-STUDY **QUIZ 5-3**

American International Group Inc.
American International Group Inc. (AIG) is a leading international insurance organization with operations in more than 130 countries and jurisdictions. Its statement of cash flows for three recent years included the following summary:

Years Ended December 31 (in millions of U.S. dollars)			
	Year 3	Year 2	Year 1
Net cash provided by (used in) operating activities	$ 35	$ 16,910	$ 18,584
Net cash provided by (used in) investing activities	36,322	(10,225)	5,778
Net cash provided by (used in) financing activities	(36,926)	(9,261)	(28,997)

What conclusions can you derive by examining the pattern of the company's cash flows during these three years?

After you complete your answers, check them with the solutions at the end of the chapter.

LO5-7

Understand the format of the statement of cash flows and additional cash flow disclosures.

COMPLETING THE STATEMENT AND ADDITIONAL DISCLOSURES

Statement Structure

Refer to the formal statement of cash flows for National Beverage that is shown in Exhibit 5.1. As you can see, it is a simple matter to construct the statement after the detailed analysis of the accounts and transactions have been completed (shown in Exhibits 5.6, 5.7, and 5.8). Exhibit 5.9 summarizes the general structure of the statement for companies that use the indirect method. As you can see, the *net increase or decrease in cash and cash equivalents* is added to the cash and cash equivalents reported on the statement of financial position at the beginning of the period, and the result equals the cash and cash equivalents reported on the same statement at the end of the period. Companies that use the direct method for computing cash flow from operations usually present a reconciliation of net earnings to cash flow from operations (the indirect method as presented in Exhibit 5.6) as a supplemental schedule. Companies must also provide two other disclosures related to the statement of cash flows.

Exhibit 5.9

Structure of the Statement of Cash Flows (Indirect Method)

Statement of Cash Flows (Indirect Method)
Operating Activities:
Net earnings
+ Depreciation and amortization expense
− Gain on sale of long-lived asset
+ Loss on sale of long-lived asset
+ Decreases in operating assets
+ Increases in operating liabilities
− Increases in operating assets
− Decreases in operating liabilities
Net Cash Flow from Operating Activities
Investing Activities:
− Purchase of property, plant, and equipment or intangible assets
+ Sale of property, plant, and equipment or intangible assets
− Purchase of investment securities
+ Sale (maturity) of investment securities
Net Cash Flow from Investing Activities
Financing Activities:
+ Borrowing from bank or other financial institution
− Repayment of loan principal
+ Issuance of long-term debt for cash
− Repayment of principal on long-term debt
+ Issuance of shares
− Repurchase (retirement) of shares
− Payment of (cash) dividends
Net Cash Flow from Financing Activities
Net Increase or Decrease in Cash and Cash Equivalents
Cash and cash equivalents at beginning of period
Cash and cash equivalents at end of period

Non-cash Investing and Financing Activities

NON-CASH INVESTING AND FINANCING ACTIVITIES are transactions that do not have direct cash flow effects; they are reported as a supplement to the statement of cash flows in narrative or schedule form.

Certain transactions are important investing and financing activities but have no cash flow effects. These are called **non-cash investing and financing activities**; they are reported as a supplement to the statement of cash flows in narrative or schedule form. For example, the purchase of a $100,000 building with a $100,000 mortgage given by the former owner does not cause either an inflow or an outflow of cash. As a result, these non-cash activities are not listed in the three main sections of the statement of cash flows. IAS 7 requires supplemental disclosure of these transactions in either narrative or schedule form. National Beverage's statement of cash flows does not list any non-cash investing and financing activities. The following excerpt from the 2015 annual report of Gildan Activewear Inc. provides examples of these non-cash transactions:

22. Supplemental cash flow disclosure (in thousands of U.S. dollars)		
	2015	**2014**
(b) Variations in non-cash transactions (partial):		
Additions to property, plant, and equipment included in accounts payable and accrued liabilities	13,993	1,754
Addition to property, plant, and equipment transferred from prepaid expenses and deposits and other non-current assets	—	5,826
Proceeds on disposal of property, plant, and equipment included in other current assets	(79)	—
Amounts payable relating to business acquisitions	(6,400)	(500)

Supplemental Cash Flow Information

Companies that use the indirect method of presenting cash flows from operations must also disclose the amounts of interest and dividends received and paid during the period, as well as cash paid for income taxes. These are normally listed in the operating activities section of the statement or in the notes.

ACCOUNTING STANDARDS FOR PRIVATE ENTERPRISES

The requirements for the reporting of cash flow information by Canadian private enterprises (Section 1540 of the *CICA Handbook*) are practically the same as the requirements for Canadian publicly accountable enterprises (IAS 7). One notable difference is the classification of interest and dividends received and paid:

Financial Reporting Issue	IFRS	ASPE
Classification of cash flows from interest and dividends		
• Interest paid	Cash payments for interest are classified as either operating (O) or financing activities (F).	Cash payments for interest are classified as an operating activity if they are included in the determination of net earnings (O).
• Dividends paid	Dividend payments to shareholders are classified as either operating (O) or financing activities (F).	Dividend payments to shareholders are classified as a financing activity (F).
• Interest and dividends received	Cash flows from interest and dividends received are classified as either operating (O) or investing activities (I).	Cash flows from interest and dividends received are classified as operating activities (O).

DEMONSTRATION **CASE**

During the year ended December 31, 2017, Old Style Brewery, a craft brewer, reported net earnings of $3,182 (all numbers in thousands) and cash and cash equivalents of $472 at the beginning and $24,676 at the end of the year. It also engaged in the following activities:

a. Paid $18,752 in principal on long-term debt.

b. Received $46,202 in cash from initial public offering of shares.

c. Incurred other non-current accrued operating expenses of $857.

d. Paid $18,193 in cash for purchase of property, plant, and equipment.

e. Accounts receivable increased by $881.

f. Borrowed $16,789 from various lenders.

g. Refundable deposits payable increased by $457.

h. Inventories increased by $574.

i. Made cash deposits on equipment of $5,830.

j. Income tax refund receivable decreased by $326.

k. Sold (issued) shares to employees for $13 in cash.

l. Accounts payable decreased by $391.

m. Received $4 from other investing activities.

n. Accrued liabilities increased by $241.

o. Prepaid expenses increased by $565.

p. Recorded depreciation of $1,324.

q. Paid $5 cash for other financing activities.

Required:
Based on this information, prepare the statement of cash flows for the year ended December 31, 2017. Use the indirect method to compute the cash flows from operating activities.

  We strongly recommend that you prepare your own answer to this requirement and then check it with the following solution.

SUGGESTED **SOLUTION**

OLD STYLE BREWERY
Statement of Cash Flows
For the Year Ended December 31, 2017
(in thousands)

Operating activities	
Net earnings	$ 3,182
Add (deduct) items not affecting cash:	
Depreciation	1,324
Other non-current accrued expenses	857
Increase in accounts receivable	(881)
Increase in inventories	(574)
Decrease in income taxes receivable	326
Increase in prepaid expenses	(565)
Decrease in accounts payable	(391)
Increase in accrued liabilities	241
Increase in refundable deposits payable	457
Net cash flows from operating activities	3,976
Investing activities	
Expenditures for property, plant, and equipment	(18,193)
Deposits on equipment	(5,830)
Other investing activities	4
Net cash flow from investing activities	(24,019)
Financing activities	
Proceeds from debt	16,789
Repayment of debt	(18,752)
Proceeds from sale of shares (IPO)	46,202
Proceeds from sale of shares (options)	1 3
Other financing activities	(5)
Net cash flow from financing activities	44,247
Increase in cash and cash equivalents	24,204
Cash and cash equivalents:	
Beginning of year	472
End of year	$24,676

APPENDIX 5A: ADJUSTMENT FOR GAINS AND LOSSES ON THE SALE OF LONG-LIVED ASSETS—INDIRECT METHOD

The operating activities section of the statement of cash flows prepared under the indirect method may include an adjustment for gains and losses on the sale of long-lived assets reported on the statement of earnings. The transactions that cause gains and losses should be classified on the statement of cash flows as operating, investing, or financing activities, depending on their dominant characteristics. For example, if the sale of a productive asset (e.g., a delivery truck) produced a gain, it would be classified as an investing activity.

An adjustment must be made in the operating activities section to avoid double counting of the gain or the loss. To illustrate, National Beverage sold equipment in 2015 for $1,905 and realized a gain of $1,188, which is the difference between the cash received and the carrying amount of the equipment sold. Based on these two numbers, the equipment's carrying amount is $717 ($1,905 − $1,188). If the equipment has an original cost of $4,625, the following entry is made to record the sale transaction:[11]

Cash (+A)	1,905		
Accumulated depreciation (−XA, +A)	3,908		
Property and equipment (−A)		4,625	
Gain on sale of assets (+Gain, +SE)		1,188	

Assets		=	Liabilities	+	Shareholders' Equity	
Cash	+1,905				Gain on sale of assets	+1,188
Accumulated depreciation	+3,908					
Property, plant, and equipment	−4,625					

The $1,905 inflow of cash is an investing cash inflow, but the gain of $1,188 is also reported on the statement of earnings. Because the gain is included in the computation of net earnings, it is necessary to subtract the $1,188 gain from the operating activities section of the statement to avoid double counting:

Cash flows from operating activities	
Net earnings	$49,311
Adjustments to reconcile net earnings to cash flow from operating activities:	
...	...
Gain on disposal of property and equipment	(1,188)
...	...
Net cash flow provided by operating activities	...
Cash flows from investing activities	
Purchases of property and equipment	...
Proceeds from disposal of property and equipment	1,905
...	...
Net cash used in investing activities	...

If the company had sold the same asset for $650 cash, the following entry would have been made:

Cash (+A)	650		
Accumulated depreciation (−XA, +A)	3,908		
Loss on sale of assets (−Loss, −SE) ($650 − $717)	67		
Property and equipment (−A)		4,625	

Assets		=	Liabilities	+	Shareholders' Equity	
Cash	+650				Loss on sale of assets	−67
Accumulated depreciation	+3,908					
Property, plant, and equipment	−4,625					

On the statement of cash flows, the loss of $67 must be removed (added to net earnings) in the computation of cash flows from operating activities, and the cash collected of $650 must be shown in the investing activities section of the statement:

Cash flows from operating activities	
Net earnings	$49,311
Adjustments to reconcile net earnings to cash flow from operating activities:	
...	...
Loss on disposal of property and equipment	67
...	...
Net cash flow provided by operating activities	...
Cash flows from investing activities	
Purchases of property and equipment	...
Proceeds from disposal of property and equipment	650
...	...
Net cash used in investing activities	...

APPENDIX 5B: REPORTING CASH FLOWS FROM OPERATING ACTIVITIES—DIRECT METHOD

Exhibit 5.3 shows National Beverage's comparative statements of financial position at the end of fiscal years 2015 and 2014 and its statement of earnings for the year 2015. Recall that the direct method reports gross cash receipts and gross cash payments related to operating activities. It presents a summary of all operating transactions that resulted in either a debit or a credit to cash.

Cash Flows from Operating Activities

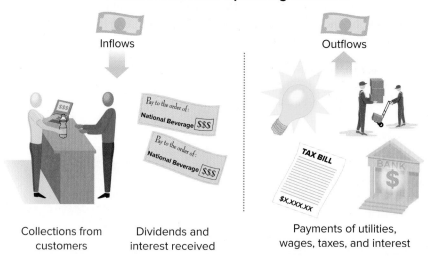

Inflows — Collections from customers — Dividends and interest received

Outflows — Payments of utilities, wages, taxes, and interest

The computation of cash receipts and payments requires adjusting each item on the statement of earnings from an accrual basis to a cash basis. To facilitate this process, the asset, liability, and equity accounts in Exhibit 5.3 that relate to operating activities have been marked with an O. These items include short-term investments, accounts receivable, inventories, prepaid expenses, accounts payable, accrued liabilities, income taxes payable, and retained earnings.

Converting Revenue and Expense Items from an Accrual Basis to a Cash Basis The computation of cash receipts and payments requires adjusting each item on the statement of earnings from an accrual basis. To facilitate this process, we analyze the change in the balance of each current asset and current liability account by examining the type of transactions that affect the account. This process helps us determine the amount of cash received or paid during the accounting period.

We will use the following relation to analyze the changes in each current asset and liability account:

| Beginning Balance | + | Increases | – | Decreases | = | Ending Balance |

Converting Revenues to Cash Inflows
When sales are recorded, accounts receivable increase, and when cash is collected, accounts receivable decrease. Hence, the change from the beginning balance of accounts receivable to the ending balance can be represented as follows:

In general	National Beverage's example
Accounts receivable, beginning (known)	$ 58,205
+ Sales revenue (known)	+ 645,825
– Cash collections from customers (computed)	– A
= Accounts receivable, ending (known)	= $ 59,951

The beginning and ending balances of accounts receivable are reported on the statement of financial position, and sales revenue is reported on the statement of earnings. However, the amount collected from customers is not reported on either statement, but can be derived from the relation above.

The beginning balance of accounts receivable increases the cash received from customers on the assumption that all amounts owed to the company at the beginning of the period are collected during the period. In contrast, the ending balance of accounts receivable is deducted from sales revenue, because these receivables have already been included in sales revenue but have not yet been collected from customers.

Using information from National Beverage's statement of earnings and statement of financial position presented in Exhibit 5.3, we can compute the cash collected from customers as follows:[12]

$$\text{Cash collections} = \$58{,}205 + \$645{,}825 - \$59{,}951 = \$644{,}079$$

Accounts Receivable (A)

Beg. bal.	58,205		
Sales	645,825	Collections	644,079
End. bal.	59,951		

Converting Cost of Sales to Cash Paid to Suppliers
The cost of sales during the accounting period may be greater or smaller than the amount of cash paid to suppliers of merchandise during the period. The computation of the cash paid to suppliers is a two-stage process. First, we analyze the change in the inventories account to determine the amount of merchandise purchases during the period, and then we analyze the change in the accounts payable account to compute the amount of cash payments to suppliers by using the following relations:

In general	National Beverage's example
Inventories, beginning (known)	$ 3,914
+ Merchandise purchases (computed)	+ A
– Cash of sales (known)	– 426,685
= Inventories, ending (known)	= $ 42,924

In general	National Beverage's example
Accounts payable, beginning (known)	$ 45,606
+ Merchandise purchases (computed)	+ A
– Cash payments to suppliers (computed)	– B
= Accounts payable, ending (known)	= $ 4,896

The beginning and ending balances of inventory and accounts payable are reported on the statement of financial position, and the cost of sales is reported on the statement of earnings. However, the amount of merchandise purchases and the payments to suppliers are not reported on either statement but can be derived from the relations above.

The ending balance of inventory is added to cost of sales to determine the cost of goods that were available for sale during the period. Given that part of the merchandise was available at the beginning of the period, it is deducted from the goods available to determine the amount of purchases during the period.

Using information from National Beverage's statement of earnings and statement of financial position presented in Exhibit 5.3, we can compute the cash paid to suppliers in two steps as follows:

$$\textbf{Merchandise purchases} = \$426{,}685 + \$42{,}924 - \$43{,}914 = \$425{,}695$$

Inventories (A)

Beg. bal.	43,914		
Purchases	425,695	Cost of sales	426,685
End. bal.	42,924		

Accounts Payable (L)

		Beg. bal.	45,606
Cash payments	426,405	Purchases	425,695
		End. bal.	44,896

The beginning balance of accounts payable is added to merchandise purchases to determine the total amount payable to suppliers. The ending balance of accounts payable is then deducted from that total because this amount has not been paid to suppliers yet:[13]

$$\textbf{Cash payments to suppliers} = \$425{,}695 + \$45{,}606 - \$44{,}896 = \$426{,}405$$

Conversion of Selling, General, and Administrative Expenses to a Cash Outflow

The total amount of any operating expense on the statement of earnings may differ from the cash payment for that expense during the accounting period. Some expenses are paid before they are recognized as expenses (e.g., prepaid rent). When prepayments are made, the balance in the prepaid expenses account increases; when prepaid expenses are used up and recognized as expenses for the period, the account balance decreases. Other expenses are paid for after they are recognized in the same or previous periods. In this case, when expenses are recorded, the balance in the accrued liabilities account increases; when payments are made, the account balance decreases. The computation of the cash paid for operating expenses is, therefore, a two-stage process. First, we analyze the change in the prepaid expenses account to determine the amount of cash paid during the period, and then we analyze the change in the accrued liabilities account to compute the amount of cash that was paid during the period for various other expenses, as shown in the following relations:

In general	National Beverage's example
Prepaid expenses, beginning (known)	$8,405
+ Cash payments for future (deferred) expenses (unknown)	+ A
− Prepaid expenses that were used up during the period (unknown)	− B
= Prepaid expenses, ending (known)	= $8,050

In general	National Beverage's example
Accrued liabilities, beginning (known)	$18,873
+ Expenses accrued during the period (unknown)	+ C
− Cash payments for accrued expenses (unknown)	− D
= Accrued liabilities, ending (known)	= $21,257

The beginning and ending balances of prepaid expenses and accrued liabilities are reported on the statement of financial position. But the prepaid expenses (B) that were used up during the period are not reported separately on the statement of earnings. Hence, we cannot compute the amount of cash (A) paid for future expenses. Similarly, the expenses (C) that accrued during the period are not reported separately on the statement of earnings, which makes it difficult to compute the amount of cash (D) paid during the period to settle accrued expenses. However, the amounts B and C are reported together on the statement of earnings as selling, general, and administrative expenses. By combining the two relations, we can then compute the sum of A and D, which represents the payments made for other expenses.

Using information from National Beverage's statement of earnings and statement of financial position presented in Exhibit 5.3, we can compute the cash paid for selling, general, and administrative expenses as follows:

Cash Paid for Other Expenses	= $134,095	(selling, general, and administrative expenses reflecting prepaid expenses that expired during the fiscal year and accrued expenses)
	+ 8,050	(prepaid expenses, end of fiscal year)
	− 8,405	(prepaid expenses, beginning of fiscal year)
	+ 18,873	(accrued liabilities, beginning of fiscal year)
	− 21,257	(accrued liabilities, end of fiscal year)
	= $131,356	

Prepaid Expenses (A)

Beg. bal.	8,405		
Cash payments unknown		Prepaid expenses that expired	unknown
End. bal.	8,050		

Accrued Liabilities (L)

		Beg. bal.	18,873
Cash payments unknown		Unpaid expenses	unknown
		End. bal.	21,257

Similar analysis can be applied to computing the cash payments for interest and income taxes. Since there is no interest payable balance, we can see that interest expense must be equal to cash payments for interest expense. National Beverage reports interest expense of $928. Since there is no interest payable balance, we can see that interest expense must be equal to cash payments for interest expense.

National Beverage's income taxes expense equals $25,402. This amount increases the balance of the income taxes payable account. In contrast, payment of income taxes reduces the balance of the account. Using information from National Beverage's statement of earnings and statement of financial position presented in Exhibit 5.3, we can compute the cash payments to the taxation authorities as follows:

$$\text{Cash paid} = \$44 + \$25,402 - \$98 = \$25,348$$

Income Taxes Payable (L)

		Beg. bal.	44
Cash payments	25,348	Income taxes payable	25,402
		End. bal.	98

The operating cash inflows and outflows are accumulated in Exhibit 5.10.

To summarize, the following adjustments must commonly be made to convert statement of earnings items to the related operating cash flow amounts:

Statement of Earnings Account	+/− Change in Statement of Financial Position Account(s)	= Operating Cash Flow
Sales revenue	+ Beginning accounts receivable − Ending accounts receivable	= Collections from customers
Cost of sales	− Beginning inventory + Ending inventory + Beginning accounts payable − Ending accounts payable	= Payments to suppliers of inventory
Selling, general, and administrative expenses	− Beginning prepaid expenses + Ending prepaid expenses + Beginning accrued liabilities − Ending accrued liabilities	= Payments to suppliers of services (e.g., rent, utilities, wages)
Interest expense	+ Beginning interest payable − Ending interest payable	= Payments for interest
Income tax expense	+ Beginning income taxes payable − Ending income taxes payable	= Payments for income taxes

Exhibit 5.10

National Beverage Inc.: Schedule of Net Cash Flows from Operating Activities—Direct Method (amounts in thousands)

Cash flows from operating activities		
Cash collected from customers		$644,079
Cash payments		
• to suppliers	426,405	
• for other operating expenses	131,356	
• for income taxes	25,348	
• for interest	928	584,037
Net cash provided by operating activities		$ 60,042

PAUSE FOR FEEDBACK

The direct method for reporting cash flows from operating activities reports gross cash receipts and gross cash payments related to operating activities. To test your understanding of this method relative to the indirect method, answer the following questions.

SELF-STUDY QUIZ 5-4

Indicate which of the following items taken from the statement of cash flows would be added (+), subtracted (−), or not included (0) in the cash flow from operations section when the direct method is used:

_____ *a.* Increase in inventories
_____ *b.* Payment of dividends to shareholders
_____ *c.* Cash collections from customers
_____ *d.* Purchase of property, plant, and equipment for cash
_____ *e.* Payment of interest to debt holders
_____ *f.* Payment of taxes to the taxation authorities

After you complete your answers, check them with the solutions at the end of the chapter.

APPENDIX 5C: T-ACCOUNT APPROACH—INDIRECT METHOD

When we began our discussion on preparing the statement of cash flows, we noted that changes in cash must equal the sum of the changes in all other statement of financial position accounts. Based on this idea, we used the following three steps to prepare the statement of cash flows:

1. Determine the change in each statement of financial position account. From this year's ending balance, subtract this year's beginning balance (i.e., last year's ending balance).

2. Identify the cash flow category or categories to which each account relates. Remember that changes in the balances of some accounts result from two types of activities. For example, the change in retained earnings is the result of adding net earnings (operating cash flow) and subtracting dividends (financing cash flow).

3. Create schedules that summarize operating, investing, and financing cash flows.

Instead of creating separate schedules for each section of the statement, many accountants prefer to prepare a single large T-account to represent the changes that have taken place in cash, subdivided into the three sections of the statement of cash flows. Such an account is presented in Panel A of Exhibit 5.11. The cash account in Panel A shows increases in cash as debits and decreases in cash as credits. Note how each section matches the three schedules that we prepared for National Beverage's cash flows presented in Exhibits 5.6, 5.7, and 5.8. Panel B includes the same T-accounts for the non-cash accounts we used in our discussion of each section of the statement of cash flows in the body of the chapter. Note how each change in the non-cash accounts has a number referencing the change in the cash account that it accompanies. The statement of cash flows presented in Exhibit 5.1 can be prepared in proper format based on the information in the cash flow T-account.

Exhibit **5.11**

T-Account Approach to Preparing the Statement of Cash Flows—Indirect Method

Panel A: Changes in Cash Account

Cash (A)

Operating			
(1) Net earnings	49,311		
(2) Depreciation and amortization expense	9,404		
		1,746	(3) Accounts receivable
(4) Inventories	990		
(5) Prepaid expenses	355		
		710	(6) Accounts payable
(7) Accrued liabilities	2,384		
(8) Income taxes payable	54		
Net cash flow from operating activities	**60,042**		
Investing			
		11,630	(9) Purchase of property, plant, and equipment
(10) Sale of property, plant, and equipment	1,905		
		6,532	(11) Purchase of short-term investments
(12) Sale of short-term investments	4,869		
		11,388	**Net cash used in investing activities**
Financing			
		18,400	(13) Payment of principal on long-term debt
		7,455	(14) Repurchase of shares
		275	(15) Payment of dividends
		26,130	**Net cash provided by financing activities**
Net increase in cash and cash equivalents	**22,524**		

Panel B: Changes in Non-cash Accounts

Accounts Receivable (A)			
Beg. bal.	58,205		
		(3) Decrease	1,746
End. bal.	59,951		

Inventories (A)			
Beg. bal.	43,914		
		(4) Decrease	990
End. bal.	42,924		

Prepaid Expenses (A)			
Beg. bal.	8,405		
		(5) Decrease	355
End. bal.	8,050		

Accounts Payable (A)			
		Beg. bal.	45,606
(6) Increase	710		
		End. bal.	44,896

Accrued Liabilities (L)			
		Beg. bal.	18,873
(7) Decrease	2,384		
		End. bal.	21,257

Income Taxes Payable (L)			
		Beg. bal.	44
		(8) Increase	54
		End. bal.	98

Property, Plant, and Equipment—Net (A)			
Beg. bal.	79,700	(2) Depreciation	9,404
(9) Purchase	11,630	(10) Sale	1,905
End. bal.	80,021		

Short-Term Investments (A)			
Beg. bal.	2,685		
(11) Purchase	6,532	(12) Sale	4,869
End. bal.	4,348		

Long-Term Debt (L)			
		Beg. bal.	52,117
(13) Payment	18,400		
		End. bal.	33,717

Contributed Capital (SE)			
		Beg. bal.	25,464
(14) Repurchase	7,455		
		End. bal.	18,009

Dividends Payable (L)			
		Beg. bal.	0
(15) Paid	275	Declared	275
		End. bal.	0

Retained Earnings (SE)			
		Beg. bal.	80,737
		(1) Net earnings	60,042
Dividends	275		
		End. bal.	129,773

CHAPTER TAKE-AWAYS

5-1. Classify cash flow items into cash flows from operating, investing, and financing activities.

The statement has three main sections: cash flows from operating activities, which are related to earning revenue from normal operations and incurring related expenses; cash flows from investing activities, which are related to the acquisition and sale of productive assets; and cash flows from financing activities, which are related to external financing of the enterprise. The net cash inflow or outflow for the year is the same amount as the increase or decrease in cash and cash equivalents for the year. Cash equivalents are highly liquid investments with original maturities of less than three months.

5-2. Report and interpret cash flows from operating activities, using the indirect method.

The indirect method for reporting cash flows from operating activities presents a conversion of net earnings (loss) to net cash flows from operating activities. The conversion involves additions and subtractions for (1) non-current accruals, including expenses (such as depreciation expense) and revenues that do not affect current assets or current liabilities, and (2) changes in each of the individual current assets (other than cash and short-term investments) and current liabilities (other than short-term borrowings from financial institutions and current portion of long-term debt, which relate to financing) that reflect differences in the timing of accrual basis earnings and cash flows.

5-3. Analyze and interpret the quality of earnings ratio.

The quality of earnings ratio (Cash flows from operating activities ÷ Net earnings) measures the portion of net earnings that was generated in cash. A higher quality of earnings ratio indicates greater ability to finance operating and other cash needs from operating cash inflows. A higher ratio also indicates that it is less likely that the company is using aggressive revenue recognition policies to increase net earnings.

5-4. Report and interpret cash flows from investing activities.

Investing activities reported on the statement of cash flows include cash payments to acquire property, plant, and equipment; intangibles; and short- and long-term investments. They also include cash proceeds from the sale of these assets.

5-5. Analyze and interpret the capital expenditures ratio.

The capital expenditures ratio (Cash flows from operating activities ÷ Cash paid for capital expenditures) reflects the portion of purchases of property, plant, and equipment; intangible assets; and acquisition of other businesses that are financed from operating activities without the need for outside debt or equity financing or the sale of other investments or other non-current assets. A high ratio is beneficial because it provides the company with opportunities for strategic acquisitions.

5-6. Report and interpret cash flows from financing activities.

Cash inflows from financing activities include cash proceeds from issuance of short- and long-term debt and contributed capital. Cash outflows include principal payments on short- and long-term debt, cash paid for the repurchase of the company's shares, and dividend payments. Cash payments associated with interest relate to either operating activities or financing activities.

5-7. Understand the format of the statement of cash flows and additional cash flow disclosures.

The statement of cash flows splits transactions that affect cash into three categories: operating, investing, and financing activities. The operating section is most often prepared using the indirect method, which begins with net earnings (loss) and adjusts the amount to eliminate non-cash transactions. Non-cash investing and financing activities are investing and financing activities that do not involve cash. They include, for example, purchases of non-current assets with long-term debt or shares, exchanges of non-current assets, and exchanges of debt for shares. These transactions are disclosed only as supplemental disclosures to the statement of cash flows along with cash paid for interest and taxes under the indirect method.

Chapters 1 through 5 discussed the important steps in the accounting process that lead to the preparation of the four basic financial statements. In Chapter 6 we begin our in-depth discussion of financial statements. We will begin with two of the most-liquid assets, cash and accounts receivable, and transactions that involve revenues and certain selling expenses. Accuracy in revenue recognition and the related recognition of cost of sales (discussed in Chapter 7) are the most important determinants of the accuracy and, thus, the usefulness of financial statement presentations. We will also introduce concepts related to the management and control of cash and receivables, which is a critical business function. A detailed understanding of these topics is crucial to future managers, accountants, and financial analysts.

KEY **RATIOS**

The quality of earnings ratio indicates what portion of net earnings was generated in cash. It is computed as follows:

$$\text{Quality of earnings ratio} = \frac{\text{Cash flows from operating activities}}{\text{Net earnings}}$$

The capital expenditures ratio measures the ability to finance purchases of property, plant, and equipment; intangibles; and other businesses from operations. It is computed as follows:

$$\text{Capital expenditures ratio} = \frac{\text{Cash flow from operating activities}}{\text{Cash paid for capital expenditures}}$$

FINDING **FINANCIAL INFORMATION**

STATEMENT OF FINANCIAL POSITION	**STATEMENT OF CASH FLOWS**
Changes in Assets, Liabilities, and Shareholders' Equity	Cash Flows from Operating Activities
	Cash Flows from Investing Activities
	Cash Flows from Financing Activities
	Separate Schedule (or note)
	Non-cash investing and financing activities
	Interest and taxes paid
	Interest, dividends, and taxes received

STATEMENT OF EARNINGS Net Earnings and Accruals	NOTES **Under Summary of Significant Accounting Policies** Definition of cash equivalents **Under Separate Note** If not listed on statement of cash flows: Non-cash investing and financing activities Interest and taxes paid Interest, dividends, and taxes received

QUESTIONS

1. Compare the purposes of the statement of earnings, the statement of financial position, and the statement of cash flows.
2. What information does the statement of cash flows report that is not reported on the other required financial statements? How do investors and creditors use that information?
3. What are cash equivalents? How are purchases and sales of cash equivalents reported on the statement of cash flows?
4. What are the major categories of business activities reported on the statement of cash flows? Define each of these activities.
5. What are the typical cash inflows from operating activities? What are the typical cash outflows for operating activities?
6. Under the indirect method, depreciation expense is added to net earnings to compute cash flows from operating activities. Does depreciation cause an inflow of cash?
7. Explain why cash paid for purchases and salaries during the period is not specifically reported as cash outflows on the statement of cash flows under the indirect method.
8. Explain why a $50,000 increase in inventory during the year must be included in developing cash flows for operating activities under the indirect method.
9. Compare the two methods of reporting cash flows from operating activities in the statement of cash flows.
10. What are the typical cash inflows from investing activities? What are the typical cash outflows for investing activities?
11. What are the typical cash inflows from financing activities? What are the typical cash outflows for financing activities?
12. What are non-cash investing and financing activities? Give two examples. How are they reported on the statement of cash flows?
13. A company used cash for both operating and investing activities, but had positive cash flow from financing activities. What does this cash flow pattern suggest about this company?
14. (Appendix 5A) How is the sale of equipment reported on the statement of cash flows, using the indirect method?
15. (Appendix 5B) How do the direct and indirect methods of determining cash flows from operating activities differ? Which method provides results that are easier to understand and why?

connect MINI-EXERCISES

LO5-1

M5-1 **Matching Items Reported to Cash Flow Statement Categories, Indirect Method**
Molson Coors Brewing Company is a leading global brewer. It brews, markets, and sells a portfolio of leading brands such as Coors Light, Coors Banquet, and Molson Canadian. Some of the items included in its recent annual consolidated statement of cash flows presented using the **indirect method** are listed below. Indicate whether each item is disclosed in the operating activities (O), investing activities (I), or financing activities (F) section of the statement, or use (NA) if the item does not appear on the statement.
____ 1. Purchase of shares (involves repurchase of the company's own shares)
____ 2. Payment on short-term borrowings
____ 3. Proceeds from sale of properties
____ 4. Inventories (decrease)
____ 5. Accounts payable (decrease)
____ 6. Depreciation and amortization

■ LO5-2   **M5-2**   **Determining the Effects of Account Changes on Cash Flow from Operating Activities, Indirect Method**

Indicate whether each item would be added (+) or subtracted (−) in the computation of cash flow from operating activities using the indirect method.

_____ 1.   Accrued liabilities (increase)
_____ 2.   Inventories (increase)
_____ 3.   Accounts receivable (decrease)
_____ 4.   Accounts payable (decrease)
_____ 5.   Depreciation, depletion, and amortization

■ LO5-1   **M5-3**   **Matching Items Reported to Cash Flow Statement Categories, Direct Method**

Lion

Lion Nathan, brewer of XXXX beer brand, Toohey's, and other well-known Australian brands, has net revenue of more than $2 billion (Australian). Some of the items included in its recent annual consolidated statement of cash flows presented using the **direct method** are listed below. Indicate whether each item is disclosed in the operating activities (O), investing activities (I), or financing activities (F) section of the statement, or use (NA) if the item does not appear on the statement.

_____ 1.   Receipts from customers
_____ 2.   Dividends paid
_____ 3.   Payment for repurchase of shares
_____ 4.   Proceeds from sale of property, plant, and equipment
_____ 5.   Repayments of borrowings
_____ 6.   Interest paid

■ LO5-3   **M5-4**   **Analyzing the Quality of Earnings Ratio**

Casey Corporation reported net earnings of $102,000, depreciation expense of $2,000, and cash flow from operations of $86,500. Compute the quality of earnings ratio. What does the ratio tell you about the company's ability to finance operating and other cash needs from operating cash inflows?

■ LO5-4   **M5-5**   **Computing Cash Flows from Investing Activities**

Compute cash flows from investing activities based on the following information.

Cash collections from customers	$550
Sale of used equipment	400
Depreciation expense	200
Purchase of short-term investments	635

■ LO5-6   **M5-6**   **Computing Cash Flows from Financing Activities**

Compute cash flows from financing activities based on the following information.

Purchase of short-term investments	$ 500
Dividends paid	700
Interest paid	300
Short-term borrowing from bank	1,200

■ LO5-7   **M5-7**   **Reporting Non-cash Investing and Financing Activities**

Which of the following transactions qualify as non-cash investing and financing activities?

_____   Purchase of building with mortgage payable.
_____   Short-term borrowing from bank.
_____   Dividends paid in cash.
_____   Purchase of equipment with short-term investments.

≡ connect EXERCISES

■ LO5-1   **E5-1**   **Matching Items Reported to Statement of Cash Flow Categories (Indirect Method)**

Lassonde Industries Inc.

Lassonde Industries Inc. is a Canadian company that develops, manufactures, and sells innovative and distinctive lines of fruit and vegetable juices and drinks that are marketed under recognized brand names such as Everfresh, Fairlee, and Oasis. Some of the items included in its recent annual consolidated statement of cash flows, presented using the indirect method, are listed below.

Indicate whether each item is disclosed in the operating activities (O), investing activities (I), or financing activities (F) section of the statement, or write not applicable (NA) if the item does not appear on the statement.

_____ 1. Dividends paid
_____ 2. Repayment of long-term debt
_____ 3. Depreciation and amortization
_____ 4. Proceeds from the issuance of shares
_____ 5. Change in accounts payable and accrued liabilities
_____ 6. Sale of intangible assets
_____ 7. Net earnings
_____ 8. Acquisition of property, plant, and equipment
_____ 9. Change in inventories

■ LO5-1

Leon's Furniture
Limited

E5-2   **Determining the Effects of Transactions on the Statement of Cash Flows**

Leon's Furniture Limited is an Ontario-based retailer of home furnishings. For each of the following first-quarter transactions, indicate whether net cash inflows (outflows) from operating activities (O), investing activities (I), or financing activities (F) are affected and whether the effect is an inflow (+) or an outflow (−), or write NE if the transaction has no effect on cash. (_Hint:_ Determine the journal entry recorded for the transaction. The transaction affects net cash flows if, and only if, the cash account is affected.)

_____ 1. Paid cash to purchase new equipment.
_____ 2. Purchased raw materials inventory on account.
_____ 3. Collected cash from customers.
_____ 4. Recorded an adjusting entry to record an accrued salaries expense.
_____ 5. Recorded and paid interest on notes payable.
_____ 6. Repaid principal on credit loan from the bank.
_____ 7. Paid rent for the following period.
_____ 8. Sold land for cash at its carrying amount.
_____ 9. Made payments to suppliers.
_____ 10. Declared and paid cash dividends to shareholders.

■ LO5-1

Dell Inc.

E5-3   **Determining the Effects of Transactions on the Statement of Cash Flows**

Dell Inc. is a leading manufacturer of personal computers and servers for the business and home markets. For each of the following transactions, indicate whether net cash inflows (outflows) from operating activities (O), investing activities (I), or financing activities (F) are affected and whether the effect is an inflow (+) or an outflow (−), or write NE if the transaction has no effect on cash. (_Hint:_ Determine the journal entry recorded for the transaction. The transaction affects net cash flows if, and only if, the cash account is affected.)

_____ 1. Recorded and paid income taxes to the federal government.
_____ 2. Issued shares for cash.
_____ 3. Paid rent for the following period.
_____ 4. Recorded an adjusting entry for expiration of a prepayment.
_____ 5. Paid cash to purchase new equipment.
_____ 6. Borrowed cash and signed notes payable in five years.
_____ 7. Collected cash from customers.
_____ 8. Purchased raw materials inventory on account.
_____ 9. Recorded and paid salaries to employees.
_____ 10. Purchased new equipment by signing a three-year note.

■ LO5-2

E5-4   **Interpreting Depreciation Expense from a Management Perspective**

QuickServe, a chain of convenience stores, was experiencing some serious cash flow difficulties because of rapid growth. The company did not generate sufficient cash from operating activities to finance its new stores, and creditors were not willing to lend money because the company had not produced any profit for the previous three years. The new controller for QuickServe proposed a reduction in the estimated life of store equipment to increase depreciation expense, saying, "We can improve cash flows from operating activities because depreciation expense is added back on the statement of cash flows." Other executives were not sure that this was a good idea, because the increase in depreciation would make it more difficult to have positive earnings: "Without profit, the bank will never lend us money."

**Required:**

What action would you recommend for QuickServe? Why?

■ LO5-2

E5-5 **Reporting and Interpreting Cash Flows from Operating Activities from an Analyst's Perspective (Indirect Method)**

Capaz Company completed its statement of earnings and statement of financial position for 2018 and provided the following information:

Statement of Earnings for 2018		
Service revenue		$53,000
Expenses		
Salaries	$41,000	
Depreciation	7,000	
Amortization of copyrights	200	
Other expenses	9,700	57,900
Net earnings (loss)		$ (4,900)

Partial Statement of Financial Position	2018	2017
Accounts receivable	$ 8,000	$15,000
Salaries payable	15,000	1,000
Other accrued liabilities	1,000	5,100

In addition, Capaz bought a small service machine for $5,000.

Required:

1. Present the operating activities section of the statement of cash flows for Capaz Company using the indirect method.

2. What were the major reasons that Capaz was able to report a net loss but positive cash flow from operations? Why are the reasons for the difference between cash flow from operations and net earnings important to financial analysts?

■ LO5-2

Apple Inc.

E5-6 **Inferring Statement of Financial Position Changes from the Statement of Cash Flows**

A statement of cash flows for Apple Inc. reported the following information (in millions of U.S. dollars):

Operating Activities	Current Year
Net earnings	$39,510
Changes in operating assets and liabilities:	
Accounts receivable, net	(4,232)
Inventories	(76)
Accounts payable	5,939
Deferred revenue	1,460
Other changes, net	17,112
Net cash provided by operations	$59,713

Required:

Based on the information reported on the statement of cash flows for Apple Inc. determine whether the following accounts increased or decreased during the year: accounts receivable, inventories, accounts payable, and deferred revenue.

■ LO5-2

Colgate-Palmolive

E5-7 **Inferring Statement of Financial Position Changes from the Statement of Cash Flows (Indirect Method)**

A recent statement of cash flows for Colgate-Palmolive reported the following information (in millions of U.S. dollars):

Operating Activities	
Net earnings	$2,339
Depreciation and amortization	442
Cash effect of changes in	
Receivables	(109)
Inventories	(60)
Accounts payable and other accruals	57
Other non-current assets and liabilities	25
Net cash provided by operations	$2,694

Required:

Based on the information reported on the statement of cash flows for Colgate-Palmolive, determine whether the following accounts increased or decreased during the period: receivables, inventories, and accounts payable and other accruals.

LO5-3

PepsiCo

E5-8   **Analyzing Cash Flows from Operating Activities: Interpreting the Quality of Earnings Ratio**

An annual report for PepsiCo contained the following information (in millions of U.S. dollars):

Net earnings	$6,558
Depreciation and amortization	2,625
Increase in accounts and notes receivable	343
Increase in inventories	111
Decrease in prepaid expenses	80
Increase in accounts payables	1,162
Increase in income taxes payable	371
Cash dividends paid	3,730
Repurchase of shares	5,022

Required:

1. Compute the cash flows from operating activities for PepsiCo by using the indirect method.
2. Compute the quality of earnings ratio.
3. What were the major reasons that PepsiCo's quality of earnings ratio did not equal 1.0?

LO5-4,5-6

E5-9   **Reporting and Interpreting Cash Flows from Investing and Financing Activities with Discussion of Management Strategy**

Crispy Chicken Inc. owns or franchises more than 90 fast food outlets. In a recent year, the Crispy Chicken reported the following information (in thousands of Canadian dollars):

Net earnings	$2,657
Purchases of property and equipment	4,310
Increase in accounts payable	1,387
Issue of shares	1,291
Depreciation and amortization	3,248
Proceeds from sale of discontinued operations	780
Repayment of long-term debt	3,077
Increase in accounts receivable	276
Payment of dividends	461

Required:

1. Based on this information, prepare the investing and financing activities sections of the statement of cash flows.
2. What do you think was management's plan for the use of the cash generated by the sale of discontinued operations?

LO5-5

Big Rock Brewery Inc.

E5-10   **Analyzing and Interpreting the Capital Expenditures Ratio**

A recent annual report for Big Rock Brewery Inc. contained the following data for the three most recent years (in thousands of Canadian dollars):

	2014	2013	2012
Cash provided (used) by operating activities	$(3,002)	$7,897	$10,454
Cash used in investing activities	(5,331)	(2,964)	(1,468)
Cash provided (used) by financing activities	7,500	(6,897)	(5,460)

Assume that all investing activities involved acquisition of new property, plant, and equipment.

Required:

1. Compute the capital expenditures ratio for the three-year period in total.
2. What portion of Big Rock Brewery's investing activities was financed from external sources or pre-existing cash balances during the three-year period?

LO5-7   **E5-11**   **Reporting Non-cash Transactions on the Statement of Cash Flows; Interpreting the Effect on the Capital Expenditures Ratio**

An analysis of Martin Corporation's operational asset accounts provided the following information:

a. Acquired a large machine that cost $26,000, paying for it by signing a $15,000, 12 percent interest-bearing note due at the end of two years, and issuing 500 shares with a market value of $22 per share.

b. Acquired a small machine that cost $8,700. Full payment was made by transferring a tract of land that had a carrying amount of $8,700.

Required:

1. Show how this information should be reported on the statement of cash flows.

2. What would be the effect of these transactions on the capital expenditures ratio? How might these transactions distort interpretation of the ratio?

LO5-S1   **E5-12**   **(Appendix 5A) Reporting and Interpreting Cash Flows from Operating Activities with Loss on Sale of Equipment (Indirect Method)**

New Vision Company completed its statement of earnings and statement of financial position for 2018 and provided the following information:

Statement of Earnings for 2018		
Service revenue		$66,000
Expenses:		
Salaries	$42,000	
Depreciation	7,300	
Utilities	7,000	
Loss on sale of equipment	1,700	58,000
Net earnings		$ 8,000

Partial Statement of Financial Position	2018	2017
Accounts receivable	$12,000	$24,000
Salaries payable	19,000	10,000
Other accrued liabilities	5,000	9,000
Land	52,000	57,000

Required:

Present the operating activities section of the statement of cash flows for New Vision Company using the indirect method. Assume a December 31 fiscal year-end.

LO5-S1   **E5-13**   **(Appendix 5A) Computing and Reporting Cash Flow Effects of Sale of Property, Plant, and Equipment**

Perez Construction Inc. provided the following information about the sale of property, plant, and equipment during two recent years:

	Year 1	Year 2
Property, plant, and equipment (at cost)	$75,000	$13,500
Accumulated depreciation on equipment disposed of	40,385	3,773
Gain (loss) on sale of equipment	(16,751)	2,436

Required:

1. Determine the cash flow from the sale of equipment that would be reported in the investing activities section of the statement of cash flows for each year.

2. Perez uses the indirect method for the operating activities section of the statement of cash flows. What amounts related to the sale of equipment would be added or subtracted in the computation of net cash flows from operating activities for each year?

LO5-S2   **E5-14**   **(Appendix 5B) Matching Items Reported on the Statement of Cash Flows to Specific Categories (Direct Method)**

BHP Billiton

The Australian company BHP Billiton is one of the world's biggest mining companies. Some of the items included in its annual consolidated statement of cash flows, presented using the direct method, are listed below.

Indicate whether each item is disclosed in the operating activities (O), investing activities (I), or financing activities (F) section of the statement, or write NA if the item does not appear on the statement:

____ 1. Dividends paid.

____ 2. Income taxes paid.

____ 3. Interest received.

____ 4. Net earnings.

____ 5. Payments for property, plant, and equipment.

____ 6. Payments in the course of operations.

____ 7. Proceeds from ordinary share issues.

____ 8. Proceeds from the sale of property, plant, and equipment.

____ 9. Receipts from customers.

____ 10. Repayment of loans.

LO5-S2   **E5-15**   **(Appendix 5B) Comparing Net Earnings and Cash Flows from Operations**

Paul's Painters, a service organization, prepared the following special report for the month of January 2018:

Service Revenue, Expenses, and Net Earnings		
Service revenue		
Cash services (per cash register tape)	$105,000	
Credit services (per charge bills; not yet collected by end of January)	30,500	$135,500
Expenses		
Salaries and wages expense (paid by cheque)	$ 50,000	
Salaries for January not yet paid	3,000	
Supplies used (taken from stock, purchased for cash during December)	2,000	
Estimated cost of using company-owned truck for the month (depreciation)	500	
Other expenses (paid by cheque)	26,000	81,500
Earnings before income tax		54,000
Income tax expense (not yet paid)		13,500
Net earnings for January		$ 40,500

Required:

1. The owner (who knows little about the financial part of the business) asked you to compute the amount by which cash had increased in January 2018 from the operations of the company. You decided to prepare a detailed report for the owner with the following major captions: cash inflows (collections), cash outflows (payments), and the difference—net increase (or decrease) in cash.

2. Reconcile the difference—net increase (or decrease) in cash—you computed in (1) with the net earnings for January 2018 by filling in the following chart:

Reconciliation with net earnings:	
Net earnings	$40,500
Deduct: Non-cash services	(?)
Add: Non-cash expenses	?
Net increase (decrease) in cash	$29,000

LO5-S2   **E5-16**   **(Appendix 5B) Reporting and Interpreting Cash Flows from Operating Activities from an Analyst's Perspective (Direct Method)**

Refer to the information for Capaz Company in Exercise 5-5.

Required:

1. Present the operating activities section of the statement of cash flows for Capaz Company using the direct method. Assume that other accrued liabilities relate to other expenses on the statement of earnings.

2. What were the major reasons that Capaz reported a net loss but positive cash flow from operations? Why are the reasons for the difference between cash flow from operations and net earnings important to financial analysts?

LO5-S2   E5-17   **(Appendix 5B) Reporting and Interpreting Cash Flows from Operating Activities from an Analyst's Perspective (Direct Method)**

Refer to the following summarized statement of earnings and additional selected information for Huanca Inc.:

Statement of Earnings	
Revenues	$146,500
Cost of sales	55,500
Gross profit	91,000
Salary expense	56,835
Depreciation and amortization	33,305
Other expenses	7,781
Net loss	$ (6,921)
Other information:	
Decrease in accounts receivable	$ 170
Decrease in inventories	643
Increase in prepaid expenses	664
Increase in accounts payable	2,282
Decrease in accrued liabilities	1,142

Required:

1. Based on this information, compute cash flow from operating activities using the direct method. Assume that prepaid expenses and accrued liabilities relate to other expenses.

2. What were the major reasons that Huanca was able to report positive cash flow from operations despite a net loss? Why are the reasons for the difference between cash flows from operations and net earnings important to financial analysts?

LO5-S3   E5-18   **(Appendix 5C) Preparing a Statement of Cash Flows, Indirect Method, Using the T-Account Method**

Golf Universe is a regional retailer of golf equipment. The company reported the following for the current year:

a. Purchased a long-term investment for cash, $15,000.

b. Paid cash dividend, $12,000.

c. Sold equipment for $6,000 cash (cost, $21,000, accumulated depreciation, $15,000).

d. Issued 500 shares at $12 per share cash.

e. Net earnings was $20,200.

f. Depreciation expense was $3,000.

Its comparative statements of financial position are presented below.

	Balances 12/31/2017	Balances 12/31/2016
Cash	$ 19,200	$ 20,500
Accounts receivable	22,000	22,000
Merchandise inventory	75,000	68,000
Investments	15,000	0
Equipment	93,500	114,500
Accumulated depreciation	(20,000)	(32,000)
Total	$204,700	$193,000
Accounts payable	$ 14,000	$ 17,000
Wages payable	1,500	2,500
Income taxes payable	4,500	3,000
Notes payable	54,000	54,000
Contributed capital	106,000	100,000
Retained earnings	24,700	16,500
Total	$204,700	$193,000

Required:

1. Following Appendix 5C, use the T-account approach to prepare the statement of cash flows for the current year.

2. Based on the cash T-account, prepare the statement of cash flows for the current year in proper format.

connect   PROBLEMS

LO5-1,5-2,5-3   P5-1
eXcel

Analyzing the Effects of Transactions on Earnings and Cash Flows, and Reporting Cash Flows from Operating Activities (Indirect Method) (AP5-1)

The following are the summary account balances from the statement of financial position of Granger Inc. as at October 31, 2017. The accounts are followed by a list of transactions for the month of November 2017. The following accounts have normal debit or credit balances. The amounts shown are in millions of dollars:

Cash	$ 88	Accounts payable	$ 315
Accounts receivable	192	Income tax payable	6
Inventories	576	Long-term debt	204
Prepaid expenses	21	Deferred income taxes (credit)	37
Property, plant, and equipment, net	982	Retained earnings	1,210
Other non-current assets	13	Contributed capital	100

The following transactions occurred in November 2017:

a. Purchased new equipment costing $50 by issuing long-term debt.

b. Received $90 on accounts receivable.

c. Received and paid the telephone bills for $1.

d. Earned $100 in sales to customers on account; the cost of sales was $60.

e. Paid employees $10 for salaries earned in November.

f. Paid half of the income taxes payable.

g. Purchased inventory for $23 on account.

h. Prepaid rent for December for a warehouse for $12.

i. Paid $10 of long-term debt and $1 in interest on the debt.

j. Purchased a patent (an intangible asset) for $8 cash.

Required:

1. Prepare a spreadsheet similar to Exhibit 5.4. Show the effects of the November 2017 transactions on the appropriate accounts, and on the three cash flow categories.

2. Prepare a table similar to Exhibit 5.5 showing both the cash and non-cash components of revenues and expenses for November 2017.

3. Prepare the operating activities section of the statement of cash flows for Granger Inc. for November 2017 using the indirect method.

4. Compute the quality of earnings ratio for November 2017, and explain why it is different from 1.0.

LO5-1,5-2,5-3,5-5,5-7
P5-2

Preparing the Statement of Cash Flows (Indirect Method) (AP5-2)

Selected financial information for Frank Corporation is presented below.
Selected 2017 transactions are as follows:

a. Purchased investment securities for $5,000 cash.

b. Borrowed $15,000 on a two-year, 8 percent interest-bearing note.

c. During 2017, sold machinery for its carrying amount; received $11,000 in cash.

d. Purchased machinery for $50,000; paid $9,000 in cash and signed a four-year note payable to the dealer for $41,000.

e. Declared and paid a cash dividend of $10,000 on December 31, 2017.

Selected account balances at December 31, 2016 and 2017, are as follows:

	December 31	
	2017	**2016**
Cash	$76,000	$21,000
Accounts receivable	17,000	12,000
Inventory	52,000	60,000
Accounts payable	7,000	10,000
Accrued wages payable	800	1,000
Income taxes payable	5,000	3,000

One-fourth of the sales and one-third of the purchases were made on credit.

FRANK CORPORATION
Statement of Earnings
For the Year Ended December 31, 2017

Sales revenue		$400,000
Cost of sales		268,000
Gross profit		132,000
Expenses		
Salaries and wages	$51,000	
Depreciation	9,200	
Rent (no accruals)	5,800	
Interest (no accruals)	12,200	
Income tax	11,800	
Total expenses		90,000
Net earnings		$42,000

Required:

1. Prepare a statement of cash flows for the year ended December 31, 2017. Use the indirect method to compute the cash flows from operating activities. Include any additional required note disclosures.
2. Compute and explain the quality of earnings ratio and the capital expenditures ratio.

LO5-2,5-7   **P5-3**   **Preparing a Statement of Cash Flows (Indirect Method)** (AP5-3)

The comparative statements of financial position of Mikos Inc. as at December 31, 2017 and 2018, and its statement of earnings for the year ended December 31, 2018, are presented below:

MIKOS INC.
Comparative Statements of Financial Position
December 31

	2018	2017
Assets		
Cash	$ 9,000	$ 17,000
Short-term investments	45,000	20,000
Accounts receivable	68,000	26,000
Inventories, at cost	54,000	40,000
Prepaid expenses	4,000	6,000
Land	45,000	70,000
Property, plant, and equipment, net	280,000	179,000
Intangible assets	24,000	28,000
	$529,000	$386,000
Liabilities and Shareholders' Equity		
Accounts payable	$ 17,000	$ 40,000
Income tax payable	6,000	1,000
Accrued liabilities	10,000	-0-
Long-term notes payable	10,000	150,000
Contributed capital	200,000	60,000
Retained earnings	186,000	135,000
	$529,000	$386,000

MIKOS INC. Statement of Earnings For the Year Ended December 31, 2018		
Sales		$850,000
Cost of sales	$430,000	
Amortization expense—intangible assets	4,000	
Depreciation expense—property, plant, and equipment	33,000	
Operating expenses	221,000	
Interest expense	12,000	700,000
Earnings before income taxes		150,000
Income tax expense		45,000
Net earnings		$105,000

Additional information is as follows:

a. Land was sold for cash at its carrying amount.

b. The short-term investments will mature in February 2019.

c. Cash dividends were declared and paid in 2018.

d. New equipment with a cost of $166,000 was purchased for cash, and old equipment was sold at its carrying amount.

e. Long-term notes of $10,000 were paid in cash, and notes of $30,000 were converted to shares.

Required:

1. Prepare a statement of cash flows for Mikos Inc. for the year ended December 31, 2018. Use the indirect method to report cash flows from operating activities.

2. Assume the role of a bank loan officer who is evaluating this company's cash flow situation. Analyze the statement of cash flows you prepared in (1.).

3. What additional information does the statement of cash flows provide that is not available on either the statement of financial position or the statement of earnings? Explain.

LO5-2

P5-4   Comparing Cash Flows from Operating Activities (Indirect Method) (AP5-4)

The accountants of National Supermarkets Inc. completed the statement of financial position at December 31, 2016, and the statement of earnings for the quarter ended on that date, and have provided the following information (in thousands of dollars):

Statement of Earnings For the Quarter Ended December 31, 2016		
Sales revenue		$470,200
Expenses		
Cost of sales	$341,600	
Selling, general, and administrative expenses, including depreciation expense of $15,500	109,900	
Interest	1,700	
Income taxes	3,400	456,600
Net earnings		$ 13,600

Selected Statement of Financial Position Accounts		
	December 31, 2016	September 30, 2016
Accounts receivable	$ 79,300	$ 74,000
Inventories	211,700	227,100
Prepaid expenses	7,200	8,700
Accounts payable	112,100	115,000
Accrued liabilities	40,100	38,300
Income taxes payable	3,300	2,200

Required:

1. Prepare the operating activities section of the statement of cash flows for the quarter ended December 31, 2016. Use the indirect method.

2. Companies that use the direct method to report cash flows from operations are also required to disclose in the notes a reconciliation of net earnings to cash flows from operating activities. What additional information does this disclosure requirement provide to users of financial statements? Explain.

LO5-2,5-3,5-5,5-S1

P5-5

(Appendix 5A) Preparing the Statement of Cash Flows with Sale of Equipment (Indirect Method) (AP5-5)

The following information has been reported by Laporte Inc. on its statements of financial position at December 31, 2016 and 2017, and on its statement of earnings for the year ended December 31, 2017. Amounts are in millions of dollars:

Statements of Financial Position		
	2017	**2016**
Cash	$ 90	$ 68
Accounts receivable	34	24
Merchandise inventory	28	32
Long-term investments	–	18
Property, plant, and equipment	196	154
Accumulated depreciation	(78)	(96)
Total assets	$270	$200
Accounts payable	$ 24	$ 38
Income taxes payable	3	4
Long-term borrowings	80	20
Contributed capital	115	100
Retained earnings	48	38
Total liabilities and shareholders' equity	$270	$200

Statement of Earnings	
Sales	$140
Cost of sales	(84)
Gross profit	56
Depreciation expense	(10)
Other operating expenses	(34)
Earnings from operations	12
Gain on sale of investments	6
Loss on sale of equipment	(2)
Earnings before income tax	16
Income tax expense	4
Net earnings	$ 12

Additional information is as follows:

a. Old equipment was sold for cash during 2017. It had an original cost of $40 and an accumulated depreciation of $28.

b. A new building was acquired during the year in exchange for a long-term note for $60, payable in five years. In addition, new equipment was purchased for cash.

Required:

1. Prepare the operating activities section of the statement of cash flows for Laporte Inc. for the year ended December 31, 2017. Use the indirect method to report the cash flow from operations.

2. Prepare the investing activities section of the statement of cash flows for Laporte Inc. for the year ended December 31, 2017.

3. Compute and explain each of the following for the year 2017: (a) quality of earnings ratio, (b) capital expenditures ratio, and (c) free cash flow.

4. Based on your answers to (1.) and (2.) above, determine the net cash flow from financing activities. (*Hint:* This can be done without preparing the financing activities section of the statement.)

5. The president of Laporte Inc., Tanya Turcotte, was provided with a copy of the operating activities section of the statement of cash flows that you prepared in (1.), and made the following comment: "This report is supposed to show operating cash inflows and outflows during the year, but I don't

see how much cash Laporte Inc. received from customers and how much it paid to trade suppliers and for income taxes. Please ask whoever prepared this statement to provide me with these numbers." Based on Tanya's comment, compute the following amounts for 2017:

a. Cash collected from customers.

b. Cash paid to trade suppliers.

c. Cash paid for income taxes.

■ LO5-S1,5-S2   **P5-6**   **(Appendices 5A and 5B) Preparing the Statement of Cash Flows with Sale of Equipment (Direct Method)** (AP5-6)

Refer to the information for Laporte Inc. in P5-5.

Required:

1. Prepare a statement of cash flows for Laporte Inc. for the year ended December 31, 2017. Use the direct method to report cash flows from operating activities.

2. What additional information does the statement of cash flows provide that is not available on either the statement of financial position or the statement of earnings?

■ LO5-S2   **P5-7**   **(Appendix 5B) Preparing a Statement of Cash Flows (Direct Method)** (AP5-7)

Refer to the information for Granger Inc. in P5-1.

Required:

1. Prepare a spreadsheet similar to Exhibit 5.4. Show the effects of the November 2017 transactions on the appropriate accounts, and on the three cash flow categories.

2. Prepare a table similar to Exhibit 5.5 showing both the cash and non-cash components of revenues and expenses for November 2017.

3. Prepare the operating activities section of the statement of cash flows for Granger Inc. for November 2017 using the direct method.

4. As a user of financial statements, would you prefer to see the cash flow from operating activities reported using the direct method or the indirect method? Justify your answer.

■ LO5-S2   **P5-8**   **(Appendix 5B) Preparing a Statement of Cash Flows (Direct Method)** (AP5-8)

Refer to the information for Frank Corporation in P5-2.

Required:

1. Prepare a statement of cash flows for the year ended December 31, 2017. Use the direct method to compute the cash flows from operating activities. Include any additional required note disclosures.

2. Is the direct method of reporting cash flows from operating activities easier to prepare than the indirect method? Explain.

3. Is the direct method of reporting cash flows from operating activities easier to understand than the indirect method? Explain.

■ LO5-S3   **P5-9**   **(Appendix 5C) Preparing a Statement of Cash Flows, Indirect Method, Using the T-Account**
eXcel   **Approach**

Hanks Company is preparing its annual financial statements at December 31, 2017. The statements are complete except for the statement of cash flows. The completed comparative statements of financial position and statement of earnings are summarized as follows:

	2017	2016
Statement of Financial Position at December 31		
Cash	$ 33,000	$ 18,000
Accounts receivable	26,000	28,000
Merchandise inventory	39,000	36,000
Property and equipment (net)	80,000	72,000
	$178,000	$154,000
Accounts payable	$ 27,000	$ 21,000
Wages payable	1,500	1,000
Note payable, long term	42,000	48,000
Contributed capital	78,500	60,000
Retained earnings	29,000	24,000
	$178,000	$154,000

Statement of Earnings for 2017	
Sales	$ 80,000
Cost of sales	(43,000)
Expenses	(30,000)
Net earnings	$ 7,000

Additional data:

a. Bought equipment for cash, $12,000.

b. Paid $6,000 on the long-term note payable.

c. Sold unissued shares for $18,500 cash.

d. Declared and paid a $2,000 cash dividend.

e. Incurred the following expenses: depreciation, $4,000; wages, $12,000; taxes, $2,000; and other, $12,000.

Required:

1. Prepare statement of cash flows T-accounts using the indirect method to report cash flows from operating activities.

2. Prepare the statement of cash flows.

3. Prepare a schedule of non-cash investing and financing activities if necessary.

ALTERNATE PROBLEMS

LO5-1,5-2,5-3   AP5-1   Analyzing the Effects of Transactions on Earnings and Cash Flows, and Reporting Cash Flows from Operating Activities (Indirect Method) (P5-1)

Ingersol Construction Supply Company is preparing its annual financial statements at December 31, 2018. The statements are complete except for the statement of cash flows. The completed comparative statement of financial position and statement of earnings are summarized as follows:

Statement of Financial Position at December 31	2018	2017
Cash	$ 34,000	$ 29,000
Accounts receivable	45,000	28,000
Merchandise inventory	32,000	38,000
Property and equipment	121,000	100,000
Less: Accumulated depreciation	(30,000)	(25,000)
	$202,000	$170,000
Accounts payable	$ 36,000	$ 27,000
Wages payable	2,200	1,400
Note payable, long term	40,000	46,000
Contributed capital	86,600	70,600
Retained earnings	37,200	25,000
	$202,000	$170,000

Statement of Earnings for 2015	
Sales	$135,000
Cost of sales	70,000
Other expenses	37,800
Net earnings	$ 27,200

The following hypothetical transactions occurred in January 2019.

a. Sold merchandise to customers, receiving $36,000 in trade receivables and $4,000 in cash. The cost of sales was $20,000.

b. Purchased new equipment costing $21,000; paid $5,000 cash and signed a long-term note for the remainder.

c. Spent $1,200 cash to maintain and repair facilities and equipment during the month.

d. Paid $29,000 on accounts payable.

e. Placed an order with suppliers for merchandise inventory costing $7,200.

f. Collected $40,000 from customers on account.

g. Paid $6,000 on long-term notes.

h. Paid $3,000 cash to rent equipment, with $2,500 for rental this month and the rest for rent for the first few days in February.

i. Issued new shares for $16,000 for cash.

j. Dividends of $15,000 were declared and paid in cash.

k. Other expenses included depreciation, $5,000; wages, $10,000; taxes, $6,000; and other, $6,800.

l. Accounts payable includes only inventory purchases made on credit. Because there are no liability accounts relating to taxes or other expenses, assume that these expenses were fully paid in cash.

Required:

1. Prepare a spreadsheet similar to Exhibit 5.4. Show the effects of the January transactions on the appropriate accounts, and on the three cash flow categories.

2. Prepare a table similar to Exhibit 5.5 showing both the cash and non-cash components of revenues and expenses for January 2019.

3. Prepare the operating activities section of the statement of cash flows for the company for January 2019 using the indirect method.

4. Compute the quality of earnings ratio for January 2019, and explain why it is different from 1.0.

LO5-1,5-2,5-3,5-5,5-7   **Preparing the Statement of Cash Flows (Indirect Method)** (P5-2)

AP5-2   Stonewall Company was organized on January 1, 2018. During the year ended December 31, 2018, the company provided the following data:

Statement of Earnings	
Sales revenue	$ 80,000
Cost of sales	(35,000)
Depreciation expense	(4,000)
Other expenses	(32,000)
Net earnings	$ 9,000
Statement of Financial Position	
Cash	$ 48,000
Accounts receivable	18,000
Merchandise inventory	15,000
Machinery (net)	25,000
Total assets	$106,000
Accounts payable	$ 10,000
Accrued liabilities	21,000
Dividends payable	2,000
Note payable, short term	15,000
Contributed capital	54,000
Retained earnings	4,000
Total liabilities and shareholders' equity	$106,000

Analysis of selected accounts and transactions follows:

a. Issued 3,000 shares for cash, at $18 per share.

b. Borrowed $15,000 on a one-year, 8 percent interest-bearing note; the note was dated June 1, 2018.

c. Paid $29,000 to purchase machinery.

d. Purchased merchandise for resale at a cost of $50,000; paid $40,000 cash and the balance on account.

e. Exchanged plant machinery with a carrying amount of $2,000 for office machines with a market value of $2,000.

f. Declared a cash dividend of $5,000 on December 15, 2018, payable to shareholders on January 15, 2016.

g. Because this is the first year of operations, all account balances are zero at the beginning of the year; therefore, the changes in the account balances are equal to the ending balances.

Required:

1. Prepare a statement of cash flows for the year ended December 31, 2018. Use the indirect method to report cash flows from operating activities.

2. Compute and explain the quality of earnings ratio and the capital expenditures ratio.

■ LO5-2,5-3   **AP5-3**   **Preparing the Statement of Cash Flows (Indirect Method)** (P5-3)

The comparative statements of financial position for Marwa Ltd. at December 31, 2018 and 2017, are presented below:

Comparative Statements of Financial Position As at December 31		
	2018	**2017**
Cash	$ 10,000	$ 56,500
Accounts receivable	35,000	20,000
Merchandise inventory	10,000	17,500
Prepaid expenses	4,000	5,000
Property, plant, and equipment, net	1,062,000	646,000
Total assets	$1,121,000	$745,000
Accounts payable	$ 23,500	$ 19,500
Income taxes payable	6,000	14,000
Note payable, due Nov. 1, 2019	22,500	52,500
Contributed capital	180,000	150,000
Retained earnings	889,000	509,000
Total liabilities and shareholders' equity	$1,121,000	$745,000

The statement of earnings for 2018 showed the following information:

Sales	$2,000,000
Gross profit	1,300,000
Operating expenses (includes depreciation of $45,000)	600,000
Interest expense	15,000
Income tax expense	160,000

As well, property, plant, and equipment were acquired for $475,000 cash during 2018. Also during 2018, property, plant, and equipment were sold at their carrying amount in exchange for cash.

Required:

1. Prepare a complete statement of cash flows for Marwa Ltd. for the year 2018. Use the indirect method for the operating section.

2. Compute the following amounts:
   a. Cash collected from customers in 2018.
   b. Cash paid to suppliers of merchandise inventory in 2018.

3. Calculate and briefly explain (*a*) the quality of earnings ratio, and (*b*) free cash flow.

■ LO5-2   **AP5-4**   **Comparing Cash Flows from Operating Activities (Indirect Method)** (P5-4)

Zena Company's accountants just completed the financial statements for the year and have provided the following information (in thousands):

Statement of Earnings for 2017		
Sales revenue		$20,600
Expenses and losses:		
Cost of sales	$9,000	
Depreciation	2,000	
Salaries	5,000	
Rent	2,500	
Insurance	800	
Utilities	700	
Interest	600	20,600
Net earnings		$ 0

Selected Statement of Financial Position Accounts		
	2017	**2016**
Merchandise inventory	$ 82	$ 60
Accounts receivable	380	450
Accounts payable	240	210
Salaries payable	29	20
Rent payable	2	6
Prepaid rent	2	7
Prepaid insurance	14	5

In addition, the company signed long-term notes for $20,000 during the year.

Required:

1. Prepare the operating activities section of the statement of cash flows for 2017 by using the indirect method.

2. As a financial analyst, would you prefer to see the cash flow from operations reported using the direct method or the indirect method? Justify your answer.

3. As the accountant who prepares the company's statement of cash flows, would you prefer to use the direct or the indirect method to report the cash flow from operations? Explain.

■ LO5-2,5-3,5-4,5-5,5-S1   **(Appendix 5A) Preparing the Statement of Cash Flows with Sale of Equipment (Indirect**
AP5-5   **Method)** (P5-5)

Mary Wong, the sole shareholder and manager of Kitchenware Inc., has approached you and asked you to prepare a statement of cash flows for her company. The company sells kitchen utensils that are used in most households. Mary is worried about the meeting that she has scheduled in two weeks with a lending officer of her bank. It is time for a review of the company's loan from the bank.

Mary provided you with the following condensed financial statements for the fiscal years ended December 31, 2016 and 2017. She assures you that the financial statements are free of any omissions or misstatements, and that they conform to IFRS.

KITCHENWARE INC.		
Statements of Financial Position as at December 31		
(in thousands of dollars)		
	2017	**2016**
Assets		
Current assets		
Cash	$ 1,000	$ 3,400
Short-term investments	2,000	8,000
Trade accounts receivable	56,300	10,600
Inventories	10,000	30,000
Furniture and fixtures, at cost	59,000	26,000
Less: Accumulated depreciation	(24,000)	(12,000)
Investments	2,000	3,000
Total assets	$106,300	$69,000
Liabilities and Shareholders' Equity		
Current liabilities		
Bank loan	$ 18,000	$ 8,000
Trade accounts payable	17,000	13,100
Dividends payable	-0-	600
Total current liabilities	35,000	21,700
Non-current liabilities		
Mortgage notes payable	28,000	-0-
Total liabilities	63,000	21,700
Shareholders' equity		
Contributed capital	24,000	22,000
Retained earnings	19,300	25,300
Total shareholders' equity	43,300	47,300
Total liabilities and shareholders' equity	$106,300	$69,000

KITCHENWARE INC.		
Statement of Earnings		
For the Years Ended December 31		
	2017	**2016**
Sales revenue	$980,000	$ 880,000
Cost of sales	(640,000)	(560,000)
Gross profit	340,000	320,000
Operating expenses:		
Depreciation	(15,200)	(12,000)
Selling and general	(298,800)	(288,000)
Earnings from operations	26,000	20,000
Interest expense	(9,600)	(3,200)
Loss on sale of furniture	(1,200)	-0-
Gain on sale of investments	800	-0-
Earnings before income taxes	6,000	16,800
Income tax expense (@ 25%)	(4,000)	(4,200)
Net earnings	$ 12,000	$ 12,600

Additional information is as follows:

a. During 2017, the company sold old furniture with an original cost of $5,000 and $3,200 of accumulated depreciation up to the date of sale.

b. During 2017, the company sold one of the non-current investments that had cost $1,000. The gain on this sale is reported on the statement of earnings.

c. The company considers short-term investments as cash equivalents.

Required:

1. Prepare a partial statement of cash flows for Kitchenware Inc. showing the operating activities section for the year ended December 31, 2017. The company uses the indirect method to report cash flows from operations.

2. Compute the following amounts:

   a. Cash collected from customers, assuming that 90 percent of the sales are on credit.

   b. Cash paid to trade suppliers of merchandise.

   c. Cash received for sale of old furniture.

3. Prepare the investing activities section of the statement of cash flows for Kitchenware Inc. for the year ended December 31, 2017.

4. Compute and explain (a) the quality of earnings ratio, and (b) free cash flow.

5. In an effort to improve the company's financial performance, Mary proposed that the furniture and fixtures be depreciated over a longer period. This change will decrease depreciation expense by $2,000 in 2016 and by $4,000 in 2017. As a professional accountant, would this proposed change be acceptable to you? Explain.

LO5-S1,5-S2 **AP5-6** **(Appendices 5A and 5B) Preparing the Statement of Cash Flows with Sale of Equipment (Direct Method)** (P5-6)
Refer to the information for Kitchenware Inc. in AP5-5.

Required:

1. Prepare a statement of cash flows for Kitchenware Inc. for the year ended December 31, 2018. Use the direct method to report cash flows from operating activities.

2. Discuss the importance of the statement of cash flows to users of financial statements. What additional information does it provide that is not reported in the other financial statements? Explain by referring to the statement that you prepared in (1.) above.

LO5-S2 **AP5-7** **(Appendix 5B) Preparing a Statement of Cash Flows (Direct Method)** (P5-7)
Refer to the information for Ingersol Construction Supply Company in AP5-1.

Required:

1. Prepare a spreadsheet similar to Exhibit 5.4. Show the effects of the January 2019 transactions on the appropriate accounts, and on the three cash flow categories.

2. Prepare a table similar to Exhibit 5.5 showing both the cash and non-cash components of revenues and expenses for January 2019.

3. Prepare the operating activities section of the statement of cash flows for Ingersol Construction Supply Company for January 2019 using the direct method.

4. As a user of financial statements, would you prefer to see the cash flow from operating activities reported using the direct method or the indirect method? Justify your answer.

LO5-S2   **AP5-8**   **(Appendix 5B) Preparing a Statement of Cash Flows (Direct Method)** (P5-8)
Refer to the information for Stonewall Company in AP5-2.

Required:

1. Prepare a statement of cash flows for the year ended December 31, 2018. Use the direct method to compute the cash flows from operating activities. Include any additional required note disclosures.

2. Is the direct method of reporting cash flows from operating activities easier to prepare than the indirect method? Explain.

3. Is the direct method of reporting cash flows from operating activities easier to understand than the indirect method? Explain.

---

connect   CASES AND PROJECTS

FINDING AND INTERPRETING FINANCIAL INFORMATION

LO5-2,5-4,5-6   **CP5-1**   **Finding Financial Information**

Go to *Connect* for the financial statements of Sears Canada Inc. and related notes.

Required:

1. Which of the two basic reporting approaches for the cash flows from operating activities did the company adopt?

2. Did the company pay for incomes taxes during the current year? If so, how much did it pay?

3. Explain why the depreciation and amortization expense of $48 million is added in the reconciliation of net loss to net cash provided by operating activities in the statement of cash flows.

4. Has the company paid cash dividends during the last two years? How do you know?

5. What was the amount of free cash flow for the year ended December 30, 2015?

LO5-2,5-4,5-6   **CP5-2**   **Finding Financial Information**

Canadian Tire
Corporation

Refer to the financial statements of Canadian Tire Corporation and related notes given in Appendix A of this book.

Required:

1. What were the three largest adjustments to reconcile net earnings from operations to the net cash provided by operating activities? Explain the direction of the effect of each adjustment in the reconciliation.

2. What were Canadian Tire Corporation's major uses of cash over the years 2014 and 2015? What were its major sources of cash for these activities?

3. What was the amount of free cash flow for the year ended January 2, 2016? What does this imply about the company's financial flexibility?

4. Canadian Tire reported a large amount of cash and cash equivalents at January 2, 2016. What type of assets does the company consider as cash equivalents?

LO5-3,5-5   **CP5-3**   **Comparing Companies within an Industry**

Canadian Tire
Corporation vs.
Sears Canada Inc.

Refer to the financial statements of Canadian Tire Corporation (Appendix A) and Sears Canada Inc. (on*Connect*), and to the Industry Ratio Report (Appendix B on *Connect*).

Required:

1. Compute the quality of earnings ratio for both companies for the current year. How might the difference in their sales growth rates explain the difference in the ratio? Sales growth rate = (Current year's sales − Prior year's sales) ÷ Prior year's sales.

2. Compare the quality of earnings ratio for both companies to the industry average. Are these companies producing more or less cash from operating activities relative to net earnings than the average company in the industry?

3. Compute the capital expenditures ratio for both companies for the current year. Compare their abilities to finance purchases of property, plant, and equipment; acquisition of intangible assets; and acquisition of other businesses with cash provided by operating activities.

FINANCIAL REPORTING AND ANALYSIS CASES

LO5-2,5-3,5-4,5-5,5-6

CP5-4

Big Rock Brewery Inc.

Using Financial Reports: Analyzing the Statement of Cash Flows of Big Rock Brewery Inc. Big Rock Brewery Inc. is a leading Canadian craft brewer that produces premium, all-natural, craft beers. Its statements of cash flows for fiscal years 2015, 2014, and 2013 are shown below:

BIG ROCK BREWERY INC. Consolidated Statements of Cash Flows For the years ended December 30 (in thousands of Canadian dollars)	2015	2014	2013
OPERATING ACTIVITIES			
Net income (loss) for the year	$(1,075)	$ 624	$2,551
Items not affecting cash:			
Depreciation and amortization	2,388	2,072	3,157
Loss (gain) on sale of assets	(111)	63	(13)
Share-based compensation	90	(190)	640
Deferred income tax expense (recovery)	(151)	46	(1,586)
Change in non-cash working capital related to operations			
Accounts payable and accrued liabilities	2,764	(4,711)	1,649
Inventory	(1,092)	(871)	884
Accounts receivable	(748)	(120)	1,005
Prepaid expenses	(904)	85	(390)
Cash provided (used) by operating activities	1,161	(3,002)	7,897
FINANCING ACTIVITIES			
Dividend payments	(1,375)	(5,181)	(4,855)
Proceeds from long-term debt	3,889	—	—
Increase in bank indebtedness	1,247	—	—
Principal repayments of long-term debt	—	—	(2,042)
Proceeds from share issuance	—	12,681	—
Cash provided by (used in) financing activities	3,761	7,500	(6,897)
INVESTING ACTIVITIES			
Purchase of property, plant, and equipment	(5,701)	(5,503)	(2,992)
Purchase of intangibles	(325)	(83)	(6)
Proceeds from sale of equipment	160	255	34
Cash used in investing activities	(5,866)	(5,331)	(2,964)
Net decrease in cash	(944)	(833)	(1,964)
Cash, beginning of year	1,484	2,317	4,281
Cash, end of year	540	1,484	2,317

Required:

1. The cash flows from operating activities show that depreciation and amortization are added to net income (loss) for the year. Is depreciation and amortization a source of cash? Explain.

2. Was the cash collected from customers during fiscal year 2015 higher or lower than Big Rock's sales revenue for that year? Explain.

3. Did Big Rock expand during 2014 and 2015? If so, how did the company pay for its expansion? Explain.

4. Compute and analyze Big Rock's quality of earnings ratio, capital expenditures ratio, and free cash flow for 2014 and 2015.

5. Analyze the company's pattern of cash flows from operating, investing, and financing activities over the three years. What conclusion can you draw from the changing pattern of cash flows? Explain.

6. Obtain a copy of Big Rock's statement of cash flows for the year 2016 through the company's website (www.sunrype.com) or the SEDAR service (www.sedar.com). Did the company's cash flow situation in 2016 improve or deteriorate relative to previous years? Explain.

7. As a potential investor in Big Rock's shares, what additional information would you need before making your decision as to whether or not to invest in this company's shares?

LO5-2,5-3,5-4,5-5,5-6

CP5-5

BlackBerry Limited

Using Financial Reports: Analyzing Blackberry's Statement of Cash Flows

Blackberry Limited is a leading designer, manufacturer, and marketer of innovative wireless solutions for the worldwide mobile communications market. Its products are used around the world and include the BlackBerry wireless platform, software development tools, and software/hardware licensing agreements. Access the company's latest annual financial statements either through the company's website (http://ca.blackberry.com/company/investors.html) or the SEDAR service (www.sedar.com) and obtain a copy of its statement of cash flows.

Required:

1. Have BlackBerry's accounts receivable increased or decreased during its most recent fiscal year? By how much have its accounts receivable changed during the past three years? Explain.

2. How does the change in inventory during the last fiscal year affect cash? Explain.

3. What conclusions can you derive by examining the pattern of the company's cash flows during these three years?

4. How did the company finance the acquisition of non-current assets during the last two fiscal years? Explain.

5. What additional information does the statement of cash flows provide that is not available on either the statement of financial position or the statement of earnings?

CRITICAL THINKING CASES

LO5-1,5-2,5-6　**CP5-6**

Enron

Ethical Decision Making: A Real-Life Example

Enron Corporation was a major U.S. energy company. Its executives engaged in a systematic accounting fraud that resulted in the company's bankruptcy in 2001. In a February 19, 2004, press release, the U.S. Securities and Exchange Commission described a number of fraudulent transactions that Enron executives concocted in an effort to meet the company's financial targets. One particularly well-known scheme was called the "Nigerian barge" transaction, which took place in the fourth quarter of 1999. According to court documents, Enron arranged to sell three electricity-generating power barges moored off the coast of Nigeria. The "buyer" was the investment banking firm Merrill Lynch. Although Enron reported this transaction as a sale in its statement of earnings, it turns out this was no ordinary sale. Merrill Lynch didn't really want the barges and had only agreed to buy them because Enron guaranteed, in a secret side deal, that it would arrange for the barges to be bought back from Merrill Lynch within six months of the initial transaction. In addition, Enron promised to pay Merrill Lynch a hefty fee for doing the deal. In an interview on National Public Radio on August 17, 2002, Carl Levin, a senator from Michigan, declared, "[T]he case of the Nigerian barge transaction was, by any definition, a loan."

Required:

1. Discuss whether the Nigerian barge transaction should have been considered a loan rather than a sale. As part of your discussion, consider the following questions. Doesn't the Merrill Lynch payment to Enron at the time of the initial transaction automatically make it a sale, not a loan? Which aspects of the transaction are similar to a loan? Which aspects suggest that the criteria for revenue recognition (discussed in Chapter 3) were not fulfilled?

2. The effect of recording the transaction as a sale rather than a loan is fairly clear: Enron was able to boost its revenues and net earnings. What is somewhat less obvious, but nearly as important, are the effects on the statement of cash flows. Describe how recording the transaction as a sale rather than as a loan would change the statement of cash flows.

3. How would the two different statements of cash flows (described in your response to (2.)) affect financial statement users?

FINANCIAL REPORTING AND ANALYSIS TEAM PROJECT

LO5-1,5-2,5-3,5-4,5-5, 5-6   **CP5-7**

Team Project: Analyzing Cash Flows

As a team, select an industry to analyze. A list of companies classified by industry can be obtained by accessing www.fpinfomart.ca and then choosing Companies by Industry. You can also find a list of industries and companies within each industry via http://ca.finance.yahoo.com/investing (click on Order Annual Reports under Tools). Each group member should acquire the annual report for a different publicly traded company in the industry. (Library files, the SEDAR service at www.sedar.com, and the company's website are good sources.)

Required:

On an individual basis, each team member should write a short report answering the following questions about the selected company. Discuss any patterns across the three companies that your team observes. Then, as a team, write a short report comparing and contrasting your companies.

1. Which of the two basic reporting approaches for cash flows from operating activities did the company adopt?

2. What is the quality of earnings ratio for the most current year? What were the major causes of differences between net earnings and cash flow from operations?

3. What is the capital expenditures ratio for the three-year period presented in total? How is the company financing its capital expenditures?

4. What portion of the cash from operations in the current year is being paid to shareholders in the form of dividends?

connect   CONTINUING CASE

LO5-1,5-2,5-4,5-6

CC5-1

Preparing the Statement of Cash Flows (Indirect Method)

Presented in alphabetical order below are the line items including the subtotals and totals from Pool Corporation's recent statement of cash flows prepared using the indirect method. Using these line items, prepare Pool Corporation's statement of cash flows, in good form, for the year ended December 31 following the format presented in Exhibit 5.1.

Accounts payable	$ 6,402
Accrued liabilities and other current liabilities	20,682
Acquisition of businesses	(5,934)
Amortization	1,559
Cash and cash equivalents at beginning of year	9,721
Cash and cash equivalents at end of year	17,487
Change in cash and cash equivalents	7,766
Depreciation expense	9,746
Loss on sale of property and equipment	263
Net cash provided by operating activities	75,103
Net cash used in financing activities	(41,759)
Net cash used in investing activities	(25,578)
Net earnings	71,993
Other financing activities	944
Other operating assets	8,635
Payment of cash dividends	(26,470)
Payments on long-term debt and other long-term liabilities	(149)
Payments on revolving line of bank credit	(700,749)
Prepaid expenses	(2,951)
Proceeds from revolving line of bank credit	749,349
Proceeds from issuance of shares under share-based compensation plans	13,085
Product inventories	(35,339)
Purchases of property and equipment	(19,844)
Repurchase of the company's shares	(77,769)
Receivables	(5,887)
Sale of property and equipment	200

SOLUTIONS TO SELF-STUDY QUIZZES

Self-Study Quiz 5-1

a. I; *b.* O; *c.* O; *d.* I; *e.* O; *f.* O; *g.* O; *h.* O; *i.* F; *j.* O

Self-Study Quiz 5-2

a. −; *b.* 0; *c.* +; *d.* +; *e.* +; *f.* −

Self-Study Quiz 5-3

AIG's pattern of cash flows in year 1 is similar to pattern 3, which indicates that the company is downsizing. In year 2, the company's cash flows are similar to pattern 2, suggesting that AIG is a mature, successful firm that is using cash generated from operations to buy non-current assets and to reduce its debt or distribute cash dividends to shareholders. Finally, the pattern of cash flows in year 3 (pattern 3) indicates that the company has downsized its operations.

Self-Study Quiz 5-4

a. NA; *b.* NA; *c.* +; *d.* NA; *e.* −; *f.* −

ENDNOTES

1. Original maturity means original maturity to the entity holding the investment. For example, both a three-month Treasury bill and a three-year Treasury note purchased three months from maturity qualify as cash equivalents. A Treasury note purchased three years ago, however, does not become a cash equivalent when its remaining maturity is three months.

2. National Beverage Corp. is a U.S. company. Even though the company uses U.S. generally accepted accounting principles instead of IFRS for financial reporting purposes, the main issues covered in this chapter are not affected by differences between US GAAP and IFRS.

3. Certain non-current assets, such as long-term receivables from customers, and non-current liabilities, such as post-retirement obligations to employees, are considered to be operating items. These items are covered in other accounting courses.

4. Examples of the accounts excluded are dividends payable, short-term borrowing (or bank indebtedness), and current portion of long-term debt (representing long-term debt with an original term longer than one year that is due within one year of the statement date).

5. Adding back depreciation and amortization to net earnings does not mean that this expense is a source of cash. In fact, depreciation and amortization are the result of a process of allocating the cost of assets over time, regardless of the timing of payment for the assets.

6. Gains and losses on sales of equipment and investments are dealt with in a similar manner and are discussed in Appendix 5A. Other similar additions and subtractions are discussed in other accounting courses.

7. Certain non-current assets, such as long-term receivables from customers, and non-current liabilities, such as post-retirement obligations to employees, are considered to be operating items. These items are covered in other accounting courses.

8. The amount of cash collected from customers is the same, regardless of the mix of cash sales and credit sales. To be sure, assume that sales are 20 percent cash and 80 percent on account, and compute the amount of cash collected from customers during the period.

9. When a loss is reported, a more negative ratio indicates greater ability to finance the company from operations.

10. An alternative definition that does not subtract dividends but adds interest after tax is often called the free cash flow of the firm. Other variations of this definition are sometimes reported by companies in the management discussion and analysis sections of their annual reports.

11. The disposal of assets and the resulting gains or losses are discussed in detail in Chapter 8.

12. We assume that all sales are made on account. However, the amount of cash collected from customers is the same, regardless of the mix of cash and credit sales. To be sure, assume that sales are 20 percent cash and 80 percent on account, and compute the amount of cash collected from customers during the period. You can use other percentages as well.

13. We assume that all purchases are made on account. However, the amount of cash paid to suppliers is the same regardless of the mix of cash and credit purchases. To be sure, assume that purchases are 10 percent cash and 90 percent on account, and compute the amount of cash paid to suppliers during the period. You can use other percentages as well.

Reporting and Interpreting Sales Revenue, Receivables, and Cash

6

After studying this chapter, you should be able to do the following:

GILDAN®

Focus Company: **Gildan Activewear Inc.**

BUILDING BRANDS TO BUILD GROSS PROFIT: MANAGING PRODUCT DEVELOPMENT, PRODUCTION, AND WORKING CAPITAL

Over the past several years, casual wear has become increasingly acceptable in the workplace as employers adopt flexible dress codes. Gildan Activewear Inc. (www.gildan.com), based in Montréal, Québec, has become a significant producer and marketer of high-quality casual wear, high-performance sports shirts, socks and sheer hosiery, and women's intimate apparel as well as of T-Shirts. More recently, Gildan has engaged in strategic pricing in one of the two business segments, printwear, which is marketed in North America, Europe, and the Asia-Pacific region. This segment designs, manufactures, and distributes undecorated activewear in large quantities, and Gildan has lowered prices to give wholesale purchasers the benefits of cost efficiencies achieved in the company. Growth in the second operating segment, branded apparel, has resulted largely from strategic acquisition of manufacturers of well-known brands of socks, underwear, and other activewear. Gildan's markets are essentially high-volume, basic, and frequently replenished non-fashion apparel that can be purchased in retail stores and at corporate, tourist, entertainment, and sports events.

Gildan started as a family operation and grew to become a publicly traded company in both Canada and the United States. Gildan's competitive strengths include its expertise in building and operating large-scale, vertically integrated, and strategically located manufacturing hubs. Gildan is successful in part because of its ongoing investments in manufacturing, which allow it to operate efficiently to reduce costs and offer competitive pricing, consistent product quality, and a reliable supply chain to service replenishment programs with short production/delivery cycle times.

Gildan has developed a significant manufacturing infrastructure in two main hubs in Central America (primarily Honduras) and the Caribbean Basin (Dominican Republic). Textiles produced in these two hubs are assembled there as well as in both Nicaragua and Haiti. Activewear is also produced and assembled in Bangladesh. Gildan sources its yarn primarily from U.S. third-party yarn suppliers as well as from its own yarn-spinning facilities in Georgia and North Carolina. With control over every important element in its supply chain, Gildan effectively profits from reliable and on-time delivery of consistent-quality products at a low cost.

Gildan's sales grew from US$224 million for fiscal year 1999 to US$2,959 million for its fiscal year ended January 3, 2016.[1] Such growth in sales could not happen if the company did not pursue specific business strategies to produce quality products, and market them effectively to targeted customers. The company's focus on low-cost manufacturing of premium-quality casual wear and its marketing philosophy of controlled distribution have been important factors in its success. The company's management recognized that its dedication to being the lowest-cost producer and leading marketer of branded basic casual wear is based on a growth strategy that comprises specific objectives, such as (1) maximizing printwear market penetration and opportunities, (2) continuing its penetration of the retail market as a full-line supplier of branded family apparel, (3) increasing capacity to support planned sales growth and generate manufacturing and distribution cost reductions, and (4) pursuing complementary acquisition opportunities. These objectives and related action plans are aimed at increasing net sales and/or decreasing the cost of sales, thereby increasing gross profit.

UNDERSTANDING THE BUSINESS

The success of each element of Gildan's strategy can be seen in the information presented in the statement of earnings excerpt in Exhibit 6.1. Net sales (revenue) is reported first, and cost of sales (cost of goods sold, cost of products sold) is set out separately from the remaining expenses. The statement of earnings then reports *gross profit (gross margin)*, which is net sales minus cost of sales.

Exhibit **6.1**

Net Sales and Gross Profit on the Statement of Earnings

REAL-WORLD EXCERPT

Gildan Activewear

ANNUAL REPORT

	2015 (15 months)	2014
Net sales	$2,959,238	$2,359,994
Cost of sales	2,229,130	1,701,311
Gross profit	730,108	658,683

*Beginning in fiscal 2015, Gildan changed the end of its fiscal year from the first Sunday following September 28 of each year to the Sunday closest to December 31 of each year because the company's business planning cycle became more aligned with the calendar year. As a result, fiscal 2015 was a transition year and included 15 months of operations, beginning on October 6, 2014, and ending on January 3, 2016. Fiscal years longer than 12 months are unusual.

Source: Gildan Activewear, Annual Report 2015.

Planning Gildan's growth strategy requires careful coordination of sales and production activities, as well as cash collection from customers. Much of this coordination involves judicious use of credit card and sales discounts, as well as prudent management of sales returns and bad debts. These activities affect *net sales revenue* on the statement of earnings and *cash* and *accounts receivable* on the statement of financial position, which are the focus of this chapter. We will introduce the gross profit percentage as a basis for evaluating changes in gross profit, as well as the receivables turnover ratio as a measure of the efficiency of credit granting and collection activities. But the cash collected from customers is a tempting target for fraud and embezzlement;

therefore, we will discuss some common controls integral to most accounting systems to minimize these misdeeds.

Lenders, shareholders, and analysts carefully monitor net sales and receivables because of their importance as predictors of the success of companies. Their importance is supported by the fact that the majority of shareholder lawsuits and enforcement actions by securities regulators against companies for misleading financial statements relate to these accounts.

ORGANIZATION OF THE CHAPTER

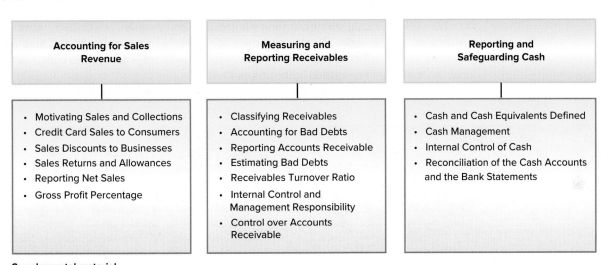

Supplemental material:
Appendix 6A: Applying the Revenue Principle in Special Circumstances

ACCOUNTING FOR SALES REVENUE

As indicated in Chapter 3, the *revenue recognition principle* requires that revenues be recorded when the following conditions are met: (1) the entity has transferred to the buyer the significant risks and rewards of ownership of the goods, (2) the entity retains neither continuing managerial involvement to the degree usually associated with ownership nor effective control over the goods sold, (3) the amount of revenue can be measured reliably, (4) it is probable that the economic benefits associated with the transaction will flow to the entity, and (5) the costs incurred or to be incurred with respect to the transaction can be measured reliably.[2] For sellers of goods, these criteria are most often met and sales revenue recorded when title and risks of ownership pass to the buyer.

The point at which title (ownership) changes hands is determined by the shipping terms in the sales contract:

- When goods are shipped *FOB (free on board) shipping point*, title changes hands at shipment, and the buyer normally pays for shipping.

- When they are shipped *FOB destination point*, title changes hands on delivery, and the seller normally pays for shipping.

Revenues from goods sold FOB shipping point are normally recognized at shipment. Revenues from goods sold FOB destination point are normally recognized at delivery.

Service companies most often record sales revenue when they have provided services to the buyer. Companies disclose the specific revenue recognition policies they use in the note to their financial statements titled "Significant Accounting Policies." Gildan reported the following in its accounting policies:

LO6-1

Apply the revenue recognition principle to determine the accepted time to record sales revenue for typical retailers, wholesalers, manufacturers, and service companies.

REAL-WORLD EXCERPT

Gildan Activewear

ANNUAL REPORT

NOTES TO CONSOLIDATED FINANCIAL STATEMENTS

1. Significant Accounting Policies

(s) Revenue recognition:

Revenue is recognized upon shipment of products to customers, since title passes upon shipment, and to the extent that the selling price is fixed or determinable. At the time of sale, estimates are made for customer price discounts and volume rebates based on the terms of existing programs. Sales are recorded net of these program costs and estimated sales returns, which are based on historical experience, current trends and other known factors, and exclude sales taxes. New sales incentive programs which relate to sales made in a prior period are recognized at the time the new program is introduced.

Source: Gildan Activewear, Annual Report 2015.

Like Gildan, many manufacturers, wholesalers, and retailers recognize revenue at shipment. This is when the title and risks of ownership pass to the buyer. Auditors expend a lot of effort to ensure that revenue recognition rules are applied consistently and revenues are recognized in the proper period.

The appropriate *amount* of revenue to record is the *cash-equivalent sales price.*

ACCELERATED REVENUE RECOGNITION IS A MATTER OF JUDGMENT   A QUESTION OF ACCOUNTABILITY

Until recently, the premature recognition of revenue was one of the most common reasons the U.S. Securities and Exchange Commission (SEC) would pursue fraud enforcement action against corporations. The issue arises because companies report revenue before it has been earned.

The new revenue recognition standard, however, does not strictly prohibit accelerated revenue recognition on consumer contracts. A familiar example is the sale of extended warranties on consumer products. A retailer will often offer the customer extended service for two or three years on a product, such as a mobile phone. If the retailer provides the service, then the amount received for the extended warranty cannot be recognized until it has been earned. If a third party (for example, the product's manufacturer) is expected to provide the service in the future, then the retailer may recognize at that time the revenue it has earned for selling the extended warranty contract to the customer. This simple example illustrates why accounting standards are subject to change and highlights the importance of the professional judgment that accountants must exercise when deciding upon the timing of revenue recognition.

Motivating Sales and Collections

Sales practices differ depending on whether sales are made to businesses or consumers. Gildan sells its products primarily through wholesale distributors, a strategy that enables the company to use a small sales force. Gildan sells its products to a network of distributors in Canada, the United States, Mexico, Europe, and Asia, which in turn resell the products to retailers and garment decorators. Consumers ultimately purchase the company's products in such venues as sports, entertainment, and corporate events as well as travel and tourism destinations. Gildan also sells its product line of activewear, underwear, and athletic socks to Canadian and U.S. retailers. Gildan recognizes revenue when it sells its products to its customers (wholesalers and retailers), not to the ultimate consumer of its products.

Gildan uses a variety of methods to motivate its customers, both businesses and consumers, to buy its products and make payment for their purchases. The principal methods include (1) allowing all customers to use credit cards to pay for purchases, (2) providing business customers direct credit and discounts for early payment, and (3) allowing returns from all customers under specific circumstances. These methods, in turn, affect the way we compute *net sales revenue.*

Credit Card Sales to Consumers

Sales to consumers are for cash or credit card (mainly Visa, MasterCard, and American Express). The seller accepts credit cards as payment for a variety of reasons:

1. Increasing customer traffic at its stores.

2. Avoiding the costs of providing credit directly to customers, including for record keeping and bad debts (discussed later).

3. Lowering losses due to bad cheques.

4. Avoiding losses from fraudulent credit card sales. (Normally, the credit card company absorbs any losses if the seller follows the credit card company's verification procedure.)

5. Receiving money faster. (Since credit card receipts can be directly deposited in its bank account, the seller receives cash payments faster than it would if it provided credit directly to consumers.)

The credit card company charges a fee for the service it provides. For example, when a seller processes the credit card payment, it might receive credit for an amount equal to only 97 percent of the sales price. The fee charged by the credit card company for its services is the **credit card discount**; 3 percent, in this case. If daily credit card sales were $3,000, Gildan would report the following:[3]

Sales revenue	$3,000
Less: Credit card discounts (0.03 × $3,000)	90
Net sales (reported on the statement of earnings)	$2,910

Gildan accounts for this sale as follows, assuming the items sold cost $2,000:

Cash (A)	2,910	
Credit card discounts (XR or E)	90	
Sales revenue (R)		3,000
Cost of sales (E)	2,000	
Inventory (A)		2,000

Assets		=	Liabilities	+	Shareholders' Equity	
Cash	+2,910				Sales revenue	+3,000
Inventory	−2,000				Credit card discounts	−90
					Cost of sales	−2,000

Gildan uses the contra-revenue account, *credit card discounts*, to keep track of the fees charged by credit card companies instead of recording the net amount received, $2,910, as sales revenue.

If a customer uses a credit card issued by the seller, such as Sears or Canadian Tire, then the sale is a credit sale resulting in credit card receivables rather than cash sales.

Sales Discounts to Businesses

Most of Gildan's sales to businesses are credit sales on open account; that is, there is no formal written promissory note indicating the amount owed to Gildan by the customer. When Gildan sells T-shirts to wholesalers on credit, credit terms are printed on each sales document and invoice (bill) sent to the customer. Often credit terms are abbreviated, using symbols. For example, if the full amount of the invoice is due within 30 days of the invoice date, the credit terms would be noted as *n/30*. Here, the *n* means the sales amount *net* of, or less, any sales returns.

A **sales (or cash) discount** is a cash discount offered to encourage prompt payment of a trade account receivable.[4] For example, Gildan may offer *standard* credit terms of 2/10, n/30, which means that the customer may deduct 2 percent from the invoice amount if cash payment is made within 10 days of the date of sale. If cash

LO6-2

Analyze the impact of credit card sales, sales discounts, and sales returns on the amounts reported as net sales.

A **CREDIT CARD DISCOUNT** is the fee charged by the credit card company for its services.

A **SALES (OR CASH) DISCOUNT** is a cash discount offered to encourage prompt payment of a trade account receivable.

payment is not made within the 10-day discount period, the full invoice amount (less any returns) is due within a maximum of 30 days.

Early Payment Incentive

Gildan offers this sales discount to encourage customers to pay more quickly. This provides two benefits to Gildan:

1. Prompt receipt of cash from customers reduces the necessity of borrowing money to meet operating needs.

2. Since customers tend to pay invoices providing discounts first, a sales discount also decreases the likelihood that the customer will run out of funds before Gildan's invoice is paid.

Companies commonly record sales discounts taken by subtracting the discount from sales if payment is made within the discount period (the usual case).[5] For example, if credit sales are recorded with terms 2/10, n/30 and payment of $980 (= $1,000 × 0.98) is made within the discount period, net sales of the following amount would be reported:

Sales revenue	$1,000
Less: Sales discounts (0.02 × $1,000)	20
Net sales (reported on the statement of earnings)	$ 980

If the items sold cost $700, the initial sales transaction and subsequent collection within the discount period would be recorded as follows:

Accounts receivable (A)		1,000	
Sales revenue (R)			1,000
Cost of sales (E)		700	
Inventory (A)			700

Assets	=	Liabilities	+	Shareholders' Equity
Accounts receivable +1,000				Sales revenue +1,000
Inventory − 700				Cost of sales − 700

Cash (A)		980	
Sales discount (XR or E)		20	
Accounts receivable (A)			1,000

Assets	=	Liabilities	+	Shareholders' Equity
Cash + 980				Sales discount −20
Accounts receivable −1,000				

If the payment is made after the discount period, $1,000 would be received in cash and reported as net sales.

Note that both the purpose of and accounting for both sales discounts and credit card discounts are similar. Both sales discounts and credit card discounts provide an attractive service to customers and promote faster receipt of cash, thereby reducing recordkeeping costs and minimizing bad debts.

TO TAKE OR NOT TO TAKE THE DISCOUNT, THAT IS THE QUESTION

FINANCIAL ANALYSIS

Customers usually pay within the discount period because the savings are substantial. With terms 2/10, n/30, 2 percent is saved by paying 20 days early (the 10th day instead of the 30th), which is equivalent to an annual interest rate of 37 percent. This annual interest rate is obtained by first computing the interest rate for the discount period. When the 2 percent discount is taken, the customer pays only 98 percent of the gross sales amount. For example, on a $100 sale with terms 2/10, n/30, $2 would be saved and $98 would be paid 20 days early. The interest rate for the 20 day discount period is

$$\text{(Amount saved} \div \text{Amount paid)} = \text{Interest rate for 20 days}$$
$$(\$2 \div \$98) = 2.04\% \text{ for 20 days, or } 0.102\% \text{ per day}$$

Given that there are 365 days in a year, the annual interest rate is then computed in the following manner:

$$\text{Annual interest rate} = 0.102\% \times 365 \text{ days} = 37.23\%$$

Credit customers would save a lot of money even if they had to borrow cash from a bank at a high rate, such as 15 percent, to take advantage of cash discounts. Normally, the bank's interest rate is less than the high interest rate associated with failing to take cash discounts.

Sales Returns and Allowances

For Gildan, prompt delivery of exactly what the customer ordered is key to maintaining good relations with the customers to whom it sells. Delivery of incorrect or damaged merchandise may cost the customer sales and can destroy these relationships. When this occurs, the customers have a right to return unsatisfactory or damaged merchandise and receive a refund or an adjustment to their bill. Such returns are often accumulated in a separate contra-revenue account called **sales returns and allowances** and must be deducted from gross sales revenue in determining net sales. This account informs Gildan's management of the volume of returns and allowances, providing an important measure of the quality of customer service. Assume, for example, that a customer bought 40 dozen T-shirts from Gildan for $2,000 on account. Before paying for the T-shirts, the customer discovered that 10 dozen T-shirts were not the colour ordered and returned them to Gildan.[6] Gildan would compute net sales as follows:

SALES RETURNS AND ALLOWANCES is a reduction of gross sales revenues for return of or allowances for unsatisfactory goods

Sales revenue	$2,000
Less: Sales returns (0.25 × $2,000)	500
Net sales (reported on the statement of earnings)	$1,500

The cost of sales related to the 10 dozen T-shirts would also be reduced.

If the items sold cost $1,400, the initial sales transaction and subsequent return of goods sold would be recorded as follows:

Accounts receivable (A)			2,000	
Sales revenue (R)				2,000
Cost of sales (E)			1,400	
Inventory (A)				1,400

Assets		**=**	**Liabilities**	**+**	**Shareholders' Equity**	
Accounts receivable	+2,000				Sales revenue	+2,000
Inventory	−1,400				Cost of sales	−1,400

Sales returns and allowances (XR)		500	
Accounts receivable (A)			500
Cost of sales (E)		350	
Inventory (A)			350

Assets		=	Liabilities	+	Shareholders' Equity	
Accounts receivable	−500				Sales returns and allowances	−500
Inventory	+350				Cost of sales	+350

If the returned merchandise is defective, then it has to be reworked before it can be restored to inventory. Accounting for returned merchandise that is either defective or damaged is discussed in other accounting courses.

Based on past experience, Gildan's management knows that some customers that purchased socks, underwear, and activewear products during the current year may return the purchased merchandise or be granted an allowance for potentially defective products in the following year. Because the expected product returns relate to sales made during the current year, Gildan estimates the potential sales returns for the year and establishes a provision for sales returns.

Reporting Net Sales

On the company's books, credit card discounts, sales discounts, and sales returns and allowances are accounted for separately to allow managers to monitor the costs of credit card use, sales discounts, and returns. Using the numbers in the preceding examples, the amount of net sales reported on the statement of earnings is computed in the following manner:[7]

Sales revenue	$6,000
Less: Credit card discounts (a contra revenue)	90
Sales discounts (a contra revenue)	20
Sales returns and allowances (a contra revenue)	500
Net sales (reported on the statement of earnings)	$5,390

Companies rarely disclose the determinants of net sales in the annual report because they may not want to reveal the effects of their credit policies to their competitors. Consequently, it is often difficult even for very knowledgeable external users to determine the effects of these deductions on net sales and net earnings. As we noted earlier, net sales less cost of sales equals the subtotal *gross profit* or *gross margin*. Analysts often examine gross profit as a percentage of net sales, called the *gross profit* or *gross margin percentage*.

GROSS PROFIT PERCENTAGE　　KEY RATIO **ANALYSIS**

LO6-3

Compute and interpret the gross profit percentage.

ANALYTICAL QUESTION → How effective is management at selling goods and services for more than the costs to purchase or produce them?

RATIO AND COMPARISONS → The gross profit percentage is helpful in answering this question. It is computed as follows:

$$\text{Gross profit percentage} = \frac{\text{Gross profit}}{\text{Net sales}}$$

The 2015† ratio for Gildan is,

$$\$687,259 \div \$2,568,618 = 0.268(26.8\%)$$

†The ratio is computed using gross profit and net sales for the calendar year 2015 instead of the corresponding values for the 15-month period. This provides a meaningful comparison of Gildan's ratio to those of competing companies,

Comparisons over Time			Comparisons with Competitors	
Gildan Activewear			Hanesbrands Inc.	Delta Apparel Inc.
2013†	2014†	2015	2015	2015
29.1%	25.3%	26.8%	37.3%	19.7%

†Consistent with the computation of the gross profit percentage for calendar year 2015, the percentages for 2013 and 2014 are also computed for the calendar years 2013 and 2014, respectively. This improves on the comparability of the ratios over time.

INTERPRETATIONS

In General → The gross profit percentage measures how much gross profit is generated from every sales dollar. It reflects the ability to charge premium prices and produce goods and services at low cost. All other things being equal, a higher gross profit results in higher net earnings.

Business strategy, as well as competition, affects the gross profit percentage. Companies pursuing a product-differentiation strategy use research and development and product promotion activities to convince customers of the superiority or distinctiveness of the company's products. This allows them to charge premium prices, producing higher gross profit percentages. Companies following a low-cost strategy rely on more-efficient management of production to reduce costs and increase the gross profit percentage. Managers, analysts, and creditors use this ratio to assess the effectiveness of the company's product development, marketing, and production strategy.

Focus Company Analysis → Gildan's gross profit percentage decreased from 29.1 percent in 2013 to 25.3 percent in 2014 and then increased to 26.8 percent in 2015. Gildan's ratio surpassed Delta Apparel's ratio for 2015, but it is below the ratio achieved by Hanesbrands. At the beginning of the chapter, we discussed key elements of Gildan's business strategy that focused on vertical integration and low-cost manufacturing of premium-quality products in Central America, its marketing philosophy, and its distribution strategy. According to Gildan's annual report for fiscal year 2015, the decline in the gross profit percentage in the last two years was primarily due to lower printwear selling prices, the decline in international currencies relative to the U.S. dollar, and an unfavourable product mix.

A Few Cautions → To assess the company's ability to sustain its gross margins, you must understand the sources of any change in its gross profit percentage. For example, an increase in margin resulting from increases in seasonal sales of high-margin products is less likely to be sustainable than one resulting from introducing new products. Also, higher prices must often be sustained with higher research and development and advertising expenses, which may reduce the operating and net profit substantially. This is why, if operating expenses do not decrease too, a small decrease in gross profit percentage can lead to a large decrease in net earnings.

SELECTED FOCUS COMPANY COMPARISONS—2015

Sears Canada 31.8%

Canadian Tire 33.7%

Danier Leather 51.8%

Reitmans 56.2%

PAUSE FOR FEEDBACK — STOP

Credit card sales, sales discounts, and sales returns all reduce the amounts reported as net sales. Both credit card discounts and sales or cash discounts promote faster receipt of cash. Sales returns and allowances include refunds and adjustments to customers' bills for defective or incorrect merchandise.

The gross profit percentage measures the ability to charge premium prices and produce goods and services at lower cost. Managers, analysts, and creditors use this ratio to assess the effectiveness of the company's product development, marketing, and production strategy.

Before you move on, complete the following questions to test your understanding of these concepts.

SELF-STUDY QUIZ 6-1

1. Assume that Sportswear Inc. sold $30,000 worth of T-shirts to various retailers with terms 1/10, n/30, and half of that amount was paid within the discount period. Gross sales at company-owned stores were $5,000 for the same period, 80 percent being paid using credit cards with a 3 percent discount and the rest in cash. Compute net sales for the period.

2. During the first quarter of fiscal year 2017, the company's net sales were $150,000 and cost of sales was $110,000. Verify that its gross profit percentage was 26.66 percent.

After you complete your answers, check them with the solutions at the end of the chapter.

MEASURING AND REPORTING RECEIVABLES

Classifying Receivables

Receivables may be classified in three common ways. First, receivables may be classified as trade or non-trade receivables. **Trade receivables** are open accounts owed to the business by trade customers and are created in the normal course of business when there is a sale of merchandise or services on credit. A *non-trade receivable* arises from transactions other than the normal sale of merchandise or services. For example, if Gildan endured an unfortunate accident and completed a successful insurance claim for reimbursement from the insurance company, then the amount of the claim would be classified as non-trade receivables.

Second, the receivable may be either an account receivable or a note receivable. An account receivable is created when there is a sale of products and services on open account to customers or when a company expects to receive payments from other parties, such as collection from an insurance company following an unfortunate accident. A **note receivable** is a written promise made by another party (e.g., a customer) to pay the company (1) a specified amount of money, called the *principal*, at a definite future date known as the *maturity date*, and (2) a specified amount of interest at one or more future dates. Interest is the amount charged for use of the principal. A note receivable is also classified as a financial asset, reflecting the contractual right to receive cash from debtors in the future. We discuss the computation of interest when we discuss notes payable in Chapter 9.

Third, in a classified statement of financial position, receivables are also classified as either *current* or *non-current* (short term or long term), depending on when the cash is expected to be collected.

Different combinations of these classifications are possible. For example, a current trade accounts receivable indicates that merchandise was sold on account and the amount is expected to be received within 12 months. Canadian companies most often report current receivables as either *trade and other receivables*, or *accounts receivable*. Gildan uses the title *trade accounts receivable*, which clearly indicates that its accounts receivable are the result of trading transactions with customers. In this book, we use the account title "accounts receivable," which is more commonly used than other titles.

TRADE RECEIVABLES are open accounts owed to the business by trade customers.

A **NOTE RECEIVABLE** is a written promise that requires another party to pay the business under specific conditions (amount, time, interest).

FOREIGN CURRENCY RECEIVABLES

INTERNATIONAL PERSPECTIVE

Selected Foreign Currency Exchange Rates (in CDN$) (as at May 20, 2016)

Chinese Yuan $0.20

American Dollar $1.31

Euro $1.47

Export (international) sales are a growing part of the Canadian economy. For example, international sales amounted to 87.4 percent of Gildan's revenues in 2015, particularly sales to the U.S. market. As is the case with domestic sales to other businesses, most export sales to businesses are on credit. When the buyer has agreed to pay in its local currency instead of Canadian dollars, Gildan cannot add accounts receivable that are denominated in a foreign currency directly to accounts receivable denominated in Canadian dollars.* Gildan's accountants must first convert the accounts receivable denominated in foreign currencies into Canadian dollars by using the end-of-period exchange rate between the two currencies. For example, if a European distributor purchased goods from Gildan for €20,000 on November 30, 2015, and each euro was worth CDN$1.42 on that date, Gildan would add $28,400 to its accounts receivable on that date. If Gildan has not collected the €20,000 by January 3, 2016, the end of its fiscal year, then the receivable should be adjusted for the change in the value of the euro, and an exchange gain or loss should be reported on the statement of earnings.

*Gildan has reported its financial statements in U.S. dollars since 2004. The use of Canadian dollars here is for illustrative purposes only.

Accounting for Bad Debts

As we noted before in the discussion of sales discounts and allowances, Gildan allows its customers (wholesalers and retailers) to purchase goods on open account because it believes that providing this service will increase sales, but it also has a cost. Gildan must pay to maintain a credit granting and collection system, because some customers may not pay their debts. Credit policies should be based on the *trade-off* between profit on additional sales and any additional bad debts. If the credit policy is too restrictive, it will result in a low rate of bad debts, but the company will turn away many good credit customers, causing a loss of sales revenue. On the other hand, if Gildan's credit policy is too liberal, then net sales will increase, but bad debts will increase because more customers will likely default on their payments, causing a write-off of (decrease in) accounts receivable.

For billing and collection purposes, Gildan keeps a separate account for each of the retailers and wholesalers that buy its products. Changes in the accounts of individual customers are recorded in a *subsidiary ledger*, which provides details of the total amount of accounts receivable reported on the statement of financial position. When Gildan extends credit to its customers, it knows that a certain amount of credit sales may not be collected in the future. The expense matching process requires the recording of bad debt expense in the *same* accounting period as the one in which the related sales are made. This presents an important accounting problem. Gildan may not learn which particular customers will not pay until the *next* accounting period. So, at the end of the period of sale, it normally does not know which customers' accounts receivable are bad debts.

Gildan resolves this problem by using the **allowance method**, which bases bad debt expense on an estimate of uncollectible accounts. There are two primary steps in applying the allowance method: (1) estimating and recording bad debts expense and (2) writing off specific accounts determined to be uncollectible during the period. The estimation of bad debts is an example of prudence, whereby Gildan deducts the estimated amount of bad debts from the ending balance of accounts receivable and reports the net realizable value of accounts receivable on the statement of financial position. Gildan's accounting policy regarding trade accounts receivable is stated in Note 3 to its financial statements for 2015:

LO6-4

Estimate, report, and evaluate the effects of uncollectible accounts receivables (bad debts) on financial statements.

The **ALLOWANCE METHOD** bases bad debt expense on an estimate of uncollectible accounts.

---

3. SIGNIFICANT ACCOUNTING POLICIES

...

(d) Trade accounts receivable:
Trade accounts receivable consist of amounts due from our normal business activities. An allowance for doubtful accounts is maintained to reflect expected credit losses. Bad debts are provided for based on collection history and specific risks identified on a customer-by-customer basis. Uncollected accounts are written off through the allowance for doubtful accounts. Trade accounts receivable are recorded net of accrued sales discounts.

Source: Gildan Activewear, Annual Report 2015.

REAL-WORLD EXCERPT

Gildan Activewear
ANNUAL REPORT

Gildan reported the following changes to its allowance for doubtful accounts account for fiscal years 2014 and 2015 in Note 7 to its financial statements:

REAL-WORLD EXCERPT

Gildan Activewear
ANNUAL REPORT

Note 7: Trade Accounts Receivable:
The movement in the allowance for doubtful accounts in respect of trade receivables was as follows:

	2015	2014
Balance, beginning of year	$4,423	$3,667
Bad debt expense (recovery)	560	2,420
Write-off of trade accounts receivable	(455)	(1,834)
Increase due to business acquisitions (note 5)	73	170
Balance, end of year	$4,601	$4,423

Source: Gildan Activewear, Annual Report 2015.

The various transactions that affected the allowance for doubtful accounts are explained below.

BAD DEBT EXPENSE (DOUBTFUL ACCOUNTS EXPENSE) is the expense associated with estimated uncollectible accounts receivable.

Recording Bad Debt Expense Estimates

Bad debt expense (doubtful accounts expense) is the expense associated with estimated uncollectible accounts receivable. It is recorded through an *adjusting journal entry at the end of the accounting period*. For the year ended January 3, 2016, Gildan estimated bad debt expense to be $560, and made the following adjusting entry:

Bad debt expense (E)		560	
Allowance for doubtful accounts (XA)			560
Assets	**= Liabilities**	**+**	**Shareholders' Equity**
Allowance for doubtful accounts −560			Bad debt expense −560

Gildan includes the bad debt expense in the category "selling" expenses on the statement of earnings. Bad debt expense decreases net earnings and shareholders' equity. Accounts receivable could not be credited in the journal entry, because it is difficult to know at that date which customers may not pay in the future. The credit is made, instead, to the account called **Allowance for doubtful accounts (Allowance for doubtful receivables, Allowance for doubtful debts)**, a contra-asset account containing the estimated uncollectible accounts receivable. As a contra asset, the balance in allowance for doubtful accounts is always subtracted from the balance of the asset accounts receivable. Thus, the entry decreases the net realizable value of accounts receivable and total assets.

ALLOWANCE FOR DOUBTFUL ACCOUNTS (ALLOWANCE FOR DOUBTFUL RECEIVABLES, ALLOWANCE FOR DOUBTFUL DEBTS) is a contra-asset account containing the estimated uncollectible accounts receivable.

For fiscal year 2015, Gildan's experience with collection from its customers resulted in an increase in the balance of the allowance account by a net amount of $178.

Writing Off Specific Uncollectible Accounts

Throughout the year, when it is determined that a customer will not pay its debt (e.g., due to bankruptcy), the write-off of that individual receivable is recorded through a journal entry. When a specific accounts receivable has been identified as uncollectible, it must be removed from the appropriate accounts receivable account. At the same time, the previously established allowance for such a doubtful receivable is no longer needed and should be removed from the allowance for doubtful accounts.

The following journal entry summarizes the write-off of $455 in accounts receivable during fiscal year 2014:

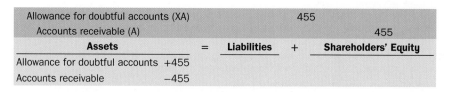

Allowance for doubtful accounts (XA)		455	
Accounts receivable (A)			455
Assets	**= Liabilities**	**+**	**Shareholders' Equity**
Allowance for doubtful accounts +455			
Accounts receivable −455			

Notice that this journal entry *did not affect any statement of earnings accounts*. The estimated bad debt expense was already recorded with an adjusting entry in the period of sale. Also, the entry *did not change the carrying amount of accounts receivable*, since the decrease in the asset account (accounts receivable) was offset by an equal decrease in the contra-asset account (allowance for doubtful accounts). Thus, it did not affect total assets.

Recovery of Accounts Previously Written Off

When a customer makes a payment on an account previously written off, the initial journal entry to write off the account is reversed for the amount that is collected, and another journal entry is made to record the collection of cash. For illustrative purposes, assume that Gildan recovered $10 from customers that had their accounts written off previously. The journal entries and transaction effects related to the recovery of bad debts are shown below:

Accounts receivable (A)	10	
Allowance for doubtful accounts (XA)		10
Cash (A)	10	
Accounts receivable (A)		10

Assets		=	Liabilities	+	Shareholders' Equity
Accounts receivable	+10				
Allowance for doubtful accounts	−10				
Cash	+10				
Accounts receivable	−10				

Notice that the net effect of the recovered amount on accounts receivable is zero. The recovered amount is first recorded in accounts receivable to reinstate the amount in the customers' accounts and show that the customers have honoured their previous commitments to pay Gildan $10.

In addition to the above transactions, Gildan increased the balance of the allowance for doubtful accounts by $170 in 2014 and $73 in 2015 because it acquired other businesses, and a portion of their accounts receivable is potentially uncollectible as well.

Summary of the Accounting Process It is important to remember that accounting for bad debts is a three-step process:

Step	Timing	Accounts Affected	Financial Statement Effects	
1. Record estimated bad debts adjustment	End of period in which sales are made	Bad debt expense (E)	↑ Net earnings	↓
		Allowance for doubtful accounts (XA)	↑ Assets (Accounts receivable, net)	↓
2. Identify and write off actual bad debts	Throughout period as bad debts become known	Accounts receivable (A)	↓ Net earnings	No effect
		Allowance for doubtful accounts (XA)	↓ Assets (Accounts receivable, net)	No effect
3. Record recovery of bad debts that were written off previously	Throughout period as bad debts are recovered	Accounts receivable (A)	↑↓ Net earnings	No effect
		Allowance for doubtful accounts (XA)	↓ Assets (Accounts receivable, net)	↓
		Cash (A)	↑ Cash	↑

Gildan's accounting for bad debts for fiscal year 2015 can now be summarized in terms of the changes in accounts receivable (gross) and the allowance for doubtful accounts:[8]

Accounts Receivable (gross) (A)

Balance at Oct. 5, 2014	358,688		
Sales on account	2,959,238	Collections on account	3,006,738
		Write-offs	455
Balance at Jan. 3, 2016	310,733		

Allowance for Doubtful Accounts (XA)

		Balance at Oct. 5, 2014	4,423
Write-offs	455	Increase due to business acquisitions	73
		Bad debt expense	560
		Balance at Jan. 3, 2016	4,601

Accounts receivable (gross) includes the total accounts receivable, both collectible and uncollectible. The balance in the allowance for doubtful accounts is the portion of the accounts receivable balance the company estimates to be uncollectible. Accounts receivable (net) reported on the statement of financial position is the portion of the accounts the company expects to collect (or its estimated net realizable value). These details are useful to external users of financial statements for assessing the quality of the company's receivables.

Reporting Accounts Receivable

Analysts who want information on Gildan's receivables will find trade accounts receivable, net of allowance for doubtful accounts (the *carrying amount*) of $306,132 and $354,265 for fiscal years 2015 and 2014, respectively, reported on the statement of financial position (Exhibit 6.2).

Exhibit 6.2

Accounts Receivable on the Statement of Financial Position

REAL-WORLD EXCERPT

Gildan Activewear

ANNUAL REPORT

CONSOLIDATED STATEMENT OF FINANCIAL POSITION (PARTIAL) January 3, 2016, and October 5, 2014 (in thousands of dollars)		
	2015	2014
Assets		
Current assets:		
Cash and cash equivalents (Note 6)	$ 50,675	$ 65,163
Trade accounts receivable (Note 7)	306,132	354,265
Income taxes receivable	–	1,439
Inventories (Note 8)	851,033	779,407
Prepaid expenses, deposits, and other current assets	42,934	41,291
Assets held for sale (Note 17)	2,840	5,839

Source: Gildan Activewear, Annual Report 2015.

Gildan disclosed details of the changes to the allowance for doubtful accounts in Note 7 to its financial statement for 2015 as indicated above.

PAUSE FOR FEEDBACK

When receivables are material, companies must employ the allowance method to account for doubtful accounts. These are the steps in the process:

a. Prepare an adjusting entry at the end of the accounting period to record the estimated bad debt expense and increase the allowance for doubtful accounts.

b. Write off specific accounts that are determined to be uncollectible during the period. This eliminates the specific uncollectible accounts receivable and reduces the allowance for doubtful accounts.

The adjusting entry reduces net earnings as well as net accounts receivable. The write-off affects neither. Before you move on, complete the following questions to test your understanding of these concepts.

SELF-STUDY QUIZ 6-2

In a recent year, Delta Apparel Inc., a Gildan competitor, had a beginning credit balance in the allowance for doubtful accounts of $851 (all numbers in thousands of U.S. dollars). It wrote off accounts receivable totalling $271 during the year and made a bad debt expense adjustment of $467 for the year.

1. Prepare the adjusting journal entry that Delta made to record bad debt expense at the end of the year.

2. Prepare the journal entry summarizing Delta's total write-offs of bad debts during the year.

3. Compute the balance in the allowance for doubtful accounts at the end of the year.

After you complete your answers, check them with the solutions at the end of the chapter.

Estimating Bad Debts

The bad debt expense recorded in the end-of-period adjusting entry is often estimated based on an aging of accounts receivable.

Aging of Accounts Receivable Method

The **aging of accounts receivable method** estimates uncollectible accounts based on the age of each account receivable. It relies on the fact that as accounts receivable become older and overdue they are usually less likely to be collectible. For example, a receivable that is due in 30 days but has not been paid after 60 days is more likely to be collected, on average, than a similar receivable that still remains unpaid after 120 days.

The **AGING OF ACCOUNTS RECEIVABLE METHOD** estimates uncollectible accounts based on the age of each account receivable.

Suppose that Amer and Ciero (a hypothetical company) split its receivables into five age categories, as presented in Exhibit 6.3. Management of the company might then *estimate* the following probable bad debt rates: 1 percent of receivables not yet due, 3 percent of receivables that are past due by 1 to 30 days, 6 percent of receivables that are past due by 31 to 60 days, and so on. The total of the amounts estimated to be uncollectible under the aging method is the balance that *should be* in the allowance for doubtful accounts at the end of the period. This is called the *estimated ending balance*. From this, the adjustment to record bad debt expense (and an increase in the allowance for doubtful accounts) for 2017 is computed.

This computation can also be illustrated in T-account form. The current credit balance in the allowance account, before the end-of-period adjustment, is $188. We insert the new ending balance from the aging schedule and then solve for the current amount of bad debt expense:

Allowance for Doubtful Accounts (XA)

		2017 Beginning balance	1,455
Write-offs (throughout the year)	1,267		
		Unadjusted balance	188
Step 2: Adjustment inferred ⟶		2017 Bad debt expense (adjustment)	1,344
Step 1: Ending balance estimated ⟶ from aging of accounts receivable		2017 Ending balance	1,532

Exhibit 6.3

Aging Analysis of Accounts Receivable

AMER AND CIERO
Analysis of Aged Trade Receivables
December 31, 2017

Customer	Not Yet Due	1–30 Days Past Due	31–60 Days Past Due	61–90 Days Past Due	Over 90 Days Past Due	Total
Adams, Inc.	$ 600					$ 600
Baker Stores	300	$ 900	$ 100			1,300
Cox Co.			400	$ 900	$ 100	1,400
Zoe Stores	2,000		1,000			3,000
Total	$17,200	$12,000	$8,000	$1,200	$1,600	$40,000
Estimated % uncollectible	1%	3%	6%	10%	25%	
Estimated uncollectible accounts	$ 172	$ 360	$ 480	$ 120	$ 400	$ 1,532

The end-of-period adjusting entry to the accounts bad debt expense and allowance for doubtful accounts is made on December 31 for $1,344.

The amount written off throughout the year may sometimes exceed the beginning balance of the allowance for doubtful accounts, which indicates that the company underestimated the amount that is potentially uncollectible. If the total amount written off equals $1,567, the allowance account will have an unadjusted *debit* balance of $112, and the bad debt expense will equal $1,644.

Gildan disclosed the aging of its accounts receivable in the management's discussion and analysis section of its annual report, as shown in Exhibit 6.4. If these receivables were due within 30 days, then the longer the receivable remains uncollected, the lower the likelihood it will be collected. Beyond 90 days, collectibility is very doubtful. The percentage of receivables past due increased from 13.8 percent in 2014 to 31.2 percent in 2015, which is not an encouraging signal. The increase in allowance for doubtful accounts from $4.4 million at October 5, 2014, to $4.6 million at January 3, 2016, reflects management's concern that a larger percentage of customers may default on their debts to Gildan. These details help shareholders, lenders, and analysts estimate future impairments of accounts receivable.

Actual Write-Offs Compared with Estimates   The amount of uncollectible accounts actually written off seldom equals the estimated amount previously recorded. This error in estimating bad debts is taken into consideration in determining the bad debt expense at the end of the next accounting period. *When estimates are found to be incorrect, financial statement values for prior annual accounting periods are* **not** *corrected.*

Exhibit **6.4**
Aging of Accounts Receivable

The aging of trade accounts receivable balances was as follows as at,

(in $ millions)	January 3, 2016	October 5, 2014
Not past due	213.9	309.2
Past due 0–30 days	63.0	33.8
Past due 31–60 days	14.8	6.1
Past due 61–120 days	14.6	6.3
Past due over 121 days	4.4	3.3
Trade accounts receivable	310.7	358.7
Less: Allowance for doubtful accounts	(4.6)	(4.4)
Total trade accounts receivable	309.1	354.3

Source: Gildan Activewear, Annual Report 2015.

SALES VERSUS COLLECTIONS: THE MARKETING– FINANCIAL MANAGEMENT CONFLICT

FINANCIAL ANALYSIS

Company managers often forget that while extending credit increases sales volume, it may also increase the volume of bad debts if proper credit checks of the customers are not made or if the company relaxes its credit policy too much. Marketing-oriented companies that emphasize sales without monitoring the collection of credit sales will soon find much of their current assets tied up in accounts receivable. On the other hand, the absence of bad debts may be the result of a very tight credit policy that reduces both sales and net earnings.

In the last decade, the leading domestic automotive companies, such as General Motors and DaimlerChrysler (now Daimler AG), contributed to sales growth by providing short- and medium-term financing to their dealers and distributors in order to encourage them to purchase their products. Financing of sales by the seller, called *vendor financing*, had become common industry practice until the risks of vendor financing came to light when demand for automobiles and auto parts weakened. Dealers and distributors started to default on their debts, and vendors were forced to absorb credit losses and increase their allowances for doubtful accounts.

When credit losses are relatively high because of vendor financing, financial analysts should be cautious in their analysis of companies' sales growth.

Prudence in the Valuation of Accounts Receivable Prudence is the exercise of care, caution, and good judgment. Creditors and analysts prefer that companies avoid overstating revenue and assets, and avoid understating expenses and liabilities. Accountants and auditors are also cautious about reporting optimistic values that overstate the company's operating performance and its financial position. For accounts receivable, the amount reported on the statement of financial position should reflect the amount most reasonably expected by a prudent accountant to be collected from customers. In this context, prudence suggests that the allowance for doubtful accounts be commensurate with the creditworthiness of the company's customers. All other things equal, a prudent measure of accounts receivable means a larger amount of bad debt expense and a larger allowance for doubtful accounts. It is better to err on the side of having a larger allowance than having a smaller one that may not be adequate to cover future bad debts.

To assess the effectiveness of overall credit granting and collection activities, managers and analysts often compute the receivables turnover ratio.

LO6-5

Compute and interpret the receivables turnover ratio and the effects of accounts receivable on cash flows.

RECEIVABLES TURNOVER RATIO

 KEY RATIO **ANALYSIS**

ANALYTICAL QUESTION → How effective are credit granting and collection activities?

RATIO AND COMPARISONS → An answer to this question is provided by the receivables turnover ratio, which is computed as follows:

$$\text{Receivables turnover ratio} = \frac{\text{Net credit sales*}}{\text{Average net accounts receivable**}}$$

*Since the amount of net credit sales is normally not reported separately, most analysts use net sales in this equation.
**Average net accounts receivable = (Beginning net accounts receivable + Ending net accounts receivable) ÷ 2

The 2015† ratio for Gildan is,

$$\frac{\$2,568,618}{(\$220,762 + \$306,132) \div 2} = 9.75$$

†The ratio is computed using net sales for the calendar year 2015 instead of the 15-month period in order to provide a meaningful comparison of Gildan's ratio to those of competing companies. Net accounts receivable is based on carrying amounts at the beginning and end of the calendar year 2015.

If Gildan's trade accounts receivable are turned over 9.75 times per year or 365 days, how many days would be needed, on average, to turn these receivables over once? This is known as the *average collection period* or *average days' sales in receivables* and is computed by dividing the receivables turnover ratio into 365 days:

$$\text{Average collection period} = \frac{365}{\text{Receivables turnover ratio}} = \frac{365}{9.75} = 37.4 \text{ days}$$

Gildan's average collection period is consistent with its credit policy, as most sales are billed to customers with credit terms of between 30 and 60 days.

Comparisons over Time			Comparisons with Competitors	
Gildan Activewear			Hanesbrands Inc.	Delta Apparel Inc.
2013†	2014†	2015	2015	2015
10.31	10.28	9.75	8.48	6.90

†Consistent with the computation of the receivables turnover ratio for 2015 based on the calendar year, the ratios for 2013 and 2014 are also computed based on the calendar years 2013 and 2014, respectively. This improves on the comparability of the ratios over time.

If Gildan's trade accounts receivable are turned over 9.75 times per year or 365 days, how many days would be needed, on average, to turn these receivables over once? This is known as the *average collection period* or *average days' sales in receivables* and is computed by dividing the receivables turnover ratio into 365 days:

$$\text{Average collection period} = \frac{365}{\text{Receivables turnover ratio}} = \frac{365}{9.75} = 37.4 \text{ days}$$

Gildan's average collection period is consistent with its credit policy, as most sales are billed to customers with credit terms of between 30 and 60 days.

Comparisons over Time			Comparisons with Competitors	
Gildan Activewear			Hanesbrands Inc.	Delta Apparel Inc.
2013†	2014†	2015	2015	2015
10.31	10.28	9.75	8.48	6.90

†Consistent with the computation of the receivables turnover ratio for 2015 based on the calendar year, the ratios for 2013 and 2014 are also computed based on the calendar years 2013 and 2014, respectively. This improves on the comparability of the ratios over time.

INTERPRETATIONS

In General → The receivables turnover ratio reflects how many times average accounts receivable are recorded and collected during the period. The higher the ratio, the faster the collection of receivables. A higher ratio benefits the company because it can invest the cash collected to earn interest income, or reduce borrowings to reduce interest expense. Overly generous payment schedules and ineffective collection methods keep the receivables turnover ratio low. Analysts and creditors watch this ratio because a sudden decline may mean that a company is extending payment deadlines in an attempt to prop up lagging sales, or even recording sales that will later be returned by customers. Many managers and analysts compute the average collection period, which indicates the average time it takes a customer to pay the amounts due.

Focus Company Analysis → Gildan's receivables turnover ratio decreased slightly, from 10.31 in 2013 to 9.75 in 2015. This indicates that the company did not turn over its accounts receivable in 2015 as quickly as it did in 2013. Its average collection period increased by two days: from 35.4 days in 2013 to 37.4 days in 2015. Gildan's ratio is higher than those of Hanesbrands and Delta Apparel. Gildan's customers are faster at paying their bills than those of Gildan's competitors. Alternatively, Gildan may have a more effective collections practice or different receivables contracts with shorter credit terms.

A Few Cautions → Since differences across industries and between firms in the manner in which customer purchases are financed can cause dramatic differences in the ratio, a particular firm's ratio should be compared only with its own prior years' figures or with other firms in the same industry following the same financing practices.

Selected Industry Comparisons: Receivables Turnover Ratio—2015

Retailing 107.16%

Food, Beverage, and Tobacco 16.98%

Paper and Forest Products 12.59%

PAUSE FOR FEEDBACK

When using the *aging of accounts receivable method*, compute the estimated ending balance in the allowance account and solve for the bad debt expense. This process involves multiplying the amount in each age category by the estimated percentage uncollectible to produce the estimated ending balance in the allowance for doubtful accounts. The difference between the estimated ending balance and the balance in the allowance account before the adjustment becomes the bad debt expense for the year. Before you move on, answer the following questions to test your understanding of this method.

1. Assume that Kleer Company reported beginning and ending balances in the allowance for doubtful accounts of $723 and $904, respectively. It also reported that write-offs of bad debts amounted to $648 (all numbers in thousands). Assuming that the company did not collect any amounts that were written off previously, what amount did the company record as bad debt expense for the period? (*Hint:* Use the allowance for doubtful accounts T-account to solve for the missing value.)

Allowance for Doubtful Accounts (XA)

2. Kleer Company reported an increase in accounts receivable for the period. Was that increase added to or subtracted from net earnings in the computation of cash flow from operations? Explain your answer.

3. Explain whether *granting longer payment deadlines* (e.g., 60 days instead of 30 days) will most likely *increase* or *decrease* the receivables turnover ratio.

After you complete your answers, check them with the solutions at the end of the chapter.

ACCOUNTS RECEIVABLE

FOCUS ON
CASH FLOWS

The change in accounts receivable can be a major determinant of a company's cash flow from operations. The statement of earnings reflects the revenues earned during the period, whereas the cash flow from operating activities reflects the cash collections from customers for the same period. Since sales on account increase the balance in accounts receivable, and cash collections from customers decrease the balance in accounts receivable, the change in accounts receivable from the beginning to the end of the period is the difference between sales and cash collections.

EFFECT ON STATEMENT OF CASH FLOWS

In General → When a net *decrease in accounts receivable* for the period occurs, the amount of cash collected from customers exceeds revenue; thus, the decrease must be *added* to revenue or to net earnings (since revenue is a component of net earnings) in computing cash flows from operations. When a net *increase in accounts receivable* occurs, cash collected from customers is less than revenue; thus, the increase must be *subtracted* from net earnings in computing cash flows from operations.

	Effect on Cash Flows
Operating activities (indirect method)	
Net earnings	$xxx
Adjusted for	
Decrease in accounts receivable	+
or	
Increase in accounts receivable	−

Focus Company Analysis → Exhibit 6.5 is the operating activities section of Gildan's statement of cash flows. The balance of Gildan's trade accounts receivable decreased during 2015. This decrease is added to net earnings in the computation of Gildan's cash flow from operations, because cash collected from customers exceeded the amount of revenues during 2015. When trade accounts receivable increase, the amount of the increase is subtracted from net earnings in determining the cash flow from operating activities, because revenues are higher than cash collected from customers.

Exhibit **6.5**

Receivables on the
Statement of Cash Flows

GILDAN ACTIVEWEAR INC. Consolidated Statements of Cash Flows Years ended January 3, 2016, and October 5, 2014 (in thousands of U.S. dollars)		
	2015 (15 months)	**2014**
Cash flows from (used in) operating activities:		
Net earnings	$304,914	$359,552
Adjustments to reconcile net earnings to cash flows from operating activities (Note 21(a)):	147,654	93,188
	452,568	452,740
Changes in non-cash working capital balances:		
Trade accounts receivable	47,893	(90,549)
Income taxes receivable	2,478	(628)
Inventories	(36,149)	(149,231)
Prepaid expenses, deposits, and other current assets	(4,290)	(10,007)
Accounts payable and accrued liabilities	(108,876)	61,775
	$353,624	$264,100

Source: Gildan Activewear, Annual Report 2015.

Internal Control and Management Responsibility

INTERNAL CONTROL refers
to the process by which the
company's board of directors,
management, and other
personnel provide reasonable
assurance regarding the
reliability of the company's
financial reporting, the
effectiveness and efficiency
of its operations, and its
compliance with applicable laws
and regulations.

The term **internal control** refers to the process by which a company's board of directors, audit committee, management, and other personnel provide reasonable assurance that the accounting system minimizes the risk of material misstatement of reported financial information.[9] In addition, the system must assure the effectiveness and efficiency of the company's operations, and its compliance with all laws and regulations. A well-designed system of internal control prevents inadvertent errors and removes opportunities for individuals to steal, misrepresent, defraud, or embezzle assets from a company. Canadian legislation prevents top executives and members of the board of directors from ignoring their management responsibility to design, supervise, and implement appropriate internal control systems.

Canadian scandals such as those involving Nortel Networks Corp. and Livent Inc. led the Canadian Securities Administrators to enact regulations regarding internal control systems, including National Instrument (NI) 52-109, which requires the corporation's chief executive officer and chief financial officer to sign form 52-109F1 (certification of annual filings), a legal document that certifies the quality of the internal control system.[10] In particular, for corporations listed on the Toronto Stock Exchange, the two officers certify the reliability of financial reporting in accordance with applicable accounting standards. Executives must also attest to the effectiveness of the internal control and financial reporting system. The annual report must disclose any deficiencies in internal control procedures, the related risks, and any plans to remedy these deficiencies. No audit is necessary, but auditors would find it unusual if an executive certified a deficient system. Auditors must correct or refuse to attest to all audited disclosure, including false claims made on form 52-109F1.

ETHICS AND THE NEED FOR INTERNAL CONTROL   A QUESTION OF ACCOUNTABILITY

Some people are bothered by the recommendation that all well-run companies should have strong internal control procedures. These people believe that control procedures suggest that the company's management does not trust its employees. Although the vast majority of employees are trustworthy, employee theft costs businesses billions of dollars each year. Interviews with convicted felons indicate that, in many cases, they stole from their employers because they thought that it was easy and that no one cared because no internal controls were present.

In their 2016 survey of Global Economic Crime (including misappropriation of assets, accounting fraud, bribery and corruption, cybercrime and money laundering) PricewaterhouseCoopers reported that 36 percent of the surveyed companies suffered economic crime in the previous two years. The main types of economic crime experienced by the surveyed companies and the percentage of companies affected are asset misappropriation (stealing), 64 percent; cybercrime, 32 percent; bribery and corruption, 24 percent; procurement fraud, 23 percent; and accounting fraud, 18 percent. Economic crime is most prevalent in Africa at 57 percent, Western Europe at 40 percent and North America at 37 percent.[11] This explains the continued emphasis by securities regulators on the validation of internal control over financial reporting.

Many companies have a formal code of ethics that requires high standards of behaviour in dealing with customers, suppliers, fellow employees, and the company's assets. Although each employee is ultimately responsible for his or her own ethical behaviour, internal control procedures can be thought of as important value statements from management. Preventing theft through strong internal control prevents people from destroying their lives if they steal and are subsequently caught and penalized for their unethical behaviour.

Control over Accounts Receivable

The internal control system must respond to different sets of activities with different types of control. Controlling and protecting cash to prevent embezzlement, for example, will be different from controlling the security and accuracy of the information system. Many managers forget that although extending credit will increase sales volume, the related receivables do not increase net earnings unless they are collected. Companies that emphasize sales without monitoring the collection of credit sales will soon find much of their current assets tied up in accounts receivable. By guarding against extending credit to non-worthy customers, the following practices can help minimize bad debts:

1. Require approval of customers' credit history by a person independent of the sales and collection functions.

2. Monitor the age of accounts receivable periodically, and contact customers with overdue payments.

3. Reward both sales and collection personnel for speedy collections so that they work as a team.

REPORTING AND SAFEGUARDING CASH

Cash and Cash Equivalents Defined

Cash is defined as money or any instrument that banks will accept for deposit and immediate credit to the company's account, such as a cheque, money order, or bank draft. Cash is usually divided into three categories: cash on hand, cash deposited in banks, and other instruments that meet the definition of cash.

International Accounting Standard 7—Statement of Cash Flows defines **cash equivalents** as short-term, highly liquid investments that are readily convertible to known amounts of cash and that are subject to an insignificant risk of change in value. Typical instruments included as cash equivalents are bank certificates of deposit and treasury bills issued by the government to finance its activities.

Even though a company may have several bank accounts and several types of cash equivalents, all cash accounts and cash equivalents are usually combined as one amount for financial reporting purposes. Gildan reports a single account, cash and cash equivalents, with a balance of $50.7 million at January 3, 2016. The company clearly specifies cash equivalents as all liquid investments with maturities of three months or less from the date of acquisition.

LO6-6

Report, control, and safeguard cash.

CASH is money or any instrument that banks will accept for deposit and immediate credit to the company's account, such as a cheque, money order, or bank draft.

A **CASH EQUIVALENT** is a short-term, highly liquid investment with an original maturity of less than three months, and subject to an insignificant risk of changes in value.

Cash Management

Many businesses receive a large amount of cash, cheques, and credit card receipts from their customers each day. Anyone can spend cash, so management must develop procedures to safeguard the cash it uses in the business. Effective cash management involves more than protecting cash from theft, fraud, or loss through carelessness. Other cash management responsibilities include the following:

1. Accurate accounting so that reports of cash flows and balances may be prepared.
2. Controls to ensure that enough cash is on hand to meet (a) current operating needs, (b) maturing liabilities, and (c) unexpected emergencies.
3. Prevention of the accumulation of excess amounts of idle cash. Idle cash earns no revenue; therefore, it is often invested in securities to earn revenue (return) until it is needed for operations.

Internal Control of Cash

Because cash is the asset most vulnerable to theft and fraud, a significant number of internal control procedures should focus on cash. You have already observed internal control procedures for cash, although you may not have known it at the time. At most movie theatres, one employee sells tickets and another employee collects them. It would be less expensive to have one employee do both jobs, but it would also be easier for that single employee to steal cash and admit a patron without issuing a ticket. If different employees perform the tasks, a successful theft requires the participation of both.

Effective internal control of cash should include the following:

1. **Separation of duties related to cash handling and recordkeeping.**

    a. Complete separation of the tasks of receiving cash and disbursing cash ensures that the individual responsible for depositing cash has no authority to sign cheques.

    b. Complete separation of the procedures of accounting for cash receipts and cash disbursements ensures, for example, that those handling sales returns do not create fictitious returns to conceal cash shortages.

    c. Complete separation of the physical handling of cash and all phases of the accounting function ensures that those either receiving or paying cash have no authority to make accounting entries.

The following diagram illustrates how the separation of duties contributes to strong internal control:

The importance of separation of individual responsibilities is that it deters theft, because it requires collusion of two or more persons to both steal cash and then conceal the theft in the accounting records.

2. Prescribed policies and procedures.

Specific policies and procedures should be established so that the work done by one individual is compared with the results reported by other individuals. Exhibit 6.6 provides a summary of typical policies and procedures to control cash.

Exhibit **6.6**
Typical Internal Controls for Cash

Internal Control Component	Prescribed Policies or Procedures
Cash budget	Prepare a monthly forecast of cash receipts, disbursements, and balances for the year, and require that managers document and justify any deviations from the budget each month. This is important in order to detect differences quickly and remedy them as soon as possible.
Cash receipts	Prepare a listing of cash receipts on a daily basis. In practice, this often takes the form of cash register receipts or a descriptive list of incoming cheques. Require that all cash receipts be deposited in a bank daily. Keep any cash on hand under strict control. In so doing, the amount of actual cash accessible is kept to a minimum each day and the loss from theft is minimized.
Cash payments	Require separate approval of the purchases and other expenditures and separate approval of the actual cash payments. Assign the cash-payment approval and the actual cheque-signing responsibilities to different individuals. Use pre-numbered cheques and pay special attention to payments by electronic funds transfers, since the bank does not process controlled documents (cheques). Once in place, this procedure will require at least four employees to collude to misappropriate funds (steal cash) from the company.
Independent internal verification	Require comparison, by an independent supervisor, of cash receipts to bank deposits and of cheques issued to invoices. Require monthly reconciliation of bank accounts with the cash accounts on the company's books (discussed in detail in the next section). This is important in order to detect differences quickly and remedy them as soon as possible.
Rotation of duties	Require that employees take vacations, and rotate their duties. Any economic crime already underway will be interrupted by an extended absence of a perpetrator; this provides an opportunity for others to detect the crime.

When procedures similar to those described in Exhibit 6.6 are followed, concealing a fraudulent cash disbursement is difficult without the collusion of two or more persons. Reconciliation of cash accounts with bank statements provides an additional control on disbursements. The level of internal control, which is reviewed by the outside independent auditor, increases the reliability of the financial statements of the business.

Reconciliation of the Cash Accounts and the Bank Statements

Content of a Bank Statement Proper use of the bank accounts of a business can be an important internal control procedure for cash. Each month, the bank provides the company (the depositor) with a **bank statement** that lists (1) each deposit recorded by the bank during the period, (2) each cheque cleared by the bank during the period, (3) other debits and credits, and (4) the running balance in the company's account. The bank statement also shows the bank charges or deductions (such as service charges) made directly to the company's account by the bank. A typical bank statement is shown in Exhibit 6.7.

A **BANK STATEMENT** is a monthly report from a bank that shows deposits recorded, cheques cleared, other debits and credits, and a running bank balance.

Exhibit **6.7**

Example of a Bank Statement

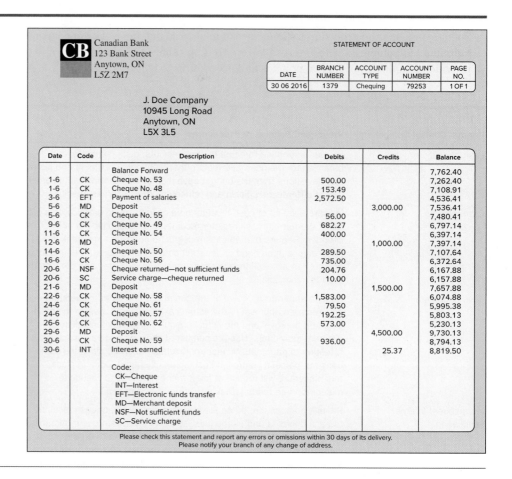

Date	Code	Description	Debits	Credits	Balance
		Balance Forward			7,762.40
1-6	CK	Cheque No. 53	500.00		7,262.40
1-6	CK	Cheque No. 48	153.49		7,108.91
3-6	EFT	Payment of salaries	2,572.50		4,536.41
5-6	MD	Deposit		3,000.00	7,536.41
5-6	CK	Cheque No. 55	56.00		7,480.41
9-6	CK	Cheque No. 49	682.27		6,797.14
11-6	CK	Cheque No. 54	400.00		6,397.14
12-6	MD	Deposit		1,000.00	7,397.14
14-6	CK	Cheque No. 50	289.50		7,107.64
16-6	CK	Cheque No. 56	735.00		6,372.64
20-6	NSF	Cheque returned—not sufficient funds	204.76		6,167.88
20-6	SC	Service charge—cheque returned	10.00		6,157.88
21-6	MD	Deposit		1,500.00	7,657.88
22-6	CK	Cheque No. 58	1,583.00		6,074.88
24-6	CK	Cheque No. 61	79.50		5,995.38
24-6	CK	Cheque No. 57	192.25		5,803.13
26-6	CK	Cheque No. 62	573.00		5,230.13
29-6	MD	Deposit		4,500.00	9,730.13
30-6	CK	Cheque No. 59	936.00		8,794.13
30-6	INT	Interest earned		25.37	8,819.50

Code:
CK—Cheque
INT—Interest
EFT—Electronic funds transfer
MD—Merchant deposit
NSF—Not sufficient funds
SC—Service charge

Please check this statement and report any errors or omissions within 30 days of its delivery.
Please notify your branch of any change of address.

Exhibit 6.7 lists four items that need explanation. Notice that the payment of salaries on June 3 is coded EFT.[12] This is the code for electronic funds transfer. Many companies pay salaries to their employees by using electronic chequing, depositing electronic payments directly into the employees' bank accounts instead of issuing paper cheques. When a company orders the electronic payment, it records this item on its books in the same manner as a paper cheque, so no additional entry is needed. Electronic funds transfer has become common among companies and individuals as they use this form of payment for utilities, telecommunication, insurance, and other recurring expenses.

Notice that on June 20, listed under debits, there is a deduction for $204.76 coded NSF. A cheque for $204.76 was received from a customer, R. Smith, and deposited by J. Doe Company with its bank, the Canadian Bank. The bank processed the cheque through banking channels to Smith's bank. Smith's account did not have sufficient funds to cover it. Therefore, Smith's bank returned it to the Canadian Bank, which then charged it back to J. Doe Company. This type of cheque is often called an *NSF cheque* (not sufficient funds). The company needs to collect the amount of the cheque again from the customer. The NSF cheque is now a receivable; consequently, J. Doe Company must make a journal entry to debit accounts receivable (R. Smith) and credit cash for the $204.76.

Notice the $10 listed under debits on June 20 and coded SC. This is the code for bank service charges. The bank statement included a memo by the bank explaining this service charge (which was not documented by a cheque). J. Doe Company must make a journal entry to reflect the $10 decrease in the bank balance as a debit to a relevant expense account, such as bank service expense, and a credit to cash.

Notice the $25.37 listed on June 30 under credits and the code INT for interest earned. The bank pays interest on chequing account balances, which increased J. Doe Company's account for interest earned during the period. The company must record the interest by making a journal entry to debit cash and credit interest revenue for the $25.37.

Need for Reconciliation   A **bank reconciliation** is the process of comparing (reconciling) and verifying the accuracy of both the ending cash balance in the company's records and the ending cash balance reported by the bank on the monthly bank statement. A bank reconciliation should be completed for each separate chequing account (i.e., for each bank statement received from each bank) at the end of each month.

A **BANK RECONCILIATION** is the process of verifying the accuracy of both the bank statement and the cash accounts of a business.

Usually, the ending cash balance as shown on the bank statement does not agree with the ending cash balance shown by the related cash ledger account on the books of the company. For example, the cash ledger account of J. Doe Company showed the following at the end of June (Doe has only one chequing account):

	Cash		
June 1 balance	6,637.14	Cheques written in June	8,714.45
June deposits	11,800.00		
Ending balance	9,722.69		

The $8,819.50 ending cash balance shown on the bank statement (Exhibit 6.7) is different from the $9,722.69 ending balance of cash shown on the books of J. Doe Company. This difference exists because (1) some transactions affecting cash were shown on the bank statement but had not been recorded in the books of the J. Doe Company, (2) some transactions were recorded in the books of J. Doe Company but were not shown on the bank statement, and (3) errors occurred in recording transactions.

The flow of documents that have not reached either the company or the bank by the end of the accounting period is illustrated below:

The most common causes of differences between the ending bank balance and the ending book balance of cash are as follows:

1. **Bank service charges.** An expense for bank services listed on the bank statement. This expense is not recorded on the company's books.

2. **NSF cheques.** A "bad cheque" or "bounced cheque" that was deposited but must be deducted from the company's cash account and recorded as a receivable.

3. **Interest.** The interest paid by the bank to the company on its bank balance.

4. **Deposits in transit.** These are deposits sent to the bank by the company and recorded in the company's ledger as debits to the cash account. The bank has not recorded these deposits (they are not shown on the bank statement as an increase in the bank balance). Deposits in transit usually happen when deposits are made one or two days before the close of the period covered by the bank statement. Deposits in transit are determined by comparing the deposits listed on the bank statement with the copies of the deposit slips retained by the company or other company records.

5. **Outstanding cheques.** These are cheques written by the company and recorded in the company's ledger as credits to the cash account that have not cleared the bank (they are not shown on the bank statement as a deduction from the bank balance). The outstanding cheques are identified by comparing the cancelled cheques that the bank returned with the record of cheques (such as cheque stubs or a journal) maintained by the company.

6. **Errors.** Both the bank and the company may make errors, especially when the volume of cash transactions is large.

Bank Reconciliation Illustrated   The company should make a bank reconciliation immediately after receiving each bank statement. The general format for the bank reconciliation follows:

Ending cash balance per books	$xxx	Ending cash balance per bank statement	$xxx
+ Collections by bank	xx	+ Deposits in transit	xx
− NSF cheques/Service charges	xx	− Outstanding cheques	xx
± Company errors	xx	± Bank errors	xx
Ending correct cash balances	$xxx	Ending correct cash balance	$xxx

J. Doe Company followed these steps in preparing the bank reconciliation:

1. **Identify bank charges and credits not recorded on the company's books.** Examination of the bank statement in Exhibit 6.7 and the company's records indicate the following:

    a. The bank deducted $204.76 for a cheque by R. Smith that was returned to the company because of insufficient funds. This amount has not been recorded on the company's books.

    b. The bank deducted $10.00 as a service charge for the returned cheque. The service charge has not been recorded on the company's books.

    c. The bank added $25.37 to the company's account as interest on the amount deposited in the bank during June. This interest revenue has not been recorded by the company yet.

    When these amounts are recorded in the company's books, the revised balance in the cash account will decrease to $9,533.30 ($9,722.69 − $204.76 − $10.00 + $25.37).

2. **Identify the deposits in transit.** A comparison of the deposit slips on hand with those listed on the bank statement revealed that a deposit of $1,800.00 made on June 30 and recorded in the company's cash account was not listed on the bank statement. It will be added by the bank when it records the deposit.

3. **Identify the outstanding cheques.** A comparison of the cancelled cheques returned by the bank with the company's records of all cheques drawn showed the following cheques still outstanding (not cleared) at the end of June:

Cheque No.	Amount
60	$ 145.00
63	815.00
64	117.20
Total	$1,077.20

    The amounts of the three cheques have already been recorded in the company's cash account but have not been entered on the bank statement, because those who received the cheques from the company have not yet presented them to the bank for clearance.

    When the bank records the deposit in transit and the outstanding cheques in the company's account, the revised bank balance will equal $9,542.30 ($8,819.50 − $1,077.20 + $1,800.00). The revised bank balance differs from the revised cash balance by $9 ($9,542.30 − $9,533.30).

4. **Determine the impact of errors.** Because the difference in the revised bank and book balances is divisible by 9, a transposition of numbers was suspected. (A transposition, such as writing 27 for 72, will always cause an error that is exactly divisible by 9.) Comparison of the cancelled cheques returned by the bank with the company's records of all cheques issued to others revealed that a cheque written for $56 as per the bank statement was recorded in the company's accounts as $65. Examination of the journal entries showed that the incorrect entry made was a debit to accounts payable and a credit to cash for $65 (instead of $56). Therefore, $9 (i.e., $65 − $56) must be added to the cash account, leading to a revised cash balance of $9,542.30.

Exhibit 6.8 shows the bank reconciliation prepared by J. Doe Company for the month of June to reconcile the ending bank balance ($8,819.50) with the ending book balance ($9,722.69). On the completed reconciliation, the correct cash balance is $9,542.30. This balance is different from both the reported bank and book balances before the reconciliation with the bank statement. This correct balance reflects the amount of cash available to J. Doe Company for use in the future and should be shown in the cash account after the reconciliation. In this example, it is also the correct amount of cash that should be reported on the statement of financial position (J. Doe Company has only one chequing account and no cash on hand).

Note that in Exhibit 6.8, the two sections of the bank reconciliation now show correct cash balances of $9,542.30. This amount will be reported as cash on a statement of financial position prepared at June 30, 2016.

A bank reconciliation like the one in Exhibit 6.8 accomplishes two major objectives:

1. Checks the accuracy of the bank balance and the company cash records, which involves developing the correct cash balance. The correct cash balance (plus cash on hand, if any) is the amount of cash that is reported on the statement of financial position.

2. Identifies any previously unrecorded transactions or changes that are necessary to cause the company's cash account(s) to show the correct cash balance. Any transactions or changes on the *company's books side* of the bank reconciliation need journal entries. Therefore, the journal entries on the next page, based on the company's books side of the bank reconciliation, must be entered into the company's records.

Exhibit 6.8

Bank Reconciliation Illustrated

J. DOE COMPANY
Bank Reconciliation
June 30, 2016

Company's Books		Bank Statement	
Ending cash balance per books	$9,722.69	Ending cash balance per bank statement	$8,819.50
Additions		Additions	
Interest earned	25.37	Deposit in transit	1,800.00
Error in recording cheque No. 55	9.00		
	9,757.06		10,619.50
Deductions		Deductions	
NSF cheque of R. Smith	204.76	Outstanding cheques	1,077.20
Bank service charges	10.00		
Ending correct cash balance	$9,542.30	Ending correct cash balance	$9,542.30

Accounts of J. Doe Company		
(a) Cash (A)	25.37	
Interest revenue (R)		25.37
To record interest on chequing account with the bank.		
(b) Accounts receivable (A)	204.76	
Cash (A)		204.76
To record NSF cheque received from R. Smith.		
(c) Accounts receivable (A)	10.00	
Cash (A)		10.00
To record service fees charged by the bank and receivable from R. Smith.		
(d) Cash (A)	9.00	
Accounts payable (L)		9.00
To correct error made in recording a cheque payable to a creditor.		

Assets		=	Liabilities	+	Shareholders' Equity
Cash (+25.37 −204.76 − 10.00 + 9.00)	−180.39		Accounts payable +9.00		
Accounts receivable	+214.76				Interest earned +25.37

The cash account prior to reconciliation was given earlier in this chapter. After the preceding journal entries are posted, the cash account is as follows:

Cash Account of J. Doe Company

Cash

June 1 Balance	6,637.14	June cheques written	8,714.45
June Deposits	11,800.00	June 30 NSF cheque*	204.76
June 30 Interest earned*	25.37	June 30 Bank service charge related to NSF cheque*	10.00
June 30 Correcting entry*	9.00		
Correct cash balance	9,542.30		

*Based on the bank reconciliation.

Notice that all of the additions and deductions on the company's books side of the reconciliation need journal entries to update the cash account. The additions and deductions on the bank statement side do not need journal entries because they will work out automatically when they clear the bank.

PAUSE FOR FEEDBACK

Cash is the most liquid of all assets, flowing continually into and out of a business. As a result, a number of critical control procedures, including the *reconciliation* of bank accounts, should be applied. Also, management of cash may be critically important to decision makers who must have cash available to meet current needs, yet must avoid excess amounts of idle cash that produce no revenue. Answer the following questions to check your understanding of the basics of bank reconciliation before you move on.

SELF-STUDY QUIZ 6-4

Indicate which of the following items discovered while preparing a company's bank reconciliation will result in adjustment of the cash balance on the statement of financial position.

1. Outstanding cheques

2. Deposits in transit

3. Bank service charges

4. NSF cheques that were deposited

After you complete your answers, check them with the solutions at the end of the chapter.

ACCOUNTING STANDARDS FOR PRIVATE ENTERPRISES

This chapter covered the revenue recognition criteria that are applicable, mainly, to the sale of merchandise. We discuss in Appendix 6A the revenue recognition methods that are applicable for companies involved in long-term contracts extending beyond one accounting period. Accounting standard setters require companies to use the percentage of completion method to recognize both revenue and expenses on long-term contracts on a gradual basis over the duration of the contract.

Financial Reporting Issue	IFRS	ASPE
Long-term contracts	Canadian publicly accountable enterprises are required to use the percentage of completion method, which is discussed in Appendix 6A.	When the percentage of completion method cannot be used, Canadian private enterprises are required to use the completed contract method, which recognizes revenue and the related expenses in the period of completion of the contract, but not in prior periods.

DEMONSTRATION CASE A

Wholesale Warehouse Stores sold $950,000 in merchandise during 2017: $400,000 was on credit with terms 2/10, n/30 (75 percent of these amounts were paid within the discount period); $500,000 was paid with credit cards (there was a 3 percent credit card discount); and the rest was paid in cash. On December 31, 2017, the accounts receivable balance was $80,000, and the allowance for doubtful accounts was $3,000 (credit balance).

Required:

1. Compute net sales for 2017, assuming that sales and credit card discounts are treated as contra-revenue accounts.

2. Assume that Wholesale uses the aging of accounts receivable method and that it estimates that $10,000 worth of current accounts are uncollectible. Record bad debt expense for 2017.

We strongly recommend that you prepare your own answers to these requirements and then check your answers with the following solution.

SUGGESTED SOLUTION

1. Both sales discounts and credit card discounts should be subtracted from sales revenues in the computation of net sales:

Sales revenue	$950,000
Less: Sales discounts (0.02 × 0.75 × $400,000)	6,000
Credit card discounts (0.03 × $500,000)	15,000
Net sales	$929,000

2. The entry made when using the aging of accounts receivable method is the estimated balance minus the unadjusted balance.

Bad debt expense (E) ($10,000 − $3,000)	7,000	
Allowance for doubtful accounts (XA)		7,000

Assets		=	Liabilities	+	Shareholders' Equity	
Allowance for doubtful accounts	−7,000				Bad debt expense	−7,000

DEMONSTRATION CASE B

Heather Ann Long, a first-year university student, has just received her first chequing account statement. This was her first chance to attempt a bank reconciliation. She had the following information to work with:

Bank balance, September 1	$1,150
Deposits during September	650
Cheques cleared during September	900
Bank service charge	5
Bank balance, October 1	$ 895

Heather was surprised that the deposit of $50 she made on September 29 had not been posted to her account and was pleased that her rent cheque of $200 had not cleared her account. Her chequebook balance was $750.

Required:

1. Complete Heather's bank reconciliation.

2. Why is it important for individuals such as Heather and businesses to do a bank reconciliation each month?

We strongly recommend that you prepare your own answers to these requirements and then check your answers with the following solution.

SUGGESTED **SOLUTION**

1. Heather's bank reconciliation:

Heather's Books		Bank Statement	
October 1 cash balance	$750	October 1 cash balance	$ 895
Additions		Additions	
None		Deposit in transit	50
Deductions		Deductions	
Bank service charge	(5)	Outstanding cheque	(200)
Correct cash balance	$745	Correct cash balance	$ 745

2. Bank statements, whether personal or business, should be reconciled each month. This process helps ensure that a correct balance is reflected in the customer's books. Failure to reconcile a bank statement increases the chance that an error will not be discovered and may result in bad cheques being written. Businesses must reconcile their bank statements for an additional reason: the correct balance that is calculated during reconciliation is reported on the statement of financial position. A bank reconciliation is an important internal control measure.

LO6-S1

Explain how revenue is recognized in special circumstances.

APPENDIX 6A: APPLYING THE REVENUE RECOGNITION PRINCIPLE IN SPECIAL CIRCUMSTANCES

The revenue recognition principle was introduced in Chapter 3. As noted earlier, application of this principle in the case of Gildan and similar companies is fairly straightforward. Such companies record revenue according to their sales contract, which specifies the point at which transfer of ownership occurs. We now expand our discussion of the revenue recognition principle and see how it is applied in business practice by companies other than typical manufacturers, wholesalers, and retailers.

Revenue Recognition before the Earnings Process Is Complete: Long-Term Construction Contracts

An important exception to the usual criteria for revenue recognition exists for companies involved in long-term construction projects, such as building an office complex for a large corporation. These projects may take a number of years to complete. As a result, if the company recorded no revenue or expenses directly related to the project during the years that it worked on the project and then recorded massive amounts of revenue and related expenses in the year that it delivered the product to the customer, the financial statements would not accurately represent the company's economic activities during the period of construction. This method of accounting, which is often referred to as the **completed contract method**, records revenue when the completed product is delivered to the customer and may be used by Canadian private enterprises under specific circumstances.

The **COMPLETED CONTRACT METHOD** records revenue when the completed product is delivered to the customer.

The **PERCENTAGE OF COMPLETION METHOD** records revenue based on a reliable measure of the percentage of work completed during the accounting period.

To deal with this unique problem for long-term construction projects, many companies use the **percentage of completion method**, which records revenue based on a reliable measure of the percentage of work completed during the accounting period, instead of the completed contract method, which records revenue when the completed product is delivered to the customer.

Under the percentage of completion method, if the contract revenue and contract costs can be estimated reliably, then both are recognized periodically as revenue and expenses during each period, based on the stage of completion of the contract activity at the end of the reporting period.[13] It also must be probable that the economic benefits of the contract will be collected. Typically, the amount of work accomplished each year is measured by the *percentage of total cost* that was incurred during the year.[14] For example, assume that the total contract price for building a bridge was $50 million and the total cost for construction was $40 million. In 2016, the construction company spent $10 million, which was 25 percent of the contract cost ($10 million ÷ $40 million).[15] This percentage of completion is then multiplied by the total contract revenue to determine the amount of revenue to be reported in 2016 (25% × $50 million = $12.5 million). The amount of expense reported in 2016 is the actual cost incurred, $10 million, and the profit is $2.5 million, the difference between revenue and expense ($12.5 million − $10 million).

Notice that the percentage of completion method does not completely satisfy the first revenue recognition criterion because revenue is reported before the significant risks and rewards of ownership are transferred to the customer. It is an acceptable method, however, because it reflects the economic substance of a company's construction activity throughout the contract period.

When the outcome of a construction contract cannot be estimated reliably, but it is probable that the costs can be collected, the amount of revenue recognized each period is limited to the contract costs that have been incurred in that period, assuming that they are recoverable from the customer. The contract costs are recognized as an expense in that period. This cost recovery method, the **zero profit method**, records revenue that is equal to the actual costs incurred during the accounting period. In the previous example, the revenue that can be recognized is exactly equal to the costs incurred in the first year of the contract. Therefore, the revenue and expenses recognized in 2016 will both equal $10 million, resulting in zero profit in that year.

> The **ZERO PROFIT METHOD** records revenue that is equal to the actual costs incurred during the accounting period.

Revenue Recognition for Service Contracts

Companies that provide services over more than one accounting period often follow revenue recognition policies similar to those followed for long-term construction contracts.[16] They recognize revenue from the completed portion of the services. For example, Federal Express, which provides air delivery service, employs the percentage of completion revenue recognition policy, as indicated in the following note:

FEDERAL EXPRESS CORPORATION AND SUBSIDIARIES

Note 1. Summary of Significant Accounting Policies

Notes to Consolidated Financial Statements

REVENUE RECOGNITION. We recognize revenue upon delivery of shipments for our transportation businesses and upon completion of services for our business services, logistics and trade services businesses.... For shipments in transit, revenue is recorded based on the percentage of service completed at the balance sheet date. Estimates of future billing adjustments to revenue and accounts receivable are recognized at the time of shipment for money-back service guarantees and billing corrections. Delivery costs are accrued as incurred.

REVENUE RECOGNITION AND FINANCIAL STATEMENT ANALYSIS

FINANCIAL **ANALYSIS**

Financial analysts cannot evaluate a company's net earnings if they do not understand how it applied the revenue recognition criteria. As a result, all companies disclose any special revenue recognition issues in the notes to their financial statements. For example, CGI Group Inc., a leading worldwide provider of information technology solutions, business process outsourcing, systems integration, and consulting, states the following in its annual report:

NOTES TO THE CONSOLIDATED FINANCIAL STATEMENTS

3. Summary of Significant Accounting Policies

Revenue recognition

...

The Company's arrangements often include a mix of the services and products. If an arrangement involves the provision of multiple components, the total arrangement value is allocated to each separately identifiable component based on its relative selling price....

Revenue from systems integration and consulting services under fixed-fee arrangements where the outcome of the arrangements can be estimated reliably is recognized using the percentage of completion method over the service periods. The Company uses the labour costs or labour hours to measure the progress towards completion. This method relies on estimates of total expected labour costs or total expected labour hours to complete the service, which are compared to labour costs or labour hours incurred to date, to arrive at an estimate of the percentage of revenue earned to date.... If the outcome of an arrangement cannot be estimated reliably, revenue is recognized to the extent of arrangement costs incurred that are likely to be recoverable....

Source: CGI Group Inc., Annual Report 2015.

This succinct explanation of the percentage of completion method is adequate for someone who has read this chapter, but it is doubtful that someone who has not studied accounting would understand its meaning. Shareholders, lenders, and analysts must examine the company's accounting policy choices for recognition of long-term contract revenue. This will assist them in understanding whether or not reported net revenues are comparable among companies operating in the same industry. Long-term contract revenue recognition is covered in detail in advanced accounting courses.

DEMONSTRATION CASE C

Assume that Landevco Inc., a major land development company, decided to subdivide a large lot of land and develop it into a commercial and residential complex. Landevco contracted with Construk Corp. for the construction of this complex, which will take three years to complete and cost Landevco $400 million, payable in three instalments of $100 million, $150 million, and $150 million at the end of years 1, 2, and 3, respectively. Construk expects to incur $300 million in total costs of construction over the three years. Construk is confident that Landevco will make the promised progress payments on time. The actual costs incurred totalled $90 million, $120 million, and $90 million for years 1, 2, and 3, respectively.

Required:

1. Assume that all the criteria for use of the percentage of completion method are met. Determine the amount that Construk should recognize as profit each year.

2. Assume also that the costs of constructing this project could not be estimated reliably. Use the zero profit method to determine the amount of revenue and profit recognized by Construk each year.

3. Assume that the costs of constructing this project could not be estimated reliably prior to starting the construction. Use the completed contract method to determine the amount of profit that would be recognized each year.

4. Compare the three revenue recognition methods with respect to the recognition of profit each year and for the three-year period as a whole.

We strongly recommend that you prepare your own answers to these requirements and then check your answers with the following solution.

1., 2., and 3.

	Year 1	Year 2	Year 3	Three-Year Period
Actual costs incurred per year	$90	$120	$90	$300
Percentage of completion method				
Percentage of work completed (= Annual cost ÷ Total costs)	30%	40%	30%	
Revenue (= Contract price × Percentage of work completed)	$120	$160	$120	$400
Profit (= Revenue − Actual costs)	30	40	30	100
Zero profit method				
Revenue (= Actual costs)	90	120	190	400
Expenses	90	120	90	300
Profit (= Revenue − Actual costs)	0	0	100	100
Completed contract method				
Revenue	0	0	400	400
Expenses*	0	0	300	300
Profit (= Revenue − Expenses)	0	0	100	100

*The costs incurred each year are accumulated in an asset account until the project is completed. They are recognized as expenses in the year of the completion of the project.

4. The percentage of completion method recognizes each year a proportion of the overall profit based on the percentage of work completed. Neither the completed contract nor the zero profit method recognizes profit during the first two years of the contract period, but both recognize the total amount of profit during the third year. These two methods differ, however, with respect to the amounts of revenue and expense recognized each year. All three methods show the same amount of profit, $100 million, over the three-year period.

CHAPTER **TAKE-AWAYS**

6-1. Apply the revenue recognition principle to determine the accepted time to record sales revenue for typical retailers, wholesalers, manufacturers, and service companies.

Revenue recognition policies are widely recognized as one of the most important determinants of the fair presentation of financial statements. For most merchandisers and manufacturers, the required revenue recognition point is the time of shipment or delivery of goods. For service companies, it is the time at which services are provided.

6-2. Analyze the impact of credit card sales, sales discounts, and sales returns on the amounts reported as net sales.

Both credit card discounts and cash discounts can be recorded either as contra revenues or as expenses. When recorded as contra revenues, they reduce net sales. Sales returns and allowances, which should always be treated as contra revenues, also reduce net sales.

6-3. Compute and interpret the gross profit percentage.

The gross profit percentage measures the ability to charge premium prices and produce goods and services at lower cost. Managers, analysts, and creditors use this ratio to assess the effectiveness of the company's product development, marketing, and production strategy.

6-4. Estimate, report, and evaluate the effects of uncollectible accounts receivable (bad debts) on financial statements.

When receivables are material, companies must employ the allowance method to account for uncollectibles. The steps in the process are as follows:
1. Prepare the end-of-period adjusting entry to record an estimate of bad debt expense.
2. Write off specific accounts determined to be uncollectible during the period.
3. Recover amounts previously written off.

The adjusting entry reduces net earnings as well as net accounts receivable. The write-off of accounts receivables affects neither.

6-5. Compute and interpret the receivables turnover ratio and the effects of accounts receivable on cash flows.

The receivables turnover ratio measures the effectiveness of credit granting and collection activities. It reflects how many times average accounts receivable were recorded and collected during the period. Analysts and creditors watch this ratio because a sudden decline may mean that a company is extending collection deadlines in an attempt to prop up lagging sales, or is even recording sales that will later be returned by customers. Alternatively, the average collection period indicates the average number of days it takes to collect from customers.

When a net decrease in accounts receivable for the period occurs, cash collected from customers exceeds revenue and cash flows from operations increase. When a net increase in accounts receivable occurs, cash collected from customers is less than revenue; thus, the cash flow from operations declines.

6-6. Report, control, and safeguard cash.

Cash is the most liquid of all assets, flowing continuously into and out of a business. As a result, a number of critical control procedures, including the reconciliation of bank accounts, should be applied. Also, management of cash may be critically important to decision makers who must have cash available to meet current needs, yet must avoid excess amounts of idle cash that produce no revenue.

The recording the cost of what was sold is closely related to recording revenue. Chapter 7 will focus on transactions related to inventory and cost of sales. This topic is important because cost of sales has a major impact on a company's gross profit and net earnings, which are watched closely by investors, analysts, and other users of financial statements. Increasing emphasis on quality, productivity, and costs has further focused production managers' attention on cost of sales and inventory. Since inventory cost figures play a major role in product introduction and pricing decisions, they are also important to marketing and general managers. Finally, since inventory accounting has a major effect on many companies' tax liabilities, this is an important place to introduce the effect of taxation on management decision making and financial reporting.

KEY **RATIOS**

The gross profit percentage measures the excess of sales prices over the costs to purchase or produce the goods or services sold, as a percentage. It is computed as follows:

$$\text{Gross profit percentage} = \frac{\text{Gross profit}}{\text{Net sales}}$$

The receivables turnover ratio measures the effectiveness of credit granting and collection activities. It is computed as follows:

$$\text{Receivables turnover ratio} = \frac{\text{Net credit sales}}{\text{Average net accounts receivable}}$$

FINDING **FINANCIAL INFORMATION**

STATEMENT OF FINANCIAL POSITION
Under Current Assets
Accounts receivable (net of allowance for doubtful accounts)

STATEMENT OF CASH FLOWS
Under Operating Activities (indirect method)
Net earnings
+ Decrease in accounts receivable (net)
− Increase in accounts receivable (net)

STATEMENT OF EARNINGS
Revenues
Net sales (sales revenue less discounts, if treated as contra-revenues, and sales returns and allowances)
Expenses
Selling expenses (including bad debt expense and discounts if treated as expenses)

NOTES
Under Summary of Significant Accounting Policies
Revenue recognition policy

QUESTIONS

1. Explain the difference between sales revenue and net sales.
2. What is gross profit or gross margin on sales? How is the gross profit ratio computed? In your explanation, assume that net sales revenue is $100,000 and cost of sales is $60,000.
3. What is a credit card discount? How does it affect amounts reported on the statement of earnings?
4. What is a sales discount? Use credit terms 1/10, n/30 in your explanation.
5. What is the distinction between sales allowances and sales discounts?
6. Differentiate accounts receivable from notes receivable.
7. Which basic accounting concept is satisfied by using the allowance method of accounting for bad debts?
8. Using the allowance method, is bad debt expense recognized in (a) the period in which sales related to the uncollectible amounts were made or (b) the period in which the seller learns that the customer is unable to pay?
9. What is the effect of the write-off of bad debts (using the allowance method) on (a) net earnings and (b) net accounts receivable?
10. Does an increase in the receivables turnover ratio generally indicate faster or slower collection of receivables? Explain.
11. Define cash and cash equivalents in the context of accounting. Indicate the types of items that should be included.
12. Summarize the primary characteristics of an effective internal control system for cash.
13. Accounts receivable are typically collected within three months from the date of sale. Can they be considered cash equivalents? Explain.
14. Why should cash-handling and cash-recording activities be separated? How is this separation accomplished?
15. What are the purposes of bank reconciliation? What balances are reconciled?
16. Briefly explain how the total amount of cash reported on the statement of financial position is computed.
17. (Appendix 6A) When is it acceptable to use the percentage of completion method?

connect MINI-EXERCISES

LO6-1

M6-1   **Interpreting the Revenue Recognition Principle**
Identify the most likely point in time when sales revenue should be recorded for each of the listed transactions.

Transaction	Point A	Point B
a. Airline tickets sold by an airline on a credit card.	___ Point of sale	___ Completion of flight
b. Computer sold by mail-order company on a credit card.	___ Shipment	___ Delivery to customer
c. Sale of inventory to a business customer on open account.	___ Shipment	___ Collection from customers

LO6-2

M6-2   **Reporting Net Sales with Sales Discounts**
Merchandise is sold for $9,500 on terms 1/10, n/30. If the buyer pays within the discount period, what amount will be reported on the statement of earnings as net sales?

LO6-2

M6-3   **Recording Sales Discounts**
A sale is made for $6,000; terms are 3/10, n/30. At what amount should the sale be recorded under the gross method of recording sales discounts? Prepare the required entry. Also give the collection entry, assuming that it is during the discount period.

LO6-2

M6-4   **Reporting Net Sales with Sales Discounts, Credit Card Discounts, and Sales Returns**
Total gross sales for the period include the following:

Credit card sales (discount 3%)	$ 9,400
Sales on account (2/15, n/60)	12,000

Sales returns related to sales on account were $650. All returns were made before payment. One-half of the remaining sales on account were paid within the discount period. The company treats all discounts and returns as contra revenues. What amount will be reported on the statement of earnings as net sales?

■ LO6-3   **M6-5**   **Recording Bad Debts**

Prepare journal entries for each transaction listed.

    a. During the period, bad debts are written off in the amount of $14,500.

    b. At the end of the period, bad debt expense is estimated to be $16,000.

■ LO6-3   **M6-6**   **Determining Financial Statement Effects of Bad Debts**

Using the following categories, indicate the effects of the following transactions. Use + for increase and − for decrease and indicate the accounts affected and the amounts.

Assets	=	Liabilities	+	Shareholders' Equity

    a. At the end of the period, bad debt expense is estimated to be $15,000.

    b. During the period, bad debts are written off in the amount of $9,500.

■ LO6-4   **M6-7**   **Determining the Effects of Credit Policy Changes on Receivables Turnover Ratio**

Indicate the most likely effect of the following changes in credit policy on the receivables turnover ratio (+ for increase, −or decrease, and N for no effect).

    a. Granted credit with shorter payment deadlines.

    b. Increased effectiveness of collection methods.

    c. Granted credit to less creditworthy customers.

■ LO6-5   **M6-8**   **Matching Reconciling Items to the Bank Reconciliation**

Indicate whether the following items would be added (+) or subtracted (−) from the company's books or the bank statement during the preparation of a bank reconciliation.

Reconciling Item	Company's Books	Bank Statement
a. Outstanding cheques		
b. Bank service charge		
c. Deposit in transit		

connect EXERCISES

■ LO6-2   **E6-1**   **Reporting Net Sales with Credit Sales and Sales Discounts**

During the months of January and February, Silver Corporation sold goods to three customers on open account. The sequence of events was as follows:

Jan.   6   Sold goods for $850 to S. Green and billed that amount subject to terms of 2/10, n/30.

      9   Sold goods to M. Munoz for $700 and billed that amount subject to terms of 2/10, n/30.

    14   Collected cash due from S. Green.

Feb.   2   Collected cash due from M. Munoz.

    28   Sold goods for $450 to R. Reynolds and billed that amount subject to terms of 2/10, n/45.

Required:

    1. Assuming that sales discounts are treated as contra revenues, compute net sales for the two months ended February 28.

    2. Prepare the journal entries to record the transactions that occurred on January 6 and 14.

■ LO6-2   **E6-2**   **Reporting Net Sales with Credit Sales, Sales Discounts, and Credit Card Sales**

The following transactions were selected from the records of Evergreen Company:

July 12   Sold merchandise to Rami, who charged the $1,000 purchase on his Visa credit card. Visa charges Evergreen a 2 percent credit card fee.

    15   Sold merchandise to Steven at an invoice price of $6,000; terms 2/10, n/30.

    20   Sold merchandise to Tania at an invoice price of $2,000; terms 2/10, n/30.

    23   Collected payment from Steven from July 15 sale.

Aug. 25   Collected payment from Tania from July 20 sale.

Required:

    1. Assuming that sales discounts are treated as contra revenues, compute net sales for the two months ended August 31.

    2. Prepare the journal entries to record the transactions that occurred on July 12, 15, and 23.

LO6-2

E6-3 **Recording Credit Sales, Sales Discounts, Sales Returns, and Credit Card Sales**

The following transactions were selected from among those completed by Hailey Retailers in 2017:

Nov. 20 Sold two items of merchandise to Baja, who charged the $450 sales amount on her Visa credit card. Visa charges Hailey a 2 percent credit card fee.

25 Sold 14 items of merchandise to Christine for $2,800; terms 2/10, n/30.

28 Sold 12 identical items of merchandise to Daoud for $7,200; terms 2/10, n/30.

30 Daoud returned one of the items purchased on the 28th; the item was defective, and credit was given to the customer.

Dec. 6 Daoud paid the account balance in full.

30 Christine paid in full the amount due for the purchase on November 25, 2017.

Required:

Prepare the appropriate journal entry for each of these transactions, assuming the company uses the gross method to record sales revenue. Do not record the cost of sales.

LO6-2

E6-4 **Reporting Net Sales with Credit Sales, Sales Discounts, Sales Returns, and Credit Card Sales**

The following transactions were selected from among those completed by Gunzo Wholesalers in 2017:

Nov. 20 Sold two items of merchandise to Brigitte, who charged the $800 sales amount on her Visa credit card. Visa charges Gunzo a 2 percent credit card fee.

25 Sold 20 items of merchandise to Clara for $5,000; terms 2/10, n/30.

28 Sold 10 identical items of merchandise to David for $6,000; terms 2/10, n/30.

30 David returned one of the items purchased on the 28th; the item was defective, and credit was given to the customer.

Dec. 6 David paid the account balance in full.

30 Clara paid in full the amount due for the purchase on November 25, 2017.

Required:

1. Assuming that sales discounts and credit card discounts are treated as contra revenues, compute net sales for the two months ended December 31, 2017.

2. Prepare the journal entries to record the transactions that occurred on November 20, November 25, and December 30.

LO6-2

E6-5 **Determining the Effects of Credit Sales, Sales Discounts, Credit Card Sales, and Sales Returns and Allowances on Statement of Earnings Categories**

Rockland Shoe Company records sales returns and allowances as contra revenues, and sales discounts and credit card discounts as selling expenses. Complete the following tabulation, indicating the effect (+ for increase, − for decrease, and N for no effect) of each transaction. Do not record the related cost of sales.

July 12 Sold merchandise to Rosa, who charged the $400 purchase on her American Express card. American Express charges a 3 percent credit card fee.

15 Sold merchandise to Thomas for $6,000; terms 2/10, n/30.

20 Collected the amount due from Thomas.

21 Lee returned shoes with an invoice price of $1,000 before he paid for them.

Transaction	Net Sales	Gross Profit	Earnings from Operations
July 12			
July 15			
July 20			
July 21			

LO6-2

E6-6 **Evaluating the Effects of Sales Returns and Allowances on Sales**

Teen World Inc. sells a wide selection of clothing items for teenage girls. The company imports merchandise from various international suppliers and distributes its merchandise to retail stores in major shopping areas. The company sells merchandise on credit, allows retailers to return incorrect or damaged merchandise within a period of two months, and grants sales allowances under certain circumstances. The company is currently reviewing its sales returns policy and provided you with the following information for the past six quarters:

Quarter	Gross Sales	Cost of Sales	Sales Returns and Allowances
Jan. 1–March 31, 2017	$1,346,300	$ 942,400	$ 53,852
April 1–June 30, 2017	1,474,500	1,042,100	76,674
July 1–Sept. 30, 2017	1,529,100	1,080,300	94,804
Oct. 1–Dec. 31, 2017	1,671,400	1,101,200	140,397
Jan. 1–March 31, 2018	1,708,800	1,103,600	153,792
April 1–June 30, 2018	1,992,700	1,317,500	219,197

Required:

1. Compute the following ratios for each of the six quarters: (a) cost of sales to net sales and (b) sales return and allowances to gross sales.

2. Comment on the ratios computed in (1.) and identify possible reasons for the increase in the amount of sales returns and allowances, and give your recommendations for controlling the amount of sales returns and allowances.

LO6-3

E6-7   **Analyzing Gross Profit Percentage on the Basis of a Multiple-Step Statement of Earnings**

The following summarized data were provided by the records of Slate Inc. for the year ended December 31, 2017:

Sales of merchandise for cash	$233,000
Sales of merchandise on credit	40,000
Cost of sales	146,000
Selling expenses	47,200
Administrative expenses	20,000
Sales returns and allowances	8,000
Bad debt expense	1,200
Items not included in the above amounts:	
Average income tax rate, 30%	
Number of common shares outstanding, 4,500	

Required:

1. Based on these data, prepare a multiple-step statement of earnings (showing both gross profit and earnings from operations).

2. What was the amount of gross profit? What was the gross profit percentage? Explain what these two numbers mean.

LO6-3

E6-8   **Analyzing Gross Profit Percentage on the Basis of a Multiple-Step Statement of Earnings and Within-Industry Comparison**

Wood Work Inc. and Modern Furniture Ltd. are two large home furnishing retailers, selling a wide range of furniture, major appliances, and home electronics. The following data were taken from the 2017 annual reports of both companies (amounts in thousands of Canadian dollars):

	Wood Work	Modern Furniture
Sales revenue	$1,341,080	$682,183
Income taxes expense	15,189	16,901
Cash dividends declared	2,443	28,047
Operating expenses	511,897	223,126
Cost of sales	748,047	398,704
Finance expense (income), net	34,272	(3,350)
Other income	2,317	–
Number of common shares outstanding (in millions)	120.8	70.0

Required:

1. Based on these data, prepare a multiple-step statement of earnings for each company for the year ending December 31, 2017 (showing both gross profit and earnings from operations).

2. Compute the gross profit and the gross profit percentage for each company. Explain what these two numbers mean. What do you believe accounts for the difference between the gross profit percentages of both companies?

LO6-4

E6-9 **Computing Bad Debt Expense by Using Aging Analysis**

Brown Cow Dairy uses the aging approach to estimate bad debt expense. The balance of each account receivable is aged on the basis of three time periods as follows: (1) not yet due, $25,000; (2) up to 120 days past due, $10,000; and (3) more than 120 days past due, $5,000. Experience has shown that, for each age group, the average bad debt rates on the receivables at year-end due to uncollectibility are (1) 2 percent, (2) 10 percent, and (3) 30 percent, respectively. At December 31, 2017 (end of the current year), the allowance for doubtful accounts balance was $600 (credit) before the end-of-period adjusting entry was made.

Required:
What amount should be recorded as bad debt expense for the current year?

LO6-4

The Nestlé Group

E6-10 **Computing Bad Debt Expense by Using Aging Analysis and Reporting Accounts Receivable**

The Nestlé Group disclosed the following analysis of its accounts receivable at December 31, 2014 (amounts in millions of Swiss francs, CHF):

Aged Accounts Receivable	Amount
Not past due	11,801
Past due 1–30 days	851
Past due 31–60 days	254
Past due 61–90 days	108
Past due 91–120 days	60
Past due more than 120 days	737
	13,811

Assume that the estimated percentages of uncollectible accounts were determined as 1 percent, 5 percent, 10 percent, 20 percent, 30 percent, and 40 percent for the six age groups, respectively. At January 1, 2014, the allowance for doubtful accounts had a balance of CHF377, and a total of CHF99 was written off as uncollectible during 2014. The company recovered CHF15 from customers whose accounts were written off in 2013.

Required:
1. Prepare the journal entries to record the receivables that were written off in 2014, the recovery of receivables written off in 2013, and the bad debt expense for 2014.
2. Show how the information related to accounts receivable is presented on the company's statement of financial position as at December 31, 2014.

LO6-4

Daimler AG

E6-11 **Interpreting Bad Debt Disclosures**

Daimler AG is a globally leading producer of premium passenger cars and the largest manufacturer of commercial vehicles in the world. Its group of businesses includes Mercedes-Benz Cars, Daimler Trucks, Daimler Financial Services, Mercedes-Benz Vans, and Daimler Buses. In a recent annual report, it disclosed the following information concerning its allowance for doubtful accounts:

Allowances. Changes in the allowance account for receivables from financial services were as follows:			
(in millions of euros)	2014	2013	2012
Balance at January 1	397	402	467
Charged to costs and expenses	73	66	61
Amounts written off	(66)	(59)	(123)
Currency translation and other changes	8	(12)	(3)
Balance at December 31	412	397	402
Source: Daimler AG, Annual Report 2014.			

Required:
1. Record summary journal entries related to bad debts for the current year. Ignore the currency translations and other changes.
2. If Daimler had written off an additional 10 million euros of accounts receivable during the period, how would net receivables and net earnings have been affected? Explain.

LO6-4

E6-12 **Interpreting Disclosures Related to Credit Card Receivables**

Wood Work Ltd. sells home furnishings, including a wide range of furniture, major appliances, and home electronics. In a recent annual report, it disclosed the following information concerning its accounts receivable.

Aging of accounts receivable, and the related impairment allowances, are provided in the following table (in thousands of dollars):

	Doubtful Accounts 2017	
Current	$19,500	$ –
31–60 days	5,000	100
61–90 days	2,300	65
91–120 days	3,400	985
	$30,200	$1,150

The changes to the allowance for doubtful accounts receivable for 2017 were as follows:

	2017
Balance at beginning of year	$1,200
Impairment losses for unrecoverable receivables	1,300
Amounts written off as uncollectible	(1,150)
Balance at end of year	$1,350

Required:

1. Compute the percentage of uncollectible accounts for each category of receivables that are past due, and comment on the results.
2. How did the company determine the losses due to unrecoverable receivables or bad debt expense?
3. Record summary journal entries related to bad debts for the current year.
4. If Wood Work had written off an amount of an additional $10,000 in accounts receivable during the period, how would net accounts receivable and net earnings have been affected? Explain.

LO6-4

Microsoft

E6-13 **Inferring Bad Debt Write-Offs and Cash Collections from Customers**

Microsoft develops, produces, and markets a wide range of computer software, including the Windows operating system. In a recent annual report, Microsoft reported the following information about accounts receivable and net sales revenue:

	Year 2	Year 1
Accounts receivable, net of allowances of $333 and $375	$14,987	$13,014
Net revenues	68,643	62,484

According to its annual report, Microsoft recorded bad debt expense of $14 during year 2 and did not reinstate any previously written-off accounts.

Required:

1. What amount of bad debts was written off during year 2?
2. Assuming that all of Microsoft's sales during the period were on open account, compute the amount of cash collected from customers for year 2.

LO6-4

Bombardier

E6-14 **Determining the Impact of Uncollectible Accounts on Net Earnings and Working Capital**

An annual report for Bombardier Inc. contained the following information at the end of its fiscal year (in millions of dollars):

	Year 2	Year 1
Accounts receivable	$1,559	$1,450
Allowance for uncollectible accounts	(34)	(42)
	$1,525	$1,408

A footnote to the financial statements disclosed that uncollectible accounts of $5 million and $17 million were written off as bad debts during years 1 and 2, respectively. Assume that the tax rate for Bombardier was 30 percent.

Required:

1. Determine the bad debt expense for year 2 based on the preceding facts.

2. Working capital is defined as current assets minus current liabilities. How was Bombardier's working capital affected by the write-off of $17 million in uncollectible accounts during year 2? What impact did the recording of bad debt expense have on working capital in year 2?

3. How was net earnings affected by the $17 million write-off during year 2? What impact did recording bad debt expense have on net earnings for year 2?

LO6-5
Samsung
Electronics

E6-15   Computing and Interpreting the Receivables Turnover Ratio

Dell Inc. is a global information technology company that offers its customers a broad range of solutions and services delivered directly by Samsung and through other distribution channels. A recent annual report contained the following data:

	(in millions of Korean won)	
	Current Year	**Previous Year**
Accounts receivable	24,972,398	25,256,207
Less: Allowance for doubtful accounts	277,788	267,675
Accounts receivable, net	24,694,610	24,988,532
Net sales (assume all on credit)	206,205,987	

Required:

1. Determine the receivables turnover ratio and average collection period for the current year.

2. Explain the meaning of each number.

LO6-5

The Second Cup

E6-16   Analyzing and Interpreting the Receivables Turnover Ratio

The Second Cup is a Canadian specialty coffee retailer with over 350 cafés that serve the needs of thousands of guests daily. Its annual reports include the following details (in thousands of Canadian dollars):

Year	2015	2014	2013	2012	2011	2010
Net sales	$37,341	$28,172	$27,188	$26,346	$25,001	$25,171
Accounts receivable	5,168	5,115	5,031	4,839	5,449	5,917
Allowance for doubtful accounts	1,734	1,089	663	223	111	74

Required:

1. Determine the receivables turnover ratio and average collection period for 2011–2015, and comment on the results.

2. Explain the meaning of the numbers that you calculated in requirement (1.).

3. Compute the ratio of allowance for doubtful accounts to accounts receivable for each of the six years, and comment on the results.

LO6-5

Air Canada
WestJet Airlines

E6-17   Comparing Receivables Turnover Ratios of Two Companies

The net revenues and balances of accounts receivable (net) for Air Canada and WestJet Airlines for 2014 and 2015 are shown below:

	Air Canada		WestJet Airlines	
	2015	**2014**	**2015**	**2014**
Net revenues	$13,868	$13,272	$4,029	$3,977
Accounts receivable (net)	654	656	82	55

Required:

1. Compute the following for each company for 2015:

   a. The receivables turnover ratio

   b. The average collection period

2. Based on your computations for (1), which company's accounts receivable appear to be the more "liquid" asset? Explain.

LO6-5

Apple Computer
Inc.

E6-18   **Interpreting the Effects of Sales Growth and Changes in Receivables on Cash Flow from Operations**

Apple Computer Inc. is best known for its iMac, iPod, iPad, and iPhone product lines. Three recent years produced a combination of dramatic increases in sales revenue and net earnings. Cash flows from operations also increased during the period. Contributing to that increasing cash flow was the change in accounts receivable. The current- and prior-year statements of financial position reported the following (in millions of U.S. dollars):

	Current Year	Previous Year
Accounts receivable, less allowance for doubtful accounts	$16,849	$17,460

Required:

1. How would the change in accounts receivable affect cash flow from operations for the current year? Explain why it would have this effect.

2. Explain how increasing sales revenue often leads to (a) increasing accounts receivable and (b) an excess of sales revenue over collections from customers.

3. The company reported $233,715 million in net sales for the current year. Compute the receivables turnover ratio and the average collection period for the current year. Are the computed numbers useful to an investor? Explain.

LO6-6

E6-19   **Identifying Strengths and Weaknesses of Internal Control**

You have been engaged to review the internal control procedures used by Data Flow Inc. During the course of your review, you note the following practices:

a. The credit manager maintains the accounts receivable records and handles all collections from customers, because the accounting department personnel are not authorized to handle cash receipts.

b. All cash received from customers is deposited daily in the company's bank account.

c. Employees who handle cash receipts are not permitted to write off accounts receivable as uncollectible.

d. Invoices that require payment are first verified by the accounting personnel for accuracy. An accounting clerk stamps them "paid" if they are cleared for payment, and sends them to the treasurer, who issues and signs the cheques.

e. The cheques issued by the company treasurer are not pre-numbered.

f. After preparing the bank reconciliation, any difference between the adjusted cash balance per the company's books and the adjusted balance per the bank statement is debited (or credited) to the cash account.

Required:

Indicate whether each of these six practices reflects a strength or a weakness of the internal control system. Provide justification for your answer.

LO6-6

E6-20   **Internal Control over Cash**

Organic Growers Inc. is a successful grower of summer fruits and vegetables. The company has a seasonal business that starts in June and ends in October. The owners use a vast agricultural terrain to grow a variety of vegetables and fruits. They employ four workers to help during the planting season and to pick the vegetables and fruits as they become ready for consumption. To save on the cost of harvesting the produce, the owners allow customers to pick the produce they like from the field and then collect the cash for the goods sold. They also have a small store where they keep small quantities of produce for sale to customers who do not wish to pick the produce themselves. Receipts for the purchased goods are given only to those who ask for them. During the summer, the owners accumulate enough cash to pay for farm supplies at the time they are delivered. They do so to avoid wasting time preparing cheques and balancing the chequebook.

Required:

How can Organic Growers strengthen its internal control over cash and improve on its overall cash management?

LO6-6

E6-21   **Reporting Cash and Cash Equivalents When There Are Several Bank Accounts**

Singh Corporation has manufacturing facilities in several cities and has cash on hand at several locations, as well as in several bank accounts. The general ledger at the end of 2017 showed the following accounts:

Cash on hand–home office	$ 700	Cash on hand–location C	$ 200
City Bank–home office	58,600	National Bank–location C	965
Cash on hand–location A	100	Petty cash fund	300
National Bank–location A	3,350	Credit Suisse–3-month certificate of deposit	5,800
Cash on hand–location B	200	FransaBank–6-month certificate of deposit	4,500
National Bank–location B	785		

The bank balances given represent the current cash balances as reflected on the bank reconciliations.

Required:

What amount of cash and cash equivalents should be reported on the company's 2017 statement of financial position? Explain the basis for your decisions on any questionable items.

■ LO6-6   **E6-22**   **Preparing Bank Reconciliation, Entries, and Reporting Cash**

The June 30, 2018, bank statement for Zoltan Company and the June ledger accounts for cash are summarized below:

Bank Statement			
	Cheques	**Deposits**	**Balance**
Balance, June 1, 2018			$ 6,900
Deposits during June		$16,200	23,100
Cheques cleared through June	$17,000		6,100
Bank service charges	40		6,060
Balance, June 30, 2018			6,060

Cash in Bank

June 1	Balance	6,900	June	Cheques written	19,000
June	Deposits	18,100			

Cash on Hand

June 30	Balance	300			

Required:

1. Reconcile the bank balance to the book balance at June 30, 2018. A comparison of the cheques written with the cheques that have cleared the bank shows outstanding cheques of $2,000. No deposits in transit were carried over from May, but a deposit is in transit at the end of June.
2. Prepare any journal entries that should be made as a result of the bank reconciliation.
3. What is the balance in the cash in bank account after the reconciliation entries?
4. What is the total amount of cash that should be reported on the statement of financial position at June 30, 2018?

■ LO6-6   **E6-23**   **Preparing Bank Reconciliation, Entries, and Reporting Cash**

The September 30, 2017, bank statement and the September ledger accounts for cash for Russell Company are summarized below:

Bank Statement			
	Cheques	**Deposits**	**Balance**
Balance, September 1, 2017			$ 6,500
Deposits recorded during September		$26,900	33,400
Cheques cleared during September	$27,400		6,000
NSF cheque–Betty Brown	170		5,830
Bank service charges	60		5,770
Balance, September 30, 2017			5,770

Cash in Bank

Sept. 1	Balance	6,500	Sept.	Cheques written	28,900
Sept.	Deposits	28,100			

Cash on Hand

Sept. 30	Balance	400			

No outstanding cheques and no deposits in transit were carried over from August; however, there are deposits in transit and cheques outstanding at the end of September.

Required:

1. Reconcile the balance in the bank account with the cash balance in the books at September 30, 2017.
2. Prepare any journal entries that should be made as a result of the bank reconciliation.
3. What should be the balance in the cash in bank account after the reconciliation entries?
4. What total amount of cash should the company report on the statement of financial position at September 30, 2017?

■ LO6-6   **E6-24**   **Preparing Bank Reconciliation, Entries, and Reporting Cash**

The bank statement for the Mini Mart Corporation shows a balance of $1,330 on June 30, but the company's cash in bank account had a balance of $499 on the same date. Comparison of the amounts reported on the bank statement with the company's records indicates (a) deposits of $160, representing cash receipts of June 30 that did not appear on the bank statement; (b) outstanding cheques totalling $240; (c) bank service charges for June amounting to $9; (d) collection of a note receivable by the bank on behalf of the company for $800 plus $40 in interest revenue; and (e) a cheque for $80 from a customer that was returned with the bank statement and marked NSF.

Required:

1. Prepare a bank reconciliation statement for Mini Mart Corporation as at June 30.
2. Prepare any journal entries that should be made as a result of the bank reconciliation.
3. Why is it important to reconcile the balance in the bank statement with the cash balance in the company's records?
4. What is the amount of cash that the company should report on its statement of financial position at June 30?

■ LO6-S1   **E6-25**   **(Appendix 7A) Determining Profit for a Construction Contract**

Blanchard Construction Company entered into a long-term construction contract with the government to build a special landing strip at an Air Force base in Saint Hubert, Québec. The project took three years and cost the government $12 million. Blanchard spent the following amounts each year: 2017, $2 million; 2018, $5 million; and 2019, $3 million. The company uses the percentage of completion method. Cost estimates equalled actual costs.

Required:

1. Determine the amount of profit that Blanchard can report each year for this project. Ignore income taxes.
2. Assume that the costs of this project could not be estimated reliably. What amount of profit should the company recognize in each of the three years? Explain.

CONNECT PROBLEMS

■ LO6-1   **P6-1**   **Applying the Revenue Principle** (AP6-1)

At what point should revenue be recognized in each of the following independent cases? Explain your answers.

Case A. For December holiday gifts, a fast-food restaurant sells coupon books for $10. Each of the $1 coupons in a book may be used in the restaurant at any time during the following 12 months. The customer must pay cash when purchasing the coupon book.

Case B. Howard Land Development Corporation sold a lot to Quality Builders to construct a new home. The price of the lot was $50,000. Quality made a down payment of $10,000 and agreed to pay the balance in six months. After making the sale, Howard learned that Quality Builders often entered into these agreements but refused to pay the balance if it did not find a customer who wanted a house built on the lot.

Case C. Driscoll Corporation has always recorded revenue at the point of sale of its refrigerators. Recently, it has extended its warranties to cover all repairs for a period of seven years. One young accountant with the company now questions whether Driscoll has completed its earning process when it sells the refrigerators. She suggests that the warranty obligation for seven years means that a significant amount of additional work must be performed in the future.

LO6-2,6-4 **P6-2** **Reporting Net Sales and Expenses with Discounts, Returns, and Bad Debts** (AP6-1)

The following data were selected from the records of Tunga Company for the year ended December 31, 2018:

Balances at January 1, 2018	
Accounts receivable (various customers)	$115,000
Allowance for doubtful accounts	4,000

The company sells merchandise for cash and on open account with credit terms 2/10, n/30. Assume a unit sales price of $500 in all transactions, and use the gross method to record sales revenue.

The following transactions occurred during 2018:

a. Sold merchandise for cash, $234,000.

b. Sold merchandise to R. Agostino on open account for $11,500.

c. Sold merchandise to K. Black on open account for $25,000.

d. Two days after purchase, R. Agostino returned one of the units purchased in (b) and received account credit.

e. Sold merchandise to B. Assaf on open account for $26,000.

f. R. Agostino paid his account in full within the discount period.

g. Collected $98,000 cash from customers for credit sales made in 2018, all within the discount periods.

h. K. Black paid the invoice in (c) within the discount period.

i. Sold merchandise to R. Fong on open account for $17,500.

j. Three days after paying the account in full, K. Black returned seven defective units and received a cash refund.

k. Collected $6,000 cash on a accounts receivable for sales made in 2017. The amount was received after the discount period.

l. Wrote off an old account of $3,000 after deciding that the amount would never be collected.

m. The company estimates that 4 percent of the accounts receivable at December 31, 2018, will be uncollectible in the future.

Required:

1. Using the following categories, indicate the dollar effect (+ for increase, − for decrease, and N for no effect) of each listed transaction, including the write-off of the uncollectible account and the adjusting entry for estimated bad debts (ignore cost of sales). The effects of the first transaction are shown as an example:

	Sales Revenue	Sales Discounts (taken)	Sales Returns and Allowances	Bad Debt Expense
a.	$234,000	N	N	N

2. Prepare the journal entries for these transactions, including the write-off of the uncollectible account and the adjusting entry for estimated bad debts. Do not record the cost of sales. Show computations for each entry.

3. Show how the accounts related to the preceding sale and collection activities should be reported on the statement of earnings for 2018. (Treat sales discounts as contra revenues.)

LO6-3 **P6-3** **Understanding the Statement of Earnings Based on the Gross Profit Percentage** (AP6-3)

The following data were taken from the year-end records of Nomura Export Company:

Statement of Earnings Items	Year 1	Year 2
Gross sales revenue	$160,000	$232,000
Sales returns and allowances	?	18,000
Net sales revenue	?	?
Cost of sales	68%	?
Gross profit	?	30%
Operating expenses	18,000	?
Earnings before income taxes	?	20,000
Income tax expense (20%)	?	?
Net earnings	?	?
Earnings per share (10,000 shares outstanding)	2.40	?

Required:

Fill in all of the missing amounts. Show computations.

LO6-4   **P6-4   Recording Bad Debts and Interpreting Disclosure of Allowance for Doubtful Accounts** (AP6-4)

Jayco Inc. started its operations in 2016. Its sales, all on account, totalled $700,000. The company collected $500,000 in cash from customers during the year and wrote off $8,000 in uncollectible accounts. The company set up an allowance for doubtful accounts at December 31, 2016, its fiscal year end, and determined the account balance to be $14,000. The unadjusted balances of selected accounts at December 31, 2017, are as follows:

Accounts receivable	$300,000
Allowance for doubtful accounts (debit)	10,000
Sales revenue (including 80 percent in sales on account)	800,000

Aging of the accounts receivable on December 31, 2017, resulted in an estimate of $11,000 in potentially uncollectible accounts.

Required:

1. Prepare the journal entries to record all the transactions during 2016 and post them to appropriate T-accounts.

2. Prepare the journal entries to record all the transactions during 2017 and post them to appropriate T-accounts.

3. Compute the receivables turnover ratio and the average collection period for 2017, and comment on the results.

4. Does the write-off of accounts receivable affect the current ratio? Explain.

5. Does the recording of bad debt expense affect the receivables turnover ratio? Explain.

LO6-4   **P6-5   Determining Bad Debt Expense Based on Aging Analysis** (AP6-5)

Green Pastures Equipment Company uses the aging approach to estimate bad debt expense at the end of each accounting year. Credit sales occur frequently on terms n/60. The balance of each accounts receivable is aged on the basis of three time periods as follows: (1) not yet due, (2) up to one year past due, and (3) more than one year past due. Experience has shown that for each age group, the average bad debt rate on the amounts receivable at year-end due to uncollectibility are (1) 1 percent, (2) 5 percent, and (3) 30 percent, respectively.

At December 31, 2017 (end of the current accounting year), the accounts receivable balance was $45,000, and the unadjusted balance of the allowance for doubtful accounts was $1,020 (credit). To simplify, the accounts of only five customers are used; the details of each are given below:

Date	Explanation	Debit	Credit	Balance
B. Brown–Account Receivable				
11/3/2016	Sale	$13,000		$13,000
30/6/2016	Collection		$4,000	9,000
31/1/2017	Collection		3,000	6,000
D. Di Lella–Account Receivable				
28/2/2017	Sale	22,000		22,000
15/4/2017	Collection		10,000	12,000
30/11/2017	Collection		7,000	5,000
N. Gidda–Account Receivable				
30/11/2017	Sale	9,000		9,000
15/12/2017	Collection		2,000	7,000
S. Kavouris–Account Receivable				
1/2/2014	Sale	19,000		19,000
1/3/2014	Collection		5,000	14,000
2/3/2015	Sale	5,000		19,000
15/4/2015	Collection		5,000	14,000
1/9/2016	Sale	10,000		24,000
15/10/2016	Collection		8,000	16,000
31/12/2017	Sale	4,000		20,000
T. Patel–Account Receivable				
30/12/2017	Sale	7,000		7,000

Required:

1. Prepare an aging analysis schedule and complete it.

2. The company determined that any receivables that date back to sales made prior to 2016 are deemed to be uncollectible. Compute the estimated uncollectible amount for each age category and in total.

3. Prepare the necessary journal entries to adjust the Accounts Receivable account and to recognize the bad debt expense at December 31, 2017.

4. Show how the amounts related to accounts receivable should be presented on the statement of earnings for 2017 and the statement of financial position at December 31, 2017.

LO6-4 **P6-6** **Determining Bad Debt Expense Based on Aging Analysis and Interpreting Ratios** (AP6-6)
IceKreme Inc. makes ice cream machines for sale to ice cream parlours. The following events occurred between April 1 and June 30, 2017:

April 10	Received an order from Peter's Appliances, a wholesaler, for 10 machines.
April 30	Sold 15 machines to Yuri Inc. on credit.
May 1	The purchasing manager of Peter's Appliances visited IceKreme's factory and purchased 12 machines instead of the 10 machines that were previously ordered.
May 5	Yuri Inc. paid for the machines purchased on April 30.
May 7	Sold 10 machines to Cheng Ltd. on credit.
May 10	Wrote off $12,000 of accounts receivable that were considered uncollectible. These receivables relate to sales made prior to April 1, 2017.
May 15	Peter's Appliances returned two defective machines and paid the amount due.
June 1	Received $80,000 from Cheng Ltd. on account.
June 30	Recovered $3,000 from the receivables that were written off on May 10.

Additional information is as follows:
- IceKreme sold all machines at $10,000 per unit.
- All of IceKreme's sales were on credit with terms 2/10, n/30.
- IceKreme's records included the following items and their balances as at March 31, 2017:

Accounts receivable	$ 60,000
Allowance of doubtful accounts (credit balance)	15,000
Net sales	600,000

Required:

1. Prepare the journal entries to record the transactions that occurred from April 1 to June 30, 2017.

2. The company uses the *aging of accounts receivable* method to determine the amount of bad debt expense. The estimated uncollectible rates for the various age groups are as follows:

	Aging of Accounts Receivable			
	Not Yet Due	1–30 Days Past Due	31–60 Days Past Due	Over 60 Days Past Due
Estimated % uncollectible	5%	10%	15%	20%

Determine the amount of receivables that may not be collectible in the future, and prepare the journal entry to record bad debt expense at June 30, 2017, the company's fiscal year-end. (*Hint*: Use a timeline to keep track of accounts receivable in order to determine the age of these receivables.)

3. IceKreme's net accounts receivable were $60,000 at June 30, 2016. Calculate IceKreme's average collection period for fiscal year 2017 and explain its meaning.

4. Evaluate IceKreme's average collection period, knowing that two major competitors, Julia Corp. and Pino Ltd., reported average collection periods of 18.3 days and 30.7 days, respectively, for fiscal year 2017.

LO6-3,6-4,6-5 **P6-7** **Recording Receivables Transactions, Determining Bad Debt Expense, and Interpreting Ratios** (AP6-7)
At December 1, 2017, Imalda Inc. reported the following information on its statement of financial position:

Accounts receivable	$154,000
Allowance for doubtful accounts	4,500 (credit balance)

The following transactions were completed during December 2017:

December 5 — Sold merchandise items for $67,000. An amount of $19,000 was received in cash and the rest on account; terms 2/10, n/60. The total cost of sales was $35,000.

December 12 — Collected cash for *half* of the credit sales made on December 5.

December 20 — Collected $90,000 in cash from customers for credit sales made in November 2017.

December 26 — One of Imalda's customers that owed $3,000 to the company experienced financial problems and was forced to close its business in December. The full amount was considered uncollectible.

Imalda uses the aging of accounts receivable method to determine bad debt expense. The aging schedule at December 31, 2017, gives the following information about the accounts receivable estimated uncollectible:

	Aging of Accounts Receivable			
	Not Yet Due	1–30 Days Past Due	31–60 Days Past Due	Over 60 Days Past Due
Total	42,000	31,500	5,000	6,500
Estimated % uncollectible	1%	2%	10%	30%

Required:

1. Prepare the journal entries to record the transactions that occurred in December 2017.

2. Using the aging schedule, compute the bad debt expense for December 2017 and prepare the related adjusting entry.

3. Compute the gross profit percentage and the receivables turnover ratio for December 2017 and explain their meaning.

LO6-4

P6-8 **Determining Bad Debts and Reporting Accounts Receivable** (AP6-8)

The bookkeeper of Vital Inc. has asked you to assist him with the preparation of information about the company's accounts receivable for presentation in the statement of financial position at December 31, 2018, the end of the company's fiscal year. The following details have been extracted from the company's files:

	Debit	Credit
Accounts receivable, January 1, 2018	$500,000	
Allowance for doubtful accounts, January 1, 2018		$25,000

Sales for 2018 totalled $1,300,000; $300,000 were in cash and the rest on account. The company collected $1,100,000 from credit customers during 2018 and wrote off $30,000 of accounts receivable as uncollectible.

Required:

1. Determine the balance of accounts receivable at December 31, 2018.

2. Vital estimates that 6 percent of the ending balance of its accounts receivable may not be collected in the future. Prepare the journal entries to record the write-off of accounts receivable and the bad debt expense for 2018.

3. Show how the information related to accounts receivable is presented on the company's statement of financial position as at December 31, 2018.

4. After you finished helping the bookkeeper with the journal entries and the statement of financial position presentation, he said, "These calculations seem to be complicated. Would it not be simpler to treat the $30,000 as bad debt expense when the company is certain that the customers are not able to pay the amount owed? That way, you record the exact amount of bad debt when it happens, and you do not have to estimate an amount of doubtful accounts and risk being incorrect." Prepare a response to the bookkeeper.

LO6-2,6-3,6-4,6-5

P6-9 **Preparing a Multiple-Step Statement of Earnings and Computing the Gross Profit Percentage and Receivables Turnover Ratio with Discounts, Returns, and Bad Debts** (AP6-9)

 eXcel

Builders Company Inc. sells heavy-construction equipment. It has 10,000 common shares outstanding and its fiscal year ends on December 31. The adjusted trial balance was taken from the general ledger on December 31, 2017:

Account Titles	Debit	Credit
Cash	$ 33,600	
Accounts receivable (net)	14,400	
Inventory, ending	52,000	
Property, plant, and equipment	40,000	
Accumulated depreciation		$ 16,800
Liabilities		24,000
Common shares		72,000
Retained earnings, January 1, 2017		9,280
Sales revenue		145,600
Sales returns and allowances	5,600	
Cost of sales	78,400	
Selling expenses	13,600	
Administrative expenses	14,400	
Bad debt expense	1,600	
Sales discounts	6,400	
Income tax expense	7,680	
Totals	$267,680	$267,680

Required:

1. Prepare a multiple-step statement of earnings (showing both gross profit and net earnings from operations). Treat sales discounts as contra revenues.

2. The beginning balance of accounts receivable (net) was $16,000. Compute the gross profit percentage and receivables turnover ratio and explain their meaning.

■ LO6-6

P6-10 **Evaluating Internal Controls** (AP6-10)

Cripple Creek Company has one trusted employee, who, as the owner said, "handles all of the bookkeeping and paperwork for the company." This employee is responsible for counting, verifying, and recording cash receipts and payments, making the weekly bank deposit, preparing cheques for major expenditures (signed by the owner), making small expenditures from the cash register for daily expenses, and collecting accounts receivable. The owner asked the local bank for a $20,000 loan. The bank asked that an audit be performed covering the year just ended. The independent auditor, in a private conference with the owner, presented some evidence of the following activities of the trusted employee during the past year:

a. Cash sales sometimes were not entered in the cash register, and the trusted employee pocketed approximately $50 per month.

b. Cash taken from the cash register (and pocketed by the trusted employee) was replaced with expense memos with fictitious signatures (approximately $12 per day). Cripple Creek is open five days per week throughout the year.

c. A $300 collection on a accounts receivable of a valued out-of-town customer was pocketed by the trusted employee and was covered by making a $300 entry as a debit to sales returns and a credit to accounts receivable.

d. An $800 collection on a accounts receivable from a local customer was pocketed by the trusted employee and was covered by making an $800 entry as a debit to allowance for doubtful accounts and a credit to accounts receivable.

Required:

1. What was the approximate amount stolen during the past year?

2. What would be your recommendations to the owner about the company's internal controls?

■ LO6-6

P6-11 **Preparing a Bank Reconciliation** (AP6-11)

The president of Kostas Fashions Ltd., Joan Kostas, has just received the monthly bank statement for June, which shows a balance of $10,517. She remembers seeing a different balance for cash at June 30 when the company accountant, Peter Wong, presented to her the monthly statement of financial position. She checks the statement of financial position and finds a cash balance of $6,518. She is not sure which amount is correct. She calls Peter and asks him why the two amounts are different. Peter takes the bank statement and related documents and promises to provide her with an explanation within a few hours. He then proceeds to prepare a bank reconciliation report for the month of June.

A review of the documents that accompanied the bank statement shows the following:

a. A credit memorandum for the collection of a note for $2,080, including $80 of interest on the note. The bank charged the company a collection fee of $25.

b. A debit memorandum for an NSF cheque for $286 from customer Rami Cossette.

c. Total service charges for June amounting to $39.

d. When comparing the bank statement with the company's records, Peter discovered the following discrepancies:

e. A deposit of $1,145 was not recorded on the bank statement.

f. Three cheques had not been presented to the bank for payment yet. The amounts of these cheques are $1,573, $679, and $1,252.

g. A deposit of $2,340 was recorded incorrectly in the books at $2,430.

Required:

1. Explain to Joan why the two balances for cash are not equal, and why it is important to prepare a bank reconciliation statement.

2. Prepare a bank reconciliation statement at June 30 and the related journal entries.

LO6-7

eXcel

P6-12   **Preparing a Bank Reconciliation and Related Journal Entries** (AP6-12)

The bookkeeper at Hopkins Company has not reconciled the bank statement with the cash account, saying instead, "I don't have time." You have been asked to prepare a reconciliation and review the procedures with the bookkeeper.

The April 30, 2018, bank statement and the April ledger accounts for cash showed the following (summarized):

Bank Statement			
	Cheques	**Deposits**	**Balance**
Balance, April 1, 2018			$31,000
Deposits during April		$36,100	67,100
Notes collected for company (including $70 interest)		1,180	68,280
Cheques cleared during April	$44,500		23,780
NSF cheque–A. B. Wright	160		23,620
Bank service charges	70		23,550
Balance, April 30, 2018			23,550

Cash in Bank

Apr. 1	Balance	23,500	Apr.	Cheques written	41,100
Apr.	Deposits	41,500			

Cash on Hand

Apr. 30	Balance	100	

A comparison of cheques written before and during April with the cheques cleared through the bank showed that cheques of $4,100 are still outstanding at April 30. No deposits in transit were carried over from March, but a deposit was in transit at April 30.

Required:

1. Prepare a detailed bank reconciliation at April 30, 2018.

2. Prepare any required journal entries as a result of the reconciliation. Why are they necessary?

3. What were the balances in the cash accounts in the ledger on May 1, 2018?

4. What total amount of cash should be reported on the statement of financial position at April 30, 2018?

ALTERNATE PROBLEMS

LO6-1

AP6-1   **Applying the Revenue Principle** (P6-1)

Review the revenue recognition practices of the following companies, and indicate at what point in time revenue should be recognized in each of these independent cases. Explain your answer.

Case A. The sales representatives of Computec Corporation are under intense pressure to achieve very high sales levels. To achieve their specific objectives, the sales representatives ask customers to order computer equipment in advance, with payment to be made later. In many cases, the company records sales on the basis of customers' orders, even though the ordered equipment may not have been manufactured yet.

Case B. Scenic Trails Inc. is a campground operator that sells annual memberships to campers. Members are allowed to pay the annual membership fees over a period of six months. The company records revenue from membership fees as soon as a new member signs the membership agreement. Members are allowed 10 days to cancel their memberships, and many members cancel their memberships within days of signing.

Case C. Educational Toys Inc. sells a wide variety of toys to distributors and allows them to return unsold merchandise within a period of three months. The company's policy encourages distributors to buy products and keep them for three months, knowing they could return any unsold merchandise during this period. The company recognizes revenue as soon as it delivers its products to distributors.

LO6-2,6-4   **AP6-2**   **Reporting Net Sales and Expenses with Discounts, Returns, and Bad Debts** (P6-2)
The following data were selected from the records of Fluwars Company for the year ended December 31, 2017:

Balances at January 1, 2017:	
Accounts receivable (various customers)	$116,000
Allowance for doubtful accounts	5,200

The company sold merchandise for cash and on open account with credit terms 1/10, n/30. Assume a unit sales price of $400 in all transactions and use the gross method to record sales revenue.
   The following transactions occurred during 2017:

a. Sold merchandise for cash, $228,000.

b. Sold merchandise to Abbey Corp; invoice amount, $12,000.

c. Sold merchandise to Brown Company; invoice amount, $23,600.

d. Abbey paid the invoice in (*b*) within the discount period.

e. Sold merchandise to Cavendish Inc.; invoice amount, $26,000.

f. Two days after paying the account in full, Abbey returned four defective units and received a cash refund.

g. Collected $89,100 cash from customers for credit sales made in 2017, all within the discount periods.

h. Three days after the purchase date, Brown returned three of the units purchased in (*c*) and received account credit.

i. Brown paid its account in full within the discount period.

j. Sold merchandise to Decca Corporation; invoice amount, $18,400.

k. Cavendish paid its account in full after the discount period.

l. Wrote off an old account of $2,400 after deciding that the amount would never be collected.

m. The estimated bad-debt rate used by the company was 5 percent of accounts receivable at December 31, 2017.

Required:

1. Using the following categories, indicate the dollar effect (+ for increase, − for decrease, and N for no effect) of each listed transaction, including the write-off of the uncollectible account and the adjusting entry for estimated bad debts (ignore the cost of sales). The effects of the first transaction are shown as an example.

	Sales Revenue	Sales Discounts (taken)	Sales Returns and Allowances	Bad Debt Expense
a.	$228,000	N	N	N

2. Prepare the journal entries for these transactions, including the write-off of the uncollectible account and the adjusting entry for estimated bad debts. Do not record the cost of sales. Show computations for each entry.

3. Show how the accounts related to the preceding sale and collection activities should be reported on the statement of earnings for 2017. (Treat sales discounts as contra-revenues.)

LO6-3   **AP6-3**   **Understanding the Statement of Earnings Based on the Gross Profit Percentage** (P6-3)
The following data were taken from the year-end records of Glare Import Company:

Statement of Earnings Items	Year 1	Year 2
Gross sales revenue	$210,000	$255,000
Sales discounts	?	5,000
Net sales revenue	207,000	?
Cost of sales	?	60%
Gross profit	40%	?
Operating expenses	42,800	?
Earnings before income taxes	?	70,000
Income tax expense (30%)	?	?
Earnings before discontinued operations	?	?
Discontinued operations, net of tax	10,000 (loss)	2,500 (gain)
Net earnings	?	?
Earnings per share (8,000 shares outstanding)	?	?

Required:

Fill in all of the missing amounts. Show computations.

LO6-4   **AP6-4**   **Recording Bad Debts and Interpreting Disclosure of Allowance for Doubtful Accounts** (P6-4)

Ratgo Corp. is a wholesaler of imported products. It reported $3,500,000 in sales for fiscal year 2017, all on account. The company collected $3,000,000 in cash from customers during the year and wrote off $17,000 in uncollectible accounts. The company's allowance for doubtful accounts had a credit balance of $18,000 at December 31, 2016, and a credit balance of $20,000 at December 31, 2017.

The unadjusted balances of selected accounts at December 31, 2018, are as follows:

Accounts receivable	$ 750,000
Allowance for doubtful accounts (debit)	5,000
Sales revenue (including 85 percent in sales on account)	4,000,000

Aging of the accounts receivable on December 31, 2018, resulted in an estimate of $25,000 in potentially uncollectible accounts.

Required:

1. Prepare the journal entries to record all the transactions during 2017 and post them to appropriate T-accounts.

2. Prepare the journal entries to record all the transactions during 2018 and post them to appropriate T-accounts.

3. Compute the receivables turnover ratio and the average collection period for 2018, and comment on the results.

4. Does the write-off of accounts receivable affect the receivables turnover ratio? Explain.

5. Does the recording of bad debt expense affect the current ratio? Explain.

LO6-4   **AP6-5**   **Determining Bad Debt Expense Based on Aging Analysis** (P6-5)

Big & Small Engines Inc. uses the aging approach to estimate bad debt expense at the end of each fiscal year. Credit sales occur frequently on terms n/45. The balance of each accounts receivable is aged on the basis of four time periods as follows: (1) not yet due, (2) up to 6 months past due, (3) 6 to 12 months past due, and (4) more than one year past due. Experience has shown that for the age groups, the average bad debt rates on the amounts receivable at year-end due to uncollectibility are (1) 1 percent, (2) 5 percent, (3) 20 percent, and (4) 50 percent, respectively.

At December 31, 2017 (end of the current fiscal year), the accounts receivable balance was $39,500, and the allowance for doubtful accounts balance was $1,550 (debit). To simplify, the accounts of only five customers are used; the details of each are given below:

Date	Explanation	Debit	Credit	Balance
R. Aouad–Account Receivable				
13/3/2017	Sale	$19,000		$19,000
12/5/2017	Collection		$10,000	9,000
30/9/2017	Collection		7,000	2,000
C. Chronis–Account Receivable				
01/06/2016	Sale	31,000		31,000
01/11/2016	Collection		20,000	11,000
01/12/2017	Collection		5,000	6,000

D. McClain–Account Receivable				
31/10/2017	Sale	12,000		12,000
10/12/2017	Collection		8,000	4,000
T. Skibinski–Account Receivable				
02/05/2017	Sale	15,000		15,000
01/06/2017	Sale	10,000		25,000
15/06/2017	Collection		15,000	10,000
15/07/2017	Collection		10,000	0
01/10/2017	Sale	26,000		26,000
15/11/2017	Collection		16,000	10,000
15/12/2017	Sale	4,500		14,500
H. Wu–Account Receivable				
30/12/2017	Sale	13,000		13,000

Required:

1. Set up an aging analysis schedule and complete it.

2. Compute the estimated uncollectible amount for each age category and in total.

3. Prepare the adjusting entry for bad debt expense at December 31, 2017.

4. Show how the amounts related to accounts receivable should be presented on the statement of earnings for 2017 and the statement of financial position at December 31, 2017.

■ LO6-3,6-4 **AP6-6** **Determining Bad Debt Expense Based on Aging Analysis and Interpreting Ratios** (P6-6)
Modern Machine Shop (MMS) Inc. manufactures special moulds that are used in the production of plastic toys. Below is MMS's accounts receivable ledger from October 1 to December 31, 2018:

General Ledger			Accounts Receivable		
Date	**Explanation**		**Debit**	**Credit**	**Balance**
Oct. 1	Balance				9,500
Oct. 8	Wrote off uncollectible accounts.			1,500	8,000
Oct. 15	Sold 10 moulds to Allen Inc.		5,000		13,000
Oct. 31	Sold 15 moulds to Machinex Ltd.		7,500		20,500
Nov. 5	Received the amount due from Machinex for moulds purchased on October 31.			7,500	13,000
Nov. 7	Sold 20 moulds to Centra Corp.		10,000		23,000
Nov. 16	Allen Inc. returned two moulds and paid the amount due for the remaining moulds purchased on October 15.			5,000	18,000
Nov. 25	Centra Corp. returned two moulds purchased on November 7.			1,000	17,000
Nov. 29	Centra Corp. made a partial payment on the moulds purchased on November 7.			5,000	12,000
Dec. 20	Recovered $500 that was written off on October 8.		500	500	12,000

Additional information is as follows:

a. MMS sold its special moulds at $500 each.

b. All sales were on credit with terms 2/10, n/30.

c. MMS's records included the following items and their balances as at September 30, 2018:

Net sales	$100,000
Accounts receivable	9,500
Allowance for doubtful accounts (credit balance)	1,300

Required:

1. Prepare the journal entries to record the transactions on October 8, November 5, November 16, and December 20.

2. MMS uses the aging of accounts receivable method to determine the amount of receivables that may not be collectible in the future. Its estimated uncollectible rates are as follows:

	Aging of Accounts Receivable			
	Not Yet Due	1–30 Days Past Due	31–60 Days Past Due	Over 60 Days Past Due
Estimated % uncollectible	1%	5%	10%	15%

Determine the amount of receivables that may not be collectible in the future, and prepare the journal entry to record bad debt expense on December 31, 2018. Show your calculations. (*Hint*: You may wish to keep track of accounts receivable in order to determine the age of these receivables.)

3. MMS's cost of sales is $60,000 for 2018. Compute and evaluate MMS's gross profit percentage for 2018. MMS's gross profit percentages were 35 percent and 40 percent for 2016 and 2017, respectively.

LO6-4,6-5   **AP6-7**   **Recording Receivables Transactions, Reporting Accounts Receivable, and Interpreting Ratios** (P6-7)

Rodamex Inc. reported the following summary transactions during the year ended December 31, 2018:

a. Sold merchandise for $5,000,000, including $500,000 cash and $4,500,000 on account, with terms net/30.

b. Sales returns and allowances, $50,000; 10 percent related to cash sales, and 90 percent related to sales on account.

c. Received $4,200,000 from customers on credit sales.

d. Wrote off $17,000 in uncollectible accounts receivable.

e. Recovered $6,000 cash from a customer whose account was previously written off.

Rodamex estimated that doubtful accounts receivable represented 2 percent of the accounts receivable balance at December 31, 2017, and 2.5 percent at December 31, 2018. The company had $700,000 in accounts receivable at December 31, 2017.

Required:

1. Prepare journal entries to record the summary transactions.

2. Show how accounts receivable would be presented on the company's comparative statement of financial position as at December 31, 2018.

3. Prepare the adjusting journal entry to record bad debt expense for 2018.

4. Compute the receivables turnover ratio for 2018. What does the result suggest about the company's ability to manage accounts receivable during 2018?

5. Compute the gross profit for 2018 assuming that the company's cost of sales averages 40 per cent of its net sales.

LO6-4   **AP6-8**   **Determining Bad Debts and Reporting Accounts Receivable** (P6-8)

Modern Kitchens Inc. (MKI) is a Montréal-based company that sells imported fancy kitchenware to retailers. Selected account balances as at September 30, 2017, are shown below:

	Debit	Credit
Accounts receivable	$119,000	
Allowance for doubtful accounts		$3,000

During October 2017, the following transactions occurred:

a. The company sold merchandise on account to various retailers for a total amount of $76,000, terms 2/10, n/30. A few retailers who purchased merchandise for a gross amount of $40,000 paid the amount due within 10 days. A total of $16,000 of the October sales remained unpaid at October 31, 2017.

b. Customers paid the company $50,000 for merchandise they purchased prior to September 30, 2017. These customers did not pay within the discount period.

c. Two of MKI's customers owed the company a total of $5,000 and were facing financial difficulties during October due to increased competition. They were forced to close their businesses before the end of October 2017. MKI does not expect to receive any money from these two customers and considers their accounts uncollectible.

d. The company received new kitchenware from a Korean supplier, Kim & Sons Ltd., for $40,000. The invoice indicated that the supplier would allow a cash discount of 1 percent if the invoice were paid before the end of October 2017. MKI paid the supplier on November 10, 2017.

MKI estimates that 4 percent of its accounts receivable at October 31, 2017, will not be collected in the future.

Required:

1. Prepare the journal entries to record the transactions that occurred in October 2017, and any related adjusting journal entries at October 31, 2017, the end of MKI's fiscal year.

2. Show how the information related to accounts receivable is presented on the company's statement of financial position at October 31, 2017.

3. The major shareholder of MKI, Michel Beauregard, was reading through the company's statement of financial position and noticed the account allowance for doubtful accounts. He called Carol Jones, MKI's accountant, and made the following statement: "Carol, I don't think we need to make a provision for doubtful accounts as it will reduce the amount of accounts receivable unnecessarily. I think we should wait until we are certain that we cannot collect from our customers before showing a reduction in the accounts receivable on the statement of financial position. This way, the accounts receivable balance will be more accurate. I would like you to make the necessary change to the financial statements before they are distributed to the other shareholders." Assume the role of Carol and prepare a response to Michel.

4. MKI had an opportunity to get a loan from the Bank of International Trade (BIT) to pay the amount due to Kim & Sons Ltd. The loan would have cost MKI $300 in interest charges. Should MKI have obtained the loan from BIT to pay its debt to Kim & Sons Ltd. before October 31, 2017?

 LO6-2,6-3,6-5 AP6-9 **Preparing a Multiple-Step Statement of Earnings and Computing the Gross Profit Percentage with Discounts, Returns, and Bad Debts** (P6-9)

Perry Corporation is a local grocery store organized seven years ago as a corporation. At that time, 10,000 common shares were issued to the three organizers. The store is in an excellent location, and sales have increased each year. At the end of 2018, the bookkeeper prepared the following statement (assume that all amounts are correct; note the incorrect terminology and format):

PERRY CORPORATION Profit and Loss December 31, 2018		
	Debit	**Credit**
Sales		$184,000
Cost of sales	$ 98,000	
Sales returns and allowances	9,000	
Selling expenses	17,000	
Administrative and general expenses	18,000	
Bad debt expense	2,000	
Sales discounts	8,000	
Income tax expense	10,900	
Net earnings	21,100	
Totals	$184,000	$184,000

Required:

1. Beginning with net sales, prepare a multiple-step statement of earnings (showing both gross profit and earnings from operations). Treat sales discounts as a contra-revenue account

2. The beginning and ending balances of accounts receivable were $16,000 and $18,000, respectively. Compute the gross profit percentage and receivables turnover ratio and explain their meaning.

 LO6-6   **AP6-10** **Evaluating Internal Controls** (P6-10)

Cory Magnum has been working for Matrix Products Inc. for five years and has gained the respect of his peers for his exemplary behaviour and work ethic. His job includes receiving cash and cheques from customers, depositing the cash receipts in the company's account at the local bank, and recording the transactions in the company's computerized accounting program. Cory was faced with personal financial problems and decided to make use of $2,000 of the company's available cash to solve them. He planned to return the money as soon as his financial situation improved. The $2,000 he took was part of the total cash sales to customers during the previous two business days. At the same time, Cory had received a cheque for $2,000 from PLC Ltd. as a partial payment on its accounts receivable.

To hide his theft, Cory deposited the cheque instead of the cash into the company's bank account and made the following journal entry:

Cash in bank	2,000	
Cash on hand		2,000

In addition, he recorded the following journal entry to credit the account of PLC Ltd. to avoid any questions from that company in the future:

| Sales returns and allowances | 2,000 | |
| Accounts receivable–PLC Ltd. | | 2,000 |

Required:

1. Assume that Matrix Products prepares financial statements on a monthly basis. Would any items on the statement of earnings or the statement of financial position be incorrect? Explain.

2. Identify the weaknesses that exist in the company's internal control system. What changes should be made to strengthen internal control over cash receipts?

LO6-6   **AP6-11**   **Preparing a Bank Reconciliation and Related Journal Entries** (P6-11)

Sergio Lucas worked long hours during the summer and saved enough money to pay his tuition and living expenses to continue his studies at the local university. On September 1, he downloaded from the bank's website his bank statement for August to make sure that the bank had not made any errors related to his bank account. Sergio has had a habit of verifying all the entries in his bank account ever since he discovered that the bank had charged him a service fee for a transaction that was unrelated to his account. After comparing the bank statement with the entries he has made in his chequebook, Sergio found that the bank statement showed a balance of $12,506.60 but his chequebook showed a balance of $12,651.65 on August 31, a difference of $145.05. He decided to compare the entries in his chequebook with those in the bank statement, hoping that the bank owes him this difference.

Sergio's review of the bank statement showed the following:

a. Three cheques (#124, #125, and #126) that he wrote in late August have not been withdrawn from his bank account yet. They totalled $619.35.

b. An automatic deduction of $44.10 was made to pay the hydro bill for August.

c. Another automatic deduction of $55.30 was made to pay for telecommunication services from Telus Corp.

d. He forgot to record in his chequebook two withdrawals from instant teller machines totalling $300.

e. A cheque for $385 that he deposited in the bank the night of August 31 did not appear on the bank statement.

f. Sergio discovered that he recorded cheque #123 as $96.25 but the correct amount that cleared his bank account was $69.25.

g. The bank charged him a service fee of $7 for August transactions.

Required:

1. Assume the role of Sergio and prepare a bank reconciliation at August 31.

2. Which amounts should Sergio enter into his chequebook to avoid making any errors in reconciling his chequebook with the bank statement for September?

LO6-6   **AP6-12**   **Computing A Outstanding Cheques and Deposits in Transit and Preparing a Bank Reconciliation and Journal Entries** (P6-12)

The August 2017 bank statement for Martha Company and the August 2017 ledger accounts for cash follow:

PB Provincial Bank 594 Water Street Faubourg, ON L2G 4S6	STATEMENT OF ACCOUNT				
	DATE	BRANCH NUMBER	ACCOUNT TYPE	ACCOUNT NUMBER	PAGE NO.
Martha Company 2784, 7th Avenue Faubourg, ON L3G 3B5	31 08 2017	815	Chequing	85157	1 OF 1

Date	Description	Debits	Credits	Balance
Aug. 1	Balance Forward			17,470
2	Cheque No. 103	300		17,170
3	Deposit		12,000	29,170
4	Cheque No. 101	400		28,770
5	Cheque No. 105	250		28,520
9	Cheque No. 102	900		27,620
10	Cheque No. 104	300		27,320
15	Deposit		4,000	31,320
21	Cheque No. 106	400		30,920
24	Cheque No. 108	21,000		9,920
25	Deposit		7,000	16,920
30	Cheque No. 109	800		16,120
30	Collection of note		2,180	18,300
30	Service charge	10		18,290
31	Interest earned		80	18,370

The amount collected on August 30 includes interest of $180.

Cash in Bank

Aug. 1	Balance	16,520	Cheques written		
Deposits			Aug. 2		300
Aug. 2		12,000	4		900
12		4,000	15		290
24		7,000	17		550
31		5,000	18		800
			20		400
			23		21,000

Cash on Hand

Aug. 31	Balance	200	

Outstanding cheques at the end of July were for $250, $400, and $300. No deposits were in transit at the end of July.

Required:

1. Compute the amount of deposits in transit at August 31, 2017.
2. Compute the amount of outstanding cheques at August 31, 2017.
3. Prepare a bank reconciliation at August 31, 2017.
4. Prepare any journal entries that the company should make as a result of the bank reconciliation. Why are they necessary?
5. After the reconciliation journal entries are posted, what balances would be reflected in the cash accounts in the ledger?
6. What total amount of cash should be reported on the August 31, 2017, statement of financial position?

connect CASES AND PROJECTS

FINDING AND INTERPRETING FINANCIAL INFORMATION

LO6-1,6-3,6-5   CP6-1   **Finding Financial Information**

Canadian Tire
Corporation

Refer to the financial statements of Canadian Tire Corporation in Appendix A of this book.

Required:

1. Does the company disclose its revenue recognition policy? What point in time does it use to recognize revenue?
2. Compute the company's gross profit percentage for the most recent two years. Has it risen or fallen? Explain the meaning of the change.
3. Does the company report an allowance for doubtful accounts in the notes to its financial statements? If so, review the details disclosed by the company and explain what they mean.
4. Compute Canadian Tire's receivables turnover ratio for 2015. Is it significantly different from the ratio computed for Gildan in the Key Ratio Analysis section in the chapter? If so, what are some possible reasons for the difference?
5. What does the company include in "cash and cash equivalents"? How close do you think the disclosed amount is to the actual fair market value of these assets?

LO6-2,6-5   CP6-2   **Finding Financial Information**

Sears Canada Inc.

Go to *Connect* for the financial statements of Sears Canada Inc.

Required:

1. What items would you expect to be subtracted from sales revenue in the computation of net sales?
2. What expenses does Sears Canada subtract from net sales in the computation of earnings before income taxes? How does this differ from Canadian Tire's practice?
3. Compute Sears Canada's receivables turnover ratio for the year ended January 30, 2016. What characteristics of its business might cause it to be so high?
4. What was the change in accounts receivable and how did it affect the cash provided by operating activities for 2015?

LO6-3,6-5   **CP6-3**   **Comparing Companies within an Industry**

Canadian Tire
Corporation
Sears Canada Inc.

Refer to the financial statements of Canadian Tire Corporation (Appendix A) and Sears Canada Inc. (on *Connect*) and the Industry Ratio Report (Appendix B on *Connect*).

Required:

1. Compute the gross profit percentage for both companies for the current year and the previous year. What do the changes in the ratios suggest?

2. Compute the receivables turnover ratio for both companies for fiscal years 2014 and 2015. Canadian Tire had $5,328.2 in receivables (trade and other receivables, and current portion of loans receivable) at January 3, 2015, and Sears Canada had $83.3 in accounts receivable (net) at January 31, 2015. What accounts for the change in these ratios?

3. Compare the receivables turnover ratio of each company for 2015 to the industry average. Are these two companies doing better or worse than the industry average? Explain.

FINANCIAL REPORTING AND ANALYSIS CASES

LO6-4   **CP6-4**   **Using Financial Reports: Interpreting Receivables Disclosures**

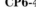

Canadian Tire
Corporation

Canadian Tire Corporation is a general retailer with nearly 1,700 retail and gasoline outlets across Canada. Canadian Tire's customers can pay for purchases using a Canadian Tire credit card. The company occasionally offers special promotions that allow customers to purchase merchandise on credit and pay after six months or one year without paying interest on the amount due. Canadian Tire refers to credit card receivables as loans receivable. Its annual report for 2015 included the following disclosures related to its loans receivables and the related allowance for credit losses:

---

11. Loans receivable

Quantitative information about the Company's loans receivable portfolio is as follows:

(in millions of dollars)	Total Principal Amount of Receivables[1]	
	2015	**2014**
Credit card loans	$4,839.4	$4,862.9
Line of credit loans	4.9	5.8
Total Financial Services' loans receivable	4,844.3	4,868.7
Dealer loans[2]	655.5	604.4
Other loans	4.1	5.5
Total loans receivable	5,503.9	5,478.6
Less: Long-term portion[3]	628.4	573.1
Current portion of loans receivable	$4,875.5	$4,905.5

1. Amounts shown are net of allowance for loan impairment.
2. Dealer loans issued by Franchise Trust (Note 24).
3. The long-term portion of loans receivable is included in long-term receivables and other assets and includes Dealer loans of $624.9 million (2014—$568.2 million).

For the year ended January 2, 2016, cash received from interest earned on credit cards and loans was $789.6 million (2014—$732.4 million).

The carrying amount of loans includes loans to Dealers that are secured by the assets of the respective Dealer corporations. The Company's exposure to loans receivable credit risk resides at Franchise Trust and at the Bank. Credit risk at the Bank is influenced mainly by the individual characteristics of each credit card customer. The Bank uses sophisticated credit scoring models, monitoring technology and collection modelling techniques to implement and manage strategies, policies, and limits that are designed to control risk. Loans receivable are generated by a large and geographically-dispersed group of customers. Current credit exposure is limited to the loss that would be incurred if all of the Bank's counterparties were to default at the same time.

A continuity schedule of the Company's allowances for loans receivable is as follows:

(in millions of dollars)	2015	2014
Balance, beginning of year	$113.2	$121.4
Impairment for credit losses	301.9	279.7
Recoveries	65.9	59.8
Write-offs	(369.5)	(347.7)
Balance, end of year	$111.5	$113.2

...

Credit card loans are considered impaired and written off when a payment is 180 days in arrears. Line of credit loans are considered impaired when a payment is over 90 days in arrears and are written off when a payment is 180 days in arrears. No collateral is held against loans receivable, except for loans to Dealers, as discussed above.

Source: Canadian Tire Corporation, Annual Report 2015.

Required:

1. What amounts did Canadian Tire report as loans receivable on its statement of financial position at the end of 2015?

2. Prepare summary journal entries to record the transactions related to loans receivable in 2015. These include the write-off of receivables, recovery of receivables written off, and bad debt expense.

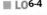

LO6-4

CP6-5   **Canadian Banks**

The global economic downturn that started in 2007 affected most sectors in the Canadian economy, particularly the financial sector, including the banking industry. For example, the common shares of Toronto Dominion Bank decreased from $68.12 per share on January 2, 2011, to $32.80 per share on February 23, 2012, before they started climbing up in March 2012 onward. Because banks lend money to individuals and companies, one would expect the banks to experience some difficulty in collecting money from their customers during an economic downturn.

Go to the websites and consult the annual reports of Scotiabank, Canadian Imperial Bank of Commerce, and Royal Bank of Canada for fiscal year 2015.

Required:

1. What is the amount of the provision for credit losses that each bank reported on its statement of earnings for both 2014 and 2015?

2. Compute the ratio Provision for credit losses/Net interest income for both 2014 and 2015. Did the ratio increase from 2014 to 2015 for each of these banks? If so, what could have caused the increase? Explain.

3. What is the amount of the allowance for loan losses that each bank reported on its statement of financial position (balance sheet) at the end of its 2015 fiscal year?

4. Compute the ratio Allowance for loan losses/Total loans receivable for both 2014 and 2015, and comment on the change in the ratio from 2014 to 2015.

CRITICAL THINKING CASES

LO6-6

CP6-6   **Making Decisions as an Independent Accountant**

Lane Manufacturing Company is a relatively small local business that specializes in the repair and renovation of antique furniture. The owner is an expert craftsperson. Although a number of skilled workers are employed, there is always a large backlog of work to be done. A long-time employee who serves as clerk-bookkeeper handles cash receipts, keeps the records, and writes cheques for disbursements. The owner signs the cheques. The clerk/bookkeeper pays small amounts in cash, subject to a month-end review by the owner. Approximately 80 regular customers are extended credit that typically amounts to less than $1,000. Although credit losses are small, in recent years the clerk/bookkeeper had established an allowance for doubtful accounts, and all write-offs were made at year-end. During January 2017 (the current year), the owner decided to start as soon as possible the construction of a building for the business that would provide many advantages over the currently rented space and would allow space to expand facilities. As a part of the considerations in financing, the financing institution asked for 2016 audited financial statements. The company statements had never been audited. Early in the audit, the independent accountant found numerous errors, and one combination of amounts in particular, that caused concern.

There was some evidence that a $2,500 job completed by Lane had been recorded as a receivable (from a new customer) on July 15, 2016. The receivable was credited for a $2,500 cash collection a few days later. The new account was never active again. The auditor also observed that shortly thereafter, three write-offs of accounts receivable balances had been made to allowance for doubtful accounts as follows: Jones, $800; Blake, $750; and Sellers, $950—all of whom were known as regular customers. These write-offs drew the attention of the auditor.

Required:

1. Explain what caused the auditor to be concerned. Should the auditor report the suspicions to the owner?

2. What recommendations would you make with respect to internal control procedures for this company?

■ LO**6-1**   **CP6-7**   **Evaluating an Ethical Dilemma: Management Incentives and Valuation of Receivables**

E.S. Bankest Capital Corp.

Accounts receivable that are reported on a statement of financial position should reflect the amount that is expected to be realized when collecting from customers. As indicated in Chapter 2, accounting information is useful if it is both relevant to a decision context and has representational faithfulness. But what if the accounts receivable are deliberately misstated? This was the case for a Florida company called E.S. Bankest Capital Corp. (ESB).

ESB was a factoring company, which means it bought accounts receivable from other companies at a discount, undertook cash collection from the companies' customers, and profited from the difference. The factoring process permits the seller of accounts receivable to collect cash immediately and shift the credit risk to the purchaser or factor. Banco Espirito Santo of Lisbon, which controls ESB, lent $140 million to ESB along with a line of credit for $30 million based on the value of ESB's accounts receivable. Banco Espirito Santo is the second-largest bank in Portugal.

ESB's management had inflated the value of the accounts receivable reported on its statement of financial position in order to obtain the loan. The reported value was $225 million when the actual value was only $5 million. The troublesome part of this fraudulent activity is that ESB's auditor, BDO Seidman, did not suspect any wrongdoing by the company and signed off on ESB's financial statements.

When the ESB fraud was disclosed in 2004, the ex-chairman of the company's board of directors, Eduardo Orlansky, was convicted of fraud, money laundering, and conspiracy and sentenced to 20 years in prison after a trial. An investigation indicated that the money borrowed from Banco Espirito Santo was deposited in various umbrella companies controlled by ESB.

Mr. Orlansky was not the only executive convicted. He was ordered to pay $165 million in restitution to Banco Espirito Santo, but the question was whether the bank would ever collect. ESB declared bankruptcy. Then Banco Espirito Santo sued BDO Seidman USA for failing to detect the fraud. The bank sued for actual losses of $170 million plus punitive damages of $351 million, and won the case in August 2007 for a total cash award of $521 million.

During the course of the trial, it was revealed that BDO Seidman was a strategic partner of one of ESB's factoring clients. BDO claimed it was fooled by ESB and that there was no conflict of interest. Although Banco Espirito Santo won the case, BDO Seidman launched and won an appeal. Ultimately, in May 2011, the two parties entered into a confidential settlement agreement.

Many articles were written about the ESB fraud in the news media. Access some of these articles to answer the following questions.

Required:

1. Preparers and auditors of financial statements are expected to exercise prudence in their valuation of assets and liabilities that are reported on the statement of financial position. Explain how the concept of prudence applies to the valuation of the accounts receivable reported by ESB.

2. In your opinion, is a confidential settlement between Banco Espirito Santo and BDO Seidman a positive event for the profession of accounting?

■ LO**6-5**   **CP6-8**   **Evaluating the Effects of Credit Policy Changes on the Receivables Turnover Ratio and Cash Flows from Operating Activities**

V. R. Rao and Company has been operating for five years as a software consulting firm specializing in the installation of industry standard products. During this period, it has experienced rapid growth in sales revenue and accounts receivable. Ms. Rao and her associates all have computer science backgrounds. This year, the company hired you as its first corporate controller. You have put into place new credit granting and collection procedures that are expected to reduce receivables by approximately one-third by year-end. You have gathered the following data related to the changes (in thousands of dollars):

	Beginning of Year	End of Year (projected)
Accounts receivable	$1,000,608	$ 660,495
Less: Allowance for doubtful accounts	36,800	10,225
Net accounts receivable	$ 963,808	$ 650,270
		Current Year (projected)
Net sales (assume all on credit)		$7,015,069

Required:

1. Compute the receivables turnover ratio based on two different assumptions:
   a. Those presented in the preceding table (a decrease in the balance in accounts receivable, net).
   b. No change in the balance of net accounts receivable; the balance was $963,808 at year-end.
2. Compute the effect (sign and amount) of the projected change in net accounts receivable on cash flow from operating activities for the year.
3. On the basis of your findings in (1) and (2), write a brief memo explaining how an increase in the receivables turnover ratio can result in an increase in cash flow from operating activities. Also explain how this increase can benefit the company.

FINANCIAL REPORTING AND ANALYSIS TEAM PROJECT

■ LO6-1,6-4,6-5   **CP6-9**   **Team Project: Analyzing Revenues and Receivables**
As a team, select an industry to analyze. A list of companies classified by industry can be obtained by accessing http://www.fpinfomart.ca and then choosing Companies by Industry. You can also find a list of industries and companies within each industry via http://ca.finance.yahoo.com/investing (click Order Annual Reports under Tools).

Each group member should acquire the annual report for a different publicly traded company in the industry. (Library files, the SEDAR service at http://www.sedar.com, and the company's website are good sources.)

Required:
On an individual basis, each team member should write a short report answering the following questions about the selected company. Discuss any patterns across the companies that you as a team observe. Then, as a group, write a short report comparing and contrasting your companies.

1. If your company lists receivables on its statement of financial position, what percentage is this asset of total assets for each of the last three years? If your company does not list receivables, discuss why this is so.
2. Perform a ratio analysis:
   a. What does the receivables turnover ratio measure in general?
   b. If your company lists receivables, compute the ratio for the last three years.
   c. What do your results suggest about the company?
   d. If available, find the industry ratio for the most recent year, compare it to your results, and discuss why you believe your company differs from or is similar to the industry ratio.
3. If your company lists receivables, determine what additional disclosure is available concerning the allowance for doubtful accounts. If the necessary information is provided, what is bad debt expense as a percentage of sales for the last three years?
4. What is the effect of the change in accounts receivable on cash flows from operations for the most recent year—that is, did the change increase or decrease operating cash flows? Explain your answer.

connect   CONTINUING CASE

■ LO6-2,6-4   **CC6-1**   **Computing Net Sales and Recording Bad Debt Estimates and Write-Offs**
Pool Corporation Inc. is the world's largest wholesale distributor of swimming pool supplies and equipment.

Required:

1. Pool Corp. reported the following information related to bad debt estimates and write-offs for the current year. Prepare journal entries for the bad debt expense adjustment and total write-offs of bad debts for the current year.

Allowance for doubtful accounts:	
Balance at beginning of year	$7,102
Bad debt expense	2,958
Write-offs	(4,160)
Balance at end of year	$5,900

2. Pool Corp. reduces net sales by the amount of sales returns and allowances, cash discounts, and credit card fees. Bad debt expense is recorded as part of selling and administrative expense. Assume that gross sales revenue for the month was $137,256, bad debt expense was $146, sales discounts were $1,134, sales returns were $856, and credit card fees were $1,849. What amount would Pool Corp. report as net sales for the month?

SOLUTIONS TO SELF-STUDY QUIZZES

Self-Study Quiz 6-1

1.

Gross Sales	$35,000
Less: Sales discounts (0.01 × 1/2 × $30,000)	150
Credit card discounts (0.03 × 0.8 × $5,000)	120
Net Sales	$34,730

2. Gross profit = $150,000 − $110,000 = $40,000
Gross profit percentage = $40,000 ÷ $150,000 = 26.66%

Self-Study Quiz 6-2

1. Bad debt expense (+E)   467
   Allowance for doubtful accounts (+XA)   467
2. Allowance for doubtful accounts (−XA)   271
   Accounts receivable (−A)   271
3. Ending balance = Beginning balance + Bad debt expense − Write-offs
         = $851 + $467 − $271 = $1,047

Self-Study Quiz 6-3

1.

Allowance for Doubtful Accounts (XA)			
		Beginning balance	723
Write-offs	648	Bad debt expense (solve)	829
		Ending balance	904

Beginning balance + Bad debt expense − Write-offs = Ending balance

$723 + X − $648 = $904; X = $829

2. The amount would be subtracted from net earnings because an increase in the accounts receivable account indicates that sales revenue was in excess of cash collected from customers for the period.

3. Granting longer payment deadlines will most likely decrease the receivables turnover ratio because later collections from customers will increase the average accounts receivable balance (the denominator of the ratio), thus decreasing the ratio.

Self-Study Quiz 6-4

3. Bank service charges are deducted from the company's account; thus, cash must be reduced and an expense must be recorded.

4. NSF cheques that were deposited were recorded on the books as increases in the cash account; thus, cash must be decreased and the related account receivable increased.

ENDNOTES

1. Gildan uses U.S. dollars as a reporting currency because a significant portion of its revenues, expenses, assets, and liabilities are denominated in U.S. dollars.

2. The International Accounting Standards Board (IASB) issued in May 2014 International Financial Reporting Standard, IFRS 15, Revenue from Contracts with Customers, which clarifies the principles for recognizing revenue. This standard supersedes both IAS 11 (Construction Contracts) and IAS 18 (Revenue). IFRS 15 will affect, among other things, how revenue is recognized for royalties arising from licensing of intellectual property and how revenue should be allocated to each component of a bundle of products and services. Individuals who have purchased mobile devices usually sign service contracts that extend beyond one year. The customer typically pays for the purchased handset and future services that are bundled together in one lump sum, which must be split into different amounts to be recognized over time as revenue is earned. Canadian publicly accountable enterprises are expected to apply the provisions of the new standard for fiscal years beginning on or after January 1, 2018.

3. Some retail businesses, such as Canadian Tire, issue their own cards and avoid credit card discounts when customers use the store's credit card to pay for their purchases.

4. It is important not to confuse a cash discount with a trade discount. Vendors sometimes use a trade discount for quoting sales prices; the sales price is the list or printed catalogue price less the trade discount. For example, an item may be quoted at $10 per unit, subject to a 20 percent trade discount, on orders of 100 units or more; thus, the price for the large order is $8 per unit. Similarly, the price on a slow-moving product line can be lowered simply by increasing the trade discount. Sales revenue should always be recorded net of trade discounts. Manufacturers also offer discounts for early order and shipment to help manage production flows.

5. We use the gross method in all examples in this textbook. Some companies use the alternative net method, which records sales revenue after deducting the amount of the cash discount. Since the choice of method has little effect on the financial statements, discussion of this method is left for other accounting courses.

6. Alternatively, Gildan might offer the customer a $200 allowance to keep the wrong-colour T-shirts. If the customer accepts the offer, Gildan would report $200 as sales returns and allowances.

7. Sales discounts and credit card discounts may also be reported as expenses on the statement of earnings.

8. This assumes that all sales are on account.

9. Internal control is defined as the "process designed, implemented and maintained by those charged with governance, management and other personnel to provide reasonable assurance about the achievement of an entity's objectives with regard to reliability of financial reporting, effectiveness and efficiency of operations, and compliance with applicable laws and regulations." *CICA Assurance Handbook*, Part 1, Glossary of Terms.

10. Canadian Securities Administrators, "National Instrument 52-109, Certification of Disclosure in Issuers' Annual and Interim Filings" (August 2008).

11. PricewaterhouseCoopers, "Global Economics Crimes Survey 2016: Adjusting the Lens on Economic Crime." The report is accessible through PwC's website, http://www.pwc.com/im/en/publications/assets/advisory/Global_Economic_Crime_Survey_%202016_Global_Report.pdf. Interested readers may also wish to consult another report by PwC, "Securing the bottom line: Canadian retail security survey 2012" (available at http://www.pwc.com/en_CA/ca/retail-consumer/publications/pwc-security-survey-2012-10-29-en.pdf), and two other reports on occupational fraud: Association of Certified Fraud Examiners (ACFE), "The 2016 Report to the Nations on Occupational Fraud and Abuse," Austin, TX (available at http://www.acfe.com/rttn2016.aspx), and Association of Certified Fraud Examiners and Dominic Peltier-Rivest, "Detecting Occupational Fraud in Canada: A Study of Its Victims and Perpetrators (available at www.acfe.com/uploadedFiles/ACFE_Website/Content/documents/rttn-canadian.pdf).

12. These codes vary among banks.

13. International Accounting Standards Board, International Accounting Standard 11—Construction Contracts: para. 22.

14. Other measures of completion include surveys of work performed or completion of a physical proportion of the contract work. See IAS 11, para. 30.

15. The difference between the expected cost and the actual cost of construction, which did not occur in this simple example, creates additional accounting problems.

16. International Accounting Standards Board, International Accounting Standard 18—Revenue: paras. 20 and 26.

Reporting and Interpreting Cost of Sales and Inventory

After studying this chapter, you should be able to:

LEARNING OBJECTIVES

LO7-1 Apply the cost principle to identify the amounts that should be included in inventory, and apply the matching process to determine the cost of sales for typical retailers, wholesalers, and manufacturers.

LO7-2 Report inventory and cost of sales by using three inventory costing methods.

LO7-3 Decide when the use of different inventory costing methods is beneficial to a company.

LO7-4 Report inventory at the lower of cost and net realizable value (LC&NRV).

LO7-5 Describe methods for controlling inventory, and analyze the effects of inventory errors on financial statements.

LO7-6 Evaluate inventory management by using the inventory turnover ratio, and analyze the effects of inventory on cash flows.

SUPPLEMENTARY MATERIAL

LO7-S1 Report inventory and cost of sales in a periodic inventory system.

LO7-S2 Compare and contrast the recording of inventory transactions in periodic and perpetual inventory systems.

Shaunl/iStockphoto.com

Focus Company: **Reitmans (Canada) Limited**

MARKETING FASHIONABLE APPAREL TO YOUNG AND CONTEMPORARY CUSTOMERS

Reitmans (Canada) Limited (www.reitmanscanadalimited.com) was founded in 1926 by Herman and Sarah Reitman. Its current management team, led by Jeremy and Stephen Reitman, grandsons of the company founders, believes it has the best specialty retailing assets in the country. Today, Reitmans operates over 800 stores across Canada and ecommerce channels under seven different banners (Reitmans, Smart Set, Penningtons, Addition Elle, RW & CO., Thyme Maternity, and Hyba) that cater to fashionable men and women, offering affordable clothing that blends the latest trends with style and quality.

With online shopping, Reitmans improves convenience, selection, and ease of purchase. Reitmans carries a large stock of products in its warehouses and stores to meet the needs of its customers. To remain a leader in its industry, Reitmans must continually introduce new products that respond to consumers' needs. It must also control the quality and cost of its inventory to enhance the profitability of its operations. Reitmans accomplishes this not only by establishing mutually beneficial relationships with its suppliers, but also by developing accounting information systems that provide real-time inventory information. The company has recently implemented new technology to manage the purchase, transportation, and distribution of apparel products that are sourced from manufacturing companies around the world. Furthermore, Reitmans's choice of accounting methods to value and report inventory can affect the amount paid in income taxes.

UNDERSTANDING THE BUSINESS

The cost and quality of inventory are concerns faced by all modern manufacturers and merchandisers, and so we turn our attention to *cost of sales* (cost of goods sold, cost of products sold) on the statement of earnings (or income statement) and *inventory* on the statement of financial position (or balance sheet). Exhibit 7.1 presents the relevant excerpts from Reitmans's financial statements that include these accounts. Note that cost of sales is subtracted from net sales to produce gross profit on Reitmans's statement of earnings. Inventory is a current asset on the statement of financial position; it is reported below cash and receivables because it is less liquid than those current assets.

Exhibit **7.1**

Excerpts from Statement of Earnings and Statement of Financial Position

REAL-WORLD EXCERPT

Reitmans (Canada) Limited

ANNUAL REPORT

REITMANS (CANADA) LIMITED
Consolidated Statement of Earnings (partial)
(in thousands of dollars)

| | YEAR ENDED | | |
	January 30, 2016	January 31, 2015	February 1, 2014
Net sales	$937,155	$939,376	$960,397
Cost of sales	410,035	372,033	377,913
Gross profit	527,120	567,343	582,484

REITMANS (CANADA) LIMITED
Consolidated Statements of Financial Position (partial)
(in thousands of dollars)

	January 30, 2016	January 31, 2015
ASSETS		
Current assets:		
Cash and cash equivalents	$118,595	$139,913
Marketable securities	45,189	57,364
Trade and other receivables	4,103	4,599
Derivative financial asset	14,405	20,635
Income taxes recoverable	3,301	1,977
Inventories	124,848	106,440
Prepaid expenses	8,921	12,148
Total current assets	$319,362	$343,076

Source: Reitmans (Canada) Limited, Annual Report 2015.

The primary goals of inventory management are to have sufficient quantities of high-quality inventory available to serve customers' needs while minimizing the costs of carrying inventory (production, storage, obsolescence, and financing). Low quality leads to customer dissatisfaction, returns, and a decline in future sales. Also, purchasing or producing too few units of a hot-selling item causes stock-outs, which mean lost sales revenue and potential customer dissatisfaction. Conversely, purchasing or producing too many units of a slow-selling item, such as light-weight uninsulated blazers, increases the storage and interest costs on short-term borrowings to finance the production or purchases. It may even lead to losses if the merchandise cannot be sold at normal prices.

Reitmans's successful management of both inventory and cost of sales requires a combined effort by human resources managers, purchasing managers, marketing managers, and accounting and financial managers. It is truly a multidisciplinary task. To meet its inventory management goals, the multidisciplinary team will forecast expected customer demand for different products, including style, size, and colour. It will also provide feedback on actual outcomes so that adjustments to purchasing schedules can be made to control the cost of sales and improve gross profit. Both cost of sales and inventory are such important determinants of a company's success that managers, investors, and financial analysts pay close attention to these financial statement items.

The accounting system plays three roles in the inventory management process. First, the system must provide accurate information necessary for preparation of periodic financial statements and reports to tax authorities.[1] Second, it must provide up-to-date information on inventory quantities and costs to facilitate ordering and warehousing decisions. Third, because inventories are subject to theft and other forms of misuse, the system must also provide the information necessary to help protect and control these important assets.

First, we discuss the components of inventory costs and how accounting systems are organized to keep track of inventory quantities and costs for decision making and control. This topic is the principal subject matter of your managerial accounting course. Then, we discuss the important choices management must make in the financial and tax reporting process, and how these choices affect the financial statements and taxes paid. Finally, we discuss how managers, investors, and financial analysts evaluate management's effectiveness at inventory management.

ORGANIZATION OF THE CHAPTER

Nature of Inventory and Cost of Sales	Inventory Costing Methods	Valuation at Lower of Cost and Net Realizable Value	Control of Inventory	Evaluating Inventory Management
• Items Included in Inventory • Costs Included in Inventory Purchases • Flow of Inventory Costs • Cost of Sales Equation • Perpetual and Periodic Inventory Systems • Recording Inventory Transactions In a Perpetual System	• Specific Identification Method • Cost Flow Assumptions (First-In, First-Out Method • Weighted-Average Cost Method • Financial Statement Effects of Inventory Costing Methods • Managers' Choice of Inventory Costing Methods		• Internal Control of Inventory • Errors in Measuring Ending Inventory	• Measuring Efficiency in Inventory Management • Inventory Turnover Ratio • Inventory and Cash Flows

Supplemental material:
Appendix 7A: Cost Flow Assumptions – Periodic Inventory System
Appendix 7B: Recording Inventory Transactions Using Periodic and Perpetual Inventory Systems

LO7-1

Apply the cost principle to identify the amounts that should be included in inventory, and apply the matching process to determine the cost of sales for typical retailers, wholesalers, and manufacturers.

INVENTORY is an asset held for sale in the ordinary course of business or used in the process of production of goods for sale or rendering of services.

MERCHANDISE INVENTORY includes goods held for resale in the ordinary course of business.

NATURE OF INVENTORY AND COST OF SALES

Items Included in Inventory

Inventory is an asset that is either (1) held for sale in the ordinary course of business or (2) used in the process of production of goods for sale or rendering of services. Inventory is reported on the statement of financial position as a current asset, because it is normally used or converted into cash within one year or within the next operating cycle of the business, whichever is longer. The types of inventory normally held depend on the characteristics of the business.

Companies that do not manufacture the products they sell, but simply purchase those products and then sell them to customers, are called *merchandisers*. Wholesale merchandisers distribute products to retail merchandisers for resale to customers through retail stores.

Merchandisers (wholesale or retail businesses) hold the following:

Merchandise inventory. These are goods (or merchandise) held for resale in the ordinary course of business. The goods are usually acquired in a finished condition and are ready for sale without further processing.

Manufacturing businesses hold the following types of inventory:

Raw materials inventory. This consists of items acquired by purchase, growth (such as food products), or extraction (natural resources) for processing into finished goods. Such items are included in raw materials inventory until used, at which point they become part of work-in-process inventory.

Work-in-process inventory. This includes goods in the process of being manufactured but not yet complete. When complete, work-in-process inventory becomes finished goods inventory.

Finished goods inventory. This consists of manufactured goods that are complete and available for sale.

Reitmans is a merchandiser of men's and women's apparel. The products that Reitmans markets in its various stores are produced by manufacturers in Canada, Europe, and Asia (primarily China). The products purchased from these contractors are shipped to Reitmans's distribution centre, located in Montreal, before they are distributed to the company's stores across Canada.

RAW MATERIALS INVENTORY includes items acquired for the purpose of processing into finished goods.

WORK-IN-PROCESS INVENTORY includes goods in the process of being manufactured.

FINISHED GOODS INVENTORY includes manufactured goods that are complete and available for sale.

Costs Included in Inventory Purchases

Goods in inventory are initially recorded at cost. The primary basis of accounting for inventory is cash-equivalent cost, which is either the price paid or consideration given to acquire an asset. Inventory cost includes the sum of the costs incurred in bringing an article to a usable or saleable condition and location.

When Reitmans purchases apparel from various manufacturers, the amount recorded should include the invoice price plus other expenditures related to the purchase, such as import duties and freight charges to deliver the items to its distribution centre (*freight-in*), as well as inspection costs. Any *purchase returns and allowances* or *purchase discounts* taken are subtracted. In general, the company should cease accumulating purchase costs when the merchandise inventory is *ready for shipment* or delivery to customers. Any additional costs related to selling the merchandise inventory to customers, such as salaries of marketing personnel, should be included in selling and marketing expenses of the period of sale, since they are incurred after the inventory is ready for sale. Direct sales to customers, by telephone or over the Internet, have reduced the need to stock inventory for long periods and, thus, reduced inventory storage costs and the cost of obsolescence.

Reitmans's accounting policy related to inventories includes the following:

NOTE 3: Significant Accounting Policies

K) INVENTORIES

... Costs include the cost of purchase, transportation costs that are directly incurred to bring inventories to their present location and condition, and certain distribution centre costs related to inventories.

Source: Reitmans (Canada) Limited, Annual Report 2015.

REAL-WORLD EXCERPT

Reitmans (Canada) Limited
ANNUAL REPORT

APPLYING THE MATERIALITY CONCEPT IN PRACTICE

FINANCIAL ANALYSIS

Incidental costs, such as inspection and preparation costs, are often not very large relative to other costs (see the discussion of materiality in Chapter 4) and do not have to be assigned to the inventory cost. Thus, for practical reasons, many companies use the invoice price, less returns and discounts, to assign a unit cost to raw materials or merchandise, and record other indirect expenditures as separate costs that are reported as expenses.

Flow of Inventory Costs

The flow of inventory costs for merchandisers (wholesalers and retailers) is relatively simple, as shown in Exhibit 7.2A. When merchandise is purchased, the merchandise inventory account is increased. When the goods are sold, the merchandise inventory is decreased and the cost of sales is increased.

The flow of inventory costs in a manufacturing environment is more complex, as diagrammed in Exhibit 7.2B. First, *raw materials* (also called *direct materials*) must be purchased. For the companies that manufacture apparel items purchased by Reitmans, these raw materials include the fabric, zippers, buckles, and buttons, among others. As materials are used in production, their cost is removed from the raw materials inventory and added to the cost of the work-in-process inventory.

Two other components of manufacturing costs, direct labour and factory overhead, are also added to the work-in-process inventory when incurred in the manufacturing process. **Direct labour** cost represents the earnings of employees who work directly on the products being manufactured. **Factory overhead** costs include all other manufacturing costs that are not raw material or direct labour costs. For example, the salary of the factory supervisor and the cost of utilities, security, and material handling are included in factory overhead.

When the apparel manufacturer completes the production of the items for delivery to Reitmans, the related costs, which have accumulated in work-in-process inventory, are transferred to finished goods inventory. When the finished goods are sold, the cost of the finished goods inventory decreases and the manufacturer's cost of sales increases. As Exhibit 7.2 indicates, there are three stages to the flow of inventory costs for both merchandisers and manufacturers. In the first stage, costs arise from purchasing and/or production activities. In the second, these activities result in additions to the costs in the inventory accounts on the statement of financial position. At the third stage, the inventory items are sold and the related costs are transferred to cost of sales on the statement of earnings. Since the flows of inventory costs for both merchandise inventory and finished goods to cost of sales are very similar, we will focus the rest of our discussion on merchandising inventory.

DIRECT LABOUR refers to the earnings of employees who work directly on the products being manufactured.

FACTORY OVERHEAD includes manufacturing costs that are not raw material or direct labour costs.

Exhibit **7.2**

Flow of Inventory Costs

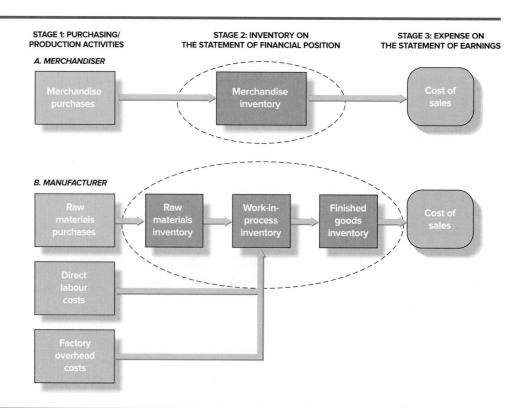

MODERN MANUFACTURING TECHNIQUES AND INVENTORY COSTS

FINANCIAL ANALYSIS

The flow of inventory costs, diagrammed in Exhibit 7.2, represents the key to manufacturing cost and quality control. The company must pay to finance the purchase and storage of apparel. In order to reduce costs, the company must minimize the quantities of these inventories and more closely match them with projected demand for the various items it sells. Reitmans works closely with its suppliers in design, production, and delivery of finished goods. In this way Reitmans ensures that quantities of inventory are received just when they are needed for sale to customers to minimize the costs of storing excess inventory. (This approach to inventory management is called *just-in-time*, or *JIT.*) Simple product design and manufacturing processes reduce costs and often lead to higher product quality and reduced scrap and rework costs, while good training of manufacturing personnel minimizes both direct labour and factory overhead costs.

Reitmans's accounting system is designed to monitor the success of changes to the various elements of its supply chain and provide information to motivate continuous improvements in purchasing and warehousing practices. The design of such systems is the subject matter of managerial accounting and cost accounting courses.

Cost of Sales Equation

Cost of sales (COS) is directly related to sales revenue. Sales revenue during an accounting period is the number of units sold multiplied by the sales price. Cost of sales is the same number of units, multiplied by their unit costs. It includes all costs of the merchandise purchased or the finished goods sold during the period.

Let us examine the relationship between cost of sales on the statement of earnings and inventory on the statement of financial position. Reitmans starts each accounting period with a stock of merchandise inventory called *beginning inventory* (BI). During the accounting period, new *purchases* (P) are added to inventory. The sum of the cost of beginning inventory and the cost of purchases (or additions to its merchandise inventory) is the **cost of goods available for sale** during that period. What remains unsold at the end of the period becomes *ending inventory* (EI) of merchandise inventory on the statement of financial position. The portion of the cost of goods available for sale that are actually sold becomes cost of sales on the statement of earnings. The ending inventory for one accounting period then becomes the beginning inventory for the next period. The relationships between these various amounts are brought together in the **cost of sales equation**: BI + P − EI = COS.

To illustrate the relationships represented by the cost of sales equation, assume that Reitmans began the period with $40,000 of men's blazers style #101 in beginning inventory,[2] purchased additional blazers during the period for $55,000, and had $35,000 in inventory at the end of the period. These amounts are combined as follows to compute the cost of sales of $60,000:

COST OF GOODS AVAILABLE FOR SALE refers to the sum of the cost of beginning inventory and the cost of purchases for the period.

The **COST OF SALES EQUATION** is BI + P − EI = COS.

Beginning inventory	$40,000
+ Purchases of merchandise during the year	55,000
Cost of goods available for sale	95,000
− Ending inventory	35,000
Cost of sales	$60,000

These same relationships are illustrated in Exhibit 7.3 and can be represented in the merchandise inventory T-account as follows:

Merchandise Inventory (A)

Beginning inventory	40,000		
Purchases of inventory	55,000	Cost of sales	60,000
Ending inventory	35,000		

Exhibit **7.3**

Nature of Cost of Sales for
Merchandise Inventory

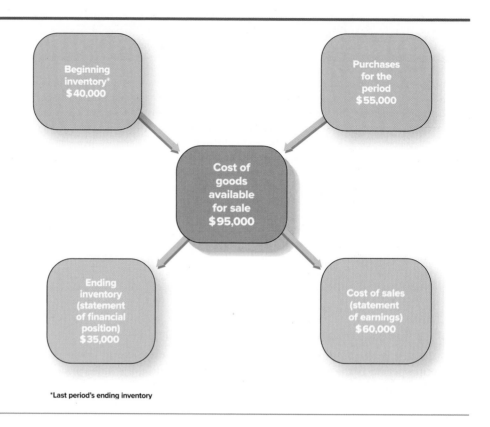

*Last period's ending inventory

If three of these four amounts are known, either the cost of sales equation or the inventory T-account can be used to solve for the fourth amount.

PAUSE FOR **FEEDBACK**

Inventory should include all items owned that are held for resale. Costs flow into inventory when goods are purchased or manufactured. They flow out (as an expense) when they are sold or disposed of. The cost of sales equation describes these flows.

SELF-STUDY **QUIZ 7-1**

Assume the following facts for blazer style #101, which Reitmans purchased and sold to customers during the year:

Beginning inventory:	200 units at unit cost of $200
Ending inventory:	1 75 units at unit cost of $200
Sales:	300 units at a sales price of $300 (cost per unit $200)

1. Using the cost of sales equation, compute the cost of purchases of blazer style #101 for the period.
2. Prepare the first three lines of a statement of earnings (showing gross profit) for blazer style #101 for the year.

After you complete your answers, check them with the solutions at the end of the chapter.

Perpetual and Periodic Inventory Systems

To compute cost of sales, three amounts must be known: (1) beginning inventory; (2) purchases of merchandise, or additions to finished goods, during the period; and (3) ending inventory. The amount of purchases for the period is always accumulated in the accounting system. The cost of sales and cost of ending inventory can be determined by using one of two different inventory systems: perpetual and periodic. To simplify the discussion of how accounting systems keep track of these amounts, we focus this discussion on blazer style #101, which Reitmans sells. Although the same general principles apply, the more complex details of manufacturing accounting systems are discussed in managerial accounting courses.

Perpetual Inventory System   All journal entries for purchase and sale transactions discussed in the text so far have been recorded using a perpetual inventory system. In a perpetual inventory system, purchase transactions are directly recorded in an inventory account. Simultaneously, when each sale is recorded, a companion cost of sales entry is made, decreasing inventory and recording cost of sales. You have already experienced the starting point for that process when your purchases are scanned at the checkout counter at Walmart or Canadian Tire. Not only does that process determine how much you must pay the cashier, it also removes the sold items from the store inventory records. As a result, information on cost of sales and ending inventory is available on a continuous (perpetual) basis.

In a **perpetual inventory system**, a detailed record is maintained for each type of merchandise stocked, showing (1) units and cost of the beginning inventory, (2) units and cost of each purchase, (3) units and cost of the goods for each sale, and (4) units and cost of the goods on hand at any point in time. This up-to-date record is maintained on a transaction-by-transaction basis and is usually necessary for purchasing, manufacturing, and distribution decisions. Most modern companies could not survive without this information. They may even share some of this information electronically with their suppliers or customers.[3] As noted at the beginning of the chapter, cost and quality pressures from increasing competition, combined with dramatic declines in the cost of computers, have made sophisticated perpetual inventory systems a minimum requirement at all but the smallest companies.[4]

> In a **PERPETUAL INVENTORY SYSTEM**, a detailed inventory record is maintained, recording each purchase and sale during the accounting period.

Periodic Inventory System   Under the **periodic inventory system**, companies do *not* maintain an ongoing record of inventory during the year; rather, an actual physical count of the goods remaining on hand is required at the end of each period. The number of units of each type of merchandise on hand is multiplied by their unit cost to compute the total cost of the ending inventory. Cost of sales is calculated by using the cost of sales equation.

Because the amount of inventory is not known until the end of the period when the physical inventory count is taken, the cost of sales cannot be determined reliably until the inventory count is completed. Inventory purchases are debited to a temporary account called purchases. Revenues are recorded at the time of each sale. However, the cost of sales is not recorded until after the inventory count is completed. At all other times, companies using a periodic system must estimate the value of inventory on hand. We briefly discuss the estimation of inventory amounts later in the chapter.

Before affordable computers and bar code readers were available, the primary reason for using the periodic inventory system was its low cost. The primary disadvantage of a periodic inventory system is the lack of timely inventory information. Managers are not informed quickly about either low stock or overstocked situations.

A perpetual inventory system provides more timely information about inventory quantities and costs than a periodic inventory system. As explained in Chapter 2, timeliness of accounting information enhances its relevance for decision-making purposes. As a consequence, we will continue to focus on perpetual inventory systems throughout the book.[5]

> In a **PERIODIC INVENTORY SYSTEM**, ending inventory and cost of sales are determined at the end of the accounting period based on a physical count.

Perpetual Inventory Records in Practice   The decision to use a perpetual versus a periodic inventory system is based on management's need for timely information for use in operating decisions and on the cost of the perpetual system. Further, the specific manner in which the perpetual system is designed will also be determined with these trade-offs in mind. Many inventory ordering and production decisions require accurate information on inventory quantities but not costs. Quantities on hand provide the information necessary for efficient management of inventory, providing delivery information to dealers and quality control.

Recording Inventory Transactions in a Perpetual System

In Chapter 6, we illustrated how sale transactions are recorded in the accounting system and reported in the financial statements of the selling company. In this chapter, we illustrate how similar transactions are recorded in the accounting system and reported in the financial statements of the purchasing company that uses a perpetual system. Appendix 7B shows how the same inventory transactions are recorded and reported under a periodic inventory system.

Sellers of merchandise or raw materials use a variety of methods to motivate their customers to buy the products they offer. The principal methods include (1) allowing customers to make purchases on account and pay later, (2) offering business customers discounts for early payment, and (3) allowing returns from all customers under specific circumstances. Recall that the amount recorded for inventory purchases should include the invoice price to be paid plus other expenditures related to the purchase, such as import duties, transportation charges (*freight-in*), as well as inspection and preparation costs. Any *purchase returns and allowances* or *purchase discounts* taken are subtracted.

Inventory Purchases   The point at which title (ownership) changes hands is determined by the shipping terms in the purchase contract, as explained in Chapter 6. When goods are shipped *FOB (free on board) destination point*, title changes hands on delivery at the buyer's location, and the seller pays the shipping costs. When they are shipped *FOB shipping point*, title changes hands on delivery at the seller's location, and the buyer pays for shipping.

If Reitmans purchases T-shirts, FOB destination point, for $1,100 on credit, the transaction would be recorded by Reitmans as follows:

Inventory (A)			1,100	
Trade payables (L)				1,100
Assets	=	**Liabilities**	+	**Shareholders' Equity**
Inventory +1,100		Trade payables +1,100		

Purchase Returns and Allowances   Goods purchased may be returned to the supplier if they do not meet specifications, arrive in damaged condition, or are otherwise unsatisfactory. Alternatively, the buyer may keep the unsatisfactory goods and benefit from a cost reduction or allowance. The effect of purchases returns or allowances on the cost of purchases must be measured. The purchaser normally receives a cash refund or a reduction in the liability owed to the supplier. Assume that Reitmans returned damaged T-shirts and received a reduction of $100 from the amount owed. The return would be recorded by Reitmans as follows:

Trade payables (L)			100	
Inventory (A)				100
Assets	=	**Liabilities**	+	**Shareholders' Equity**
Inventory −100		Trade payables −100		

PURCHASE RETURNS AND ALLOWANCES are a reduction in the cost of purchases associated with unsatisfactory goods.

Purchase returns and allowances are treated as a reduction in the cost of inventory purchases associated with unsatisfactory goods.

Purchase Discounts   Cash discounts must be accounted for by both the buyer and the seller (accounting by the seller was discussed in Chapter 6). When inventory is purchased on credit, terms such as 2/10, n/30 are sometimes specified. These terms mean that if payment is made within 10 days from the date of purchase, the buyer can deduct a 2 percent **purchase discount** for prompt payment. If payment is not made within the discount period, the amount owed to the supplier (net of purchases returns and allowances) is due 30 days after the date of purchase.

PURCHASE DISCOUNT is a cash discount received for prompt payment of an account.

Assume that Reitmans purchased the T-shirts with credit terms 2/10, n/30 and paid the amount owed within 10 days. The payment would be recorded as follows:

Trade payables (L)		1,000	
Inventory (A)			20
Cash (A)			980
Assets	**=**	**Liabilities**	**+**	**Shareholders' Equity**
Inventory	−20	Trade payables	−1,000	
Cash	−980			

If for any reason Reitmans does not pay within the 10-day discount period, it must pay $1,000 to the supplier instead of $980.[6]

The net cost of the T-shirts, $980, will gradually become cost of sales on the statement of earnings when T-shirts are sold to customers. What remains unsold at the end of the period becomes part of the ending inventory on the statement of financial position.

STRETCHING OUT THE PAYABLES

A QUESTION OF ACCOUNTABILITY

Hoffa Shoes has been incurring significant interest charges (10 percent) on short-term borrowing from its bank.* Hoffa normally purchases shoes from suppliers on terms 1/10, n/30. The annual rate of interest earned by taking the discount is 18.43 percent, computed as follows:

(Amount saved ÷ Amount paid) = Interest rate for 20 days

($1 ÷ $99) = 1.01% for 20 days, or 0.0505 per day

Annual interest rate = 0.0505% × 365 days = 18.43%

Hoffa's policy had been to take all purchase discounts even if it had to borrow at 10 percent to make the early payment. Management reasoned that the company earned 8.43 percent more than it paid in interest (18.43 percent − 10 percent).

A new employee suggested a new plan. Records indicated that, even though the terms of Hoffa's agreement with its suppliers (1/10, n/30) required payment of the full amount within a maximum of 30 days, the suppliers would not complain as long as payment was made within 55 days of the purchase date, since they normally did not send out a second bill until 60 days after the purchase date. She reasoned that Hoffa would be better off foregoing the discount and paying on the 55th day after the purchase date. She argued that, since Hoffa would now be paying within 55 days instead of 10 days of the purchase, not taking the discount would be borrowing for 45 days, not the 20 days used in the former analysis. The analysis supporting the proposal is as follows:

(Amount saved ÷ Amount paid) = Interest rate for 45 days

($1 ÷ $99) = 1.01% for 45 days, or 0.02244%

Annual interest rate = 0.02244% × 365 days = 8.19%

In effect, her plan allows Hoffa to borrow from suppliers at 8.19 percent instead of the bank's rate of 10 percent, saving 1.81 percent. When she presented this plan to the management for discussion, the purchasing manager agreed with the arithmetic presented but objected nonetheless. Since the plan violated its agreement with suppliers, the purchasing manager thought it was unethical. Many ethical dilemmas in business involve trade-offs between monetary benefits and potential violations of moral values.

*Hoffa Shoes is a fictitious company, but most companies face this dilemma.

LO7-2

Report inventory and cost of sales by using three inventory costing methods.

INVENTORY COSTING METHODS

In the Reitmans example presented earlier, the cost of all units of blazer style #101 was the same: $200. If inventory costs do not change, this would be the end of our discussion. As we are all aware, however, the prices of most goods do change. In recent years, the costs of many manufactured items, such as automobiles and motor-cycles, have risen gradually. In other high-technology industries, such as the computer industry, however, costs of production have dropped dramatically, along with retail prices.

When inventory costs change, the determination of the cost of sales and the cost of ending inventory can turn net earnings into losses (and vice versa) and cause companies to pay or save millions in taxes. A simple example will illustrate these dramatic effects. Do not let the simplicity of our example mislead you. It applies broadly to actual company practices.

The example is based on the following data for Reitmans during the first quarter of the current year, assuming for simplicity that Reitmans purchases and sells only blazer style #101:

Date	Transaction or Event	Number of Blazers	Number of Blazers on Hand	Cost per Blazer	Sale Price per Blazer
January 1	Beginning inventory	800	800	$200	
January 31	Sale to customers	(600)	200		$279
February 5	Purchase	800	1,000	210	
February 28	Sale to customers	(900)	100		295
March 10	Purchase	900	1,000	220	
March 31	Sale to customers	(200)	800		299
Total number of blazers sold = 600 + 900 + 200 = 1,700					
Ending inventory = 800 blazers					

Note that the cost per blazer increased between January and March. Sales were made on January 31, February 28, and March 31. What amount would the accountant record as cost of sales for each of the sale transactions? The answer depends on which specific goods we assume are sold. Three generally accepted inventory costing methods are available to determine the cost of sales:[7]

1. Specific identification

2. First-in, first-out (FIFO)

3. Weighted average

The three inventory costing methods are alternative ways to assign the total cost of goods available for sale between (1) ending inventory and (2) cost of sales. International Accounting Standard 2 requires only that the inventory costing method used be rational and systematic. The selected inventory costing method should be the one that provides the best correspondence between expenses and revenues. The first method identifies individual items that remain in inventory or are sold. The remaining two methods assume that inventory items follow a particular physical flow. As you proceed through the various illustrations, keep in mind that the three inventory costing methods are simply methods of allocating the total cost of goods available for sale to cost of sales on the statement of earnings and ending inventory on the statement of financial position.

Specific Identification Method

SPECIFIC IDENTIFICATION METHOD identifies the cost of the specific item that was sold.

When the **specific identification method** is used, the cost of each item sold is individually identified and recorded as cost of sales. Without electronic tracking, the method may be manipulated when the units are identical, because one can affect the cost of sales and the ending inventory accounts by picking and choosing from among the several available unit costs. For this reason, IFRS prohibit the use of this method when there are large numbers of inventory items that are interchangeable, such as blazers of the same size and style.

The specific identification method is impractical when large quantities of similar items are kept in stock. It is appropriate, however, when dealing with very expensive items, such as broadband telecommunications systems, aircraft, yachts, fine art objects, buildings, luxury cars, and fine jewellery, because each item tends to differ from the other items. This method requires keeping track of the purchase cost of each item. This is done by either (1) coding the purchase cost on each unit before placing it in stock or (2) keeping a separate record of the unit and identifying it with a serial number.

The technology of bar code scanning and radio frequency identification is a simple and cost-effective method to keep track of inventory items at all times, even for items with low unit costs. The scanner transmits cost and quantity information to a company's central database, thereby creating a perpetual record of inventory costs. This affects the computation of the cost of sales and the cost of ending inventory. To compute the cost of sales, the bar code identifies the specific unit that is sold and matches it to the recorded cost through the scanning process. The recorded cost of all units that remain unsold at March 31 represents the cost of ending inventory.

Cost Flow Assumptions

Most inventory items are accounted for by using one of two cost flow assumptions. The *choice of an inventory costing method is NOT based on the physical flow of goods* on and off the shelves. That is why the methods are called *cost flow assumptions*. A useful visual learning tool for representing inventory cost flows is a stack of inventory units. The different inventory costing methods can then be visualized as flows of inventory costs in and out of the stack. Each blazer represents the cost of purchase when entering and held in inventory, then the cost of sales when sold to the customer and exiting the inventory.

The oldest blazers are placed at the top of the stack because they are typically sold first. The purchase and sale transactions in our example are presented on the time line in Exhibit 7.4, which shows the flow of blazers over time.

Transaction Date	Jan.1	Sale Jan.31	Purchase Feb. 5	Sale Feb.28	Purchase Mar. 10	Sale Mar. 31
Number of blazers	800	(600)	800	(900)	900	(200)
Cost per blazer purchased	$200		$210		$220	
Sale price per blazer		$279		$295		$299
Cost of blazers sold		?		?		?
The main objective in this illustration is to determine the cost of blazers sold on each of the three dates.						

Exhibit **7.4**
Flow of Goods over Time

First-In, First-Out Method The **first-in, first-out (FIFO) method** assumes that the earliest goods purchased (the first ones in) are the first units sold (the first ones out) and the last goods purchased remain in ending inventory. First, each purchase is treated as if it were added to the stack in sequence (800 blazers of beginning inventory at $200 each, followed by a first purchase on February 5 of 800 blazers at $210 each, and a second purchase on March 10 of 900 blazers at $220 each). Each of the 1,700 blazers sold is then removed from the stack in the same sequence it was added (800 units at $200, 800 units at $210, and 100 units at $220); first in is first out. FIFO allocates the oldest unit costs to cost of sales and the newest unit costs to ending inventory. We assume that physical inventory is taken at March 31, the end of the first quarter, to determine the number of blazers unsold, and that the number of blazers in stock is the same under both inventory control systems without any shrinkage or impairment in inventory value.

FIRST-IN, FIRST-OUT (FIFO) METHOD assumes that the oldest units (the first costs in) are the first units sold.

When using the perpetual inventory system, Reitmans must compute the cost of sales for each sales transaction to continuously update its inventory records. In Exhibit 7.5, the cost of sales is computed after each sales transaction. The graphic depicts the purchase and sale transactions to help you visualize how the cost of sales is computed under this system. The 600 blazers sold on January 31 are taken from the beginning inventory of 800 blazers at a cost of $200 per blazer. When Reitmans sold 900 blazers on February 28, the company shipped to customers the remaining 200 blazers at a cost of $200 each, plus 700 blazers from the 800 units purchased on February 5 at a cost of $210 each. The remaining 100 blazers were then sold to customers on March 31, along with an additional 100 blazers taken from the 900 blazers purchased on March 10 at a cost of $220 each. This leaves 800 blazers in ending inventory. The total cost of sales is $350,000, and the cost of ending inventory is $176,000.

Exhibit **7.5**

FIFO Inventory Flows—
Perpetual Inventory System

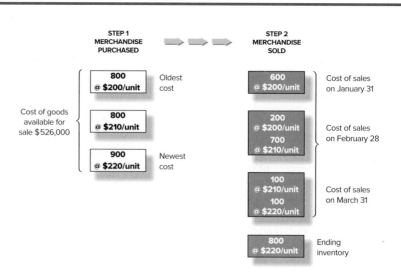

Cost of Sales Calculation (FIFO Perpetual) Cost of blazers purchased and sold							
Date			**Units**		**Cost**		**Total**
January 1	Beginning inventory	Oldest cost	800	×	$200	=	$160,000
January 31	Cost of sales		(600)	×	$200	=	(120,000)
	Cost of remaining inventory		200	×	$200	=	40,000
February 5	Purchases		800	×	$210	=	168,000
	Cost of goods available for sale		1,000				208000
February 28	Cost of sales (900 units)		(200)	×	$200	=	(40,000)
			(700)	×	$210	=	(147,000)
	Cost of remaining inventory		100	×	$210	=	21,000
March 10	Purchases	Newest cost	900	×	$220	=	198,000
	Cost of goods available for sale		1,000				219,000
March 31	Cost of sales (200 units)		(100)	×	$210	=	(21,000)
			(100)	×	$220	=	(22,000)
	Ending inventory		800	×	$220	=	176,000
	Cost of sales						$350,000

Weighted-Average Cost Method

Weighted-Average Cost Method The **weighted-average cost method** requires computation of the weighted-average unit cost of the goods available for sale.

As indicated before, when a perpetual inventory system is used, the inventory records are updated after every purchase and sale transaction in order to keep track of the number of inventory items on hand. The 600 blazers sold on January 31 are taken from the beginning inventory of 800 blazers at a cost of $200 per unit, for a total cost of $120,000. The cost of the remaining 200 blazers is then added to the cost of the 800 blazers purchased on February 5 to compute a new weighted-average unit cost of $208 per blazer, as shown in Exhibit 7.6.

The **WEIGHTED-AVERAGE COST METHOD** uses the weighted-average unit cost of the goods available for sale for both cost of sales and ending inventory.

Exhibit **7.6**

Weighted-Average Inventory Flows—Perpetual Inventory System

Cost of Sales Calculation (Weighted-Average Perpetual) Cost of blazers purchased and sold							
Date	**Transaction**	**Units**		**Cost**		**Total**	
January 1	Beginning inventory	800	×	$200	=	$160,000	
January 31	Sale	(600)	×	$200	=	(120,000)	
		200	×	$200	=	40,000	
February 5	Purchase	800	×	$210	=	168,000	
	Number of units available for sale (NUAS) =	1,000				$208,000	Cost of goods available for sale (COGAS)
February 28	Sale	(900)	×	$208		(187,200)	
		100	×	$208		20,800	
March 10	Purchase	900	×	$220		198,000	
	Number of units available for sale (NUAS) =	1,000				$218,800	Cost of goods available for sale (COGAS)
March 31	Sale	(200)	×	$218.8	=	(43,760)	
		800	×	$218.8	=	175,040	
		800	×	$218.8	=	175,040	

First weighted-average cost per unit $= \dfrac{\text{COGAS}}{\text{NUAS}} = \dfrac{\$208,000}{1,000} = \$208$

Second weighted-average cost per unit $= \dfrac{\text{COGAS}}{\text{NUAS}} = \dfrac{\$218.800}{1,000} = \$218.8$

This average cost is then used to compute the cost of the 900 blazers sold on February 28; that is, 900 × $208, or $187,200. The cost of the remaining 100 blazers is then added to the cost of the 900 blazers purchased on March 10 to compute a third weighted-average cost of $218.80 per blazer. This average cost is then used to compute the cost of the 200 blazers sold on March 31; that is, 200 × $218.80, or $43,760. Since the average cost changed three times, this method is called the *moving weighted-average cost* method. The total cost of sales during the quarter is $350,960 ($120,000 + $187,200 + $43,760), and the cost of ending inventory is $175,040.

Financial Statement Effects of Inventory Costing Methods

Each of the three alternative inventory costing methods is in conformity with IFRS. To understand why managers choose between FIFO and weighted-average cost methods in different circumstances, we must first understand their effects on the statement of earnings and statement of financial position. Exhibit 7.7 summarizes the financial statement effects of the FIFO and weighted-average cost methods using the perpetual inventory system. Remember that the methods differ only in the portion of goods available for sale allocated to cost of sales versus ending inventory. For that reason, the method that gives the highest cost of ending inventory also gives the lowest cost of sales and the highest gross profit, income tax expense, and net earnings amounts, and vice versa.

Exhibit 7.7

Financial Statement Effects of Inventory Costing Methods—Perpetual Inventory System

	Inventory Costing Method	
	FIFO	**Weighted Average**
Cost of Sales Calculation		
Beginning inventory	$160,000	$160,000
Add: Purchases	366,000	366,000
Cost of goods available for sale	526,000	526,000
Deduct: Ending inventory (to statement of financial position)	176,000	175,040
Cost of sales (to statement of earnings)	$350,000	$350,960
Effect on the statement of earnings		
Sales	$492,700*	$492,700
Cost of sales	350,000	350,960
Gross profit	$142,700	$141,740
Effect on the statement of financial position		
Inventory	$176,000	$175,040

*(600 × $279) + (900 × $295) + (200 × $299)

In our example, recall that unit costs were increasing. *Assuming the price to the customer is constant, when unit costs are rising, the weighted-average cost method produces lower net earnings and a lower inventory valuation than FIFO. When unit costs are declining, the weighted-average cost method produces higher net earnings and a higher inventory valuation than FIFO.* These effects are summarized in the following table:

	Normal Financial Statement Effects of			
	Rising Costs		**Declining Costs**	
	FIFO	**Weighted Average**	**FIFO**	**Weighted Average**
Cost of sales	Lower	Higher	Higher	Lower
Gross profit	Higher	Lower	Lower	Higher
Net earnings	Higher	Lower	Lower	Higher
Ending inventory	Higher	Lower	Lower	Higher

These effects occur because the weighted-average cost method causes the newer unit costs, which are highest, to be reflected in cost of sales on the statement of earnings; FIFO causes the older unit costs, which are lowest, to be reflected in cost of sales on the statement of earnings. In contrast, on the statement of financial position, the ending inventory amount under the weighted-average cost method reflects a mix of unit costs, which may be an unrealistic valuation, whereas FIFO ending inventory is based on the newest costs, thus assisting the user in predicting the amount of cash needed to replace the inventory.

DIFFERENT INVENTORY COSTING METHODS AND INTERNATIONAL COMPARISONS

INTERNATIONAL PERSPECTIVE

While most countries have harmonized or will shortly harmonize their accounting standards with IFRS, the United States has delayed its harmonization process. The Financial Accounting Standards Board (FASB) in the United States permits a fourth method: last-in, first-out (LIFO). LIFO assumes that the most recently purchased items (the last ones in) are sold first and the oldest items are left in inventory. LIFO allocates the newest unit costs to cost of sales and the oldest unit costs to ending inventory. Because, in general, prices rise rather than fall, the effect is to increase cost of sales and, therefore, decrease taxable income. Reducing income tax payable retains more cash in a corporation to finance future growth or payout to existing debtors and shareholders.

The use of LIFO by U.S. companies for some or all of their inventories creates comparability problems when one attempts to compare companies across international borders. For example, Toyota Motor Corporation (of Japan) uses the average-cost method, except for the cost of finished products carried by certain subsidiary companies, which is determined based on the specific identification method or LIFO. Managers, investors, and financial analysts who read audited financial statements must also carefully read the significant accounting policies that companies use in preparing their financial statements and related note disclosures.

Consistency in Use of Inventory Costing Methods It is important to remember that regardless of the physical flow of goods, a company can use either the weighted-average or the FIFO inventory costing method. Companies are expected to select the most representationally faithful inventory costing method. Each component of inventory value is supposed to reflect most accurately the anticipated benefit that will eventually be realized from either the use or the sale of the inventory. Therefore, a company is not required to use the same inventory costing method for all inventory items. The justification arises from the pervasive principle of economic substance over form. For example, Telestra Corporation uses FIFO cost for valuation of raw materials and weighted-average cost for other inventory items.

To enhance comparability, accounting rules require companies to apply their accounting methods on a consistent basis. A company is not permitted to use FIFO one period, weighted average the next, and then FIFO the next. A change in method is allowed only if the change will improve the measurement of financial results and financial position. Changing from one inventory costing method to another is a significant event. Such a change requires full disclosure about the reason for the change and the accounting effects.

Managers' Choice of Inventory Costing Methods

What motivates companies to choose different inventory costing methods? In principle, managers should choose the method that best reflects the company's economic circumstances for financial reporting purposes. In practice, most managers choose generally accepted accounting methods based on two factors:

1. Effect on net earnings (managers prefer to report higher earnings for their companies).
2. Effect on income taxes (managers prefer to pay the least amount of taxes allowed by law, as late as possible: the *least—latest rule*).

LO7-3

Decide when the use of different inventory costing methods is beneficial to a company.

Because accounting standards and tax laws differ, management must also choose an inventory costing method to use on the company's tax return (for tax purposes). In general, most companies choose to use the same inventory costing method for both financial reporting and tax reporting purposes.

The income tax effects associated with FIFO and weighted average for companies facing rising costs can be illustrated by continuing our simple Reitmans example. Using the data from Exhibit 7.7 and assuming expenses other than cost of sales are $42,700 and that the tax rate is 25 percent, the following differences in taxes result:

	Inventory Costing Method	
	FIFO	**Weighted Average**
Sales	$492,700*	$492,700
Cost of sales	350,000	350,960
Gross net earnings	142,700	141,740
Other expenses	42,700	42,700
Net earnings before income taxes	100,000	99,040
Income tax expense (at 25%)	25,000	24,760
Net earnings	$ 75,000	$ 74,280

*(600 × $279) + (900 × $295) + (200 × $299)

For this illustration, the use of the weighted-average cost method produces a lower amount of income taxes than the FIFO method, but the difference in income taxes is not material. Many high-technology companies enjoy declining costs for basic commodities, such as computer chips. In such circumstances, the FIFO method—in which the oldest, most expensive goods become cost of sales—produces the largest cost of sales, the lowest gross profit, and, thus, the lowest income tax liability.

Most Canadian companies use the perpetual inventory system and either FIFO or moving weighted average for inventory costing. The choice of either method affects both the reported cost of inventory on the statement of financial position and net earnings and cash flows. The reported amounts also affect the calculation of several financial ratios. When prices are rising, companies that wish to minimize their income taxes would logically choose weighted-average cost rather than FIFO, because the weighted-average cost method produces lower earnings before income taxes. The lower net earnings reduces profitability and other ratios. However, management may be interested in maximizing net earnings and the reported inventory value to satisfy restrictions imposed by creditors in lending agreements. While companies are expected to adopt the inventory costing method that provides the best representation of the flow of costs during the period, the choice of a specific accounting method is influenced, in some cases, by management's objectives and the effects of the chosen method on the reported results.

INVENTORY COSTING AND CONFLICTS BETWEEN MANAGERS' AND OWNERS' INTERESTS

A QUESTION OF ACCOUNTABILITY

We have seen that the selection of an inventory method can have significant effects on financial statements. Company managers may have an incentive to select a particular method that may not be consistent with the objectives of the owners. For example, the use of weighted-average cost during a period of rising prices may be in the best interests of the owners, because the weighted-average cost method often reduces the company's tax liability. If managers' compensation is tied to reported net earnings, they may prefer FIFO, which typically results in higher net earnings.

A well-designed compensation plan should reward managers for acting in the best interests of the owners, but, unfortunately, this is not always the case. Clearly, a manager who selects an accounting method that is not optimal for the company, solely to increase his or her compensation, has engaged in questionable ethical behaviour.

PAUSE FOR
FEEDBACK

Three different inventory costing methods may be used to allocate costs between the units remaining in inventory and the units sold, depending on economic circumstances. The methods are specific identification, FIFO, and weighted-average cost. Each of the inventory costing methods conforms to IFRS. Remember that the cost flow assumption need not match the physical flow of inventory. The following questions test your understanding of the FIFO and weighted-average cost methods.

SELF-STUDY **QUIZ 7-2**

Assume that a company began operations this year. Its purchases for the year were as follows:

January	10 units @ $10 each
May	5 units @ $11 each
November	5 units @ $13 each

During the year, 10 units were sold for $20 each in June, and 5 units were sold in December for $23 each. Operating expenses other than cost of sales totalled $100.

1. Compute cost of sales and pretax earnings for the year under the FIFO and weighted-average cost methods, assuming the use of a perpetual inventory system.

2. Which method would you recommend that the company adopt? Why?

After you complete your answers, check them with the solutions at the end of the chapter.

INVENTORY COSTING METHODS AND FINANCIAL STATEMENT ANALYSIS

FINANCIAL
ANALYSIS

Critics of multiple inventory valuation methods argue that the existence of alternatives is inconsistent with the comparability characteristic of high-quality, useful accounting information. This quality is needed so that managers, investors, and financial analysts can compare information for a company with that of other companies for the same period. These types of comparisons are more difficult when companies use different accounting methods. Often, it is impossible to convert, for example, a FIFO-based inventory value to a weighted-average cost of inventory because the data needed for the conversion are unavailable. In reality, however, a particular method may result in a better representation of the economic substance of inventory transactions than their legal form might. Absolute standardization based on one inventory costing method could readily result in formal comparability that fails to inform users of the best estimate of either cost of sales or inventory value.

Users of financial statements must be certain that their decisions are based on real differences, not artificial differences created by alternative accounting methods. For this reason, users must be knowledgeable about alternative accounting methods and how they affect financial statements. This is why accounting standards require companies to inform external users when the method of inventory valuation has changed and to restate the prior year's information—not only must a change in method be communicated, but also the reasons the alternative now in place provides an improved reflection of economic substance must be revealed.

VALUATION AT LOWER OF COST AND NET REALIZABLE VALUE

Inventories should be measured at their acquisition cost, in conformity with the cost principle. However, the cost of inventories may *not* be recoverable if their selling prices have declined, they are damaged, or they have become obsolete. The lower

LO7-4

Report inventory at the lower of cost and net realizable value (LC&NRV).

amount should be used as the inventory valuation because it faithfully represents that inventory values cannot exceed the amount that can be obtained from selling the inventory. For the purpose of inventory valuation, market value refers to the **net realizable value** of the inventory, which is essentially an estimate of the amount that a company expects to receive for selling its inventory in the ordinary course of business, net of estimated selling expenses. This valuation rule, a departure from the cost principle, is known as measuring inventories at the **lower of cost and net realizable value (LC&NRV)**.

This departure from the cost principle is particularly important for two types of companies: (1) high-technology companies, such as BlackBerry, that manufacture goods for which the cost of production and the selling price are declining and (2) companies like Reitmans that sell seasonal goods, such as clothing, the value of which drops dramatically at the end of each selling season (fall or spring).

Under LC&NRV, companies recognize a loss in the period in which the net realizable value of an item drops rather than in the period in which the item is sold. The loss is the difference between the purchase cost and the net realizable value and is added to the cost of sales of the period. To illustrate, assume that Reitmans had the following items in the current period's ending inventory:

NET REALIZABLE VALUE is the expected sales price less estimated selling costs.

LOWER OF COST AND NET REALIZABLE VALUE (LC&NRV) is a valuation method departing from the cost principle; it serves to recognize a loss when the net realizable value of inventory drops below its cost.

Item	Quantity	Cost per Item	Net Realizable Value (NRV) per Item	LC&NRV per Item	Total LC&NRV
Blazers style #101	100	$220	$200	$200	100 × $200 = $20,000
Coats style #305	400	100	130	100	400 × $100 = 40,000

The 100 blazers should be recorded in the ending inventory at their net realizable value ($200), which is lower than their cost ($220). Reitmans makes the following journal entry to record the write-down:[8]

Cost of sales (E) (100 × $20)	2,000	
Allowance for write-down of inventory to NRV (XA)		2,000

Assets	=	Liabilities	+	Shareholders' Equity
Allowance for write-down of inventory to NRV −2,000				Cost of sales −2,000

This allowance account to record the decline in the value of its inventory is similar to using an allowance for doubtful accounts to record the estimated doubtful accounts. Alternatively, the inventory account could have been directly reduced by $2,000.

Since the net realizable value of the coats ($130) is higher than their original cost ($100), no write-down is necessary. The coats remain on the books at their cost of $100 per unit ($40,000 in total). Recognition of holding gains on inventory is not permitted by IFRS.

The write-down of the inventory of blazers to net realizable value produces the following financial statement effects:

	Effects of LC&NRV Write-Down	
	Current Period	Period of Sale
Cost of sales	Increase $20,000	Decrease $20,000
Pretax earnings	Decrease $20,000	Increase $20,000
Ending inventory on statement of financial position	Decrease $20,000	Unaffected

The LC&NRV rule accounts for the added expense in the current period, not in the period of sale. Consequently, pretax earnings are reduced by $20,000 in the period in which the net realizable value drops, rather than in the next period when the blazers are sold. Since the cost of sales for the current period increases by $20,000 and the cost of sales for the next period decreases by $20,000, the total cost of sales (and earnings before taxes) for the two periods combined does not change. On the statement of financial position, the $20,000 loss in the current period reduces the amount of inventory reported at year-end.

If the net realizable value of the inventory items that were written down increases in a subsequent accounting period because of changed economic circumstances, then the amount of the write-down is reversed up to the original cost, so that the new carrying amount of the inventory is the lower of the cost and the revised net realizable value. Normally, a reversal of a previous write-down occurs when an inventory item that is carried at net realizable value is still on hand in a subsequent period when its selling price has increased.

Under IFRS, the LC&NRV rule must be applied to all inventories, item by item, regardless of the inventory costing methods that a company uses.[9] For example, in the excerpt below, Reitmans reports the use of the lower of cost (weighted average) and net realizable value rule for financial statement purposes.

REAL-WORLD EXCERPT

*Reitmans (Canada)
Limited*
ANNUAL REPORT

NOTES TO THE CONSOLIDATED FINANCIAL STATEMENTS

NOTE 3. Significant Accounting Policies

K) INVENTORIES

Merchandise inventories are measured at the lower of cost, determined on an average basis, and net realizable value. Costs include the cost of purchase, transportation costs that are directly incurred to bring inventories to their present location and condition, and certain distribution centre costs related to inventories. The Company estimates net realizable value as the amount that inventories are expected to be sold, in the ordinary course of business, less the estimated costs necessary to make the sale, taking into consideration fluctuations of retail prices due to seasonality.

Source: Reitmans (Canada) Limited, Annual Report 2015.

Reitmans also reports the write-down to its inventories in Note 5 below. These details inform the financial statement users that a loss of $13,014 thousand was made at the end of fiscal year 2015. The amount of the write-downs represents 10.4 percent of the carrying amount of inventories on that date.

REAL-WORLD EXCERPT

*Reitmans (Canada)
Limited*
ANNUAL REPORT

NOTES TO THE CONSOLIDATED FINANCIAL STATEMENTS

5. INVENTORIES

During the year ended January 30, 2016, inventories recognized as cost of goods sold amounted to $397,021 (January 31, 2015—$363,350). In addition, the Company recorded $13,014 (January 31, 2015—$8,683) of inventory write-downs as a result of net realizable value being lower than cost which were recognized in cost of goods sold, and no inventory write-downs recognized in previous periods were reversed.

Source: Reitmans (Canada) Limited, Annual Report 2015.

CONTROL OF INVENTORY

Internal Control of Inventory

In general, inventory is the asset second-most vulnerable to theft after cash. Efficient management of inventory to avoid the cost of stock-outs and overstock situations is also crucial to the profitability of most companies. Consequently, a number of control features focus on safeguarding inventories and providing up-to-date information for management decisions. To assure shareholders that the reported inventory costs are free from material error, Reitmans must also safeguard the reporting of inventory costs. The following are the most important control features:

1. Separation of responsibilities for inventory accounting and physical handling of inventory.

LO7-5

Describe methods for controlling inventory, and analyze the effects of inventory errors on financial statements.

2. Storage of inventory in a manner that protects it from theft and damage.

3. Limiting access to inventory to authorized employees.

4. Maintaining perpetual inventory records (described below).

5. Comparing perpetual records to periodic physical counts of inventory.

The first three features protect inventory while the last two ensure the accuracy of reporting inventory costs.

Errors in Measuring Ending Inventory

As the cost of sales equation indicates, a direct relationship exists between the cost of ending inventory and the cost of sales, because items not in the ending inventory are assumed to have been sold. Thus, the measurement of ending inventory quantities and costs affects both the statement of financial position (assets) and the statement of earnings (cost of sales, gross profit, and net earnings). The measurement of ending inventory affects not only the net earnings for that period but also the net earnings for the next accounting period. This two-period effect occurs because the ending inventory for one accounting period is the beginning inventory for the next.

Greeting card maker Gibson Greeting Inc. (now owned by American Greetings Corporation) overstated its net earnings by 20 percent, because one division overstated ending inventory for the year. You can compute the effects of the error on both the current year's and next year's earnings before taxes using the cost of sales equation. Assume that the ending inventory was inadvertently overstated by $10,000 because of a clerical error that was not discovered. This error would have the following effects in the current year and next year:

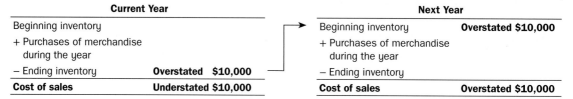

Current Year		Next Year	
Beginning inventory		Beginning inventory	**Overstated $10,000**
+ Purchases of merchandise during the year		+ Purchases of merchandise during the year	
− Ending inventory	**Overstated $10,000**	− Ending inventory	
Cost of sales	**Understated $10,000**	**Cost of sales**	**Overstated $10,000**

Because the cost of sales was understated, earnings before taxes would be *overstated* by $10,000 in the *current year*. Consequently, income tax expense, income tax payable, and net earnings would be overstated. And, since the current year's ending inventory becomes next year's beginning inventory, it would have the following effects: cost of sales would be overstated and earnings before taxes would be *understated* by the same amount in the *next year*. Furthermore, income tax expense, income tax payable, and net earnings would be understated. If there are no other changes, an overstatement during one time period will reverse to an identical understatement in the next.

Each of these errors would flow into retained earnings so that, at the end of the current year, retained earnings would be overstated by $10,000 (less the related income tax expense). This error would be offset in the next year, and retained earnings and inventory at the end of next year would be correct.

Exhibit 7.8 shows how an error that understates the cost of ending inventory affects other elements of financial statements during the year of the error and the following year. An error that overstates ending inventory would have exactly the opposite effects on the financial statement items shown in Exhibit 7.8.

Exhibit **7.8**

Effect of Understatement in Ending Inventory on Selected Financial Statement Items

ERROR: UNDERSTATEMENT OF ENDING INVENTORY

	Year of the Error	Following Year
Beginning inventory	NE*	U
Ending inventory	U	NE
Cost of sales	O	U
Gross profit	U	O
Earnings before income tax	U	O
Income tax expense	U	O
Net earnings	U	O
Retained earnings, end of year	U	NE

*U = Understated; O = Overstated; NE = No Effect

PAUSE FOR FEEDBACK STOP

A company can keep track of the ending inventory and cost of sales for the period using (1) the perpetual inventory system, which is based on the maintenance of detailed and continuous inventory records, or (2) the periodic inventory system, which is based on a physical count of ending inventory and use of the cost of sales equation to determine cost of sales. An error in the measurement of ending inventory affects cost of sales on the current period's statement of earnings and ending inventory on the statement of financial position. Because this year's ending inventory becomes next year's beginning inventory, it also affects cost of sales in the following period by the same amount but in the opposite direction. These relationships can be seen through the cost of sales equation (BI + P − EI = COS).

SELF-STUDY QUIZ 7-3

Sarlos Ltd. provided the following summary statement of earnings for fiscal years 2017 and 2018. Assume that an error in the inventory count at December 31, 2017, resulted in an overstatement of ending inventory by $10,000:

SARLOS LTD.
Statement of Earnings
For the Years Ended December 31

	With Inventory Error 2018	With Inventory Error 2017	Without Inventory Error 2018	Without Inventory Error 2017
Sales	$600,000	$500,000	$600,000	$500,000
Cost of sales	350,000	300,000	?	?
Gross profit	250,000	200,000	?	?
Selling, general, and administrative expenses	120,000	100,000	?	?
Earnings before income tax	130,000	100,000	?	?
Income tax expense (at 40%)	52,000	40,000	?	?
Net earnings	$ 78,000	$ 60,000	?	?

1. Complete the statement of earnings above for 2017 and 2018, assuming that the inventory error was discovered at the end of 2018.

2. Compute the combined net earnings for both 2017 and 2018. Would the inventory error at December 31, 2017, affect the financial statements for 2019? Explain.

After you complete your answers, check them with the solutions at the end of the chapter.

EVALUATING INVENTORY MANAGEMENT

Measuring Efficiency in Inventory Management

As noted at the beginning of the chapter, the primary goals of inventory management are to have sufficient quantities of high-quality inventory available to serve customers' needs while minimizing the costs of carrying inventory (production, storage, obsolescence, and financing). The inventory turnover ratio is an important measure of the company's success in balancing these conflicting goals.

LO7-6

Evaluate inventory management by using the inventory turnover ratio and the effects of inventory on cash flows.

INVENTORY TURNOVER RATIO

ANALYTICAL QUESTION → How efficient are inventory management activities?

RATIO AND COMPARISONS → The answer to this question is facilitated by the computation of the inventory turnover ratio as follows:

$$\text{Inventory turnover ratio} = \frac{\text{Cost of sales}}{\text{Average inventory*}}$$

*Average inventory = (Beginning inventory + Ending inventory) ÷ 2

The 2015 inventory turnover ratio for Reitmans is,

$$\frac{\$410,035}{(\$106,440 + \$124,848) \div 2} = 3.55$$

Comparisons over Time				Comparisons with Competitors	
Reitmans				Le Château Inc.	Hudson's Bay Company
2013	2014	2015		2015	2015
3.72	3.44	3.55		0.74	2.31

INTERPRETATIONS

In General → The inventory turnover ratio reflects how many times the average inventory was purchased and sold during the period. A higher ratio indicates that inventory moves more quickly through the operating cycle, reducing storage and obsolescence costs. If less money is tied up in inventory, then any excess can be invested to earn interest income or to reduce borrowings, which reduces interest expense. More-efficient purchasing practices, such as just-in-time inventory, as well as high product demand and matching of supply to demand will result in a higher ratio. Inefficient purchasing techniques and poor matching of supply to customer demand will result in a low ratio. Analysts and creditors watch this ratio because a sudden decline may mean that a company is facing an unexpected decrease in demand for its products or is becoming sloppy in its inventory management. Many managers and analysts compute the related number of average days to sell inventory, which, for Reitmans, is equal to

$$\text{Average days to sell inventory} = \frac{365}{\text{Inventory turnover ratio}} = \frac{365}{3.55} = 102.8 \text{ days}$$

This number indicates the average time it takes the company to purchase and deliver inventory to customers.

Focus Company Analysis → Reitmans's inventory turnover ratio decreased during 2014 but partially recovered the level achieved in 2013. This decrease over the three-year period reflects a steady decrease in sales caused by increased competition from other companies entering the market. In comparison, Le Château's inventory turnover ratio is significantly lower than Reitmans's because it experienced a decrease in sales and a concurrent buildup of inventory. Hudson's Bay also has a lower ratio than Reitmans because it carries other products with lower turnover.

A Few Cautions → Differences across industries in purchasing, production, and sales processes cause dramatic differences in the ratio. For example, restaurants, such as Pizza Hut, which must turn over their perishable inventory very quickly, tend to have much higher inventory turnover than automakers, such as Toyota. A particular firm's ratio should be compared only with its prior years' figures or with other firms in the same industry. Financial statement users need to interpret the ratios carefully because companies may use different accounting methods.

**SELECTED FOCUS
COMPANY INVENTORY
TURNOVER
RATIOS—2015**

Sears Canada   3.29%

Gildan Activewear 2.73%

Canadian Tire 4.81%

Inventory and Cash Flows

When companies expand production to meet increases in demand, this increases the amount of inventory reported on the statement of financial position. However, when companies overestimate demand for a product, they usually produce too many units of the slow-moving item. This increases storage costs as well as the interest costs on short-term borrowings that finance the inventory. It may even lead to losses if the excess inventory cannot be sold at normal prices. The statement of cash flows often provides the first sign of such problems.

| FOCUS ON |
| **CASH FLOWS** |

INVENTORY

As with the change in trade receivables, the change in inventories can be a major determinant of a company's cash flow from operations. The statement of earnings reflects the cost of sales during the period, whereas the statement of cash flows should reflect the cash payments to suppliers for the same period. Cost of sales may be more or less than the amount of cash paid to suppliers during the period. Since most inventory is purchased on open credit (borrowing from suppliers is normally called *trade payables*), reconciling cost of sales with cash paid to suppliers requires consideration of the changes in both the inventory and trade payables accounts.

The simplest way to think about the effects of changes in inventory is to realize that buying (increasing) inventory eventually decreases cash, and selling (decreasing) inventory eventually increases cash. Similarly, borrowing from suppliers, which increases trade payables, increases cash; paying suppliers, which decreases trade payables, decreases cash.

Effect on Statement of Cash Flows

In General → A *decrease in inventory* for the period indicates that the cost of sales exceeded the cost of goods purchased; thus, the decrease in inventory must be *added* to net earnings to reflect the cost of goods purchased.

An *increase in inventory* for the period indicates that the cost of goods purchased exceeded the cost of sales; thus, the increase in inventory must be *subtracted* from net earnings to reflect the cost of goods purchased.

A *decrease in trade payables* for the period indicates that the payments to suppliers exceeded the cost of goods purchased; thus, the decrease in trade payables must be *subtracted* from net earnings in computing cash flows from operations.

An *increase in trade payables* for the period indicates that the cost of goods purchased exceeded the payments to suppliers; thus, the increase in trade payables must be *added* to net earnings in computing cash flows from operations.

	Effect on Cash Flows
Operating activities (indirect method)	
Net earnings	$xxx
Adjusted for	
Add inventory *decrease*	+
or	
Subtract inventory *increase*	−
Add trade payables *increase*	+
or	
Subtract trade payables *decrease*	−

Focus Company Analysis → Exhibit 7.9 is the operating activities section of Reitmans's statement of cash flows. When the inventory balance increases during the period, as was the case at Reitmans for the fiscal year ended January 31, 2015, the company has purchased more inventory than it sold during the period. Thus, the increase in inventory is subtracted from net earnings in the computation of cash flow from operations. Conversely, when the inventory balance decreases during the period, as was the case at Reitmans for the fiscal year ended January 30, 2016, the company has sold more inventory than it purchased, and the decrease in inventory is added to net earnings in the computation of cash flow from operations. When the trade payables balance decreases during the period, as was the case at Reitmans during fiscal year 2015, the company has paid more to its suppliers than it purchased on credit. Thus, the decrease is subtracted from net earnings in the computation of cash flow from operations. Conversely, when the trade payables balance increases during the period, as was the case at Reitmans during fiscal year 2016, the company has purchased on credit from its suppliers more than it paid them. Thus, the increase is added to net earnings in the computation of cash flow from operations.

Exhibit **7.9**

Inventories on the
Statement of Cash Flows

*Reitmans (Canada)
Limited*
ANNUAL REPORT

CONSOLIDATED STATEMENTS OF CASH FLOWS (thousands of Canadian dollars)		
	Years Ended	
	January 30, 2016	**January 31, 2015**
Cash Flows from Operating Activities		
Net earnings (loss)	$(24,703)	$13,415
Adjustments for various non-cash items (summarized)	46,487	61,540
Changes in Working Capital Items:		
Trade and other receivables	(223)	713
Inventories	(18,408)	3,161
Prepaid expenses	3,227	364
Trade and other payables	6,099	(3,007)
Deferred revenue	(1,748)	1,075
Cash from operating activities	$35,434	$63,846

Source: Reitmans (Canada) Limited, Annual Report 2015.

STOP PAUSE FOR FEEDBACK

The inventory turnover ratio measures the efficiency of inventory management. It reflects how many times average inventory was produced and sold during the period. Analysts and creditors watch this ratio because a sudden decline may mean that a company is facing an unexpected drop in demand for its products or is becoming sloppy in its production management. Before you move on, complete the following questions to test your understanding of these concepts.

SELF-STUDY **QUIZ 7-4**

Reitmans reported the following cost of sales and ending inventory for a recent six-year period (amounts in millions of dollars):

Year	2015	2014	2013	2012	2011	2010
Cost of sales	$410.0	$372.0	$365.5	$372.1	$363.3	$350.7
Ending inventory	124.8	106.4	109.6	93.3	93.2	73.2

1. Compute the inventory turnover ratios for 2011 through 2015. Is Reitmans managing its inventory efficiently?

2. If Reitmans had been able to manage its inventory more efficiently and decreased purchases and ending inventory by $10 million in 2015, would its inventory turnover ratio for 2015 have increased or decreased? Explain.

3. If Reitmans had decreased its trade payables, would its cash flow from operations have increased or decreased?

After you complete your answers, check them with the solutions at the end of this chapter.

ACCOUNTING STANDARDS FOR PRIVATE ENTERPRISES

The accounting standards related to measuring and reporting of inventories by Canadian private enterprises are very similar to those included in IAS 2–Inventories, which Canadian publicly accountable enterprises must use. The ASPE do not allow, however, the reversal of write-down of inventory.

DEMONSTRATION **CASE A**

This case reviews the application of the inventory costing methods and the inventory turnover ratio.

Balent Appliances distributes a number of high-cost household appliances. One product, microwave ovens, has been selected for case purposes. Assume that the following summarized transactions were completed during the accounting period in the order given:

	Units	Unit Cost
a. Beginning inventory	11	$200
b. Inventory purchases	9	220
c. Sales (at $420 per unit)	8	?
d. Inventory purchases	10	210
e. Sales (at $420 per unit)	11	?

Required:

1. Compute the following amounts in accordance with each of the inventory costing methods, assuming that a periodic inventory system is used.

2. Compute the inventory turnover ratio for the current period by using each of the inventory costing methods. What does this ratio mean? Which inventory costing method provides the higher ratio? Is this true in all situations? Explain.

3. Will the choice of inventory costing method affect cash flow from operations? Explain.

	Ending Inventory		Cost of Sales	
	Units	Dollars	Units	Dollars
a. FIFO				
b. Weighted average				

We strongly recommend that you prepare your own answers to these requirements and then check your answers with the following solution.

SUGGESTED **SOLUTION**

1.

	Ending Inventory		Cost of Sales	
	Units	Dollars	Units	Dollars
a. FIFO	11	$2,320	19	$3,960
b. Weighted average	11	2,303	19	3,977

Computations

Cost of goods available for sale = Beginning inventory + Purchases
$$= (11 \text{ units} \times \$200) + (9 \text{ units} \times \$220 + 10 \text{ units} \times \$210)$$
$$= \$6,280$$

FIFO Cost

Ending inventory = (10 units × $210 + 1 unit × $220) = $2,320
Cost of sales = $6,280 − $2,320 = $3,960

Weighted-Average Cost

Average cost = $6,280 ÷ 30 units = $209.33
Ending inventory = 11 units × $209.33 = $2,303
Cost of sales = $6,280 − $2,303 = $3,977

2. Inventory turnover ratio = Cost of sales ÷ Average inventory
FIFO $3,960 ÷ [($2,200 + $2,320) ÷ 2] = 1.75
Weighted average $3,977 ÷ [($2,200 + $2,303) ÷ 2] = 1.7

The inventory turnover ratio reflects how many times the average inventory was purchased and sold during the period. Thus, Balent Appliances purchased and sold its average inventory fewer than two times during the period.

The weighted-average costing method provides the higher inventory turnover ratio. This is generally true when the prices of inventory items increase over time, because the cost of sales reflects more recent, higher prices and ending inventory includes older, lower prices than FIFO.

3. The choice of an inventory costing method does not affect the total amount of purchases and the amount paid to suppliers. It simply allocates the purchases differently between cost of sales and ending inventory. However, the method chosen affects the computation of cost of sales, gross profit, and earnings before income taxes. Hence, the amount of income taxes payable is affected by the inventory costing method.

DEMONSTRATION CASE B

Metal Products Inc. has been operating for three years as a distributor of a line of metal products. It is now the end of 2017, and for the first time, the company will undergo an audit by an external auditor. The company uses a periodic inventory system. The annual statements of earnings prepared by the company are as follows:

	For the Year Ended December 31			
	2017		**2016**	
Sales revenue		$800,000		$750,000
Cost of sales				
Beginning inventory	$ 40,000		$ 45,000	
Add purchases	484,000		460,000	
Cost of goods available for sale	524,000		505,000	
Deduct ending inventory	60,000		40,000	
Cost of sales		464,000		465,000
Gross margin on sales		336,000		285,000
Operating expenses		306,000		275,000
Pretax earnings		30,000		10,000
Income tax expense (20%)		6,000		2,000
Net earnings		$ 24,000		$ 8,000

During the early stages of the audit, the external auditor discovered that the ending inventory for 2016 was understated by $15,000.

Required:

1. Based on the preceding statement of earnings amounts, compute the gross profit percentage on sales for each year. Do the results suggest an inventory error? Explain.

2. Correct and reconstruct the two statements of earnings.

3. Answer the following questions:
   a. What are the correct gross profit percentages?
   b. What effect did the $15,000 understatement of the ending inventory have on the pretax earnings for 2016? Explain.
   c. What effect did the inventory error have on the pretax income for 2017? Explain.
   d. How did the inventory error affect the income tax expense?

We strongly recommend that you prepare your own answers to these requirements and then check your answers with the following solution.

SUGGESTED SOLUTION

1. The gross profit percentages as reported are as follows:

   2013: $285,000 ÷ $750,000 = 38%
   2014: $336,000 ÷ $800,000 = 42%

   The change in the gross profit percentage from 38% to 42% suggests the possibility of an inventory error in the absence of any other explanation.

2. The corrected statements of earnings follow:

For the Year Ended December 31				
	2017		**2016**	
Sales revenue		$800,000		$750,000
Cost of sales				
Beginning inventory	$ 55,000*		$ 45,000	
Add purchases	484,000		460,000	
Cost of goods available for sale	539,000		505,000	
Deduct ending inventory	60,000		55,000*	
Cost of sales		479,000		450,000
Gross margin on sales		321,000		300,000
Operating expenses		306,000		275,000
Pretax earnings		15,000		25,000
Income tax expense (20%)		3,000		5,000
Net earnings		$ 12,000		$ 20,000

*Increased by $15,000.

3. a. The correct gross profit percentages are as follows:

   2013: $300,000 ÷ $750,000 = 40.0%
   2014: $321,000 ÷ $800,000 = 40.1%

   The inventory error of $15,000 was responsible for the difference in the gross profit percentages reflected in (1). The error in the 2016 ending inventory affected the gross margin for both 2016 and 2017 by the same amount, $15,000, but in the opposite direction.

   b. Effect on pretax earnings in 2016: The understatement ($15,000) of ending inventory caused an understatement of pretax earnings by the same amount.

   c. Effect on pretax earnings in 2017: The understatement of beginning inventory (by the same $15,000 since the inventory amount is carried over from the prior period) caused an overstatement of pretax earnings by the same amount.

   d. The total income tax expense for 2016 and 2017 combined was the same ($8,000) regardless of the error. However, there was a shift of $3,000 ($15,000 × 20%) in income tax expense from 2013 to 2017.

OBSERVATION An ending inventory error in one year affects pretax earnings by the amount of the error and in the same direction. It affects pretax earnings again in the following year by the same amount but in the opposite direction.

APPENDIX 7A: COST FLOW ASSUMPTIONS—PERIODIC INVENTORY SYSTEM

LO7-S1

Report inventory and cost of sales in a periodic inventory system.

When a periodic inventory system is used, the cost of merchandise sold is not recorded every time a sale is made. Instead, the cost of all the goods sold during the period is recorded at year-end. The cost of ending inventory is first determined based on an actual physical count of the number of units of each type of merchandise on hand, multiplied by their unit cost. The cost of sales equation is then used to calculate the cost of sales.

Would the computation of cost of ending inventory and cost of sales change if Reitmans used a periodic inventory system instead of a perpetual inventory system? The answer depends on the cost flow assumption that management chooses.

First-In, First-Out Method When the FIFO method is used, the order of costs in and out of inventory is identical for both the perpetual and the periodic inventory systems. Therefore, the cost of ending inventory and cost of sales will be the same under both systems. Exhibit 7A.1 summarizes the flow of goods. The table at the bottom of Exhibit 7A.1 shows the flow of units and costs during the period. Notice that purchases are accumulated until the end of the period when the physical inventory count is taken and the cost of ending inventory is determined. The cost of sales is calculated at that time as the difference between the cost of goods available for sale (beginning inventory plus purchases) and the cost of ending inventory.

Exhibit **7A.1**

FIFO Inventory Flows—
Periodic Inventory System

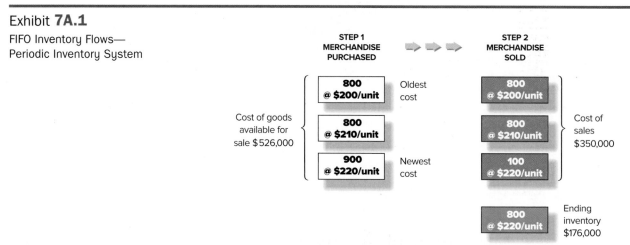

Cost of Sales Calculation (FIFO Periodic) Cost of blazers purchased and sold						
Date			**Units**	**Cost**	**Total**	
January 1	Beginning inventory	**Oldest cost**	800	× $200	= $160,000	
February 5	Purchase		800	× $210	= 168,000	
March 10	Purchase	**Newest cost**	900	× $220	= 198,000	
	Number of units available for sale		2,500		$526,000	**Cost of goods available for sale**
	Number of units in ending inventory		800	× $220	= 176,000	**Cost of ending inventory**
	Number of units sold		1,700		$350,000	**Cost of sales**

The total cost of sales is $350,000, the same amount computed under the perpetual inventory system. This is not surprising, because the old units that are in inventory at any date are assumed to be sold first before the new units are sold. Under both the perpetual and periodic systems, the 800 units in beginning inventory, the 800 units purchased on February 5, and 100 of the 900 units purchased on March 10 are assumed to be sold.

Weighted-Average Cost Method   As indicated before, when a periodic inventory system is used, the cost of ending inventory and cost of sales are computed at the end of the accounting period. The average cost is calculated by dividing the cost of goods available for sale by the total units available for sale. For our example, the weighted-average unit cost for the quarter is computed as indicated in Exhibit 7A.2.

In these circumstances, the cost of sales and the ending inventory are assigned the same weighted-average cost of $210.40 per blazer. The cost of the ending inventory is $168,320 (800 blazers at $210.40 each) compared to $175,040 under the perpetual inventory system, and the cost of sales is $357,680 compared to $350,960 under the perpetual system. The periodic cost of sales is always higher than the perpetual cost of sales in a period of rising prices, because the periodic average cost per unit includes the cost of all units available for sale during the accounting period, whereas the perpetual average cost method considers only the cost of units available for sale at different dates in the accounting period. This change in the cost of blazers explains why Reitmans must retain a consistent inventory costing method to ensure that users of its financial statements have comparable estimates of the cost of sales and ending inventory from one year to the next.

Weighted-Average Inventory Flows—Periodic Inventory System

Cost of Sales Calculation (Weighted-Average Periodic)
Cost of blazers purchased and sold

Date		Units		Cost		Total	
January 1	Beginning inventory	800	×	$200	=	$160,000	
February 5	Purchase	800	×	$210	=	168,000	
March 10	Purchase	900	×	$220	=	198,000	
Number of units available for sale (NUAS):		2,500				$526,000	**Cost of goods available for sale (COGAS)**
Number of units in ending inventory:		800	×	$210.4	=	168,320	**Cost of ending inventory**
Number of units sold:		1,700	×	$210.4	=	$357,680	**Cost of sales**

$$\text{Weighted-average cost per unit} = \frac{\text{COGAS}}{\text{NUAS}} = \frac{\$526,000}{2,500} = \$210.40^{10}$$

METHODS FOR ESTIMATING INVENTORY— THE GROSS PROFIT METHOD

FINANCIAL ANALYSIS

When a periodic inventory system is used and detailed perpetual inventory records are not kept, the cost of sales and the amount of ending inventory can be directly computed only when a physical inventory count is taken. Because taking a physical inventory count is expensive, it is normally done only once each year. In these circumstances, managers who wish to prepare monthly or quarterly financial statements for internal use often estimate the cost of sales and cost of ending inventory by using the *gross profit method*. The gross profit method uses the historical gross profit percentage (introduced in Chapter 6) to estimate cost of sales.

For example, if Reitmans's historical gross profit percentage on blazer style #101 is 30 percent and $500,000 worth of this model is sold in January, it will estimate the cost of sales to be $350,000 ($500,000 × [100% − 30%]) for the month. If Reitmans keeps track of purchases and other additions to inventory, it can then use the cost of sales equation to solve for an estimate of ending inventory. Retailers often take their physical inventory counts based on the retail price instead of cost and then use a similar method (called the *retail method*) to estimate cost. Methods for estimating inventory and cost of sales are discussed in detail in intermediate accounting courses.

Comparison of Perpetual and Periodic Systems The differences between the perpetual and periodic inventory systems are highlighted in italics in Exhibit 7A.3.

Comparison of Perpetual and Periodic Inventory Systems

Perpetual	**Periodic**
Beginning inventory (carried over from prior period)	Beginning inventory (carried over from prior period)
+ Purchases for the period (accumulated in an *inventory* account)	+ Purchases for the period (accumulated in a *purchases* account)
= Cost of goods available for sale	= Cost of goods available for sale
− *Cost of sales (measured at every sale, based on perpetual record)*	− *Ending inventory (measured at end of period, based on physical inventory count)*
= *Ending inventory (perpetual record updated at every sale)*	= *Cost of sales (computed as a residual amount)*
EI = BI + PUR − COS	COS = BI + PUR − EI

Compare and contrast the recording of inventory transactions in periodic and perpetual inventory systems.

APPENDIX 7B: RECORDING INVENTORY TRANSACTIONS USING PERIODIC AND PERPETUAL INVENTORY SYSTEMS

The recording of the purchase and sales transactions summarized in Exhibit 7.4 are presented in Exhibit 7B.1 using the first-in, first-out (FIFO) method, assuming that all transactions are on account. The journal entries under the periodic inventory system are contrasted with those recorded under the perpetual system.

Exhibit **7B.1**

Comparison of Journal Entries under the Periodic and Perpetual Inventory Systems

Periodic Records (FIFO Costing Method)	**Perpetual Records (FIFO Costing Method)**
1. Record all transactions in chronological order. Record all purchases in the *purchases* account and all sales in the sales revenue account.	1. Record all transactions in chronological order. Purchases should be recorded in the *inventory* account and in a detailed perpetual inventory record. Sales should be recorded in sales revenue, and the cost of sales should be recognized on the date of sale.

January 31:

Trade receivables (A)	167,400	
Sales revenue (R) (600 units × $279)		167,400
Cost of sales (E)	120,000	
Inventory (A) (600 units × $200)		120,000

January 31:

Trade receivables (A)	167,400	
Sales revenue (R) (600 units × $279)		167,400

February 5:

Inventory (A) (800 units × $210)	168,000	
Trade payables (L)		168,000

February 5:

Purchases* (T) (800 units × $210)	168,000	
Trade payables (L)		168,000

*Purchases is a temporary account (T) closed to Ccost of sales at the end of the period.

February 28:

Trade receivables (A)	265,500	
Sales revenue (R) (900 units × $295)		265,500
Cost of sales (E)	187,000	
Inventory (A)		187,000
(200 units 3 $200 1 700 units × $210)		

February 28:

Trade receivables (A)	265,500	
Sales revenue (R) (900 units × $295)		265,500

March 10:

Inventory (A) (900 units × $220)	198,000	
Trade payables (L)		198,000

March 10:

Purchases (T) (900 units × $220)	198,000	
Trade payables (L)		198,000

March 31:

Trade receivables (A)	59,800	
Sales revenue (R) (200 units × $299)		59,800
Cost of sales (E)	43,000	
Inventory (A)		43,000
(100 units × $210 1 100 units × $220)		

March 31:

Trade receivables (A)	59,800	
Sales revenue (R) (200 units × $299)		59,800

Periodic Records (FIFO Costing Method)	**Perpetual Records (FIFO Costing Method)**

Periodic Records (FIFO Costing Method)

2. At March 31, end of period: Use the cost of sales and inventory amounts. It is not necessary to compute the cost of sales because, under the perpetual inventory system, the cost of sales account is up to date. The balance in the cost of sales account is reported on the statement of earnings. Also, the inventory account shows the ending inventory amount reported on the statement of financial position. A physical inventory count is still necessary to assess the accuracy of the perpetual records and to assess theft and other forms of misuse (called shrinkage).

Cost of Sales (E)

Jan. 31 sale	120,000
Feb. 28 sale	187,000
Mar. 31 sale	43,000
End.	350,000

Inventory (A)

Jan. 1 bal.	160,000	Jan. 31 sale	120,000
Feb. 5 purchase	168,000	Feb. 28 sale	187,000
Mar. 10 purchase	198,000	Mar. 31 sale	43,000
End.	176,000		

March 31:

No entry

Perpetual Records (FIFO Costing Method)

2. At March 31, end of period:
   a. Count the number of units on hand.
   b. Compute the cost of the ending inventory.
   c. Compute and record the cost of sales.

Beginning inventory (last periods ending inventory)	$160,000
Add purchases (balance in the purchases account)	366,000
Cost of goods available for sale	526,000
Deduct ending inventory	
(physical count: 800 units at $220)	176,000
Cost of sales	$350,000

March 31:

Transfer beginning inventory and purchases to the cost of sales account:

Cost of sales (E)	526,000	
Inventory (A) (beginning)		160,000
Purchases (T)		366,000

Transfer the ending inventory amount from the cost of sales account to determine the cost of sales and establish the ending inventory balance:

Inventory (A) (ending)	176,000	
Cost of sales (E)		176,000

Notice that the cost of ending inventory and cost of sales are the same when the FIFO method is used. If the average-cost method is used, the journal entries to record the transactions during the three-month period and the adjustments at March 31 are similar to those that are presented in Exhibit 7B.1, except for the differences in cost of sales and inventory amounts.

CHAPTER **TAKE-AWAYS**

7-1. Apply the cost principle to identify the amounts that should be included in inventory, and the matching process to determine the cost of sales for typical retailers, wholesalers, and manufacturers.

Inventory should include all of the items owned that are held for resale. Costs flow into inventory when goods are purchased or manufactured. They flow out (as an expense) when the goods are sold or otherwise disposed of. In conformity with the matching process, the total cost of sales during the period must be related to the sales revenue earned during the period. A company can keep track of the ending inventory and cost of sales for the period using (1) the perpetual inventory system, which is based on the maintenance of detailed and continuous inventory records, and (2) the periodic inventory system, which is based on a physical count of ending inventory and uses of the cost of sales equation to determine cost of sales.

7-2. Report inventory and cost of sales by using three inventory costing methods.

The chapter discussed three different inventory costing methods used to allocate costs between the units remaining in inventory and the units sold, and their applications in different economic circumstances. The methods discussed were specific identification, FIFO, and weighted-average cost. Each of the inventory costing methods is in conformity with IFRS. Remember that the cost flow assumption need not match the physical flow of inventory.

7-3. Decide when the use of different inventory costing methods is beneficial to a company.

The selection of a method of inventory costing is important because it will affect reported net earnings, income tax expense (and, hence, cash flow), and the inventory valuation reported on the statement of financial position. In a period of rising prices, FIFO results in higher earnings than does weighted-average cost. In a period of falling prices, the opposite result occurs.

7-4. Report inventory at the lower of cost and net realizable value (LC&NRV).

Ending inventory should be measured based on the lower of actual cost and net realizable value (LC&NRV basis). This practice can have a major effect on the statements of companies facing declining costs. Damaged, obsolete, and out-of-season inventory should also be written down to its current estimated net realizable value if that is below cost. The LC&NRV adjustment increases cost of sales, decreases net earnings, and decreases reported inventory.

7-5. Describe methods for controlling inventory, and analyze the effects of inventory errors on financial statements.

Various control procedures can limit inventory theft or mismanagement. An error in the measurement of ending inventory affects the cost of sales on the current period's statement of earnings and ending inventory on the statement of financial position. It also affects the cost of sales in the following period by the same amount, but in the opposite direction, because this year's ending inventory becomes next year's beginning inventory. These relationships can be seen through the cost of sales equation, $BI + P - EI = COS$.

7-6. Evaluate inventory management by using the inventory turnover ratio and analyze the effects of inventory on cash flows.

The inventory turnover ratio measures the efficiency of inventory management. It reflects how many times the average inventory was produced and sold during the period. Analysts and creditors watch this ratio because a sudden decline in this ratio may mean that a company is facing an unexpected decline in demand for its products or is becoming sloppy in its production management. When a net *decrease in inventory* for the period occurs, sales are more than purchases; thus, the decrease must be *added* to net earnings in computing cash flows from operations. When a net *increase in inventory* for the period occurs, sales are less than purchases; thus, the increase must be *subtracted* from net earnings in computing cash flows from operations.

In this and previous chapters, we discussed the current assets of a business. These assets are critical for the operations of a business, but, in general, they produce value only when they are sold. In Chapter 8, we will discuss the property, plant, and equipment; natural resources; and intangibles that are the elements of productive capacity. Many of the capital assets produce value, such as a factory that manufactures cars. These assets present some interesting accounting problems because they benefit a number of accounting periods.

KEY **RATIOS**

The inventory turnover ratio measures the efficiency of inventory management. It reflects how many times the average inventory was produced and sold during the period:

$$\text{Inventory Turnover Ratio} = \frac{\text{Cost of Sales}}{\text{Average Inventory}}$$

FINDING **FINANCIAL INFORMATION**

STATEMENT OF FINANCIAL POSITION
Reported in Current Assets:
Inventory

STATEMENT OF EARNINGS
Expenses
Cost of sales

STATEMENT OF CASH FLOWS
Reported in Operating Activities (indirect method):
+ decrease in inventory
− increase in inventory
+ increase in trade payables
− decrease in trade payables

NOTES
Reported in Summary of Significant Accounting Policies:
Description of management's choice of inventory accounting policy (FIFO, weighted-average cost, LC&NRV, etc.)
Reported in a Separate Note:
If not listed on the statement of financial position, components of inventory (merchandise, raw materials, work-in-process, finished goods)

QUESTIONS

1. Why is inventory an important item to both internal (management) and external users of financial statements?
2. What are the general guidelines for deciding which items should be included in inventory?
3. Explain the application of the cost principle to an item in the ending inventory.
4. Define cost of goods available for sale. How does it differ from cost of sales?
5. Define beginning inventory and ending inventory.
6. The chapter discussed three inventory costing methods. List the three methods and briefly explain each.
7. Explain how net earnings can be manipulated when the specific identification inventory costing method is used.
8. Contrast the effects of weighted average versus FIFO on reported assets (i.e., the ending inventory) when (*a*) prices are rising and (*b*) prices are falling.
9. Contrast the statement of earnings effect of weighted average versus FIFO (i.e., on earnings before income taxes) when (*a*) prices are rising and (*b*) prices are falling.
10. Contrast the effects of weighted average versus FIFO on cash outflow and inflow.
11. Explain briefly the application of the LC&NRV concept to the ending inventory and its effect on the statement of earnings and statement of financial position when the net realizable value of inventory is lower than its cost.
12. Explain the difference between a reversal of a write-down and a holding gain.
13. (Appendix 7A) When a perpetual inventory system is used, unit costs of the items sold are known at the date of each sale. In contrast, when a periodic inventory system is used, unit costs are known only at the end of the accounting period. Why are these statements correct?
14. (Appendix 7A) The periodic inventory calculation is BI + P − EI = COS. The perpetual inventory calculation is BI + P − COS = EI. Explain the significance of the difference between these two calculations.
15. (Appendix 7B) Identify the differences in the recording of inventory transactions under both the periodic and perpetual inventory systems and explain these differences.

connect   MINI-EXERCISES

LO7-1   **M7-1**   **Matching Inventory Items to Type of Business**
Match the type of inventory with the type of business in the following matrix:

	TYPE OF BUSINESS	
Type of Inventory	**Merchandising**	**Manufacturing**
Work in process		
Finished goods		
Merchandise		
Raw materials		

LO7-1   **M7-2**   **Recording the Cost of Purchases for a Merchandiser**
Elite Apparel purchased 80 new shirts for cash and recorded a total cost of $2,620, determined as follows:

Invoice amount	$2,180
Shipping charges	175
Import taxes and duties	145
Interest paid in advance on loan to finance the purchase	120
	$2,620

Required:
Make the needed corrections in this calculation. Prepare the journal entry or entries to record this purchase in the correct amount, assuming a perpetual inventory system. Show computations.

LO7-1   **M7-3**   **Identifying the Cost of Inventories for a Manufacturer**
Operating costs incurred by a manufacturing company become either (1) part of the cost of inventory to be expensed as cost of sales at the time the finished goods are sold or (2) expenses at the time they are incurred. Indicate whether each of the following costs belongs in category (1) or (2).
___ *a.* Wages of factory workers
___ *b.* Costs of raw materials purchased
___ *c.* Sales salaries
___ *d.* Heat, light, and power for the factory building
___ *e.* Heat, light, and power for the headquarters office building

LO7-1   **M7-4**   **Inferring Purchases Using the Cost of Goods Sold Equation**
Sears Canada Inc. is a major retailer, with department stores in all provinces. The dominant portion of the company's business consists of providing merchandise and services to consumers through department stores that include catalog departments. In a recent annual report, Sears reported cost of sales of $3,424.5 million, ending inventory for the current year of $641.4 million, and ending inventory for the previous year of $774.6 million.

Required:
Is it possible to develop a reasonable estimate of the merchandise purchases for the year? If so, prepare the estimate; if not, explain why.

LO7-2   **M7-5**   **Matching Financial Statement Effects to Inventory Costing Methods**
Indicate whether the FIFO or the average cost inventory costing method normally produces each of the following effects under the listed circumstances.

a. Declining costs
   Highest net earnings _____
   Highest inventory _____
b. Rising costs
   Highest net earnings _____
   Highest inventory _____

LO7-3

M7-6 **Matching Inventory Costing Method Choices to Company Circumstances**
Indicate whether the FIFO or the average cost inventory costing method would normally
be selected when inventory costs are rising. Explain why.

LO7-4

M7-7 **Reporting Inventory under Lower of Cost and Net Realizable Value**
Wood Company had the following inventory items on hand at the end of the year:

	Quantity	Cost per Item	Net Realizable Value per Item
Item A	70	$110	$100
Item B	30	60	85

Required:
Compute the lower of cost and net realizable value on an item-by-item basis, and determine
the amount that would be reported for inventory on the statement of financial position.

LO7-5

M7-8 **Determining the Financial Statement Effects of Inventory Errors**
Assume the 2017 ending inventory was understated by $50,000. Explain how this error would
affect the 2017 and 2018 pretax earnings amounts. What would be the effects if the 2017 ending
inventory were overstated by $50,000 instead of being understated by the same amount?

LO7-6

M7-9 **Determining the Effects of Inventory Management Changes on Inventory Turnover Ratio**
Indicate the most likely effect of the following changes in inventory management on the inventory
turnover ratio (use + for increase, − for decrease, and N for no effect).
___ *a.* Have parts inventory delivered daily by suppliers instead of weekly.
___ *b.* Extend payments for inventory purchases from 15 days to 30 days.
___ *c.* Shorten the production process from 10 days to 8 days.

connect EXERCISES

LO7-1

E7-1 **Identifying Items to Be Included in Inventory**
Boilard Inc. planned to report inventory of $50,000 based on its physical count of inventory in its
warehouse at year-end, December 31, 2016. During the audit, the auditor developed the following
additional information:

a. Goods from a supplier costing $300 are in transit with Canada Post on December 31, 2016. The
terms are F.O.B. shipping point. Because these goods had not arrived, they were excluded from
the physical inventory count.

b. Boilard delivered samples costing $400 to a customer on December 27, 2016, with the
understanding that they would be returned to Boilard on January 18, 2017. Because these goods
were not on hand, they were excluded from the physical inventory count.

c. On December 31, 2016, goods in transit to customers, with terms F.O.B. shipping point, amounted
to $2,000 (the expected delivery date was January 10, 2017). Because the goods had been shipped,
they were excluded from the physical inventory count.

d. On December 31, 2016, goods in transit to a customer, F.O.B. destination, amounted to $1,000 and
are not expected to arrive at their destination before January 10, 2017. Because the goods had
been shipped, they were not included in the physical inventory count.

Required:
Boilard is required to include in inventory all goods for which it has title. Note that the point where
title (ownership) changes hands is determined by the shipping terms in the sales contract. When
goods are shipped "F.O.B. shipping point," title changes hands at shipment and the buyer normally
pays for shipping. When they are shipped "F.O.B. destination," title changes hands on delivery,
and the seller normally pays for shipping. Begin with the $50,000 inventory amount, and compute
the correct amount for the ending inventory. Explain the basis for your treatment of each of the
preceding items. (*Hint:* Set up three columns: item, amount, and explanation.)

LO7-1

E7-2 **Inferring Missing Amounts Based on Statement of Earnings Relationships**
Supply the missing dollar amounts for the 2018 statement of earnings of Laurin Retailers for each of
the following independent cases:

Case	Sales Revenue	Beginning Inventory	Purchases	Total Available	Ending Inventory	Cost of Sales	Gross Profit	Operating Expenses	Pretax Earnings or (Loss)
A	$1,300	$200	$1,400	$?	$1,000	$?	$?	$400	$?
B	900	200	800	?	?	?	?	150	0
C	?	300	?	?	600	400	800	200	?
D	800	?	600	?	250	?	?	250	100
E	2,000	?	1,800	2,200	?	?	1,000	?	(100)

■ LO**7-1**   **E7-3**   **Inferring Missing Amounts Based on Statement of Earnings Relationships**

Supply the missing dollar amounts for the 2017 statement of earnings of Kwan Company for each of the following independent cases:

	Case A	Case B	Case C
Sales revenue	$ 8,000	$ 6,000	$?
Sales returns and allowances	150	?	275
Net sales revenue	?	?	5,920
Beginning inventory	11,000	6,500	4,000
Purchases	5,000	?	9,420
Transportation—in	?	120	170
Purchase returns	350	600	?
Cost of goods available for sale	?	14,790	13,370
Ending inventory	10,000	10,740	?
Cost of sales	?	?	5,400
Gross profit	?	1,450	?
Expenses (operating)	1,300	?	520
Pretax earnings (loss)	$ 800	$ (500)	$ 0

■ LO**7-1**   **E7-4**   **Inferring Merchandise Purchases**

Le Château Inc.

Le Château Inc. is a Canadian specialty retailer and manufacturer of contemporary fashion apparel, accessories, and footwear for women and men of all ages. Its products are sold in over 200 retail locations across Canada. Assume that you are employed as a stock analyst and your boss has just completed a review of the new annual report. She provided you with her notes, but they are missing some information that you need. Her notes show that the ending inventory for Le Château in the current year was $115,357,000 and in the previous year was $124,878,000. Net sales for the current year were $250,210,000. Gross profit was $51,545,000; net loss was $38,676,000. For your analysis, you determine that you need to know the cost of sales and the amount of purchases for the year.

Required:

Explain how you can develop the information from her notes. Show calculations. (*Hint*: Use the cost of sales equation or the inventory T-account to solve for the missing value.

■ LO**7-1**   **E7-5**   **Recording Sales and Purchases with Cash Discounts**

A. The Cycle Shop sells merchandise on credit terms of 2/10, n/30. Merchandise that cost $900 was sold to Claudette Labelle on February 1, 2018, at $1,600. The company uses the perpetual inventory system.

Required:

1. Prepare the journal entry to record the credit sale.

2. Prepare the journal entry to record the collection of cash from C. Labelle (*a*) on February 9, 2018, and (*b*) on March 2, 2018.

B. On March 4, 2018, the Cycle Shop purchased bicycles and accessories from a supplier on credit for $8,000; the terms were 1/15, n/30. The company uses the net method to record purchases. (The net method is explained in endnote 5).

Required:

3. Prepare the journal entry to record the purchase on credit.

4. Prepare the journal entry to record the payment of the invoice (*a*) on March 12, 2018, and (*b*) on March 28, 2018.

LO7-2,7-3   **E7-6**   **Analyzing and Interpreting the Financial Statement Effects of the FIFO and Weighted-Average Cost Methods**

Lunar Company uses a perpetual inventory system. The company's accounting records provided the following information for Product 2:

Transactions	Units	Unit Cost
a. Inventory, December 31, 2016	3,000	$12
For the year 2017:		
b. Purchase, April 11	9,000	10
c. Sale, May 1 ($30 each)	5,000	
d. Purchase, June 1	8,000	13
e. Sale, July 3 ($30 each)	6,000	
f. Operating expenses (excluding income tax expense), $85,000		

Required:

1. Prepare a statement of earnings for 2017, through pretax earnings, showing the detailed computation of cost of sales for two cases:

   a. Case A—FIFO

   b. Case B—Weighted average

   For each case, show the computation of the ending inventory. (*Hint:* Set up adjacent columns, one for each case.)

2. Compare the pretax earnings and the ending inventory amounts between the two cases. Explain the similarities and differences.

3. Which inventory costing method may be preferred for income tax purposes? Explain.

4. Prepare journal entries to record transactions (*b*) through (*e*), as well as the cost of sales at December 31, 2017, assuming that Lunar uses FIFO for inventory costing.

LO7-2,7-3   **E7-7**   **Analyzing and Interpreting the Financial Statement Effects of FIFO and Weighted-Average Cost Methods**

Scoresby Inc. uses a perpetual inventory system. At December 31, 2018, the company's accounting records provided the following information for Product B:

Transactions	Units	Unit Cost
a. Inventory, December 31, 2017	7,000	$ 8
For the year 2018:		
b. Purchase, March 5	19,000	9
c. Sale, June 15 ($29 each)	10,000	
d. Purchase, September 19	8,000	11
e. Sale, November 20 ($31 each)	16,000	
f. Operating expenses (excluding income tax expense), $500,000		

Required:

1. Prepare a statement of earnings for 2018 through pretax earnings, showing the detailed computation of cost of sales for two cases:

   a. Case A—FIFO

   b. Case B—Weighted average

2. For each case, show the computation of the ending inventory. (*Hint:* Set up adjacent columns, one for each case.)

3. Compare the two cases with regard to the pretax earnings and the ending inventory amounts. Explain the similarities and differences.

4. Which inventory costing method may be preferred for income tax purposes? Explain.

5. Prepare journal entries to record transactions (*b*) through (*e*), assuming that Scoresby uses FIFO for inventory costing.

LO7-4   **E7-8**   **Reporting Inventory at Lower of Cost and Net Realizable Value**

Peterson Company is preparing the annual financial statements dated December 31, 2017. Ending inventory information about the five major items stocked for regular sale follows:

	Ending Inventory		
Item	**Quantity on Hand**	**Unit Cost When Acquired (FIFO)**	**Net Realizable Value at Year-End**
A	50	$15	$12
B	80	30	40
C	10	45	52
D	30	25	30
		Ending Inventory	
E	350	10	5

Required:

1. Compute the value of the 2017 ending inventory by using the LC&NRV rule applied on an item-by-item basis. (*Hint:* Set up columns for item, quantity, total cost, total net realizable value, and LC&NRV valuation.)

2. What will be the effect of the write-down of inventory to LC&NRV on cost of sales for the year 2017?

3. Assume that 20 units of item E had not been sold by December 31, 2018, and that the net realizable value of that item increased to $7.50 per unit. How would this information be reflected in Peterson's statement of earnings for 2018 and its statement of financial position at year-end? Explain.

■ LO7-4   **E7-9**   **Reporting Inventory at Lower of Cost and Net Realizable Value**

Fine Leather Ltd. had the following inventory at December 31, 2017:

		Per Unit	
Item	**Quantity**	**Cost**	**Net Realizable Value**
Leather blazers			
Model 154	20	$100	$120
Model 160	15	180	168
Model 165	10	250	260
Handbags			
Model 11	60	30	35
Model 12	40	45	42
Model 13	25	65	63

Required:

1. Determine the value of ending inventory that should be reported on the statement of financial position by applying the LC&NRV rule to,

   a. Each item of inventory

   b. Each major category of inventory

   c. Total inventory

2. Which of the computations in (1) results in the lowest net earnings for 2017? Explain.

3. Which level of inventory aggregation (individual item basis, major categories, or total inventory) is permitted by IFRS? Why are the other levels of aggregation not acceptable? Explain.

■ LO7-4   **E7-10**   **Interpreting Disclosures Related to Inventory**

Le Château Inc.

Le Château Inc. manufactures and sells fashion apparel, accessories, and footwear at various retail locations across Canada. Its annual report for the year ended January 31, 2015, included the following note:

8. INVENTORIES			
(in thousands of dollars)	**Jan. 31, 2015**	**Jan. 25, 2014**	**Jan. 26, 2013**
Raw materials	$ 6,141	$ 8,181	$ 9,033
Work-in-process	2,187	2,782	2,745
Finished goods	101,062	107,523	106,017
Finished goods in transit	5,967	6,392	5,423
	$115,397	$124,878	$123,218

The cost of inventory recognized as an expense and included in cost of sales for the year ended January 31, 2015, is $98.7 million (2014, $101.8 million), including write-downs recorded of

$5.5 million (2014, $5.3 million), as a result of net realizable value being lower than cost and reversals of inventory write-downs recognized in prior periods of $216,000 (2014, $483,000).

Required:

1. Explain each of the inventory items listed in the note.

2. Assume that the write-downs and the reversal of write-downs relate to the values of specific items of inventory. Prepare the journal entry to record both the write-downs and the reversal of write-downs of inventory costs. Le Château uses a perpetual inventory system.

3. Assume that some of the raw materials that were written down on January 31, 2015, were not used for production purposes by January 30, 2016, the end of its 2016 fiscal year. The inventory items that were written down had an original cost of $2.3 million, and their net realizable value was $1.7 million. Changes in market conditions increased the net realizable value of these items to $2.4 million, which exceeded their original cost. How would this information be reflected in Le Château's statement of earnings for fiscal year 2016 and its statement of financial position as at January 30, 2016? Explain.

LO7-5

E7-11 **Analyzing the Effects of an Error in Recording Purchases**

Garraway Ski Company mistakenly recorded purchases of inventory on account received during the last week of December 2017 as purchases during January of 2018 (this is called a *purchases cut-off error*). Garraway uses a periodic inventory system, and ending inventory was correctly counted and reported each year. Assuming that no correction was made in 2017 or 2018, indicate whether each of the following financial statement amounts will be understated, overstated, or correct:

1. Net earnings for 2017.

2. Net earnings for 2018.

3. Retained earnings at December 31, 2017.

4. Retained earnings at December 31, 2018.

LO7-5

Gibson Greeting
Cards

E7-12 **Analyzing the Effect of an Inventory Error Disclosed in an Actual Note to a Financial Statement**

Several years ago, the financial statements of Gibson Greeting Cards (now owned by American Greetings Corporation) contained the following note:

> On July 1, the Company announced that it had determined that the ending inventory... had been overstated... The overstatement of inventory... was $8,806,000.

Gibson reported net earnings of $25,852,000 for the year in which the error occurred, and its income tax rate was 39.3 percent.

Required:

1. Compute the amount of net earnings that Gibson reported after correcting the inventory error. Show computations.

2. Assume that the inventory error was not discovered. Identify the financial statement accounts that would have been incorrect for the year the error occurred and for the subsequent year. State whether each account was understated or overstated.

LO7-5

E7-13 **Analyzing and Interpreting the Impact of an Inventory Error**

Dalez Corporation prepared the following two statements of earnings (simplified for illustrative purposes):

	First Quarter 2017		Second Quarter 2017	
Sales revenue		$11,000		$18,000
Cost of sales				
Beginning inventory	$4,000		$ 3,800	
Purchases	3,000		13,000	
Cost of goods available for sale	7,000		16,800	
Ending inventory	3,800		9,000	
Cost of sales		3,200		7,800
Gross profit		7,800		10,200
Expenses (operating)		5,000		6,000
Pretax earnings		$ 2,800		$ 4,200

During the third quarter, it was discovered that the ending inventory for the first quarter should have been $4,200.

Required:

1. What effect did this error have on the pretax earnings of each quarter and of the two quarters combined? Explain.

2. Did this error affect the earnings per share amounts for each quarter? (See the discussion of earnings per share in Chapter 6.) Explain.

3. Prepare corrected statements of earnings for each quarter.

4. Set up a schedule with the following headings to reflect the comparative effects of the correct and incorrect amounts on the statement of earnings:

Statement of earnings item		1st Quarter		2nd Quarter	
Incorrect amount	Correct amount	Error (if any)	Incorrect amount	Correct amount	Error (if any)

LO7-6

Sony Corporation

E7-14   **Evaluating Inventory Management by Using the Inventory Turnover Ratio**

Sony Corporation manufactures and sells cellphones directly to mobile telecommunications service suppliers. The company reported the following amounts for fiscal year 2014 (in billions of yen):

Net sales revenue	6,682
Cost of sales	5,140
Beginning inventory	710
Ending inventory	734

Required:

1. Compute the inventory turnover ratio and the average days to sell inventory for the current year.

2. Explain the meaning of each of the amounts computed in (1).

3. Indicate whether the inventory turnover ratio will increase, decrease, or remain unchanged as a result of the following changes in inventory management. Justify your answers.

   a. Have parts inventory delivered daily by suppliers instead of weekly.

   b. Extend payments for inventory purchases from 30 days to 45 days.

   c. Shorten the production process from 10 days to 8 days.

LO7-6

E7-15   **Analyzing and Interpreting the Effects of the FIFO/Weighted-Average Choice on the Inventory Turnover Ratio**

The records at the end of January 2017 for All Star Company showed the following for a particular kind of merchandise:

Inventory, December 31, 2016, at FIFO: 19 units @ $12 = $228
Inventory, December 31, 2016, at weighted average: 19 units @ $10 = $190

Transactions	Units	Unit Cost	Total Cost
Purchase, January 9, 2017	25	15	$375
Purchase, January 20, 2017	50	16	800
Sale, January 11, 2017 (at $38 per unit)	40		
Sale, January 27, 2017 (at $39 per unit)	28		

Required:

Compute the inventory turnover ratio under the FIFO and weighted-average inventory costing methods and a perpetual inventory system (show computations and round to the nearest dollar). Explain which method you believe is the better indicator of the efficiency of inventory management.

LO7-6

Performance Sports Group Ltd.

E7-16   **Interpreting the Effect of Changes in Inventories and Trade Payables on Cash Flow from Operations**

Performance Sports Group Ltd. is a leading developer and manufacturer of ice hockey, roller hockey, and lacrosse equipment as well as related apparel. Its products are marketed under the Bauer Hockey, Mission Roller Hockey, and Maverik Lacrosse brand names throughout the world. A recent annual report included the following on its statement of financial position (amounts in thousands of dollars):

CONSOLIDATED STATEMENTS OF FINANCIAL POSITION		
Item	Current Year	Previous Year
......		
Inventory	157,429	109,747
......	...	...
Trade payables	42,116	22,548

Required:

Explain the effects of the changes in inventory and trade payables on cash flow from operating activities for the current year.

LO7-S1   **E7-17   (Appendix 7A) Calculating Ending Inventory and Cost of Sales Under FIFO and Weighted-Average Cost Methods—Periodic System**

Clor Company uses a periodic inventory system. At December 31, 2017, the accounting records provided the following information for Product 1:

	Units	Unit Cost
Inventory, December 31, 2016	3,000	$8
For the year 2017:		
Purchases, March 31	5,000	9
Purchases, August 1	2,000	7
Inventory, December 31, 2017	4,000	

Required:

Compute the cost of sales and the ending inventory under the FIFO and weighted-average costing methods. (*Hint:* Set up adjacent columns for the two methods.)

LO7-S1   **E7-18   (Appendix 7A) Deciding between Two Alternative Inventory Costing Methods Based on Cash Flow and Net Earnings Effects under a Periodic System**

Courtney Company uses a periodic inventory system. Data for 2017 are as follows: beginning merchandise inventory (December 31, 2016), 3,000 units at $35; purchases, 12,000 units at $38; operating expenses (excluding income taxes), $213,000; ending inventory per physical count at December 31, 2017, 2,700 units; sales price per unit, $70; and average income tax rate, 30 percent.

Required:

1. Prepare statements of earnings under the FIFO and weighted-average costing methods. Use a format similar to the following:

		Inventory Costing Method	
Statement of Earnings	Units	FIFO	Weighted Average
Sales revenue	_____	$_____	$_____
Cost of sales			
Beginning inventory	_____	_____	_____
Purchases	_____	_____	_____
Cost of goods available for sale	_____	_____	_____
Ending inventory	_____	_____	_____
Cost of sales	_____	_____	_____
Gross profit		_____	_____
Expenses (operating)		_____	_____
Pretax earnings		_____	_____
Income tax expense		_____	_____
Net earnings			

2. Which method, FIFO or weighted-average cost, is preferable in terms of (*a*) net earnings and (*b*) cash flow? Explain.

3. What would be your answer to (2), assuming that prices were falling? Explain.

LO7-S1

E7-19   **(Appendix 7A) Deciding between Two Alternative Inventory Costing Methods Based on Cash Flow Effects under a Periodic System**

Following is partial information for the statement of earnings of Timber Company under two different inventory costing methods, assuming the use of a periodic inventory system:

	FIFO	Weighted Average
Unit sales price, $50		
Cost of sales		
Beginning inventory (400 units)	$13,600	$13,600
Purchases (475 units)	17,100	17,100
Cost of goods available for sale		
Ending inventory (545 units)		
Cost of sales		
Operating expenses	1,700	1,700

Required:

1. Compute the cost of sales under the FIFO and weighted-average inventory costing methods.

2. Prepare a statement of earnings through pretax earnings for each method.

3. Rank the two methods with regard to favourable cash flow, and explain the basis for your ranking.

LO7-S2

E7-20   **(Appendix 7B) Recording Purchases and Sales under Periodic and Perpetual Inventory Systems**

Demski Company reported beginning inventory of 600 units at a unit cost of $10. It engaged in the following purchase and sale transactions during 2017:

Jan. 14   Sold 120 units at unit sales price of $20 on open account.
April 9   Purchased 90 additional units at unit cost of $10 on open account.
Sept. 2   Sold 270 units at sales price of $25 on open account.

At the end of 2017, a physical count showed that Demski Company had 300 units of inventory still on hand.

Required:

Record each transaction, assuming that Demski Company uses (*a*) a periodic inventory system and (*b*) a perpetual inventory system (including any necessary entries at December 31, the end of the accounting period). Demski Company uses the FIFO inventory costing method.

connect PROBLEMS

LO7-1

P7-1   **Identifying Items to Be Included in Inventory**

Reggie Company has just completed a physical inventory count at year-end, December 31, 2017. Only the items on the shelves, in storage, and in the receiving area were counted and costed on a FIFO basis. The inventory amounted to $65,000. During the audit, the auditor developed the following additional information:

a. Goods costing $750 were being used by a customer on a trial basis and were excluded from the inventory count at December 31, 2017.

b. Goods costing $900 were in transit to Reggie on December 31, 2017, with terms F.O.B. destination (explained below). Because these goods had not arrived, they were excluded from the physical inventory count.

c. On December 31, 2017, goods in transit to customers, with terms F.O.B. shipping point, amounted to $1,300 (the expected delivery date was January 10, 2018). Because the goods had been shipped, they were excluded from the physical inventory count.

d. On December 28, 2017, a customer purchased goods for $2,650 cash and left them "for pick-up on January 3, 2018." The cost of sales totalled $1,590 and was included in the physical inventory count because the goods were still on hand.

e. On the date of the inventory count, the company received notice from a supplier that goods ordered earlier at a cost of $2,550 had been delivered to the transportation company on December 27, 2017; the terms were F.O.B. shipping point. Because the shipment had not arrived by December 31, 2017, it was excluded from the physical inventory count.

f. On December 31, 2017, the company shipped goods to a customer, F.O.B. destination. The goods, which cost $850, are not expected to arrive at their destination before January 8, 2018. Because the goods were not on hand, they were not included in the physical inventory count.

g. One of the items sold by the company has such a low volume that the management planned to drop it last year. To induce Reggie Company to continue carrying the item, the manufacturer-supplier provided the item on a consignment basis. This means that the manufacturer-supplier retains ownership of the item, and Reggie Company (the consignee) has no responsibility to pay for the items until they are sold to customers. Each month, Reggie Company sends a report to the manufacturer on the number sold and remits cash for the cost. At the end of December 2017, Reggie Company had five of these items on hand; therefore, they were included in the physical inventory count at $950 each.

Required:

Reggie is required to include in inventory all goods for which it has title. Note that the point where title (ownership) changes hands is determined by the shipping terms in the sales contract. When goods are shipped "F.O.B. shipping point," title changes hands at shipment and the buyer normally pays for shipping. When they are shipped "F.O.B. destination," title changes hands on delivery, and the seller normally pays for shipping. Begin with the $65,000 inventory amount and compute the correct amount for the ending inventory. Explain the basis for your treatment of each of the preceding items. (*Hint:* Set up three columns: item, amount, and explanation.)

LO7-2,7-3
eXcel

P7-2 Evaluating Three Alternative Inventory Methods Based on Net Earnings and Cash Flow

At the end of January 2018, the records of Regina Company showed the following for a particular item that sold at $18 per unit:

Transaction	Units	Amount
Inventory, January 1, 2018	500	$2,500
Sale, January 10	(400)	
Purchase, January 12	600	3,600
Sale, January 17	(300)	
Purchase, January 26	160	1,280

Required:

1. Assuming the use of a perpetual inventory system, prepare a summarized statement through gross profit on sales under each of the following inventory costing methods: (*a*) weighted-average cost, (*b*) FIFO, and (*c*) specific identification, assuming that the company is permitted to use this method. For specific identification, assume that the first sale was out of the beginning inventory and the second sale was out of the January 12 purchase. Show the inventory computations in detail.

2. Which method would result in
   a. the highest pretax earnings?
   b. the lowest income tax expense?
   c. the most favourable cash flow?
   Explain.

3. Prepare journal entries to record the transactions that occurred in January 2018, assuming that FIFO is used for inventory costing.

LO7-2,7-3

P7-3 Comparing and Contrasting the Effects of Inventory Costing Methods on Financial Statement Elements (AP7-1)

Neverstop Corporation sells item A as part of its product line. Information about the beginning inventory, purchases, and sales of item A are given in the following table for the first six months of 2017. The company uses a perpetual inventory system:

	Purchases		Sales	
Date	Number of Units	Unit Cost	Number of Units	Sales Price
January 1 (beginning inventory)	500	$2.50		
January 24			300	$4.00
February 8	600	$2.60		
March 16			560	$4.20
June 11	300	$2.75		

Required:

1. Compute the cost of ending inventory by using the weighted-average costing method.

2. Compute the gross profit for the first six months of 2017 by using the FIFO costing method.

3. Would the gross profit be higher, lower, or the same if Neverstop used the weighted-average costing method rather than the FIFO method? Explain. No calculations are required.

4. Prepare journal entries to record the purchase and sale transactions, as well as the cost of sales, assuming that the weighted-average method is used.

5. Assume that because of a clerical error, the ending inventory is reported to be 440 units rather than the actual number of units (540) on hand. If FIFO is used, calculate the amount of the understatement or overstatement in

   a. the cost of sales for the first six months of 2017.

   b. the current assets at June 30, 2017.

■ LO7-3,7-6   **P7-4**   **Reporting the Effects of Inventory Costing Methods on Financial Statement Elements and Evaluating Inventory Management** (AP7-2)

Kramer Corp. reported the following sale and purchase transactions related to a specific product in January 2017:

Date	Transaction	Quantity	Unit Cost	Unit Sales Price
Jan. 1	Beginning inventory	5 units	$90	
Jan. 3	Sale on account	3 units		$120
Jan. 6	Purchase on account	11 units	95	
Jan. 8	Sale on account	4 units		120
Jan. 9	Sale on account	5 units		120
Jan. 15	Sales returned due to damage, $240 (two units that were sold on January 9). The units were in very poor condition and were destroyed.			

Kramer Corp. uses a perpetual inventory system and the FIFO inventory costing method.

Required:

1. Compute net sales and gross profit for January 2017.

2. Determine the inventory turnover ratio and the average days to sell inventory for January 2017, and explain what the numbers mean.

3. Prepare the journal entries to record the purchase transaction on January 6, the sale transaction on January 8, and the sales return on January 15.

4. Compute the cost of sales for January 2017, assuming for this part only that Kramer uses the weighted-average cost method.

■ LO7-5   **P7-5**   **Analyzing and Interpreting the Effects of Inventory Errors** (AP7-3)

eXcel

The statements of earnings for Pruitt Company summarized for a four-year period show the following (amounts in thousands of dollars):

	2018	2017	2016	2015
Sales revenue	$2,025	$2,450	$2,700	$2,975
Cost of sales	1,505	1,627	1,782	2,113
Gross profit	520	823	918	862
Operating expenses	490	513	538	542
Pretax earnings	30	310	380	320
Income tax expense (30%)	9	93	114	96
Net earning	$ 21	$ 217	$ 266	$ 224

An audit revealed that in determining these amounts, the ending inventory for 2016 was understated by $22.

Required:

1. Revise these statements of earnings to reflect the correct amounts.

2. Did the error affect the cumulative net earnings for the four-year period? Explain.

3. What effect did the error have on the income tax expense for 2016 and 2017?

LO7-5

P7-6

Reporting the Statement of Earnings and Cash Flow Effects of Lower of Cost and Net Realizable Value

Smart Company prepared its annual financial statements dated December 31, 2017. The company applies the FIFO inventory costing method; however, the company neglected to apply the LC&NRV valuation to the ending inventory. The preliminary 2017 statement of earnings follows:

Sales revenue		$280,000
Cost of sales		
Beginning inventory	$ 31,000	
Purchases	184,000	
Cost of goods available for sale	215,000	
Ending inventory (FIFO cost)	46,500	
Cost of sales		168,500
Gross profit		111,500
Operating expenses		62,000
Pretax earnings		49,500
Income tax expense (30%)		14,850
Net earnings		$ 34,650

Assume that you have been asked to restate the 2017 financial statements to incorporate the LC&NRV inventory valuation rule. You have developed the following data relating to the ending inventory at December 31, 2017:

		Acquisition Cost		
Item	Quantity	Unit	Total	Net Realizable Value
A	3,050	$3	$ 9,150	$4
B	1,500	5	7,500	3.5
C	7,100	1.5	10,650	3.5
D	3,200	6	19,200	4
			$46,500	

Required:

1. Restate the statement of earnings to reflect the valuation of the ending inventory on December 31, 2017, at the LC&NRV. Apply the LC&NRV rule on an item-by-item basis and show computations.

2. Compare and explain the LC&NRV effect on each amount that was changed in (1).

3. What is the conceptual basis for applying LC&NRV to merchandise inventories?

4. What effect (increase, decrease, no effect) did the LC&NRV rule have on the cash flow for 2017? What will be the long-term effect on cash flow (increase, decrease, no effect)? Computations are not necessary.

LO7-6

P7-7

Evaluating the Effects of Manufacturing Changes on the Inventory Turnover Ratio and Cash Flows from Operating Activities

H. T. Tan and Company has been operating for five years as an electronics component manufacturer specializing in cellphone components. During this period, it has experienced rapid growth in sales revenue and inventory. Mr. Tan and his associates have hired you as the company's first corporate controller. You have put into place new purchasing and manufacturing procedures that are expected to reduce inventories by approximately one-third by year-end. You have gathered the following data related to the changes (in thousands):

Item	Beginning of Year	End of Year (projected)
Inventory	$495,700	$304,310
		Current Year (projected)
Cost of sales		$7,008,984

Required:

1. Compute the inventory turnover ratio based on two different assumptions:

   a. Those presented in the preceding table (a decrease in the balance in inventory).

   b. No change from the beginning of the year in the inventory balance.

2. Compute the effect of the projected change in the balance in inventory on cash flow from operating activities for the year (show the sign and amount of the effect).

3. On the basis of the preceding analysis, write a brief memo explaining how an increase in inventory turnover can result in an increase in cash flow from operating activities. Also explain how this increase can benefit the company.

LO7-1,7-2,7-4,7-5

P7-8 **Recording Inventory Transactions, Computing Ending Inventory and Cost of Sales, and Determining the Effects of LC&NRV Rule on the Inventory Turnover Ratio** (AP7-4)

Sokos Corporation sells item A as part of its product line. Transactions related to this product during December 2017 are summarized below.

Date	Transaction	Units	Amount per Unit
Dec. 1	Inventory	50	$30.00
Dec. 4	Sale	40	36.00
Dec. 11	Purchase	75	33.00
Dec. 13	Sale	60	37.50
Dec. 20	Purchase	80	34.00
Dec. 27	Sale	50	40.00

Sokos uses a perpetual inventory system and makes its inventory purchases on account. It uses the FIFO inventory costing method and the lower of cost and net realizable value rule on an individual item basis. Its fiscal year ends on December 31 each year. All sales are on account.

Required:

1. Prepare journal entries to record the transactions on December 4 and December 11.

2. Compute the cost of ending inventory at December 31, 2017 and cost of sales for the month of December 2017.

3. Would the cost of ending inventory increase or decrease if Sokos used the weighted-average cost method instead of FIFO. Explain without re-computing the cost of ending inventory.

4. The net realizable value of Item A is $30 per unit at December 31, 2017. Prepare the adjusting entry to reflect the application of the LC&NRV rule.

5. Assume that the Company's accountant ignored the LC&NRV rule. How would this error affect the Company's inventory turnover ratio? Explain.

LO7-S1

P7-9 **(Appendix 7A) Analyzing the Effects of Three Alternative Inventory Methods and Deciding on the Preferred Method** (AP7-5)

All Signs Company uses a periodic inventory system. The company's accounting records for the most popular item in inventory showed the following details:

Transactions	Units	Unit Cost
Beginning inventory, April 1, 2018	800	$15
Transactions during 2018:		
a. Purchase, May 20	1,200	16
b. Sale, July 1 ($46 each)	(1,400)	
c. Purchase, September 30	1,000	18
d. Sale, November 1 ($46 each)	(200)	
e. Sales return November 5 (relating to Transaction [d])	40	

Required:

Compute (a) the cost of goods available for sale during 2018, (b) the cost of ending inventory at December 31, 2018, and (c) the cost of sales for 2018, under each of the following inventory costing methods (show computations and round to the nearest dollar):

1. Weighted-average cost.

2. FIFO.

3. Specific identification, assuming that the company is permitted to use it and that half of the units sold on June 1, 2018, were selected from the beginning inventory and the other half was taken from the purchase of May 20, 2018. Assume that the sale of November 1, 2018, was selected from the purchase of September 30, 2018.

4. As a shareholder, which of these three methods would you prefer?

■ LO7-S1

eXcel

P7-10   **(Appendix 7A) Evaluating the FIFO/Weighted-Average Choice When Costs Are Rising and Falling**

Net earnings is to be evaluated under four different situations as follows:

i. Prices are rising: Situation A—FIFO is used. Situation B—Weighted average is used.

ii. Prices are falling: Situation C—FIFO is used. Situation D—Weighted average is used.

The basic data common to all four situations are sales, 500 units for $15,000; beginning inventory, 300 units; purchases, 400 units; ending inventory, 200 units; and operating expenses, $4,000. The following tabulated statements of earnings for each situation have been set up for analytical purposes:

| | Prices Rising | | Prices Falling | |
| | Situation A | Situation B | Situation C | Situation D |
Statement of Earnings	**FIFO**	**Weighted Average**	**FIFO**	**Weighted Average**
Sales revenue	$15,000	$15,000	$15,000	$15,000
Cost of sales				
Beginning inventory	3,300	?	?	?
Purchases	4,800	?	?	?
Cost of goods available for sale	8,100	?	?	?
Ending inventory	2,400	?	?	?
Cost of sales	5,700	?	?	?
Gross profit	9,300	?	?	?
Operating expenses	4,000	4,000	4,000	4,000
Pretax earnings	5,300	?	?	?
Income tax expense (30%)	1,590			
Net earnings	$ 3,710	?	?	?

Required:

1. Compute the missing values for each situation. In Situations A and B (prices rising), assume the following: beginning inventory, 300 units at $11 = $3,300; purchases, 400 units at $12 = $4,800. In Situations C and D (prices falling), assume the opposite; that is, beginning inventory, 300 units at $12 = $3,600; purchases, 400 units at $11 = $4,400. Use periodic inventory procedures.

2. Compare and contrast the relative effects on pretax earnings and on net earnings as demonstrated by (i) when prices are rising and (ii) when prices are falling.

3. Compare and contrast the relative effects, if any, on the cash position for each situation.

4. Would you recommend the FIFO method or the weighted-average cost method? Explain.

■ LO7-S2

P7-11   **(Appendix 7B) Recording Sales and Purchases with Cash Discounts and Returns** (AP7-6)

Campus Stop Inc. is a student co-op. On January 1, 2017, the beginning inventory was $150,000, the trade receivables balance was $4,000, and the allowance for doubtful accounts had a credit balance of $800. Campus Stop uses a perpetual inventory system.

The following transactions (summarized) occurred during 2017:

a. Sold merchandise for $275,000 cash; the cost of sales is $137,500.

b. Received merchandise returned by customers as unsatisfactory and paid a cash refund of $1,600; the returned merchandise had cost $800.

c. Purchased merchandise from vendors on credit, terms 3/10, n/30, as follows:

   i. August Supply Company, invoice price, $5,000.

   ii. Other vendors, invoice price, $120,000.

d. Purchased equipment for use in store for cash, $2,200.

e. Purchased office supplies for future use in the store; paid cash, $700.

f. Paid freight on merchandise purchased, $400 cash.

g. Paid trade payables in full during the period as follows:

   i. Paid August Supply Company after the discount period, $5,000.

   ii. Paid other vendors within the discount period, $116,400.

Required:

Prepare journal entries for each of the preceding transactions.

ALTERNATE PROBLEMS

LO7-2,7-3   AP7-1   Comparing and Contrasting the Effects of Inventory Costing Methods on Financial Statement Elements (P7-3)

The Sportex Company, a diversified distribution outlet for sporting goods, purchases cartons of tennis balls from the Ball Corporation and markets the balls under the Sportex name. Purchases and sales data for January 2019, the first month of operations, are provided below:

Date	Transaction	Number of Cartons	Total Cost	Amount of Invoice
January 2	Purchase	800	$16,000	
January 5	Sale	500		$20,000
January 19	Purchase	600	13,200	
January 21	Sale	700		29,200
January 29	Purchase	500	11,000	

Sportex uses a perpetual inventory system.

Required:

1. Compute the cost of sales for January 2019 by using the FIFO method.

2. Compute the cost of ending inventory at January 31, 2019, assuming that Sportex uses the weighted-average cost method. (Round your calculation of the average cost to the nearest cent.)

3. Would the gross profit be higher, lower, or the same if Sportex used the weighted-average costing method rather than the FIFO method? Explain. No calculations are required.

4. Prepare journal entries to record the purchase and sale transactions, as well as the cost of sales, assuming that the FIFO method is used.

5. Assume that a purchase of 100 units costing $2,200 made on January 31, 2019, FOB shipping point, omitted from the inventory count because the merchandise had not arrived at the Company's warehouse yet. If FIFO is used, compute the amount of the understatement or overstatement in

    a. the cost of sales for the month of January 2019.

    b. the current assets at January 31, 2019.

LO7-3   AP7-2   Reporting the Effects of Inventory Costing Methods on Financial Statement Elements and Evaluating Inventory Management (P7-5)

The following details were extracted on November 30, 2017, from the records of Seema Company for a specific product:

Date	Quantity	Unit Cost	Unit Sale Price
Beginning inventory, January 1	300	$ 9	
Purchase, February 10	400	10	
Sale, April 7	300	9	$15
Purchase, August 20	300	11	
Sale, November 29	350	10	16

On December 21, 2017, Seema sold 200 units to a customer at $18 per unit. Assume that the company uses a perpetual inventory system and that its fiscal year ends on December 31, 2017.

Required:

1. Which inventory costing method does Seema use? Explain.

2. Prepare the journal entries to record the purchase transaction on August 20 and the sale transaction on December 21, assuming that both are cash transactions.

3. Compute the inventory turnover ratio during 2017, and briefly explain what the amount means.

4. Assume that the demand for this product slowed down during December 2017, and its net realizable value dropped to $9.5 per unit at December 31, 2017. Seema reports its ending inventory at the LC&NRV. Prepare the journal entry that should be recorded at December 31, 2017.

5. Compute the cost of sales for 2017, assuming for this part only that Seema uses the weighted-average cost method.

LO7-5   AP7-3   Analyzing and Interpreting the Effects of Inventory Errors (P7-5)

The statements of earnings for four consecutive years for Colca Company reflected the following summarized amounts:

	2019	2018	2017	2016
Sales revenue	$58,000	$62,000	$51,000	$50,000
Cost of sales	37,000	43,000	35,000	32,500
Gross profit	21,000	19,000	16,000	17,500
Operating expenses	12,000	14,000	12,000	10,000
Pretax earnings	$ 9,000	$ 5,000	$ 4,000	$ 7,500

Subsequent to the development of these amounts, it has been determined that the physical inventory taken on December 31, 2017, was understated by $3,000.

Required:

1. Revise the statements of earnings to reflect the correct amounts, taking into consideration the inventory error.
2. Compute the gross profit percentage for each year (*a*) before the correction and (*b*) after the correction. Do the results lend confidence to your corrected amounts? Explain.
3. What effect would the error have had on the income tax expense, assuming an average tax rate of 30 percent?

■ LO7-1,7-2,7-4,7-5

AP7-4

Recording Inventory Transactions, Computing Ending Inventory and Cost of Sales, and Determining the Effects of LC&NRV Rule on the Inventory Turnover Ratio (P7-8)

Chaiz Inc. specializes in importing furniture for commercial use. Chaiz reported the following information (all transactions are on account) for the quarter ending September 30, 2018:

Date	Transaction	Units	Amount per Unit
July 1	Inventory	224	$36.0
July 13	Purchase	152	35.5
July 29	Sale	242	49.5
August 3	Purchase	112	34.5
August 16	Purchase	204	32.5
September 21	Sale	134	49.0

Chaiz uses the perpetual inventory system and the FIFO method for inventory costing.

Required:

1. Prepare journal entries to record the transactions on July 13 and July 29.
2. Compute the cost of ending inventory at September 30, 2018, and the cost of sales, gross profit, and gross profit percentage for the quarter ending September 30, 2018.
3. Would Chaiz's gross profit increase or decrease if it uses the weighted-average cost method instead of FIFO? Explain without re-computing the gross profit.
4. Chaiz is required to report its ending inventory at the lower of cost and net realizable value. The net realizable value of chairs decreased to $33 per unit on September 30, 2018. Prepare the adjusting entry to reflect the application of the LC&NRV rule.
5. Assume that Chaiz's accountant did not apply the LC&NRV rule, and that the company inventory turnover for the quarter ended September 30, 2018, is 1.45. Re-compute the inventory turnover using the correct value for ending inventory.

■ LO7-S1

AP7-5

(Appendix 7A) Analyzing the Effects of Three Alternative Inventory Methods and Deciding on the Preferred Method (P7-9)

Yared Company uses a periodic inventory system. The company's accounting records for the most popular item in inventory showed the following details:

Transaction	Units	Unit Cost
Beginning Inventory, January 1, 2018	1,800	$2.50
Transactions during 2018:		
a. Purchase, January 30	2,500	3.10
b. Sale, March 14 ($5 each)	(1,450)	
c. Purchase, May 1	1,200	4.00
d. Sale, August 31 ($5 each)	(1,900)	

Required:

Compute (*a*) the cost of goods available for sale during 2018, (*b*) the cost of ending inventory at December 31, 2018, and (*c*) the cost of sales for 2018, under each of the following inventory costing methods (show computations and round to the nearest dollar):

1. Weighted-average cost.

2. FIFO.

3. Specific identification, assuming that the company is permitted to use it and that two-fifths of the units sold on March 14, 2018, were selected from the beginning inventory and three-fifths from the purchase of January 30, 2018. Assume that the sale of August 31, 2018, was selected from the remainder of the beginning inventory, with the balance from the purchase of May 1, 2018.

4. As a shareholder, which of these three methods would you prefer? Explain.

 LO7-S2   **AP7-6**   **(Appendix 7B) Recording Sales and Purchases with Cash Discounts and Returns** (P7-11)
The following transactions were selected from those occurring during the month of January 2017 for Dan's Store Inc. A wide variety of goods is offered for sale. Credit sales are extended to a few select customers; the usual credit terms are n/EOM (end of the month). The cost of sales is always one-half of the gross sales price.

a. Sales to customers:
Cash, $228,000
Credit, $72,000

b. Unsatisfactory merchandise returned by customers:
Cash, $3,000
Credit, $2,000

c. Purchased merchandise from vendors on credit, with terms 2/10, n/30:
    i. Amount billed by Amy Supply Company, $4,000
    ii. Amount billed by other vendors, $68,000

d. Paid freight on merchandise purchased, $1,500 cash

e. Collections on trade receivables, $36,000

f. Paid trade payables in full during the period as follows:
    i. Amy Supply Company after the discount period, $4,000
    ii. Paid other vendors within the discount period, $66,640

g. Paid $1,000 for two new laptop computers for the office

Required:

Prepare journal entries for these transactions, assuming that a periodic inventory system is used.

---

connect   **CASES AND PROJECTS**

FINDING AND INTERPRETING FINANCIAL INFORMATION

 LO7-1,7-2   **CP7-1**   **Finding Financial Information**
Go to *Connect* for the financial statements of Sears Canada Inc.

Sears Canada Inc.

1. How much inventory does the company own at the end of the current year?

2. Estimate the amount of inventory that the company purchased during the current year. (*Hint:* Use the cost of sales equation.)

3. What method does the company use to determine the cost of its inventory?

4. Compute the inventory turnover ratio for the current year. What does an inventory turnover ratio tell you?

5. What was the change in inventory? How did it affect net cash provided by operating activities for the current year?

LO7-1,7-2,7-6 **CP7-2**   **Finding Financial Information**
Refer to the financial statements of Canadian Tire Corporation given in Appendix A at the end of this book.

Canadian Tire Corporation

1. What method does the company use to determine the cost of its inventory?

2. Did the company write down its inventory at year-end? If so, what is the amount of the write-down?

3. Compute Canadian Tire's inventory turnover ratio for the year ended January 2, 2016. What does this ratio tell you?

4. If the company overstated ending inventory by $10 million for the year ended January 2, 2016, what would be the correct value for earnings before income taxes?

■ LO7-6

Canadian Tire
Corporation
Sears Canada Inc.

CP7-3 **Comparing Companies within an industry**

Refer to the financial statements of Canadian Tire Corporation (Appendix A) and Sears Canada Inc. (on *Connect*) and the Industry Ratio Report (Appendix B on *Connect*).

Required:

1. Compute the inventory turnover ratio for both companies for the current year. What would you infer from the difference?

2. Compare the inventory turnover ratio for both companies to the industry average. Are these two companies doing better or worse than the industry average in turning over their inventory?

FINANCIAL REPORTING AND ANALYSIS CASES

■ LO6-4,6-6,7-4,7-5

CP7-4

Review of Business Operations and Preparation of a Correct Statement of Earnings (A Comprehensive and Challenging Case)[10]

It is July 15, 2017. You, a junior accountant at a small accounting firm, go over your notes from your afternoon meeting with Marco Douga. Marco came to your office looking for help with his business, Marco's Professional Print Shop Ltd. (MPP). Marco is the owner-manager of MPP, a copy and print shop located in Newville. He recently approached a bank for a loan.

At his last meeting with the bank, the bank manager indicated that the loan is almost approved and told Marco that he needed to examine MPP's 2016 financial statements. In your file, you have the following information:

Exhibit I: Summary notes of the discussion with Marco Douga.

Exhibit II: Statement of earnings for the years ended December 31, 2016 and 2015, prepared by the client.

Your supervisor is eager to see a draft statement of earnings for the year ended December 31, 2016, based on the information you have thus far.

Required:

1. Identify any areas of concern that you may have about the operation of the business, particularly the proper accounting for revenue and expenses, and the control of operations.

2. Prepare a revised statement of earnings based on the information that you gathered during your meeting with Marco.

3. Identify the weaknesses in MPP's internal control of operations. What changes would you recommend? Explain.

EXHIBIT I

Summary Notes of the Discussion with Marco Douga

MPP provides copying and small print job services from a single location close to a university. The business was organized in January 2015 to meet the needs of companies, the university, and students in the area. At the time, there were no copying businesses in the area, and Marco saw this as an opportunity to become his own boss after many years of working as a mechanic for the local bus company.

Marco re-mortgaged his home for $55,000. This money was invested in the share capital of MPP. He also borrowed money from relatives to get the business started. With the money, Marco was able to purchase the computers, printers, copiers, and scanners needed to provide the full range of quality services that he thought his customers would need. Most of the equipment he purchased was used, which greatly reduced start-up costs. He also purchased the furniture and fixtures needed to set up a functional and attractive place for the business. As of December 31, 2016, MPP still owed Marco's relatives $100,000. Marco personally paid $3,800 interest for each of the last two years on the additional mortgage on his home. MPP now needs a loan for two reasons. First, some of Marco's relatives want their loans repaid. Since the business is now on its way, Marco thinks MPP can repay some of the money it owes. Second, Marco would like to upgrade some of MPP's equipment and obtain some additional pieces of equipment.

In addition to providing copying and printing services, MPP sells a variety of stationery and office products, and provides assistance in designing documents and other printed materials. MPP operates long hours to provide high-quality customer service, as well as to complete customer orders. More than one person has to be on duty at all times to ensure that production can be done while customers are being served, and so that pick-ups from and deliveries to customers can be made. Marco tries to be in the store as much as possible, but he is not able to be there all the time. His wife, Carla, works in the store about 15 hours per week. The store is operated by employees only (when neither Marco nor his wife is present) for about 25 hours per week, mostly at non-peak times.

Marco spends a lot of time trying to attract new customers. He regularly visits businesses in the area to meet the decision makers, often treating them to an evening out or a meal. About 40 percent of the advertising and promotion budget goes toward this type of activity. The remaining money is spent on advertising in community newspapers, sponsorship of various community activities, and printing and delivering flyers to businesses in the vicinity.

Marco is satisfied with the performance of his business. He thinks that it has grown nicely since its inception and anticipates that it will be profitable soon. Carla performs MPP's accounting and prepares a yearly statement of earnings, but she has little training in accounting.

Customers can pay by cash or credit card, or MPP will provide credit to any customers who ask. About 25 percent of MPP's business is for cash, 25 percent is on credit cards, and the remainder is on credit offered by MPP. MPP asks customers to pay within 10 days, but often they do not. When a sale is completed, it is rung up on the cash register. When Marco and Carla are in the store, they are the only ones who operate the register. Marco admits that, because he is in too much of a hurry, he sometimes puts the cash in his pocket rather than take the time to ring up the sale. Having cash in hand allows him to pay his babysitter and other personal expenses. Though it was hard for him to be certain, Marco estimated that transactions worth about $10,000 each year have been handled in this way. When Marco and Carla are out of the store, the cash is controlled by one of the employees. That employee is required to lock up for the day, count the cash in the register, and then lock the cash in a drawer in Marco's office. Marco has a lot of confidence in his employees, most of whom are students attending university and working part-time to make money.

Carla records the revenue by adding up the deposits made to the company's bank account during the year. Amounts owed by customers are recorded at the time of delivery, on a specially designated sheet of paper kept by the cash register. As cash is received, the related balance on the list is reduced. The accounts receivable balance on December 31 is the total amount on the list on that date. On December 31, 2016, there was $16,200 on the list and on December 31, 2015, the amount was $11,505. When Carla prepared the statement of earnings, she included a bad debt expense of $1,955 in 2015 and $2,754 in 2016, the amounts being estimated at 17 percent of the accounts receivable balance.

Marco obtained a corporate credit card on which he makes MPP's purchases. Items purchased on the credit card are expensed in the year as long as a statement is received from the credit card company before Carla prepares the year-end statement of earnings. If the statement comes in after that time, the expenses will get picked up the following year. Marco sometimes makes personal purchases on the corporate credit card if he thinks he is too close to his credit limit on his personal credit card. Marco estimates that he charged about $4,000 of personal expenses to the corporate credit card in each of the last two years. In addition, Marco has taken about $25,000 in cash each year from the business for personal reasons. Carla included these amounts in the "Payments to employees" item on the statement of earnings.

MPP maintains supplies of paper, toner, bindings, and other materials used to meet customers' printing and photocopying needs. In addition, there is an inventory of merchandise that MPP sells to customers. Marco determines what he needs for inventory by doing a visual check of the storeroom every few days. When he needs particular items, he calls the suppliers, who are usually able to deliver the goods within a few days. On occasion, Marco has to go to a large business supply store, because he has run out of needed stock before the supplier can deliver the goods, and he pays for these purchases with the corporate credit card. Carla determines the cost of merchandise sold during a year by adding up the amounts on the invoices received from the suppliers.

The amount of inventory on hand at the end of each year is counted so that Marco can get a clear idea of what he has on hand. Marco was told that management needed the inventory value on December 31, 2016, and 2015. He determined the value of the inventory by using the list of what was in the stockroom on December 31 and by applying prices from the most recent supplier price lists. On December 31, 2016, MPP had inventory of $12,222, and on December 31, 2015, the balance was $8,200.

Marco pays suppliers' invoices in full as soon as they are received. Marco explained that he is afraid to miss a payment because suppliers may stop supplying. He figures that paying the bills as soon as they are received is the best way of avoiding the problem.

Employees are paid minimum wage. Since it is easier for Carla, employees are paid their gross earnings by cheque at the end of each week.

EXHIBIT II

Statement of earnings supplied by the client

MARCO'S PROFESSIONAL PRINT SHOP LTD. STATEMENT OF EARNINGS For the year ended December 31		
	2016	**2015**
Sales	$360,547	$260,034
Cost of merchandise sold	124,984	96,212
Selling, general, and administrative	42,204	35,249
Payments to employees	90,099	83,740
Computers, printers, copiers, and scanners	10,000	85,000
Furniture and fixtures	—	15,000
Advertising and promotion	34,727	29,503
Utilities	18,300	17,900
Interest on loans from relatives	5,000	5,000
Bank charges	2,000	1,500
Rent	22,000	22,000
Bad debt expense	2,754	1,955
Other expenses	16,618	12,444
	368,686	405,503
Net loss	$ (8,139)	$(145,469)

LO7-6

Reitmans (Canada) Limited

CP7-5 **Using Financial Reports: Analyzing Inventory and Gross Profit for a Seasonal Business**

Reitmans (Canada) Limited manufactures and sells a variety of fashionable women's apparel and accessories. The company's business is seasonal, as are most retail businesses. Historically, more than 25 percent of the company's total annual sales have been generated during its second fiscal quarter (February–April). The company's results of operations depend significantly upon the sales generated during this period. A variety of factors affect sales, including fashion trends, competition, economic conditions, the timing of merchandise releases and promotional events, changes in merchandise assortment, success of marketing programs, cross-border shopping, and weather conditions, among others. The following table provides selected financial information for two recent years. All amounts are in thousands:

Time Period	Net Sales	Cost of Sales	Ending Inventory
Fiscal year 2013			**$109,601**
First quarter 2014	$206,478	$ 83,733	120,742
Second quarter 2014	258,326	104,545	112,455
Third quarter 2014	238,295	92,462	124,324
Fourth quarter 2014	236,277	91,293	106,440
Fiscal year 2014	**939,376**	**372,033**	**106,440**
First quarter 2015	201,731	81,636	134,977
Second quarter 2015	252,998	113,835	131,488
Third quarter 2015	240,270	102,236	142,617
Fourth quarter 2015	242,156	112,328	124,848
Fiscal Year 2015	**937,155**	**410,035**	**124,848**

Required:

1. Compute the gross profit and the inventory turnover ratio for fiscal years 2014 and 2015.

2. Compute the company's gross profit for each quarter. What does the seasonal pattern of the gross profit reveal?

3. Is there a seasonal pattern in inventory balances? Would Reitmans' choice of fiscal year-end affect the inventory turnover ratio computed in (1)? Explain.

4. Re-compute Reitmans' inventory turnover ratios for 2015 based on the average of the quarterly balances of ending inventory instead of the annual balances. Is there a significant difference between this ratio and the ratio computed in (1)? Explain.

LO7-2,7-5,7-6   CP7-6   Using Financial Reports: Analyzing Reported Information

Alimentation
Couche-Tard

Alimentation Couche-Tard is the second-largest convenience store operator in North America. It has more than 9,000 outlets: Couche-Tard in Quebec; Mac's in central and western Canada; and Circle K in the United States. The following table includes selected information from its financial statements (amounts in millions of U.S. dollars):

	Year Ended April 26, 2015	Year Ended April 27, 2014	Year Ended April 28, 2013
Revenues	34,529.9	37,956.6	35,543.4
Cost of sales	29,261.9	32,965.3	30,933.8
Earnings before income taxes	1,239.7	946.4	646.7
Income tax expense	306.2	134.2	73.9
Trade accounts receivable	486.1	904.6	935.4
Inventories	859.6	848.0	846.0
Trade payables	1,348.8	1,547.3	1,386.1

Required:

1. Compute the following amounts for each of the fiscal years 2014 and 2015:

    a. Collections from customers.

    b. Purchases of merchandise from suppliers.

    c. Payments to suppliers.

    d. The trade receivables turnover ratio and the average collection period.

    e. The inventory turnover ratio and the average period to sell inventory.

    f. The average period for conversion of inventories into cash.

2. The company uses the indirect method to report its cash flows from operations. How would the changes in trade accounts receivable, inventory, and trade payables be reported in the operating activities section of its statement of cash flows for 2015?

3. In the notes to its financial statements, the company states that the cost of merchandise in its distribution centres is determined according to the FIFO method. Would you expect the company's net earnings to increase or decrease if it used the weighted-average costing method instead of FIFO? Explain.

4. Assume that the company purchased canned products from a local supplier on April 26, 2015, with terms F.O.B. shipping point. The merchandise, at a cost of $1.4 million, had not arrived at the company's warehouse until April 30, and was not included in the inventory count at year-end. What effect would this error have on the company's net earnings for 2015? Show calculations.

LO7-2,7-5,7-6   CP7-7   Using Financial Reports: Analyzing Reported Information

Geox S.p.A.

Geox S.p.A. is an Italy-based company active in the footwear and apparel manufacturing industry, which includes classic, casual, and sports footwear, as well as apparel for men, women, and children. The company's products are sold in more than 70 countries worldwide through a widespread distribution network. Geox prepares its financial statements in accordance with IFRS. The following table includes selected information from its financial statements (amounts in millions of euros):

	2015	2014	2013
Net sales	874.3	824.2	754.2
Cost of sales	423.5	420.5	402.7
Earnings (loss) before income taxes	19.1	(1.4)	(38.5)
Income tax expense	9.1	(1.5)	8.7
Trade receivables	113.0	106.5	100.8
Inventories	304.8	287.7	281.9
Trade payables	224.0	167.6	169.1

Required:

1. Compute the following amounts for each of the fiscal years 2014 and 2015:

    a. Collections from customers.

    b. Purchases of merchandise from suppliers. Assume for simplicity that the company buys its products from other manufacturers.

    c. Payments to suppliers.

      d. Trade receivables turnover ratio and the average collection period.

      e. Inventory turnover ratio and the average period to sell inventory.

      f. Average period for conversion of inventories into cash.

2. The company uses the indirect method to report its cash flows from operations. How would the changes in trade receivables, inventory, and trade payables be reported in the operating activities section of its statement of cash flows for 2015?

3. In the notes to its financial statements, the company states that the cost of merchandise is determined by using the weighted-average costing method. Would you expect the company's net earnings to increase or decrease if it used FIFO instead of weighted-average cost? Explain.

4. Assume that the company purchased goods from a supplier in Asia with terms F.O.B. destination. These goods, which cost €1.2 million, were shipped on December 24, 2015, but had not arrived by December 31. The company's accountant included the cost of these goods in inventory at year-end. Is that an error? If so, what effect would this error have on the company's net earnings for 2015? Show calculations.

CRITICAL THINKING CASES

LO7-5

CP7-8 **Evaluating the Use of a Perpetual Inventory System to Control Theft**

The president of National Wholesalers suspects that employees are stealing several items of merchandise, particularly items that are small enough to hide in clothing. The president's suspicions resulted from complaints made in April by several retailers who claimed that shortages were frequently found when orders of financial and programmable calculators were inspected upon receipt.

    The assistant controller was asked to provide whatever information might prove helpful in identifying the extent of any problem that might have developed since the end of the previous fiscal year on December 31. The following report was submitted on May 1:

	Financial Calculators	Programmable Calculators
Number of units in inventory on December 31, per physical count	19,600	7,600
Cost per unit	$ 8.40	$ 29.25
Number of units purchased since January 1:		
January	4,200	1,400
February	3,600	3,100
March	5,100	2,700
April	2,700	1,800
Total	15,600	9,000
Average cost per unit of purchases since January 1	$ 8.40	$ 30.00
Average gross profit percentage on merchandise billed to retailers	30%	25%
Sales recorded from January 1 to April 30	$343,200	$496,400
Number of units physically counted in the warehouse on April 30	6,400	3,900

Required:

1. Compute the number of units of each type of merchandise that are unaccounted for on May 1. The company uses a periodic inventory system and the weighted-average inventory costing method.

2. Determine the monetary value of the apparent loss.

3. Assuming that the apparent loss realized during the period January 1–April 30 is representative of the loss that might be realized on these two items during an entire year, would you recommend that (*a*) a new inventory system be installed in the warehouse at an annual cost of $4,000 to maintain perpetual inventory records of these two items of merchandise and (*b*) a quarterly physical inventory count of these items be implemented at an additional cost of $1,000 per quarterly count? Show supporting computations.

LO7-5

Caterpillar Inc.

CP7-9 **Evaluating an Acquisition: Effect of Inventory Valuation on Earnings and Management Bonuses**

Caterpillar Inc. is the largest manufacturer of construction equipment in the world. In the course of growing its business, the company often purchased other companies. ERA Mining Machinery Limited (Siwei) was one such purchase. In June 2012, Caterpillar paid US$653.4 million, including US$475 million in cash, for all of Siwei's shares. Often when companies such as Caterpillar acquire other companies, they pay a premium over the fair value of the net assets acquired. The premium is called goodwill and the goodwill, associated with the Siwei acquisition was reported by Caterpillar at US$625 million.

By November 2012, Caterpillar disclosed its concerns regarding accounting fraud and, in particular, the misrepresentation of the value of inventory reported by Siwei. Siwei undertook improper cost allocation and revenue recognition methods as well, leading to an overstatement of net earnings as well as assets, including an overstatement of inventory by US$17 million. Caterpillar discovered the discrepancy following a physical inventory count after it had purchased Siwei. Caterpillar's chief financial officer noted publicly that a physical count was not a normal part of due diligence. This led some observers to conclude that in China, a physical inventory count should become part of the due diligence process.

The fraud appears to have been deliberate and occurred over several years. Siwei manufactures hydraulic roof supports to prevent the roofs of coal mines from collapsing. Caterpillar announced a write-down of US$580 million in the value of Siwei, which affected its earnings for the fourth quarter of 2012.

Caterpillar conducted its own internal investigation and subsequently dismissed all the senior management at Siwei, replacing them with management personnel from Caterpillar. Deloitte and Ernst & Young were the auditors acting for Caterpillar during the acquisition of Siwei, and RSM Nelson Wheeler of Hong Kong was Siwei's auditor.

The chief executive officer of Caterpillar, Mr. Doug Oberhelman, has taken full responsibility for the current situation. The company is considering what steps it should take to recover losses and enforce accountability on those responsible for the alleged fraud.

Required:

A number of news articles have been written about this alleged fraud. Access some of these articles to answer the following questions.

1. As a new staff member at Caterpillar Inc.'s auditing firm, you are assigned to write a memo on the effect of the overstatement of the value of inventory. Illustrate this effect with the use of adjusting entries to the appropriate financial statement accounts. Assume that Caterpillar is subject to an income tax rate of 30 percent.

2. Assume that both the CFO and the CEO of Caterpillar receive cash bonuses based on net earnings at the end of the year. What effect, if any, did the write-down of US$580 million have on the net earnings of Caterpillar Inc.? What effect, if any, did the write-down have on the share price?

FINANCIAL REPORTING AND ANALYSIS TEAM PROJECT

LO7-3

  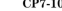

CP7-10   **Team Project: Analyzing Inventories**

As a team, select an industry to analyze. A list of companies classified by industry can be obtained by accessing www.fpinfomart.ca and then choosing "Companies by Industry." You can also find a list of industries and companies within each industry via http://ca.finance.yahoo.com/investing (click on "Order Annual Reports" under "Tools"). Each team member should acquire the annual report for one publicly traded company in the industry, with each member selecting a different company. (Library files, the SEDAR service at www.sedar.com, and the company website are good sources.)

Required:

On an individual basis, each team member should then write a short report answering the following questions about the selected company. Discuss any patterns across the companies that you as a team observe. Then, as a group, write a short report comparing and contrasting your companies.

1. If your company lists inventories on its statement of financial position, what percentage is this asset of total assets for each of the last three years? If your company does not list inventories, discuss why this is so.

2. If your company lists inventories, what inventory costing method does it use? What do you think motivated this choice?

3. Perform a ratio analysis:
   - *a.* What does the inventory turnover ratio measure in general?
   - *b.* If your company reports inventories, compute the ratio for the last three years.
   - *c.* What do your results suggest about the company?
   - *d.* If available, find the industry ratio for the most recent year, compare it to your results, and discuss why you believe your company differs or is similar to the industry ratio.

4. What is the effect of the change in inventories on cash flows from operations for the most recent year; that is, did the change increase or decrease operating cash flows? Explain your answer.

LO7-2,7-3   **CC7-1**   **Evaluating the Choice of Inventory Method When Costs Are Rising and Falling**

Pool Corporation Inc. reported in its recent annual report that the industry experienced some price deflation one year followed by more normalized price inflation of approximately 2 percent overall despite price deflation for certain chemical products. This suggests that in some years Pool's overall inventory costs rise, and in some years they fall. Furthermore, in many years, the costs of some inventory items rise while others fall. Assume that Pool has only two product items in its inventory this year. Purchase and sale information are presented below. Pool uses a perpetual inventory system.

Transaction	Inventory Item A		Inventory Item B	
	Units	Unit Cost	Units	Unit Cost
Beginning inventory	40	$6	40	$6
Purchases, February 7	80	8	80	5
Sales, February 28	50		70	
Purchases, March 16	100	9	100	3
Sales, April 28	110		90	

Required:

1. Compute the cost of sales for each of the two items separately using the FIFO and weighted-average cost inventory costing methods.

2. Prepare the journal entries to record the transactions of February 7 and February 28, using the FIFO method. Pool sold Item A for that $12 and Item B for $8.

3. Which of these two methods is preferable in terms of (*a*) net earnings and (*b*) income taxes paid (cash flow)? Answer the question for each item separately. Explain.

SOLUTIONS TO SELF-STUDY QUIZZES

Self-Study Quiz 7-1

1.
$$BI + P - EI = COS$$
$$200 \times \$200) + P - (175 \times \$200) = 300 \times \$200$$
$$P = \$55,000$$

2.

Net sales	$90,000
Cost of sales	60,000
Gross profit	$30,000

Self-Study Quiz 7-2

1. FIFO cost of sales = $(10 \times \$10) + (5 \times \$11) = \$155$

Average cost prior to sale in June = $[\$100 + \$55]/[10 + 5] = \$10.33$

Average cost prior to sale in December = $[5 \text{ (unsold units)} \times \$10.33 + \$65 \text{ (new purchases)}]/[5 + 5]$
$$= \$11.665$$

Cost of sales = $10 \times \$10.33 + 5 \times \$11.665 = \$161.625$ (rounded to $162)

	FIFO	Weighted Average
Sales revenue (15 × $20)	$300	$300
Cost of sales	155	162
Gross profit	145	138
Other expenses	100	100
Pretax earnings	$ 45	$ 38

2. The weighted-average cost would be recommended because it produces lower pretax earnings and lower income taxes. The FIFO method would be recommended if the company's objective is to report higher net earnings.

Self-Study Quiz 7-3

1.

	SARLOS LTD. STATEMENTS OF EARNINGS For the Years Ended December 31			
	With Inventory Error		**Without Inventory Error**	
	2018	**2017**	**2018**	**2017**
Sales	$600,000	$500,000	$600,000	$500,000
Cost of sales	350,000	300,000	340,000	310,000
Gross profit	250,000	200,000	260,000	190,000
Selling, general, and administrative expenses	120,000	100,000	120,000	100,000
Earnings before income tax	130,000	100,000	140,000	90,000
Income tax expense (at 40%)	52,000	40,000	56,000	36,000
Net earnings	$ 78,000	$ 60,000	$ 84,000	$ 54,000

2. The combined net earnings for both 2017 and 2018 is $138,000. The effects of the inventory error at the end of 2014 cancel out after two years. The 2017 error would not affect the financial statements for 2019.

Self-Study Quiz 7-4

1.

Year	2015	2014	2013	2012	2011
Average inventory	115.6	106.5	101.3	93.25	83.2
Inventory turnover	3.55	3.49	3.61	3.99	4.37

These ratios show that efficiency in managing inventory deteriorated steadily from 2011 to 2014 and improved slightly in 2015.

2. Both the ending inventory and the cost of sales will decrease by $10 million, but the rate of decrease of cost of sales, the numerator (= $10 ÷ $410.0 = 0.024), is much smaller than the decrease in the denominator, ending inventory (= $10 ÷ $124.8 = 0.008). This will cause the inventory turnover ratio to increase.

$$\text{Inventory turnover ratio} = \$400.0/[(\$106.4 + \$114.8)] = 3.62$$

3. A decrease in trade payables would have decreased cash flow from operations because Reitmans would have paid its vendors more than the cost of purchases made on account during the period.

ENDNOTES

1. Tax reports often differ from the statements prepared for shareholders and other external users.
2. Although Reitmans sells mostly women's apparel, its RW&CO sells a variety of men's apparel. We focus our attention on a specific type of product to illustrate the main concepts of inventory costing. Reitmans attributes a style number to each type of blazer. The number 101 does not refer to any specific style.
3. Many companies, such as Gildan Activewear Inc., provide product information to their current and potential customers. The website http://www.mygildan.com/store/my/inventory/ distributorMap.jsp allows Gildan's customers to find out how many units of each product are available at each location that distributes its products in Canada, the United States, Mexico, Europe, or the Asia-Pacific region.
4. A perpetual inventory system is also preferred over a periodic system because internal control procedures have gained more importance in the past few years with legislation requiring chief executive officers (CEOs) and chief financial officers (CFOs) of all companies listed on Canadian stock exchanges to certify the quality of internal control systems.
5. An alternative to recording the purchase transaction, called the net method, consists of debiting the inventory account initially for $1,078 (invoice price, $1,100 – purchase discount, $22), assuming that Reitmans will pay the supplier within 10 days. The sales return would be recorded at $98, net of the related purchase discount. The net amount owed to the supplier, $980, is then paid

within 10 days of the purchase date. If payment is made after the discount period, then a discount lost account is debited for $20, the difference between the cash paid ($1,000) and the amount that Reitmans would have owed the supplier if it had paid within 10 days ($980). The balance of the discount lost account highlights the potential savings from early payments to suppliers that Reitmans has forgone. The balance of the discount lost account is added to the inventory account at year end.

6. A fourth method—last-in, first-out (LIFO)—is accepted in the United States but is prohibited under International Accounting Standard 2—Inventories.

7. The loss could be debited to a separate account, such as loss due to write-down of inventory, which is closed to cost of sales at the end of the accounting period.

8. IAS 2 states that in some cases it may be appropriate to group similar or related items. This may occur when "items of inventory relating to the same product line that have similar purposes or end uses, are produced and marketed in the same geographical area, and cannot be practicably evaluated separately from other items in that product line." (para. 29)

9. Notice that the simple average of the unit costs is $210 [($200 + $210 + $220)/3], but the weighted average is $210.40, because the latter considers the number of units purchased at each unit cost. Beware of using a simple average.

10. Adapted with permission from Canadian Institute of Chartered Accountants, *Filling the GAAP to IFRS: Teaching Supplements for Canada's Accounting Academics, CD3—Questions and Answers Pack*, 2008. Toronto: CICA. Any changes to the original material are the sole responsibility of the author and have not been reviewed or endorsed by the CICA.

CHAPTER 8

Reporting and Interpreting Property, Plant, and Equipment; Natural Resources; and Intangibles

After studying this chapter, you should be able to do the following:

LEARNING OBJECTIVES

LO8-1 Define, classify, and explain the nature of long-lived assets, and interpret the fixed asset turnover ratio.

LO8-2 Apply the cost principle to measure the acquisition and maintenance of property, plant, and equipment.

LO8-3 Apply various depreciation methods as assets are held and used over time.

LO8-4 Explain the effect of asset impairment on the financial statements.

LO8-5 Analyze the disposal of property, plant, and equipment.

LO8-6 Apply measurement and reporting concepts for natural resources and intangible assets.

LO8-7 Explain the impact on cash flows of the acquisition, use, and disposal of long-lived assets.

Chris Parypa Photography/Shutterstock.com

Focus Company: **WestJet Airlines**

MANAGING EARNINGS THROUGH CONTROL OF PRODUCTIVE CAPACITY

WestJet Airlines (www.westjet.com), Canada's second-largest airline, has provided low-fare, friendly service to customers since its first flight took off in 1996. Clive Beddoe, along with a small team of Calgary entrepreneurs, started up WestJet with 220 employees and three Boeing 737-200 aircraft serving five destinations. By the end of 2015, the company employed over 11,000 people, had 140 aircraft, and served more than 100 destinations in North America, Central America, the Caribbean, and Europe. WestJet plans to expand its fleet of Boeing 737, 767, and Bombardier Q400s to 225 aircraft by 2027. Investment in new aircraft allows WestJet to operate one of the youngest and highly fuel-efficient fleets of any large North American commercial airline, and illustrates one way of responding to environmental concerns.

WestJet is a capital-intensive company, with more than $3,473 million in property and equipment reported on its statement of financial position at December 31, 2015, representing 68 percent of its total assets. In fiscal year 2015, WestJet spent $841.5 million on aircraft additions, compared to approximately $694.2 million in 2014. Because the demand for air travel is seasonal, with peak demand occurring during specific times of the year, planning for optimal productive capacity in the airline industry is very difficult. WestJet's managers must determine how many aircraft are needed in which cities at what points in time to fill all seats demanded. Otherwise, the company loses revenue (not enough seats to meet demand) or incurs higher costs (too many seats unfilled and unpaid for).

UNDERSTANDING THE BUSINESS

Running a business—such as an airline, resource extraction and processing organization, or pharmaceutical company—means acquiring adequate property, plant facilities, and equipment that will provide the capacity to serve the customers' current and future needs. Capital-intensive companies must pay large sums for their capacity, with the expectation of regaining that money over time, plus all operating costs and a reasonable profit. This explains why property, plant, and equipment of this type are referred to as either long-lived assets or fixed assets.

Non-current assets are acquired for corporate operations intended to generate and protect financial benefits well into the company's future. For airlines, the aircraft, spare engines and parts, hangars, flight simulators, buildings, and equipment are all fixed assets. In comparison, resource extraction, processing, and distribution companies require the property (land) from which to extract raw resources, the plant facilities to process raw materials into refined products, and a distribution system to bring the refined products to the point of sale.

For high technology and pharmaceutical companies, of equal importance to property, plant, and equipment, is the existing and new knowledge (i.e., intellectual capital) generated by scientists and engineers. These companies expand and thrive by inventing, developing, and successfully distributing new products and systems. Intellectual property is an important asset that cannot be directly seen or touched and is, therefore, an example of an intangible asset. The value of this type of asset is often protected either by patents, which provide legal protection for a limited time period, or through agreements of confidentiality, which provide unlimited protection against copying and theft.

One of the major challenges facing managers of most businesses is forecasting the level of long-lived productive capacity they will need in order to produce forecasted revenue streams. On the one hand, if managers underestimate the level of capacity needed in the future, the company will not be able to produce goods or services that are in demand, and will miss the opportunity to earn revenue. On the other hand, if managers overestimate the productive capacity needed, the company will incur excessive costs that will reduce its profitability.

The airline industry provides an outstanding example of the difficulty associated with planning for and analyzing the capacity to produce service revenue. If an aircraft destined for Toronto takes off from Calgary with empty seats, the economic value associated with those seats is lost for that flight. There is obviously no way to sell the seat to a customer after the aircraft has left the gate. Unlike a manufacturer, an airline cannot place seats in inventory for use on future flights.

Likewise, if an unexpectedly large number of people want to board a flight, the airline must turn away some customers if seats are not available. You might be willing to buy a television set from Sears even if you are told that it is out of stock and there will be a one-week delay in delivery. But you probably won't fly home for a holiday on an airline that would have you wait one week because no seats were available on its flights when you wanted to fly. You would simply pick another airline or choose a different mode of transportation.

The battle for passengers in the airline industry is fought in terms of property, plant, and equipment. Customers expect security and user-friendly as well as accessible reservation, hospitality, entertainment, and communication services. Passengers also want convenient schedules (which require a large number of aircraft), and they want to fly in new, modern aircraft. Because airlines have such a large investment in equipment with no opportunity to hold unused seats in inventory, they work hard to fill aircraft to capacity for each flight.

In summary, issues related to property, plant, and equipment have a pervasive impact on a company in terms of strategy, pricing decisions, and profitability. Business managers devote considerable time to planning optimal levels of productive capacity that are adequate to meeting expected future demand. Accountants estimate and report the cost of using these assets throughout their productive lives, taking into consideration applicable income tax laws and regulations, and financial analysts closely review financial statements to determine the impact of management decisions on the company's profitability and financial condition.

This chapter is organized according to the life cycle of long-lived assets—acquisition, use, and disposal. First, we will discuss the measuring and reporting issues related to land, buildings, and equipment. Then we will discuss the measurement and reporting issues for natural resources and intangible assets. Among the issues we will discuss are maintaining, using, and disposing of property and equipment over time, and measuring and reporting assets considered impaired in their ability to generate future cash flows.

ORGANIZATION OF THE CHAPTER

Acquisition and Maintenance of Property, Plant, and Equipment	Use, Impairment, and Disposal of Property, Plant, and Equipment	Natural Resources and Intangible Assets
• Classification of Long-Lived Assets • Fixed Asset Turnover Ratio • Measuring and Recording Acquisition Cost • Various Acquisition Methods • Repairs, Maintenance, and Betterments	• Depreciation Concepts • Alternative Depreciation Methods • Changes in Depreciation Estimates • Managers' Selection among Accounting Alternatives • Measuring Asset Impairment • Disposal of Property, Plant, and Equipment	• Acquisition and Depletion of Natural Resources • Acquisition and Amortization of Intangible Assets • Examples of Intangible Assets

LO8-1

Define, classify, and explain the nature of long-lived assets, and interpret the fixed asset turnover ratio.

ACQUISITION AND MAINTENANCE OF PROPERTY, PLANT, AND EQUIPMENT

Exhibit 8.1 shows the asset section of WestJet's statement of financial position at December 31, 2015. More than 67 percent of WestJet's total assets are property and equipment. The company's annual report contains additional information about the acquisition cost of property and equipment owned or controlled by WestJet, and related depreciation; the amount of new investment in equipment during the year; and the amount of equipment that was sold or retired, as well as details of other long-lived assets with probable long-lived benefits. Let us begin by classifying these long-lived assets.

Classification of Long-Lived Assets

LONG-LIVED ASSETS are tangible or intangible resources owned by a business and used in its operations to produce benefits over several years.

Accountants use the terms **long-lived assets** to identify property, plant, equipment, and intangible properties held for production, rental to others, or administrative purposes, as well as the development, construction, maintenance, or repair of other assets. Long-lived assets are acquired, constructed, or developed for use on a continuing basis. They are not normally sold to generate revenue, although the normal course of business for real estate companies is the purchase and sale of long-lived assets, such as land and buildings. Long-lived assets, which are listed as non-current assets on the statement of financial position, can be tangible or intangible and have the following characteristics:

WESTJET AIRLINES LTD. Consolidated Statement of Financial Position December 31, 2015, and 2014 (in thousands of dollars)			
	Note	2015	2014
Assets			
Current assets:			
Cash and cash equivalents	4	$1,183,797	$1,358,071
Restricted cash	5	68,573	58,149
Accounts receivable	17	82,136	54,950
Prepaid expenses, deposits, and other	17	131,747	144,192
Inventory	17	36,018	36,658
Assets held for sale		–	78,306
		1,502,271	1,730,326
Non-current assets:			
Property and equipment	6	3,473,262	2,793,194
Intangible assets	7	63,549	60,623
Other assets	17	89,942	62,290
Total assets		$5,129,024	$4,646,433

Source: WestJet Airlines Ltd., Annual Report 2015.

Exhibit 8.1

WestJet Airlines Asset Section of the Statement of Financial Position

REAL-WORLD EXCERPT

WestJet Airlines Ltd.

ANNUAL REPORT

1. **Tangible assets** (or fixed assets) can be touched because they have physical substance. This classification is most often called *property, plant, and equipment*. The four kinds of tangible assets held for use in operations are as follows:

   a. *Land,* which is reported on the statement of financial position as a separate item if it has a material value. Unlike aircraft or patents on pharmaceutical products, land does not become obsolete; therefore, it is never depreciated. It may, however, be impaired in value.

   b. *Buildings, fixtures,* and *equipment,* which are reported as a separate item on the statement of financial position or in the notes. For WestJet, this category includes aircraft, deposits on aircraft, spare engines, buildings, ground property and equipment, and leasehold improvements.

   c. *Biological assets,* which are living animals or plants, such as sheep, dairy cattle, pigs, bushes, vines, and fruit trees. For example, Andrew Peller Limited, which produces wine, reports the grapevines controlled by the company as biological assets.

   d. *Natural resources,* which include mineral deposits, such as gold or diamonds, oil wells, and reserves. Corporations such as Barrick Gold, Lucara Diamond Corp., and Suncor Energy Inc. extract natural resources.

2. **Intangible assets** have no physical substance. Historically, they were called "intangibles and other nothings." WestJet's intangible assets include computer software and landing rights, which give the airline the exclusive right for departure and landing at specific time periods. Intangible assets frequently arise from intellectual effort and are known as *intellectual property.* Examples include copyrights, patents, licences, trademarks, software, franchises, and subscription lists.

TANGIBLE ASSETS have physical substance.

Property, Plant, and Equipment as a Percentage of Total Assets for Selected Focus Companies—2015

Reitmans 26.1%

Canadian Tire 27.5%

BCE 45.1%

INTANGIBLE ASSETS have property ownership rights but not physical substance.

FIXED ASSET TURNOVER RATIO

ANALYTICAL QUESTION → How effectively is management utilizing its property, plant, and equipment to generate revenues?

RATIO AND COMPARISONS → The fixed asset turnover ratio is useful in answering this question. It is computed as follows:

$$\text{Fixed asset turnover ratio} = \frac{\text{Net sales (or operating revenues)}}{\text{Average net fixed assets}^*}$$

*[Beginning + Ending balances of Property, plant, and equipment (net of accumulated depreciation)] ÷ 2

The 2015 ratio for WestJet is,

$$\frac{\$4,209,265}{(3,473,262 + 2,793,194)/2} = 1.34 \text{ times}$$

Comparisons over Time			Comparisons with Competitors	
WestJet Airlines			Southwest Airlines	Ryanair
2013	2014	2015	2015	2015
1.64	1.51	1.34	1.33	1.07

INTERPRETATIONS

In General → The fixed asset turnover ratio measures the sales dollars generated by each dollar of fixed assets used. A high ratio normally suggests effective management. An increasing ratio over time signals more-efficient use of fixed assets. Creditors and security analysts use this ratio to assess a company's effectiveness at generating sales from its long-lived assets.

Focus Company Analysis → WestJet's fixed asset turnover ratio has decreased over 2013–2015 as the company replaced aging assets. When compared to two other companies in the industry, WestJet appears to be more efficient at utilizing its fixed assets than both Southwest Airlines and Ryanair. Interestingly, Southwest has purchased some of WestJet's older aircraft. WestJet can further improve on its ratio by increasing its revenues from flights, either by increasing the number of flights or by increasing the number of paying passengers for existing flights.

A Few Cautions → A lower or declining ratio may indicate that a company is expanding (by acquiring additional productive assets) in anticipation of higher sales in the future. An increasing ratio could also signal that a firm has cut back on capital expenditures because it anticipates a downturn in business. As a consequence, appropriate interpretation of the fixed asset turnover ratio requires an investigation of related activities.

SELECTED FOCUS COMPANIES' FIXED ASSET TURNOVER RATIOS—2015

BCE   1.00%

Canadian Tire 3.07%

Reitmans   5.68%

LO8-2

Apply the cost principle to measure the acquisition and maintenance of property, plant, and equipment.

Measuring and Recording Acquisition Cost

The *cost principle* requires that all reasonable and necessary costs incurred in acquiring a long-lived asset, placing it in its operational setting, and preparing it for use should be recorded in a designated asset account. We say that the costs are *capitalized* when they are recorded as assets on the statement of financial position instead of as expenses on the statement of earnings in the current period. These costs, including any sales taxes, legal fees, transportation costs, and installation costs, are added to the purchase price of the asset. Special discounts and interest charges associated with the purchase should not, however, be included in the cost of the asset. Interest charges should be reported as interest expense.

In addition to purchasing buildings and equipment, a company may acquire undeveloped land, typically with the intent to build a new factory or office building. When a company purchases land, all of the incidental costs paid by the purchaser—such as title fees, sales commissions, legal fees, title insurance, delinquent taxes, and surveying fees—should be included in its cost. Because land is not subject to depreciation, it must be recorded as a separate asset.

Sometimes, a company purchases an old building or used machinery for use in its business operations. Renovation and repair costs incurred by the purchaser prior to the asset's use should be included as a part of its cost.

Assume that WestJet purchased one new Q400 aircraft from Bombardier on January 1, 2017 (the beginning of WestJet's 2017 fiscal year), for a list price of $27.5 million. Also assume that Bombardier offered WestJet a discount of $800,000 for signing the purchase agreement. This means that the price of a new airplane to WestJet is $26.7 million. In addition, WestJet paid $300,000 to have the airplane delivered and $1,000,000 to prepare the airplane for use. The amount recorded for the purchase, called the **acquisition cost**, is the net cash amount paid or, when non-cash assets are used up as payment, the fair market value of the asset given or asset received, whichever can be more clearly determined (called the *cash-equivalent price*). WestJet would calculate the acquisition cost of the aircraft as follows:

> The **ACQUISITION COST** is the net cash-equivalent amount paid or to be paid for the asset.

Invoice price	$27,500,000
Deduct: Discount from Bombardier	800,000
Net cash invoice price	26,700,000
Add: Transportation charges paid by WestJet	300,000
Preparation costs paid by WestJet	1,000,000
Cost of the aircraft (added to the asset account)	$28,000,000

Various Acquisition Methods

For Cash   Assuming that WestJet paid cash for the aircraft and related transportation and preparation costs, the transaction is recorded as follows:

Aircraft (A)		28,000,000		
Cash (A)				28,000,000

Assets	=	**Liabilities**	+	**Shareholders' Equity**
Aircraft	+28,000,000			
Cash	−28,000,000			

It might seem unusual for WestJet to pay cash to purchase new assets that cost $28 million, but this is often the case. When it acquires productive assets, a company may pay with cash that was either generated from operations or recently borrowed. Notice that WestJet's cash balance at December 31, 2015, is approximately $1.2 billion. It also is possible for the seller to finance the purchase on credit.

For Debt   Now let's assume that WestJet signed a note payable for the aircraft and paid cash for the transportation and preparation costs. WestJet would record the following journal entry:

Aircraft (A)		28,000,000	
Cash (A)			1,300,000
Note payable (L)			26,700,000

Assets	=	**Liabilities**		+	**Shareholders' Equity**
Aircraft +28,000,000		Note payable	+26,700,000		
Cash −1,300,000					

Commercial airlines often utilize financing schemes that include leasing aircraft. Shorter-term leases, called an **operating lease**, provide airlines with flexibility in managing fleet size and obsolescence, which can occur with changes in environmental and noise-level laws in various countries. Operating leases are not reported on the statement of financial position as liabilities and the assets are not included in fixed assets. On the other hand, longer-term leases, called a **finance lease**, or capital lease, are in essence the acquisition of assets that are reported on the statement of financial

> An **OPERATING LEASE** does not transfer substantially all the risks and rewards of ownership from the lessor to the lessee.

> A **FINANCE LEASE** transfers substantially all the risks and rewards of ownership from the lessor to the lessee.

position along with the lease obligations. At December 31, 2015, WestJet Airlines disclosed the following regarding its leasing commitments:

> **Management's Discussion and Analysis of Financial Results 2015**
>
> **OFF BALANCE SHEET ARRANGEMENTS**
>
> Aircraft operating leases
>
> We currently have 44 Boeing 737 aircraft under operating leases. Future cash flow commitments in connection with these aircraft totaled US$466.6 million at December 31, 2015 (December 31, 2014 —US$542.7 million) which we expect to fund through cash from operations.
>
> *Source:* WestJet Airlines Ltd., Annual Report 2015.

Additional discussion of leases is provided in Chapter 9.

For Equity (or Other Non-cash Consideration)

Any non-cash consideration, such as a company's common shares or a right given by the company to the seller to purchase the company's goods or services at a special price, might be part of the transaction. When a non-cash consideration is included in the purchase of an asset, the cash-equivalent cost (fair market value of the asset given or received) is determined.

Assume that WestJet gave Bombardier 1,000,000 of its common shares, with a market value of $23 per share (the approximate stock price on the date of the transaction), and paid the balance in cash, including cash for the transportation and preparation costs. The journal entry and transaction effects follow:

Aircraft (A)				28,000,000	
Cash (A)					5,000,000
Common shares (SE)					23,000,000

Assets		=	**Liabilities**	+	**Shareholders' Equity**	
Aircraft	+28,000,000				Common shares	+23,000,000
Cash	−5,000,000					

By Construction

In some cases, a company may construct an asset for use instead of buying it from a manufacturer. The acquisition cost of this self-constructed asset will include all direct and indirect costs of construction, including interest on any loans obtained to construct the asset. As soon as the asset is available for use, the accumulated construction costs will be depreciated over its productive life. The amount of interest that is included in the cost of the construction is called **capitalized interest**, which reduces the company's total interest expense every year until the facility is ready for use. Once the construction of the facility is completed, any interest costs on construction loans, however, must be expensed. The complex computation of interest capitalization is discussed in other accounting courses.

For example, in 2009, WestJet completed the construction of its new head office in Calgary, which the company refers to as its Campus facility. Because the company had the asset built for its own use, the cost includes necessary costs of construction, such as labour and materials, as well as overhead costs directly attributable to the construction activity. The costs also include the interest expense incurred during the construction period, based on the amount of funds invested in the construction of the Campus. WestJet added the interest incurred to the other construction costs of the new building until it was ready for use in operations.

Capitalizing labour, materials, and a portion of interest expense increases assets, decreases expenses, and increases net earnings. Let us assume the new Campus cost WestJet $600,000 in labour costs, $1,300,000 in materials and supplies, as well as interest expense of $100,000 incurred during the construction project. WestJet would record the following journal entry:

CAPITALIZED INTEREST represents interest on borrowed funds directly attributable to construction until the asset is ready for its intended use.

Building (A)				2,000,000	
Cash (A)					2,000,000
Assets	=	**Liabilities**	+	**Shareholders' Equity**	
Building	+2,000,000				
Cash	−2,000,000				

As a Basket Purchase of Assets

When several long-lived assets, such as land, building, and equipment, are acquired in a single transaction and for a single lump sum, known as a **basket purchase**, the cost of each asset must be measured and recorded separately. This is true because land is not depreciated but buildings and equipment are, although at different rates. The purchase price must be apportioned among the land, the building, and the equipment, on a rational basis.

> A **BASKET PURCHASE** is an acquisition of two or more assets in a single transaction for a single lump sum.

Accountants use current market values of the acquired assets on the date of acquisition to apportion the single lump sum to the various assets in the basket. Assume that WestJet paid $3,000,000 cash to purchase a building and the land on which the building is located. As the current market values of the building and land were not known, a professional appraisal was obtained. This appraisal, totalling $3,150,000, indicated the following estimated market values: $1,890,000 for the building and $1,260,000 for the land. The total purchase price is then apportioned on the basis of relative market values, as follows:

Building	**Land**
$\dfrac{\text{Market value}}{\text{Total market value}} = \dfrac{\$1,890,000}{\$3,150,000} = 60\%$	$\dfrac{\text{Market value}}{\text{Total market value}} = \dfrac{\$1,260,000}{\$3,150,000} = 40\%$
60% × $3,000,000 Total cost = $1,800,000	40% × $3,000,000 Total cost = $1,200,000

The cost of the building is determined by multiplying the total cost of $3,000,000 by the ratio of the market value of the building to the total market value ($1,890,000 ÷ $3,150,000 = 60 percent). Similarly, the cost of the land is determined by multiplying the total cost by the ratio of the market value of the land to the total market value ($1,260,000 ÷ $3,150,000 = 40 percent). Assuming that WestJet purchases the assets with cash, the journal entry and effects are as follows:

Land (A)				1,200,000	
Building (A)				1,800,000	
Cash (A)					3,000,000
Assets	=	**Liabilities**	+	**Shareholders' Equity**	
Land	+1,200,000				
Building	+1,800,000				
Cash	−3,000,000				

PAUSE FOR FEEDBACK

In general, all necessary and reasonable costs to prepare the asset for its intended use are part of the cost of the asset. Assets can be acquired with cash, with debt, or with the company's shares (at market value). Before you move on, complete the following questions to test your understanding of this concept.

SELF-STUDY QUIZ 8-1

McDonald's Corporation

In a recent year, McDonald's Corporation purchased buildings and equipment priced at $1.8 billion. Assume that the company also paid $8 million for transportation costs, $1.3 million for installation and preparation of the buildings and equipment before use, and $100,000 in maintenance contracts to cover repairs to the buildings and equipment during use.

1. Compute the acquisition cost for the buildings and equipment.

2. For each situation below, indicate the effects of this acquisition on the following financial statement categories. Use "+" for increase and "−" for decrease, and indicate the accounts and amounts.

	Assets	Liabilities	Shareholders' Equity
a. Paid 30 percent in cash and signed a note payable for the balance.			
b. Issued 10 million shares at a market price of $105 per share and paid the balance in cash.			

After you complete your answers, check them with the solutions at the end of the chapter.

Repairs, Maintenance, and Betterments

Most assets require substantial expenditures during their useful lives to maintain or enhance their productive capacity. These expenditures include cash outlays for ordinary repairs and maintenance, major repairs, replacements, and additions. Remember that the terms *expenditure* and *expense* are not synonymous. An expenditure is the payment of money to acquire goods or services. These goods and services may be recorded as either assets or expenses, depending on whether they benefit future periods or only the current period. Expenditures that are made after an asset is acquired are classified as follows:

ORDINARY REPAIRS AND MAINTENANCE are expenditures for normal operating upkeep of long-lived assets.

REVENUE EXPENDITURES maintain the productive capacity of the asset during the current accounting period only and are recorded as expenses.

1. **Ordinary repairs and maintenance** or **revenue expenditures**—expenditures that maintain the productive capacity of the asset during the current accounting period only. These cash outlays are recorded as *expenses* in the current period. Ordinary repairs and maintenance are expenditures for the normal maintenance and upkeep of long-lived assets. These expenditures are recurring in nature, involve relatively small amounts at each occurrence, and do not directly lengthen the useful life of the asset.

    In the case of WestJet, the most significant component of its revenue expenditures is the routine maintenance work on aircraft engines, landing gear, airframes, and other aircraft equipment. Although the cost of individual ordinary repairs is relatively small, in the aggregate these expenditures can be substantial. In 2015, WestJet reported $164.3 million in maintenance expenses on its consolidated statement of earnings.

EXTRAORDINARY REPAIRS are infrequent expenditures that increase the asset's economic usefulness in the future.

BETTERMENTS are costs incurred to enhance the productive or service potential of a long-lived asset.

2. **Extraordinary repairs** and **betterments**—expenditures that increase the productive life, operating efficiency, or capacity of the asset. These **capital expenditures**, which provide benefits to the company over a number of accounting periods, are added to the appropriate *asset* accounts. They occur infrequently, involve large amounts of money, and increase an asset's economic usefulness in the future through either increased efficiency or longer life. Examples include additions, complete reconditioning, and major overhauls and replacements, such as the complete replacement of an engine on an aircraft.

CAPITAL EXPENDITURES increase the productive life, operating efficiency, or capacity of the asset and are recorded as increases in asset accounts, not as expenses.

An example of a betterment is WestJet's installation of blended winglets on its aircraft to improve the aerodynamic performance and handling design of the 737-800s. From a maintenance perspective, winglets help aircraft achieve better climb performance, allowing lower thrust settings, which extends engine life and reduces costs. The aircraft itself also uses less fuel, helping WestJet implement its greener air strategy.

In many cases, no clear line distinguishes capital expenditures (assets) from revenue expenditures (expenses). In these situations, accountants must exercise professional judgment and make subjective decisions. Many managers prefer to classify an item as a capital expenditure for financial reporting, because it reduces expenses and increases net earnings for the period. Of course, most managers prefer to classify the expenditure as a deductible expense on the income tax return, to pay lower taxes in the current period. Because the decision to capitalize or expense is subjective, auditors closely review the items reported as capital and revenue expenditures.

To avoid spending too much time on classifying capital and revenue expenditures, some companies develop simple policies that govern the accounting for these expenditures. For example, one large computer company expenses all individual items that cost less than $1,000. These policies are acceptable because immaterial (relatively small dollar) amounts will not affect users' decisions when analyzing financial statements.

LIVENT: HIDING HUNDREDS OF MILLIONS IN EXPENSES THROUGH CAPITALIZATION

A QUESTION OF ACCOUNTABILITY

When expenditures that should be recorded as current-period expenses are improperly capitalized as part of the cost of an asset, the effects on the financial statements can be enormous. In one of the largest Canadian accounting frauds in history, Livent inflated its net earnings and cash flows from operations by hundreds of millions of dollars in just such a scheme. This fraud turned Livent's actual losses into earnings. For example, in 1997 an actual $8 million loss was reported as net earnings of $4.3 million. Charges were initially brought in 1999 in the United States after the former chief financial officer informed a new manager of the fraud. The founders, Myron Gottlieb and Garth Drabinsky, were finally convicted and sentenced for forgery and fraud in February 2009.

The forgery pertained primarily to invoices of an engineering firm, which actually did fulfill its contractual obligations to construct the sets for Livent's productions. In essence, Livent reported expenses incurred to prepare for the production of its musicals on Broadway as if they were long-lived assets. These false additions to long-lived assets were then depreciated and a fraction of their total cost reported on the statement of earnings as depreciation expense, instead of their full cost. In combination, the accounting statements were materially misleading and over-stated the financial health of Livent.

PAUSE FOR FEEDBACK   STOP

A corporation maintains and improves on the ability of its long-lived assets to generate future benefits in a variety of ways: repairing or maintaining (expensed in current period) or adding to or improving (capitalized as part of the cost of the asset).

SELF-STUDY QUIZ 8-2

A building that originally cost $400,000 has been used over the past 10 years and needs continuous maintenance and repairs. Indicate whether each of the following expenditures should be expensed in the current period or capitalized as part of the cost of the asset.

		EXPENSE OR CAPITALIZE?
1.	Major replacement of electrical wiring throughout the building.	_____
2.	Repairs to the front door of the building.	_____
3.	Annual cleaning of the filters on the building's air conditioning system.	_____
4.	Significant repairs due to damage from an unusual flood.	_____

After you complete your answers, check them with the solutions at the end of the chapter.

USE, IMPAIRMENT, AND DISPOSAL OF PROPERTY, PLANT, AND EQUIPMENT

LO8-3

Apply various depreciation methods as assets are held and used over time.

Depreciation Concepts

All long-lived assets, such as aircraft purchased by WestJet, have limited useful lives, except land. Long-lived assets represent the prepaid cost of a bundle of future services or benefits. A portion of an asset's acquisition cost must be allocated as an expense to the periods in which revenue is earned as a result of its use. WestJet earns revenue when it provides air travel service, and incurs an expense when using its aircraft to generate the revenue.

The term used to identify and allocate the acquisition cost of using buildings and equipment that generate revenue over time is depreciation. Thus, **depreciation** is the process of allocating the acquisition cost of buildings and equipment over their productive lives by using a systematic and rational method.[1]

Students are often confused about the concept of depreciation as accountants define it. In accounting, depreciation is a process of *cost allocation*, not a process of determining an asset's current market value or worth. Depreciation is not a cash expense but a distribution of the acquisition cost over the same time period in which the asset is expected to generate revenue. When an asset is depreciated, the amount remaining on the statement of financial position *does not represent its current market value*. Under the cost principle, the cost of a long-lived asset is recorded at its current market value only on the acquisition date. At subsequent dates, the undepreciated cost is not measured on a market value basis. WestJet reported in its statement of earnings a depreciation and amortization expense of $264,921,000 for the year 2015. The journal entry and transaction effects, including the contra-asset account (XA), follow:

Depreciation expense (E)			264,921,000	
Accumulated depreciation (XA)				264,921,000
Assets	**=**	**Liabilities**	**+**	**Shareholders' Equity**
Accumulated depreciation (XA)				Depreciation expense (E)
−264,921,000				−264,921,000

The periodic depreciation expenses throughout the asset's useful life are accumulated in accumulated depreciation, the contra-asset account, and deducted from the related asset's acquisition cost. The acquisition cost minus accumulated depreciation and any write-downs in asset value is called the **carrying amount (or book value)** and appears on the statement of financial position. In addition, companies like WestJet disclose information about the long-lived assets they own or control, and the related accumulated depreciation, in a note to the financial statements.

NOTES TO CONSOLIDATED FINANCIAL STATEMENTS
6. Property and Equipment

December 31, 2015	Cost	Accumulated Depreciation	Net Book Value
Aircraft	$3,912,617	$(1,170,643)	$2,741,974
Ground property and equipment	183,828	(111,652)	72,176
Spare engines and rotables	240,893	(73,447)	167,446
Deposits on aircraft	319,019	–	319,019
Buildings	136,783	(30,419)	106,364
Leasehold improvements	22,104	(11,730)	10,374
Assets under development	55,909	–	55,909
	4,871,153	(1,397,891)	3,473,262

December 31, 2014	Cost	Accumulated Depreciation	Net Book Value
Aircraft	3,024,219	(1,090,933)	1,933,286
Ground property and equipment	158,078	(97,926)	60,152
Spare engines and rotables	216,051	(72,016)	144,035
Deposits on aircraft	509,684	–	509,684
Buildings	136,338	(26,904)	109,434
Leasehold improvements	19,768	(9,308)	10,460
Assets under development	26,143	–	26,143
	4,090,281	(1,297,087)	2,793,194

Source: WestJet Airlines Ltd., Annual Report 2015.

DEPRECIATION is the process of allocating the acquisition cost of buildings and equipment over their useful lives by using a systematic and rational method.

The **CARRYING AMOUNT** (or **BOOK VALUE**) is the acquisition cost of an asset less accumulated depreciation and any write-downs in asset value.

REAL-WORLD EXCERPT

WestJet Airlines Ltd.

2015 ANNUAL REPORT

CARRYING AMOUNT AS AN APPROXIMATION OF REMAINING LIFE

FINANCIAL ANALYSIS

Some analysts compare the carrying amount of assets to their original cost as an approximation of their remaining life. If the carrying amount of an asset is 100 percent of its cost, it is a new asset; if the carrying amount is 25 percent of its cost, the asset has about 25 percent of its estimated life remaining. In WestJet's case, the carrying amount of its aircraft is approximately 71 percent of the original cost. This compares with 63 percent for Southwest Airlines and 71 percent for Ryanair.

Based on the information WestJet provided in its Note 1 (j) and Note 7, the carrying amount for aircraft can be used to estimate the asset's remaining useful life, assuming an average useful life of 18 years.[2] You simply compute the ratio of carrying amount to acquisition cost, and multiply this by the asset's estimated useful life. Consider, for example, WestJet's aircraft:

$$\frac{\text{Carrying amount}}{\text{Acquisition cost}} \times \text{Estimated useful life} = \frac{\$3,473,262}{\$4,871,153} \times 18 = 12.8 \text{ years}$$

The useful life of WestJet's important assets can be analyzed in this manner, and comparisons can be made to other companies in the industry. This is, however, only a rough approximation, because the carrying amount of long-lived assets depends on the estimates of useful life and residual value, as well as the specific depreciation method used.

The calculation of depreciation expense requires three amounts for each depreciable asset:

1. Acquisition cost
2. *Estimated* useful life to the company
3. *Estimated* residual (or salvage) value at the end of the asset's useful life to the company

Two of these three amounts are estimates. Therefore, *depreciation expense is an estimate.*

Estimated useful life represents management's estimate of the asset's useful *economic life* to the company, rather than of its total economic life to all potential users. The asset's expected physical life is often longer than the company intends to use the asset. Economic life may be expressed in terms of years or units of capacity, such as the number of hours a machine is expected to operate or units it can produce. WestJet plans to use its aircraft over a period of 15 to 20 years, whereas its buildings are expected to last for 40 years. The subsequent owner of the aircraft would use an estimated useful life based on its own policies.

The determination of estimated useful life of a long-lived asset must conform to the *continuity assumption.* This assumption holds that the business will continue to pursue its commercial objectives and will not liquidate in the foreseeable future. In Note 1 to its financial statements, WestJet, as do other companies, discloses the useful lives of its long-lived assets and the methods used to depreciate them. We will use the same estimates in our illustrations, where appropriate.

Carrying Amount/ Original Cost—2015

Ryanair 71%

Southwest Airlines 63%

WestJet 71%

ESTIMATED USEFUL LIFE is the expected service life of an asset to the current owner.

NOTES TO CONSOLIDATED FINANCIAL STATEMENTS

1. Statement of Significant Accounting Policies

(j) Property and equipment:

Property and equipment is stated at cost and depreciated to its estimated residual value. Expected useful lives and depreciation methods are reviewed annually.

Asset Class	Basis	Rate
Aircraft, net of estimated residual value	Straight-line	15 to 20 years
Engine, airframe, and landing gear overhaul	Straight-line	3 to 12 years
Ground property and equipment	Straight-line	3 to 25 years
Spare engines and rotables, net of estimated residual value	Straight-line	15 to 20 years
Buildings	Straight-line	40 years
Leasehold improvements	Straight-line	5 years/Term of lease

Estimated residual values of the Corporation's aircraft range between $2,500 and $6,000 per aircraft. Spare engines have a residual value equal to 10% of the original purchase price. Residual values, where applicable, are reviewed annually against prevailing market rates at the consolidated statement of financial position date.

Major overhaul expenditures are capitalized and depreciated over the expected life between overhauls. All other costs relating to the maintenance of fleet assets are charged to the consolidated statement of earnings on consumption or as incurred.

Rotable parts are purchased, depreciated, and disposed of on a pooled basis. When parts are purchased, the cost is added to the pool and depreciated over its useful life of 15 to 20 years. The cost to repair rotable parts is recognized in maintenance expense as incurred.

Source: WestJet Airlines Ltd., Annual Report 2015.

RESIDUAL (or SALVAGE) VALUE is the estimated amount to be recovered, less disposal costs, at the end of the estimated useful life of an asset.

Residual (or salvage) value represents management's estimate of the amount the company expects to recover upon disposal of the asset at the end of its estimated useful life. The residual value may be the estimated value of the asset as salvage or scrap, or its expected value if sold to another user.

Residual value is the estimated amount to be recovered, less any estimated costs of dismantling, disposal, and sale. In many cases, disposal costs may approximately equal the gross residual value. Therefore, many depreciable assets are assumed to have no residual value. In the case of aircraft owned by WestJet, the company uses third-party industry market valuations, recommendations from the aircraft manufacturer, and actual experience to estimate useful life and expected residual value. WestJet explains that revisions will arise from changes to both market prices of used aircraft and utilization of the aircraft.

DIFFERENCES IN ESTIMATED LIVES WITHIN A SINGLE INDUSTRY

FINANCIAL ANALYSIS

Notes to actual financial statements of companies in the airline industry reveal the following estimates for estimated lives of new aircraft:

Company	Estimated Life (in years)	Residual Value
Lufthansa Group	20	5 percent of cost
Emirates Airlines	15	10 percent of cost
JetBlue Airways	25	20 percent of cost
Southwest Airlines	23–25	2–20 percent of cost

The differences in estimated lives may be attributable to a number of factors, such as type of aircraft used by each company, equipment replacement plans, differences in operations, and the degree of management prudence in setting its accounting policies. In addition, given the same type of aircraft, companies that plan to use the equipment over fewer years may estimate higher residual values than do companies that plan to use the equipment longer.

Differences in estimated lives and residual values of assets used by specific companies can have a significant impact on a comparison of the profitability of the competing companies. Analysts must be certain that they identify the causes for the differences in depreciable lives.

Individual items of property, plant, and equipment may include various significant parts that have different useful lives. For this reason, IFRS require that companies allocate the acquisition cost of each item of property, plant, and equipment to its component parts, and that each significant part be depreciated separately over its useful life.[3] In an aircraft, the airframe, engines, and landing gear may have different useful lives. It is, therefore, appropriate to allocate specific costs to these aircraft components and depreciate them separately. This is known as componentization of assets.

NOTES TO CONSOLIDATED FINANCIAL STATEMENTS

1. Statement of Significant Accounting Policies
(r) Critical accounting judgments and estimates
Judgments
(i) Componentization

The componentization of the Corporation's assets, namely aircraft, are based on management's judgment of what components constitute a significant cost in relation to the total cost of an asset and whether these components have similar or dissimilar patterns of consumption and useful lives for purposes of calculating depreciation and amortization. Management has considered market values, depreciation rates and industry practices in determining the level of componentization.

Source: WestJet Airlines Ltd., Annual Report 2015.

REAL-WORLD EXCERPT

WestJet Airlines Ltd.
2015 ANNUAL REPORT

Alternative Depreciation Methods

Accountants agree that there is no single best method of depreciation, because the cost of using long-lived assets to generate revenue differs significantly among companies. Thus, managers may choose from among different acceptable depreciation methods.

Exhibit 8.2
Illustrative Data for Computing Depreciation under Alternative Methods

WESTJET AIRLINES	
Acquisition cost of aircraft, purchased on January 1, 2017	$28,000,000
Estimated useful life (in years)	20
Estimated residual value	$6,000,000
Estimated useful life (in flights)	40,000 flights
Actual flights in Year: 2017 2,100 flights	
Year: 2018 1,950 flights	
Year: 2019 2,050 flights	

Their decision should reflect the anticipated reduction in future cash flow as a result of the wear and tear from using the asset over time. Once selected, the depreciation method should be applied consistently over time to enhance comparability of financial information to users. We will discuss the three most common depreciation methods:

1. Straight line
2. Units of production
3. Declining (or diminishing) balance

The hypothetical data shown in Exhibit 8.2 will be used to illustrate each of the three methods of calculating depreciation expense for one Q400 aircraft purchased on January 1, 2017.[4]

Straight-Line Method More companies, including WestJet, use straight-line depreciation in their financial statements than all other methods combined. Under **straight-line depreciation**, an equal portion of an asset's depreciable cost is allocated to each accounting period over its estimated useful life. The formula to estimate annual depreciation expense follows:

STRAIGHT-LINE DEPRECIATION
is the method that allocates the cost of an asset in equal periodic amounts over its useful life.

Straight-Line Formula

$$\underbrace{(\text{Cost} - \text{Residual Value})}_{\substack{\text{Depreciable} \\ \text{Cost}}} \times \underbrace{1/\text{Useful Life}}_{\substack{\text{Straight-Line} \\ \text{Rate}}} = \text{Depreciation Expense}$$

In this formula, "cost minus residual value" is the amount to be depreciated, also called *depreciable cost*. The term "1 ÷ useful life" is the straight-line rate. Using the data provided in Exhibit 8.2, the depreciation expense is computed as follows:

$$(\$28{,}000{,}000 - \$6{,}000{,}000) \times 1/20 = \$1{,}100{,}000$$

	Amount for the adjusting entry: reported on the statement of earnings (closed at year-end)↓	Balance in the contra-asset account after the adjusting entry↓	Cost less accumulated depreciation: reported on the statement of financial position↓

		Straight-Line Method		
Year	**Computation** (Cost − Residual value) × 1/Useful Life	**Depreciation Expense**	**Accumulated Depreciation**	**Carrying Amount**
At acquisition:				
2017	($28,000,000 − $6,000,000) × 1/20	$1,100,000	$1,100,000	$26,900,000
2018	($28,000,000 − $6,000,000) × 1/20	1,100,000	2,200,000	25,800,000
2019	($28,000,000 − $6,000,000) × 1/20	1,100,000	3,300,000	24,700,000
	Total	$3,300,000		

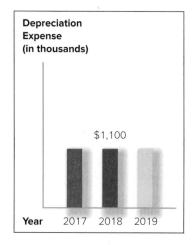

Depreciation Expense (in thousands)

$1,100

Year   2017   2018   2019

Notice the following items:

- Depreciation expense is a constant amount for each year.
- Accumulated depreciation increases by an equal amount each year.
- Carrying amount decreases by the same amount each year until it equals the estimated residual value.

This is the reason for the name *straight-line method*. Notice, too, that the adjusting entry can be prepared from this schedule, and the effects on the statement of earnings and ending balance on the statement of financial position are known. WestJet uses the straight-line method for all of its long-lived assets. Most companies in the airline industry use the straight-line method. Depreciation expense, accumulated depreciation, and carrying amount decrease systematically from period to period at a constant rate each year. The depreciation expense is said to be a *fixed expense* because it is constant each year, regardless of the actual air miles flown by the aircraft.

UNITS-OF-PRODUCTION DEPRECIATION is a method to allocate the cost of an asset over its useful life based on the relation of its periodic output to its total estimated output.

Units-of-Production (Activity) Method   Assume WestJet uses the **units-of-production depreciation** method, which allocates the cost of an asset over its useful life based on the relation of its periodic output to its total estimated output. The formula to estimate annual depreciation expense under this method follows:

Units-of-Production Formula

Depreciation rate per unit

$$\overbrace{\frac{(\text{Cost} - \text{Residual value})}{\text{Estimated total production}}} \times \frac{\text{Actual}}{\text{production}} = \text{Depreciation expense}$$

Dividing the depreciable amount by the estimated total production yields the depreciation rate per unit of production (or activity), which is then multiplied by the actual annual production (or activity) to determine depreciation expense. Using the information in Exhibit 8.2, the computation of the depreciation rate per unit follows:

$$\frac{\$28{,}000{,}000 - \$6{,}000{,}000}{40{,}000 \text{ flights}} = \$550 \text{ per flight}$$

For every flight, WestJet would record depreciation expense of $550. The depreciation schedule for the years 2017, 2018, and 2019 under the units-of-production method follows:

Units-of-Production Method				
Year	Computations	Depreciation Expense	Accumulated Depreciation	Carrying Amount
At acquisition				$28,000,000
2017	$550 × 2,100 flights	$1,155,000	$1,155,000	26,845,000
2018	550 × 1,950 flights	1,072,500	2,227,500	25,772,500
2019	550 × 2,050 flights	1,127,500	3,355,000	24,645,000
	Total	$3,355,000		

When the units-of-production method is used, depreciation expense is said to be a *variable expense* because it varies directly with production, or use. The carrying amount and the amount of accumulated depreciation will also fluctuate from year to year.

You might wonder what happens if the total estimated productive output differs from actual output. Remember that the estimate is management's best guess of total output. If any difference occurs at the end of the asset's life, the final adjusting entry to depreciation expense should be for the amount needed to cause the asset's carrying amount to equal the asset's estimated residual value.

The units-of-production method is based on an estimate of an asset's total productive capacity or output that is difficult to determine. This is another example of the degree of subjectivity inherent in accounting.

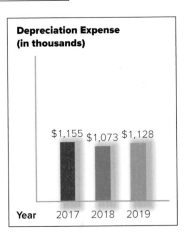

Depreciation Expense (in thousands)

$1,155 $1,073 $1,128

Year   2017   2018   2019

Declining-Balance Method   If the asset is considered to be more efficient or productive in its earliest years, with a levelling off in later years, managers might choose the **declining-balance depreciation** method to reflect a sharper reduction in the economic benefits (cash flow) expected to be derived from the asset in the earlier rather than later years. This is called *accelerated depreciation*. Special equipment acquired to produce a patented drug is an example. The drug faces little or no competition in its early years. Therefore, the producer can demand a higher price and derive more benefits from the equipment. In later years, as products mimicking the benefits of the drug are developed and brought to market, the asset's economic benefits will drop because of competition. Finally, when the drug is no longer protected by the patent, manufacturers of generic products can flood the market at very low prices. While the therapeutic benefits of the drug will not change, the economic benefits to the pharmaceutical company will be relatively low. Hence, a declining-balance method is used to better reflect the decline of economic benefits over time.

DECLINING-BALANCE DEPRECIATION is the method that allocates the cost of an asset over its useful life based on a multiple of the straight-line rate (often two times).

The relationship between accelerated depreciation expense, repair expense, and the total expense of using the asset is shown in Exhibit 8.3. Although accelerated methods are seldom used for financial reporting purposes, the method that is used more frequently than others is the declining-balance method.

Declining-balance depreciation is based on multiplying the asset's carrying amount by a fixed rate that exceeds the straight-line (SL) rate. The rate is often double (two times) the SL rate and is called the *double declining-balance rate*. For example, if the estimated useful life of an asset is 10 years and the SL rate is 10 percent (1 ÷ 10), then the declining-balance rate is 20 percent (2 × the SL rate of 10 percent). Other typical acceleration rates are 1.5 times and 1.75 times. The double declining-balance (DDB) rate is adopted most frequently by companies utilizing the accelerated method, and it will be used in our illustration.

To calculate depreciation expense under the double declining-balance method, the carrying amount of the asset is multiplied by the DDB rate as follows:

Double Declining-Balance Formula

$$\underbrace{(\text{Cost} - \text{Accumulated depreciation})}_{\text{Carrying amount}} \times \underbrace{\frac{2}{\text{Useful life}}}_{\substack{\text{Declining-}\\\text{Balance rate}}} = \text{Depreciation expense}$$

Exhibit **8.3**

The Relationship among
Depreciation Expense, Repair
Expense, and Total Expense

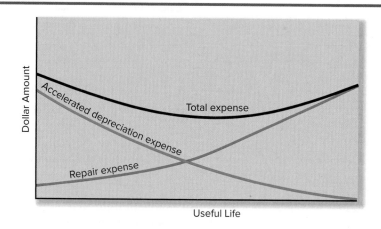

There are two important differences between this method and the others described previously:

- Notice that accumulated depreciation, not residual value, is included in the formula. Since accumulated depreciation increases each year, carrying amount (cost − accumulated depreciation) decreases. The DDB rate is applied to a lower carrying amount each year, resulting in a decline in depreciation expense over time.

- An asset's carrying amount cannot be depreciated below residual value. Therefore, if the annual computation reduces carrying amount below residual value, a lower amount of depreciation expense must be recorded so that carrying amount equals residual value. No additional depreciation expense is computed in subsequent years.

Computation of DDB depreciation expense is illustrated using the data given in Exhibit 8.2 (amounts in thousands of dollars):

	Double Declining-Balance Method			
Year	Computation (Cost − Accumulated Depreciation) × 1/Useful Life	Depreciation Expense	Accumulated Depreciation	Carrying Amount
At acquisition:				$28,000,000
2017	($28,000,000 − $0) × 2/20	$2,800,000	$2,800,000	25,200,000
2018	($28,000,000 − $2,800,000) × 2/20	2,520,000	5,320,000	22,680,000
2019	($28,000,000 − $5,320,000) × 2/20	2,268,000	7,588,000	20,412,000
	Total	$7,588,000		

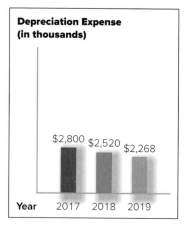

**Depreciation Expense
(in thousands)**

$2,800 $2,520 $2,268

Year 2017 2018 2019

The calculated depreciation expense for this asset differs depending upon the depreciation method used. Using the straight-line method, the annual expense is $1,100,000 each year of the aircraft's 20-year useful life. Using the units-of-production method, annual depreciation expense varies each year from a low of $1,072,500 in 2018 to a high of $1,155,000 in 2017. Finally, using the double declining-balance method, depreciation expense declines every year from $2,800,000 in 2017 to $2,268,000 in 2019. This, in part, explains why an analyst must be careful when using the carrying amount to estimate the remaining useful life of an asset. Using our example, we obtain different estimates for the remaining useful life for the same aircraft after three years, depending on the depreciation method used.

Depreciation Method	Estimated Remaining Useful Life
Straight line	($24,700,000/$28,000,000) × 20 = 17.64 years, or approximately 18 years
Units of production	($24,645,000/$28,000,000) × 20 = 17.60 years, or approximately 18 years
Double declining balance	($20,412,000/$28,000,000) × 20 = 14.58 years, or approximately 15 years

This example illustrates why care must be taken to read the notes to the financial statements of any company to identify the accounting policies it uses before comparing its financial results to those of other companies.

The depreciation method that is selected by management informs external users of management's expectation of the pattern of economic benefits that the company will derive from the using the asset in its business operations over time. Companies will use different depreciation methods for different types of assets, but they are expected to apply the same methods to each type of assets to maintain comparability of information over time.

In the previous illustration, we assumed that the aircraft was purchased at the beginning of the year. In reality, however, companies purchase assets at any date during the year, which complicates the computation of depreciation expense for the first year of acquisition. For practical purposes, acquisitions made during the year are depreciated in a convenient manner during the asset's first year of operation. Depreciation expense can be computed for the number of months the asset is actually in use, or it can be computed for half a year using the half-year convention.

For example, if WestJet acquired the aircraft on October 1, 2017, instead of January 1, 2017, the annual straight-line depreciation expense could be pro-rated by determining the monthly depreciation expense and multiplying the monthly depreciation by the number of months WestJet flew this aircraft during 2017 (three months in this case):

$$\text{Depreciation expense} = (\$1,100,000 \div 12) \times 3 \text{ months} = \$275,000$$

Alternatively, companies that acquire many long-lived assets during the year may use the half-year rule, which implies that similar long-lived assets, such as office equipment, that are acquired at different dates throughout the year can be assumed to have been purchased around the middle of the year. Thus, all the office equipment acquired during the fiscal year is depreciated for one-half of a year at the end of the year of acquisition. This practical rule is acceptable as long as the amount of depreciation expense for the year is not materially misstated.

In Summary The following table summarizes the three depreciation methods and computations for each method. Exhibit 8.4 shows, graphically, the differences in depreciation expense over time for each method.

Method	Computation	Depreciation Expense
Straight line	$(\text{Cost} - \text{Residual value}) \times \dfrac{1}{\text{Useful life}}$	Equal amounts each year
Units of production	$\dfrac{(\text{Cost} - \text{Residual value})}{\text{Estimated total production}} \times \text{Annual production}$	Varying amounts based on production level
Double declining balance	$(\text{Cost} - \text{Accumulated depreciation}) \times \dfrac{2}{\text{Useful life}}$	Declining amounts over time

Exhibit **8.4**
Differences in Depreciation
Methods over Time

IMPACT OF ALTERNATIVE DEPRECIATION METHODS

FINANCIAL ANALYSIS

Assume that you are analyzing two companies that are identical except that one uses accelerated depreciation and the other uses the straight-line method. Which company would you expect to report higher net earnings? Actually, the question is tricky; you cannot say for certain which company's net earnings would be higher.

The accelerated methods report higher depreciation expense and, therefore, lower net earnings during the early years of the life of an asset. In later years, this effect reverses. Therefore, companies that use accelerated depreciation report lower depreciation expense and higher net earnings during the later years of an asset's life compared to those using the straight-line method. The graph in Exhibit 8.4 shows the pattern of depreciation over the life of an asset for the straight-line and declining-balance methods discussed in this chapter. When the curve for the accelerated method falls below the curve for the straight-line method, the accelerated method produces higher net earnings than the straight-line method. The total depreciation of the asset over its useful life should be the same for each method.

The depreciation method that a company uses to allocate the cost of an asset over time should faithfully represent the economic decline in the ability of the asset to generate economic benefits in the future. Furthermore, the chosen method should be used consistently from one period to the next. Users of financial statements must understand that differences in depreciation methods rather than real economic differences can cause significant variations in reported net earnings. For example, the Japanese company Sony Corporation changed its depreciation method for property, plant, and equipment for fiscal year 2013 from the declining-balance method the straight-line method, because the company "believes that the straight-line method better reflects the pattern of consumption of the estimated future benefits to be derived from those assets being depreciated and provides a better matching of costs and revenues over the assets' estimated useful lives."[5] This change in depreciation methods resulted in a decrease in depreciation expense and an increase in net earnings. The change in method coincided with Sony's reporting of net losses for fiscal years 2012 and 2013. The decrease in depreciation expense reduced the net loss for fiscal year 2013, although the effect of the change is relatively small (approximately 3 percent of the total amount of depreciation and amortization expense).

PAUSE FOR
FEEDBACK

Three cost allocation methods are discussed in this section:

- Straight line: (Cost − Residual value) × 1/Useful life

- Units of production: [(Cost − Residual value)/Estimated total production] × Annual production

- Double declining balance: (Cost − Accumulated depreciation) × 2/Useful life

Practise these methods using the following information.

SELF-STUDY **QUIZ 8-3**

Assume that WestJet acquired new computer equipment at a cost of $240,000. The equipment has an estimated life of six years (and an estimated operating life of 50,000 hours) with an estimated residual value of $30,000. Determine the depreciation expense for the first full year under each of the following methods:

1. Straight line

2. Double declining balance

3. Units of production (assuming the equipment ran for 8,000 hours in the first year)

After you complete your answers, check them with the solutions at the end of the chapter.

Changes in Depreciation Estimates

Depreciation is based on two estimates—useful life and residual value. These estimates are made at the time a depreciable asset is acquired. As experience with the asset accumulates, one or both of these initial estimates may have to be revised to more faithfully represent the economic effect of using the asset in operations. In addition, extraordinary repairs and betterments may be added to the original acquisition cost at some time during the asset's use. When it is clear that either estimate should be revised to a material degree or the asset's cost has been changed, the undepreciated asset balance (less any residual value at that date) should be apportioned over the remaining estimated life from the current year into the future. This is called a *change in estimate*.

To compute the new depreciation expense resulting from a change in estimate for any of the depreciation methods described in this chapter, substitute the carrying amount for the original acquisition cost, the new residual value for the original amount, and the estimated remaining useful life for the original estimated useful life. As an illustration, the computation using the straight-line method is as follows.

Assume the following for an aircraft owned by WestJet:

Cost of aircraft when acquired	$28,000,000
Estimated useful life	20 years
Estimated residual value	$6,000,000
Accumulated depreciation through year 5	
($28,000,000 − $6,000,000) × 1/20 = $1,100,000 per year × 5 years = $5,500,000	

Shortly after the start of year 6, WestJet changed the initial estimated useful life to 25 years and lowered the estimated residual value to $4,000,000. At the end of year 6, the computation of the new amount for depreciation expense is as follows:

Acquisition cost	$28,000,000
Less: Accumulated depreciation (years 1–5)	5,500,000
Carrying amount	22,500,000
Less: New residual value	4,000,000
New depreciable amount	$18,500,000
Annual depreciation based on remaining life:	
$18,500,000 ÷ 20 years (25 − 5 years) =	$ 925,000 per year

Companies may also change depreciation methods (e.g., from declining balance to straight line), although such change requires significantly more disclosure since the comparability of information over time is compromised. Changes in accounting estimates and depreciation methods should be made only when the new estimate or accounting method "better measures" the periodic net earnings of the business.

PAUSE FOR FEEDBACK

When management changes an estimate used in a depreciation computation, the carrying amount of the asset at the time of the change minus any expected residual value is allocated over the remaining life of the asset. Before you move on, practice the depreciation computation using the following information.

SELF-STUDY QUIZ 8-4

Assume that WestJet Airlines owned a service truck that originally cost $100,000. When purchased, the truck had an estimated useful life of 10 years, with no residual value. After operating the truck for five years, WestJet determined that the remaining life was only two more years. Based on this change in estimate, what amount of annual depreciation should be recorded over the remaining life of the asset? WestJet uses the straight-line method.

After you complete your answer, check it with the solution at the end of the chapter.

Managers' Selection among Accounting Alternatives

Financial Reporting For financial reporting purposes, corporate managers must select the depreciation method that provides the best matching of revenues and expenses for any given asset. If the asset is expected to provide benefits evenly over time, then the straight-line method is preferred. Managers also find this method easy to use and explain. If no other method provides improved faithful representation, then the straight-line method is selected. Also, during the early years of an asset's life, the straight-line method reports higher net earnings than the accelerated methods do. For these reasons, the straight-line method is by far the most common.

However, certain assets produce more revenue in their early lives because they are more efficient then than in later years. In this case, managers select an accelerated method to allocate cost. In addition, as the asset ages, repair costs are likely to increase. Thus, the total of the depreciation expense and repair expense for any given period is likely to provide a nearly constant amount of expenses each period.

In addition to selecting a method of depreciation subsequent to the acquisition of property, plant, and equipment, managers must decide if they wish to measure these assets at historical cost (adjusted for depreciation) or to revalue them to their fair value at the end of the fiscal year. The primary argument in favour of revaluation is that the historical cost of an asset purchased 15 or 20 years ago is not meaningful because of the impact of inflation. For example, most people would not compare the original purchase price of a house acquired in 1987 to the purchase price for the identical house next door acquired in 2017, because the price of houses has changed dramatically between those years. A primary argument against the revaluation of property, plant, and equipment is the lack of objectivity involved in estimating an asset's current cost. Consequently, most companies use the cost method for financial reporting purposes.

Tax Reporting   WestJet Airlines, like most public companies, must prepare two sets of reports. One set is prepared under IFRS for reporting to shareholders. The other set is prepared to determine the company's tax obligation and is computed in conformity with the tax rules enacted by the tax authorities of the country where the company has been legally established. Canadian corporations must compute their tax obligations in accordance with the Income Tax Act. The reason that the two sets of rules are different is simple— the objectives of financial reporting and tax reporting differ.

Financial Reporting (IFRS)	Tax Reporting
The objective of financial reporting is to provide financial information about the reporting entity that is useful to existing and potential investors, lenders, and other creditors in making decisions about providing resources to the entity.	The objective of the Income Tax Act is to raise sufficient revenues to pay for the expenditures of the federal government, with many provisions designed to encourage certain behaviours that are thought to benefit society (e.g., contributions to charities are tax-deductible to encourage people to support worthy programs).

It is easy to understand why two sets of accounting reports are permitted, but perhaps the more interesting aspect concerns the reason why managers incur the extra cost of preparing two sets of reports. In some cases, differences between the Income Tax Act and IFRS leave the manager no choice but to have separate reports. In other cases, the explanation is an economic one, called the *least and the latest rule*. In general, taxpayers want to pay the lowest amount of tax that is legally permitted at the latest possible date. If you had the choice of paying $100,000 to the federal government at the end of this year or at the end of next year, you would choose the end of next year. By doing so, you would be able to invest the $100,000 saved for an extra year and earn a return on the investment.

By complying with the requirements of the Income Tax Act, corporations can defer (delay) paying millions and sometimes billions of dollars in taxes. The following companies, which prepare their financial statements in compliance with IFRS, reported material amounts of deferred tax obligations in a recent year. The deferral of payment of income tax to future years was in large part due to differences between the depreciation methods used for financial reporting versus tax reporting.

Company	Deferred Tax Liabilities Due to Applying Different Depreciation Methods
WestJet Airlines Ltd.	$ 327 million
Canadian National Railway Company	8,105 million
Suncor Energy Inc.	11,983 million

The depreciation methods discussed in the previous section are not acceptable for federal income tax reporting. One objective of domestic tax law is to provide an incentive for existing Canadian companies to invest in modern property, plant, and equipment in order to retain their global competitiveness. Governments around the world also compete to attract production facilities by using their tax laws to support their domestic economic growth. More production usually means more employment for Canadians, and economic growth.

Corporations that are subject to taxation in Canada must apply capital cost allowance (CCA) to tangible assets, as determined by the schedules provided by the tax authorities. The CCA schedules must be used to calculate the maximum annual expense used in computing taxable income according to the tax rules and regulations. These schedules classify capital assets into different classes and stipulate the maximum CCA rate (a declining-balance rate) for each class. For example, aircraft is currently Class 9, with a CCA rate of 25 percent per year.

CCA does not attempt to match the cost of an asset with the revenue it produces over its useful life, in conformity with the matching process. Instead, CCA provides for accelerated depreciation of an asset over a period that is usually much shorter than the asset's estimated useful life. Because CCA is based on an accelerated method, the high expense reported under CCA reduces a corporation's taxable income more in the early years of a long-lived asset than in later years. For example, the straight-line depreciation expense related to the Q400 aircraft is $1,100,000 for 2017, but the corresponding CCA will be $7,000,000 ($28,000,000 × 25 percent), of which half may be deducted in the first year the asset is acquired. The difference between the CCA deduction of $3,500,000 and the depreciation expense of $1,100,000 reduces taxable income by $2,400,000. This will reduce the amount of income tax payable, leaving WestJet with more cash available to finance its growth. Chapter 9 provides further discussion on this topic.

TWO SETS OF REPORTS

A QUESTION OF ACCOUNTABILITY

When they first learn that companies prepare two sets of reports, some people question the ethics or the legality of the practice. In reality, *it is both legal and ethical to prepare separate reports for tax and financial reporting purposes. However, these reports must reflect the same transactions.* The amounts reported for tax purposes are essentially adjustments to amounts recorded in the accounting system for financial reporting purposes. Understating revenues or overstating expenses on a tax return can result in financial penalties and/or imprisonment. Accountants who aid tax evaders can also be fined or imprisoned, and can lose their professional licences.

DEPRECIATION METHODS IN OTHER COUNTRIES

INTERNATIONAL PERSPECTIVE

With the severe and extreme economic contraction in 2008 and 2009, many countries worldwide relaxed either their accounting or their tax regulations in an effort to stimulate their domestic economies. Austria, for example, has permitted accelerated depreciation up to 30 percent of either acquisition or construction costs for property, plant, and equipment, such as aircraft, for assets acquired in 2009 and 2010, while the United States enacted the American Recovery and Reinvestment Act of 2009, thereby extending a 50 percent acceleration provision to include properties placed into service in 2009 as well as those already available for 2008.

While accounting methods remain unchanged, tax regulations in some countries have changed to reduce the cash burden of tax payments on capital-intensive industries and stimulate investment in new long-lived assets. The economic goal is to sustain economic growth and retain jobs. When users of financial statements for airlines compare reported net earnings for companies operating in these three countries, knowing the income tax regimes are comparable is as important as knowing the accounting methods are comparable as well.

LO8-4

Explain the effect of asset impairment on the financial statements.

Measuring Asset Impairment

Canadian corporations are required to review the carrying amount of their tangible and intangible assets for possible impairment. Assets can have different values that are used for different purposes. Historical acquisition costs are essential for verifiability of past transactions. These costs are then adjusted for systematic depreciation over their useful lives. However, adjusted historical costs are not relevant for investment decisions that rely on expectations of future cash flows. Consequently, investors and creditors may be interested in the asset's *fair value*, which reflects the amount at which an asset can be bought or sold between two knowledgeable, willing parties in an arm's-length transaction. However, companies usually acquire long-lived assets for use in their production processes, and not for resale to others. Therefore, a long-lived asset has *value in use*, which is measured as the present value (or current cash equivalent) of future cash flows expected to be derived from use of the asset over time.

Subsequent to acquisition, the economic benefits or future cash flows associated with assets do change for a variety of reasons. Adverse changes to future benefits may be triggered, for example, by reduced market price for the asset, contraction in the economy, ongoing evidence of operating cash flow losses, and technological obsolescence. Consequently, assets should then be assessed for possible impairment. Two steps are necessary:

> **Step 1: Test for impairment**
>
> Impairment occurs when events or changed circumstances cause the carrying amount of these assets to exceed their recoverable amount, which is the higher of its value in use and its fair value less costs to sell.
>
> **If Carrying amount > Recoverable amount, then the asset is impaired**
>
> **Step 2: Computation of impairment loss**
>
> For any asset considered to be impaired, companies recognize a loss for the difference between the asset's carrying amount and its recoverable amount.
>
> **Impairment loss = Carrying amount − Recoverable amount**

That is, the asset is *written down* to its recoverable amount.

A simple illustration will help in understanding how this concept is applied. Assume that WestJet has an old aircraft that is still in good working condition. This aircraft has a carrying amount of $15 million. Because of an economic downturn, its current market price has dropped to $13 million, and the company will incur $0.5 million in costs to sell this aircraft to an interested buyer. At the same time, the value in use of the aircraft or current cash equivalent of future net cash flows expected to be derived from using it is $14 million. In this case, the test for impairment indicates that this aircraft is impaired by $1 million, which is determined as follows:

> **Step 1: Test**
>
> | Fair value less costs to sell | $12,500,000 | } Recoverable amount = $14,000,000 |
> |---|---|---|
> | Value in use | 14,000,000 | |
> | Carrying amount | 15,000,000 | |
>
> **Step 2: Impairment loss** = $15,000,000 − $14,000,000 = $1,000,000

If the aircraft's value in use is greater than $15 million, then the aircraft is not impaired and there is no need, in this case, to determine the aircraft's fair value less costs to sell.

Fair values can be determined based on quoted market prices. If there is no current market price, then fair values can be based on prices of similar assets for which a recent transaction occurred, on an arm's-length appraisal value, or by using specific valuation techniques.

In the previous example, the recoverable amount was determined for one asset—an aircraft. Sometimes, however, an asset does not generate cash inflows that are largely independent from other assets or groups of assets. In this case, the asset would be grouped with other assets that would form a cash-generating unit. The recoverable amount would then be determined for the cash-generating unit as a whole instead of the individual assets to which it belongs.

Although WestJet reported no impairment losses to its property, plant, and equipment, let us assume that a review of WestJet's aircraft indicated that an asset group of aircraft has a carrying amount of $132 million. The value in use of this asset group was estimated at $120 million, and fair value less costs to sell was estimated at $125 million by using published sources of market prices of used aircraft as well as third-party bids. These aircraft are, therefore, impaired because their recoverable amount, $125 million, is lower than their carrying amount. The following journal entry would be recorded:

Loss due to impairment of assets (SE)			7,000,000	
Aircraft (A)				7,000,000
Assets	=	**Liabilities**	+	**Shareholders' Equity**
Aircraft −7,000,000				Loss due to impairment −7,000,000

An impairment loss recognized in a prior period can be reversed in the future if there has been a change in the estimates used to determine the asset's recoverable amount since the impairment loss was recognized. In this case, the increased carrying amount of the asset shall not exceed the carrying amount that would have been determined (net of depreciation) had no impairment loss been recognized for the asset in prior years.

Companies that recognize impairment losses or reversal of prior impairment losses are required to disclose in the notes to their financial statements specific details about each material impairment loss recognized or reversed during the period, either for an individual asset or for a cash-generating unit. The disclosures include the nature of the asset or the cash-generating unit, the events and circumstances that led to the recognition or reversal of the impairment loss, the amount of the impairment loss recognized or reversed, and the methods used to determine the recoverable amount.

For example, in 2015, Bombardier Inc., the world's leading manufacturer of both planes and trains, reported in great detail the sources of impairment charges of $4,290 million on its Areospace Program Tooling, including impairment of $3,070 million on the *C Series* aircraft program as explained below in Note 21 to its financial statements:

REAL-WORLD EXCERPT

Bombardier Inc.

ANNUAL REPORT

NOTES TO THE CONSOLIDATED FINANCIAL STATEMENTS

21. INTANGIBLE ASSETS

...

C Series aircraft program

In October 2015, the Corporation entered into a memorandum of understanding for the C Series aircraft program with the Government of Québec. Following the completion of an in-depth review of the C Series aircraft program as well as discussions with the Government of Québec which resulted in the memorandum of understanding, the Corporation performed an impairment test on the C Series aircraft program cash generating unit (the "C Series aircraft program") which principally consists of capitalized development costs. The Corporation determined that the C Series aircraft program carrying amount exceeded its recoverable amount, and accordingly recorded an impairment charge of $3,070 million, in special items, related to the C Series aircraft program development costs in fiscal year 2015. After the impairment charge, the remaining balance of the C Series aerospace program tooling is $1,850 million as at December 31, 2015.

Source: Bombardier Inc., Annual Report 2015.

The complex nature of testing for asset impairment is covered in advanced accounting courses.

LO8-5

Analyze the disposal of property, plant, and equipment.

Disposal of Property, Plant, and Equipment

In some cases, a business may *voluntarily* decide not to hold a long-lived asset for its entire life. The company may drop a product from its line and no longer need the equipment that was used to produce the product, or managers may want to replace a machine with a newer, more efficient one. These disposals include sale, trade-in, and retirement. When WestJet disposes of an old aircraft, it may sell it to a cargo airline or regional airline. A business may also dispose of an asset *involuntarily* as a result of a casualty, such as a storm, fire, or accident.

Disposals of long-lived assets seldom occur on the last day of the accounting period. Therefore, depreciation must be updated to the date of disposal. The disposal of a depreciable asset usually requires two entries:

1. An adjusting entry to update the depreciation expense and accumulated depreciation accounts.

2. An entry to record the disposal. The cost of the asset and any accumulated depreciation at the date of disposal must be removed from the accounts. The difference between any resources received on disposal of an asset and its carrying amount at the date of disposal is a gain or loss on disposal of the asset. This gain (or loss) is revenue (or expense) from "peripheral or incidental" activities rather than from normal operations. Gains and losses from disposals are usually shown separately on the statement of earnings after earnings from operations.

Assume that at the end of 2016 WestJet sold an aircraft that was no longer needed because of the elimination of service to a small city. The original cost of the aircraft was $2.6 million. The unrecorded depreciation expense for the year was $71,000.[6] The aircraft was sold for $1.9 million in cash and had accumulated depreciation of $224,000 at the beginning of 2016. The loss on the sale of this aircraft is $405,000, calculated as follows:

Cash received		$1,900,000
Original cost	$2,600,000	
Less: Accumulated depreciation	295,000	
Carrying amount		2,305,000
Loss on disposal		$ (405,000)

The entries and effects of the transaction on the date of the sale are as follows:

1. Depreciation expense (E)	71,000	
Accumulated depreciation—Aircraft (XA)		71,000
2. Cash (A)	1,900,000	
Accumulated depreciation—Aircraft (XA)	295,000	
Loss on sale of asset (SE)	405,000	
Aircraft (A)		2,600,000

Assets	=	Liabilities	+	Shareholders' Equity
1. Accumulated depreciation −71,000				1. Depreciation expense −71,000
2. Cash +1,900,000				2. Loss on sale of asset −405,000
Accumulated depreciation + 295,000				
Aircraft −2,600,000				

A gain or loss on disposal occurs because (1) depreciation expense is based on estimates that may differ from actual experience and (2) depreciation is based on original cost, not current market value. Because the gain or loss on disposal is not part of the continuing operating activities of a company, it is usually shown as a separate line item on the statement of earnings. In 2015, for example, WestJet sold property and equipment and reported a net loss of $1,860,000 as a separate item on its consolidated statement of earnings.

When disposing of a long-lived asset, a company must first record depreciation expense for usage of the asset since the last time it was recorded. Then, the asset at cost and its related accumulated depreciation are eliminated. The difference between the cash received, if any, and the carrying amount of the asset is either a gain or a loss on disposal.

SELF-STUDY QUIZ 8-5

Now let us assume the same facts as above, except that the aircraft was sold for $2,500,000 cash. Prepare the two entries on the date of the sale.

1. Update the depreciation expense for the year.

2. Record the sale.

After you complete your answers, check them with the solutions at the end of the chapter.

Companies may also trade in an old asset in exchange for a new asset and pay cash to cover the difference in the assets' values. Let us assume that an old vehicle, originally acquired at $20,000 with $16,000 of accumulated depreciation, has a fair market value of $3,000. The company exchanges this vehicle in partial payment for computer hardware and pays an additional amount of $1,600 in cash. This trade-in transaction includes a non-cash consideration. Hence, the computer hardware is recorded at its fair market value, unless the fair market value of the old vehicle is more objectively determinable. Notice that the carrying amount of the vehicle is $4,000 and the total payment for the computer hardware is $4,600, which is equal to the fair market value of the vehicle plus the cash consideration. Assuming that the fair market value of the vehicle is more objectively determinable, the journal entry and effects of the trade-in transaction are as follows:[7]

Computer hardware (A)	4,600	
Accumulated depreciation—Vehicle (XA)	16,000	
Loss on disposal of assets (SE)	1,000	
Vehicle (A)		20,000
Cash (A)		1,600

In certain situations, the company may dispose of an old, unusable asset if it cannot sell it to another party. The abandonment or retirement of an asset results in a loss that is equal to the asset's carrying amount. The journal entry to record the retirement of an asset is similar to the case of a sale or a trade-in, except that the cash account is not affected.

LO8-6

Apply measurement and reporting concepts for natural resources and intangible assets.

NATURAL RESOURCES are assets that occur in nature, such as mineral deposits, timber, oil, and gas.

NATURAL RESOURCES AND INTANGIBLE ASSETS

Acquisition and Depletion of Natural Resources

You may be familiar with some large companies that develop raw materials and products from **natural resources**—assets that occur in nature, such as oil, diamonds, gold, and iron ore (e.g., Suncor Energy Inc., Barrick Gold Corporation). These resources are often called *wasting assets* because they are depleted (i.e., physically used up). Companies that develop natural resources are critical to the economy because they produce essential items, such as lumber for construction and fuel for heating and transportation. Such companies attract considerable public attention because of the significant effect they can have on the environment.

It may surprise you to know that, in Canada, natural resource companies do not own the land from which they extract oil or minerals. They acquire mineral rights from the government to explore, develop, and extract minerals from the land, but they do not own the land itself. When the rights to explore and develop natural resources are acquired, they are recorded in conformity with the cost principle. The land remains the common property of Canadians. This is one reason why concerned citizens often read financial statements from companies involved in mineral exploration, development, and extraction to determine the amount of money spent to protect and remediate any damage done to the environment.

Through exploration, the company estimates the value of the resources extracted and sold throughout their productive lives. The quantity of resources in the reserve is carefully surveyed by using sophisticated geological engineering methods. The initial reserve value is then depleted, or allocated on a systematic and rational basis to match the expected revenue generated from the sale of the resources, known as **depletion**.[8]

> **DEPLETION** is the systematic and rational allocation of the cost of a natural resource over the period of exploitation.

Often these companies keep the reserve value separate from other property, plant, and equipment values incurred, because the companies may have to construct special roads and erect housing, buildings, and facilities in remote locations to extract the resources. When the site is put into production, these accumulated costs will be depreciated over the productive life of the site. Thus, natural resource companies amortize the acquisition costs of intangible mineral rights, deplete their reserve values, and depreciate exploration and development costs as well as self-constructed extraction facilities.

Assume that an oil company determined the depletion of one of its oil reserves to be $6,000,000 for the current year. The journal entry to record the depletion of oil reserves, and the transaction effects are as follows:

Oil inventory (A)		6,000,000		
Oil reserves (A)			6,000,000	
(or Accumulated depletion XA)				
Assets	**=**	**Liabilities**	**+**	**Shareholders' Equity**
Oil inventory +6,000,000				
Oil reserves −6,000,000				
(or Accumulated depletion)				

Note that the amount of the natural resource that is depleted is capitalized as inventory, not expensed. When the inventory is sold, the cost of sales is then included as an expense on the statement of earnings.

A *depletion rate* is computed by dividing the total acquisition and development cost (less any estimated residual value, which is rare) by the estimated units that can be withdrawn, economically, from the resource. The depletion rate is multiplied each period by the actual number of units withdrawn during the accounting period. This procedure is the same as the units-of-production method of calculating depreciation.

When buildings and similar improvements are acquired for the development and exploitation of a natural resource, they should be recorded in separate asset accounts and depreciated—not depleted. Their estimated useful lives cannot be longer than the time needed to exploit the natural resource, unless they have a significant use after the source is depleted.

Acquisition and Amortization of Intangible Assets

Intangible assets are increasingly important resources for organizations. An intangible asset has value because of certain rights and privileges conferred by law on its owner. An intangible asset has no material or physical substance. Examples include mineral rights to explore and develop land, landing rights for time slots at airports, patents, trademarks, and licences. Intangible assets are usually evidenced by a legal document. The growth in the importance of intangible assets has resulted from the tremendous expansion in computer information systems and Web technologies. In fact, many lawyers specialize in finding potential targets for patent infringement lawsuits for their clients.

Intangible assets are recorded at historical cost only if they are purchased. If an intangible asset is developed internally, the cost of development is normally recorded as an expense. Upon acquisition of intangible assets, managers determine whether the separate intangibles have definite or indefinite lives.

Definite Life   The cost of an intangible with a definite life is allocated on a straight-line basis each period over its useful life in a process called **amortization** that is similar to depreciation and depletion. However, most companies do not estimate a residual value for their intangible assets. Let us assume a company purchases a patent for $800,000 and intends to uses it for 20 years. The adjusting entry to record $40,000 in patent amortization expense ($800,000 ÷ 20 years) is as follows:

> **AMORTIZATION** is the systematic and rational allocation of the acquisition cost of an intangible asset over its useful life.

Patent amortization expense (E)	40,000	
Patent (A) (or Accumulated amortization XA)		40,000

Amortization expense is included on the statement of earnings, and the intangible assets are reported at cost less accumulated amortization on the statement of financial position.

Indefinite Life   Intangible assets with indefinite lives are *not amortized*. Instead, these assets are to be tested at least annually for possible impairment, and the asset's carrying amount is written down (decreased) to its recoverable amount if impaired. The two-step process is similar to that used for other long-lived assets, including intangibles with definite lives.

Let us assume a company purchases for $120,000 cash a copyright that is expected to have an indefinite life. At the end of the current year, management determines that the fair value of the copyright is $90,000. The $30,000 loss ($120,000 carrying amount less $90,000 fair value) is recorded as follows:

Loss due to impairment (SE)	30,000	
Copyright (A)		30,000

Examples of Intangible Assets

Many Canadian companies disclose information about goodwill and other intangible assets in their annual reports. These intangibles include broadcast rights, publishing rights, trademarks, patents, licences, customer lists, franchises, and purchased research and development. For example, WestJet provided the following details on its intangible assets of $63.5 million in the notes to its 2015 annual report:

NOTES TO CONSOLIDATED FINANCIAL STATEMENTS

7. Intangible assets

December 31, 2015	Cost	Accumulated Amortization	Net Book Value
Software	85,348	(55,707)	29,641
Landing rights	17,781	(3,186)	14,595
Other	5,836	(227)	5,609
Assets under development	13,704	–	13,704
	122,669	(59,120)	63,549

Source: WestJet Airlines Ltd., Annual Report 2015.

> For accounting purposes, **GOODWILL (COST IN EXCESS OF NET ASSETS ACQUIRED)** is the excess of the purchase price of a business over the market value of its identifiable assets and liabilities.

Goodwill   By far, the most frequently reported intangible asset is **goodwill (cost in excess of net assets acquired)**. The term *goodwill*, as used by most business people, means the favourable reputation that a company has with its customers. Goodwill arises from factors such as customer confidence, reputation for good service and quality products, and financial standing. For example, WestJet's promise to deliver no-frills, friendly, reliable transportation combines factors that produce customer loyalty and repeated travel. From its first day of operations, a successful business continuously builds its own goodwill through a combination of factors that cannot be sold separately. In this context, goodwill is said to be internally generated and is not reported as an asset.

The only way to report goodwill as an asset is to purchase another business. Often, the purchase price of a business exceeds the fair market value of all of the identifiable assets owned by the business minus all of the identifiable liabilities owed to others. Why would a company pay more to acquire a business as a whole than it would pay if it bought the assets individually? The answer is to obtain its goodwill. It may be easy for a company to buy a fleet of aircraft, but it would not generate the same level of revenue flying the same routes as if it acquired the goodwill associated with WestJet's brand name.

For accounting purposes, goodwill is defined as the difference between the purchase price of a company as a whole and the fair market value of its net assets (all identifiable assets minus all identifiable liabilities):

Purchase price
− Fair market value of identifiable assets and liabilities
Goodwill to be reported

In many acquisitions, the amount recorded as goodwill can be very large. For example, CGI Group Inc., a leading provider of information technology and business solutions, has completed several acquisitions over the years. The company reported an amount of $7,137 million for goodwill as at September 30, 2015, representing 60.5 percent of its total assets at that time.

Companies that reported goodwill related to acquisitions prior to July 1, 2001, were required to amortize it over an estimated useful life (not to exceed 40 years) by using the straight-line method. IFRS consider goodwill to have an indefinite life, but any subsequent impairment in its value should be written down. This leads to the recognition of a loss that is reported as a separate item on the statement of earnings in the year the impairment occurs.

Trademarks A **trademark** is an exclusive legal right to use a name, image, or slogan identified with a product or a company. For example, banks such as the Bank of Montreal, auto manufacturers such as Toyota and General Motors, and fast-food restaurant chains such as Pizza Hut have familiar trademarks. Trademarks are protected by law when they are registered at the Canadian Intellectual Property Office of Industry Canada. The protection of a trademark provides the registered holder with exclusive rights to the trademark and can be renewed every 15 years throughout its life. Trademarks are often some of the most valuable assets that a company can own, but they are rarely seen on statements of financial position. The reason is simple—intangible assets are not recorded unless they are purchased. Companies often spend millions of dollars developing trademarks, but these expenditures are recorded as expenses and not capitalized. Purchased trademarks that have definite lives are amortized on a straight-line basis over their estimated useful life, up to a maximum period of 40 years.

> A **TRADEMARK** is an exclusive legal right to use a special name, image, or slogan.

Patents A **patent** is an exclusive right granted by the Canadian Intellectual Property Office of Industry Canada for a period of 20 years. It is typically granted to a person who invents a new product or discovers a new process. The patent enables the owner to use, manufacture, and sell both the subject of the patent and the patent itself. Without the protection of a patent, inventors would likely be unwilling to develop new products. The patent prevents a competitor from simply copying a new invention or discovery until the inventor has had a period of time to earn an economic return on the new product.

> A **PATENT** is granted by the federal government for an invention; it is an exclusive right given to the owner to use, manufacture, and sell the subject of the patent.

A patent that is *purchased* is recorded at cost. An *internally developed* patent is recorded at only its registration and legal costs because IFRS require the immediate expensing of research and development costs. Development costs can, however, be capitalized if specific conditions are satisfied. In conformity with the matching process, the cost of a patent must be amortized over the shorter of its economic life and its remaining legal life.

Eastman Kodak Company, a pioneer in the photography business, has developed many patents since it was formed in 1889. These internally developed patents have been quite valuable to the company, but they are not reported as assets on its statements of financial position because their valuation would have been subjective in the absence of an exchange transaction or an active market for such patents. In February 2013, the company sold its digital imaging patents for approximately US$530 million in order to reduce its debt.

A **COPYRIGHT** is the exclusive right to publish, use, and sell a literary, musical, or artistic work.

Copyrights   **Copyright** protection is also granted by the Canadian Intellectual Property Office. It gives the owner the exclusive right to publish, use, and sell a literary, musical, or artistic piece of work for a period not exceeding 50 years after the author's death. The book that you are reading has a copyright to protect the publisher and the authors. It is illegal, for example, for an instructor to copy several chapters from this book and hand them out in class. The same principles, guidelines, and procedures used in accounting for the cost of patents are also used for copyrights.

A **FRANCHISE** is a contractual right to sell certain products or services, use certain trademarks, or perform activities in a geographical region.

Franchises   A **franchise** is a contractual right to sell certain products or services, use certain trademarks, or perform activities in a geographical region. Franchises may be granted by either the government or other businesses for a specified period and purpose. A city may grant one company a franchise to distribute gas to homes for heating purposes, or a company may sell franchises, such as the right for a local outlet to operate a Quiznos restaurant. Franchise agreements are contracts that can have a variety of provisions. They usually require an investment by the franchisee; therefore, they should be accounted for as intangible assets. The life of the franchise agreement depends on the contract. It may be for a single year or an indefinite period.

The Second Cup, for example, had 278 franchisee-operated and 32 company-operated cafés by the end of fiscal year 2015. The company provides franchisees with training, products, services, and operational support to enable them to maximize their business potential. In exchange for the services it provides to franchisees, the company collects royalty payments consisting of a specific percentage of the gross sales reported by the franchisees.

TECHNOLOGY includes costs for computer software and Web development.

Technology   The number of companies reporting a **technology** intangible asset has increased significantly in recent years. Computer software and Web development costs are becoming increasingly significant as companies modernize their processes and make greater use of advances in information and communication technology. For example, internally developed and externally acquired software represented about 47 percent of the carrying amount of intangibles reported by WestJet Airlines as at December 31, 2015.

LICENCES AND OPERATING RIGHTS, obtained through agreements with governmental units and agencies, permit owners to use public property in performing their services.

Licences and Operating Rights   **Licences and operating rights** are typically obtained through agreements with governmental units or agencies, and permit the holders to use public property in performing their services. For airline companies, the operating rights are authorized landing slots that are regulated by the government and are in limited supply at many airports. They are intangible assets that can be bought and sold by the airlines. Other types of licences that grant permission to companies include airwaves for radio and television broadcasts, and land for cable and telephone lines.

Research and Development Expense—Not an Intangible Asset   If an intangible asset is developed internally, the cost of research is recorded as an expense. When a company can demonstrate that technical and commercial feasibility of the resulting product or service has been established, then development costs can be deferred and amortized over the lifetime of the commercialized product. For example, Bombardier, a Canadian manufacturer of planes and trains, capitalized in 2015 an amount of $1.624 million in development expenditures related to its aerospace program tooling:

REAL-WORLD EXCERPT

Bombardier
ANNUAL REPORT

NOTES TO THE CONSOLIDATED FINANCIAL STATEMENTS

2. Summary of Significant Accounting Policies

Intangible assets

Internally generated intangible assets include development costs (mostly aircraft prototype design and testing costs) and internally developed or modified application software. These costs are capitalized when certain criteria for deferral such as proven technical feasibility are met. The costs of internally generated intangible assets include the cost of materials, direct labour, manufacturing overheads, and borrowing costs.

Source: Bombardier Inc., Annual Report 2015.

Leaseholds   A **Leasehold** is the right granted in a contract called a *lease* to use a specific asset. Leasing is a common type of business contract. For a consideration called *rent*, the owner (lessor) extends to another party (lessee) certain rights to use specified property. Leases may vary from simple arrangements, such as the month-to-month (*operating*) lease of an office or the daily rental of an automobile, to long-lived (*capital*) leases having complex contractual arrangements.

A **LEASEHOLD** is the right granted to a lessee under a lease contract.

Lessees sometimes make significant improvements to a leased property when they enter into a long-term lease agreement. A company that agrees to lease office space on a 15-year lease may install new fixtures or move walls to make the space more useful. These improvements are called *leasehold improvements* and are recorded as an asset by the lessee despite the fact that the lessor usually owns the leasehold improvements at the end of the lease term. The cost of leasehold improvements should be amortized over the estimated useful life of the related improvements or the remaining life of the lease, whichever is shorter.

PRODUCTIVE ASSETS AND DEPRECIATION

FOCUS ON
CASH FLOWS

Effect on Statement of Cash Flows

The indirect method for preparing the operating activities section of the statement of cash flows involves reconciling net earnings (reported on the statement of earnings) to cash flows from operations. This means that, among other adjustments, (1) revenues and expenses that do not affect cash and (2) gains and losses that relate to investing or financing activities (not operations) should be eliminated. When depreciation is recorded, no cash payment is made (i.e., there is no credit to cash). Since depreciation expense (a non-cash expense) is subtracted from revenues in calculating net earnings, it must be added back to net earnings to eliminate its effect.

Gains and losses on disposal of long-lived assets represent the difference between cash proceeds and the carrying amount of the assets disposed of. Hence, gains and losses are non-cash amounts that do not relate to operating activities, but they are included in the computation of net earnings. Therefore, gains are subtracted from net earnings and losses are added to net earnings in the computation of cash flow from operations.

Effect on Statement of Cash Flows

IN GENERAL → Acquiring, selling, and depreciating long-lived assets affect a company's cash flows as indicated in the following table:

LO8-7

Explain the impact on cash flows of the acquisition, use, and disposal of long-lived assets.

	Effect on Cash Flows
Operating activities (indirect method)	
Net earnings	$xxx
Adjusted for:	
Depreciation expense	+
Gains on disposal of long-lived assets	−
Losses on disposal of long-lived assets	+
Losses due to asset impairment write downs	+
Investing activities	
Purchase of long-lived assets	−
Sale of long-lived assets	+

FOCUS COMPANY ANALYSIS → Exhibit 8.5 shows a condensed version of WestJet's statement of cash flows prepared using the indirect method. Buying and selling long-lived assets are investing activities. In 2015, WestJet used $906,280,000 in cash to purchase aircraft and other property and equipment. Since selling long-lived assets is not an operating activity, any gains (losses) on the sale of long-lived assets that are included in net earnings are deducted from (added to) net earnings in the operating activities section to eliminate the effect of the sale. Unless they are large, these gain and loss adjustments are normally not specifically highlighted on the statement of cash flows. WestJet reports a loss of $1,860,000 on its statement of cash flows for 2015.

Finally, in capital-intensive industries such as airlines, depreciation and amortization expense is a significant non-cash expense. In WestJet's case, depreciation and amortization expense is the single largest adjustment to net earnings in determining cash flows from operations. It was 39.3 percent of operating cash flows in 2014 but dropped to 30.2 percent in 2015.

Exhibit 8.5

WestJet Statement of Cash Flows

REAL-WORLD EXCERPT

WestJet Airlines Ltd.

2015 ANNUAL REPORT

Consolidated Statement of Cash Flows
For the years ended December 31
(in thousands of Canadian dollars)

	2015	2014
Operating activities:		
Net earnings	$367,530	$283,957
Items not involving cash:		
Depreciation and amortization	264,921	226,740
Change in maintenance provisions	35,786	8,413
Loss (gain) on disposal of property and equipment	1,860	48,332
Other adjustments (summarized)	206,344	9,221
	876,441	576,663
Investing activities:		
Aircraft additions	(841,491)	(694,200)
Aircraft disposals	83,348	75,655
Other property and equipment and intangible additions	(64,789)	(46,586)
	(822,932)	(665,131)

Source: WestJet Airlines Ltd., Annual Report 2015.

A MISINTERPRETATION

FINANCIAL ANALYSIS

Some analysts misinterpret the meaning of a non-cash expense and often say that "cash is provided by depreciation." Although depreciation is added in the operating section of the statement of cash flows, *depreciation is not a source of cash*. Cash from operations can be provided only by selling goods and services. A company with a large amount of depreciation expense does not generate more cash compared with a company that reports a small amount of depreciation expense, assuming that they are exactly the same in every other respect. While depreciation expense reduces the amount of reported net earnings for a company, it does not reduce the amount of cash generated by the company, because it is a non-cash expense. Remember that the effects of recording depreciation are a reduction in shareholders' equity (debit to depreciation expense) and in long-lived assets (credit to accumulated depreciation), not in cash. That is why, on the statement of cash flows, depreciation expense is added back to net earnings (on an accrual basis) to compute cash flows from operations (net earnings on a cash basis).

Although depreciation is a non-cash expense, the *depreciation method used for tax purposes can affect a company's cash flows*. For tax purposes, the Income Tax Act requires companies to use a capital cost allowance (CCA), a form of depreciation based on the declining-balance method. The higher the amount of CCA reported by a company for tax purposes, the lower the taxable income and the income taxes it must pay. Because taxes must be paid in cash, a reduction in the tax obligation of a company reduces the company's cash outflows.

The maximum deduction for CCA for each class of assets is based on rates specified by the Canada Revenue Agency, but corporations may choose to deduct lower amounts for CCA during periods of losses or low earnings before taxes, and postpone CCA deductions to future years to minimize their income tax obligations.

ACCOUNTING STANDARDS FOR PRIVATE ENTERPRISES

Accounting standards for private enterprises differ from IFRS in two main areas: (1) measurement of property, plant, and equipment and (2) measurement of impairment losses.

Financial Reporting Issue	IFRS	ASPE
Measurement of property, plant, and equipment	Canadian publicly accountable enterprises may use either the cost model or the revaluation model to measure property, plant, and equipment subsequent to acquisition. Increases in fair value are recorded if the revaluation model is used. However, most companies use the cost model.	The cost model must be used to report property, plant, and equipment, and increases in their fair values are not recorded.
Measurement of impairment of long-lived assets	The asset's carrying amount is compared to its recoverable amount (the higher of the asset's value in use and its fair value less costs to sell) to determine if an impairment has occurred.	The asset's carrying amount is compared to its fair value less costs to sell to determine if impairment occurred.
	An impairment loss can be reversed if the asset's recoverable amount subsequently increases.	An impairment loss cannot be reversed if the asset's fair value subsequently increases.
	Impairment testing is required for each reporting date.	Impairment testing is required only if impairment is suspected.

DEMONSTRATION CASE A

Diversified Industries started as a residential construction company. In recent years, it expanded into heavy construction, ready-mix concrete, construction supplies, and earth-moving services.

The following transactions were selected from those completed during 2017. They focus on the primary issues discussed in this chapter.

2017

January 1	Management decided to buy a building that was about 10 years old. The location was excellent, and there was adequate parking. The company bought the building and the land on which it was situated for $305,000. It paid $100,000 in cash and signed a mortgage note payable for the rest. A reliable appraiser provided the following market values: land, $132,300, and building, $182,700.
January 12	Paid renovation costs on the building of $38,100, prior to use.
July 10	Paid $1,200 for ordinary repairs on the building.
Dec. 31	Year-end adjustments:

   a. The building will be depreciated on a straight-line basis over an estimated useful life of 30 years. The estimated residual value is $35,000.

   b. The company owns a patent right that is used in operations. On January 1, 2017, the patent account had a balance of $3,300. The patent has an estimated remaining useful life of six years (including 2017).

   c. At the beginning of the year, the company owned equipment with a cost of $650,000 and a carrying amount of $500,000. The equipment is being depreciated by using the double-declining-balance method, with a useful life of 20 years with no residual value.

   d. At year-end, the company identified a piece of old excavation equipment with a cost of $156,000 and remaining carrying amount of $120,000. Due to its smaller size and lack of safety features, the old equipment has limited use. The company reviewed the asset for possible impairment of value. The equipment's fair value less costs to sell is $40,000, and its value in use was determined at $38,000.

Required:

1. Indicate the accounts affected and the amount and direction (+ for increase and − for decrease) of the effect for each of the preceding events on the basic accounting equation. Use the following headings:

Date	Assets	=	Liabilities	+	Shareholders' Equity

2. Record the adjusting journal entries based on the information for December 31 ([a] and [b] only).

3. Show the December 31, 2017, statement of financial position classifications and amount for each of the following items:

   Property, plant, and equipment—land, building, and equipment

   Intangible asset—patent

4. Assuming that the company had sales of $1,000,000 for the year and a carrying amount of $500,000 for property, plant, and equipment at the beginning of the year, compute the fixed asset turnover ratio. Explain its meaning.

We strongly recommend that you prepare your own answers to these requirements and then check your answers with the following solution.

SUGGESTED **SOLUTION**

1.

Date	Assets		Liabilities		Shareholders Equity	
Jan. 1 (1)	Cash	−100,000	Note payable	+205,000		
	Land	+128,100				
	Building	+176,900				
Jan. 12 (2)	Cash	−38,100				
	Building	+38,100				
July 10 (3)	Cash	−1,200			Repairs expense	−1,200
Dec. 31 a (4)	Accumulated depreciation	−6,000			Depreciation expense	−6,000
Dec. 31 b (5)	Patent	−550			Amortization expense	−550
Dec. 31 c (6)	Accumulated depreciation	−50,000			Depreciation expense	−50,000
Dec. 31 d (7)	Equipment	−80,000			Loss due to asset impairment	−80,000

(1)

	Land		Building		Total
Market	$132,300	+	$182,700	=	$315,000
Percentage of total	42%	+	58%	=	100%
Cost	$128,100	+	$176,900	=	$305,000

(2) Capitalize the expenditure of $38,100 because it is necessary to prepare the asset for use.

(3) This is a natural resource.

(4) This is an ordinary repair (revenue expenditure) that should be expensed.

(5)

Cost of building		Straight-line depreciation
Initial payment	$176,900	Depreciation = ($215,000 − $35,000)/30 years
Repairs prior to use	38,100	= $6,000 annually
Acquisition cost	$215,000	

(6)

Straight-line depreciation

Unamortized cost of patent	$3,300
Remaining useful life	÷ 6 years
	$ 550

(7)

Asset impairment

Carrying amount of old equipment	$120,000
Recoverable amount	−40,000
Loss due to impairment	$ 80,000

2. Adjusting entries December 31, 2017:

a.	Depreciation expense, building (E)	6,000	
	Accumulated depreciation (XA)		6,000
b.	Depreciation expense, building (E)	50,000	
	Accumulated depreciation (A)		50,000

3. Statement of financial position, December 31, 2017:

Assets		
Property, plant, and equipment		
Land		$128,100
Building	$215,000	
Less: Accumulated depreciation	6,000	209,000
Equipment ($650,000 − $80,000)	570,000	
Less: Accumulated depreciation ($150,000 + $50,000)	200,000	370,000
Total		707,100
Intangible asset		
Patent ($3,300 − $550)		2,750

4. Fixed asset turnover ratio:

$$\frac{\text{Net sales}}{\text{Average net fixed assets}} = \frac{\$1,000,000}{(\$500,000 + \$707,100) \div 2} = 1.66$$

This construction company is capital intensive. The fixed asset turnover ratio measures the company's efficiency at using its investment in property, plant, and equipment to generate sales.

DEMONSTRATION CASE B

In 2018, Diversified Industries, a residential construction company, acquired a gravel pit (designated Gravel Pit No. 1) to support its construction operations. The company completed the following transactions during 2018 related to the gravel pit. Amounts have been simplified and the company's fiscal year ends on December 31.

June 19	Bought Gravel Pit No. 1 for $50,000 cash. The location had been carefully surveyed. It was estimated that 100,000 cubic metres of gravel could be removed from the deposit.
August 1	Paid $10,000 for costs of preparing the new gravel pit for exploitation.
November 10	12,000 cubic metres of gravel were removed from Gravel Pit No. 1 to be sold in 2019.

Required:

Record the transactions that occurred on June 19, August 1, and November 10.

We strongly recommend that you prepare your own answers to these requirements and then check your answers with the following solution.

SUGGESTED **SOLUTION**

Date	Accounts	Debit	Credit
June 19	Gravel Pit No. 1 (A)	50,000	
	Cash (A)		50,000
Aug. 1	Gravel Pit No. 1 (A)	10,000	
	Cash (A)		10,000
Nov. 10*	Inventory – gravel (A)	7,200	
	Gravel Pit No. 1 (A)		7,200

*Cost of gravel pit		Units-of-production depletion
Initial purchase price	$50,000	Depletion rate = $60,000/100,000 = $0.60 per cubic metre
Preparation costs	10,000	Depletion amount = 12,000 × $0.60 = $7,200
Total cost	$60,000	Capitalize this amount to gravel inventory.

CHAPTER **TAKE-AWAYS**

8-1. Define, classify, and explain the nature of long-lived assets, and interpret the fixed asset turnover ratio.

a. Non-current assets are those that a business retains for long periods of time, for use in the course of normal operations rather than for sale. They may be divided into tangible assets (land, buildings, equipment, natural resources) and intangible assets (including goodwill, patents, and franchises).

b. The cost allocation method utilized affects the amount of net property, plant, and equipment that is used in the computation of the fixed asset turnover ratio. Accelerated methods reduce book value and increase the turnover ratio.

8-2. Apply the cost principle to measure the acquisition and maintenance of property, plant, and equipment.

The acquisition cost of property, plant, and equipment is the cash-equivalent purchase price plus all reasonable and necessary expenditures made to acquire and prepare the asset for its intended use. These assets may be acquired by using cash, debt, or equity, or through self-construction. Expenditures made after the asset is in use are either capital expenditures or revenue expenditures:

a. Capital expenditures provide benefits for one or more accounting periods beyond the current period. Amounts are debited to the appropriate asset accounts and depreciated or depleted over their useful lives.

b. Revenue expenditures provide benefits during the current accounting period only. Amounts are debited to appropriate current expense accounts when the expenses are incurred.

8-3. Apply various depreciation methods as assets are held and used over time.

Cost allocation methods: In conformity with the matching process, cost (less any estimated residual value) is allocated to periodic expense over the periods benefited. Because of

depreciation, the carrying amount of an asset declines over time and net earnings is reduced by the amount of the expense. Common depreciation methods include straight line (a constant amount over time), units of production (a variable amount over time), and double declining balance (a decreasing amount over time).
- Depreciation—buildings and equipment
- Depletion—natural resources
- Amortization—intangibles

8-4. Explain the effect of asset impairment on the financial statements.

When events or changes in circumstances reduce the estimated future cash flows of long-lived assets below their carrying amounts, the carrying amounts should be written down (by recording a loss) to the fair value of the assets.

8-5. Analyze the disposal of property, plant, and equipment.

When assets are disposed of through sale or abandonment,
- Record additional depreciation since the last adjustment was made.
- Remove the cost of the old asset and its related accumulated depreciation or depletion.
- Recognize the cash proceeds.
- Recognize any gains or losses when the asset's carrying amount is not equal to the cash received.

8-6. Apply measurement and reporting concepts for natural resources and intangible assets.

The cost principle should be applied in recording the acquisition of natural resources and intangible assets. Natural resources should be depleted (usually by the units-of-production method) with the amount of the depletion expense usually capitalized to an inventory account. Intangibles with definite useful lives are amortized by using the straight-line method. Intangibles with indefinite useful lives, including goodwill, are not amortized, but are reviewed at least annually for impairment. Intangibles are reported at their carrying amount on the statement of financial position.

8-7. Explain the impact on cash flows of the acquisition, use, and disposal of long-lived assets.

Depreciation expense is a non-cash expense that has no effect on cash. It is added back to net earnings on the statement of cash flows to determine cash from operations. Acquiring and disposing of long-lived assets are investing activities.

In the previous chapters, we discussed business and accounting issues related to the assets a company holds. In Chapters 9, 10, and 11, we shift our focus to the other side of the statement of financial position to see how managers finance the operations of their business and the acquisition of productive assets. We discuss various types of liabilities in Chapters 9 and 10 and examine owners' equity in Chapter 11.

KEY **RATIO**

The fixed asset turnover ratio measures how efficiently a company utilizes its investment in property, plant, and equipment over time. The company's ratio can be compared to the ratio of its competitors. It is computed as follows):

$$\text{Fixed asset turnover ratio} = \frac{\text{Net sales (or operating revenues)}}{\text{Average net fixed assets}}$$

FINDING **FINANCIAL INFORMATION**

STATEMENT OF FINANCIAL POSITION	**STATEMENT OF EARNINGS**
Under Long-Lived Assets	**Under Operating Expenses**
Property, plant, and equipment (net of accumulated depreciation)	Depreciation, amortization, and depletion expense *or* as part of
Natural resources (net of accumulated depletion)	Selling, general, and administrative expenses and
Intangibles (net of accumulated amortization)	Cost of sales (with the amount of depreciation expense disclosed in a note)

STATEMENT OF CASH FLOWS
Under Operating Activities (indirect method)
Net earnings
+ Depreciation and amortization expense
− Gains on sales of assets
+ Losses on sales of assets
Under Investing Activities
+ Sales of assets for cash
− Purchases of assets for cash

NOTES
Under Summary of Significant Accounting Policies
Description of management's choice of depreciation methods, including useful lives, and the amount of annual depreciation expense, if not listed on the statement of earnings
Under a Separate Footnote
If not specified on the statement of financial position, a listing of the major classifications of long-lived assets at cost and the balance in accumulated depreciation, amortization, and depletion

QUESTIONS

1. Define long-lived assets. Why are they considered a "bundle of future services"?
2. How is the fixed asset turnover ratio computed? Explain its meaning.
3. What are the classifications of long-lived assets? Explain each.
4. Relate the cost principle to accounting for long-lived assets. Under the cost principle, what amounts should usually be included in the acquisition cost of a long-lived asset?
5. Describe the relationship between the matching process and accounting for long-lived assets.
6. What is a basket purchase? What measurement problem does it pose?
7. Distinguish between
    a. Capital expenditures and revenue expenditures. How is each accounted for?
    b. Ordinary and extraordinary repairs. How is each accounted for?
8. Distinguish between depreciation and depletion.
9. In computing depreciation, three values must be known or estimated; identify and explain the nature of each.
10. Estimated useful life and residual value of a long-lived asset relate to the current owner or user rather than all potential users. Explain this statement.
11. What type of depreciation expense pattern is provided under each of the following methods? When is the use of each method appropriate?
    a. Straight line
    b. Units of production
    c. Double declining balance
12. Over what period should an addition to an existing long-lived asset be depreciated? Explain.
13. What is an asset impairment? How is it accounted for?
14. What is componentization and how is it used?
15. Define intangible asset. What period should be used to amortize an intangible asset?
16. Define goodwill. When is it appropriate to record goodwill as an intangible asset?
17. Explain how research and development expenditures should be accounted for.
18. Why is depreciation expense added to net earnings on the statement of cash flows when using the indirect method of reporting cash flow from operations?

connect MINI-EXERCISES

LO8-1,8-3,8-6 **M8-1** **Classifying Long-Lived Assets and Related Cost Allocation Concepts**
For each of the following long-lived assets, indicate its nature and the related cost allocation concept. Use the following symbols:

Nature		Cost Allocation Concept	
L	Land	DR	Depreciation
B	Building	DP	Depletion
E	Equipment	A	Amortization
NR	Natural resource	NO	No cost allocation
I	Intangible	O	Other
O	Other		

Asset	Nature	Cost Allocation	Asset	Nature	Cost Allocation
(1) Tractors			(6) Operating license		
(2) Land in use			(7) Production plant		
(3) Timber tract			(8) Trademark		
(4) Warehouse			(9) Silver mine		
(5) New engine for old machine			(10) Land held for sale		

LO8-1

M8-2 Computing and Evaluating the Fixed Asset Turnover Ratio

The following information was reported by Young's Air Cargo Service for 2015:

Net fixed assets (beginning of year)	$1,500,000
Net fixed assets (end of year)	2,300,000
Net sales for the year	3,600,000
Net earnings for the year	1,600,000

Compute the company's fixed asset turnover ratio for the year. What can you say about Young's ratio when compared to WestJet's 2015 ratio?

LO8-2

M8-3 Identifying Capital Expenditures and Expenses

For each of the following items, enter the correct letter to the left to show the type of expenditure. Use the following:

Type of Expenditure	Transactions
C Capital expenditure	— (1) Purchased a patent, $4,300 cash.
	— (2) Paid $10,000 for monthly salaries.
E Expense	— (3) Paid cash dividends, $20,000.
N Neither	— (4) Purchased a machine, $7,000; signed a long-term note.
	— (5) Paid premium for a three-year insurance policy, $900.
	— (6) Paid for routine maintenance, $200.
	— (7) Paid $400 for ordinary repairs.
	— (8) Paid $6,000 for improvements that lengthened the asset's productive life.
	— (9) Paid $20,000 cash for addition to old building.

LO8-3

M8-4 Computing Carrying Amount (Straight-Line Depreciation)

Compute the carrying amount of a three-year-old machine that has a cost of $31,000, an estimated residual value of $1,000, and an estimated useful life of five years. The company uses straight-line depreciation.

LO8-3

M8-5 Computing Carrying Amount (Double-Declining-Balance Depreciation)

Compute the carrying amount of a three-year-old machine that has a cost of $55,000, an estimated residual value of $5,000 and an estimated useful life of five years. The company uses double-declining-balance depreciation. Round to the nearest dollar.

LO8-3

M8-6 Computing Carrying Amount (Units-of-Production Depreciation)

Compute the carrying amount of a three-year-old machine that has a cost of $26,000, an estimated residual value of $1,000, and an estimated useful life of 50,000 machine hours. The company uses units-of-production depreciation and ran the machine 3,200 hours in year 1; 7,050 hours in year 2; and 7,500 hours in year 3.

■ LO8-4   **M8-7   Identifying Asset Impairment**

For each of the following scenarios, indicate whether an asset has been impaired (Y for yes and N for no) and, if so, the amount of loss that should be recorded.

		Carrying Amount	Value in Use	Fair Value Less Costs to Sell	Is Asset Impaired?	Amount of Loss
a.	Machine	$ 15,500	$ 10,000	$ 9,500		
b.	Copyright	31,000	41,000	37,900		
c.	Factory building	58,000	29,000	27,000		
d.	Building	227,000	227,000	200,000		

■ LO8-5   **M8-8   Recording the Disposal of a Long-Lived Asset (Straight-Line Depreciation)**

As part of a major renovation at the beginning of the year, Bonham's Bakery sold shelving units (store fixtures) for $1,800 cash. The shelving units that were 10 years old, had a original cost of $6,500 with an estimated residual value of $800 and they had been depreciated on a straight-line basis over an estimated useful life of 12 years. Prepare the journal entry to record the sale of the shelving units.

■ LO8-6   **M8-9   Computing Goodwill and Patents**

Elizabeth Pie Company has been in business for 50 years and has developed a large group of loyal restaurant customers. Giant Bakery Inc. has made an offer to buy Elizabeth Pie Company for $5,000,000. The carrying amount of Elizabeth Pie's recorded assets and liabilities on the date of the offer is $4,300,000 with a fair value of $4,500,000. Elizabeth Pie also holds a patent for a pie crust fluting machine that the company invented. The patent, with a fair value of $300,000, was never recorded by Elizabeth Pie because it was developed internally. The company estimates goodwill from loyal customers to be $310,000 (also never recorded by the company). Should Elizabeth Pie Company management accept Giant Bakery's offer of $5,000,000? If so, compute the amount of goodwill that Giant Bakery should record on the date of the purchase.

■ LO8-7   **M8-10   Preparing the Statement of Cash Flows**

Garrett Company had the following activities for the year ended December 31, 2015: Sold land that cost $20,000 for $20,000 cash; purchased $181,000 of equipment, paying $156,000 in cash and signing a note payable for the rest; and recorded $5,500 in depreciation expense for the year. Net earnings for the year were $18,000. Prepare the operating and investing activities sections of a statement of cash flows for the year based on the data provided.

connect **EXERCISES**

■ LO8-1   **E8-1   Preparing a Partial Classified Statement of Financial Position**

Ballard Power Systems Inc.

The following is a list of account titles and amounts (in thousands) reported by Ballard Power Systems Inc., a leading developer and manufacturer of fuel cells, an alternative power source for automobiles:

Raw materials	$ 8,353	Work in progress	$ 1,820
Leasehold improvements	7,518	Accumulated amortization—Intangibles	41,194
Prepaid expenses	934	Fuel cell technology	43,443
Trade receivables	17,164	Cash and cash equivalents	20,316
Finished goods	3,441	Computer equipment	6,339
Furniture and fixtures	741	Building	15,846
Land	1,220	Short-term investments	25,878
Other long-term assets	1,126	Production and test equipment	47,460
Goodwill	48,106	Accumulated depreciation—Property, plant, and equipment	48,399

Required:

Prepare the asset section of the statement of financial position for Ballard Power Systems Inc., classifying the assets into current assets; property, plant and equipment (net); and other assets.

LO8-1

Apple Inc.

E8-2   **Computing and Interpreting the Fixed Asset Turnover Ratio from a Financial Analyst's Perspective**

The following data were disclosed in the annual reports of Apple Inc., which designs, manufactures, and markets mobile communication and media devices, personal computers, and portable digital music players. Its products include Mac, iPod, iPhone, and iPad, among others.

(in millions of US dollars)	2015	2014	2013	2012	2011
Net sales	$223,715	$182,795	$170,910	$156,508	$108,249
Net property, plant, and equipment	22,471	20,624	16,597	15,452	7,777

Required:

1. Compute Apple's fixed asset turnover ratio for the four years 2012 through 2015.

2. How might a financial analyst interpret the results?

LO8-2

E8-3   **Determining Financial Statement Effects of Acquisition of Several Assets in a Basket Purchase**

Kline Corporation acquired additional land and a building that included several pieces of equipment, for $600,000. The acquisition was settled as follows: cash, $120,000; issuance of Kline's common shares, $120,000; and signing of a long-term note, $360,000. An appraiser estimated the market values to be $200,000 for the land, $500,000 for the building, and $100,000 for the equipment. Indicate the accounts affected and the amount and direction (+ for increase and − for decrease) of the effect of this acquisition on the accounting equation. Use the following headings:

Assets	=	Liabilities	+	Shareholders' Equity

LO8-2,8-3

E8-4   **Computing and Recording Cost and Depreciation of Assets in a Basket Purchase (Straight-Line Depreciation)**

Zeidler Company bought a building and the land on which the building is located for a total cash price of $356,000. The company paid transfer costs of $4,000. Renovation costs on the building were $46,000. An independent appraiser provided market values for the land, $100,000, and building, $300,000 before renovation.

Required:

1. Apportion the cost of the property on the basis of the appraised values. Show computations.

2. Prepare the journal entry to record the purchase of the building and land, including all expenditures. Assume that all transactions were for cash and that all purchases occurred at the start of the year.

3. Compute depreciation of the building at the end of one year, using the straight-line method. Assume an estimated useful life of 12 years and an estimated residual value of $28,000.

4. What would be the carrying amount of the property (building and land) at the end of year 2?

LO8-2,8-3

E8-5   **Determining Financial Statement Effects of an Asset Acquisition and Depreciation (Straight-Line Depreciation)**

The following transactions related to a machine purchased by Ashkar Company in 2018:

March 1	Purchased the machine at an invoice price of $21,000; paid $6,000 cash and signed a note for the balance, payable on October 1, 2018, with annual interest at a rate of 6 percent.
March 3	Paid freight of $1,000.
March 5	Paid installation costs of $2,500.
October 1	Paid the balance due plus the related interest.
December 31	Recorded straight-line depreciation on the machine based on an estimated useful life of 10 years and an estimated residual value of $4,000.

Required (round all amounts to the nearest dollar):

1. Indicate the accounts affected and the amount and direction (+ for increase and − for decrease) of the effect of each transaction (March 1, 3, 5, and October 1) on the accounting equation. Use the following headings:

Date	Assets	=	Liabilities	+	Shareholders' Equity

2. Compute the acquisition cost of the machine.

3. Compute the depreciation expense to be reported for 2018.

4. What is the impact on the cost of the machine of the interest paid on the note? Under what circumstances can interest expense be included in an asset's acquisition cost?

5. What would be the carrying amount of the machine at the end of 2019?

LO8-1, 8-2

Air Canada

E8-6   **Evaluating the Impact of Capitalized Interest on Cash Flows and the Fixed Asset Turnover Ratio from an Analyst's Perspective**

You are a financial analyst charged with evaluating the asset efficiency of companies in the airline industry. The financial statements for Air Canada include the following note:

> **U) INTEREST CAPITALIZED**
>
> Borrowing costs are expensed as incurred. For borrowing costs attributable to the acquisition, construction, or production of an asset that necessarily takes a substantial period of time to get ready for its intended use, in which case they are capitalized as part of the cost of that asset. Capitalization of borrowing costs commences when expenditures for the asset and borrowing costs are being incurred and the activities to prepare the asset for its intended use are in progress. Borrowing costs are capitalized up to the date when the project is completed and the related asset is available for its intended use.

Required:

1. Assume that Air Canada followed this policy for a major construction project this year. What is the direction of the effect of Air Canada's policy on the following? Use + for increase, − for decrease, and NE for no effect.

   a. Cash flows

   b. Fixed asset turnover ratio

2. Normally, how would your answer to (1*b*) affect your evaluation of Air Canada's effectiveness in utilizing property, plant, and equipment?

3. If the fixed asset turnover ratio changes because of interest capitalization, does this change indicate a real change in efficiency? Why or why not?

LO8-3

E8-7   **Recording Depreciation and Repairs (Straight-Line Depreciation), and Determining Financial Statement Effects**

Stacey Company operates a small manufacturing facility as a supplement to its regular service activities. At the beginning of 2018, an asset account for the company showed the following balances:

Manufacturing equipment	$100,000
Accumulated depreciation through 2017	54,000

In early January 2018, the following expenditures were incurred for repairs and maintenance:

Routine maintenance and repairs on the equipment	$ 1,000
Major overhaul of the equipment	12,000

The equipment is being depreciated on a straight-line basis over an estimated life of 15 years, with a $10,000 estimated residual value. The company's fiscal year ends on December 31.

Required:

1. Compute the depreciation expense for the manufacturing equipment for 2017.

2. Prepare the journal entries to record the two expenditures that occurred during 2018.

3. Prepare the adjusting entry at December 31, 2018, to record the depreciation of the manufacturing equipment, assuming no change in the estimated life or residual value of the equipment. Show computations.

4. Indicate the accounts affected, amounts, and direction (+ for increase and − for decrease) of the effects of the journal entries you prepared for (1) to (3) on the accounting equation. Use the following headings:

Date	Assets	=	Liabilities	+	Shareholders' Equity

LO8-3

E8-8 **Computing Depreciation under Alternative Methods**

Purity Ice Cream Company bought a new ice cream maker at the beginning of the year at a cost of $10,000. The estimated useful life was four years, and the residual value was $1,000. Assume that the estimated productive life of the machine was 9,000 hours. Actual annual usage was 3,600 hours in year 1; 2,700 hours in year 2; 1,800 hours in year 3; and 900 hours in year 4.

Required:

1. Complete a separate depreciation schedule for each of the alternative methods. Round your computations to the nearest dollar.

   a. Straight line

   b. Units of production

   c. Double declining balance

Method: _____				
Year	**Computation**	**Depreciation Expense**	**Accumulated Depreciation**	**Carrying Amount**
At acquisition				
1				
2				
Etc.				

2. Assuming that the machine was used directly in the production of one of the products that the company manufactures and sells, what factors might management consider in selecting a preferable depreciation method in conformity with the matching process?

LO8-3

E8-9 **Computing Depreciation under Alternative Methods**

Sterling Steel Company purchased a new stamping machine at the beginning of the year at a cost of $580,000. The estimated residual value was $60,000. Assume that the estimated useful life was five years and the estimated productive life of the machine was 260,000 units. Actual annual production was as follows:

Year	1	2	3	4	5
Units	73,000	62,000	30,000	53,000	42,000

Required:

1. Complete a separate depreciation schedule for each of the alternative methods. Round your computations to the nearest dollar.

   a. Straight line

   b. Units of production

   c. Double declining balance

Method: _____				
Year	**Computation**	**Depreciation Expense**	**Accumulated Depreciation**	**Carrying Amount**
At acquisition				
1				
2				
Etc.				

2. Assuming that the machine was used directly in the production of one of the products that the company manufactures and sells, what factors might management consider in selecting a preferable depreciation method in conformity with the matching process?

LO8-3

General Motors
Corporation

E8-10 **Explaining Depreciation Policy**

The 2011 annual report for General Motors Corporation contained the following note:

> **Note 4. Significant Accounting Policies**
>
> *Property, net*
>
> Property, plant, and equipment, including internal use software, is recorded at cost. Major improvements that extend the useful life or add functionality of property are capitalized. The gross amount of assets under capital leases is included in property, plant, and equipment. Expenditures for repairs and maintenance are charged to expense as incurred. We depreciate all depreciable property using the straight-line method. Leasehold improvements are amortized over the period of lease or the life of the asset, whichever is shorter. For depreciable property placed in service before January 2001, Old GM used accelerated depreciation methods. For depreciable property placed in service after January 2001, Old GM used the straight-line method. The amortization of the assets under capital leases is included in depreciation expense. Upon retirement or disposition of property, plant and equipment, the cost and related accumulated depreciation are removed from the accounts and any resulting gain or loss is recorded in earnings. Impairment charges related to property are recorded in automotive cost of sales or GM Financial operating and other expenses.

Required:

Why do you think the company changed its depreciation method for depreciable property placed in service after January 1, 2001, and subsequent years?

LO8-3

FedEx Corporation

E8-11   Interpreting Management's Choice of Different Depreciation Methods for Tax and Financial Reporting

An annual report for FedEx Corporation included the following information:

> For financial reporting purposes, we record depreciation and amortization of property and equipment on a straight-line basis over the asset's service life or the related lease term. For income tax purposes, depreciation is generally computed using accelerated methods when applicable.

Required:

Explain why FedEx uses different methods of depreciation for financial reporting and tax purposes.

LO8-3,8-7

E8-12   Computing Depreciation and Carrying Amount for Two Years by Using Alternative Depreciation Methods, and Interpreting the Impact on Cash Flows

Schrade Company bought a machine for $96,000 cash. The estimated useful life was four years, and the estimated residual value was $6,000. Assume that the estimated useful life is 120,000 units. Units actually produced were 43,000 in year 1 and 45,000 in year 2.

Required:

1. Determine the appropriate amounts to complete the following schedule. Show computations, and round to the nearest dollar.

Method of Depreciation	Depreciation Expense for		Carrying Amount at the End of	
	Year 1	Year 2	Year 1	Year 2
Straight line				
Units of production				
Double declining balance				

2. Which method would result in the lowest earnings per share for year 1? For year 2?

3. Which method would result in the highest amount of cash outflows in year 1? Why?

4. Indicate the effects of (a) acquiring the machine and (b) recording annual depreciation on the operating and investing activities on the statement of cash flows for year 1. Assume that straight-line depreciation is used.

LO8-4,8-5

E8-13   Inferring Asset Impairment and Recording Disposal of Assets

Fashion House Ltd. designs, manufactures, and markets clothing products for both women and men. The company conducted an impairment test for its property and equipment at December 31, 2016, the end of its fiscal year, and determined that the property and equipment were impaired. The effects of the company's transactions related to property and equipment during 2016 and the impairment losses are reflected in the following information.

	Dollars in Thousands
Cost of property and equipment, January 1, 2016	$43,742
Cost of property and equipment, December 31, 2016	42,846
Additions to property and equipment during the year	3,974
Accumulated depreciation and impairment losses, January 1, 2016	29,338
Accumulated depreciation and impairment losses, December 31, 2016	27,834
Depreciation expense during the year	3,300
Cost of equipment sold during the year	4,870
Accumulated depreciation on equipment sold	4,870
Cash received on equipment sold	65

Required:

1. Reconstruct the journal entry for the disposal of equipment during the year.

2. Compute the amount of property and equipment that Fashion House Ltd. wrote off as impaired during the year. Fashion House records impairment losses as adjustments to accumulated depreciation. (*Hint:* Set up T-accounts.)

■ LO8-5   **E8-14**   **Recording the Disposal of an Asset and Financial Statement Effects**

FedEx Corporation

FedEx Corporation is a global leader in express distribution. It has the world's largest fleet of all-cargo aircraft and thousands of vehicles and trailers to pick up and deliver packages. Assume that FedEx sold a small delivery truck that had been used in the business for three years. The records of the company reflect the following:

Delivery truck	$38,000
Accumulated depreciation	23,000

Required:

1. Prepare the journal entry to record the disposal of the truck and the related transaction effects, assuming that the sales price was (a) $15,000, (b) $15,600, and (c) $14,600.

2. Based on the three preceding situations, explain the effects of the disposal of an asset on financial statements.

■ LO8-5   **E8-15**   **Recording the Disposal of an Asset at Three Different Sale Prices**

Marriott International

Marriott International is a worldwide operator and franchisor of hotels and related lodging facilities totalling over $1.4 billion in property and equipment. It also develops, operates, and markets time-share properties totalling nearly $2 billion. Assume that Marriott replaced furniture that had been used in the business for five years. The records of the company reflected the following regarding the sale of the existing furniture:

Furniture (cost)	$6,000,000
Accumulated depreciation	5,500,000

Required:

1. Prepare the journal entry for the disposal of the furniture, assuming that it was sold for,
   a. $500,000 cash
   b. $1,600,000 cash
   c. $400,000 cash

2. Based on the three preceding situations, explain the effects of the disposal of an asset.

■ LO8-5   **E8-16**   **Inferring Asset Age and Recording Accidental Loss on a Long-Lived Asset (Straight-Line Depreciation)**

On January 1, 2018, the records of Smita Corporation showed the following:

Truck (estimated residual value, $3,000)	$18,000
Accumulated depreciation (straight line, two years)	6,000

On September 30, 2018, the delivery truck was a total loss as a result of an accident. As the truck was insured, the company collected $7,600 cash from the insurance company on October 5, 2018.

Required:

1. Based on the data given, compute the estimated useful life of the truck.
2. Prepare all journal entries to record the events that occurred on September 30 and October 5, 2018, and the related adjustments to the accounts on December 31, 2018. Show computations.

LO8-3   **E8-17**   **Inferring Asset-Related Information from Incomplete Data**

The following table includes specific details related to four different assets owned by Shabra Ltd. as at December 31, 2017.

	Land	Building	Machine	Truck
Date of purchase	A	F	July 2, 2014	January 1, 2011
Acquisition cost	B	$640,000	$60,000	$50,000
Useful life	indefinite	40 years	10 years	J
Depreciation method	C	straight line	double declining balance	straight line
Accumulated depreciation	D	$128,000	H	$35,000
Carrying amount	E	G	I	K

Shabra's fiscal year ends on December 31. The land and building were purchased on the same date for an aggregate price of $700,000. The company does not use the units-of-production method for depreciation, and assumes that the residual value or each asset is zero.

Required:

Determine the missing values in the above table (i.e., cells A through K).

LO8-6   **E8-18**   **Computing the Acquisition and Depletion of a Natural Resource**

Freeport-McMoRan Copper & Gold Inc. is a natural resources company involved in the exploration, development, and extraction of natural resources, with the majority of its resources in Indonesia. Annual revenues exceed $21 billion. Assume that in February 2017, Freeport-McMoRan paid $7,000,000 for a mineral deposit in Indonesia. During March, it spent $740,000 in preparing the deposit for exploitation. It was estimated that 9,000,000 cubic yards could be extracted economically. During 2017, 720,000 cubic yards were extracted and sold. During January 2018, the company spent another $60,000 for additional developmental work. After conclusion of the latest work, the estimated remaining recovery was increased to 12,200,000 cubic yards over the remaining life. During 2018, 600,000 cubic yards were extracted.

Required:

1. Compute the acquisition cost of the deposit in 2017.
2. Compute the depletion expense for 2017.
3. Compute the carrying amount of the deposit after payment of the January 2018 developmental costs.
4. Compute the depletion expense for 2018.
5. Prepare the journal entries to record the acquisition of the deposit in 2017 and the depletion expense for 2017.

LO8-6   **E8-19**   **Computing and Reporting the Acquisition and Amortization of Four Different Intangible Assets**

Wyatt Company had four intangible assets at the end of 2018 (end of the fiscal year):

a. Computer software and Web development technology purchased on January 1, 2018, for $70,000. The technology is expected to have a useful life of four years.

b. A patent purchased from R. Jay on January 1, 2018, for a cash cost of $6,000. Jay had registered the patent with the Canadian Intellectual Property Office seven years earlier on January 1, 2008. The cost of the patent is amortized over its legal life.

c. A lease on some property for a five-year term beginning January 1, 2018. The company immediately spent $7,800 cash for long-lived improvements (estimated useful life, eight years; no residual value). At the termination of the lease, there will be no recovery of these improvements.

d. A trademark that was internally developed and registered with the Canadian government for $13,000 on November 1, 2017. Management decided that the trademark has an indefinite life.

Required:

1. What is the acquisition cost of each intangible asset?

2. Compute the amortization of each intangible asset at December 31, 2018. The company does not use contra accounts.

3. Show how these assets and any related expenses should be reported on the statement of financial position at December 31, 2018, and on the statement of earnings for 2018.

LO8-6
Tim Hortons Inc.

E8-20

Recording Rent Paid in Advance, Leasehold Improvements, Periodic Rent, and Related Amortization

Tim Hortons Inc. is Canada's leading chain of quick-service restaurants, offering a variety of coffees, donuts, and other baked goods. Assume that Tim Hortons planned to open a new store on St. George Street near the University of Toronto and obtained a 15-year lease starting January 1, 2018. Although a serviceable building was on the property, the company had to build an additional structure for storage. The 15-year lease required an $18,000 cash advance payment plus cash payments of $5,000 per month during occupancy. During January 2018, the company spent $90,000 cash to build the structure. The new structure has an estimated life of 18 years with no residual value.

Required:

1. Prepare the journal entries for the company to record the payment of the $18,000 advance on January 1, 2018, and the first monthly rental.

2. Prepare the journal entry to record the construction of the new structure.

3. Prepare any adjusting entries required at December 31, 2018, the end of the company's fiscal year, with respect to (a) the advance payment and (b) the new structure. Assume that straight-line depreciation is used. Show computations.

4. Compute the total expense resulting from the lease for 2018.

LO8-1,8-2,8-3,8-4,8-5,
8-6,8-7

E8-21

Finding Financial Information as a Potential Investor

You are considering investing the cash gifts you received for graduation in shares of various companies. You visit the websites of major companies, searching for relevant information.

Required:

For each of the following, indicate where you would locate the information in an annual report. (*Hint:* The information may be in more than one location.)

1. The detail on major classifications of long-lived assets.

2. The accounting method(s) used for financial reporting purposes.

3. Whether the company has had any capital expenditures for the year.

4. The net amount of property, plant, and equipment.

5. Policies on amortizing intangibles.

6. Depreciation expense.

7. Any significant gains or losses on disposals of long-lived assets.

8. Accumulated depreciation of property, plant, and equipment at the end of the last fiscal year.

9. The amount of assets written off as impaired during the year.

LO8-2,8-3

E8-22

Recording and Explaining Depreciation, Extraordinary Repairs, and Changes in Estimated Useful Life and Residual Value (Straight-Line Depreciation)

The records of Luci Company reflected the following details for Machine A at December 31, 2018, the end of the company's fiscal year:

Cost when acquired	$30,000
Accumulated depreciation	10,200

During January 2019, the machine was renovated at a cost of $15,500. As a result, the estimated life increased from five years to eight years and the residual value increased from $4,500 to $6,500. The company uses straight-line depreciation.

Required:

1. Prepare the journal entry to record the renovation.

2. How old was the machine at the end of 2018?

3. Prepare the adjusting entry at the end of 2019 to record straight-line depreciation for the year.

4. Explain the rationale for your entries in (1) and (3).

LO8-3,8-7

E8-23 **Computing the Effect of a Change in Useful Life and Residual Value on Financial Statements and Cash Flows (Straight-Line Depreciation)**

Dustin Company owns the office building occupied by its administrative office. The office building was reflected in the accounts at the end of last year as follows:

Acquisition cost	$330,000
Accumulated depreciation (based on straight-line depreciation, an estimated life of 50 years, and a residual value of $30,000)	78,000

Following a careful study, management decided in January of this year that the total estimated useful life should be changed to 30 years (instead of 50) and the residual value reduced to $22,500 (from $30,000). The depreciation method will not change.

Required:

1. Compute the annual depreciation expense prior to the change in estimates.

2. Compute the annual depreciation expense after the change in estimates.

3. What will be the net effect of changing the estimates on the statement of financial position, net earnings, and cash flows for the year?

LO8-3

AMERCO

E8-24 **Preparing a Depreciation Schedule Using Two Different Methods for the Same Asset**

AMERCO, the holding company for U-Haul International Inc., included the following note in its annual report for the fiscal year ending on March 31, 2016:

> **Note 3. Accounting Policies**
> **Property, Plant, and Equipment**
>
> ....
>
> Management determined that additions to the fleet resulting from purchases should be depreciated on an accelerated method based upon a declining formula. Under the declining balances method (2.4 times declining balance), the book value of a rental truck is reduced approximately 16%, 13%, 11%, 9%, 8%, 7%, and 6% during years one through seven, respectively, and then reduced on a straight line basis to a salvage value of 20% by the end of year 15. Beginning in October 2012, new purchased rental equipment subject to this depreciation schedule is depreciated to a salvage value of 15%. Comparatively, a standard straight line approach would reduce the book value by approximately 5.7% per year over the life of the truck.

Assume that the company purchased a truck on January 1, 2014, for $50,000.

Required:

1. Verify that the use of a declining balance with a multiple of 2.4 reduces the book value (carrying amount) of the truck by 16% by December 31, 2014.

2. Prepare a depreciation schedule that shows the annual depreciation expense, accumulated depreciation and carrying amount of the truck throughout its 15 years of service using the declining balance method. Use a multiple rate of 2.4.

3. Prepare a depreciation schedule that shows the annual depreciation expense, accumulated depreciation and carrying amount of the truck throughout its 15 years of service using the company's depreciation policy. Compare the depreciation expenses for the years 2021 to 2028 to those you computed in requirement 2 and explain why the company changes its depreciation method after year 7 (2020).

Mc Graw Hill connect **PROBLEMS**

LO8-3

P8-1 **Understanding the Nature of Depreciation**

At the beginning of his first year at university, Georgio Labos bought a used combination colour television and stereo system for $960. He estimates that these two items will be almost worthless by the time he graduates in four years and plans to abandon them then.

Required:

1. Assume that Georgio expects to receive four years of entertainment services for the $960. What is the carrying amount of these items after one year? Use straight-line depreciation with no residual value.

2. The university's academic year lasts a total of 30 weeks, from early September to late April. Georgio does not take the TV and stereo system with him on vacations. During the academic year,

he participates in many activities, so he averages three hours per week of watching television and listening to music. What is the average cost per hour of use? (Ignore costs of electricity and repairs.)

3. Georgio is disturbed by the answer to (2). He complains to a friend that this amount exceeds the hourly cost of going to the movies on specific days of the week. His friend suggests that he could lower the average cost by leaving the TV set on whenever he goes to class. Georgio attends classes for 12 hours per week. Comment on this suggestion.

4. After owning the TV set and stereo system for one year, Georgio became curious about the price he could get for selling these items. He discovered that the most he could receive is $600. He does not plan to sell them but the information distresses him. What amount should he associate with the TV set and stereo system after one year? Explain.

▨ LO8-1,8-2,8-3,8-5

P8-2

Determining the Acquisition Cost and the Financial Statement Effects of Depreciation, Extraordinary Repairs, and Asset Disposal (AP8-1)

On January 2, 2015, Athol Company bought a machine for use in operations. The machine has an estimated useful life of eight years and an estimated residual value of $2,600. The company provided the following information:

a. Invoice price of the machine, $82,000.

b. Freight paid by the vendor per sales agreement, $1,000.

c. Installation costs, $2,400 cash.

d. Cost of cleaning up the supplies, boxes, and other garbage that remained after the installation of the machine, $100 cash.

e. Payment of the machine's price was made as follows:

January 2:

- Issued 2,000 common shares of Athol Company at $3.50 per share.
- Signed a $45,000 note payable due April 16, 2015, plus 8 percent interest.
- Balance of the invoice price to be paid in cash. The invoice allows for a 2 percent cash discount if the cash payment is made by January 11.
  January 15: Paid the balance of the invoice price in cash.
  April 16:   Paid the note payable and interest in cash.

f. On June 30, 2017, the company completed the replacement of a major part of the machine that cost $18,575. This expenditure is expected to reduce the machine's operating costs, increase its estimated useful life by two years, and decrease its estimated residual value to $2,000.

g. Assume that on October 1, 2022, the company decided to replace the machine with a newer, more efficient model. It then sold the machine to Sako Ltd. on that date for $30,000 cash.

Required:

1. Compute the acquisition cost of the machine, and explain the basis for including certain costs in the determination of the machine's acquisition cost.

2. Indicate the accounts affected, amounts, and direction (+ for increase and − for decrease) of the effects of the purchase and subsequent cash payments on the accounting equation. Use the following headings:

Date	Assets	=	Liabilities	+	Shareholders' Equity

3. Prepare the journal entries to record the purchase of the machine and subsequent cash payments on January 15 and April 16, 2015.

4. Compute the depreciation expense for each of the years 2015, 2016, and 2017, assuming the company's fiscal year ends on December 31. Use the straight-line depreciation method.

5. Prepare the journal entry to record the sale of the machine on October 1, 2022. (*Hint:* First determine the balance of the accumulated depreciation account on that date.)

▨ LO8-2,8-3

P8-3

Analyzing the Effects of Repairs, a Betterment, and Depreciation (AP8-2)

A recent annual report for Swifty Air Cargo Company states the following:

Property, Plant, and Equipment

Expenditures for major additions, improvements, flight equipment modifications, and specific equipment overhaul costs are capitalized when such costs are determined to extend the useful life of the asset or are part of acquiring the asset. Maintenance and repairs are charged to expense as incurred.

Assume that Swifty made extensive repairs on an existing building and added a new section. The building is a garage and repair facility for delivery trucks that serve the local area. The existing building originally cost $820,000, and by the end of 2016, it was half depreciated on the basis of a useful life of 20 years and no residual value. Assume straight-line depreciation was used. During 2017, the following expenditures related to the building were made:

a. Ordinary repairs and maintenance expenditures for the year, $17,000 paid in cash.

b. Extensive and major repairs to the roof of the building, $120,000 paid in cash. These repairs were completed on December 31, 2017.

c. The new section, completed on December 31, 2017, at a cost of $230,000 paid in cash, has an estimated useful life of nine years and no residual value.

Required:

1. Applying the policies of Swifty, complete the following schedule, indicating the effects of the preceding expenditures. If there is no effect on an account, write N on the line (amounts in thousands):

	Building	Accumulated Depreciation	Depreciation Expense	Repairs Expense	Cash
Balance January 1, 2017	$820,000	$410,000			
Depreciation for 2017		_____	_____		_____
Balance prior to expenditures	820,000	_____	_____		
Expenditure a	_____	_____	_____	_____	_____
Expenditure b	_____	_____	_____	_____	_____
Expenditure c	_____	_____	_____	_____	_____
Balance December 31, 2017	_____	_____	_____	_____	_____

2. What was the carrying amount of the building at December 31, 2017?

3. Compute the depreciation expense for 2018, assuming no additional capital expenditures on this building in 2018.

4. Explain the effect of depreciation on cash flows.

■ LO8-2,8-3
eXcel

P8-4   **Computing a Basket Purchase Allocation, and Recording Depreciation under Three Alternative Methods** (AP8-3)

At the beginning of the year, Wong's Martial Arts Centre bought three used fitness machines from Hangar Inc. for a total cash price of $38,000. Transportation costs on the machines were $2,000. The machines were immediately overhauled and installed, and started operating. The machines were different; therefore, each had to be recorded separately in the accounts. An appraiser was requested to estimate their market value at the date of purchase (prior to the overhaul and installation). The carrying amounts shown on Hangar's books are also available. The carrying amounts, appraisal results, installation costs, and renovation expenditures follow:

	Machine A	Machine B	Machine C
Carrying amount on Hangar's books	$8,000	$29,000	$6,000
Appraisal value	9,500	32,000	8,500
Installation costs	300	500	200
Renovation costs prior to use	2,000	400	600

By the end of the first year, each machine had been operating 8,000 hours.

Required:

1. Compute the cost of each machine by making a supportable allocation of the total cost to the three machines. Explain the rationale for the allocation basis used.

2. Prepare the entry to record depreciation expense at the end of year 1, assuming the following:

Machine	Estimates		Depreciation Method
	Life	Residual Value	
A	5 years	$1,500	Straight line
B	40,000 hours	900	Units of production
C	4 years	2,000	Double declining balance

LO8-1,8-3

Performance Sports
Group Ltd.

P8-5 **Inferring Depreciation Amounts, and Determining the Effects of a Depreciation Error on Key Ratios** (AP8-4)

Performance Sports Group Ltd. is a leading developer and manufacturer of ice hockey, roller hockey, and lacrosse equipment as well as related apparel. The following information was reported in Note 5 to the company's financial statements for fiscal year 2015 (in thousands of US dollars):

5. Property, Plant, and Equipment, Net

Property, plant, and equipment, net, consisted of the following:

	May 31, 2015	May 31, 2014
Buildings	$ 14,737	$ 7,553
Machinery and equipment	10,946	9,691
Computer software and equipment	25,681	16,452
Furniture and fixtures	5,605	5,483
Leasehold improvements	3,874	3,801
Construction in progress	5,545	600
	66,388	43,580
Less: Accumulated depreciation	(19,337)	(18,258)
Total property, plant, and equipment, net	$ 47,051	$ 25,322

Required:

1. Assuming that the company did not sell any property, plant, and equipment in 2015, what was the amount of depreciation expense recorded in 2015?

2. Assume that the company failed to record depreciation in 2015. Indicate the effect of the error (i.e., overstated or understated) on the following ratios: (a) earnings per share, (b) fixed asset turnover ratio, (c) current ratio, and (d) return on equity. Computations are not required.

LO8-1,8-3

Bombardier Inc.

P8-6 **Evaluating the Effect of Alternative Depreciation Methods on Key Ratios from an Analyst's Perspective**

Bombardier Inc. is one of the largest manufacturers of planes and trains in the world. The company's long-lived assets exceed $20 billion. As a result, depreciation is a significant item on Bombardier's statement of earnings. You are a financial analyst for Bombardier and have been asked to determine the impact of alternative depreciation methods. For your analysis, you have been asked to compare methods based on a machine that cost $106,000. The estimated useful life is 13 years, and the estimated residual value is $2,000. The machine has an estimated useful life in productive output of 200,000 units. Actual output was 20,000 in year 1 and 16,000 in year 2.

Required:

1. For years 1 and 2 only, prepare a separate depreciation schedule for each of the following alternative methods. Round your computations to the nearest dollar.

    a. Straight line

    b. Units of production

    c. Double declining balance

Method: _____				
Year	Computation	Depreciation Expense	Accumulated Depreciation	Carrying Amount
At acquisition				
1				
2				

2. Evaluate each method in terms of its effect on cash flow, fixed asset turnover ratio, and earnings per share (EPS). Assuming that Bombardier is most interested in reducing taxes and maintaining a high EPS for year 1, which method of depreciation would you recommend to management? Would your recommendation change for year 2? Why or why not?

LO8-5,8-7

Mattel Inc.

P8-7 **Inferring Asset Age, and Determining Financial Statement Effects of a Long-Lived Asset Disposal (A Challenging Problem)** (AP8-5)

Mattel Inc. is the leading toy maker in the world. The company's revenues exceed $6 billion. In the toy business, it is very difficult to determine the life expectancy of a product. Products that children love one year may sit on the shelf the following year. As a result, companies in the toy business often sell productive assets that are no longer needed. Assume that on December 31, 2017, the end of the company's fiscal year, Mattel's records showed the following data about a machine that was no longer needed to make a toy that was popular last year:

Machine, original cost	$104,000
Accumulated depreciation	55,000*

*Based on an estimated useful life of eight years, a residual value of $16,000, and straight-line depreciation.

On April 1, 2018, the machine was sold for $52,000 cash.

Required:

1. How old was the machine on January 1, 2018? Show computations.

2. Indicate the effect (i.e., the amount and direction, increase or decrease) of the sale of the machine on April 1, 2018, on the following (ignore income taxes):

   a. Total assets

   b. Net earnings

   c. Cash flows (by each section of the statement: operating, investing, and financing activities)

■ **LO8-5,8-7**   **P8-8**

Singapore Airlines

Inferring Activities Affecting Property, Plant, and Equipment from Notes to the Financial Statements, and Analyzing the Impact of Depreciation on Cash Flows (AP8-6)

Singapore Airlines reported the following information in the notes to a recent annual report (in Singapore dollars):

SINGAPORE AIRLINES
Notes to the Accounts
21. Property, plant, and equipment (in $ million)

	Beginning of Year	Additions	Impairment Loss	Disposals/ Transfers	End of Year
Cost					
Aircraft	$18,748.4	$ 748.4		$(278.0)	$19,218.8
Other property, plant, and equipment (summarized)	5,059.9	2,432.7		(1,795.7)	5,696.9
Accumulated depreciation					
Aircraft	8,960.0	1,410.1	$29.0	(812.6)	9,586.5
Other fixed assets (summarized)	1,821.6	128.7	2.7	(147.0)	1,806.0

Singapore Airlines also reported the following cash flow details:

Cash Flow from Operating Activities (in $ million)

	The Company	
	Current Year	**Prior Year**
Earnings before income taxes	$ 442.9	$ 367.9
Adjustments for:		
Depreciation of property, plant, and equipment	1,538.8	1,575.5
Loss (Gain) on disposal of property, plant, and equipment	(51.9)	(51.2)
Other adjustments (summarized)	137.4	205.9
Net cash provided by operating activities	$2,067.2	$2,098.1

Required:

1. Reconstruct the information in Note 21 into T-accounts for property, plant, and equipment and accumulated depreciation:

Property, Plant, and Equipment		Accumulated Depreciation	
Beg. balance			Beg. balance
Acquisitions	Disposals/transfers	Disposals/transfers	Depreciation expense
			Impairment loss
End. balance			End. balance

2. Compute the amount of cash the company received for disposals and transfers. Show computations.

3. Compute the percentage of depreciation expense to cash flows from operations. How do you interpret this percentage?

LO8-5   **P8-9**   **Recording and Interpreting the Disposal of Three Long-Lived Assets** (AP8-7)

During 2018, Côté Company disposed of three different assets. On January 1, 2018, prior to the disposal of the assets, the accounts reflected the following:

Asset	Original Cost	Residual Value	Estimated Life	Accumulated Depreciation (straight line)
Machine A	$20,000	$2,000	8 years	$13,500 (6 years)
Machine B	41,000	4,000	10 years	29,600 (8 years)
Machine C	75,000	3,000	12 years	60,000 (10 years)

The machines were disposed of in the following ways:

a. Machine A: Sold on January 1, 2018, for $7,200 cash.

b. Machine B: Sold on April 1, 2018, for $8,500; received cash, $2,500, and a note receivable for $6,000, due on March 31, 2016, plus 6 percent interest.

c. Machine C: Suffered irreparable damage from an accident on July 2, 2018. On July 10, 2018, a salvage company removed the machine immediately at no cost. The machine was insured, and $18,000 cash was collected from the insurance company.

Required:

1. Prepare all journal entries related to the disposal of each machine in 2018.

2. Explain the accounting rationale for the way that you recorded each disposal.

LO8-6   **P8-10**   **Determining Financial Statement Effects of Activities Related to Various Long-Lived Assets** (AP8-8)

BSP Company completed the following transactions during fiscal year 2017:

January 1	Purchased a patent for $28,000 cash, with an estimated useful life of seven years.
April 1	Purchased the assets (not detailed) of another business for $164,000 cash, including $10,000 for goodwill. The company assumed no liabilities. Goodwill has an indefinite life.
October 15	Paid $5,500 for regular maintenance and ordinary repairs.
December 31	Constructed a storage shed on land leased from D. Heald at a cost of $15,600. The lease will expire in three years. (Amounts spent to enhance leased property are capitalized as intangible assets called leasehold improvements.)
December 31	Sold Machine A for $6,000 cash. The machine was purchased on January 1, 2014, for $25,000. It had a useful life of five years and a residual value of $5,000. Its accumulated depreciation totalled $12,000 as at December 31, 2016.
December 31	Paid $5,200 for a complete reconditioning of Machine B, which was acquired on January 1, 2016, for $31,000. The machine had a useful life of 15 years and a residual value of $7,000.

The company uses the straight-line method of depreciation and amortization.

Required:

1. Indicate the accounts affected, amounts, and direction of the effects (+ for increase, – for decrease, and NE for no effect) of each transaction on the accounting equation. Use the following structure:

Date	Assets	=	Liabilities	+	Shareholders' Equity

2. Compute the amount of depreciation expense for Machine B to be recorded at December 31, 2018, the company's year-end.

LO8-6   **P8-11**   **Computing Goodwill from the Purchase of a Business and Related Amortization** (AP8-9)

Lassonde Industries Inc.

Lassonde Industries Inc. is a North American leader in the development, manufacture, and sale of innovative and distinctive lines of fruit and vegetable juices and drinks marketed under recognized brands such as Everfresh, Fairlee, Flavür, Fruité, Graves, Oasis, and Rougemont.

The notes to the company's financial statements for 2015 indicate that it acquired the remaining outstanding shares of Apple & Eve, LLC on July 3, 2014. The purchase price was $158,296,000 and the fair market value of identifiable assets acquired and liabilities assumed are as follows (in thousands of dollars):

Current assets	$45,309
Property, plant, and equipment	642
Intangible assets	99,441
Current liabilities	(23,802)

Required:

1. Compute the amount of goodwill resulting from the purchase.

2. Compute the adjustments that Lassonde Industries would make at the end of its fiscal year, December 31, 2014, for depreciation and amortization of all the long-lived assets it acquired. The intangible assets include four major categories that have different useful lives as follows:

Intangible Asset	Acquisition Cost	Estimated Useful Life
Client relationships	$62,368	15 years
Trademarks and trade name	36,469	20 years
Software	419	3 years
Non-compete agreements	185	1 year

Assume that all the acquired long-lived assets have no residual value and that property, plant, and equipment have an estimated useful life of 10 years. The company uses the straight-line depreciation method and does not amortize goodwill.

■ LO8-6   **P8-12**   **Determining the Financial Statement Effects of the Acquisition and Amortization of Intangibles**

Figg Company, with a fiscal year ending December 31, acquired three intangible assets during 2018. For each of the following transactions, indicate the accounts affected and the amounts and direction of the effects (+ for increase, − for decrease, and N for no effect) on the accounting equation. Use the following headings:

Date	Assets	=	Liabilities	+	Shareholders' Equity

a. On January 1, 2018, the company purchased a patent from Ullrich Ltd. for $6,000 cash. Ullrich had developed the patent and registered it with the Canadian Intellectual Property Office on January 1, 2013.

b. On January 1, 2018, the company purchased a copyright for a total cash cost of $12,000; the remaining legal life was 25 years. Company executives estimated that the copyright would have no value by the end of 20 years.

c. The company purchased another company in January 2018 at a cash cost of $130,000. Included in the purchase price was $30,000 for goodwill; the balance was for plant, equipment, and fixtures (no liabilities were assumed).

d. On December 31, 2018, the company amortized the patent over its remaining legal life.

e. On December 31, 2018, the company amortized the copyright over the appropriate period.

■ LO8-4,8-6   **P8-13**   **Computing Amortization, Carrying Amount, and Asset Impairment Related to Different Intangible Assets** (AP8-10)

Havel Company has five different intangible assets to be accounted for and reported on the financial statements. Management is concerned about the amortization of the cost of each of these intangibles. Facts about each intangible follow:

a. *Patent.* The company purchased a patent at a cash cost of $54,600 on January 1, 2018. The patent had a legal life of 20 years from the date of registration with the Canadian Intellectual Property Office, which was January 1, 2011. It is amortized over its remaining legal life.

b. *Copyright.* On January 1, 2018, the company purchased a copyright for $22,500 cash. The legal life remaining from that date is 30 years. It is estimated that the copyrighted item will have no value by the end of 25 years.

c. *Franchise.* The company obtained a franchise from McKerma Company to make and distribute a special item. It obtained the franchise on January 1, 2018, at a cash cost of $14,400 for a 12-year period.

d. *Licence.* On January 1, 2017, the company secured a licence from the city to operate a special service for a period of five years. Total cash expended to obtain the licence was $14,000.

e. Goodwill. The company started business in January 2016 by purchasing another business for a cash lump sum of $400,000. Included in the purchase price was $60,000 for goodwill. Company executives stated that "the goodwill is an important long-lived asset to us." It has an indefinite life.

Required:

1. Compute the amount of amortization that should be recorded for each intangible asset at the end of the fiscal year, December 31, 2018.
2. Compute the carrying amount of each intangible asset on December 31, 2019.
3. Assume that on January 2, 2020, the copyrighted item was impaired in its ability to continue to produce strong revenues. The other intangible assets were not affected. Havel estimated that the copyright will be able to produce future cash flows of $18,000. The fair value of the copyright is determined to be $16,000. Compute the amount, if any, of the impairment loss to be recorded.

■ LO8-3
e**X**cel

P8-14 **Analyzing and Recording Entries Related to a Change in Estimated Life and Residual Value**

Rungano Corporation is a global publisher of magazines, books, and music, as well as video collections, and it is one of the world's leading direct-mail marketers. Many direct-mail marketers use high-speed Didde press equipment to print their advertisements. These presses can cost more than $1 million. Assume that Rungano owns a Didde press acquired at an original cost of $1,200,000. It is being depreciated on a straight-line basis over a 20-year estimated useful life and has a $150,000 estimated residual value. At the end of 2018, the press had been depreciated for eight years. In January 2019, a decision was made, on the basis of improved maintenance procedures, that a total estimated useful life of 25 years and a residual value of $219,000 would be more realistic. The fiscal year ends December 31.

Required:

1. Compute (a) the amount of depreciation expense recorded in 2018 and (b) the carrying amount of the printing press at the end of 2018.
2. Compute the amount of depreciation that should be recorded in 2019. Show computations.
3. Prepare the adjusting entry to record depreciation expense at December 31, 2019.

■ LO8-2,8-3,8-5,8-7
P8-15

Determining the Acquisition Cost and the Financial Statement Effects of Depreciation, Extraordinary Repairs, and Asset Disposal; and Analyzing the Impact of Depreciation on Cash Flows

On July 1, 2014, Sampras Corp. purchased property that includes land, buildings and equipment for $5.5 million. The company paid half of this amount using cash and signed a two-year note for the remainder. Principal and interest at the rate of 5 percent are due at maturity. The fair market value of these assets are as follows: land, $1,750,000; building, $2,800,000; and equipment, $2,450,000.

The company also paid in cash $180,000 for legal fees, $220,000 for commissions, and $100,000 for appraisal fees.

Additional information:

a. The building has an estimated residual value of $150,000 and is depreciated over 10 years using the straight-line method.
b. The equipment has an estimated useful life of four years and an estimated salvage value of $300,000. It is depreciated using the double-declining-balance method.
c. Sampras Corp. started renovating the building on January 1, 2017, and paid $120,000 for new decorations. In addition, it spent $400,000 on new construction, which increased the building's useful life by three years, and its residual value by $100,000. The renovation on the building was completed by June 30, 2017.
d. Sampras Corp. sold the building on January 1, 2018, for $2,500,000 cash.

Required:

1. Identify the expenses (both type of expense and amount) that Sampras Corp. would report on its statement of earnings for the fiscal year ended June 30, 2015.
2. Show how the purchase transaction on July 1, 2014, and related adjustments at June 30, 2015, would be presented on a partial statement of cash flows for the year ended June 30, 2015. Show all relevant calculations and all the effects on cash flows. The company uses the indirect method of reporting cash from operating activities.
3. Prepare the journal entries to record the disposal of the building on January 1, 2018.

ALTERNATE PROBLEMS

■ LO8-1,8-2,8-3,8-5

AP8-1

Determining the Acquisition Cost and the Financial Statement Effects of Depreciation, Extraordinary Repairs, and Asset Disposal (P8-2)

On July 1, 2015, the Fitzgerald Corp. bought a machine for use in operations. The machine has an estimated useful life of six years and an estimated residual value of $2,500. The company provided the following information:

a. Invoice price of the machine, $60,000.

b. Freight paid by the vendor per sales agreement, $650.

c. Installation costs, $2,500 cash.

d. Payment of the machine's price was made as follows:

July 1:

- Fitzgerald Corp. issued 2,000 common shares at $5 per share.

- Signed an interest-bearing note for the balance of the invoice price, payable on September 1, 2015, plus 9 percent interest.

October 1: Paid the note payable and related interest in cash.

e. On June 30, 2018, the company completed the replacement of a major part of the machine that cost $11,500. This expenditure is expected to reduce the machine's operating costs and increase its estimated useful life by two years. At the same time, the machine's estimated residual value was reduced to $2,000.

f. Assume that on July 1, 2022, the company decided to dispose of the machine by selling it to Ayad Inc. on that date for $16,000 cash.

Required:

1. Compute the acquisition cost of the machine, and explain the basis for including certain costs in the determination of the machine's acquisition cost.

2. Indicate the accounts affected and the amounts and direction (+ for increase and − for decrease) of the effects of the purchase and subsequent cash payment on the accounting equation. Use the following headings:

Date	Assets	=	Liabilities	+	Shareholders' Equity

3. Prepare the journal entries to record the purchase of the machine and subsequent cash payments on September 1, 2015.

4. Compute the depreciation expense for each of the years 2015 and 2018, assuming the company's fiscal year ends on December 31. Use the straight-line depreciation method.

5. Prepare the journal entry to record the sale of the machine on July 1, 2022. (*Hint:* First determine the balance of the accumulated depreciation account on that date.)

■ LO8-2,8-3

AMERCO

AP8-2

Analyzing the Effects of Repairs, a Betterment, and Depreciation (AP8-3)

A recent annual report for AMERCO, the holding company for U-Haul International Inc., included the following note:

> **Property, Plant, and Equipment**
> Property, plant, and equipment are stated at cost. Interest costs incurred during the initial construction of buildings or rental equipment are considered part of the cost. Depreciation is computed for financial reporting purposes principally using the straight-line method over the following estimated useful lives: rental equipment 2–20 years, building and non-rental equipment 3–55 years. Major overhauls to rental equipment are capitalized and are depreciated over the estimated period benefited. Routine maintenance costs are charged to operating expense as they are incurred.

AMERCO subsidiaries own property, plant, and equipment that provide offices for U-Haul and that are utilized in the manufacture, repair, and rental of U-Haul equipment. Assume that AMERCO made extensive repairs on an existing building and added a new wing. The building is a garage and repair facility for rental trucks that serve the Vancouver area. The existing building originally cost $460,000, and by December 31, 2014 (5 years), it was one-quarter depreciated on the basis of a 20-year estimated useful life and no residual value. Assume straight-line depreciation, computed to the nearest month. During 2018, the following expenditures related to the building were made:

a. Ordinary repairs and maintenance expenditures for the year, $10,000 paid in cash.

    b. Extensive and major repairs to the roof of the building, $34,000 paid in cash. These repairs were completed on June 30, 2018.

    c. The new wing was completed on June 30, 2018, at a cash cost of $173,000. By itself, the wing had an estimated useful life of 15 years and no residual value. The company intends to sell the building and wing at the end of the building's useful life.

Required:

1. Applying the policies of AMERCO, complete the following schedule, indicating the effects of the preceding expenditures. If there is no effect on an account, write N on the line:

	Building	Accumulated Depreciation	Depreciation Expense	Repairs Expense	Cash
Balance, January 1, 2018	$460,000	$115,000			
Depreciation January 1–June 30		___	___		___
Balance prior to expenditures	460,000	___	___		
Expenditure *a*	___	___	___	___	___
Expenditure *b*	___	___	___	___	___
Expenditure *c*	___	___	___	___	___
Depreciation July 1–December 31:					
Existing building		___	___		___
Major repairs and betterments		___	___		___
Balance, December 31, 2018	___	___	___	___	___

2. What was the carrying amount of the building on December 31, 2018?

3. Explain the effect of depreciation on cash flows.

LO8-2,8-3   **AP8-3**   **Computing a Basket Purchase Allocation, and Recording Depreciation under Three Alternative Methods** (P8-4)

At the beginning of the year, Labinski Inc. bought three used machines from Santoro Corporation for a total cash price of $62,000. Transportation costs on the machines were $3,000. The machines were immediately overhauled and installed, and started operating. The machines were different; therefore, each had to be recorded separately in the accounts. An appraiser was requested to estimate their market value at the date of purchase (prior to the overhaul and installation). The carrying amounts shown on Santoro's books are also available. The carrying amounts, appraisal results, installation costs, and renovation expenditures follow:

	Machine A	Machine B	Machine C
Carrying amount on Santoro's books	$10,500	$28,000	$26,000
Appraisal value	11,500	32,000	28,500
Installation costs	800	1,100	1,100
Renovation costs prior to use	600	1,400	1,600

By the end of the first year, each machine had been operating 7,000 hours.

Required:

1. Compute the cost of each machine by making a supportable allocation of the total cost to the three machines (round your calculations to two decimal places). Explain the rationale for the allocation basis used.

2. Prepare the entry to record depreciation expense at the end of year 1, assuming the following:

Machine	Estimates Life	Estimates Residual Value	Depreciation Method
A	4 years	$1,000	Straight line
B	35,000 hours	2,000	Units of production
C	5 years	1,500	Double declining balance

LO8-1,8-3   **AP8-4**   **Inferring Depreciation Amounts and Determining the Effects of a Depreciation Error on Key Ratios** (P8-5)

Gildan Activewear Inc.

Gildan Activewear Inc. is a Canadian vertically integrated manufacturer and marketer of quality branded basic family apparel, including T-shirts, fleece, sport shirts, socks, and underwear. The following information was reported in Note 9 to the company's financial statements for fiscal year 2014:

	October 5, 2014	September 29, 2013
Land	$ 45,541	$ 39,922
Buildings and improvements	314,823	249,230
Manufacturing equipment	687,369	532,557
Other equipment	129,688	114,628
Assets not yet utilized in operations	166,872	114,030
	1,344,293	1,050,365
Less accumulated depreciation	470,567	394,498
Carrying amount	$ 873,726	$ 655,869

Required:

1. Assuming that Gildan did not have any asset impairment losses and did not sell any property, plant, and equipment in fiscal year 2014, what was the amount of depreciation expense recorded in 2014?

2. Assume that Gildan failed to record depreciation in 2014. Indicate the effect of the error (i.e., overstated or understated) on the following: (a) earnings per share, (b) fixed asset turnover ratio, (c) current ratio, and (d) return on equity. Computations are not required.

■ LO8-5,8-7 **AP8-5** **Inferring Asset Age and Determining Financial Statement Effects of a Long-Lived**
Hasbro Inc. **Asset Disposal (A Challenging Problem)** (P8-7)

Hasbro Inc. designs, manufactures, and markets high-quality toys, games, and infant products. The company's revenues exceed $4.0 billion. In the toy business, it is very difficult to determine the life expectancy of a product. Products that children love one year may sit on the shelf the following year. As a result, companies in the toy business often sell productive assets that are no longer needed. Assume that on December 31, 2017, the end of the company's fiscal year, Hasbro's records showed the following data about a machine that was no longer needed to make a toy that was popular last year:

Machine, original cost	$214,000
Accumulated depreciation	128,000*
*Based on an estimated useful life of six years, a residual value of $22,000, and straight-line depreciation.	

On July 1, 2018, the machine was sold for $76,000 cash.

Required:

1. How old was the machine on January 1, 2018? Show computations.

2. Indicate the effect (i.e., the amount and direction increase or decrease) of the sale of the machine on July 1, 2018, on

   a. Total assets.

   b. Net earnings.

   c. Cash flows (for each section of the statement: operating, investing, and financing activities).

■ LO8-5,8-7 **AP8-6** **Inferring Activities Affecting Fixed Assets from Notes to the Financial Statements and**

 Analyzing the Impact of Depreciation on Cash Flows (P8-8)

The Emirates Group **Analyzing the Impact of Depreciation on Cash Flows** (P8-8)

The Emirates Group reported the following information in the notes to the financial statements of its 2015–2016 annual report (in millions of United Arab Emirates Dirham (AED):

EMIRATES GROUP		
Notes to the Accounts		
11. Property, plant, and equipment		
(in millions of AED)	**Acquisition Cost**	**Accumulated Depreciation**
Balance, April 1, 2015	105,914	25,370
Additions	16,349	
Depreciation expense		7,900
Disposals/write-offs	(9,467)	(3,308)
Other changes (summarized)	12	10
Balance, March 31, 2016	112,808	29,972

The Emirates Group also reported the following cash flow details for fiscal years ending March 31:

Cash Flow from Operating Activities (in millions of AED)		
	2016	**2015**
Earnings from operations	7,318	4,728
Adjustments for:		
Depreciation	8,000	7,446
(Gain)/Loss on sale of property, plant, and equipment	(367)	(132)
Other adjustments (summarized)	(846)	1,223
Cash generated from operating activities	14,105	13,265

Required:

1. Reconstruct the information in Note 11 into T-accounts for property, plant, and equipment and for accumulated depreciation.

Property, Plant, and Equipment		**Accumulated Depreciation**	
Beg. balance			Beg. balance
Additions	Disposals	Disposals	Depreciation expense
	Other adjustments		Other adjustments
End. balance			End. balance

2. Compute the amount of cash the company received for disposals during fiscal year 2015–2016. Show computations.

3. Compute the percentage of depreciation expense to cash flows from operations for fiscal year 2015–2016. How do you interpret this percentage?

LO8-3,8-5   **AP8-7**   **Recording and Interpreting the Disposal of Three Long-Lived Assets** (P8-9)

During 2018, Callaway Company disposed of three different assets. On January 1, 2018, prior to the disposal of the assets, the accounts reflected the following:

Asset	Original Cost	Residual Value	Estimated Life	Accumulated Depreciation (straight line)
Machine A	$24,000	$2,000	5 years	$17,600 (4 years)
Machine B	16,500	5,000	10 years	8,050 (7 years)
Machine C	59,200	3,200	14 years	48,000 (12 years)

The machines were disposed of in the following ways:

a. Machine A: Sold on January 1, 2018, for $6,250 cash.

b. Machine B: Sold on July 1, 2018, for $9,500; received cash, $4,500, and a $5,000 interest-bearing (10 percent) note receivable due at the end of 12 months.

c. Machine C: Suffered irreparable damage from an accident on October 2, 2018. On October 10, 2018, a salvage company removed the machine immediately at a cost of $500. The machine was insured, and $11,500 cash was collected from the insurance company.

Required:

1. Prepare all journal entries related to the disposal of each machine.

2. Explain the accounting rationale for the way that you recorded each disposal.

LO8-3,8-5   **AP8-8**   **Determining Financial Statement Effects of Activities Related to Various Long-Lived Assets** (P8-10)

Zhou Corporation completed the following transactions during fiscal year 2019:

January 1	Purchased a license for $7,200 cash with an estimated useful life of four years.
January 1	Repaved the parking lot of the building leased from H. Lane for $17,800. The lease will expire in 10 years, but the estimated useful life of the parking lot is five years with no residual value. (Amounts spent to enhance leased property are capitalized as intangible assets called leasehold improvements.)
July 1	Purchased another business for $120,000 cash. The transaction included $115,000 for the assets and $24,000 for the liabilities assumed by Zhou. The remainder was goodwill with an indefinite life.
November 30	Paid $6,700 for ordinary repairs and regular maintenance of the building.

December 31   Sold Machine A for $6,000 cash. The machine was acquired for $21,500 on January 1, 2016, and had a useful life of four years and a residual value of $3,500. Its accumulated depreciation totalled $13,500 at December 31, 2018.

December 31   Paid $7,000 for a complete reconditioning of Machine B, which was acquired on July 1, 2015, for $18,000. By December 31, 2018, accumulated depreciation totalled $7,000. Zhou expected to use the machine for eight years and then sell it for $2,000 at the end of its useful life.

The company uses the straight-line method of depreciation and amortization.

Required:

1. For each of these transactions, indicate the accounts affected and the amounts and direction of the effects (+ for increase and – for decrease) on the accounting equation. Use the following structure:

Date	Assets	=	Liabilities	+	Shareholders' Equity

2. Compute the amount of depreciation and amortization expense for Machine B to be recorded at December 31, 2020, the company's year-end.

■ **LO8-6**   **AP8-9**   **Computing Goodwill from the Purchase of a Business and Related Amortization** (P8-11)
Weebok Corporation acquired Sport Shoes on January 2, 2017. Weebok acquired the name of the company and all of its assets, except cash, for $450,000 cash. Weebok did not assume the liabilities. On January 2, 2017, the statement of financial position of Sport Shoes reflected the following carrying amounts, and an independent appraiser estimated the following market values for the assets:

January 2, 2017	Carrying Amount	Market Value
Trade receivables, net	$ 45,000	$ 45,000
Inventory	220,000	210,000
Property, plant, and equipment, net	32,000	60,000
Other assets	3,000	10,000
Total assets	300,000	
Liabilities	$ 60,000	
Shareholders' equity	240,000	
Total liabilities and shareholders' equity	$300,000	

Required:

1. Compute the amount of goodwill resulting from the purchase. (*Hint:* Assets are purchased at market value, which is their cost at the date of acquisition.)

2. Compute the adjustments that Weebok would make at the end of its fiscal year, December 31, 2017, for depreciation of all long-lived assets (straight line), assuming an estimated remaining useful life of 15 years and no residual value. The company does not amortize goodwill.

■ **LO8-4,8-6**   **AP8-10**   **Computing Amortization, Carrying Amount, and Asset Impairment Related to Different Intangible Assets** (P8-13)
Theriault Corporation has five different intangible assets to be accounted for and reported on the financial statements. The management is concerned about the amortization of the cost of each of these intangibles. Facts about each intangible follow:

a. *Patent.* The company purchased a patent at a cash cost of $18,600 on January 1, 2018. The patent had a legal life of 20 years from the date of registration with the Canadian Intellectual Property Office, which was January 1, 2016. It is amortized over its remaining legal life.

b. *Copyright.* On January 1, 2018, the company purchased a copyright for $24,750 cash. The legal life remaining from that date is 30 years. It is estimated that the copyrighted item will have no value by the end of 15 years.

c. *Franchise.* The company obtained a franchise from Farrell Company to make and distribute a special item. It obtained the franchise on January 1, 2018, at a cash cost of $19,200 for a 12-year period.

d. *Licence.* On January 1, 2017, the company secured a licence from the city to operate a special service for a period of seven years. Total cash expended to obtain the licence was $21,000.

 e. *Goodwill.* The company started business in January 2016 by purchasing another business for a cash lump sum of $650,000. The purchase price included $75,000 for goodwill. Company executives stated that "the goodwill is an important long-lived asset to us." It has an indefinite life.

Required:

1. Compute the amount of amortization expense that should be recorded for each intangible asset at the end of the fiscal year, December 31, 2018.
2. Compute the carrying amount of each intangible asset on January 1, 2021.
3. Assume that on January 2, 2021, the franchise was impaired in its ability to continue to produce strong revenues. The other intangible assets were not affected. Theriault estimated that the franchise will be able to produce future cash flows of $16,500, with a fair value of $15,000. Compute the amount, if any, of the impairment loss to be recorded.

 CASES AND PROJECTS

FINDING AND INTERPRETING FINANCIAL INFORMATION

LO8-1,8-3   **CP8-1**   **Finding Financial Information**

Sears Canada Inc.

Go to *Connect* for the financial statements of Sears Canada Inc.

Required:
Answer each of the following questions and indicate where you located the information to answer the question. (*Hint:* Use the notes to the financial statements for some of these questions.)

1. What method(s) of depreciation of property, plant, and equipment and amortization of intangible assets does the company use?
2. What types of property, plant, and equipment does Sears Canada own or control as at January 30, 2016?
3. What types of intangible assets does Sears Canada own as at January 30, 2016?
4. What is the amount of accumulated depreciation on the company's buildings as at January 30, 2016?
5. What amount of depreciation and amortization expense was reported for the 2015 fiscal year?
6. Did Sears Canada acquire any businesses during fiscal year 2015? If so, what was the total cost of acquisition and what percentage of that cost was attributed to goodwill?
7. What is the fixed asset turnover ratio for the 2015 fiscal year? What does it suggest?

LO8-1,8-3   **CP8-2**   **Finding Financial Information**

Canadian Tire Corporation

Refer to the financial statements and accompanying notes of Canadian Tire Corporation given in Appendix A at the end of this book.

Required:
Answer each of the following questions and indicate where you located the information to answer the question. (*Hint:* Use the notes to the financial statements for some of these questions.)

1. How much did the company spend on property and equipment (capital expenditures) in fiscal 2015?
2. What is the estimated useful life of leasehold improvements for depreciation purposes?
3. What was the historical cost of fixtures and equipment held by the company at the end of the 2015 fiscal year?
4. What proportion of the cost of buildings has been depreciated as at January 2, 2016? Is it possible to estimate how old the buildings are, on average?
5. What amount of depreciation of property, plant, and equipment and amortization of intangible assets was reported as an expense for the 2015 fiscal year?
6. What is the company's fixed asset turnover ratio for fiscal 2015? What does it suggest?

LO8-1,8-3   **CP8-3**   **Comparing Companies within an Industry**

Canadian Tire Corporation vs. Sears Canada Inc.

Refer to the financial statements of Canadian Tire Corporation (Appendix A) and Sears Canada Inc. (on *Connect*) and the Industry Ratio Report (Appendix B on *Connect*).

Required:

1. Compute the ratio of property, plant, and equipment (net) to total assets, for both companies each year. Why might the companies' ratios differ?

2. Compute the percentage of the gross amount of property, plant, and equipment that has been depreciated for each company for the most recent year. Why do you think the percentages differ?

3. Compute the fixed asset turnover ratio for the most recent year presented for both companies. Which has the higher efficiency in using assets? Why?

4. Compare the fixed asset turnover ratio for both companies to the industry average. Are these companies doing better or worse than the industry average in asset efficiency?

FINANCIAL REPORTING AND ANALYSIS CASES

 LO8-3

CP8-4

Using Financial Reports: Analyzing the Age of Assets

Grandma's Pizza Inc. is a growing chain of pizza restaurants. A note to the Company's financial statements for 2016 contained the following information (in thousands of dollars):

	2016	**2015**
Land	$ 32,795	$ 32,880
Buildings and improvements	87,010	86,892
Leasehold improvements	110,903	110,323
Equipment and other	333,884	320,480
Construction in progress	10,970	6,466
	575,562	557,041
Less accumulated depreciation and amortization	(361,518)	(337,584)
Net property and equipment	$214,044	$219,457

Depreciation and amortization expense charged to operations was $40,307 in the current year and $39,965 in the previous year. Depreciation is generally computed by using the straight-line method for financial reporting purposes.

Required:

1. What is your best estimate of the average expected life for Grandma's Pizza's depreciable assets?

2. What is your best estimate of the average age of Grandma's Pizza's depreciable assets?

   LO8-1,8-3,8-6,8-7

CP8-5

Shaw
Communications
Inc.

Using Financial Reports: Analyzing Fixed Asset Turnover Ratio and Cash Flows

Shaw Communications Inc. is a diversified Canadian communications and media company, providing consumers with broadband cable television, high-speed Internet, home phone, telecommunications, and satellite direct-to-home services. Selected data from a recent annual report are as follows (in millions of dollars):

Property, plant, and equipment, and intangibles	Current Year	Prior Year
From the consolidated statement of financial position and notes		
Property, plant, and equipment, net	$4,220	$3,652
Intangible assets with indefinite lives	7,938	7,268
Intangible assets with finite lives, net	1,042	645
From the consolidated statement of earnings		
Revenue	$5,488	$5,241
From the consolidated statement of cash flows		
Net earnings for the year	$ 880	$ 887
Adjustments:		
Depreciation and amortization	899	768
Other adjustments, net	(142)	(131)
Cash provided by operations	$1,637	$1,524
From the notes to the financial statements		
Accumulated depreciation on property and equipment	$3,588	$3,343

Required:

1. Compute the cost of the property, plant, and equipment at the end of the current year. Explain your answer.

2. What is your best estimate of the average expected life of Shaw's property, plant, and equipment? What was the approximate age of the property, plant, and equipment at the end of the current year? Assume that Shaw uses straight-line depreciation.

3. Compute the fixed asset turnover ratio for the current year. Explain your results.

4. On the consolidated statement of cash flows, why are the depreciation and amortization amounts added to net earnings for the year?

CRITICAL THINKING CASES

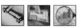

LO8-1,8-2,8-7 CP8-6

Marriott
International Inc.

Evaluating the Impact of Capitalized Interest on Cash Flows and Fixed Asset Turnover from an Analyst's Perspective

You are a financial analyst charged with evaluating the asset efficiency of companies in the hotel industry. Recent financial statements for Marriott International Inc. include the following note:

> **12. Property and Equipment**
>
> We record property and equipment at cost, including interest and real estate taxes we incur during development and construction. Interest we capitalized as a cost of property and equipment totalled $9 million in 2015, $33 million in 2014, and $31 million in 2013.

Required:

1. Assume that Marriott followed this policy for a major construction project this year. How does Marriott's policy affect the following (use + for increase, – for decrease, and N for no effect)?

    a. Cash flows

    b. Fixed asset turnover ratio

2. Normally, how would your answer to requirement (1b) affect your evaluation of Marriott's effectiveness in utilizing fixed assets?

3. If the fixed asset turnover ratio decreases due to interest capitalization, does this change indicate a real decrease in efficiency? Why or why not?

LO8-3,8-7 CP8-7

Evaluating an Ethical Dilemma: Analyzing an Accounting Change

The interim report for the fourth quarter of 2016 for Norwood Corporation included the following information:

> **Note 2. Changes in Accounting Policies and Significant Accounting Estimates**
>
> **Property, Plant, and Equipment**
>
> … The Company had utilized the straight line method of depreciation for production equipment, which allocates cost equally to each period. In a period of fluctuating production levels, the straight line depreciation method does not result in rational allocation of the cost of equipment to production. Consequently, effective July 1, 2016, the Company changed to the unit of production depreciation method for its production assets. This method allocates the equipment costs to the actual units produced based on estimated annual capacity over the remaining useful life of the assets. The impact of this change has been applied prospectively as a change in an estimate, and it resulted in a $12 million reduction in depreciation expense in 2016.

Required:

1. What was the stated reason for the change in depreciation method? What other factors do you think management considered when it decided to make this accounting change?

2. Do you think this is an ethical decision?

3. Who were affected by the change, and how were they benefited or harmed?

4. What impact did this change have on cash flows for Norwood?

5. As an investor, how would you react to the fact that Norwood's depreciation expense will decrease by $12 million?

LO8-1,8-2 CP8-8

Evaluating an Ethical Dilemma: A Real-Life Example

Assume you work as a staff member in a large accounting department for a multinational public company. Your job requires you to review documents relating to the company's equipment purchases. Upon verifying that purchases are properly approved, you prepare journal entries to record the equipment purchases in the accounting system. Typically, you handle equipment purchases costing $100,000 or less.

This morning, you were contacted by the executive assistant to the chief financial officer (CFO). She says that the CFO has asked to see you immediately in his office. Although your boss's boss has attended a few meetings where the CFO was present, you have never met the CFO during your three years with the company. Needless to say, you are anxious about the meeting.

Upon entering the CFO's office, you are warmly greeted with a smile and friendly handshake. The CFO compliments you on the great work that you have been doing for the company. You soon feel a little more comfortable, particularly when the CFO mentions that he has a special project for you. He states that he and the CEO have negotiated significant new arrangements with the company's equipment suppliers, which require the company to make advance payments for equipment to be purchased in the future. The CFO says that, for various reasons that he did not want to discuss, he will be processing the payments through the operating division of the company rather than the equipment accounting group. Given that the payments will be made through the operating division, they will initially be classified as operating expenses of the company. He indicates that clearly these advance payments for property and equipment should be recorded as assets, so he will be contacting you at the end of every quarter to make an adjusting journal entry to capitalize the amounts inappropriately classified as operating expenses. He advises you that a new account, called prepaid equipment, has been established for this purpose. He quickly wraps up the meeting by telling you that it is important that you not talk about the special project with anyone. You assume he doesn't want others to become jealous of your new important responsibility.

A few weeks later, at the end of the first quarter, you receive a voicemail from the CFO stating, "The adjustment that we discussed is $771,000,000 for this quarter." Before deleting the message, you replay it to make sure you heard it right. Your company generates over $8 billion in revenues and incurs $6 billion in operating expenses every quarter, but you have never made a journal entry for that much money. So, just to be sure there is not a mistake, you send an e-mail to the CFO confirming the amount. He phones you back immediately to abruptly inform you, "There's no mistake. That's the number." Feeling embarrassed that you may have annoyed the CFO, you quietly make the adjusting journal entry.

For each of the remaining three quarters in that year and for the first quarter in the following year, you continue to make these end-of-quarter adjustments. The "magic number," as the CFO liked to call it, was $560,000,000 for Q2, $742,745,000 for Q3, $941,000,000 for Q4, and $818,204,000 for Q1 of the following year. During this time, you have had several meetings and lunches with the CFO where he provides you the magic number, sometimes supported with nothing more than a Post-it note with the number written on it. He frequently compliments you on your good work and promises that you will soon be in line for a big promotion.

Despite the CFO's compliments and promises, you are growing increasingly uncomfortable with the journal entries that you have been making. Typically, whenever an ordinary equipment purchase involves an advance payment, the purchase is completed a few weeks later. At that time, the amount of the advance is removed from an equipment deposit account and transferred to the appropriate equipment account. This has not been the case with the CFO's special project. Instead, the prepaid equipment account has continued to grow, now standing at over $3.8 billion. There has been no discussion about how or when this balance will be reduced, and no depreciation has been recorded for it.

Just as you begin to reflect on the effect the adjustments have had on your company's fixed assets, operating expenses, and earnings from operations, you receive a call from the vice-president for internal audit. She needs to talk with you this afternoon about "a peculiar trend in the company's fixed asset turnover ratio and some suspicious journal entries that you have been making."

Required:

1. Complete the following table to determine what the company's accounting records would have looked like had you not made the journal entries as part of the CFO's special project. Comment on how the decision to capitalize amounts, which were initially recorded as operating expenses, has affected the level of earnings from operations in each quarter.

(amounts in millions of U.S. dollars)	Q1 Year 1 (March 31)		Q2 Year 1 (June 30)		Q3 Year 1 (September 30)		Q4 Year 1 (December 31)		Q1 Year 2 (March 31)	
	With Entries	Without Entries	With Entries	Without Entries	With Entries	Without Entries	With Entries	Without Entries	With Entries	Without Entries
Property and equipment, net	$38,614	$	$35,982	$	$38,151	$	$38,809	$	$39,155	$
Sales revenues	8,825	8,825	8,910	8,910	8,966	8,966	8,478	8,478	8,120	8,120
Operating expenses	7,628		8,526		7,786		7,725		7,277	
Earnings from operations	1,197		384		1,180		753		843	

2. Using the publicly reported numbers (which include the special journal entries that you recorded), compute the fixed asset turnover ratio (rounded to two decimal places) for the periods ended

Q2–Q4 of year 1 and Q1 of year 2. What does the trend in this ratio suggest to you? Is this consistent with the changes in earnings from operations reported by the company?

3. Before your meeting with the vice-president for internal audit, you think about the above computations and the variety of peculiar circumstances surrounding the "special project" for the CFO. What in particular might have raised your suspicion about the real nature of your work?

4. Your meeting with internal audit was short and unpleasant. The vice-president indicated that she had discussed her findings with the CFO before meeting with you. The CFO claimed that he too had noticed the peculiar trend in the fixed asset turnover ratio, but that he had not had a chance to investigate it further. He urged internal audit to get to the bottom of things, suggesting that perhaps someone might be making unapproved journal entries. Internal audit had identified you as the source of the journal entries and had been unable to find any documents that approved or substantiated the entries. She ended the meeting by advising you to find a good lawyer. Given your current circumstances, describe how you would have acted earlier had you been able to foresee where it might lead you.

5. In the real case on which this one is based, the internal auditors agonized over the question of whether they had actually uncovered a fraud or whether they were jumping to the wrong conclusion. *The Wall Street Journal* mentioned this on October 30, 2002, by stating, "it was clear… that their findings would be devastating for the company. They worried about whether their revelations would result in layoffs. Plus, they feared that they would somehow end up being blamed for the mess." Beyond the personal consequences mentioned in this quote, describe other potential ways in which the findings of the internal auditors would likely be devastating for the publicly traded company and those associated with it.

WorldCom Verizon

Epilogue: This case is based on a fraud committed at WorldCom (now called Verizon). The case draws its numbers, the nature of the unsupported journal entries, and the CFO's role in carrying out the fraud from a report issued by WorldCom's bankruptcy examiner. Year 1 in this case was actually 2001 and year 2 was 2002. This case excludes other fraudulent activities that contributed to WorldCom's $11 billion fraud. The 63-year-old CEO was sentenced to 25 years in prison for planning and executing the biggest fraud in the history of American business. The CFO, who cooperated in the investigation of the CEO, was sentenced to five years in prison.

FINANCIAL REPORTING AND ANALYSIS TEAM PROJECT

LO8-3,8-7 **CP8-9**

Team Project: Analyzing Long-Lived Assets

As a team, select an industry to analyze. A list of companies classified by industry can be obtained by accessing www.fpinfomart.ca and then choosing Companies by Industry. You can also find a list of industries and companies within each industry via http://ca.finance.yahoo.com/investing (click on Order Annual Reports under Tools).

Each group member should acquire the annual report for a different publicly traded company in the industry. (Library files, the SEDAR service at www.sedar.com, and the company's website are good sources.)

Required:

On an individual basis, each team member should then write a short report answering the following questions about the selected company. Discuss any patterns across the companies that you as a team observe. Then, as a group, write a short report comparing and contrasting your companies.

1. List the accounts and amounts of the company's long-lived assets (land, buildings, equipment, intangible assets, natural resources, and other).
   a. What is the percentage of each to total assets?
   b. What do the results of your analysis suggest about the strategy your company has followed with respect to investing in long-lived assets?

2. What cost allocation method(s) and estimates does the company use for each type of long-lived asset?

3. Compute the approximate average remaining useful life of property, plant, and equipment overall.

4. What does the company disclose regarding asset impairment? What was its impairment loss, if any, in the most recent year?

5. Perform a ratio analysis:
   a. What does the fixed asset turnover ratio measure in general?
   b. Compute the ratio for the last three years.

    c. What do your results suggest about the company?

    d. If available, find the industry ratio for the most recent year, compare it to your results, and discuss why you believe your company differs from or is similar to the industry ratio.

6. What was the effect of depreciation expense on cash flows from operating activities? Compute the ratio of depreciation expense to cash flows from operating activities for each of the past three years.

7. Refer to the statement of cash flows and identify the capital expenditures that the company made over the last three years. Did the company sell any long-lived assets?

▨ connect CONTINUING CASE

LO8-2,8-3,8-5 CC8-1   **Asset Acquisition, Depreciation, and Disposal**

Pool Corporation Inc. is the world's largest wholesale distributor of swimming pool supplies and equipment. Assume Pool Corporation purchased, for cash, new loading equipment for the warehouse on January 1, 2017, at an invoice price of $72,000. It also paid $2,000 for freight on the equipment, $1,300 to prepare the equipment for use in the warehouse, and $800 for insurance to cover the equipment during operation in 2017. The equipment was estimated to have a residual value of $3,300 and be used over three years or 24,000 hours.

Required:

1. Record the purchase of the equipment, freight, preparation costs, and insurance on January 1, 2017.

2. Create a depreciation schedule assuming Pool Corporation uses the straight-line method.

3. Create a depreciation schedule assuming Pool Corporation uses the double declining-balance method. Round answers to the nearest dollar.

4. Create a depreciation schedule assuming Pool Corporation uses the units-of-production method, with actual production of 8,000 hours in 2017, 7,400 hours in 2018, and 8,600 hours in 2019.

5. On December 31, 2018, the equipment was sold for $22,500. Record the sale of the equipment assuming the company used the straight-line method.

SOLUTIONS TO SELF-STUDY QUIZZES

Self-Study Quiz 8-1

1. (Amounts in thousands)

Property, Plant, and Equipment (PPE)	
Acquisition cost	$1,800,000
Transportation	8,000
Installation	1,300
Total	$1,809,300

The maintenance contracts are not necessary for making the assets ready for use and, therefore, are not included in the acquisition cost.

2. (Amounts in thousands)

	Assets	Liabilities		Shareholders' Equity	
a. PPE	+ 1,809,300	Note payable	+ 1,266,510		
Cash	− 542,790				
b. PPE	+ 1,809,300			Share capital	+ 1,050,000
Cash	− 759,300				

Self-Study Quiz 8-2

1. Capitalize
2. Expense
3. Expense
4. Capitalize

Self-Study Quiz 8-3

1. ($240,000 − $30,000) × 1/6 = $35,000
2. ($240,000 − 0) × 2/6 = $80,000
3. [($240,000 − $30,000) ÷ 50,000] × 8,000 = $33,600

Self-Study Quiz 8-4

Depreciation expense = $50,000 (carrying amount after 5 years) ÷ 2 years (remaining life) = $25,000

Self-Study Quiz 8-5

1.	Depreciation expense (E)	71,000	
	Accumulated depreciation—aircraft (XA)		71,000
2.	Cash (A)	2,500,000	
	Accumulated depreciation—aircraft (XA)	295,000	
	Gain on sale of asset (+ Gain, + SE)		195,000
	Aircraft (A)		2,600,000

ENDNOTES

1. The term "depletion" most often refers to the allocation of the acquisition cost of natural resources, while the term "amortization" is often used in reference to the allocation of the acquisition cost of intangible assets. These terms are discussed later in this chapter.

2. WestJet Airlines reported in Note 1(j) that its aircraft have expected useful lives ranging from 15 to 20 years. We assume a weighted average useful life of 18 years instead of a simple average of 17.5 years.

3. International Accounting Standard Board, International Accounting Standard 16-Property, Plant and Equipment: paras. 43–47.

4. Most of the examples that we discuss in this chapter assume that assets were acquired on the first day of the year and depreciated for the entire year. In practice, assets are purchased at various times during the year. Most companies adopt a policy to cover partial-year depreciation, such as "to the nearest full month" or "half year in the year of acquisition."

5. Sony Corporation, Annual Report 2014.

6. Sale of the aircraft during the year requires updating the accumulated depreciation account to the date of sale by computing depreciation for a fraction of the year. The depreciation expense could be based on the number of months of depreciation, or 50 percent of the annual depreciation if the company uses the half-year rule.

7. The same analysis applies when a company exchanges an old asset for a new asset of the same kind, such as an old vehicle for a newer model.

8. Consistent with the procedure for recording depreciation, an accumulated depletion account may be used. In practice, most companies credit the asset account directly for the periodic depletion. This procedure is also typically used for intangible assets, which are discussed in the next section.

Reporting and Interpreting Current Liabilities

After studying this chapter, you should be able to do the following:

LEARNING OBJECTIVES

LO9-1 Define, measure, and report current liabilities.

LO9-2 Compute and interpret the quick ratio.

LO9-3 Compute and interpret the accounts payable turnover ratio.

LO9-4 Report notes payable, and explain the time value of money.

LO9-5 Report contingent liabilities.

LO9-6 Explain the importance of working capital and its impact on cash flows.

SUPPLEMENTARY MATERIAL

LO9-S1 Compute and report deferred income taxes.

LO9-S2 Compute and report present values of future cash flows.

LO9-S3 Compute and report future value of a single amount. (Online)

LO9-S4 Compute and report future value of an annuity. (Online)

IVY PHOTOS/Shutterstock.com

Focus Company: **Sears Canada Inc.**

MANAGING CAPITAL STRUCTURE

Sears Canada Inc. (www.sears.ca) offers Canadian consumers a diverse array of shopping options, with department and specialty stores, Canada's most extensive general merchandise catalogue, a comprehensive website, and a broad range of home-related services from coast to coast across Canada. The company offers a wide range of general merchandise through its department stores. Home furnishings, major appliances, and home electronics are offered through Sear Home stores. In small communities, Sears offers a wide assortment of products through locally owned Hometown Dealer Stores. Its parent company, Sears Holdings Corporation, also owns Kmart Holding Corporation and Sears, Roebuck and Co. Holdings. Important brand names include DieHard® (T-shirts and hoodies), Kenmore® (appliances), and Craftsman® (tools).

The progression of the Internet and advances in mobile technology, social networking, and social media are reshaping the relationship of Sears with its customers. The company continues to shift its strategy to its core customers, developing a membership model of business that provides them with convenience and products of value through the proprietary Shop Your Way® membership platform. The parent company has invested in online ecommerce platforms, the membership program, and the technology to support this strategy.

In Canada, the effect of this shift in the retailing model has established four areas of focus: product, operations, infrastructure, and network. The goal is to provide Canadians with fashionable, high-quality materials and great service using the Canada's Best brand to signify the best value in products Sears sells. In operations, the company is focused on improving its cost-efficient inventory and supply chain, not only for products but financial services also.

To achieve its goal of being a multi-channel retailer, maximizing online as well as traditional walk-in and catalogue access to its services, Sears has upgraded its infrastructure and technology. Its goal is to deliver a unified brand story as an authentically Canadian retailer throughout all its purchasing channels. The transition at Sears will lead to some divestment of unprofitable operations that are not essential to its core retail operations.

In addition to operating activities, management must focus on a number of critical financing activities to ensure that the company remains profitable and is able to generate sufficient resources to meet its goals. The financing activities for Sears generate funds to serve two important purposes: (1) finance the current operating activities of the business and (2) acquire long-lived assets that permit the company to grow in the future.

UNDERSTANDING THE BUSINESS

Businesses finance the acquisition of their assets from two sources: funds supplied by creditors (debt) and funds provided by owners (equity). The mixture of debt and equity used by a business to finance its short- and long-term operating requirements is called its **capital structure**. In addition to choosing a capital structure, management can select from a variety of sources when borrowing money, as illustrated in the liabilities section of the statement of financial position for Sears in Exhibit 9.1.

CAPITAL STRUCTURE is the mixture of debt and equity that finances the short-and long-term operating requirements of a company.

SEARS CANADA INC. Consolidated Statements of Financial Position (Partial) (in millions of Canadian dollars)			
	Notes	As at January 30, 2016	As at January 31, 2015
LIABILITIES			
Current liabilities			
Accounts payable and accrued liabilities	14, 15	$ 332.7	$ 359.4
Deferred revenue	13	158.3	171.2
Provisions	16	75.8	58.6
Income taxes payable	22	2.6	—
Other taxes payable		17.3	34.6
Current portion of long-term obligations	14, 17, 19, 24	4.0	4.0
Total current liabilities		590.7	627.8
Non-current liabilities			
Long-term obligations	14, 17, 19, 24	20.2	24.1
Deferred revenue	13	74.2	76.8
Retirement benefit liability	14, 20.1	326.9	407.4
Deferred tax liabilities	22	—	3.4
Other long-term liabilities	16, 18	67.0	63.8
Total non-current liabilities		488.3	575.5
Total liabilities		$1,079.0	$1,203.3

Source: Sears Canada Inc., Annual Report 2015.

Exhibit 9.1

Liabilities of Sears Canada Inc.

REAL-WORLD EXCERPT

Sears Canada Inc.

ANNUAL REPORT

In deciding how best to finance its projects, Sears's management must consider two key factors: the financial risk associated with the source of financing and the cost. From the firm's perspective, debt capital is riskier than equity, because interest and principal payments on debt are legal obligations that must be paid. If a company cannot meet a required debt payment because of a temporary cash shortage, creditors may force the company into bankruptcy and require the sale of assets to satisfy the debt obligations. As with any business transaction, borrowers and lenders attempt to negotiate the most favourable terms possible. Managers devote considerable effort to analyzing alternative borrowing arrangements.

In contrast, dividend payments to shareholders are not legal obligations until declared by the board of directors. Therefore, equity offers lower financial risk to the issuing corporation. While companies may suspend or reduce the amount of dividends during periods of financial difficulty, they may not suspend the payment of principal and interest owed to creditors without negative consequences.

Companies that include debt in their capital structure must also make strategic decisions concerning the proper balance between short-term and long-term debt. To evaluate a company's capital structure, financial analysts calculate a number of accounting ratios. In this chapter, we primarily discuss current (short-term) liabilities, as well as some important accounting ratios. We will also introduce present value concepts in Appendix 9B. In the next chapter, we discuss special types of long-term debt.

ORGANIZATION OF THE CHAPTER

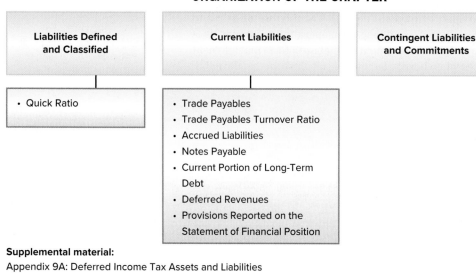

| Liabilities Defined and Classified | Current Liabilities | Contingent Liabilities and Commitments | Working Capital Management |

- Quick Ratio

- Trade Payables
- Trade Payables Turnover Ratio
- Accrued Liabilities
- Notes Payable
- Current Portion of Long-Term Debt
- Deferred Revenues
- Provisions Reported on the Statement of Financial Position

Supplemental material:

Appendix 9A: Deferred Income Tax Assets and Liabilities

Appendix 9B: Present Value Concepts

Appendix 9C: Present Value Tables

Appendix 9D: Present Value Computations Using Excel (on *Connect*)

Appendix 9E: Future Value Concepts (on *Connect*)

LIABILITIES DEFINED AND CLASSIFIED

LO9-1

Define, measure, and report current liabilities.

LIABILITIES are present debts or obligations arising from an entity's past transactions that will be paid with assets or services.

Most people have a reasonable understanding of the definition of the word *liability*. Accountants formally define **liabilities** as present debts or obligations arising from an entity's past transactions that will be paid with assets or services. As Exhibit 9.1 shows, Sears reported current and non-current liabilities of $1,079.0 million as at January 30, 2016. Sears has borrowed money in the past from creditors and purchased goods and services on credit (past transactions), promising its creditors to pay cash (an asset) at some point in the future, based on the terms of its debt agreements.

When a liability is first recorded, it is measured in terms of its current cash equivalent, which is the cash amount that a creditor would accept to settle the liability immediately. Although Sears had current and non-current debt of $24.2 million as at January 30, 2016, it will repay much more than that, because the company must also pay interest on the debt. Interest payable in the future is not included in the amount of the liability because it accrues and becomes a liability with the passage of time. For fiscal year 2015, the company reported $6.3 million of interest expense in Note 17 to its financial statements.

Like most businesses, Sears has several kinds of liabilities and a wide range of creditors. The list of liabilities on the statement of financial position differs from one company to the next, because different operating activities result in different types of liabilities. The liability section of Sears's statement of financial position begins with the caption "Current liabilities." **Current liabilities** are defined as short-term obligations that will be settled within the coming year by providing cash, goods, other current assets or services. If the entity's operating cycle is longer than one year, then obligations that will be settled within the operating cycle are classified as current liabilities. Because most companies have an operating cycle that is shorter than one year, current liabilities can normally be defined simply as liabilities that are due within one year. Non-current liabilities include all other liabilities.

Information about current liabilities is very important to managers and analysts because these obligations must be paid in the near future. Companies that do not settle their current obligations in a timely manner quickly find that suppliers of goods and services may not be prepared to grant them credit for their purchases, and they may be forced to seek short-term financing through banks. Analysts say that a company has **liquidity** if it has the ability to pay its current obligations. A number of financial ratios are useful in evaluating liquidity, including the current ratio (discussed in Chapter 2), the quick ratio, and the dollar amount of working capital (defined as current assets minus current liabilities). Working capital is a margin of safety indicating that a company can meet its short-term obligations. Sears reported current assets of $1,133.7 million as at January 30, 2016, which is almost double its current liabilities of $590.7 million. The quick ratio is a conservative measure of liquidity, comparing only the most-liquid assets (cash, short-term investments, and net receivables) to current liabilities. In contrast, the current ratio includes all current assets in the numerator of the ratio.

Working capital management involves a delicate balance. On the one hand, working capital provides liquidity and a margin of safety. If sales activity slows, for example, working capital provides resources to maintain business operations during a period in which there are reduced cash inflows from customers. On the other hand, excess money tied up in bank accounts or inventory is not productive because it does not generate profits. Companies have become very sophisticated in managing working capital to provide needed liquidity without tying up excessive amounts of money in nonproductive assets. One example is the just-in-time (JIT) inventory method, which uses statistical methods to maintain optimal levels of inventory based on forecasted needs.

CURRENT LIABILITIES are short-term obligations that will be settled within the coming year by providing cash, goods, other current assets or services.

LIQUIDITY is the ability to pay current obligations.

QUICK RATIO

KEY RATIO ANALYSIS

ANALYTICAL QUESTION → Does the company currently have the resources to pay its short-term debt?

RATIO AND COMPARISONS → Analysts use the *quick ratio* as an indicator of the amount of quick assets (cash, short-term investments, and net receivables) available to satisfy current liabilities. It is computed as follows:

Quick ratio = Quick assets ÷ Current liabilities

The 2015 ratio for Sears Canada Inc. is,

$409,200,000 ÷ $590,700,000 = 0.69

LO9-2

Compute and interpret the quick ratio.

Comparisons over Time			Comparisons with Competitors	
Sears Canada			Hudson's Bay	Canadian Tire
2013	2014	2015	2015	2015
0.70	0.73	0.69	0.30	1.75

INTERPRETATIONS

In General → A high ratio normally suggests good liquidity, but too high a ratio suggests inefficient use of resources. Many strong companies use sophisticated management techniques to minimize funds invested in current assets, and as a result, have quick ratios that are very low.

Focus Company Analysis → Sears's quick ratio in 2015 indicates that the company has $0.69 to pay each $1.00 in current liabilities. It is relatively stable over the three-year period 2013–2015. In comparison to Sears's ratio, Hudson's Bay's ratio is much lower as most of its current assets are comprised of inventories, whereas Canadian Tire's is more than double that of Sears due to its sizable portfolio of short-term loans receivable.

A Few Cautions → The quick ratio may be a misleading measure of liquidity because it can be influenced by small variations in the flow of transactions. The repayment of a large bank loan could have a big impact on the ratio. Analysts recognize that managers can manipulate the quick ratio by engaging in particular types of transactions just before the close of the fiscal year. For example, the quick ratio can be improved by paying creditors immediately prior to the preparation of financial statements.

PAUSE FOR FEEDBACK

Companies incur current liabilities that require settlement within a short period of time. These liabilities are usually settled through cash payments. The quick ratio indicates whether quick assets are sufficient to pay current liabilities. Before you move on, complete the following questions to test your understanding of this ratio.

SELF-STUDY QUIZ 9-1

The quick ratio for Sears was 0.69 at January 30, 2016. For each of the following events, indicate whether the quick ratio will increase or decrease, and provide an explanation.

1. Sears signs a note, payable in six months, in exchange for new equipment that costs $250,000.
2. The company borrows $1,000,000 in long-term debt.
3. The company pays income taxes payable in the amount of $550,000.
4. The company finances a new building with long-term debt.

After you complete your answers, check them with the solutions at the end of the chapter.

Liabilities are very important from an analytical perspective, because they affect a company's future cash flows and risk characteristics. Current liabilities are usually grouped according to type of creditor, separating liabilities owed to trade suppliers and other creditors (accounts payable) from those owed to providers of services (accrued liabilities), customers (deferred revenue), banks (short-term borrowings), governments (taxes payable), and others. For many types of liabilities, the amount of the debt is determined based on contractual agreements between the company and suppliers of goods, services, or funds. Most of these liabilities are recorded as they occur during the accounting period, as in the case of trade payables for merchandise purchases, loans from banks, and notes payable to creditors. However, specific liabilities that can be determined with accuracy, such as salaries payable and interest payable, require accrual through adjusting entries at the end of the accounting period, prior to the preparation of financial statements.

For other types of liabilities, the exact amounts will not be known with certainty until a future event, but they must be estimated and recorded if they relate to transactions that occurred during the accounting period. For example, a liability for a product warranty will not be known until the repair work is carried out in the future. But the matching process requires that warranty costs be recognized as an expense during the same period in which the product was sold. Because these costs and the related liability are not known, they must be estimated based on past experience or some reasonable basis and recorded through adjusting entries. Most often, the estimate of future warranty costs is based on a percentage of net sales. Such liabilities are referred to *provisions* on the statement of financial position.

In particular cases, it may not be possible to provide a reasonable estimate of a potential future liability that is contingent on a future event. Relevant information about contingent liabilities must, therefore, be disclosed in notes to the financial statements.

CURRENT LIABILITIES

Many current liabilities have a direct relationship to the operating activities of a business. In other words, specific operating activities are financed, in part, by a related current liability. Some examples from the Sears annual report (Exhibit 9.1) are as follows:

Operating Activity		Current Liability
Purchase home appliances	$\longrightarrow$	Accounts payable
Service performed by employees	$\longrightarrow$	Accrued liabilities
Cash received from customers for future delivery of merchandise	$\longrightarrow$	Deferred revenue
Provide warranty on products sold	$\longrightarrow$	Provisions

By understanding the relationship between operating activities and current liabilities, an analyst can easily explain changes in the various current liability accounts.

We will now discuss the current liability accounts that are found on most statements of financial position.

Accounts Payable

Most companies do not produce all the goods and services they use in their basic operations. Instead, they purchase goods and services from other businesses. Typically, these transactions are made on credit, with cash payments occurring after the goods and services have been provided. As a result, these transactions create *accounts payable*, also called *trade accounts payable*.

For many companies, trade credit is a relatively inexpensive way to finance the purchase of inventory, because interest does not normally accrue on accounts payable. As an incentive to encourage more sales, some vendors may offer very generous credit terms that allow the buyer to possibly resell merchandise and collect cash before payment must be made to the original vendor. For example, Apple Inc. maintains an efficient cash management system by collecting cash from its credit customers before it pays its trade suppliers. In fiscal year 2015, Apple collected cash from customers after 27 days, on average, but paid its trade suppliers after 86 days, on average.

Some managers may be tempted to delay payment to suppliers for as long as possible to conserve cash. Normally, this strategy is not advisable. Most successful companies develop positive working relationships with their suppliers to ensure that they receive quality goods and services. Managers can destroy good supplier relationships if they are slow to pay. In addition, financial analysts become concerned if a business does not meet its obligations to trade creditors on a timely basis, because delayed payment often indicates that the company is experiencing financial difficulties. Both managers and analysts use the trade payables turnover ratio to evaluate effectiveness in managing payables.

ACCOUNTS PAYABLE TURNOVER RATIO

**KEY RATIO
ANALYSIS**

LO9-3

LO9-3

Compute and interpret the accounts payable turnover ratio.

ANALYTICAL QUESTION → How efficient is management at meeting its obligations to suppliers?

RATIO AND COMPARISONS → The *accounts payable turnover ratio* is a measure of how quickly management is paying trade suppliers. Analysts use this ratio as a measure of liquidity. It is computed as follows:

$$\text{Accounts payable turnover ratio} = \frac{\text{Cost of sales}}{\text{Average accounts payable}}$$

The 2015 ratio for Sears Canada Inc. is,

$$\frac{\$1,943.8}{\$184.1^*} = 10.56$$

$$*\frac{(\$205.7 + \$162.5)}{2} = \$184.1 \text{ (based on Note 15 of Sears's financial statements)}$$

In reality, the numerator of this ratio should be net credit purchases, not cost of sales, assuming the accounts payable relate to purchases from trade suppliers. Because credit purchases are not usually reported in financial statements, we use total purchases of merchandise inventory as a rough approximation, assuming that all purchases are made on credit. For merchandising companies, we compute purchases by adjusting the cost of sales for the change in inventory during the period, as follows:[1]

Purchases = Cost of sales + Ending inventory − Beginning inventory

For Sears, purchases for fiscal year 2015 equalled $1,876.2, and the accounts payable turnover ratio for 2015 would have decreased to 7.88 if the amount of purchases was substituted for cost of sales in the numerator. The decrease in the ratio from 8.43 to 7.88 is not significant. For most companies, inventories do not change significantly over time; hence, the cost of sales can be used instead of purchases in computing this ratio.

Comparisons over Time			Comparisons with Competitors	
Sears Canada			Hudson's Bay	Canadian Tire
2013	2014	2015	2015	2015
7.82	8.43	10.56	5.44	8.07*

*Canadian Tire reported trade payables and accrued liabilities as one item. Trade payables were estimated as 55 percent of the total amount based amounts reported by Sears and Hudson's Bay for these liabilities.

If the accounts payable of Sears are turned over 10.56 times per year, or every 365 days, how many days would be needed, on average, to turn these payables once? This is known as the *average age of payables* and is computed by dividing 10.56 into 365 days:

$$\text{Average age of payables} = \frac{365}{\text{Accounts payable turnover ratio}}$$

The average age of payables for Sears in 2015 is,

$$\frac{365 \text{ days}}{10.56} = 34.6 \text{ days}$$

INTERPRETATIONS

In General → A high turnover ratio normally suggests that a company is paying its suppliers in a timely manner.

A Few Cautions → The accounts payable turnover ratio is an average associated with all accounts payable. The ratio might not reflect reality if a company pays some creditors on time but is late with others. The ratio is also subject to manipulation. Managers could be late with payments to creditors during the entire year but catch up at year-end so that the ratio is at an acceptable level. A low ratio can indicate either liquidity problems (i.e., the company is not able to generate sufficient cash to meet its obligations) or aggressive cash management (i.e., the company maintains only the minimum amount of cash necessary to support its operating activities). The first is a problem; the second is a strength. Analysts would have to study other factors, such as the quick ratio and the amount of cash flows generated from operating activities, to fully explain the result.

Accrued Liabilities

In many situations, a business incurs an expense in one accounting period and makes cash payment for the expense in a subsequent period. **Accrued liabilities** are expenses that have been incurred before the end of an accounting period but have not yet been paid. These expenses include such items as employee salaries and wages, rent, interest, and income taxes. They are recorded as adjusting entries at year-end.

Income Taxes Payable Like individuals, corporations must pay tax at the appropriate federal and provincial rates on income from active business operations, property income, and capital gains arising from the sale of assets. Federal income tax rates change over time because of changes in governmental tax policies, and provincial income tax rates vary across Canadian provinces. In general, the combined corporate income tax rate is in the range of 30 to 35 percent.

Sears reported an income tax recovery of $338.8 million for 2014 and $67.9 million for 2015 because of the net losses reported for both years, as shown in the following excerpt from its consolidated statement of net loss:

> **ACCRUED LIABILITIES** are expenses that have been incurred but have not been paid at the end of the accounting period.

> **REAL-WORLD EXCERPT**
>
> *Sears Canada Inc.*
>
> ANNUAL REPORT

SEARS CANADA INC. **Consolidated Statements of Net Loss** **For the 52-week periods ended January 30, 2016 and January 31, 2015**		
(in millions of Canadian dollars)	2015	2014
Earnings (loss) before income taxes	$(62.7)	$(360.0)
Income tax (expenses) recovery		
Current	(8.1)	74.7
Deferred	2.9	(53.5)
	(5.9)	21.2
Net earnings (loss)	$(67.9)	$(338.8)

Source: Sears Canada Inc., Annual Report 2015.

Notice that the income tax expense or recovery for each year has two components: a current portion and a deferred portion. The current portion is payable or recoverable within prescribed time limits, but the deferred portion arises because of differences between the accounting rules used for financial reporting and the tax rules corporations must use to determine their taxable income, as explained in Chapter 8.[2]

Taxes Other Than Income Taxes In addition to paying taxes on income, companies are often required to collect and pay other types of taxes and fees, depending on the specific industry and geographical location in which they operate. These taxes add to the cost of producing and selling goods and services and are eventually passed on to customers through higher sales prices.[3] Typically, the prices of goods and services are increased by the federal Goods and Services Tax (GST), currently set at 5 percent, and a Provincial Sales Tax (PST) that varies between 0 and 10 percent, depending on the province, or a combined federal and provincial sales tax called the Harmonized Sales Tax (HST).[4]

The GST and PST, or HST, amounts are added to the sales price, collected from customers, and then remitted to the federal and provincial governments. In this respect, the seller acts as an intermediary between the customer and the federal and provincial governments and facilitates the collection of sales taxes from customers. When a company sells goods and services, the applicable sales taxes, if any, are added to the sales price, but they are not revenue for the seller. The sales taxes collected from customers represent liabilities that are remitted periodically (monthly or quarterly) to the respective governments. For example, if a Sears store in British Columbia sold apparel to a customer for $40, the total cash paid by the customer includes a GST of $2.00 ($40 × 5%) and a PST of $2.80 ($40 × 7%). The journal entry to record this transaction, and the transaction effects, are, as follows:

Cash (A)		44.80	
Sales revenue (R)			40.00
GST payable (L)			2.00
PST payable (L)			2.80

Assets		=	Liabilities		+	Shareholders' Equity	
Cash	+44.80		GST payable	+2.00		Sales revenue	+40.00
			PST payable	+2.80			

All of the GST and PST collected from customers is accumulated in these two liability accounts and then remitted to the federal and provincial governments on a monthly or quarterly basis. The unpaid amounts at year-end are included in current liabilities.

PAUSE FOR FEEDBACK

Customers are required to pay sales taxes on most of the goods and services they acquire. They pay these taxes to the companies that sell these goods and services. Companies serve as agents of the federal and provincial governments in collecting these taxes and then remitting them to the government authorities. Before you move on, complete the following question to test your understanding of sales taxes.

SELF-STUDY QUIZ 9-2

Assume that the sale of apparel for $40 cash was made in a Sears store located in Toronto, where sales of apparel are subject to a harmonized sales tax of 13 percent. Prepare the journal entry to record the sale transaction.

After you complete your answer, check it with the solution at the end of the chapter.

Payroll Liabilities   At the end of each accounting period, employees will usually have earned salaries that have not been paid. Unpaid salaries may be reported as a separate item or as part of accrued liabilities, as is the case with Sears. In addition to reporting salaries that have been earned but are unpaid, companies must also report the cost of unpaid benefits, which include retirement programs, vacation time, employment insurance, health insurance, and many others. Employers must also remit income tax and other social benefit contributions on behalf of their employees to the appropriate government agencies. While we will look at only the three largest deductions for most people, reporting is similar for each type of payroll tax.

Employee Deductions   Federal and provincial laws require the employer to deduct an appropriate amount of income tax each period from the gross earnings of each employee. Employee income tax is usually the largest amount withheld from wages and salaries by the employer. The amount of income tax withheld from the employee's salary is recorded by the employer as a current liability between the date of deduction and the date on which the amount held is remitted to the government. If you have been employed and received a paycheque, you have probably noticed that additional amounts were deducted from your gross earnings for Employment Insurance (EI); for contributions to the Canada Pension Plan (CPP), or Quebec Pension Plan (QPP) in the province of Quebec; for future retirement benefits; for health insurance; and for other contributions that you and your employer must remit to the appropriate agencies.

In general, employers match the employee's CPP remittance, but they are required by Canada Revenue Agency to pay $1.40 for every $1.00 remitted by the employee for EI. Other deductions, such as union dues and workers' compensation, depend on the terms of employment and will result in a future obligation for the employer to remit these amounts to the legal recipient. In total, the employer's share of contributions remitted by a corporation on behalf of its employees to other parties can add up to 20 percent of the employee's gross earnings.

Compensation expense for employee services includes all funds earned by the employee as well as funds that must be paid to others on behalf of employees (i.e., benefits). To illustrate, let us assume that Sears's operations accumulated the following information in their detailed payroll records for the first two weeks of January 2017:

Salaries and wages earned	$18,000,000
Income taxes withheld	4,500,000
CPP contributions	710,000
EI contributions	350,000

The entry to record the payroll and employee deductions, and the related transaction effects, follow:

Compensation expense (E)	18,000,000	
Liability for income taxes withheld (L)		4,500,000
CPP payable (L)		710,000
EI payable (L)		350,000
Cash (A)		12,440,000

Assets	=	Liabilities	+	Shareholders' Equity
Cash −12,440,000		Liability for income taxes withheld +4,500,000		Compensation expense −18,000,000
		CPP payable +710,000		
		EI payable +350,000		

The employer must also contribute an equal amount of CPP contributions and 1.40 times the employees' contributions to EI. The second entry records the taxes that employers must pay from their own funds:

Compensation expense (E)	1,200,000	
CPP payable (L)		710,000
EI payable (L)		490,000

Assets	=	Liabilities	+	Shareholders' Equity
		CPP payable +710,000		Compensation expense −1,200,000
		EI payable +490,000		

The compensation expense ($18,000,000 + $1,200,000) includes salaries and wages earned, as well as the employer's share of CPP and EI contributions. The cash paid to employees ($12,440,000) is less than the total amount earned ($18,000,000) because the employer must withhold both income taxes ($4,500,000) and the employees' share of CPP and EI contributions ($1,060,000). The CPP and EI payable reflect both the employees' share and the employer's share.

The current liabilities of Sears include $170.2 million in accrued liabilities. The various items that make up this amount are disclosed in Note 15 to the company's financial statements for 2015.

NOTES TO THE CONSOLIDATED FINANCIAL STATEMENTS

15. Accounts payable and accrued liabilities

The components of "Accounts payable and accrued liabilities" as included in the Consolidated Statements of Financial Position were as follows:

(in millions of Canadian dollars)	As at January 30, 2016	As At January 31, 2015
Total accounts payable	$162.5	$205.7
Accrued liabilities		
Payroll and employee benefits	29.0	26.6
Merchandise accruals	65.5	48.5
Short-term leasehold inducements	8.3	8.6
Advertising accruals	11.9	7.4
Other accrued liabilities	55.4	62.6
Total accrued liabilities	170.2	153.7
Total accounts payable and accrued liabilities	$332.7	$359.4

Source: Sears Canada Inc., Annual Report 2015.

REAL-WORLD EXCERPT

Sears Canada Inc.
ANNUAL REPORT

Notes Payable

LO9-4

Report notes payable, and explain the time value of money.

The **TIME VALUE OF MONEY** is interest that is associated with the use of money over time.

Most companies need to borrow money to finance their operations. When a company borrows money, a formal written contract is usually prepared. Obligations supported by these written notes are typically called *notes payable*. A note payable specifies the amount borrowed, the date by which it must be paid, and the interest rate associated with the borrowing.

Creditors are willing to lend cash because they will earn interest as compensation for giving up the use of their money for a period. This simple concept, called the **time value of money**, is interest that is associated with the use of money over time. The longer the borrowed money is held, the larger is the dollar amount of interest expense. Interest at a given interest rate on a two-year loan is more than interest on a one-year loan. To the *borrower*, interest is an expense; to the *creditor*, interest is revenue.

To calculate interest, three variables must be considered: (1) the principal (i.e., the cash that was borrowed), (2) the annual interest rate, and (3) the time period for the loan. The interest formula is

$$\textbf{Interest} = \textbf{Principal} \times \textbf{Annual interest rate} \times \textbf{Time}$$

To illustrate the accounting for a note payable, assume that on December 1, 2017, Sears borrowed $100,000 cash on a one-year, 6 percent note payable. The interest is payable on May 31, 2018, and November 30, 2018. The principal is payable at the maturity date of the note, November 30, 2018. The note is recorded in the accounts as follows:

Cash (A)				100,000	
Note payable, short term (L)					100,000
Assets	=	**Liabilities**	+	**Shareholders' Equity**	
Cash +100,000		Notes payable +100,000			

Interest on this note is incurred as long as the debt is outstanding. Interest expense is recorded when it is incurred rather than when the cash is actually paid. Because the company uses the money for two months during fiscal year 2017, it records interest expense in 2017 for two months, even though cash is not paid until May 31, 2018.

The computation of interest expense for fiscal year 2017 is as follows:[5]

$$\textbf{Interest} = \textbf{Principal} \times \textbf{Annual interest rate} \times \textbf{Time}$$
$$\textbf{Interest} = \$100{,}000 \times 6\% \times 2/12 = \$1{,}000$$

Note that interest expense is calculated for a specific accounting period, which varies from one month up to one year. The entry to record interest expense on January 31, 2018, is as follows:

Interest expense (E)				1,000	
Interest payable (L)					1,000
Assets	=	**Liabilities**	+	**Shareholders' Equity**	
		Interest payable +1,000		Interest expense −1,000	

On May 31, 2018, Sears would pay $3,000 in interest, which includes the $1,000 accrued and reported in fiscal year 2017, plus the $2,000 interest accrued in the first four months of fiscal year 2018. The following journal entry would be made:

Interest expense (E)				2,000	
Interest payable (L)				1,000	
Cash (A)					3,000
Assets	=	**Liabilities**	+	**Shareholders' Equity**	
Cash −3,000		Interest payable −1,000		Interest expense −2,000	

PAUSE FOR **FEEDBACK** STOP

When a company borrows money from a creditor, it must pay interest on the amount borrowed. Interest is incurred over time, and the amount payable depends on the amount borrowed, the interest rate, and how long the loan was outstanding. Before you move on, complete the following questions to test your understanding of this concept.

SELF-STUDY **QUIZ 9-3**

In the previous example, we assumed that the $100,000 note payable by Sears required payment of interest on May 31 and November 30. Assume that the one-year note payable was signed on October 1, 2017, and required payment of interest every three months, starting on December 31, 2017.

1. What adjusting entry should Sears make at the end of its fiscal year for 2017?

2. What entry should the company make on March 31, 2018?

3. What entry should the company make on June 30, 2018?

After you complete your answers, check them with the solutions at the end of the chapter.

Current Portion of Long-Term Debt

The distinction between current and long-term debt is important for both managers and analysts. Because current debt must be paid within the next year, companies must have sufficient cash to repay currently maturing debt. To provide accurate information concerning current liabilities, a company must reclassify long-term debt within a year of its maturity date as a current liability. Assume that Sears signed a note payable of $5 million on June 1, 2016. Repayment is required on May 31, 2019. The statements of financial position at February 3, 2018, and February 2, 2019, would report the following:

February 3, 2018

Non-current liabilities	
Note payable	$5,000,000

February 2, 2019

Current liabilities	
Current portion of long-term note	$5,000,000

An example of this type of disclosure can be seen in Exhibit 9.1. Notice that Sears reported $4 million as the current portion of long-term obligations at January 30, 2016. This portion is payable in full during fiscal year 2016. In some cases, companies will refinance debt when it comes due rather than pay out cash currently on hand.

Deferred Revenues

In most business transactions, cash is paid after the product or service has been delivered. In some cases, cash is paid before delivery. You have probably paid for magazines that you will receive at some time in the future. The publisher collects money for your subscription in advance, before the magazine is published or posted online. When a company collects cash before the related revenue has been earned, the cash received represents **deferred revenues**.

Sears offers a broad range of merchandise from apparel and home fashions to appliances through many department stores and online, and it also sells extended warranty services on the products it sells. Should the product break down, Sears will provide repair services within its contractual obligations. More frequently, however, the product will function properly and no service is required. Sears defers revenue

DEFERRED REVENUES are previously recorded liabilities that need to be adjusted at the end of the accounting period to reflect the amount of revenues earned.

from selling extended warranties and then recognizes the revenue earned gradually over the duration of the contracts or when the service is completed. Sears included the following details in its 2015 annual report:

REAL-WORLD EXCERPT

Sears Canada Inc.

ANNUAL REPORT

NOTES TO THE CONSOLIDATED FINANCIAL STATEMENTS
13. Deferred revenue
The components of deferred revenue were, as follows:

(in millions of Canadian dollars):	Fiscal Year Ended	
	As at January 30, 2016	**As at January 31, 2015**
Arising from extended warranty service contracts[(i)]	**$131.2**	$134.8
Arising from unshipped sales[(ii)]	**50.8**	57.2
Arising from customer loyalty program[(iii)]	**34.1**	36.8
Arising from gift card issuances[(iv)]	**10.7**	15.0
Other[(v)]	**5.7**	4.2
Total deferred revenue	**$232.5**	$248.0
Current	**158.3**	271.2
Non-current	**74.2**	76.8
Total deferred revenue	**$232.5**	$248.0

The following explanations describe the Company's deferred revenue:
 (i) Deferred revenue arising from the sale of extended warranty service contracts, which provide coverage for product repair services over the term of the contracts.
 (ii) Deferred revenue arising from the sale of merchandise which has not yet been delivered to or picked up by the customer. The revenue is recognized once the merchandise is delivered to the customer.
 (iii) Deferred revenue arising from the Company's Sears Club loyalty program.
 (iv) Deferred revenue arising from the purchase of gift cards by customers that have not yet been redeemed for merchandise. The revenue is recognized primarily upon redemption of the gift card.
 (v) Other includes deferred revenue for goods that have not yet been fully delivered or services not yet rendered. The revenue is recognized when the goods have been delivered or by reference to the stage of completion of the service.

Source: Sears Canada Inc., Annual Report 2015.

Deferred revenue is reported as a liability because cash has been collected but the related revenue has not been earned by the end of the accounting period. The obligation to provide the services or goods in the future still exists. These obligations are classified as current or long term, depending on when they must be settled.

The information disclosed in this note indicates that Sears has engaged in transactions that resulted in different types of deferred revenue.

Assume that Sears signed new extended warranty contracts for appliances sold during fiscal year 2017 and received $81.6 million from customers in advance. The journal entry to record the deferred revenue for these contracts, and related transaction effects, follow:

Cash (A)		81.6	
Deferred extended warranty revenue (L)			81.6

Assets	=	Liabilities	+	Shareholders' Equity
Cash +81.6		Deferred extended warranty revenue +81.6		

As time passes, Sears earns a portion of the deferred revenue on the new contracts as well as part of the deferred revenue recorded in previous accounting periods. Assuming that a total of $74.7 million was earned during fiscal year 2017, the entry to record the earned revenue would be as follows:

Deferred extended warranty revenue (L)		74.7	
Revenue from extended warranties (R)			74.7

Gift cards and prepaid cards have become popular ways of selling merchandise or service for future delivery. These cards are usually purchased as gifts to others for special occasions. When a store sells a gift card, the amount received is a liability until the store delivers merchandise or service in the future. When the recipient of the gift card presents it to the store for redemption, the amount redeemed is recorded as revenue, the deferred revenue account is reduced, and the cost of merchandise given or service rendered is recorded as an expense. Sears sells gift cards throughout the fiscal year, particularly during the end-of-year holiday shopping season. The information disclosed in Note 13 to its annual report for fiscal year 2015 indicates that gift cards worth $10.7 million had not been redeemed by January 30, 2016, but would likely be presented for redemption within a short period of time.

Provisions Reported on the Statement of Financial Position

The liabilities discussed so far reflect specific amounts to be paid to identifiable parties by certain dates. When either the amount or the timing of the liability is uncertain, it is referred to as a **provision**. A provision must be recognized when the following conditions are met: (1) an entity has a present obligation as a result of a past event, (2) it is probable that cash or other assets will be required to settle the obligation, and (3) a reliable estimate can be made of the amount of the obligation. For example, an estimated liability is created when a company offers a warranty with the products it sells. The cost of providing repair work must be estimated and recorded as a liability (and expense) in the period in which the product is sold. Most companies quickly refund money for any defective products that they sell. The following disclosures from Sears's annual report provide additional information about its provisions, including warranty liabilities.

A **PROVISION** is a liability of uncertain timing or amount.

NOTES TO THE CONSOLIDATED FINANCIAL STATEMENTS

16. Provisions

The following is a continuity which shows the change in provisions during fiscal year 2015:

(in millions of dollars)	As at Jan. 31, 2015	Additional Provisions	Release of Provisions	Reversed Provisions	As at Jan. 30, 2016
Insurance(i)	$13.7	$ 3.2	$ (4.8)	$ —	$12.1
Returns and allowances(ii)	12.0	6.5	(7.4)	—	11.1
Warranties(iii)	8.2	0.6	(3.6)	—	5.2
Sales tax(iv)	6.0	22.1	(1.4)	—	26.7
Severance(v)	11.9	28.7	(18.3)	(5.9)	16.4
Environmental(vi)	6.1	2.7	(2.1)	(0.3)	6.4
Other provisions	5.5	—	(2.4)	(0.2)	2.9
Total provisions	$63.4	$63.8	$(40.0)	$(6.4)	80.8
Current	58.6	63.6	(40.0)	(6.4)	75.8
Non-current(iii)	4.8	0.2	—	—	5.0
Total provisions	$63.4	$63.8	$(40.0)	$(6.4)	$80.8

The following explanations describe the Company's provisions:

(i) The provision for insurance, or general liability claims, represents the Company's best estimate of the future outflow of economic resources due to automobile, product and other general liability claims. Insurance claims relating to this provision are expected to be paid over the next several years; however, as the Company has no unconditional right to defer the settlement past at least 12 months, this provision is considered to be current. In estimating the obligation associated with incurred losses, the Company utilizes actuarial methodologies validated by an independent third party. These actuarial methodologies utilize historical data to project future incurred losses. Loss estimates are adjusted based on reported claims and actual settlements.

(ii) The provision for returns and allowances represents the Company's best estimate of the future outflow of economic resources due to merchandise returns and allowances. Returns and allowances relating to this provision are expected to be realized over the next 12 months. Uncertainty exists relating to the amount and timing of returns and allowances, therefore, historical data has been used to arrive at this estimate.

(iii) The provision for warranty claims represents the Company's best estimate of the future outflow of economic resources that will be required due to the Company's warranty obligations. Uncertainty exists relating to the number of incidents requiring merchandise repair and the related costs. This provision is estimated based on historical warranty trends and costs. The amount of expected reimbursements from vendors recorded as at January 30, 2016 was $0.2 million (January 31, 2015: $0.2 million) and is reflected in "Accounts receivable, net" and "Other long-term assets" in the Consolidated Statements of Financial Position. The provision for warranty claims is primarily expected to be realized within 72 months, with the balance included in "Provisions" and "Other long-term liabilities" in the Consolidated Statements of Financial Position.

(iv) The Company maintains provisions for sales tax assessments under active discussion, audit, dispute or appeal with tax authorities. These provisions represent the Company's best estimate of the amount expected to be paid based on qualitative and quantitative assessments. Though uncertainty exists around the timing of settlement of the disputes or appeals with tax authorities, the Company expects that sales tax provisions will be settled within 4 years. However, as the Company has no unconditional right to defer the settlement of these provisions past at least 12 months, these provisions are classified as current.

(v) The provision for severance represents the Company's best estimate of the future outflow of payments to terminated employees. Uncertainty exists in certain cases relating to the amount of severance that will be awarded in court proceedings. As the Company has no unconditional right to defer these payments past at least 12 months, this provision is classified as current.

(vi) The environmental provision primarily represents the costs to remediate environmental contamination associated with decommissioning auto centres to meet regulatory requirements. The provision is based on assessments conducted by third parties as well as historical data. The timing of payments to remediate is uncertain and as the Company has no unconditional right to defer these payments past at least 12 months, the balance is included primarily in "Provisions", with the remainder of the balance included in "Other long-term liabilities" in the Consolidated Statements of Financial Position.

Source: Sears Canada Inc., Annual Report 2015.

Sears determines its warranty liability based on number of units sold, historical and anticipated rates of warranty claims on those units, and cost per claim to satisfy Sears's warranty obligation. Sears's estimate of the warranty expenses incurred in fiscal year 2015 as a result of the period's sales is $0.6 million. The journal entry to record the estimated liability at year-end follows:

| Warranty expense (E) | 800,000 | |
| Provision for product warranty (L) | | 800,000 |

Assets	=	Liabilities	+	Shareholders' Equity
		Provision for product warranty +800,000		Warranty expense −800,000

When the company receives units that require repair under the warranty, its employees repair the defective product, replace component parts as needed, and return the units to customers. The costs Sears incurred during fiscal year 2015 to satisfy its warranty obligations total $3.6 miliion. Sears refers to this amount as "utilizations" of the warranty. It is recorded as follows:

| Provision for product warranty (L) | 3,600,000 | |
| Cash (A) | | 3,600,000 |

This journal entry assumes that Sears paid cash to satisfy the warranty. If the product is exchanged for another one, then the inventories account is credited instead of cash. The warranty expense is not affected by the costs incurred under the warranty because the warranty expense is recognized separately, based on the volume of sales made during the fiscal year.

In addition to estimated liabilities for warranties, provisions are usually made for product returns and allowances; legal and tax disputes that arise in the ordinary course of business; closing of stores or specific operations; and restructuring of production, sales, or administrative structures. Information on provisions for items such as store closures helps potential and existing creditors, investors, and analysts to understand the implications of these liabilities.

OVERSTATEMENT OF LIABILITIES AND MANAGEMENT INCENTIVES

A QUESTION OF ACCOUNTABILITY

The amount of liabilities that companies are expected to pay in the future is not always known with certainty. As we indicated above, estimates of potential liabilities are often made when companies accrue expenses associated with specific accounting periods. The methods of estimating such expenses and liabilities often lead to imprecise amounts of future payments. The imprecise nature of the estimation process leads to either an overstatement or an understatement of the correct amount of the liability. An overstatement of expenses leads to an understatement of net earnings in the estimation period, and a subsequent overstatement of net earnings in the next account-ing period. Occasionally, managers may rely on the inaccurate nature of estimated liabilities to manipulate net earnings in ways that serve their self-interests. For example, the key executives of Nortel, which was one of the top global makers of telecommunication equipment in North America, overstated accrued liabilities during the years 2000 to 2002. In the first quarter of 2003, Nortel's executives reduced the overstated accrued liabilities, which had the effect of turning a loss for that quarter into a net earnings figure. Since the compensation of key executives was related to the company's financial performance, the key executives, who decided to reduce the balance of accrued liabilities in order to increase net earnings, received bonus payments from the company because the reported net earnings figure was then sufficiently large to cause a distribution of bonuses to key management personnel. When such an action was later uncovered by auditors, the company's board of directors fired the three top executives who had overall responsibility for the company's financial statements.

CONTINGENT LIABILITIES

Most students have an intuition about contingent liabilities. If you believe that failure to study may lead to failing a course, then you understand the concept of contingent liability. The actual failure in a course will be a liability because the student will incur additional costs for repeating the course. A student may not know, however, whether he or she failed the course until the final grade has been reported, but students know that it is possible to fail the course if they do not study. Their actions prior to the final assessment and subsequent reporting of their grades may lead to failure and addi-tional costs, which makes the failure to study a contingent liability.

Each of the liabilities that we have discussed is reported on the statement of finan-cial position with a specific monetary value, because each involves the *probable* future sacrifice of economic benefits. Some transactions or events create only a possible (but not probable) future sacrifice of economic benefits. These situations create contin-gent liabilities, which are possible liabilities that arise from past events and whose existence will be confirmed only by the occurrence or non-occurrence of one or more uncertain future events not entirely under the control of the company. In some cases, it is not probable that cash of other assets will be required to settle the obligation, or, in others, the amount of the obligation cannot be measured with sufficient reliability.[6] A **contingent liability** is a possible liability that is created as a result of a past event, and which may or may not become a recorded liability, depending on future events.

LO9-5

Report contingent liabilities.

A **CONTINGENT LIABILITY** is a possible liability that is created as a result of a past event; it is not an effective liability until some future event occurs.

Contingent Liability Examples

Lawsuits   Environmental problems   Tax disputes

Whether a situation produces a provision or a contingent liability relates to two factors: the probability of the future economic sacrifice and the ability of management to estimate the amount of the liability reliably. The following table offers scenarios of past events that result in a present obligation, or a possible obligation that depend on the occurrence, or not, of specific future events:

Level of certainty of the present or possible obligation	Should a liability be recognized?	Disclosure requirements
There is a present obligation that probably requires an outflow of resources.		
1. The amount of the liability can be estimated reliably.	A provision must be recognized.	Disclosure of the provision is required.
2. The amount of the liability cannot be estimated reliably.	No provision shall be recognized.	Disclosure is required for the contingency.
There is either a present or a possible obligation that may, but probably will not, require an outflow of resources.	No provision shall be recognized.	Disclosure is required for the contingency.
There is either a present or a possible obligation where the likelihood of an outflow of resources is remote.	No provision shall be recognized.	Disclosure is not required.

The notes to Sears's financial statements include a note that specifies the type of contingencies that the company may face in the future. The excerpt below provides a list of contingencies that are typical for many companies.

REAL-WORLD EXCERPT

Sears Canada Inc.

ANNUAL REPORT

NOTES TO THE CONSOLIDATED FINANCIAL STATEMENTS

21. Contingent liabilities

21.1 Legal Proceedings

The Company is involved in various legal proceedings incidental to the normal course of business. The Company takes into account all available information, including guidance from experts (such as internal and external legal counsel) at the time of reporting to determine if it is probable that a present obligation (legal or constructive) exists, if it is probable that an outflow of resources embodying economic benefit will be required to settle such obligation and whether the Company can reliably measure such obligation at the end of the reporting period. The Company is of the view that, although the outcome of such legal proceedings cannot be predicted with certainty, the final disposition is not expected to have a material adverse effect on the consolidated financial statements, including its Consolidated Statements of Financial Position, Consolidated Statements of Net Loss and Comprehensive Loss, and Consolidated Statements of Cash Flows.

Source: Sears Canada Inc., Annual Report 2015.

Sears reported not only its contingent liabilities related to legal proceedings but also its commitments and guarantees to pay specific amounts in the future. Commitments reflect contractual agreements to enter into transactions with other parties. Commitments to buy or sell goods and services or to make specific payments are not normally recorded in the accounting system, as long as there is no exchange transaction. Commitments to pay or receive cash are relevant to financial statement users and help them in predicting the company's future cash flows.

WORKING CAPITAL MANAGEMENT

Working capital is defined as the difference between current assets and current liabilities. It is important to both managers and financial analysts because it has a significant impact on the health and profitability of a company.

The working capital accounts are actively managed to achieve a balance between costs and benefits. On the one hand, if a business has too little working capital, it runs the risk of not being able to meet its obligations to creditors. On the other hand, too much working capital may tie up resources in unproductive assets and incur additional costs. Excess inventory, for example, ties up funds that could be invested more profitably elsewhere in the business, and incurs additional costs associated with storage and deterioration.

Changes in working capital accounts are also important to managers and analysts because they have a direct impact on the cash flows from operating activities reported on the statement of cash flows.

LO9-6

Explain the importance of working capital and its impact on cash flows.

WORKING CAPITAL is the difference between current assets and current liabilities.

WORKING CAPITAL AND CASH FLOWS

FOCUS ON
CASH FLOWS

Many working capital accounts have a direct relationship to income-producing activities. Trade receivables, for example, are related to sales revenue; trade receivables increase when sales are made on credit. Cash is collected when the customer pays the bill. Similarly, trade payables increase when an expense is incurred without a cash payment. A cash outflow occurs when the account is paid. Changes in working capital accounts that are related to income-producing activities must be considered when computing cash flows from operating activities.

EFFECT ON THE STATEMENT OF CASH FLOWS

In General → On the statement of cash flows, the net earnings figure is adjusted (under the indirect method) to compute cash flows from operating activities. As explained in Chapter 5, changes in working capital accounts (other than cash) affect cash flows from operations as shown in the following table:

	Effect on Cash Flows
Operating activities (indirect method)	
Net earnings	$xxx
Adjusted for:	
Decreases in current assets* or increases in current liabilities	+
Increases in current assets* or decreases in current liabilities	−
*Other than cash	

Focus Company Analysis → A segment of Sears's consolidated statement of cash flows for fiscal year 2015, prepared using the indirect method, follows:

REAL-WORLD EXCERPT

Sears Canada Inc.

ANNUAL REPORT

SEARS CANADA INC.			
Consolidated Statement of Cash Flows			
For the 52-week periods ended January 30, 2016, and January 31, 2015			
(in millions of Canadian dollars)	Notes	**2015**	2014
Cash flow used for operating activities:			
Net loss		**$ (67.9)**	$(338.8)
Adjustments for items not affecting cash (summarized)		**(57.6)**	111.3
Changes in non-cash working capital balances	33	**(64.3)**	(67.3)
Changes in non-cash long-term assets and liabilities	34	**(11.7)**	30.2
Net cash from (used in) operating activities		**$(201.5)**	$(264.6)

33. Changes in non-cash working capital balances

Cash (used for) generated from non-cash working capital balances were made up of the following:

	2015	2014
Accounts receivable, net	**$ 12.5**	$ 10.0
Inventories	**(23.4)**	133.2
Prepaid expenses	**(2.3)**	(5.6)
Derivative financial assets	**1.3**	1.0
Accounts payable and accrued liabilities	**(35.3)**	(74.0)
Deferred revenue	**(12.9)**	(16.5)
Provisions	**17.2**	(50.8)
Income and other taxes payable and recoverable	**(18.1)**	(62.5)
Effect of foreign exchange rates	**(3.3)**	(2.1)
Cash used for non-cash working capital balances	**$(64.3)**	$(67.3)

Source: Sears Canada Inc., Annual Report 2015.

Recall from our previous discussions of the statement of cash flows that revenues and expenses reported on the statement of earnings include both cash and non-cash components, and that changes in working capital accounts (other than cash and cash equivalents) reflect non-cash revenues and expenses during the accounting period. The disclosed information shows that changes in non-cash working capital items decreased cash flows from operating activities by $64.3 million in 2015. The changes in working capital items help users evaluate how well Sears is managing the sources and uses of its operating cash flows.

PAUSE FOR **FEEDBACK**

The excerpt from the notes to Sears's financial statements shows the effects of changes in non-cash working capital items on cash flow from operations. Before you move on, complete the following questions to test your understanding of this concept.

SELF-STUDY **QUIZ 9-4**

For each of the following events, state whether working capital will increase, decrease, or not change, and identify the effect, if any, of each event on cash flow from operating activities.

1. Sears purchases office equipment on account for $250,000.

2. The company borrows $1,000,000 in long-term debt.

3. The company pays income taxes payable in the amount of $750,000.

4. The company finances a new building with long-term debt.

After you complete your answers, check them with the solutions at the end of the chapter.

ACCOUNTING STANDARDS
FOR PRIVATE ENTERPRISES

Accounting standards for private enterprises do not differ much from IFRS in reporting the common types of current liabilities. Two notable differences in the standards relate to recognition of contingent liabilities and accounting for income taxes.

Financial Reporting Issue	IFRS	ASPE
Recognition of contingent liabilities	A contingent liability is recognized if the occurrence of the future event is both *probable* and measurable. An event is probable if it more likely to occur than not. This leads to the recognition of more contingent liabilities than under ASPE.	A contingent liability is recognized if the occurrence of the future event is both *likely* (that is, highly probable) and measurable.
Accounting for income taxes	Canadian publicly accountable enterprises are required to report both the current and deferred portions of the income taxes that result from differences between IFRS and income tax laws.	Users of the financial statements of Canadian private enterprises remain unconvinced of the incremental value of information conveyed by deferred income taxes. For this reason, Canadian private enterprises may report an income tax expense that simply equals the income tax payable.

DEMONSTRATION **CASE**

Hull Construction completed several transactions during the year. In each case, decide if a liability should be recorded and, if so, determine the amount. Assume the current date is December 31, 2017. Review Appendix 9B before determining the amount of the liabilities in transactions 5 and 6.

1. Employees earned salaries of $100,000 that have not been paid. This amount included $30,000 of employee income taxes withheld, $4,500 in contributions to the Canada Pension Plan, and $1,500 in Employment Insurance contributions.

2. The company borrowed $100,000 on June 30 at an annual interest rate of 7 percent. No payments associated with this loan have been made.

3. A customer made a $75,000 down payment on a construction project. Work will begin next month.

4. The company lost a lawsuit for $250,000 but plans to appeal.

5. On December 31, 2017, a bank lent money to Hull. The company agreed to repay the bank $100,000 on December 31, 2018. The bank charges an annual interest rate of 5 percent.

6. The company signed a loan agreement that requires it to pay $50,000 per year for 20 years. The annual interest rate is 8 percent.

We strongly recommend that you prepare your own answers to these requirements and then check your answers with the following solution.

SUGGESTED **SOLUTION**

1. Four liability accounts should be increased: liability for income taxes withheld, $30,000; CPP payable, $9,000 ($4,500 + $4,500); EI payable, $3,600 ($1,500 + $1,500 × 1.40); and salaries payable, $64,000 ($100,000 − $30,000 − $4,500 − $1,500).

2. The amount borrowed ($100,000) should be recorded as a liability on June 30. In addition, interest accrued but not paid should be recorded as a liability at year-end. This amount is $100,000 × 7% × 6/12 = $3,500.

3. The customer deposit ($75,000) is a liability until work is performed and the related revenue earned.

4. Most likely, the $250,000 should be recorded as a liability, unless the grounds for appeal significantly reduce the probability that the $250,000 will eventually be paid.

5. A liability should be recorded for the present value of the obligation. The amount is determined by using the present value factor from Table 9C.1 for $n = 1$, $i = 5\%$: $100,000 × 0.9524 = $95,240.

6. A liability should be recorded for the present value of the obligation. The amount is determined by using the present value factor from Table 9C.2 for $n = 20$, $i = 8\%$: $50,000 × 9.8181 = $490,905.

APPENDIX 9A: DEFERRED INCOME TAX ASSETS AND LIABILITIES

LO9-S1

Compute and report deferred income taxes.

In previous chapters, we made simplifying assumptions concerning income tax expense. We often provided the amount of income tax expense (e.g., $100,000) and prepared a journal entry similar to the following:

Income tax expense (E)	100,000	
Income tax payable (L)		100,000

Assets	=	Liabilities	+	Shareholders' Equity
		Income tax payable +100,000		Income tax expense −100,000

However, separate rules govern the preparation of financial statements (IFRS) and tax returns (Income Tax Act). Specifically, some types of revenue are exempt from tax while other types of expenses are not deductible in computing taxable income. These *permanent differences* do not cause much complication in accounting for income taxes. However, *temporary differences* of the following types result in complex accounting:

1. Product warranty costs that are recognized as a liability and an expense for financial reporting purposes when the related products are sold, but they are deductible for tax purposes only when payments under the warranty are made.

2. Long-lived assets, including development costs, which are usually depreciated by using the straight-line method for financial reporting purposes, are depreciated on an accelerated basis (capital cost allowance) for tax purposes.

The differences between depreciation expense and capital cost allowance (CCA) are by far the most common source of temporary differences, which disappear over the long run. Assuming the corporation is a going concern, a specific long-lived asset will eventually be unable to generate further benefits to the corporation and will be fully depreciated. Similarly, the cost of this asset would have been deducted over the years as CCA for tax purposes. So the main issue is timing of the recognition of revenues and expenses for financial reporting versus tax purposes. These temporary differences cause the income tax expense (which is based on earnings before taxes reported on the statement of earnings) to be different from the income tax payable (which is based on taxable income computed on the income tax return).

This difference creates an interesting accounting problem; should the tax liability reported on the statement of financial position be the amount of income taxes currently payable based on the tax return, or should the liability include deferred tax effects that exist because of differences between IFRS and the income tax rules? Accountants have resolved this issue by recording the "economic" liability, which includes income taxes currently payable, adjusted for the effects of temporary differences between IFRS and the income tax rules.

The difference between the amounts of income tax expense and income taxes payable is called *deferred income tax*. Deferred income tax items exist because of temporary differences caused by reporting revenues and expenses on a company's statement of earnings in conformity with IFRS, and on the tax return in accordance with the Income Tax Act. In practice, deferred income taxes can be either assets (such as taxes related to cash collected from a customer, which is taxable before it is reported as a revenue on the statement of earnings) or liabilities (such as taxes related to depreciation and amortization, reported on the tax return on an accelerated basis and on the statement of earnings on a straight-line basis).

To illustrate, let us consider one item that gives rise to deferred income taxes. Assume that a Canadian company uses straight-line depreciation for its financial statements and CCA for its tax return. As a result, it reports lower income on its tax return than on its statement of earnings, because CCA reported on the tax return exceeds depreciation expense reported on the statement of earnings. Assume that the company computed income taxes payable of $8,000,000 based on the numbers reported on the tax return, and reported income tax expense of $10,000,000 on its statement of earnings. The company records its tax obligation as follows:

Income tax expense (E)	10,000,000	
Deferred income taxes (L)		2,000,000
Income tax payable (L)		8,000,000

Assets	=	Liabilities	+	Shareholders' Equity
		Deferred income taxes		Income tax expense
		+2,000,000		−10,000,000
		Income tax payable +8,000,000		

The deferred income tax amount is settled when the difference between CCA and depreciation expense "reverses" in the future. This happens when the CCA recorded on the tax return becomes lower than the straight-line depreciation reported on the statement of earnings (remember from Chapter 9 that declining depreciation, such as CCA, causes higher depreciation expense than straight-line depreciation in the early years of an asset's life and lower depreciation in the later years). When a temporary difference reverses, the deferred income tax amount is reduced.

In reality, although temporary differences reverse in theory, new temporary differences are created as companies purchase new long-lived assets, offsetting the reversing differences. Consequently, the deferred income tax liabilities reported by most companies may not result in significant cash outflows in the foreseeable future.

As indicated earlier, the deferred income tax liability arises primarily from differences between depreciation expense and CCA. What if companies used CCA for reporting purposes instead of straight-line depreciation? In this case, most of the temporary differences would disappear and the deferred income tax asset or liability would be reduced to a relatively small amount, thus reducing the significance of this item on the statements of financial position of most companies. However, the use of CCA for financial reporting purposes increases the depreciation expense, thus reducing net earnings. Managers may not favour this outcome if it affects their remuneration and the market value of the company's shares, even though the use of CCA instead of straight-line depreciation does not affect cash outflows for income tax purposes.

The computation of deferred income taxes involves some complexities that are discussed in advanced accounting courses. At this point, you need to understand only that deferred income tax assets and liabilities are caused by temporary differences related to the recognition of revenues and expenses for financial reporting versus income tax reporting purposes. Each temporary difference has an impact on the statement of earnings in one accounting period and on the tax return in another.

APPENDIX 9B: PRESENT VALUE CONCEPTS

The concept of *present value* (PV) is based on the time value of money. It provides a foundation for measuring and reporting long-term notes and bonds. **Present value** is the current cash equivalent of an amount to be received in the future, or a future amount discounted for compound interest. Quite simply, money received today is worth more than money to be received one year from today (or at any other future date) because it can be used to earn interest. If you invest $1,000 today at 4 percent, you will have $1,040 in one year. The difference between the $1,000 and the $1,040 is interest that can be earned during the year. In contrast, if you receive $1,000 one year from today, you will lose the opportunity to earn the $40 interest revenue.

In one of your mathematics courses, you have probably already solved some problems involving the time value of money. In the typical problem, you were told a certain dollar amount had been deposited in a savings account earning a specific rate of

LO9-S2

Compute and report present values of future cash flows.

PRESENT VALUE is the current cash equivalent of an amount to be received in the future, or a future amount discounted for compound interest.

interest. You were asked to determine the dollar amount that would be in the savings account after a certain number of years. In this appendix, we will show you how to solve problems that are the opposite of the ones you have worked with. In present value problems, you are told a dollar amount to be received in the future (such as the balance of a savings account after five years) and asked to determine the present value of the amount (the amount that must be deposited in the savings account today).

The value of money changes over time because money can earn interest. With a present value problem, you know the dollar amount of a cash flow that will occur in the future and need to determine its value now. The opposite situation occurs when you know the dollar amount of a cash flow that occurs today and need to determine its value at some point in the future. These problems are called *future value* problems. **Future value** is the sum to which an amount will increase as a result of compound interest. The following illustrates the basic difference between present value and future value problems:

	Now	Future
Present value	?	$1,000
Future value	$1,000	?

Present and future value problems may involve two types of cash flow: a single payment or an annuity (a series of cash payments).[7] Thus, four different situations are related to the time value of money:

1. Present value of a single payment
2. Future value of a single payment
3. Present value of an annuity
4. Future value of an annuity

Present value problems involving single amounts and annuities are discussed below. Future value problems are covered in an online appendix to this chapter (Appendix 9E on *Connect*).

Present Value of a Single Amount

The present value of a single amount is the amount of cash you are willing to accept today in lieu of a cash receipt at some date in the future. You might be offered the opportunity to invest in a debt instrument paying you $10,000 in 10 years. Before you decided whether to invest, you would want to determine the present value of the instrument. Graphically, the present value of $1 due at the end of the third period with an interest rate of 4 percent can be represented as follows:

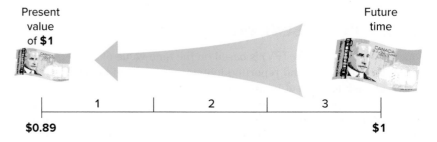

To compute the present value of an amount to be received in the future, we subtract interest that is earned over time from the amount to be received in the future. For example, if you place $100 in a savings account that earns 2 percent, you will have $102 at the end of a year. In a present value problem, you are told that you have $102 at the end of the year and must compute the amount to be deposited at the beginning of the year. To solve this type of problem, you must discount the amount to be received in the future at interest rate i for n periods. The formula to compute the present value of a single amount is

$$\text{Present value} = \frac{1}{(1 + i)^n} \times \text{Amount}$$

The formula is not difficult to use, but most analysts use calculators, Excel, or present value tables for computations. We will illustrate how to use present value tables. Assume that today is January 1, 2017, and you have the opportunity to receive $1,000 cash on December 31, 2019. At an interest rate of 4 percent per year, how much is the $1,000 payment worth to you on January 1, 2017? You could discount the amount year by year,[8] but it is easier to use Table 9C.1, "Present Value of $1," in Appendix 9C. For $i = 4\%$, $n = 3$, we find that the present value of $1 is 0.8890. The present value of $1,000 to be received at the end of three years can be computed as follows:

$1,000 × 0.8890 (From Table 9C.1, $i = 4\%$, $n = 3$) = $889.00

Learning how to compute a present value amount is not difficult, but it is more important that you understand what it means. The $889.00 is the amount that you would pay to have the right to receive $1,000 at the end of three years, assuming an interest rate of 4 percent. Conceptually, you would be indifferent about having $889.00 today and receiving $1,000 in three years, because you can use financial institutions to convert dollars from the present to the future, and vice versa. If you had $889.00 today but preferred $1,000 in three years, you could simply deposit the money into a savings account that paid annual interest at 4 percent and it would grow to $1,000 in three years. Alternatively, if you had a contract that promised you $1,000 in three years, you could sell it to an investor for $889.00 cash today because it would permit the investor to earn the difference in interest.

PAUSE FOR FEEDBACK **STOP**

There are two types of payments when you compute present values. So far, we have discussed single payments. In the next section, we will discuss annuities. Before you move on, complete the following questions to test your understanding of these concepts.

SELF-STUDY QUIZ 9-5

1. If the interest rate in a present value problem increases from 4 percent to 5 percent, will the present value increase or decrease? Explain.

2. What is the present value of $10,000 to be received 10 years from now if the interest rate is 6 percent compounded annually?

After you complete your answers, check them with the solution at the end of this chapter.

Present Value of an Annuity

Many business problems involve multiple cash payments over a number of periods instead of a single payment. An **annuity** is a series of consecutive payments characterized by

An **ANNUITY** is a series of equal amounts of cash that are paid or received at equally distant points in time

1. An equal dollar amount each interest period.

2. Interest periods of equal length (year, half-year, quarter, or month).

3. An equal interest rate each interest period.

Examples of annuities include monthly payments on an automobile or a home loan, annual contributions to a savings account, and monthly retirement benefits.

The present value of an annuity is the value now of a series of equal amounts to be received (or paid) each period for some specified number of periods in the future. It is computed by discounting each of the equal periodic amounts. A good example of this type of problem is a retirement program that offers the retiree a monthly income after retirement. The present value of an annuity of $1 for three periods at 4 percent may be represented graphically, as follows:

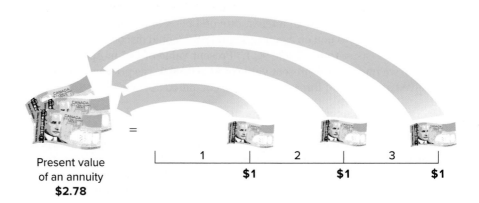

Present value
of an annuity
$2.78

Assume you are to receive $1,000 cash on each December 31, 2014, 2018, and 2019. How much would the sum of these three $1,000 future amounts be worth on January 1, 2017, assuming an interest rate of 4 percent per year? We could use Table 9C.1 in Appendix 9C to calculate the present value as follows:

| | | Factor from Table 9C.1 | | |
Year	Amount	Appendix 9C, $i = 4\%$		Present Value
1	$1,000	× 0.9615 ($n = 1$)	=	$ 961.50
2	$1,000	× 0.9246 ($n = 2$)	=	924.60
3	$1,000	× 0.8890 ($n = 3$)	=	889.00
		Total present value	=	$2,775.10

We can compute the present value of this annuity more easily, however, by using Table 9C.2 in Appendix 9C as follows:

$$\$1{,}000 \times 2.7751 \ (\textbf{From Table 9C.2, } i = 4\%, n = 3) = \$2{,}775.10$$

Exhibit 9B.3 provides a graphical illustration of the present value computations discussed above.

Interest Rates and Interest Periods   The preceding illustrations assumed annual periods for compounding and discounting. Although interest rates are almost always quoted on an annual basis, most interest-compounding periods encountered in business are less than one year (semi-annually or quarterly). When interest periods are less than a year, the values of n and i must be restated to be consistent with the length of the interest period.

To illustrate, 4 percent interest compounded annually for five years requires use of $n = 5$ and $i = 4\%$. If compounding is quarterly, the interest period is one-quarter of a year (i.e., four periods per year), and the quarterly interest rate is one-quarter of the annual rate (i.e., 1 percent per quarter). Therefore, 4 percent interest compounded quarterly for five years requires use of $n = 20$ and $i = 1\%$.

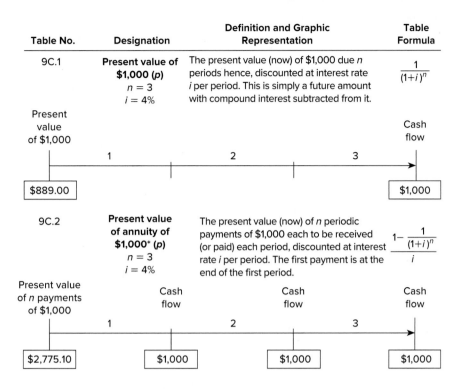

Exhibit **9B.3**
Overview of Present Value Computations

Table No.	Designation	Definition and Graphic Representation	Table Formula
9C.1	**Present value of $1,000 ($p$)** $n = 3$ $i = 4\%$	The present value (now) of $1,000 due n periods hence, discounted at interest rate i per period. This is simply a future amount with compound interest subtracted from it.	$\dfrac{1}{(1+i)^n}$

Present value of $1,000

	1		2		3	Cash flow

$889.00 $1,000

| 9C.2 | **Present value of annuity of $1,000* ($p$)** $n = 3$ $i = 4\%$ | The present value (now) of n periodic payments of $1,000 each to be received (or paid) each period, discounted at interest rate i per period. The first payment is at the end of the first period. | $\dfrac{1- \dfrac{1}{(1+i)^n}}{i}$ |

Present value of n payments of $1,000

	Cash flow		Cash flow		Cash flow
	1	2	3		

$2,775.10 $1,000 $1,000 $1,000

*Notice that these are ordinary annuities; that is, they are often called *end-of-period annuities*. Thus, the table values for p, the present value, are at the beginning of the period of the first payment. Annuities due assume the opposite; that is, they are *beginning-of-period annuities*. Ordinary annuity values can be converted into annuities due simply by multiplication of $(1 + i)$.

TRUTH IN ADVERTISING

A QUESTION
OF ACCOUNTABILITY

A number of advertisements in newspapers, in magazines, on television, and on the Internet can easily be misinterpreted if the consumer does not understand present value concepts. We discuss two examples.

Most car companies offer seasonal promotions with special financing incentives. A car dealer may advertise 1.9 percent interest on car loans when banks are charging 6 percent. Typically, the lower interest rate is not a special incentive because the dealer simply charges a higher price for cars that the dealership finances. It may be better to borrow from the bank and "pay cash" at the dealership to negotiate a lower price. Customers should use the present value concepts illustrated in this chapter to compare financing alternatives.

Another misleading advertisement is one that promises a chance to become an instant millionaire. The fine print discloses that the winner will receive $25,000 for 40 years, which is $1,000,000 (40 × $25,000), but the present value of this annuity at 8 percent is only $298,000. Most winners are happy to get the money, but they are not really millionaires.

Some consumer advocates criticize businesses that use these types of advertisements. They argue that consumers should not have to study present value concepts to understand advertisements. Some of these criticisms may be valid, but the quality of information contained in advertisements that include interest rates has improved during the past few years.

Accounting Applications of Present Values

Many business transactions require the use of present value concepts. We illustrate two such cases so that you can test your understanding of these concepts.

Case A   On January 1, 2017, Nesca Corp. bought some new equipment. The company signed a note and agreed to pay $200,000 for the equipment on December 31, 2018. The market interest rate for this note was 6 percent. The $200,000 represents the cash-equivalent price of the equipment and the interest that will be earned for two years.

1. How should the accountant record the purchase?

   Answer: This case requires application of the present value of a single amount. In conformity with the cost principle, the cost of the equipment is its current cash-equivalent price, which is the present value of the future payment. The problem can be shown graphically as follows:

January 1, 2017	December 31, 2017	December 31, 2018
?		$200,000

   The present value of the $200,000 is computed as follows:

   $$\$200,000 \times 0.8900 \text{ (From Table 9C.1, } i = 6\%, n = 2 \text{)} = \$178,000$$

   Therefore, the journal entry is, as follows:

Equipment (A)		178,000	
Note payable (L)			178,000

Assets	=	**Liabilities**	+	**Shareholders' Equity**
Equipment +178,000		Note payable +178,000		

   Some companies prefer to record the following journal entry:

Equipment (A)		178,000	
Discount on notes payable (XL)		22,000	
Note payable (L)			200,000

Assets	=	**Liabilities**	+	**Shareholders' Equity**
Equipment +178,000		Note payable +200,000		
		Discount on notes payable		
		−22,000		

   The discount account is a contra-liability account that represents the interest that will accrue on the note over its life.

2. What journal entry should be made at the end of the first and second years for interest expense?

   Answer: The following schedule shows the computation of interest expense for the two years.

Date	Interest Expense Unpaid Balance × 6%	Unpaid Balance of Note Payable
January 1, 2017		$178,000
December 31, 2017	$178,000 × 6% = $10,680	188,680
December 31, 2018	188,680 × 6% = 11,320*	200,000

   *The exact computation is $11,320.80, which is rounded down to $11,320 to ensure that the unpaid balance of the note does not exceed $200,000.

Each year's interest expense is recorded in an adjusting entry, as follows:

Dec. 31, 2017	Interest expense (E)		10,680	
	Note payable (L)			10,680
Assets	=	**Liabilities**	+	**Shareholders' Equity**
		Note payable +10,680		Interest Expense −10,680

Dec. 31, 2018	Interest expense (E)		11,320	
	Note payable (L)			11,320
Assets	=	**Liabilities**	+	**Shareholders' Equity**
		Note payable +11,320		Interest Expense −11,320

Notice that interest of $10,680 accrued during 2017 but was not paid. It is, therefore, added to the balance of the note payable account. This interest amount has itself earned interest during 2018.

3. What journal entry should be made on December 31, 2018, to record the payment of the debt?

Answer: At this date, the amount to be paid is the note payable balance, which is the same as the maturity amount on the due date. The journal entry to record full payment of the debt follows:

Note payable (L)		200,000	
Cash (A)			200,000
Assets	=	**Liabilities**	+	**Shareholders' Equity**
Cash −200,000		Note payable −200,000		

Case B   On January 1, 2017, Nesca bought new research equipment. The company elected to finance the purchase with a note to be paid in three equal annual instalments of $146,886. Each instalment includes principal plus interest on the unpaid balance at 5 percent per year. The annual instalments are due on December 31, 2017, 2018, and 2019. This problem can be shown graphically, as follows:

January 1, 2017	December 31, 2017	December 31, 2018	December 31, 2019
?	$146,886	$146,886	$146,886

1. What is the amount of the note?

Answer: The note is the present value of each instalment payment, $i = 5\%$ and $n = 3$. This is an annuity because payment is made in three equal instalments. The amount of the note is computed as follows:

$$\$146,886 \times 2.7232 \text{ (From Table 9C.2, } i = 5\%, n = 3) = \$400,000$$

The acquisition is recorded, as follows:

Research equipment (A)		400,000	
Cash (A)			400,000
Assets	=	**Liabilities**	+	**Shareholders' Equity**
Research equipment +400,000		Note payable +400,000		

2. What was the total amount of interest expense in dollars?
Answer:

$$\$146,886 \times 3 - \$400,000 = \$40,658$$

3. Prepare a debt payment schedule that shows the entry for each payment and the effect on interest expense and the unpaid amount of principal each period.

Answer:

	Debt Payment Schedule			
Date	**Cash Payment (Credit)**	**Interest Expense (Unpaid Principal × 5%) (Debit)**	**Decrease in Principal (Debit)**	**Unpaid Principal**
1/1/2017				$400,000
31/12/2017	$146,886	$400,000 × 5% = $20,000	$126,886ᵃ	273,114ᵇ
31/12/2018	146,886	273,114 × 5% = 13,656	133,230	139,884
31/12/2019	146,886	139,884 × 5% = 7,002*	139,884	0
Total	$440,658		$40,658*	$400,000

*To accommodate rounding error.

Computations: ᵃ$146,886 − $20,000 = $126,886
ᵇ$400,000 − $126,886 = $273,114

Notice in the debt payment schedule that with each successive payment the payment on principal increases and interest expense decreases. This effect occurs because the interest each period is based on a lower amount of the unpaid principal. When an annuity is involved, schedules such as this one are often useful analytical tools.

4. What journal entry should be made at the end of each year to record the payments on this note?

Answer:

Dec. 31, 2017	Note payable (L)	126,886	
	Interest expense (E)	20,000	
	Cash (A)		146,886

Assets	=	**Liabilities**	+	**Shareholders' Equity**
Cash −146,886		Note payable −126,886		Interest Expense −20,000

Dec. 31, 2018	Note payable (L)	133,230	
	Interest expense (E)	13,656	
	Cash (A)		146,886

Assets	=	**Liabilities**	+	**Shareholders' Equity**
Cash −146,886		Note payable −133,230		Interest Expense −13,656

Dec. 31, 2019	Note payable (L)	139,884	
	Interest expense (E)	7,002	
	Cash (A)		146,886

Assets	=	**Liabilities**	+	**Shareholders' Equity**
Cash −146,886		Note payable −139,884		Interest Expense −7,002

APPENDIX 9C: PRESENT VALUE TABLES

Table **9C.1**

Present Value of $1,
$p = 1/(1 + i)^n$

Periods	1.5%	1.75%	2%	2.25%	2.5%	2.75%	3%	3.25%	3.5%
1	0.9852	0.9828	0.9804	0.9780	0.9756	0.9732	0.9709	0.9685	0.9662
2	0.9707	0.9659	0.9612	0.9565	0.9518	0.9472	0.9426	0.9380	0.9335
3	0.9563	0.9493	0.9423	0.9354	0.9286	0.9218	0.9151	0.9085	0.9019
4	0.9422	0.9330	0.9238	0.9148	0.9060	0.8972	0.8885	0.8799	0.8714
5	0.9283	0.9169	0.9057	0.8947	0.8839	0.8732	0.8626	0.8522	0.8420
6	0.9145	0.9011	0.8880	0.8750	0.8623	0.8498	0.8375	0.8254	0.8135
7	0.9010	0.8856	0.8706	0.8558	0.8413	0.8270	0.8131	0.7994	0.7860
8	0.8877	0.8704	0.8535	0.8369	0.8207	0.8049	0.7894	0.7742	0.7594
9	0.8746	0.8554	0.8368	0.8185	0.8007	0.7834	0.7664	0.7499	0.7337
10	0.8617	0.8407	0.8203	0.8005	0.7812	0.7624	0.7441	0.7263	0.7089
11	0.8489	0.8263	0.8043	0.7829	0.7621	0.7420	0.7224	0.7034	0.6849
12	0.8364	0.8121	0.7885	0.7657	0.7436	0.7221	0.7014	0.6813	0.6618
13	0.8240	0.7981	0.7730	0.7488	0.7254	0.7028	0.6810	0.6598	0.6394
14	0.8118	0.7844	0.7579	0.7323	0.7077	0.6840	0.6611	0.6391	0.6178
15	0.7999	0.7709	0.7430	0.7162	0.6905	0.6657	0.6419	0.6189	0.5969
16	0.7880	0.7576	0.7284	0.7005	0.6736	0.6479	0.6232	0.5995	0.5767
17	0.7764	0.7446	0.7142	0.6851	0.6572	0.6305	0.6050	0.5806	0.5572
18	0.7649	0.7318	0.7002	0.6700	0.6412	0.6137	0.5874	0.5623	0.5384
19	0.7536	0.7192	0.6864	0.6552	0.6255	0.5972	0.5703	0.5446	0.5202
20	0.7425	0.7068	0.6730	0.6408	0.6103	0.5813	0.5537	0.5275	0.5026
30	0.6398	0.5942	0.5521	0.5130	0.4767	0.4431	0.4120	0.3831	0.3563
40	0.5513	0.4996	0.4529	0.4106	0.3724	0.3379	0.3066	0.2782	0.2526
50	0.4750	0.4200	0.3715	0.3287	0.2909	0.2576	0.2281	0.2021	0.1791
Periods	**3.75%**	**4%**	**4.5%**	**5%**	**6%**	**7%**	**8%**	**9%**	**10%**
1	0.9639	0.9615	0.9569	0.9524	0.9434	0.9346	0.9259	0.9174	0.9091
2	0.9290	0.9246	0.9157	0.9070	0.8900	0.8734	0.8573	0.8417	0.8264
3	0.8954	0.8890	0.8763	0.8638	0.8396	0.8163	0.7938	0.7722	0.7513
4	0.8631	0.8548	0.8386	0.8227	0.7921	0.7629	0.7350	0.7084	0.6830
5	0.8319	0.8219	0.8025	0.7835	0.7473	0.7130	0.6806	0.6499	0.6209
6	0.8018	0.7903	0.7679	0.7462	0.7050	0.6663	0.6302	0.5963	0.5645
7	0.7728	0.7599	0.7348	0.7107	0.6651	0.6227	0.5835	0.5470	0.5132
8	0.7449	0.7307	0.7032	0.6768	0.6274	0.5820	0.5403	0.5019	0.4665
9	0.7180	0.7026	0.6729	0.6446	0.5919	0.5439	0.5002	0.4604	0.4241
10	0.6920	0.6756	0.6439	0.6139	0.5584	0.5083	0.4632	0.4224	0.3855
11	0.6670	0.6496	0.6162	0.5847	0.5268	0.4751	0.4289	0.3875	0.3505
12	0.6429	0.6246	0.5897	0.5568	0.4970	0.4440	0.3971	0.3555	0.3186
13	0.6197	0.6006	0.5643	0.5303	0.4688	0.4150	0.3677	0.3262	0.2897
14	0.5973	0.5775	0.5400	0.5051	0.4423	0.3878	0.3405	0.2992	0.2633
15	0.5757	0.5553	0.5167	0.4810	0.4173	0.3624	0.3152	0.2745	0.2394
16	0.5549	0.5339	0.4945	0.4581	0.3936	0.3387	0.2919	0.2519	0.2176
17	0.5348	0.5134	0.4732	0.4363	0.3714	0.3166	0.2703	0.2311	0.1978
18	0.5155	0.4936	0.4528	0.4155	0.3503	0.2959	0.2502	0.2120	0.1799
19	0.4969	0.4746	0.4333	0.3957	0.3305	0.2765	0.2317	0.1945	0.1635
20	0.4789	0.4564	0.4146	0.3769	0.3118	0.2584	0.2145	0.1784	0.1486
30	0.3314	0.3083	0.2670	0.2314	0.1741	0.1314	0.0994	0.0754	0.0573
40	0.2293	0.2083	0.1719	0.1420	0.0972	0.0668	0.0460	0.0318	0.0221
50	0.1587	0.1407	0.1107	0.0872	0.0543	0.0339	0.0213	0.0134	0.0085

Table 9C.2

Present Value of Annuity of $1, $p = [1 - 1/(1 + i)^n]/i$

Periods*	1.5%	1.75%	2%	2.25%	2.5%	2.75%	3%	3.25%	3.5%
1	0.9852	0.9828	0.9804	0.9780	0.9756	0.9732	0.9709	0.9685	0.9662
2	1.9559	1.9487	1.9416	1.9345	1.9274	1.9204	1.9135	1.9066	1.8997
3	2.9122	2.8980	2.8839	2.8699	2.8560	2.8423	2.8286	2.8151	2.8016
4	3.8544	3.8309	3.8077	3.7847	3.7620	3.7394	3.7171	3.6950	3.6731
5	4.7826	4.7479	4.7135	4.6795	4.6458	4.6126	4.5797	4.5472	4.5151
6	5.6972	5.6490	5.6014	5.5545	5.5081	5.4624	5.4172	5.3726	5.3286
7	6.5982	6.5346	6.4720	6.4102	6.3494	6.2894	6.2303	6.1720	6.1145
8	7.4859	7.4051	7.3255	7.2472	7.1701	7.0943	7.0197	6.9462	6.8740
9	8.3605	8.2605	8.1622	8.0657	7.9709	7.8777	7.7861	7.6961	7.6077
10	9.2222	9.1012	8.9826	8.8662	8.7521	8.6401	8.5302	8.4224	8.3166
11	10.0711	9.9275	9.7868	9.6491	9.5142	9.3821	9.2526	9.1258	9.0016
12	10.9075	10.7395	10.5753	10.4148	10.2578	10.1042	9.9540	9.8071	9.6633
13	11.7315	11.5376	11.3484	11.1636	10.9832	10.8070	10.6350	10.4669	10.3027
14	12.5434	12.3220	12.1062	11.8959	11.6909	11.4910	11.2961	11.1060	10.9205
15	13.3432	13.0929	12.8493	12.6122	12.3814	12.1567	11.9379	11.7249	11.5174
16	14.1313	13.8505	13.5777	13.3126	13.0550	12.8046	12.5611	12.3244	12.0941
17	14.9076	14.5951	14.2919	13.9977	13.7122	13.4351	13.1661	12.9049	12.6513
18	15.6726	15.3269	14.9920	14.6677	14.3534	14.0488	13.7535	13.4673	13.1897
19	16.4262	16.0461	15.6785	15.3229	14.9789	14.6460	14.3238	14.0119	13.7098
20	17.1686	16.7529	16.3514	15.9637	15.5892	15.2273	14.8775	14.5393	14.2124
30	24.0158	23.1858	22.3965	21.6453	20.9303	20.2493	19.6004	18.9819	18.3920
40	29.9158	28.5942	27.3555	26.1935	25.1028	24.0781	23.1148	22.2084	21.3551
50	34.9997	33.1412	31.4236	29.8344	28.3623	26.9972	25.7298	24.5518	23.4556

Periods*	3.75%	4%	4.5%	5%	6%	7%	8%	9%	10%
1	0.9639	0.9615	0.9569	0.9524	0.9434	0.9346	0.9259	0.9174	0.9091
2	1.8929	1.8861	1.8727	1.8594	1.8334	1.8080	1.7833	1.7591	1.7355
3	2.7883	2.7751	2.7490	2.7232	2.6730	2.6243	2.5771	2.5313	2.4869
4	3.6514	3.6299	3.5875	3.5460	3.4651	3.3872	3.3121	3.2397	3.1699
5	4.4833	4.4518	4.3900	4.3295	4.2124	4.1002	3.9927	3.8897	3.7908
6	5.2851	5.2421	5.1579	5.0757	4.9173	4.7665	4.6229	4.4859	4.3553
7	6.0579	6.0021	5.8927	5.7864	5.5824	5.3893	5.2064	5.0330	4.8684
8	6.8028	6.7327	6.5959	6.4632	6.2098	5.9713	5.7466	5.5348	5.3349
9	7.5208	7.4353	7.2688	7.1078	6.8017	6.5152	6.2469	5.9952	5.7590
10	8.2128	8.1109	7.9127	7.7217	7.3601	7.0236	6.7101	6.4177	6.1446
11	8.8798	8.7605	8.5289	8.3064	7.8869	7.4987	7.1390	6.8052	6.4951
12	9.5227	9.3851	9.1186	8.8633	8.3838	7.9427	7.5361	7.1607	6.8137
13	10.1424	9.9856	9.6829	9.3936	8.8527	8.3577	7.9038	7.4869	7.1034
14	10.7396	10.5631	10.2228	9.8986	9.2950	8.7455	8.2442	7.7862	7.3667
15	11.3153	11.1184	10.7395	10.3797	9.7122	9.1079	8.5595	8.0607	7.6061
16	11.8702	11.6523	11.2340	10.8378	10.1059	9.4466	8.8514	8.3126	7.8237
17	12.4050	12.1657	11.7072	11.2741	10.4773	9.7632	9.1216	8.5436	8.0216
18	12.9205	12.6593	12.1600	11.6896	10.8276	10.0591	9.3719	8.7556	8.2014
19	13.4173	13.1339	12.5933	12.0853	11.1581	10.3356	9.6036	8.9501	8.3649
20	13.8962	13.5903	13.0079	12.4622	11.4699	10.5940	9.8181	9.1285	8.5136
30	17.8292	17.2920	16.2889	15.3725	13.7648	12.4090	11.2578	10.2737	9.4269
40	20.5510	19.7928	18.4016	17.1591	15.0463	13.3317	11.9246	10.7574	9.7791
50	22.4345	21.4822	19.7620	18.2559	15.7619	13.8007	12.2335	10.9617	9.9148

*There is one payment each period.

Available on *Connect*: APPENDIX 9D: PRESENT VALUE COMPUTATIONS USING EXCEL

Available on *Connect*: APPENDIX 9E: FUTURE VALUE CONCEPTS

CHAPTER **TAKE-AWAYS**

9-1. Define, measure, and report current liabilities.

Strictly speaking, accountants define liabilities as obligations arising from past transactions that will be settled in the future by some transfer or use of assets or provision of services. They are classified on the statement of financial position as either current or non-current. Current liabilities are short-term obligations that will be paid within the normal operating cycle of the business or within one year of the statement of financial position date, whichever is longer. Non-current liabilities are all obligations not classified as current.

9-2. Compute and interpret the quick ratio.

The quick ratio is a comparison of the most liquid or quick assets (cash, short-term investments, and net receivables) to current liabilities. Analysts use this ratio to assess the liquidity of a company.

9-3. Compute and interpret the trade payables turnover ratio.

This ratio is computed by dividing cost of sales by average trade payables. It shows how quickly management is paying its trade creditors and is considered to be a measure of liquidity.

9-4. Report notes payable, and explain the time value of money.

A note payable specifies the amount borrowed, when it must be repaid, and the interest rate associated with the debt. Accountants must report the debt and the interest as it accrues. The time value of money refers to the fact that interest accrues on borrowed money with the passage of time.

9-5. Report contingent liabilities.

A contingency is a possible liability that has arisen as a result of a past event. Such contingencies are disclosed in a note if it is not probable that cash or other assets will be required to settle the obligation, or if the amount of the obligation cannot be measured with sufficient reliability.

9-6. Explain the impact of changes in current liabilities on cash flows.

Changes in trade payables and accrued liabilities affect cash flows from operating activities. Cash flows are increased when trade payables and accrued liabilities increase, and vice versa.

In this chapter, we focused on current liabilities and introduced present value concepts. In the next chapter, we will discuss non-current liabilities in the context of the capital structure of the company.

KEY **RATIOS**

The quick ratio measures the ability of a company to pay its current obligations. It is computed as follows:

$$\text{Quick ratio} = \frac{\text{Quick assets}}{\text{Current liabilities}}$$

The accounts payable turnover ratio and its companion average age of payables are measures of how quickly a company pays its creditors. They are computed as follows:

$$\text{Accounts payable turnover ratio} = \frac{\text{Cost of sales}}{\text{Average net accounts payable}}$$

$$\text{Average age of payables} = \frac{365}{\text{Accounts payable turnover ratio}}$$

FINDING **FINANCIAL INFORMATION**

STATEMENT OF FINANCIAL POSITION
Under Current Liabilities
Liabilities listed by account title, such as
  Accounts payable
  Accrued liabilities
  Notes payable
  Deferred income taxes
Under Non-current Liabilities
Liabilities listed by account title, such as
  Long-term debt
  Deferred income taxes

STATEMENT OF EARNINGS
Liabilities are shown only on the statement of financial position, never on the statement of earnings. Transactions affecting liabilities often affect a statement of earnings account. For example, accrued salary compensation affects a statement of earnings account (compensation expense) and a statement of financial position account (salaries payable).

STATEMENT OF CASH FLOWS
Under Operating Activities (indirect method)
Net earnings
+ Increases in most current liabilities
− Decreases in most current liabilities

NOTES
Under Summary of Significant Accounting Policies
Description of pertinent information concerning the accounting treatment of liabilities. Normally, there is minimal information.
Under a Separate Note
If not listed on the statement of financial position, a listing of the major classifications of liabilities with information about maturities and interest rates appears in a note. Information about contingent liabilities is reported in the notes.

QUESTIONS

1. Define *liability*. Differentiate between a current liability and a non-current liability.
2. How can external parties be informed about the liabilities of a business?
3. Liabilities are measured and reported at their current cash-equivalent amount. Explain.
4. A *liability* is a known obligation of either a definite or an estimated amount. Explain.
5. Define *working capital*. How is it computed?
6. What is the quick ratio? How is it related to the classification of liabilities?
7. Define *accrued liability*. What type of entry usually reflects an accrued liability?
8. Define *deferred revenue*. Why is it a liability?
9. Define *note payable*. What other liability is associated with a note payable? Explain.
10. Define *provisions*. How do they differ from other liabilities?
11. What is a contingent liability? How is a contingent liability reported?
12. Compute interest expense for the following note: face value, $4,000; 6 percent interest; date of note, April 1, 2017. Assume that the fiscal year ends on December 31, 2017.
13. Explain the concept of the time value of money.
14. (Appendix 9B) Explain the basic difference between future value and present value.
15. (Appendix 9B) What is an annuity?

■ connect MINI-EXERCISES

LO9-3 **M9-1** **Computing Interest Expense**
Karek Company borrowed $600,000 on a 90-day note at 5 percent interest. The money was borrowed for 30 days in 2017 and 60 days in 2018; the note and interest are payable upon maturity in 2018. How much interest expense, if any, would be reported in 2017 and in 2018?

LO9-3 **M9-2** **Recording a Note Payable**
Wygant Corporation borrowed $290,000 on October 1, 2017. The note carried a 6 percent interest rate with the principal and interest payable on May 1, 2018. Prepare the journal entry to record the note on October 1. Prepare the adjusting entry to record accrued interest on December 31.

■ LO9-1,9-2,9-5 **M9-3** **Finding Financial Information**

For each of the following items, specify whether the information would be found in the statement of financial position, the statement of earnings, the statement of cash flows, the notes to the financial statements, or not at all.

1. The amount of working capital.

2. The total amount of current liabilities.

3. Information concerning company pension plans.

4. The accounts payable turnover ratio.

5. Information concerning the impact of changes in working capital on cash flows for the period.

■ LO9-1 **M9-4** **Computing Working Capital**

The statement of financial position for Stavro Corporation reported the following: non-current assets, $240,000; total assets, $360,000; non-current liabilities, $176,000; total shareholders' equity, $94,000. Compute Stavro's working capital.

■ LO9-1 **M9-5** **Analyzing the Impact of Transactions on Liquidity**

Ospry Inc. has a quick ratio of 0.80 and working capital in the amount of $1,240,000. For each of the following transactions, determine whether working capital will increase, decrease, or remain the same.

a. Paid accounts payable; $50,000.

b. Recorded accrued salaries; $100,000.

c. Borrowed $250,000 from a local bank, to be repaid in 90 days.

d. Purchased $20,000 of new inventory on credit.

■ LO9-4 **M9-6** **Reporting Contingent Liabilities**

Buzz Coffee Shops is famous for its large servings of hot coffee. After a well-known case involving McDonald's, the lawyer for Buzz warned management (in 2017) that it could be sued if someone were to spill hot coffee and be burned: "With the temperature of your coffee, I can guarantee it's just a matter of time before you're sued for $1,000,000." Unfortunately, in 2018 the prediction came true when a customer filed suit. The case went to trial in 2019, and the jury awarded the customer $400,000 in damages, which the company immediately appealed. During 2020, the customer and the company settled their dispute for $150,000. What is the proper reporting of this liability each year?

■ LO9-S2 **M9-7** **(Appendix 9B) Computing the Present Value of a Single Payment**

What is the present value of $500,000 to be paid in 10 years with an interest rate of 8 percent?

■ LO9-S2 **M9-8** **(Appendix 9B) Computing the Present Value of an Annuity**

What is the present value of 10 equal payments of $15,000 with an interest rate of 6 percent?

■ LO9-S2 **M9-9** **(Appendix 9B) Computing the Present Value of a Complex Contract**

As a result of a slowdown in operations, Global Stores is offering employees who have been terminated a severance package of $118,000 cash, another $129,000 to be paid in one year, and an annuity of $27,500 to be paid each year for six years beginning in one year. What is the present value of the package, assuming an interest rate of 5 percent?

■■ connect EXERCISES

■ LO9-1 **E9-1** **Identifying Current Liabilities**

A current liability is a short-term obligation that is normally expected to be settled within one year. For each of the following events and transactions that occurred in November 2017, indicate the title of the current liability account that is affected and the amount that would be reported on a statement of financial position prepared on December 31, 2017. If an event does not result in a current liability, explain why.

a. A customer purchases a ticket from WestJet Airlines for $470 cash to travel in January 2018. Answer from WestJet's standpoint.

b. Hall Construction Company signs a contract with a customer for the construction of a new $500,000 warehouse. At the signing, Hall receives a cheque for $50,000 as a deposit on the future construction. Answer from Hall's standpoint.

c. On November 1, 2017, a bank lends $10,000 to a company. The loan carries a 5 percent annual interest rate, and the principal and interest are due in a lump sum on October 31, 2018. Answer from the company's standpoint.

d. A popular ski magazine company receives a total of $17,800 from subscribers on December 31, the last day of its fiscal year. The subscriptions begin in the next fiscal year. Answer from the magazine company's standpoint.

e. On November 20, the campus bookstore receives 900 accounting textbooks at a cost of $70 each. The terms indicate that payment is due within 30 days of delivery. Answer from the bookstore's standpoint.

f. Ziegler Company, a farm equipment company, receives its phone bill at the end of January 2018 for $2,300 for January calls. The bill has not been paid to date.

LO9-1,9-2

E9-2 **Computing Shareholders' Equity and Working Capital: Explaining the Quick Ratio and Working Capital**

Dumont Corporation is preparing its 2017 statement of financial position. The company records show the following related amounts at the end of the fiscal year, December 31, 2017:

Cash	$ 25,000	Liability for withholding taxes	$ 6,000
Short-term investments	54,000	Deferred rent revenue	14,000
Trade receivables	147,000	Bonds payable (due in 15 years)	180,000
Inventories	110,000	Wages payable	14,000
Prepayments	2,000	Property taxes payable	6,000
Non-current assets	296,200	Note payable (6%; due in 6 months)	24,000
Notes payable (8%, due in 5 years)	30,000	Interest payable	3,200
Trade payables	119,000	Shareholders' equity	200,000
Income taxes payable	28,000		

Required:

1. Compute (a) the amount of working capital and (b) the quick ratio (show computations). Why is working capital important to management? How do financial analysts use the quick ratio?

2. Would your computations be different if the company reported $250,000 worth of contingent liabilities in the notes to its financial statements? Explain.

LO9-1

E9-3 **Recording Payroll Costs with Discussion**

Matyas Company completed the salary and wage payroll for April 2017. The payroll provided the following details:

Salaries and wages earned	$224,000
Employee income taxes withheld	55,000
CPP contributions*	11,100
EI contributions	4,000
Union dues withheld	3,000
Insurance premiums withheld	1,000

*$11,100 each for employer and employees. Employment Insurance, employees' share.

Required:

1. Prepare the journal entry to record the payroll for April, including employee deductions.

2. Prepare the journal entry to record the employer's additional payroll expenses.

3. Prepare a combined journal entry to show the payment of amounts owed to governmental agencies and other organizations.

4. What was the total compensation expense for the company? Explain. What percentage of the payroll was take-home pay? From the employers' perspective, does an economic difference between the cost of salaries and the cost of benefits exist? From the employees' perspective, does a difference exist?

LO9-1   **E9-4**   **Computing Payroll Costs; Discussion of Labour Costs**

Riverside Ltd. has completed the payroll for January 2018, reflecting the following data:

Salaries and wages earned	$69,000
Employee income taxes withheld	16,900
CPP contributions*	3,415
EI contributions	1,242
Union dues withheld	1,200

*$3,415 each for employer and employee. Employment Insurance, employees' share.

Required:

1. What amount of additional compensation expense must be paid by the company? What was the amount of the employees' take-home pay?

2. List the liabilities that are reported on the company's statement of financial position at January 31, 2018. The employees' take-home pay was paid on that day.

3. Would employers react differently to a 4 percent increase in the employer's share of CPP than to a 4 percent increase in the basic level of salaries? Would financial analysts react differently?

LO9-1, 9-4   **E9-5**   **Recording a Note Payable through Its Time to Maturity with Discussion of Management Strategy**

Sears Canada Inc.

Many businesses borrow money during periods of increased business activity to finance inventory and trade receivables. Sears Canada Inc. is one of Canada's largest general merchandise retailers. Each year, Sears Canada builds up its inventory to meet the needs of December holiday shoppers. A large portion of these holiday sales are on credit. As a result, Sears Canada often collects cash from the sales several months after the December holidays. Assume that on November 1, 2017, Sears Canada borrowed $4.5 million cash from the bank for working capital purposes and signed an interest-bearing note due in six months. The interest rate was 5 percent per annum, payable at maturity. Assume that the fiscal year of Sears Canada ends on December 31.

Required:

1. Prepare the journal entry to record the note on November 1, 2017.

2. Prepare any adjusting entry required at December 31, 2017.

3. Prepare the journal entry to record payment of the note and interest on the maturity date, April 30, 2018.

4. If Sears Canada needs extra cash for every December holiday season, should management borrow money on a long-term basis to avoid the necessity of negotiating a new short-term loan each year?

LO9-1, 9-4   **E9-6**   **Determining Financial Statement Effects of Transactions Involving Notes Payable**

Refer to the previous exercise.

Sears Canada Inc.

Required:

1. Determine the financial statement effects for each of the following transactions: (*a*) issuance of the note on November 1, 2017, (*b*) impact of the adjusting entry at December 31, 2017, and (*c*) the payment of the note and interest on April 30, 2018. Indicate the accounts affected, amounts, and direction of the effects (+ for increases and − for decreases) on the accounting equation. Use the following headings:

Date	Assets	=	Liabilities	+	Shareholders' Equity

2. If Sears needs extra cash during every Christmas season, should management borrow money on a long-term basis to avoid the necessity of negotiating a new short-term loan each year?

LO9-1   **E9-7**   **Reporting Warranty Liability**

Gonzales Co. provides warranties for many of its products. Its estimated warranty liability account had a balance of $140,800 at January 1, 2017. Based on an analysis of warranty claims during the past several years, the warranty expense for 2017 was established at 0.4 percent of sales. During 2017, the actual cost of servicing products under warranty was $64,400, and sales were $14,400,000.

Required:

1. Compute the warranty expense that should appear on the company's statement of earnings for the year ended December 31, 2017.

2. What amount will be reported in the estimated warranty liability account on the statement of financial position as at December 31, 2017?

■ LO9-1   **E9-8**   **Reporting Warranty Liability**

Amster Corp. produces and sells a single product that requires considerable servicing and adjustment during the first two years after sale. The company offers a warranty for two years covering most service requirements. The product's price ranges from $900 to $1,200, depending on the particular model produced. Warranty work costs $100 per product, regardless of the model. This amount has been quite stable for several years. Most of the warranty work occurs between the 6th and the 18th month after sale. The company's sales have been expanding, from approximately 9,000 units in 2012 to approximately 12,000 units in 2017.

Required:

How should Amster Corp. account for warranty costs, and how should the information be reported on its financial statements?

■ LO9-1, 9-2, 9-6   **E9-9**   **Determining the Impact of Transactions, Including Analysis of Cash Flows**

Diego Company sells a wide range of goods through two retail stores operating in adjoining cities. Most purchases of goods for resale are on account. Occasionally, a short-term note payable is used to obtain cash for current use. The following transactions were selected from those occurring during 2018:

a. On January 10, 2018, purchased merchandise on credit, $18,000; the company uses a perpetual inventory system.

b. On March 1, 2018, borrowed $100,000 cash from the bank and signed an interest-bearing note payable at the end of one year, with an annual interest rate of 4 percent payable at maturity.

c. On April 5, 2018, sold merchandise on credit, $33,900; this amount included GST of $1,500 and PST of $2,400. The cost of sales represents 70 percent of the sales invoice.

Required:

1. Describe the financial statement effects of these transactions. Indicate the accounts affected and the amounts and direction of the effects (+ for increases and − for decreases) on the accounting equation. Use the following headings:

Date	Assets	=	Liabilities	+	Shareholders' Equity

2. What amount of cash is paid on the maturity date of the note?

3. Discuss the impact of each transaction on Diego's cash flows.

4. Discuss the impact of each transaction on the quick ratio. Assume that the quick ratio is greater than 1.0 before considering each transaction.

■ LO9-S1   **E9-10**   **(Appendix 9A) Computing Deferred Income Tax: One Temporary Difference, with Discussion**

The comparative statements of earnings of Martin Corporation for fiscal years 2017 and 2018 showed the following summarized pretax data:

	2017	2018
Sales revenue	$55,000	$63,000
Expenses (excluding income tax)	39,000	43,000
Pretax earnings	$16,000	$20,000

The expenses in 2017 included an amount of $4,000 that was deductible for tax purposes in 2018. The average income tax rate was 32 percent. Taxable income from the income tax returns was $20,000 for 2017 and $16,000 for 2018.

Required:

1. For each year, compute (*a*) the income taxes payable and (*b*) the deferred income tax. Is the deferred income tax a liability or an asset? Explain.

2. Show what amounts related to income taxes should be reported each year on the statement of earnings and the statement of financial position. Assume that the income tax is paid on March 1 of the next year.

3. Explain why income tax expense is not simply the amount of cash paid during the year.

LO9-S1   **E9-11**   **(Appendix 9A) Recording Deferred Income Tax: One Temporary Difference; Discussion of Management Strategy**

The comparative statement of earnings for Chung Corporation for fiscal years 2016 and 2017 provided the following summarized pretax data:

	2016	2017
Revenue	$750,000	$820,000
Expenses (excluding income tax)	540,000	580,000
Pretax earnings	$210,000	$240,000

The expenses for 2017 included an amount of $30,000 that was deductible only on the 2016 income tax return. The average income tax rate was 30 percent. Taxable income shown in the tax returns was $180,000 for 2016 and $270,000 for 2017.

Required:

1. For each year, compute (*a*) the income taxes payable and (*b*) the deferred income tax. Is the deferred income tax a liability or an asset? Explain.

2. Prepare the journal entry for each year to record the income taxes payable, the deferred income tax, and the income tax expense.

3. Show the tax-related amounts that should be reported each year on the statement of earnings and the statement of financial position. Assume that income tax is paid on March 1 of the next year.

4. Why would management want to incur the cost of preparing separate tax and financial accounting reports to defer the payment of taxes?

LO9-S1   **E9-12**   **(Appendix 9A) Computing and Reporting Deferred Income Tax: Depreciation**

Amber Corporation reported the following summarized pretax data at the end of each year:

Statement of Earnings for the Year	**2016**	**2017**	**2018**
Revenues	$170,000	$182,000	$195,000
Expenses (including depreciation*)	125,500	126,000	122,500
Pretax earnings	$ 44,500	$ 56,000	$ 72,500

*Straight-line depreciation expense on a machine purchased January 1, 2016, for $75,000. The machine has a three-year estimated life and no residual value. The company used capital cost allowance on the income tax return as follows: 2016, $37,500; 2017, $25,000; and 2018, $12,500. The average income tax rate is 28 percent for each of the three years.

Taxable income from the income tax return was as follows: 2016, $32,000; 2017, $56,000; and 2018, $85,000.

Required:

1. For each year, compute (*a*) the income taxes payable and (*b*) the deferred income tax. Is the deferred income tax a liability or an asset? Explain.

2. Show the tax-related amounts that should be reported each year on the statement of earnings and the statement of financial position.

LO9-S2   **E9-13**   **(Appendix 9B) Computing Present Values**

On January 1, 2017, Shannon Company completed the following transactions (assume a 6 percent annual interest rate):

a. Bought a delivery truck and agreed to pay $50,000 at the end of three years.

b. Rented an office building and was given the option of paying $10,000 at the end of each of the next three years or paying $28,000 immediately.

c. Established a savings account by depositing a single amount that will increase to $90,000 at the end of seven years.

d. Decided to deposit a single sum in the bank that will provide 10 equal annual year-end payments of $40,000 to a retired employee (payments starting December 31, 2017).

Required (show computations and round to the nearest dollar):

1. In (*a*), what is the cost of the truck that should be recorded at the time of purchase?
2. In (*b*), which option for the office building should the company select?
3. In (*c*), what single amount must be deposited in this account on January 1, 2017?
4. In (*d*), what single sum must be deposited in the bank on January 1, 2017?

LO9-S2

E9-14 **(Appendix 9B) Computing Growth for a Savings Fund with Periodic Deposits**
On January 1, 2017, you plan to take a trip around the world upon graduation four years from now. Your grandmother wants to deposit sufficient funds for this trip in a savings account for you. On the basis of a budget, you estimate that the trip currently would cost $24,000. To be generous, your grandmother decides to deposit $5,500 in the fund at the end of each of the next four years, starting on December 31, 2017. The savings account will earn 4 percent annual interest, which will be added to the savings account at each year-end.

Required (show computations and round to the nearest dollar):

1. How much money will you have for the trip at the end of year 4 (i.e., after four deposits)?
2. What is the interest for the four years?
3. How much interest revenue did the fund earn in 2017, 2018, 2019, and 2020?

LO9-S2

E9-15 **(Appendix 9B) Computing the Value of an Asset Based on Present Value**
Quetario Company is considering purchasing a machine that would save the company $13,500 in cash per year for six years, at the end of which the machine would be retired with no residual value. The firm wishes to earn a minimum return of 8 percent, compounded annually, on any such investment. Assume that the cash savings occur at year-end, and ignore income taxes.

Required:

1. What is the maximum amount that the firm should be willing to pay for this machine? Show your computations.
2. Would the maximum amount be different if the machine is expected to have a residual value of $4,000 at the end of six years? Explain.
3. As an alternative to the scenario in (2), the company could buy a machine that had no residual value and offered no cost savings for the first five years, but this machine would offer cost savings of $113,561 at the end of the sixth year. If the company can buy only one machine, which one should it be? Defend your answer.

LO9-S2

E9-16 **(Appendix 9B) Reporting a Mortgage Note**
On January 1, 2018, Wong Corporation signed a mortgage note for $5,000,000 at 8 percent for a term of five years. Mortgage payments are made semi-annually on June 30 and on December 31. Each mortgage payment is a blend of interest on the unpaid amount and a partial repayment of the principal loan.

Required:

1. Compute the amount of each mortgage payment.
2. Record the mortgage payments on June 30, 2018, and December 31, 2018.
3. What is the current portion of the mortgage at December 31, 2018? What portion of the mortgage would appear as long-term debt on the statement of financial position at that same date?

connect PROBLEMS

LO9-1, 9-2

P9-1 **Recording and Reporting Current Liabilities with Discussion of the Effects on the Quick Ratio** (AP9-1)
Dumax Company completed the following transactions during 2018. The company's fiscal year ends on December 31, 2018.

Jan. 2   Paid accrued interest in the amount of $52,000.
Apr. 30   Borrowed $550,000 from Commerce Bank; signed a 12-month, 6 percent interest-bearing note.
May 20   Sold merchandise for $6,000 cash plus harmonized sales tax at 14 percent, and realized a gross profit of 40 percent of sales.

June 3 Purchased merchandise for resale at a cost of $75,800; terms 2/10, n/30.

July 5 Paid the invoice received on June 3.

Aug. 31 Signed a contract to provide security service to a small apartment complex and collected $6,840 of fees for six months in advance, including HST at the rate of 14 percent. (Record the collection in a way that will not require an adjusting entry at year-end.)

Dec. 31 Reclassified a long-term debt in the amount of $100,000 to a current liability.

31 Determined that salary and wages earned but not yet paid on December 31 totalled $85,000. Ignore payroll taxes.

31 Recorded income tax expense for the year in the amount of $125,000. The current income taxes payable were $93,000.

Required:

1. Prepare journal entries to record each of these transactions, assuming that a perpetual inventory system is used.

2. Prepare all adjusting and reclassification entries required on December 31, 2018.

3. Show how all of the current liabilities arising from these transactions are reported on the statement of financial position at December 31, 2018.

4. For each transaction and entry, state whether the quick ratio is increased, decreased, or remains unchanged. Assume that the quick ratio is less than 1.0 prior to each transaction.

LO9-1, 9-6 **P9-2 Determining Financial Effects of Transactions Affecting Current Liabilities with Discussion of Cash Flow Effects** (AP9-2)

Refer to the previous problem.

Required:

1. For each transaction (including adjusting entries) listed in the previous problem, indicate the accounts affected, amounts, and direction of the effects (+ for increases and − for decreases) on the accounting equation. Use the following headings:

Date	Assets	=	Liabilities	+	Shareholders' Equity

2. For each transaction and related adjusting entry, state whether cash flow from operating activities is increased, decreased, or unchanged.

LO9-1 **P9-3 Recording and Reporting Accrued Liabilities and Deferred Revenue and Financial Statement Effects with Discussion**

During 2018, Riverside Company completed the following two transactions. The company's fiscal year ends on December 31.

a. Paid and recorded wages of $130,000 during 2018; however, at the end of December 2018, wages of $1,300 for three days are unpaid and unrecorded because the next weekly pay day is January 6, 2019.

b. Rented office space to another party and collected $3,000 on December 10, 2018. The rent collected was for 30 days from December 12, 2018, through January 10, 2019, and was credited in full to rent revenue.

Required:

1. Prepare (a) the adjusting entry required on December 31, 2018, and (b) the journal entry on January 6, 2019, to record the payment of any unpaid wages from December 2018.

2. Prepare (a) the journal entry for the collection of rent on December 10, 2018, and (b) the adjusting entry on December 31, 2018.

3. Determine the financial statement effects for each of the journal entries you prepared in (1) and (2). Indicate the accounts affected, amounts, and direction of the effects (+ for increases and − for decreases) on the accounting equation. Use the following headings:

Date	Assets	=	Liabilities	+	Shareholders' Equity

4. Show how the liabilities related to these transactions should be reported on the company's statement of financial position at December 31, 2018.

5. Explain why the accrual method of accounting provides more relevant information to financial analysts than the cash method.

■ LO9-1, 9-2, 9-4   **P9-4**

Leon's Furniture Limited

The Walt Disney Company

Brunswick Corporation

Alcoa

Determining Financial Statement Effects of Various Liabilities (AP9-3)

1. Leon's Furniture Limited is one of Canada's largest home furnishing retailers, with a network of 75 stores selling a wide range of furniture, major appliances, and home electronics. Its annual report contained the following note:

> **Unpaid warranty claims**
>
> Warranty repairs related to warranty plans sold separately are recorded as claims expense at the time the customer reports a claim. For these warranties, a provision for unpaid warranty claims is established for unpaid reported claims. The provision for unpaid claims is based on estimates, and may differ from actual claims paid.
>
> The Company also provides a standard warranty for certain products. For these warranties, a provision for warranty claims is recognized when the underlying products are sold. The amount of the provision is estimated using historical experience and may differ from actual claims paid.

Required:

Assume that estimated warranty costs for 2016 were $1 million and that the warranty work was performed during 2017. Describe the financial statement effects for each year.

2. Walt Disney is a well-recognized brand in the entertainment industry, with products ranging from broadcast media to parks and resorts. The following note is from its annual report:

> **Walt Disney**
>
> **Revenue Recognition**
>
> Revenues from advance theme park ticket sales are recognized when the tickets are used. Revenues from expiring multi-use tickets are recognized ratably over the estimated usage period. For non-expiring, multi-day tickets, revenues are recognized over a five-year time period based on estimated usage. The estimated usage periods are derived from historical usage patterns.

Required:

Assume that Disney collected $100 million in 2016 for multi-year tickets that will be used in future years. For 2017, the company estimates that 70 percent of the tickets will be used, and the remaining 30 percent will be used in 2018. Describe the financial statement effects for each year.

3. Brunswick Corporation is a multinational company that manufactures and sells marine and recreational products. Its annual report contained the following information:

> **Litigation**
>
> A jury awarded $44.4 million in damages in a suit brought by Independent Boat Builders Inc., a buying group of boat manufacturers and its 22 members. Under the antitrust laws, the damage award has been tripled, and the plaintiffs will be entitled to their attorney's fees and interest.
>
> The Company has filed an appeal contending the verdict was erroneous as a matter of law, both as to liability and damages.

Required:

How should Brunswick report this litigation in its financial statements?

4. Alcoa is involved in the mining and manufacturing of aluminum. Its products can become an advanced alloy for the wing of a Boeing 787 or a common, recyclable Coca-Cola can. The annual report for Alcoa stated the following:

> **Environmental Expenditures**
>
> Liabilities are recorded when remediation costs are probable and the costs can be reasonably estimated.

Required:

In your own words, explain Alcoa's accounting policy for environmental expenditures. What is the justification for this policy?

■ LO9-1   **P9-5**

Bombardier Inc.

Recording and Reporting Product Warranties

Bombardier Inc. specializes in manufacturing transportation products (aircraft, railway equipment, snowmobiles, and watercraft). The company offers warranties on all of its products. Note 2 to Bombardier's financial statements for fiscal year 2015 stated the following:

Product warranties typically range from one to five years, except for aircraft and bogie structural warranties that extend up to 20 years.

Selected information from Bombardier's annual reports follows (amounts in millions of U.S. dollars):

	2015	2014	2013
Revenues	18,172	20,111	18,151
Provision for product warranties at year-end	725	773	863

During fiscal year 2015, Bombardier paid $224 million to customers in exchange for returned products under the warranty.

Required:

1. Compute the amount of warranty expense for fiscal year 2015.

2. Prepare journal entries to record both the warranty expense for the year and the payments made under the warranty.

3. Compute the ratio of the warranty liability to revenues for the three years. Has the ratio increased or decreased during the three-year period?

4. Based on the limited information available about the warranty expense and payments in 2015, should Bombardier increase the balance of the warranty liability in future years? Explain.

■ LO9-1

IBM

P9-6 **Defining and Analyzing Changes in Current Liabilities**

International Business Machines (IBM) is a leading provider of computer products and services. The company is known for its hardware products but has focused on providing information technology services in recent years. IBM provides standard warranties and extended warranties with the sale of its products. The company's note on significant accounting policies is as follows:

> The company offers warranties for its hardware products that generally range up to three years, with the majority being either one or three years. Estimated costs for warranty terms standard to the deliverable are recognized when revenue is recorded for the related deliverable. The company estimates its warranty costs standard to the deliverable based on historical warranty claim experience and estimates of future spending, and applies this estimate to the revenue stream for products under warranty. subsequently recognized on a straight-line basis over the delivery period.
>
> ....

Revenue from separately priced extended warranty contracts is initially recorded as deferred income and subsequently recognized on a straight-line basis over the delivery period.

Selected information related to warranties provided by IBM follows (in millions of U.S. dollars):

	2015	2014	2013
Net revenues	$81,741	$92,793	$98,367
Standard warranty liability, end of year	181	197	376
Settlements made during the year	196	298	387
Extended warranty deferred revenue, end of year	538	536	579
Additions to extended warranty deferred revenue during the year	286	298	305

Required:

1. Compute the amount of warranty expense for 2014 and 2015.

2. Prepare journal entries to record both the warranty expense for 2015 and the payments made under the warranty during the year.

3. Compute the ratio of the warranty expense to net revenues for the three years. Has the ratio increased or decreased during the three-year period? Provide possible reasons for the changes in the ratio. The Standard warranty liability had a balance of $394 at the beginning of 2013.

4. Based on the limited information available about the warranty expense and settlements during these three years, should IBM reduce the ratio of the warranty expense to net sales in future years? Explain.

5. Compute the extended warranty revenue recognized during 2014 and 2015, and prepare the journal entry to record the revenue recognized in 2015.

■ LO9-1   **P9-7**   **Determining Financial Statement Effects of Deferred Revenues**

A. Deferred revenues—customer deposits

Eastern Brewing Company (EBC) distributes its products in an aluminum keg. Customers are charged a deposit of $25 per keg, and deposits received from customers are recorded in the keg deposits account.

Required:

1. Where on the statement of financial position will the keg deposits account be found? Explain.
2. A production specialist who works for EBC estimates that 50 kegs for which deposits were received during the year will never be returned. How would the deposits related to these 50 kegs be reflected in the company's financial statements?

B. Deferred revenues—rent

On September 1, 2017, Noreen Ltd. collected $72,000 in cash from its tenant as an advance rent payment on its store location. The six-month lease period ends on February 28, 2018, at which time the lease contract may be renewed. Noreen's fiscal year ends on December 31.

Required:

1. Prepare journal entries to record the collection of rent on September 1, 2017, and the related adjustment for the amount of rent earned during 2017.
2. If the amount received on September 1, 2017, had covered a period of 18 months, how should Noreen report the deferred rent amount on its statement of financial position as at December 31, 2017?

C. Deferred revenues—subscription fees

Tremblay Inc. publishes a monthly newsletter for retail marketing managers and requires its subscribers to pay $60 in advance for a one-year subscription. During the month of April 2018, Tremblay Inc. sold 150 one-year subscriptions and received payments in advance from all new subscribers. Only 90 of the new subscribers paid their fees in time to receive the April newsletter. The other subscribers received the newsletter in May.

Required:

Prepare journal entries to record the subscription fees received in advance during April 2018, and the related adjusting entry to recognize the subscription revenue earned during April 2018.

■ LO9-1   **P9-8**   **Defining and Analyzing Changes in Current Liabilities** (AP9-4)

Leon's Furniture Limited

Leon's Furniture Limited is one of Canada's largest home furnishing retailers, with a network of 75 stores selling a wide range of furniture, major appliances, and home electronics. The company reported the following items in its statement of financial position dated December 31, 2015 (in thousands of Canadian dollars):

	December 31, 2015	December 31, 2014
Current liabilities		
Trade and other payables	$206,076	$197,044
Customers' deposits	112,446	97,705
Dividends payable	7,141	7,106
Deferred warranty plan revenue	49,380	51,111

Required:

1. Define each of the current liabilities and identify the types of transactions that cause each liability to change (increase, decrease).
2. The company reported that $43,335 of deferred warranty plan revenue was earned during fiscal year 2015. Determine the amount that was collected in advance from customers during 2015, and prepare the related journal entry.
3. The company's board of directors declared dividends of $28,501 during 2015. Prepare the journal entries to record the declaration and payment of dividends during 2015.

■ LO9-1, 9-5   **P9-9**   **Making a Decision as Chief Financial Officer: Contingent Liabilities**

For each of the following situations, determine whether the company should (*a*) report a liability on the statement of financial position, (*b*) disclose a contingent liability, or (*c*) not report the situation. Justify and explain your conclusions.

1. An automobile company introduces a new car. Past experience demonstrates that lawsuits will be filed as soon as the new model is involved in any accidents. The company can be certain that at least one jury will award damages to people injured in an accident.

2. A research scientist determines that your company's bestselling product may infringe on another company's patent. If the other company discovers the infringement and files a lawsuit, your company could lose millions of dollars.

3. As part of land development for a new housing project, your company has polluted a natural lake. Under provincial law, you must clean up the lake once you complete the development. The development project will take five to eight years to complete. Current estimates indicate that it will cost $2 to $3 million to clean up the lake.

4. Your company has just been notified that it lost a product liability lawsuit for $1 million that it plans to appeal. Management is confident that the company will win on appeal, but the lawyers believe that it will lose.

5. A key customer is unhappy with the quality of a major construction project. The company believes that the customer is being unreasonable but, to maintain goodwill, has decided to do $250,000 in repairs next year.

■ LO9-2,9-3　　**P9-10**　**Analyzing and Interpreting the Quick Ratio and the Trade Payables Turnover Ratio** (AP9-5)

 e**X**cel

Clearwater
Seafoods Inc.

Clearwater Seafoods Inc. is a leader in the global seafood market. Its main operations include harvesting, processing, distributing, and marketing of seafood products primarily in Canada, the United States, Europe, and Asia. Selected financial statement information for the company over the four-year period 2012–2015 is presented below (amounts in thousands of Canadian dollars):

	2015	2014	2013	2012
Quick assets	$132,840	$ 97,410	$ 90,689	$ 84,935
Current liabilities	167,631	85,213	62,574	64,169
Cost of sales	372,757	341,908	301,291	276,190
Trade payables	82,870	52,308	40,760	44,633
Increase (decrease) in inventories	24,966	(6,831)	(4,806)	(9,846)

Required:

1. Compute the quick ratio for each of the four years, and comment on the four-year trend of the ratio.

2. Compute the trade payables turnover ratio and the average age of payables for the years 2012–2015. Did the company's management of its trade payables improve over time? Explain.

3. In computing the trade payables turnover ratio, it is preferable to use purchases instead of cost of sales in the numerator. Re-compute the ratio for each of the years 2012–2015 using purchases in the numerator. Do the new ratios differ significantly from those computed in (2)? Explain.

■ LO9-6　　**P9-11**　**Determining Cash Flow Effects** (AP9-6)

For each of the following transactions, determine whether cash flows from operating activities will increase, decrease, or remain the same:

a. Purchased merchandise on credit.

b. Paid a trade payable.

c. Accrued payroll for the month but did not pay it.

d. Borrowed money from the bank. The term of the note is 90 days.

e. Reclassified a long-term note as a current liability.

f. Paid accrued interest expense.

g. Recorded a liability based on a pending lawsuit.

h. Paid back the bank for money borrowed in (*d*), along with related interest.

i. Collected cash from a customer for services that will be performed in the next accounting period.

j. Paid GST to the federal government. The amount was previously collected from customers.

■ LO9-S1   **P9-12**   **(Appendix 9A) Recording and Reporting Deferred Income Tax: Depreciation** (AP9-7)

At December 31, 2017, the records of Pearson Corporation provided the following information:

Statement of Earnings	
Revenues	$160,000
Depreciation expense (straight line)	(11,000)
Other expenses (excluding income tax)	(90,000)
Earnings before income taxes	$ 59,000

Additional information is as follows:

a. Revenues include $20,000 interest on tax-free municipal bonds.

b. Depreciation expense relates to equipment acquired on January 1, 2017, at a cost of $44,000, with no salvage value and an estimated useful life of four years.

c. The accelerated depreciation (capital cost allowance) used on the tax return is as follows: 2017, $17,600; 2018, $13,200; 2019, $8,800; and 2020, $4,400.

d. The company is subject to an income tax rate of 30 percent. Assume that 85 percent of the income tax liability is paid in the year incurred.

e. The income tax return for 2017 shows a taxable income of $32,400.

Required:

1. Compute the income taxes payable and the deferred income tax for 2017. Is the deferred income tax a liability or an asset? Explain.

2. Prepare the journal entry to record income taxes for 2017.

3. Show how the tax-related amounts should be reported on the statement of earnings for 2017 and the statement of financial position at December 31, 2017.

■ LO9-S2   **P9-13**   **(Appendix 9B) Computing Present Values** (AP9-8)

On January 1, 2017, Bianca Company completed the following transactions (use a 7 percent annual interest rate for all transactions):

a. Borrowed $115,000 for seven years. Interest of $6,000 will be paid at the end of each year and the loan of $115,000 will be paid at the end of the 7th year.

b. Established a plant addition fund of $490,000 to be available at the end of year 8. A single sum that will grow to $490,000 will be deposited on January 1, 2017.

c. Agreed to pay a severance package to a discharged employee. The company will pay $75,000 at the end of the first year, $112,500 at the end of the second year, and $150,000 at the end of the third year.

d. Purchased a $170,000 machine on January 1, 2017, and paid cash, $34,000. A five-year note payable is signed for the balance. The note will be paid in five equal year-end payments starting on December 31, 2017.

Required (show computations and round to the nearest dollar):

1. In transaction (*a*), determine the present value of the debt.

2. In transaction (*b*), determine the amount that the company must deposit on January 1, 2017? What is the total amount of interest revenue that will be earned?

3. In transaction (*c*), determine the present value of this obligation.

4. In transaction (*d*), determine the amount of each of the equal annual payments that will be paid on the note? What is the total amount of interest expense that will be incurred?

■ LO9-S2   **P9-14**   **(Appendix 9B) Comparing Options by Using Present Value Concepts** (AP9-9)

After hearing a knock at your front door, you are surprised to see the Prize Patrol from a large, well-known magazine subscription company. It has arrived with the good news that you are the big winner, having won $20 million. Later, after consulting with a lawyer, you discover that you have three options: (1) you can receive $1 million per year for the next 20 years (starting one year from now), (2) you can have $8 million today, or (3) you can have $2 million today and receive $700,000 for each of the next 20 years. Your investment adviser tells you that it is reasonable to expect to earn 5 percent annual compound interest on investments. Which option do you prefer? What factors influenced your decision?

LO9-S2

P9-15 **(Appendix 9B) Computing Equal Periodic Debt Payments, and Completing a Schedule** (AP9-10)

On January 1, 2017, you bought a new Toyota automobile for $30,000. You made a $5,000 cash down payment and signed a $25,000 note, payable in four equal instalments on each December 31, the first payment to be made on December 31, 2017. The interest rate is 8 percent per year on the unpaid balance. Each payment will include payment on principal plus the interest.

Required:

1. Compute the amount of the equal payments that you must make.
2. What is the total amount of interest that you will pay during the four years?
3. Complete the following schedule:

Debt Payment Schedule				
Date	Cash Payment	Interest Expense	Decrease in Principal	Unpaid Principal
1/1/2017				
31/12/2017				
31/12/2018				
31/12/2019				
31/12/2020				
Totals				

4. Explain why the amount of interest expense decreases each year.
5. To reduce the total amount of interest paid on this note, you considered the possibility of making equal payments every three months (four payments per year). Compute the amount of the equal payments that you must make, and the amount of interest that will be saved over the life of the note.

LO9-S2

P9-16 **(Appendix 9B) Analyzing and Reporting Sale of Used Asset and Financing the Purchase of New Asset** (AP9-11)

Toronto Taxi Inc. owns a van that was purchased on January 1, 2011, for $45,000. The van has been depreciated using the straight-line method over 10 years and has a residual value of $5,000. On September 30, 2019, the company sold it for $7,000 cash and bought a new vehicle for $50,000 and signed a 4 percent note, payable in four equal annual instalments on September 30 of each year, with the first payment due on September 30, 2020. The company made the following additional payments in cash: $1,500 for a one-year insurance policy and $3,000 for preparation charges (i.e., registration, licence plate). The company depreciates the new van using the double-declining-balance method over five years. The new vehicle has an estimated residual value of $6,000.

Required:

1. Compute the gain or loss on the sale of the old van and prepare the journal entry to record this transaction.
2. Prepare the journal entries to record all the transactions that occurred on September 30, 2019.
3. Compute the amount of the annual instalment on the note payable and prepare the journal entry to record the payment of the first instalment.
4. Prepare the necessary adjusting entries at December 31, 2019, the end of the company's fiscal year.

LO9-S2

P9-17 **(Appendix 9B) Computing Amounts for a Debt Fund with Journal Entries**

On December 31, 2016, Post Company decided to invest a sufficient amount of cash to pay the principal amount of a $160,000 debt due on December 31, 2019. The company will make four equal annual deposits on December 31 of the years 2016 through 2019. The fund will earn 7 percent compound annual interest, which will be added to the balance at each year-end. The fund trustee will pay the loan principal (to the creditor) upon receipt of the last fund deposit. The company's fiscal year ends on December 31. The four annual deposits have a present value of $122,064 on December 31, 2016.

Required (show computations and round to the nearest dollar):

1. How much cash must be deposited each December 31?
2. What amount of interest will be earned on the four deposits until December 31, 2019?
3. How much interest revenue will the fund earn each year?

4. Prepare journal entries for the company to record the following transactions:

   a. The first deposit on December 31, 2016.

   b. The deposit at December 31, 2017, and interest revenue for 2017.

   c. The payment of the debt on December 31, 2019.

5. Show how the effect of the fund will be reported on the statement of earnings for 2017 and the statement of financial position at December 31, 2017.

ALTERNATE PROBLEMS

 LO^{9-1,9-2,9-6} **AP9-1** **Recording and Reporting Current Liabilities with Discussion of the Effects on the Quick Ratio** (P9-1)

Computek Ltd. completed the following transactions during 2018. The company's fiscal year ends on December 31, 2018.

  Jan. 8 Purchased on account merchandise for resale at a cost of $14,500, with terms 2/10, n/30. The company uses a periodic inventory system.

      19 Paid the invoice received on January 8.

  Mar. 10 Sold merchandise on credit for a total amount of $11,300, which included GST at 5 percent and PST at 8 percent of the sales amount.

  Apr. 1 Borrowed $35,000 from the bank for general use; signed a 12-month, 6 percent interest-bearing note.

  June 3 Purchased merchandise for resale at a cost of $16,420.

  July 5 Paid the invoice received on June 3.

  Aug. 1 Rented a small office in a building owned by the company and collected $6,000 for six months' rent in advance. Ignore sales taxes. (Record the collection in a way that will not require an adjusting entry at year-end.)

  Dec. 20 Received a $100 refundable deposit from a customer as a guarantee to return a large trailer "borrowed" for 30 days.

      31 Determined that wages earned but not yet paid on December 31 amounted to $9,500. Ignore payroll taxes.

Required:

1. Prepare the journal entry for each of these transactions.

2. Prepare the adjusting entry (entries) required on December 31, 2018.

3. Show how all of the liabilities arising from these transactions are reported on the statement of financial position at December 31, 2018.

4. For each transaction and related adjusting entry, state whether the quick ratio increases, decreases, or remains the same. Assume that the quick ratio is less than 1.0 before considering each transaction.

 LO^{9-1,9-6} **AP9-2** **Determining Financial Effects of Transactions Affecting Current Liabilities with Discussion of Cash Flow Effects** (P9-2)

Refer to the previous problem.

Required:

1. For each transaction (including adjusting and reclassification entries), indicate the accounts affected, amounts, and direction of the effects (+ for increases and − for decreases) on the accounting equation. Use the following headings:

Date	Assets	=	Liabilities	+	Shareholders' Equity

2. For each transaction, state whether cash flow from operating activities is increased, decreased, or unchanged.

 LO^{9-1,9-2} **AP9-3** **Determining Financial Statement Effects of Various Liabilities** (P9-4)

Ford Motor Company

1. Ford Motor Company is one of the world's largest companies, with annual sales of cars and trucks in excess of $120 billion. Its annual report contained the following note:

> **Warranties**
>
> Estimated warranty costs are accrued for at the time the vehicle is sold to a dealer. Estimates for warranty costs are made based primarily on historical warranty claim experience.

Required:

This year, Ford reported claims amounting to $4.0 billion and accrued expenses for warranties in the amount of $3.9 billion. Describe the financial statement effects for this year.

Carnival Cruise Lines

2. Carnival Cruise Lines operates cruise ships in Alaska, the Caribbean, the South Pacific, and the Mediterranean. Some cruises are brief; others can last for several weeks. The company does more than $1 billion in cruise business each year. The following note is from its annual report:

> **Revenue and Expense Recognition**
>
> Guest cruise deposits represent unearned revenues and are initially recorded as customer deposit liabilities when received. Customer deposits are subsequently recognized as cruise revenues, together with revenues from onboard and other activities, and all associated direct costs and expenses of a voyage are recognized as cruise costs and expenses, upon completion of voyages with durations of 10 nights or less and on a pro rata basis for voyages in excess of 10 nights.

Required:

In your own words, explain how deferred revenue is reported on the statement of financial position for Carnival. Assume that Carnival collected $15 million in 2017 for cruises that will be completed in the following year. Of that amount, $3 million was related to cruises of 10 or fewer nights that were not complete; $7 million to cruises of more than 10 nights that, on average, were 60 percent complete; and $5 million was related to cruises that had not yet begun. What is the amount of deferred revenue that should be reported on the 2017 statement of financial position?

Exxon Mobil Corporation

3. An annual report for Exxon Mobil Corporation reported a quick ratio of 0.45. For the previous year, the ratio was 0.70. Based on this information, do you think that Exxon Mobil is experiencing financial difficulty? What other information would you want to consider in making this evaluation?

Brunswick Corporation

4. Brunswick Corporation is a multinational company that manufactures and sells marine and recreational products. Its annual report contained the following information:

> **Environmental Matters**
>
> The environmental remediation and clean-up projects in which the Company is involved have an aggregate estimated range of exposure of approximately $40.0 million to $64.2 million as of December 31, 2015. At December 31, 2015 and 2014, the Company had reserves for environmental liabilities of $40.0 million and $39.9 million, respectively, reflected in Accrued expenses and Other long-term liabilities in the Consolidated Balance Sheets. The Company recorded environmental provisions of $1.4 million, $1.0 million and $0.5 million for the years ended December 31, 2015, 2014 and 2013, respectively.

Required:

In your own words, explain Brunswick's accounting policy for environmental expenditures. What is the justification for this policy?

■ LO9-1   **AP9-4**   **Defining and Analyzing Changes in Current Liabilities** (P9-8)

WestJet Airlines Ltd.

WestJet Airlines Ltd. is a Canadian airline that offers scheduled flights, cargo services, and vacation packages to many destinations in North America, Central America, the Caribbean, and Europe. The company reported the following current liabilities in its statement of financial position dated December 31, 2015, and related note disclosures (in thousands of Canadian dollars):

	December 31, 2015	December 31, 2014
Accounts payable and accrued liabilities	$545,438	$415,562
Advance ticket sales	620,216	575,781
Deferred rewards program	117,959	86,870
Non-refundable guest credits	40,921	45,434
Current portion of maintenance provisions	85,819	54,811

In the notes to its financial statements, WestJet indicates that it has a rewards program that allows passengers to accumulate credits that they can use towards future flights and vacation packages. The company also issues future non-refundable travel credits to passengers (guests) in case of flight cancellations or changes.

Required:

1. Define each of the current liabilities and identify the types of transactions that cause each liability to change (increase, decrease).

2. Assume that the company received $3,575,494 from passengers in advance of their flights. Determine the amount of advanced ticket sales that the company earned during fiscal year 2015, and prepare the related journal entries to record the transactions that affected this account.

LO9-2,9-3   AP9-5   Analyzing and Interpreting the Quick Ratio and the Trade Payables Turnover Ratio (P9-10)

Potash Corporation of Saskatchewan is the world's largest fertilizer company, producing the three primary crop nutrients: potash, phosphate, and nitrogen. Potash Corp. is a major player in meeting the growing challenge of feeding the world, and has operations and business interests in seven countries. Selected financial statement information for this company over the most recent four-year period is shown below (in millions of U.S. dollars):

	2015	2014	2013	2012
Quick assets	$ 731	$1,244	$1,380	$1,651
Current liabilities	1,747	2,198	2,113	1,854
Cost of sales	3,522	3,859	3,943	4,023
Trade payables	426	457	450	623

Required:

1. Compute the quick ratio for each of the four years, and comment on the four-year trend of the ratio.

2. Compute the trade payables turnover ratio and the average age of payables for the years 2012–2015. Did the company improve on its management of trade payables? Explain.

LO9-4   AP9-6   Determining Cash Flow Effects (P9-11)

For each of the following transactions, determine whether cash flows from operating activities will increase, decrease, or remain the same:

a. Purchased merchandise for cash.

b. Paid salaries and wages for the last month of the previous accounting period.

c. Paid PST to the provincial government, based on collections from customers.

d. Borrowed money from the bank. The term of the note is two years.

e. Withheld CPP contributions from employees' pay cheques and immediately paid these to the government.

f. Recorded accrued interest expense.

g. Paid cash as a result of losing a lawsuit. A liability had been recorded.

h. Paid salaries and wages for the current month.

i. Performed services for a customer who had paid for them in the previous accounting period.

LO9-1,9-5   AP9-7   (Appendix 9A) Recording and Reporting Deferred Income Taxes: Two Temporary Differences (P9-12)

The records of Calib Corporation provided the following summarized data for 2017 and 2018:

Year-End December 31		
	2017	2018
Statement of Earnings		
Revenues	$210,000	$218,000
Expenses (excluding income tax)	130,000	133,000
Earnings before income taxes	$ 80,000	$ 85,000

a. Calib is subject to an income tax rate of 35 percent. Assume that 80 percent of the income taxes payable are paid in the current year and 20 percent on February 28 of the next year.

b. The temporary differences resulted from the following:

i. The 2018 expenses include an amount of $8,000 that must be deducted only in the 2017 tax return.

ii. The 2018 revenues include an amount of $6,000 that was taxable only in 2019.

iii. The taxable income shown in the tax returns was $72,000 for 2017 and $87,000 for 2018.

Required:

1. For each year, compute (a) the income taxes payable and (b) the deferred income taxes. Identify whether the deferred income tax amounts are assets or liabilities. Explain.

2. Prepare the journal entry for each year to record income taxes payable, deferred income taxes, and income tax expense.

3. Show the tax-related amounts that should be reported each year on the statement of earnings and the statement of financial position.

4. As a financial analyst, would you evaluate differently a deferred income tax liability compared with income taxes currently payable?

LO9-S2   **AP9-8**   **(Appendix 9B) Computing Present Values** (P9-13)

On January 1, 2018, Brunet Company completed the following transactions (use an 8 percent annual interest rate for all transactions):

a. Borrowed $2,000,000 to be repaid in five years. Agreed to pay $150,000 interest each year for the five years.

b. Established a plant addition fund of $1,000,000 to be available at the end of year 10. A single sum that will grow to $1,000,000 will be deposited on January 1, 2018.

c. Purchased a $750,000 machine on January 1, 2019, for $400,000, paid in cash. A four-year note payable is signed for the balance. The note will be paid in four equal year-end payments starting on December 31, 2018.

Required (show computations and round to the nearest dollar):

1. In transaction (a), determine the present value of the obligation.

2. In transaction (b), determine the amount that the company must deposit on January 1, 2018? What is the total amount of interest revenue that will be earned?

3. In transaction (c), determine the amount of each of the equal annual payments that will be made on the note? What is the total amount of interest expense that will be incurred?

LO9-S2   **AP9-9**   **(Appendix 9B) Comparing Options by Using Present Value Concepts** (P9-14)

After completing a long and successful career as senior vice-president for a large bank, you are preparing for retirement. After visiting the human resources office, you have found that you have several retirement options: (1) you can receive an immediate cash payment of $7,000,000, (2) you can receive $600,000 per year for life (you have a life expectancy of 20 years), or (3) you can receive $600,000 per year for 10 years and then $700,000 per year for life (this option is intended to give you some protection against inflation). You have determined that you can earn 5 percent compounded annually on your investments. Which option do you prefer and why?

LO9-S2   **AP9-10**   **(Appendix 9B) Computing Equal Periodic Debt Payments, and Completing a Schedule with Journal Entries** (P9-15)
eXcel

On January 1, 2017, Ontario Company sold a new machine to Canada Company for $70,000. Canada Company made a cash down payment of $20,000 and signed a $50,000, 8 percent note for the balance due. The note is payable in three equal instalments due on December 31, 2017, 2018, and 2019. Each payment includes principal plus interest on the unpaid balance. Canada Company recorded the purchase as follows:

Jan. 1, 2017		
Machinery	70,000	
Cash		20,000
Note payable		50,000

Required (show computations and round to the nearest dollar):

1. What is the amount of the equal annual payments that Canada Company must make?

2. What is the total interest on the note over the three years?

3. Complete the following debt payment schedule:

Debt Payment Schedule				
Date	Cash Payment	Interest Expense	Decrease in Principal	Unpaid Principal
1/1/2017				
31/12/2017				
31/12/2018				
31/12/2019				
Total				

4. Prepare the journal entry for each of the three payments.

5. Explain why interest expense decreased in amount each year.

■ LO9-S2   **AP9-11**   **(Appendix 9B) Analyzing and Reporting Sale of Used Asset and Financing the Purchase of New Asset** (P9-16)

Sandox Corp. owns equipment that was purchased on January 1, 2014, for $90,000. The equipment has been depreciated using the straight-line method over five years and has a residual value of $10,000. On July 1, 2018, the company sold it for $14,000 cash and purchased new equipment for $100,000. Sandox paid $20,000 in cash and signed a 5 percent note, payable in five equal annual instalments on June 30 of each year, starting on June 30, 2019. The company made the following additional payments in cash: $1,500 for a one-year insurance policy and $3,000 for installation of the equipment. Sandox decided to depreciate the new equipment using the double-declining-balance method over five years. The equipment has an estimated residual value of $12,000.

Required:

1. Compute the gain or loss on the sale of the old equipment and prepare the journal entry to record this transaction.

2. Prepare the journal entries to record all the transactions that occurred on July 1, 2018.

3. Compute the amount of the annual instalment on the note payable and prepare the journal entry to record the payment of the first instalment.

4. Prepare the necessary adjusting entries at December 31, 2018, the end of the company's fiscal year.

 CASES AND PROJECTS

FINDING AND INTERPRETING FINANCIAL INFORMATION

■ LO9-1,9-3,9-4   **CP9-1**   **Finding Financial Information**

Canadian Tire
Corporation

Refer to the financial statements of Canadian Tire Corporation in Appendix A of this book.

Required:

1. Does Canadian Tire report income taxes payable as a separate account on its statement of financial position at the end of the current year? If not, where would this account be included on Canadian Tire's statement of financial position?

2. How did changes in trade and other payables affect cash flows from operating activities in the current year?

3. What is the amount of non-current liabilities at the end of the current year?

4. What amounts of deferred income tax assets and liabilities are reported on the statement of financial position at the end of the current year?

5. Does the company disclose information on contingent liabilities?

■ LO9-1,9-4   **CP9-2**   **Finding Financial Information**

Sears Canada Inc.

Go to *Connect* for the financial statements of Sears Canada Inc.

Required:

1. What is the amount of accounts payable at the end of the current year? (*Hint:* Refer to the notes to the financial statements for details.)

2. How did changes in accounts payable and accrued liabilities affect cash flows from operating activities in the current year?

3. The company's liabilities include deferred revenue. Refer to the notes to the financial statements for details of deferred revenue, and describe the types of transactions that would cause each type of deferred revenue to change.

4. What is the amount of long-term debt at the end of the current year?

5. Does the company have any contingent liabilities?

■ LO9-2,9-3   **CP9-3**   **Comparing Companies within an Industry**

Canadian Tire vs.
Sears Canada Inc.

Refer to the financial statements of Canadian Tire Corporation (Appendix A) and Sears Canada Inc. (*Connect*), and the Industry Ratio Report (Appendix B on *Connect*).

Required:

1. Compute the quick ratio for each company for each year shown in the financial statements.

2. Compare the most recent quick ratio for each company to the industry average from the Industry Ratio Report. Based solely on the quick ratio, are these companies more or less liquid than the average company in their industry?

3. Compute the accounts payable turnover ratio for each company for each year.

4. Using this information and any other data from the annual report, write a brief assessment of the liquidity of the two companies.

FINANCIAL REPORTING AND ANALYSIS CASES

LO9-1

Southwest Airlines

CP9-4 **Explaining a Note: Accrued Liability for a Frequent Flyer Program**

Most major airlines have frequent flyer programs that permit passengers to earn free tickets based on the number of reward miles they have flown. A Southwest Airlines annual report contained the following note:

> **Frequent Flyer Awards**
>
> The Company records a liability for the estimated incremental cost of providing free travel under its frequent flyer program for all amounts earned from flight activity that are expected to be redeemed for future travel. The estimated incremental cost includes direct passenger costs such as fuel, food, and other operational costs, but does not include any contribution to overhead or profit.

Required:

1. What cost measures other than incremental cost could Southwest use?

2. What account should Southwest debit when it accrues this liability?

LO9-2, 9-9

Maple Leaf Foods Inc.

CP9-5 **Using Financial Reports: Evaluating Cash Management**

Maple Leaf Foods Inc. is one of Canada's largest meat processors. It produces fresh and processed pork and poultry products under the Maple Leaf and Schneiders brands. Selected financial information is presented below for the period 2012–2015 (in millions of dollars):

	2015	2014	2013	2012
Net sales	$3,293	$3,157	$2,958	$4,865
Net accounts receivable	58	60	111	71
Inventories	258	270	288	302
Cost of sales	2,912	2,939	2,774	4,097
Accounts payable	256	275	650	447

Required:

1. Compute the following ratios for each of the years 2012–2015:

   a. Accounts payable turnover

   b. Inventory turnover

   c. Accounts receivable turnover

2. One of the measures of a company's effectiveness in utilizing cash resources is the cash conversion cycle, which is the difference between the average number of days needed to convert inventory to cash and the average number of days to pay trade suppliers. Compute the cash conversion cycle for each of the years 2012–2015. Did the company improve on its management of cash? Explain.

LO9-S2

CP9-6 **(Appendix 9B) Analyzing Hidden Interest in a Real Estate Deal: Present Value**

Many advertisements contain offers that seem too good to be true. A few years ago, an actual newspaper ad offered "a $150,000 house with a zero interest rate mortgage" for sale. If the purchaser made monthly payments of $3,125 for four years ($150,000 ÷ 48 months), then there would be no charge for interest. When the offer was made, mortgage interest rates were 12 percent. Present value for $n = 48$, and $i = 1\%$ is 37.9740.

Required:

1. Did the builder actually provide a mortgage at zero interest?

2. Estimate the true price of the home that was advertised. Assume that the monthly payment was based on an implicit interest rate of 12 percent.

CRITICAL THINKING CASES

■ LO9-1, 9-2   **CP9-7**   **Making Decisions as a Manager: Liquidity**

In some cases, a manager can engage in transactions that improve the appearance of financial reports without affecting the underlying economic reality. In this chapter, we discussed the importance of liquidity as measured by the quick ratio and working capital. For each of the following transactions, (*i*) determine whether reported liquidity, as measured by the quick ratio and working capital, is improved and (*ii*) state whether you believe that the fundamental liquidity of the company has been improved. Assume that the company has positive working capital and a quick ratio of 0.5 immediately prior to each transaction.

- *a.* Borrowed $1 million from the bank, payable in 90 days.
- *b.* Borrowed $10 million with a long-term note, payable in five years.
- *c.* Reclassified the current portion of long-term debt as long term as a result of a new agreement with the bank that guarantees the company's ability to refinance the debt when it matures.
- *d.* Paid $100,000 of the company's accounts payable.
- *e.* Entered into a borrowing agreement that allows the company to borrow up to $10 million when needed.
- *f.* Required all employees to take accrued vacation to reduce its liability for vacation compensation.

■ LO9-2   **CP9-8**   **Evaluating an Ethical Dilemma: Managing Reported Results**

The president of a regional wholesale distribution company planned to borrow a significant amount of money from the bank at the beginning of the next fiscal year. He knew that the bank placed a heavy emphasis on the liquidity of potential borrowers. To improve the company's quick ratio, the president told his employees to stop shipping new merchandise to customers and to stop accepting merchandise from suppliers for the last three weeks of the fiscal year. Is this behaviour ethical? Would your answer be different if the president had been concerned about reported net earnings and asked all of the employees to work overtime to ship out merchandise that had been ordered at the end of the year?

FINANCIAL REPORTING AND ANALYSIS TEAM PROJECT

■ LO9-1, 9-2, 9-3, 9-4   **Team Project: Examining an Annual Report**

CP9-9   As a team, select an industry to analyze. A list of companies classified by industry can be obtained by accessing www.fpinfomart.ca and then choosing "Companies by Industry." You can also find a list of industries and companies within each industry via http://ca.finance.yahoo.com/investing (click on Order Annual Reports under Tools).

Each group member should acquire the annual report for a different publicly traded company in the industry. (Library files, the SEDAR service at www.sedar.com, and the company's website are good sources.)

Required:

On an individual basis, each team member should then write a short report answering the following questions about the selected company. Discuss any patterns across the companies that you as a team observe. Then, as a group, write a short report comparing and contrasting your companies.

1. List the accounts and amounts of the company's current liabilities for the last three years.
   - *a.* What is the percentage of each to the respective year's total liabilities?
   - *b.* What do the results of your analysis suggest about the strategy your company has followed with respect to borrowed funds overall and over time?
2. What, if any, contingent liabilities are reported by the company for the most recent year, and what is your assessment of the risk of each after reading the note(s)?
3. Perform a ratio analysis:
   - *a.* What does the quick ratio measure in general?
   - *b.* Compute the ratio for the last three years.
   - *c.* What do your results suggest about the company?
   - *d.* If available, find the industry ratio for the most recent year, compare it to your results, and discuss why you believe the ratio for your company differs from or is similar to the industry ratio.

4. Perform another ratio analysis:

    a. What does the accounts payable turnover ratio measure in general?

    b. Compute the ratio for the last three years.

    c. What do your results suggest about the company?

    d. If available, find the industry ratio for the most recent year, compare it to your results, and discuss why you believe the ratio for your company differs from or is similar to the industry ratio.

5. What is the effect of the change in accounts payable on cash flows from operating activities for the most recent year; that is, did the change increase or decrease operating cash flows? Explain your answer.

connect CONTINUING CASE

LO9-1

CC9-1

Recording and Reporting Liabilities

Pool Corporation Inc. is the world's largest wholesale distributor of swimming pool supplies and equipment. It is a publicly traded corporation that trades on the NASDAQ exchange under the symbol POOL. It sells these products to swimming pool repair and service businesses, swimming pool builders, and retail swimming pool stores. The majority of these customers are small, family-owned businesses. Pool Corporation completed the following transactions during 2017. The annual accounting period ends December 31, 2017.

September 15   Purchased and paid for merchandise for resale at an invoice cost of $125,000. The company uses a periodic inventory system.

October 1   Borrowed $900,000 from First National Bank for general use; signed an 11 month, 5 percent interest-bearing note payable.

October 5   Received a $40,000 customer deposit from Joe Lipscomb for services to be performed in the future.

October 15   Performed $18,000 of the services paid for by Mr. Lipscomb.

December 12   Received utility bill for $12,000. Pool will pay it in early January.

        31   Determined wages of $52,000 earned but not yet paid on December 31 (disregard payroll taxes).

Required:

1. Prepare journal entries for each of these transactions.

2. Prepare all adjusting entries required on December 31, 2017.

SOLUTIONS TO SELF-STUDY QUIZZES

Self-Study Quiz 9-1

Effect on quick ratio:

1. Decrease, because the current liabilities will increase but the quick assets will remain the same.

2. Increase, because cash will increase but current liabilities will not change.

3. Increase, because the relative decrease in current liabilities is greater than the relative decrease in quick assets.

4. No change, because this transaction affects only *non-current* assets and *non-current* liabilities.

Self-Study Quiz 9-2

Cash	45.20	
Sales revenue		40.00
HST payable		5.20

Self-Study Quiz 9-3

1.

Interest expense	1,000	
Interest payable		1,000

2.

Interest expense	2,000	
Interest payable	1,000	
Cash		3,000

3.

Interest expense	3,000	
Cash		3,000

Self-Study Quiz 9-4

1. Decrease; no effect on cash flow from operating activities.
2. Increase; no effect on cash flow from operating activities. This is a financing activity.
3. No change; cash flow from operating activities will decrease.
4. No change; this is a non-cash transaction with no effect on cash flows.

Self-Study Quiz 9-5

1. The present value will decrease. With a higher interest rate, more interest will accumulate over time, so the initial amount needed at the start will be smaller because the interest component will be larger.
2. $10,000 \times 0.5584 = \$5,584$

ENDNOTES

1. For manufacturing companies, the purchases consist primarily of raw materials used in the production of finished goods. The computation of raw materials purchased is discussed in cost accounting courses.
2. Appendix 9A provides further details on the current and deferred components of income tax expense.
3. To highlight the relative significance of the taxes and fees imposed on the airline industry, WestJet Airlines offered to sell one-way tickets for $3 on flights between Calgary and Edmonton on June 30, 2002. However, the price of a $6 return ticket quickly rose to $89.27 when all of the applicable fees and taxes were added! See P. Fitzpatrick, "WestJet Launches $3 Ticket Protest," *National Post* (Financial Post), June 21, 2002: FP1.
4. The provinces of New Brunswick, Newfoundland and Labrador, Nova Scotia, Ontario, and Prince Edward Island have harmonized sales taxes. The provinces of British Columbia, Manitoba, Quebec, and Saskatchewan have separate provincial sales taxes. The province of Alberta, and the three territories—Northwest Territories, Nunavut, and Yukon—do not have provincial sales taxes. At the time of writing this text, sales taxes ranged from a GST rate of 5 percent in Alberta and the three territories to an HST rate of 15 percent in Nova Scotia.
5. To simplify the interest calculation, we assume that Sears's fiscal year for 2017 ends on January 31, 2018 instead of February 3, 2018.
6. International Accounting Standards Board, International Accounting Standard 37—Provisions, Contingent Liabilities and Contingent Assets: para. 10.
7. Present value and future value problems involve cash flows. The basic concepts are the same for cash inflows (receipts) and cash outflows (payments). No fundamental differences exist between present value and future value calculations for cash payments versus cash receipts.
8. The detailed discounting is as follows:

Periods	Interest for the Year	Present Value*
1.	$1,000.00 − ($1,000.00 × 1/1.04) = $38.46	$1,000.00 − $38.46 = $961.54
2.	$ 961.54 − ($ 961.54 × 1/1.04) = $36.98	$ 961.54 − $36.98 = $924.56
3.	$ 924.56 − ($ 924.56 × 1/1.04) = $35.56†	$ 924.56 − $35.56 = $889.00

*Verifiable in Table 10C.1.
†Adjusted for rounding.

Reporting and Interpreting Non-current Liabilities

After studying this chapter, you should be able to do the following:

LEARNING OBJECTIVES

LO10-1 Describe the characteristics of long-term notes and bonds payable.

LO10-2 Report notes payable and related interest expense.

LO10-3 Report bonds payable and interest expense for bonds sold at par, at a discount, or at a premium.

LO10-4 Compute and interpret the times interest earned ratio.

LO10-5 Report the early retirement of bonds.

LO10-6 Describe other non-current liabilities.

LO10-7 Compute and interpret the debt-to-equity ratio.

LO10-8 Explain how financing activities are reported on the statement of cash flows.

SUPPLEMENTARY MATERIAL

LO10-S1 Compute the present value of a bond using Excel.

LO10-S2 Report the carrying amount of a bond without using a bond discount or premium account.

LO10-S3 Report interest expense using the straight-line method amortization method.

Martin Good/Shutterstock.com

Focus Company: **Bell Canada Enterprises (BCE)**

FINANCING GROWTH WITH LONG-TERM DEBT

ell Canada Enterprises (BCE) Inc. (www.bce.ca) is Canada's largest communications company. The core business of BCE is delivering wired or wireless telecommunication services across any screen the customer chooses, from smartphone to television.

The technology and infrastructure necessary to support the telecommunications industry could not have been developed without billions of dollars of investment. One of the strengths of our economic system is the ability of corporations to raise large amounts of money from owners and creditors. In this chapter, we will discuss money raised from creditors by the issuance of long-term debt, and in the next chapter we will look at the issuance of shares to owners.

Bell is a familiar name in the telecommunications industry. If you are one of the 21 million subscribers to its network, you may have already texted a message today using BCE's network. The company is large by any measure. It employs over 50,000 people and reported over $21 billion in revenue last year. In order for BCE to maintain its position as an industry leader, it must reinvest large amounts of money in its business. In 2015, the company spent over $134 million on research and development and $4.16 billion on investments in both tangible and intangible assets.

Management of capital-intensive businesses face a number of challenges. Large investments must be made based on estimates of customer demand many years into the future. If management does not make sufficient investments, customers will be lost to other companies. If an over-investment is made, money will be tied up in assets that do not generate revenue and earnings will suffer.

In addition to deciding upon the proper level of investment in long-lived assets, management must decide on the optimal mix of sources of financing for those assets. BCE finances its investments in long-lived assets from three sources: internally generated funds, investments by owners, and borrowings from long-term creditors.

UNDERSTANDING THE BUSINESS

Non-current liabilities include all of the entity's obligations that are not classified as current liabilities, such as long-term notes and bonds payable. Typically, a non-current liability will require payment more than one year in the future. These obligations may be created by borrowing money, or they may result from other activities.

BCE reports its non-current liabilities on the statement of financial position, after current liabilities, as shown in Exhibit 10.1. Details of the long-term debt, deferred tax liabilities, post-employment benefit obligations, and other non-current liabilities are disclosed separately and explained in the notes.

In Chapter 9, we introduced the term *capital structure*, the mix of debt and equity that is used to finance a company's growth. Almost all companies employ some debt in their capital structure. Indeed, large corporations need to borrow billions of dollars, which makes borrowing from individual creditors impractical. Instead, these corporations issue long-term notes and bonds to raise debt capital.

Bonds are securities that corporations and governmental units issue when they borrow large amounts of money. After bonds have been issued, they can be traded on established exchange markets. The ability to sell a bond on the bond exchange is a significant advantage for creditors because it provides them with liquidity, or the ability to convert their investments into cash. If you lend money directly to a corporation for 20 years, you must wait that long before your cash investment is repaid. If you lend money by purchasing a bond, you can always sell it to another creditor if you need cash before it matures.

The liquidity of publicly traded bonds offers an important advantage to corporations. Because most creditors are reluctant to lend money for long periods with no opportunity to receive cash prior to maturity, they demand a higher interest rate for long-term loans. By issuing more-liquid debt, corporations can reduce the cost of long-term borrowing.

This chapter provides a basic understanding of the management, accounting, and financial issues associated with long-term notes and bonds. We begin with a description of long-term notes and bonds payable. Then we see how transactions affecting these liabilities are analyzed and recorded. We also describe other typical non-current liabilities and examine how the reported debt and supplementary disclosures are used by analysts to make informed judgments about investment and credit risk.

Exhibit 10.1
Non-current Liabilities

REAL-WORLD EXCERPT

BCE Inc.

ANNUAL REPORT

CONSOLIDATED STATEMENTS OF FINANCIAL POSITION As at December 31			
(in millions of Canadian dollars)	Note	2015	2014
LIABILITIES			
Current Liabilities			
Trade payable and other liabilities	18	$ 4,287	$ 4,398
Interest payable		148	145
Dividends payable		576	534
Current tax liabilities		86	269
Debt due within one year	19	4,895	3,743
Total current liabilities		9,992	9,089
Non-current liabilities			
Long-term debt	20	15,390	16,355
Deferred tax liabilities	9	1,824	1,321
Post-employment benefit obligations	21	2,038	2,772
Other non-current liabilities	22	1,420	1,521
Total non-current liabilities		20,672	21,969
Total liabilities		$30,664	$31,058

Source: BCE Inc., Annual Report 2015.

ORGANIZATION OF THE CHAPTER

Supplemental material:

Appendix 10A: Bond calculations using Excel

Appendix 10B: Reporting bond transactions: A simplified approach

Appendix 10C: Reporting Interest Expense on Bonds by Using the Straight-Line Amortization Method

CHARACTERISTICS OF LONG-TERM NOTES AND BONDS PAYABLE

The use of long-term debt offers significant advantages to companies such as BCE:

1. *Shareholders maintain control.* Debt does not dilute ownership and control of the company, because debtholders participate neither in the management of operations nor in the eventual distribution of retained earnings to shareholders.

2. *Interest expense is tax deductible.* The deductibility of interest for tax purposes reduces the net cost of borrowing. This is an advantage compared to dividends paid on shares that are not tax deductible.

3. *The impact on earnings is positive.* Money can often be borrowed at a low interest rate and invested at a higher rate. Assume that Maple Leaf Sports and Entertainment owns a store selling apparel with logos of Toronto's sports teams on it. The company has shareholders' equity of $500,000 invested in the store and generates $100,000 in earnings before interest and taxes per year. Management plans to open a new store that will also cost $500,000 and generate $100,000 in earnings before interest and taxes per year. Should management issue new shares or borrow the money at an interest rate of 8 percent? The following analysis for both stores shows that the use of debt will increase the return to the owners:

	Option 1 Equity	Option 2 Debt
Earnings before interest and income taxes	$ 200,000	$200,000
Interest expense	–0–	40,000
	200,000	160,000
Income tax expense (at 35%)	70,000	56,000
Net earnings	$ 130,000	$104,000
Owners' equity	$1,000,000	$500,000
Return on equity (net earnings/owners' equity)	13%	20.8%

Unfortunately, long-term debt carries higher risk than equity. The following are the major disadvantages associated with issuing long-term debt:

1. *Risk of bankruptcy.* Interest payments to the debtholders must be made each period whether the corporation generates net earnings or incurs a loss.

2. *Negative impact on cash flows.* Debt must be repaid at a specific time in the future. Management must be able to generate sufficient cash to repay the debt or have the ability to refinance it.

LO10-1

Describe the characteristics of long-term notes and bonds payable.

Sound business practice requires maintaining an appropriate balance between debt and equity capital.

The types of long-term debt available to a company of BCE's size are not available to students and professors, or even to small and medium-sized corporations. Because of its size and the predictability of its revenue, BCE can borrow from a single lender or it may issue debt to many lenders. Single-lender debt is typically in the form of a note or a mortgage note, whereas multiple-lender debt is typically in the form of a debenture or a bond.

Companies can raise long-term debt directly from a number of financial service organizations, including banks, insurance companies, and pension fund companies. Raising debt from one of these organizations is known as *private placement*. This type of debt is often called a *note payable*, which is a written promise to pay a stated sum of money at one or more specified future dates, called the *maturity date(s)*.

In many cases, a company's need for debt capital exceeds the financial capability of any single creditor. In these situations, the company may issue publicly traded debt called *bonds*. The bonds can be traded in established markets that provide bondholders with liquidity (i.e., the ability to sell the bond and receive cash quickly). BCE borrows billions of dollars or other currencies in long-term debt to develop and provide communications services to its various customers reliably and quickly at a cost they are willing to pay. In exchange for the borrowed money, BCE signs debt agreements in the form of loans, notes, or mortgage notes with banks and other institutional lenders. Loans and notes are often for terms of five years or less, while mortgage terms can exceed 25 years.

Lenders often protect their interests by requesting that the debt be secured rather than unsecured. If you have a credit card, a student loan, or perhaps an automobile loan, you may have read the terms of the debt contract, which indicate whether or not the debt is secured. In the case of a personal credit card, the debt is unsecured, which means that if a debtor fails to make the required payment, or *defaults*, the lender cannot repossess any specific asset of the cardholder. In the case of a large, personal long-term loan, such as an automobile loan, lenders will insist on the right to repossess the automobile in the event of default. Repossession allows the lender to sell the automobile and recover all or part of the unpaid loan.

Corporations such as BCE can secure their notes and bonds payable by using revenue, inventory, property, equipment, and buildings. Secured debt provides the creditor with the right to foreclose on the debt and repossess the assets, or collateral, pledged by the company as security should the company violate the terms of its debt contract. BCE has disclosed information concerning its long-term debt, as shown in Exhibit 10.2. The note lists the different types of notes and bonds that BCE's subsidiaries have issued in the past. After studying this chapter, you will understand the terms used in the note related to long-term debt, particularly the accounting and financial issues associated with bonds.

All debentures and subordinated debentures have been issued in Canadian dollars and bear a fixed rate of interest.

A bond usually requires the payment of interest over its life, with the repayment of principal on the maturity date. The **bond principal** is (1) the amount payable at the maturity date and (2) the basis for computing periodic cash interest payments. The principal also is called the **par value and face amount**, or *maturity value*. All bonds have a par value, which is the amount that will be paid when the bond matures. For most Canadian bonds, the par value is $1,000, but it can be any amount.

A bond always specifies the **stated rate** of interest and the timing of periodic cash interest payments, usually annually or semi-annually. Each periodic interest payment is equal to the principal times the stated interest rate. The selling price of a bond does not affect the periodic cash payment of interest. For example, a $1,000, 6 percent bond always pays cash interest of $60 on an annual basis, or $30 on a semi-annual basis.

The **BOND PRINCIPAL** is the amount payable at the maturity of the bond. It is also the basis for computing periodic cash interest payments.

PAR VALUE and **FACE AMOUNT** are other names for bond principal or the maturity value of a bond.

The **STATED RATE** is the rate of interest per period specified in the bond contract.

Exhibit **10.2**

Note 20:
Long-Term Debt

REAL-WORLD EXCERPT

BCE Inc.

ANNUAL REPORT

	Note	Weighted Average Interest Rate	Maturity	December 31, 2015	December 31, 2014
Bell Canada					
Debentures					
1997 trust indenture		4.34%	2016–2045	$13,400	$12,900
1976 trust indenture		9.54%	2021–2054	1,100	1,100
Subordinated debentures		8.21%	2026–2031	386	275
Finance leases		6.77%	2016–2047	2,260	2,129
Unsecured committed term credit facility (Astral)		1.29%	2016	526	1,018
Other				141	219
Total debt				17,702	17,773
Net unamortized premium/discount				24	30
Unamortized debt issuance costs				(38)	(40)
Less: Amount due within one year				(2,298)	(1,368)
Total long-term debt				$15,390	$16,355

Restrictions

Some of the debt agreements:

- require us to meet specific financial ratios
- impose covenants, maintenance tests and new issue tests
- require us to make an offer to repurchase certain series of debentures upon the occurrence of a change of control event as defined in the relevant debt agreements

We are in compliance with all conditions and restrictions under such debt agreements.

BELL CANADA

All outstanding debentures are issued under trust indentures and are unsecured. All debentures are issued in series and certain series are redeemable at Bell Canada's option prior to maturity at the prices, times and conditions specified in each series.

2015

In 2015, Bell Canada repaid approximately $500 million ($395 million U.S. dollars) of the borrowings under its unsecured committed term credit facility that was used to partially fund the acquisition of Astral.

On November 2, 2015, Bell Canada redeemed early its 3.60% Series M-21 medium term notes (MTN) debentures, issued under its 1997 trust indenture, having an outstanding principal amount of $1 billion which were due on December 2, 2015.

On October 1, 2015, Bell Canada issued 3.00% Series M-40 MTN debentures under its 1997 trust indenture, with a principal amount of $1 billion, which mature on October 3, 2022.

On March 30, 2015, Bell Canada issued 4.35% Series M-39 MTN debentures under its 1997 trust indenture, with a principal amount of $500 million, which mature on December 18, 2045.

Subsequent to year end, on January 11, 2016, Bell Canada redeemed, prior to maturity, its 4.64% Series M-19 MTN debentures, having an outstanding principal amount of $200 million which were due on February 22, 2016, as well as its 3.65% Series M-23 MTN debentures, having an outstanding principal amount of $500 million which were due on May 19, 2016.

In addition, on February 29, 2016, Bell Canada issued 3.55% Series M-41 MTN debentures under its 1997 trust indenture, with a principal amount of $750 million, which mature on March 2, 2026.

Source: BCE Inc., Annual Report 2015.

Different types of bonds have different characteristics, primarily because individual creditors have different types of risk and return preferences. A retired person, for example, may be willing to receive a lower interest rate in return for greater security. This type of creditor might want a mortgage bond that pledges a specific asset as security if the company is unable to repay the bond. Another creditor might be willing to accept higher risk with a low interest rate and an unsecured status if the company provides the opportunity to convert the bond into common shares at some point in the future. Companies design bond features that are attractive to different groups of creditors, just as automobile manufacturers try to design cars that appeal to different groups of consumers. Important types of bonds are shown in the illustration below:

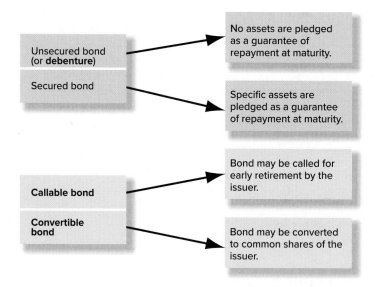

Telecommunication companies often need to build research and communication facilities to implement the most up-to-date high-speed communications services, such as BCE's 4G LTE wireless network. One possibility is for BCE to finance the project by issuing bonds that are secured by the assets that will be in place once the project is finished. Another possibility is to issue bonds secured by the amount of revenues expected from the completed project. The company could also issue debentures that are unsecured, depending on how much risk the debenture holders are willing to take.

When a company decides to issue new bonds, it prepares a bond, or trust, **indenture** (bond contract) that specifies the legal provisions of the bonds. These provisions include the maturity date, rate of interest to be paid, date of each interest payment, and any conversion privileges. The indenture also contains covenants designed to protect the creditors. Typical covenants include limitations on new debt that the company might issue in the future, limitations on the payment of dividends, and required minimum levels of certain accounting ratios, such as the current ratio. Managers prefer covenants that are less restrictive because they may limit the company's future actions. Creditors, however, prefer more-restrictive covenants that reduce the risk of losing their investment. As with any business transaction, the final result is achieved through a process of negotiation.

Bond covenants are usually reported in the notes to the financial statements. For example, the note disclosures in Exhibit 10.2 indicate that some of the debt agreements that either BCE or its subsidiaries have signed require BCE to meet specific financial ratios.

The disclosures in Exhibit 10.2 also provide specific information about the characteristics of the bonds, debentures, and notes issued by BCE and its subsidiaries. For example, all outstanding debentures of Bell Canada are unsecured. They are issued in series, and certain series are redeemable at Bell Canada's option prior to maturity at the prices, times, and conditions specified in each series. The bond issuer also prepares a prospectus, which is a legal document given to potential bond investors. The prospectus describes the company, the bond, and how the proceeds of the bond will be used.[1]

When a bond is issued, the investor receives a **bond certificate**. All of the bond certificates for a single bond issue are identical. The face of each certificate shows the same maturity date, interest rate, interest dates, and other provisions. An independent party, called the **trustee**, is usually appointed to represent the bondholders. A trustee's duties are to ascertain whether the issuing company fulfills all of the provisions of the bond indenture.

An **INDENTURE** is a bond contract that specifies the legal provisions of a bond issue.

A **BOND CERTIFICATE** is the bond document that each bondholder receives.

A **TRUSTEE** is an independent party appointed to represent the bondholders.

Players in the Bond Market

Most companies work with an underwriter that either buys the entire issue of bonds and then resells them to individual creditors (called a *firm commitment underwriter*), or an underwriter that simply sells the bonds or notes without any obligation to purchase them (called a *best efforts underwriter*). It is not uncommon for companies to use several underwriters to sell a large bond issue. For example, Canadian underwriters that help companies sell notes, debentures, and bonds include BMO Nesbitt Burns Inc., CIBC World Markets Inc., Desjardins Securities Inc., National Bank Financial Inc., RBC Dominion Securities Inc., Scotia Capital Inc., and TD Securities Inc., among others.

Bond dealers typically sell bonds to institutional investors, such as banks, insurance companies, and mutual and pension funds. They also create a secondary market for bonds by trading them for their own account in response to supply and demand by institutional investors. Almost all trades occur by telephone, known as an over-the-counter (OTC) market, not through a formal bond exchange. The market for bonds exceeds, by far, the value of stocks traded on a typical day because of the high value of each trade. A bond trade of $200 million would not be unusual in this market.[2]

Because of the complexities associated with bonds, several agencies exist to evaluate the probability that a bond issuer will not be able to meet the requirements specified in the indenture. This risk is called *default risk*. In general, the higher the risk of default, the higher will be the interest rate required to successfully persuade investors to purchase the bond. To protect the bondholder, the covenants will be more restrictive on the borrower. Dominion Bond Rating Service (DBRS), Moody's Investor Services Inc. (Moody's), Fitch Inc., and Standard and Poor's Rating Services (S&P) each assesses the default risk for every issue of corporate debentures and bonds.[3] Their ratings range from investment grade (low default risk) to extremely speculative junk bonds (high default risk). If it becomes apparent that there has been a change in default risk for any debt already issued, each rating service will issue a public bulletin that upgrades or downgrades the credit rating, along with reasons for the change.[4]

Bond prices change for two main reasons: changes in creditworthiness of the bond issuer and changes in market interest rates. The company's creditworthiness depends on the operating, investing, and financing decisions made by management. However, interest rates are not within the control of corporations but depend on the supply and demand for money. The most important interest rate is the rate at which the federal government can borrow money for the long term. This is the benchmark risk-free rate of return on bonds, because purchasers believe that the federal government will never fail to repay, or default, on its debts. The interest rates of all other debt instruments are established relative to this risk-free rate. The difference between the interest rate on debt instruments and the risk-free rate is called the *spread*. The size of the spread depends upon the perceived additional risk that the company will default on either its interest or principal payments on the debt.

REPORTING NOTE TRANSACTIONS

BCE borrows billions of dollars in long-term debt to develop technologies that will expand its business and allow it to successfully compete against other companies. When individual lenders, such as a bank, are willing to provide the required amount of money at a reasonable interest rate and repayment conditions, BCE signs a loan, a note, or a mortgage note and receives the necessary funds to purchase specific assets. For example, in Exhibit 10.2, the explanatory note related to the debenture, notes, and bonds issued by Bell Canada indicates it issued 3.00 percent medium-term debentures with a principal amount of $1 billion, payable on October 3, 2022.

The terms of a debt agreement are negotiated between the lender and the borrower and depend on the size of the debt and the creditworthiness of the borrower. The debt contract specifies the interest rate on the debt and the dates of payment of both interest and principal. In the case of notes payable, the lender and the borrower may agree

LO10-2

Report notes payable and related interest expense.

that the principal will be paid at a specific date in the future (the maturity date), plus annual or semi-annual interest payments. Alternatively, they may agree that equal portions of the principal are payable annually along with interest on the debt, or that equal payments covering both principal and interest (i.e., *blended* payments) will be made periodically until the principal is fully paid at the maturity date.

In the following illustration, we assume that on January 1, 2017, a company borrowed $100,000 from a local bank, to be repaid over a period of five years, plus interest at the rate of 6 percent per year. We consider three possible repayment schedules:

1. Payment of the principal on December 31, 2021, with interest payable annually on December 31.

2. Payment of one-fifth of the principal annually on December 31, with interest payable annually on that date.

3. Payment of five equal annual amounts that include both principal and interest each December 31.

Exhibit 10.3 shows the computation of the payments of principal and interest on an annual basis under each of the three alternatives. Notice that the company pays the largest amount of interest under option 1 because the principal is not repaid until the end of year 5. Under both options 2 and 3, interest expense decreases over time because part of the principal is paid every year. A summary of the journal entries related to the issuance of the notes and payment of principal and interest is presented in Exhibit 10.4.

Exhibit 10.3
Note-Repayment Schedule

Date	Cash Payment (Credit)	Interest Expense: Unpaid Principal × 6% (Debit)	Payment of Principal (Debit)	Carrying Amount (Unpaid Balance)
Option 1: Principal paid at the maturity date; interest paid annually on December 31				
1/1/2017				$100,000
31/12/2017	$ 6,000	$ 6,000	–0–	100,000
31/12/2018	6,000	6,000	–0–	100,000
31/12/2019	6,000	6,000	–0–	100,000
31/12/2020	6,000	6,000	–0–	100,000
31/12/2021	106,000	6,000	$100,000	–0–
	$130,000	$30,000	$100,000	
Option 2: Interest and one-fifth of the principal paid annually on December 31				
1/1/2017				$100,000
31/12/2017	$ 26,000	$ 6,000	$ 20,000	80,000
31/12/2018	24,800	4,800	20,000	60,000
31/12/2019	23,600	3,600	20,000	40,000
31/12/2020	22,400	2,400	20,000	20,000
31/12/2021	21,200	1,200	20,000	–0–
	$118,000	$18,000	$100,000	
Option 3: Equal amounts including both principal and interest paid annually on December 31				
1/1/2017				$100,000
31/12/2017	$ 23,739*	$ 6,000	$ 17,739	82,261
31/12/2018	23,739	4,936	18,803	63,458
31/12/2019	23,739	3,807	19,932	43,526
31/12/2020	23,739	2,612	21,127	22,399
31/12/2021	23,739	1,340†	22,399	–0–
	$118,695	$18,695	$100,000	

*The $100,000 represents the present value of an annuity of five payments at an interest rate of 6 percent:
Annuity × $P_{i=6\%, n=5}$ (Table 9C.2, Appendix 9C, 4.2124) = $100,000
Annuity = $100,000 ÷ 4.2124 = $23,739.40, rounded down to $23,739 for simplicity.
†The calculated interest is reduced by $4 to remove the effect of rounding down the annuity payments over the five years.

Date	Journal entry	Option 1		Option 2		Option 3	
1/1/2017	Cash	100,000		100,000		100,000	
	Note payable		100,000		100,000		100,000
12/31/2017	Note payable			20,000		17,739	
	Interest expense	6,000		6,000		6,000	
	Cash		6,000		26,000		23,739
(See note below)							
12/31/2021	Note payable	100,000		20,000		22,399	
	Interest expense	6,000		1,200		1,340	
	Cash		106,000		21,200		23,739

Note: Similar journal entries are recorded at December 31, 2018, 2019 and 2020 with different amounts.

Exhibit 10.4

Summary of Journal Entries to Record the Note-Related Transactions

---

PAUSE FOR FEEDBACK 🛑 STOP

Companies that borrow money from creditors make different arrangements to repay the amount borrowed and related interest. Exhibit 10.3 shows three different alternatives for repayment of debt. Study this exhibit carefully before attempting the self-study quiz.

SELF-STUDY QUIZ 10-1

Refer to Exhibit 10.3, option 3, and answer the following requirements:

1. Prepare the journal entry to record the payment at December 31, 2019. Show the effects of this transaction on the accounting equation.

2. Assume that the company agreed to repay the loan of $100,000 in 10 equal semi-annual payments instead of five equal annual payments. Compute the amount of the semi-annual payment and the total interest payable over the five-year period. (*Hint:* Use $i = 3\%$ [6% ÷ 2] and $n = 10$ [5 years × 2] to compute the semi-annual payment.)

3. Explain why the total amount of interest is lower than $18,695, the amount that is shown in Exhibit 10.3.

After you complete your answers, check them with the solutions at the end of the chapter.

In the previous illustration, we assumed that the company borrowed $100,000 on January 1, 2017, and paid interest and/or principal at the end of the fiscal year. In practice, however, companies borrow money or incur debt whenever the need arises during the year. In this case, the interest expense that is not paid by the end of the fiscal year should be accrued and reported as interest payable (or accrued liability) on the statement of financial position.

Repayment schedules such as Exhibit 10.3 are useful in that they allow the borrower to predict the cash flows needed for principal and interest payments on an annual basis and permit the accountant to compute the interest expense that should be recognized periodically, as well as the reduction of the note payable, if applicable. The schedule also allows for the splitting of the long-term debt between the current and long-term portions for the purposes of classifying and reporting the debt on the statement of financial position. For example, under option 3, the remaining principal of $43,526 at December 31, 2019, would be split into two amounts: $21,127, which is reported as the current portion of long-term debt (payable within one year), and $22,399, which is reported as long-term debt.

To assist financial statement users in assessing a company's financial position and future cash flow commitments on its existing long-term debt, companies are required to disclose the total amount of expected payments in each of the next five years to meet scheduled repayments of the principal amount of the debt. BCE provided such details in the management discussion and analysis (MD&A) section of its annual report.

BCE Inc.

ANNUAL REPORT

MANAGEMENT DISCUSSION AND ANALYSIS							
Contractual Obligations							
The following table is a summary of our contractual obligations at December 31, 2015, that are due in each of the next five years and thereafter.							
(in millions of dollars)	**2016**	**2017**	**2018**	**2019**	**2020**	**Thereafter**	**Total**
Recognized financial liabilities							
Long-term debt	1,899	1,107	1,731	1,309	1,401	7,995	15,442
Notes payable	1,666	–	–	–	–	–	1,666
Minimum future lease payments under finance leases	544	484	337	261	240	1,199	3,065
Loans secured by trade receivables	931	–	–	–	–	–	931
Interest payable on long-term debt notes payable and loan secured by trade receivables	728	639	575	506	457	5,077	7,982
MLSE financial liability	–	135	–	–	–	–	135
Net interest receipts on derivatives	(25)	(12)	–	–	–	–	(37)
Commitments (off-balance sheet)							
Operating leases	287	257	206	178	154	814	1,896
Commitments for property, plant, and equipment and intangible assets	946	650	570	497	448	1,373	4,484
Purchase obligations	1,140	578	541	525	452	1,645	4,881
National expansion of TMN[1]	190	–	–	–	–	–	190
Total	8,306	3,838	3,960	3,276	3,152	18,103	40,635

REPORTING BOND TRANSACTIONS

The **COUPON RATE** is the stated rate of interest on bonds.

Exhibit 10.2 shows that Bell Canada issued debentures for a total face value of $14.775 billion as at December 31, 2015. Each trust indenture specifies two types of cash payments:

1. *Principal.* This is usually a single payment made when the bond matures. It is also called the *par* or *face value*.

2. *Cash interest payments.* These payments are computed by multiplying the principal amount times the interest rate, called the **coupon rate**, or contract or stated rate, of interest stated in the bond contract. The bond contract specifies whether these payments are made quarterly, semi-annually, or annually.

Neither the company nor the underwriter determines the price at which the bonds sell. Instead, the market determines the current cash equivalent of future interest and principal payments by using present value concepts covered in Chapter 9. To determine the present value of the bond, compute the present value of the principal (a single payment) and the present value of the interest payments (an annuity) and add the two amounts.

The **MARKET INTEREST RATE** is the current rate of interest on a debt when incurred; also called the **YIELD** or **EFFECTIVE-INTEREST RATE**.

Creditors demand a certain rate of interest to compensate them for the risks related to bonds, called the **market interest rate** (also known as the *yield,* or *effective-interest rate*). Because the market rate is the interest rate on a debt when it is incurred, it should be used in computing the present value of the bond.

The **BOND PREMIUM** is the difference between the selling price and par when the bond is sold for more than par.

The present value of a bond may be the same as par, above par (**bond premium**), or below par (**bond discount**). If the stated and the market interest rates are the same, a bond sells at par. If a bond pays a stated interest rate that is lower than the market rate that creditors demand, they will not buy it unless its price is reduced (i.e., a discount must be provided). If a bond pays a stated rate that is higher than the market rate that creditors demand, they will be willing to pay a premium to buy it.

The **BOND DISCOUNT** is the difference between the selling price and par when the bond is sold for less than par.

This relationship can be shown graphically, as follows:[5]

Bond Contract	Market Rate	Bond Price
Coupon interest rate is 6%	4%	Premium
	6%	Par
	8%	Discount

Basically, corporations and creditors are indifferent to whether a bond is issued at par, at a discount, or at a premium, because bonds are always priced to provide the market rate of interest. To illustrate, consider a corporation that issues three separate bonds on the same day. The bonds are exactly the same except that one has a stated interest rate of 6 percent, another 7 percent, and a third at 8 percent. If the market rate of interest was 7 percent, the first would be issued at a discount, the second at par, and the third at a premium, but a creditor who bought any one of the bonds would earn the market interest rate of 7 percent.

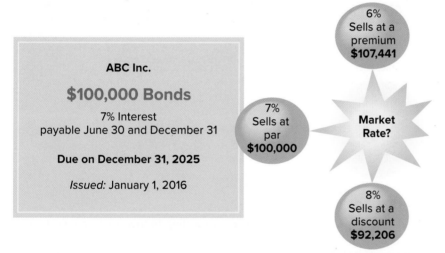

ABC Inc.

$100,000 Bonds

7% Interest
payable June 30 and December 31

Due on December 31, 2025

Issued: January 1, 2016

6%
Sells at a premium
$107,441

7%
Sells at par
$100,000

Market Rate?

8%
Sells at a discount
$92,206

BOND INFORMATION FROM THE BUSINESS PRESS

FINANCIAL ANALYSIS

Bond prices are reported each day in the business press based on transactions that occurred in the market on the previous trading day. The following is typical of the information you will find:

			March 17, 2016		March 18, 2016	
Bond	**Coupon**	**Maturity Date**	**Bid $**	**Yield %**	**Bid $**	**Yield %**
Bell Canada	4.40	March 16, 2018	105.18	1.73	105.20	1.72
Suncor Energy Inc.	5.39	March 26, 2037	96.06	5.71	96.02	5.72

Source: http://www.financialpost.com/markets/data/bonds-canadian.html.

Bell Canada's bond, highlighted above, has a coupon rate of 4.40 percent and will mature on March 16, 2018. The bond's yield was 1.73 percent on March 17, 2016, and its price was 105.18 percent of its par value, or $1,051.80. Market conditions caused the yield to decrease to 1.72 percent the following day, but the coupon rate remains fixed at 4.40 percent. As the yield decreased relative to the fixed coupon rate, the price increased from $105.18 on March 17, 2016, to $105.20 on March 18, 2016, which illustrates the inverse relationship between the yield and the bond price.

Bell Canada's bond sold on March 17, 2016, at a premium because the market rate demanded by buyers is lower than the coupon rate offered by the company. In comparison, Suncor's bond sold at a discount of 3.94 percent of its face value on the same date, because it offers a coupon rate of 5.39 percent that is lower than the market interest rate of 5.71 percent on that date. Notice that the yields for these bonds are significantly different because of the specific characteristics of these bonds that affect their riskiness.

Changes in the daily bond prices do not affect the company's financial statements. For financial reporting purposes, the company uses the interest rates that existed when the bonds were first sold to the public. Subsequent changes do not affect the company's accounting for the bonds.

PAUSE FOR FEEDBACK

Your study of bonds will be easier if you understand the terminology that has been introduced in this chapter. Let us review some of those terms.

SELF-STUDY QUIZ 10-2

Define the following:

1. Market interest rate. Identify synonyms for *market interest rate*.

2. Coupon interest rate. Identify synonyms for *coupon interest rate*.

3. Bond discount.

4. Bond premium.

After you complete your answers, check them with the solutions at the end of the chapter.

Bonds Issued at Par

Bonds sell at their par value when buyers are willing to invest in them at the interest rate stated on the bond. To illustrate, let us assume that on January 1, 2016, Mobile Services Corporation (MSC), a hypothetical Canadian company, issued 6 percent bonds with a par value of $400,000 and received $400,000 in cash (which means that the bonds sold at par). The bonds were dated to start earning interest on January 1, 2016, and will pay interest each June 30 and December 31. The bonds mature in 10 years, on December 31, 2025.

The amount of money a corporation receives when it sells bonds is the present value of the future cash flows associated with them. When MSC issued its bonds, it agreed to make two types of payments in the future: a single payment of $400,000 when the bond matures in 10 years and an annuity of $12,000 payable twice each year for 10 years. The bond payments can be shown graphically, as follows:

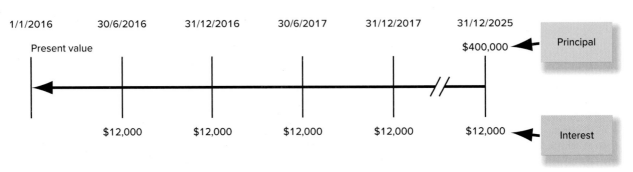

The present value of the bond payments can be computed with the tables contained in Appendix 9C by using the factor for 20 periods and an interest rate of 3 percent (6 percent ÷ 2):

	Present Value
a. Single payment: $400,000 × 0.5537	$221,480
b. Annuity: $12,000 × 14.8775	178,120*
Issue price of MSC's bonds	$400,000
*Rounded	

When the effective rate of interest equals the stated rate of interest, the present value of the future cash flows associated with a bond always equals the bond's par value. Remember that a bond's selling price is determined by the present value of its future cash flows, not the par value. On the date of issue, bond liabilities are recorded at the present value of future cash flows, as follows:

Cash (A)		400,000		
Bonds payable (L)				400,000
Assets	=	**Liabilities**	+	**Shareholders' Equity**
Cash +400,000		Bonds payable +400,000		

Companies rarely issue bonds at par. One example is the issuance at par of US$900 million, 100-year notes by Canadian Pacific Railway Company that pay interest at the rate of 6.125 percent annually and mature on September 15, 2115.

Reporting Interest Expense on Bonds Issued at Par   The creditors who bought the bonds did so with the expectation that they would earn interest over the life of the bond. MSC will pay interest at 3 percent (i.e., 6 percent per year) on the par value of the bonds each June 30 and December 31 until the bond's maturity date. The amount of interest each period will be $12,000 (3% × $400,000). The entry to record the interest payments follows:

Bond interest expense (E)		12,000		
Cash (A)				12,000
Assets	=	**Liabilities**	+	**Shareholders' Equity**
Cash −12,000				Bond interest expense −12,000

Bond interest payment dates rarely coincide with the last day of a company's fiscal year. Interest expense incurred but not paid must be accrued with an adjusting entry. If MSC's fiscal year ended on May 31, the company would accrue interest for five months and record interest expense and interest payable.

PAUSE FOR **FEEDBACK**

Calculation of the present value of the principal and interest payments is straightforward. Practice the mechanics of computing the present value of a bond issue before moving on.

SELF-STUDY QUIZ 10-3

Assume that MSC issued $100,000 bonds that will mature in 10 years. The bonds pay interest at the end of each year at an annual rate of 4 percent. They were sold when the market rate was 4 percent. Determine the selling price of the bonds.

After you complete your answer, check it with the solution at the end of the chapter.

Bonds Issued at a Discount

Bonds sell at a discount when the market rate of interest demanded by the buyers is higher than the stated interest rate offered by the issuer. Assume that the market rate of interest was 8 percent when MSC sold its bonds (which have a par value of $400,000). The bonds have a stated rate of 6 percent, payable semi-annually, which is less than the market rate on that date. Therefore, the bonds sold at a *discount*. This usually occurs when the market rate of interest increases after the company determines the coupon rate on the bonds.

To compute the issue price of the bonds, we need to compute the present value of the future cash flows specified on the bond. As in the previous example, the number of periods is 20, but we must use an interest rate of 4 percent (8 percent ÷ 2), which is the market rate of interest. Thus, the issue price of MSC's bonds is computed as follows:

	Present Value
a. Principal: $400,000 × 0.4564	$182,560
b. Interest: $12,000 × 13.5903	163,084
Issue (sale) price of MSC's bonds	$345,644*
*Discount: $400,000 − $345,644 = $54,356	

The cash price of the bonds issued by MSC is $345,644. Some people refer to this price as 86.4, which means that the bonds were sold at 86.4 percent of their par value ($345,644 ÷ $400,000).

When a bond is sold at a discount, the bonds payable account is credited for the par value, and the discount is recorded as a debit to discount on bonds payable. The issuance of MSC's bonds at a discount is recorded as follows:[6]

Cash (A)	345,644	
Discount on bonds payable (XL)	54,356	
Bonds payable (L)		400,000

Assets	=	Liabilities	+	Shareholders' Equity
Cash +345,644		Bonds payable +400,000		
		Discount on bonds payable −54,356		

Note that the discount is recorded in a separate contra-liability account (discount on bonds payable) as a debit. The statement of financial position reports the bonds payable at their carrying amount, which is their maturity amount less any unamortized discount. MSC, like most companies, does not separately disclose the amount of unamortized discount (or premium) when the amount is small relative to other amounts reported on the statement of financial position.

Although MSC received only $345,644 when it sold the bonds, it must repay $400,000 when the bonds mature. This extra cash that must be paid is an adjustment to the interest payments, ensuring that creditors earn the market rate of interest on the bonds. To compute the interest expense, the borrower apportions, or amortizes, the bond discount to each semi-annual interest period as an increase to the interest payment. Therefore, the amortization of bond discount is an increase in bond interest expense. Canadian publicly accountable enterprises are required to use the effective-interest method to amortize bond discount or premium. An alternative method, straight-line amortization, which may be used by Canadian private enterprises, is discussed in Appendix 10C.

BCE uses the effective-interest method to amortize any discount or premium on its long-term debt:

Exhibit 10.2 lists all the outstanding long-term debt issued by BCE and Bell Canada. Some of these bonds, debentures, and notes were sold at a discount while others were sold at a premium. The net unamortized premium or discount on long-term debt amounted to $24 million at December 31, 2015.

Reporting Interest Expense on Bonds Issued at a Discount by Using Effective-Interest Amortization

Under the **effective-interest method**, interest expense for a bond is computed by multiplying the current unpaid balance (or carrying amount) by the market rate of interest that existed on the date the bonds were sold. The periodic amortization of a bond discount or premium is then calculated as the difference between interest expense and the amount of cash paid or accrued. This process can be summarized as follows:

The **EFFECTIVE-INTEREST METHOD** amortizes a bond discount, or premium, on the basis of the effective-interest rate.

Step 1: Compute the interest expense:

Internet expense = Unpaid balance × Effective interest rate × n/12

n = Number of months in each interest period

Step 2: Compute the amortization amount:

Amortization of bond discount = Interest expense − Interest paid (or accrued)

The first interest payment on MSC's bonds is on June 30, 2016. Interest expense at the end of the first six months is calculated by multiplying the unpaid balance of the debt by the market rate of interest for six months ($345,644 × 8% × 6/12 = $13,826). This represents the amount of interest revenue that bondholders expected to earn on their investment during this six-month period when they decided to purchase the bonds. The amount of cash paid is calculated by multiplying the principal by the stated rate of interest for six months ($400,000 × 6% × 6/12 = $12,000). The difference between the interest expense and the cash paid (or accrued) is the amount of discount that has been amortized ($13,826 − $12,000 = $1,826).

The journal entry to record the periodic interest expense is as follows. Effective-interest amortization causes these amounts to change each period.

Bond interest expense (E)	13,826	
Discount on bonds payable (XL)		1,826
Cash (A)		12,000

Assets	=	Liabilities	+	Shareholders' Equity
Cash −12,000		Discount on bonds payable +1,826		Bond interest expense −13,826

Each period, the amortization of the bond discount increases the bond's carrying amount (or unpaid balance). The amortization of bond discount can be thought of as interest that was earned by the bondholders but not paid to them. During the first six months of 2016, the bondholders earned interest of $13,826 but received only $12,000 in cash. The additional $1,826 was added to the carrying amount of the bond and will be paid when the bond matures.

Interest expense for the second half of 2016 is calculated by multiplying the carrying amount on June 30, 2016, by the market rate of interest for six months ($347,470 × 8% × 6/12 = $13,899). The amortization of the bond discount in the second period is $1,899.

Bond interest expense (E)			13,899	
Discount on bonds payable (XL)				1,899
Cash (A)				12,000

Assets		=	**Liabilities**	+	**Shareholders' Equity**	
Cash	−12,000		Discount on bonds payable	+1,899	Bond interest expense	−13,899

Notice that interest expense for the second half of 2016 is greater than the amount for the first six months of the year. This is logical, because MSC effectively borrowed more money during the second half of the year (i.e., the $1,826 unpaid interest). Interest expense increases each year during the life of the bond, because the amortized bond discount reflects unpaid interest on an increasing amount. This process can be illustrated with the amortization schedule shown below for the first two years and the last year of the bond's life:

Amortization Schedule: Bond Discount (Effective Interest)				
Date	(a) Interest to Be Paid [$400,000 × 3%]	(b) Interest Expense [4% × (d) Carrying Amount, Beginning of Period]	(c) Amortization [(b) − (a)]	(d) Carrying Amount [Beginning Carrying Amount + (c)]
1/1/2016				$345,644
30/6/2016	$12,000	$13,826	$1,826	347,470
31/12/2016	12,000	13,899	1,899	349,369
30/6/2017	12,000	13,975	1,975	351,344
31/12/2017	12,000	14,054	2,054	353,398
.	.	.	.	.
.	.	.	.	.
30/6/2025	12,000	15,699	3,699	396,164
31/12/2025	12,000	15,836*	3,836	400,000

*The interest expense of $15,847 was rounded down by $11 so that the carrying amount does not exceed $400,000.

Interest expense (column b) is computed by multiplying the market rate of interest by the carrying amount at the beginning of the period (column d). Amortization is computed by subtracting interest paid (column a) from interest expense (column b). The carrying amount (column d) is computed by adding amortization of bond discount (column c) to the carrying amount at the beginning of the period.

Bonds payable are reported on the statement of financial position at their carrying amount—that is, the maturity amount less any unamortized bond discount (or plus any unamortized bond premium). The carrying amount reflects the present value of remaining payments using the effective-interest rate at the date of issue. It increases over time as the amortized bond discount is added to the initial bond issue price. At the maturity date of the bonds, the unamortized discount (i.e., the balance in the discount on bonds payable account) is zero. At that time, the maturity value of the bonds and the carrying amount are the same (i.e., $400,000).

PAUSE FOR FEEDBACK   STOP

We have computed interest expense using the effective-interest method of amortization and determined the carrying amount of the bond after each interest payment date. Practice these computations before moving on.

SELF-STUDY QUIZ 10-4

Assume that MSC issued $100,000 bonds that will mature in 10 years. The bonds pay interest twice each year at an annual rate of 7 percent. They were sold when the market rate was 8 percent.

1. What amount of interest expense would be reported at the end of the first year?

2. What is the carrying amount of the bonds at the end of the first year?

After you complete your answers, check them with the solutions at the end of the chapter.

Bonds are recorded at the present value of their future cash flows using an interest rate determined by the market on the date the bonds were sold. The accounting for the bonds is not affected by subsequent changes in the market rate of interest. This interest rate is based on the terms of the debt issue and the risk characteristics of the debt.

ZERO COUPON BONDS

FINANCIAL ANALYSIS

So far, we have discussed common bonds that are issued by many corporations. For a number of reasons, corporations may issue bonds with unusual features. The concepts you have learned will help you understand these bonds. For example, a corporation might issue a bond that does not pay periodic cash interest. These bonds are often called zero coupon bonds. Why would an investor buy a bond that did not pay interest? Our discussion of bond discounts has probably given you a good idea of the answer. The coupon interest rate on a bond can be virtually any rate, and the price of the bond will be adjusted so that investors earn the market rate of interest. A bond with a zero coupon interest rate is simply a deeply discounted bond that will sell for substantially less than its maturity value.

Let us use the $400,000 MSC bond to illustrate a zero coupon rate. Assume that the market rate of interest is 6.5 percent and the bond pays no cash interest. The bond matures in 10 years. The selling price of the bond is the present value of the maturity amount, because no other cash payments will be made over the life of the bond. We can compute the present value with the tables in Appendix 9C, using the present value factor for 20 periods and an interest rate of 3.25 percent, assuming semi-annual compounding:

	Present Value
Single payment: $400,000 × 0.5275	$211,000

Accounting for a zero coupon bond is not different from accounting for other bonds sold at a discount, except that the amount of the discount is much larger and there are no periodic interest payments. For example, AT&T Inc. issued in 2007 a zero-coupon bond that has a redemption value of US$1,030 million in 2022, but received only US$500 million at that time. The discount on the bond, which reflects interest over a period of 15 years, is a massive US$530 million.

Bonds Issued at a Premium

Bonds sell at a premium when the market rate of interest is lower than the stated interest rate. Assume that the market rate of interest is 4 percent while MSC's bonds pay interest of 6 percent semi-annually. In this case, the bonds sell at a premium. The issue price for MSC's bonds is computed as follows:

	Present Value
a. Principal: $400,000 × 0.6730	$269,200
b. Interest: $12,000 × 16.3514	196,217
Issue (sale) price of MSC's bonds	$465,417

When a bond is sold at a premium, the bonds payable account is credited for the par value, and the premium is recorded as a credit to premium on bonds payable, an adjunct-liability account. The issuance of MSC's bonds at a premium is recorded as follows:

Cash (A)	465,417	
Premium on bonds payable (L)		65,417
Bonds payable (L)		400,000

Assets	=	Liabilities	+	Shareholders' Equity
Cash +465,417		Premium on bonds payable +65,417		
		Bonds payable +400,000		

The carrying amount of the bond is the sum of the balances of the two accounts, premium on bonds payable and bonds payable, or $465,417.

Reporting Interest Expense on Bonds Issued at a Premium by Using Effective-Interest Amortization

The effective-interest method is basically the same for a discount or a premium. In either case, interest expense for a bond is computed by multiplying the carrying amount (i.e., the unpaid balance) by the market rate of interest on the date the bonds were sold. The periodic amortization of a bond premium or discount is then calculated as the difference between interest expense and the amount of cash paid or accrued.

The first interest payment on MSC's bonds is made on June 30, 2016. The interest expense at the end of the first six months is calculated by multiplying the unpaid balance of the debt by the market rate of interest for six months ($465,417 × 4% × 6/12 = $9,308). It also represents the interest revenue that bondholders expected to earn on their investment during this six-month period when they decided to purchase the bonds. The amount of cash paid is calculated by multiplying the principal by the stated rate of interest for six months ($400,000 × 6% × 6/12 = $12,000). The difference between the interest expense and the cash paid (or accrued) is the amount of premium that has been amortized ($12,000 − $9,308 = $2,692). Thus, the amount of cash paid to bondholders includes two components: interest expense of $9,308, reflecting interest revenue to the bondholders for the first six-month period, and an amortized premium of $2,692, representing a partial payment of the premium that bondholders paid initially when they purchased the bonds.

The payment of interest on the bonds is recorded, as follows:

Bond interest expense (E)	9,308	
Premium on bonds payable (L)	2,692	
Cash (A)		12,000

Assets	=	Liabilities	+	Shareholders' Equity
Cash −12,000		Premium on bonds payable −2,692		Bond interest expense −9,308

The basic difference between effective-interest amortization of a bond discount and a bond premium is that the amortization of a discount *increases* the carrying amount of the liability and the amortization of a premium *reduces* it. The following schedule illustrates amortization of the bond premium for the first two years and the last year of the bond's life:

		Amortization Schedule: Bond Premium (Effective Interest)		
Date	**(a) Interest to Be Paid [$400,000 × 3%]**	**(b) Interest Expense [2% × (d) Carrying Amount, Beginning of Period]**	**(c) Amortization [(a) − (b)]**	**(d) Carrying Amount [Beginning Carrying Amount − (c)]**
1/1/2016				$465,417
30/6/2016	$12,000	$9,308	$2,692	462,725
31/12/2016	12,000	9,255	2,745	459,980
30/6/2017	12,000	9,200	2,800	457,179
31/12/2017	12,000	9,144	2,856	454,323
.	.	.	.	.
.	.	.	.	.
30/6/2025	12,000	8,156	3,844	403,938
31/12/2025	12,000	8,063*	3,937	400,000

*The interest expense of $8,079 was rounded down by $16 so that the carrying amount does not exceed $400,000.

Interest expense (column b) is computed by multiplying the market rate of interest by the carrying amount at the beginning of the period (column d). Amortization is computed by subtracting interest expense (column b) from interest paid (column a). The carrying amount (column d) is computed by subtracting amortization of bond premium (column c) from the carrying amount at the beginning of the period.

In summary, interest expense changes each accounting period as the effective amount of the liability changes. As in the case of a bond discount, the carrying amount of the bonds reflects the present value of remaining payments using the effective-interest rate at the date of issue.

PAUSE FOR FEEDBACK

The use of an amortization schedule facilitates the computation of interest expense, amortization of the premium on bonds payable, and the carrying amount of the bonds over the bond's life. Practice these computations before moving on.

SELF-STUDY **QUIZ 10-5**

Refer to the amortization schedule above and answer the following requirements:

1. Complete the schedule for three additional semi-annual payments of interest until June 30, 2019.

2. Compute the unpaid balance of the bonds at June 30, 2019. Can you think of another way of computing this balance? If so, show your computations.

After you complete your answers, check them with the solutions at the end of the chapter.

Interest expense is reported on the statement of earnings. Because interest is related to financing activities rather than operating activities, it is normally not included in operating expenses on the statement of earnings. Instead, interest expense is reported as a deduction from the earnings from operations account. BCE Inc. reports interest expense of $909 million for 2015, as shown in Exhibit 10.4.

Exhibit **10.4**

Consolidated Statement
of Earnings

REAL-WORLD EXCERPT

BCE Inc.

ANNUAL REPORT

Consolidated Income Statement For the Year Ended December 31

(in millions of Canadian dollars)	Note	2015	2014
...			
Earnings before finance costs and income taxes		4,685	4,635
Finance costs			
Interest expense	7	(909)	(929)
Interest on post-employment benefit obligations	21	(110)	(101)
Other income	8	(12)	42
Earnings before income taxes		3,654	3,647
Income taxes	9	(924)	(929)
Net earnings		2,730	2,718

Source: BCE Inc., Annual Report 2015.

Interest payments are legal obligations for the borrower; therefore, financial analysts, investors, and creditors want to be certain that a business is generating sufficient resources to meet its obligations. The times interest earned ratio is useful when making this assessment.

TIMES INTEREST EARNED RATIO

KEY RATIO ANALYSIS

LO10-4

Compute and interpret the times interest earned ratio.

ANALYTICAL QUESTION → Is the company generating sufficient resources (added value) from its profit-making activities to meet its current obligations associated with debt?

RATIO AND COMPARISONS → The times interest earned ratio is helpful in answering this question. It is computed as follows:

$$\text{Times interest earned ratio} = \frac{\text{Net earnings} + \text{Interest expense} + \text{Income tax expense}}{\text{Interest expense}}$$

The 2015 ratio for the BCE Inc. is,

$$\frac{\$2,370 + \$909 + \$924}{\$909} = 5.02$$

Comparisons over Time				Comparisons with Competitors	
BCE				Rogers Communications	TELUS
2013	2014	2015		2015	2015
5.45	5.93	5.02		3.39	5.16

INTERPRETATIONS

In General → A high ratio is viewed more favourably than a low ratio. Basically, the ratio shows the amount of earnings before interest and income tax that is generated relative to interest expense. A high ratio shows an extra margin of protection in case profitability deteriorates. Analysts are particularly interested in a company's ability to meet its required interest payments, because failure to do so could result in bankruptcy.

Focus Company Analysis → In 2015, BCE's profit-making activities generated $5.02 for each $1.00 of interest expense. BCE's net earnings could fall substantially before the company would appear to have trouble meeting its interest obligations with resources generated by normal operations. BCE's ability to repay its creditors dropped slightly in 2015 relative to the previous two years. Its ratio is slightly lower than TELUS's but higher than Rogers's.

A Few Cautions → The times interest earned ratio is often misleading for new or rapidly growing companies that tend to invest considerable resources to build capacity for future operations. In such cases, the times interest earned ratio will reflect significant amounts of interest expense associated with the new capacity but not the earnings that will be generated with the new capacity. Analysts should consider the company's long-term strategy when using this ratio. While this ratio is widely used, some analysts prefer to compare interest expense to the amount of cash that a company can generate, because creditors cannot be paid with "net earnings" that are generated. The cash coverage ratio addresses this concern and is discussed in Chapter 12.

Early Retirement of Debt

LO10-5

Report the early retirement of bonds.

Bonds are normally issued for long periods, such as 20 or 30 years. As mentioned earlier, bondholders who need cash prior to the maturity date can simply sell the bonds to another investor. This transaction does not affect the books of the company that issued the bonds.

As mentioned earlier, each bond issue has characteristics specified in the bond indenture. The issuing company often adds special characteristics to a bond to make it more attractive to investors, who normally have a large number of investment alternatives from which to select.

Bonds sometimes offer different features with respect to early retirement. Callable (redeemable) bonds may be called for early retirement at the option of the issuer. **Retractable bonds** may be turned in for early retirement at the option of the bondholder. Convertible bonds may be converted to other securities of the issuer (usually common shares) at the option of the bondholder. These features are normally present for debt issues that are marketable.

RETRACTABLE BONDS may be turned in for early retirement at the option of the bondholder.

Assume that MSC's bonds are redeemable. Typically, the bond indenture would include a call premium for redeemable bonds.

Assume that the $400,000 face-value bonds that were issued by MSC on January 1, 2016, at a discount in the previous illustration were called by the company on December 31, 2021, at 101 percent of par, four years before their maturity. The company's decision to call these bonds is typically made when the market rate of interest decreases to the point where the market value of the bonds exceeds the call price. MSC would issue new bonds that pay a lower interest rate than the outstanding bonds, thus saving on interest payments.

If the market rate of interest drops to 4 percent, then MSC can issue new bonds that pay interest of 4 percent instead of 6 percent. Semi-annual interest payments would then be reduced from $12,000 to $8,000 ($400,000 × 0.02). The cash savings of $4,000 every six months is equivalent to $29,302 ($4,000 × 7.3255[7]) at December 31, 2021. Redemption of the bonds requires MSC to pay a premium of $4,000 ($400,000 × 0.01), but it saves the company $29,302. It is, therefore, a sound economic decision.

However, the early retirement of these bonds would result in an accounting loss that equals the difference between the redemption amount and the carrying amount of the bonds. At December 31, 2021, the carrying amount of the bond is $373,072, representing the present value of the remaining future principal and interest payments.[8] This amount is then compared to the redemption amount of $404,000 ($400,000 × 1.01), resulting in a loss of $30,928. The company's accountants would make the following journal entry to record the bond redemption:

Bonds payable (L)	400,000	
Loss on redemption of bonds (SE)	30,928	
Discount on bonds payable (XL)		26,928
Cash (A)		404,000

Assets	=	**Liabilities**	+	**Shareholders' Equity**
Cash −404,000		Bonds payable		Loss on redemption of bonds
		−400,000		−30,928
		Discount on bonds		
		payable +26,927		

The bond redemption results in an economic gain but also in an accounting loss, because the carrying amount of the bonds is not adjusted over time to reflect changes in the market value of these bonds.

In some cases, a company may elect to retire debt early by purchasing it on the open market, just as an investor would. This approach is necessary when the bonds do not have a call feature. It might also be an attractive approach if the price of the bonds fell after the date of issue. What could cause the price of a bond to fall? The most common cause is a rise in interest rates. As you may have noticed during our discussion of present value concepts, bond prices move in the opposite direction of interest rates. If interest rates go up, bond prices fall, and vice versa. When interest rates go up, a company wanting to retire a bond before maturity may find that buying the bond on the open market is less expensive than paying a call premium.

When interest rates increase, the market value of the bonds decreases, and the redemption or repurchase of the bonds in the open market results in a gain. The gain increases the company's net earnings, which reflects positively on the performance of management. However, if the company needs to reissue bonds at a higher interest rate, then the gain on redemption or repurchase of the bonds is misleading, because the company will need to make higher interest payments on the refinanced debt. In contrast, when interest rates decrease, the refinancing of long-term debt by retiring old debt and issuing new debt will result in a loss on debt retirement, but it will reduce the amount of periodic interest payments. Hence, management may be inclined to retire debt prematurely in order to show improved financial performance, but this decision may affect cash flows negatively in the future.

BORROWING IN FOREIGN CURRENCIES

INTERNATIONAL PERSPECTIVE

Many corporations with foreign operations elect to finance those operations with foreign debt to lessen the exchange rate risk. This type of risk exists because the relative value of each nation's currency varies virtually on a daily basis due to various economic factors. As this book is being written, the U.S. dollar is worth approximately $1.2967. A year earlier, it was worth $1.2300. A Canadian company that owed debt denominated in U.S. dollars would experience a loss from this increase in the value of the U.S. dollar relative to the value of the Canadian dollar.

A Canadian corporation that conducts business operations in the United States might decide to borrow money in U.S. dollars to finance its operations. If it has operations in Europe, it may borrow in euros to finance its European operations. The cash flows from the business will be in euros, which can be used to pay off the debt, which is in euros. If the business generated cash flows in euros but paid off debt in Canadian dollars, it would be exposed to exchange rate risk because the value of the Canadian dollar fluctuates relative to the euro.

For reporting purposes, accountants must convert, or translate, foreign debt into a single currency. Conversion rates for all major currencies are published in most newspapers and on the Internet. To illustrate foreign currency translation, assume that BCE borrowed US$1 million. For reporting purposes, the accountant must use the conversion rate at December 31, 2015, which was USD 1 = CAD 1.3840. The equivalent of the US$1,000,000 debt is CAD$1,384,000 (US$1,000,000 × 1.3840). As you can see, the Canadian dollar equivalent of foreign debt will change if the conversion rate changes, even when no additional borrowings or repayments occur. Changes in conversion rates result in foreign exchange gains or losses that are covered in advanced accounting courses.

Borrowing in foreign currencies gives rise to foreign exchange risk, whereby a decrease in the value of the Canadian dollar relative to the foreign currency would require a larger amount of Canadian dollars to settle the foreign debt. The reverse is true if the Canadian dollar appreciates relative to foreign currency. A variety of risk reduction techniques can be undertaken by BCE to limit the potential increase in Canadian dollars it may have to pay. These include currency forwards, futures, swaps, and options, which are different types of financial instruments. Accounting for financial instruments is taught in advanced accounting courses

OTHER NON-CURRENT LIABILITIES

L0 10-6

Describe other non-current liabilities.

In addition to long-term debt, companies report a number of other non-current liabilities that result from their operating, investing, and financing activities. Typical non-current liabilities are lease obligations, asset retirement obligations, accrued retirement benefits liability, and deferred income taxes (covered in Appendix 9A).

Lease Liabilities

Companies often lease rather than purchase assets. For example, renting extra delivery trucks during a busy period is more economical than owning them if they are not needed during the rest of the year. When a company leases an asset on a short-term basis, the agreement, called an **operating lease**, does not transfer substantially the risks and rewards of ownership from the lessor to the lessee. No liability is recorded when an operating lease is created. Instead, a company records rent expense as it uses the asset. Assume that on December 15, 2017, a company signed an operating lease contract to rent five large trucks during January 2018. No liability is recorded in 2017. Rent expense is recorded during January 2018 as the trucks are actually used.

An **OPERATING LEASE** does not transfer substantially all the risks and rewards of ownership from the lessor to the lessee.

For a number of reasons, a company may prefer to lease an asset on a long-term basis rather than purchase it. If control of the leased asset has been transferred to the lessee along with the risks and rewards of ownership, then the lease is called a **finance lease**, regardless of the contractual form of the obligation the two parties signed. In essence, a finance lease contract represents the purchase and financing of an asset even though it is legally a lease agreement. Unlike an operating lease, finance leases are accounted for as if an asset has been purchased, by recording an asset and a liability.

A **FINANCE LEASE** transfers substantially all the risks and rewards of ownership from the lessor to the lessee.

Because of the significant differences in accounting for operating and finance leases, guidelines have been established to distinguish between them. A finance lease would normally satisfy one or more of the following situations:[9]

- Ownership of the asset is transferred to the lessee at the end of the lease term.

- The lease contract provides the lessee with an option to purchase the asset in the future at a price that is expected to be sufficiently lower than its fair market value at the time the option becomes exercisable.

- The lease term is for the major part of the asset's economic life even if title is not transferred.

- The present value of the minimum lease payments is substantially all of the fair value of the leased asset when the lease is signed.

- The leased assets are of such a specialized nature that only the lessee can use them without major modifications.

The accounting for leases as finance leases reflects the economic substance of the transaction, which is in essence a purchase of an asset with long-term financing, rather than the legal form of the commitment to make specific payments in the future. As a result, the financial statements should faithfully represent the economic nature of the transaction. If managers have a choice of recording a lease as operating or finance, most would prefer to record it as an operating lease. By doing so, the company is able to report less debt on its statement of financial position.

In contrast, the accounting for finance leases requires reporting a non-current liability, thereby increasing the debt-to-equity ratio (discussed later in this chapter). Furthermore, the current portion of the lease liability increases current liabilities, reduces working capital, and lowers the current ratio. Companies avoid these undesirable consequences if finance leases are accounted for as operating leases. It is important to note, however, that the cash outflows are not affected by the classification of leases. Many financial analysts are concerned that companies can avoid reporting debt associated with finance leases by structuring the lease agreement in a manner that meets the requirements for recording it as an operating lease.[10]

To record a finance lease, it is necessary to determine the current cash equivalent of the required lease payments. Assume that BCE signs a lease for new telecommunications equipment. The accountant has determined that the lease is a finance lease with a current cash equivalent of $25 million. Once the lease is signed, the transaction is recorded in a manner similar to the actual purchase of telecommunications equipment:

Leased equipment (A)	25,000,000		
Lease payable (L)		25,000,000	
Assets	**= Liabilities**	**+**	**Shareholders' Equity**
Leased equipment	Lease payable		
+25,000,000	+25,000,000		

BCE Inc. leases assets for use in its operations. Some of the lease contracts are accounted for as finance leases, while others qualify as operating leases, as disclosed in the following excerpts from the notes to the financial statements:

NOTES

2. Significant Accounting Policies

i) Property, Plant and Equipment—Leases

Leases of property, plant, and equipment are recognized as finance leases when we obtain substantially all the risks and rewards of ownership of the underlying assets. At the inception of the lease, we record an asset together with a corresponding long-term lease liability at the lower of the fair value of the leased asset or the present value of the minimum lease payments. If there is reasonable certainty that the lease transfers ownership of the asset to us by the end of the lease term, the asset is amortized over its useful life. Otherwise, the asset is amortized over the shorter of its useful life and the lease term. The long-term lease liability is measured at amortized cost using the effective interest method.

All other leases are classified as operating leases. Operating lease payments are expensed on a straight-line basis over the term of the lease.

Source: BCE Inc., Annual Report 2015.

NOTES

13. PROPERTY, PLANT, AND EQUIPMENT

Finance Leases

BCE's significant finance leases are for satellites and office premises. The office leases have a typical lease term of 25 years. The leases for satellites, used to provide programming to our Bell TV customers, have lease terms of 15 years. The satellite leases are non-cancellable.

...

The following table provides a reconciliation of our minimum future lease payments to the present value of our finance lease obligations.

December 31, 2015	Note	2016	2017	2018	2019	2020	Thereafter	Total
Minimum future lease payments	23	544	484	337	261	240	1,199	3,065
Less								
Future finance costs		(139)	(125)	(111)	(98)	(86)	(246)	(805)
Present value of future lease obligations		405	359	226	163	154	953	2,260

27. COMMITMENTS AND CONTINGENCIES

Commitments

The following table is a summary of our contractual obligations at December 31, 2015, that are due in each of the next five years and thereafter.

December 31, 2015	2016	2017	2018	2019	2020	Thereafter	Total
Operating leases	287	257	206	178	154	814	1,896

...

BCE's significant operating leases are for office premises, cellular tower sites and retail outlets with lease terms ranging from 1 to 42 years. These leases are non-cancellable and are renewable at the end of the lease period. Rental expense relating to operating leases was $340 million in 2015 and $335 million in 2014.

Source: BCE Inc., Annual Report 2015.

BCE discloses the cash payments it is expected to make over each of the next five years under both the operating and finance leases. For the finance leases, BCE also discloses the finance costs (interest expense) and present value of future obligations in addition to the cash payments.

Provisions

In Chapter 9, we indicated that companies establish provisions when either the amount or the timing of the liability is uncertain. In many cases, companies make investing or operating decisions resulting in future obligations that may not be determinable with accuracy, particularly if the amount of the obligation is dependent on the timing of future events. Examples include restructuring of the company's operations; legal disputes; and the dismantlement, removal, and restoration of property, plant, and equipment.

Employee Retirement Benefits

Most employers provide retirement programs for their employees. In a *defined contribution* program, the employer makes cash payments to an investment fund. When employees retire, they are entitled to a portion of the fund. If the investment strategy of the fund is successful, the retirement income for the employees will be larger. If the strategy is not successful, it will be lower. In other words, the employees bear the risk associated with the investments in the plan. The employer's only obligation is to make the required annual payments to the fund, which are recorded as pension expense.

Other employers offer *defined benefit* programs. Under these programs, an employee's retirement benefits are based on a percentage of his or her pay at retirement or a certain amount of money for each year of employment. In these cases, the amount of pension expense that must be accrued each year is the change in the current cash value of the employee's retirement package. The current cash value changes each year for a variety of reasons. For example, it changes (1) as employees get closer to receiving benefits, (2) as employees' retirement benefits increase because of higher pay or longer service, or (3) if the employees' life expectancies change. The company must report a pension liability based on any portion of the current cash value of the retirement program that has not actually been funded. For example, if the company transferred $8 million to the pension fund manager but the current cash value of the pension program was $10 million, the company would report a $2 million pension liability on its statement of financial position.

For many corporations, especially those with a unionized workforce, the financial obligation associated with defined benefit retirement programs can be very large, because the risk associated with investments in the pension plan is borne by the employer, which must cover any shortfall between the investment income and the payments to retirees. For this reason, companies have been moving away from defined benefit pension plans in favour of defined contribution pension plans.

In addition to defined benefit or defined contribution pension plans, employers may offer other post-employment benefits to their employees, such as healthcare and life insurance benefits for some employees. In recent years, employer-provided healthcare benefits have been the subject of much discussion. These have often been referred to in the financial press as legacy costs. As more people retire and live longer, these legacy costs will increase. Moreover, large companies pay for a portion of their employees' post-retirement health insurance costs. The issue arises because these potential future payments are recorded as an expense in the current accounting period.

The cost of these future benefits must be estimated and recorded as an expense in the periods when the employees perform services. The recording of future healthcare costs for retired employees is an excellent example of the use of estimates in accounting. Imagine the difficulty of estimating future healthcare costs when you do not know how long employees will live or how healthy they will be during their lives.

BCE offers its employees both defined benefit and defined contribution pension plans. In addition, it provides healthcare and life insurance benefits to some employees during retirement. Because defined benefit plans are costly to employers, new BCE employees can generally participate only in defined contribution plans. In 2015, the pension and other employment benefit plans cost BCE $250 million, and its post-employment benefit obligations amounted to $2,038 million at December 31, 2015, as reported in Exhibit 10.1.

Accounting for retirement benefits is a complex topic that is discussed in detail in subsequent accounting courses. We introduce the topic at this point as another example of the application of the matching process, which requires that expenses be recorded in the year in which the benefit is received. The benefit in this case is the work performed by the employees, and all costs incurred to compensate employees for their work must be recorded regardless of the timing of pension payments. This accounting procedure also avoids creating improper incentives for managers. If the future cost of retirement benefits was not included in the period in which work was performed, managers might have the incentive to offer employees increases in their retirement benefits instead of increases in their salaries. In this manner, managers could understate the true cost of employee services and make their companies appear more profitable.

DEBT-TO-EQUITY RATIO

KEY RATIO ANALYSIS

LO10-7

Compute and interpret the debt-to-equity ratio.

SELECTED FOCUS COMPANIES DEBT-TO-EQUITY RATIOS—2015

Reitmans 0.39%

National Beverage 0.68%

WestJet Airlines 1.62%

Companies raise large amounts of money to acquire additional assets by issuing shares to investors and borrowing funds from creditors. These additional assets are used to generate more earnings. However, since debt must be repaid, taking on increasing amounts of debt carries increased risk. The debt-to-equity ratio provides one measure for analysts to examine the company's financing strategy.

ANALYTICAL QUESTION → As an investor who must decide whether or not to buy shares, it is important to know how much of the company's assets is financed by creditors and how much is financed by owners. The debt-to-equity ratio is used to assess the debt capacity of a business. It is computed as follows:

$$\text{Debt-to-equity ratio} = \frac{\text{Total liabilities}}{\text{Shareholders' equity}}$$

The 2015 ratio for BCE is,

$$\frac{\$30,664}{\$17,329} = 1.77$$

RATIO AND COMPARISONS

Comparisons over Time			Comparisons with Competitors	
BCE			Rogers Communications	TELUS
2013	2014	2015	2015	2015
1.79	2.04	1.77	4.08	2.44

INTERPRETATIONS

In General → The debt-to-equity ratio indicates how much debt has been used to finance the company's acquisition of assets relative to equity financing that is supplied by shareholders. A high ratio normally suggests that a company relies heavily on funds provided by creditors. Managers use the ratio to decide whether they should finance any additional acquisitions by using debt. Creditors use this ratio to assess the risk that a company may not be able to meet its financial obligations during a business downturn. Investors use it to assess the level of financial risk associated with the expected cash flows from their investment (dividends and appreciation in share value).

Focus Company Analysis → The debt-to-equity ratio for BCE increased in 2014 relative to 2013, and then decreased in 2015. BCE recognized massive impairment losses in the past resulting from overpayment for acquisitions. The asset write-down resulted in a significant deficit, which is being reduced over time as the company continues to report net earnings year after year. It is also important to note, however, that BCE's ratio is better than those of its competitors.

A Few Cautions → The debt-to-equity ratio tells only part of the story with respect to risks associated with debt. The ratio is a good indication of debt capacity, but it does not help the investor understand whether the company's operations can support the amount of debt that it has. Remember that debt carries with it the obligation to make cash payments for interest and principal. As a result, most investors would evaluate the debt-to-equity ratio within the context of the amount of cash the company is able to generate from operating activities.

PAUSE FOR FEEDBACK

We learned how to compute two ratios: the times interest earned ratio and the debt-to-equity ratio. Check your understanding of these ratios before you move on.

SELF-STUDY QUIZ 10-6

Which company has a higher level of risk: a company with a high debt-to-equity ratio and a high interest coverage ratio or a company with a low debt-to-equity ratio and a low interest coverage ratio?

After you have completed your answer, check it with the solution at the end of the chapter.

FINANCING ACTIVITIES ON THE STATEMENT OF CASH FLOWS

FOCUS ON CASH FLOWS

BONDS PAYABLE

The issuance of long-term debt is reported as a cash inflow from financing activities. The repayment of principal is reported as an outflow from financing activities. As noted in Chapter 5, interest paid may be reported in either the operating or the financing section of the statement of cash flows.

EFFECT ON STATEMENT OF CASH FLOWS

In General → As we saw in Chapter 9, transactions involving short-term creditors (e.g., accounts payable) affect working capital and are, therefore, reported in the operating activities section of the statement of cash flows. Cash received from long-term creditors is reported as an inflow from financing activities. Cash payments made to long-term creditors are reported as outflows from financing activities. Examples are shown in the following table:

Financing Activity	Effect on Cash Flows
Issuance of bonds	+
Debt retirement	−
Repayment of bond principal upon maturity	−

LO10-8

Explain how financing activities are reported on the statement of cash flows.

REAL-WORLD EXCERPT

BCE Inc.

ANNUAL REPORT

Focus Company Analysis → A segment of BCE's statements of cash flows for the years 2014 and 2015 follows:

Consolidated cash flow statement for the year ended 31 December 2015			
In millions of Canadian dollars	Note	2015	2014
Cash flows used in financing activities			
Increase in notes payable and bank advances		$ 76	$ 469
Issue of long-term debt	20	1,498	1,428
Repayment of long-term debt	20	(2,084)	(1,113)
Privatization of Bell Aliant	24	–	(989)
Issue of common shares	25	952	49
Issue of equity securities by subsidiaries to non-controlling interest	25	(35)	–
Repurchase of common shares	26	(138)	
Cash dividends paid on common shares		(2,169)	(1,893)
Cash dividends paid on preferred shares		(150)	(134)
Cash dividends paid by subsidiaries to non-controlling interest		(41)	(145)
Other financing activities		(22)	(108)
Cash flows used in financing activities		$(2,113)	$(2,440)

Source: BCE Inc., Annual Report 2015.

SELECTED FOCUS COMPANY COMPARISONS: CASH FLOWS FROM FINANCING ACTIVITIES (IN MILLIONS OF DOLLARS)—2015

WestJet Airlines −259

Gildan Activewear 59

Reitmans −21.5

In 2015, the company raised a substantial amount of long-term debt ($1,498 million). It also reduced its long-term debt by $2,084 million. Repayments of long-term debt are made when the debt matures or when a company decides to redeem the outstanding debt prematurely in order to take advantage of lower interest rates.

Analysts are particularly interested in the financing activities section of the statement of cash flows because it provides important insights about the future capital structure for the company. Rapidly growing companies typically report significant amounts of funds in this section of the statement.

ACCOUNTING STANDARDS FOR PRIVATE ENTERPRISES

The accounting standards for private enterprises differ from IFRS in measuring and reporting specific types of long-term debt.

Financial Reporting Issue	IFRS	ASPE
Measurement of long-term debt	Canadian publicly accountable enterprises generally measure their long-term debt at amortized cost, but they are required to use the effective-interest method of amortization.	Canadian private enterprises generally measure their long-term debt at amortized cost. They may use the effective-interest method or the simpler straight-line method to amortize any discount or premium on debt issuance, particularly if the two methods do not usually produce significant differences in the carrying amounts of long-term debt.
Classification of redeemable long-term debt	Publicly accountable enterprises must classify such debt as a current liability.	If long-term bonds, debentures, or notes become redeemable (callable) as a result of a violation of a debt covenant, a private enterprise may continue to classify the debt as long term if the enterprise succeeds in renegotiating the debt agreement prior to releasing its financial statements.
Classification of finance leases	The criteria for classification of finance leases allow for some flexibility in implementation.	ASPE provide guidance as to the minimum percentages that constitute a major portion of the economic life of the leased asset (75%) or a substantial portion of the fair value of a leased asset (90%).

DEMONSTRATION CASE

To raise funds to build a new plant, Reed Company management issued bonds. The bond indenture specified the following:

> Par value of the bonds ($1,000 bonds): $600,000
>
> Date of issue: February 1, 2017; due in 10 years on January 31, 2027
>
> Stated interest rate: 6.5 percent per annum, payable semi-annually on July 31 and January 31

The market interest rate was 6 percent when the bonds were sold on February 1, 2017. The fiscal year for Reed Company ends on December 31.

Required:

1. How much cash did Reed Company receive from the sale of the bonds on February 1, 2017? Show your computations.

2. Prepare the journal entry on February 1, 2017, to record the sale and issuance of the bonds payable.

3. Prepare the journal entry for the payment of interest and amortization of the premium for the first interest payment on July 31, 2017. The company uses the effective-interest method.

4. Prepare the adjusting entry required on December 31, 2017, the end of the fiscal year.

5. Prepare the journal entry to record the second interest payment and the amortization of the premium on January 31, 2018.

6. Show how bond interest expense and bonds payable are reported on the financial statements at December 31, 2017.

We strongly recommend that you prepare your own answers to these requirements and then check your answers with the following solution.

SUGGESTED **SOLUTION**

1. The sale price of the bonds is the present value of future payments:

Principal $600,000 × 0.5537 (Table 9C.1, $n = 20$, $i = 3$):	$332,220
Interest ($600,000 × 6.5% × 1/2) × 14.8775 (Table 9C.2, $n = 20$, $i = 3$):	290,111
	$622,331

2. February 1, 2017 (issuance date):

Cash (A)	622,331	
Premium on bonds payable (L)		22,331
Bonds payable (L)		600,000
To record sale of bonds payable.		

3. July 31, 2017 (first interest payment date):

Bond interest expense (E) ($622,331 × 3%)	18,670	
Premium on bonds payable (L)	830	
Cash (A) ($600,000 × 3.25%)		19,500
To record payment of semi-annual interest.		

4. December 31, 2017 (end of the accounting period):

Bond interest expense (E) [($622,331 − $830) × 6% × 5/12]	15,538	
Premium on bonds payable (L)	712	
Bond interest payable (L) ($600,000 × 6.5% × 5/12)		16,250
Adjusting entry for five months' interest accrued plus		
amortization of the premium, August 1 to December 31, 2017.		

5. January 31, 2018 (second interest date):

Bond interest payable (L)	16,250	
Bond interest expense (E) [($622,331 − $830) × 6% × 1/12]	3,108	
Premium on bonds payable (L)	142	
Cash (A)		19,500
To record payment of semi-annual interest.		

6. Interest expense reported on the 2017 statement of earnings should be for 11 months, February 1 through December 31. Interest expense, per these entries, is $18,670 + $15,538 = $34,208.

Statement of Earnings for 2017:	
Interest expense	$ 34,208
Statement of Financial Position, December 31, 2017:	
Non-current liabilities:	
Bonds payable, 6% (due January 31, 2027)	$600,000
Add unamortized premium*	20,789
	$620,789

*$22,331 − ($830 + $712) = $20,789

APPENDIX 10A: BOND CALCULATIONS USING EXCEL

Instead of using the present value tables in Appendix 9C, most analysts and accountants use Excel to do the financial computations that are necessary when working with bonds. In Chapter 9, we showed you how to use Excel to compute the present value of both single payment and annuity problems. Because a bond involves both types of payments, you can use that process to compute the present value of each type of payment and add them together. Alternatively, you can use a single Excel process to compute the present value of a bond. We will illustrate the Excel process by using the bond example from this chapter. Assume that BCE issued a $100,000 bond that matured in two years and paid $10,000 interest twice per year (four payments of $5,000 each.)

LO10-S1

Compute the present value of a bond using Excel.

When the bond was issued, the market rate of interest was 12 percent. The present value of this bond can be computed as follows:

- **Determine the present value of a bond.** The present value of a bond can be computed using an Excel function (you don't have to enter the formula yourself). On the toolbar, click on the insert function button (f.x). A dropdown box called Insert Function will appear. You will be asked to type a brief description of what you want to do and click GO. You should enter "present value" and click the GO button. A new screen will appear and you should highlight PV, and click OK. A new dropdown box will appear. Enter the amounts from the problem in this box: Rate is the market rate of interest per period. For this problem, enter 0.06. Nper is the number of periods. You should enter 4. Pmt is the cash interest payment per period, which is $5000 for this problem. Fv is the maturity value of the bond, or $100000, in this case. Notice that when using Excel, amounts must be entered as negative numbers because they represent payments. Also, you should not enter a comma between the digits. The final box is Type, which permits you to do problems involving payments at either the beginning or end of the period. Most problems involve payments at the end of the period, so you do not need to enter anything in this box because the default is for end-of-period problems. Once you have entered the required data, enter OK and Excel will compute this value as $96,534.89 and show it on your spreadsheet. Notice that this amount is slightly different from the amount computed using present value tables because the table numbers have been rounded. An Excel screen with the data entered follows:

APPENDIX 10B: REPORTING BOND TRANSACTIONS: A SIMPLIFIED APPROACH

LO10-S2

Report the carrying amount of a bond without using a bond discount or premium account.

For financial reporting purposes, it is not necessary to use a discount or premium account when recording bonds sold at a discount or premium. This appendix discusses an alternative way of recording the bond transactions and reporting the bond's carrying amount using the same illustrations presented in the chapter.

Bonds Issued at a Discount

Bonds sell at a discount when the market rate of interest demanded by the buyers is higher than the stated interest rate offered by the issuer. Assume that the market rate of interest was 8 percent when MSC sold its bonds (which have a par value of $400,000). The bonds have a stated rate of 6 percent, payable semi-annually, which is less than the market rate on that date. Therefore, the bonds sold at a *discount*. This usually occurs when the market rate of interest increases after the company determines the coupon rate on the bonds.

To compute the cash issue price of the bonds, we can use the tables in Appendix 9C. As in the chapter example, the number of periods is 20 and we use an interest rate of 4 percent per period, which is the market rate of interest. The cash issue price of MSC's bonds is computed as follows:

	Present Value	To compute the present
a. Principal: $400,000 × 0.4564	$182,560	value using Excel, enter:
b. Interest: $12,000 × 13.5903	163,084	$f_x = PV(0.04, 20, -5000,$
Issue (sale) price of MSC's bonds	$345,644*	$-100000)$

*Discount: $400,000 − $345,644 = $54,356

The cash price of the bonds issued by MSC is $345,644. Some people refer to this price as 86.4, which means that the bonds were sold at 86.4 percent of their par value ($345,644 ÷ $400,000).

The issuance of MSC's bonds at a discount is recorded as follows:

Cash (A)				345,644	
Bonds payable (L)					345,644
Assets	=	**Liabilities**		+	**Shareholders' Equity**
Cash −345,644		Bonds payable +345.644			

Although MSC received only $345,644 when it sold the bonds, it must repay $400,000 when the bonds mature. This extra cash that must be paid is an adjustment to the interest payments, ensuring that creditors earn the market rate of interest on the bonds. To compute the interest expense, the borrower apportions, or amortizes, the bond discount to each semi-annual interest period as an increase to the interest payment. Therefore, the amortization of bond discount is an increase in bond interest expense.

Reporting Interest Expense on Bonds Issued at a Discount by Using Effective-Interest Amortization
Under the **effective-interest method**, interest expense for a bond is computed by multiplying the current unpaid balance (or carrying amount) by the market rate of interest that existed on the date the bonds were sold. The periodic amortization of a bond discount, or premium, is then calculated as the difference between interest expense and the amount of cash paid or accrued. This process can be summarized as follows:

The **EFFECTIVE-INTEREST METHOD** amortizes a bond discount, or premium, on the basis of the effective-interest rate.

Step 1:   Compute the interest expense:

Internet expense = Unpaid balance × Effective interest rate × *n*/12
n = Number of months in each interest period

Step 2:   Compute the amortization amount:

Amortization of bond discount = Interest expense − Interest paid (or accrued)

The first interest payment on MSC's bonds is on June 30, 2016. Interest expense at the end of the first six months is calculated by multiplying the unpaid balance of the debt by the market rate of interest for six months ($345,644 × 8% × 6/12 = $13,826). This represents the amount of interest revenue that bondholders expected to earn on their investment during this six-month period when they decided to purchase the bonds. The amount of cash paid is calculated by multiplying the principal by the stated rate of interest for six months ($400,000 × 6% × 6/12 = $12,000). The difference between the interest expense and the cash paid (or accrued) is the amount of discount that has been amortized ($13,826 − $12,000 = $1,826).

The journal entry to record the periodic interest expense is as follows. Effective-interest amortization causes these amounts to change each period.

Bond interest expense (E)			13,826	
Bonds payable (XL)				1,826
Cash (A)				12,000

Assets	=	Liabilities	+	Shareholders' Equity	
Cash −12,000		Bonds payable +1,826		Bond interest expense	−13,826

Each period, the amortization of the bond discount increases the bond's carrying amount (or unpaid balance). The amortization of bond discount can be thought of as interest that was earned by the bondholders but not paid to them. During the first six months of 2016, the bondholders earned interest of $13,826 but received only $12,000 in cash. The additional $1,826 was added to the carrying amount of the bond and will be paid when the bond matures.

Interest expense for the second half of 2016 is calculated by multiplying the carrying amount on June 30, 2016, by the market rate of interest for six months ($347,470 × 8% × 6/12 = $13,899). The amortization of the bond discount in the second period is $1,899:

Bond interest expense (E)			13,899	
Bonds payable (XL)				1,899
Cash (A)				12,000

Assets	=	Liabilities	+	Shareholders' Equity	
Cash −12,000		Bonds payable +1,899		Bond interest expense	−13,899

Notice that interest expense for the second half of 2016 is greater than the amount for the first six months of the year. This is logical, because MSC effectively borrowed more money during the second half of the year (i.e., the $1,826 unpaid interest). Interest expense increases each year during the life of the bond, because the amortized bond discount reflects unpaid interest on an increasing amount. This process can be illustrated with the amortization schedule shown below for the first two years and the last year of the bond's life:

		Amortization Schedule: Bond Discount (Effective Interest)		
Date	**(a) Interest to Be Paid [$400,000 × 3%]**	**(b) Interest Expense [4% × (d) Carrying Amount, Beginning of Period]**	**(c) Amortization [(b) − (a)]**	**(d) Carrying Amount [Beginning Carrying Amount + (c)]**
1/1/2016				$345,644
30/6/2016	$12,000	$13,826	$1,826	347,470
31/12/2016	12,000	13,899	1,899	349,369
30/6/2017	12,000	13,975	1,975	351,344
31/12/2017	12,000	14,054	2,054	353,398
.	.	.	.	.
30/6/2025	12,000	15,699	3,699	396,164
31/12/2025	12,000	15,836*	3,836	400,000

*The interest expense of $15,847 was rounded down by $11 so that the carrying amount does not exceed $400,000.

Interest expense (column b) is computed by multiplying the market rate of interest by the carrying amount at the beginning of the period (column d). Amortization is computed by subtracting interest paid (column a) from interest expense (column b).

The carrying amount (column d) is computed by adding amortization of bond discount (column c) to the carrying amount at the beginning of the period.

Bonds payable are reported on the statement of financial position at their carrying amount—that is, the maturity amount less any unamortized bond discount (or plus any unamortized bond premium). The carrying amount reflects the present value of remaining payments using the effective-interest rate at the date of issue. It increases over time as the amortized bond discount is added to the initial bond issue price until it reaches the maturity value at the end of the bond's life. At that time, the maturity value of the bonds and the carrying amount are the same (i.e., $400,000).

The same process applies if the market rate of interest was lower than the stated interest rate when MSC sold its bond. The premium that results from the sale of the bond would be amortized over time. The interest that is payable each six months exceeds the amount of interest required by the bondholders, indicating that MSC is effectively paying back part of cash received initially from the bondholders. This causes a reduction in the carrying amount of the bond over time until it reaches $400,000 at the maturity date of the bond.

PAUSE FOR FEEDBACK [STOP]

We have shown a simplified approach to recording bond interest expense and reporting the carrying amount of bonds when they are issues at a discount. Apply the same approach to a bond sold at a premium.

SELF-STUDY QUIZ 10-7

Assume that MSC issued on January 1, 2017, $100,000 bonds that will mature in 10 years. The bonds pay interest twice each year on July 1 and January 1 at an annual rate of 7 percent. They were sold when the market rate was 6 percent.

1. Determine the selling price of the bonds.

2. Prepare the journal entry to record interest expense at December 31, 2017, using the effective-interest method to amortize the bond premium.

3. Determine the carrying amount of the bonds as at December 31, 2017.

After you complete your answers, check them with the solutions at the end of the chapter.

APPENDIX 10C: REPORTING INTEREST EXPENSE ON BONDS BY USING THE STRAIGHT-LINE AMORTIZATION METHOD

LO10-S3

Report interest expense using the straight-line method amortization method.

While the effective-interest method is the preferred method to amortize bond discount or premium, Canadian private enterprises may use **straight-line amortization**, which allocates an equal amount to each interest period, because it is relatively easy to compute the required numbers. You may wonder why private enterprises are permitted to use a method that is not conceptually correct. The answer is *materiality*. Private enterprises are permitted to use the straight-line method because the amortized discounts or premiums that result from the two methods are normally not materially different. We use the examples in the chapter to illustrate the amortization of a bond discount as well as of a bond premium.

STRAIGHT-LINE AMORTIZATION of a bond discount or premium is a simplified method that allocates an equal amount to each interest period.

Bonds Issued at a Discount Refer to the illustration in the chapter, in which MSC's $400,000 bond issue was sold at a discount of $54,356. To amortize the bond discount over the life of MSC's bonds by using straight-line amortization, an equal amount is allocated to each interest period. MSC's bonds have 20 six-month interest periods. Therefore, the amount amortized on each semi-annual interest date is $2,718 ($54,356 ÷ 20 periods). This amount is added to the interest paid ($12,000) to compute interest expense for the period ($14,718).

The journal entry to record the interest payment each period is as follows:

Bond interest expense (E)		14,718	
Discount on bonds payable (XL)			2,718
Cash (A)			12,000

Assets	=	Liabilities	+	Shareholders' Equity
Cash −12,000		Discount on bonds payable +2,718		Bond interest expense −14,718

Comparison of Discount Amortization Methods

Interest expense (y-axis: 13,000 to 16,000)
Payment Period (x-axis: 1 3 5 7 9 11 13 15 17 19)

- Effective-interest amortization
- Straight-line amortization

Bonds payable are reported on the statement of financial position at their carrying amount—that is, the maturity amount less any unamortized bond discount (or plus any unamortized bond premium). At June 30, 2016, the carrying amount of MSC's bonds is more than the original issue price. The carrying amount increases to $348,362 ($345,644 + $2,718) because of the amortization of the discount. In each interest period, the carrying amount of the bonds increases by $2,718 because the unamortized discount decreases by $2,718. At the maturity date of the bonds, the unamortized discount (i.e., the balance in the discount on bonds payable account) is zero. At that time, the maturity amount of the bonds and the carrying amount are the same (i.e., $400,000). The process can be seen in the following amortization schedule, which shows the first two years and the last year of the bond's life. Compare it to the amortization schedule based on the effective-interest method:

	Amortization Schedule: Bond Discount (Straight Line)			
Date	(a) Interest to Be Paid [$400,000 × 3%]	(b) Interest Expense [(a) + (c)]	(c) Amortization [$54,356 ÷ 20 periods]	(d) Carrying Amount [Beginning Carrying Amount + (c)]
1/1/2016				$345,644
30/6/2016	$12,000	$14,718	$2,718	348,361
31/12/2016	12,000	14,718	2,718	351,079
30/6/2017	12,000	14,718	2,718	353,797
31/12/2017	12,000	14,718	2,718	356,515
.	.	.	.	.
.	.	.	.	.
30/6/2025	12,000	14,718	2,718	397,282
31/12/2025	12,000	14,718	2,718	400,000

Under the straight-line method, interest expense remains constant over the life of the bond, but it increases when the effective-interest method is used. The graph above illustrates these differences. However, both methods amortize the same historic discount and do not reflect current market values.

PAUSE FOR FEEDBACK

We have computed interest expense using the straight-line method of amortization of the bond discount and determined the carrying amount of the bond after each interest payment date. Practice these computations before moving on.

SELF-STUDY QUIZ 10-8

Assume that MSC issued $100,000 bonds that will mature in 10 years. The bonds pay interest twice each year at an annual rate of 7 percent. They were sold when the market rate was 8 percent.

1. Determine the selling price of the bonds.

2. What amount of interest was paid at the end of the first year?

3. What amount of interest expense would be reported at the end of the first year using straight-line amortization of bond discount?

After you complete your answers, check them with the solutions at the end of the chapter.

Bonds Issued at a Premium Refer to the illustration in the chapter, in which MSC's $400,000 bond issue was sold at a premium of $65,417. The premium recorded by MSC must be apportioned to each of the 20 interest periods. Using the straight-line method, the premium that is amortized in each semi-annual interest period is $3,271 ($65,417 ÷ 20 periods). This amount is subtracted from the interest payment ($12,000) to calculate the interest expense ($8,729). Thus, amortization of the bond premium decreases interest expense.

The payment of interest on the bonds is recorded as follows:

Bond interest expense (E)	8,729	
Premium on bonds payable (L)	3,271	
Cash (A)		12,000

Assets	=	Liabilities	+	Shareholders' Equity
Cash −12,000		Premium on bonds payable −3,271		Bond interest expense −8,729

Notice that the $12,000 cash paid each period includes $8,729 interest expense and $3,271 premium amortization. Thus, the cash payment to the investors includes the current interest they have earned, plus a return of part of the premium they paid when they bought the bonds.

The carrying amount of the bonds is the amount in the bonds payable account plus any unamortized premium. On June 30, 2016, the carrying amount of the bonds is $462,146 ($400,000 + $65,417 − $3,271). A partial amortization schedule follows:

	Amortization Schedule: Bond Discount (Straight Line)			
Date	(a) Interest to Be Paid [$400,000 × 2%]	(b) Interest Expense [(a) − (c)]	(c) Amortization [$65,417 ÷ 20 periods]	(d) Carrying Amount [Beginning Carrying Amount − (c)]
1/1/2016				$465,417
30/6/2016	$12,000	$8,729	$3,271	462,146
31/12/2016	12,000	8,729	3,271	458,875
30/6/2017	12,000	8,729	3,271	455,604
31/12/2017	12,000	8,729	3,271	452,333
.	.	.	.	.
.	.	.	.	.
30/6/2025	12,000	8,729	3,271	403,271
31/12/2025	12,000	8,729	3,271	400,000

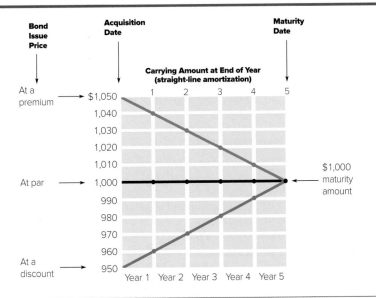

Exhibit 10.5

Amortization of Bond Discount and Premium Compared— Straight-Line Amortization

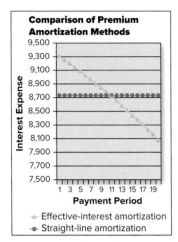

Comparison of Premium Amortization Methods

-▲- Effective-interest amortization
-■- Straight-line amortization

At the maturity date, after the last interest payment, the bond premium is fully amortized, and the maturity amount equals the carrying amount of the bonds. When the bonds are paid off in full, the same entry will be made whether the bond was originally sold at par, at a discount, or at a premium. Exhibit 10.5 compares the effects of the amortization of bond discount and bond premium on a $1,000 bond.

Under the straight-line method, interest expense remains constant over the life of the bond, but it decreases when the effective-interest method is used. The graph in the margin illustrates these differences.

STOP PAUSE FOR FEEDBACK

We have computed interest expense using the straight-line method of amortization of the bond premium. Practice these computations before moving on.

SELF-STUDY QUIZ 10-9

Assume that MSC issued $100,000 bonds that will mature in 10 years. The bonds pay interest twice each year at an annual rate of 9 percent. They were sold when the market rate was 8 percent.

1. Determine the selling price of the bonds.

2. What amount of interest was paid at the end of the first year?

3. What amount of interest expense would be reported at the end of the first year using straight-line amortization?

After you complete your answers, check them with the solutions at the end of the chapter.

CHAPTER TAKE-AWAYS

10-1. Describe the characteristics of long-term notes and bonds payable.

Long-term notes and bonds payable have a number of characteristics designed to meet the needs of the issuing corporation and the creditor. Corporations use debt to raise long-term capital. Long-term debt offers a number of advantages compared to equity, including financial leverage, the tax deductibility of interest, and the fact that control of the company is not diluted. Long-term debt carries additional risk because interest and principal payments are not discretionary.

10-2. Report notes payable and related interest expense.

A note or mortgage payable requires periodic payment of interest and repayment of the principal amount. The principal is typically repaid in blended payments of both principal and interest over the life of the note. The interest portion of the payment should be separated from the principal repayment for proper recording of the interest and the reduction of the liability.

10-3. Report bonds payable and interest expense for bonds sold at par, at a discount, or at a premium.

Three types of events must be recorded over the life of a typical bond: (1) the receipt of cash when the bond is first sold, (2) the periodic payment of interest, and (3) the repayment of principal upon the maturity of the bond. Bonds are sold at a discount whenever the coupon interest rate is less than the market rate of interest. A discount is the difference between the par value of the bond and its selling price. The discount is recorded as a contra liability when the bond is sold and is amortized over the life of the bond as an adjustment to interest payment. Bonds are sold at a premium whenever the coupon interest rate is higher than the market rate of interest. A premium is the difference between the selling price of the bond and its par value.

The premium is recorded as a liability when the bond is sold and is amortized over the life of the bond as an adjustment to interest payment.

10-4. Compute and interpret the times interest earned ratio.

This ratio measures the ability of a company to meet its interest obligations with resources from its profit-making activities. The ratio is computed by comparing interest expense to earnings before interest expense and income taxes.

10-5. Report the early retirement of bonds.

A corporation may retire bonds before their maturity date. The difference between the carrying amount and the amount paid to retire the bonds is reported as a gain or a loss, depending on the circumstances.

10-6. Describe other non-current liabilities.

In addition to long-term debt, companies report a number of other non-current liabilities that result from their operating, investing, and financing activities. Typical non-current liabilities include lease obligations, provisions, retirement benefit obligations, and deferred income taxes.

10-7. Compute and interpret the debt-to-equity ratio.

The debt-to-equity ratio (total liabilities ÷ shareholders' equity) measures the relationship between total liabilities and the shareholders' capital that finances the assets. The higher the ratio, the more debt is used to finance assets. As the ratio (and thus debt) increases, risk increases.

10-8. Explain how financing activities are reported on the statement of cash flows.

Cash flows associated with transactions involving long-term creditors are reported in the financing activities section of the statement of cash flows. Interest paid may be reported in either the operating activities section or the financing activities section.

The capital structure of a business is made up of funds supplied by both the creditors and the owners. In this chapter, we discussed the role of bonds payable in the capital structure of a business. In the next chapter, we will discuss shareholders' equity.

KEY **RATIOS**

The times interest earned ratio measures a company's ability to generate resources from current operations to meet its interest obligations. The computation of this ratio follows:

$$\text{Times interest earned} = \frac{\text{Net earnings} + \text{Interest expense} + \text{Income tax expense}}{\text{Interest expense}}$$

The debt-to-equity ratio measures the relationship between liabilities and the shareholders' capital that finances the assets. The higher the ratio, the more debt is assumed by the company to finance assets. The ratio is computed as follows:

$$\text{Debt-to-equity ratio} = \frac{\text{Total liabilities}}{\text{Shareholders' equity}}$$

FINDING **FINANCIAL INFORMATION**

STATEMENT OF FINANCIAL POSITION

Under Current Liabilities

Notes, bonds, and debentures are normally listed as non-current liabilities. An exception occurs when these liabilities are within one year of maturity. Such debts are reported as current liabilities with the following title:

Current portion of long-term debt

Under Non-current Liabilities

Notes, bonds, and debentures are listed under a variety of titles, depending on the characteristics of the debt. Titles include,

Notes payable

Bonds payable

Debentures

Financial liabilities

STATEMENT OF EARNINGS

Interest expense associated with long-term debt is reported on the statement of earnings. Most companies report interest expense as part of finance costs in a separate category on the statement of earnings.

STATEMENT OF CASH FLOWS
Under Financing Activities
+ Cash inflows from long-term creditors
− Cash outflows to long-term creditors
(including interest paid)
Under Operating Activities
Interest paid if classified as an operating
activity

NOTES
**Under Summary of Significant Accounting
Policies**
Description of pertinent information concerning
the accounting treatment of liabilities. Normally,
there is minimal information. Some companies
report the method used to amortize bond
discounts and premiums.
Under a Separate Note
Most companies include a separate note called
"Long-term debt" that reports information about
each major debt issue, including amount and
interest rate. The note may also provide detail
concerning debt characteristics and covenants.

QUESTIONS

1. What are the primary characteristics of a bond? For what purposes are bonds usually issued?
2. What is the difference between a bond indenture and a bond certificate?
3. Differentiate secured debt from unsecured debt.
4. Differentiate among redeemable, retractable, and convertible bonds.
5. From the perspective of the issuer, what are some advantages of using debt instead of issuing shares?
6. As the tax rate increases, the net cost of borrowing money decreases. Explain.
7. At the date of issuance, bonds are recorded at their current cash-equivalent amount. Explain.
8. Explain the nature of the discount and premium on bonds payable.
9. Explain the difference between the stated interest rate and the effective-interest rate on a bond.
10. Differentiate between the stated and effective rates of interest on a bond sold (*a*) at par, (*b*) at a discount, and (*c*) at a premium.
11. What is the carrying amount of a bond payable?
12. If a company issues a bond at a discount, will interest expense each period be more or less than the cash payment for interest? If another company issues a bond at a premium, will interest expense be more or less than the cash payment for interest? Is your answer to either question affected by the method used to amortize the discount or premium?
13. (Appendix 10C) Explain the basic difference between the straight-line and effective-interest methods of amortizing bond discount or premium. Explain when the straight-line method may be used.

connect   MINI-EXERCISES

LO10-3   **M10-1**   **Finding Financial Information**
For each of the following items, specify whether the information would be found in the statement of financial position, the statement of earnings, the statement of cash flows, the notes to the statements, or not at all.
1. The amount of a bond liability.
2. Interest expense for the period.
3. Cash interest paid for the period.
4. Interest rates for specific bond issues.
5. The names of major holders of bonds.
6. The maturity date of specific bond issues.

LO10-2   **M10-2**   **Computing Issuance Price of a Note**
Willams Company borrowed $600,000 from a local bank to be repaid in 20 semi-annual instalments, including interest at an annual rate of 6 percent. Determine the amount of each instalment and the interest paid with the first instalment.

LO10-3   **M10-3**   **Computing Bond Issuance Price**

Tran Company issued $900,000, 10-year, 6 percent bonds on July 1, 2017. Interest is payable semi-annually on June 30 and December 31. Determine the issuance price of the bonds assuming a market yield of 5 percent.

LO10-3   **M10-4**   **Understanding Effect of Discount or Premium on Interest Expense**

If a company issues a bond at a discount, will interest expense each period be more or less than the cash payment for interest? If another company issues a bond at a premium, will interest expense be more or less than the cash payment for interest? Is your answer to either question affected by the method used to amortize the discount or premium?

LO10-3   **M10-5**   **Recording the Issuance of a New Bond and the Payment of Interest (Effective-Interest Amortization)**

Coffman Company issued $1,000,000, 10-year, 4.5 percent bonds on January 1, 2018. The bonds sold for $940,000. Interest is payable semi-annually each June 30 and December 31. Record the sale of the bonds on January 1, 2018, and the payment of interest on June 30, 2018, using effective-interest amortization. The yield on the bonds is 5 percent.

LO10-3   **M10-6**   **Recording the Issuance of a New Bond and the Payment of Interest**

RKO Company issued $850,000, 10-year, 8 percent bonds on January 1, 2018. The bonds sold for $910,000. Interest is payable annually each December 31. Record the sale of the bonds on January 1, 2018, and the payment of interest on December 31, 2018, using the effective-interest method of amortization. The yield on the bonds is 7 percent.

LO10-4,10-7   **M10-7**   **Understanding Financial Ratios**

The debt-to-equity and times interest earned ratios were discussed in this chapter. Which is a better indicator of a company's ability to meet its required interest payment? Explain.

LO10-5   **M10-8**   **Determining Financial Statement Effects of an Early Retirement of Debt**

If interest rates fell after the issuance of a bond and the company decided to retire the debt, would you expect the company to report a gain or loss on debt retirement? Describe the financial statement effects of a debt retirement under these circumstances.

LO10-8   **M10-9**   **Reporting Cash Flow Effects**

In what section of the statement of cash flows would you find cash paid to retire bonds? In what section would you find cash paid for interest?

LO10-S3   **M10-10**   **(Appendix 10C) Recording the Issuance of a New Bond and the Payment of Interest (Straight-Line Amortization)**

Wagdy Company issued $600,000, 10-year, 6 percent bonds on July 1, 2017. The bonds sold for $580,000. Interest is payable semi-annually each June 30 and December 31. Record the sale of the bonds, and the payment of interest on December 31, 2017, using straight-line amortization.

connect EXERCISES

LO10-1   **E10-1**   **Bond Terminology: Fill in the Blanks**

1. The _____ is the amount (a) payable at the maturity of the bond and (b) on which the periodic cash interest payments are computed.

2. _____ is another name for bond principal, or the maturity amount for a bond.

3. The _____ is the rate of cash interest per period stated in the bond contract.

4. A _____ is an unsecured bond; no assets are specifically pledged to guarantee repayment.

5. _____ may be called for early retirement at the option of the issuer.

6. _____ may be converted to other securities of the issuer (usually common shares).

LO10-1,10-3,10-7

E10-2

Determining Financial Statement Effects for Long-Term Note and First Interest Payment, with Premium

Grocery Corporation sold $500,000, 7 percent notes on January 1, 2017, at a market rate of 8 percent. The notes were dated January 1, 2017, with interest to be paid each December 31; they mature 10 years from January 1, 2017. Use effective-interest amortization.

Required:

1. How are the financial statements affected by the issuance of the notes? Describe the impact on the debt-to-equity and times interest earned ratios, if any.

2. How are the financial statements affected by the payment of interest on December 31? Describe the impact on the debt-to-equity and times interest earned ratios, if any.

3. Show how the interest expense, interest payment, and notes payable should be reported on the financial statements for 2017.

LO10-1   **E10-3**

Shaw
Communications
Inc.

Explaining Why Debt Is Sold at a Discount

A recent annual report of Shaw Communications Inc. contained the following note:

> **10. LONG-TERM DEBT**
>
> On December 7, 2010, the Company issued $500,000,000 senior notes at a rate of 5.50% due December 7, 2020. The effective rate is 5.55% due to the discount on the issuance.

After reading this note, one student asked why Shaw didn't simply sell the notes for an effective yield of 5.55 percent and avoid having to account for a very small discount over the life of the notes. Prepare a written response to this question.

LO10-1   **E10-4**

Enbridge Pipelines
Inc.

Interpreting Information Reported in the Business Press

The business press reported the following information concerning a bond issued by Enbridge Pipelines Inc.:

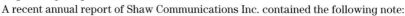

Bonds	Coupon	Maturity	Bid $	Yield %
Enbridge Pipelines Inc.	5.33	April 6, 2040	109.45	4.67

Required:

1. Explain the meaning of the reported information. If you bought Enbridge Pipelines bonds with $10,000 face value, how much would you pay (based on the information reported above)?

2. Assume that the bond was originally sold at par. What impact would the increase in value have on the financial statements for Enbridge Pipelines?

LO10-1,10-3   **E10-5**

The Walt Disney
Company

Explaining an International Transaction

A Walt Disney annual report contained the following note:

> The Company issued 100 billion (approximately $920 million) of Japanese yen bonds through a public offering in Japan. The bonds are senior, unsecured debt obligations of the Company, which mature in June 2019. Interest on the bonds is payable semi-annually at a fixed interest rate of 5% per year through maturity. The bonds provide for principal payments in dollars and interest payment in Japanese yen.

Required:

1. Describe how this bond would be reported on the statement of financial position.

2. Explain why you think management borrowed money in this manner.

LO10-1,10-4,10-7   **E10-6**

Analyzing Financial Ratios

You have just started your first job as a financial analyst for a large investment company. Your boss, a senior analyst, has finished a detailed report evaluating bonds issued by two different companies. She stopped by your desk and asked for help: "I have compared two ratios for the companies and found something interesting." She went on to explain that the debt-to-equity ratio for Applied Technologies Inc. is much lower than the industry average and that the one for Innovative Solutions Inc. is much higher. On the other hand, the times interest earned ratio for Applied Technologies is much higher than the industry average, and the ratio for Innovative Solutions is much lower. Your boss then asked you to explain what the ratios indicate about the two companies so that she could include the explanation in her report. How would you respond to your boss?

LO10-2   **E10-7**   **Comparing Different Options to Repay a Note Payable**

On October 1, 2017, Rocco Inc. purchased new equipment for $50,000 and was considering three different options for payment of this amount:

1. Pay the full amount on September 30, 2021, along with annual interest, payable each September 30.

2. Pay one quarter of this amount each September 30 along with the interest that would have accrued on the unpaid amount until that date.

3. Pay four equal annual instalments that include both interest and a partial repayment of the full amount, starting on September 30, 2018.

The equipment vendor would charge Rocco an annual interest rate of 5 percent for any of the three options.

Required:

Which of these three options would result in the lowest amount of interest payments over the four years? Support your answer with computations.

LO10-2   **E10-8**   **Computing the Issue Price of a Note Payable**

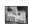

On January 1, 2017, Kaizen Corporation issued a $500 million note that matures in 10 years. The note has a stated interest rate of 6 percent. When the note was issued, the market rate was 6 percent. The note pays interest twice per year, on June 30 and December 31. At what price was the note issued?

LO10-3,10-8   **E10-9**   **Computing the Issue Price of a Bond with Analysis of Net Earnings and Cash Flow Effects**

Imai Company issued a $1 million bond that matures in five years. The bond has a 9 percent coupon rate. When the bond was issued, the market rate was 8 percent. The bond pays interest twice per year, on June 30 and December 31. Record the issuance of the bond on June 30. Was the bond issued at a discount or at a premium? How will the discount or premium affect future net earnings and future cash flows?

LO10-3   **E10-10**   **Computing Issue Prices of Bonds for Three Cases**

Thompson Corporation is planning to issue $100,000, five-year, 6 percent bonds. Interest is payable semi-annually each June 30 and December 31. All of the bonds will be sold on July 1, 2017; they mature on June 30, 2022.

Required:

Compute the issue (sale) price on July 1, 2017, if the yield is (*a*) 6 percent, (*b*) 5 percent, and (*c*) 7 percent. Show computations.

LO10-3   **E10-11**   **Recording Bond Issue and First Interest Payment with Premium (Effective-Interest Amortization)**

On January 1, 2018, Bochini Corporation sold a $10 million, 8.25 percent bond issue. The bonds were dated January 1, 2018, had a yield of 8 percent, pay interest each December 31, and mature 10 years from the date of issue.

Required:

1. Prepare the journal entry to record the issuance of the bonds.

2. Prepare the journal entry to record the interest payment on December 31, 2018. Use effective-interest amortization.

3. Show how the bond interest expense and the bonds payable should be reported on the annual financial statements for 2018.

LO10-3   **E10-12**   **Determining Financial Statement Balance with the Effective-Interest Amortization of a Bond Discount**

Eagle Corporation issued $10,000,000, 6.5 percent bonds dated April 1, 2018. The market rate of interest was 7 percent, with interest paid each March 31. The bonds mature in three years, on March 31, 2021. Eagle's fiscal year ends on December 31.

Required:

1. What was the issue price of these bonds?

2. Compute the bond interest expense for fiscal year 2018. The company uses the effective-interest method of amortization.

3. Show how the bonds should be reported on the statement of financial position at December 31, 2018.

4. What amount of interest expense will be recorded on March 31, 2019? Is this amount different from the amount of cash that is paid? If so, why?

LO10-3   E10-13   Analyzing a Bond Amortization Schedule: Reporting Bonds Payable

Stein Corporation issued a $1,000 bond on January 1, 2017. The bond specified an interest rate of 9 percent payable at the end of each year. The bond matures at the end of 2019. It was sold at a market rate of 11 percent per year. The following schedule was completed:

	Cash Paid	Interest Expense	Amortization	Carrying Amount
January 1, 2017 (issuance)				$ 951
End of year 2017	?	$105	$15	966
End of year 2018	?	106	16	982
End of year 2019	?	108	18	1,000

Required:

1. What was the bond's issue price?
2. Did the bond sell at a discount or a premium? How much was the premium or discount?
3. What amount of cash was paid each year for bond interest?
4. What amount of interest expense should be shown each year on the statement of earnings?
5. What amount(s) should be shown on the statement of financial position for bonds payable at each year-end? (For 2019, show the balance just before repayment of the bond.)
6. What method of amortization was used?
7. Show how the following amounts were computed for 2018: (*a*) $106, (*b*) $16, and (*c*) $982.
8. Is the method of amortization that was used preferable? Explain why.

LO10-3   E10-14   Preparing a Debt Payment Schedule with the Effective-Interest Method of Amortization, and Determining Reported Amounts

Shuttle Company issued $5,000,000, three-year, 4.1 percent bonds on January 1, 2017. The bond interest is paid each December 31, the end of the company's fiscal year. The bond was sold to yield 4 percent.

Required:

1. Complete a bond payment schedule. Use the effective-interest method.
2. What amounts will be reported on the financial statements (statement of financial position, statement of earnings, and statement of cash flows) for 2017, 2018, and 2019?

LO10-5   E10-15   Reporting the Retirement of a Bond with Discount

The Nair Company issued a $5 million bond at a discount five years ago. The current carrying amount of the bond is $4.75 million. The company now has excess cash and decides to retire the bond. The bond is callable at 101 percent of its face value.

Required:

Prepare the journal entry to record the retirement of the bond.

LO10-8   E10-16   Determining Effects on the Statement of Cash Flows

The effects of specific events that occur over the life of a bond are reported on the statement of cash flows. Determine whether each of the following events affects the statement of cash flows. If so, describe the impact and specify where the effect is reported on the statement.

1. A $1,000,000 bond is issued at a discount in 2016. The carrying amount of the bond reported on the statement of financial position on that date is $985,000, before any amortization of bond discount.
2. At year-end, accrued interest amounts to $50,000, and $1,000 of the bond discount is amortized by using the effective-interest method.
3. Early in 2017, the accrued interest is paid. At the same time, $8,000 of interest that accrued in 2017 is paid.

LO10-6   E10-17   Evaluating Lease Alternatives

As the new vice-president for consumer products at Acme Manufacturing, you are attending a meeting to discuss a serious problem associated with delivering merchandise to customers. Bob Vargas, director of logistics, summarized the problem, saying, "It's easy to understand; we just don't have enough delivery trucks given our recent growth." Barb Belini from the accounting department responded, "Maybe it's easy to understand, but it's impossible to do anything. Because of Bay Street's concern about the amount of debt on our statement of financial position, we're under a freeze and can't borrow money to acquire new assets. There's nothing we can do."

On the way back to your office after the meeting, your assistant offers a suggestion, "Why don't we just lease the trucks we need? That way we can get the assets we want without having to record a liability on the statement of financial position."

How would you respond to this suggestion?

LO10-6   **E10-18**   **Reporting a Liability**

McDonald's Corporation

McDonald's Corporation is one of the world's most popular fast-food restaurants, offering good food at convenient locations. Effective management of its properties is a key to its success. McDonald's both owns and leases property, as the following note in a recent annual report indicates:

> The Company owns and leases real estate primarily in connection with its restaurant business. The Company identifies and develops sites that offer convenience to customers and long-term sales and profit potential to the Company. The Company generally owns the land and building or secures long-term leases for restaurant sites, which ensures long-term occupancy rights and helps control related costs.

Required:

Should McDonald's report finance leases on its statement of financial position? Explain. If the obligation should be reported as a liability, how should the amount be measured?

LO10-6,10-7   **E10-19**   **Reporting Retirement Benefits and Effect on the Debt-to-Equity Ratio**

Sears Canada Inc.

Sears Canada Inc. offers Canadian consumers a diverse array of shopping options, with department and specialty stores, a comprehensive website, and a broad range of home-related services. At February 2, 2016, Sears had approximately 35,000 associates (or employees) helping customers through their personal shopping and catalogue ordering. The company's annual report for 2015 included the following information:

> **NOTES TO CONSOLIDATED FINANCIAL STATEMENTS**
>
> **20. Retirement benefit plans**
>
> The Company currently maintains a defined benefit registered pension plan and a defined contribution registered pension plan which covers eligible, regular full-time employees as well as some of its part-time employees. The defined benefit plan provides pensions based on length of service and final average earnings....
>
> In July 2008, the Company amended its pension plan and introduced a defined contribution component. The defined benefit component continues to accrue benefits related to future compensation increases although no further service credit is earned. In addition, the Company no longer provides medical, dental and life insurance benefits at retirement for associates who had not achieved the eligibility criteria for these non-pension, post-retirement benefits as at December 31, 2008.
>
> *Source:* Sears Canada Inc., Annual Report 2015.

Required:

1. Compare and contrast defined benefit and defined contribution pension plans.
2. What change did Sears introduce to its employee retirement program in July 2008? What is the main reason for this change? Explain.

LO10-6   **E10-20**   **Reporting a Liability, with Discussion**

Air Canada

An annual report for Air Canada contained the following information:

> **9. PENSION AND OTHER BENEFIT LIABILITIES**
>
> The Corporation maintains several defined benefit and defined contribution plans providing pension, other post-retirement and post-employment benefits to its employees and former employees for whom the related pension assets and liabilities have not yet been settled.
>
> ...
>
> The other employee benefits include health, life, and disability. These benefits consist of both post-employment and post-retirement benefits. The post-employment benefits relate to disability benefits available to eligible active employees, while the post-retirement benefits are comprised of health care and life insurance benefits available to eligible retired employees.

Required:

Should Air Canada report a liability for these benefits on its statement of financial position? Explain.

■ LO10-S2   **E10-21**   **(Appendix 10B) Reporting Bonds Payable – Simplified Approach**
Refer to E10-13. Use the approach presented in Appendix 10B.

Required:

1. Prepare the journal entries to record all the transactions related to the bond.
2. Show how the interest expense and the bond payable should be reported on the December 31, 2018, annual financial statements.

■ LO10-S2   **E10-22**   **(Appendix 10B) Recording the Issuance of a Bond, Preparing a Debt Payment Schedule with the Effective-Interest Method of Amortization, and Determining Reported Amounts – Simplified Approach**
Refer to E10-14. Use the approach presented in Appendix 10B.

Required:

1. Prepare the journal entry to record the issuance of the bond.
2. Complete a bond payment schedule. Use the effective-interest method.
3. What amounts will be reported on the financial statements (statement of financial position, statement of earnings, and statement of cash flows) for 2017, 2018, and 2019?

■ LO10-1,10-S3   **E10-23**   **(Appendix 10C) Computing the Issue Price of a Bond, with Discussion**
Charger Corporation issued a $250,000 bond that matures in five years. The bond has a stated interest rate of 7 percent and pays interest on February 1, May 1, August 1, and November 1. When the bond was issued, the market rate of interest was 8 percent. Record the issuance of the bond on February 1. Also record the payment of interest on May 1 and August 1. Use the straight-line method for amortization of any discount or premium. Explain why someone would buy a bond that did not pay the market rate of interest.

■ LO10-S3   **E10-24**   **(Appendix 10C) Recording Bond Issue and First Interest Payment with Discount (Straight-Line Amortization)**
On January 1, 2018, Seton Corporation sold a $10,000,000, 5.5 percent bond issue. The bonds were dated January 1, 2018, had a yield of 6 percent, pay interest each December 31, and mature 10 years from January 1, 2018.

Required:

1. Prepare the journal entry to record the issuance of the bonds.
2. Prepare the journal entry to record the interest payment on December 31, 2018. Use straight-line amortization.
3. Show how the bond interest expense and the bonds payable should be reported on the financial statements for 2018.

■ LO10-S3   **E10-25**   **(Appendix 10C) Recording Bond Issue: Entries for Issuance and Interest**
Northland Corporation had $400,000, 10-year bonds outstanding on December 31, 2017 (end of the fiscal year). Interest is payable each December 31. The bonds were issued (sold) on January 1, 2017. The 2017 annual financial statements showed the following:

Statement of earnings	
Bond interest expense (straight-line amortization)	$ 33,200
Statement of financial position	
Bonds payable (net liability)	389,200

Required (show computations):

1. What was the issue price of the bonds? Prepare the journal entry to record the issuance of the bonds on January 1, 2017.
2. What was the coupon rate on the bonds? Prepare the entry to record interest expense for 2017.

■ LO10-S3   **E10-26**   **(Appendix 10C) Determining Financial Statement Effects of Long-Term Debt and Related Interest**

Chamandy Corporation issued a $25,000,000, 7 percent note on July 1, 2018, at a market rate of 6 percent. The note was dated July 1, 2018, with interest to be paid each June 30. The note matures in 10 years. The company's fiscal year ends on December 31.

Required:

1. How are the financial statements affected by the issuance of the note? Describe the impact on the debt-to-equity and the times interest earned ratios, if any.

2. How are the financial statements affected by the payment of interest on June 30, 2018? Describe the impact on the debt-to-equity and the times interest earned ratios, if any.

3. Show how the interest expense and the note payable should be reported on the December 31, 2018, annual financial statements. Use the straight-line method to amortize any discount or premium.

connect PROBLEMS

LO10-1,10-3 **P10-1**

Bell Canada

Recording Issuance of Note and Computation of Interest (AP10-1)

Bell Canada issued 3.55 percent, Series M-41 MTN debentures on February 28, 2016.[11] The debentures have the following specifications:

Principal amount	$750 million
Maturity date	March 1, 2026
Issue price	99.624% of principal amount
Coupon rate	3.55%
Effective-interest rate	3.595%
Interest payment dates	March 1 and September 1
Initial interest payment date	September 1, 2016
Amount of first interest payment	$13,458,390.41

Required:

1. Prepare a journal entry to record the sale of these debentures on March 1, 2016.

2. Prepare the journal entry to record the payment of interest and amortization of the discount on September 1, 2016. The company uses the effective-interest method of amortization. (Assume there are 30 days in a month and 360 days in a year.)

3. Compute the interest expense that accrued from September 1, 2016, to December 31, 2016, the end of Bell's fiscal year, and prepare the adjusting journal entry on December 31, 2016, to record interest expense and amortization of the discount on the debentures.

4. Show the amounts that should be reported on Bell's financial statements for 2016.

5. Compute the total amount of interest expense over the life of the notes.

6. After looking at the issue price, a student asked why Bell did not simply sell the notes at 100 percent of the principal amount instead of selling them at a discount. How would you respond to this question?

LO10-2 **P10-2**

eXcel

Computing Equal Periodic Debt Payments, and Completing a Schedule (AP10-2)

On June 1, 2017, you bought a new sports car for $60,000. You made a $10,000 cash down payment and signed a $50,000 note, payable in four equal instalments on each June 1, with the first payment to be made on June 1, 2018. The interest rate is 6 percent per year on the unpaid balance. Each payment will include payment on principal plus interest.

Required:

1. Compute the amount of the equal payments that you must make.

2. What is the total amount of interest that you will pay during the four years?

3. Complete the following schedule:

Debt Payment Schedule				
Date	Cash Payment	Interest Expense	Decrease in Principal	Unpaid Principal
1/6/2017				
1/6/2018				
1/6/2019				
1/6/2017				
1/6/2018				
Totals				

4. Explain why the amount of interest expense decreases each year.

5. To reduce the total amount of interest paid on this note, you considered the possibility of making equal payments every three months (four payments per year). Compute the amount of the equal payments that you must make and the amount of interest that will be saved over the life of the note.

LO10-2

eXcel

P10-3   **Computing Equal Periodic Debt Payments, and Completing a Schedule**

Alimentex Inc. develops, manufactures, and markets a wide range of fruit and vegetable juices and drinks as well as specialty food products, such as fondue broths and sauces, soups, sauces and gravies, pestos, and sauces for pasta and pizza.

The company's long-term debt includes the following obligations:

Long-Term Debt	As at Dec. 31, 2016	As at Dec. 31, 2015
	(In thousands of dollars)	
1. Obligation related to the acquisition of equipment, 5.5%, payable starting in December 2014 in eight equal annual blended instalments of $262,212 through 2021.	$1,120	$1,310
2. Obligation under a finance lease for distribution equipment, 9.7%, payable starting in November 2015 in 11 equal semi-annual blended instalments of $44,998, through November 2020.	293	350

Required:

1. Assume that the equipment related to the first obligation was acquired on January 1, 2014, and that the first payment of $262,212 was made on December 31, 2014. Verify that the carrying amount reported by the company as at December 31, 2016, represents the present value of the remaining annual payments. (Note: Tables 9C.1 and 9C.2 in Chapter 9 do not include the 5.5 percent interest rate. Use Microsoft Excel or a calculator to compute the present value of future payments.)

2. How much interest will the company pay as part of the five remaining instalments on the 5.5 percent obligation? (*Hint:* You may find it helpful to prepare a schedule similar to Exhibit 10.3, option 3.)

3. Prepare the journal entry to record payment of the instalment on December 31, 2017.

4. Assume that the obligation under the finance lease was signed on June 1, 2015, and that the first semi-annual instalment was made on November 30, 2015. Verify that the carrying amount reported by the company as at December 31, 2016, represents the present value of the remaining semi-annual payments. Use a calculator or Microsoft Excel to compute the present value of future payments.

LO10-3,10-4,10-7

P10-4

Recording Bond Issuance and Interest Payment with Explanation of Bond Premium and Discussion of Management Strategy (AP10-3)

On March 1, 2017, Catalin Corporation issued $40 million in bonds that mature in 10 years. The bonds have a stated interest rate of 5.8 percent and pay interest on March 1 and September 1. When the bonds were sold, the market rate of interest was 6 percent. Catalin uses the effective-interest method. By December 31, 2017, the market interest rate had increased to 6.5 percent.

Required:

1. Record the issuance of the bond on March 1, 2017.

2. Compute the present value of the difference between the interest paid each six months ($40 million × 5.8% × 6/12 = $1.16 million) and the interest demanded by the market ($40 million × 6% × 6/12 = $1.2 million). Use the market rate of interest and the 10-year life of the bond in your present value computation. What does this amount represent? Explain.

3. Record the payment of interest on September 1, 2017.

4. Record the adjusting entry for accrued interest on December 31, 2017.

5. Why does interest expense change each year when the effective-interest method is used?

6. Compute the present value of Catalin's bonds, assuming that they had a 7-year life instead of a 10-year life. Compare this amount to the carrying amount of the bond at March 1, 2017. What does this comparison demonstrate?

7. Determine the impact of these transactions at year-end on the debt-to-equity ratio and the times interest earned ratio.

■ LO10-3
eXcel

P10-5   **Recording Bond Issuance and Interest Payments (Effective-Interest Method)** (AP10-4)

Nordic Company issued bonds with the following provisions:

Maturity value: $60,000,000

Interest: 7.9 percent per annum payable semi-annually each June 30 and December 31

Terms: Bonds dated January 1, 2017, due five years from that date

The company's fiscal year ends on December 31. The bonds were sold on January 1, 2017, at a yield of 8 percent.

Required:

1. Compute the issue (sale) price of the bonds (show computations).
2. Prepare the journal entry to record the issuance of the bonds.
3. Prepare the journal entries at the following dates: June 30, 2017; December 31, 2017; and June 30, 2018. Use the effective-interest method to amortize bond discount or premium.
4. How much interest expense would be reported on the statement of earnings for 2017? Show how the liability related to the bonds should be reported on the statement of financial position at December 31, 2017.

■ LO10-3

P10-6   **Completing an Amortization Schedule (Effective-Interest Amortization)**

Berj Corporation issued bonds and received cash in full for the issue price. The bonds were dated and issued on January 1, 2016. The coupon rate was payable at the end of each year. The bonds mature at the end of four years. The following schedule has been partially completed (amounts in thousands):

Date	Cash Paid	Interest Expense	Amortization	Carrying Amount
January 1, 2017				$6,101
End of year 2017	$450	$427	$23	6,078
End of year 2018	450	?	?	6,053
End of year 2019	450	?	?	?
End of year 2020	450	?	?	6,000

Required:

1. Complete the amortization schedule.
2. What was the maturity amount of the bonds?
3. How much cash was received at the date of issuance (sale) of the bonds?
4. What was the amount of discount or premium on the bond?
5. How much cash will be disbursed for interest each period and in total for the full life of the bond issue?
6. What method of amortization is being used? Explain.
7. What is the coupon rate of interest?
8. What is the effective rate of interest?
9. What amount of interest expense should be reported on the statement of earnings each year?
10. Show how the bonds should be reported on the statement of financial position at the end of each year (show the last year immediately before repayment of the bonds).

■ LO10-3
eXcel

P10-7   **Recording Bond Issuance, Interest Expense, and Effects of Bond Redemption of Financial Statements (Effective-Interest Method)** (AP10-5)

Nguyen Corporation issued a $8,000,000, 6 percent bond on August 1, 2017. The market interest rate was 7 percent on that date and the bond matures in eight years. Interest on these bonds is payable annually on August 1. The company uses the effective interest method and its fiscal year ends on November 30.

Required:

1. Compute the issue price of the bond on August 1, 2017.
2. Prepare the journal entries on November 30, 2017, and on August 1, 2018, to record interest expense.
3. Assume that the company redeems 40 percent of the original bond at 103 on August 1, 2018, after the payment of interest. Show the accounts and amounts that the company should report on its statement of financial position as at August 1, 2018, after the redemption of the bonds.

4. How would the effect of the redemption transaction be reported on the statement of earnings and the statement of cash flows for the year ending November 30, 2018? The company uses the indirect method to prepare the operating section of the statement of cash flows. Show details.

LO10-5

P10-8   **Understanding the Early Retirement of Debt** (AP10-6)

CM Entertainment Inc. owns and operates movie theatres. The company sold 6.5 percent bonds for $105,000,000 and used the cash proceeds to retire bonds with a face value of $100,000,000 with a coupon rate of 8 percent. At that time, the old bonds had a carrying amount of $99,547,000.

Required:

1. Why did the company issue new bonds to retire the old bonds?
2. Prepare the journal entries to record the issuance of the new bonds and the early retirement of the old bonds.
3. How should CM Entertainment report the gain or loss on retirement of the old bonds?

LO10-S2

P10-9   **(Appendix 10B) Reporting Bonds Payable – Simplified Approach** (AP10-7)

Refer to P10-6. Use the approach presented in Appendix 10B.

Required:

1. Prepare the journal entry to record the issuance of the bond.
2. Prepare the journal entry to record the payment of interest at the end of 2018. Use the effective-interest method.
3. What amounts will be reported on the financial statements (statement of financial position, statement of earnings, and statement of cash flows) for 2017?

LO10-S3

P10-10   **(Appendix 10C) Comparing Bonds Issued at Par, Discount, and Premium**

Sikes Corporation, whose fiscal year ends on December 31, issued the following bonds:

Date of bonds: January 1, 2018

Maturity amount and date: $10 million due in 10 years (December 31, 2024)

Interest: 5 percent per annum payable each December 31

Date of sale: January 1, 2018

Required:

1. Provide the following amounts to be reported on the 2018 financial statements (use straight-line amortization and show amounts in thousands):

	Issued at Par	at 96	at 102
	Case A	Case B	Case C
a. Interest expense	$	$	$
b. Bonds payable			
c. Unamortized premium or discount			
d. Carrying amount of bonds			
e. Stated rate of interest			
f. Cash paid for interest			

2. For each of cases B and C, explain why interest expense is different from cash paid for interest.
3. Assume that you are an investment adviser and a retired person has written to you asking, "Why should I buy a bond at a premium when I can find one at a discount? Isn't that stupid? It's like paying the list price for a car instead of negotiating a discount." Write a brief letter in response to the question.

LO10-S3

P10-11   **(Appendix 10C) Completing a Schedule Comparing Bonds Issued at Par, Discount, and Premium** (AP10-8)

Quartz Corporation sold a $50 million, 7 percent bond issue on January 1, 2018. The bonds pay interest each December 31 and mature 10 years from January 1, 2018. For comparative study and analysis, assume three independent selling scenarios: case A, bonds sold at par; case B, bonds sold at 98; case C, bonds sold at 102. Use straight-line amortization and disregard income tax unless specifically required.

Required:

1. Complete the following schedule to analyze the differences among the three cases.

	Case A (Par)	Case B (at 98)	Case C (at 102)
a. Cash inflow at the date of issue (sale)			
b. Total cash outflow through the maturity date			
c. Net cash outflow = total interest expense over the life of the bonds			
d. Total interest expense, net of income tax (25 percent)			
Statement of earnings for 2018			
e. Bond interest expense			
Statement of financial position at December 31, 2018, non-current liabilities			
f. Bonds payable, 7 percent			
g. Unamortized discount			
h. Unamortized premium			
i. Net liability			

2. For each case, explain why the amounts in items (c), (d), and (e) of (1) are the same or different.

LO10-S3   P10-12   (Appendix 10C) Computing Amounts for Bond Issue, and Comparing Amortization Methods (AP10-9)

eXcel

Dektronik Corporation manufactures electrical test equipment. The company's board of directors authorized a bond issue on January 1, 2016, with the following terms:

Maturity (par) value: $800,000

Interest: 7.5 percent per annum payable each December 31

Maturity date: December 31, 2020

Effective-interest rate when sold: 8 percent

Required:

1. Compute the bond issue price. Explain why both the stated and effective-interest rates are used in this computation.

2. Assume that the company used the straight-line method to amortize the discount or premium on the bond issue. Compute the following amounts for each year (2016–2020):

   a. Cash payment for bond interest.

   b. Amortization of bond discount or premium.

   c. Bond interest expense.

   d. Carrying amount of the bond.

   e. Interest expense as a percentage of the carrying amount at the beginning of the year.

   The straight-line method is theoretically deficient when interest expense is related to the carrying amount of the debt. Explain.

3. Assume instead that the company used the effective-interest method to amortize the discount or premium. Prepare an effective-interest bond amortization schedule similar to the one in the text. The effective-interest method provides a constant interest rate when interest expense is related to the carrying amount (unpaid balance). Explain by referring to the bond amortization schedule.

4. Which method should the company use to amortize the bond discount or premium? As a financial analyst, would you prefer one method over the other? If so, why?

ALTERNATE PROBLEMS

LO10-1,10-3   AP10-1   Recording Issuance of Note and Computation of Interest (P10-1)

Shaw Communications Inc.

Shaw Communications Inc. is a diversified Canadian communications company that provides cable television, Internet, digital phone, telecommunications, and satellite direct-to-home services to more than 3 million customers. On February 19, 2016, the company sold long-term notes with the following specifications:

Principal amount	$300 million
Maturity date	February 19, 2021
Issue price	99.890% of principal amount
Coupon rate	3.15%
Effective interest rate	3.174%
Interest payment dates	February 19 and August 19

Required:

1. Prepare the journal entries to record the sales of the notes on February 19, 2016.

2. Prepare the journal entries to record the payment of interest and amortization of the discount on August 19, 2016. The company uses the effective-interest method to amortize the discount.

3. Compute the interest expense that accrued from August 19 to December 31, 2016, the end of Shaw's fiscal year, and prepare the adjusting journal entries on (1) December 31, 2016, to record interest expense and amortization of the discount on the notes and (2) on February 19, 2017 to record the interest payment. (Assume there are 30 days in a month and 360 days in a year.)

4. Show the amounts that should be reported on Shaw's financial statements for 2016.

5. Compute the total amount of interest expense over the life of the notes.

6. After looking at the issue price, a student asked why the management of Shaw Communications did not simply sell the notes at 100 percent of the principal amount instead of selling them at a discount. How would you respond to this question?

LO10-2
eXcel

AP10-2   **Computing Equal Periodic Debt Payments, and Completing a Schedule with Journal Entries** (P10-2)

On January 1, 2018, Ontario Company sold a new machine to Canada Company for $70,000. Canada Company made a cash down payment of $20,000 and signed a $50,000, 8 percent note for the balance due. The note is payable in three equal instalments due on December 31, 2018, 2019, and 2020. Each payment includes principal plus interest on the unpaid balance. Canada Company recorded the purchase as follows:

January 1, 2018		
Machinery	70,000	
Cash		20,000
Note payable		50,000

Required (show computations and round to the nearest dollar):

1. What is the amount of the equal annual payments that Canada Company must make?
2. What is the total interest on the note over the three years?
3. Complete the following debt payment schedule:

Debt Payment Schedule				
Date	Cash Payment	Interest Expense	Decrease in Principal	Unpaid Principal
1/1/2018				
31/12/2018				
31/12/2019				
31/12/2020				
Total				

4. Prepare the journal entries for each of the three payments.
5. Explain why interest expense decreased in amount each year.

LO10-3,10-4,10-7

AP10-3

Using the Effective-Interest Method with Explanation of Bond Premium and Discussion of Management Strategy (P10-4)

On March 1, 2018, Carter Corporation issued $15,000,000 in bonds that mature in 10 years. The bonds have a coupon rate of 6.3 percent and pay interest on March 1 and September 1. When the bonds were sold, the market rate of interest was 6 percent. Carter uses the effective-interest method to amortize bond discount or premium. By December 31, 2018, the market interest rate had increased to 7 percent.

Required:

1. Record the issuance of the bond on March 1, 2018.
2. Compute the present value of the difference between the interest paid each six months ($472,500) and the interest demanded by the market ($15 million × 6% × 6/12 = $450,000). Use the market rate of interest and the 10-year life of the bond in your present value computation. What does this amount represent? Explain.
3. Record the payment of interest on September 1, 2018.
4. Record the adjusting entry for accrued interest on December 31, 2018.
5. Why does interest expense change each year when the effective-interest method is used?
6. Compute the present value of Carter's bonds, assuming that they had a 7-year life instead of a 10-year life. Compare this amount to the carrying amount of the bond at March 1, 2021. What does this comparison demonstrate?
7. Determine the impact of the transactions at year-end on the debt-to-equity ratio and the times interest earned ratio.

■ **LO10-3**
e**X**cel

AP10-4 **Computing the Issue Price of Bonds, and Recording Issuance and Interest Payments** (P10-5)

Jaymar Company issued bonds with the following provisions:

Maturity value: $100,000,000

Interest: 8.1 percent per annum payable semi-annually each June 30 and December 31

Terms: Bonds dated January 1, 2018, due 10 years from that date

The company's fiscal year ends on December 31. The bonds were sold on January 1, 2018, at a yield of 8 percent.

Required:

1. Compute the issue (sale) price of the bonds. Show computations.
2. Prepare the journal entry to record the issuance of the bonds.
3. Prepare the journal entries at the following dates: June 30, 2018; December 31, 2018; and June 30, 2019. Use the effective-interest method to amortize bond discount or premium.
4. How much interest expense would be reported on the statement of earnings for 2018? Show how the liability related to the bonds should be reported on the statement of financial position at December 31, 2018.

■ **LO10-3**
e**X**cel

AP10-5 **Recording Bond Issuance, Interest Expense, and Effects of Bond Redemption of Financial Statements (Effective-Interest Method)** (P10-7)

Ashraf Ltd. sold on June 30, 2017, $4,000,000, 20-year bonds, paying a nominal interest rate of 6.5 percent. The bonds were issued at 105.7344 percent with a yield of 6 percent. The bonds pay annual interest on June 30. The company uses the effective interest method and its fiscal year ends on December 31.

Required:

1. Prepare the journal entry to record the issuance of the bond.
2. Show how the liability for bonds payable would be presented on the statement of financial position as at December 31, 2017.
3. Prepare the journal entry to record the first interest payment on June 30, 2018.
4. Ashraf Ltd. decided on June 30, 2018, to redeem the outstanding bonds at 102 percent, after paying interest to bondholders. Show how the effects of this transaction would be reported on the statement of earnings and the statement of cash flows for the year ended June 30, 2018. The company uses the indirect method to prepare the operating section of the statement of cash flows.
5. Why would Ashraf Ltd. engage in an early redemption of its bonds? Explain.

■ **LO10-1,10-5** **AP10-6**
Thomson Reuters
Corporation

Understanding the Difference between Carrying Amount and Market Value (P10-8)

Thomson Reuters Corporation is the world's leading source of electronic information and services to businesses and professionals in various fields, such as media, financial services, tax and accounting, and healthcare and science. The company's annual report for 2015 indicates that the carrying amount of long-term debt is $6,829 million, but its fair value is $6,366 million. The fair value of debt is estimated based on either quoted market prices for similar issues or current rates offered to the company for debt of the same maturity.

Required:

What is meant by "fair value"? Explain why there is a difference between the carrying amount and the fair value of the long-term debt for Thomson Reuters. Assume that Thomson Reuters decided to retire all of its long-term debt for cash (a very unlikely event). Prepare the journal entry to record the transaction.

LO10-S2   **AP10-7**   **(Appendix 10B) Reporting Bonds Payable – Simplified Approach** (P10-9)

Refer to AP10-5. Use the approach presented in Appendix 10B.

Required:

1. Prepare the journal entry to record the issuance of the bond.
2. Prepare the journal entries to record the accrual of interest expense on December 31, 2017, and the payment of interest at June 30, 2018.
3. What amounts will be reported on the financial statements (statement of financial position, statement of earnings, and statement of cash flows) for 2017?

LO10-S3   **AP10-8**   **(Appendix 10C) Completing a Schedule That Involves a Comprehensive Review of the Issuance of Bonds at Par, Discount, and Premium, Including Cash Flows** (P10-11)

 eXcel

On January 1, 2016, Ontec Corporation sold and issued $100 million, five-year, 10 percent bonds. The bond interest is payable annually each December 31. Assume three separate and independent selling scenarios: case A, bonds sold at par; case B, bonds sold at 90; and case C, bonds sold at 110.

Required:

1. Complete a schedule similar to the following for each separate case, assuming straight-line amortization of discount and premium. Disregard income tax. Show all dollar amounts in millions.

	At Start of 2016	At End of 2016	At End of 2017	At End of 2018	At End of 2019	At End of 2020 Prior to Payment of Principal	At End of 2020 Payment of Principal
Case A: sold at par (100)	$	$	$	$	$	$	$
Cash inflow							
Cash outflow							
Interest expense on statement of earnings							
Carrying amount on statement of financial position							
Case B: sold at a discount (90)							
Cash inflow							
Cash outflow							
Interest expense on statement of earnings							
Carrying amount on statement of financial position							
Case C: sold at a premium (110)							
Cash inflow							
Cash outflow							
Interest expense on statement of earnings							
Carrying amount on statement of financial position							

2. For each separate case, calculate the following:
   a. Total cash outflow.
   b. Total cash inflow.
   c. Net cash outflow.
   d. Total interest expense over the life of the bonds.
3. a. Explain why the net cash outflows differ among the three cases.
   b. For each case, explain why the net cash outflow is the same as total interest expense.

LO10-S3   **AP10-9**   **(Appendix 10C) Straight-Line versus Effective-Interest Methods of Amortizing Bond Discount, with Discussion** (P10-12)

Canadian Products Corporation manufactures office equipment and supplies. The company authorized a bond issue on January 1, 2016, with the following terms:

Maturity (par) value: $120,000,000

Interest: 7.9 percent per annum payable each December 31

Maturity date: December 31, 2020

Effective-interest rate when sold: 8 percent

Required:

1. Compute the bond issue price. Explain why both the stated and effective-interest rates are used in this computation.

2. Prepare the entry to record this bond issue.

3. Assume that the company used the straight-line method to amortize the discount or premium on the bond issue. Compute the following amounts for each year (2016–2020):

    a. Interest paid.

    b. Amortization of bond discount or premium.

    c. Bond interest expense.

    d. Carrying amount of the bond.

    e. Interest expense as a percentage of the carrying amount at the beginning of the year.

    The straight-line method is theoretically deficient when interest expense is related to the carrying amount of the debt. Explain.

4. Assume instead that the company used the effective-interest method to amortize the discount or premium. Prepare an effective-interest bond amortization schedule similar to the one in the text. The effective-interest method provides a constant interest rate when interest expense is related to the net liability. Explain by referring to the bond amortization schedule.

5. Which method should the company use to amortize the bond discount or premium? As a financial analyst, would you prefer one method over the other? If so, why?

≡ connect   CASES AND PROJECTS

FINDING AND INTERPRETING FINANCIAL INFORMATION

LO10-3,10-7,10-8   **Finding Financial Information**

CP10-1   Refer to the financial statements of Canadian Tire Corporation given in Appendix A of this book.

Canadian Tire Corporation

Required:

1. How much did the company report for finance costs, and how much cash was paid for interest during the year ended January 2, 2016? Where did you find the information?

2. Review the company's note on long-term debt, and identify the different types of debt that the company has issued in the past, as well as the characteristics of the various debt issues.

3. Does the company report other long-term liabilities? If so, identify these liabilities.

LO10-3,10-7,10-8   **Finding Financial Information**

CP10-2   Go to *Connect* for the financial statements of Sears Canada Inc.

Sears Canada Inc.

Required:

1. How much cash was paid for interest during the year ended January 30, 2016?

2. Review the company's note on long-term debt. Does the company provide details about its debt issues? If so, identify the characteristics of one of the debt issues.

3. Describe the company's established arrangements, if any, that permit it to borrow money if needed.

4. Does the company report other non-current liabilities? If so, identify these liabilities.

■ LO10-1,10-4,10-6

Canadian Tire
Corporation vs.
Sears Canada Inc.

CP10-3

Comparing Companies

Refer to the financial statements of Canadian Tire Corporation (Appendix A) and Sears Canada Inc. (on *Connect*).

Required:

1. Examine the statements of cash flows for both companies. What are the primary sources of cash flows for both companies for fiscal year 2015?

2. Two financial ratios (the debt-to-equity ratio and the times interest earned ratio) are discussed in this chapter. Compute these ratios for both companies for fiscal year 2015. Are they relevant for these companies? Explain.

FINANCIAL REPORTING AND ANALYSIS CASES

■ LO10-1

CP10-4

Analyzing the Use of Debt

Cricket Corporation's financial statements for 2017 showed the following:

Statement of Earnings	
Revenues	$300,000
Expenses	(198,000)
Interest expense	(2,000)
Pretax earnings	100,000
Income tax (30%)	(30,000)
Net earnings	$ 70,000
Statement of Financial Position	
Assets	$300,000
Liabilities (average interest rate, 10%)	20,000
Share capital	200,000
Retained earnings	80,000
	$300,000

Notice that the company had a debt of only $20,000 compared with share capital of $200,000. A consultant recommended the following: debt, $100,000 (at 10 percent) instead of $20,000, and share capital of $120,000 (12,000 shares) instead of $200,000 (20,000 shares). That is, the company should finance the business with more debt and less owner contribution.

Required (round to the nearest percent):

1. You have been asked to develop a comparison between (*a*) the actual results and (*b*) the results based on the consultant's recommendation. To do this, you decided to develop the following schedule:

Item	Actual Results for 2017	Results with an $80,000 Increase in Debt and an $80,000 Decrease in Equity
a. Total debt		
b. Total assets		
c. Total shareholders' equity		
d. Interest expense		
e. Net earnings		
f. Return on total assets		
g. Earnings available to shareholders:		
(1) Amount		
(2) Per share		
(3) Return on shareholders' equity		

2. Based on the completed schedule in (1), provide a comparative analysis and interpretation of the actual results and the consultant's recommendation.

CRITICAL THINKING CASES

LO10-1 **CP10-5** **Making a Decision as a Financial Analyst**

You are working for a large mutual fund company as a financial analyst. You have been asked to review two competitive companies in the same industry. Both have similar cash flows and net earnings, but one has no debt in its capital structure while the other has a debt-to-equity ratio of 1.2. Based on this limited information, which company would you prefer? Justify your conclusion. Would your preference be influenced by the companies' industry?

LO10-1 **CP10-6** **Evaluating an Ethical Dilemma**

You work for a small company considering investing in a new Internet business. Financial projections suggest that the company will be able to earn in excess of $20 million per year on an investment of $100 million. The company president suggests borrowing the money by issuing bonds that will carry a 7 percent interest rate. He says, "This is better than printing money! We won't have to invest a penny of our own money, and we get to keep $13 million per year after we pay interest to the bondholders." As you think about the proposed transaction, you feel a little uncomfortable about taking advantage of the creditors in this fashion. You feel that it must be wrong to earn such a high return by using money that belongs to other people. Is this an ethical business transaction?

LO10-1 **CP10-7** **Evaluating an Ethical Dilemma**

Many retired people invest a significant portion of their money in bonds of corporations because of the relatively low level of risk. During the 1980s, significant inflation caused some interest rates to rise to as high as 15 percent. Retired people who bought bonds that paid only 6 percent continued to earn at the lower rate. During the 1990s, inflation subsided and interest rates declined. Many corporations took advantage of call options on bonds and refinanced high interest rate debt with low interest rate debt. In your judgment, is it ethical for corporations to continue paying low interest rates when rates increase but to call bonds when rates decrease?

LO10-1 **CP10-8** **Evaluating an Ethical Dilemma**

Assume that you are a portfolio manager for a large insurance company. The majority of the money you manage is from retired schoolteachers who depend on the income you earn on their investments. You have invested a significant amount of money in the bonds of a large corporation and have just received a call from the company's president explaining that it is unable to meet its current interest obligations because of deteriorating business operations related to increased international competition. The president has a recovery plan that will take at least two years. During that time, the company will not be able to pay interest on the bonds, and, she admits, if the plan does not work, bondholders will probably lose more than half of their money. As a creditor, you can force the company into immediate bankruptcy and probably get back at least 90 percent of the bondholders' money. You also know that your decision will cause at least 10,000 people to lose their jobs if the company ceases operations. Given only these two options, what should you do?

FINANCIAL REPORTING AND ANALYSIS TEAM PROJECT

LO10-1,10-3,10-4,
10-7,10-8 **CP10-9**

Team Project: Examining an Annual Report

As a team, select an industry to analyze. A list of companies classified by industry can be obtained by accessing www.fpinfomart.ca and then choosing "Companies by Industry." You can also find a list of industries and companies within each industry via http://ca.finance.yahoo.com/investing (click on "Order Annual Reports" under "Tools").

Each group member should acquire the annual report for a different publicly traded company in the industry. (Library files, the SEDAR service at www.sedar.com, and the company's website are good sources.)

Required:

On an individual basis, each team member should then write a short report answering the following questions about the selected company. Discuss any patterns across the companies that you, as a team, observe. Then, as a group, write a short report comparing and contrasting your companies.

1. Has your company issued any long-term bonds or notes? If so, read the related note and list any unusual features (e.g., callable, convertible, secured by specific collateral).

2. If your company issued any bonds, were they issued at either a premium or a discount? If so, does the company use the straight-line or effective-interest amortization method?

3. Perform a ratio analysis:

   a. What does the times interest earned ratio measure, in general?

   b. Compute the ratio for the last three years.

   c. What do your results suggest about the company?

   d. If available, find the industry ratio for the most recent year, compare it with your results, and discuss why you believe your company differs from or is similar to the industry ratio.

4. Ratio analysis:

   a. What does the debt-to-equity ratio measure, in general?

   b. Compute the ratio for the last three years.

   c. What do your results suggest about the company?

   d. If available, find the industry ratio for the most recent year, compare it with your results, and discuss why you believe your company differs from or is similar to the industry ratio.

5. During the recent year, how much cash did the company receive on issuing debt? How much did it pay on debt principal? What does management suggest were the reasons for issuing and/or repaying debt during the year?

▦ connect   CONTINUING CASE

▦ **LO10-3**   **CC10-1**   **Recording and Reporting Liabilities**

Pool Corporation Inc. is the world's largest wholesale distributor of swimming pool supplies and equipment. It is a publicly traded corporation that trades on the NASDAQ exchange under the symbol POOL. It sells these products to swimming pool repair and service businesses, swimming pool builders, and retail swimming pool stores. The majority of these customers are small, family-owned businesses. The current financial statements for Pool show that the company borrowed approximately $750,000,000 during 2017. For purposes of this case, assume that Pool borrowed the money on January 1, 2017, at an interest rate of 3.95 percent when the market rate was also 4 percent. The debt matures in 10 years. Pool pays interest on this debt on June 30 and December 31 of each year.

Required:

1. What was the issue price on January 1, 2017?

2. What amounts of interest expense should be recorded on June 30, 2017, and on December 31, 2017?

3. Determine the carrying amounts of the bonds at December 31, 2017, and December 31, 2018.

SOLUTIONS TO SELF-STUDY QUIZZES

Self-Study Quiz 10-1

1.

Note payable (L)	19,932	
Interest expense (E)	3,807	
Cash (A)		23,739

Assets	=	**Liabilities**	+	**Shareholders' Equity**	
Cash −23,739		Note payable −19,932		Interest expense	−3,807

2. Annuity $\times P_{i=3\%, n=10}$ (Table 9C.2, Appendix 9C, 8.5302) = $100,000

   Annuity = $100,000 ÷ 8.5302 = $11,723.05

   Total amount of annuity payments = $11,723.05 × 10 semi-annual periods = $117,230.50

   Total interest paid over the five-year period = $117,230.50 − $100,000 = $17,230.50

3. The total interest paid in this case is lower than $18,699 because a portion of the principal amount is paid every six months instead of once per year. This allows the borrower to save on interest on the remaining unpaid portion of the principal.

Self-Study Quiz 10-2

1. The market rate is the interest rate demanded by creditors. It is the rate used in the present value computations to discount future cash flows. The market interest rate is also called yield, or effective-interest rate.
2. The coupon interest rate is the stated rate on the bonds. It is also called stated rate and contract rate.
3. A bond that sells for less than par is sold at a discount. This occurs when the stated rate is lower than the market rate.
4. A bond that sells for more than par is sold at a premium. This occurs when the coupon rate is higher than the market rate.

Self-Study Quiz 10-3

Principal:	$100,000	×	0.6756	= $ 67,560
Interest:	4,000	×	8.1109	= 32,444
				$100,004

The additional $4 is due to rounding errors.

Self-Study Quiz 10-4

1.

Principal:	$100,000	×	0.4564	= $45,640
Interest:	3,500	×	13.5903	= 47,566
				$93,206

Interest expense, first semi-annual period = $93,206 × (0.08 ÷ 2) = $3,728
Amortization of bond discount = $3,728 − $3,500 = $228
Carrying amount, end of first semi-annual period = $93,206 + $228 = $93,434
Interest expense, second semi-annual period = $93,434 × (0.08 ÷ 2) = $3,737
Interest expense for the first year = $3,728 + $3,737 = $7,465

2. Carrying amount, end of second semi-annual period = $93,434 + $228 = $93,662

Self-Study Quiz 10-5

1.

Amortization Schedule: Bond Premium (effective interest)				
Date	**(a) Interest to Be Paid [$400,000 × 3%]**	**(b) Interest Expense (2% × Carrying Amount, Beginning of Period)**	**(c) Amortization [(a) − (b)]**	**(d) Carrying Amount**
31/12/2017				$454,323
30/6/2018	$12,000	$9,086	$2,914	451,409
31/12/2018	12,000	9,028	2,972	448,437
30/6/2019	12,000	8,969	3,031	445,406

2. The carrying amount at June 30, 2019, is $445,406. This amount is the unpaid balance of the bonds and represents the present value of the remaining payments using the market rate of interest when the bonds were issued. At June 30, 2019, there are 13 interest payments remaining and the principal of the bonds. Their present value is,

Present value = $400,000 × 0.7730 (Table 9C.1, Appendix 9C)
    + $12,000 × 11.3484 (Table 9C.2, Appendix 9C)
    = $445,380 (The difference of $26 is due to rounding.)

Self-Study Quiz 10-6

A company can be forced into bankruptcy if it does not meet its interest obligations to creditors. Many successful companies borrow very large amounts of money without creating unreasonable risk, because they generate sufficient funds from normal operations to meet their obligations. Even a small amount of debt can be a problem if a company does not generate funds to meet current interest obligations. Usually, the company with a high interest coverage ratio (even if it has a high debt-to-equity ratio) is viewed as being less risky than one with a low interest coverage ratio.

Self-Study Quiz 10-7

1. (Amounts are rounded to the nearest dollar.)

Principal:	$100,000	×	0.5537	=	$ 55,370
Interest:	3,500	×	14.8775	=	52,071
					$107,441

2. Interest expense, first semi-annual period = $107,441 × (0.06 ÷ 2) = $3,223.

Bond interest expense (E)	3,223	
Bonds payable (XL)	277	
Cash (A)		3,500

3. Carrying amount, July 1, 2017 = $107,441 − $227 = $107,214
   Interest expense, July 1–December 31, 2017 = $107,214 × (0.06 ÷ 2) = $3,216
   Carrying amount, December 31, 2017 = $107,214 − ($3,500 − $3,216) = $106,930

Self-Study Quiz 10-8

1.

Principal:	$100,000	×	0.4564	=	$45,640
Interest:	$ 3,500	×	13.5903	=	47,566
					$93,206

2. Interest paid = $100,000 × 0.07 = $7,000

3. Interest expense = Interest payment + Amortization of bond discount = $7,000 + $6,794/10
   = $7,679.40

Self-Study Quiz 10-9

1.

Principal:	$100,000	×	0.4564	=	$ 45,640
Interest:	$ 4,500	×	13.5903	=	61,156
					$106,796

2. Interest paid = $100,000 × 0.09 = $9,000

3. Interest expense = Interest payment − Amortization of bond premium = $9,000 − $6,796/10
   = $8,320.40

ENDNOTES

1. An example of a prospectus issued by Bell Canada is available on the SEDAR system (www.sedar.com). Access the website, search for Bell Canada under B, view the documents filed by the company, and select Prospectus supplement—English, dated February 29, 2016.

2. Further details about the bond market are available at www.investinginbonds.com.

3. Standard & Poor's (S&P) has a useful website at www.standardandpoors.com for those interested in learning about the credit ratings used by this credit rating agency.

4. The details of how default risk is rated vary slightly from one agency to another. You can view a sample of these descriptions in detail at www.dbrs.com.

5. The difference between the coupon interest rate and the market interest rate is often very small, usually a fraction of 1 percent, when the bonds are sold. Companies try to sell their bonds at prices close to their par value. However, the market rate of interest continuously changes as a result of such factors as inflation expectations and the level of business activity. It is, therefore, virtually impossible to issue a bond at a point when the coupon rate and the market rate are exactly the same.

6. Alternatively, the bonds payable account could be credited for $345,644, thus eliminating the need to use the discount on bonds payable account. In this case, the bonds payable account is credited periodically for the amount of interest expense that is not paid or accrued (which equals the amortized discount). Appendix 10B provides details of this approach.

7. From Table 9C.2, Chapter 9, the present value of an annuity of $1 discounted at 2 percent for 8 periods.

8. The carrying amount is the present value of the remaining cash payments (eight interest payments and the principal amount), which equals $400,000 × 0.7307 + $12,000 × 6.7327 or $373,072.

9. International Accounting Standards Board, International Accounting Standard 17, Leases (2009): para. 10.

10. The current standard related to lease accounting (IAS 17) has been criticized because the distinction between operating leases and finance leases and the reporting of leases in financial statements does not always provide a faithful representation of leasing arrangements. For this reason, a new international financial reporting standard, IFRS 16 – Leases, will practically eliminate the distinction between operating and finance leases and require the lessees to report the leased property as an asset and the corresponding lease payments as liabilities on their statements of financial position. IFRS 16 is effective for annual periods beginning on or after January 1, 2019.

11. In reality, the debentures were issued on February 29, 2016, they mature on March 2, 2026, and interest payment dates are March 2 and September 2. These dates were changed slightly to simplify the computation of interest accrual.

Reporting and Interpreting Shareholders' Equity

After studying this chapter, you should be able to do the following:

Courtesy of BCE Inc.

Focus Company: **BELL CANADA ENTERPRISES, INC.**

FINANCING CORPORATE GROWTH WITH CAPITAL SUPPLIED BY OWNERS

ell Canada Enterprises Inc. (BCE) (www.bce.ca) is Canada's largest communications company. It provides voice, data, and image communications services to millions of global customers. BCE has achieved its current size and profitability through investments in and acquisitions of other companies. But the business continues to change rapidly as customers demand different and more services at competitive prices.

In order to continue to thrive and grow, BCE has invested more in state-of-the-art fibre and mobile networks and product research and development in order to expand its broadband access to all of BCE's services on any screen the customer chooses. The company closely manages its statement of financial position and, in particular, its capital structure—that is, the proportion of debt and equity used to finance its growth. BCE wants to ensure a strong credit profile in order both to encourage new investment and to increase the dividends paid to its shareholders.

In Chapters 9 and 10, we discussed the role of liabilities in the capital structure of a company. In this chapter, we study both the role that shareholders' equity plays in building a successful business and the strategies that managers use to maximize shareholders' wealth.

UNDERSTANDING THE BUSINESS

To some people, the words *corporation* and *business* are almost synonymous. You have probably heard friends refer to a career in business as "the corporate world." Equating business and corporations is understandable, because corporations are the dominant form of business organization in terms of volume of operations. If you were to write the names of 50 familiar companies on a piece of paper, probably all of them would be corporations.

The popularity of the corporate form can be attributed to a critical advantage that corporations have over sole proprietorships and partnerships. They can raise large amounts of capital because both large and small investors can easily participate in their ownership. This ease of participation is related to three important factors:

- Shares can be purchased in small amounts. You could buy a single share of BCE for approximately $43 at the time of writing this chapter and become one of the owners of this company.

- Ownership interest can easily be transferred through the sale of shares on established markets, such as the Toronto Stock Exchange (TSX).

- Stock ownership provides investors with limited liability.[1]

Many Canadians own shares, either directly or indirectly through a mutual fund or pension program. Share ownership offers them the opportunity to earn higher returns than they otherwise could on deposits to bank accounts or investments in corporate bonds. Unfortunately, share ownership also involves higher risk of loss of the investment in shares. The proper balance between risk and the expected return on an investment depends on individual preferences.

BCE's statement of financial position at December 31, 2015, reports total equity of $17,329 million, as indicated in Exhibit 11.1. For most corporations, shareholders' equity includes two primary sources:

Exhibit 11.1

Shareholders' Equity Sections of Consolidated Statements of Financial Position

REAL-WORLD EXCERPT

BCE Inc.

ANNUAL REPORT

CONSOLIDATED STATEMENTS OF FINANCIAL POSITION (PARTIAL) SHAREHOLDERS' EQUITY At December 31			
(in millions of Canadian dollars)	Note	2015	2014
Equity attributable to BCE shareholders			
Preferred shares	24, 25	$ 4,004	$ 4,004
Common shares	24, 25	18,100	16,717
Shares subject to cancellation			
Contributed surplus	24, 25	1,150	1,141
Accumulated other comprehensive income (loss)		119	97
Deficit	24	(6,350)	(7,013)
Total equity attributable to BCE shareholders		17,023	14,946
Non-controlling interest	24, 29	306	293
Total equity		17,329	15,239
Total liabilities and equity		47,993	46,297

Source: BCE Inc., Annual Report 2015.

1. *Contributed capital*, which reflects the amount invested by shareholders, has two distinct components: (*a*) amounts initially received from the sale of shares and (*b*) contributed surplus that reflects contributions made by shareholders in excess of the amounts credited to share capital accounts. BCE's contributed capital accounts are preferred shares, common shares, and contributed surplus.

2. *Retained earnings* are generated by the profit-making activities of the company. This is the cumulative amount of net earnings since the corporation's organization, less the cumulative amount of dividends paid by the corporation since organization.[2]

Most companies generate a significant portion of their shareholders' equity from retained earnings rather than from capital raised through the sale of shares. In the case of BCE, Exhibit 11.1 shows a negative amount, a deficit, which suggests that BCE has not been a profitable company. We will address this interesting issue as well as other details of Exhibit 11.1 later in this chapter.

Exhibit 11.2 reports the changes that occurred to the various components of shareholders' equity during fiscal year 2015. This exhibit looks fairly complicated, but the main changes that took place in 2015 relate to issuance of common shares, reporting of net earnings, and distribution of dividends. We will refer to this exhibit for specific transactions throughout the chapter.

Exhibit **11.2**

Consolidated Statements of Changes in Equity

REAL-WORLD EXCERPT

BCE Inc.

ANNUAL REPORT

For the Year Ended December 31, 2015 (In millions of Canadian dollars)	Note	CONSOLIDATED STATEMENTS OF CHANGES IN EQUITY ATTRIBUTED TO BCE SHAREHOLDERS						Non-controlling Interest	Total Equity
		Preferred Shares	Common Shares	Contributed Surplus	Accumulated Other Comprehensive Income	Deficit	Total		
Balance at January 1, 2015		4,004	16,717	1,141	97	(7,013)	14,946	293	15,239
Net earnings		–	–	–	–	2,678	2,678	52	2,730
Other comprehensive income		–	–	–	22	429	451	2	453
Total comprehensive income		–	–	–	22	3,107	3,129	54	3,183
Common shares issued under employee stock option plan	25	–	96	(7)	–	–	89	–	89
Common shares issued under employee savings plan	25	–	128	–	–	–	128	–	128
Other share-based compensation		–	–	16	–	(53)	(37)	–	(37)
Dividends declared on BCE common and preferred shares		–	–	–	–	(2,365)	(2,365)	–	(2,365)
Dividends declared by subsidiaries to non-controlling interest		–	–	–	–	–	–	(41)	(41)
Common shares issued under bought deal offering	25	–	863	–	–	(26)	837	–	837
Common shares issued for the acquisition of Glentel Inc.	3, 25	–	296	–	–	–	296	–	296
Balance at December 31, 2015		4,004	18,100	1,150	119	(6,350)	17,023	306	17,329

Source: BCE Inc., Annual Report 2015.

ORGANIZATION OF THE CHAPTER

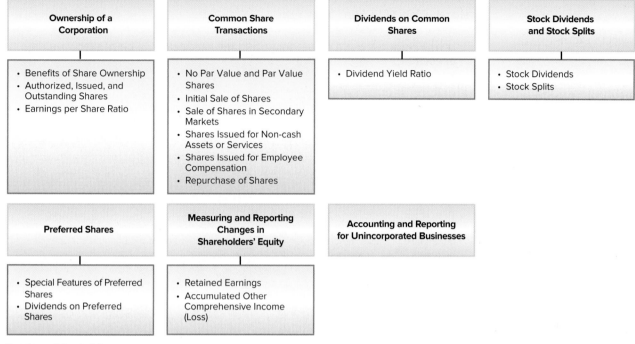

Supplemental material:

Appendix 11A: Accounting for Owners' Equity for Sole Proprietorships and Partnerships

OWNERSHIP OF A CORPORATION

The corporation is the only business form that the law recognizes as a separate entity. As a distinct entity, the corporation enjoys a continuous existence, separate and apart from its owners. It may own assets, incur liabilities, expand and contract in size, sue others, be sued, and enter into contracts independent of the shareholders.

To protect everyone's rights, both the creation and governance of corporations are tightly regulated by law. Corporations are created by making application to the federal government or a provincial government. The Canada Business Corporations Act (CBCA) outlines all of the legal requirements of federal incorporation (www.laws. justice.gc.ca).

To create a corporation, an application for a charter must be submitted to the appropriate government authorities. The application must specify the name of the corporation, the purpose (type of business), the types and number of shares authorized, and a minimum amount of capital that the owners must invest at the date of organization. Upon approval of the application, the government issues a charter, sometimes called the *articles of incorporation*. Each corporation is governed by a board of directors elected by the shareholders.

Benefits of Share Ownership When you invest in a corporation, you are known as a *shareholder*, or *stockholder*. As a shareholder, you receive shares that you can subsequently sell on established stock exchanges without affecting the corporation.

Owners of common shares receive the following benefits:

1. **A voice in management.** They may vote at the shareholders' meeting (or by proxy) on major issues concerning management of the corporation.[3]

2. **Dividends.** They receive a proportionate share of the distribution of the corporation's net earnings.

3. **Residual claim.** They may receive a proportionate share of the distribution of remaining assets upon the liquidation of the company.

LO11-1

Explain the role of share capital in the capital structure of a corporation.

Owners, unlike creditors, are able to vote at the annual shareholders' meeting. The following notice of the annual and special meeting of shareholders was sent to all shareholders of BCE in March 2016.

LETTER FROM THE CHAIR OF THE BOARD AND THE PRESIDENT AND CHIEF EXECUTIVE OFFICER

Dear fellow shareholders,

It is our pleasure to invite you to BCE's 2015 Annual General Shareholder Meeting to be held at 9:30 a.m. on Thursday, April 30, 2015, at the Design Exchange in Toronto.

If you are unable to attend in person, a live webcast of the meeting will be available on our website at BCE.ca.

As a shareholder, you have the right to vote your shares on all items that come before the meeting. Your vote is important and we encourage you to exercise your right in the manner that suits you best. We facilitate this process by enabling you to vote by proxy on the Internet, by phone, by fax or by mail. You can also vote in person at the meeting.

This circular provides details about all the items for consideration at the meeting, including information about nominated directors and their compensation, the auditors, our corporate governance practices, reports from the four standing committees of the Board, and shareholder proposals. It also contains detailed information about our philosophy, policies and programs for executive compensation and how your Board receives input from shareholders on these matters.

At the meeting, we will review our financial position, business operations and the value we are delivering to shareholders. We also look forward to responding to your questions.

Thank you for your support and continued confidence in BCE. We look forward to seeing you at this year's meeting.

Sincerely,

Thomas C. O'Neill   George A. Cope
Chair of the Board   President and CEO

March 5, 2015

Source: BCE Inc., Notice of 2015 Annual General Shareholder Meeting and Management Proxy Circular.

The notice of the annual meeting was accompanied by a *management information* (or *proxy*) *circular* that contained several pages of information concerning the people who were nominated to be members of the board of directors. Since most owners do not actually attend the annual meeting, the notice included a proxy card, which is similar to an absentee ballot. Each owner may complete the proxy and mail it to the company, which will include it in the votes at the annual meeting.

Shareholders have ultimate authority in a corporation, as shown in Exhibit 11.3. The board of directors and, indirectly, all the employees are accountable to the shareholders. The organizational structure shown in Exhibit 11.3 is typical of most corporations, but the specific structure depends on the nature of the company's business.

Authorized, Issued, and Outstanding Shares

The **AUTHORIZED NUMBER OF SHARES** is the maximum number of shares that a corporation can issue, as specified in the charter.

When a corporation is created, its corporate charter specifies the type and maximum number of shares that it can sell to the public. This maximum is called the **authorized number of shares**. Typically, the corporate charter authorizes a larger number of shares than the corporation expects to issue initially. This strategy provides future flexibility for the issuance of additional shares without the need to amend the charter. In the case of BCE, the number of authorized common shares is unlimited.

The term **ISSUED SHARES** refers to the number of shares that have been issued.

The term **OUTSTANDING SHARES** refers to the total number of shares that are owned by shareholders on any particular date.

The number of **issued shares** and the number of **outstanding shares**—that is, the total number of shares that are owned by shareholders on any particular date—are determined by the corporation's equity transactions. For BCE, the numbers of issued shares and outstanding shares are the same; at December 31, 2015, this number was 865.6 million. The number of issued shares may differ from the number of outstanding shares if the company has bought back some of its shares from shareholders. If a corporation needs to sell more shares than its charter authorizes, it must seek permission from the current shareholders to modify the charter.

Exhibit 11.4 defines and illustrates the terms usually used in relation to corporate shares.

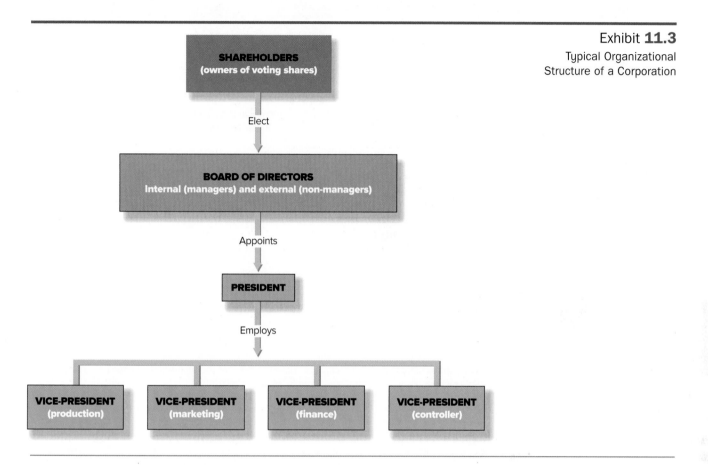

Exhibit **11.3**
Typical Organizational
Structure of a Corporation

Exhibit **11.4**
Authorized, Issued, and
Outstanding Shares

Definitions	Illustrations		
Authorized number of shares:			
The maximum number of shares that can be issued, as specified in the charter of the corporation.	The charter specifies "an unlimited number of common shares."		
Issued number of shares:			
The total number of shares that the corporation has issued to date.	To date, XYZ Corporation has sold and issued 30,000 common shares.		
Un-issued number of shares:			
The number of authorized shares that have never been issued to date.	Authorized shares Issued shares Un-issued shares	100,000 (30,000) 70,000	
Treasury shares:*			
Shares that have been issued to investors and then reacquired by the issuing corporation.	To date, XYZ Corporation has repurchased 1,000 previously issued shares.		
Outstanding number of shares:			
The number of shares currently owned by shareholders–that is, the number of shares authorized, minus the total number of un-issued shares, minus the number of treasury shares.	Authorized shares Treasury shares Un-issued shares Outstanding shares	100,000 (1,000) (70,000) 29,000	

*Notice that when treasury shares are held, the number of shares issued and the number outstanding differ by the number of treasury shares held (treasury shares are included in "issued" but not in "outstanding").

EARNINGS PER SHARE RATIO

KEY RATIO ANALYSIS

LO11-2

Analyze the earnings per share ratio.

ANALYTICAL QUESTION → How profitable is a company?

RATIO AND COMPARISONS → The *earnings per share* (EPS) is a measure of the return on investment that is based on the number of shares outstanding instead of the dollar amounts reported on the statement of financial position. In simple situations, it is computed as follows:

$$\text{Earnings per share} = \frac{\text{Net earnings available to common shareholders}}{\text{Average number of common shares outstanding}}$$

The 2015 ratio for BCE is,

$$\frac{\$2,526}{847.1} = \$2.98$$

Comparisons over Time			Comparisons with Competitors	
BCE			Rogers Communications	TELUS
2013	**2014**	**2015**	**2015**	**2015**
$2.55	$2.98	$2.98	$2.68	$2.29

INTERPRETATIONS

In General → All analysts and investors are interested in a company's earnings. You have probably seen newspaper headlines announcing a company's earnings. Notice that those news stories normally report EPS. The reason is simple. Numbers are much easier to compare on a per share basis. For example, in 2015, BCE reported $2,526 million of earnings attributable to common shareholders compared to $2,363 million in 2014. If we make that comparison on a per share basis, EPS did not change. It remained at $2.98 because of the proportional increase in the number of common shares outstanding during the year.

Focus Company Analysis → BCE has a strategy of growth and reinvestment of earnings. Analysts are watching EPS to be sure the company will achieve its strategy. BCE's EPS increased from $2.55 in 2013 to $2.98 in 2015. Its EPS in 2015 exceeds the EPS figures of its competitors. However, comparison of the EPS figures for the three companies may not be very informative as a measure of profitability of shareholders' investments in these companies. The reason is simple: shares of different companies are likely to have different prices, which makes EPS comparisons less meaningful than other measures of profitability.

A Few Cautions → While EPS is an effective and widely used measure of profitability, it can be misleading if there are significant differences in the market values of the shares being compared. Two companies earning $1.50 per share might appear to be comparable, but if shares in one company cost $10 while shares of the other cost $175, they are not comparable. For example, BCE's stock price was $38.6 at December 31, 2015. But the stock price of Rogers Communications was $47.7 at that date, even though BCE has a higher EPS figure. Obviously, investors expect a large EPS number for companies with higher stock prices.

COMMON SHARE TRANSACTIONS

LO11-3

Describe the characteristics of common shares, and analyze transactions affecting common shares.

COMMON SHARES are the basic voting shares issued by a corporation; called *residual equity* because they rank after preferred shares for dividend and liquidation distributions.

Corporations issue two types of shares: common shares and preferred shares. All corporations issue common shares, while only some issue preferred shares, which grant preferences that the common shares do not have. In this section, we discuss common shares, and in a subsequent section we discuss preferred shares.

Common shares are the basic voting shares issued by a corporation. They are often called the *residual equity* because they rank after the preferred shares for dividend and asset distribution upon liquidation of the corporation. The dividend rate for common shares is determined by the board of directors based on the company's profitability, unlike the dividend rate on preferred shares which is determined by contract. When the company is not profitable, the board may cut or eliminate dividends on common shares, but in most cases it cannot reduce preferred dividends.

No Par Value and Par Value Shares

Par value is the nominal value per share established in the charter of a corporation. It has no relationship to the market value per share. The CBCA and most provincial corporation acts prohibit the issuance of par value shares. The few Canadian companies that still have par value shares outstanding issued them before the CBCA was amended in 1985. For this reason, the remainder of this chapter focuses on **no par value shares**, which do not have an amount per share specified in the corporate charter. In contrast, most U.S. corporations issue par value shares.

The original purpose of requiring corporations to specify a par value per share was to establish a minimum permanent amount of capital that the owners could not withdraw as long as the corporation existed. Thus, owners could not withdraw all of their capital in anticipation of a bankruptcy, which would leave creditors with an empty corporate shell. This permanent amount of capital is called **legal capital**. The requirement that shares not be issued for less than their par value often resulted in par values that were too small to be effectively meaningful. This notion of legal capital has lost its significance over time, because the par values of shares have been set at very low amounts by issuing corporations. In contrast, when a corporation issues no par value shares, the legal capital is the initial amount received from shareholders.

BCE's corporate charter authorizes the issue of no par value common shares. However, its preferred shares have a stated value upon which the dividend payments are based. This stated value has no relationship to the market value of the preferred shares.

PAR VALUE is the nominal value per share specified in the charter; it serves as the basis for legal capital.

NO PAR VALUE SHARES are shares that have no par value specified in the corporate charter.

LEGAL CAPITAL is the permanent amount of capital defined by law that must remain invested in the business; it serves as a cushion for creditors.

Initial Sale of Shares

Two names are applied to transactions involving the initial sale of a company's shares to the public. An *initial public offering*, or *IPO*, involves the very first sale of a company's shares to the public (i.e., when the company first "goes public"). You have probably heard the story of Facebook, for example, whose shares decreased dramatically in value after its IPO. While investors sometimes earn significant returns on IPOs, they also take significant risks. Once the shares of a company are traded on established markets, additional sales of new shares to the public are called *seasoned new issues* or *secondary share offerings*.

As was the case with debt (discussed in Chapter 10), most companies use an underwriter to assist in the sale of shares. The underwriter is usually an investment bank that acts as an intermediary between the corporation and the investors. The underwriter advises the corporation on matters concerning the sale and is directly involved in the sale of shares to the public.

Most sales of shares to the public are cash transactions. To illustrate accounting for an initial sale of shares, assume that BCE sold 100,000 common shares for $45 per share. The company records the following journal entry:

Cash (A) (100,000 × $45)			4,500,000	
Common shares (SE)				4,500,000
Assets	**=**	**Liabilities**	**+**	**Shareholders' Equity**
Cash +4,500,000				Common shares +4,500,000

In 2015, BCE issued new shares for $1,383 million, as shown in Exhibit 11.2. These shares were issued for various purposes, including the exercise of stock options, as explained later in the chapter.

Sale of Shares in Secondary Markets

When a company sells shares to the public, the transaction is between the issuing corporation and the buyer. Subsequent to the initial sale, investors can sell shares to other investors without directly affecting the corporation. For example, if investor

Eric Mortisson sold 1,000 of BCE's common shares to Jennifer Hussein, BCE does not record a journal entry on its books. Eric received cash for the shares he sold, and Jennifer received shares for the cash she paid. BCE itself did not receive or pay anything because of this transaction.

Each business day, the financial information service providers, such as bloomberg. com, reuters.com, finance.yahoo.com, and money.msn.com, report the results of thousands of transactions between investors in the secondary markets, where trading of shares takes place. These markets include the Toronto Stock Exchange (TSX) and TSX Venture Exchange in Canada; the New York Stock Exchange (NYSE), American Stock Exchange, and NASDAQ in the United States; and similar markets in other countries.

Managers of corporations closely follow the movements in the price of their company's shares. Shareholders expect to earn money on their investment from both dividends and increases in the share (or stock) price. In many instances, senior management has been replaced because of poor performance of the shares in the secondary markets. Although managers watch the share price on a daily basis, it is important to remember that the transactions between investors do not directly affect the company's financial statements.

GOING PUBLIC

FINANCIAL ANALYSIS

As noted earlier, an IPO is the first sale of shares to the public. Prior to that sale, the company is a private company. A company might want to go public for one of two common reasons. In some cases, for the company to grow and meet consumer demand, it must expand its productive capacity. The need for new capital may be beyond the capability of the private owners. By going public, the company can raise the funds needed to expand.

In other cases, the company may not need significant funds, but the current owners may want to create a market for its shares. Often, selling shares is difficult if the company is not listed on a major stock exchange. By going public, a company can increase the marketability of its shares.

IPOs often create a lot of interest among investors. Some good opportunities are available to earn excellent returns by investing in growing companies. Substantial risk is also associated with many IPOs.

In recent years, much interest has surrounded Internet companies that have gone public. For example, Facebook Inc., which allows people to communicate with each other, post photos, and share information through a mobile application, had an IPO of its shares in May 2012 at an initial price of $29.6. Since then, Facebook's share price increased significantly, reaching $114.4 by June 2016 because of investors' expectations of the company's future profitability.

There are countless stories of people in their 20's and 30's who have become instant millionaires after the IPO of a new Internet company. Less well publicized, however, are the stories of individuals who have lost money investing in shares of new and unproven businesses.

Shares Issued for Non-cash Assets or Services

Small companies are playing an increasingly important role in the North American economy. Often, they are private enterprises that account for a large percentage of the new jobs that have been created in the past decade. Many of today's corporate giants were small start-up companies just a few years ago. Companies such as Dell, Microsoft, Amazon.com, Google Inc., and Facebook Inc. began, literally, as basement operations in the homes of their founders.

One feature common to all start-up companies is a shortage of cash. Because these companies often cannot afford to pay cash for needed assets and services, they sometimes issue shares to people who can supply these assets and services. Many executives, for instance, will join start-up companies for very low salaries because they also earn compensation in the form of common shares. An executive who was granted Google shares during its early days would be very wealthy today.

When a company issues shares to acquire assets or services, the acquired items are recorded at the *market value* of the shares issued at the date of the transaction, in accordance with the *cost principle*. If the market value of the shares issued cannot be determined, the market value of the consideration received should be used.

To illustrate, assume that during its early years of operation, BCE was unable to pay cash for needed legal services. The company issued 10,000 shares to a law firm when a share was selling for $15. At that time, the company recorded the following journal entry:

Legal fees (E)	150,000	
Common shares (SE)		150,000

Assets	=	Liabilities	+	Shareholders' Equity	
				Legal fees	−150,000
				Common shares	+150,000

Notice that the value of the legal services received is assumed to be the same as the value of the shares that were issued. This assumption is reasonable, because two independent parties usually keep negotiating a deal until the value of what is given up equals the value of what is received.

Shares Issued for Employee Compensation

One of the advantages of the corporate form is the possibility to separate the management of a business from its ownership. This separation can also be a disadvantage because some managers may not act in the best interests of shareholders. This problem can be overcome in a number of ways. Compensation packages can be developed to reward managers for meeting goals that are important to shareholders. Another strategy is to offer managers *stock options*, which permit them to buy shares at a fixed price.

The holder of a stock option has an interest in a company's performance in the same manner as a shareholder. Stock option plans have become an increasingly common form of compensation over the past few years. However, the excessive use of stock options as a form of compensating key executives led the executives of some companies to manipulate reported financial information in an effort to increase the share price, allowing them to benefit by buying shares at a fixed price and selling them at a higher price for a profit.

The BCE annual report provides the following disclosures with respect to its future contractual obligations related to stock options:

NOTES TO CONSOLIDATED FINANCIAL STATEMENTS

Note 24. Share-Based Payments

The following table summarizes BCE's outstanding stock options at December 31, 2015 and 2014.

	Note	2015		2014	
		Number of Options	Weighted Average Exercise Price ($)	Number of Options	Weighted Average Exercise Price ($)
Outstanding, January 1		9,278,190	$43	7,870,231	$40
Granted		2,835,667	$56	2,915,361	$48
Exercised[1]	25	(2,289,677)	$39	(1,372,006)	$36
Forfeited		(157,276)	$49	(135,396)	$44
Outstanding, December 31		9,666,904	$48	9,278,190	$43
Exercisable, December 31		1,174,191	$38	865,600	$36

(1) The weighted average share price for options exercised was $56 and $49 in 2015 and 2014, respectively.

Source: BCE Inc., Annual Report 2015.

The options issued by BCE specify that shares could be bought at a predetermined exercise price. Granting a stock option is a form of compensation even if the exercise price and the current share price are the same.

Stock options are a widely used form of executive compensation. Most companies offer them with an exercise price equal to the current market price per share. For example, assume that BCE granted a key employee options to purchase a total of 10,000 common shares in the future at an average price of $40, which equals the market price per share on the date of the grant. The option holder would benefit from the stock option in a few years if the market price per share exceeded $40, presumably because the increase in BCE's market value would be partially attributed to the employee's managerial skills. Undoubtedly, the difference between the increased market price and the exercise price of $40 is a form of taxable compensation to the employee. Exhibit 11.2 shows that BCE issued common shares for $96 million on exercise of stock options during 2015.

When the options are exercised, BCE receives $40 per common share, while it could have obtained a higher price if it sold the same shares in the market to other investors. Clearly, the exercise of employee stock options entails a cost to BCE that should be measured and reported. The more interesting issue, however, is whether BCE incurs a cost at the time of granting the options. In general, a fair value of the options can be estimated by using specific valuation methods and then comparing with the exercise price to determine the additional compensation expense for the period.

In 2015, BCE granted its key employees 2,835,667 stock options at a weighted-average exercise price of $56 per share, and 2,289,677 stock options were exercised by employees during that year.

The measurement and reporting of the cost of stock options has been hotly debated by accounting standard setters and company executives. Many companies rely on stock options to compensate their employees and key executives, especially in the technology, energy, and gold mining sectors. Companies in these sectors have lobbied against reporting the cost of stock options as an expense on the statement of earnings, because it lowers their net earnings, and may even turn net earnings into losses.

Canadian companies must estimate and report compensation expense associated with stock options. The specific procedures to compute the compensation expense are covered in intermediate accounting courses.

Repurchase of Shares

A corporation may want to purchase its own shares from existing shareholders for a number of reasons. One common reason is to increase the market price per share and EPS that result from the reduction in the number of outstanding shares.

Most Canadian companies cancel their shares when they buy them back from shareholders. When shares are cancelled, the appropriate share capital account is reduced by an amount that reflects the average issuance price per share. If the purchase price is less than the average issuance price, the difference is credited to contributed surplus. For example, if BCE purchases 50,000 common shares in the open market at $30 per share and the average price of the previously issued common shares is $34,[4] the journal entry and the transaction effects will be as follows:

Common shares (SE) (50,000 × $34)	1,700,000	
Cash (A)		1,500,000
Contributed surplus (SE)		200,000

Assets	=	Liabilities	+	Shareholders' Equity	
Cash	−1,500,000			Common shares	−1,700,000
				Contributed surplus	+200,000

Repurchases of shares at prices lower than the average issue price do not result in profit for the issuing company because they are capital transactions, not operating transactions. Companies profit from buying and selling shares issued by other companies, but not their own shares.[5]

Assume, further, that BCE subsequently purchased 50,000 of its own common shares when the price per share was $40. In this case, the excess of the purchase price over the issuance price is $6 per share for a total of $300,000. This difference is debited first to contributed surplus to the extent of $200,000 (the account balance), and the remaining amount of $100,000 is debited to retained earnings. The retained earnings account is reduced, because the excess of the purchase price over the contribution made previously by shareholders reflects the company's profitable operations, which resulted in net earnings and caused an increase in share price. Hence, the $100,000 is viewed as a distribution of accumulated net earnings, or retained earnings, to shareholders who sold their shares to the company. The journal entry and the transaction effects follow:

Common shares (SE) (50,000 × $34)	1,700,000	
Contributed surplus (SE)	200,000	
Retained earnings (SE)	100,000	
Cash (A)		2,000,000

Assets		=	Liabilities	+	Shareholders' Equity	
Cash	−2,000,000				Common shares	−1,700,000
					Contributed surplus	−200,000
					Retained earnings	−100,000

Contributed surplus related to one class of shares, such as common shares, can be used only for share transactions involving the same class of shares.

The disclosures in Exhibit 11.2 show that BCE did not repurchase common shares in 2015. The last share repurchase transactions occurred in 2012 and resulted in cash payment of $107 million with reductions of $46 million in the common shares account, $3 million in the contributed surplus account, and $58 million in the retained earnings account (increase in deficit).

PAUSE FOR FEEDBACK

We have looked at several transactions involving the sale and repurchase of common shares. In the next section, we will discuss dividends. Before you move on, complete the following questions to test your understanding of share repurchase transactions.

SELF-STUDY QUIZ 11-1

A recent annual report for BCE Inc. included the following statement:

> During the year, BCE repurchased and cancelled a total of 3,500,466 common shares for a total cost of $143 million. Of the total cost, $61 million represents stated capital and $4 million represents the reduction of the contributed surplus attributable to these common shares. The remaining $78 million was charged to the deficit.

1. Use the information above to reconstruct the journal entry to record the repurchase transaction.

2. Compute the average issuance price of BCE's common shares prior to the repurchase transaction.

After you complete your answers, check them with the solutions at the end of the chapter.

DIVIDENDS ON COMMON SHARES

Investors buy common shares because they expect a return on their investment. This return can come in two forms: appreciation of the share price, and dividends. Some investors prefer to buy shares that pay little or no dividends, because companies that

LO11-4

Discuss dividends, and analyze related transactions.

reinvest the majority of their earnings tend to increase their future earnings potential, along with their stock price. Wealthy investors in high tax brackets prefer to receive their return on equity investments in the form of higher stock prices, because capital gains may be taxed at a lower rate than dividend income. Other investors, such as retired people who need a steady income, prefer to receive their return on an investment in the form of dividends. These people often seek shares that will pay very high dividends, such as shares of utility companies.

A corporation does not have a legal obligation to pay dividends. While creditors can force a company into bankruptcy if it does not meet required interest payments on debt, shareholders do not have a similar right if a corporation is unable to pay dividends. Although a corporation does not have a legal obligation to pay a dividend, a liability is created when the board of directors approves (i.e., declares) a dividend.

Without a qualifier, the term *dividend* means a cash dividend, but dividends can also be paid in assets other than cash or by issuing additional shares. The most common type of dividend is a cash dividend.

A dividend declaration by BCE's board of directors includes three important dates:

> The **DECLARATION DATE** is the date on which the board of directors officially approves a dividend.

1. The **declaration date** is the date on which the board of directors officially approved the dividend. As soon as it makes the declaration, it creates a dividend liability.

> The **DATE OF RECORD** is the date on which the corporation prepares the list of current shareholders as shown on its records; dividends can be paid only to the shareholders who own shares on that date.

2. The **date of record** follows the declaration; it is the date on which the corporation prepares the list of current shareholders, based on its shareholder records. The dividend is payable only to those names listed on the record date. No journal entry is made on this date.

> The **PAYMENT DATE** is the date on which a cash dividend is paid to the shareholders of record.

3. The **payment date** is the date on which the cash is disbursed to pay the dividend liability. It follows the date of record as specified in the dividend announcement.

BCE pays cash dividends on its outstanding common shares on a quarterly basis. The quarterly dividend on common shares is often increased when the company's profitability increases. For example, BCE increased its dividend per common share from $0.34 in 1998 to $0.6825 in 2016. In some cases, however, a corporation may reduce or even suspend dividend payments to common shareholders if its financial situation deteriorates. BCE provides details of the quarterly dividends on its preferred and common shares on its website. For example, details related to the cash dividends on common shares declared during 2016 are as follows:

REAL-WORLD EXCERPT

BCE Inc.

DIVIDEND INFORMATION

Date of Declaration	Date of Record	Date of Payment	Amount of Dividend
February 3, 2016	March 15, 2016	April 15, 2016	$0.6825
April 27, 2016	June 15, 2016	July 15, 2016	$0.6825
August 3, 2016	September 15, 2016	October 15, 2016	$0.6825
November 2, 2016	December 15, 2016	January 15, 2017	$0.6825

Source: www.bce.ca/investors/dividendinfo/dividenddates

For instructional purposes, the time lag between the date of declaration and the date of payment may be ignored because it does not pose any substantive issues. When all three dates fall in the same accounting period, a single entry on the date of payment may be made for purely practical reasons.

Assume, for simplicity, that BCE had 875 million common shares outstanding on November 2, 2016. The total amount of cash dividends paid on January 15, 2017, is therefore $587,187,500.

The declaration of dividends creates a liability on November 2, 2016, that is recorded as follows:

Dividends declared—Common (SE)	587,187,500	
Dividend payable—Common (L)		587,187,500

Assets	=	**Liabilities**	+	**Shareholders' Equity**
		Dividends payable—Common		Dividends declared—Common
		+587,187,500		−587,187,500

The payment of the dividends on common shares on January 15, 2017, is recorded as follows:

Dividends payable—Common (L)		587,187,500		
Cash (A)				587,187,500
Assets	**=**	**Liabilities**	**+**	**Shareholders' Equity**
Cash		Dividends payable—Common		
−587,187,500		+587,187,500		

Notice that the declaration and payment of a cash dividend have two impacts: they reduce assets (cash) and shareholders' equity (retained earnings) by the same amount. This observation explains the two fundamental requirements for the payment of a cash dividend:

1. *Sufficient retained earnings.* The corporation must have accumulated a sufficient amount of retained earnings to cover the amount of the dividend. Incorporation laws often limit cash dividends to the balance in the retained earnings account. BCE reports a deficit instead of retained earnings in its statement of financial position, as shown in Exhibit 11.2, yet it has declared cash dividends to its shareholders during 2015. How is that possible? According to section 42 of the CBCA, a corporation may declare and pay dividends if payment of the dividend does not place the company into a position that would prevent it from paying its liabilities as they become due. BCE's statement of financial position at December 31, 2015, shows that the carrying amount of its assets far exceeds the carrying amount of its liabilities. In addition, BCE's statement of cash flows shows that the company generated $6.3 billion from operating activities in 2015. BCE's liquidity position allowed its board of directors to declare and pay dividends even though its retained earnings account has a debit balance.

2. *Sufficient cash.* The corporation must have access to sufficient cash to pay the dividend and to meet the operating needs of the business. The mere fact that the retained earnings account has a large credit balance does not mean that the board of directors can declare and pay a cash dividend. The cash generated in the past by earnings represented in the retained earnings account may have been expended to acquire inventory, buy operational assets, and pay liabilities. Consequently, no necessary relationship exists between the balance of retained earnings and the balance of cash on any particular date. Quite simply, retained earnings is not cash.

Exhibit 11.2 indicates that BCE declared dividends on preferred and common shares for a total amount of $2,365 million in 2015, which is less than the net earnings for 2015.

The company has established a dividend reinvestment plan that allows shareholders to receive additional common shares instead of cash dividends. It also encourages its employees to purchase BCE common shares through an employee savings plan, whereby employees can use a percentage of their salaries to buy BCE common shares through regular payroll deductions.

IMPACT OF DIVIDENDS ON SHARE PRICE

FINANCIAL
ANALYSIS

When a company declares a dividend, it is important to establish which shareholders receive the dividend. For this reason, the stock exchanges set an *ex-dividend date*, which is normally two business days before the date of record, to make certain that dividend cheques are sent to the right shareholders. If you buy shares before the ex-dividend date, you receive the dividend. If you buy the shares on the ex-dividend date or later, the previous shareholder receives the dividend. While this date is important in understanding dividends, it has no accounting implications.

If you follow share prices, you will notice that the price of a company's common share often falls on the ex-dividend date. The reason is simple. On that date, the share is worth less because it no longer includes the right to receive the next dividend.

PAUSE FOR FEEDBACK

One of the reasons that investors buy common shares is to earn dividends. We have looked at dividends paid in cash. In the next section, we will look at dividends paid in shares. Before you move on, complete the following questions to test your understanding of cash dividends.

SELF-STUDY QUIZ 11-2

The board of directors of TELUS Corporation declared on May 5, 2016, a quarterly dividend of $0.46 per share on issued and outstanding common shares, payable on July 4, 2016, to holders of record at the close of business on June 10, 2016. Assume that TELUS had 603 million common shares outstanding on the declaration date. Answer the following questions concerning this dividend:

1. On which date is a liability created?

2. On which date does a cash outflow occur?

3. Prepare the journal entry to record the payment of the dividend.

4. What are the three fundamental requirements for the payment of a dividend?

After you complete your answers, check them with the solutions at the end of this chapter.

Because of the importance of dividends to many investors, analysts often compute the dividend yield ratio to evaluate a corporation's dividend policy.

DIVIDEND YIELD RATIO

KEY RATIO ANALYSIS

LO11-5

Analyze the dividend yield ratio.

ANALYTICAL QUESTION → Investors in common shares expect to earn a return on their investment. A portion of this return comes in the form of dividends. How much do investors earn on their investment based on dividends?

RATIO AND COMPARISONS → The *dividend yield ratio* is a measure of the percentage return that shareholders earn from the dividends they receive. Potential investors often use this ratio to help select among alternative investment opportunities. In 2015, BCE declared four quarterly dividends of $0.65 per share for a total of $2.60 per share. The ratio is computed as follows:

$$\text{Dividend yield ratio} = \frac{\text{Dividends per share}}{\text{Market price per share}}$$

The 2015 ratio for BCE is

$$\frac{\$2.60}{\$53.46} = 0.049, \text{ or } 4.9\%$$

Comparisons over Time				Comparisons with Competitors	
BCE				Rogers Communications*	TELUS*
2013	**2014**	**2015**		**2015**	**2015**
5.1%	4.6%	4.9%		4.0%	6.1%

*The fiscal years of both Rogers Communications and TELUS ended on January 30, 2016.

INTERPRETATIONS

In General → Investors in common shares earn a return from dividends and capital appreciation (increases in the market price of the shares they own). Growth-oriented companies often pay out very small amounts of dividends and rely on increases in their market price to provide a return to investors. Others pay out large dividends but have more stable market prices. Each type of share appeals to different types of investors with different risk and return preferences.

Focus Company Analysis → During the three years 2013 through 2015, BCE distributed annual dividends of $2.33, $2.47, and $2.60 per share, respectively. Its share price was $46.0, $53.28, and $53.46 on December 31, 2013, 2014, and 2015, respectively. BCE's dividend yield was relatively stable over the three-year period, and between those of Rogers Communications and TELUS.

A Few Cautions → Remember that the dividend yield ratio tells only part of the return on investment story. Often, potential capital appreciation is a much more important consideration. When analyzing changes in the ratio, it is important to understand the cause. For example, a company might pay out $2 per share in dividends each year. If the market price of its shares is $100 per share, the yield is 2 percent. If the market price per share falls to $25 the following year and the company continues to pay out $2 per share in dividends, the dividend yield ratio will "improve" to 8 percent. Most analysts would not interpret this change as being favourable.

STOCK DIVIDENDS AND STOCK SPLITS

Stock Dividends

A **stock dividend** is a distribution of additional shares of a corporation's own share capital to its shareholders on a pro rata basis, at no cost to the shareholder. Stock dividends usually consist of additional common shares issued to the holders of common shares. The term "pro rata basis" means that each shareholder receives additional shares equal to the percentage of shares already held. A shareholder with 10 percent of the outstanding shares receives 10 percent of any additional shares issued as a stock dividend.

The term "stock dividend" is sometimes misused in annual reports and news articles. A recent *Wall Street Journal* headline announced that a particular company had just declared a "stock dividend." A close reading of the article revealed that the company had declared a cash dividend on the shares.

The value of a stock dividend is the subject of much debate. In reality, a stock dividend has no economic value. All shareholders receive a pro rata distribution of shares, which means that each shareholder owns exactly the same portion of the company as before. The value of an investment is determined by the percentage of the company that is owned, not the number of shares that are held. If you get change for a dollar coin, you are not wealthier because you hold *four* quarters instead of only *one* dollar coin. Similarly, if you own 10 percent of a company, you are not wealthier simply because the company declares a stock dividend and gives you (and all other shareholders) more shares.

At this point, you may still wonder why having extra shares does not make an investor wealthier. The reason is simple: the stock market reacts immediately when a stock dividend is issued, and the share price falls proportionally. Theoretically, if the share price was $60 before a stock dividend, normally (in the absence of events affecting the company) the price will fall to $30 if the number of shares is doubled. Thus, an investor could own 100 shares worth $6,000 before the stock dividend (100 × $60) and 200 shares worth $6,000 after the stock dividend (200 × $30).

In reality, the fall in price is not exactly proportional to the number of new shares that are issued. In some cases, the stock dividend makes the stock more attractive to new investors. Many investors prefer to buy shares in round lots, which are multiples of 100 shares. An investor with $10,000 might not buy a share selling for $150 because she cannot afford to buy 100 shares. She might buy the share, however, if the price is less than $100 as a result of a stock dividend. In other cases, stock dividends are accompanied by an announcement of increases in cash dividends, which are attractive to some investors.

When a common stock dividend occurs, the company must transfer from retained earnings an additional amount into the common shares account to reflect the additional shares that have been issued. The amount transferred should reflect the fair market value per share at the declaration date, as recommended in the CBCA.

LO11-6

Discuss the purpose of stock dividends and stock splits, and report transactions.

A **STOCK DIVIDEND** is a distribution of additional shares of a corporation's own equity.

For small stock dividends that are less than 20–25 percent of the outstanding shares, the amount transferred from the retained earnings account to the common shares account is based on the market price per share at the date of declaration. If the company declared a cash dividend instead of a stock dividend, and the shareholders used the cash they received to buy additional shares, the shareholders would be paying the market price to acquire additional shares. This assumption is valid if the stock dividend is relatively small so that it will not cause a significant change in the market price. For larger stock dividends, the market price per share will drop significantly, so it will not be an appropriate basis for transferring an amount from retained earnings to common shares. In this case, the amount transferred is based on the average issue price per share. In either situation, the stock dividend does not change total shareholders' equity. It changes only the balances of specific shareholders' equity accounts.

Let us assume that a company declared on July 25, 2017, a 10 percent stock dividend on common shares to be issued on August 25, 2017, to shareholders of record on August 10, 2017. The company had 100,000 shares outstanding, and the market price per share was $20 on the date of declaration. The declaration of the stock dividend requires the following journal entry on July 25, 2017:

Dividends declared—Common (SE)	200,000	
(100,000 × 10% × $20)		
Stock dividend to be issued (SE)		200,000

Assets	=	Liabilities	+	Shareholders' Equity	
				Dividends declared—Common	−200,000
				Stock dividend to be issued	+200,000

The equity account "Stock dividend to be issued" is credited, instead of the "Common shares account," until the shares are issued. The issuance and distribution of the additional shares on August 25, 2017, is recorded as follows:

Stock dividend to be issued (SE)	200,000	
Common shares (SE)		200,000

Assets	=	Liabilities	+	Shareholders' Equity	
				Stock dividend to be issued	−200,000
				Common shares	+200,000

If the company had declared a 50 percent stock dividend, the average price received for issuing all of the common shares would be used instead of the market price per share as a basis for the reduction of retained earnings. If the average issue price per share is $15, the "Dividends declared—Common" account would be reduced by $750,000 (100,000 × 50% × $15) and the "Common shares" account would be increased by the same amount.

Stock Splits

Stock splits are *not* dividends. They are similar to a stock dividend but are quite different in terms of their impact on the shareholders' equity accounts. In a **stock split**, the *total* number of authorized, issued, and outstanding shares is increased by a specified number, such as a two-for-one split. In this instance, each share held is called in, and two new shares are issued in its place.

A **STOCK SPLIT** is an increase in the total number of authorized shares by a specified ratio; it does not decrease retained earnings.

BCE has had three stock splits over the years. A four-for-one split occurred on October 4, 1948, followed by a three-for-one split on April 26, 1979. The last split was a two for one, executed on May 14, 1997. In summary, a common share issued prior to October 4, 1948, has already split into 24 shares. If these stock splits did not occur, BCE's share price would have been $1,422 at the time of writing this book.

In both a stock dividend and a stock split, the shareholder receives more shares but does not pay to acquire the additional shares. A stock dividend requires a journal entry; a stock split does not require one but is disclosed in the notes to the financial statements. The comparative effects of a stock dividend versus a stock split may be summarized as follows:

Shareholders' Equity	Before	After a 100% Stock Dividend	After a 2-for-1 Stock Split
Contributed capital			
Number of shares outstanding	30,000	60,000	60,000
Issue price per share	$ 10	$ 10	$ 5
Common shares	300,000	600,000	300,000
Retained earnings	650,000	350,000	650,000
Total shareholders' equity	$950,000	$950,000	$950,000

PAUSE FOR FEEDBACK

We have concluded our discussion of common shares by looking at stock dividends and stock splits. In the next section, we will examine preferred shares. Before you move on, complete the following questions to test your understanding of stock dividends.

SELF-STUDY QUIZ 11-3

Barton Corporation issued 100,000 new common shares as a result of a stock dividend when the market value was $30 per share. The average issue price is $10 per share.

1. Record this transaction, assuming that it was a small stock dividend.

2. Record this transaction, assuming that it was a large stock dividend.

3. What journal entry is required if the transaction is a stock split?

After you complete your answers, check them with the solutions at the end of the chapter.

PREFERRED SHARES

In addition to common shares, some corporations issue *preferred shares*. **Preferred shares** differ from common shares because of a number of rights granted to the preferred shareholders. The most significant differences are as follows:

- **Preferred shares do not grant voting rights.** As a result, they do not appeal to investors who want some control over the operations of the corporation. Indeed, this is one of the main reasons some corporations issue preferred shares to raise equity capital. Preferred shares permit them to raise funds without diluting common shareholders' control of the company.

- **Preferred shares are less risky than common shares.** Preferred shareholders have a priority over common shareholders for the receipt of dividends and in the distribution of assets if the corporation goes out of business. Usually, a specified amount per share must be paid to preferred shareholders upon dissolution before any remaining assets can be distributed to the common shareholders.

- **Preferred shares typically have a fixed dividend rate.** Preferred shares typically have no par value but, unlike common shares, they often carry a nominal value called the *stated value*. BCE's preferred shares have a stated value of $25 per share. Most preferred shares have fixed dividend rates, or amounts per share. The fixed dividend is attractive to certain investors who want a stable income from their investment.

Special Features of Preferred Shares

Some corporations issue **convertible preferred shares**, which provide preferred shareholders the option to exchange their preferred shares for a different series of

LO11-7

Describe the characteristics of preferred shares, and analyze transactions affecting preferred shares.

PREFERRED SHARES are shares that have specified rights over common shares.

CONVERTIBLE PREFERRED SHARES are preferred shares that are convertible to common shares at the option of the holder.

preferred shares or for common shares of the corporation. The terms of the conversion specify the conversion dates and a conversion ratio.

The classification of preferred shares as equity or debt depends upon the terms of the preferred equity issue. Preferred shares may be *redeemable* or *callable* at some future date at the option of the issuing corporation. Corporations are unlikely to redeem preferred shares if conditions are financially unfavourable to the company. Such redeemable shares are classified as equity, because the issuing corporation can choose not to redeem the shares. However, preferred shares that have fixed redemption dates are classified as debt, because the issuing corporation has a future financial liability. Moreover, dividends on these shares are treated as expenses, much like the interest expense related to long-term debt.

Some preferred share issues are *retractable* at the option of the shareholder. In that case, preferred shareholders have the right to receive the redemption price from the corporation at a specific future date. Thus, retractable preferred shares represent a contractual obligation to deliver cash or another financial asset at a future date under conditions that may be unfavourable to the issuing corporation. Consequently, retractable preferred shares are classified as debt.

The notes to BCE's consolidated financial statements for 2015 provide a considerable amount of detail regarding its preferred shares.

REAL-WORLD EXCERPT

BCE Inc.

ANNUAL REPORT

NOTE 25: SHARE CAPITAL

Preferred Shares

BCE Inc.'s articles of amalgamation provide for an unlimited number of First Preferred Shares and Second Preferred Shares, all without par value. The terms set out in the articles authorize BCE's directors to issue the shares in one or more series and to set the number of shares and conditions for each series.

The following table is a summary of the principal terms of BCE Inc.'s First Preferred Shares. There were no Second Preferred Shares issued and outstanding at December 31, 2015. BCE Inc.'s articles of amalgamation, as amended, describe the terms and conditions of these shares in detail.

Series	Annual Dividend Rate	Convertible Into	Conversion Date	Redemption Date	Redemption Price	Number of Shares Authorized	Issued and Outstanding	At December 31 2015	At December 31 2014
Q	Floating	Series R	December 1, 2025	At any time		8,000,000	—	—	—
R	4.13%	Series Q	December 1, 2020	December 1, 2020	$25.00	8,000,000	8,000,000	200	200
S	Floating	Series T	November 1, 2016	At any time	$25.50	8,000,000	3,606,225	90	90
T	3.393%	Series S	November 1, 2016	November 1, 2016	$25.00	8,000,000	4,393,775	110	110
Y	Floating	Series Z	December 1, 2017	At any time	$25.50	10,000,000	8,772,468	219	219
Z	3.152%	Series Y	December 1, 2017	December 1, 2017	$25.00	10,000,000	1,227,532	31	31
AA	3.45%	Series AB	September 1, 2017	September 1, 2017	$25.00	20,000,000	10,144,302	259	259
AB	Floating	Series AA	September 1, 2017	At any time	$25.50	20,000,000	9,855,698	251	251
AC	3.55%	Series AD	March 1, 2018	March 1, 2018	$25.00	20,000,000	5,069,935	129	129
AD	Floating	Series AC	March 1, 2018	At any time	$25.50	20,000,000	14,930,065	381	381
AE	Floating	Series AF	February 1, 2020	At any time	$25.50	24,000,000	9,292,133	232	36
AF	3.11%	Series AE	February 1, 2020	February 1, 2020	$25.00	24,000,000	6,707,867	168	364
AG	4.50%	Series AH	May 1, 2016	May 1, 2016	$25.00	22,000,000	10,841,056	271	271
AH	Floating	Series AG	May 1, 2016	At any time	$25.50	22,000,000	3,158,944	79	79
AI	4.15%	Series AJ	August 1, 2016	August 1, 2016	$25.00	22,000,000	10,754,990	269	269
AJ	Floating	Series AI	August 1, 2016	At any time	$25.50	22,000,000	3,245,010	81	81
AK	4.15%	Series AL	December 31, 2016	December 31, 2016	$25.00	25,000,000	25,000,000	625	625
AL	Floating	Series AK	December 31, 2021			25,000,000		—	—
AM	4.85%	Series AN	March 31, 2016	March 31, 2016	$25.00	30,000,000	11,500,000	263	263
AN	Floating	Series AM	March 31, 2021			30,000,000			
AO	4.55%	Series AP	March 31, 2017	March 31, 2017	$25.00	30,000,000	4,600,000	118	118
AP	Floating	Series AO	March 31, 2022			30,000,000			
AQ	4.25%	Series AR	September 30, 2018	September 30, 2018	$25.00	30,000,000	9,200,000	228	228
AR	Floating	Series AQ	September 30, 2023			30,000,000		—	—
								4,004	4,004

Source: BCE Inc. Annual Report 2015.

BCE has also disclosed details of the specific features of each series of preferred shares. All of its outstanding preferred shares at December 31, 2015, are non-voting, except under special circumstances, when the holders are entitled to one vote per share. Holders of Series R, T, Z, AA, AC, AF, AG, AI, AK, AM, AO, and AQ shares are entitled to fixed cumulative quarterly dividends, which are reset every five years, whereas holders of Series S, Y, AB, AD, AE, AH, AJ, AL, AN, AP, and AR shares are entitled to floating adjustable cumulative monthly dividends with a floating dividend rate that is calculated every month. All of these preferred shares are convertible at the holder's option into another associated series of preferred shares on a one-for-one basis. In addition, BCE may redeem each of the preferred shares in the first series above at $25.00 per share on the applicable redemption date and every five years after that date, whereas each preferred share in the second series may be redeemed at any time at $25.50 per share.[6]

PAUSE FOR **FEEDBACK** STOP

We have listed the various types of preferred shares that BCE Inc. has issued over time. Each series of preferred shares has specific characteristics. In the next section, we will discuss dividends on preferred shares. Before you move on, complete the following questions to test your understanding of preferred shares.

SELF-STUDY **QUIZ 11-4**

Refer to the previous table showing a summary of BCE's preferred shares, and answer the following questions related to Preferred Shares, Series R.

1. What is the total amount of dividends payable on Series R per year?

2. What is meant by *redemption date*?

3. What is the earliest date that BCE can redeem its Series R shares?

After you complete your answers, check them with the solutions at the end of the chapter.

Dividends on Preferred Shares

Investors who purchase preferred shares give up certain advantages that are available to investors in common shares. Generally, preferred shareholders do not have the right to vote at the annual meeting, nor do they share in increased earnings if the company becomes more profitable. To compensate these investors, preferred shares offer a dividend preference. The two most common dividend preferences are

1. Current dividend preference and

2. Cumulative dividend preference.

Current Dividend Preference Preferred shares always carry a **current dividend preference**, which requires that the current preferred dividend be paid before any dividends are paid on the common shares. When the current dividend preference has been met and there are no other preferences, dividends can then be paid to the common shareholders.

Declared dividends must be allocated between the preferred and common shares. First, dividends are allocated to the preferred shares, and then the remainder of the total dividend is allocated to the common shares. Exhibit 11.5 illustrates the allocation of the current dividend preference under three different assumptions concerning the total amount of dividends to be paid.

CURRENT DIVIDEND PREFERENCE is the feature of preferred shares that grants preferred shareholders priority for dividends over common shareholders.

Exhibit **11.5**

Dividends on Preferred Shares:
Current Dividend Preference
Only

Preferred shares outstanding, $1.20; 2,000 shares.

Common shares outstanding; 5,000 shares.

Allocation of dividends between preferred and common shares assuming current dividend preference only:

Assumptions	Total Dividends Paid	$1.20 Preferred Shares (2,000 shares)*	Common Shares (5,000 shares)
No. 1	$ 2,000	$2,000	0
No. 2	3,000	2,400	$ 600
No. 3	18,000	2,400	15,600

*Preferred dividends = 2,000 × $1.20 = $2,400

CUMULATIVE DIVIDEND PREFERENCE is the feature of preferred shares that requires specified current dividends not paid in full to accumulate for every year in which they are not paid. These cumulative preferred dividends must be paid before any common dividends can be paid

DIVIDENDS IN ARREARS are dividends on cumulative preferred shares that have not been declared in prior years.

Cumulative Dividend Preference   The **cumulative dividend preference** states that if all or a part of the current dividend is not paid in full, the unpaid amount, known as **dividends in arrears**, must be paid before any common dividends can be paid. Of course, if the preferred shares are non-cumulative, dividends cannot be in arrears; any dividends that are not declared are permanently lost by the preferred shareholders. Because preferred shareholders are not willing to accept this unfavourable feature, preferred shares are usually cumulative.

The allocation of dividends between cumulative preferred shares and common shares is illustrated in Exhibit 11.6 under four different assumptions concerning the total amount of dividends to be paid. Notice that the dividends in arrears are paid first, then the current dividend preference is paid, and, finally, the remainder is paid to the common shareholders.

Exhibit **11.6**

Dividends on Preferred Shares:
Cumulative Dividend Preference

Preferred shares outstanding, $1.20; 2,000 shares.

Common shares outstanding; 5,000 shares.

Dividends are in arrears for the two preceding years.

Allocation of dividends between preferred and common shares, assuming cumulative preference:

Assumptions (dividends in arrears, 2 years)	Total Dividends Paid	$1.20 Preferred Shares (2,000 shares)*	Common Shares (5,000 shares)
No. 1	$ 2,400	$2,400	0
No. 2	7,200	7,200	0
No. 3	8,000	7,200	$ 800
No. 4	30,000	7,200	22,800

*Current dividend preference, 2,000 × $1.20 = $2,400; dividends in arrears preference, $2,400 × 2 years = $4,800; and current dividend preference plus dividends in arrears = $7,200.

MEASURING AND REPORTING CHANGES IN SHAREHOLDERS' EQUITY

LO11-8

Measure and report changes in shareholders' equity.

Exhibit 11.2 discloses the balances of the various components of BCE's shareholders' equity at January 1, 2015, and December 31, 2015, as well as the changes that occurred to each component over these two years. While we provided explanations for many changes that occurred in 2015, two components of shareholders' equity deserve further discussion: retained earnings and accumulated other comprehensive income (loss).

Retained Earnings

Retained earnings represent net earnings less dividends that have been declared since the first day of the company's operations. Most companies report retained earnings on their statements of financial position. In BCE's case, its retained earnings turned into a deficit in 2003 after a massive write-off of the value of BCE's investments in other companies. Its deficit of $5,830 million on December 31, 2003, was reduced each year and reached $1,299 million by December 31, 2009. However, the transition from using Canadian generally accepted accounting principles to IFRS caused a reduction in the carrying amounts of BCE's assets and an increase in its liabilities, with a net decrease in shareholders' equity that increased the deficit from $1,299 million to $7,508 million as at January 1, 2010, but it was later reduced to $6,350 million by December 31, 2015. The gradual reduction of this deficit will allow BCE to report retained earnings in future years.

Under rare circumstances, you may see a statement that includes an adjustment to the beginning balance of retained earnings resulting from a correction of a material accounting error that occurred in the financial statements of a prior period.

If an accounting error from a previous period is corrected by making an adjustment to the current statement of earnings, net earnings for the current period will be improperly measured. To avoid this problem, the financial statements of the prior period in which the error occurred are restated to reflect the correction of the error. The nature of the prior-period error should be disclosed along with the effect of the correction on each financial statement item that is affected by the error. To the extent that prior-period errors affect specific statement of earnings items, retained earnings of the prior period will also be affected.

Adjustments to the financial statements of prior periods should also be made if the entity changes its accounting policies, such as a change from the FIFO method of inventory valuation to the weighted-average cost method, or when companies are required to adopt new accounting standards. In these cases, the entity adjusts the opening balance of each affected component of equity, including retained earnings.

PROPER ACCOUNTING FOR PRIOR-PERIOD ERRORS

A QUESTION OF ACCOUNTABILITY

Adjustments related to errors made in prior periods should not affect the current-period earnings, particularly when compensation of key management personnel is tied to measures of profitability, such as net earnings. In the case of Nortel, which was one of the top global makers of telecommunications equipment in North America, provisions were made for such items as inventory write-downs and contract disputes that lacked proper justification. These provisions, which reflected overstated expenses, were reversed in a subsequent accounting period. The excessive amount of the reversed provisions turned the net loss of one accounting period into a net earnings figure that was sufficiently large to trigger payment of bonuses to key management personnel. This inaccurate accounting for the effect of prior errors was subsequently discovered, and key management personnel were accused of management fraud. The reversal of the erroneous provisions should have been reported as an adjustment to the earnings of prior periods and should not have affected the current period's earnings. Had the accounting been done properly, bonuses would not have been paid to key management personnel and accusations of management fraud could have been avoided.

Accumulated Other Comprehensive Income (Loss)

IFRS require Canadian publicly accountable enterprises to report accumulated other comprehensive income (loss). This equity item reflects the financial effect of events that cause changes in shareholders' equity, other than investments by shareholders or distributions to shareholders. Such changes in equity result from unrealized gains or losses related to the valuation of specific assets and liabilities at fair value. For BCE, these changes include such items as unrealized gains or losses on available-for-sale assets, unrealized gains or losses on derivatives transactions that are designated as cash flow hedges, and unrealized gains or losses on translating the financial statements of companies that have operations in other countries but are controlled by the Canadian reporting entity. The unrealized gains and losses resulting from these changes are not reported on the statement of earnings because they have not been realized yet. Measurement of the unrealized gains and losses related to these and similar items is fairly complex and is covered in intermediate and advanced accounting courses.

RESTRICTIONS ON THE PAYMENT OF DIVIDENDS

FINANCIAL
ANALYSIS

Two common constraints on the ability of a corporation to pay dividends are the existence of debt covenants and preferred stock dividends in arrears. For additional security, some creditors include a debt covenant that limits the amount of dividends a corporation can pay. These debt covenants often include a limit on borrowing and require a minimum balance of cash or working capital. If debt covenants are violated, the creditor can demand immediate repayment of the debt. The disclosure principle requires disclosure of debt covenants, typically in a separate note to the financial statements.

The existence of dividends in arrears on preferred shares can also limit a company's ability to pay dividends to its common shareholders and can affect a company's future cash flows. Dividends are never an actual liability until the board of directors declares them. Hence, dividends in arrears are not reported on the statement of financial position but are disclosed in the notes to the statements. The following note from Lone Star Industries is typical if a company has dividends in arrears:

> The total of dividends in arrears on the $13.50 preferred shares at the end of the year was $11,670,000. The aggregate amount of such dividends must be paid before any dividends are paid on common shares.

Analysts are particularly interested in information concerning these restrictions because of the impact they have on the company's dividend policy.

FINANCING ACTIVITIES

FOCUS ON
CASH FLOWS

LO11-9

Discuss the impact of share capital transactions on cash flows.

Transactions involving share capital have a direct impact on the capital structure of a business. Because of the importance of these transactions, they are reported in a separate section of the statement called "cash flows from financing activities." Examples of cash flows associated with share capital are included in the statements of cash flows for BCE shown in Exhibit 11.7. Remember that shares issued in exchange for assets do not impact cash flow and are disclosed in a note to the statement of cash flows.

EFFECT ON STATEMENT OF CASH FLOWS

IN GENERAL → Cash received from owners is reported as an inflow. Cash paid to owners is reported as an outflow. Examples are shown in the following table:

SELECTED FOCUS COMPANY COMPARISONS: CASH FLOWS FROM FINANCING ACTIVITIES—2015
(in millions)

Sears Canada Inc. −$5.8

Reitmans Ltd. −$21.5

WestJet Airlines Ltd. −$259

	Effect on Cash Flows
Financing activities	
Issuance of shares	+
Repurchase of shares	−
Payment of cash dividends	−

FOCUS COMPANY ANALYSIS → BCE has issued both preferred and common shares during 2015, but did not repurchase any common shares for cancellation during that year. It paid dividends on both common and preferred shares during 2015.

Exhibit **11.7**
Excerpt from Statements of
Cash Flows for BCE Inc.

REAL-WORLD EXCERPT

BCE Inc.

ANNUAL REPORT

CONSOLIDATED STATEMENTS OF CASH FLOWS For the Years Ended December 31			
(in $ millions)	Note	2015	2014
Cash flows used in financing activities			
Increase in notes payable		76	469
Issue of long-term debt	20	1,498	1,428
Repayment of long-term debt	20	(2,084)	(1,113)
Privatization of Bell Aliant	24	—	(989)
Issue of common shares	25	952	49
Common shares issuance cost		(35)	—
Repurchase of shares for settlement of share-based payments		(138)	(83)
Cash dividends paid on common shares		(2,169)	(1,893)
Cash dividends paid on preferred shares		(150)	(134)
Cash dividends/distributions paid by subsidiaries to non-controlling interest		(41)	(145)
Other financing activities		(22)	(29)
Cash flows used in financing activities		(2,113)	(2,440)

Source: BCE Inc., Annual Report 2015.

ACCOUNTING AND REPORTING FOR UNINCORPORATED BUSINESSES

In this book, we emphasize the corporate form of business because it plays a dominant role in our economy. In fact, there are three forms of business organizations: corporations, sole proprietorships, and partnerships. As we have seen in this chapter, a corporation is a legal entity, separate and distinct from its owners. It can enter into contracts in its own name, it can be sued, and it is taxed as a separate entity. A *sole proprietorship* is an unincorporated business owned by one individual. If you started a lawn care business in the summer by yourself, it would be a sole proprietorship. It is not necessary to file any legal papers to create a proprietorship. A *partnership* is an unincorporated business owned by two or more people. Again, it is not necessary to file legal papers to create a partnership, but it is certainly a good idea to have a lawyer draw up a contract between the partners.

Neither partnerships nor proprietorships are separate legal entities. As a result, owners may be directly sued and are individually taxed on the earnings of the business.

The fundamentals of accounting and reporting for unincorporated businesses are the same as for a corporation, except for shareholders' equity. Typical account structures for the three forms of business organizations are outlined in Exhibit 11.8.

Accounting for sole proprietorships and partnerships is discussed in Appendix 11A.

Typical Account Structure		
Corporation (Shareholders' Equity)	**Sole Proprietorship (Owner's Equity)**	**Partnership (Partners' Equity)**
Share capital, contributed surplus	Doe, capital	Able, capital; Baker, capital
Retained earnings	Not used	Not used
Dividends paid	Doe, drawings	Able, drawings; Baker, drawings
Revenues, expenses, gains, and losses	Same	Same
Assets and liabilities	Same	Same

ACCOUNTING STANDARDS
FOR PRIVATE ENTERPRISES

Canadian private enterprises do not issue shares to the public. To finance their growth, most private enterprises turn to banks and other creditors as sources of financing. Because the external users of financial statements prepared by private enterprises are primarily creditors, the Canadian accounting standards for private enterprises have been simplified relative to IFRS. The main differences in accounting standards related to the equity section of the statement of financial position are summarized below:

Financial Reporting Issue	IFRS	ASPE
Reporting of changes in equity	Canadian publicly accountable enterprises are required to prepare a statement of changes in equity that includes the changes in all equity accounts.	Canadian private enterprises prepare a statement of retained earnings and disclose all other changes in equity in the notes to their financial statements.
Measurement of share-based compensation expense	Publicly accountable enterprises must use specific valuation models to measure share-based compensation expense.	Canadian private enterprises are permitted to use a simplified valuation model to measure the value of share-based compensation because of the difficulty in determining a fair value for shares that have no public market.
Reporting of EPS	Publicly accountable enterprises must report EPS on the statement of earnings.	Canadian private enterprises are not required to report EPS because external users do not believe this information is useful. Users, in particular creditors, are most interested in cash flows from operating activities.

DEMONSTRATION **CASE**

DEMONSTRATION CASE

This case focuses on the organization and operations for the first year of Mera Corporation, which was organized on January 2, 2017. The laws specify that the legal capital for no par value shares is the full amount of the shares. The corporation was organized by 10 local entrepreneurs for the purpose of operating a business to sell various supplies to hotels. The charter authorized the following share capital:

- Common shares, no par value, unlimited number of shares.

- Preferred shares, 5 percent, $25 par value, 10,000 shares (cumulative, non-convertible, and non-voting; liquidation value, $26).

The following summarized transactions, selected from 2017, were completed during the months indicated:

a.	January 5	Sold a total of 7,500 shares of no par value common shares to the 10 entrepreneurs for cash at $52 per share. Credit the common shares account for the total issue amount.
b.	February 1	Sold 7,560 preferred shares at $25 per share; cash collected in full.
c.	March 10	Purchased land for a store site and made full payment by issuing 400 preferred shares. Early construction of the store is planned. Debit land account (store site). The preferred share is selling at $25 per share.
d.	April 15	Paid $2,000 cash for organization costs. Debit the intangible asset account organization costs.
e.	May 25	Issued 40 preferred shares to A. B. Cain in full payment of legal services rendered in connection with organization of the corporation. Assume that the preferred share is selling regularly at $25 per share. Debit organization costs.
f.	June 10	Sold 500 no par value common shares for cash to C. B. Abel at $54 per share.
g.	November 30	The company's board of directors declared the annual dividends on the preferred shares, and a dividend of $0.50 per common share. The dividends are payable on December 20 to shareholders of record at December 15.
h.	December 20	Paid the declared dividends on preferred and common shares.
i.	December 31	Purchased equipment for $600,000; paid cash. No depreciation expense should be recorded in 2017.
j.	December 31	Borrowed $20,000 cash from the City Bank on a one-year, interest-bearing note. Interest is payable at a 12 percent rate at maturity.
k.	December 31	Calculated the following for the year: gross revenues, $129,300; expenses, $98,000, including corporation income tax but excluding amortization of organization costs. Assume that these summarized revenue and expense transactions involved cash. Because the equipment and the bank loan transactions were on December 31, no related adjusting entries at the end of 2017 are needed.
l.	December 31	Decided that a reasonable amortization period for organization costs, starting as of January 1, 2017, is 10 years. This intangible asset must be amortized to expense.

Required:

1. Prepare appropriate journal entries, with a brief explanation, for each of these transactions.

2. Prepare the required adjusting entry for 2017 to amortize organization costs.

3. Prepare appropriate closing entries at December 31, 2017.

4. Prepare a statement of financial position for Mera Corporation at December 31, 2017. Emphasize full disclosure of shareholders' equity.

5. Assume that, instead of issuing common shares in January for $390,000, the company issued shares for $260,000 and borrowed an amount of $130,000 from its bank, signing a note, payable on December 31, 2016. Interest on the note is 10 percent, payable on December 31 of each year. Is borrowing from the bank more beneficial to the common shareholders, compared with issuing additional common shares? Explain. For the purpose of this analysis, use an income tax rate of 40 percent.

We strongly recommend that you prepare your own answers to these requirements, and then check your answers with the following solution.

SUGGESTED **SOLUTION**

1. Journal entries:

a.	January 5	Cash (A)	390,000	
		Common shares (SE)		390,000
		Sale of no par value common shares ($52 × 7,500 shares = $390,000).		
b.	February 1	Cash (A)	189,000	
		Preferred shares, 5% (SE)		189,000
		Sale of preferred shares ($25 × 7,560 shares = $189,000).		
c.	March 10	Land (A)	10,000	
		Preferred shares, 5% (SE)		10,000
		Purchased land for future store site; paid in full by issuance of 400 preferred shares ($25 × 400 shares = $10,000).		
d.	April 15	Organization costs (A)	2,000	
		Cash (A)		2,000
		Paid organization costs.		
e.	May 25	Organization costs (A)	1,000	
		Preferred shares 5% (SE)		1,000
		Organization costs (legal services) paid by issuance of 40 preferred shares. The implied market value is $25 × 40 shares = $1,000.		
f.	June 10	Cash (A)	27,000	
		Common shares (500 shares) (SE)		27,000
		Sold 500 no par value common shares ($54 × 500 shares = $27,000).		
g.	November 30	Dividends declared—Preferred (SE)	10,000	
		Dividends declared—Common (SE)	4,000	
		Dividends payable—Preferred (L)		10,000
		Dividends payable—Common (L)		4,000
		Declaration of the annual dividend on preferred shares (8,000 × $25 × 0.05) and a dividend of $0.50 per common share.		
h.	December 20	Dividends payable—Preferred (L)	10,000	
		Dividends payable—Common (L)	4,000	
		Cash (A)		14,000
		Payment of the declared dividends.		
i.	December 31	Equipment (A)	600,000	
		Cash (A)		600,000
		Purchased equipment.		
j.	December 31	Cash (A)	20,000	
		Note payable (L)		20,000
		Borrowed cash and signed a one-year, 12 percent interest-bearing note.		

k.   December 31   Cash (A)   129,300

                       Revenues (E)   129,300

               Expenses (E)   98,000

                       Cash (A)   98,000

               To record summarized revenues and expenses.

2.

December 31   Expenses (E)   300

                       Organization costs (A)   300

               Adjusting entry to amortize organization costs for one year [($2,000 + $1,000) ÷ 10 years = $300].

3. Closing entries:

December 31   Revenues (R)   129,300

                       Income summary   129,300

               Income summary   98,300

                       Expenses ($98,000 + $300) (E)   98,300

               Income summary   31,000

                       Retained earnings (SE)   31,000

4. Statement of Financial Position:

MERA CORPORATION
Statement of Financial Position at December 31, 2017

Assets		
Current assets		
Cash		$ 41,300
Tangible assets		
Land	$ 10,000	
Equipment (no depreciation assumed in the problem)	600,000	610,000
Intangible assets		
Organization costs (cost, $3,000 less amortization, $300)		2,700
Total assets		$654,000
Liabilities		
Current liabilities		
Note payable, 12%		$ 20,000
Shareholders' Equity		
Contributed capital		
Preferred shares, 5% (par value $25; authorized 10,000 shares, issued and outstanding 8,000 shares)	$200,000	
Common shares (no par value; authorized unlimited, issued, and outstanding 8,000 shares)	417,000	
Total contributed capital	617,000	
Retained earnings	17,000	
Total shareholders' equity		634,000
Total liabilities and shareholders' equity		$654,000

5. Interest on the loan equals $13,000 ($130,000 × 10%) for 2017. This expense will reduce the income tax expense by $5,200 ($13,000 × 40%). The net earnings of $31,000 will then be reduced by $7,800 ($13,000 − $5,200) for a revised net earnings of $23,200. Net earnings available to common shareholders equals $13,200 after deducting $10,000 of dividends on preferred shares. The return on common shareholders' equity, therefore, equals 4.7 percent ($13,200 ÷ $278,100, which is the average common shareholders' equity = [$260,000 + ($260,000 + $270,000 + $13,200 − $4,000)]/2).

Without the $130,000 loan, the return on common shareholders' equity is 5.1 percent ([$31,000 − $10,000]/[($390,000 + $434,000*)/2]). This shows that borrowing an amount of $130,000 at 10 percent is not preferable to issuing additional common shares in this particular case.

*$390,000 + $27,000 + $31,000 − $14,000

APPENDIX 11A: ACCOUNTING FOR OWNERS' EQUITY FOR SOLE PROPRIETORSHIPS AND PARTNERSHIPS

Proprietorships and partnerships are private enterprises that do not issue shares for sale to the public. They normally report their financial information in accordance with the accounting standards for private enterprises. These standards are less complicated than the IFRS that publicly accountable enterprises must use. For example, private enterprises are not required to report other comprehensive income.

The use of accounting standards for private enterprises does not mean, however, that the standards are less rigorous than those used by publicly accountable enterprises. This simplified set of standards makes the preparation and audit of financial statements affordable for smaller business entities. All of the principles, such as economic substance over form and the excess of benefit over cost, guided the production of these standards.

LO11-S1

Report owners' equity for sole proprietorships and partnerships.

Owner's Equity for a Sole Proprietorship

A sole proprietorship is an unincorporated business owned by one person. Only two owner's equity accounts are needed: a capital account for the proprietor (J. Doe, capital) and a drawing (or withdrawal) account for the proprietor (J. Doe, drawings).

The capital account of a sole proprietorship serves two purposes: to record investments by the owner and to accumulate periodic net earnings or loss. The drawing account is used to record the owner's withdrawals of cash or other assets from the business. The drawing account is closed to the capital account at the end of each accounting period. The capital account reflects the cumulative total of all investments by the owner, plus all earnings of the entity, less all withdrawals of resources from the entity by the owner.

In most respects, the accounting for a sole proprietorship is the same as for a corporation. Exhibit 11.9 presents the recording of selected transactions and the owner's equity section of the statement of financial position of Doe Retail Store to illustrate the accounting for owner's equity for a sole proprietorship.

Selected Transactions during 2017

January 1, 2017

J. Doe started a retail store by investing $150,000 of personal savings. The journal entry for the business is as follows:

Cash (A)	150,000	
J. Doe, capital (OE)		150,000
Assets	= **Liabilities**	+ **Owner's Equity**
Cash +150,000		J. Doe, capital +150,000

During 2017

Each month during the year, Doe withdrew $1,000 cash from the business for personal living expenses. Accordingly, the following journal entry was made each month:

J. Doe, drawings (OE)	1,000	
Cash (A)		1,000
Assets	= **Liabilities**	+ **Owner's Equity**
Cash −1,000		J. Doe, drawings −1,000

Note: At December 31, 2017, after the last withdrawal, the drawings account will reflect a debit balance of $12,000.

Exhibit 11.9

Accounting for Owner's Equity for a Sole Proprietorship

December 31, 2017

The store's operations for the year resulted in revenues of $128,000 and expenses of $110,000. The revenue and expense accounts are closed to the capital account at the end of the year. The closing entry follows:

Individual revenue accounts (R)			128,000	
Individual expense accounts (E)				110,000
J. Doe, capital (OE)				18,000

Assets	=	Liabilities	+	Owner's Equity	
				Revenues	−128,000
				Expenses	+110,000
				J. Doe, capital	+18,000

December 31, 2017

The journal entry required to close the drawings account follows:

| J. Doe, capital (OE) | | | 12,000 | |
| J. Doe, drawings (OE) | | | | 12,000 |

Assets	=	Liabilities	+	Owner's Equity	
				J. Doe, capital	−12,000
				J. Doe, drawings	+12,000

Statement of Financial Position, December 31, 2017 (partial)	
Owner's equity	
J. Doe, capital, January 1, 2017	$150,000
Add: Net earnings for 2017	18,000
Total	168,000
Deduct: Withdrawals for 2017	(12,000)
J. Doe, capital, December 31, 2017	$156,000

A sole proprietorship does not pay income taxes. Therefore, its financial statements do not reflect income tax expense or income taxes payable. Instead, the net earnings of a sole proprietorship are taxed when it is included on the owner's personal income tax return. Because an employer/employee contractual relationship cannot exist with only one party involved, a "salary" to the owner is not recognized as an expense of a sole proprietorship. The owner's salary is accounted for as a distribution of net earnings (i.e., a withdrawal).

Owners' Equity for a Partnership

Small businesses and professionals such as accountants, doctors, and lawyers may use the partnership form of business. It is formed by two or more persons reaching mutual agreement about the terms of the partnership. The law does not require an application for a charter as it does in the case of a corporation. Instead, the agreement between the partners constitutes a legally enforceable partnership contract. The agreement should specify matters such as division of net earnings, management responsibilities, transfer or sale of partnership interests, disposition of assets upon liquidation, and procedures to be followed in case of the death of a partner. If the partnership agreement does not specify these matters, the applicable provincial laws are binding.

The primary advantages of a partnership are (1) ease of formation, (2) complete control by the partners, and (3) lack of income taxes on the business itself. The primary disadvantage is the unlimited liability of each partner for the partnership's liabilities. If the partnership does not have sufficient assets to satisfy outstanding debt, its creditors can seize the partners' personal assets.

As with a sole proprietorship, accounting for transactions undertaken by a partnership follows the same underlying fundamentals as any other form of business organization, except for those entries that directly affect owners' equity.

Accounting for partners' equity follows the same pattern as illustrated earlier for a sole proprietorship, except that separate partner capital and drawings accounts must be established for each partner. Investments by each partner are credited to the partner's capital account, and withdrawals from the partnership by each partner are debited to the respective drawings accounts. The net earnings for a partnership are divided between the partners in the profit ratio specified in the partnership agreement, and credited to each partner's account. The respective drawings accounts are closed to the partner capital accounts. After the closing process, each partner's capital account reflects the cumulative total of all investments of that individual partner, plus the partner's share of all partnership earnings, less all the partner's withdrawals.

Exhibit 11.10 presents selected journal entries and partial financial statements for AB Partnership to illustrate the accounting for the distribution of net earnings and partners' equity.

		Exhibit **11.10**
Selected Transactions during 2017		Accounting for Partners' Equity

January 1, 2017

A. Able and B. Baker organized AB Partnership on this date. Able contributed $60,000 and Baker $40,000 cash to the partnership and agreed to divide profit (and loss) 60 percent and 40 percent, respectively. The journal entry for the business to record the investment follows:

Cash (A)			10,000	
A. Able, capital (OE)				60,000
B. Baker, capital (OE)				40,000
Assets	**=**	**Liabilities**	**+**	**Owner's Equity**
Cash +100,000				A. Able, capital +60,000
				B. Baker, capital +40,000

During 2017

The partners agreed that Able would withdraw $1,000 and Baker $650 per month in cash. Accordingly, the following journal entry for the withdrawals was made each month:

A. Able, drawings (OE)			1,000	
B. Baker, drawings (OE)			650	
Cash (A)				1,650
Assets	**=**	**Liabilities**	**+**	**Owner's Equity**
Cash -1,650				A. Able, drawings -1,000
				B. Baker, drawings -650

December 31, 2017

Assume that the normal closing entries for the revenue ($150,000) and expense accounts ($120,000) resulted in net earnings of $30,000 that was distributed between the two partners. The closing entry is as follows:

Individual revenue accounts (R)			150,000	
Individual expense accounts (E)				120,000
A. Able, capital (OE)				18,000
B. Baker, capital (OE)				12,000
Assets	**=**	**Liabilities**	**+**	**Owner's Equity**
				Revenues -150,000
				Expenses +120,000
				A. Able, capital +18,000
				B. Baker, capital +12,000

Net earnings are divided as follows:

A. Able, $30,000 × 60%	$18,000
B. Baker, $30,000 × 40%	12,000
Total	$30,000

December 31, 2017

The journal entry required to close the drawings accounts follows:

A. Able, capital (OE)	12,000	
B. Baker, capital (OE)	7,800	
A. Able, drawings (OE)		12,000
B. Baker, drawings (OE)		7,800

Assets	=	Liabilities	+	Owner's Equity	
				A. Able, capital	−12,000
				B. Baker, capital	−7,800
				A. Able, drawings	+17,000
				B. Baker, drawings	+7,800

A separate statement of partners' capital, similar to the following, is customarily prepared to supplement the statement of financial position:

AB PARTNERSHIP
Statement of Partners' Capital
For the Year Ended December 31, 2017

	A. Able	B. Baker	Total
Investment, January 1, 2017	$60,000	$40,000	$100,000
Add: Additional investments during the year	–0–	–0–	–0–
Net earnings for the year	18,000	12,000	30,000
Totals	78,000	52,000	130,000
Deduct: Drawings during the year	(12,000)	(7,800)	(19,800)
Partners' equity, December 31, 2017	$66,000	$44,200	$110,200

The financial statements of a partnership follow the same format as those for a corporation, except that (1) the statement of earnings includes an additional section titled distribution of net earnings, (2) the partners' equity section of the statement of financial position is detailed for each partner, (3) a partnership has no income tax expense because partnerships do not pay income tax (each partner must report his or her share of the partnership net earnings on his or her individual tax return), and (4) salaries paid to partners are not recorded as expense but are treated as a distribution of net earnings (withdrawals).

CHAPTER **TAKE-AWAYS**

11-1. Explain the role of share capital in the capital structure of a corporation.

The law recognizes corporations as separate legal entities. Owners invest in a corporation and receive shares that can be traded on established stock exchanges. Shares provide a number of rights, including the right to receive dividends.

11-2. Analyze the earnings per share ratio.

The EPS ratio facilitates the comparison of a company's earnings over time or with other companies' earnings at a single point in time. By expressing earnings on a per share basis, differences in the size of companies become less important.

11-3. Describe the characteristics of common shares, and analyze transactions affecting common shares.

A common share is the basic voting share issued by a corporation. Usually, it has no par value, but par value shares can also be issued. Preferred shares are issued by some corporations. These shares contain some special rights and may appeal to certain investors. A number of key transactions involve share capital: (1) initial sale of shares, (2) cash dividends, (3) stock dividends and stock splits, and (4) repurchase of shares. Each is illustrated in this chapter.

11-4. Discuss dividends, and analyze related transactions.

The return associated with an investment in shares comes from two sources: appreciation of share price and dividends. Dividends are recorded as a liability when they are declared by the board of directors (i.e., on the date of declaration). The liability is satisfied when the dividends are paid (i.e., on the date of payment).

11-5. Analyze the dividend yield ratio.

The dividend yield ratio measures the percentage of return on investment from dividends. For most companies, the return associated with dividends is very small.

11-6. Discuss the purpose of stock dividends, stock splits, and report transactions.

Stock dividends are distributions of a company's shares to existing shareholders on a pro rata basis. The transaction involves transferring an additional amount into the common shares account from the retained earnings account. A stock split also involves the distribution of additional shares to shareholders, but no additional amount is transferred into the common shares account from the retained earnings account.

11-7. Describe the characteristics of preferred shares, and analyze transactions affecting preferred shares.

Preferred shares provide investors certain advantages, including dividend preferences and a preference on asset distributions in the event the corporation is liquidated.

11-8. Measure and report changes in shareholders' equity.

The shareholders' equity section of the statement of financial position is affected by many changes that occur over time. These changes are reported in a separate statement of changes in equity that discloses a summary of the effects of transactions and events that affected the various components of equity, including share capital, contributed surplus, retained earnings, and accumulated other comprehensive income (loss).

11-9. Discuss the impact of share capital transactions on cash flows.

Both inflows (e.g., issuance of share capital) and outflows (e.g., repurchase of shares) are reported in the financing activities section of the statement of cash flows. The payment of dividends is reported as an outflow in this section.

Throughout the preceding chapters, we emphasized the conceptual basis of accounting. An understanding of the rationale underlying accounting is important for both preparers and users of financial statements. In Chapter 12, we discuss the important players in communicating accounting information to external users, and the process, manner, and timing of the transmission of this information to users. We also bring together our discussion of the major users of financial statements and how they analyze and use them. We discuss and illustrate many widely used analytical techniques discussed in earlier chapters, as well as additional techniques. These discussions will help you consolidate much of what you have learned about the financial reporting process from previous chapters. As you study Chapter 12, you will see that an understanding of accounting rules and concepts is essential for effective analysis of financial statements.

KEY **RATIOS**

The earnings per share ratio states the net earnings of a corporation on a per common share basis. The ratio is computed as follows:

$$\text{Earnings per share} = \frac{\text{Net earnings available to common shareholders}}{\text{Average number of common shares outstanding}}$$

The dividend yield ratio measures the dividend return on the current share price. The ratio is computed as follows:

$$\text{Dividend yield ratio} = \frac{\text{Dividends per share}}{\text{Market price per share}}$$

FINDING **FINANCIAL INFORMATION**

STATEMENT OF FINANCIAL POSITION
Under Current Liabilities
Dividends, once declared by the board of directors, are reported as a liability (usually current).
Under Non-current Liabilities
Transactions involving share capital do not usually generate non-current liabilities.
Under Shareholders' Equity
Typical accounts include
   Preferred shares
   Common shares
   Contributed surplus
   Retained earnings
   Accumulated other comprehensive income (loss)

STATEMENT OF CHANGES IN SHAREHOLDERS' EQUITY
This statement reports detailed information concerning shareholders' equity, including,
(1) amounts in each equity account,
(2) number of shares outstanding, and
(3) impact of transactions such as declaration of dividends and repurchase of shares.

STATEMENT OF EARNINGS
Share capital is never shown on the statement of earnings. Dividends are not an expense. They are a distribution of net earnings and are, therefore, not reported on the statement of earnings.

STATEMENT OF CASH FLOWS
Under Financing Activities
+ Cash inflows from initial sale of shares
− Cash outflows for dividends
− Cash outflows for repurchase of shares

NOTES
Under Summary of Significant Accounting Policies
Usually, very little information concerning share capital is provided in this summary.
Under a Separate Note
Most companies report information about their stock option plans and information about major transactions such as stock dividends. A historical summary of dividends paid per share is typically provided.

QUESTIONS

1. Define *corporation* and identify its primary advantages.
2. What is the charter of a corporation?
3. Explain each of the following terms: (a) *authorized shares*, (b) *issued shares*, and (c) *outstanding shares*.
4. Name three rights of shareholders. Which of these is most important in your mind? Why?
5. Differentiate between common shares and preferred shares.
6. Explain the distinction between par value shares and no par value shares.
7. What are the usual characteristics of preferred shares?
8. What are the two basic sources of shareholders' equity? Explain each.
9. Shareholders' equity is accounted for by source. What does *source* mean?

10. What are the two basic requirements to support the declaration of a cash dividend? What are the effects of a cash dividend on assets and shareholders' equity?

11. Differentiate between cumulative and non-cumulative preferred shares.

12. Define *stock dividend*. How does it differ from a cash dividend?

13. What are the primary purposes of issuing a stock dividend?

14. Identify and explain the three important dates with respect to dividends.

15. Define *retained earnings*. What are the primary components of retained earnings at the end of each period?

16. Define *prior-period errors*. How are they reported?

17. Define *accumulated other comprehensive income (loss)*. Why is it a separate component of shareholders' equity?

connect MINI-EXERCISES

LO11-1   **M11-1**   **Evaluating Shareholders' Rights**

Name three rights of common shareholders. Which of these is most important in your opinion? Why?

LO11-3   **M11-2**   **Recording the Sale of Common Shares**

To expand operations, Aragon Consulting issued 170,000 previously unissued common shares. The selling price was $21 per share. Record the issuance of these shares.

LO11-3,11-7   **M11-3**   **Comparing Common Shares and Preferred Shares**

Your parents have just retired and have asked you for some financial advice. They have decided to invest $100,000 in a company very similar to BCE. The company has issued both common and preferred shares. What factors would you consider in giving them advice? Which type of shares would you recommend?

LO11-4   **M11-4**   **Determining the Amount of a Dividend**

Cole Company has been authorized to issue a maximum of 288,000 common shares, but issued only 260,000 shares. The company's board of directors has declared a dividend of 65 cents per share. What is the total amount of the dividend that will be paid?

LO11-4   **M11-5**   **Recording Dividends**

On April 15, 2017, the board of directors for Auction.com declared a cash dividend of 65 cents per share payable to shareholders of record on May 20. The dividends are payable on June 14. The company has 100,000 common shares outstanding. Prepare any necessary journal entries for each date.

LO11-6   **M11-6**   **Determining the Impact of Stock Dividends and Stock Splits**

Reliable Tools Inc. announced a 100 percent stock dividend. Determine the impact (increase, decrease, no change) of this dividend on the following:

1. Total assets
2. Total liabilities
3. Common shares
4. Total shareholders' equity
5. Market value per share of common share

Assume that the company announced a 2-for-1 stock split. Determine the impact of the stock split.

LO11-6   **M11-7**   **Recording a Stock Dividend**

University Food Systems Inc. has issued a 40 percent stock dividend. The company has 752,000 common shares authorized and 200,000 shares issued and outstanding. The common shares account had a balance of $2,200,000 on the date of declaration of the stock dividend, and the market value was $13 per share. Record the issuance of this stock dividend.

LO11-7   **M11-8**   **Determining the Amount of a Preferred Dividend**

Lipscomb Inc. has 200,000 cumulative preferred shares outstanding. The preferred shares are entitled to a dividend of $2 per share but, because of cash flow problems, the company did not pay any dividends last year. The board of directors plans to pay $1.4 million in dividends this year. What amount will go to the preferred shareholders?

■ connect EXERCISES

■ LO11-1,11-3,11-7

E11-1

Determining the Effects of the Issuance of Common and Preferred Shares

Kelly Incorporated was issued a charter on January 15, 2017, that authorized the following share capital:

Common shares, no par value, 100,000 shares.

Preferred shares, $1.50, no par value, 5,000 shares. (*Note:* $1.50 is the dividend rate.)

During 2017, the following selected transactions occurred:

a. Sold and issued 20,000 common shares at $18 cash per share.

b. Sold and issued 3,000 preferred shares at $25 cash per share.

At the end of 2017, the company's net earnings equalled $40,000.

Required:

1. Prepare the shareholders' equity section of the statement of financial position at December 31, 2017.

2. Assume that you are a common shareholder. If Kelly needed additional capital, would you prefer to have it issue additional common or preferred shares? Explain.

■ LO11-2,11-8 **E11-2**

Reporting Shareholders' Equity

The financial statements of Planet Media Inc. included the following selected information at December 31, 2018:

Common shares	$1,600,000
Retained earnings	900,000
Net earnings	1,000,000
Dividends declared	800,000

The common shares were sold at $20 per share.

Required:

1. What was the amount of retained earnings at the beginning of 2018?

2. Compute earnings per share.

3. Prepare the shareholders' equity section of the company's statement of financial position at December 31, 2018.

■ LO11-1,11-3 **E11-3**

Reporting Shareholders' Equity, and Determining Dividend Policy

Sampson Corporation was organized in 2017 to operate a financial consulting business. The charter authorized the issue of 12,000 common shares. During the first year, the following selected transactions were completed:

a. Sold and issued 6,000 common shares for cash at $22 per share.

b. Sold and issued 600 common shares for a piece of land to be used for a facilities site; construction began immediately. Assume that the market price per share was $22 on the date of issuance. Debit the land account.

c. Sold and issued 1,000 common shares for cash at $23 per share.

d. At year-end, the statement of earnings showed a loss of $7,000. Because a loss was incurred, no income tax expense was recorded.

Required:

1. Prepare the journal entry required for each of these transactions.

2. Prepare the shareholders' equity section as it should be reported on the statement of financial position at year-end, December 31, 2017.

3. Can Sampson pay dividends at year-end? Explain.

■ LO11-1,11-3,11-7

E11-4

Determining the Effects of Transactions on Shareholders' Equity

Quick Fix-it Corporation was organized in January 2018 to operate several car repair businesses in a large metropolitan area. The charter issued by the government authorized the following no par value shares:

Common shares, 200,000 shares

Preferred shares, 50,000 shares

During January and February 2018, the following transactions were completed:

a. Collected $80,000 cash from shareholders and issued 4,000 common shares.

b. Sold and issued 2,000 preferred shares at $25 per share; collected the cash.

c. Sold and issued 500 common shares to a new investor at $25 per share; collected the cash.

The company's operations resulted in net earnings of $40,000 for 2018. The board of directors declared cash dividends of $25,000 that were paid in December 2018. The preferred shares have a dividend rate of $1 per share.

Required:

1. Prepare the shareholders' equity section of the statement of financial position at December 31, 2018.

2. Why would an investor prefer to buy a preferred share rather than a common share?

3. Is it ethical to sell shares to outsiders at a higher price than the amount paid by the organizers?

 LO11-1,11-3   E11-5   **Recording Shareholders' Equity Transactions, Including Non-cash Consideration**
Teacher Corporation obtained a charter at the start of 2017 that authorized 50,000 no par value common shares and 40,000, $1, no par value preferred shares. The corporation was organized by four individuals who "reserved" 51 percent of the common shares for themselves. The remaining shares were to be sold to other individuals at $50 per share on a cash basis. During 2017, the following selected transactions occurred:

a. Collected $25 per share cash from three of the organizers and received two adjoining lots of land from the fourth organizer. Sold and issued 3,000 common shares to each of the four organizers and received title to the land.

b. Sold and issued 6,000 common shares to an investor at $50 cash per share.

c. Sold and issued 8,000 preferred shares at $25 cash per share.

d. At the end of 2017, the accounts reflected net earnings of $42,000.

Required:

1. Prepare the journal entries to record each of these transactions.

2. Write a brief memo to explain the basis that you used to determine the cost of the land.

3. Is it ethical to sell shares to outsiders at a higher price than the amount paid by the organizers?

 LO11-1,11-4,11-5

E11-6   **Determining the Ending Balance of Retained Earnings, and Evaluating Dividend Policy**
The following account balances were selected from the records of Blake Corporation at December 31, 2017, after all adjusting entries were completed:

Common shares (no par value; authorized 100,000 shares, issued 34,000 shares)	$680,000
Contributed surplus	163,000
Dividends declared in 2017	18,000
Retained earnings, January 1, 2017	75,000
Correction of prior-period accounting error (a debit, net of income tax)	8,000
Income summary for 2017 (credit balance)	28,000

The stock price was $22.63 per share on that date.

Required:

1. Identify the amounts that would be reported in the retained earnings column of the statement of changes in equity for 2017.

2. Prepare the shareholders' equity section of the statement of financial position at December 31, 2017.

3. Compute and evaluate the dividend yield ratio.

 **LO11-4,11-6   E11-7**   **Analyzing the Impact of Dividend Policy**
McDonald and Associates is a small manufacturer of electronic connections for local area networks. Consider three independent situations.

Case 1: McDonald increases its cash dividends by 50 percent, but no other changes occur in the company's operations.

Case 2: The company's net earnings and cash flows increase by 50 percent, but this does not change its dividends.

Case 3: McDonald issues a 50 percent stock dividend, but no other changes occur.

Required:

1. How do you think each situation would affect the company's stock price?

2. If the company changed its accounting policies and reported higher net earnings, would the change have an impact on the stock price?

▨ LO11-4   **E11-8**   **Computing Dividends on Preferred Shares, and Analyzing Differences**

The records of Hoffman Company reflected the following balances in the shareholders' equity accounts at December 31, 2017:

Common shares, no par value, 40,000 shares outstanding	$800,000
Preferred shares, $2, no par value, 6,000 shares outstanding	150,000
Retained earnings	235,000

On September 1, 2018, the board of directors was considering the distribution of a $62,000 cash dividend. No dividends were paid during 2013 and 2017. You have been asked to determine dividend amounts under two independent assumptions (show computations):

a. The preferred shares are non-cumulative.

b. The preferred shares are cumulative.

Required:

1. Determine the total amounts that would be paid to the preferred shareholders and to the common shareholders under the two independent assumptions.

2. Write a brief memo to explain why the dividend per common share was less under the second assumption.

3. Why would an investor buy Hoffman's common shares instead of its preferred shares if they pay a lower dividend per share? Explain. The market prices of the preferred and common shares were $25 and $40, respectively, on September 1, 2018.

▨ LO11-4,11-6,11-7   **Determining the Impact of Dividends**

E11-9   Average Corporation has the following shares outstanding at the end of 2016:

Preferred shares, $3, no par value; 8,000 outstanding shares

Common shares, no par value; 30,000 outstanding shares

On October 1, 2017, the board of directors declared dividends as follows:

Preferred shares: Full dividend amount, payable December 20, 2017

Common shares: 10 percent common stock dividend (i.e., one additional share for each 10 held), issuable December 20, 2017

On December 20, 2017, the market prices were $50 per preferred share and $32 per common share.

Required:

Explain the effect of each of the dividends on the assets, liabilities, and shareholders' equity of the company at each of the specified dates.

▨ LO11-4   **E11-10**   **Recording the Payment of Dividends**

Sun Life Financial Inc.

Sun Life Financial Inc. disclosed the following information in a press release:

> **TORONTO, May 10, 2016/CNW/**—The Board of Directors of Sun Life Financial Inc. (TSX: SLF) (NYSE: SLF) today announced an increase of 4% or 1.5 cents per share to the dividend to be paid on its common shares, rising to $0.405 per common share, payable June 30, 2016, to shareholders of record at the close of business on June 1, 2016.
>
> The Board also announced that the following quarterly dividends on its Class A Non-cumulative Preferred Shares are payable on June 30, 2016, to shareholders of record at the close of business on June 1, 2016:
>
> | | |
> |---|---|
> | Series 1 | $0.296875 per share |
> | Series 2 | $0.30 per share |
> | Series 3 | $0.278125 per share |
> | Series 4 | $0.278125 per share |
> | Series 5 | $0.28125 per share |
> | Series 8R | $0.142188 per share |
> | Series 9QR | $0.116679 per share |
> | Series 10R | $0.24375 per share |
> | Series 12R | $0.26563 per share |

Required:

1. Prepare the journal entries to record the declaration and payment of dividends to common shareholders. Assume that there were 612 million common shares outstanding on May 10, 2016.

2. Prepare the journal entries to record the declaration and payment of dividends to the holders of 8 million Series 10R preferred shares.

3. All the preferred shares were sold and issued on different dates between 2005 and 2015 at $25 per share. Why does Sun Life pay different dividend amounts for the different series?

LO11-6   **E11-11**   **Analyzing Stock Dividends**

On December 31, 2018, the shareholders' equity section of the statement of financial position of R & B Corporation reflected the following:

Common shares (no par value, authorized 60,000 shares, outstanding 30,000 shares)	$360,000
Contributed surplus	12,000
Retained earnings	175,000
Accumulated other comprehensive income	28,000

On February 1, 2019, the board of directors declared a 10 percent stock dividend to be issued April 30, 2019. The market value per share was $18 on the declaration date.

Required:

1. For comparative purposes, prepare the shareholders' equity section of the statement of financial position (*a*) before the stock dividend and (*b*) after the stock dividend. (*Hint:* Use two columns for this requirement.)

2. Explain the effects of this stock dividend on the company's assets, liabilities, and shareholders' equity.

LO11-6   **E11-12**   **Analyzing Stock Dividends**

At the beginning of 2018, the shareholders' equity section of the statement of financial position of Ponti Corporation reflected the following:

Common shares, no par value, authorized unlimited number of shares, issued and outstanding 36,000 shares	$360,000
Retained earnings	750,000

On February 1, 2018, the board of directors declared a 100 percent stock dividend to be issued on April 30, 2018. The price per common share was $18 on February 1, 2018.

Required:

1. For comparative purposes, prepare the shareholders' equity section of the statement of financial position (*a*) before the stock dividend and (*b*) after the stock dividend. (*Hint:* Use two columns to show amounts for this requirement.)

2. Explain the effects of this stock dividend on assets, liabilities, and shareholders' equity.

LO11-6   **E11-13**   **Determining the Impact of Stock Dividends and Stock Splits**

Milano Tools Inc. announced a 100 percent stock dividend.

Required:

1. Determine the impact (increase, decrease, no change) of this dividend on the following:

    a. Total assets

    b. Total liabilities

    c. Common shares

    d. Total shareholders' equity

    e. Market value per common share

2. Now assume that the company announced a 2-for-1 stock split. Determine the impact of the stock split on the five items above. Explain why the accounting for stock dividends differs from that of the stock split.

LO11-4   **E11-14**   **Evaluating Dividend Policy**

H&R Block

H&R Block is a well-known name, especially during income tax time each year. The company serves more than 25 million taxpayers in more than 10,000 offices in Canada, Australia, England, and the United States. The company's news releases for 2016 contained the following announcement:

H&R Block Announces Quarterly Cash Dividend

KANSAS CITY, MO—(MARKETWIRE)—March 2, 2016—H&R Block, Inc. (NYSE: HRB), the world's largest consumer tax services provider, today announced that its Board of Directors declared a quarterly cash dividend of 20 cents per share, payable April 1, 2016, to shareholders of record as of March 15, 2016.

Source: H&R Block News Release.

The following day, March 3, 2016, the Company announced a loss from continuing operations of US$79 million for the third fiscal quarter ending on January 31, 2016.

Required:

1. Explain why H&R Block can pay dividends despite the loss that it announced for the previous quarter.
2. What factors did the board of directors consider when it declared the dividends?

■ LO11-3 **E11-15** **Analyzing the Repurchase of Shares**

Dorel Industries Inc.

Dorel Industries Inc. manufactures and markets juvenile products, bicycles, and a wide assortment of both domestically produced and imported furniture products, principally within North America. The company's annual report for 2014 included the following information (dollar amounts are in thousands):

On May 12, 2014, the Company announced that it had decided to implement a new normal course issuer bid (the "2014 NCIB"). As approved by the TSX, under the 2014 NCIB, the Company is entitled to repurchase for cancellation up to 500,000 Class "B" Subordinate Voting Shares during the period of May 14, 2014, to May 13, 2015, or until such earlier time as the bid is completed or terminated at the option of the Company. Any shares the Company purchases under the 2014 NCIB will be purchased on the open market plus brokerage fees through the facilities of the TSX at the prevailing market price at the time of the transaction. Shares acquired under the 2014 NCIB will be cancelled. In accordance with the 2014 NCIB, the Company did not repurchase any Class "B" Subordinate Voting Shares during the year ended December 30, 2014.

During the year ended December 30, 2013, in accordance with its previous normal course issuer bid which ended on May 1, 2014, the Company repurchased a total of 10,000 Class "B" Subordinate Voting Shares for a cash consideration of $321. The excess of the shares' repurchase value over their carrying amount of $253 was charged to retained earnings as share repurchase premiums.

Required:

1. Determine the average issuance price per Class "B" Subordinate Voting Share in 2013.
2. Determine the impact of this transaction on the financial statements.
3. Why do you think the board decided to repurchase the company's shares?
4. What impact will this purchase have on Dorel's future dividend obligations?

connect PROBLEMS

■ LO11-3,11-4,11-6 **Missing Amounts** (AP11-1)

P11-1 At December 31, 2017, the records of Nortech Corporation provided the following selected and incomplete data:

Common shares, no par value	
Shares authorized, 200,000	
Shares issued, __?__ ; issue price $17 per share; cash collected in full	$2,125,000
Net earnings for 2017	118,000
Dividends declared and paid during 2017	75,000
Prior-period error, correction of 2016 accounting error (a credit, net of income tax)	9,000
Retained earnings balance, January 1, 2017	155,000

Required:

1. Complete the following tabulation:
   Shares authorized, _____.
   Shares issued, _____.
   Shares outstanding, _____.
2. EPS, $_____.

3. Dividend paid per common share, $ _____.

4. The prior-period error should be reported on the _____ as an addition to _____ (or a deduction from _____).

5. The amount of retained earnings available for dividends on January 1, 2017, was $ _____.

6. Assume that the board of directors voted a 100 percent stock split (the number of shares will double). After the stock split, the average issue price per share will be $_____ and the number of outstanding shares will be _____.

7. Assume that the company declared a 100 percent stock dividend instead of the 100 percent stock split. Compare and contrast the stock dividend and the stock split with regard to their effects on shareholders' equity components.

LO11-3,11-7,11-8

P11-2

Recording Transactions Affecting Shareholders' Equity (AP11-2)

King Corporation began operations in January 2018. The charter authorized the following share capital:

Preferred shares: 5 percent, $25 par value, authorized 40,000 shares

Common shares: no par value, authorized 100,000 shares

During 2018, the following transactions occurred in the order given:

a. Sold and issued 20,000 common shares to each of the three organizers. Collected $9 cash per share from two of the organizers, and received a plot of land with a small building on it in full payment for the shares of the third organizer and issued the shares immediately. Assume that 30 percent of the non-cash payment received applies to the building.

b. Sold and issued 6,000 preferred shares at $25 per share. Collected the cash and issued the shares immediately.

c. Sold and issued 2,000 preferred shares at $25 and 2,000 common shares at $12 per share. Collected the cash and issued the shares immediately.

d. The operating results at the end of 2018 were as follows:

Revenues	$330,000
Expenses, including income taxes	240,000

Required:

1. Prepare the journal entries to record each of these transactions and to close the accounts.

2. Write a brief memo explaining how you determined the cost of the land and the building in the first journal entry.

3. Prepare the shareholders' equity section of the statement of financial position for King Corporation as at December 31, 2018.

LO11-3,11-4,11-6,11-8

P11-3

Preparing the Shareholders' Equity Section after Selected Transactions (AP11-3)

Eddie Edwards Limited, a public company, was formed on January 2, 2017, with the following authorized capital structure:

Preferred shares: No par value, $1.00 per share quarterly cumulative dividend, callable at 103, 100,000 shares

Common shares: Unlimited number of shares

The following selected transactions occurred during the first six months of operations:

January 2	Sold and issued 100,000 common shares in exchange for land and building with a combined appraised value of $2,200,000. Sixty percent of the acquisition cost is attributable to the building.
January 3	Sold and issued 50,000 preferred shares for $1,250,000 cash.
April 1	Declared the quarterly cash dividend on the preferred shares, payable on April 25.
April 10	Declared and distributed a 5 percent common stock dividend on all outstanding common shares as of March 31. The market price of the common shares on March 31 was $24 per share.
April 25	Paid the preferred dividend that was declared on April 1.

Required:

1. Prepare journal entries to record the above transactions.

2. Prepare the shareholders' equity section of the statement of financial position for Eddie Edwards Limited as at June 30, 2017. Assume that the company recorded net earnings of $500,000 for its first six months.

LO11-4,11-6   **P11-4**   **Comparing Stock and Cash Dividends** (AP11-4)

e**X**cel

Calgate Company had the following shares outstanding and retained earnings at December 31, 2017:

Preferred shares, 4% (par value $25; outstanding, 10,000 shares)	$250,000
Common shares (outstanding, 30,000 shares)	600,000
Retained earnings	281,000

The board of directors is considering the distribution of a cash dividend to the two groups of shareholders. No dividends were declared during 2015 or 2016. Three independent cases are assumed:

Case A: The preferred shares are non-cumulative; the total amount of dividends is $51,000.

Case B: The preferred shares are cumulative; the total amount of dividends is $60,000.

Case C: Same as case B, except the amount is $96,000.

Required:

1. Compute the amount of dividends, in total and per share, that would be payable to each class of shareholders for each case. Show computations.

2. Assume that the company issued a 10 percent common stock dividend on the outstanding common shares when the market value per share was $24. Complete the following comparative schedule for common shares only, including explanation of the differences.

	Amount of Dollar Increase (Decrease)	
Item	**Cash Dividend—Case C**	**Stock Dividend**
Assets	$_____	$_____
Liabilities	$_____	$_____
Shareholders' equity	$_____	$_____

LO11-4,11-8   **P11-5**   **Analyzing Dividend Policy**

Dana and David, two young financial analysts, were reviewing financial statements for Smart Phone Limited (SPL), a manufacturer of wireless mobile communication devices. Dana noted that the company did not report any dividends in the financing activity section of the statement of cash flows and said, "I have heard that SPL is one of the best performing companies. If it's so good, I wonder why it isn't paying any dividends." David wasn't convinced that Dana was looking in the right place for dividends but didn't say anything.

Dana continued the discussion and noted, "Sales are up by nearly 50 percent over the previous two years. While net earnings are up over $600 million compared to last year, cash flow from operating activities increased by nearly $1,500 million compared to the previous year."

At that point, David noted that the statement of cash flows reported that the company had repurchased nearly $800 million in common shares. He commented, "No wonder it can't pay dividends. With cash flows being used to repurchase shares, the board is probably reluctant to oblige itself to dividends."

Required:

1. Correct any misstatements that either Dana or David made. Explain.

2. Which of the factors presented in the case help you understand the company's dividend policy?

LO11-4,11-6,11-7   **Determining the Financial Statement Effects of Dividends**

P11-6   Uno Company has outstanding 52,000 common shares and 25,000, $2, preferred shares. On December 1, 2017, the board of directors voted to distribute a $2 cash dividend per preferred share and a 5 percent common stock dividend on the common shares. At the date of declaration, the common share was selling at $40 and the preferred share at $25. The dividends are to be paid, or issued, on February 15, 2018. The company's fiscal year ends on December 31.

Required:

Explain the comparative effects of the two dividends on the assets, liabilities, and shareholders' equity (*a*) through December 31, 2017, (*b*) on February 15, 2018, and (*c*) overall from December 1, 2017, through February 15, 2018. A schedule similar to the following might be helpful:

	Comparative Effects Explained	
Item	**Cash Dividend on Preferred**	**Stock Dividend on Common**
1. Through December 31, 2017: Assets, etc.		

■ LO11-4,11-6   **P11-7**   **Recording Dividends**

UBL Financial Group provides personal and commercial banking, wealth management services, insurance, and corporate and investment banking. On March 3, 2017, the company announced that its board of directors had declared a stock dividend, which has the same effect as a two-for-one split of its common shares. The board of directors also declared a quarterly common share cash dividend of $0.52 per share, which represents $0.26 per share on a post-stock dividend basis. This dividend of $0.26 per share was payable on May 24, 2017, to common shareholders of record on April 25, 2017.

Required:

1. Prepare any journal entries that UBC Financial should make as the result of information in the preceding report. Assume that the company has 1.3 million shares outstanding with a market value of $13.25 per share and an average issue price of $5.60.
2. What factors did the board of directors consider in making this decision?

■ LO11-8   **P11-8**   **Determining the Balance of Retained Earnings, and Preparing the Shareholders' Equity Section**

The annual report of Prodimax Ltd. for fiscal year 2017 included the financial statements for fiscal year 2016, which were restated to reflect the effects of a fraudulent action by a former employee. The restated financial statements included the following items and their account balances:

Share capital	$ 7,375	
Retained earnings, beginning of year	74,494	
Net earnings	8,467	
Dividends declared	3,108	
Effect of prior-period error	593	Debit balance

Required:

1. Determine the balance of retained earnings for the year ending October 31, 2016, and prepare the shareholders' equity section of the statement of financial position as at October 31, 2016.
2. The company provided the following explanation for the prior-period error. Use the amounts shown in the "Adjustment" column below to reconstruct the journal entry that was prepared to record the effect of the alleged fraud on the identified financial statement accounts:

PRIOR-PERIOD ERROR

During fiscal 2017, management uncovered evidence of a misappropriation of certain assets (related to an alleged fraud by a former non-executive employee). As a result, management determined that certain costs, which previously had been included in the cost of inventories, should have been expensed. In addition, certain costs previously included in cost of goods sold have been reclassified as unusual items. Accordingly, the consolidated financial statements for the fiscal year ended October 31, 2016, have been restated as follows from the amounts previously reported:

	As Previously Reported	Adjustment	As Restated
Cost of sales	$96,660	$(1,058)	$95,602
Unusual items	—	1,173	1,173
Income tax expense	4,730	(44)	4,686
Net earnings	8,538	(71)	8,467
Inventories	62,045	(1,072)	60,973
Income taxes recoverable	693	408	1,101
Retained earnings as at October 31, 2016	79,924	(664)	79,260
Retained earnings as at October 31, 2015	74,494	(593)	73,901

■ LO11-8   **P11-9**   **Determining the Balance of Retained Earnings, and Preparing the Statement of Changes in Equity** (AP11-5)

Thomson Reuters
Corporation

The consolidated statements of changes in equity of Thomson Reuters Corporation for fiscal years 2015 and 2014 included the following items and their account balances at December 31, 2015 and 2014 (in millions of U.S. dollars). This list shows the balances of the various components of shareholders' equity at the beginning of each year, and changes that affected these components during the year. These changes are presented in a random order:

	2015	2014
Share capital, beginning of year	9,976	10,170
Contributed surplus, beginning of year	181	177
Retained earnings, beginning of year	7,450	7,303
Accumulated other comprehensive income (loss), beginning of year	(4,380)	(1,614)
Shares issued under stock compensation plan	147	129
Net earnings (loss)	1,255	1,909
Shares issued under dividend reinvestment plan	33	33
Other comprehensive income (loss), net	(494)	(1,866)
Dividends declared—common and preferred	1,048	1,069
Contributed surplus—stock compensation plans	(15)	4
Shares purchased for cancellation	470	356
Excess of purchase price over carrying value of shares repurchased and cancelled	996	693

Required:

Prepare a statement of changes in equity for fiscal years 2015 and 2014, similar to the statement that appears in Exhibit 11.2. Include the following headings: share capital, contributed surplus, retained earnings, and accumulated other comprehensive income.

■ LO11-3   P11-10   **Analyzing the Repurchase of Shares** (AP11-6)

Canadian Tire Corporation

Canadian Tire Corporation offers a range of retail goods and services, including general merchandise, apparel, sporting goods, petroleum, and financial services. Its annual report for fiscal year 2015 included the following:

---

28. Share Capital

During 2015 and 2014, the Company issued and repurchased Class A Non-Voting Shares. The following transactions occurred with respect to Class A Non-Voting Shares during 2015:

(C$ in millions)	Number	$
Shares outstanding at beginning of the year	74,023,208	695.3
Issued		
Dividend reinvestment plan	65,760	8.3
Repurchased	(3,450,981)	(434.6)
Excess of issue price over repurchase price	–	402.0
Shares outstanding at end of the year	70,637,987	671.0

Conditions of Class A Non-Voting Shares and Common Shares

The holders of Class A Non-Voting Shares are entitled to receive a preferential cumulative dividend at the rate of $0.01 per share per annum. After payment of preferential cumulative dividends at the rate of $0.01 per share per annum on each of the Class A Non-Voting Shares with respect to the current year and each preceding year and payment of a non-cumulative dividend on each of the Common Shares with respect to the current year at the same rate, the holders of the Class A Non-Voting Shares and the Common Shares are entitled to further dividends declared and paid in equal amounts per share without preference or distinction or priority of one share over another.

Required:

1. Why do you think Canadian Tire's board of directors decided to repurchase the company's Class A non-voting shares?

2. Prepare the journal entry to record a summary of the repurchase transactions.

3. Compute the repurchase price and weighted-average issuance price of the repurchased Class A shares. Explain why the difference between the repurchase price and the issuance price is not recorded as a gain on repurchase of shares.

4. Assume that Canadian Tire had 3,423,366 common shares and 70,637,987 Class A non-voting shares when the board of directors declared that a total of $28.5 million will be paid as dividends to both classes of shares. Assume further that Canadian Tire did not declare dividends in 2014 and 2015. Allocate the total amount of dividends between the two classes of shares.

■ LO11-3,11-4 P11-11
WestJet Airlines

Analyzing the Repurchase of Shares and Retained Earnings (AP11-7)

The following information is extracted from the statements of financial position of WestJet Airlines. All amounts are in thousands of Canadian dollars.

	December 31, 2015	December 31, 2014
Shareholders' Equity		
Share capital	$ 582,796	$ 603,287
Retained earnings	1,292,581	1,102,300
Other components	84,626	71,915
Total shareholders' equity	$1,959,993	$1,777,502

Net earnings for the year ended December 31, 2015, is $367,530.

WestJet reported the following information in the notes to its 2015 financial statements:

> During the year ended December 31, 2015, the Corporation purchased and cancelled a total of 4,719,690 shares (December 31, 2014 – 1,435,150) for total consideration of $123,813 (December 31, 2014 – $39,431). The average book value of the shares repurchased was $4.73 per share (December 31, 2014 – $4.70) and was charged to share capital. The excess of the market price over the average book value, including transaction costs, was $101,489 (December 31, 2014 – $32,680) and was charged to retained earnings.

Required:

1. Prepare the journal entry to record the share repurchase transaction.
2. Why do you think WestJet decided to repurchase the shares? Explain.
3. Did WestJet declare any dividends during fiscal year 2015? If so, compute the amount of dividends declared by the company?

■ LO11-S1   P11-12
eXcel

(Appendix 11A) Comparing Owners' Equity Sections for Alternative Forms of Organization

Assume for each of the following independent cases that the accounting period for NewBiz ends on December 31, 2018, and that the income summary account at that date reflected a debit balance (loss) of $20,000:

Case A: Assume that NewBiz is a *sole proprietorship* owned by Proprietor A. Prior to the closing entries, the capital account reflected a credit balance of $50,000 and the drawings account a balance of $8,000.

Case B: Assume that NewBiz is a *partnership* owned by Partner A and Partner B. Prior to the closing entries, the owners' equity accounts reflected the following balances: A, capital, $40,000; B, capital, $38,000; A, drawings, $5,000; and B, drawings, $9,000. Net earnings and losses are divided equally.

Case C: Assume that NewBiz is a *corporation*. Prior to the closing entries, the shareholders' equity accounts showed the following: share capital, authorized 30,000 shares, outstanding 15,000 shares, $150,000; contributed surplus, $5,000; retained earnings, $65,000.

Required:

1. Prepare all of the closing entries indicated at December 31, 2018, for each of the three separate cases.
2. Show for each case how the owners' equity section of the statement of financial position would appear at December 31, 2018.

ALTERNATE PROBLEMS

■ LO11-3,11-4,11-6
AP11-1

Finding Missing Amounts (P11-1)

At December 31, 2018, the records of Kozmetsky Corporation provided the following selected and incomplete data:

Common shares, no par value	
Shares authorized, unlimited	
Shares issued, ____?___ ; issue price $10 per share	
Net earnings for 2018	$4,800,000
Common shares account	2,000,000
Dividends declared and paid during 2018	$2 per share
Retained earnings balance, January 1, 2018	71,900,000

Required:

1. Complete the following tabulation:
   Shares issued, _____.
   Shares outstanding, _____.

2. Earnings per share, $_____.

3. Total dividends paid on common shares during 2018, $_____.

4. Assume that the board of directors voted a 100 percent stock split (the number of shares will double). After the stock split, the average issue price per share will be $_____ and the number of outstanding shares will be _____.

5. Disregard the stock split assumed in (4). Assume instead that a 10 percent stock dividend was declared and issued when the market price of the common shares was $91. Explain how the shareholders' equity will change.

■ LO11-3,11-7 **AP11-2**   **Recording Transactions Affecting Shareholders' Equity** (P11-2)

Peterson Company was granted a charter that authorized the following share capital:

   Preferred shares: 8 percent, par value $25, 20,000 shares

   Common shares: No par value, 100,000 shares

During the first year, 2017, the following selected transactions occurred in the order given:

a. Sold 30,000 common shares at $35 cash per share and 5,000 preferred shares at $25 cash per share. Collected cash and issued the shares immediately.

b. Sold and issued 2,000 preferred shares as full payment for a plot of land to be used as a future plant site. Assume that the share was selling at $25.

c. Declared and paid the quarterly cash dividend on the preferred shares.

d. At December 31, 2017, the income summary account has a credit balance of $76,000.

Required:

1. Prepare the journal entries to record each of these transactions.

2. Explain the economic difference between acquiring an asset for cash and acquiring it by issuing shares. Is it "better" to acquire a new asset without having to give up another asset?

■ LO11-3,11-4,11-6,11-8 **AP11-3**   **Preparing the Shareholders' Equity Section after Selected Transactions** (P11-3)

The shareholders' equity accounts of Gennar Inc. at January 2, 2017, are as follows:

Preferred shares, no par value, cumulative, 4,000 shares issued	$ 200,000
Common shares, no par value, 125,000 shares issued	2,500,000
Retained earnings	1,600,000

The following transactions occurred during the year:

March 10	Purchased a building for $3,000,000. The seller agreed to receive 20,000 preferred shares and 15,000 common shares of Gennar in exchange for the building. The preferred shares were trading in the market at $50 per share on that day.
July 1	Declared a semi-annual cash dividend of $1.00 per common share and the required amount of dividends on preferred shares, payable on August 1, 2017, to shareholders of record on July 21, 2017. The annual dividend of $2 per preferred share had not been paid in either 2013 or 2017.
August 1	Paid the cash dividend declared on July 1 to both common and preferred shareholders.
December 31	Determined that net earnings for the year were $385,000.

Required:

1. Prepare journal entries to record the above transactions.

2. Prepare the shareholders' equity section of Gennar's statement of financial position as at December 31, 2017.

LO11-4,11-6 **AP11-4** **Comparing Stock and Cash Dividends** (P11-4)

Ritz Company had the following shares outstanding and retained earnings at December 31, 2018:

Preferred shares, 8% (par value $25; outstanding, 9,000 shares)	$225,000
Common shares (outstanding, 5,000 shares)	800,000
Retained earnings	720,000

The board of directors is considering the distribution of a cash dividend to the two groups of shareholders. No dividends were declared during 2013 or 2017. Three independent cases are assumed:

Case A: The preferred shares are non-cumulative; the total amount of dividends is $25,000.

Case B: The preferred shares are cumulative; the total amount of dividends is $36,000.

Case C: Same as case B, except the amount is $77,500.

Required:

1. Compute the amount of dividends, in total and per share, payable to each class of shareholders for each case. Show computations.

2. Assume that the company issued a 10 percent common stock dividend on the outstanding common shares when the market value per share was $47. Complete the following comparative schedule for common shares only, including an explanation of the differences.

Item	Amount of Dollar Increase (Decrease)	
	Cash Dividend—Case C	Stock Dividend
Assets	$_____	$_____
Liabilities	$_____	$_____
Shareholders' equity	$_____	$_____

LO11-8 **AP11-5** **Determining the Balance of Retained Earnings, and Preparing the Statement of Changes in Equity** (P11-9)

Alimentation Couche-Tard Inc.

The consolidated statements of changes in equity of Alimentation Couche-Tard Inc. for fiscal years 2015 and 2014 included the following items and their account balances at April 26, 2015, and April 27, 2014 (in millions of Canadian dollars). This list shows the balances of the various components of shareholders' equity at the beginning of each year, and the changes that affected these components during the year. These changes are presented in a random order:

	2015	2014
Share capital, beginning of year	$ 686.5	$ 670.4
Contributed surplus, beginning of year	11.6	16.5
Retained earnings, beginning of year	3,090.6	2,344.0
Accumulated other comprehensive income, beginning of year	186.9	185.8
Stock option–based compensation expense	6.0	1.8
Net earnings	932.8	811.2
Other comprehensive income (loss), net	(925.5)	1.1
Dividends declared	86.9	64.6
Initial fair value of stock options exercised	6.9	6.7
Cash received on exercise of options	3.8	9.4

Required:

1. Compute the balance of retained earnings at April 26, 2015.

2. Prepare a statement of changes in equity for fiscal years 2015 and 2014, similar to the statement that appears in Exhibit 11.2.

LO11-3 **AP11-6** **Analyzing the Repurchase of Shares** (P11-10)

Jean Coutu Group

The Jean Coutu Group operates a network of franchised stores in Canada, located in the provinces of Québec, New Brunswick, and Ontario under the banners of PJC Jean Coutu, PJC Clinique, PJC Santé, and PJC Santé Beauté, and employs more than 17,000 people. Its annual report for fiscal year 2015 included the following:

22. Capital Stock

...

Changes that occurred in capital stock are presented as follows:

	2015		2014	
	Shares		**Shares**	
	(in millions)	**$**	**(in millions)**	**$**
Class A subordinate voting shares				
Outstanding shares, beginning of year	85.2	422.1	100.0	537.1
Exercise of exchange privilege	0.5	—	10.4	—
Repurchased and cancelled	(2.6)	(12.7)	(26.2)	(129.4)
Repurchased and not cancelled	—	—	—	(1.5)
Stock options exercised	0.4	6.6	1.0	14.4
Outstanding shares, end of year	83.5	416.0	85.2	422.1

a) Substantial Repurchase under the normal course issuer bid

On October 8, 2013, the Corporation announced an offer to repurchase for cancellation up to 22,000,000 Class "A" subordinate voting shares of the Corporation at a price of $18.50 per share (the "Offer"). In accordance with the Offer, the Corporation repurchased 22,000,000 Class "A" subordinate voting shares at a price of $18.50 per share for a total consideration of $407.5 million including related costs during the fiscal year 2014. An amount of $299.8 million representing the excess of the purchase price over the carrying value of the repurchased shares was included in retained earnings for the fiscal year ended March 1, 2014.

b) Repurchase under the normal course issuer bid

For the years ended February 28, 2015, and March 1, 2014, the Corporation repurchased 2,574,100 and 4,093,300 Class "A" subordinate voting shares at an average price of $21.62 and $17.17 per share for a total consideration of $55.6 million and $70.3 million including related costs, respectively. Amounts of $42.9 million and $48.6 million representing the excess of the purchase price over the carrying value of the repurchased shares were included in retained earnings for the years ended February 28, 2015, and March 1, 2014, respectively. The shares repurchased during fiscal year ended February 28, 2015, and March 1, 2014, were cancelled during these same periods.

Required:

1. Why do you think Jean Coutu's board of directors decided to repurchase the company's shares?
2. Prepare the journal entries to record summaries of the repurchase transactions that occurred in fiscal years 2014 and 2015.
3. Compute the weighted-average issuance price per common share when the shares were repurchased, and explain why Jean Coutu paid a much higher price for repurchasing its own shares.
4. What impact will this transaction have on Jean Coutu's future dividend obligations?

LO11-3,11-4 AP11-7   Analyzing the Repurchase of Shares and Retained Earnings (P11-11)
The following information is extracted from the statement of financial position of Dollarama Inc. All amounts are in thousands of Canadian dollars.

	February 1, 2015	February 2, 2014
Shareholders' Equity		
Share capital	$462,734	$493,602
Contributed surplus	15,338	10,884
Retained earnings	196,112	346,478
Accumulated other comprehensive income	66,296	13,202
Total shareholders' equity	$740,480	$864,166

Net earnings for the year ended December 31, 2015, is $295,410.

WestJet reported the following information in the notes to its 2015 financial statements:

Taking into account the Share Split, the total number of common shares repurchased for cancellation under the 2013–2014 NCIB and the 2014–2015 NCIB during the year ended February 1, 2015, amounted to 9,272,672 common shares (February 2, 2014—7,440,836 common shares under the 2013–2014 NCIB) for a total cash consideration of $436,221 (February 2, 2014—$293,201). For the year ended February 1, 2015, the Corporation's share capital was reduced by $32,937 (February 2, 2014—$26,460) and the remaining $403,284 (February 2, 2014—$266,741) was accounted for as a reduction of retained earnings.

Required:

1. Prepare the journal entry to record the share repurchase transaction.
2. Why do you think Dollarama decided to repurchase the shares? Explain.
3. Did Dollarama declare any dividends during fiscal year 2015? If so, compute the amount of dividends declared by the company?

🔲 connect CASES AND PROJECTS

FINDING AND INTERPRETING FINANCIAL INFORMATION

LO11-3,11-4,11-6

CP11-1

Canadian Tire
Corporation

Finding Financial Information

Refer to the financial statements of Canadian Tire Corporation given in Appendix A of this book.

Required:

1. Identify the types of shares that Canadian Tire is authorized to issue, and their characteristics. Do all types of shares have the same voting rights? If not, explain why.
2. Did the company repurchase shares during 2015? If so, how many shares were repurchased? Reconstruct a summary journal entry to record the share repurchase transactions.
3. Does the company provide stock options to senior executives? If so, describe the plan that is currently in effect. How many stock options were granted in 2015, and how many were exercised during the same year? What was the compensation expense related to the stock option plan for 2015?
4. Identify all the cash flows related to issuance of shares, repurchase of shares, and payment of dividends during fiscal year 2015.
5. The company declared dividends on the different types of outstanding shares during 2015. How much cash did the company pay in 2015 in dividends? Why is this amount different from the dividends declared by the board of directors?
6. Has the company ever issued a stock dividend or declared a stock split? If so, describe the procedure. (*Hint:* Access the following link for details: http://investors.canadiantire.ca/English/investors/investor-resources/faqs/default.aspx)

LO11-3,11-4,11-6

CP11-2

Sears Canada Inc.

Finding Financial Information

Go to *Connect* for the financial statements of Sears Canada Inc.

Required:

1. Identify the types of shares that Sears Canada is authorized to issue, and their characteristics. Do all types of shares have the same voting rights? If not, explain why.
2. Does the company have any treasury shares at January 30, 2016? If so, how many shares?
3. Did the company repurchase shares during fiscal year 2015? If so, how many shares were repurchased? Reconstruct the journal entry to record the share repurchase transactions.
4. Does the company provide stock options to senior executives? If so, describe the plan that is currently in effect. How many stock options were granted in 2015, and how many were exercised during the same year? What was the compensation expense related to the stock option plan for 2015?
5. Identify all the cash flows related to issuance of shares, repurchase of shares, and payment of dividends during fiscal year 2015.

LO11-4,11-5,11-6

CP11-3

Canadian Tire
Corporation vs.
Sears Canada Inc.

Comparing Companies within an Industry

Refer to the financial statements of Canadian Tire Corporation (Appendix A) and Sear Canada Inc. (on *Connect*) and the Industry Ratio Report (Appendix B on *Connect*).

Required:

1. Canadian Tire Corporation split its stock in the past. Describe the impact that the split would have on the market value of the stock compared to a company that did not split its stock. Why do some companies elect to split their stock?
2. Calculate the dividend yield ratios for Canadian Tire (assume a market price of $118.15 per share) and Sears Canada (assume a market price of $6.15 per share) for the most recent reporting year.

3. Why would an investor choose to invest in a corporation whose board of directors does not declare and pay dividends?

4. Using the information from the following table, compare the dividend-related industry average ratios for the retailing industry to the media industry and the utilities industry. What type of investor would be interested in buying shares in a utility instead of a retailing company? Why?

DIVIDEND RATIOS FOR VARIOUS INDUSTRIES

Industry	Example Company	Dividend Yield
Media	Cineplex Inc.	1.60%
Retailing	Sears Canada Inc.	1.16%
Utilities	ATCO Ltd.	4.00%

FINANCIAL REPORTING AND ANALYSIS CASES

LO11-2,11-3,11-4

CP11-4

Procter & Gamble

Finding Information Missing from an Annual Report

Procter & Gamble is a multi-billion dollar company that sells a variety of consumer products, such as Mr. Clean, Cheer, Crest, Vicks, Scope, Pringles, Folgers, Vidal Sassoon, and Zest. The company's annual report contained the following information (in millions except per share data):

a. Retained earnings at June 30, 2015, totalled $75,349.

b. Net earnings for the year ended June 30, 2015, was $10,756.

c. The number of common shares outstanding at June 30, 2015, was 4,008.4 shares.

d. Dividends declared on common shares equalled $2.14 per share.

Required:

1. Compute the total amount of dividends declared by the company.

2. A shareholder observed that P&G has a sizable amount of retained earnings and wondered why the company accumulated this amount instead of distributing it to its shareholders. Write a brief memo to explain why earnings have been retained by the company.

3. Compute the company's earnings per share (EPS), assuming that P&G had not issued preferred shares. Is EPS a useful measure of performance? Explain.

LO11-3   **CP11-5**

Power Financial Corporation

Characteristics of Preferred Shares

Power Financial Corporation is a Canadian diversified international management company that holds interests, directly or indirectly, in companies that are active in the financial services industry in Canada, the United States, and Europe. The company included the following information about specific issues of preferred shares in a recent annual report:

> The Corporation issued 11,200,000 4.40% Non-Cumulative 5-Year Rate Reset First Preferred Shares, Series P for cash proceeds of $280 million. The 4.40% Non-Cumulative First Preferred Shares, Series P are entitled to fixed non-cumulative preferential cash dividends at a rate equal to $1.10 per share per annum. On January 31, 2016, and on January 31 every five years thereafter, the Corporation may redeem for cash the Series P First Preferred Shares in whole or in part, at the Corporation's option, at $25.00 per share plus all declared and unpaid dividends to the date fixed for redemption, or the Series P First Preferred Shares are convertible to Non-Cumulative Floating Rate First Preferred Shares, Series Q, at the option of the holders on January 31, 2016, or on January 31 every five years thereafter. Transaction costs incurred in connection with the Series P First Preferred Shares of $8 million were charged to retained earnings.

Required:

1. Identify the various characteristics of these preferred shares.

2. Based on the characteristics of these shares, should they be classified as debt or equity? Explain.

LO11-5,11-6 CP11-6

Royal Bank of Canada

Analyzing Dividend Policy

Royal Bank of Canada (RY on TSX and NYSE) is Canada's largest bank at the time of writing this book, and one of the largest banks in the world, based on market capitalization. It is one of North America's leading diversified financial services companies that provide personal and commercial banking, wealth management services, insurance, investor services, and capital markets products and services on a global basis. RBC employs over 78,000 employees who serve more than 16 million personal, business, public sector, and institutional clients through offices in Canada, the United States, and 37 other countries.

	2015*	2014	2013	2012	2011
Dividends	$ 4,443	$ 4,097	$ 3,651	$ 3,291	$ 2,979
Net income (net earnings)	10,026	9,004	8,342	7,539	6,444
Dividends per common share	3.08	2.84	2.53	2.28	2.08
Market price per share	74.77	80.01	70.02	56.94	48.62
Dividend yield	4.10%	3.80%	4.00%	4.50%	3.90%

*RBC's fiscal year starts on November 1 and ends on October 31. The information under this column refers essentially to fiscal year 2015 (November 1, 2014–October 31, 2015). It is labelled as 2015 because this period includes 10 months in 2015.

Assume that you are a financial analyst preparing a forecast of RBC's operating results for fiscal year 2017. Because of a number of factors, you believe that net earnings for 2017 will be in the range of $10,000 million to $11,000 million. To complete your financial forecast, you now need to estimate the total amount of dividends that RBC will pay.

Required:

1. Based on the information above, describe the dividend policy of RBC, and estimate the dividends that the company will pay in 2017. (*Hint:* The ratio of dividends to net earnings, called the *dividend payout ratio,* may provide useful information about the company's dividend policy.)

2. RBC's board of directors has increased dividends per share continuously over the past five years. What is your expectation of dividends per share for fiscal year 2017? Justify your answer.

3. The dividend yield has fluctuated over the past five years. What should be the market price per share for the dividend yield to reach 4.50 percent, assuming a dividend of $3.17 per share? Explain.

CRITICAL THINKING CASES

LO11-5,11-6

CP11-7

Evaluating an Ethical Dilemma

You are a member of the board of directors of a large company that has been in business for more than 100 years. The company is proud of the fact that it has paid dividends every year that it has been in business. Because of this stability, many retired people have invested large portions of their savings in the company's common stock. Unfortunately, the company has struggled for the past few years as it tries to introduce new products and is considering not paying a dividend this year. The president wants to skip the dividend in order to have more cash to invest in product development, saying, "If we don't invest this money now, we won't get these products to market in time to save the company. I don't want to risk thousands of jobs." One of the most senior board members speaks next: "If we don't pay the dividend, thousands of retirees will be thrown into financial distress. Even if you don't care about them, you have to recognize our stock price will crash when they all sell." The company treasurer proposes this alternative: "Let's skip the cash dividend and pay a stock dividend. We can still say we've had a dividend every year." The entire board now turns to you for your opinion. What should the company do?

LO11-4

CP11-8

Evaluating an Ethical Dilemma

You are the president of a very successful Internet company that has had a remarkably profitable year. You have determined that the company has more than $10 million in cash generated by operating activities not needed in the business. You are thinking about paying it out to shareholders as a special dividend. You discuss the idea with your vice-president, who reacts angrily to your suggestion, declaring, "Our stock price has gone up by 200 percent in the last year alone. What more do we have to do for the owners? The people who really earned that money are the employees who have been working 12 hours a day, six or seven days a week to make the company successful. Most of them didn't even take vacations last year. I say we have to pay out bonuses and nothing extra for the shareholders." As president, you know that you are hired by the board of directors, which is elected by the shareholders. What is your responsibility to both groups? To which group would you give the $10 million?

FINANCIAL REPORTING AND ANALYSIS TEAM PROJECT

LO11-1,11-3,11-4,11-7

CP11-9

Team Project: Examining an Annual Report

As a team, select an industry to analyze. A list of companies classified by industry can be obtained by accessing www.fpinfomart.ca and then choosing Companies by Industry. You can also find a list of industries and companies within each industry via http://ca.finance.yahoo.com/investing (click on Order Annual Reports under Tools).

Each group member should acquire the annual report for a different publicly traded company in the industry. (Library files, the SEDAR service at www.sedar.com, and the company's website are good sources.)

Required:

On an individual basis, each team member should then write a short report answering the following questions about the selected company. Discuss any patterns across the companies that you as a team observe. Then, as a team, write a short report comparing and contrasting your companies.

1. *a.* List the accounts and amounts of the company's shareholders' equity.

     b. From the notes to financial statements, identify any unusual features in the contributed capital accounts (e.g., convertible preferred, non-voting common), if any.

2. Identify the cash flows related to share capital transactions. You will need to refer to the statement of cash flows.

3. If new shares were issued during the year, what was the average price per share at the time of issuance?

4. Reconstruct the journal entry for the issuance of shares.

5. What type of dividends did the company declare during the year? How much was paid in cash?

⬛ connect   CONTINUING CASE

LO11-3,11-4 CC11-1   **Recording and Reporting Shareholders' Equity Transactions**

Pool Corporation Inc. is the world's largest wholesale distributor of swimming pool supplies and equipment. It is a publicly traded corporation that trades on the NASDAQ exchange under the symbol POOL. It sells these products to swimming pool repair and service businesses, swimming pool builders, and retail swimming pool stores. The majority of these customers are small, family-owned businesses. The company issued the following press release:

> *COVINGTON, La., Feb. 26, 2016 (GLOBE NEWSWIRE) — Pool Corporation (NASDAQ:POOL) announced today that its Board of Directors has authorized an additional $150.0 million under its existing share repurchase program for the purchase of the Company's stock in the open market at prevailing market prices or in privately negotiated transactions.*
>
> *The Company also announced that the Board has declared a quarterly cash dividend of $0.26 per share. The dividend is payable on March 30, 2016 to stockholders of record on March 16, 2016.*

Assume that the company repurchased 1,448,000 shares for cancellation during the first quarter of 2016 and paid a total amount of $99,219,000. The average issuance price per common share is $8.76.

Required:

1. Prepare the journal entry to record the repurchase of shares by Pool.

2. Prepare all necessary journal entries associated with the dividend. Pool has 100 million shares authorized with 42.7 million issued and outstanding. Assume that the dividend was paid after the repurchase of shares took place.

SOLUTIONS TO SELF-STUDY QUIZZES

Self-Study Quiz 11-1

1.

Common shares	61	
Contributed surplus	4	
Deficit	78	
Cash		143

2. Average issuance price = ($61,000,000 + $4,000,000)/3,500,466 = $18.57

Self-Study Quiz 11-2

1. The liability is created on the declaration date, May 5, 2016.
2. The cash outflow occurs on the payment date, July 4, 2016.
3.

Dividends payable	277,380,000	
Cash (603,000,000 × $0.46)		277,380,000

4. The fundamental requirements are availability of retained earnings, declaration by the board of directors, and availability of cash. However, if a corporation reports a deficit, it may declare and pay dividends if payment of the dividend does not place the company into a position that would prevent it from paying its liabilities as they become due.

Self-Study Quiz 11-3

1.

Retained earnings	3,000,000	
Common shares		3,000,000

2.

Retained earnings	1,000,000	
Common shares		1,000,000

3. No journal entry is required in the case of a stock split.

Self-Study Quiz 11-4

1. Total annual dividends = Number of shares × Dividend per share
   = 8,000,000 × ($25 × 4.13%) = $33,040,000
2. The redemption date is the earliest date when BCE can call Series R back from shareholders and pay them $25.00 per share.
3. The earliest redemption date is December 1, 2020.

ENDNOTES

1. If a corporation becomes insolvent, creditors have recourse for their claims only to the corporation's assets. Thus, shareholders stand to lose only their equity in the corporation. In the case of a partnership or sole proprietorship, creditors have recourse to the owners' personal assets if the assets of the business are insufficient to meet its debts.
2. Publicly accountable enterprises are required to report a third component of equity called accumulated other comprehensive income (loss). We discuss this component briefly later in this chapter.
3. A voting proxy is written authority by a shareholder that gives another party the right to vote the shareholder's shares in the annual meeting of the shareholders. Typically, proxies are solicited by and given to the president of the corporation.
4. The average issue price per share equals the balance of the common shares account divided by the number of common shares outstanding.
5. Assume that a company issues shares at $10 per share and then buys them back from some shareholders at $9 per share. If the difference of $1 is treated as profit, then the company will have to pay income tax, causing a reduction in cash. If it continues with similar transactions, then it will pay income taxes on earnings that did not result from operating transactions. The decrease in cash causes a decrease in the company's assets, which depresses the company's market value and causes further deterioration in the share price. No one would want to invest in such a company. Earnings are generated from operating activities, not capital transactions.
6. Further details about each series of BCE's preferred shares are available on its website at www.bce.ca/investors/preferredshares.

Communicating Accounting Information and Analyzing Financial Statements

After studying this chapter, you should be able to do the following:

LEARNING OBJECTIVES

LO12-1 Recognize the roles of people involved in the accounting communication process (regulators, managers, board of directors, auditors, information intermediaries, and users), and the guidance they receive from legal and professional standards.

LO12-2 Identify the steps in the accounting communication process, including the issuance of press releases, annual reports, quarterly reports, and documents filed with securities commissions.

LO12-3 Explain how a company's business strategy affects financial analysis.

LO12-4 Discuss how analysts use financial statements.

LO12-5 Compute and interpret component percentages.

LO12-6 Compute and interpret profitability ratios.

LO12-7 Compute and interpret liquidity ratios.

LO12-8 Compute and interpret solvency ratios.

LO12-9 Compute and interpret market test ratios.

SUPPLEMENTARY MATERIAL

LO12-S1 Evaluate a company's performance using the expanded DuPont model.

Vale Stock/Shutterstock.com

Focus Company: **Canadian Tire Corporation, Limited**

FINANCIAL ANALYSIS: BRINGING IT ALL TOGETHER

The history of Canadian Tire Corporation Ltd. (www.canadiantire.ca) is an unusual success story. Founded in 1923 by two brothers, John W. and Alfred J. Billes, in Toronto, Canadian Tire has become one of Canada's most-shopped-at general retailers, with nearly 1,700 retail and gasoline outlets across Canada offering automotive and hardware products, sporting goods, clothes for work or play, convenient gas bars, and everything needed for the home. Canadian Tire's financial statements are presented in Exhibit 12.1.

Canadian Tire operates businesses that offer a wide variety of products and services. These include Canadian Tire Financial Services Limited, Canadian Tire Bank, Canadian Tire Real Estate Limited, FGL Sports Ltd., and Mark's Work Wearhouse Ltd. Canadian Tire and its subsidiaries employed more than 68,000 full-time and part-time employees as of December 31, 2015. Canadian Tire's net revenues grew at an average rate of 4.6 percent per year during the 10-year period 2006–2015, and its earnings grew at an average annual rate of 9.1 percent during the same period.

As a publicly traded company listed on the Toronto Stock Exchange, Canadian Tire is required to provide detailed information in regular filings with the Ontario Securities Commission. Integrity in communicating with investors and other users of financial statements is key to maintaining relationships with providers of capital. Furthermore, clear and timely communication of the company's financial situation enables Canadian Tire to comply with exchange rules and securities commission regulations. It also informs the company's investors, creditors, and other users of financial statements of the company's success in implementing its business strategy.

Exhibit **12.1**
Canadian Tire Financial
Statements

REAL-WORLD EXCERPT

Canadian Tire

ANNUAL REPORT

CANADIAN TIRE CORPORATION LTD.
Consolidated Balance Sheets

As at (C$ in millions)	January 2, 2016	January 3, 2015
ASSETS		
Cash and cash equivalents (Note 8)	$ 900.6	$ 662.1
Short-term investments (Note 9)	96.1	289.1
Trade and other receivables (Note 10)	915.0	880.2
Loans receivable (Note 11)	4,875.5	4,905.5
Merchandise inventories	1,764.5	1,623.8
Income taxes recoverable	42.2	31.9
Prepaid expenses and deposits	96.1	104.5
Assets classified as held for sale (Note 12)	2.3	13.1
Total current assets	8,692.3	8,510.2
Long-term receivables and other assets (Note 13)	731.2	684.2
Long-term investments	153.4	176
Goodwill and intangible assets (Note 14)	1,246.8	1,251.7
Investment property (Note 15)	137.8	148.6
Property and equipment (Note 16)	3,978.2	3,743.1
Deferred income taxes (Note 18)	48.1	39.4
Total assets	$14,987.8	$14,553.2
LIABILITIES		
Bank indebtedness (Note 8)	$ –	$ 14.3
Deposits (Note 19)	880.7	950.7
Trade and other payables (Note 20)	1,957.1	1,961.2
Provisions (Note 21)	216.1	206
Short-term borrowings (Note 23)	88.6	199.8
Loans payable (Note 24)	655.5	604.4
Income taxes payable	61.5	54.9
Current portion of long-term debt (Note 25)	24.3	587.5
Total current liabilities	3,883.8	4,578.8
Long-term provisions (Note 21)	45.7	44.1
Long-term debt (Note 25)	2,971.4	2,131.6
Long-term deposits (Note 19)	1,372.2	1,286.2
Deferred income taxes (Note 18)	111.1	93.9
Other long-term liabilities (Note 26)	813.9	787.8
Total liabilities	9,198.1	8,922.4
EQUITY		
Share capital (Note 28)	671.2	695.5
Contributed surplus	2.9	2.9
Accumulated other comprehensive income	148.1	82.0
Retained earnings	4,172.0	4,075.1
Equity attributable to shareholders of Canadian Tire Corporation	4,994.2	4,855.5
Non-controlling interests (Note 17)	795.5	775.3
Total equity	5,789.7	5,630.8
Total liabilities and equity	$14,987.8	$14,553.2

The related notes form an integral part of these consolidated financial statements.

Source: Canadian Tire Corporation Ltd., Annual Report 2015.

CANADIAN TIRE CORPORATION LTD.
Consolidated Satatements of Income

For the years ended (C$ in millions, except per-share amounts)	January 2, 2016	January 3, 2015
Revenue (Note 30)	$12,279.6	$12,462.9
Cost of producing revenue (Note 31)	8,144.3	8,416.9
Gross margin	4,135.3	4,046.0
Other (income)	(54.9)	(11.0)
Selling, general, and administrative expenses (Note 32)	3,096.1	3,052.9
Net finance costs (Note 33)	92.8	108.9
Change in fair value of redeemable financial instrument (Note 35)	—	17.0
Income before income taxes	1,001.3	878.2
Income taxes (Note 18)	265.4	238.9
Net income	$ 735.9	$ 639.3
Net income attributable to:		
Shareholders of Canadian Tire Corporation	$ 659.4	$ 604.0
Non-controlling interests (Note 17)	76.5	35.3
	$ 735.9	$ 639.3
Basic EPS	$ 8.66	$ 7.65
Diluted EPS	$ 8.61	$ 7.59
Weighted average number of Common and Class A Non-voting Shares outstanding:		
Basic	76,151,321	78,960,025
Diluted	76,581,602	79,612,957

The related notes form an integral part of these consolidated financial statements.

Source: Canadian Tire Corporation Ltd., Annual Report 2015.

CANADIAN TIRE CORPORATION LTD.
Consolidated Statements of Cash Flows

For the years ended (C$ in millions, except per-share amounts)	January 2, 2016	January 3, 2015
Cash generated from (used for):		
Operating activities		
Net income	$ 735.9	$ 639.3
Adjustments for:		
Depreciation of property and equipment and investment property (Notes 31 and 32)	312.8	279.2
Income tax expense	265.4	238.9
Net finance costs	92.8	108.9
Amortization of intangible assets (Note 32)	111.9	93.1
Changes in fair value of derivative instruments	6.9	(33.9)
(Gain) on disposal of property and equipment, investment property, assets held for sale, intangible assets, and lease terminations	(43.9)	9.0
Change in fair value of redeemable financial instrument (Note 35)	–	17.0
Interest paid	(101.4)	(122.0)
Interest received	8.4	10.4
Income taxes paid	284.0	(256.5)
Other	14.6	25.0
	1,119.4	990.4
Changes in working capital and other (Note 34)	(115.3)	(83.5)
Change in loans receivable	(25.2)	(332.4)
Cash generated from operating activities	978.9	574.5

Investing activities		
Additions to property and equipment and investment property	**(515.9)**	(538.6)
Additions to intangible assets	**(94.7)**	(150.1)
	(610.6)	(688.7)
Acquisition of short-term investments	**(177.4)**	(431.6)
Proceeds from the maturity and disposition of short-term investments	**426.6**	665.3
Acquisition of long-term investments	**35.0**	(155.8)
Proceeds from the disposition of long-term investments	**–**	7.6
Proceeds on disposition of property and equipment, investment property, and assets held for sale	**101.5**	21.3
Long-term receivables and other assets	**0.1**	3.1
Other	**(4.2)**	(10.7)
	311.6	99.2
Cash (used for) investing activities	**(299.0)**	(589.5)
Financing activities		
Dividends paid	**(152.2)**	(141.4)
Distributions paid to non-controlling interests	**(53.8)**	(19.5)
	(206.0)	(160.9)
Net (repayment) issuance of short-term borrowings	**(111.2)**	79.4
Issuance of loans payable	**270.1**	235.6
Repayment of loans payable	**(219.0)**	(242.4)
Issuance of long-term debt (Note 25)	**856.1**	563.7
Repayment of long-term debt and finance lease liabilities (Note 25)	**(588.5)**	(474.0)
Payment of transaction costs related to long-term debt	**(6.5)**	(2.0)
	201.0	160.3
Repurchase of share capital (Note 28)	**(434.6)**	(290.6)
Proceeds on sale of ownership interests in the Financial Services business	**–**	500.0
Transaction costs on sale of ownership interests in the Financial Services business	**–**	(23.2)
	(434.6)	186.2
Change in deposits	**12.5**	(97.0)
Cash generated from (used for) financing activities	**(427.1)**	88.6
Cash generated in the period	**252.8**	73.6
Cash and cash equivalents, net of bank indebtedness, beginning of period	**647.8**	574.2
Cash and cash equivalents, net of bank indebtedness, end of period (Note 8)	**$ 900.6**	$ 647.8

The related notes form an integral part of these consolidated financial statements.

Source: Canadian Tire Corporation Ltd., Annual Report 2015.

Financial analysts evaluate Canadian Tire's historical performance to determine whether they should recommend that their clients purchase its shares. The analysts want some reasonable assurance that the company will continue to thrive. As a result, the company's share price is expected to increase, thereby benefiting their clients who own shared of Canadian Tire. Two analysts looking at the same company, however, may arrive at different conclusions, depending in part on the investors' investment objectives: growth or safety. Some analysts may reject Canadian Tire because it is too risky relative to other investment opportunities, whereas others may recommend the investment because Canadian Tire has grown quickly relative to the risk in its business.

As you analyze Canadian Tire's financial results, it is important to remember that any analysis is understood in the context of what an investor wants to accomplish. Your analysis, in itself, will present neither a good nor a bad picture of Canadian Tire's performance. This assessment must be made in the context of not only the investor's goals but also the industry's performance and the economic environment.

Would you want to buy shares in Canadian Tire? To make a rational decision, you want to consider more factors than just the company's rapid growth in profitability and the recommendation of a financial analyst. The information contained in Canadian Tire's financial statements and the analytical tools discussed in this chapter provide an important framework to help you decide whether to invest in Canadian Tire shares.

UNDERSTANDING THE BUSINESS

Successful companies such as Canadian Tire ensure that their financial reporting reflects their business strategies. Canadian Tire's investments in new businesses; the results of operating, investing, and financing activities; and the company's financial condition are communicated to shareholders, creditors, and other interested parties through press releases, conference calls with shareholders, financial analysts, and periodic reporting of financial information.

CORPORATE GOVERNANCE refers to the procedures designed to ensure that the company is managed in the interests of the shareholders.

Canadian Tire is committed to high standards of **corporate governance**, the procedures designed to ensure that the company is managed in the interests of the shareholders. Its corporate governance practices are generally consistent with the best-practice guidelines of the Canadian securities regulatory authorities.[1] Good corporate governance can ease a company's access to capital, lowering both the cost of borrowing (interest rates) and the perceived riskiness of investment in its shares.

In an attempt to restore investor confidence following the scandals at Enron and WorldCom, the U.S. Congress passed the *Public Accounting Reform and Investor Protection Act* (the *Sarbanes-Oxley Act*), which strengthened financial reporting and corporate governance provisions for public companies. Compliance with the provisions of this act has also affected Canadian companies that are publicly traded on U.S. stock exchanges. In light of the U.S. experience, the Canadian Securities Administrators, which coordinates and harmonizes regulation of the Canadian capital markets among the 13 securities regulators of Canada's provinces and territories, has imposed requirements on all publicly traded companies to bolster investors' confidence in financial reporting. Even with these added safeguards, the wisdom of famed analyst Jack Ciesielski's warning to financial statement users is still relevant:

> One usual answer to the question "why does accounting matter?" is that it helps to avoid "blow-ups": the unpleasant outcome when a stock crashes because the firm's management engaged in accounting chicanery that subsequently becomes visible. … the analyst who understands accounting matters will know precisely where the "soft spots" are in financial reporting, the ones that can be manipulated in order to meet an expected earnings target or avoid breaking a loan covenant.

Source: The Analyst's Accounting Observer, www.accountingobserver.com.

Companies spend billions of dollars each year preparing, auditing, and publishing their financial statements. These statements are then mailed to current and prospective investors. Most companies also make financial information available to investors on the Internet. Canadian Tire has a particularly interesting website that contains current financial statements, recent news articles about the company, and a variety of other relevant information.

The reason that Canadian Tire and other companies spend so much money providing information to investors is simple: financial statements help people make better economic decisions. Two broad groups of people use financial statements. One group is the management of the business; it relies on accounting data to make important operating decisions, such as the pricing of products or expansion of productive capacity. The second group is the external decision makers, who rely on accounting information to make important investment and credit decisions. In fact, the conceptual framework of accounting unequivocally states that the objective of financial reporting is to communicate information primarily to meet the needs of external decision makers, including present and potential owners, investment analysts, and creditors.

Users of financial statements are interested in three types of information:

1. *Information about past performance.* Information concerning items such as net earnings, sales volume, cash flows, and return earned on the investment helps people assess the success of the business and the effectiveness of its management. Such information also helps the decision maker compare one company with others.

2. *Information about the present condition of a business.* This type of information helps answer the following questions: What types of assets are owned? How much debt does the business owe, and when is it due? What is its cash position? What are its EPS, return on investment, and debt-to-equity ratios? What is the inventory position? Answers to these and similar questions help people assess the successes and failures of the past. More important, they provide information that is useful in assessing the cash flow and earnings potentials of the business.

3. *Information about the future performance of the business.* Decision makers select from among several alternative courses of action. Because all decisions are future oriented, financial statements based on historical cost are not an ideal basis upon which to forecast future performance. Investors are most interested in risk and the potential rewards for accepting risk. In general, as risk in the business environment increases, investors demand higher future returns on their investments to compensate them for that increased risk. Investors prefer to earn maximum return for minimum risk when choosing companies in which to invest.

Reliable accounting measures of past performance are one source of information upon which investors base their assessments of risk and potential return. Analysis of reliable measures indicating financial trends for each company is, therefore, very important. If investors can reasonably assume that important business factors will in the future be very similar to the current situation, then a reliable historical trend is often a satisfactory basis upon which to predict future financial performance. For example, the recent sales and earnings trends of a business are usually good indicators of what might be expected in the future. In other words, investors must know where the company has been in order to predict where it is likely to go.

In this chapter, we will take a more detailed look at those responsible for regulating and governing the preparation and communication of accounting information to statement users in the Internet age. One outcome of the process is assurance that the disclosure faithfully represents what it is supposed to represent. We will also examine financial disclosure to help you learn how to find relevant information. In addition, we discuss and illustrate many widely used analytical techniques discussed in earlier chapters, as well as additional techniques. These discussions will help you consolidate much of what you have learned about the financial reporting process from previous chapters.

ORGANIZATION OF THE CHAPTER

Supplemental material:
Appendix 12A: Expanding the Dupont Model—The Scott Formula (on *Connect*)

PLAYERS IN THE ACCOUNTING COMMUNICATION PROCESS

LO12-1

Recognize the roles of people involved in the accounting communication process (regulators, managers, board of directors, auditors, information intermediaries, and users), and the guidance they receive from legal and professional standards.

Exhibit 12.2 summarizes the major actors involved in assuring the integrity of the financial reporting process.

Regulators (CSA, AcSB, AASB, Stock Exchanges)

The financial information reported by Canadian companies is subject to strict regulations and standards issued by government regulators and private standard-setting organizations. Canadian publicly traded corporations must comply with provincial securities regulations that are coordinated by the Canadian Securities Administrators (CSA). The CSA is a forum for the 13 securities regulators of Canada's provinces and territories that was established to harmonize regulation of the Canadian capital markets.

Exhibit **12.2**
Ensuring the Integrity of
Financial Position

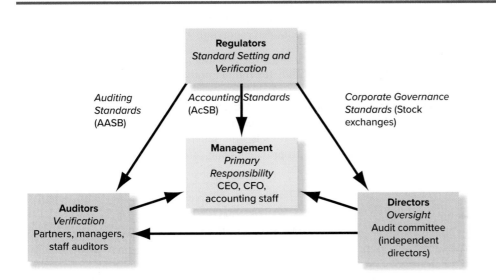

Securities regulators work closely with the Accounting Standards Board (AcSB), which is responsible for establishing standards of accounting and reporting by Canadian companies. External auditors ensure that companies prepare their financial reports in accordance with these standards, and their audit work is guided by International Standards on Auditing, which have been adopted by the Canadian Auditing and Assurance Standards Board (AASB) as Canadian Auditing Standards.

Stock exchanges also provide an essential quality assurance service to listed companies by undertaking ongoing surveillance of their reporting and trading activities. When they suspect non-compliance with accounting standards, the stock exchanges undertake independent investigations and share information with securities commissions; the Canada Revenue Agency (CRA), which collects income taxes from corporations; and other law enforcement agencies, such as the Royal Canadian Mounted Police (RCMP). As intermediaries, the stock exchanges may also enforce their rules through penalties ranging from temporary cease-trade orders to fines and delisting of companies.

Managers (CEO, CFO, and Accounting Staff)

The primary responsibility for the information in Canadian Tire's financial statements and related disclosures lies with both the highest officer in the company, often called the chief executive officer (CEO), and the highest officer associated with the financial and accounting side of the business, often called the chief financial officer (CFO). At Canadian Tire and all Canadian publicly accountable enterprises, these two officers must personally certify the following:

- Each report filed with the regulatory authorities does not contain any untrue statement of a material fact or omit to state a material fact, and fairly presents, in all material respects, the financial condition, financial performance, and cash flows of the company.

- There are no significant deficiencies and material weaknesses in the design or operation of internal controls over financial reporting that are reasonably likely to adversely affect the company's ability to record, process, summarize, and report financial information.

- They have disclosed to the auditors and the audit committee of the board any weaknesses in internal controls or any fraud involving management or other employees who have a significant role in financial reporting.

The members of the *accounting staff* who actually prepare the details of the reports also have professional responsibility for the accuracy of this information, although their legal responsibility is smaller. Their future professional success depends heavily on their reputations for honesty and competence. Accounting managers responsible for financial statements with material errors are routinely dismissed from their positions—subject to professional review and sanction, which may include permanent curtailment of their license to practice—and often have difficulty finding other employment.

Board of Directors (Audit Committee)

The **BOARD OF DIRECTORS**, elected by the shareholders to represent their interests, is responsible for maintaining the integrity of the company's financial reports.

The **board of directors**, elected by the shareholders to represent their interests, is responsible for maintaining the integrity of the company's financial reports. Canadian Tire's corporate governance guidelines state that the board of directors is responsible for reviewing and overseeing the integrity of Canadian Tire with respect to its compliance with applicable audit, accounting, and financial reporting requirements. The audit committee of the board, which must be composed of non-management (independent) financially literate directors, is responsible for hiring the company's independent auditors. They also meet separately with the auditors to discuss management's compliance with their financial reporting responsibilities. This structure complies with both U.S. and Canadian best practices.

Recent changes to securities regulations have increased the burden of responsibility for accurate financial disclosure. If any company listed on a stock exchange is found guilty of knowingly violating any disclosure regulation, not only the company but also members of its board of directors and audit committee can be sued. If experts, such as accountants or financial analysts, who relied on the company's financial reports also issued disclosure that misrepresented the company, they too may be individually sued by users who seek to recover some or all of their financial losses, which may have resulted from relying on such misleading information.

Auditors

The provincial securities commissions require that publicly traded companies have their statements audited by professional independent accountants in accordance with International Standards on Auditing. Many privately owned companies also have their statements audited. An **unqualified (clean) audit opinion** is the auditors' declaration that the financial statements are fair presentations in all material respects in conformity with IFRS. By signing an unqualified audit opinion, the audit firm assumes part of the financial responsibility for the fairness of the financial statements and related presentations. This opinion, which adds credibility to the statements, is also often required by agreements with lenders and private investors.[2] Subjecting the company's statements to independent verification reduces the risk that the company's condition is misrepresented in the statements. As a consequence, rational investors and lenders should lower the rate of return (interest) they charge for providing capital.

An **UNQUALIFIED (CLEAN) AUDIT OPINION** is the auditors' declaration that the financial statements are fair presentations in all material respects in conformity with **IFRS**.

Deloitte is currently Canadian Tire's auditor. Deloitte, Ernst & Young, KPMG, and PricewaterhouseCoopers are the largest audit firms, employing thousands of professional accountants practicing in offices throughout the world. They audit a majority of publicly traded companies and many privately held companies. Some public companies and most private companies are audited by audit firms of smaller size.

WHERE WERE THE AUDITORS?

A QUESTION OF ACCOUNTABILITY

Most professional accountants act in an honest and ethical manner, abiding by the codes of ethics developed by the professional accounting organizations. Nevertheless, a few accountants act in their own interest and disregard ethical conduct. They even become accomplices in spectacular fraud cases and subsequent company bankruptcies. For example, Enron Corp., a U.S. energy trading company, intentionally inflated its net earnings by hiding assets and related debts from 1997 to 2001. Throughout this period, the audit firm Arthur Andersen LLP, a global accounting services company with revenues in excess of $500 million, should have known that the financial statements issued by Enron's management were fraudulent.

The collapse of Enron, the largest unexpected bankruptcy in U.S. history at that time, caused tremendous losses to the company's shareholders, creditors, employees, and other stakeholders. Furthermore, Enron's bankruptcy in December 2001 caused the collapse of Arthur Andersen. More than 300 clients left the firm within 90 days, taking $250 million of potential revenue with them to other audit firms. This audit failure led to calls for improved accountability by managers and auditors, thereby generating considerable discussion among securities regulators, financial analysts, investors, and creditors regarding stricter regulation of the accounting profession.

The Sarbanes-Oxley Act (SOX), approved by the U.S. Congress in July 2002, was a direct response to the Enron scandal and others that occurred in the United States. This law has set higher standards of responsibility for the officers and directors of publicly listed companies as well as for auditors. Canadian companies that are listed on U.S. stock exchanges must also comply with the SOX requirements.

Information Intermediaries: Analysts and Information Services

Students often view the communication process between companies and financial statement users as a simple process of making the report available to individual shareholders who read the report and then make investment decisions based on what they have learned. This simple picture is far from today's reality. Now, most investors rely on sophisticated financial analysts and information services to gather and analyze information. Exhibit 12.3 summarizes this process.

Exhibit **12.3**
Using Financial Reports

Management
Primary Responsibility
CEO, CFO, accounting staff

Information Intermediaries
Analysis & Advice
Financial analysts, information services

Users
Analysis & Decisions
Institutional and private investors, lenders, suppliers, customers, etc.

Financial Analysts Financial analysts receive accounting reports and other information about the company from electronic information services. They also gather information through conversations with company executives and visits to company facilities and competitors. The results of their analyses are combined into analysts' reports.

Analysts' reports normally include forecasts of share price and future quarterly and annual earnings per share; a buy, sell, or hold recommendation for the company shares; and explanations for these judgments. In making these **earnings forecasts**, predictions of earnings for future accounting periods, the analysts rely heavily on their knowledge of how the accounting system translates business events into the numbers on a company's financial statements, which are the subject matter of this text. Individual analysts often specialize in particular industries (such as sporting goods or energy companies). Analysts are regularly evaluated based on the accuracy of their forecasts, as well as the profitability of their stock picks.

Analysts often work in the research departments of brokerage and investment banking houses such as RBC Dominion Securities, mutual fund companies such as the Investors Group, and investment advisory services such as Standard & Poor's, which sell their advice to others. Through their reports and recommendations, analysts transfer their knowledge of accounting, the company, and the industry to others who lack this expertise. Many believe that investment decisions, which are based on analysts' advice, cause stock market prices to react quickly to information in financial statements. A quick, unbiased reaction to information is called *market efficiency* in finance. It is highly unlikely that unsophisticated investors can glean more information from financial statements than what the sophisticated analysts have already learned. Careful analysis does not lead all analysts to the same conclusions, however. These differences of opinion are reflected in the following earnings (per share) forecasts for Canadian Tire Corporation and stock recommendations made by a number of analysts at the date indicated below.

EARNINGS FORECASTS are predictions of earnings for future accounting periods.

REAL-WORLD EXCERPT

Thomson Reuters Corporation

ANALYSTS' EARNINGS FORECASTS

CANADIAN TIRE CORPORATION Analysts' Earnings Forecasts (as of April 2, 2016)		
	For Fiscal 2016	**For Fiscal 2017**
Average forecast	$8.72	$ 9.55
Lowest forecast	8.39	9.25
Highest forecast	9.24	10.02
Number of analysts	13	12

Source: www.reuters.com/finance/stocks/analyst?symbol=CTCa.TO

Company managers provide analysts with information for their analysis. Optimistic earnings forecasts, however, put additional pressure on management to meet and even exceed analysts' forecasts to please investors. The drive to meet analysts' earnings expectations has led the management of some companies to adopt accounting policies that result in premature recognition of revenue or deferral of expenses, or both, to increase reported earnings.

The information services discussed next allow investors to gather their own information about the company and to monitor the recommendations of analysts.

Information Services Canadian companies file financial statements and other securities-related forms electronically with SEDAR (System for Electronic Document Analysis and Retrieval), which is the official site for the filing of documents by public companies as required by securities laws in Canada.[3] SEDAR is currently a free service available on the Internet at www.sedar.com.[4] Many companies also provide access to their financial statements and other information over the Internet.

Financial analysts and other sophisticated users obtain much of the information they use from the wide variety of commercial online information services. Services such as Lexis-Nexis (lexisnexis.ca); S&P Capital IQ (capitaliq.com); Westlaw Business, which is owned by Thomson Reuters (business.westlaw.com); and Can

West Interactive Inc. (fpinfomart.ca) provide broad access to financial statements and related news information. They also allow users to search the database by keyword, including various financial statement terms.

More-general information services include Factiva (dowjones.com/factiva), Bloomberg (bloomberg.com), and Thomson Reuters Eikon thomsonreuterseikon.com), as well as the financial sections of national newspapers such as *The Globe and Mail* and the *National Post*. Factiva provides access to news stories about companies and company press releases, including the initial announcements of annual and quarterly financial results. The Bloomberg service and Thomson Reuters Eikon also provide the ability to combine these sources of information in sophisticated analyses.

A growing number of other resources offer a mixture of free and fee-based information regarding many companies on the Internet. These include reuters.com, hoovers.com, finance.yahoo.com, google.com/finance, and www.marketwatch.com.

INFORMATION SERVICES AND JOB SEARCHES

FINANCIAL ANALYSIS

Information services have become the primary tool for professional analysts who use them. Information services are an important source of information for job seekers, as potential employers expect top job applicants to demonstrate knowledge about their companies during an interview, and electronic information services are an excellent source of company information. The best place to learn about your potential employers is their websites. Be sure to read the material in the employment section and the investor relations section of the site. To learn more about electronic information services, contact the business or reference librarian at your college or university library, or explore some of the websites mentioned earlier.

Users: Institutional and Private Investors, Creditors, and Others

Institutional investors include private pension funds (associated with unions and employees of specific companies), public pension funds (for provincial and municipal employees), mutual funds, endowments and trust funds (e.g. to fund a university or college), and charitable foundations. These institutional investors usually employ their own analysts who also rely on the information intermediaries just discussed. Institutional investors often control the majority of publicly traded shares of Canadian companies. This is not the case with Canadian Tire, as institutional investors hold only about 2 percent of the company's outstanding shares.

Private investors include individuals who purchase shares in companies; for example, individuals making large investments as well as small retail investors who, like most individuals, buy a relatively small number of shares of publicly traded companies through brokers, such as BMO Nesbitt Burns. Private investors normally lack the expertise to understand financial statements and the resources to gather data efficiently. As a consequence, they often rely on the advice of information intermediaries or turn their money over to the management of mutual and pension funds (institutional investors).

Lenders (creditors) include suppliers, banks, commercial credit companies, and other financial institutions that lend money to companies. Lending officers and financial analysts in these organizations use these same public sources of information. In addition, when companies borrow money from financial institutions, they often agree to provide additional financial information (e.g., monthly statements) as part of the lending contract. Lenders are often the primary external user group for financial statements of private companies. Institutional and private investors also become creditors when they buy a company's publicly traded bonds and debentures.

Financial statements play an important role in the relationships between customers and suppliers. Customers evaluate the financial health of suppliers to determine

INSTITUTIONAL INVESTORS are managers of pension funds, mutual funds, endowment funds, and other funds that invest on behalf of others.

PRIVATE INVESTORS include individuals who purchase shares in companies.

LENDERS (CREDITORS) include suppliers and financial institutions that lend money to companies.

whether they will be reliable, up-to-date sources of supply. Suppliers evaluate their customers to estimate their future needs and ability to pay debts. Competitors also attempt to learn useful information about a company from its statements. The potential loss of competitive advantage is one of the costs to the preparer of public financial disclosures. Accounting regulators consider these costs as well as the direct costs of preparation when they require new disclosures.

THE DISCLOSURE PROCESS

LO12-2

Identify the steps in the accounting communication process, including the issuance of press releases, annual reports, quarterly reports, and documents filed with securities commissions, as well as the guiding principles in communicating useful information.

A **PRESS RELEASE** is a written public news announcement normally distributed to major news services.

As noted in our discussion of information services and information intermediaries, the accounting communication process includes more steps and participants than one would envision in a world in which annual and quarterly reports are simply mailed to shareholders.

Press Releases

To provide timely information to external users and to limit the possibility of selective leakage of information, Canadian Tire and most public companies announce quarterly and annual earnings through a **press release**: a written public news announcement normally distributed to major news services as soon as the figures are available. Canadian Tire normally issues its annual earnings press releases about five weeks after the end of its fiscal year. The announcements are sent electronically to the major print and electronic news services, including Reuters and Bloomberg, which make them immediately available to subscribers. Exhibit 12.4 shows an excerpt of a typical quarterly press release for Canadian Tire that includes key financial figures and an invitation to interested parties to access a live webcast concerning the company's quarterly results. The press release also includes condensed, unaudited financial statements that form part of the formal quarterly report to shareholders, distributed after the press release.

Exhibit **12.4**

Earnings Press Release for Canadian Tire Corporation

REAL-WORLD EXCERPT

Canadian Tire Corporation

PRESS RELEASE

Canadian Tire Corporation Delivers Strong Q1 Results

TORONTO, May 12, 2016—CNW/—Canadian Tire Corporation, Limited (TSX:CTC, TSX:CTC.A) today released first quarter results for the period ended April 2, 2016.

"Once again, our results demonstrate continued strong execution by all of our retail businesses with solid same-store sales and impressive margin and expense management, even in a quarter with unseasonable weather," said Michael Medline, President and CEO, Canadian Tire Corporation.

"We have also taken a meaningful step in driving our innovation agenda forward with the very successful launch of our new digital catalogue—the Canadian Tire WOW Guide—a great example of how we're bridging the gap between the physical and digital worlds," continued Medline.

CONSOLIDATED OVERVIEW

- Consolidated retail sales increased $19.5 million, or 0.8%, in the first quarter including a 9.0% decline in Petroleum retail sales due to lower gas prices and gas volumes. Excluding Petroleum, consolidated retail sales were up 3.0% over the same period last year.
- Excluding Petroleum, consolidated revenue increased $91.9 million, or 4.3% in the quarter, primarily due to higher shipments at Canadian Tire and increased sales at FGL Sports and Mark's, partially offset by decreased revenue at Financial Services. Consolidated revenue increased 1.8% over the same period last year.
- Diluted EPS was $0.90 in the quarter, an increase of $0.02 per share, or 2.6%, over the first quarter of 2015.

…

CONFERENCE CALL

Canadian Tire will conduct a conference call to discuss information included in this news release and related matters at 2:00 p.m. ET on May 12, 2016. The conference call will be available simultaneously and in its entirety to all interested investors and the news media through a webcast at http://corp.canadiantire.ca/EN/investors, and will be available through replay at this website for 12 months.

…

Source: http://corp.canadiantire.ca/EN/NewsRoom/NewsReleases/Pages/default.aspx

Many companies, including Canadian Tire, follow these press releases with a webcast conference call at which senior managers (often the CEO and/or CFO) present the results and then answer questions from analysts about the results. These calls are open to the investing public. Listening to these calls (which are often archived on a company's website for a period of time afterwards) is a good way to learn about a company's business strategy and its expectations for the future, as well as key factors that analysts consider when they evaluate a company.

HOW DOES THE STOCK MARKET REACT TO EARNINGS ANNOUNCEMENTS?

FINANCIAL **ANALYSIS**

For actively traded shares, such as those of Canadian Tire, most of the stock market reaction (share price increases and decreases from investor trading) to the news in the press release usually occurs quickly. Recall that a number of analysts follow Canadian Tire and regularly predict the company's earnings. When the actual earnings are published, the market reacts not to the amount of earnings but to the difference between actual earnings and expected earnings. This amount is called unexpected earnings.

Companies such as Canadian Tire issue press releases concerning other important events, including announcements of new services or the material acquisition of new companies. Press releases related to annual earnings often precede the issuance of the annual report by 15 to 45 days. This time is necessary in order to prepare the additional detail and to print and distribute those reports. The time difference between quarterly earnings press releases and the filing of quarterly reports is usually a shorter period.

Annual Reports

For privately held companies, *annual reports* are relatively simple documents photocopied on white paper. They normally include the following:

1. Basic financial statements: statement of earnings, statement of financial position, statement of changes in equity, and statement of cash flows.

2. Related notes.

3. Report of independent accountants (auditor's opinion).

The annual reports of public companies are significantly more elaborate, both because of additional reporting requirements imposed on these companies by securities commissions and because many companies use their annual reports as public relations tools to communicate non-accounting information to shareholders, customers, the press, and others.

The annual reports of public companies are normally split into two sections. The first, *non-financial*, section usually includes a letter to shareholders from the chairperson and CEO, along with descriptions of the company's management philosophy, products, successes (and occasionally failures), and exciting prospects and challenges for the future. Beautiful photographs of products, facilities, and personnel are often included. The second, *financial*, section includes the core of the report. Securities regulators set minimum disclosure standards for the financial section of the annual reports of public companies. The principal components of the financial section follow:

1. Summarized financial data.

2. Management's discussion and analysis covering financial condition and results of operations.

3. Report of the independent accountants (Auditor's Opinion) and the management report.

4. The basic financial statements.

5. Notes to the financial statements.

The order of these components varies.

Most of these components, except for management's discussion and analysis (MD&A), have been discussed in earlier chapters. The MD&A includes management's discussion and explanation of key figures in the financial statements and risks the company faces in the future. The MD&A section contains important non-financial and strategic information to help users interpret the financial statements. Unlike the annual financial statements and related notes, information in the MD&A section is not audited. The securities commissions in Canada and the United States have noted that the intent of the MD&A is to clearly convey an interpretation of how all of the important factors combined to generate the reported results of a company. Many companies devote a sizable portion of their annual reports to the MD&A section. For example, Canadian Tire devoted fifty pages of its 2015 annual report to a detailed analysis of the company's results of operations and its various business segments. Canadian Tire's MD&A section also includes a review of the company's liquidity, capital resources, and contractual obligations.

Quarterly Reports

Quarterly reports normally begin with a short letter to shareholders. This is followed by a condensed statement of earnings for the quarter, which often shows less detail than the annual statement of earnings, and a condensed statement of financial position dated at the end of the quarter (e.g., March 31 for the first quarter). These condensed financial statements are not audited and so are marked "unaudited." Often, the statement of cash flows, the statement of changes in equity, and some notes to the financial statements are omitted. Private companies also normally prepare quarterly reports for lenders. Companies issue their quarterly reports about five weeks after the end of each quarter.

Reports to Securities Commissions

Public companies must also file periodic reports with the OSC and other provincial securities commissions. These reports include the annual report, quarterly reports, an annual information form, and an information circular.

The annual information form provides a more detailed description of the business, including such items as the company's corporate structure, the industry in which it operates, the products and services it offers, product and project development, sales and marketing, manufacturing, and competition. The form also lists the properties owned and leased by the company, and significant contracts that the company has signed.

The information circular is a legal document that is forwarded to the company's shareholders prior to the annual general or special meeting of shareholders. It provides information about the items that the shareholders will be asked to consider and vote on during the meeting, including election of new directors, appointment of independent auditors, and other matters of a legal nature. The circular also provides details of the compensation of the CEO, CFO, and other key executive officers as well as information about the company's corporate governance practices.

In addition to these periodic reports, companies file other types of reports as the need arises. These include a short-form prospectus providing details of the equity and/ or debt securities that they plan to issue to investors, and press releases concerning new developments. The SEDAR website, www.sedar.com, lists all of the reports, documents, and news items that Canadian Tire and other corporations have filed.[5]

THE INVESTMENT DECISION

Of the people who use financial statements, current and potential investors are perhaps the single largest group. They often rely on the advice of professional analysts who develop recommendations on widely held stocks, such as Canadian Tire stock.

Most individual investors use analysts' reports, tracking their recommendations. As this book was being written, professional analysts issued the following investment recommendations for Canadian Tire:

Analyst Ratings: Canadian Tire	Current Month	Last Month	Two Months Ago	Three Months Ago
1—Buy	1	1	1	1
2—Outperform	9	9	9	9
3—Hold	3	4	4	3
4—Underperform	0	0	0	1
5—Sell	0	0	0	0
Source: www.reuters.com/finance/stocks/analyst?symbol=CTCa.TO. Accessed December 10, 2016.				

What do these recommendations mean? It is clear that analysts reach different conclusions despite access to the same set of financial information. Notice also that analysts' recommendations shift over time as new information is released and actual performance becomes observable.

Analysts are expected to have a good understanding of financial statements and the standards that imbue these reports with both relevance and faithful representation. They may disagree, however, on how to interpret the results of their analyses of a company's past performance. Analysts' differing opinions affect their predictions of the future operating performance to the extent that their analyses of a company's past performance are relevant to formulating their predictions. The level of disagreement among financial analysts shows that financial statement analysis is part art and part science.

In addition to analyzing a company's financial statements, analysts consider other factors that might affect the future operating performance of the company and its financial situation. These include global, economic, and industry factors that are not controllable by the company, and management's ability to adapt its business plans in response to the uncertainties and risks associated with these uncontrollable factors. Management success at containing the effects of uncontrollable risks and managing in the face of uncertainties plays a role in analysts' predictions of the future economic health of a specific company. Regardless of how careful an analyst is, however, the truth about predictions is that they often prove to be inaccurate.

When considering an investment in shares, the investor should evaluate the future net earnings and growth potential of the business on the basis of three factors:

1. *Economy-wide factors.* The overall health of the economy has a direct impact on the performance of an individual business. Prudent investors must consider data such as the unemployment rate, the general inflation rate, and changes in interest rates. For example, increases in interest rates often slow economic growth because consumers are less willing to buy merchandise on credit when interest rates are high. Furthermore, companies that wish to expand their operations will find it too expensive to borrow funds.

2. *Industry factors.* Certain events have a major impact on each company within an industry but have only a minor impact on other companies outside the industry. For example, a major drought will be devastating for food-related industries but will have no effect on the electronics industry.

3. *Individual company factors.* To properly analyze a company, you should learn as much as you can about it. Good analysts do not rely solely on the information contained in the financial statements. They visit the company, buy its products, and read about it in the business press. For example, if you evaluate McDonald's, it is equally important to assess the quality of its statement of financial position and the quality of its I'm Greek-ing Out salad.

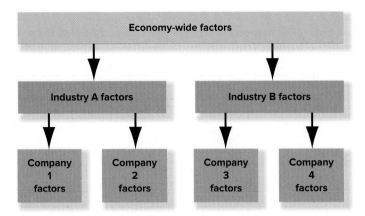

Besides considering these factors, investors should understand a company's business strategy when evaluating its financial statements. Before discussing analytical techniques, we will show you how business strategy affects financial statement analysis.

UNDERSTANDING A COMPANY'S STRATEGY

Financial statement analysis involves more than just "crunching numbers." Before you start looking at numbers, you should know what you are looking for. While financial statements report on transactions, each of these transactions is the result of a company's operating decisions as it implements its business strategy.

A useful starting point for financial statement analysis is the return on equity (ROE), or *DuPont model.* The DuPont model helps us analyze the profitability of a business and demonstrates that a variety of strategies can result in high levels of profitability. The model follows:

A key insight provided by the DuPont model is that companies can be profitable by achieving high profit margins or a rapid turnover of assets (or a combination of both). Businesses can earn a high rate of return for the owners (i.e., a high ROE) by following different strategies. There are two fundamental strategies:

1. *Product differentiation.* Under this strategy, companies offer products with unique benefits, such as high quality or unusual features or style. These unique benefits allow a company to charge higher prices. In general, higher prices result in higher profit margins, which lead to higher returns on equity (as shown in the DuPont model).

2. *Cost advantage.* Under this strategy, companies selling similar products attempt to operate more efficiently than their competitors, allowing them to offer lower prices to attract customers. The efficient use of resources is captured in the total asset turnover ratio, and as the ROE model illustrates, a high total asset turnover ratio leads to higher return on investment.

You can probably think of a number of companies that have followed one of these two basic strategies:

Differentiation on Quality	Differentiation on Cost
Cars:	**Cars:**
Cadillac	Hyundai Accent
Mercedes	Chevrolet Spark
Lincoln	Toyota Yaris
Retail Stores:	**Retail Stores:**
Cartier	Target
Holt Renfrew	Walmart

The best place to start your analysis is with a solid understanding of a company's business strategy. To evaluate how a company is doing, you must know what managers are trying to do. You can learn a lot about a company's strategy by reading its complete annual report, especially the letter from the president. It also is useful to read articles about the company in the business press.

Canadian Tire's business strategy is described in its annual report as follows:

REAL-WORLD EXCERPT
Canadian Tire
ANNUAL REPORT

6.2 2016 Strategic imperatives

For 2016, the Company will pursue the following strategic imperatives and key initiatives, which are aligned with its vision to ultimately become the most innovative retailer in the world, and support the achievement of the three year (2015–2017) financial aspirations.

1. Strengthen brands and enhance customer experiences (connections)

The Company is committed to being a "brand-led" organization and being the conduit between target customers and the best portfolio of retail brands.

2. Transition to the new world of omni-retail where digital complements the physical

In order to compete on a global basis and continue to be relevant and engaged with its customers, the Company must invest in the future of digital retailing to both enhance its physical store networks and eCommerce capabilities.

3. Drive growth and productivity in core businesses

The Company continues to focus on driving organic growth and productivity within its four core banners: Canadian Tire, FGL Sports, Mark's, and Financial Services.

4. Create an agile and high-performing corporate culture

The Company is committed to attracting, developing, and retaining world-class talent that will drive growth in the business.

Source: Canadian Tire Corporation, Limited, Annual Report 2015.

This description of Canadian Tire's strategy serves as a guide for our financial analysis. By understanding what management is trying to accomplish, we are better able to evaluate its progress in meeting its goals.

With these implications in mind, we can attach more meaning to the information contained in Canadian Tire's financial statements.

As the preceding discussion indicates, a company can take different actions to try to affect each of the ratios in the DuPont model. To understand the impact of these actions, financial analysts disaggregate each of the ratios into more detailed ratios. For example, the total asset turnover ratio is further disaggregated into turnover ratios for specific assets, such as accounts receivable, inventory, and fixed assets. We have developed our understanding of these ratios in previous chapters, but we will bring them together in the next few sections as part of a comprehensive review of ratio analysis.

LO12-4

Discuss how analysts use
financial statements.

FINANCIAL STATEMENT ANALYSIS

Analyzing financial data without a basis of comparison is impossible. For example, would you be impressed with a company that earned $1 million last year? You are probably thinking, "It depends." Earnings of $1 million might be very good for a company that lost money the year before, but not good for a company that earned $500 million during the previous year. It might be good for a small company but not good for a very large company. And, it might be good if all the other companies in the industry lost money, but not good if they all earned much more.

As you can see from this simple example, financial results cannot be evaluated in isolation. To properly analyze the information reported in financial statements, you must develop appropriate comparisons. The task of finding appropriate benchmarks requires judgment, and it is not always an easy task. For this reason, financial analysis is a sophisticated skill, not a mechanical process.

There are two types of benchmarks for making financial comparisons: time series and comparisons with other companies.

1. *Time series analysis.* In this type of analysis, information for a single company is compared over time. For example, a key measure of performance for a retail company is the change in sales volume each year for its existing stores. The time series chart below shows that Canadian Tire's sales were volatile over the 12-year period, 2004–2015, with sales growth in existing stores in the last three years:[6]

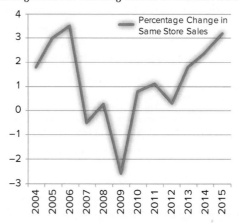

2. *Comparison with similar companies.* Financial results are often affected by industry- and economy-wide factors. By comparing a company with another one in the same line of business, an analyst can obtain better insight into its performance. For example, the comparison of profit margin (net earnings as a percentage of sales) for 2015 and the change in sales for Canadian Tire, Sears Canada, and Hudson's Bay Company from the previous year shows that Hudson's Bay Company had the highest increase in sales, but Canadian Tire reported the highest profit margin ratio. While Hudson's Bay Company was able to increase its sales significantly, it appears that Canadian Tire was more effective at controlling its expenses relative to the increase in its sales:

Finding comparable companies is often very difficult. Canadian Tire's products include petroleum products, which are not sold by either Sears Canada or Hudson's Bay Company. No single retailer competes directly with Canadian Tire across the wide variety of products and services that the company offers.

Care must be exercised when selecting comparable companies from the same basic industry. Days Inn, Four Seasons, Hilton, Holiday Inn, and Marriott are all in the hotel industry, but not all could be considered comparable companies for the purpose of financial analysis. These hotels offer different levels of quality and appeal to different types of customers.

The governments of the United States, Canada, and Mexico developed the North American Industry Classification System for use in reporting economic data. The system assigns a specific industry code to each corporation, based on its business operations. Analysts often use these six-digit codes to identify companies that have similar business operations. Financial information services, such as Standard & Poor's, provide averages for many common accounting ratios for various industries as defined by the industrial classification codes. Because of the diversity of companies included in each industry classification, these data should be used with great care. For this reason, some analysts prefer to compare two companies that are very similar instead of using industry-wide comparisons.

RATIO AND PERCENTAGE ANALYSES

All financial analysts use ratio analysis, or **percentage (ratio) analysis**, when they review companies. A ratio, or percentage, expresses the proportional relationship between two different amounts, allowing for easy comparisons. Assessing a company's profitability is difficult if you know only that it had net earnings of $500,000. Comparing net earnings to other numbers, such as shareholders' equity, provides additional insights. If shareholders' equity is $5 million, the relationship of net earnings to shareholder investment is $500,000 ÷ $5,000,000 = 10 percent. This measure indicates a different level of performance than would be the case if shareholders' equity were $50 million. Ratio analysis condenses the large volume of raw financial data and helps decision makers identify significant relationships and make meaningful comparisons between companies.

Ratios may be computed by using amounts in one statement, such as the statement of earnings, or in two different statements, such as the statement of earnings and the statement of financial position. In addition, amounts on a single statement may be expressed as a percentage of a base amount.

PERCENTAGE (RATIO) ANALYSIS is an analytical tool designed to identify significant relationships; it measures the proportional relationship between two financial statement amounts.

Component Percentages

Analysts often compute a **component percentage**, which expresses each item on a financial statement as a percentage of a single *base amount*, the denominator of the ratio. To compute component percentages for the statement of earnings, the base amount is net sales revenue. Each expense is expressed as a percentage of net sales revenue. On the statement of financial position, the base amount is total assets; each element of the statement of financial position is divided by total assets. This is also known as creating a common-size financial statement.

Discerning important relationships and trends in Canadian Tire's statement of earnings shown in Exhibit 12.1 is difficult without using component percentages. Net earnings increased by 15.1 percent between 2014 and 2015, which appears to be good; but it is difficult for an analyst to evaluate the operating efficiency of Canadian Tire based on the reported numbers on the statement of earnings.

Exhibit 12.2 shows a component percentage analysis for Canadian Tire's statement of earnings (from Exhibit 12.1). One additional year, 2013, is presented for comparative purposes. If you simply reviewed the dollar amounts on the statement of earnings, you might be concerned about several significant dCifferences. For example,

LO12-5

Compute and interpret component percentages.

A **COMPONENT PERCENTAGE** expresses each item on a particular financial statement as a percentage of a single base amount.

net finance costs decreased by $16.1 million between 2014 and 2015. Is this decrease reasonable, relative to the decrease in sales? Should you be concerned, as an analyst? The component percentage indicates that net finance costs actually decreased slightly as a percentage of sales revenue during that period. In other words, net finance costs decreased in proportion to sales revenue.

Exhibit **12.5**

Component Percentages for Canadian Tire

Statement of Earnings	Component Percentages		
	2015	**2014**	**2013**
Revenue	100.0%	100.0%	100.0%
Cost of producing revenue	66.3	67.5	68.4
Gross margin	33.7	32.5	31.6
Other (income)	0.5	(0.1)	(0.0)
Selling, general, and administrative expenses	(25.2)	(24.5)	(24.0)
Net finance costs	0.8	0.9	0.9
Change in fair value of redeemable financial instrument	–	0.1	–
Income before income taxes	8.2	7.1	6.7
Income taxes	(2.2)	(1.9)	(1.9)
Net income	6.0	5.1	4.8

The component analysis for Canadian Tire shown in Exhibit 12.5 helps highlight several additional issues:

1. Net earnings (net income) increased from $639.3 million in 2013 to $735.9 million in 2015. Gross margin also increased during the same period, from 5.1 percent to 6.0 percent, indicating that expenses decreased at a faster rate than sales revenue.

2. Some of the changes in percentages may seem immaterial, but they involve very significant amounts of money. The decrease in the ratio of net finance costs as a percentage of sales from 0.9 percent in 2014 to 0.8 percent in 2015 represents $16.1 million.

3. The gross profit as a percentage of sales increased between 2013 and 2015. The company attributes this increase to productivity initiatives focused on optimizing assortments, improving sales mix, and reducing product costs.

4. Significant stability in all of the statement of earnings relationships indicates a well-run company. Notice that most of the individual statement of earnings items changed by less than 1.5 percentage points over a three-year period, except for the cost of producing revenue, which decreased by 2.1 percent. The more stable these relationships are over a long time period, particularly during economic turbulence, the more confidence analysts will have in their predictions of the company's future, based on relationships among the various elements of the company's financial statements.

Exhibit 12.6, similar to Exhibit 12.5, shows a component percentage analysis for Canadian Tire's statement of financial position covering a period of four years. If you simply reviewed the dollar amounts on the statement of earnings, you might be concerned about several significant differences. For example, total liabilities increased by $275.7 million between 2014 and 2015. Is this increase reasonable, relative to the increase in assets during 2015? Should you be concerned, as an analyst? The component percentage indicates that total liabilities actually decreased slightly as a percentage of total assets. In other words, total liabilities have decreased proportionally to total assets.

Statement of Financial Position	Component Percentages				
	2015	**2014**	**2013**	**2012**	
ASSETS					
Current Assets:					
Cash and cash equivalents	6.0	4.6	4.7	7.7	
Short-term investments	0.6	2.0	3.1	1.3	
Trade and other receivables	6.1	6.0	5.6	5.7	
Loans receivable	32.5	33.7	33.5	32.3	
Merchandise inventories	11.8	11.2	10.9	11.4	
Income taxes recoverable	0.3	0.2	0.2	0.4	
Prepaid expenses and deposits	0.6	0.7	0.5	0.3	
Assets classified as held for sale	0.0	0.1	0.1	0.0	
Total current assets	58.0	58.5	58.5	58.9	
Long-term receivables and other assets	4.9	4.7	5.0	5.2	
Long-term investments	1.0	1.2	1.0	1.4	
Goodwill and intangible assets	8.3	8.6	8.7	8.2	
Investment property	0.9	1.0	0.7	0.7	
Property and equipment	26.5	25.7	25.8	25.3	
Deferred income taxes	0.3	0.3	0.3	0.3	
Total assets	100.0	100.0	100.0	100.0	
LIABILITIES					
Current Liabilities:					
Bank indebtedness	—	0.1	0.5	0.6	
Deposits	5.9	6.5	8.7	9.9	
Trade and other payables	13.1	13.5	13.3	12.3	
Provisions	1.4	1.4	1.4	1.4	
Short-term borrowings	0.6	1.4	0.9	0.9	
Loans payable	4.4	4.2	4.5	4.7	
Income taxes payable	0.4	0.4	0.4	0.4	
Current portion of long-term debt	0.2	4.0	2.0	5.0	
Total current liabilities	25.9	31.5	31.7	35.3	
Long-term provisions	0.3	0.3	0.3	0.4	
Long-term debt	19.8	14.7	17.2	17.7	
Long-term deposits	9.2	8.8	8.5	8.4	
Deferred income taxes	0.7	0.7	0.7	0.6	
Other long-term liabilities	5.4	5.4	1.7	1.6	
Total liabilities	61.4	61.3	60.0	64.0	
SHAREHOLDERS' EQUITY					
Share capital	4.5	4.8	4.3	5.2	
Contributed surplus	0.0	0.0	0.1	0.0	
Accumulated other comprehensive income (loss)	1.0	0.6	0.4	−0.0	
Retained earnings	27.8	28.0	33.2	30.8	
Equity attributable to shareholders of Canadian Tire Corporation	33.3	33.4	37.9	36.0	
Non-controlling interests	5.3	5.3	2.1	—	
Total shareholders' equity	38.7	38.7	40.0	36.0	
Total liabilities and shareholders' equity	100.0	100.0	100.0	100.0	

Exhibit **12.6**

Component Percentages for Canadian Tire

The component analysis for Canadian Tire shown in Exhibit 12.6 provides several additional insights:

1. Receivables and merchandise inventories represent approximately 50 percent of the total assets, and this percentage has been relatively stable over time.

2. Total liabilities have declined slightly over the past few years but are relatively stable. They make up about 61 percent of the financing of total assets. However, current liabilities decreased by 10 percentage points over the four-year period while non-current liabilities increased by 8 percentage points approximately over the same period.

3. The various percentages indicate, generally, that the financial situation of Canadian Tire is relatively stable over time despite significant changes in the dollar value of certain elements of the statement of financial position.

Many analysts use graphics software in their study of financial results. Graphic representation is especially useful when communicating findings during meetings or in printed form. Graphic summaries of key 2015 data from Exhibits 12.5 and 12.6 are shown below.

In addition to component percentages, analysts use ratios to compare related items from the financial statements. Of the many ratios that can be computed from a single set of financial statements, analysts use only those that are relevant to the analysis of a given situation. Comparing cost of sales to property, plant, and equipment is never useful because these items have no natural relationship. Instead, an analyst will often compute certain widely used ratios and then decide which additional ratios are relevant to the particular decision. For example, research and development costs as a percentage of sales is not a commonly used ratio, but it is useful when analyzing companies that depend on new products, such as pharmaceutical or technology firms.

When you compute ratios, remember a basic fact about financial statements: statement of financial position amounts relate to an instant in time, and statement of earnings amounts relate to a specified period. Therefore, when a statement of earnings amount is compared with a statement of financial position amount, you should express the statement of financial position amount as an average of the beginning and ending balances. In practice, many analysts simply use the ending statement of financial position amount. This approach is appropriate only if no significant changes have occurred in statement of financial position amounts. For consistency, we always use average amounts.

Financial statement analysis is a process that requires judgment. Not all ratios are relevant to the analysis of a given situation. We will discuss several ratios that are appropriate to most situations. They can be grouped into the four categories shown in Exhibit 12.7.

Tests of Profitability

Profitability is a primary measure of the overall success of a company. Indeed, it is necessary for a company's survival. Investors and creditors prefer a single measure of profitability that is meaningful in all situations. Unfortunately, no single measure can be devised to meet this comprehensive need. Several **tests of profitability** focus on measuring the adequacy of net earnings by comparing it to other items reported on the financial statements.

1. Return on Equity (ROE)

Return on equity (also called *return on owners' investment*) relates net earnings to the investment made by the owners. It reflects the simple fact that investors expect to earn more money if they invest more money. Two investments that offer a return of $10,000 are not comparable if one requires an investment of $100,000 and the other requires an investment of $250,000. The ROE is computed as follows:[7]

LO12-6

Compute and interpret profitability ratios.

TESTS OF PROFITABILITY compare net earnings with one or more primary activities.

Exhibit **12.7**
Widely Used Accounting Ratios

Ratio		Basic Computation
Tests of Profitability		
1. Return on equity (ROE)	Chapter 4	$\dfrac{\text{Net earnings}}{\text{Average shareholders' equity}}$
2. Return on assets (ROA)	Chapter 3	$\dfrac{\text{Net earnings} + \text{Interest expense (net of tax)}}{\text{Average total assets}}$
Financial leverage percentage	Chapter 12	Return on equity − Return on assets
3. Earnings per share (EPS) ratio	Chapter 11	$\dfrac{\text{Net earnings available to common shareholders}}{\text{Average number of common shares outstanding}}$
4. Quality of earnings	Chapter 5	$\dfrac{\text{Cash flows from operating activities}}{\text{Net earnings}}$
5. Net profit margin ratio	Chapter 4	$\dfrac{\text{Net earnings}}{\text{Net sales}}$
6. Fixed asset turnover ratio	Chapter 8	$\dfrac{\text{Net sales}}{\text{Average net fixed assets}}$
Tests of Liquidity		
7. Cash ratio	Chapter 12	$\dfrac{\text{Cash} + \text{Cash equivalents}}{\text{Current liabilities}}$
8. Current ratio	Chapter 2	$\dfrac{\text{Current assets}}{\text{Current liabilities}}$
9. Quick ratio	Chapter 9	$\dfrac{\text{Quick assets}}{\text{Current liabilities}}$
10. Receivables turnover ratio	Chapter 6	$\dfrac{\text{Net credit sales}}{\text{Average net trade receivables}}$
11. Inventory turnover ratio	Chapter 7	$\dfrac{\text{Cost of sales}}{\text{Average inventory}}$
12. Accounts payable turnover ratio	Chapter 9	$\dfrac{\text{Cost of sales}}{\text{Average net trade payables}}$
Tests of Solvency		
13. Times interest earned ratio	Chapter 10	$\dfrac{\text{Net earnings} + \text{Interest expense} + \text{Income tax expense}}{\text{Interest expense}}$
14. Cash coverage ratio	Chapter 12	$\dfrac{\text{Cash flows from operating activities (before interest and taxes)}}{\text{Interest paid}}$
15. Debt-to-equity ratio	Chapter 10	$\dfrac{\text{Total liabilities}}{\text{Shareholders' equity}}$
Market Tests		
16. Price/earnings ratio	Chapter 12	$\dfrac{\text{Current market price per share}}{\text{Earnings per share}}$
17. Dividend yield ratio	Chapter 11	$\dfrac{\text{Dividends per share}}{\text{Market price per share}}$

Note: Most of these ratios have been discussed in previous chapters. The specific chapter appears next to the ratio.

$$\text{Return on equity} = \frac{\text{Net earnings}}{\text{Average shareholders' equity}}$$

$$\text{Canadian Tire, 2015} = \frac{\$735.9}{\$5,710.3^*} = 12.9\%$$

*($5,789.7 + $5,630.8) ÷ 2

Canadian Tire earned 12.9 percent on the owners' investment. Was that return high or low? We can answer this question by comparing Canadian Tire's ROE with the ratios of similar companies. The ROEs for two of Canadian Tire's competitors, Sears Canada and Hudson's Bay Company, are −3 percent and 10.5 percent, respectively. Clearly, Canadian Tire produced a better ROE than Sears Canada but lags behind Hudson's Bay Company.

We gain additional insight by examining Canadian Tire's ROE over time:

	2015	2014	2013
ROE	12.9	11.5	11.1

This comparison shows that Canadian Tire's performance, as measured by ROE, improved over the three years, primarily because of the relative decrease operating expenses.

Return on Equity for Selected Industries—2014
Paper and forest products 7.4%
Gold −15.1%
Retailing −1.7%
Telecommunications services 15.6%

2. Return on Assets (ROA)   Another test of profitability compares net earnings to the total assets (i.e., total investment) used to generate the net earnings. Many analysts consider the *return on assets* (ROA) to be a better measure of management's ability to utilize assets effectively, because it is not affected by the way in which the assets were financed. For example, the ROE could be very large for a company that has a large amount of debt compared to a company that earned the same return based on the same amount of assets but borrowed less money. The ROE measures profitability from the perspective of the shareholders, whereas the ROA takes into consideration the resources contributed by both shareholders and creditors. For this reason, the return to shareholders, net earnings, is augmented by the return to creditors, which is interest expense. Interest expense is measured net of income tax, because it represents the net cost of the funds provided by creditors to the corporation.[8]

The ROA is computed as follows:

$$\text{Return on assets} = \frac{\text{Net earnings} + \text{Interest expense}^9 \text{ (net of tax)}}{\text{Average total assets}}$$

$$\text{Canadian Tire, 2015} = \frac{\$735.9 + \$106.9 \times (1 - 0.265^*)}{\$14,770.5^\dagger} = 5.44\%$$

*Income tax rate = Income tax expense ÷ Earnings before income taxes = $265.4 ÷ $1,001.3 = 0.265
†($14,987.8 + $14,553.2) ÷ 2

Canadian Tire earned 5.4 percent on the total resources it used during the year. The company achieved a better return on assets than both Hudson's Bay (2.8%) and Sears Canada (−3.99%).

Financial Leverage Percentage   The *financial leverage percentage* measures the advantage or disadvantage that occurs when a company's ROE differs from its ROA (i.e., ROE − ROA ≠ 0). In the DuPont model discussed earlier in this chapter, financial leverage was defined as the proportion of assets acquired with funds supplied by owners. The financial leverage percentage measures a related but different concept. It describes the relationship between the ROE and the ROA. Leverage is positive when the rate of return on a company's assets exceeds the average after-tax interest rate on its borrowed funds. Basically, the company borrows at one rate and earns a higher rate of return on its investments. Most companies have positive leverage.

Financial leverage percentage can be measured by comparing the return on investment ratios as follows:

Financial leverage percentage = Return on equity − Return on assests

Canadian Tire, 2015 = 12.9% − 5.4% = 7.5%

When a company is able to borrow funds at an after-tax interest rate and invest those funds to earn a higher after-tax rate of return, the difference benefits the owners. The notes to Canadian Tire's annual report indicate that the company has borrowed money at rates ranging from 2.238 percent to 6.445 percent, with a weighted-average interest rate of 4.34 percent before tax. This cost of debt would be reduced to 3.191 percent [= 4.34 % × (1 − 0.265)]. The borrowed money is invested in assets earning 5.4 percent. The difference between the income earned on the money it has borrowed and the interest it has paid to creditors is available for Canadian Tire's shareholders. This benefit of financial leverage is the primary reason that most companies obtain a significant amount of their resources from creditors rather than from the sale of shares. Notice that financial leverage can be enhanced either by investing effectively (i.e., earning a high return on investment) or by borrowing effectively (i.e., paying a low rate of interest).

A negative financial leverage percentage means that ROE has decreased relative to ROA or that ROA has increased relative to ROE. ROE decreases when net earnings decrease, either as a signal of a deterioration in the company's profitability or when equity increases through the issuance of additional shares. An inflow of cash from a new equity issue may indicate that the company is entering a growth phase that is expected to increase net earnings. Another possibility is that ROA may have increased substantially relative to ROE because of an increase in after-tax interest expense and in the cost of debt financing. Without careful interpretation of relevant information available on a specific company, investors cannot accurately interpret a decrease in ROE as either good news or bad news.

In general, if a decrease in ROE signals future growth despite a temporarily negative financial leverage percentage, investors may not be too alarmed by negative leverage. If, however, an increase in ROA is the result of borrowing at high interest rates, investors could well interpret negative leverage as reflecting bad news. It is, therefore, important for investors to be cautious when interpreting any increase or decrease in ratios.

Canadian Tire's financial leverage percentage is higher than Sears Canada's (1 percent) but significantly lower than the ratio of Hudson's Bay Company (7.7 percent).

3. Earnings per Share Ratio *Earnings per share* (EPS) is a measure of the return on investment that is based on the number of shares outstanding instead of the dollar amounts reported on the statement of financial position. In simple situations, EPS is computed as follows:

$$\text{Earnings per share ratio} = \frac{\text{Net earnings available to common shareholders}}{\text{Average number of common shares outstanding}}$$

$$\text{Canadian Tire, 2015} = \frac{\$659.4}{76.15^*} = \$8.66$$

*Reported on the statement of earnings

This computation of EPS is based on information reported on the statement of earnings. The additional complexities in the computation of EPS are discussed in advanced accounting courses.

EPS is probably the single most widely watched ratio. Companies' announcements of their net earnings each quarter during the fiscal year are normally reported in the business press. The following news story by Reuters concerning Canadian Tire's earnings results for the fourth quarter of 2015 illustrates the importance of EPS.

REAL-WORLD EXCERPT

Canadian Tire Corporation

EARNINGS ANNOUNCEMENT
BY BUSINESS NEWS NETWORK
(BNN)

The Canadian Press, February 18, 2016

Canadian Tire Corp. Ltd. (CTCa.TO) overcame a number of negative factors to grow its profit in its fourth quarter, including lower prices for the gasoline it sells and unusually warm weather that depressed sales of some seasonal products, especially at its Mark's clothing chain.

The Toronto-based company had $241.5 million or $3.01 per share of net income in the quarter ended Jan. 2.

That was up about 17 per cent from $206.6 million or $2.44 per share a year earlier, when several expenses were higher.

Its retail revenue fell 7.4 per cent to $3.38 billion from $3.65 billion, but that was partly due to one less week of selling in the latest quarter and also because of the warm weather, the downturn in the Alberta economy and lower gasoline prices.

Excluding petroleum sales, Canadian Tire's overall revenue was $3 billion — down 5.8 per cent from a year earlier.

Same-store sales at Mark's were down 5.2 per cent and down 0.4 per cent at FGL Sports overall, although up 1.6 per cent at the Sport Chek stores. Canadian Tire same-store sales were up 2.0 per cent from the year-earlier quarter.

For the full year ended Jan. 2, 2016, the company had $735.9 million of net income, up from $639.3 million in fiscal 2015. Revenue was $12.3 billion, down from $12.5 billion.

Source: http://www.bnn.ca/News/2016/2/18/Canadian-Tire-sees-growth-in-fourth-quarter-.aspx. Accessed April 2, 2016.

4. Quality of Earnings Ratio   Most financial analysts are concerned about the quality of a company's earnings because the use of some accounting procedures can result in higher earnings reports. For example, a company that uses short estimated lives for non-current assets will report lower earnings than will a similar company that uses longer estimated lives. One method of evaluating the quality of a company's earnings is to compare its reported earnings to its cash flows from operating activities, as follows:

$$\text{Quality of earnings ratio} = \frac{\text{Cash flows from operating activities}}{\text{Net earnings}}$$

$$\text{Canadian Tire, 2015} = \frac{\$978.9}{\$735.9} = 1.33$$

A quality of earnings ratio higher than 1 is considered to indicate higher-quality earnings, because each dollar of net earnings is supported by at least one dollar of cash flow. Recall that net earnings include both cash and non-cash components that result from accrual of revenues and expenses that will affect cash in future accounting periods. A ratio below 1 indicates that accruals represent a significant portion of net earnings, which suggests that earnings are of lower quality than if the ratio exceeded 1. Hudson's Bay Company had a quality of earnings ratio of 0.05 and Sears Canada's ratio was 2.97, but its positive ratio is misleading because it reported net cash outflow from operations and a net loss, two negative amounts that resulted in a positive ratio.

5. Net Profit Margin Ratio   The *net profit margin ratio* measures the percentage of each sales dollar, on average, that represents net earnings. It is computed as follows:

$$\text{Net profit margin ratio} = \frac{\text{Net earnings}}{\text{Net sales}}$$

$$\text{Canadian Tire, 2015} = \frac{\$735.9}{\$12,279.6} = 6.0\%$$

During 2015, each dollar of Canadian Tire's sales generated 6.0 cents of net earnings. Care must be used in analyzing the net profit margin ratio, because it does not consider the amount of resources employed (i.e., total investment) to generate net earnings. For example, the hypothetical statements of earnings of Canadian Tire and Hudson's Bay Company might show the following:

	Hudson's Bay Company	Canadian Tire
a. Sales revenue	$500,000	$150,000
b. Net earnings	25,000	7,500
c. Net profit margin ratio (b ÷ a)	5%	5%
d. Total investment	$250,000	$125,000
e. Return on total investment* (b ÷ d)	10%	6%
*Assuming no interest expense.		

In this example, both companies reported the same profit margin (5 percent). Hudson's Bay Company, however, appears to be performing much better, because it is earning a 10 percent return on the total investment versus the 6 percent earned by Canadian Tire. The profit margin percentages do not reflect the effect of the $250,000 total investment in Hudson's Bay Company compared to the $125,000 total investment in Canadian Tire. Thus, the net profit margin ratio omits one of the two important factors that should be used in evaluating return on the investment.

It is very difficult to compare profit margins for companies in different industries. For example, profit margins are low in the food industry, but they are high in the jewellery business. Both types of businesses can be quite profitable, however, because a high sales volume can compensate for a low profit margin. Grocery stores have low profit margins but generate a large sales volume from their relatively inexpensive stores and inventory. Although jewellery stores generate more net earnings from each sales dollar, they require a large investment in luxury stores and very expensive inventory.

The trade-off between profit margin and sales volume can be stated in very simple terms: would you prefer to have 5 percent of $1,000,000 or 10 percent of $100,000? As you can see, a larger percentage is not always better.

The operating strength of Canadian Tire (6.0 percent) is better than Hudson's Bay Company's operating performance (3.5 percent), and both are stronger than Sears Canada (−0.21 percent) when you compare their net profit margin ratios for 2015.

6. Fixed Asset Turnover Ratio

Another measure of operating efficiency is the fixed asset turnover ratio, which compares sales volume with a company's investment in fixed assets. The term *fixed assets* is synonymous with *property, plant, and equipment*. The ratio is computed as follows:

$$\text{Fixed asset turnover ratio} = \frac{\text{Net sales}}{\text{Average net fixed assets}}$$

$$\text{Canadian Tire, 2015} = \frac{\$11,427.2}{\$3,354.7^*} = 3.41/\$3.07$$

*($3,891.7 + $4,116) ÷ 2

The fixed asset turnover ratio for Canadian Tire is lower than the ratio for Sears Canada (6.64) but higher than Hudson's Bay's ratio (2.29). In simple terms, this means that Sears Canada as a competitive advantage over Canadian Tire in terms of its ability to effectively utilize fixed assets to generate revenue. For each dollar that Canadian Tire invested in investment property and property, plant, and equipment, it was able to earn $6.64 in sales revenue, while Hudson's Bay Company earned $2.29.

The fixed asset turnover ratio is widely used to analyze capital-intensive companies, such as airlines and electric utilities. For companies that have large amounts of inventory and trade receivables, analysts often prefer to use the total asset turnover ratio, which is based on total assets rather than fixed assets:

$$\text{Total asset turnover ratio} = \frac{\text{Net sales}}{\text{Average total assets}}$$

$$\text{Canadian Tire, 2015} = \frac{\$12,279.6}{\$14,770.5^*} = 0.83$$

*($14,987.8 + $14,553.2) ÷ 2

In 2015, Canadian Tire was able to generate $0.83 in revenue for each dollar invested in the company's assets. This ratio does not compare favourably to the ratio of either Sears Canada (1.85) or Hudson's Bay Company (0.98).

As we showed with the ROE model earlier in this chapter, one strategy to improve ROE is to generate more revenue from the company's assets. Many analysts consider this type of improvement to be an important indication of the quality of the company's management.

PAUSE FOR FEEDBACK

We have discussed several measures of profitability. Next we will discuss tests of liquidity. Before you move on, complete the following questions to test your understanding of these ratios.

SELF-STUDY QUIZ 12-1

Dollarama Inc. reported the following data in a recent annual report (in millions of dollars):

	Current Year	Last Year
Net earnings	$ 385.1	
Net sales	2,650.3	
Interest expense (net of tax)	5.8	
Shareholders' equity	466.9	$ 740.5
Total assets	1,813.8	1,700.8

1. Compute the following ratios:
   a. Return on equity
   b. Return on assets
   c. Net profit margin
2. Does the company use debt effectively to generate returns to shareholders? Explain.

After you complete your answers, check them with the solutions at the end of this chapter.

The DuPont Analysis

Exhibit 12.8 shows a decomposition of Canadian Tire's ROE, which was presented earlier in this chapter. This analysis shows the sources of the change in ROE and can provide useful insights into Canadian Tire's business strategy.

Exhibit 12.8 shows a decrease in profit margin for fiscal years 2014 and 2015. The component percentages (see Exhibit 12.5) suggest that this decrease was caused mainly by an increase in the cost of sales (cost of producing revenue) in 2014 and an increase in sales and marketing expenses in 2015 that outpaced the increase in revenues for these years. The company improved on its utilization of assets to generate revenue, but its financial leverage decreased in 2014 and increased slightly in 2015. The increase in the total asset turnover ratio was not significant enough to offset the decreases in the other two components of the DuPont model.[10] This decomposition of the ROE highlights the areas that require further analysis in order to increase the return on shareholders' equity.

	Fiscal Year Ended		
	January 2, 2016	**January 3, 2015**	**December 28, 2013**
Net earnings	$ 735.9	$ 639.3	$ 564.4
Net sales	12,279.6	12,462.9	11,785.6
Average total assets	14,770.5	14,091.6	13,429.3
Average shareholders' equity	5,710.3	5,540.4	5,107.1
DuPont model			
Net earnings/Net sales	0.060	0.051	0.048
× Net sales/Avg. total assets	0.831	0.884	0.878
× Avg. total assets/Avg. shareholders' equity	2.587	2.543	2.630
= Net earnings/Avg. shareholders' equity	0.129	0.115	0.111

Exhibit **12.8**
Canadian Tire ROE Decomposition

PAUSE FOR FEEDBACK STOP

We used ROE analysis in Exhibit 12.8 to understand how Canadian Tire's ROE had changed over the fiscal years 2013–2015. This type of analysis is often called *time series analysis*. ROE analysis can also be used to explain why a company has an ROE that is different from its competitors' at a single point in time. This type of analysis is called *cross-sectional analysis*. Before you move on, complete the following analysis to test your understanding of the DuPont model.

SELF-STUDY QUIZ 12-2

Google Inc. and Yahoo Inc. both supply Internet search services. Both companies have developed reputations for good service. The following is an analysis of their ROEs for a recent year. Using the DuPont analysis, explain how Google produced its higher ROE.

DuPont model	Google	Yahoo
Net earnings/Net sales	0.257	0.213
÷ Net sales/Average total assets	0.581	0.335
÷ Average total assets/Average shareholders' equity	1.249	1.180
= Net earnings/Average shareholders' equity	0.187	0.084

After you complete your answer, check it with the solution at the end of this chapter.

Tests of Liquidity

Liquidity refers to a company's ability to meet its currently maturing debts. **Tests of liquidity** focus on the relationship between current assets and current liabilities and measure a company's ability to meet its currently maturing obligations. A company's ability to pay its current liabilities is an important factor in evaluating its short-term financial strength. For example, a company that does not have cash available to pay for purchases on a timely basis will lose its cash discounts and run the risk of having its credit discontinued by vendors. Three ratios are used to measure liquidity: cash ratio, current ratio, and quick ratio.

7. Cash Ratio Cash is the lifeblood of a business. Without cash, a company cannot pay employees or meet obligations to its creditors. Even a profitable business will fail

LO12-7

Compute and interpret liquidity ratios.

TESTS OF LIQUIDITY are ratios that measure a company's ability to meet its currently maturing obligations without sufficient cash. One measure of the adequacy of available cash, called the *cash ratio*, is computed as follows:

$$\text{Cash ratio} = \frac{\text{Cash + Cash equivalents}}{\text{Current liabilities}}$$

$$\text{Canadian Tire, 2015} = \frac{\$900.6}{\$3,883.8} = 0.23$$

Analysts often use this ratio to compare similar companies. Sears Canada has a ratio (0.53) that exceeds the ratios of both Canadian Tire and Hudson's Bay Company (0.15), indicating that Sears Canada has a larger cash reserve compared to current liabilities.

Would analysts be concerned about a low cash ratio for Canadian Tire? Probably not, because there are other factors to consider. The statement of financial position for Canadian Tire shows that the company has a sizeable portfolio of loans receivable that can be sold to a financial institution for cash should the company need to pay current liabilities. Most analysts believe that the cash ratio should not be too high, because holding excess cash is usually uneconomical. It is far better to invest the cash in productive assets or reduce debt.

Some analysts do not use this ratio because it is very sensitive to small events. The collection of a large trade receivable, for example, would have a significant positive effect on the cash ratio. The current ratio and the quick ratio are much less sensitive to the timing of cash collections from customers.

8. Current Ratio The *current ratio* measures the relationship between current assets and current liabilities at a specific date. It is computed as follows:

$$\text{Current ratio} = \frac{\text{Current assets}}{\text{Current liabilities}}$$

$$\text{Canadian Tire, 2015} = \frac{\$8,692.3}{\$3,883.8} = 2.24$$

The current ratio measures the cushion of working capital that companies maintain to allow for the inevitable unevenness in the flow of funds through the working capital accounts. At the end of 2015, Canadian Tire had $2.24 in current assets for each $1 of current liabilities. Most analysts would judge the ratio to be very strong, given Canadian Tire's ability to generate cash. By comparison, both Sears Canada (1.92) and Hudson's Bay Company (1.36) have ratios that are lower than Canadian Tire's.

To properly use the current ratio, analysts must understand the nature of a company's business. Many manufacturing companies have developed sophisticated systems to minimize the amount of inventory they must hold. These systems, called *just-in-time inventory*, are designed so that an inventory item will arrive just as it is needed. While these systems work well in manufacturing processes, they do not work as well in retailing. Customers expect to find merchandise when they want it, and it has proven difficult to precisely forecast consumer behaviour. As a result, most retailers have comparatively large current ratios because they must carry large inventories. Most companies use a systems approach to inventory management that improves on the distribution of merchandise throughout their supply chains. For example, Canadian Tire has implemented state-of-the-art and innovative technologies, including dimensioner technology, voice pick technology, and automated guided vehicle technology, which replaces traditional human-operated forklifts. These processes allow improved transportation, simplified order processing at suppliers, and reduced lead time for identification of the products needed by specific stores to replenish inventories.

Analysts consider a current ratio of 2 to be financially conservative. Indeed, most companies have current ratios that are below 2. The optimal level for a current ratio depends on the business environment in which a company operates. If cash flows are predictable and stable, as they are for a utility company, the current ratio can even be lower than 1. For a business with highly variable cash flows, such as an airline, a ratio exceeding 1 may be desirable.

Analysts become concerned if a company's current ratio is high compared to those of other companies. A firm is operating inefficiently when it ties up too much money in inventory or trade receivables. There is no reason, for instance, for a Canadian Tire store to hold 1,000 tires in stock if it sells only 100 tires a month.

9. Quick (Acid Test) Ratio The *quick ratio* is a more stringent test of short-term liquidity than the current ratio. The quick ratio compares quick assets, defined as *cash and near-cash assets*, to current liabilities. Quick assets include cash, short-term investments, and trade receivables (net of the allowance for doubtful accounts). Inventories are omitted from quick assets because of the uncertainty of the timing of cash flows from their sale. Prepayments are also excluded from quick assets. Thus, the quick, or acid test, ratio is a more severe test of liquidity than the current ratio. It is computed as follows:

$$\text{Quick ratio} = \frac{\text{Quick assets}}{\text{Current liabilities}}$$

$$\text{Canadian Tire, 2015} = \frac{\$6,787.2}{\$3,883.8} = 1.75$$

The quick ratio is a measure of the safety margin that is available to meet a company's current liabilities. Canadian Tire has $1.75 in cash and near-cash assets for every $1 in current liabilities. This value is relatively high because Canadian Tire carries a relatively large amount of credit card receivables that resulted from customers' use of Canadian Tire's credit card. As a result, both Sears Canada (0.69) and Hudson's Bay Company (0.30) have much smaller ratios than does Canadian Tire.

> **Current Ratio for Selected Industries—2014**
>
> Telecommunications services 1.06
>
> Paper and forest products 2.53
>
> Metals and mining 3.68
>
> Biotechnology 4.51
>
> Gold 4.81

PAUSE FOR FEEDBACK STOP

We have discussed three measures of liquidity: the cash ratio, the current ratio, and the quick ratio. Next, we will discuss additional measures of liquidity. Before you move on, complete the following question to test your understanding of these ratios.

SELF-STUDY QUIZ 12-3

The following quick ratios, presented in random order, pertain to the five industries noted above:

	Industries				
	1	**2**	**3**	**4**	**5**
Quick ratio	2.61	0.92	3.43	0.80	3.19

Of these five industries, one is telecommunications services and another is paper and forest products. Identify the ratio associated with each of these two industries. On average, the quick assets for the telecommunications services industry represent over 85 percent of the industry's current assets.

After you complete your answer, check it with the solution at the end of this chapter.

---

10. Receivables Turnover Ratio Trade receivables are closely related to both short-term liquidity and operating efficiency. A company that can quickly collect cash from its customers has good liquidity and does not needlessly tie up funds in unproductive assets. The receivables turnover ratio is computed as follows:

$$\text{Receivables turnover ratio} = \frac{\text{Net credit sales*}}{\text{Average net accounts receivable}}$$

$$\text{Canadian Tire, 2015} = \frac{\$12,279.6}{\$5,821.2} = 2.11$$

*Since the amount of net credit sales is normally not reported separately, most analysts use net sales in this equation: ($5,464.9 + $6,177.5) ÷ 2

This ratio is called a *turnover* because it reflects how many times the trade receivables were recorded and collected, and then new receivables recorded again during the period (i.e., turned over). Receivables turnover expresses the relationship of the average balance in accounts receivable to the transactions (i.e., credit sales) that created those receivables. This ratio measures the effectiveness of the company's credit granting and collection activities. A high receivables turnover ratio suggests effective collection activities. Granting credit to poor credit risks and making ineffective collection efforts cause this ratio to be low. A very low ratio is obviously a problem, but a very high ratio can also be troublesome because it suggests an overly stringent credit policy that could cause lost sales and net earnings.

The receivables turnover ratio is often converted to a time basis known as the *average age of trade receivables*. The computation is as follows:

$$\textbf{Average age of receivables} = \frac{\textbf{Days in a year}}{\textbf{Receivables turnover ratio}}$$

$$\textbf{Canadian Tire, 2015} = \frac{365}{2.11} = \textbf{173 days}$$

The effectiveness of credit and collection activities is sometimes judged by the general rule that the average collection period should not exceed 1.5 times the credit terms. For example, if the credit terms require payment in 30 days, the average collection period should not exceed 45 days (i.e., not more than 15 days past due). Like all rules, this one has many exceptions.

When you evaluate financial statements, you should always think about the reasonableness of the numbers you compute. We computed the average age of receivables for Canadian Tire as 173 days; about six months. Is that number reasonable? To entice customers to buy products from their stores, companies often use special promotions, offering interest-free credit for 90 to 180 days on large purchases made on the credit cards they issue to their customers. For example, Canadian Tire offers deferred payments for six months on any Canadian Tire store purchase over $200. This is why Canadian Tire refers to its credit card receivables as loans receivable, since they are essentially interest-free short-term loans to customers. Given this fact, an average collection period of 159 days seems reasonable for Canadian Tire.

In contrast, the average collection periods for Sears Canada and Hudson's Bay Company are 7.7 days and 30.8 days, respectively. Do these average collection periods seem reasonable? Probably not. Because we did not know each company's credit sales, we used total sales as an approximation. Think about the last time you watched a customer buying merchandise on credit in a retail store. Most customers use a bank credit card, such as MasterCard or Visa. From the seller's perspective, a sales transaction involving a bank credit card is recorded in virtually the same manner as a cash sale. A credit sale involving a credit card does not create a trade receivable on the seller's books. Instead, the trade receivable is recorded on the books of the credit card company.

11. Inventory Turnover Ratio   Like the receivables turnover ratio, the *inventory turnover ratio* is a measure of both liquidity and operating efficiency. It reflects the relationship of inventory to the volume of sales during the period. It is computed as follows:

$$\textbf{Inventory turnover ratio} = \frac{\textbf{Cost of sales}}{\textbf{Average inventory}}$$

$$\textbf{Canadian Tire, 2015} = \frac{\$8,144.3}{\$1,694.2^*} = \textbf{4.81 times}$$

*($1,623.8 + $1,764.5) ÷ 2

Because a company normally realizes profit each time the inventory is sold, an increase in the ratio is usually favourable. If the ratio is too high, however, it may be an indication that sales were lost because desired items were not in stock. The cost of a lost sale is often much higher than the lost profit. When a business is out of stock on an item desired by a customer, the individual will often go to a competitor to find it. That visit may help the competitor establish a business relationship with the customer. Thus, the cost of being out of stock may be all future profits of a lost customer.

On average, Canadian Tire's inventory was acquired and sold to customers five times during the year. The inventory turnover ratio is critical for companies that have adopted Canadian Tire's business strategy. They want to be able to offer the customer the right product when it is needed at a price that beats the competition. If Canadian Tire does not effectively manage its inventory levels, it will incur extra costs that must be passed on to the customer. Canadian Tire has a higher inventory turnover ratio than both Sears Canada (3.29) and Hudson's Bay Company (2.31) do.

Inventory turnover ratios vary significantly from one industry to the next. Companies in the food industry (grocery stores and restaurants) have high inventory turnover ratios because their inventory is subject to rapid deterioration in quality. Companies that sell expensive merchandise (automobiles and high-fashion clothes) have much lower ratios because sales of these items are infrequent but customers want to have a selection to choose from when they do buy.

The inventory turnover ratio is often converted to a time basis called the *average days' supply in inventory*. The computation is as follows:

$$\text{Average day's supply in inventory} = \frac{\text{Days in year}}{\text{Inventory turnover ratio}}$$

$$\text{Canadian Tire, 2015} = \frac{365}{4.81} = 75.9 \text{ days}$$

12. Accounts Payable Turnover Ratio The *accounts payable turnover ratio* evaluates the company's effectiveness in managing payables to trade creditors. It is computed as follows:

$$\text{Accounts payables turnover ratio} = \frac{\text{Cost of sales}}{\text{Average net accounts payables}}$$

In reality, the numerator of this ratio should be net credit purchases, not cost of sales. Because credit purchases are not usually reported in financial statements, we use total purchases of merchandise inventory as a rough approximation, assuming that all purchases are made on credit. For merchandising companies, we compute purchases by adjusting the cost of sales for the change in inventory during the period as follows:[11]

Purchases = Cost of sales + Ending inventory − Beginning inventory

For Canadian Tire, purchases for fiscal year 2015 equal $8,285 million ($8,144.3 + $1,764.5 − $1,623.8). For most companies, inventories do not change significantly over time. In fact, Canadian Tire's inventories increased by 8.7 percent in 2015; hence, the cost of sales represents a reasonable approximation of the cost of purchases and can be used instead of purchases in computing this ratio.

The computation of the accounts payable turnover ratio for Canadian Tire follows:

$$\text{Canadian Tire, 2015} = \frac{\$8,144.3}{\$1,694.2^*} = 4.44 \text{ times}$$

*($1,834.9 + $1,836.9) ÷ 2

This ratio reflects how many times the accounts payable were recorded and paid, and then new payables recorded again during the period. The accounts payable turnover ratio expresses the relationship of the average balance in accounts payable to the purchase transactions that created those payables. Usually, a low ratio raises questions concerning a company's liquidity. It could also reflect aggressive cash management. By conserving cash with slow payments to trade suppliers, the company minimizes the amount of money it must borrow, and the related interest. The accounts payable turnover ratio is often converted to a time basis known as the *average age of payables*. The computation is as follows:

$$\text{Average age of payables} = \frac{\text{Days in a year}}{\text{Accounts payables turnover ratio}}$$

$$\text{Canadian Tire, 2015} = \frac{365}{4.44} = 82.2 \text{ days}$$

The accounts payable turnover ratio can be subject to manipulation. Managers may delay payment to creditors during the entire year but catch up at year-end so that the ratio is at an acceptable level. The accounts payable turnover ratio of Sears Canada (3.28) indicates that it pays its trade suppliers much later than Canadian Tire, but Hudson's Bay's ratio (5.44) suggests that the company pays its trade suppliers faster than Canadian Tire does. Their average ages of payables are 111.3 days and 67 days, respectively.

Using Ratios to Analyze the Operating Cycle   In Chapter 3, we introduced the concept of the operating cycle, which is the time it takes for a company to pay cash to its suppliers, sell goods to its customers, and collect cash from its customers. Analysts are interested in the operating cycle because it helps them evaluate a company's cash needs and is a good indicator of management efficiency.

The operating cycle for most companies involves three distinct phases: acquisition of inventory, sale of inventory, and collection of cash from customers. We have discussed three ratios that are helpful in evaluating a company's operating cycle. They are the accounts payable turnover ratio, the inventory turnover ratio, and the receivables turnover ratio. Each of these ratios measures the number of days it takes to complete an operating activity. The lengths of the component parts for Canadian Tire's operating cycle are as follows:

Ratio	Operating Activity	Time
Accounts payable turnover ratio	Purchase of inventory	82 days
Inventory turnover ratio	Sale of inventory	76 days
Receivables turnover ratio	Collection of cash from customers	173 days

The component parts of the operating cycle help us understand the cash needs of the company. Canadian Tire, on average, pays for its inventory 82 days after it receives it. It takes, on average, 249 days (76 + 173) for Canadian Tire to sell the inventory and collect cash from customers. Therefore, Canadian Tire must invest cash in its operating activities for nearly 167 days between the time it pays its vendors and the time it collects from its customers. Companies prefer to minimize the time between paying vendors and collecting cash from customers, because it frees up cash for other productive purposes. Canadian Tire could reduce this time by increasing the inventory turnover or changing its credit policy to speed up collection from customers, but that may cause a decrease in sales.

PAUSE FOR FEEDBACK

We have discussed several measures of liquidity. Next we will discuss tests of solvency. Before you move on, complete the following questions to test your understanding of these measures.

SELF-STUDY QUIZ 12-4

Dollarama Inc. reported the following data in a recent annual report (in millions of dollars):

Cash and cash equivalents	$ 59.2
Accounts receivable	11.1
Inventories	470.2
Other current assets	66.6
Current liabilities	227.0

Compute the following ratios:

1. Current ratio
2. Quick ratio
3. Cash ratio

After you complete your answers, check them with the solutions at the end of this chapter.

Tests of Solvency

LO12-8

Compute and interpret solvency ratios.

Solvency refers to a company's ability to meet its long-term obligations. **Tests of solvency**, which are measures of a company's ability to meet these obligations, include the times interest earned, cash coverage, and debt-to-equity ratios.

TESTS OF SOLVENCY are ratios that measure a company's ability to meet its long-term obligations.

13. Times Interest Earned Ratio   Interest payments are a definite obligation of the borrowing company. If a company fails to make required interest payments, creditors may force it into bankruptcy. Because of the importance of interest payments, analysts often compute a ratio called the *times interest earned ratio*:

$$\text{Times interest earned ratio} = \frac{\text{Net earnings + Interest expense + Income tax expense}}{\text{Interest expense}}$$

$$\text{Canadian Tire, 2015} = \frac{\$735.9 + \$106.9 + \$265.4}{\$106.9} = 10.37 \text{ times}$$

This ratio compares the earnings that a company generated during one period—before deducting interest and income tax expenses—to its interest expense for the same period. It represents a margin of protection for the creditors. In 2015, Canadian Tire generated nearly $10.37 in earnings before interest and taxes for each $1 of interest expense, a ratio that indicates a secure position for creditors. Canadian Tire's ratio is higher than those of Hudson's Bay Company (4.05) and Sears Canada, which reported a loss before interest and income taxes.

Some analysts prefer to calculate this ratio based on all contractually required payments, including principal payments and rent obligations under lease contracts. Other analysts believe that this ratio is flawed, because interest expense and other obligations are paid in cash, not with net earnings. These analysts prefer to use the *cash coverage ratio*.

14. Cash Coverage Ratio   Given the importance of cash flows and required interest payments, it is easy to understand why many analysts use the *cash coverage ratio*. It is computed as follows:

$$\text{Cash coverage ratio} = \frac{\text{Cash flows from operating activities before interest and taxes}}{\text{Interest paid (from statement of cash flows)}}$$

$$\text{Canadian Tire, 2015} = \frac{\$1,364.3}{\$101.4} = 13.45 \text{ times}$$

The cash coverage ratio compares the cash generated with the cash obligations of the period. Analysts are concerned about a company's ability to make required interest payments. The cash coverage ratio for Canadian Tire shows that the company generated $13,45 in cash from operations for every $1 of interest paid, which is good coverage. Canadian Tire's cash coverage ratio is much higher than Hudson's Bay's ratio (1.13). In contrast to both companies, Sears Canada reported a net cash outflow from operations, but the interest it paid is relatively low. Note that the numerator and the denominator of the cash coverage ratio use *interest paid and income taxes paid* from the statement of cash flows instead of *interest expense and income taxes expense* from the statement of earnings. Accrued interest and interest payments are normally similar in amount, but are not always the same.

15. Debt-to-Equity Ratio   The *debt-to-equity ratio* expresses a company's debt as a proportion of its shareholders' equity.[12] It is computed as follows:

$$\text{Debt-to-equity ratio} = \frac{\text{Total liabilities}}{\text{Shareholders' equity}}$$

$$\text{Canadian Tire, 2015} = \frac{\$9,198.1}{\$5,789.7} = 1.59$$

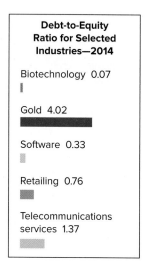

In 2015, for each $1 of shareholders' equity, Canadian Tire had $1.59 of liabilities. By comparison, Sears Canada and Hudson's Bay Company's debt-to-equity ratios were 1.95 and 3.08, respectively.

Debt is risky for a company because specific interest payments must be made even if the company has not generated sufficient net earnings. In contrast, dividends are always at the company's discretion and are not legally enforceable until they are declared by the board of directors. Thus, equity capital is usually considered much less risky than debt.

Despite the risk associated with debt, most companies obtain significant amounts of resources from creditors because of the advantages of financial leverage discussed earlier. In addition, interest paid is a deductible expense on the corporate income tax return. In selecting a capital structure, a company must balance the higher returns available through leverage against the higher risk associated with debt. Because of the importance of this risk–return relationship, most analysts consider the debt-to-equity ratio to be a key part of any company evaluation.

Market Tests

LO12-9

Compute and interpret market test ratios.

MARKET TESTS are ratios that tend to measure the market worth of a common share.

Several ratios, often called **market tests**, relate the current market price per share to the return that accrues to investors. Many analysts prefer these ratios because they are based on the current value of an owner's investment in a company.

16. Price/Earnings (P/E) Ratio The *price/earnings (P/E) ratio* measures the relationship between the current market price per share and its EPS. Recently, when the price of a Canadian Tire common share was $69.11, EPS was $6.13, as calculated earlier. The P/E ratio for the company is computed as follows:

$$\text{Price/earnings ratio} = \frac{\textbf{Current market price per share}}{\textbf{Earnings per share}}$$

$$\text{Canadian Tire, 2015} = \frac{\$105.35}{\$8.66} = 12.2$$

The P/E ratio indicates that Canadian Tire's shares were selling at a price that was 12.2 times its EPS. The P/E ratio reflects the stock market's assessment of the company's future business performance. A high ratio indicates that the market expects earnings to grow rapidly. Canadian Tire's P/E ratio is reasonable and higher than that of Hudson's Bay Company (8.1), whereas Sears reports a loss per share for fiscal year 2015.

Sometimes, the components of the P/E ratio are inverted, giving the *capitalization rate*, a rate at which the stock market is apparently capitalizing the current earnings. The capitalization rate for Canadian Tire is $8.66 ÷ $105.35 = 8.2 percent.

In economic terms, the share price is related to the present value of the company's future earnings. Thus, a company that expects to increase its earnings in the future is worth more than one that cannot grow its earnings (assuming other factors are the same). But while a high P/E ratio and good growth prospects are considered favourable, there are risks. When a company with a high P/E ratio does not meet the level of earnings expected by the market, the negative impact on its share price can be dramatic.

17. Dividend Yield Ratio When investors buy shares, they expect returns from two sources: dividend income and price appreciation. The *dividend yield ratio* measures the relationship between the dividend per share paid to shareholders and the current market price per share. Canadian Tire paid a dividend of $2.15 per share when the market price per share was $105.35. Its dividend yield ratio is computed as follows:

$$\text{Dividend yield ratio} = \frac{\textbf{Dividend per share}}{\textbf{Market price per share}}$$

$$\text{Canadian Tire, 2015} = \frac{\$2.15}{\$105.35} = 2.0\%$$

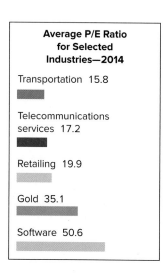

The dividend yield ratio for shares of most companies is not high compared with returns on alternative investments. Investors may accept low dividend yields if they expect that the price of a company's shares will increase while they own it. Clearly, investors who bought Canadian Tire's common shares did so with the expectation that their price would increase. In contrast, companies with low growth potential tend to offer much higher dividend yields than do companies with high growth potential. These latter companies usually appeal to retired investors who need current income rather than future growth potential.

The dividend yields for both Sears Canada (0 percent) and Hudson's Bay Company (1.2 percent) are lower than that for Canadian Tire. The chart shows dividend yields for a selection of companies.

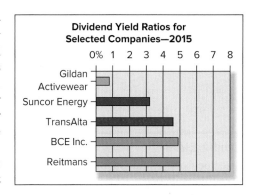

PAUSE FOR FEEDBACK STOP

We have discussed several measures of solvency and two market tests. Next, we will discuss important analytical considerations. Before you move on, complete the following questions to test your understanding of these measures.

SELF-STUDY QUIZ 12-5

Dollarama Inc. reported the following data in a recent annual report (in millions of dollars):

Total liabilities	$1,347.00
Shareholders' equity	466.90
Earnings before interest and taxes	549.40
Interest expense	21.40
Earnings per share	3.03
Share price at year-end	79.95

Compute the following ratios:

1. Debt-to-equity

2. Times interest earned ratio

3. P/E ratio

After you complete your answers, check them with the solutions at the end of this chapter.

INTERPRETING RATIOS AND OTHER ANALYTICAL CONSIDERATIONS

Except for EPS, the computation of financial ratios has not been standardized by the accounting profession or security analysts. Thus, users of financial statements should compute the various ratios in accordance with their decision objectives. Before using ratios computed by others, the analyst should determine the computational approach that was used.

Ratios can best be interpreted only by comparing them to other ratios or to some threshold value. For example, a very low current ratio may indicate an inability to meet maturing debts, and a very high current ratio may indicate an unprofitable use of funds. Furthermore, an optimal ratio for one company may not be optimal for another. Comparisons of ratios for different companies are appropriate only if the companies are indeed comparable in terms of industry, nature of operations, size, and accounting policies.

Because ratios are based on the aggregation of information, they may obscure underlying factors that are of interest to the analyst. For example, a current ratio that is considered optimal may obscure a short-term liquidity problem if the company has a very large amount of inventory but a minimal amount of cash with which to pay debts as they mature. Careful analysis can uncover this type of problem.

In other cases, analysis cannot uncover obscured problems. For example, consolidated statements include financial information about the parent and its subsidiaries. The parent company may have a high current ratio and the subsidiary a low ratio. When the statements are consolidated, the current ratio may fall within an acceptable range. The fact that the subsidiary could have a serious liquidity problem is obscured in this case.

Exhibit **12.9**

Selected Financial Ratios for Braniff International

	Years before Bankruptcy				
	5	**4**	**3**	**2**	**1**
Current ratio	1.20	0.91	0.74	0.60	0.49
Debt-to-equity ratio	2.03	2.45	4.88	15.67	N/A*

*In the year before bankruptcy, Braniff reported negative owners' equity as a result of a large net loss that produced a negative balance in retained earnings. Total liabilities exceeded total assets.

Despite limitations, ratio analysis is a useful analytical tool. For instance, financial ratios are effective for predicting bankruptcy. Exhibit 12.9 gives the current and debt-to-equity ratios for Braniff International Corporation (an airline company in the United States) for each year before it filed for bankruptcy. Notice the deterioration of these ratios each year. Analysts who studied the financial ratios were probably not surprised by Braniff's bankruptcy. After selling many of its assets and undergoing a complete financial restructuring, Braniff was able to resume limited flight operations but was forced to file for bankruptcy for a second time after additional financial difficulty.

Financial statements provide information to all investors, both sophisticated and unsophisticated. However, users who understand basic accounting principles and terminology are able to more effectively analyze the information in the financial statements. For example, unsophisticated users who do not understand the cost principle might believe that assets are reported on the statement of financial position at their fair market value. Interpreting accounting numbers without an understanding of the concepts that were used to develop them is impossible.

In analyzing different companies, you will find that they rarely use exactly the same accounting policies. Comparisons among companies are appropriate only if the analyst who is making them understands the impact of various accounting alternatives. For example, one company may be prudent in selecting accounting alternatives, such as declining depreciation, while another may use profit-maximizing alternatives, such as straight-line depreciation. Those who do not understand the different effects of accounting methods are very likely to misinterpret financial results. Perhaps the most important first step in analyzing financial statements is a review of the company's accounting policies, which are disclosed in a note to the statements.

Other Financial Information

The ratios we have discussed are useful for most analytical purposes. Because each company is different, you must exercise professional judgment when you conduct each financial analysis. To illustrate, let us look at some special factors that might affect our analysis of Canadian Tire.

1. *Rapid growth.* Growth in total sales volume does not always indicate that a company is successful. Sales volume from new stores may obscure the fact that existing stores are not meeting customer needs and are experiencing declining sales. In robust economic times, the retail industry often undertakes long-term expansion plans, which rapidly become unprofitable if the economy slows. For example, Canadian Tire's earnings releases report that the company posted same-store sales increases ranging from 1.4 percent to 4.7 percent between 2001 and 2006, but

with the economic recession, this growth slowed down or changed to decreases in comparable store sales between 2007 and 2012. Nevertheless, the management of Canadian Tire continued to report net earnings throughout this turbulent period. Same-store sales increased again during the period 2013–2015.

2. *Uneconomical expansion.* Some growth-oriented companies open stores in less-than-desirable locations if good locations cannot be found. These poor locations can cause the company's average productivity to decline. One measure of productivity in the retail industry is sales volume per square foot of selling space. For The Home Depot, which is a competitor in the home renovation industry, productivity decreased from 2007 to 2009 before showing signs of gradual improvement in later years. In response to economic hard times that started in 2008, The Home Depot has considerably decreased its new store openings in an effort to improve its productivity:

Year	Sales per Square Foot
2015	$370
2014	352
2013	334
2012	319
2011	299
2010	288
2009	279
2008	298
2007	332
2006	358
2005	377

3. *Subjective factors.* Remember that some vital information about a company is not contained in the annual report. The best way to evaluate Canadian Tire's innovation through introducing new products, programs, and services to customers is to visit its stores and those of competitors.

As these examples illustrate, no single approach can be used to analyze all companies. Furthermore, an effective analyst will look beyond the information contained in an annual report.

INSIDER INFORMATION

A QUESTION OF ACCOUNTABILITY

Financial statements are an important source of information for investors. Announcement of an unexpected earnings increase or decrease can cause a substantial movement in the price of a company's shares.

A company's accountants are often aware of important financial information before it is made available to the public. This is called *insider information*. Some people may be tempted to buy or sell shares based on insider information, but to do so is a serious criminal offence. Securities commissions have brought charges against a number of individuals who traded on insider information. Their conviction resulted in large fines and time served in jail.

In some cases, it may be difficult to determine whether something is insider information. For example, an individual may simply overhear a comment made in the company elevator by two executives. A well-respected Wall Street investment banker gave good advice when dealing with such situations: "If you are not sure if something is right or wrong, apply the newspaper headline test. Ask yourself how you would feel to have your family and friends read about what you had done in the newspaper." Interestingly, many people who spent time in jail and lost small fortunes in fines because of insider trading convictions say that the most difficult part of the process was telling their families.

To uphold the highest ethical standard, many public accounting firms have rules that prevent members of their professional staff from investing in companies that the firm audits. These rules are designed to ensure that the company's auditors cannot be tempted to engage in insider trading and to maintain independence from the audited firm.

Information in an Efficient Market

Considerable research has been done on the way in which stock markets react to new information. Much of this evidence supports the view that the markets react very quickly to new information in an unbiased manner (i.e., the market does not systematically overreact or under react to new information). A market that reacts to information in this manner is called an *efficient market*. In **efficient markets**, the price of a security fully reflects all publicly available information.

It is not surprising that the stock markets react quickly to new information. Many professional investors manage stock portfolios valued in the hundreds of millions of dollars. These investors have a large financial incentive to discover new information about a company and trade quickly based on that information.

The research on efficient markets has important implications for financial analysis. It is probably not beneficial to study old information (e.g., an annual report that was released six months earlier) in an effort to identify an undervalued stock. In an efficient market, the price of the stock reflects all of the information contained in the report shortly after it was released. Furthermore, a company cannot manipulate the price of its stock by manipulating its accounting policy. The market should be able to differentiate between a company with increasing earnings because of improved productivity and one that has increased its earnings by changing from prudent to liberal accounting policies.

EFFICIENT MARKETS are securities markets in which prices fully reflect all publicly available information.

ACCOUNTING STANDARDS FOR PRIVATE ENTERPRISES

As we noted in previous chapters, the Accounting Standards for Canadian Private Enterprises differ from IFRS with respect to measurement and reporting of specific elements of financial statements, even though both sets of standards are derived from the same conceptual framework for accounting. When analyzing financial statements, users should be aware of the measurement rules that underlie the values reported on these statements, particularly if comparisons are being made between private enterprises and publicly accountable enterprises that use different sets of financial reporting standards.

CHAPTER **TAKE-AWAYS**

12-1. Recognize the roles of people involved in the accounting communication process (regulators, managers, board of directors, auditors, information intermediaries, and users), and the guidance they receive from legal and professional standards.
Management of the reporting company must decide on the appropriate format (categories) and level of detail to present in its financial reports. Independent audits increase the credibility of the information. Financial statement announcements from public companies are usually first transmitted to users through electronic information services. The securities commission staff review public reports for compliance with legal and professional standards, investigate irregularities, and punish violators. Analysts play a major role in making financial statements and other information available to average investors through their stock recommendations and earnings forecasts.

12-2. Identify the steps in the accounting communication process, including the issuance of press releases, annual reports, quarterly reports, and documents filed with securities commissions.
Earnings are first made public in press releases. Companies follow these announcements with annual and quarterly reports containing statements, notes, and additional information. Public companies must also file additional reports, containing more details about the company, with the securities commissions (e.g., OSC, SEC).

12-3. Explain how a company's business strategy affects financial analysis.
In simple terms, a business strategy establishes the objectives a business is trying to achieve. Performance is best evaluated by comparing the financial results to the objectives that the

business was working to achieve. In other words, an understanding of a company's strategy provides the context for conducting financial statement analysis.

12-4. Discuss how analysts use financial statements.

Analysts use financial statements to understand present conditions and past performance, as well as to predict future performance. Financial statements provide important information to help users understand and evaluate corporate strategy. The data reported on statements can be used for either time series analysis (evaluating a single company over time) or in a comparison with similar companies at a single point in time. Most analysts compute component percentages and ratios when using statements.

12-5. Compute and interpret component percentages.

To compute component percentages for the statement of earnings, the base amount is net sales revenue. Each expense is expressed as a percentage of net sales revenue. On the statement of financial position, the base amount is total assets; the balance of each account is divided by total assets. Component percentages are evaluated by comparing them over time for a single company or by comparing them with percentages for similar companies.

12-6. Compute and interpret profitability ratios.

Several tests of profitability focus on measuring the adequacy of net earnings by comparing it to other items reported on the financial statements. Exhibit 12.7 lists these ratios and shows how to compute them. Profitability ratios are evaluated by comparing them over time for a single company or by comparing them with ratios for similar companies.

12-7. Compute and interpret liquidity ratios.

Tests of liquidity measure a company's ability to meet its current maturing debt. Exhibit 12.7 lists these ratios and shows how to compute them. Liquidity ratios are evaluated by comparing them over time for a single company or by comparing them with ratios for similar companies.

12-8. Compute and interpret solvency ratios.

Solvency ratios measure a company's ability to meet its long-term obligations. Exhibit 12.7 lists these ratios and shows how to compute them. Solvency ratios are evaluated by comparing them over time for a single company or by comparing them with ratios for similar companies.

12-9. Compute and interpret market test ratios.

Market test ratios relate the current price per share to the return that accrues to investors. Exhibit 12.7 lists these ratios and shows how to compute them. Market test ratios are evaluated by comparing them over time for a single company or by comparing them with ratios for similar companies.

FINDING **FINANCIAL INFORMATION**

STATEMENT OF FINANCIAL POSITION

Analysts use information reported on the statement of financial position to compute many ratios. Most analysts use an average of the beginning and ending amounts for statement of financial position accounts when the ratio calculation also includes an amount reported on the statement of earnings.

STATEMENT OF CASH FLOWS

Some ratios use amounts reported on this statement.

STATEMENT OF EARNINGS

EPS is the only ratio that is required to be reported on the financial statements. It is usually reported at the bottom of the statement of earnings.

STATEMENT OF CHANGES IN EQUITY

Ratios are not reported on this statement.

NOTES

Under Summary of Significant Accounting Policies

This note has no information pertaining directly to ratios, but it is important to understand differences in accounting policies if you are comparing two companies.

Under a Separate Note

Most companies include a 5-year or a 10-year financial summary as a separate note. This summary includes data for significant financial statement items, some accounting ratios, and non-accounting information.

QUESTIONS

1. Describe the roles and responsibilities of management, the board of directors, and independent auditors in the financial reporting process.
2. Define the following three users of financial accounting disclosures and the relationships among them: *financial analysts*, *private investors*, and *institutional investors*.
3. Briefly describe the role of information services in the communication of financial information.
4. What are three fundamental uses of external financial statements by decision makers?
5. What are some of the primary items on financial statements about which creditors are usually concerned?
6. Why are the notes to the financial statements important to decision makers?
7. What is the primary purpose of comparative financial statements?
8. Why are statement users interested in financial summaries covering several years? What is the primary limitation of a 5-year or a 10-year financial summary?
9. What is ratio analysis? Why is it useful?
10. What are component percentages? Why are they useful?
11. Explain the two concepts of return on investment.
12. What is financial leverage? How is it measured as a percentage?
13. Is profit margin a useful measure of profitability? Explain.
14. Compare and contrast the current ratio and the quick ratio.
15. What does the debt-to-equity ratio reflect?
16. What are market tests?
17. Identify three factors that limit the effectiveness of ratio analysis.
18. Dimitri Company has prepared draft financial results now being reviewed by the accountants. You notice that the financial leverage percentage is negative. You also note that the current ratio is 2.4 and the quick ratio is 3.7. You remember that these financial relationships are unusual. Does either imply that a mistake has been made? Explain.

▩ connect   MINI-EXERCISES

▩ LO12-1   **M12-1**   **Matching Players in the Accounting Communication Process with Their Definitions**
Match each player with the related definition by entering the appropriate letter in the space provided.

Players	Definitions
___ (1) Independent auditor	A. Adviser who analyzes financial and other economic information to form forecasts and stock recommendations.
___ (2) CEO and CFO	
___ (3) Users	B. Institutional and private investors and creditors (among others).
___ (4) Financial analyst	C. Chief executive officer and chief financial officer who have primary responsibility for the information presented in financial statements.
	D. Independent CPA who examines financial statements and attests to their fairness.

▩ LO12-5   **M12-2**   **Inferring Financial Information Using Component Percentages**
A large retailer reported revenue of $1,665,000. The company's gross profit percentage was 44 percent. What amount of cost of sales did the company report?

▩ LO12-5   **M12-3**   **Inferring Financial Information Using Component Percentages**
A consumer products company reported a 5.4 percent increase in sales from 2017 to 2018. Sales in 2017 were $29,600. In 2018, the company reported cost of sales in the amount of $9,107. What was the gross profit percentage in 2018?

LO12-6   **M12-4**   **Computing the Return on Owners' Equity Ratio**

Compute the return on equity ratio for 2018 given the following data:

	2018	2017
Net earnings	$ 183,000	$ 159,000
Shareholders' equity	1,100,000	1,250,000
Total assets	2,460,000	2,630,000
Interest expense	42,000	32,000

LO12-6   **M12-5**   **Inferring Financial Information**

Compute the financial leverage percentage for 2018 given the following data:

	2018	2017
Return on equity	21%	26%
Return on assets	6%	8%
Profit margin	12%	12%

LO12-7   **M12-6**   **Analyzing the Inventory Turnover Ratio**

A manufacturer reported an inventory turnover ratio of 8.6 during 2017. During 2018, management introduced a new inventory control system that was expected to reduce average inventory levels by 25 percent without affecting sales volume. Given these circumstances, would you expect the inventory turnover ratio to increase or decrease during 2018? Explain.

LO12-7   **M12-7**   **Inferring Financial Information Using a Ratio**

Stacy Company reported total assets of $1,400,000 and non-current assets of $480,000. The company also reported a current ratio of 3.5. What amount of current liabilities did the company report?

LO12-8   **M12-8**   **Analyzing Financial Relationships**

Ramesh Company has prepared draft financial results now being reviewed by the accountants. You notice that the financial leverage percentage is negative. You also note that the current ratio is 2.4 and the quick ratio is 3.7. You recognize that these financial relationships are unusual. Does either imply that a mistake has been made? Explain.

LO12-9   **M12-9**   **Inferring Financial Information Using a Ratio**

In 2017, Pringle Company reported earnings per share of $9.50 when its common shares were selling for $228 each. In 2018, its earnings increased by 13 percent. If all other relationships remain constant, what would be the price per share?

LO12-9   **M12-10**   **Inferring Financial Information Using a Ratio**

An Internet company earned $6.50 per share and paid dividends of $3.50 per common share. The company reported a dividend yield of 5 percent. What was the price per share?

LO12-9   **M12-11**   **Analyzing the Impact of Accounting Alternatives**

Youngstown Corporation is considering changing its inventory method from FIFO to weighted average and wants to determine the impact on selected accounting ratios. In general, what impact would you expect on these ratios—profit margin, fixed asset turnover ratio, current ratio, and quick ratio—assuming that prices are rising over time?

connect EXERCISES

LO12-3   **E12-1**   **Matching Players in the Accounting Communication Process with Their Definitions**

Match each player with the related definition by entering the appropriate letter in the space provided.

Players	Definitions
____ (1) Financial analyst	A. Financial institution or supplier that lends money to the company.
____ (2) Creditor	
____ (3) Independent auditor	B. Chief executive officer and chief financial officer, who have primary responsibility for the information presented in financial statements.
____ (4) Private investor	
____ (5) CSA	C. Manager of pension, mutual, and endowment funds who invests on behalf of others.
____ (6) Information service	
____ (7) Institutional investor	D. Canadian Securities Administrators, which harmonizes securities regulations in the Canadian capital markets.
____ (8) CEO and CFO	
	E. Company that gathers, combines, and transmits (paper and electronic) financial and related information from various sources.
	F. Adviser who analyzes financial and other economic information to make forecasts and stock recommendations.
	G. Individual who purchases shares in companies.
	H. Independent CPA who examines financial statements and attests to their fairness.

LO12-4   **E12-2**   **Finding Financial Information: Matching Information Items to Financial Reports**

Following are information items that are included in various financial reports. Match each information item with the report(s) where it would most likely be found by entering the appropriate letter(s) in the space provided.

Information Item	Report
____ (1) Summarized financial data for 5- or 10-year period.	A. Annual report
____ (2) Initial announcement of quarterly earnings.	B. Annual information form
____ (3) Complete quarterly statement of earnings, statement of financial position, and statement of cash flows.	C. Press release
____ (4) Basic financial statements for the year.	D. Quarterly report
____ (5) Detailed discussion of the company's competition.	E. None of the above
____ (6) Notes to financial statements.	
____ (7) Identification of those responsible for the financial statements.	
____ (8) Initial announcement of hiring of new vice-president of sales.	

LO12-4   **E12-3**   **Understanding the Disclosure Process through the Le Château Website**

Le Château

Using your Web browser, access Le Château at http://lechateau.com/style/company/links/investor.jsp. Examine the most recent quarterly earnings press release and the related interim report.

Required:

Based on the information provided on the site, answer the following questions:

1. What were the release dates of the quarterly earnings press release and the interim report?
2. What additional information was provided in the interim report that was not reported in the earnings press release?

■ LO12-4,12-5 **E12-4** **Researching Information Provided on Company Websites**

Canadian Tire
Corporation

Using your Web browser, visit Canadian Tire Corporation at www.corp.canadiantire.ca.

Required:

Based on the information provided on the site, answer the following questions:

1. Which document(s) provided the most recent information on quarterly earnings?

2. For the most recent quarter, what was the change in sales revenue compared with the same quarter one year earlier? What was management's explanation for the change (if any)?

3. What were the annual earnings per share and stock price per share on the day of the most recent fourth-quarter earnings press release?

■ LO12-3 **E12-5** **Understanding Earnings per Share and Stock Prices**

Apple Inc.

REAL-WORLD EXCERPT

Apple Inc.

EARNINGS RELEASES

The following is an excerpt from an earnings release of Apple Inc., the maker of iMac, iPod, iPad and iPhone products, related to the results of its operations for the first quarter of fiscal year 2016.

> **Apple Reports Record First Quarter Results**
>
> CUPERTINO, California—January 26, 2016—Apple® today announced financial results for its fiscal 2016 first quarter ended December 26, 2015. The Company posted record quarterly revenue of $75.9 billion and record quarterly net income of $18.4 billion, or $3.28 per diluted share. These results compare to revenue of $74.6 billion and net income of $18 billion, or $3.06 per diluted share, in the year-ago quarter. Gross margin was 40.1 percent compared to 39.9 percent in the year-ago quarter. International sales accounted for 66 percent of the quarter's revenue.
>
> *Source:* https://www.apple.com/pr/library/2016/01/26Apple-Reports-Record-First-Quarter-Results.html. Accessed April 10, 2017.

Despite the increase in Apple's revenues and earnings over the same quarter of the previous year, its shares fell from US$97.34 on January 29, 2016, to US$96.43 on February 1, 2016.

Required:

Explain why the price per share decreased even though the company announced an increase in its earnings per share.

■ LO12-5 **E12-6** **Preparing a Schedule by Using Component Percentages**

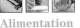

Alimentation
Couche-Tard Inc.

Alimentation Couche-Tard Inc. is a leading convenience store operator in Canada, with Couche-Tard stores in Québec and Mac's stores in central and western Canada. It also operates Circle K shops in the United States. Complete the component percentage analysis on the company's statement of earnings that follows. Discuss the insights provided by this analysis:

CONSOLIDATED STATEMENTS OF EARNINGS			
For the years ended April 25, 2015, April 27, 2014, and April 28, 2013			
(in millions of U.S. dollars, except per share amounts)			
	2015	**2014**	**2013**
Revenues	$34,529.9	$37,962.1	$35,543.4
Cost of sales	29,261.9	32,974.0	30,933.8
Gross profit	5,268.0	4,988.1	4,609.6
Operating, selling, administrative, and general expenses (Note 8)	3,376.9	3,419.9	3,239.6
Restructuring and integration costs (Notes 4 and 23)	30.3	—	34.0
Loss on disposal of aviation fuel business (Note 5)	11.0	—	—
Curtailment gain on defined benefits pension plans obligation (Notes 5 and 27)	(2.6)	(0.9)	(19.4)
Negative goodwill (Note 4)	(1.2)	(48.4)	(4.4)
Depreciation, amortization and impairment of property and equipment, intangible assets, and other assets	530.4	583.2	521.1
	3,944.8	3,953.8	3,770.9
Operating income	1,323.2	1,034.3	838.7
Share of earnings of joint venture accounted for using the equity method (Note 6)	21.9	22.7	15.8
Net financial (revenues) expenses	105.4	110.6	207.8
Earnings before income taxes	1,239.7	946.4	646.7
Income taxes	306.2	134.2	73.9
Net earnings	933.5	812.2	572.8

LO12-7   **E12-7**   **Analyzing the Impact of Selected Transactions on the Current Ratio**

Current assets for JC Inc. totalled $54,000, and the current ratio was 1.8. Assume that the following transactions were completed: (1) purchased merchandise for $6,000 on short-term credit and (2) purchased a delivery truck for $20,000—paid $4,000 cash and signed a two-year interest-bearing note for the balance.

Required:

Compute the current ratio after each transaction.

LO12-7   **E12-8**   **Analyzing the Impact of Selected Transactions on Accounts Receivable and Inventory Turnover**

Procter & Gamble

Procter & Gamble is a multinational corporation that manufactures and markets many products that are probably in your home. Last year, sales for the company were $76,279 (all amounts in millions of U.S. dollars). The annual report did not disclose the amount of credit sales, so we will assume that 30 percent of sales were on credit. The average gross margin rate was 50 percent on sales. Account balances follow:

	Beginning	Ending
Accounts receivables (net)	$4,861	$6,836
Inventory	5,454	6,759

Required:

Compute the turnover ratios for the accounts receivable and inventory, the average age of receivables, and the average days' supply of inventory.

LO12-6,12-7   **E12-9**   **Analyzing the Impact of Specific Events on Selected Ratios**

Consider the following two independent situations:

1. A manufacturer reported an inventory turnover ratio of 8.6 during 2016. During 2017, management introduced a new inventory control system that was expected to reduce average inventory levels by 25 percent without affecting sales volume. Given these circumstances, would you expect the inventory turnover ratio to increase or decrease during 2017? Explain.

2. Lexis Corporation is considering changing its inventory method from weighted average cost to FIFO and wants to determine the impact on selected accounting ratios. In general, what would be the impact of this change on the following ratios, assuming that prices have been increasing over time: net profit margin ratio, fixed asset turnover ratio, current ratio, and quick ratio?

LO12-6   **E12-10**   **Computing Financial Leverage**

Nokia Corporation

Nokia Corporation is a global leader in providing integrated communications and electronic solutions for businesses. Its financial statements reported the following at year-end (in millions of euros):

Average total assets	35,738
Average total debt (2% interest)	20,989
Net earnings (average tax rate 30%)	260

Required:

Compute the financial leverage percentage. Was it positive or negative?

LO12-7   **E12-11**   **Analyzing the Impact of Selected Transactions on the Current Ratio**

Current assets for GK Company totalled $100,000, and the current ratio was 1.5. Assume that the following transactions were completed: (1) paid $6,000 for merchandise purchased on short-term credit, (2) purchased a delivery truck for $20,000 cash, (3) wrote off a bad accounts receivable for $1,000, and (4) paid previously declared dividends in the amount of $20,000.

Required:

Compute the current ratio after each transaction.

LO12-5   **E12-12**   **Inferring Financial Information**

Dollarama

Dollarama is the leading dollar store operator in Canada with over 800 locations in all provinces. In a recent year, the company reported average inventories of $439.6 million and an inventory turnover ratio of 3.68. Average total fixed assets were $622.8 million, and the fixed asset turnover ratio was 4.26. Determine the gross profit for Dollarama.

LO12-7 **E12-13** **Computing Selected Ratios**

Sales for the year for RK Ltd. were $1,500,000, of which one-half was on credit. The average gross margin rate was 40 percent on sales. Account balances follow:

	Beginning	Ending
Accounts receivable (net)	$150,000	$180,000
Inventory	150,000	90,000

Required:
Compute and comment on the turnover ratios for the accounts receivable and inventory, the average age of receivables, and the average days' supply of inventory.

LO12-7 **E12-14** **Analyzing the Impact of Selected Transactions on the Current Ratio**

Current assets for Clarke Inc. totalled $1,000,000, the current ratio was 2.0, and the company uses the periodic inventory method. Assume that the following transactions were completed: (1) sold $26,000 in merchandise on account, (2) declared but did not pay dividends of $40,000, (3) paid rent in advance in the amount of $24,000, (4) paid previously declared dividends in the amount of $40,000, (5) collected a accounts receivable in the amount of $20,000, and (6) reclassified $90,000 of long-term debt as a short-term liability.

Required:
Compute the current ratio after each transaction.

LO12-7 **E12-15** **Computing Liquidity Ratios**

Cintas

Cintas designs, manufactures, and implements corporate identity uniform programs that it rents or sells to customers throughout the United States and Canada. The company's stock is traded on the NASDAQ and has provided investors with significant ROEs over the past few years. Selected information from the company's statement of financial position follows. The company reported revenue of $4,476,886 and cost of sales of $2,555,549 for fiscal year 2015:

CINTAS Statement of Financial Position As of May 31,		
(amounts in thousands)	**2015**	**2014**
Cash and cash equivalents	$417,073	$513,288
Short-term investments	16,081	—
Accounts receivable, less allowance of $15,674 and $14,906, respectively	496,130	508,427
Inventories, net	226,211	251,239
Prepayments	24,030	26,190
Accounts payable	109,607	150,070
Accrued compensation and related liabilities	88,423	85,026
Income taxes, current	—	5,960
Long-term debt due within one year	—	503

Required:
Compute the current ratio, quick ratio, inventory turnover ratio, and receivables turnover ratio (assuming that 60 percent of sales was on credit) for 2015, and comment on the liquidity position of the company.

LO12-8 **E12-16** **Determining the Impact of Selected Transactions on Measures of Solvency**

Three commonly used measures of solvency are the debt-to-equity ratio, the times interest earned ratio, and the cash coverage ratio. For each of the following transactions, determine whether the measure will increase, decrease, or not change. Assume that all ratios are higher than 1.

a. Issued shares in exchange for equipment for $500,000.

b. Issued bonds at par for $1 million cash.

c. Previously declared dividends are paid in cash.

d. Accrued interest expense is recorded.

e. A customer pays money on his account receivable.

■ LO12-5,12-6,12-7,12-8   **Using Financial Information to Identify Mystery Companies**
E12-17   The following selected financial data pertain to four unidentified companies:

a. Retail fur store

b. Advertising agency

c. Wholesale candy company

d. Car manufacturer

	Company			
	1	**2**	**3**	**4**
Statement of Financial Position Data				
(component percentage)				
Cash	3.5	4.7	8.2	11.7
Accounts receivable	16.9	28.9	16.8	51.9
Inventory	46.8	35.6	57.3	4.8
Property, plant, and equipment	18.3	21.7	7.6	18.7
Statement of Earnings Data				
(component percentage)				
Gross profit	22.0	22.5	44.8	N/A*
Net earnings before taxes	2.1	0.7	1.2	3.2
Selected Ratios				
Current ratio	1.3	1.5	1.6	1.2
Inventory turnover ratio	3.6	9.8	1.5	N/A
Debt-to-equity ratio	2.6	2.6	3.2	3.2
*N/A = Not applicable				

Required:

Match each company with its financial information. Support your choices.

■ LO12-5,12-6,12-7,12-8   **Using Financial Information to Identify Mystery Companies**
E12-18   The following selected financial data pertain to four unidentified companies:

a. Travel agency

b. Hotel

c. Meat packer

d. Drug company

	Company			
	1	**2**	**3**	**4**
Statement of Financial Position Data				
(component percentage)				
Cash	7.3	21.6	6.1	11.3
Accounts receivable	28.2	39.7	3.2	22.9
Inventory	21.6	0.6	1.8	27.5
Property, plant, and equipment	32.1	18.0	74.6	25.1
Statement of Earnings Data				
(component percentage)				
Gross profit	15.3	N/A*	N/A	43.4
Earnings before income taxes	1.7	3.2	2.4	6.9
Selected Ratios				
Current ratio	1.5	1.2	0.6	1.9
Inventory turnover ratio	27.4	N/A	N/A	3.3
Debt-to-equity ratio	1.7	2.2	5.7	1.3
*N/A = Not applicable				

Required:

Match each company with its financial information. Support your choices.

LO12-5,12-6,12-7,12-8

E12-19

Using Financial Information to Identify Mystery Companies

The following selected financial data pertain to four unidentified companies:

a. Cable TV company

b. Grocery store

c. Accounting firm

d. Retail jewellery store

	Company			
	1	**2**	**3**	**4**
Statement of Financial Position Data				
(component percentage)				
Cash	5.1	8.8	6.3	10.4
Accounts receivable	13.1	41.5	13.8	4.9
Inventory	4.6	3.6	65.1	35.8
Property, plant, and equipment	53.1	23.0	8.8	35.7
Statement of Earnings Data				
(component percentage)				
Gross profit	N/A*	N/A	45.2	22.5
Earnings before income taxes	0.3	16.0	3.9	1.5
Selected Ratios				
Current ratio	0.7	2.2	1.9	1.4
Inventory turnover	N/A	N/A	1.4	15.5
Debt-to-equity	2.5	0.9	1.7	2.3
*N/A = Not applicable				

Required:

Match each company with its financial information. Support your choices.

LO12-5,12-6,12-7,12-8

E12-20

Using Financial Information to Identify Mystery Companies

The following selected financial data pertain to four unidentified companies:

a. Full-line department store

b. Wholesale fish company

c. Automobile dealership (new and used cars)

d. Restaurant

	Company			
	1	**2**	**3**	**4**
Statement of Financial Position Data				
(component percentage)				
Cash	11.6	6.6	5.4	7.1
Accounts receivable	4.6	18.9	8.8	35.6
Inventory	7.0	45.8	65.7	26.0
Property, plant, and equipment	56.0	20.3	10.1	21.9
Statement of Earnings Data				
(component percentage)				
Gross profit	56.7	36.4	14.1	15.8
Earnings before income taxes	2.7	1.4	1.1	0.9
Selected Ratios				
Current ratio	0.7	2.1	1.2	1.3
Inventory turnover ratio	30.0	3.5	5.6	16.7
Debt-to-equity ratio	3.3	1.8	3.8	3.1

Required:

Match each company with its financial information. Support your choices.

■ LO12-3   **E12-21   Inferring Information from the DuPont Model**
In this chapter, we discussed the DuPont model. Using that framework, find the missing amount in each case below:

Case 1: ROE is 10 percent; net earnings are $300,000; total asset turnover ratio is 5; and net sales are $1,000,000. What is the amount of average shareholders' equity?

Case 2: Net earnings are $440,000; net sales are $8,000,000; average shareholders' equity is $2,000,000; ROE is 22 percent; and total asset turnover ratio is 8. What is the amount of average total assets?

Case 3: ROE is 15 percent; net profit margin ratio is 10 percent; total asset turnover ratio is 5; and average total assets are $1,000,000. What is the amount of average shareholders' equity?

Case 4: Net earnings are $150,000; ROE is 15 percent; total asset turnover ratio is 5; net sales are $1,000,000; and financial leverage is 2. What is the amount of average total assets?

connect PROBLEMS

■ LO12-5   **P12-1   Analyzing Comparative Financial Statements by Using Percentages** (AP12-1)
eXcel   The comparative financial statements prepared at December 31, 2017, for Goldfish Company showed the following summarized data:

	2017	2016
Statement of Earnings		
Sales revenue	$195,000*	$165,000
Cost of sales	120,000	100,000
Gross margin	75,000	65,000
Operating expenses and interest expense	60,000	53,000
Earnings before income taxes	15,000	12,000
Income tax expense	4,000	3,000
Net earnings	$ 11,000	$ 9,000
Statement of Financial Position		
Cash	$ 4,000	$ 8,000
Accounts receivable (net)	15,000	18,000
Inventory	40,000	35,000
Property, plant, and equipment (net)	45,000	38,000
	$104,000	$ 99,000
Current liabilities (no interest)	$ 16,000	$ 19,000
Non-current liabilities (10% interest)	45,000	39,000
Common shares (6,000 shares)	30,000	30,000
Retained earnings†	13,000	11,000
	$104,000	$ 99,000

*One-third was credit sales.
†During 2017, cash dividends amounting to $9,000 were declared and paid.

Required:

1. Complete the following columns for each item in the preceding comparative financial statements:

Increase (Decrease) 2017 over 2016	
Amount	Percentage

2. Answer the following:
   a. By what amount did working capital change?
   b. What was the percentage change in the average income tax rate?
   c. What was the amount of cash inflow from revenues for 2017?
   d. What was the percentage change for the average markup realized on sales?

LO12-5,12-6,12-7,12-8

P12-2

Analyzing Comparative Financial Statements by Using Percentages and Selected Ratios (AP12-2)

Use the data given in P12-1 for Goldfish Company.

Required:

1. Present component percentages for 2017 only.

2. Answer the following for 2017:

   a. What was the average percentage markup on sales?

   b. What was the average income tax rate?

   c. Compute the net profit margin ratio. Was it a good or poor indicator of performance? Explain.

   d. What percentage of total resources was invested in property, plant, and equipment?

   e. Compute the debt-to-equity ratio. Does it look good or bad? Explain.

   f. What was the ROA?

   g. What was the ROE?

   h. Compute the financial leverage percentage. Did borrowing from creditors benefit shareholders? Explain.

 LO12-6,12-7,12-8,12-9

P12-3

Sears Canada Inc. and Canadian Tire Corporation

Analyzing Ratios (AP12-3)

Sears Canada Inc. and Canadian Tire Corporation are two giants of the Canadian retail industry. Both offer full lines of moderately priced merchandise. Annual sales for Sears total $3.1 billion. Canadian Tire is somewhat larger, with $12.2 billion in revenues. Compare the two companies as potential investments based on the following ratios:

Ratio	Sears Canada	Canadian Tire
P/E	13.3	14.0
Net profit margin ratio	4.5%	3.9%
Quick ratio	1.02	1.54
Current ratio	1.8	1.99
Debt-to-equity	1.05	1.38
ROE	14.9%	9.2%
ROA	7.6%	5.2%
Dividend yield	0%	0%
EPS	$ 2.18	$ 4.10
Price per share at year-end	$29.0	$57.5
Dividends per share	$ 0	$ 0.84

 LO12-6,12-7,12-8,12-9

P12-4

Analyzing a Financial Statement by Using Several Ratios

Summer Corporation has just completed its comparative statements for the year ended December 31, 2015. At this point, certain analytical and interpretive procedures are to be undertaken. The completed statements (summarized) are as follows:

	2018	2017
Statement of Earnings		
Sales revenue	$960,000[a]	$840,000[a]
Cost of sales	540,000	460,000
Gross margin	420,000	380,000
Operating expenses (including interest on bonds)	342,000	336,000
Pretax earnings	78,000	44,000
Income tax expense	24,000	12,000
Net earnings	$ 54,000	$ 32,000
Statement of Financial Position		
Cash	$ 13,600	$ 7,800
Accounts receivable (net)	84,000	56,000
Merchandise inventory	50,000	40,000
Prepayments	400	200
Property, plant, and equipment (net)	260,000	240,000
	$408,000	$344,000

	2018	2017
Accounts payable	$ 34,000	$ 36,000
Income taxes payable	2,000	4,000
Bonds payable (5% interest rate)	140,000ᵇ	100,000
Common shares (40,000 shares)	200,000ᶜ	200,000
Retained earnings	32,000ᵈ	4,000
	$408,000	$344,000

ᵃCredit sales totalled 40 percent of total sales.
ᵇ$40,000 of bonds were issued on January 2, 2018.
ᶜThe market price of the stock at the end of 2018 was $18 per share.
ᵈDuring 2018, the company declared and paid a cash dividend of $26,000.

Required:

1. Compute appropriate ratios for 2018 and explain the meaning of each.
2. Answer the following for 2018:
   a. Evaluate the financial leverage percentage. Explain its meaning by using the computed amount(s).
   b. Evaluate the net profit margin ratio and explain how a shareholder might use it.
   c. Explain to a shareholder why the current ratio and the quick ratio are different. Do you observe any liquidity problems? Explain.
   d. Assuming that credit terms are 1/10, n/30, do you perceive an unfavourable situation for the company related to credit sales? Explain.
   e. By how much should the balance of accounts receivable decrease if the company wishes to reduce its average collection period to 30 days?

■ LO12-6,12-7,12-8,12-9   **Comparing Alternative Investment Opportunities** (AP12-4)

P12-5   The 2017 financial statements for Armstrong and Blair companies are summarized below:

	Armstrong Company	Blair Company
Statement of Earnings		
Cash	$ 17,500	$ 11,000
Accounts receivable (net)	20,000	15,000
Inventory	50,000	20,000
Property, plant, and equipment (net)	70,000	200,000
Other non-current assets	42,500	154,000
Total assets	$200,000	$400,000
Current liabilities	$ 50,000	$ 25,000
Long-term debt (10%)	30,000	35,000
Share capital	75,000	250,000
Contributed surplus	15,000	55,000
Retained earnings	30,000	35,000
Total liabilities and shareholders' equity	$200,000	$400,000
Statement of Earnings		
Sales revenue (1/3 on credit)	$225,000	$405,000
Cost of sales	(122,500)	(202,500)
Expenses (including interest and income tax)	(80,000)	(157,500)
Net earnings	$ 22,500	$ 45,000

Selected data from the 2016 statements follows:

Accounts receivable (net)	$10,000	$20,000
Inventory	46,000	24,000
Long-term debt	30,000	35,000
Other data:		
Share price at end of 2017	$ 18	$ 15
Income tax rate	30%	30%
Dividends declared and paid in 2017	$18,000	$75,000
Number of common shares during 2017	7,500	25,000

The companies are in the same line of business and are direct competitors in a large metropolitan area. Both have been in business approximately 10 years, and each has had steady growth. The management of each has a different viewpoint in many respects. Blair Company is more conservative, and as its president said, "We avoid what we consider to be undue risk." Neither company is publicly held. Armstrong Company has an annual audit by an independent auditor, but Blair Company does not.

Required:

1. Complete a schedule that reflects a ratio analysis of each company. Compute the ratios discussed in the chapter. Use ending balances if average balances are not available.

2. A client of yours has the opportunity to buy 10 percent of the shares in one or the other company at the share prices given. Based on the data given, prepare a comparative written evaluation of the ratio analyses (and any other available information) and give your recommended choice with supporting explanation.

 LO12-6,12-7,12-8

P12-6

Analyzing the Impact of Alternative Inventory Methods on Selected Ratios

Company A uses the FIFO method to cost inventory, and Company B uses the weighted-average method. The two companies are exactly alike except for the difference in inventory costing methods. Costs of inventory items for both companies have been rising steadily in recent years, and each company has increased its inventory each year. Each company has paid its tax liability in full for the current year (and all previous years), and each company uses the same accounting methods for both financial reporting and income tax reporting, except for inventory valuation.

Required:

Identify which company will report the higher amount for each of the following ratios. If this is not possible, explain why.

1. Current ratio
2. Quick ratio
3. Debt-to-equity ratio
4. ROE
5. EPS

 LO12-2,12-4 **P12-7**

WestJet Airlines Ltd.

Using Financial Reports: Interpreting Financial Statement Information and Analyzing and Interpreting Ratios (AP12-5)

WestJet Airlines Ltd. was founded in 1996 by a team of Calgary entrepreneurs and as of December 31, 2015, has grown from serving five western Canadian destinations with three aircraft to serving more than 100 destinations in North America, Central America, and the Caribbean with 140 aircraft. WestJet's financial statements for 2015 and 2014 and excerpts from selected notes to its financial statements are shown below:

CONSOLIDATED STATEMENTS OF FINANCIAL POSITION WestJet Airlines Ltd. December 31, 2015 and 2014 (stated in thousands of Canadian dollars)			
	Note	2015	2014
Assets			
Current assets:			
Cash and cash equivalents	4	$1,183,797	$1,358,071
Restricted cash	5	68,573	58,149
Accounts receivable	17	82,136	54,950
Prepaid expenses, deposits, and other	17	131,747	144,192
Inventory	17	36,018	36,658
Assets held for sale		–	78,306
		1,502,271	1,730,326
Non-current assets:			
Property and equipment	6	3,473,262	2,793,194
Intangible assets	7	63,549	60,623
Other assets	17	89,942	62,290
Total assets		$5,129,024	$4,646,433

	Note	2015	2014
Liabilities and shareholders' equity			
Current liabilities:			
Accounts payable and accrued liabilities	17	$ 545,438	$ 415,562
Advance ticket sales		620,216	575,781
Deferred rewards program		117,959	86,870
Non-refundable guest credits		40,921	45,434
Current portion of long-term debt	8	85,819	54,811
Current portion of maintenance provisions	9	141,572	159,843
		1,551,925	1,338,301
Non-current liabilities:			
Maintenance provisions	8	243,214	191,768
Long-term debt	9	1,033,261	1,028,820
Other liabilities	17	13,603	13,150
Deferred income tax	10	327,028	296,892
Total liabilities		3,169,031	2,868,931
Shareholders' equity:			
Share capital	11	582,796	603,287
Equity reserves		82,713	75,094
Hedge reserves		1,903	(3,179)
Retained earnings		1,292,581	1,102,300
Total shareholders' equity		1,959,993	1,777,502
Total liabilities and shareholders' equity		$5,129,024	$4,646,433

The accompanying notes are an integral part of the consolidated financial statements.

Source: WestJet Airlines Ltd., Annual Report 2015.

CONSOLIDATED STATEMENTS OF EARNINGS
WestJet Airlines Ltd.
Years Ended December 31, 2015 and 2014
(stated in thousands of Canadian dollars, except per share amounts)

	Notes	2015	2014
Revenues:			
Guest		$3,557,222	$3,599,157
Other		472,043	377,395
		4,029,265	3,976,552
Expenses:			
Aircraft fuel		814,498	1,090,330
Salaries and benefits		801,715	724,941
Rates and fees		562,745	520,340
Sales and marketing		325,127	325,370
Depreciation and amortization		264,921	226,740
Aircraft leasing		174,089	182,450
Maintenance		164,305	126,761
Other		251,147	253,362
Employee profit share		100,965	68,787
		3,459,512	3,501,081
Earnings from operations		569,753	475,471
Non-operating income (expense):			
Finance income		15,529	17,070
Finance costs		(53,665)	(51,838)
Gain on foreign exchange		(10,326)	(2,064)
Gain (loss) on disposal of property and equipment		(1,860)	(48,332)
Gain on derivatives		827	–
		(49,495)	(85,164)
Earnings before income taxes		520,258	390,307
Income tax expense:			
Current	10	123,939	114,521
Deferred	10	28,789	(8,171)
		152,728	106,350
Net earnings		$ 367,530	$ 283,957

	Notes	2015	2014
Earnings per share:			
Basic	13	2.94	2.22
Diluted	13	2.92	2.20

The accompanying notes are an integral part of the consolidated financial statements.

Source: WestJet Airlines Ltd., Annual Report 2015.

CONSOLIDATED STATEMENTS OF CASH FLOWS
WestJet Airlines Ltd.
Years Ended December 31, 2015 and 2014
(stated in thousands of Canadian dollars)

	Notes	2015	2014
Operating activities			
Net earnings		$367,530	$283,957
Items not involving cash:			
Depreciation and amortization		264,921	226,740
Change in maintenance provisions		35,786	8,413
Change in other liabilities		(3,192)	(529)
Amortization of transaction costs		4,503	5,015
Amortization of hedge settlements		1,390	1,400
Gain on derivatives		(827)	–
(Gain) loss on disposal of property and equipment		1,860	48,332
Stock-based payment expense	11	17,254	18,626
Deferred income tax expense (recovery)		28,789	(8,171)
Unrealized foreign exchange (gain) loss		(938)	(10,634)
Change in non-cash working capital		199,706	21,349
Change in restricted cash		(10,424)	(43)
Change in other assets		(15,912)	(6,833)
Purchase of shares pursuant to compensation plans		(14,005)	(10,989)
		876,441	576,633
Investing activities:			
Aircraft additions		(841,491)	(694,200)
Aircraft disposals		83,348	75,655
Other property and equipment and intangible additions		(64,789)	(46,586)
		(822,932)	(665,131)
Financing activities			
Increase in long-term debt		153,112	613,885
Repayment of long-term debt		(171,490)	(308,588)
Shares repurchased		(123,813)	(39,431)
Dividends paid	12	(69,711)	(61,313)
Issuance of shares pursuant to compensation plans		156	96
Cash interest paid		(47,305)	(39,507)
Change in non-cash working capital		21	4,866
		(259,030)	170,008
Cash flow from operating, investing, and financing activities		(205,521)	81,510
Effect of foreign exchange on cash and cash equivalents		31,247	20,556
Net change in cash and cash equivalents		(174,274)	102,066
Cash and cash equivalents, beginning of year		1,358,071	1,256,005
Cash and cash equivalents, end of year		$1,183,797	$1,358,071
Supplemental disclosure of operating cash flows			
Cash interest received		16,349	17,243
Cash taxes paid, net		(114,752)	(204,489)

The accompanying notes are an integral part of the consolidated financial statements.

Source: WestJet Airlines Ltd., Annual Report 2015.

NOTES TO CONSOLIDATED FINANCIAL STATEMENTS

1. Statement of significant accounting policies:

...

(d) Revenue recognition

(i) Guest revenue, including the air component of vacation packages, are recognized when air transportation is provided. Tickets sold but not yet used are reported in the consolidated statement of financial position as advance ticket sales.

...

Source: WestJet Airlines Ltd., Annual Report 2015.

Required:

1. Examine WestJet's statements of financial position. The company's assets increased in 2015. Which asset shows the largest increase?

2. WestJet's current liabilities include the advance ticket sales account with a balance of $620,216. What does this account represent, and what type of transactions would cause an increase or a decrease in the account balance? Explain.

3. Compute the total asset turnover ratio, return on assets, return on equity, and net profit margin ratio for both 2014 and 2015. Comment on the profitability of WestJet's operations in both years. WestJet's total assets and shareholders' equity at December 31, 2013, amounted to $4,143,463 and $1,589,840, respectively.

4. WestJet's operations generated significant amounts of cash during both 2014 and 2015. The company also made significant investments in new aircraft in 2015. How did the company finance the acquisition of additional aircraft?

5. Compute and interpret the quality of earnings ratio and the capital expenditures ratio for both 2014 and 2015. (*Note:* Include property and equipment and intangible assets in your computation of the ratio.)

6. Access one of the online information services listed in the chapter, search for WestJet Airlines Ltd. (WJA.TO), and look for earnings estimates. What is the average analysts' estimate of WestJet's earnings per share (EPS) for the next two fiscal years? Do analysts expect WestJet's EPS to increase or decrease in the future? What information did the analysts take into consideration in computing their EPS estimates for the next two years?

■ LO12-6,12-7,12-8,12-9

P12-8

🖊️ 🎨 e**X**cel

MTY Food Group
Inc.

Analyzing Financial Statements by Using Appropriate Ratios (AP12-6)

MTY Food Group Inc. is a Canadian franchisor and operator of numerous quick service restaurants operating under 40 brand names such as Thai Express, Mucho Burrito, Sushi Shop, Jugo Juice and Manchu Wok. Its annual report for 2015 included the following:

MTY FOOD GROUP INC.
Consolidated Statement pof Earnings
For the years ended November 30,
(in thousands of Canadian dollars, except per share amounts)

	2015	2014
Revenue	$145,203	$115,177
Expenses		
Depreciation—property, plant and equipment	1,535	1,091
Amortization—intangible assets	6,744	5,985
Interest on long-term debt	436	422
	103,236	80,016
Other income (charges)		
Foreign exchange gain	64	106
Interest income	144	118
Gain on preferred share redemption	–	100
Impairment charge of intangible assets and goodwill	(8,093)	(2,356)
Gain on disposal of property, plant, and equipment and intangible assets	1,821	1,179
	(6,064)	(853)
Income before taxes	35,903	34,308

	2015	2014
Income taxes		
Current	10,454	8,820
Deferred	(774)	303
	9,680	9,123
Net income	$ 26,223	$ 25,185
Earnings per share		
Basic	1.36	1.32
Diluted	1.36	1.32

Source: MTY Food Group Inc. Annual Report 2015.

MTY FOOD GROUP INC.
Consolidated Statement of Financial Position
At the years ended November 30,
(in thousands of Canadian dollars)

	2015	2014
Assets		
Current assets		(restated)
Cash	$ 33,417	$ 6,701
Accounts receivable	18,417	16,809
Inventories	2,208	2,294
Loans receivable	240	181
Prepaid expenses	620	1,045
	55,219	27,030
Loans receivable	217	505
Property and equipment	10,506	9,855
Goodwill	103,925	107,484
Intangible assets	55,520	54,574
	$225,387	$199,448
Liabilities and shareholders' equity		
Liabilities		
Current liabilities		
Line of credit	$ 6,300	$ 11,750
Accounts payable and accrued liabilities	24,361	14,151
Provisions	3,468	3,053
Income taxes payable	2,334	716
Deferred revenue and deposits	5,660	3,709
Current portion of long-term debt	6,344	6,548
	48,467	40,233
Long-term debt	1,612	3,814
Deferred income taxes	6,099	5,930
	56,178	49,977
Shareholders' Equity		
Equity attributable to owners		
Capital stock	19,792	19,792
Contributed surplus	481	481
Accumulated other comprehensive income	(111)	(14)
Retained earnings	146,492	124,331
	166,654	144,590
Equity attributable to non-controlling interest	2,555	4,881
	169,209	149,471
	$225,387	$199,448

Source: MTY Food Group Inc. Annual Report 2015.

Additional information related to 2013 at year-end is as follows:

Shareholders' equity	$130,809
Total assets	173,044
Property, plant, and equipment	6,213
Accounts receivable	13,452
Inventories	1,029
Trade and other payables	11,903

The market price per share was $34.29 at November 28, 2014,* and $31.24 at November 30, 2015.

*November 28 was the Friday, therefore stock markets were closed on November 30.

Required:

1. For MTY Food Group Inc.'s past two years, compute the ratios discussed in this chapter. If there is insufficient information, describe what is missing and explain what you would do.

2. Assume that you work in the loan department of National Bank, and you are evaluating an application from MTY Food Group Inc. for a credit facility of $300 million to purchase the shares of another competing company. What specific ratios would you consider in your evaluation, and would you lend MTY Food Group Inc. the requested amount?

■ LO12-7,12-8,12-9

P12-9

Analyzing an Investment by Comparing Selected Ratios (AP12-7)

You have the opportunity to invest $10,000 in one of two companies from a single industry. The only information you have follows. The word *high* refers to the top third of the industry, *average* is the middle third, and *low* is the bottom third. Which company would you select? Write a brief report justifying your recommendation.

Ratio	Company A	Company B
Current	High	Average
Quick	Low	Average
Debt-to-equity	High	Average
Inventory turnover	Low	Average
P/E	Low	Average
Dividend yield	High	Average

■ LO12-7,12-8,12-9

P12-10

Analyzing an Investment by Comparing Selected Ratios (AP12-8)

You have the opportunity to invest $10,000 in one of two companies from a single industry. The only information you have is shown below. The word *high* refers to the top third of the industry, *average* is the middle third, and *low* is the bottom third. Which company would you select? Write a brief report justifying your recommendation.

Ratio	Company A	Company B
Current	Low	Average
Quick	Average	Average
Debt-to-equity	Low	Average
Inventory turnover	High	Average
P/E	High	Average
Dividend yield	Low	Average

■ LO12-5,12-9   **P12-11**

Analyzing Financial Statements by Using Appropriate Ratios

Morksen Corp. has enjoyed modest success in penetrating the personal electronic devices market since it began operations a few years ago. A new line of devices introduced recently has been well-received by customers. However, the company president, who is knowledgeable about electronics but not accounting, is concerned about the future of the company.

Although the company has a line of credit with the local bank, it currently needs cash to continue operations. The bank wants more information before it extends the company's credit line. The president has asked you, as the company's chief accountant, to evaluate the company's performance by using appropriate financial statement analysis, and to recommend possible courses of action for the company. In particular, the president wants to know how the company can obtain additional cash. Summary financial statements for the past three years are available below.

Required:

1. Evaluate the company's performance and its financial condition for the past two years. Select six appropriate ratios to analyze the company's profitability, liquidity, and solvency for 2016 and 2017, and explain to the company's president the meaning of each ratio you calculate.

2. Based on your analysis of the ratios that you computed in (1), what recommendation would you make to the president for obtaining additional cash?

MORKSEN CORP.
Consolidated Statements of Earnings
For the Years Ended December 31,

(in thousands of dollars)	2017	2016	2015
Sales	$64,000	$56,000	$46,800
Cost of sales	50,000	43,000	36,000
Gross profit	14,000	13,000	10,800
Operating expenses before interest and income taxes	8,000	7,400	6,620
Interest expense	1,780	1,220	—
Earnings before income taxes	4,220	4,380	4,180
Income tax expense	1,900	2,040	1,940
Net earnings	$ 2,320	$ 2,340	$ 2,240

MORKSEN CORP.
Consolidated Statements of Financial Position
At December 31,

(in thousands of dollars)	2017	2016	2015
Assets			
Current assets			
Cash	$ 380	$ 480	$ 1,000
Short-term investments	740	740	740
Accounts receivable	10,880	8,400	5,140
Merchandise inventory	16,660	10,060	7,220
Total current assets	28,660	19,680	14,100
Property, plant, and equipment			
Land	4,000	4,000	2,000
Buildings and equipment	26,000	26,000	18,000
	30,000	30,000	20,000
Less: accumulated depreciation	8,940	7,440	5,760
Net property, plant, and equipment	21,060	22,560	14,240
Total assets	$49,720	$42,240	$28,340
Liabilities and Shareholders' Equity			
Current liabilities			
Bank loan	$16,500	$11,400	$ —
Accounts payable	6,000	4,300	2,880
Other liabilities	1,640	1,600	1,500
Income tax payable	960	1,040	1,000
Total current liabilities	25,100	18,340	5,380
Shareholders' equity			
Common shares	20,000	20,000	20,000
Retained earnings	4,140	3,520	2,640
Other comprehensive income	480	380	320
Total shareholders' equity	24,620	23,900	22,960
Total liabilities and shareholders' equity	$49,720	$42,240	$28,340

ALTERNATE PROBLEMS

LO12-3   AP12-1   **Analyzing Financial Statements by Using Ratios and Percentage Changes** (P12-1)

Taber Company has just prepared the following comparative annual financial statements for 2018:

TABER COMPANY
Comparative Statement of Earnings
For the Years Ended December 31,

	2018	2017
Sales revenue (one-half on credit)	$110,000	$100,000
Cost of sales	52,000	49,000
Gross margin	58,000	51,000
Expenses (including $4,000 interest expense each year)	40,000	37,000
Pretax earnings	18,000	14,000
Income tax expense (30%)	5,400	4,200
Net earnings	$ 12,600	$ 9,800

TABER COMPANY
Comparative Statement of Financial Position
At December 31,

	2018	2017
Assets		
Cash	$ 49,500	$ 18,000
Accounts receivable (net; terms 1/10, n/30)	37,000	32,000
Inventory	25,000	38,000
Property, plant, and equipment (net)	95,000	105,000
Total assets	$206,500	$193,000
Liabilities		
Accounts payable	$ 42,000	$ 35,000
Income taxes payable	1,000	500
Note payable, long term	40,000	40,000
Shareholders' equity		
Share capital (9,000 shares)	90,000	90,000
Retained earnings	34,900	25,400
Other comprehensive income (loss)	(1,400)	2,100
Total liabilities and shareholders' equity	$206,500	$193,000

Required (round percentages and ratios to two decimal places):

1. For 2018, compute the tests of (a) profitability, (b) liquidity, (c) solvency, and (d) market. Assume that the quoted price of the stock was $23 per share for 2018. Dividends declared and paid during 2018 were $5,200.

2. Answer the following for 2018:

   a. Compute the percentage changes in sales, net earnings, cash, inventory, and debt.

   b. What is the pretax interest rate on the note payable?

3. Identify at least two problems facing the company that are suggested by your responses to (1) and (2).

LO12-5,12-6,12-7   **Using Ratios to Analyze Several Years of Financial Data** (P12-2)

AP12-2   The following information was contained in the annual financial statements of Pine Company, which started business January 1, 2016 (assume account balances only in cash and share capital on this date; all amounts are in thousands of dollars):

	2016	2017	2018	2019
Accounts receivable (net; terms n/30)	$11	$12	$18	$24
Merchandise inventory	12	14	20	30
Net sales (three-fourths on credit)	44	66	80	100
Cost of sales	28	40	55	62
Net earnings (loss)	(8)	5	12	11

Required (show computations and round to two decimal places):

1. Complete the following tabulation:

Items	2016	2017	2018	2019
a. Profit margin–percentage				
b. Gross profit percentage				
c. Expenses as percentage of sales, excluding cost of sales				
d. Inventory turnover ratio				
e. Days' supply in inventory				
f. Receivables turnover ratio				
g. Average collection period				

2. Evaluate the results of the related ratios *a*, *b*, and *c* to identify the favourable or unfavourable factors. Give your recommendations to improve the company's operations.

3. Evaluate the results of the last four ratios (*d, e, f,* and *g*), and identify any favourable or unfavourable factors. Give your recommendations to improve the company's operations.

 LO12-6,12-9 AP12-3

Coca-Cola and
PepsiCo

Analyzing Ratios (P12-3)

Coke and Pepsi are well-known international brands. Coca-Cola sells more than $46 billion worth of beverages each year, while annual sales of Pepsi products exceed $65 billion. Compare the two companies as potential investments based on the following ratios:

Ratio	Coca-Cola	PepsiCo
P/E ratio	19.3	17.8
Gross profit percentage	64.2	53.5
Net profit margin ratio	22.0%	13.7%
Quick ratio	0.7	0.5
Current ratio	1.3	1.4
Debt-to-equity ratio	0.9	1.3
ROE	29.5%	39.8%
ROA	15.9%	16.4%
Dividend yield	2.9%	2.9%

LO12-6,12-7,12-8,12-9
AP12-4

 e**X**cel

Comparing Loan Requests from Two Companies by Using Several Ratios (P12-5)

The 2017 financial statements for Rand and Tand companies are summarized below:

	Rand Company	Tand Company
Statement of Financial Position		
Cash	$ 25,000	$ 45,000
Accounts receivable (net)	55,000	5,000
Inventory	110,000	25,000
Property, plant, and equipment (net)	550,000	160,000
Other assets	140,000	57,000
Total assets	$880,000	$292,000
Current liabilities	$120,000	$ 15,000
Long-term debt (12%)	190,000	55,000
Share capital	480,000	210,000
Contributed surplus	50,000	4,000
Retained earnings	38,000	7,000
Other comprehensive income	2,000	1,000
Total liabilities and shareholders' equity	$880,000	$292,000
Statement of Earnings		
Sales revenue (on credit)	(½) $800,000	(¼) $280,000
Cost of sales	(480,000)	(150,000)
Expenses (including interest and income tax)	240,000	(95,000)
Net earnings	$ 80,000	$ 35,000

	Rand Company	Tand Company
Selected Data from the 2016 Statements		
Accounts receivable, net	$ 47,000	$11,000
Long-term debt (12%)	190,000	55,000
Inventory	95,000	38,000
Other Data		
Share price at end of 2017	$ 14.00	$ 11.00
Income tax rate	30%	30%
Dividends declared and paid in 2017	$ 20,000	$ 9,000
Number of common shares during 2017	24,000	10,500

These two companies are in the same line of business and in the same province but in different cities. Each company has been in operation for about 10 years. Rand Company is audited by a national accounting firm; Tand Company is audited by a local accounting firm. Both companies received an unqualified opinion (i.e., the independent auditors found nothing wrong) on the financial statements. Rand Company wants to borrow $75,000 cash, and Tand Company needs $30,000. The loans will be for a two-year period and are needed for working capital purposes.

Required:

1. Complete a schedule that reflects a ratio analysis of each company. Compute the ratios discussed in the chapter.

2. Assume that you work in the loans department of a local bank. You have been asked to analyze the situation and recommend which loan is preferable. Based on the data given, your analysis prepared in (1), and any other information, give your choice and provide a supporting explanation.

■ LO12-2,12-4 **AP12-5**

Leon's Furniture
Limited

Using Financial Reports: Interpreting Financial Statement Information and Analyzing and Interpreting Ratios (P12-7)

Leon's Furniture Limited is a leading Canadian full-line furniture retailer. The company sells home furnishings, major appliances, and home electronics through more than 75 company-owned and franchised stores across Canada. Its sales grew from $289 million when it became a public company in 1996 to $2 billion in 2015. Leon's financial statements for 2011 and 2012 are shown on the next few pages.

Required:

1. Examine Leon's statements of financial position. Identify the four largest changes in the carrying amount of assets, liabilities, and shareholders' equity between the statements of financial position dates. What type of transactions could have caused the changes in the carrying amount of these items?

2. The carrying amounts of the assets and liabilities reported on the company's statements of financial position reflect a mix of historical acquisition costs, amortized costs, and fair values. Refer to the notes to the company's financial statements for fiscal year 2015 that are available on its website (www.leons.ca/investorrelations.aspx) and identify the valuation bases used by the company for financial reporting purposes.

3. Using information from the company's statements of financial position and statement of earnings for 2015, can you determine the amount of cash flow generated from operations? If not, where can you find such information? The company's notes to its financial statements indicate that depreciation of property, plant, and equipment as well as investment properties for 2015 is $33,694, and that amortization of intangible assets totalled $8,044.

4. Compute the following ratios for fiscal years 2015 and 2014: total asset turnover ratio, return on assets, return on equity, and net profit margin ratio. Use the results of your computations to comment on the company's financial situation and profitability of its operations in both years. Leon's total assets and shareholders' equity at December 31, 2013, amounted to $1,682,174 and $496,555, respectively.

5. Suppose that you are evaluating Leon's financial statements for a potential investment in the company's shares. To what extent is the information contained in these financial statements relevant for your decision? What additional information would you require before making your decision?

LEON'S FURNITURE INC.
Consolidated Statements of Financial Position
As at December 31,
(thousands of dollars)

	2015	2014
ASSETS		
Current		
Cash and cash equivalents (Notes 5 and 22)	$ 7,589	$ 45,900
Restricted marketable securities (Note 22)	18,691	18,310
Available-for-sale financial assets (Note 22)	22,960	22,358
Trade receivables (Note 22)	117,832	112,171
Income taxes recoverable	24,920	—
Inventories (Note 6)	303,961	266,628
Deferred acquisition costs (Note 7)	8,329	4,957
Deferred financing costs	473	923
Total current assets	505,025	471,247
Other assets	6,214	6,192
Deferred acquisition costs (Note 7)	13,093	11,093
Property, plant, and equipment, net (Note 8)	323,218	334,052
Investment properties (Note 9)	18,496	21,992
Intangible assets, net (Note 10)	318,214	321,302
Goodwill (Note 10)	390,120	390,120
Deferred income tax assets (Note 20)	9,083	7,478
Total assets	$1,583,463	$1,563,476
LIABILITIES AND SHAREHOLDERS' EQUITY		
Current		
Trade and other payables (Note 11)	$ 206,076	$ 197,044
Provisions (Note 12)	5,343	4,576
Income taxes payable	7,266	34,773
Customers' deposits	112,446	97,705
Finance lease liabilities (Note 13)	1,954	2,002
Dividends payable (Note 16)	7,141	7,105
Deferred warranty plan revenue	49,380	51,111
Loans and borrowings (Note 14)	50,000	30,000
Total current liabilities	439,606	424,316
Loans and borrowings (Note 14)	237,357	285,363
Convertible debentures (Note 14)	92,628	91,773
Finance lease liabilities (Note 13)	11,895	13,849
Deferred warranty plan revenue	95,775	92,254
Redeemable share liability (Note 15)	880	401
Deferred rent liabilities and lease inducements	8,858	6,794
Deferred income tax liabilities (Note 20)	96,062	99,621
Total liabilities	983,061	1,014,371
Commitments and contingencies (Note 18)		
Shareholders' equity		
Common shares (Note 16)	34,389	31,169
Equity component of convertible debentures (Note 14)	7,089	7,089
Retained earnings	558,526	510,398
Accumulated other comprehensive income	398	449
Total shareholders' equity	600,402	549,105
Total liabilities and shareholders' equity	$1,583,463	$1,563,476

The accompanying notes are an integral part of these consolidated financial statements.

Source: Leon's Furniture, Annual Report 2015.

LEON'S FURNITURE INC.
Consolidated Statements of Income
Years Ended December 31,
(thousands of dollars)

	2015	2014
Revenue (Note 17)	$2,031,718	$2,008,480
Cost of sales (Note 6)	1,145,593	1,131,651
Gross profit	886,125	876,829
Selling, general, and administrative expenses (Note 18)	767,079	756,936
Operating profit	119,046	119,893
Net finance costs (Note 19)	(17,627)	(16,759)
Profit before income taxes	101,419	103,134
Income tax expense (Note 20)	24,790	27,610
Net income	$ 76,629	$ 75,524
Weighted average number of common shares outstanding		
Basic	71,217,958	70,898,590
Diluted	82,364,539	82,177,519
Earnings per share (Note 21)		
Basic	$ 1.08	$ 1.07
Diluted	$ 0.97	$ 0.96

The accompanying notes are an integral part of these consolidated financial statements.

Source: Leon's Furniture, Annual Report 2015.

LO12-5,12-6,12-7,12-8, 12-9   **AP12-6**

eXcel

Lassonde Industries Inc.

Analyzing Financial Statements by Using Appropriate Ratios (P12-8)

Lassonde Industries Inc. manufactures and sells fruit and vegetable juices and drinks, as well as specialty food products under such brand names as Oasis, Fruité, Fairlee, and Canadian Club. The company's products are distributed to wholesalers, supermarkets, and food service providers. The following information was reported in a recent annual report:

LASSONDE INDUSTRIES INC.
Consolidated Statement of Income
For the Years ended December 31,
(in thousands of Canadian dollars)

	2015	2014
Sales	$1,449,287	$1,181,026
Cost of sales	1,039,637	851,240
Selling and administrative expenses	298,179	241,333
(Gains) losses on capital assets	219	94
	1,338,035	1,092,667
Operating profit	111,252	88,359
Financial expenses	27,841	23,301
Other (gains) losses	(2,979)	(1,810)
Profit before income taxes	86,390	66,868
Income tax expense	26,179	19,472
Profit	$ 60,211	$ 47,396
Attributable to:		
Company shareholders	56,979	45,242
Non-controlling interest	3,232	2,154
	$ 60,211	$ 47,396
Basic and diluted earnings per share (in $)	$ 8.15	$ 6.47
Weighted average number of shares outstanding (in thousands)	6,988	6,988

LASSONDE INDUSTRIES INC.
Consolidated Statement of Financial Position
For the Years Ended December 31,
(in thousands of Canadian dollars)

	2015	2014
Assets		
Current		
Cash and cash equivalent	$ 524	$ 345
Accounts receivable	141,882	121,615
Income tax recoverable	2,191	1,368
Inventories	222,065	194,631
Other current assets	12,230	13,836
Derivative instruments	10,858	7,690
Total current assets	389,750	339,485
Derivative instruments	—	48
Property, plant, and equipment	271,341	251,847
Other intangible assets	260,200	237,742
Net defined benefit asset	2,302	1,710
Other long-term assets	831	1,009
Goodwill	219,424	184,861
Total assets	$1,143,848	$1,016,702
Liabilities		
Current		
Bank overdraft	$ 9,513	$ 17,433
Accounts payable and accrued liabilities	183,711	146,156
Income tax payable	1,495	4,427
Other current liabilities	13,456	9,566
Derivative instruments	—	969
Current portion of long-term debt	14,828	10,862
Total current liabilities	223,003	189,413
Derivative instruments	843	—
Net defined benefit liability	2,009	499
Long-term debt	326,239	359,221
Deferred tax liabilities	43,006	32,744
Other long-term liabilities	5,948	4,068
Total liabilities	601,048	585,945
Shareholders' equity		
Share capital	48,864	48,864
Contributed surplus	1,382	1,382
Accumulated other comprehensive income	99,082	39,744
Retained earnings	351,705	308,695
Non-controlling interest	41,767	32,072
Total shareholders' equity	542,800	430,757
Total liabilities and shareholders' equity	$1,143,848	$1,016,702

LASSONDE INDUSTRIES INC.
Consolidated Statement of Cash Flows
For the Years Ended December 31,
(in thousands of Canadian dollars) (audited)

	2015	2014
Operating activities		
Profit	$ 60,211	$ 47,396
Adjustments for:		
Income tax expense	26,179	19,472
Interest income and expense	22,918	19,838
Depreciation and amortization	42,562	34,704
Amortization of unearned discounts and unused tax credits	(700)	(401)
Change in fair value of financial instruments	5,548	3,189
Cost of the defined benefit plans recognized in profit or loss, net of contributions	(2,732)	2,362
(Gains) losses on capital assets	219	94
Unrealized foreign exchange (gains) losses	(261)	(647)
	153,944	126,007
Change in non-cash operating working capital items	6,686	(14,482)
Income tax received	558	1,284
Income tax paid	(22,761)	(16,574)
Interest received	34	227
Interest paid	(20,081)	(16,204)
Settlements of derivative instruments	(1,546)	(1,175)
Net cash provided by operating activities	116,834	79,083
Financing activities		
Change related to the revolving operating credit, net of transaction costs	(32,758)	56,558
Increase in long-term debt, net of transaction costs	(53)	78,835
Repayment of long-term debt	(44,117)	(50,286)
Dividends paid on Class A shares	(5,274)	(5,142)
Dividends paid on Class B shares	(6,116)	(5,967)
Investment of the non-controlling interest	—	8,053
Settlement of retractable financial instruments	—	(11,818)
Increase in other long-term liabilities	—	1,812
Net cash invested by financing activities	(88,318)	72,045
Investing activities		
Consideration received (paid) on business combinations, net of acquired cash on hand	531	(159,990)
Acquisitions of property, plant, and equipment	(19,569)	(16,103)
Acquisitions of other intangible assets	(556)	(4,612)
Net proceeds from the disposal of property, plant, and equipment	256	24
Net cash invested by investing activities	(19,338)	(180,681)
Increase (decrease) in cash and cash equivalents	9,178	(29,553)
Cash and cash equivalents at beginning	(17,088)	12,636
Impact of exchange rate changes on cash and cash equivalents	(1,079)	(171)
Cash and cash equivalents at end	$ (8,989)	$(17,088)

Additional cash flow information is presented in Note 23.

Source: Lassonde Industries Inc., Annual Report 2015.

Additional information related to 2013 at year-end is as follows:

Shareholders' equity	$362,073
Total assets	796,849
Property, plant, and equipment	248,428
Accounts receivable	97,303
Inventories	146,338
Accounts payable and accrued liabilities	118,725

The company declared and paid a dividend of $1.62 per share during fiscal year 2015 and $1.60 per share during fiscal year 2014. The market price per share was $130.00 at December 31, 2014, and $162.00 at December 31, 2015.

Required:

1. Compute the ratios discussed in this chapter for the last two years. If there is insufficient information, describe what is missing and explain what you would do.

2. Assume the role of an investment adviser. A client of yours has the opportunity to invest $1 million in shares of international companies. Prepare a written evaluation of relevant ratios and indicate whether you would recommend to your client that the $1 million be invested in the shares of Lassonde Industries.

 LO12-8,12-9 **AP12-7** **Analyzing an Investment by Comparing Selected Ratios** (P12-9)
You have the opportunity to invest $10,000 in one of two companies from a single industry. The only information you have is shown below. The word *high* refers to the top third of the industry, *average* is the middle third, and *low* is the bottom third. Which company would you select? Write a brief report justifying your recommendation.

Ratio	Company A	Company B
EPS	High	Low
ROA	Low	High
Debt-to-equity	High	Average
Current	Low	Average
P/E	Low	High
Dividend yield	High	Average

 **LO**12-6,12-7,12-8,12-9
AP12-8 **Analyzing an Investment by Comparing Selected Ratios** (P12-10)
You have the opportunity to invest $10,000 in one of two companies from a single industry. The only information you have follows. The word *high* refers to the top third of the industry, *average* is the middle third, and *low* is the bottom third. Which company would you select? Write a brief report justifying your recommendation.

Ratio	Company A	Company B
ROA	High	Average
Net profit margin	High	Low
Financial leverage	High	Low
Current	Low	High
P/E	High	Average
Debt-to-equity	High	Low

connect **CASES AND PROJECTS**

FINDING AND INTERPRETING FINANCIAL INFORMATION

 LO12-6,12-7,12-8,12-9
CP12-1

Canadian Tire
Corporation

Analyzing Financial Statements
Refer to the financial statements of Canadian Tire Corporation given in Appendix A of this book. From the list of ratios that were discussed in this chapter, select and compute the ratios that will help you evaluate the company's operations for fiscal year 2015. Assume a market price of $200 per share.

 LO12-6,12-7,12-8,12-9
CP12-2

Sears Canada Inc.

Analyzing Financial Statements
Go to *Connect* for the financial statements of Sears Canada Inc. From the list of ratios that were discussed in this chapter, select and compute the ratios that will help you evaluate the company's operations for fiscal year 2015. Assume a market price of $6 per share.

■ LO12-6,12-7,12-8,12-9

CP12-3

Canadian Tire
Corporation
Sears Canada Inc.

Comparing Companies within an Industry

Refer to the financial statements of Canadian Tire Corporation (Appendix A), to *Connect* for the financial statements of Sears Canada Inc., and to the Industry Ratio Report (Appendix B on *Connect*). Compute the following ratios for fiscal year 2015: ROE, EPS, net profit margin, current ratio, inventory turnover, debt-to-equity, P/E, and dividend yield. Assume the stock price is $200 for Canadian Tire Corporation and $6 for Sears Canada Inc. Compare the ratios for each company to the industry average ratios.

FINANCIAL REPORTING AND ANALYSIS CASE

■ LO12-3

CP12-4

Interpreting Financial Results Based on Corporate Strategy

In this chapter, we discussed the importance of analyzing financial results based on an understanding of the company's business strategy. Using the DuPont model, we illustrated how different strategies could earn high returns for investors. Assume that two companies in the same industry adopt fundamentally different strategies. One manufactures high-quality consumer electronics. Its products employ state-of-the-art technology, and the company offers a high level of customer service both before and after the sale. The other company emphasizes low cost with good performance. Its products utilize well-established technology but are never innovative. Customers buy these products at large, self-service warehouses and are expected to install the products by using information contained in printed brochures. Which of the ratios discussed in this chapter would you expect to differ for these companies as a result of their different business strategies?

CRITICAL THINKING CASES

■ LO12-6,12-7,12-8,12-9

CP12-5

Analyzing the Impact of Alternative Depreciation Methods on Ratio Analysis

Speedy Company uses the double-declining-balance method to depreciate its property, plant, and equipment, and Turtle Company uses the straight-line method. Both companies use declining-balance depreciation for income tax purposes. The two companies are exactly alike except for the difference in depreciation methods.

Required:

1. Identify the financial ratios discussed in this chapter that are likely to be affected by the difference in depreciation methods.

2. Which company will report the higher amount for each ratio that you have identified? If you cannot be certain, explain why.

■ LO12-6,12-7   **CP12-6**

Analyzing the Impact of Alternative Accounting Methods on Ratios

The ratios computed for Canadian Tire Corporation in this chapter are compared with those of Sears Canada Inc. and Hudson's Bay Company Ltd. The comparison of ratios across these three companies assumes that they use the same accounting methods in reporting the various elements of their financial statements.

Required:

1. Access the annual reports of the three companies through their respective websites and identify the method(s) each company uses to do each of the following:

   a. Depreciate its property, plant, and equipment

   b. Value its inventory at year-end

2. Are the methods used by these companies similar or different? Explain.

3. If two of these companies used different accounting methods, what impact would the different methods have on the following ratios:

   a. Net profit margin

   b. ROE

   c. Current ratio

   d. Debt-to-equity

■ LO12-6   **CP12-7**

Evaluating an Ethical Dilemma

Bianca Company requested a sizeable loan from Provincial Bank to acquire a large tract of land for future expansion. Bianca reported current assets of $1,900,000 ($430,000 in cash) and current liabilities of $1,075,000. Provincial denied the loan request for a number of reasons, including the fact that the current ratio was below 2. When Bianca was informed of the loan denial, the controller of the company immediately paid $420,000 that was owed to several trade creditors. The controller then asked Provincial to reconsider the loan application. Based on these abbreviated facts, would you recommend that Provincial approve the loan request? Why? Are the controller's actions ethical?

FINANCIAL REPORTING AND ANALYSIS TEAM PROJECT

LO12-3,12-5,12-6,12-7,   **Team Project: Examining an Annual Report**
12-8,12-9   **CP12-8**   As a team, select an industry to analyze. A list of companies classified by industry can be obtained

by accessing www.fpinfomart.ca and then choosing Companies by Industry. You can also find a list of industries and companies within each industry via http://ca.finance.yahoo.com/investing (click on Order Annual Reports under Tools).

Using a Web browser, each team member should acquire the annual report for one publicly traded company in an industry, with each member selecting a different company. (Library files, the SEDAR service at www.sedar.com, and the company website are good resources.)

Required:
On an individual basis, each team member should write a short report providing the following information about the selected company. Discuss any patterns across the companies that you as a team observe. Then, as a team, write a short report comparing and contrasting your companies.

Compute and interpret each of the ratios discussed in this chapter. The most frequently used sections will be the financial statements. Also, you may want to review the notes, the summary of financial information (usually for the past 5 to 10 years), and management's discussion and analysis.

📶 connect   CONTINUING CASE

LO12-6,12-7,12-8,12-9   **Computing Selected Financial Ratios**
CC12-1   Pool Corporation Inc. is the world's largest wholesale distributor of swimming pool supplies and equipment. It is a publicly traded corporation which trades on the NASDAQ exchange under the symbol POOL. It sells these products to swimming pool repair and service businesses, swimming pool builders, and retail swimming pool stores. The majority of these customers are small, family-owned businesses.

Required:
1. Access the company's most recent annual report from its website www.poolcorp.com.
2. Compute the following ratios:
   a. Return on assets
   b. Profit margin
   c. Current ratio
   d. Inventory turnover
   e. Cash coverage ratio
   f. Debt-to-equity ratio
   g. Price/earnings ratio (*Hint:* You will need to go to another source to get the market price per share at year end.)

SOLUTIONS TO SELF-STUDY QUIZZES

Self-Study Quiz 12-1
1. a. ROE = Net earnings/Average shareholders' equity
      = $385.1/[($740.5 + $466.9)/2] = 0.638, or 63.8%
   b. ROA = (Net earnings + Interest expense, net of tax)/Average total assets
      = ($385.1 + $5.8)/[($1,700.8 + $1,813.8)/2] = 0.223, or 22.3%
   c. Profit margin = Net earnings/Net sales = $385.1/$2,650.3 = 0.145, or 14.5%
2. The company uses debt effectively to generate return to shareholders. Its ROE exceeds its ROA.

Self-Study Quiz 12-2

Google's profit margin ratio is higher than that of Yahoo, and its total asset turnover ratio is also significantly higher than Yahoo's. Google is more efficient at controlling costs relative to revenue. Its financial leverage percentage is slightly higher than Yahoo's. Overall, Google has a faster total asset turnover ratio, higher net profit margin ratio, and higher leverage, which explains why its ROE is twice as high as Yahoo's.

Self-Study Quiz 12-3

The quick ratio should be lower than the current ratio, because the numerator of the quick ratio includes only part of the current assets. Three of the quick ratios, 2.61, 3.43, and 3.19 are greater than the current ratios of both the telecommunications services and paper and forest products industries, so they cannot be associated with any of these two industries. Consequently, the quick ratios 0.92 and 0.80 must be associated with these two industries. The quick assets for the telecommunications services industry exceeds 85 percent of its current assets, and a quick ratio of 0.80 does not meet this requirement. As a result, the quick ratio of 0.92 belongs to the telecommunications services industry.

Self-Study Quiz 12-4

1. Current ratio = Current assets/Current liabilities = $607.1/$227.0 = 2.67
2. Quick ratio = Quick assets/Current liabilities = $70.3/$227.0 = 0.31
3. Cash ratio = (Cash + Cash equivalents)/Current liabilities = $59.2/$227.0 = 0.26

Self-Study Quiz 12-5

1. Debt-to-equity ratio = Total liabilities/Shareholders' equity
    = $1,347.0/$466.9 = 2.88
2. Times interest earned ratio = Earnings before interest and taxes/Interest expense
    = $549.4/$21,4 = 25.67 times
3. P/E ratio = Market price/Earnings per share
    = $79.95/$3.03 = 26.38

ENDNOTES

1. Details of Canadian Tire's corporate governance structure and activities can be found at http://investors.canadiantire.ca/English/investors/corporate-governance/overview/default.aspx.

2. In some cases, the auditor may not be satisfied that the company's financial statements are in compliance with IFRS. A qualified opinion is then issued if the company's management is not willing to modify the financial reports as per the auditor's recommendation. If the exceptions to IFRS are very serious, then the auditor may issue an adverse opinion, if the company's management cannot be persuaded to rectify the problems to avoid such an opinion. In extreme cases, the auditor may deny the issuance of an opinion if insufficient information is available to express an opinion. These latter types of opinions are rarely issued by auditors.

3. Canadian companies that have shares traded on U.S. stock exchanges can file SEC forms electronically with EDGAR (Electronic Data Gathering and Retrieval), a site sponsored by the SEC.

4. To look at SEDAR, just type the address on your Web browser. Select French or English, depending on your preference, and then select Company Profiles, followed by the letter of the alphabet that corresponds to the first letter of the company's name. You will then see a list of companies that includes the selected company. Many of the financial statement examples used in this book were downloaded from this website.

5. U.S., Canadian, and international companies that have shares trading on U.S. securities exchange markets are required to file a number of reports with the SEC. These forms for U.S. companies include Form 10-K, an annual report that provides a detailed description of the business and more detailed schedules concerning various figures reported in the annual financial statements, and Form 10-Q, which is essentially a quarterly report to shareholders. Canadian companies listed in the United States typically file their annual reports with the SEC on Form 40-F, and they furnish their quarterly reports, press releases, and other periodic disclosures on Form 6-K.

6. The percentage change in sales for existing stores is computed as follows:

$$\text{Percentage change} = \left[\frac{\text{Sale}_{\text{Current year}} - \text{Sale}_{\text{Previous year}}}{\text{Sale}_{\text{Previous year}}} \times 100 \right]$$

Similar percentage changes can be computed for various elements of financial statements.

7. The figures for Canadian Tire used throughout the following ratio examples are taken from the financial statements in Exhibit 12.1.

8. To illustrate the net cost of using debt, assume that a company earned $100 in revenue and incurred $70 in operating expenses. Consider two scenarios: (1) the company uses long-term debt that cost $10 in interest expense and (2) the company does not use debt.

   The deduction of interest expense from earnings before interest and taxes reduced the income tax expense from $12 to $8, and net earnings decreased by only $6. Therefore, the net cost of using debt in this case is $6, or $10 × (1 × 0.4, the tax rate).

	Debt Financing	Equity Financing
Earnings before interest and taxes	$30	$30
Interest expense	(10)	0
Earnings before income taxes	$20	$30
Income tax expense (@40 percent)	(8)	(12)
Net earnings	$12	$18

9. IFRS require companies to report interest expense and other financing-related expenses as "finance costs" on the statement of earnings. Details of the finance costs are reported in Note 33 to the financial statements. The finance costs of Canadian Tire are, essentially, interest expense.

10. An expanded version of the DuPont model is provided by the Scott formula. Interested readers are referred to Appendix 12A on *Connect* for a detailed application of the Scott formula to the financial statements of Canadian Tire Corporation, Limited.

11. For manufacturing companies, the purchases consist primarily of raw materials used in the production of finished goods. The computation of raw materials purchased is discussed in cost accounting courses.

12. Alternatively, the relationship between debt and owners' equity may be calculated with the following ratio:

$$\text{Total liabilities to Total equities} = \frac{\text{Total liabilities}}{\text{Total liabilities and Shareholders' equity}}$$

$$\text{Canadian Tire, 2015} = \frac{\$9,198.1}{\$14,987.8} = 61.4\%$$

This ratio is one of those readily available through the component percentage analysis in Exhibit 12.3.

Reporting and Interpreting Investments in Other Corporations

C H A P T E R

13

After studying this chapter, you should be able to do the following:

LEARNING OBJECTIVES

LO13-1 Analyze and report investments in debt securities held to maturity.

LO13-2 Analyze and report passive investments in securities using the fair value method.

LO13-3 Analyze and report investments involving significant influence using the equity method.

LO13-4 Analyze and report investments in controlling interests.

JE Whyte/iStockphoto.com

Focus Company: **BCE Inc.**

INVESTMENT STRATEGIES AND DIVERSIFICATION

Bell Canada Enterprises (BCE) Inc. (www.bce.ca), Canada's largest communications company, employs approximately 50,000 people in the various companies under its control. Historically, BCE grew through careful investment in the shares of other companies that have operations in the telecommunications industry. Today, BCE's core business is carried out through its wholly owned subsidiaries, Bell Canada, Bell Mobility, and Bell Media.

The company's investment portfolio consists of $1,119 million worth of shares in other companies. BCE's recent history of investments includes the acquisition of equity interests in Maple Leaf Sports & Entertainment Ltd., which owns several sports teams as well as real estate and entertainment properties; Glentel Inc., a Canadian-based dual-carrier, multi-brand mobile products distributor; Q9 Networks Inc., a provider of outsourced data centre solutions, such as hosting, co-location, and cloud services; the Montréal Canadiens Hockey Club; the Bell Centre in Montréal; and the Toronto Argonauts Football Club.

UNDERSTANDING THE BUSINESS

Many strategic factors motivate managers to invest in securities. A company that has extra cash and simply wants to earn a return on the idle funds can invest those funds in the shares and bonds issued by other companies, either long or short term. We say that these investments are passive, because the managers are not interested in influencing or controlling the other companies. The assets section of BCE's 2015 statement of financial position, shown in Exhibit 13.1, reflects non-current investments in financial instruments, which are included in other non-current assets.[1]

Sometimes, a company decides to make a significant investment in another company for the purpose of influencing that company's policies and activities. BCE's statement of financial position (balance sheet) reports these types of investments as "Investments in associates and joint ventures." Finally, managers may determine that controlling another company, either by purchasing it directly or becoming the majority shareholder, is desirable. If the acquired company ceases to exist, its assets and liabilities are added at fair value to the assets and liabilities of the buyer. If the acquired company continues as a separate legal entity, then the financial reports of both companies are combined into a set of consolidated financial statements, as BCE has done.

In this chapter, we discuss the accounting for four types of investments. First, we discuss the use of the amortized cost method to account for passive investments in bonds. Second, we examine the fair value method of accounting for passive investments in shares.[2] Third, we present the equity method of accounting for investments, which permits the investor to exert significant influence over the strategic operating and financing decisions of the investee. The chapter closes with a discussion of accounting for mergers and consolidated statements.

BCE Inc. Consolidated Statements of Financial Position			
(in millions of Canadian dollars)	Note	December 31, 2015	December 31, 2014
ASSETS			
Current			
Cash		$ 100	$ 142
Cash equivalents		513	424
Trade and other receivables	11	3,009	3,069
Prepaid expenses		393	379
Other current assets		377	201
Total current assets		4,808	4,548
Non-current assets			
Property, plant, and equipment	13	21,630	21,327
Intangible assets	14	1,176	10,224
Deferred tax assets	9	89	162
Investments in associates and joint ventures	3, 15	1,119	776
Other non-current assets	16	794	875
Goodwill	17	8,337	8,385
Total non-current assets		43,185	41,749
Total assets		$47,993	$46,297

Source: BCE Inc., 2015 Annual Report.

Exhibit 13.1

Consolidated Statements of Financial Position (Assets Section)

REAL-WORLD EXCERPT

BCE Inc.

CONSOLIDATED STATEMENTS OF FINANCIAL POSITION

ORGANIZATION OF THE CHAPTER

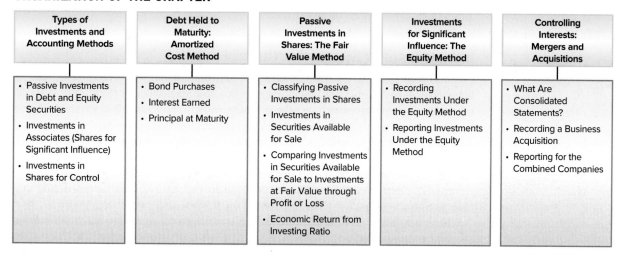

Types of Investments and Accounting Methods	Debt Held to Maturity: Amortized Cost Method	Passive Investments in Shares: The Fair Value Method	Investments for Significant Influence: The Equity Method	Controlling Interests: Mergers and Acquisitions
• Passive Investments in Debt and Equity Securities • Investments in Associates (Shares for Significant Influence) • Investments in Shares for Control	• Bond Purchases • Interest Earned • Principal at Maturity	• Classifying Passive Investments in Shares • Investments in Securities Available for Sale • Comparing Investments in Securities Available for Sale to Investments at Fair Value through Profit or Loss • Economic Return from Investing Ratio	• Recording Investments Under the Equity Method • Reporting Investments Under the Equity Method	• What Are Consolidated Statements? • Recording a Business Acquisition • Reporting for the Combined Companies

TYPES OF INVESTMENTS AND ACCOUNTING METHODS

The accounting methods used to record and report investments depend on whether the investor intends to hold the investment for strategic or non-strategic reasons, and the extent of the investor's influence over the strategic operating and financing decisions of the investee.

Passive Investments in Debt and Equity Securities

Passive investments are made to earn a rate of return on funds that may be needed for future short- or long-term purposes. The classification and valuation of passive investments depend on the nature of the investment as well as management's intent. Investments are classified as cash equivalents if they consist of highly liquid investments with original maturities of three months or less at the date of purchase, such as treasury bills issued by the federal government and certificates of deposit. These are reported at cost plus accrued interest, which approximates fair market value.

Passive investments include investments in both debt (treasury bills, bonds,[3] and notes) and equity securities (shares). Debt securities are always considered passive investments, but this does not mean there is no risk to the investor. Investors holding municipal bonds for the city of Detroit, for example, will most probably not recover the cost of their investment because the city filed for bankruptcy in July 2013. In this type of situation, the investor must report an impairment loss on the financial asset. If the company intends to hold the securities until they reach their maturity dates, the investments are measured and reported at amortized cost. If the investor intends to resell the securities before their maturity, then they are reported at their fair value.

For investments in equity securities, the investment is presumed passive if the investing company owns less than 20 percent of the outstanding voting shares of the other company. The fair value method is used to measure and report such investments.

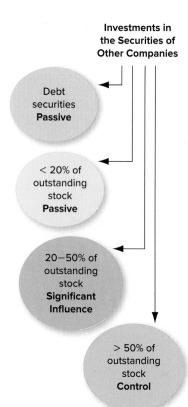

Investments in the Securities of Other Companies

Debt securities **Passive**

< 20% of outstanding stock **Passive**

20–50% of outstanding stock **Significant Influence**

> 50% of outstanding stock **Control**

Investments in Associates (Shares Acquired for Significant Influence)

Significant influence is the ability to have an important impact on the strategic operating and financing policies of another company in which the investor owns voting shares. Significant influence is presumed if the investing company owns from 20 to 50 percent of the outstanding voting shares of the other company. However, other factors may also indicate that significant influence exists, such as membership on the board of directors of the other company, participation in the policy-making processes, evidence of material transactions between the two companies, an interchange of management personnel, or technological dependency. The equity method is used to measure and report this category of investments.

Investments in Shares for Control

According to IFRS 10—Consolidated Financial Statements, an investor controls an investee when it not only has power over the investee and exposure to rights to variable returns from its involvement with the investee, but also has the ability to use its power to affect the investee's returns. Determining power depends on the interaction among four factors, the scope of the investor's authority to make decisions for the investee, the authority relative to other investors, the strength of the link between remuneration and return on the investment for the investor, and the investor's exposure to variable returns. The extent of the investor's power must be continuously assessed, and any change must be reflected when accounting for the investment.

These categories and the appropriate measuring and reporting methods can be summarized as follows:

Investment Category	Investment in Debt Securities of Another Entity		Investment in the Voting Common Shares of Another Entity		
	Passive		Passive	Significant Influence	Control
Level of Ownership	Per held to maturity	Not held to maturity	< 20% of outstanding voting shares	20–50% of outstanding voting shares	> 50% of outstanding voting shares
Measuring and Reporting Method	Amortized cost method	Fair value method		Equity method	Consolidation method

DEBT HELD TO MATURITY: THE AMORTIZED COST METHOD

When management plans to hold a bond (or note) until its maturity date (when the principal is due), it is reported in an account appropriately called **held-to-maturity investments**. Bonds should be classified as held-to-maturity investments if management has the intent and the ability to hold them until maturity. These investments in debt instruments are listed at cost, adjusted for the amortization of any bond discount or premium (**amortized cost method**). Changes in the fair value of these investments are not recognized in the company's accounting records.

We now illustrate accounting for investments in bonds issued by another company.

Bond Purchases

On the date of purchase, a bond may be acquired at the maturity amount (at *par*), for less than the maturity amount (at a *discount*), or for more than the maturity amount (at a *premium*).[4] The total cost of the bond, including all incidental acquisition costs, such as transfer fees and broker commissions, is debited to the held-to-maturity investments account.

To illustrate accounting for bond investments, assume that on July 1, 2016, BCE paid the par value[5] of $100,000 for 4 percent bonds that mature on June 30, 2021. The 4 percent interest is paid each June 30 and December 31. Management plans to hold the bonds for five years, until maturity.

The journal entry to record the purchase of the bonds follows:

Held-to-maturity investments (A)		100,000		
Cash (A)				710,000
Assets	=	**Liabilities**	+	**Shareholders' Equity**
Held-to-maturity investments +100,000				
Cash −100,000				

Interest Earned

The bonds in the illustration were purchased at par, or face value. Since no premium or discount needs to be amortized, the carrying amount remains constant over the life of the investment. In this situation, revenue earned from the investment each period is measured as the amount of interest collected in cash or accrued at year-end. The following journal entry records the receipt of $2,000 ($100,000 × 4% × 6/12) in interest on June 30:

Cash (A)		2,000		
Interest revenue (R, SE)				2,000
Assets	=	**Liabilities**	+	**Shareholders' Equity**
Cash +2,000				Interest revenue +2,000

The same entry is made on succeeding interest payment dates.

LO13-1

Analyze and report investments in debt securities held to maturity.

HELD-TO-MATURITY INVESTMENTS are investments in bonds that management has the intent and ability to hold until maturity.

The **AMORTIZED COST METHOD** reports investments in debt securities held to maturity at cost, net of any discount or premium.

PAUSE FOR FEEDBACK

Accounting for debt held to maturity is relatively simple when the debt is purchased at its face value. Realistically, bonds sell at either a discount or premium, as discussed in Chapter 10. Check your understanding of accounting for a purchase of bonds at a premium before you move on.

SELF-STUDY QUIZ 13-1

Quartz Company purchased bonds on July 1, 2017, for $5,009,289. The bonds have a face value of $5,000,000, mature on June 30, 2019, have a nominal interest rate of 4.1 percent, and pay interest semi-annually on December 31 and June 30. The effective interest rate was 4 percent when the bonds were purchased. Quartz Company plans to hold the bonds until maturity.

1. Record the purchase of the bonds.

2. Record the receipt of interest on December 31, 2017.

After you complete your answers, check them with the solutions at the end of the chapter.

Principal at Maturity

When the bonds mature on June 30, 2018, the journal entry to record receipt of the principal payment will be as follows:

Cash (A)				100,000	
Held-to-maturity investments (A)					100,000
Assets		=	**Liabilities**	+	**Shareholders' Equity**
Cash	+100,000				
Held-to-maturity investments	−100,000				

If the bond investment must be sold before maturity, any difference between the market value of the bond (the proceeds from the sale) and its carrying amount would be reported as a gain or loss on sale. If management intends to sell the bonds before the maturity date, they are treated in the same manner as investments in shares classified as securities available for sale, as discussed in the next section.

PASSIVE INVESTMENTS IN SHARES: THE FAIR VALUE METHOD

LO13-2

Analyze and report passive investments in securities using the fair value method.

The **FAIR VALUE METHOD** is used to report investments at their fair value (the amount that would be received in an orderly sale).

When the investing company owns less than 20 percent of the outstanding voting shares of another company, the investment is considered passive. Passive investments in securities are reported according to the **fair value method**; that is, reported at the fair value on the date of the statement of financial position. Before we discuss the specific accounting for these investments, we should consider the implications of using fair value:

1. **Why are passive investments reported at fair value on the statement of financial position?**

   Two primary factors determine the answer to this question:

   - **Relevance**—Analysts who study financial statements often attempt to forecast a company's future cash flows. They want to know how a company can generate cash for purposes such as expansion of the business, payment of dividends, or survival during a prolonged economic downturn. One source of cash is the sale of shares from the company's portfolio of passive investments. The best estimate of the cash that could be generated by the sale of these securities is their fair value.

   - **Measurability**—Accountants record, with a high degree of reliability (an unbiased and verifiable measurement), any item that can be measured in monetary terms. Determining the fair value of most assets is very difficult because they are not actively traded. For example, the head office building of the Toronto Dominion Bank is an important part of the Toronto skyline. The statement of financial position of the Toronto Dominion Bank reports the building in terms of its original cost less accumulated depreciation, in part because of the difficulty in determining an objective market value for it. Contrast the difficulty of determining the value of a building with the ease of determining the value of securities that Toronto Dominion Bank may own. A quick look at the financial section of a newspaper or an Internet financial service is all that is necessary to determine the current price of shares issued by many companies (e.g., Thomson Reuters Inc., WestJet Airlines Ltd.) because these securities are traded each day on established stock exchanges.

2. **When an investment account is adjusted to reflect changes in fair value, what other account is affected when the asset account is increased or decreased?** Under the double-entry method of accounting, every journal entry affects at least two accounts. The first account is the investments account. The other account affected is the **unrealized holding gains or losses** that are recorded whenever the fair value of investments changes. The gains or losses are unrealized because no actual sale has taken place; the value of the investment has changed while the shares are being held by the investing company. If the value of the investments increased by $100,000 during the year, an adjusting journal entry records the increase in the investments account and an unrealized holding gain of $100,000. If the value of the investments decreased by $75,000 during the year, an adjusting journal entry records the decrease in the investments account and an unrealized holding loss of $75,000. The unrealized holding gains or losses should be reported in the statement of earnings, except in certain circumstances that are specified below.

> **UNREALIZED HOLDING GAINS OR LOSSES** are amounts associated with price changes of securities that are currently held.

Classifying Passive Investments in Shares

Passive investments may be classified as investments at fair value through profit or loss or as investments available for sale, depending on management's intent.

Investments at Fair Value through Profit or Loss Investments are classified as **investments at fair value through profit or loss** (FVTPL) if they are actively traded with the objective of generating profits on short-term changes in the price of the securities. This approach is similar to the one taken by many mutual funds. The portfolio manager actively seeks opportunities to buy and sell securities. These investments are initially recorded at fair value. Subsequent to initial recognition, they are measured at fair value at each reporting date. Fair value adjustments or unrealized holding gains or losses are recognized in the statement of earnings. Securities held for trading are classified as *current assets* on the statement of financial position because they are intended to be sold within one year.

> **INVESTMENTS AT FAIR VALUE THROUGH PROFIT OR LOSS** are all investments in shares or bonds held primarily for the purpose of active trading (buying and selling) in the near future (classified as current).

Investments in Securities Available for Sale Most companies do not actively trade the securities of other companies. Instead, they invest to earn a return on funds they may need for future operating purposes. These investments are called **investments in securities available for sale** (SAS).[6] They reflect financial assets that are designated by the company on initial recognition as being available for sale. They are classified as current or non-current assets on the statement of financial position, depending on whether management intends to sell the securities during the next year.

> **INVESTMENTS IN SECURITIES AVAILABLE FOR SALE** are all passive investments other than securities held for trading (classified as current or non-current).

Investments at FVTPL are most commonly reported by financial institutions that actively buy and sell short-term investments to maximize returns. Most corporations, however, invest in short- and long-term SAS. We will focus on this category in the next section by analyzing BCE's investing activities.

BCE disclosed in the notes to its financial statements the various types of financial assets and liabilities, as well as their classification and measurement:

Notes to consolidated financial statements

2—Significant accounting policies

...

(o) Financial instruments

TRADE AND OTHER RECEIVABLES

Trade and other receivables, which include trade receivables and other short-term receivables, are measured at amortized cost using the effective interest method, net of any allowance for doubtful accounts. An allowance for doubtful accounts is established based on individually significant exposures or on historical trends. Factors considered when establishing an allowance include current economic conditions, historical information and the reason for the delay in payment. Amounts considered uncollectible are written off.

AVAILABLE FOR SALE (AFS) FINANCIAL ASSETS

Our portfolio investments in equity securities are classified as AFS and are presented in our statements of financial position as *other non-current assets*. They have been designated as such based on management's intentions or because they are not classified in any other categories. These securities are recorded at fair value on the date of acquisition, including related transaction costs, and are adjusted to fair value at each reporting date. The corresponding unrealized gains and losses are recorded in other comprehensive income and are reclassified to other (expense) income in the income statements when realized or when an impairment is determined.

OTHER FINANCIAL LIABILITIES

Other financial liabilities, which include trade payables and accruals, compensation payable, obligations imposed by the Canadian Radio-television and Telecommunications Commission (CRTC), interest payable and long-term debt, are recorded at amortized cost using the effective interest method.

Source: BCE Inc., 2015 Annual Report.

Investments in Securities Available for Sale

For simplification, let us assume that BCE had no passive investments at December 31, 2015. The following example illustrates the accounting and reporting for SAS.

Purchase of Shares   Suppose that on January 1, 2016, the start of the 2016 fiscal year, BCE purchases 10,000 common shares of Green Web Apps Inc. (GWA), a fictitious company, for $60 per share. GWA has 100,000 outstanding shares, so BCE owns 10 percent (10,000 ÷ 100,000) of GWA's shares, which is treated as a passive investment. Such investments are recorded as follows:

Investments in SAS (A)		600,000		
Cash (A)				600,000
Assets		**= Liabilities**	**+**	**Shareholders' Equity**
Investments in SAS	+600,000			
Cash	−600,000			

Dividends Earned   Investments in equity securities earn a return from two sources: (1) dividend income and (2) price appreciation. Dividends earned are reported as investment income on the statement of earnings and are included in the computation of net earnings for the period.

Assume that during the fourth quarter of fiscal 2016, BCE received a cash dividend of $1 per share from GWA that totals $10,000 ($1 × 10,000 shares). The journal entry and transaction effects are as follows:

Cash (A)		10,000		
Investment income (R, SE)				10,000
Assets	**=**	**Liabilities**	**+**	**Shareholders' Equity**
Cash	+10,000			Investment income +10,000

This entry is the same for financial assets that are either held for trading or available for sale. Price increases (or decreases) are analyzed both at year-end and when a security is sold.

Year-End Valuation   At the end of the accounting period, passive investments are reported on the statement of financial position at fair value, the amount that would be received in an orderly sale.

For fiscal year 2016:

Assume that GWA had a market value of $58 per share at the end of the year; that is, the investment has lost $2 ($60 − $58) per share. However, the loss is not realized since the investment has not been sold. It simply resulted from holding the shares while their fair value changed.

Reporting the investments in SAS at fair value requires adjusting the carrying amount to fair value at the end of each period.[7] The adjusting entry recognizes the *unrealized* holding gain or loss and adjusts the carrying amount of the investments accordingly. The net unrealized gains and losses on these investments are reported in the statement of comprehensive income as part of other comprehensive income, which affects shareholders' equity, but not net earnings. As noted in Chapter 11, other comprehensive income reflects the financial effect of events that cause changes in shareholders' equity other than investments by shareholders or distributions to shareholders. Hence, other comprehensive income includes unrealized gains and losses on investments that are available for sale. When the investment is sold, the net unrealized gains or losses are transferred from other comprehensive income directly to the statement of earnings.

The following chart is used to compute any unrealized gain or loss on the investments in the SAS portfolio:

Fiscal Year	Fair Value	−	Carrying Amount before Adjustment	=	Amount for Adjusting Entry
2016	$580,000	−	$600,000	=	$20,000
	($58 × 10,000)		($60 × 10,000)		An **unrealized loss** for the period

As indicated in Note 3 to BCE's financial statements for fiscal year 2016, the company reports changes in the fair value of investments in SAS in other comprehensive income. The adjusting entry at the end of fiscal year 2016 is recorded as follows:

Investments in SAS (A)

1/1/16	600,000		
		20,000	AJE
12/31/16	580,000		

Net unrealized losses/gains—Investments in SAS (OCI, SE)   20,000
    Investments in SAS (A)   20,000

Assets	=	Liabilities	+	Shareholders' Equity
Investments in SAS −20,000				Net unrealized losses/gains– Investments in SAS −20,000

If management of BCE intends to hold the investment in these securities for the long term, it would be reported on the company's statement of financial position at December 31, 2016, the end of the 2016 fiscal year, at $580,000. An unrealized loss of $20,000 on investments in SAS would also be reported under other comprehensive income in the statement of comprehensive income as well as the statement of changes in equity, thus affecting the balance of accumulated other comprehensive income, which is a component of shareholders' equity. The only item reported on the statement of earnings for 2016 would be investment income of $10,000 from the dividends earned, classified under other non-operating items:

On the 2016 Statement of Financial Position

Assets

Investments in SAS $580,000

On the 2016 Statement of Changes in Equity

Other comprehensive income

Net unrealized loss   (20,000)

For fiscal year 2017:

Let us assume that BCE held the GWA shares through fiscal year 2017, and that the price per share was $61 at year-end. The year-end adjustment would be computed as follows:

Fiscal Year	Fair Value	–	Carrying Amount before Adjustment	=	Amount for Adjusting Entry
2017	$610,000	–	$580,000	=	$30,000
	($61 × 10,000)		($58 × 10,000)		An **unrealized gain** for the period

The adjusting entry at the end of fiscal year 2017 is recorded as follows:

Investments in SAS (A)				30,000	
Net unrealized losses/gains—Investments in SAS (OCI, SE)					30,000
Assets	**=**	**Liabilities**	**+**	**Shareholders' Equity**	
Investments in SAS +30,000				Net unrealized losses/gains– Investments in SAS +30,000	

Net Unrealized Losses/Gains (SE)			**Investments in SAS (A)**		
1/1/16	–0–		1/1/2016	600,000	
AJE	20,000			20,000	AJE
12/31/16	20,000		12/31/16	580,000	
		30,000 AJE		30,000	
		10,000 2/31/17	12/31/17	610,000	

On the statement of financial position at December 31, 2017, the end of the 2017 fiscal year, BCE would report, under assets, an investment in SAS of $610,000 and, under other comprehensive income, its net unrealized gain of $10,000 (fair value – cost) on these investments:

On the 2017 Statement of Financial Position

Assets

Investments in SAS $610,000

On the 2017 Statement of Changes in Equity

Other comprehensive income

Net unrealized gain   10,000

Sale of Shares   When available-for-sale investments are sold, cash is increased and *two* accounts are eliminated:

- Investments in SAS (A)
- Net unrealized losses/gains (OCI, SE)

Let us assume that BCE sold its investment in GWA on May 15, 2018, for $62.50 per share. The company would receive $625,000 in cash ($62.50 × 10,000) for shares that have a carrying amount of $610,000 on December 31, 2017. The gain of $15,000 is realized and recognized in the statement of earnings. In addition, the credit balance of net unrealized losses/gains—investments in SAS is recognized as gain on sale of the investment. The initial investment of $600,000 has been sold for $625,000 and the gain of $25,000 has been realized and recognized in the statement of earnings. The sale and related gain are recorded through two journal entries:

Net Unrealized Losses/Gains (SE)

1/1/16	–0–		
AJE	20,000		
12/31/16	20,000		
		30,000	AJE
		10,000	12/31/17
Closing	10,000		
5/15/18	–0–		

(1) Cash (A)	625,000	
Gain on sale of investments in SAS (Gain, SE)		15,000
Investments in SAS (A)		610,000
(2) Net unrealized losses/gains—Investments in SAS (OCI, SE)	10,000	
Gain on sale of investments in SAS (Gain, SE)		10,000

Assets		=	Liabilities	+	Shareholders' Equity	
Cash	+625,000				Gain on sale of investments in SAS	+15,000
Investments in SAS	–610,000				Net unrealized losses/gains– Investments in SAS	–10,000
					Gain on sale of investments in SAS	+10,000

BCE's consolidated statements of comprehensive income include unrealized gains on financial assets that are available for sale as shown in Exhibit 13.2.

Exhibit **13.2**
Consolidated Statements of Comprehensive Income

REAL-WORLD EXCERPT

BCE Inc.
ANNUAL REPORT

(in millions of Canadian dollars)	December 31, 2015	December 31, 2014
Net earnings	**$2,730**	**$2,718**
Other comprehensive income (loss), net of income taxes		
Items that will be subsequently reclassified to net earnings		
Net change in value of available-for-sale (AFS) financial assets, net of income taxes of nil for 2015 and 2014	23	58
Net change in value of derivatives designated as cash flow hedges, net of income taxes of ($2) million and ($13) million for 2015 and 2014, respectively	1	34
Items that will not be reclassified to net earnings		
Actuarial gains (losses) on defined benefit plans net of income taxes of ($161) million and $253 million for 2015 and 2014, respectively	429	(685)
Other comprehensive income (loss)	453	(593)
Total comprehensive income	**$3,183**	**$2,125**
...		

Source: BCE Inc. 2015 Annual Report.

Comparing Investments in Securities Available for Sale to Investments at Fair Value through Profit or Loss

The reporting impact of unrealized holding gains or losses depends on the classification of the investment.

Portfolio of Investments in SAS As we learned in the previous section, the balance in net unrealized holding gains and losses is reported as a separate component of shareholders' equity (under accumulated other comprehensive income). It is not reported on the statement of earnings and does not affect net earnings. At the time of sale, both the investment in SAS and net unrealized losses/gains—investments in SAS are eliminated, and the net realized gain or loss that resulted from the change in the fair value of the investment since acquisition is reflected in the statement of earnings.

Portfolio of investments at FVTPL   For investments at FVTPL, the amount of the adjustment to record net unrealized holding gains and losses is included in each period's statement of earnings. Net holding gains increase net earnings and net holding losses decrease it. This also means that the amount recorded as net unrealized gains and losses on these investments is closed to retained earnings at the end of the period. Thus, when selling a security, cash and only *one* other statement of financial position account are affected: investments at FVTPL. The gain or loss on sale of investments at FVTPL is the difference between the cash proceeds from the sale and the carrying amount of the investment.

Exhibit 13.3 provides comparative journal entries and financial statement balances for the transactions illustrated for BCE from January 1, 2016, to May 15, 2018. *Note that the total gain reported for the three years is the same, $35,000, for both types of securities.* The only difference relates to the reporting of net unrealized gains and losses. For investments measured at FVTPL, the net unrealized gains or losses are reported on the statement of earnings, whereas net unrealized gains and losses related to investments in SAS are reported as an adjustment to equity (accumulated other comprehensive income) on the statement of financial position:

Income in	Investments at FVTPL	Investments in SAS
2016	$10,000 dividends	$10,000 dividends
	(20,000) unrealized loss	–
2017	30,000 unrealized gain	–
2018	15,000 realized gain	25,000 realized gain
Total	$35,000	$35,000

PAUSE FOR FEEDBACK

Passive investments other than debt held to maturity are recorded at fair value and adjusted to fair value at year-end. The resulting unrealized gains or losses are recorded.

- For investment at FVTPL, the net unrealized gains and losses are reported in net earnings.
- For SAS, the net unrealized gains and losses are reported as a component of shareholders' equity in accumulated other comprehensive income.

Any dividends earned are reported as income. Check your understanding of accounting and reporting of passive investments before you move on.

SELF-STUDY QUIZ 13-2

In 2017, Rosa Food Corporation acquired 5,000 (10 percent) of the outstanding voting shares of another company for $100,000, to be held as a long-term investment available for sale. At the end of 2017, the fair value per share was $22. At the end of 2018, the fair value per share dropped to $17. On January 2, 2019, Rosa Food sold the entire investment for $120,000 cash.

1. Record the purchase.
2. Record the adjusting entry at the end of 2017. What would be reported for the investment
   - *a.* on the statement of financial position?
   - *b.* on the statement of earnings?
3. Record the adjusting entry at the end of 2018.
4. Record the sale in 2019.
5. If the investment was measured at FVTPL, what would be reported for this investment
   - *a.* on the statement of financial position at the end of 2017?
   - *b.* on the 2017 statement of earnings?

After you complete your answers, check them with the solutions at the end of the chapter.

Exhibit **13.3**

Comparison of Accounting for Investments at FVTPL and Investments in SAS

Part A: Entries

	Investments at FVTPL		Investments in SAS	
Fiscal Year 2016:				
• Purchase (for $600,000 cash)	Investments at FVTPL (A)	600,000	Investments in SAS (A)	600,000
	Cash (A)	600,000	Cash (A)	600,000
• Receipt of dividends ($10,000 cash)	Cash (A)	10,000	Cash (A)	10,000
	Investment income (R, SE)	10,000	Investment income (R, SE)	10,000
• Year-end adjustment to fair value (= $580,000)	Net unrealized losses/gains— Investments at FVTPL (Loss, SE)	20,000	Net unrealized losses/gains— Investments in SAS (OCI, SE)	20,000
	Investments at FVTPL (A)	20,000	Investments in SAS (A)	20,000
Fiscal Year 2017:				
• Year-end adjustment to fair value (= $610,000)	Investments at FVTPL (A)	30,000	Investments in SAS (A)	30,000
	Net unrealized losses/gains— Investments at FVTPL (Gain, SE)	30,000	Net unrealized losses/gains— Investments in SAS (OCI, SE)	30,000
Fiscal Year 2018:				
• Sale (for $625,000)	*One statement of financial position account is eliminated:*		*Two statements of financial position accounts are eliminated:*	
	Cash (A)	625,000	Cash (A)	625,000
	Investments at FVTPL (A)	610,000	**Investments at SAS (A)**	610,000
	Gain on sale of investment (Gain, SE)	15,000	Gain on sale of investment (Gain, SE)	15,000
			Net unrealized losses/gains— Investments in SAS (OCI, SE)	15,000
			Gain on sale of investment (Gain, SE)	15,000

Part B: Financial Reporting

	Investments at FVTPL				Investments in SAS			
Statement of Financial Position:	**Assets**	**2018**	**2017**	**2016**	**Assets**	**2018**	**2017**	**2016**
	Investments at FVTPL	—	600,000	600,000	Investments in SAS	—	600,000	600,000
	Changes in fair value	—	10,000	(20,000)	Changes in fair value	—	10,000	(20,000)
	Investments at FVTPL	—	610,000	580,000	Investments in SAS	—	610,000	580,000
					Shareholders' Equity			
					Accumulated other comprehensive income:			
					Net unrealized losses/gains		10,000	(20,000)
					Retained earnings	25,000		
Statement of Earnings:		**2018**	**2017**	**2016**		**2018**	**2017**	**2016**
	Investment income	—	—	10,000	Investment income	—	—	10,000
	Gain on sale	15,000	—	—	Gain on sale	25,000	—	—
	Net unrealized losses/gains — Investments at FVTPL	—	30,000	(20,000)				

ECONOMIC RETURN FROM INVESTING

Both corporate and individual investors need to monitor the performance of their securities portfolios. Normally, this is done using the economic return from investing ratio, which provides a percentage of what was earned plus any realized and/or unrealized gains or losses on the portfolio.

ANALYTICAL QUESTION

During the period, how much was earned per dollar invested in securities?

$$\text{Economic return from investing} = \frac{\text{Dividends and interest received} + \text{Change in fair value*}}{\text{Fair value of investments (beginning of period)}}$$

*Beginning balance of investments − Ending balance of investments

RATIO AND COMPARISONS

The 2016 ratio for our hypothetical investment is,

$$\frac{\$10, \text{Dividends} - \$20, \text{Unrealized loss}}{\$600,000} = -0.017, \text{ or } -1.7\%$$

The 2017 ratio for our hypothetical investment is,

$$\frac{\$0 \text{ Dividends} + \$30,000 \text{ Unrealized gain}}{\$580,000} = +0.052, \text{ or } +5.2\%$$

The 2018 ratio for our hypothetical investment is,

$$\frac{\$0 \text{ Dividends} + \$15,000 \text{ Realized gain}}{\$610,000} = +0.025, \text{ or } +2.5\%$$

INTERPRETATIONS

In General → Economic investment returns contain two parts: the effect of dividends received, called the dividend yield, and the effect of the change in fair value, called the capital gain or loss. Note that from an economic standpoint, the investor earns the capital gain or loss whether the securities are sold or not, since the investor has the opportunity to convert the gain or loss into cash by selling the investment. If you look at the numerator of the ratio each year, you will see that it matches the amount of earnings reported each year under investments at FVTPL in Exhibit 13.3, Part B. This is why many analysts believe that the accounting for investments at FVTPL better reflects the economics of investing,

A Few Cautions → Computations for realistic portfolios are more complex if securities are bought and sold throughout the year. This affects the computation of the denominator of the ratio.

INVESTMENTS FOR SIGNIFICANT INFLUENCE: THE EQUITY METHOD

LO13-3

Analyze and report investments involving significant influence using the equity method.

BCE invests cash in specific financial assets as passive investments. In some situations, BCE's management may want to exercise significant influence over the strategic operating, investing, and financing policies of other companies (presumed by owning 20 to 50 percent of the outstanding voting shares of the investee company) without becoming the controlling shareholder (presumed when owning more than 50 percent of the voting shares). This allows BCE to influence decisions made by the investee's board of directors. Examples follow:

- A retailer may want to influence a manufacturer in order to be sure that it can obtain certain products designed to its specifications.

- A manufacturer may want to influence a computer consulting firm to ensure that it can incorporate the consulting firm's cutting-edge technology in its manufacturing processes.

- A manufacturer may recognize that a parts supplier lacks experienced management and could prosper with additional managerial support.

BCE provided in its 2015 annual information form a list of its investments in associated companies and in joint ventures.

> **3. Description of our business**
>
> **3.1 General summary**
>
> ...
>
> In addition to our operating segments, we also hold investments in a number of other assets, including:
>
> - a 28% indirect equity interest in Maple Leaf Sports & Entertainment Ltd. (MLSE), a sports and entertainment company that owns several sports teams as well as real estate and entertainment assets in Toronto
> - a 50% indirect equity interest in Glentel Inc. (Glentel), a Canadian-based dual-carrier, multi-brand mobile products distributor
> - a 35.4% indirect equity interest in Q9 Networks Inc. (Q9), a provider of outsourced data centre solutions, such as hosting, co-location and cloud services
> - an 18.4% indirect equity interest in entities that operate the Montréal Canadiens Hockey Club and the Bell Centre in Montréal
> - a 50% indirect equity interest in the Toronto Argonauts Football Club
>
> ...
>
> *Source:* BCE Annual Information Form for the year ended December 31, 2015, p. 3.

The **equity method** must be used when an investor can exert significant influence over an investee.[8] On the statement of financial position, these non-current investments are reported as **investments in associates** and joint ventures. BCE reported the following accounting policy about its investments in associates:

The **EQUITY METHOD** is used when an investor can exert significant influence over an investee; the method permits recording the investor's share of the investee's profit.

INVESTMENTS IN ASSOCIATES are investments in shares held for the purpose of influencing the operating and financing strategies of the entity for the long term.

> **Notes to consolidated financial statements**
>
> **2—Significant accounting policies**
>
> **(I) Investments in associates and joint arrangements**
>
> Our financial statements incorporate our share of the results of our associates and joint ventures using the equity method of accounting, except when the investment is classified as held for sale.
>
> Equity income from investments is recorded in other (expense) income in the income statements. Investments in associates and joint ventures are recognized initially at cost and adjusted thereafter to include the company's share of income or loss and comprehensive income on an after-tax basis. Investments are reviewed for impairment at each reporting period by comparing their recoverable amount to their carrying amount.
>
> *Source:* BCE Inc., 2015 Annual Report.

Recording Investments under the Equity Method

With a passive investment, an investor usually cannot influence the associate's operating and investment activities; for example, by compelling the associate to pay dividends. So any dividends the investor receives from the associate are reported as dividend income.

Under the equity method, however, the investor's 20 to 50 percent ownership in a company presumes significant influence over the associate's operating and financing policies. Often, the associate's board of directors may include a representative of the investor that influences the associate's board to declare dividends, among other decisions. Because of this influence, the investment is accounted for as if the two companies were one. That is, the net earnings reported by the associate increases the associate's net assets (assets minus liabilities). Likewise, the investor should report a portion of the associate's profit as its profit, along with an increase in the investment account. Dividends paid by the associate decrease the associate's net assets. Similarly, the receipt of dividends by the investor is treated as a reduction of the investment account, not income. A summary follows:

- **Net earnings of associate:** If the associate reports positive results of operations for the year, the investor then records investment income equal to its percentage share of the associate's net earnings and increases its asset account investments in Associated Companies. If the associate reports a net loss, the investor records the opposite effect.

- **Dividends paid by associate:** If the associate declares and pays dividends during the year (a financing decision), the investor reduces its investment account and increases cash when it receives its share of the dividends.

Investment in Associated Companies

Beginning balance	
Purchases of shares	Sales of shares
Company's % share of associate's net earnings (credit Equity in Earnings of Associates)	Company's % share of associate's net loss (debit Equity in Associate's Earnings)
	Company's % share of associate's dividends declared for the period (debit Cash)
Ending balance	

Purchase of Shares   For simplification, let us assume that at the beginning of fiscal year 2016 BCE had no non-current investments in companies over which it exerted significant influence. Suppose that in 2016 BCE purchased 40,000 of the outstanding voting common shares of GWA for $400,000 in cash. Since GWA had 100,000 common shares outstanding, BCE acquired 40 percent and was presumed to have significant influence over the investee. Therefore, BCE must use the equity method to account for this investment. The purchase of the asset would be recorded at cost:

Investments in associates (A)		400,000	
Cash (A)			400,000
Assets	=	**Liabilities** +	**Shareholders' Equity**
Investments in associates	+400,000		
Cash	−400,000		

Earnings and Other Comprehensive Income of Associates   Because the investor can influence the process of generating earnings for the associate, the investor company bases its investment income on the associate's earnings rather than on the dividends it pays. Suppose that during 2016 GWA reported profit of $500,000 for the year. BCE's percentage share of GWA's profit would be $200,000 (40% × $500,000) and would be recorded as follows:

Investments in associates (A)		200,000	
Equity in associate earnings (R, SE)			200,000
Assets	=	**Liabilities** +	**Shareholders' Equity**
Investments in associates			Equity in earnings of associates
+200,000			+200,000

If the associate reports a loss for the period, the investor records its percentage share of the loss by decreasing the investment account and recording an "equity in associate" loss. The equity in earnings (or loss) of associates is usually reported as a separate item in the non-operating section of the statement of earnings, with interest revenue, interest expense, and gains and losses on sales of assets. BCE reports its share of earnings from its investments accounted for at equity in Note 8 to its financial statements:

Notes to consolidated financial statements
Note 8. Other (expense) income

For the year ended December 31	2015	2014
Losses on disposal/retirement of software, plant, and equipment	(55)	(51)
Impairment of assets	(49)	(105)
Equity (losses) income from investments in associates and joint ventures		
Loss on investment	(54)	–
Operations	5	(12)
Early debt redemption costs	(18)	(29)
Gains on investments	72	10
Net mark-to-market gains on derivatives used as economic hedges	54	134
Dividend income from assets held for sale	–	42
Other	33	53
Total other (expense) income	(12)	42

Source: BCE Inc., 2015 Annual Report.

Dividends Received   Because BCE can influence the dividend policies of its associates, any dividends it receives should not be recorded as investment income. Instead, dividends received reduce its investment account. Suppose that, during 2016, GWA declared and paid a cash dividend of $2 per share. BCE would receive $80,000 in cash ($2 × 40,000 shares) from GWA:

Cash (A)	80,000	
Investments in associates (A)		80,000

Assets	=	Liabilities	+	Shareholders' Equity
Cash	+80,000			
Investments in associates	−80,000			

In summary, the effects for 2016 are reflected in the following T-accounts:

Investments in Associates (A)

1/1/16	0		
Purchase	400,000		
Share of associate's net earnings	200,000	80,000	Share of associate's dividends
31/12/16	520,000		

Equity in Earnings of Associates (R)

	0		1/1/16
	200,000	Share of associate's net earnings	
	200,000		

Reporting Investments under the Equity Method

The investments in associates account is reported on the statement of financial position as a non-current asset. However, as these last two entries show, the balance of the investment account does not reflect either the cost of the investment or its fair value. Instead, the following occurs:

- The investment account is increased by the cost of shares that were purchased and the proportional share of the associate's net earnings.

- The account is reduced by the amount of dividends received from the associate and the proportional share of any losses reported by the associate.

- The account is adjusted for the proportionate share of the associated company's other comprehensive income (loss).

When the securities are sold, the difference between the cash received and the carrying amount of the investment is recorded as a gain or loss on the sale of the asset and reported on the statement of earnings in the non-operating section.

Subsequent to the acquisition of equity investments and recognition of the associate's net earnings or loss, the investor must test for impairment of the value of the investment. For the purpose of impairment testing, the carrying amount of the investment is compared to its recoverable amount.[9] An impairment loss is recognized through the statement of earnings. An impairment loss can be reversed in the future if the recoverable amount increases in subsequent periods. BCE provided a summary of its investments in associated companies and joint ventures in Note 15 to its financial statements. These investments were not profitable during 2015; BCE's share of the losses reported by the investee companies is $49 million.

REAL-WORLD EXCERPT

BCE Inc.

ANNUAL REPORT

Notes to consolidated financial statements

Note 15. Investments in associates and joint ventures

The following table provides summarized financial information in respect to BCE's associates and joint ventures. For a list of associates and joint ventures please see Note 28, Related party transactions.

For the year ended December 31	Note	2015	2014
Assets		5,067	3,910
Liabilities		(2,699)	(2,202)
Total Net assets		2,368	1,708
BCE's share of net assets		1,119	776
Revenues		2,125	871
Expenses		(2,261)	(918)
Total net losses		(136)	(47)
BCE's share of net losses	8	(49)	(12)

Source: BCE Inc., Consolidated Financial Statements 2015.

STRUCTURING INVESTMENT TRANSACTIONS AND SELECTING ACCOUNTING METHODS FOR INVESTMENTS   A QUESTION OF ACCOUNTABILITY

Managers can choose between FIFO and weighted-average cost, or accelerated depreciation and straight-line depreciation. In the case of minority (≤ 50 percent owned) investments, investments of less than 20 percent of a company's outstanding voting shares are usually accounted for under the fair value method, and the purchase of 20 to 50 percent of the outstanding voting shares of a corporation is accounted for under the equity method.

However, managers may be able to structure the acquisition of shares in a manner that permits them to use the accounting method that they prefer. For example, a company that wants to use the fair value method could purchase only 19.9 percent of the outstanding voting shares of another company and achieve the same investment goals as they would with a 20 percent investment. Why might managers want to avoid using the equity method? Most managers prefer to minimize variations in reported earnings. If a company were planning to buy shares in a firm that reported large earnings in some years and large losses in other years, it might want to use the fair value method to avoid reporting its share of the associate's net earnings and losses.

Analysts who compare several companies must understand management's reporting choices and the way in which differences between the fair value and equity methods can affect earnings.

STOP   PAUSE FOR FEEDBACK

Significant influence over an associate's operating and financing policies is presumed when an investor owns between 20 and 50 percent of the outstanding voting shares of the associate. Such investments are reported using the equity method. Under the equity method, the investor records the investment at cost on the acquisition date. Each period thereafter, the investment amount is increased (or decreased) by the proportionate interest in the net earnings (or loss) reported by the associate and decreased by the proportionate share of the dividends declared by that corporation. Test your understanding of the equity method before you move on.

Answer the following questions using the T-accounts to help you infer the amounts. Dollar amounts are in thousands.

Investments in Associates (A)

1/1/2017	246.3		
Purchase of shares	157.0		
Share of associates' net earnings	?	16.6	Share of associates' dividends
31/12/2017	419.7		

Equity in Earnings of Associates (R)

		0	1/1/2017
		?	Share of associates' net earnings
		?	31/12/2017

a. Purchased investments in associated companies for cash. Record the purchase.

b. Received cash dividends on the investments. Record the receipt of dividends.

c. At year-end, the investments in associated companies had a fair value of $434.0; the associates also reported $110.0 in net earnings for the year. Prepare the adjusting entry.

d. What information related to the investments in associates would be reported on the statement of financial position at December 31, 2017? What amounts would be reported on the statement of earnings for 2017?

After you complete your answers, check them with the solutions at the end of the chapter.

INVESTMENTS

FOCUS ON
CASH FLOWS

Many of the effects from measuring passive investments at fair value, and from using the equity method to account for investments held to exercise significant influence in associated companies, affect net earnings but not cash flows. These items require adjustments under the indirect method when converting net earnings to cash flows from operating activities.

In General → Investments have a number of effects on the statement of cash flows:

1. The cash resulting from the sale or purchase of investments is reflected in the investing activities section.

2. In the operating activities section, there are a number of adjustments to net earnings:

   a. Any gain (loss) on the sale of investments is subtracted from (added to) net earnings.

   b. Any unrealized holding gain (loss) on investments at FVTPL is subtracted from (added to) net earnings.

   c. Equity in net earnings (losses) of associates is subtracted from (added to) net earnings because no cash was involved in the recording of the investment income under the equity method.

   d. Any dividends received from an associate are added to net earnings because, when cash was received, no income was recorded under the equity method.

Effect on Statement of Cash Flows

	Effect on Cash Flows
Operating Activities	
Net earnings	$xxx
Adjusted for	
Gains/losses on sale of investments	−/+
Equity in net earnings/losses of associates	−/+
Net unrealized holding gains/losses on investments at FVTPL	−/+
Dividends received from associates	+
Investing Activities	
Purchase of investments	−
Sale of investments	+

Focus Company Analysis → A partial statement of cash flows for BCE for fiscal year 2015 follows. In the operating activities section, BCE did not report separately the adjustments made to net earnings as a result of it investments. In the investing activities section, BCE reported new business acquisitions. It also divested from other businesses which resulted in cash inflows that exceeded the cash paid for business acquisitions in both 2015 and 2014.

Consolidated Statements of Cash Flows for the year ended December 31

(in millions of Canadian dollars)	Note	2015	2014
Cash flows from operating activities			
Net earnings		2,730	2,718
Adjustments for:			
Severance, acquisition, and other costs	6	446	216
Depreciation and amortization	13, 14	3,420	3,452
Post-employment benefit plans cost	21	391	377
Net interest expense		900	921
Gains on investments	8	(72)	(10)
Income taxes	9	924	929
Contributions to post-employment benefit plans	21	(566)	(683)
Payments under other post-employment benefit plans	21	(75)	(73)
Severance and other costs paid		(190)	(190)
Interest paid		(911)	(907)
Income taxes paid (net of refunds)		(672)	(743)
Acquisition and other costs paid		(292)	(131)
Net change in operating assets and liabilities		241	365
Cash flows from operating activities		6,274	6,241
Cash flows used in investing activities			
Capital expenditures	4	(3,626)	(3,717)
Business acquisitions	3	(311)	(18)
Business dispositions	3	409	720
Acquisition of spectrum licenses	14	(535)	(566)
Other investing activities		(51)	11
Cash flows used in investing activities		(4,114)	(3,570)

Source: BCE Inc., Consolidated Financial Statements 2015.

CONTROLLING INTERESTS: MERGERS AND ACQUISITIONS

Before we discuss financial reporting issues for situations in which a company owns more than 50 percent of the voting rights of another entity, we should consider management's reasons for acquiring this level of ownership. The following are some of the reasons for acquiring control of another corporation:

1. **Vertical integration**—In this type of acquisition, a company acquires another at a different level in the channels of distribution.

2. **Horizontal growth**—These acquisitions involve companies at the same level in the channels of distribution.

3. **Synergy**—The operations of two companies together may be more profitable than the combined profitability of the companies as separate entities.

Understanding why one company has acquired control over other companies is a key factor in understanding the company's overall business strategy.

What Are Consolidated Statements?

The **PARENT COMPANY** is the entity that gains control over another company.

The **SUBSIDIARY COMPANY** is the entity that is acquired by the parent.

Any corporate acquisition involves two companies. The **parent company** is the company that gains control over the other company. The **subsidiary company** is the company that the parent acquires. When one company acquires control over another, **consolidated financial statements** must be presented. These statements combine the operations of the parent and its subsidiaries into a single set of statements. Basically, consolidated statements can be thought of as the adding together of the separate financial statements for two or more companies to make it appear as if a single company exists. Thus, the cash accounts for each company are added together, as are the inventory accounts, land accounts, and others.

The notes to BCE's 2015 annual report provide the following information:

REAL-WORLD EXCERPT

BCE Inc.

ANNUAL REPORT

Notes to consolidated financial statements

2—Significant accounting policies

(b) Basis of consolidation

We consolidate the financial statements of all of our subsidiaries. Subsidiaries are entities we control, where control is achieved when the company is exposed or has the right to variable returns from its involvement with the investee and has the current ability to direct the activities of the investee that significantly affect the investee's returns.

The results of subsidiaries acquired during the year are consolidated from the date of acquisition and the results of subsidiaries sold during the year are deconsolidated from the date of disposal. Where necessary, adjustments are made to the financial statements of acquired subsidiaries to conform their accounting policies to ours. All intercompany transactions, balances, income, and expenses are eliminated on consolidation.

Changes in BCE's ownership interest in a subsidiary that do not result in a change of control are accounted for as equity transactions, with no effect on net earnings or on other comprehensive income.

Source: BCE Inc., 2015 Annual Report.

As the note indicates, eliminating any intercompany items is necessary when consolidated statements are prepared. *Remember that consolidated statements make it appear as though a single company exists when in fact there are two or more separate legal entities.* Consolidation is an example of accounting for the economic substance of transactions rather than the legal form. Intercompany items do not exist for a single corporation. For example, a debt owed by BCE (the parent) to its subsidiary Bell Media Inc. is not reported on a consolidated statement because a company cannot owe itself money.

Recording a Business Acquisition

We learned that consolidated statements are presented in such a way that two companies appear to have combined into one. In fact, the simplest way to understand the statements that result from the consolidation process is to consider the case of a company that purchases all of the net assets (assets minus liabilities) of another, and the target company ceases to exist as a separate company. In such a situation, the purchasing company records the net assets of the target company at their fair value along with goodwill, if any.

To illustrate, we will use simplified data for BCE (the purchaser) and GWA (the hypothetical target). Let us assume that on January 1, 2016, BCE paid $100 (all numbers in millions) in cash to acquire the net assets of GWA. It then combines GWA's operations into its own operations, and GWA ceases to exist as a separate legal entity. Exhibit 13.4 presents BCE and GWA's statements of financial position and fair value data for GWA's assets and liabilities immediately *before* the acquisition.

Note that BCE paid $100 for 100 percent of GWA even though the total carrying amount of GWA's net assets was only $80 ($90 assets − $10 liabilities). This is not surprising, because *the carrying amounts of a company's net assets are not the same as their fair value.* We will assume that an analysis of GWA's assets and liabilities on the date of acquisition revealed the following facts:

- GWA's plant and equipment had a fair value of $35 million (net carrying amount of $30 million).

- The carrying amounts of other non-current assets ($60 million) and current liabilities ($10 million) on GWA's statement of financial position were equal to their fair values.

- GWA had developed a good reputation with an important group of investors, which increased GWA's overall value. For these reasons, BCE was willing to pay an additional $15 million to acquire GWA. The $15 million difference between the purchase price of the company and the fair value of its net assets is called **goodwill (cost in excess of net assets acquired)**. It may be computed as follows (amounts in millions):

> For accounting purposes, **GOODWILL (COST IN EXCESS OF NET ASSETS ACQUIRED)** is the excess of the purchase price of a business over the market value of its identifiable assets and liabilities.

Purchase price for GWA	$100
Less: Net assets purchased, at fair value ($35 + $60 − $10)	85
Goodwill purchased	$ 15

As noted, the assets and liabilities of GWA are recorded by BCE on its books at the purchase price (fair value) on the date of acquisition. This method of recording acquisitions, called the **acquisition method**, is the only method allowed under IFRS. BCE would record the acquisition as follows:

> The **ACQUISITION METHOD** records assets and liabilities acquired at their fair values.

Exhibit 13.4

Statements of Financial Position Immediately before the Acquisition

(In millions of dollars)		**GWA**	
	BCE	**Carrying Amount**	**Fair Value**
Assets			
Cash and other current assets	$1,960		
Plant and equipment (net)	2,703	$30	$35
Other non-current assets	2,477	$60	$60
Total assets	$7,140	$90	
Liabilities and Shareholders' Equity			
Current liabilities	$1,925	$10	$10
Non-current liabilities	1,457		
Shareholders' equity	3,758	$80	
Total liabilities and shareholders' equity	$7,140	$90	

Plant and equipment (net) (A)	35	
Other non-current assets (A)	60	
Goodwill (A)	15	
Current liabilities (L)		10
Cash (A)		100

Assets		=	**Liabilities**	+	**Shareholders' Equity**
Plant and equipment (net)	+35		Current liabilities +10		
Other non-current assets	+60				
Goodwill	+15				
Cash	−100				

It is important to remember that goodwill can be reported on the statement of financial position *only if it is the result of a business acquisition*.

Reporting for the Combined Companies

Post-acquisition Statement of Financial Position   The post-acquisition statement of financial position shown in Exhibit 13.5 was prepared by combining the preceding journal entry with BCE's statement of financial position shown in Exhibit 13.4. Remember the following:

1. GWA's assets and liabilities are added at their fair values, not their carrying amounts.

2. Goodwill = Purchase price − Net assets purchased (at their fair prices).

3. The cash payment made for the acquisition is subtracted from cash on the statement of financial position.

Post-acquisition Statement of Earnings After the merger, BCE's accounting system will capture all of the revenues and expenses of the combined company. The resulting statement of earnings is presented in Exhibit 13.6. The combined amounts include the following:

1. Revenues that would have been recorded in the separate accounting systems had the combination not taken place (BCE's $17,613 + GWA's $120 = $17,733).

2. Expenses that would have been recorded in the separate accounting systems had the combination not taken place (BCE's $17,219 + GWA's $106 = $17,325).

3. Additional expenses related to the recording of GWA's assets and liabilities at fair value; $1 additional depreciation expense, assuming a five-year useful life ($5 excess of fair value of additional plant and equipment over their carrying amounts ÷ 5 years = $1 per year).[10]

Exhibit **13.5**

BCE's Statement of Financial Position Immediately after the Acquisition

(in millions of dollars)	BCE
Assets	
Cash and other current assets (1,960 − 100)	$1,860
Plant and equipment (net) (2,703 + 35)	2,738
Other assets (2,477 + 60)	2,537
Goodwill (100 − 85)	15
Total assets	**$7,150**
Liabilities and shareholders' equity	
Current liabilities (1,925 + 10)	$1,935
Non-current liabilities	1,457
Shareholders' equity	3,758
Total liabilities and shareholders' equity	**$7,150**

Exhibit **13.6**

BCE's Statement of Earnings for the Year Following Acquisition

(in millions of dollars)	BCE
Revenues (17,613 + 120)	$17,733
Expenses (17,219 + 106 + 1)	17,326
Net earnings	$ 407

Again, it is important to remember that the statement of earnings would be the same if BCE and GWA continued as separate legal entities after the acquisition and consolidated statements were prepared.

As we noted in Chapter 8, goodwill is considered to have an indefinite life. As a consequence, it is not amortized, but like all long-lived assets, goodwill is reviewed for possible impairment of value. Recording an impairment loss would increase expenses for the period and reduce the amount of goodwill on the statement of financial position. BCE described its accounting for goodwill in its recent annual report:

REAL-WORLD EXCERPT

BCE Inc.

ANNUAL REPORT

Notes to consolidated financial statements

n) Impairment of non-financial assets

...

GOODWILL IMPAIRMENT TESTING

We perform an annual test for goodwill impairment in the fourth quarter for each of our cash generating units (CGUs) or groups of CGUs to which goodwill is allocated, and whenever there is an indication that goodwill might be impaired.

A CGU is the smallest identifiable group of assets that generates cash inflows that are independent of the cash inflows from other assets or groups of assets.

We identify any potential impairment by comparing the carrying value of a CGU or group of CGUs to its recoverable amount. The recoverable amount of a CGU or group of CGUs is the higher of its fair value less costs of disposal and its value in use. Fair value less costs of disposal is based on estimates of discounted future cash flows or other valuation methods. Cash flows are projected based on past experience, actual operating results and business plans. When the recoverable amount of a CGU or group of CGUs is less than its carrying value, the recoverable amount is determined for its identifiable assets and liabilities. The excess of the recoverable amount of the CGU or group of CGUs over the total of the amounts assigned to its assets and liabilities is the recoverable amount of goodwill.

An impairment charge is deducted from earnings for any excess of the carrying value of goodwill over its recoverable amount. For purposes of impairment testing of goodwill, BCE's CGUs or groups of CGUs correspond to our reporting segments as disclosed in Note 4, Segmented information.

Source: BCE Inc., 2015 Annual Report.

PAUSE FOR FEEDBACK

Purchase of the net assets of another business must be accounted for using the acquisition method. The acquired company's assets and liabilities are measured at their fair values. Any amount paid above the fair value of the net assets is reported as goodwill by the buyer. To make sure you understand how to apply these concepts, answer the following questions.

SELF-STUDY **QUIZ 13-4**

Lexis Corporation purchased the net assets of Nexis Company for $9 million. On the date of the acquisition, the fair value of Nexis's other assets account was $11, and the carrying amounts of Nexis's liabilities were equal to their fair values. The summary statements of financial position of the two companies appeared as follows immediately *before* the acquisition:

	Lexis	Nexis
Cash	$10	
Other assets	90	$10
Liabilities	30	4
Shareholders' equity	70	6

Compute the balances of the following accounts of Lexis Corporation after the acquisition is recorded:

1. Goodwill

2. Shareholders' equity

3. Other assets (excluding goodwill)

After you complete your answers, check them with the solutions at the end of this chapter.

ACCOUNTING STANDARDS
FOR PRIVATE ENTERPRISES

Unlike Canadian publicly accountable enterprises, which are required to comply with IFRS, Canadian private enterprises may use simplified accounting and reporting requirements when accounting for investments in shares of other corporations. The main differences in accounting standards related to the accounting and reporting of investments in other corporations are summarized below:

Financial Reporting Issue	IFRS	ASPE
Changes in fair values of investments	Publicly accountable enterprises must report such changes in the financial statements.	Private enterprises need only report changes in fair values of equity securities if they are traded on exchange markets.
Reporting of investments with significant influence	Corporations must account for their investments in associates using the equity method.	Investments in associates may be accounted for using either the equity method or the fair value method. If the associate's shares are not traded on exchange markets, the cost method may be used instead of the fair value method.
Consolidation of financial statements	Publicly accountable enterprises must consolidate the financial statements of all the subsidiaries that are under their control.	Canadian private enterprises may choose not to consolidate the financial statements of the companies that they control. They may opt for simpler financial reporting methods (cost method, equity method, or fair value method) because it is not clear whether the reporting requirements prescribed by IFRS would provide useful information to users of the financial statements of private enterprises.

DEMONSTRATION **CASE A**

Howell Equipment Corporation sells and services a major line of farm equipment. Both sales and service operations have been profitable. The following transactions affected the company during 2017:

Jan. 1   Purchased 2,000 common shares of Dear Company at $40 per share to be held as SAS. This purchase represented 1 percent of Dear's outstanding shares.
Dec. 28   Received $4,000 cash dividend on the Dear Company shares.
Dec. 31   Determined that the market price of Dear's common shares was $39.

Required:

1. Prepare the journal entry for each of these transactions.

2. What accounts and amounts will be reported on the statement of financial position at the end of 2017? On the statement of earnings for 2017?

3. Assuming management intends to trade these shares actively instead of holding them as SAS, what accounts and amounts will be reported on the statement of financial position at the end of 2017? On the statement of earnings for 2017?

We strongly recommend that you prepare your own answers to these requirements and then check your answers with the following solution.

SUGGESTED **SOLUTION**

1.

Jan. 1	Investments in SAS (+A)	80,000	
	Cash (−A) (2,000 shares × $40)		80,000
Dec. 28	Cash (+A)	4,000	
	Investment income (+R, +SE)		4,000
Dec. 31	Net unrealized gains/losses–Investments in SAS (+Loss, −SE)	2,000	
	Investments in SAS (−A)		2,000

Fiscal Year	Fair Value	−	Carrying Amount before Adjustment	=	Amount for Adjusting Entry
2017	$78,000	−	$80,000	=	$(2,000)
	($39 × 2,000)		($40,000 × 2,000)		An unrealized loss for the period

2.

On the Statement of Financial Position:		**On the Statement of Earnings:**	
Current or Non-current Assets		*Other Non-operating Items*	
Investments in SAS	$78,000	Investment income	$4,000
($80,000 cost – $2,000 adjustment)			
Shareholders' Equity			
Accumulated other comprehensive income			
Net unrealized loss	($2,000)		

3.

On the Statement of Financial Position:		**On the Statement of Earnings:**	
Current Assets		*Other Non-operating Items*	
Investments at FVTPL	$78,000	Investment income	$4,000
($80,000 cost – $2,000 adjustment)		Net unrealized loss on investments at FVTPL	(2.000)

DEMONSTRATION **CASE B**

On January 1, 2018, Connaught Company purchased 40 percent of the outstanding voting shares of London Company on the open market, for $85,000 cash. London declared $10,000 in cash dividends and reported net earnings of $60,000 for the year.

Required:

1. Prepare the journal entries for 2018.

2. What accounts and amounts will be reported on the statement of financial position at the end of 2018? On the statement of earnings for 2018?

We strongly recommend that you prepare your own answers to these requirements and then check your answers with the following solution.

SUGGESTED **SOLUTION**

1.

Jan. 1	Investments in associates (A)	85,000	
	Cash (A)		85,000
Dividends	Cash (A) ($10,000 × 40%)	4,000	
	Investments in associates (A)		4,000
Dec. 31	Investments in associates (A) ($60,000 × 40%)	24,000	
	Equity in earnings of associates (R, SE)		24,000

2.

On the Statement of Financial Position:		**On the Statement of Earnings:**	
Non-current assets		*Other Non-operating items*	
Investments in associates	$105,000	Equity in earnings of associates	$24,000
($85,000 – $4,000 + $24,000)			

DEMONSTRATION **CASE C**

On January 1, 2018, Hilton Company purchased the net assets of Paris Company in the open market for $85,000 cash. On the date of acquisition, the fair value of Paris Company's property, plant, and equipment was $89,000 and the fair value of a note payable was $10,000. Hilton had no other assets or liabilities.

Required:

1. Analyze the acquisition to determine the amount of goodwill purchased.

2. Prepare the journal entry that Hilton Company should make on the date of the acquisition.

3. Should Paris Company's assets be included on Hilton's statement of financial position at their carrying amounts or fair values?

We strongly recommend that you prepare your own answers to these requirements and then check your answers with the following solution.

SUGGESTED **SOLUTION**

1.

Purchase price for Paris Company	$85,000
Less: Fair value of net assets purchased	79,000
Goodwill	$ 6,000

2.

Jan. 1, 2018	Property, plant, and equipment (A)	89,000	
	Goodwill (A)	6,000	
	Note payable (L)		10,000
	Cash (A)		85,000

3. Paris Company's assets should be included on the post-acquisition statement of financial position at their fair values as of the date of acquisition.

CHAPTER **TAKE-AWAYS**

13-1. Analyze and report bond investments in debt securities held to maturity.

When management intends to hold a bond investment until it matures, the held-to-maturity bond is recorded at cost when acquired and reported at amortized cost on the statement of financial position. Any interest earned during the period is reported on the statement of earnings.

13-2. Analyze and report passive investments in securities using the fair value method.

Acquiring less than 20 percent of the outstanding voting shares of an investee's common shares is presumed to be a passive investment. Passive investments may be classified in one of two categories depending on management's intent: investments at FVTPL (actively traded to maximize return) or available-for-sale investments (earn a return but are not as actively traded).

- The investments are recorded at cost and adjusted to fair value at year-end. The investments account is increased or decreased to arrive at their fair value, and an unrealized holding gain or loss is recorded.
- For investments at FVTPL, the net unrealized gains and losses are reported on the statement of earnings.
- For available-for-sale investments, the net unrealized gains and losses are reported as a component of shareholders' equity in other comprehensive income.

Any dividends earned are reported as income, and any gains or losses on sales of passive investments are reported on the statement of earnings.

13-3. Analyze and report investments involving significant influence using the equity method.

If between 20 and 50 percent of the outstanding voting shares are owned, significant influence over the investee firm's operating and financing policies is presumed, and the equity method is applied. Under the equity method, the investor records the investment at cost on the acquisition date. Each period thereafter, the investment amount is increased (or decreased) by the proportionate interest in the net earnings (or loss) reported by the associated corporation and decreased by the proportionate share of the dividends declared by the associated corporation.

The investing activities section of the statement of cash flows discloses purchases and sales of investments. In the operating section, net earnings are adjusted for any gains or losses on sales of investments and equity in the earnings of associated corporations (net of dividends received).

13-4. Analyze and report investments in controlling interests.

Acquisition of a controlling interest of another corporation (more than 50 percent of the outstanding voting shares) must be accounted for using the acquisition method. The acquired company's assets and liabilities are measured at their fair values. Any amount paid above the fair value of the net assets is reported as goodwill by the investor. The concept of consolidation is based on the view that a parent company and its subsidiaries constitute one economic entity. Therefore, the separate statement of earnings, statements of financial position, and statements of cash flows should be combined each period on an item-by-item basis as a single set of consolidated financial statements. Consolidated statements are the same as those that result from a business acquisition, when all of the assets and liabilities are acquired and the target company ceases to exist.

KEY **RATIO**

Economic return from investing measures the performance of a company's securities portfolio. Investment returns include both dividends received and any change in the fair value of the securities. A high or rising ratio suggests that a firm's securities portfolio is improving. It is computed as follows:

$$\text{Economic return from investing} = \frac{\text{Dividends and interest received} + \text{Change in fair value*}}{\text{Fair value of investments (beginning of period)}}$$

*Beginning balance of investments − Ending balance of investments

FINDING **FINANCIAL INFORMATION**

STATEMENT OF FINANCIAL POSITION
Current Assets
Investments at FVPTL
Investments in SAS
Non-current Assets
Investments in SAS
Shareholders' Equity
Accumulated other comprehensive income:
Net unrealized gains and losses on investments in SAS

STATEMENT OF EARNINGS
Under "Non-operating Items"
Investment income
Loss or gain on sale of investments
Net unrealized gains and losses on investments at FVPTL
Equity in net earnings (or losses) of associates

STATEMENT OF CASH FLOWS
Operating Activities
Net earnings adjusted for:
Gains/losses on sale of investments
Equity in earnings/losses of associates
Dividends received from associates
Net unrealized gains/losses on investments at FVTPL

NOTES
In Various Notes
Accounting policies for investments
Details on passive investments and investments in associates

QUESTIONS

1. Explain the difference between a short-term and a long-term investment.
2. Explain the difference in accounting methods used for passive investments, investments in which the investor can exert significant influence, and investments in which the investor has control over another entity.
3. Explain how bonds held to maturity are reported on the statement of financial position.
4. Explain the application of the cost principle to the purchase of common shares in another company.
5. When and how does the investor company measure investment income under the fair value method?
6. When the equity method is used, why does the investor company measure investment income on a proportionate basis when net earnings is reported by the associated corporation rather than when dividends are declared?

7. When the equity method is used, dividends received from the associated corporation are not recorded as investment income. To record dividends as revenue involves double counting. Explain.

8. When one company acquires control of another, how are the acquired company's assets and liabilities recorded?

9. What is goodwill?

10. What is a parent–subsidiary relationship?

11. Explain the basic concept underlying consolidated statements.

12. What is the basic element that must be present before consolidated statements are appropriate?

connect MINI-EXERCISES

LO13-1,13-2,13-3,13-4

M13-1

Matching Measurement and Reporting Methods

Match the following. Answers may be used more than once:

Measurement Method

A. Amortized cost	___ 1. Less than 20 percent ownership.
B. Equity method	___ 2. Current fair value.
C. Purchase method and consolidation	___ 3. More than 50 percent ownership.
	___ 4. At least 20 percent but not more than 50 percent ownership.
D. Fair value method	___ 5. Bonds held to maturity.
	___ 6. Original cost less any amortization of premium or discount with the purchase.
	___ 7. Original cost plus proportionate part of the earnings of the associate, less proportionate part of the dividends declared by the associate.

LO13-1

M13-2

Recording a Bond Investment

James Company purchased $800,000, 8 percent bonds issued by Heidi Company on January 1, 2017. The purchase price of the bonds was $900,000. Interest is payable semi-annually each June 30 and December 31. Record the purchase of the bonds on January 1, 2017.

LO13-2

M13-3

Recording Available-for-Sale Securities Transactions

During 2017, Jamar Company acquired some of the 50,000 outstanding common shares of Anglis Corporation as investments available for sale. The accounting period for both companies ends December 31. Prepare the journal entries for each of the following transactions that occurred during 2017:

Dec. 2 Purchased 6,250 shares of Anglis common shares at $15 per share.

Dec. 15 Anglis Corporation declared and paid a cash dividend of $2 per share.

Dec. 31 Determined the current market price of Anglis's shares to be $12 per share.

LO13-2

M13-4

Recording Trading Securities Transactions

Using the data in M13-3, assume that Jamar Company purchased the voting shares of Anglis Corporation for the portfolio of securities held for trading instead of holding them in their portfolio of investments available for sale. Prepare the journal entries for each of the transactions listed. M13-3, assume that Jamar Company purchased the voting shares of Anglis Corporation for the portfolio of securities held for trading instead of holding them in their portfolio of investments available for sale. Prepare the journal entries for each of the transactions listed.

LO13-2

M13-5

Determining Financial Statement Effects of Available-for-Sale Securities Transactions

Using the following categories, indicate the effects of the transactions listed in M13-3 assuming the securities are available for sale. Use + for increase and − for decrease, and indicate the amounts.

	Statement of Financial Position			Statement of Earnings		
Transaction	Assets	Liabilities	Shareholders' Equity	Revenues/ Gains	Expenses/ Losses	Net Earnings

LO13-2

M13-6

Determining Financial Statement Effects of Trading Securities Transactions

Using the following categories, indicate the effects of the transactions listed in M13-3 assuming the securities are trading securities. Use + for increase and − for decrease and indicate the amounts.

	Statement of Financial Position			Statement of Earnings		
Transaction	Assets	Liabilities	Shareholders' Equity	Revenues/ Gains	Expenses/ Losses	Net Earnings

LO13-3 **M13-7** **Recording Equity Method Securities Transactions**

On January 1, 2018, PurchaseAgent.com acquired 35 percent (800,000 shares) of the common shares of E-Transaction Corporation. The accounting period for both companies ends December 31. Prepare the journal entries for each of the following transactions that occurred during 2018 for PurchaseAgent.com:

July 2   E-Transaction declared and paid a cash dividend of $5 per share.

Dec. 31   E-Transaction reported net earnings of $400,000.

LO13-3 **M13-8** **Determining Financial Statement Effects of Equity Method Securities**

Using the following categories, indicate the effects of the transactions listed in M13-7. Use + for increase and − for decrease and indicate the amounts.

	Statement of Financial Position			Statement of Earnings		
Transaction	Assets	Liabilities	Shareholders' Equity	Revenues/ Gains	Expenses/ Losses	Net Earnings

LO13-4 **M13-9** **Recording a Merger**

England Textile Company acquired Belgium Fabric Company for $660,000 cash when Belgium's only assets, property and equipment, had a book value of $660,000 and a fair value of $750,000. England also assumed Belgium's bonds payable of $175,000. After the merger, Belgium would cease to exist as a separate legal entity. Record the acquisition.

LO13-4 **M13-10** **Computing and Interpreting Economic Return from Investing Ratio**

N.M.S. Company held available-for-sale securities and reported the following information at the end of each year:

Year	Dividend Revenue	Ending Fair Value of Investments
2017	$1,500	$64,000
2018	3,000	70,000
2019	4,200	82,000
2020	3,500	80,000

Compute the economic return from investing ratio for 2018, 2019, and 2020. What do the results suggest about N.M.S. Company?

LO13-4 **M13-11** **Interpreting Goodwill Disclosures**

The Walt Disney Company owns theme parks, movie studios, television and radio stations, newspapers, and television networks, including ABC and ESPN. Its statement of financial position recently reported goodwill in the amount of $24 billion, which is almost 35 percent of the company's total assets. This percentage is very large compared to that of most companies. Explain why you think Disney has such a large amount of goodwill reported on its statement of financial position.

connect EXERCISES

LO13-1 **E13-1** **Recording Bonds Held to Maturity**

Canadian Tire Corporation

Canadian Tire Corporation is Canada's largest retailer of sporting goods, offering a comprehensive assortment of products, operating stores from coast to coast under the names Sport Chek, Sports Experts, Coast Mountain Sports, Sport Mart, and National Sports. Revenues from selling sporting goods are in excess of $1.6 billion each year.

Assume that as part of its cash management strategy, Canadian Tire purchased $10 million in bonds at par for cash on July 1, 2018. The bonds pay 5 percent interest each June 30 and December 31 and mature in 10 years. Canadian Tire plans to hold the bonds until maturity.

Required:

1. Record the purchase of the bonds on July 1, 2018.

2. Record the receipt of interest on December 31, 2018.

LO13-2,13-3   **E13-2**   **Comparing Fair Value and Equity Methods**

Company A purchased a certain number of Company B's outstanding voting shares at $19 per share as a non-current investment. Company B had 20,000 shares outstanding. Complete the following matrix relating to the measurement and reporting by Company A after acquisition of the shares of Company B:

Question	Fair Value Method	Equity Method
a. What is the applicable level of ownership by Company A of Company B to apply the method?	____ %	____ %
For (b), (e), (f), and (g), assume the following:		
Number of Company B shares acquired	1,000	5,000
Net earnings reported by Company B in the first year	$50,000	$50,000
Dividends declared by Company B in the first year	10,000	10,000
Market price per share at end of first year, Company B	15	15

b. At acquisition, the debit to the investment account on the books of Company A should equal.

$_____ $_____

c. When should Company A recognize income earned on the investment in shares of Company B? Explain.

_____   _____

d. After the acquisition date, how should Company A change the balance of the investment account with respect to the shares owned in Company B (other than for disposal of the investment)? Explain.

_____   _____

e. What is the net balance in the investment account on the statement of financial position of Company A at the end of the first year?

_____   _____

f. What amount of income from the investment in Company B should Company A report at the end of the first year?

_____   _____

g. What amount of unrealized loss should Company A report at the end of the first year?

_____   _____

LO13-2   **E13-3**   **Recording Transactions in the Portfolio of Securities Held for Trading**

On June 30, 2017, MetroMedia Inc. purchased 10,000 of Mitek's common shares for $20 per share. Management purchased the shares for speculative purposes and designated them as investments at FVPTL. The following information pertains to Mitek's price per share:

Date	Price
31/12/2017	$24
31/12/2018	31
31/12/2019	25

MetroMedia sold its investment in Mitek's shares on February 14, 2020, at a price of $22 per share. Prepare any journal entries that are required by the facts presented in this case.

LO13-2   **E13-4**   **Recording Transactions in the Portfolio of SAS**

Using the data in E13-3, assume that MetroMedia management designated Mitek's shares as an investment in SAS instead of investments at FVTPL. Prepare any journal entries that are required by the facts presented in the case.

LO13-2   **E13-5**   **Recording Passive Investments in Securities and Determining Financial Statement Effects**

On June 30, 2017, Forlini Company acquired some of the 50,000 outstanding common shares of Como Corporation. The fiscal years for both companies end on December 31. The following transactions occurred during 2017:

Dec. 2   Purchased 8,000 shares of Como common stock at $28 per share.

Dec. 15   Como Corporation declared and paid a cash dividend of $2 per share.

Dec. 31   Determined that the current market price of Como stock was $25 per share.

Required:

1. Assume that Forlini Company purchased Como's shares for trading purposes. Prepare the journal entries to record each of the transactions listed above.

2. Assume that Forlini Company purchased Como's shares for inclusion in its available-for-sale portfolio. Prepare the journal entries for the same transactions above.

3. Using the following categories, indicate the effects of each transaction assuming that Como's shares are (a) held for trading and (b) purchased as an investment of SAS.

Transaction	Statement of Financial Position			Statement of Earnings		
	Assets	Liabilities	Shareholders' Equity	Revenues	Expenses	Net Earnings
Shares at FVTPL						
Dec. 2						
Dec. 15						
Dec. 31						
Shares available for sale						
Dec. 2						
Dec. 15						
Dec. 31						

LO13-2   **E13-6**   **Reporting Gains and Losses in Passive Investments in Securities**

On March 10, 2017, General Solutions Inc. purchased 5,000 of MicroTech's common shares for $50 per share. The following information pertains to MicroTech's price per share:

Date	Price
31/12/2017	$55
31/12/2018	40
31/12/2019	42

General Solutions sold its investment in MicroTech's shares on September 12, 2020, at a price of $39 per share.

Required:

1. Assume that management purchased the shares for speculative purposes and recorded this transaction as an investment at FVTPL. Prepare any journal entries that are required by the facts presented in this case.

2. Assume that management classified MicroTech's shares as an investment available for sale. Prepare any journal entries that are required by the facts presented in this case.

LO13-3   **E13-7**   **Recording and Reporting an Equity Method Security**

Felicia Company acquired some of the 60,000 outstanding common shares of Nueces Corporation during 2017, as a non-current investment. The fiscal year for both companies ends December 31. The following transactions occurred during 2017:

Jan. 10   Purchased 21,000 of Nueces common shares at $12 per share.

Dec. 31   *a.* Received the 2017 financial statements of Nueces Corporation that reported net earnings of $90,000.

           b. Nueces Corporation declared and paid a cash dividend of $0.60 per share.

           c. Determined the market price of Nueces stock to be $11 per share. The decrease in price is not considered an impairment in the value of the investment.

Required:

1. What accounting method should the company use? Why?

2. Prepare the journal entries for each of these transactions. If no entry is required, explain why.

3. Show how the non-current investment and the related revenue should be reported on the 2017 financial statements (statement of financial position and statement of earnings) of the company.

LO13-3   **E13-8**   **Interpreting the Effects of Equity Method Investments on Cash Flow from Operations**
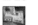

Use the data in E13-7 to answer the following questions.

Required:

1. How would the investing section of the statement of cash flows for 2017 be affected by the preceding transactions?

2. How would the equity in the earnings of Nueces Corporation and the dividends received from Nueces Corporation affect the operating section of the statement of cash flows for 2017, using the indirect method? Explain the reasons for the effects.

■ LO13-4

Alimentation
Couche-Tard Inc.

E13-9 **Determining the Appropriate Accounting Treatment for an Acquisition**

The notes to the 2015 financial statements of Alimentation Couche-Tard contained the following information:

> **4. Business Acquisitions**
>
> On March 16, 2015, the Corporation acquired 100% of the outstanding shares of the The Pantry through an all-cash transaction valued at $36.75 per share. The Corporation financed this transaction using its existing credit facility, as modified on May 16, 2014, December 1, 2014, and March 16, 2015. The Pantry operates over 1,500 convenience stores in 13 U.S. states, the majority of which dispense road transportation fuel. The Corporation owns the land and buildings for 409 sites, leases the land and owns the buildings for 52 sites and leases same assets for the remaining sites.

Assume that Alimentation Couche-Tard acquired 100 percent of the fair value of the net assets of The Pantry for $850.7 million in cash. The Pantry's assets at the time of the acquisition had a carrying amount of $1,056.9 million and a fair value of $1,349 million. Alimentation Couche-Tard also assumed The Pantry's liabilities, which had a carrying amount of $1,053.9 million and a fair value of $1,157 million.

Required:

Prepare the journal entry to record the acquisition of the net assets of The Pantry.

■ LO13-2

E13-10 **Analyzing and Interpreting the Economic Return from Investing Ratio**

Kukenberger Inc., reported the following in its portfolio of SAS:

Year	Dividends Received	Ending Fair Value of Investment Portfolio
2017	$24,550	$836,451
2018	23,906	759,999
2019	24,399	806,345
2010	25,538	845,160

Required:

1. Determine the economic return from investing ratio for 2018, 2019, and 2020.
2. What do your results suggest about Kukenberger's investment portfolio?

connect PROBLEMS

■ LO13-1

Starbucks
Corporation

P13-1 **Determining Financial Statement Effects for Bonds Held to Maturity** (AP13-1)

Starbucks Corporation provides high-quality coffee products. Assume that as part of its expansion strategy, Starbucks plans to open numerous new stores internationally over the next five years. The company has US$5 million to support the expansion and has decided to invest the funds in corporate bonds until the money is needed. Assume that Starbucks purchased bonds with US$5 million face value at par for cash on July 1, 2017. The bonds pay 8 percent interest each June 30 and December 31 and mature in five years. Starbucks plans to hold the bonds until maturity.

Required:

1. What accounts are affected when the bonds are purchased on July 1, 2017?
2. What accounts are affected when interest is received on December 31, 2017?
3. Should Starbucks prepare a journal entry if the market value of the bonds decreases to US$4 million on December 31, 2017? Explain.

■ LO13-2

eXcel

P13-2 **Recording Passive Investments** (AP13-2)

On March 1, 2017, HiTech Industries purchased 10,000 common shares of Integrated Services Company for $20 per share. The following information applies to Integrated's price per share:

Date	Price
31/12/2017	$17
31/12/2018	24
31/12/2019	31

Required:

1. Prepare journal entries to record the facts in the case, assuming that HiTech purchased the shares for the portfolio of securities held for trading.

2. Prepare journal entries to record the facts in the case, assuming that HiTech purchased the shares as an investment available for sale.

LO13-2	**P13-3**	**Recording Passive Investments**

Below are selected T-accounts for the RunnerTech Company.

Statement of Financial Position Accounts

(In Other Investments) Investments in SAS				(In Other Comprehensive Income) Net Unrealized Gains (Losses)—SAS		
1/1	5,587				1,556	1/1
Purchase	19,000		Sale	?	?	AJE
AJE	?	15,239 Sale			5,683	12/31
12/31	14,558					

Statement of Earnings Accounts

Dividend Revenue			Gain on Sale of Investments		
	? Earned			2,384	Sale
	7,771 12/31			2,384	12/31

Required:

1. Prepare journal entries to record the following transactions:

    a. Purchase of securities for the portfolio of investments in SAS for cash.

    b. Receipt of cash dividends on the investments.

    c. Sale of investments in SAS at a gain.

2. At year-end, the investments in SAS had a fair value of $14,558. Prepare the adjusting entry.

3. At what amount would the investments in SAS be reported on the statement of financial position as at December 31?

4. What amount(s) would be reported on the statement of earnings for the year?

5. How would year-end reporting change if the securities were categorized as investments in FVTPL instead of investments in SAS?

LO13-2	**P13-4**	**Reporting Passive Investments** (AP13-3)

During January 2017, Ka-Shing Company purchased shares of the following companies as a non-current investment:

Company and Type of Share	Number of Shares Outstanding	Purchase	Cost per Share
Q Corporation—Common	90,000	12,600	$ 5
R Corporation—Preferred, non-voting	20,000	12,000	30

Subsequent to acquisition, the following data were available:

	2017	2018
Net earnings reported at December 31:		
Q Corporation	$30,000	$36,000
R Corporation	40,000	48,000
Dividends declared and paid during the year (per share):		
Q Corporation—Common	$ 0.85	$ 0.90
R Corporation—Preferred	1.00	1.10
Market value per share at December 31:		
Q Corporation—Common	$ 4.00	$ 4.00
R Corporation—Preferred	29.00	30.00

Required:

1. What accounting method should be used for the investment in Q Corporation's common shares? R Corporation's preferred shares? Why?

2. Prepare the journal entries to record the following events for each year using parallel columns (if no entry is required, explain why):

    a. Purchase of the investments.

    b. Income reported by Q and R Corporations.

    c. Dividends received from Q and R Corporations.

    d. Fair value effects at year-end.

3. For each year, show how the following amounts should be reported on the financial statements of Ka-Shing Company:

    a. Non-current investment.

    b. Shareholders' equity—net unrealized gains and losses.

    c. Investment income.

LO13-2,13-3   **P13-5**   **Recording Passive Investments and Investments for Significant Influence**

e**X**cel

On August 4, 2016, Osaka Corporation purchased 1,000 common shares of Tremblay Ltée for $45,000. The following information applies to Tremblay's shares:

Date	Price
31/12/2016	$52
31/12/2017	47
31/12/2018	38

Tremblay declares and pays cash dividends of $2 per share on June 1 of each year.

Required:

1. Prepare journal entries to record the facts in the case, assuming that Osaka purchased the shares for the portfolio of securities held for trading.

2. Prepare journal entries to record the facts in the case, assuming that Osaka purchased the shares for the portfolio of SAS.

3. Prepare journal entries to record the facts in the case, assuming that Osaka used the equity method to account for the investment. Osaka owns 30 percent of Tremblay, and Tremblay reported $50,000 in net earnings each year.

LO13-2,13-3   **P13-6**   **Comparing Methods to Account for Various Levels of Ownership of Voting Shares**

e**X**cel

Company C had outstanding 30,000 common shares. On January 1, 2018, Company D purchased some of these shares as a non-current investment at $25 per share. At the end of 2018, Company C reported the following: profit, $50,000, and cash dividends declared and paid during the year, $25,500. The market value of Company C stock at the end of 2018 was $22 per share.

Required:

1. For each of the following cases (in the tabulation), identify the method of accounting that Company D should use. Explain why.

2. Prepare the journal entries for Company D at the dates indicated for each of the two independent cases, assuming that the investments will be held long term. If no entry is required, explain why. Use the following format:

Tabulation of Items	Case A: 3,600 Shares Purchased	Case B: 10,500 Shares Purchased
1. Accounting method:		
2. Journal entries:		
a. To record the acquisition at January 1, 2018.		
b. To recognize the income reported by Company C for 2018.		
c. To recognize the dividends declared and paid by Company C.		
d. To recognize fair value effect at end of 2018.		

3. Complete the following schedule to show the separate amounts that should be reported on the 2018 financial statements of Company D:

	Dollar Amounts	
	Case A	Case B
Statement of Financial Position		
Investments		
Shareholders' equity		
Statement of Earnings		
Investment income		
Equity in earnings of investee		

LO13-2,13-3   **P13-7**   **Comparing the Fair Value and Equity Methods** (AP13-4)

eXcel

Ship Corporation had outstanding 100,000 common shares. On January 10, 2017, Shore Company purchased a block of these shares in the open market at $20 per share for long-term investment purposes. At the end of 2017, Ship reported net earnings of $300,000 and cash dividends of $0.60 per share. At December 31, 2017, Ship's stock was selling at $18 per share. This problem involves two separate cases:

Case A   Purchase of 10,000 of Ship's common shares.

Case B   Purchase of 40,000 of Ship's common shares.

Required:

1. For each case, identify the accounting method that the company should use. Explain why.
2. For each case, in parallel columns, prepare the journal entries for each of the following (if no entry is required, explain why):
   a. Acquisition
   b. Revenue recognition
   c. Dividends received
   d. Fair value effects
3. For each case, show how the following should be reported on the 2017 financial statements:
   a. Non-current investments
   b. Shareholders' equity
   c. Investment income

LO13-3   **P13-8**   **Recording Investments for Significant Influence**

Below are selected T-accounts for the Brunet Company.

Investments in Associates				Equity in Associate Earnings		
1/1	56,685					1,556 1/1
Purchase	15,685			Sale	?	? AJE
Share of associate net earnings	?	8,564	Share of associate dividends			5,683 12/31
12/31	67,450					

Required:

1. Prepare journal entries to record the following transactions:
   a. Purchase of additional investments in associated companies for cash.
   b. Receipt of cash dividends on the investments.
2. At year-end, the investments in associates had a fair value of $62,000; the associates also reported $8,120 in net earnings for the year. Prepare the adjusting entry.
3. At what amount would the investments in associates be reported on the statement of financial position as at December 31?
4. What amount(s) would be reported on the statement of earnings for the year?

LO13-3   **P13-9**   **Determining Cash Flow Effects of Investments for Significant Influence** (AP13-5)

During 2018, Oscar Company purchased some of the 90,000 common shares of Selma Inc. as a non-current investment. The fiscal year for each company ends on December 31. The following transactions occurred during 2018:

Jan. 7   Purchased 40,500 of Selma's shares at $33 per share.

Dec. 31   a. Received the 2017 financial statements of Selma, which reported net earnings of $220,000.
         b. Selma declared and paid a cash dividend of $2 per share.
         c. Determined that the current market price of Selma's stock was $40 per share.

Required:

Indicate how the operating activities and investing activities sections of the statement of cash flows (indirect method) will be affected by each transaction.

LO13-4   **P13-10**   **Analyzing Goodwill and Reporting a Merger** (AP13-6)

On January 4, 2018, Pronti Company acquired all of the net assets of Scott Company for $120,000 cash. The statements of financial position for each company prior to the acquisition follow:

Statement of Financial Position at January 4, 2018	Pronti Company	Scott Company
Assets		
Cash	$118,000	$23,000
Property, plant, and equipment (net)	132,000	65,000*
Total assets	$250,000	$88,000
Liabilities	$ 27,000	$12,000
Shareholders' equity		
Common shares	120,000	40,000
Retained earnings	103,000	36,000
Total liabilities and shareholders' equity	$250,000	$88,000

*Determined by Pronti Company to have a fair value of $72,000 at the date of acquisition.

Required:

1. How much goodwill was involved in this acquisition? Show computations.
2. Record the acquisition by Pronti Company on January 4, 2018.
3. Prepare a statement of financial position immediately after the acquisition.

LO13-2   **P13-11**   **Interpreting the Economic Return from Investing Ratio** (AP13-7)

Mobile Services Inc. provides wireless communications services to a variety of customers. The following information relates to the company's investments in SAS in 2018 and 2017:

	2018	2017
	(in thousands of dollars)	
Investment portfolio	$1,328	$1,538
Investment income	282	211

Required:

1. Compute the economic return from investing ratio for 2018.
2. What do the results in requirement (1) suggest about Mobile Services?

ALTERNATE PROBLEMS

LO13-1   **AP13-1**   **Determining Financial Statement Effects for Bonds Held to Maturity** (P13-1)

Krispy Kreme
Doughnuts Inc.

Krispy Kreme operates and franchises a worldwide chain of quick-service drive-in doughnut stores. Customers drive up to a parking space and order doughnuts through an intercom speaker system. The ordered quantity is then delivered to the customer. Assume that Krispy Kreme Doughnuts Inc. has $15 million in cash to support future expansion and has decided to invest the funds in corporate bonds until the money is needed. Krispy Kreme purchases bonds with $15 million face value for $15.7 million cash on January 1, 2018. The bonds pay 6 percent interest each June 30 and December 31 and mature in four years. Krispy Kreme plans to hold the bonds until maturity.

Required:

1. What accounts were affected when the bonds were purchased on January 1, 2018?
2. What accounts were affected when interest was received on June 30, 2018?
3. Should Krispy Kreme prepare a journal entry if the market value of the bonds decreases to $16.3 million on December 31, 2018? Explain.

LO13-2   **AP13-2**   **Recording Passive Investments** (P13-2)

eXcel

On September 15, 2017, MultiMedia Corporation purchased 10,000 common shares of Community Broadcasting Company for $32 per share. The following information applies to Community Broadcasting's price per share:

Date	Price
31/12/2017	$34
31/12/2018	24
31/12/2019	21

Required:

1. Prepare journal entries to record the facts in the case, assuming that MultiMedia purchased the shares for the portfolio of securities held for trading.

2. Prepare journal entries to record the facts in the case, assuming that MultiMedia purchased the shares as an investment available for sale.

LO13-2   **AP13-3**   **Reporting Passive Investments** (P13-4)

During January 2017, Hexagon Company purchased 12,000 of the 200,000 outstanding common shares of Smiley Corporation at $30 per share. This block of shares was purchased as a long-term investment. Assume that the fiscal year for each company ends on December 31. Subsequent to acquisition, the following data were available:

	2017	2018
Profit reported by Smiley Corporation at December 31	$40,000	$60,000
Cash dividends declared and paid by Smiley Corporation during the year	60,000	80,000
Market price of Smiley Corporation's share at December 31	28	29

Required:

1. What accounting method should Hexagon Company use to record the investment in Smiley Corporation's common shares? Why?

2. Prepare the journal entries to record the following events for each year using parallel columns (if no entries are required, explain why):

   a. Acquisition of Smiley Corporation's shares.

   b. Net earnings reported by Smiley Corporation.

   c. Dividends received from Smiley Corporation.

   d. Fair value effects at year-end.

3. For each year, show how the following amounts should be reported on the financial statements of Hexagon Company:

   a. Non-current investment.

   b. Shareholders' equity—net unrealized gains and losses.

   c. Revenues.

LO13-2,13-3   **AP13-4**   **Comparing the Fair Value and Equity Methods** (P13-7)

Packer Company purchased, as a long-term investment, some of the 200,000 outstanding shares of Buenos Corporation. The fiscal year of each company ends on December 31. The following transactions occurred during 2018:

Jan. 10   Purchased common shares of Buenos at $15 per share as follows:
          Case A—30,000 shares.
          Case B—80,000 shares.

Dec. 31   a. Received the 2018 financial statements of Buenos Corporation; the reported net earnings was $90,000.
          b. Received a cash dividend of $0.60 per share from Buenos Corporation.
          c. Determined that the current market price of Buenos stock was $9 per share.

Required:

1. For each case, identify the accounting method that the company should use. Explain why.

2. Prepare the journal entries for each case for these transactions. If no entry is required, explain why. (*Hint:* Use parallel columns for Case A and Case B.)

3. Determine the amounts for each case that should be reported on the 2018 financial statements. Use the following format:

	Dollar Amounts	
	Case A	Case B
Statement of Financial Position (Partial)		
Investments		
Investments in common shares, Buenos Corporation		
Shareholders' equity		
Net unrealized gain or loss		
Statement of Earnings (Partial)		
Investment income		
Equity in earnings of associated company		

LO13-2,13-3 AP13-5 **Determining Cash Flow Effects of Passive Investments and Investments for Significant Influence** (P13-9)

For each of the transactions in AP13-4, indicate how the operating activities (indirect method) and investing activities sections of the statement of cash flows will be affected.

LO13-4 **AP13-6** **Analyzing Goodwill and Reporting an Acquisition** (P13-10)

On June 1, 2017, Kappa Company acquired all of the net assets of Delta Company for $120,000 cash. The statements of financial position for both companies prior to the acquisition follow:

Statement of Financial Position at June 1, 2017	Kappa Company	Delta Company
Assets		
Cash	$176,000	$ 13,000
Property, plant, and equipment (net)	352,000	165,000*
Total assets	$528,000	$178,000
Liabilities	$ 93,000	$ 82,000
Shareholders' equity		
Common shares	250,000	65,000
Retained earnings	185,000	31,000
Total liabilities and shareholders' equity	$528,000	$178,000

*Determined by Kappa Company to have a fair value of $180,000 at the date of acquisition.

Required:

1. How much goodwill was involved in this merger? Show computations.

2. Record the merger by Kappa Company on June 1, 2017.

3. Prepare a statement of financial position immediately after the acquisition.

LO13-2 **AP13-7** **Interpreting the Economic Return from Investing Ratio** (P13-10)

Selma International, Inc., reported the following information regarding its investment portfolio in the company's 2017 annual report:

	2017	2016
	(in thousands of dollars)	
Investment portfolio	$8,942	$8,903
Dividend revenue	696	362

Required:

1. Compute the economic return from investing ratio for 2017.

2. What do the results in (1) suggest about Selma International?

CASES AND PROJECTS

FINDING AND INTERPRETING FINANCIAL INFORMATION

LO13-2,13-3,13-4 **Finding Financial Information**

CP13-1 Refer to the consolidated financial statements of Canadian Tire Corporation in Appendix A at the end of this book.

Required:

Identify all the items that appear on Canadian Tire's financial statements for fiscal year 2015 (consolidated balance sheets, consolidated statements of income, consolidated statements of comprehensive income, and consolidated statements of cash flows) in relation to its investments in other companies, and explain what each item means. (*Hint:* The notes to the financial statements may be helpful to answer this requirement.)

FINANCIAL REPORTING AND ANALYSIS CASE

LO13-2,13-3 CP13-2 **Using Financial Reports: Analyzing the Financial Effects of the Fair Value and Equity Methods**

On January 1, 2017, Woodrow Company purchased 30 percent of the outstanding common shares of Trevor Corporation at a total cost of $560,000. Management intends to hold the stock for the long term. The investment in Trevor Corporation was reported at $720,000 on the statement of financial position at December 31, 2017. No additional Trevor shares were purchased during the year.

The company received $80,000 in cash dividends that were declared and paid by Trevor during 2017. The company used the equity method to account for its investment in Trevor. The market price of Trevor's shares increased during 2017 to a total value of $600,000.

Required:

1. Explain why the investment account balance increased from $560,000 to $720,000 during 2017.

2. What amount of revenue from the investment was reported during 2017?

3. If Woodrow did not have significant influence over Trevor and used the fair value method, what amount of revenue from the investment should have been reported in 2017?

4. If Woodrow did not have significant influence over Trevor and used the fair value method, what amount should be reported as the investment in Trevor Corporation on the statement of financial position at December 31, 2017?

CRITICAL THINKING CASES

LO13-4   **CP13-3**   **Evaluating an Ethical Dilemma: Using Inside Information**

Assume that you are on the board of directors of a company that has decided to buy 80 percent of the outstanding shares of another company within the next three or four months. The discussions have convinced you that this company is an excellent investment opportunity, so you decide to buy $10,000 worth of the company's shares for your personal portfolio. Is there an ethical problem with your decision? Would your answer be different if you planned to invest $500,000? Are there different ethical considerations if you don't buy the shares but recommend that your brother do so?

LO13-4   **CP13-4**   **Evaluating an Acquisition from the Standpoint of a Financial Analyst**

Assume that you are a financial analyst for a large investment banking firm. You are responsible for analyzing companies in the retail sales industry. You have just learned that a large west coast retailer has acquired a large east coast retailer for a price more than the net book value of the acquired company. You have reviewed the separate financial statements for the two companies before the announcement of the acquisition. Write a brief report explaining what will happen when the financial results of the companies are consolidated under the acquisition method.

FINANCIAL REPORTING AND ANALYSIS TEAM PROJECT

LO13-2,13-3,13-4   **Team Project: Examining an Annual Report**

CP13-5   As a team, select an industry to analyze. A list of companies classified by industry can be obtained by accessing www.fpinfomart.ca and then choosing Companies by Industry.

Each group member should acquire the annual report for a different publicly traded company in the industry. (Library files, the SEDAR service at www.sedar.com, and the company's website are good sources.)

Required:

On an individual basis, each team member should write a short report answering the following questions about the selected company. Discuss any patterns across the companies that you as a team observe. Then, as a team, write a short report comparing and contrasting your companies.

 a. Determine whether the company prepared consolidated financial statements. If so, did it use the purchase method? How do you know?

 b. Does the company use the equity method for any of its investments?

 c. Does the company hold any investments in securities? If so, what is their fair value? Does the company have any unrealized gains or losses?

 d. Identify the company's lines of business. Why does management want to engage in these business activities?

connect   CONTINUING CASE

LO13-2   **CC13-1**   **Accounting for Passive Investments**

Pool Corporation Inc. is the world's largest wholesale distributor of swimming pool supplies and equipment. Assume Pool Corporation purchased for cash 400,000 shares of The Walt Disney Company on November 21, 2014, at $88 per share as an investment. The following information applies to the stock price of Disney:

	Price per Share
12/31/2014	$105
12/31/2015	95
12/31/2016	98

On September 15, 2017, Pool Corporation sold all of the Disney securities at $100 per share.

Required:

1. Prepare journal entries to record the facts in the case, assuming that Pool Corporation purchased the shares for its portfolio of securities held for trading.
2. Prepare journal entries to record the facts in the case, assuming that Pool Corporation purchased the shares for its portfolio of securities available for sale.

SOLUTIONS TO SELF-STUDY QUIZZES

Self-Study Quiz 13-1

1. Journal entry to record the purchase of the bonds:

Held-to-maturity investments (A)	5,009,289	
Cash (A)		5,009,289

Verification of bond price = $5,000,000 × 0.9238(PV of principal) + $102,500 × 3.8077(PV of interest)
= $5,009,289

2. Journal entry to record the receipt of interest:

Cash (A)	102,500	
Held-to-maturity investments (A)		2,314
Interest revenue (R, SE) [$5,009,289 × 4% × (6/12)]		108,186

Note: The amount $2,314 represents a reduction of the premium of $9,289 that the company paid when it purchased the bonds.

Self-Study Quiz 13-2

1.

Investments in SAS (A)	100,000	
Cash (A)		100,000

2.

Investments in SAS (A)	10,000	
Net unrealized losses/gains (OCI, SE)		10,000
[$110,000 fair value − $100,000 cost = +$10,000]		

    a. **Non-current assets**:

Investments in SAS	$110,000

    Shareholders' equity:

(Accumulated other comprehensive income) Net unrealized gain	$ 10,000

    b. No dividend revenue or realized gains and losses from sale of investments would be reported on the statement of earnings.

3.

Net unrealized losses/gains (OCI, SE)	25,000	
Investments in SAS (A)		25,000
Unrealized loss = [($17 × 5,000 shares) − $110,000 book value]		

4.

Cash (A)	120,000	
Investments in SAS (A)		85,000
Net unrealized losses/gains (OCI, SE)		35,000
Net unrealized losses/gains (OCI, SE)	20,000	
Gain on sale of investment (SE)		20,000

The balance of net unrealized losses/gains is the gain realized on the sale of the investment. It is reported in the statement of earnings.

5. *a.* **Current assets:**

Investments in SAS	$110,000

  b. **Other items:**

Net unrealized gain	$ 10,000

There were no dividends reported.

Self-Study Quiz 13-3

a.	Investments in associates (+A)	157.0	
	Cash (−A)		157.0
b.	Cash (+A)	16.6	
	Investments in associates (−A)		16.6
c.	Investments in associates (+A)	33.0	
	Equity in earnings of associates (+R, +SE)		33.0

The investments in associates are not impaired because their fair value exceeds their carrying amount.

  d. **Statement of financial position**

Non-current assets

Investments in associates	$419.7

Statement of earnings

Other Non-operating items

Equity in earnings of associates	$33.0

Self-Study Quiz 13-4

1. Goodwill = Purchase price ($10) − Fair value of net assets ($11 − $4) = $3.
2. Lexis's shareholders' equity is unchanged, remaining at $70.
3. Lexis's other assets + Nexis's other assets (at fair value) = $90 + $11 = $101.

ENDNOTES

1. A financial instrument is defined as "any contract that gives rise to a financial asset of one entity and a financial liability or equity instrument of another entity." IAS 32—Financial Instruments: Presentation: para. 11.

2. Fair value is defined as "the price that would be received to sell an asset or paid to transfer a liability in an orderly transaction between market participants at the measurement date" (IFRS 13—Fair Value Measurement: para. 9).

3. A bond is a long-term debt requiring repayment of principal at a specific date, along with periodic interest payments. Accounting for bonds is covered in Chapter 10.

4. The determination of the price of the bond is based on the present value techniques discussed in Chapter 9. Many analysts refer to a bond price as a *percentage of par*. For example, an online financial advisory service might report that a bond issued by Bell Canada with a par value of $1,000 is selling at 109.50. This means it would cost $1,095 (109.50 percent of $1,000) to buy the bond.

5. When bond investors accept a rate of interest on a bond investment that is the same as the stated rate of interest on the bonds, the bonds will sell at par (i.e., at 100 or 100 percent of face value).

6. This classification of investments in securities will disappear when publicly accountable enterprises implement IFRS 9—Financial Instruments, which is effective for fiscal years starting on or after January 1, 2018. All investments in securities will then be classified as investments at FVTPL.

7. Companies often keep the asset value at cost and record the change in fair value in a related valuation allowance that is added or subtracted from the asset. This does not change the financial statement presentation.

8. The equity method must also be used to account for joint ventures, which are joint arrangements whereby the parties that have joint control of the arrangement have rights to the net assets of the arrangement. Joint ventures are discussed in other accounting courses.

9. The recoverable amount of an asset is the higher of its value in use or its fair value less costs to sell, as explained in Chapter 8.

10. Ignoring income taxes.

Financial Statements of the Canadian Tire Corporation, Limited

This appendix includes the financial statements of the Canadian Tire Corporation, Limited, for 2015, and selected notes to these financial statements. Notes 4, 5, 6, 12, 35, 36, 38, and 39, and sections of Notes 2, 11, and 29, were omitted because of space limitations. The complete set of the Canadian Tire Corporation's financial statements and related notes are available on *Connect.*

Canadian Tire Corporation

2015 Report to Shareholders

MANAGEMENT'S RESPONSIBILITY FOR FINANCIAL STATEMENTS

The Management of Canadian Tire Corporation, Limited, is responsible for the accompanying consolidated financial statements. The financial statements have been prepared by Management in accordance with International Financial Reporting Standards, which recognize the necessity of relying on some best estimates and informed judgments. All financial information in our Management's Discussion and Analysis is consistent with the consolidated financial statements.

To discharge its responsibilities for financial reporting and safeguarding of assets, Management depends on the Company's systems of internal control. These systems are designed to provide reasonable assurance that the financial records are reliable and form a proper basis for the timely and accurate preparation of financial statements. Management meets the objectives of internal control on a cost-effective basis through the prudent selection and training of personnel, adoption, and communication of appropriate policies, and employment of an internal audit program.

The Board of Directors oversees Management's responsibilities for the consolidated financial statements primarily through the activities of its Audit Committee, which is composed solely of directors who are neither officers nor employees of the Company. This Committee meets with Management and the Company's independent auditors, Deloitte LLP, to review the consolidated financial statements and recommend approval by the Board of Directors. The Audit Committee is also responsible for making recommendations with respect to the appointment of and for approving remuneration and the terms of engagement of the Company's auditors. The Audit Committee also meets with the auditors, without the presence of Management, to discuss the results of their audit.

The consolidated financial statements have been audited by Deloitte LLP, who were appointed by shareholder vote at the annual shareholders' meeting. Their report is presented below.

Michael B. Medline
President and
Chief Executive Officer

Dean McCann
Executive Vice-President and
Chief Financial Officer

February 17, 2016

INDEPENDENT AUDITOR'S REPORT

To the Shareholders of Canadian Tire Corporation, Limited

We have audited the accompanying consolidated financial statements of Canadian Tire Corporation, Limited, which comprise the consolidated balance sheets as at January 2, 2016, and January 3, 2015, and the consolidated statements of income, consolidated statements of comprehensive income, consolidated statements of cash flows, and consolidated statements of changes in equity for the years ended January 2, 2016, and January 3, 2015, and a summary of significant accounting policies and other explanatory information.

Management's Responsibility for the Consolidated Financial Statements

Management is responsible for the preparation and fair presentation of these consolidated financial statements in accordance with International Financial Reporting Standards, and for such internal control as management determines is necessary to enable the preparation of consolidated financial statements that are free from material misstatement, whether due to fraud or error.

Auditor's Responsibility

Our responsibility is to express an opinion on these consolidated financial statements based on our audits. We conducted our audits in accordance with Canadian generally accepted auditing standards. Those standards require that we comply with ethical requirements and plan and perform the audit to obtain reasonable assurance about whether the consolidated financial statements are free from material misstatement.

An audit involves performing procedures to obtain audit evidence about the amounts and disclosures in the consolidated financial statements. The procedures selected depend on the auditor's judgment, including the assessment of the risks of material misstatement of the consolidated financial statements, whether due to fraud or error. In making those risk assessments, the auditor considers internal control relevant to the entity's preparation and fair presentation of the consolidated financial statements in order to design audit procedures that are appropriate in the circumstances, but not for the purpose of expressing an opinion on the effectiveness of the entity's internal control. An audit also includes evaluating the appropriateness of accounting policies used and the reasonableness of accounting estimates made by management, as well as evaluating the overall presentation of the consolidated financial statements.

We believe that the audit evidence we have obtained in our audits is sufficient and appropriate to provide a basis for our audit opinion.

Opinion

In our opinion, the consolidated financial statements present fairly, in all material respects, the financial position of Canadian Tire Corporation, Limited, as at January 2, 2016, and January 3, 2015, and its financial performance and its cash flows for the years then ended in accordance with International Financial Reporting Standards.

Deloitte LLP

Chartered Professional Accountants
Licensed Public Accountants

February 17, 2016
Toronto, Ontario

CONSOLIDATED BALANCE SHEETS

As at

(C$ in millions)	January 2, 2016	January 3, 2015
ASSETS		
Cash and cash equivalents (Note 8)	$ 900.6	$ 662.1
Short-term investments (Note 9)	96.1	289.1
Trade and other receivables (Note 10)	915.0	880.2
Loans receivable (Note 11)	4,875.5	4,905.5
Merchandise inventories	1,764.5	1,623.8
Income taxes recoverable	42.2	31.9
Prepaid expenses and deposits	96.1	104.5
Assets classified as held for sale (Note 12)	2.3	13.1
Total current assets	8,692.3	8,510.2
Long-term receivables and other assets (Note 13)	731.2	684.2
Long-term investments	153.4	176.0
Goodwill and intangible assets (Note 14)	1,246.8	1,251.7
Investment property (Note 15)	137.8	148.6
Property and equipment (Note 16)	3,978.2	3,743.1
Deferred income taxes (Note 18)	48.1	39.4
Total assets	$14,987.8	$14,553.2
LIABILITIES		
Bank indebtedness (Note 8)	$ –	$ 14.3
Deposits (Note 19)	880.7	950.7
Trade and other payables (Note 20)	1,957.1	1,961.2
Provisions (Note 21)	216.1	206.0
Short-term borrowings (Note 23)	88.6	199.8
Loans payable (Note 24)	655.5	604.4
Income taxes payable	61.5	54.9
Current portion of long-term debt (Note 25)	24.3	587.5
Total current liabilities	3,883.8	4,578.8
Long-term provisions (Note 21)	45.7	44.1
Long-term debt (Note 25)	2,971.4	2,131.6
Long-term deposits (Note 19)	1,372.2	1,286.2
Deferred income taxes (Note 18)	111.1	93.9
Other long-term liabilities (Note 26)	813.9	787.8
Total liabilities	9,198.1	8,922.4
EQUITY		
Share capital (Note 28)	671.2	695.5
Contributed surplus	2.9	2.9
Accumulated other comprehensive income	148.1	82.0
Retained earnings	4,172.0	4,075.1
Equity attributable to shareholders of Canadian Tire Corporation	4,994.2	4,855.5
Non-controlling interests (Note 17)	795.5	775.3
Total equity	5,789.7	5,630.8
Total liabilities and equity	$14,987.8	$14,553.2

The related notes form an integral part of these consolidated financial statements.

Maureen J. Sabia
Director

Diana L. Chant
Director

CONSOLIDATED STATEMENTS OF INCOME

For the years ended (C$ in millions, except per share amounts)	January 2, 2016	January 3, 2015
Revenue (Note 30)	$12,279.6	$12,462.9
Cost of producing revenue (Note 31)	8,144.3	8,416.9
Gross margin	4,135.3	4,046.0
Other (income)	(54.9)	(11.0)
Selling, general and administrative expenses (Note 32)	3,096.1	3,052.9
Net finance costs (Note 33)	92.8	108.9
Change in fair value of redeemable financial instrument (Note 35)	–	17.0
Income before income taxes	1,001.3	878.2
Income taxes (Note 18)	265.4	238.9
Net income	$ 735.9	$ 639.3
Net income attributable to:		
Shareholders of Canadian Tire Corporation	$ 659.4	$ 604.0
Non-controlling interests (Note 17)	76.5	35.3
	$ 735.9	$ 639.3
Basic EPS	$ 8.66	$ 7.65
Diluted EPS	$ 8.61	$ 7.59
Weighted average number of Common and Class A Non-Voting Shares outstanding:		
Basic	76,151,321	78,960,025
Diluted	76,581,602	79,612,957

The related notes form an integral part of these consolidated financial statements.

CONSOLIDATED STATEMENTS OF COMPREHENSIVE INCOME

For the years ended (C$ in millions)	January 2, 2016	January 3, 2015
Net income	$735.9	$639.3
Other comprehensive income		
Items that may be reclassified subsequently to net income:		
Cash flow hedges:		
Gains	275.6	114.0
Reclassification of gains to non-financial assets	(207.4)	(77.5)
Reclassification of gains to income	(3.0)	(1.5)
Available-for-sale financial assets:		
(Losses)	(0.5)	(0.1)
Reclassification of gains to income	–	(0.1)
Item that will not be reclassified subsequently to net income:		
Actuarial gains (losses)	0.8	(13.2)
Other comprehensive income	65.5	21.6
Other comprehensive income attributable to:		
Shareholders of Canadian Tire Corporation	$ 68.0	$ 21.5
Non-controlling interests	(2.5)	0.1
	$ 65.5	$ 21.6
Comprehensive income	$801.4	$660.9
Comprehensive income attributable to:		
Shareholders of Canadian Tire Corporation	$727.4	$625.5
Non-controlling interests	74.0	35.4
	$801.4	$660.9

The related notes form an integral part of these consolidated financial statements.

CONSOLIDATED STATEMENTS OF CASH FLOWS

For the years ended (C$ in millions)	January 2, 2016	January 3, 2015
Cash generated from (used for):		(Note 39)
Operating activities		
Net income	$735.9	$639.3
Adjustments for:		
Depreciation of property and equipment and investment property (Notes 31 and 32)	312.8	279.2
Income tax expense	265.4	238.9
Net finance costs	92.8	108.9
Amortization of intangible assets (Note 32)	111.9	93.1
Changes in fair value of derivative instruments	6.9	(33.9)
(Gain) on disposal of property and equipment, investment property, assets held for sale, intangible assets, and lease terminations	(43.9)	(9.0)
Change in fair value of redeemable financial instrument (Note 35)	–	17.0
Interest paid	(101.4)	(122.0)
Interest received	8.4	10.4
Income taxes paid	(284.0)	(256.5)
Other	14.6	25.0
	1,119.4	990.4
Change in operating working capital and other (Note 34)	(115.3)	(83.5)
Change in loans receivable	(25.2)	(332.4)
Cash generated from operating activities	978.9	574.5
Investing activities		
Additions to property and equipment and investment property	(515.9)	(538.6)
Additions to intangible assets	(94.7)	(150.1)
	(610.6)	(688.7)
Acquisition of short-term investments	(177.4)	(431.6)
Proceeds from the maturity and disposition of short-term investments	426.6	665.3
Acquisition of long-term investments	(35.0)	(155.8)
Proceeds from the disposition of long-term investments	–	7.6
Proceeds on disposition of property and equipment, investment property, and assets held for sale	101.5	21.3
Long-term receivables and other assets	0.1	3.1
Other	(4.2)	(10.7)
	311.6	99.2
Cash (used for) investing activities	(299.0)	(589.5)
Financing activities		
Dividends paid	(152.2)	(141.4)
Distributions paid to non-controlling interests	(53.8)	(19.5)
	(206.0)	(160.9)
Net (repayment) issuance of short-term borrowings	(111.2)	79.4
Issuance of loans payable	270.1	235.6
Repayment of loans payable	(219.0)	(242.4)
Issuance of long-term debt (Note 25)	856.1	563.7
Repayment of long-term debt and finance lease liabilities (Note 25)	(588.5)	(474.0)
Payment of transaction costs related to long-term debt	(6.5)	(2.0)
	201.0	160.3
Repurchase of share capital (Note 28)	(434.6)	(290.6)
Proceeds on sale of ownership interests in the Financial Services business	–	500.0
Transaction costs on sale of ownership interests in the Financial Services business	–	(23.2)
	(434.6)	186.2
Change in deposits	12.5	(97.0)
Cash (used for) generated from financing activities	(427.1)	88.6
Cash generated in the period	252.8	73.6
Cash and cash equivalents, net of bank indebtedness, beginning of period	647.8	574.2
Cash and cash equivalents, net of bank indebtedness, end of period (Note 8)	$900.6	$647.8

The related notes form an integral part of these consolidated financial statements.

CONSOLIDATED STATEMENTS OF CHANGES IN EQUITY

(C$ in millions)	Share capital	Contributed surplus	Cashflow hedges	Fair value changes in available-for-sale financial assets	Total accumulated other comprehensive income	Retained earnings	Equity attributable to shareholders of Canadian Tire Corporation	Equity attributable to non-controlling interests	Total equity
					Total accumulated other comprehensive income				
Balance at January 3, 2015	$ 695.5	$ 2.9	$ 81.8	$ 0.2	$ 82.0	$ 4,075.1	$ 4,855.5	$775.3	$ 5,630.8
Net income	–	–	–	–	–	659.4	659.4	76.5	735.9
Other comprehensive income (loss)	–	–	66.6	(0.5)	66.1	1.9	68.0	(2.5)	65.5
Total comprehensive income (loss)	–	–	66.6	(0.5)	66.1	661.3	727.4	74.0	801.4
Contributions by and distributions to shareholders of Canadian Tire Corporation									
Issuance of Class A Non-voting Shares (Note 28)	8.3	–	–	–	–	–	8.3	–	8.3
Repurchase of Class A Non-voting Shares (Note 28)	(434.6)	–	–	–	–	–	(434.6)	–	(434.6)
Excess of purchase price over average cost (Note 28)	402.0	–	–	–	–	(402.0)	–	–	–
Dividends	–	–	–	–	–	(162.4)	(162.4)	–	(162.4)
Contributions by and distributions to non-controlling interests									
Issuance of trust units to non-controlling interests, net of transaction costs	–	–	–	–	–	–	–	1.8	1.8
Distributions and dividends to non-controlling interests	–	–	–	–	–	–	–	(55.6)	(55.6)
Total contributions and distributions	(24.3)	–	–	–	–	(564.4)	(588.7)	(53.8)	(642.5)
Balance at January 2, 2016	$ 671.2	$ 2.9	$ 148.4	$ (0.3)	$148.1	$ 4,172.0	$4,994.2	$ 795.5	$ 5,789.7
Balance at December 28, 2013	$ 712.9	$ 2.4	$ 47.0	$ 0.4	$ 47.4	$ 4,404.6	$ 5,167.3	$ 282.6	$ 5,449.9
Net income	–	–	–	–	–	604.0	604.0	35.3	639.3
Other comprehensive income (loss)	–	–	34.8	(0.2)	34.6	(13.1)	21.5	0.1	21.6
Total comprehensive income (loss)		–	34.8	(0.2)	34.6	590.9	625.5	35.4	660.9
Contributions by and distributions to shareholders of Canadian Tire Corporation									
Issuance of Class A Non-voting Shares (Note 28)	6.9	–	–	–	–	–	6.9	–	6.9
Repurchase of Class A Non-voting Shares (Note 28)	(290.6)	–	–	–	–	–	(290.6)	–	(290.6)
Excess of purchase price over average cost (Note 28)	266.3	–	–	–	–	(266.3)	–	–	–
Dividends	–	–	–	–	–	(154.1)	(154.1)	–	(154.1)
Issuance of redeemable financial instrument (Note 35)						(500.0)	(500.0)		(500.0)
Contributed surplus arising on sale of property to CT REIT	–	0.5	–	–	–	–	0.5	–	0.5
Contributions by and distributions to non-controlling interests									
Sale of ownership interests in the Financial Services business, net of transaction costs	–	–	–	–	–	–	–	476.8	476.8
Issuance of trust units to non-controlling interests, net of transaction costs	–	–	–	–	–	–	–	1.8	1.8
Distributions to non-controlling interests	–	–	–	–	–	–	–	(21.3)	(21.3)
Total contributions and distributions	(17.4)	0.5	–	–	–	(920.4)	(937.3)	457.3	(480.0)
Balance at January 3, 2015	$ 695.5	$ 2.9	$ 81.8	$ 0.2	$ 82.0	$4,075.1	$4,855.5	$775.3	$5,630.8

The related notes form an integral part of these consolidated financial statements.

1. The Company and its operations

Canadian Tire Corporation, Limited, is a Canadian public company primarily domiciled in Canada. Its registered office is located at 2180 Yonge Street, Toronto, Ontario, M4P 2V8, Canada. It is listed on the Toronto Stock Exchange (TSX—CTC, CTC.A). Canadian Tire Corporation, Limited, and entities it controls are together referred to in these consolidated financial statements as the "Company" or "Canadian Tire Corporation." Refer to Note 17 for the Company's major subsidiaries.

The Company comprises three main business operations, which offer a range of retail goods and services, including general merchandise, apparel, sporting goods, petroleum, financial services including a bank, and real estate operations. Details of its three reportable operating segments are provided in Note 6.

2. Basis of preparation

Fiscal year

The fiscal year of the Company consists of a 52- or 53-week period ending on the Saturday closest to December 31. The fiscal years for the consolidated financial statements and notes presented for 2015 and 2014 are the 52-week period ended January 2, 2016, and the 53-week period ended January 3, 2015, respectively.

Statement of compliance

These consolidated financial statements have been prepared in accordance with International Financial Reporting Standards ("IFRS") and using the accounting policies described herein.

These consolidated financial statements were authorized for issuance by the Company's Board of Directors on February 17, 2016.

Basis of presentation

These consolidated financial statements have been prepared on the historical cost basis, except for the following items, which are measured at fair value:

* financial instruments at fair value through profit or loss ("FVTPL");
* derivative financial instruments;
* available-for-sale financial assets;
* liabilities for share-based payment plans; and
* initial recognition of assets acquired and liabilities assumed in a business combination.

In addition, the post-employment defined benefit obligation is recorded at its discounted present value.

Functional and presentation currency

These consolidated financial statements are presented in Canadian dollars ("C$"), the Company's functional currency.

Judgments and estimates

The preparation of these consolidated financial statements in accordance with IFRS requires Management to make judgments and estimates that affect:

* the application of accounting policies;
* the reported amounts of assets and liabilities;
* disclosures of contingent assets and liabilities; and
* the reported amounts of revenue and expenses during the reporting periods.

Actual results may differ from estimates made in these consolidated financial statements.

Judgments are made in the selection and assessment of the Company's accounting policies. Estimates are used mainly in determining the measurement of recognized transactions and balances. Estimates are based on historical experience and other factors, including expectations of future events that are believed to be reasonable under the circumstances. Judgments and estimates are often interrelated. The Company's judgments and estimates are continually re-evaluated to ensure they remain appropriate. Revisions to accounting estimates are recognized in the period in which the estimates are revised and in future periods affected.

The following are the accounting policies that are subject to judgments and estimates that the Company believes could have the most significant impact on the amounts recognized in these consolidated financial statements.

Impairment of assets

Judgment—The Company uses judgment in determining the grouping of assets to identify its Cash Generating Units ("CGUs") for purposes of testing for impairment of property and equipment and goodwill and intangible assets. The Company has determined that its Retail CGUs comprise individual stores or groups of stores within a geographic market. In testing for impairment, goodwill acquired in a business combination is allocated to the CGUs that are expected to benefit from the synergies of the business combination. In testing for impairment of intangibles with indefinite lives, these assets are allocated to the CGUs to which they relate. Furthermore, on a quarterly basis, judgment has been used in determining whether there has been an indication of impairment, which would require the completion of a quarterly impairment test, in addition to the annual requirement.

Estimation—The Company's estimate of a CGU's or group of CGUs' recoverable amount based on value in use ("VIU") involves estimating future cash flows before taxes. Future cash flows are estimated based on multi-year extrapolation of the most recent historical actual results or budgets and a terminal value calculated by discounting the final year in perpetuity. The growth rate applied to the terminal value is based on the Bank of Canada's target inflation rate or Management's estimate of the growth rate specific to the individual item being tested. The future cash flow estimates are then discounted to their present value using an appropriate pre-tax discount rate that incorporates a risk premium specific to each business. The Company's determination of a CGU's or group of CGUs' recoverable amount based on fair value less cost to sell uses factors such as market rental rates for comparable assets.

Fair value measurement of redeemable financial instrument

Judgment—The Company uses judgment in determining the fair value measurement of the redeemable financial instrument issued in conjunction with the sale of a 20 percent equity interest in the Company's Financial Services business. In calculating the fair value, judgment is used when determining the discount and growth rates applied to the forecasted earnings in the discounted cash flow valuation. Refer to Note 35 for further information regarding this financial instrument.

Estimation—The inputs to determine the fair value are taken from observable markets where possible, but where they are unavailable, assumptions are required in establishing fair value. The fair value of the redeemable financial instrument is determined based on the Company's best estimate of forecasted normalized earnings attributable to the Financial Services business, adjusted for any undistributed earnings.

Merchandise inventories

Estimation—Merchandise inventories are carried at the lower of cost and net realizable value. The estimation of net realizable value is based on the most reliable evidence available of the amount the merchandise inventories are expected to realize. Additionally, estimation is required for inventory provisions due to shrinkage.

Income and other taxes

Judgment—In calculating current and deferred income and other taxes, the Company uses judgment when interpreting the tax rules in jurisdictions where the Company operates. The Company also uses judgment in classifying transactions and assessing probable outcomes of claimed deductions, which considers expectations of future operating results, the timing and reversal of temporary differences, and possible audits of income tax and other tax filings by tax authorities.

Consolidation

Judgment—The Company uses judgment in determining the entities that it controls and accordingly consolidates. An entity is controlled when the Company has power over an entity, exposure or rights to variable returns from its involvement with the entity, and is able to use its power over the entity to affect its return from the entity. The Company has power over an entity when it has existing rights that give it the current ability to direct the relevant activities, which are the activities that significantly affect the investee's returns. Since power comes from rights, power can result from contractual arrangements. However, certain contractual arrangements contain rights that are designed to protect the Company's interest, without giving it power over the entity.

Loans receivable
Estimation—The Company's estimate of allowances on credit card loans receivable is based on a roll-rate methodology that employs statistical analysis of historical data and experience of delinquency and default, to estimate the amount of loans that will eventually be written off as a result of events occurring before the reporting date, with certain adjustments for other relevant circumstances influencing the recoverability of these loans receivable. Default rates, loss rates, and the expected timing of future recoveries are regularly benchmarked against actual outcomes to ensure that they remain appropriate. Future customer behaviour may be affected by a number of factors, including changes in interest and unemployment rates and program design changes.

Post-employment benefits
Estimation—The accounting for the Company's post-employment benefit plan requires the use of assumptions. The accrued benefit liability is calculated using actuarial determined data and the Company's best estimates of future salary escalations, retirement ages of employees, employee turnover, mortality rates, market discount rates, and expected health and dental care costs.

Other
Other estimates include determining the useful lives of property and equipment, investment property, and intangibles assets for the purposes of depreciation and amortization; in accounting for and measuring items such as deferred revenue, customer loyalty and other provisions, and purchase price adjustments on business combinations; and in measuring certain fair values, including those related to the valuation of business combinations, share-based payments, and financial instruments.

3. Significant accounting policies

The accounting policies set out below have been applied consistently to all periods presented in these consolidated financial statements and have been applied consistently throughout the Company.

Basis of consolidation
These consolidated financial statements include the accounts of Canadian Tire Corporation and entities it controls. An entity is controlled when the Company has the ability to direct the relevant activities of the entity, has exposure, or rights, to variable returns from its involvement with the entity, and is able to use its power over the entity to affect its returns from the entity.

The results of certain subsidiaries that have different year-ends have been included in these consolidated financial statements for the 52-week period ended January 2, 2016, and the 53-week period ended January 3, 2015. The year-end of CTFS Holdings, Limited, and its subsidiaries, Franchise Trust, and CT Real Estate Investment Trust ("CT REIT") is December 31.

Income or loss and each component of OCI are attributed to the shareholders of the Company and to the non-controlling interests. Total comprehensive income is attributed to the shareholders of the Company and to the non-controlling interests even if this results in the non-controlling interests having a deficit balance on consolidation.

Business combinations
The Company applies the acquisition method in accounting for business combinations.

The Company measures goodwill as the difference between the fair value of the consideration transferred, including the recognized amount of any non-controlling interests in the acquiree, and the net recognized amount (generally fair value) of the identifiable assets acquired and liabilities assumed, all measured as at the acquisition date.

Consideration transferred includes the fair value of the assets transferred (including cash), liabilities incurred by the Company on behalf of the acquiree, the fair value of any contingent consideration, and equity interests issued by the Company.

Where a business combination is achieved in stages, previously held interests in the acquired entity are remeasured to fair value at the acquisition date, which is the date control is obtained, and the resulting gain or loss, if any, is recognized in net income. Amounts arising from interests in the acquiree prior to the acquisition date that have previously been recognized in OCI are reclassified to net income.

The fair values of property and equipment recognized as a result of a business combination is based on either the cost approach or market approaches, as applicable. The market value of property is the estimated amount for which a property could be exchanged on the date of valuation between a willing buyer and a willing seller in an arm's length transaction, after proper marketing wherein the parties each act knowledgeably and willingly. For the cost approach, the current replacement cost or reproduction cost for each major asset is calculated.

The fair values of banners and trademarks acquired in a business combination are determined using an income approach. The "relief from royalty" method has been applied to forecast revenue using an appropriate royalty rate. This results in an estimate of the value of the intangible assets acquired by the Company.

The fair values of franchise agreements and other intangibles, such as customer relationships, are determined using an income approach or multi-period excess earnings approach. This method is based on the discounted cash flows expected to be derived from ownership of the assets. The present value of the cash flows represents the value of the intangible asset. The fair value of off-market leases acquired in a business combination is determined based on the present value of the difference between market rates and rates in the existing leases.

The fair values of inventories acquired in a business combination is determined based on the estimated selling price in the ordinary course of business less the estimated costs of sale, and a reasonable profit margin based on the effort required to complete and sell the inventories.

Transaction costs that the Company incurs in connection with a business combination are expensed immediately.

Joint arrangement
A joint arrangement is an arrangement in which two or more parties have joint control. Joint control is the contractually agreed sharing of control whereby decisions about relevant activities require unanimous consent of the parties sharing control. A joint arrangement is classified as a joint operation when the parties that have joint control have rights to the assets and obligations for the liabilities related to the arrangement. The Company records its share of a joint operation's assets, liabilities, revenues, and expenses.

Foreign currency translation
Transactions in foreign currencies are translated into Canadian dollars at rates in effect at the date of the transaction. Monetary assets and liabilities in foreign currencies are translated into Canadian dollars at the closing exchange rate at the balance sheet date. Non-monetary items that are measured in terms of historical cost are translated into Canadian dollars at the exchange rate at the date of the original transaction. Exchange gains or losses arising from translation are recorded in Other income or Cost of producing revenue as applicable in the Consolidated Statements of Income.

Financial instruments

Recognition and measurement
Financial assets and financial liabilities, including derivatives, are recognized in the Consolidated Balance Sheets when the Company becomes a party to the contractual provisions of a financial instrument or non-financial derivative contract. All financial instruments are required to be measured at fair value on initial recognition. Subsequent measurement of these assets and liabilities is based on either fair value or amortized cost using the effective interest method, depending upon their classification.

Transaction costs that are directly attributable to the acquisition or issue of financial assets and financial liabilities (other than financial assets and financial liabilities classified as FVTPL) are added to or deducted from the fair value of the financial assets or financial liabilities, as appropriate, on initial recognition. Transaction costs directly attributable to the acquisition of financial assets or financial liabilities classified as FVTPL are recognized immediately in net income.

The Company classifies financial instruments, at the time of initial recognition, according to their characteristics and Management's choices and intentions related thereto for the purposes of ongoing measurement. Classification choices for financial assets include a) FVTPL, b) held to maturity, c) available for sale, and d) loans and receivables. Classification choices for financial liabilities include a) FVTPL and b) other liabilities.

The Company's financial assets and financial liabilities are generally classified and measured as follows:

Asset/Liability	Category	Measurement
Cash and cash equivalents	Loans and receivables	Amortized cost
Short-term investments[1]	Available for sale	Fair value
Trade and other receivables[2]	Loans and receivables	Amortized cost
Loans receivable	Loans and receivables	Amortized cost
Deposits (recorded in prepaid expenses and deposits)	Loans and receivables	Amortized cost
Long-term receivables and other assets[2]	Loans and receivables	Amortized cost
Long-term investments[3]	Available for sale	Fair value
Bank indebtedness	Other liabilities	Amortized cost
Deposits	Other liabilities	Amortized cost
Trade and other payables[2]	Other liabilities	Amortized cost
Short-term borrowings	Other liabilities	Amortized cost
Loans payable	Other liabilities	Amortized cost
Long-term debt	Other liabilities	Amortized cost
Redeemable financial instrument (recorded in other long-term liabilities)	FVTPL	Fair value

[1]Certain short-term investments are classified as FVTPL and measured at fair value.
[2]Includes derivatives that are classified as FVTPL or are effective hedging instruments, and measured at fair value as well as share-based payables which are carried at fair value.
[3]Certain long-term investments are classified as FVTPL and measured at fair value.

Financial instruments at fair value through profit or loss

Financial instruments are classified as FVTPL when the financial instrument is either held for trading or designated as such upon initial recognition. Financial instruments are classified as held for trading if acquired principally for the purpose of selling in the near future or if part of an identified portfolio of financial instruments that the Company manages together and has a recent actual pattern of short-term profit-making. Derivatives are classified as FVTPL unless they are designated as effective hedging instruments.

Financial instruments classified as FVTPL are measured at fair value, with changes in fair value recorded in net income in the period in which they arise.

Available-for-sale

Financial assets classified as available-for-sale are measured at fair value with changes in fair value recognized in OCI until realized through disposal or other than temporary impairment, at which point the change in fair value is recognized in net income. Dividend income from available-for-sale financial assets is recognized in net income when the Company's right to receive payments is established. Interest income on available-for-sale financial assets, calculated using the effective interest method, is recognized in net income.

Loans and receivables

Loans and receivables are financial assets with fixed or determinable payments that are not quoted in an active market. Subsequent to initial recognition, loans and receivables are measured at amortized cost using the effective interest method, less any impairment, with gains and losses recognized in net income in the period that the asset is derecognized or impaired.

Cash and cash equivalents

Cash and cash equivalents are defined as cash plus highly liquid and rated certificates of deposit or commercial paper with an original term to maturity of three months or less.

Short-term investments

Short-term investments are investments in highly liquid and rated certificates of deposit, commercial paper or other securities, primarily Canadian and United States ("U.S.") government securities, and notes of other creditworthy parties, with an original term to maturity of more than three months and remaining term to maturity of less than one year.

Trade and other receivables

The allowance for impairment of trade and other receivables is established when there is objective evidence that the Company will not be able to collect all amounts due according to the original terms of the receivables. Significant financial difficulties of the debtor, probability that the debtor will enter bankruptcy or financial reorganization, and default or delinquency in payments are considered indicators that the trade receivable is impaired. The amount of the allowance is calculated as the difference between the asset's carrying amount and the present value of estimated future cash flows, discounted at the original effective interest rate. The carrying amount of the asset is reduced through the use of an allowance account, and the amount of the loss is recognized in Selling, general and administrative expenses in the Consolidated Statements of Income. When a trade receivable is deemed uncollectible, it is written off against the allowance account. Subsequent recoveries of amounts previously written off are recognized as a recovery in Selling, general and administrative expenses, in the Consolidated Statements of Income.

Loans receivable

Loans receivable consists of credit card and line of credit loans, as well as loans to Associate Dealers ("Dealers"), who are independent third-party operators of Canadian Tire Retail stores. Loans receivable are recognized when cash is advanced to the borrower. They are derecognized when the borrower repays its obligations, the loans are sold or written off, or substantially all of the risks and rewards of ownership are transferred.

Losses for impaired loans are recognized when there is objective evidence that impairment of the loans has occurred. Impairment allowances are calculated on individual loans and on groups of loans assessed collectively. Impairment losses are recorded in Cost of producing revenue in the Consolidated Statements of Income. The carrying amount of impaired loans in the Consolidated Balance Sheets is reduced through the use of impairment allowance accounts. Losses expected from future events are not recognized.

All individually significant loans receivable are assessed for specific impairment. All individually significant loans receivable found not to be specifically impaired are then collectively assessed for any impairment that has been incurred but not yet identified. Loans receivable that are not individually significant are collectively assessed for impairment by grouping together loans receivable with similar risk characteristics.

The Company uses a roll-rate methodology to calculate allowances for credit card and line of credit loans. This methodology employs statistical analysis of historical data and experience of delinquency and default, to estimate the amount of loans that will eventually be written off as a result of events occurring before the reporting date, with certain adjustments for other relevant circumstances influencing the recoverability of the loans receivable. The estimated loss is the difference between the present value of the expected future cash flows, discounted at the original effective interest rate of the portfolio, and the carrying amount of the portfolio. Default rates, loss rates, and the expected timing of future recoveries are regularly benchmarked against actual outcomes to ensure that they remain appropriate.

Merchandise inventories

Merchandise inventories are carried at the lower of cost and net realizable value.

Cash consideration received from vendors is recognized as a reduction to the cost of related inventory, unless the cash consideration received is either a reimbursement of incremental costs incurred by the Company or a payment for assets or services delivered to the vendor.

The cost of merchandise inventories is determined based on weighted average cost and includes costs incurred in bringing the merchandise inventories to their present location and condition. All inventories are finished goods.

Net realizable value is the estimated selling price of inventory during the normal course of business less estimated selling expenses.

Long-term investments

Investments in highly liquid and rated certificates of deposit, commercial paper, or other securities with a remaining term to maturity of greater than one year are classified as long-term investments. The Company's exposure to credit, currency, and interest rate risks related to other investments is disclosed in Note 5.

Assets under finance leases are recognized as assets of the Company at their fair value or, if lower, at the present value of the minimum lease payments, each determined at the inception of the lease. The corresponding liability is included in the Consolidated Balance Sheets as a finance lease obligation. Lease payments are apportioned between finance costs and reduction of the lease obligations, so as to achieve a constant rate of interest on the remaining balance of the liability.

Sale and leaseback

The accounting treatment of a sale and leaseback transaction is assessed based upon the substance of the transaction and whether the sale is made at the asset's fair value.

For sale and finance leasebacks, any gain or loss from the sale is deferred and amortized over the lease term. For sale and operating leasebacks, the assets are sold at fair value and, accordingly, the gain or loss from the sale is recognized immediately in net income.

Impairment of assets

The carrying amounts of property and equipment, investment property, and intangible assets with finite useful lives are reviewed at the end of each reporting period to determine whether there are any indicators of impairment. Indicators of impairment may include a significant decline in asset market value, material adverse changes in the external operating environment which affect the manner in which the asset is used or is expected to be used, obsolescence, or physical damage of the asset. If any such indicators exist, then the recoverable amount of the asset is estimated. Goodwill and intangible assets with indefinite useful lives and intangible assets not yet available for use are not amortized but are tested for impairment at least annually or whenever there is an indicator that the asset may be impaired.

Cash generating units

When it is not possible to estimate the recoverable amount of an individual asset, the Company estimates the recoverable amount of the CGU to which the asset belongs. The CGUs correspond to the smallest identifiable group of assets whose continuing use generates cash inflows that are largely independent of the cash inflows from other assets or groups of assets.

Goodwill acquired in a business combination is allocated to each of the CGUs (or groups of CGUs) expected to benefit from the synergies of the combination. Intangible assets with indefinite useful lives are allocated to the CGU to which they relate.

Determining the recoverable amount

An impairment loss is recognized when the carrying amount of an asset, or of the CGU to which it belongs, exceeds the recoverable amount. The recoverable amount of an asset or CGU is defined as the higher of its fair value less costs to sell ("FVLCS") and its VIU.

In assessing VIU, the estimated future cash flows are discounted to their present value. Cash flows are discounted using a pre-tax discount rate that includes a risk premium specific to each line of business. The Company estimates cash flows before taxes based on the most recent actual results or budgets. Cash flows are then extrapolated over a period of up to five years, taking into account a terminal value calculated by discounting the final year in perpetuity. The growth rate applied to the terminal values is based on the Bank of Canada's target inflation rate or a growth rate specific to the individual item being tested based on Management's estimate.

Recording impairments and reversals of impairments

Impairments and reversals of impairments are recognized in Other income in the Consolidated Statements of Income. Any impairment loss is allocated first to reduce the carrying amount of any goodwill allocated to the CGU and then to the other assets of the CGU. Impairments of goodwill cannot be reversed. Impairments of other assets recognized in prior periods are assessed at the end of each reporting period to determine if the indicators of impairment have reversed or no longer exist. An impairment loss is reversed if the estimated recoverable amount exceeds the carrying amount. The increased carrying amount of an asset attributable to a reversal of impairment may not exceed the carrying amount that would have been determined had no impairment been recognized in prior periods.

Assets classified as held for sale

Non-current assets and disposal groups are classified as assets held for sale when their carrying amount is to be recovered principally through a sale transaction rather than through continuing use. This condition is regarded as met only when the sale is highly probable and the asset (or disposal group) is available for immediate sale in its present condition. Management must be committed to the sale, and it should be expected to qualify for recognition as a completed sale within one year from the date of classification. Assets (and disposal groups) classified as held for sale are measured at the lower of the carrying amount or FVLCS and are not depreciated. The fair value measurement of assets held for sale is categorized within Level 2 of fair value hierarchy (refer to Note 35.4 for definition of levels).

Borrowing costs

Borrowing costs directly attributable to the acquisition or construction of a qualifying asset are capitalized. Qualifying assets are those that require a minimum of three months to prepare for their intended use. All other borrowing costs are recognized in Cost of producing revenue or in Net finance costs in the Consolidated Statements of Income in the period in which they are incurred.

Employee benefits

Short-term benefits

Short-term employee benefit obligations are measured on an undiscounted basis and are expensed as the related service is provided.

The Company recognizes a liability and an expense for short-term benefits such as bonuses, profit-sharing, and employee stock purchases if the Company has a present legal obligation or constructive obligation to pay this amount, as a result of past service provided by the employees and the obligation can be estimated reasonably.

Post-employment benefits

The Company provides certain health care, dental care, life insurance, and other benefits, but not pensions, for certain retired employees pursuant to Company policy. The Company accrues the cost of these employee benefits over the periods in which the employees earn the benefits. The cost of employee benefits earned by employees is actuarially determined using the projected benefit method pro-rated on length of service and Management's best estimate of salary escalation, retirement ages of employees, employee turnover, life expectancy, and expected health and dental care costs. The costs are discounted at a rate that is based on market rates as at the measurement date. Actuarial gains and losses are immediately recorded in OCI.

The Company also provides post-employment benefits with respect to contributions to a Deferred Profit Sharing Plan ("DPSP").

Termination benefits

Termination benefits are payable when employment is terminated by the Company before the normal retirement date or whenever an employee accepts voluntary redundancy in exchange for these benefits. The Company recognizes a provision for termination benefits when it is demonstrably committed to either terminating the employment of current employees according to a detailed formal plan, without possibility of withdrawal, or providing termination benefits as a result of an offer made to encourage voluntary redundancy.

Share-based payments

Stock options with tandem stock appreciation rights ("stock options") are granted with a feature that enables the employee to exercise the stock option or receive a cash payment equal to the difference between the market price of the Company's Class A Non-Voting Shares as at the exercise date and the exercise price of the stock option. These stock options are considered to be compound instruments. The fair value of compound instruments is measured at each reporting date, taking into account the terms and conditions on which the rights to cash or equity instruments are granted. As the fair value of the settlement in cash is the same as the fair value of the settlement as a traditional stock option, the fair value of the stock option is the same as the fair value of the debt component. The corresponding expense and liability are recognized over the respective vesting period.

The fair value of the amount payable to employees with respect to share unit plans and trust unit plans, which are settled in cash, is recorded as the services are provided over the vesting period. The fair value of the liability is remeasured at each reporting date with the change in the liability being recognized in Selling, general and administrative expenses in the Consolidated Statements of Income.

Insurance reserve

Included in trade and other payables is an insurance reserve that consists of an amount determined from loss reports and individual cases and an amount, based on past experience, for losses incurred but not reported. These estimates are continually reviewed and are subject to the impact of future changes in such factors as claim severity and frequency. While Management believes that the amount is adequate, the ultimate liability may be in excess of or less than the amounts provided, and any adjustment will be reflected in net income during the periods in which they become known.

The Company uses actuarial valuations in determining its reserve for outstanding losses and loss-related expenses using an appropriate reserving methodology for each line of business. The Company does not discount its liabilities for unpaid claims.

Provisions

A provision is recognized if, as a result of a past event, the Company has a present legal or constructive obligation that can be estimated reliably and it is probable that an outflow of economic benefits will be required to settle the obligation. The amount recognized as a provision is the best estimate of the consideration required to settle the present obligation at the end of the reporting period, taking into account risks and uncertainty of cash flows. Where the effect of discounting is material, provisions are determined by discounting the expected future cash flows at a pre-tax rate that reflects current market assessments of the time value of money and the risks specific to the liability.

Sales and warranty returns

The provision for sales and warranty returns relates to the Company's obligation for defective goods in current store inventories and defective goods sold to customers that have yet to be returned, after sales service for replacement parts, and future corporate store sales returns. Accruals for sales and warranty returns are estimated on the basis of historical returns and are recorded so as to allocate them to the same period the corresponding revenue is recognized. These accruals are reviewed regularly and updated to reflect Management's best estimate; however, actual returns could vary from these estimates.

Site restoration and decommissioning

Legal or constructive obligations associated with the removal of underground fuel storage tanks and site remediation costs on the retirement of certain property and equipment and with the termination of certain lease agreements, are recognized in the period in which they are incurred, when it is probable that an outflow of resources embodying economic benefits will be required and a reasonable estimate of the amount of the obligation can be made. The obligations are initially measured at the Company's best estimate, using an expected value approach, and are discounted to present value.

Onerous contracts

A provision for onerous contracts is recognized when the expected benefits to be derived by the Company from a contract are lower than the unavoidable costs of meeting its obligations under the contract. The provision is measured at the present value of the lower of the expected cost of terminating the contract or the expected net cost of continuing with the contract.

Customer loyalty

An obligation arises from the "My Canadian Tire 'Money'™" customer loyalty program when the Company issues e-Canadian Tire "Money" and when the Dealers pay the Company to acquire paper-based Canadian Tire "Money," as the Dealers retain the right to return paper-based Canadian Tire Money to the Company for refund in cash. These obligations are measured at fair value by reference to the fair value of the awards for which they could be redeemed and based on the estimated probability of their redemption. The expense is recorded in Selling, general and administrative expenses in the Consolidated Statements of Income.

Debt

Debt is classified as current when the Company expects to settle the liability in its normal operating cycle, it holds the liability primarily for the purpose of trading, the liability is due to be settled within 12 months after the date of the Consolidated Balance Sheets, or it does not have an unconditional right to defer settlement of the liability for at least 12 months after the date of the Consolidated Balance Sheets.

Share capital

Shares issued by the Company are recorded at the value of proceeds received. Repurchased shares are removed from equity. No gain or loss is recognized in net income on the purchase, sale, issue, or cancellation of the Company's shares.

Share repurchases are charged to share capital at the average cost per share outstanding and the excess between the repurchase price and the average cost is first allocated to contributed surplus, with any remainder allocated to retained earnings.

Dividends

Dividends declared and payable to the Company's shareholders are recognized as a liability in the Consolidated Balance Sheets in the period in which the dividends are approved by the Company's Board of Directors.

Distributions

Distributions to non-controlling interests are recognized as a liability in the Consolidated Balance Sheets in the period in which the distributions are declared.

Revenue

The Company recognizes revenue when the amount can be reliably measured, when it is probable that future economic benefits will flow to the entity, and when specific criteria have been met for each of the Company's activities as described below.

Sale of goods

Revenue from the sale of goods includes merchandise sold to Dealers and Mark's Work Wearhouse Ltd. ("Mark's") and FGL Sports Ltd. ("FGL Sports") franchisees, the sale of gasoline through agents, and the sale of goods by Mark's, PartSource, and FGL Sports corporately-owned stores to the general public. This revenue is recognized when the goods are delivered, less an estimate for the sales and warranty returns. Revenue from the sale of goods is measured at the fair value of the consideration received less an appropriate deduction for actual and expected returns, discounts, rebates, and warranty and loyalty program costs, net of sales taxes.

If there is any uncertainty regarding the right of a customer to return goods, no revenue is recognized until the uncertainty is resolved. However, in the case of warranties, if warranty claims can be reasonably estimated, revenue is then recorded for the net amount.

Customer loyalty programs

Loyalty award credits issued as part of a sales transaction relating to the Company's Gas Advantage, Cash Advantage, and Sport Chek MasterCard Rewards credit card programs result in revenue being deferred until the loyalty award is redeemed by the customer. The portion of the revenue that is deferred is the fair value of the award. The fair value of the award takes into account the amount for which the award credits could be sold separately, less the proportion of the award credits that are not expected to be redeemed by customers.

Interest income on loans receivable

Interest income includes interest charged on loans receivable and fees that are an integral part of the effective interest rate on financial instruments, such as annual credit card fees. Interest income on financial assets that are classified as loans and receivables is determined using the effective interest method.

Services rendered

Service revenue includes Roadside Assistance Club membership revenue; insurance premiums and reinsurance revenue; extended warranty contract fees; merchant, interchange, and processing fees; cash advance fees; foreign exchange fees; and service charges on the loans receivable of the Financial Services operating segment, as well as Mark's clothing alteration revenue. Service revenue is recognized according to the contractual provisions of the arrangement, which is generally when the service is provided or over the contractual period.

Merchant, interchange, and processing fees, cash advance fees, and foreign exchange fees on credit card transactions are recognized as revenue at the time transactions are completed. Revenue from separately priced extended warranty contracts is recorded on a straight-line basis over the term of the contracts.

Reinsurance premiums are recorded on an accrual basis and are included in net income on a pro rata basis over the life of the insurance contract, with the unearned portion deferred in the Consolidated Balance Sheets. Premiums that are subject to adjustment are estimated based on available information. Any variances from the estimates are recorded in the periods in which they become known.

Royalties and licence fees

Royalties and licence fees include licence fees from petroleum agents and Dealers, and royalties from Mark's and FGL Sports franchisees. Royalties and licence fee revenues are recognized as they are earned in accordance with the substance of the relevant agreement and are measured on an accrual basis.

Rental income

Rental income from operating leases where the Company is the lessor is recognized on a straight-line basis over the terms of the respective leases.

Vendor rebates

The Company records cash consideration received from vendors as a reduction in the price of vendors' products and recognizes it as a reduction to the cost of related inventory or, if the related inventory has been sold, to the cost of producing revenue. Certain exceptions apply where the cash consideration received is either a reimbursement of incremental selling costs incurred by the Company or a payment for assets or services delivered to the vendor, in which case the cost is reflected as a reduction in selling, general and administrative expenses.

The Company recognizes rebates that are at the vendor's discretion when the vendor either pays the rebates or agrees to pay them and payment is considered probable and reasonably estimable.

Net finance costs

Finance income comprises interest income on funds invested (including available-for-sale financial assets). Interest income is recognized as it accrues using the effective interest method.

Finance costs comprises interest expense on borrowings (including borrowings relating to the Dealer Loan Program), unwinding of the discount on provisions, and is net of borrowing costs that have been capitalized. Interest on deposits is recorded in Cost of producing revenue in the Consolidated Statements of Income.

Income taxes

The income tax expense for the year comprises current and deferred income tax. Income tax expense is recognized in net income except to the extent that it relates to items recognized either in OCI or directly in equity. In this case, the income tax expense is recognized in OCI or in equity, respectively.

The income tax expense is calculated on the basis of the tax laws enacted or substantively enacted at the date of the Consolidated Balance Sheets in the countries where the Company operates and generates taxable income.

Deferred income tax is recognized using the liability method for unused tax losses, unused tax benefits, and temporary differences arising between the tax bases of assets and liabilities and their carrying amounts in these consolidated financial statements. However, deferred income tax is not accounted for if it arises from the initial recognition of goodwill or the initial recognition of an asset or liability in a transaction, other than a business combination, that at the time of the transaction affects neither accounting nor taxable income. Deferred income tax is determined using tax rates (and laws) that have been enacted or substantively enacted at the date of the Consolidated Balance Sheets and are expected to apply when the related deferred income tax asset is realized or the deferred income tax liability is settled.

Deferred income tax assets are recognized only to the extent that it is probable that future taxable income will be available against which the temporary differences can be utilized. Deferred income tax liabilities are provided on temporary differences arising on investments in subsidiaries and associates, except where the timing of the reversal of the temporary difference is controlled by the Company and it is probable that the temporary difference will not reverse in the foreseeable future.

Earnings per share

Basic earnings per share ("Basic EPS") is calculated by dividing the net income attributable to the shareholders of the Company by the weighted average number of Common and Class A Non-Voting shares outstanding during the reporting period. Diluted earnings per share ("Diluted EPS") is calculated by adjusting the net income attributable to the shareholders of the Company and the weighted average number of shares outstanding for the effects of all potentially dilutive equity instruments, which comprise employee stock options. Net income attributable to the shareholders of the Company is the same for both the Basic EPS and Diluted EPS calculations.

Non-controlling interests

When the proportion of the equity held by non-controlling interests changes, the Company adjusts the carrying amounts of the controlling and non-controlling interests to reflect the changes in their relative interest in the subsidiary. The Company recognizes directly in equity any difference between the amount by which the non-controlling interests are adjusted and the fair value of the consideration paid or received, and attribute it to the shareholders of the Company.

Operating segments
An operating segment is a component of the Company that engages in business activities from which it may earn revenues and incur expenses, including revenues and expenses that relate to transactions with any of the Company's other operations, and for which discrete financial information is available.

7. Joint arrangement and business combinations

7.1 Joint arrangement of Canada Square
On July 17, 2014, CT REIT acquired a one-third interest in Canada Square, a mixed-use commercial development in Toronto, pursuant to a co-ownership arrangement (the "Co-ownership"). The Co-ownership is a joint arrangement as the material decisions about relevant activities require unanimous consent of the co-owners. This joint arrangement is a joint operation as each co-owner has rights to the assets and obligations relating to the Co-ownership. Accordingly, CT REIT recognizes its proportionate share of the assets, liabilities, revenue, and expenses of the Co-ownership in its financial statements.

7.2 Other business combinations
During the year ended January 2, 2016, the Company acquired various franchise operations for total consideration of $3.2 million, of which $2.3 million was payable at January 2, 2016. The fair value of the net assets acquired was $2.8 million, resulting in goodwill recognized of $0.4 million.

During the year ended January 3, 2015, the Company acquired various franchise operations for total consideration of $7.3 million, of which $1.0 million was payable at January 3, 2015. The fair value of the net assets acquired was $3.3 million, resulting in goodwill recognized of $4.0 million.

8. Cash and cash equivalents
Cash and cash equivalents comprise the following:

(C$ in millions)	2015	2014
Cash	$ 192.2	$ 134.5
Cash equivalents	698.6	521.0
Restricted cash and cash equivalents[1]	9.8	6.6
Total cash and cash equivalents[2]	900.6	662.1
Bank indebtedness	–	(14.3)
Cash and cash equivalents, net of bank indebtedness	$ 900.6	$ 647.8

[1]Relates to GCCT and is restricted for the purpose of paying out note holders and additional funding costs.
[2]Included in cash and cash equivalents are amounts held in reserve in support of Financial Services' liquidity and regulatory requirements. Refer to Note 34.1.

9. Short-term investments

Short-term investments include the following:

(C$ in millions)	2015	2014
Short-term investments[1]	$ 95.4	$287.5
Restricted short-term investments[2]	0.7	1.6
	$ 96.1	$289.1

[1]Included in short-term investments are amounts held in reserve in support of Financial Services' liquidity and regulatory requirements. Refer to Note 34.1.
[2]Relates to GCCT and is restricted for the purpose of paying out note holders and additional funding costs.

10. Trade and other receivables

Trade and other receivables include the following:

(C$ in millions)	2015	2014
Trade and other receivables	$ 673.6	$ 736.8
Derivatives (Note 35)	241.4	143.4
Total financial assets	$ 915.0	$ 880.2

Trade receivables are primarily from Dealers and franchisees, a large and geographically dispersed group whose receivables, individually, generally comprise less than one percent of the total balance outstanding.

Receivables from Dealers are in the normal course of business, and include cost-sharing and financing arrangements. The net average credit period on sale of goods is between 14 and 120 days.

11. Loans receivable

Quantitative information about the Company's loans receivable portfolio is as follows:

(C$ in millions)	Total principal amount of receivables[1]		Average balance[1]	
	2015	2014	2015	2014
Credit card loans	$ 4,839.4	$ 4,862.9	$ 4,722.7	$ 4,563.4
Line of credit loans	4.9	5.8	5.4	6.1
Total Financial Services' loans receivable	$ 4,844.3	$ 4,868.7	$ 4,728.1	$ 4,569.5
Dealer loans[2]	655.5	604.4		
Other loans	4.1	5.5		
Total loans receivable	5,503.9	5,478.6		
Less: long-term portion[3]	628.4	573.1		
Current portion of loans receivable	$ 4,875.5	$ 4,905.5		

[1]Amounts shown are net of allowance for loan impairment.
[2]Dealer loans issued by Franchise Trust (refer to Note 24).
[3]The long-term portion of loans receivable is included in long-term receivables and other assets and includes Dealer loans of $624.9 million (2014 – $568.2 million).

For the year ended January 2, 2016, cash received from interest earned on credit cards and loans was $789.6 million (2014 – $732.4 million).

The carrying amount of loans includes loans to Dealers that are secured by the assets of the respective Dealer corporations. The Company's exposure to loans receivable credit risk resides at Franchise Trust and at the Bank. Credit risk at the Bank is influenced mainly by the individual characteristics of each credit card customer. The Bank uses sophisticated credit scoring models, monitoring technology and collection modelling techniques to implement and manage strategies, policies, and limits that are designed to control risk. Loans receivable are generated by a large and geographically-dispersed group of customers. Current credit exposure is limited to the loss that would be incurred if all of the Bank's counterparties were to default at the same time.

A continuity schedule of the Company's allowances for loans receivable[1] is as follows:

(C$ in millions)	2015	2014
Balance, beginning of year	$ 113.2	$ 121.4
Impairments for credit losses, net of recoveries	301.9	279.7
Recoveries	65.9	59.8
Write-offs	(369.5)	(347.7)
Balance, end of year	$ 111.5	$ 113.2

[1]Loans include credit card loans and line of credit loans. No allowances for credit losses have been made with respect to Franchise Trust and FGL Sports loans receivable.

The Company's allowances for credit losses are maintained at levels that are considered adequate to absorb future credit losses.

The Company's aging of the loans receivable that are past due, but not impaired, is as follows:

(C$ in millions)	2015			2014		
	1–90 days	**>90 days**	**Total**	1–90 days	>90 days	Total
Loans receivable	**$ 306.3**	**$ 62.8**	**$ 369.1**	$ 342.9	$ 60.4	$ 403.3

Credit card loans are considered impaired and written off when a payment is 180 days in arrears. Line of credit loans are considered impaired when a payment is over 90 days in arrears and are written off when a payment is 180 days in arrears. No collateral is held against loans receivable, except for loans to Dealers, as discussed above.

13. Long-term receivables and other assets

Long-term receivables and other assets include the following:

(C$ in millions)	2015	2014
Loans receivable (Note 11)	**$ 628.4**	$ 573.1
Mortgages receivable	**28.0**	32.5
Derivatives (Note 35)	**50.2**	58.3
Other receivables	**5.1**	4.8
Total financial assets	**711.7**	668.7
Other	**19.5**	15.5
	$ 731.2	$ 684.2

14. Goodwill and intangible assets

The following table presents the changes in cost and accumulated amortization and impairment of the Company's intangible assets:

						2015
	Indefinite-life intangible assets and goodwill			Finite-life intangible assets		
(C$ in millions)	Goodwill	Banners and trademarks	Franchise agreements and other intangibles	Software	Other intangibles	Total
Cost						
Balance, beginning of year	$ 438.5	$ 266.6	$ 156.9	$ 1,158.1	$ 23.1	$ 2,043.2
Additions internally developed	–	–	–	109.1	–	109.1
Additions related to business combinations	0.4	–	2.0	–	–	2.4
Other additions	–	0.8	–	–	–	0.8
Disposals/retirements	–	–	–	0.9	–	0.9
Other movements and transfers	–	–	–	(0.4)	–	(0.4)
Balance, end of year	$ 438.9	$ 267.4	$ 158.9	$ 1,267.7	$ 23.1	$ 2,156.0
Accumulated amortization and impairment						
Balance, beginning of year	$ (1.9)	$ –	$ –	$ (775.3)	$ (14.3)	$ (791.5)
Amortization for the year	–	–	–	(109.8)	(2.1)	(111.9)
Impairment	–	–	–	–	–	–
Disposals/retirements	–	–	–	(4.5)	–	(4.5)
Other movements and transfers	–	–	–	–	(1.3)	(1.3)
Balance, end of year	$ (1.9)	$ –	$ –	$ (889.6)	$ (17.7)	$ (909.2)
Net carrying amount, end of year	$ 437.0	$ 67.4	$ 158.9	$ 378.1	$ 5.4	$ 1,246.8

						2014
	Indefinite-life intangible assets and goodwill			Finite-life intangible assets		
(C$ in millions)	Goodwill	Banners and trademarks	Franchise agreements and other intangibles	Software	Other intangibles	Total
Cost						
Balance, beginning of year	$ 434.5	$ 245.2	$ 154.3	$ 1,027.1	$ 23.1	$ 1,884.2
Additions internally developed	–	–	–	134.2	–	134.2
Additions related to business combinations	4.0	–	2.6	–	–	6.6
Other additions	–	21.4	–	–	–	21.4
Disposals/retirements	–	–	–	(2.6)	–	(2.6)
Other movements and transfers	–	–	–	(0.6)	–	(0.6)
Balance, end of year	$ 438.5	$ 266.6	$ 156.9	$ 1,158.1	$ 23.1	$ 2,043.2
Accumulated amortization and impairment						
Balance, beginning of year	$ (1.6)	$ –	$ –	$ (686.9)	$ (10.2)	$ (698.7)
Amortization for the year	–	–	–	(90.9)	(2.2)	(93.1)
Impairment	(0.3)	–	–	–	–	(0.3)
Disposals/retirements	–	–	–	2.5	–	2.5
Other movements and transfers	–	–	–	–	(1.9)	(1.9)
Balance, end of year	$ (1.9)	$ –	$ –	$ (775.3)	$ (14.3)	$ (791.5)
Net carrying amount, end of year	$ 436.6	$ 266.6	$ 156.9	$ 382.8	$ 8.8	$ 1,251.7

The following table presents the details of the Company's goodwill:

(C$ in millions)	2015	2014
FGL Sports	$ 356.9	$ 356.9
Mark's	56.7	56.3
Canadian Tire	23.4	23.4
Total	$ 437.0	$ 436.6

Banners and trademarks include FGL Sports and Mark's store banners, which represent legal trademarks of the Company with expiry dates ranging from 2016 to 2030. In addition, banners and trademarks include FGL Sports and Mark's private-label brands that have legal expiry dates. As the Company currently has no approved plans to change its store banners and intends to continue to renew all trademarks and private-label brands at each expiry date for the foreseeable future, there is no foreseeable limit to the period over which the assets are expected to generate net cash inflows. Therefore, these intangible assets are considered to have indefinite useful lives.

Franchise agreements have expiry dates with options to renew or have indefinite lives. As the Company intends to renew these agreements at each renewal date for the foreseeable future, there is no foreseeable limit to the period over which the franchise agreements and franchise locations will generate net cash inflows. Therefore, these assets are considered to have indefinite useful lives.

Finite-life intangible assets include FGL Sports customer relationships, certain private-label brands, and off-market leases that the Company has assessed as having limited life terms. These assets are amortized over a term of five to seven years. Off-market leases are amortized over the term of the lease to which they relate.

The amount of borrowing costs capitalized in 2015 was $3.4 million (2014 – $3.2 million). The capitalization rate used to determine the amount of borrowing costs capitalized during the year was 6.0 percent (2014 – 5.7 percent).

Amortization expense of software and other finite-life intangible assets is included in Selling, general and administrative expenses in the Consolidated Statements of Income.

Impairment of intangible assets and subsequent reversal

The Company performed its annual impairment test on goodwill and indefinite-life intangible assets for all CGUs based on VIU using after-tax discount rates ranging from 7.2 to 10.0 percent and growth rates ranging from 1.0 to 12.1 percent per annum.

The amount of impairment of intangible assets in 2015 was $nil (2014 – $0.3 million). There was no reversal of impairments in 2015 or 2014. The impairment on goodwill in 2014 pertains to the Company's Retail operating segment and is reported in Other Income in the Consolidated Statements of Income.

For all goodwill and intangible assets, the estimated recoverable amount is based on VIU exceeding the carrying amount. There is no reasonable possible change in assumptions that would cause the carrying amount to exceed the estimated recoverable amount.

15. Investment property

The following table presents changes in the cost and the accumulated depreciation and impairment on the Company's investment property:

(C$ in millions)	2015	2014
Cost		
Balance, beginning of year	$ 178.8	$ 123.9
Additions	11.0	32.9
Disposals/retirements	(3.8)	(3.7)
Reclassified to/from held for sale	(6.1)	(3.3)
Reclassified to/from property and equipment	(10.1)	–
Other movements and transfers	2.6	29.0
Balance, end of year	$ 172.4	$ 178.8
Accumulated depreciation and impairment		
Balance, beginning of year	$ (30.2)	$ (30.4)
Depreciation for the year	(4.0)	(3.5)
Impairment	–	(1.6)
Disposal/retirements	1.1	2.3
Reclassified to/from held for sale	2.8	5.1
Reclassified to/from property and equipment	(4.1)	–
Other movements and transfers	(0.2)	(2.1)
Balance, end of year	$ (34.6)	$ (30.2)
Net carrying amount, end of year	$ 137.8	$ 148.6

The investment properties generated rental income of $19.2 million (2014 – $16.9 million).

Direct operating expenses (including repairs and maintenance) arising from investment property recognized in net income were $9.7 million (2014 – $8.8 million).

The estimated fair value of investment property was $228.2 million (2014 – $230.7 million). This recurring fair value measurement is categorized within Level 3 of the fair value hierarchy (refer to Note 35.4 for definition of levels). The Company determines the fair value of investment property by applying a pre-tax capitalization rate to the annual rental income for the current leases. The capitalization rate ranged from 5.3 percent to 11.0 percent (2014 – 5.8 percent to 11.0 percent). The cash flows are for a term of five years, including a terminal value. The Company has real estate management expertise that is used to perform the valuation of investment property and has also completed independent appraisals on certain investment property owned by CT REIT.

Impairment of investment property and subsequent reversal

Any impairment or reversals of impairment are reported in Other income in the Consolidated Statements of Income.

16. Property and equipment

The following table presents changes in the cost and the accumulated depreciation and impairment on the Company's property and equipment:

(C$ in millions)	Land	Buildings	Fixtures and equipment	Leasehold improve- ments	Assets under finance lease	Construction in progress	2015 Total
Cost							
Balance, beginning of year	$ 861.0	$ 2,857.7	$ 1,071.9	$ 1,001.1	$ 256.5	$ 224.3	$ 6,272.5
Additions	9.1	63.3	165.8	155.6	14.0	163.2	571.0
Disposals/retirements	(4.2)	(10.5)	(21.4)	(6.7)	(8.0)	(26.3)	(77.1)
Reclassified to/from held for sale	(0.4)	(5.8)	(0.5)	–	–	–	(6.7)
Reclassified to/from investment property	0.9	9.2	–	–	–	–	10.1
Other movements and transfers	8.0	2.0	0.8	(9.3)	0.3	(1.8)	–
Balance, end of year	$ 874.4	$ 2,915.9	$ 1,216.6	$ 1,140.7	$ 262.8	$ 359.4	$ 6,769.8
Accumulated depreciation and impairment							
Balance, beginning of year	$ (4.4)	$(1,289.8)	$ (712.0)	$ (365.7)	$ (157.5)	$ –	$(2,529.4)
Depreciation for the year	–	(108.4)	(103.8)	(80.0)	(16.5)	–	(308.7)
Impairment	–	(0.2)	(0.2)	–	–	–	(0.4)
Reversal of impairment losses	–	–	0.1	0.1	–	–	0.2
Disposals/retirements	0.1	4.8	18.6	7.1	7.4	–	38.0
Reclassified to/from held for sale	–	4.0	0.3	–	–	–	4.3
Reclassified to/from investment property	–	4.1	–	–	–	–	4.1
Other movements and transfers	(2.3)	(0.3)	2.2	2.3	(1.6)	–	0.3
Balance, end of year	$ (6.6)	$(1,385.8)	$ (794.8)	$ (436.2)	$ (168.2)	$ –	$(2,791.6)
Net carrying amount, end of year	$ 867.8	$ 1,530.1	$ 421.8	$ 704.5	$94.6	$ 359.4	$ 3,978.2

(C$ in millions)	Land	Buildings	Fixtures and equipment	Leasehold improve- ments	Assets under finance lease	Construction in progress	2014 Total
Cost							
Balance, beginning of year	$ 815.0	$ 2,750.8	$ 938.8	$ 882.3	$ 276.6	$ 179.1	$ 5,842.6
Additions	49.8	141.2	139.8	145.2	19.4	59.3	554.7
Disposals/retirements	–	(4.8)	(35.2)	(23.4)	(10.5)	–	(73.9)
Reclassified to/from held for sale	(3.2)	(15.9)	(0.5)	(2.5)	–	–	(22.1)
Other movements and transfers	(0.6)	(13.6)	29.0	(0.5)	(29.0)	(14.1)	(28.8)
Balance, end of year	$ 861.0	$ 2,857.7	$ 1,071.9	$ 1,001.1	$ 256.5	$ 224.3	$ 6,272.5
Accumulated depreciation and impairment							
Balance, beginning of year	$ (0.3)	$(1,201.0)	$ (641.3)	$ (316.5)	$ (167.4)	$ –	$(2,326.5)
Depreciation for the year	–	(102.4)	(80.1)	(74.9)	(18.3)	–	(275.7)
Impairment	(4.1)	(0.6)	(0.2)	–	(0.1)	–	(5.0)
Disposals/retirements	–	3.8	27.0	23.2	10.5	–	64.5
Reclassified to/from held for sale	–	8.3	0.3	2.5	–	–	11.1
Other movements and transfers	–	2.1	(17.7)	–	17.8	–	2.2
Balance, end of year	$ (4.4)	$(1,289.8)	$ (712.0)	$ (365.7)	$ (157.5)	$ –	$(2,529.4)
Net carrying amount, end of year	$ 856.6	$ 1,567.9	$ 359.9	$ 635.4	$ 99.0	$ 224.3	$ 3,743.1

The Company capitalized borrowing costs of $11.8 million (2014 – $7.7 million) on indebtedness related to property and equipment under construction. The rate used to determine the amount of borrowing costs capitalized during the year was 6.0 percent (2014 – 5.7 percent).

The carrying amount of assets under finance leases at January 2, 2016, comprises $39.3 million (2014 – $44.9 million) in buildings and $55.3 million (2014 – $54.1 million) in fixtures and equipment.

Impairment of property and equipment and subsequent reversal
The impairment of property and equipment pertain to the Company's Retail operating segment. Any impairment or reversal of impairment is reported in Other income in the Consolidated Statements of Income.

17. Subsidiaries

17.1 Control of subsidiaries and composition of the Company

These consolidated financial statements include entities controlled by Canadian Tire Corporation. Control exists when Canadian Tire Corporation has the ability to direct the relevant activities and the returns of an entity. The financial statements of these entities are included in these consolidated financial statements from the date that control commences until the date that control ceases. Details of the Company's significant entities are as follows:

			Ownership Interest	
Name of subsidiary	Principal activity	Country of incorporation and operation	**2015**	2014
CTFS Holdings Limited[1]	Marketing of insurance products, processing credit card transactions at Canadian Tire stores, banking and reinsurance	Canada	**80.0%**	80.0%
Canadian Tire Real Estate Limited	Real estate	Canada	**100.0%**	100.0%
CT Real Estate Investment Trust	Real estate	Canada	**83.8%**	83.2%
FGL Sports Ltd.	Retailer of sporting equipment, apparel, and footwear	Canada	**100.0%**	100.0%
Franchise Trust[2]	Canadian Tire Dealer Loan Program	Canada	**0.0%**	0.0%
Glacier Credit Card Trust[3]	Financing program to purchase co-ownership interests in Canadian Tire Bank's credit card loans	Canada	**0.0%**	0.0%
Mark's Work Wearhouse Ltd.	Retailer of clothing and footwear	Canada	**100.0%**	100.0%

[1] Legal entity CTFS Holdings Limited, incorporated in 2014, is the parent company of CTB and CTFS Bermuda Holdings Limited. CTB's principal activity is banking, marketing of insurance products, and processing credit card transactions at Canadian Tire stores. CTFS Bermuda Holdings Limited owns 100.0 percent of CTFS Bermuda Ltd., whose principal activity is reinsurance.

[2] Franchise Trust is a legal entity sponsored by a third-party bank that originates loans to Dealers under the Dealer Loan Program. The Company does not have any share ownership in Franchise Trust. However, the Company has determined that it has the ability to direct the relevant activities and returns on the silo of assets and liabilities of Franchise Trust that relate to the Canadian Tire Dealer Loan Program. As the Company has control over this silo of assets and liabilities, it is consolidated in these financial statements.

[3] GCCT was formed to meet specific business needs of the Company, namely to buy co-ownership interests in the Company's credit card loans. GCCT issues debt to third-party investors to fund its purchases. The Company does not have any share ownership in GCCT. However, the Company has determined that it has the ability to direct the relevant activities and returns of GCCT. As the Company has control over GCCT, it is consolidated in these financial statements.

17.2 Details of non–wholly owned subsidiaries that have non-controlling interests

The portion of net assets and income attributable to third parties is reported as non-controlling interests and net income attributable to non-controlling interests in the Consolidated Balance Sheets and Consolidated Statements of Income, respectively. The non-controlling interests of CT REIT and CTFS Holdings Limited were initially measured at fair value on the date of acquisition.

The following table summarizes the information relating to non-controlling interests:

				2015
(C$ in millions)	CT REIT[1]	CTFS Holdings Limited[2]	Other[3]	Total
Non-controlling interests	16.2%	20.0%	50.0%	
Current assets	$ 29.3	$5,364.2	$13.2	$5,406.7
Non-current assets	4,321.6	209.9	32.2	4,563.7
Current liabilities	245.2	1,226.3	4.3	1,475.8
Non-current liabilities	1,892.4	3,305.8	25.6	5,223.8
Net assets	2,213.3	1,042.0	15.5	3,270.8
Revenue	$ 378.2	$1,165.2	$181.4	$1,724.8
Net income attributable to non-controlling interests	$ 20.6	$ 53.0	$ 2.9	$ 76.5
Equity attributable to non-controlling interests	286.5	504.3	4.7	795.5
Distributions to non-controlling interests	(20.3)	(33.6)	(1.7)	(55.6)

[1] Net income attributable to non-controlling interests is based on net income of CT REIT adjusted to convert to the Company's cost method, including recording of depreciation.

[2] Net income attributable to non-controlling interests is based on the net income of CTFS Holdings Limited adjusted for contractual requirements as stipulated in the Universal Shareholder agreement.

[3] Net income attributable to non-controlling interests is based on net income of the subsidiary adjusted for contractual requirements as stipulated in the ownership agreement.

				2014
(C$ in millions)	CT REIT[1]	CTFS Holdings Limited[2]	Other[3]	Total
Non-controlling interests	16.8%	20.0%	50.0%	
Current assets	$ 15.1	$ 5,326.1	$ 9.0	$ 5,350.2
Non-current assets	4,002.3	222.9	34.1	4,259.3
Current liabilities	(310.2)	(1,846.9)	(2.8)	(2,159.9)
Non-current liabilities	(1,705.1)	(2,699.5)	(26.7)	(4,431.3)
Net assets	2,002.2	1,002.6	13.6	3,018.4
Revenue	$ 344.8	$ 241.6	$ 187.8	$ 774.2
Net income attributable to non-controlling interests	$ 19.9	$ 10.3	$ 5.1	$ 35.3
Equity attributable to non-controlling interests	284.4	487.3	3.6	775.3
Distributions to non-controlling interests	(19.8)	–	(1.5)	(21.3)

[1]Net income attributable to non-controlling interests is based on net income of CT REIT adjusted to convert to the Company's cost method, including recording of depreciation.
[2]Net income attributable to non-controlling interests is based on the net income of CTFS Holdings Limited adjusted for contractual requirements as stipulated in the Universal Shareholder agreement.
[3]Net income attributable to non-controlling interests is based on net income of the subsidiary adjusted for contractual requirements as stipulated in the ownership agreement.

17.3 Continuity of non-controlling interests

(C$ in millions)	2015	2014
Balance at beginning of year	$ 775.3	$ 282.6
Sale of ownership interests, net of transaction costs	–	476.8
Comprehensive income attributable to non-controlling interests for the year[1]	74.0	35.4
Issuance of trust units to non-controlling interests, net of transaction costs	1.8	1.8
Distributions	(55.6)	(21.3)
Balance at end of year	$ 795.5	$ 775.3

[1]Includes $(2.5) million (2014 – $0.1 million) from the Consolidated Statements of Comprehensive Income.

18. Income taxes

18.1 Deferred income tax assets and liabilities

The amount of deferred tax assets or liabilities recognized in the Consolidated Balance Sheets and the corresponding movement recognized in the Consolidated Statements of Income, Consolidated Statements of Changes in Equity, or resulting from a business combination is as follows:

							2015
(C$ in millions)	Balance, beginning of year	Recognized in profit or loss	Recognized in other comprehensive income	Recognized in equity	Acquired in business combination	Other adjustments	Balance, end of year
Provisions, deferred revenue and reserves	$ 139.3	$ 4.5	$ –	$ –	$ –	$ –	$ 143.8
Property and equipment	(56.7)	12.9	–	–	–	–	(43.8)
Intangible assets	(147.5)	(5.7)	–	–	(0.3)	–	(153.5)
Employee benefits	36.4	1.3	(0.2)	–	–	–	37.5
Cash flow hedges	(29.5)	–	(23.8)	–	–	–	(53.3)
Finance lease assets and obligations	13.9	(1.9)	–	–	–	–	12.0
FVTPL financial asset	(18.7)	5.9	–	–	–	–	(12.8)
Tax losses	3.5	(0.6)	–	–	–	0.8	3.7
Other	4.8	(1.3)	–	–	(0.1)	–	3.4
Net deferred tax asset (liability)[1]	$ (54.5)	$ 15.1	$(24.0)	$ –	$(0.4)	$0.8	$ (63.0)

[1]Includes the net amount of deferred tax assets of $48.1 million and deferred tax liabilities of $111.1 million.

(C$ in millions)	Balance, beginning of year	Recognized in profit or loss	Recognized in other compre-hensive income	Recognized in equity	Acquired in business combination	Other adjustments	Balance, end of year
							2014[1]
Provisions, deferred revenue and reserves	$ 123.5	$ 15.8	$ –	$ –	$ –	$ –	$ 139.3
Property and equipment	(53.8)	(2.9)	–	–	–	–	(56.7)
Intangible assets	(152.2)	4.8	–	–	–	–	(147.4)
Employee benefits	30.5	1.2	4.7	–	–	–	36.4
Cash flow hedges	(17.0)	–	(12.5)	–	–	–	(29.5)
Finance lease assets and obligations	10.8	3.1	–	–	–	–	13.9
FVTPL financial asset	(10.6)	(8.1)	–	–	–	–	(18.7)
Tax Losses	1.7	1.8	–	–	–	–	3.5
Other	3.1	1.1	–	0.5	–	–	4.7
Net deferred tax asset (liability)[2]	$ (64.0)	$ 16.8	$ (7.8)	$ 0.5	$ –	$ –	$ (54.5)

[1]Note the prior year balances have been reclassified to align to the current year presentation, which more clearly describes the categories of temporary tax differences.
[2]Includes the net amount of deferred tax assets of $39.4 million and deferred tax liabilities of $93.9 million.

No deferred tax is recognized on the amount of temporary differences arising from the difference between the carrying amount of the investment in subsidiaries, branches and associates, and interests in joint arrangements accounted for in the financial statements and the cost amount for tax purposes of the investment. The Company is able to control the timing of the reversal of these temporary differences and believes it is probable that they will not reverse in the foreseeable future. The amount of these taxable temporary differences was approximately $2.6 billion at January 2, 2016 (2014 – $2.5 billion).

18.2 Income tax expense

The following are the major components of income tax expense:

(C$ in millions)	2015	2014
Current tax expense		
Current period	$ 258.9	$ 248.5
Adjustments in respect of prior years	21.6	7.2
	$ 280.5	$ 255.7
Deferred tax (benefit) expense		
Deferred income tax (benefit) relating to the origination and reversal of temporary differences	$ (0.3)	$ (7.9)
Deferred income tax (benefit) adjustments in respect of prior years	(16.6)	(8.9)
Deferred income tax expense resulting from change in tax rate	1.8	–
	(15.1)	(16.8)
Total income tax expense	$ 265.4	$ 238.9

Income tax expense (benefit) recognized in Other Comprehensive Income was as follows:

(C$ in millions)	2015	2014
Gains on derivatives designated as cash flow hedges	$ 100.0	$ 40.4
Reclassification of gains to non-financial assets on derivatives designated as cash flow hedges to non-financial assets	(74.9)	(27.2)
Reclassification of gains to income on derivatives designated as cash flow hedges to income	(1.1)	(0.6)
(Losses) on available-for-sale financial assets	(0.2)	(0.1)
Reclassification of gains to income on available-for-sale financial assets to income	–	–
Actuarial gains (losses)	0.2	(4.7)
Total income tax expense	$ 24.0	$ 7.8

Reconciliation of income tax expense

Income taxes in the Consolidated Statements of Income vary from amounts that would be computed by applying the statutory income tax rate for the following reasons:

(C$ in millions)	2015	2014
Income before income taxes	$1,001.3	$ 878.2
Income taxes based on the applicable statutory tax rate of 26.56% (2014 – 26.50%)	$ 266.0	$ 232.7
Adjustment to income taxes resulting from:		
Non-taxable portion of capital gains	(6.8)	–
Income attributable to non-controlling interest in flow-through entities	(6.3)	(6.6)
Adjustments of tax estimates	7.3	5.9
Non-deductibility of stock option expense	2.5	10.5
Prior years' tax settlements	(2.3)	(7.6)
Changes in tax rates	1.8	–
Higher (lower) income tax rates on earnings of foreign subsidiaries	0.3	(0.5)
Non-deductibility of change in fair value of redeemable financial instrument	–	4.5
Other	2.9	–
Income tax expense	$ 265.4	$ 238.9

The applicable statutory tax rate is the aggregate of the Canadian federal income tax rate of 15.0 percent (2014 – 15.0 percent) and the provincial income tax rate of 11.6 percent (2014 – 11.5 percent). The increase in the applicable rate from 2014 is primarily due to an increase in the provincial tax rates in the year.

In the ordinary course of business, the Company is subject to ongoing audits by tax authorities. While the Company has determined that its tax filing positions are appropriate and supportable, from time to time certain matters are reviewed and challenged by the tax authorities.

The 2015 tax expense has been reduced by $2.3 million (2014 – $7.6 million) due to prior years' tax settlements and increased by $7.3 million (2014 – $5.9 million) due to adjustments to tax estimates.

The Company regularly reviews the potential for adverse outcomes with respect to tax matters. The Company believes that the ultimate disposition of these will not have a material adverse effect on its liquidity, consolidated financial position, or net income because the Company has determined that it has adequate provision for these tax matters. Should the ultimate tax liability materially differ from the provision, the Company's effective tax rate and its earnings could be affected positively or negatively in the period in which the matters are resolved.

19. Deposits

Deposits consist of broker deposits and retail deposits.

Cash from broker deposits is raised through sales of GICs through brokers rather than directly to the retail customer. Broker deposits are offered for varying terms ranging from 30 days to five years and issued broker GICs are non-redeemable prior to maturity (except in certain rare circumstances). Total short-term and long-term broker deposits outstanding at January 2, 2016, were $1,548.5 million (2014 – $1,534.6 million).

Retail deposits consist of HIS deposits, retail GICs, and TFSA deposits. Total retail deposits outstanding at January 2, 2016, were $704.4 million (2014 – $702.3 million).

For repayment requirements of deposits refer to Note 5.4. The following are the effective rates of interest:

	2015	2014
GIC deposits	2.84%	3.00%
HIS account deposits	1.52%	1.53%

20. Trade and other payables

Trade and other payables include the following:

(C$ in millions)	2015	2014
Trade payables and accrued liabilities	$ 1,836.9	$ 1,834.9
Derivatives (Note 35)	0.7	–
Total financial liabilities	1,837.6	1,834.9
Deferred revenue	38.4	39.3
Insurance reserve	16.9	16.8
Other	64.2	70.2
	$ 1,957.1	$ 1,961.2

Deferred revenue consists mainly of unearned insurance premiums, unearned roadside assistance revenue, and unearned revenue related to gift cards.

Other consists primarily of sales taxes payable.

The credit range period on trade payables is three to 180 days (2014 – four to 120 days).

21. Provisions

The following table presents the changes to the Company's provisions:

(C$ in millions)	2015					
	Sales and warranty returns	Site restoration and decom- missioning	Onerous contracts	Customer loyalty	Other	Total
Balance, beginning of year	$ 115.6	$ 38.4	$ 1.1	$ 79.9	$ 15.1	$ 250.1
Charges, net of reversals	296.5	(0.7)	3.9	153.6	4.9	458.2
Utilizations	(292.3)	(1.1)	(3.4)	(147.3)	(5.4)	(449.5)
Unwinding of discount	0.6	0.7	–	–	0.3	1.6
Change in discount rate	0.1	1.0	0.1	–	0.2	1.4
Balance, end of year	$ 120.5	$ 38.3	$ 1.7	$ 86.2	$ 15.1	$ 261.8
Current provisions	115.9	4.0	1.3	86.2	8.7	216.1
Long-term provisions	$ 4.6	$ 34.3	$ 0.4	$ –	$ 6.4	$ 45.7

22. Contingencies

Legal and regulatory matters

The Company is party to a number of legal and regulatory proceedings. The Company believes that each such proceeding constitutes a routine matter incidental to the business conducted by the Company. The Company cannot determine with certainty the ultimate outcome of all the outstanding claims but believes that the ultimate disposition of the proceedings will not have a material adverse effect on its consolidated earnings, cash flow, or financial position.

23. Short-term borrowings

Short-term borrowings include commercial paper notes and bank line of credit borrowings. Short-term borrowings may bear interest payable at maturity or be sold at a discount and mature at face value.

The commercial paper notes are short-term notes issued with varying original maturities of one year or fewer, typically 90 days or fewer, at interest rates fixed at the time of each renewal, and are recorded at amortized cost. As at January 2, 2016, $88.6 million (2014 – $121.8 million) of commercial paper notes were issued by the Company.

As at January 2, 2016, $nil (2014 – $78.0 million) of bank line of credit borrowings had been drawn on CT REIT's Bank Credit Facility.

24. Loans payable

Franchise Trust, an SPE, is a legal entity sponsored by a third-party bank that originates loans to Dealers. Loans payable are the loans that Franchise Trust incurs to fund loans to Dealers. These loans are not direct legal liabilities of the Company but have been consolidated in the accounts of the Company as the Company effectively controls the silo of Franchise Trust containing the Dealer Loan Program.

Loans payable, which are initially recognized at fair value and are subsequently measured at amortized cost, are due within one year.

25. Long-term debt

Long-term debt includes the following:

(C$ in millions)	2015		2014	
	Face value	Carrying amount	Face value	Carrying amount
Senior notes[1]				
Series 2010-1, 3.158%, November 20, 2015	$ –	$ –	$ 250.0	$ 249.7
Series 2012-1, 2.807%, May 20, 2017	200.0	199.7	200.0	199.4
Series 2012-2, 2.394%, October 20, 2017	400.0	399.2	400.0	398.7
Series 2013-1, 2.755%, November 20, 2018	250.0	249.1	250.0	248.9
Series 2014-1, 2.567%, September 20, 2019	472.5	470.7	472.5	470.2
Series 2015-1, 2.238%, September 20, 2020	465.0	462.9	–	–
Subordinated notes[1]				
Series 2010-1, 4.128%, November 20, 2015	–	–	14.6	14.6
Series 2012-1, 3.827%, May 20, 2017	11.6	11.6	11.6	11.6
Series 2012-2, 3.174%, October 20, 2017	23.3	23.3	23.3	23.3
Series 2013-1, 3.275%, November 20, 2018	14.6	14.6	14.6	14.6
Series 2014-1, 3.068%, September 20, 2019	27.5	27.5	27.5	27.5
Series 2015-1, 3.237%, September 20, 2020	35.0	35.0	–	–
Medium-term notes and debentures				
4.95% due June 1, 2015	–	–	300.0	299.3
2.85% due June 9, 2022	150.0	149.2	–	–
3.53% due June 9, 2025	200.0	198.8	–	–
6.375% due April 13, 2028	150.0	148.5	150.0	149.6
6.445% due February 24, 2034	200.0	198.0	200.0	199.5
5.61% due September 4, 2035	200.0	199.3	200.0	199.5
Finance lease obligations	145.9	145.9	153.0	153.0
Mortgages	60.0	60.1	58.3	58.5
Promissory note	2.3	2.3	1.2	1.2
Total debt	$ 3,007.7	$ 2,995.7	$ 2,726.6	$ 2,719.1
Current	$ 24.3	$ 24.3	$ 587.5	$ 587.5
Non-current	2,983.4	2,971.4	2,139.1	2,131.6

[1]Senior and subordinated notes are those of GCCT.

The carrying amount of long-term debt is net of debt issuance costs of $12.0 million (2014 – $7.5 million).

Senior and subordinated notes

Asset-backed series senior and subordinated notes issued by the Company are recorded at amortized cost using the effective interest method.

Subject to the payment of certain priority amounts, the series senior notes have recourse on a priority basis to the related series ownership interest. The series subordinated notes have recourse to the related series ownership interests on a subordinated basis to the series senior notes in terms of the priority of payment of principal and, in some circumstances, interest. The series notes, together with certain other permitted obligations of GCCT, are secured by the assets of GCCT. The entitlement of note holders and other parties to such assets is governed by the priority and payment provisions set forth in the GCCT Indenture and the related series supplements under which these series of notes were issued.

Repayment of the principal of the series 2012-1, 2012-2, 2013-1, 2014-1, and 2015-1 notes is scheduled to commence and be completed on the expected repayment dates indicated in the preceding table. Subsequent to repayment, collections distributed to GCCT with respect to the related ownership interest will be applied to pay principal owing. This process is applied to principal owing for series subordinated notes and in some circumstances interest for the series senior notes.

Principal repayments may commence earlier than these scheduled commencement dates if certain events occur including:
- the Bank failing to make required distributions to GCCT or failing to meet covenant or other contractual terms;
- the performance of the receivables failing to achieve set criteria; and
- insufficient receivables in the pool.

None of these events occurred in the year ended January 2, 2016.

Medium-term notes and debentures
Medium-term notes and debentures are unsecured and are redeemable by the Company, in whole or in part, at any time, at the greater of par or a formula price based upon interest rates at the time of redemption.

On June 25, 2014, the Company redeemed $200.0 million of medium-term notes, which were to mature on June 1, 2016, and bore interest at 5.65 percent. Upon redemption, the Company paid a redemption premium of $15.0 million, which was included in net finance costs.

Finance lease obligations
Finance leases relate to distribution centres, fixtures, and equipment. The Company generally has the option to renew such leases or purchase the leased assets at the conclusion of the lease term. During 2015, interest rates on finance leases ranged from 0.81 percent to 11.35 percent. Remaining terms at January 2, 2016, were one to 144 months.

Finance lease obligations are payable as follows:

(C$ in millions)	2015			2014		
	Future minimum lease payments	Interest	Present value of future minimum lease payments	Future minimum lease payments	Interest	Present value of future minimum lease payments
Due in less than one year	$ 27.8	$ 8.2	$ 19.6	$ 29.7	$ 9.0	$ 20.7
Due between one year and two years	24.5	7.2	17.3	25.0	8.0	17.0
Due between two years and three years	21.0	6.5	14.5	21.0	7.0	14.0
Due between three years and four years	18.5	5.8	12.7	18.4	6.3	12.1
Due between four years and five years	16.7	5.1	11.6	16.1	5.6	10.5
More than five years	85.0	14.8	70.2	98.8	20.1	78.7
	$ 193.5	$ 47.6	$ 145.9	$ 209.0	$ 56.0	$ 153.0

Mortgages
Mortgages bear interest rates ranging from 2.50 percent to 3.60 percent and have maturity dates ranging from May 2016 to December 2019.

Promissory notes
Promissory notes were issued as part of franchise acquisitions (Refer to Note 7.2). These notes are non-interest-bearing.

Debt covenants
The Company has provided covenants to certain of its lenders. The Company was in compliance with all of its covenants as at January 2, 2016.

26. Other long-term liabilities

Other long-term liabilities include the following:

(C$ in millions)	2015	2014
Redeemable financial instrument[1]	$ 517.0	$ 517.0
Employee benefits (Note 27)	141.2	137.5
Deferred gains	16.8	18.1
Derivatives (Note 35)	12.9	–
Deferred revenue	8.8	13.2
Other	117.2	102.0
	$ 813.9	$ 787.8

[1] A financial liability; refer to Note 35 for further information on the redeemable financial instrument.

Deferred gains relate to the sale and leaseback of certain distribution centres. The deferred gains are amortized over the terms of the leases.

Other includes the long-term portion of share-based payment transactions, unearned insurance premiums, unearned roadside assistance revenue, deferred lease inducements, and off-market leases.

27. Post-employment benefits

Profit-sharing program

The Company has a profit-sharing program for certain employees. The amount awarded to employees is contingent on the Company's profitability. A portion of the award ("Base Award") is contributed to a DPSP for the benefit of the employees. The maximum amount of the Company's Base Award contribution to the DPSP per employee per year is subject to limits set by the Income Tax Act. Each participating employee is required to invest and maintain 10 percent of the Base Award in a Company share fund of the DPSP. The share fund holds both Common Shares and Class A Non-Voting Shares. The Company's contributions to the DPSP in respect of each employee vest 20 percent after one year of continuous service and 100 percent after two years of continuous service.

In 2015, the Company contributed $22.1 million (2014 – $20.5 million) under the terms of the DPSP.

Defined benefit plan

The Company provides certain health care, dental care, life insurance, and other benefits for certain retired employees pursuant to Company policy. The Company does not have a pension plan. Information about the Company's defined benefit plan is as follows:

(C$ in millions)	2015	2014
Change in the present value of defined benefit obligation		
Defined benefit obligation, beginning of year	$ 137.5	$ 115.4
Current service cost	2.3	1.9
Interest cost	5.4	5.6
Actuarial gain arising from changes in demographic assumptions	(0.2)	(0.3)
Actuarial (gain) loss arising from changes in financial assumptions	(4.6)	18.6
Actuarial loss (gain) arising from changes in experience assumptions	3.8	(0.4)
Benefits paid	(3.0)	(3.3)
Defined benefit obligation, end of year[1]	$ 141.2	$ 137.5

[1] The accrued benefit obligation is not funded because funding is provided when benefits are paid. Accordingly, there are no plan assets.

(C$ in millions)	2015	2014
Components of non-pension post-retirement benefit cost		
Amounts recognized in net income:		
Current service cost	$ 2.3	$ 1.9
Interest cost	5.4	5.6
Total recognized in net income	$ 7.7	$ 7.5
Amount recognized in other comprehensive income:		
Actuarial gain arising from changes in demographic assumptions	$ 0.2	$ 0.3
Actuarial gain (loss) arising from changes in financial assumptions	4.6	(18.6)
Actuarial (loss) gain arising from changes in experience assumptions	(3.8)	0.4
Total recognized in other comprehensive income	$ 1.0	$(17.9)

Significant actuarial assumptions used:

	2015	2014
Defined benefit obligation, end of year:		
Discount rate	4.10%	4.00%
Net benefit plan expense for the year:		
Discount rate	4.00%	4.90%

For measurement purposes, a 4.91 percent weighted average health care cost trend rate is assumed for 2015 (2014 – 6.12 percent). The rate is assumed to decrease gradually to 2.91 percent for 2032 (2014 – decrease gradually to 4.50 percent for 2032) and remain at that level thereafter.

The most recent actuarial valuation of the obligation was performed as of January 2, 2016. The next required valuation will be as of December 29, 2018.

The cumulative amount of actuarial losses before tax recognized in equity at January 2, 2016, was $44.1 million (2014 – $45.1 million).

Sensitivity analysis:

The following tables provide the sensitivity of the defined benefit obligation and defined benefit cost relating to post-employment benefits provided by the Company to the health care cost trend rate, the discount rate, and the life expectancy assumptions. For each sensitivity test, the impact of a reasonably possible change in a single factor is shown with other assumptions left unchanged.

(C$ in millions)				2015
	Total of current service and interest cost		Accrued benefit obligation	
Sensitivity analysis				
A fifty basis point change in assumed discount rates	Increase	Decrease	Increase	Decrease
	$(0.1)	$ 0.1	$(11.0)	$ 12.4
A one-percentage-point change in assumed health care cost trend rates	0.8	(0.6)	12.9	(10.8)
A one year change in assumed life expectancy	(0.2)	0.2	(3.0)	3.0

The weighted average duration of the defined benefit plan obligation at January 2, 2016 is 16.5 years (2014 – 17.5 years).

28. Share capital

Share capital consists of the following:

(C$ in millions)	2015	2014
Authorized		
3,423,366 Common Shares		
100,000,000 Class A Non-Voting Shares		
Issued		
3,423,366 Common Shares (2014 – 3,423,366)	$ 0.2	$ 0.2
70,637,987 Class A Non-Voting Shares (2014 – 74,023,208)	671.0	695.3
	$ 671.2	$ 695.5

All issued shares are fully paid. The Company does not hold any of its Common or Class A Non-Voting Shares. Neither the Common nor Class A Non-Voting Shares have a par value.

During 2015 and 2014, the Company issued and repurchased Class A Non-Voting Shares.

The following transactions occurred with respect to Class A Non-Voting Shares during 2015 and 2014:

(C$ in millions)	2015		2014	
	Number	$	Number	$
Shares outstanding at beginning of the year	74,023,208	$ 695.3	76,560,851	$ 712.7
Issued under the dividend reinvestment plan	65,760	8.3	62,357	6.9
Repurchased[1]	(3,450,981)	(434.6)	(2,600,000)	(290.6)
Excess of purchase price over average cost	–	402.0	–	266.3
Shares outstanding at end of the period	70,637,987	$ 671.0	74,023,208	$ 695.3

[1]Repurchased shares have been restored to the status of authorized but unissued shares. The Company records shares repurchased on a transaction date basis.

Conditions of Class A Non-Voting Shares and Common Shares

The holders of Class A Non-Voting Shares are entitled to receive a fixed cumulative preferential dividend at the rate of $0.01 per share per annum. After payment of fixed cumulative preferential dividends at the rate of $0.01 per share per annum on each of the Class A Non-Voting Shares with respect to the current year and each preceding year, and payment of a non-cumulative dividend on each of the Common Shares with respect to the current year at the same rate, the holders of the Class A Non-Voting Shares and the Common Shares are entitled to further dividends declared and paid in equal amounts per share without preference or distinction or priority of one share over another.

In the event of the liquidation, dissolution, or winding-up of the Company, all of the property of the Company available for distribution to the holders of the Class A Non-Voting Shares and the Common Shares shall be paid or distributed equally, share for share, to the holders of the Class A Non-Voting Shares, and to the holders of the Common Shares without preference or distinction or priority of one share over another.

The holders of Class A Non-Voting Shares are entitled to receive notice of and to attend all meetings of the shareholders; however, except as provided by the *Business Corporations Act* (Ontario) and as hereinafter noted, they are not entitled to vote at those meetings. Holders of Class A Non-Voting Shares, voting separately as a class, are entitled to elect the greater of (i) three Directors or (ii) one-fifth of the total number of the Company's Directors.

The holders of Common Shares are entitled to receive notice of, to attend, and to have one vote for each Common Share held at all meetings of holders of Common Shares, subject only to the restriction on the right to elect those directors who are elected by the holders of Class A Non-Voting Shares as set out above.

Common Shares can be converted, at any time and at the option of each holder of Common Shares, into Class A Non-Voting Shares on a share-for-share basis. The authorized number of shares of either class cannot be increased without the approval of the holders of at least two-thirds of the shares of each class represented and voted at a meeting of the shareholders called for the purpose of considering such an increase. Neither the Class A Non-Voting Shares nor the Common Shares can be changed in any manner whatsoever whether by way of subdivision, consolidation, reclassification, exchange, or otherwise unless at the same time the other class of shares is also changed in the same manner and in the same proportion.

Should an offer to purchase Common Shares be made to all, or substantially all of the holders of Common Shares, or be required by applicable securities legislation or by the Toronto Stock Exchange to be made to all holders of Common Shares in Ontario and should a majority of the Common Shares then issued and outstanding be tendered and taken up pursuant to such offer, the Class A Non-Voting Shares shall thereupon and thereafter be entitled to one vote per share at all meetings of the shareholders and thereafter the Class A Non-Voting Shares shall be designated as Class A Shares. The foregoing voting entitlement applicable to Class A Non-Voting Shares would not apply in the case where an offer is made to purchase both Class A Non-Voting Shares and Common Shares at the same price per share and on the same terms and conditions.

The foregoing is a summary of certain conditions attached to the Class A Non-Voting Shares of the Company and reference should be made to the Company's articles of amendment dated December 15, 1983, for a full statement of such conditions.

As of January 2, 2016, the Company had dividends declared and payable to holders of Class A Non-Voting Shares and Common Shares of $42.6 million (2014 – $40.7 million) at a rate of $0.575 per share (2014 – $0.525 per share).

On February 17, 2016, the Company's Board of Directors declared a dividend of $0.575 per share payable on June 1, 2016, to shareholders of record as of April 30, 2016.

Dividends per share declared were $2.1500 in 2015 (2014 – $1.9625).

Dilutive effect of employee stock options is 430,281 (2014 – 652,932).

29. Share-based payments

The fair value of employee stock options and performance share units ("PSUs") is measured using the Black-Scholes formula. Measurement inputs include the share price on the measurement date, exercise price of the instrument, expected volatility (based on weighted average historical volatility adjusted for changes expected based on publicly available information), weighted average expected life of the instruments (based on historical experience and general option holder behaviour), expected dividends, and the risk-free interest rate (based on government bonds). Service and non-market performance conditions attached to the transactions are not taken into account in determining fair value. The fair value of deferred share units ("DSUs") is equal to the traded price of a Class A Non-Voting Share.

The Company's share-based payment plans are described below. There were no cancellations or significant modifications to any of the plans during 2015.

Stock options

The Company has granted stock options to certain employees that enable such employees to exercise their stock options and subscribe for Class A Non-Voting Shares, or receive a cash payment equal to the difference between the daily weighted average share price of the Company's Class A Non-Voting Shares on the exercise date and the exercise price of the stock option. The exercise price of each option equals the weighted average closing price of Class A Non-Voting Shares on the Toronto Stock Exchange for the 10-calendar day period ending on the last day immediately preceding the date of grant. Stock options granted from 2008 to 2011 generally vested on the third anniversary of their grant and were exercisable over a term of seven years. Stock options granted from 2012 to 2015 generally vest on a graduated basis over a three-year period and are exercisable over a term of seven years. At January 2, 2016, the aggregate number of Class A Non-Voting Shares that were authorized for issuance under the stock option plan was 3.4 million.

Compensation expense, net of hedging arrangements, recorded for stock options for the year ended January 2, 2016, was $14.0 million (2014 – $10.7 million).

Stock option transactions during 2015 and 2014 were as follows:

	2015		2014	
	Number of options	**Weighted average exercise price**	Number of options	Weighted average exercise price
Outstanding at beginning of year	1,526,343	$ 72.21	1,986,354	$ 64.26
Granted	387,234	129.14	330,879	99.81
Exercised and surrendered	(823,888)	65.69	(747,768)	63.17
Forfeited	(79,446)	92.53	(35,810)	74.90
Expired	–	–	(7,312)	71.90
Outstanding at end of year	1,010,243	$ 97.75	1,526,343	$ 72.21
Stock options exercisable at end of year	243,240		538,667	

[1]The weighted average market price of the Company's shares when the options were exercised in 2015 was $127.12 (2014 – $105.37).

The following table summarizes information about stock options outstanding and exercisable at January 2, 2016:

Range of exercise prices	Options outstanding			Options exercisable	
	Number of outstanding options	Weighted average remaining contractual life[1]	Weighted average exercise price	Number of exercisable options	Weighted average exercise price
$129.14	362,669	6.19	$129.14	–	$ –
99.72 to 103.61	267,707	5.20	99.83	73,101	99.85
69.01	258,080	4.18	69.01	48,352	69.01
40.04 to 63.67	121,787	2.44	60.64	121,787	60.64
$ 40.04 to 129.14	1,010,243	4.96	$ 97.75	243,240	$74.09

[1]Weighted average remaining contractual life is expressed in years.

30. Revenue

Revenue consists of the following:

(C$ in millions)	2015	2014
Sale of goods	$ 10,649.9	$ 10,890.6
Interest income on loans receivable	852.1	784.6
Royalties and license fees	375.6	363.2
Services rendered	342.6	372.2
Rental income	59.4	52.3
	$ 12,279.6	$ 12,462.9

Major customers

The Company does not rely on any one customer.

31. Cost of producing revenue

Cost of producing revenue consists of the following:

(C$ in millions)	2015	2014
Inventory cost of sales[1]	$ 7,747.1	$ 8,033.2
Net impairment loss on loans receivable	297.1	274.7
Finance costs on deposits	54.5	57.6
Other	45.6	51.4
	$ 8,144.3	$ 8,416.9

[1]Inventory cost of sales includes depreciation for the year ended January 2, 2016 of $8.9 million (2014 – $7.0 million).

Inventory writedowns as a result of net realizable value being lower than cost, recognized in the year ended January 2, 2016 were $33.9 million (2014 – $40.2 million).

Inventory writedowns recognized in previous periods and reversed in the year ended January 2, 2016 were $5.7 million (2014 – $14.5 million). The reversal of writedowns was the result of actual losses being lower than previously estimated.

The writedowns and reversals are included in inventory cost of sales.

32. Selling, general, and administrative expenses

Selling, general, and administrative expenses consist of the following:

(C$ in millions)	2015	2014
Personnel expenses	$ 1,127.9	$ 1,140.7
Occupancy	648.6	625.1
Marketing and advertising	365.3	381.4
Depreciation of property and equipment and investment property[1]	303.9	272.2
Amortization of intangible assets	111.9	93.1
Other	538.5	540.4
	$ 3,096.1	$ 3,052.9

[1]Refer to Note 31 for depreciation included in cost of producing revenue.

33. Net finance costs

Net finance costs consists of the following:

(C$ in millions)	2015	2014
Finance income		
Short- and long-term investments	$ 8.0	$ 10.4
Mortgages	5.6	7.9
Tax instalments	–	0.1
Other	0.5	0.5
Total finance income	**$ 14.1**	**$ 18.9**
Finance costs		
Subordinated and senior notes	$ 50.2	$ 40.0
Medium-term notes	45.9	69.3
Loans payable	11.1	12.2
Finance leases	9.0	9.4
Short-term borrowings	1.2	1.3
Other[1]	7.4	6.8
	124.8	139.0
Less: Capitalized borrowing costs	17.9	11.2
Total finance costs	**$106.9**	**$127.8**
Net finance costs	**$ 92.8**	**$108.9**

[1]Includes $1.8 million of amortization of debt issuance costs (2014 – $2.1 million).

34. Notes to the consolidated statements of cash flows

Change in operating working capital and other comprise the following:

(C$ in millions)	2015	2014
Change in operating working capital		
Trade and other receivables	$ 83.1	$ (38.1)
Merchandise inventories	(147.3)	(146.6)
Income taxes	(0.6)	(1.9)
Prepaid expenses and deposits	8.3	(36.1)
Trade and other payables	(80.9)	86.9
Total	(137.4)	(135.8)
Change in other		
Provisions	12.7	17.1
Long-term provisions	(0.4)	(3.2)
Other long term liabilities	9.8	38.4
Total	22.1	52.3
Change in operating working capital and other	$ (115.3)	$ (83.5)

34.1 Cash and marketable investments held in reserve

Cash and marketable investments includes reserves held by the Financial Services segment in support of its liquidity and regulatory requirements. As at January 2, 2016, reserves held by Financial Services totaled $275.1 million (2014 – $344.5 million) and includes restricted cash and short-term investments disclosed in Notes 8 and 9.

34.2 Supplementary information

During the year ended January 2, 2016, the Company acquired property and equipment and investment property at an aggregate cost of $582.0 million (2014 – $587.6 million). During the year ended January 2, 2016, intangible assets were internally developed or acquired at an aggregate cost of $109.9 million (2014 – $155.6 million).

The amount related to property and equipment and investment property acquired that is included in trade and other payables at January 2, 2016, is $104.1 million (2014 – $71.7 million). The amount related to intangible assets that is included in trade and other payables at January 2, 2016, is $38.0 million (2014 – $22.8 million).

During the year ended January 2, 2016, the Company also included in the property and equipment, investment property, and intangible assets acquired non-cash items relating to finance leases, asset retirement obligations, and capitalized interest in the amount of $33.7 million (2014 – $37.3 million).

37. Guarantees and commitments

Guarantees

In the normal course of business, the Company enters into numerous agreements that may contain features that meet the definition of a guarantee. A guarantee is defined to be a contract (including an indemnity) that contingently requires the Company to make payments to the guaranteed party based on (i) changes in an underlying interest rate, foreign exchange rate, equity or commodity instrument, index or other variable that is related to an asset, a liability or an equity security of the counterparty; (ii) failure of another party to perform under an obligating agreement; or (iii) failure of a third party to pay its indebtedness when due.

The Company has provided the following significant guarantees and other commitments to third parties:

Standby letters of credit

Franchise Trust, a legal entity sponsored by a third-party bank, originates loans to Dealers for their purchase of inventory and fixed assets. While Franchise Trust is consolidated as part of these financial statements, the Company has arranged for several major Canadian banks to provide standby LCs to Franchise Trust to support the credit quality of the Dealer loan portfolio. The banks may also draw against the LCs to cover any shortfalls in certain related fees owing to it. In any case where a draw is made against the LCs, the Company has agreed to reimburse the banks issuing the standby LCs for the amount so drawn. The Company has not recorded any liability for these amounts due to the credit quality of the Dealer loans and to the nature of the underlying collateral represented by the inventory and fixed assets of the borrowing Dealers. In the unlikely event that all the LCs had been fully drawn simultaneously, the maximum payment by the Company under this reimbursement obligation would have been $151.0 million at January 2, 2016 (2014 – $144.6 million).

The Company has obtained documentary and standby letters of credit aggregating $32.3 million (2014 – $38.5 million) related to the importation of merchandise inventories and to facilitate various real estate activities.

Business and property dispositions

In connection with agreements for the sale of all or part of a business or property and in addition to indemnifications relating to failure to perform covenants and breach of representations and warranties, the Company has agreed to indemnify the purchasers against claims from its past conduct, including environmental remediation. Typically, the term and amount of such indemnification will be determined by the parties in the agreements. The nature of these indemnification agreements prevents the Company from estimating the maximum potential liability it would be required to pay to counterparties. Historically, the Company has not made any significant indemnification payments under such agreements, and no amount has been accrued in the consolidated financial statements with respect to these indemnification agreements.

Lease agreements guarantees

The Company has guaranteed leases on certain franchise stores in the event the franchisees are unable to meet their remaining lease commitments. These lease agreements have expiration dates through November 2023. The maximum amount that the Company may be required to pay under these agreements was $5.3 million (2014 – $6.4 million). In addition, the Company could be required to make payments for percentage rents, realty taxes, and common area costs. No amount has been accrued in the consolidated financial statements with respect to these lease agreements.

Third-party financial guarantees

The Company has guaranteed the debts of certain Dealers. These third-party financial guarantees require the Company to make payments if the Dealer fails to make scheduled debt payments. The majority of these third-party financial guarantees have expiration dates extending up to and including July 2016. The maximum amount that the Company may be required to pay under these debt agreements was $50.0 million (2014 – $50.0 million), of which $32.3 million (2014 – $38.5 million) was issued at January 2, 2016. No amount has been accrued in the consolidated financial statements with respect to these debt agreements.

The Company has entered into agreements to buy back franchise-owned merchandise inventory should the banks foreclose on any of the franchisees. The terms of the guarantees range from less than a year to the lifetime of the particular underlying franchise agreement. The Company's maximum exposure as at January 2, 2016, was $88.0 million (2014 – $70.0 million).

Indemnification of lenders and agents under credit facilities

In the ordinary course of business, the Company has agreed to indemnify its lenders under various credit facilities against costs or losses resulting from changes in laws and regulations that would increase the lenders' costs and from any legal action brought against the lenders related to the use of the loan proceeds. These indemnifications generally extend for the term of the credit facilities and do not provide any limit on the maximum potential liability. Historically, the Company has not made any significant indemnification payments under such agreements, and no amount has been accrued in the consolidated financial statements with respect to these indemnification agreements.

Other indemnification agreements

In the ordinary course of business, the Company provides other additional indemnification agreements to counterparties in transactions such as leasing transactions, service arrangements, investment banking agreements, securitization agreements, indemnification of trustees under indentures for outstanding public debt, director and officer indemnification agreements, escrow agreements, price escalation clauses, sales of assets (other than dispositions of businesses discussed above), and the arrangements with Franchise Trust discussed above. These additional indemnification agreements require the Company to compensate the counterparties for certain amounts and costs incurred, including costs resulting from changes in laws and regulations (including tax legislation) or as a result of litigation claims or statutory sanctions that may be suffered by a counterparty as a consequence of the transaction.

The terms of these additional indemnification agreements vary based on the contract and do not provide any limit on the maximum potential liability. Historically, the Company has not made any significant payments under such additional indemnifications, and no amount has been accrued in the consolidated financial statements with respect to these additional indemnification commitments.

The Company's exposure to credit risks related to the above noted guarantees are disclosed in Note 5.

Capital commitments

As at January 2, 2016, the Company had capital commitments for the acquisition of property and equipment, investment property, and intangible assets for an aggregate cost of approximately $120.2 million (2014 – $164.6 million).

Sixth Canadian Edition Focus Companies

	CHAPTER	FOCUS COMPANY	MANAGERIAL FOCUS	CONTRAST COMPANIES	KEY RATIOS
1	Financial Statements and Business Decisions	Canadian Tire Corporation Limited (Household goods and automotive supplies)	Valuing an investment		
2	Investing and Financing Decisions and the Statement of Financial Position	Canadian Tire Corporation Limited (Household goods and automotive supplies)	Investing and financing decisions	Hudson's Bay Company Sears Canada	**Current Ratio**
3	Operating Decisions and Statement of Earnings	Canadian Tire Corporation Limited (Household goods and automotive supplies)	Operating decisions	Hudson's Bay Company Sears Canada	**Total Asset Turnover Return on Assets**
4	Adjustments, Financial Statements, and the Quality of Earnings	Canadian Tire Corporation Limited (Household goods and automotive supplies)	Year-end accounting activities	Hudson's Bay Company Sears Canada	**Net Profit Margin Return on Equity**
5	Reporting and Interpreting Cash Flows	National Beverage Corp. (Manufacturer of soft and energy drinks)	Management of cash	Coca-Cola PepsiCo	**Quality of Earnings Capital Expenditures**
6	Reporting and Interpreting Sales Revenue, Receivables, and Cash	GILDAN Gildan Activewear Inc. (High-quality casual wear)	Marketing strategy	Hanesbrands Delta Apparel	**Gross Profit Percentage Receivables Turnover**
7	Reporting and Interpreting Cost of Sales and Inventory	REITMANS CANADA LTÉE/LTD Reitmans (Canada) Limited (Clothing retiler)	Inventory management	Le Château Hudson's Bay Company	**Inventory Turnover**

	CHAPTER	FOCUS COMPANY	MANAGERIAL FOCUS	CONTRAST COMPANIES	KEY RATIOS
8	Reporting and Interpreting Property, Plant, and Equipment; Natural Resources; and Intangibles	**WEST JET** WestJet Airlines Ltd. (Major Canadian airline)	Planning productive capacity	Southwest Airlines Ryanair	**Fixed Asset Turnover**
9	Reporting and Interpreting Current Liabilities	**SEARS** Sears Canada Inc. (Department and specialty stores)	Capital structure	Hudson's Bay Company Canadian Tire Corporation	**Quick Ratio** **Accounts Payable Turnover**
10	Reporting and Interpreting Non-Current Liabilities	**BCE** Bell Canada Enterprises Inc. (Communications company)	Long-term debt financing	Rogers Communications TELUS	**Times Interest Earned** **Debt-to-Equity**
11	Reporting and Interpreting Shareholders' Equity	**BCE** Bell Canada Enterprises Inc. (Communications company)	Corporate ownership	Rogers Communications TELUS	**Earnings per Share** **Dividend Yield**
12	Communicating Accounting Information and Analyzing Financial Statements	Canadian Tire Corporation Limited (Household goods and automotive supplies)	Financial statement analysis	Hudson's Bay Company Sears Canada	**Ratio Summary**
13	Reporting and Interpreting Investments in Other Corporations (Online)	**BCE** Bell Canada Enterprises Inc. (Communications company)	Investment strategies		**Economic Return from Investing**

Index